HMH | into **Literature**™

TEACHER'S EDITION

GRADE 8

Program Consultants:

Kylene Beers

Martha Hougen

Elena Izquierdo

Carol Jago

Erik Palmer

Robert E. Probst

Front Cover Photo Credits: (outer ring): ©Alexy Lisovoy/Shutterstock, (inner ring): ©Joseph Sohm-Visions of America/Getty Images, (c): ©Carrie Garcia/Houghton Mifflin Harcourt, (c overlay): ©Eyewire/Getty Images, (bc overlay): ©elenamiv/Shutterstock

Back Cover Photo Credits: (Units 1-6): ©Syda Productions/Shutterstock; ©PeopleImages/DigitalVision/Getty Images; ©Jason Donnelly/Shutterstock; Library of Congress Prints & Photographs Division [LC-DIG-ppmsca-34584]; ©David Schaffer/Caiaimage/Getty Images; ©Tim de Waele/Corbis via Getty Images

Printed in the U.S.A.

ISBN 978-1-328-47486-5

1 2 3 4 5 6 7 8 9 10 0690 27 26 25 24 23 22 21 20 19 18

4500718807   A B C D E F G

Teacher's Edition Table of Contents

Image Credit: (r): ©kanetmark/Shutterstock

PROGRAM CONSULTANTS

Kylene Beers

Nationally known lecturer and author on reading and literacy; coauthor with Robert Probst of *Disrupting Thinking, Notice & Note: Strategies for Close Reading,* and *Reading Nonfiction;* former president of the National Council of Teachers of English. Dr. Beers is the author of *When Kids Can't Read: What Teachers Can Do* and coeditor of *Adolescent Literacy: Turning Promise into Practice*, as well as articles in the Journal of Adolescent and Adult Literacy. Former editor of *Voices from the Middle,* she is the 2001 recipient of NCTE's Richard W. Halley Award, given for outstanding contributions to middle school literacy. She recently served as Senior Reading Researcher at the Comer School Development Program at Yale University as well as Senior Reading Advisor to Secondary Schools for the Reading and Writing Project at Teachers College.

Martha Hougen

National consultant, presenter, researcher, and author. Areas of expertise include differentiating instruction for students with learning difficulties, including those with learning disabilities and dyslexia; and teacher and leader preparation improvement. Dr. Hougen has taught at the middle school through graduate levels. In addition to peer-reviewed articles, curricular documents, and presentations, Dr. Hougen has published two college textbooks: *The Fundamentals of Literacy Instruction and Assessment Pre-K–6* (2012) and *The Fundamentals of Literacy Instruction and Assessment 6–12* (2014). Dr. Hougen has supported Educator Preparation Program reforms while working at the Meadows Center for Preventing Educational Risk at The University of Texas at Austin and at the CEEDAR Center, University of Florida.

Elena Izquierdo

Nationally recognized teacher educator and advocate for English language learners. Dr. Izquierdo is a linguist by training, with a Ph.D. in Applied Linguistics and Bilingual Education from Georgetown University. She has served on various state and national boards working to close the achievement gaps for bilingual students and English language learners. Dr. Izquierdo is a member of the Hispanic Leadership Council, which supports Hispanic students and educators at both the state and federal levels. She served as Vice President on the Executive Board of the National Association of Bilingual Education and as Publications and Professional Development Chair.

Carol Jago

Teacher of English with 32 years of experience at Santa Monica High School in California; author and nationally known lecturer; former president of the National Council of Teachers of English. Ms. Jago currently serves as Associate Director of the California Reading and Literature Project at UCLA. With expertise in standards assessment and secondary education, Ms. Jago is the author of numerous books on education, including *With Rigor for All* and *Papers, Papers, Papers,* and is active with the California Association of Teachers of English, editing its scholarly journal *California English* since 1996. Ms. Jago also served on the planning committee for the 2009 NAEP Readig Framework and the 2011 NAEP Writing Framework.

Erik Palmer

Veteran teacher and education consultant based in Denver, Colorado. Author of *Well Spoken: Teaching Speaking to All Students* and *Digitally Speaking: How to Improve Student Presentations with Technology.* His areas of focus include improving oral communication, promoting technology in classroom presentations, and updating instruction through the use of digital tools. He holds a bachelor's degree from Oberlin College and a master's degree in curriculum and instruction from the University of Colorado.

Robert E. Probst

Nationally respected authority on the teaching of literature; Professor Emeritus of English Education at Georgia State University. Dr. Probst's publications include numerous articles in *English Journal* and *Voices from the Middle,* as well as professional texts including (as coeditor) *Adolescent Literacy: Turning Promise into Practice* and (as coauthor with Kylene Beers) *Disrupting Thinking, Notice & Note: Strategies for Close Reading,* and *Reading Nonfiction.* He regularly speaks at national and international conventions including those of the International Literacy Association, the National Council of Teachers of English, the Association for Supervision and Curriculum Development, and the National Association of Secondary School Principals. He has served NCTE in various leadership roles, including the Conference on English Leadership Board of Directors, the Commission on Reading, and column editor of the NCTE journal *Voices from the Middle.* He is also the 2007 recipient of the CEL Outstanding Leadership Award.

Lead and Learn

Students who communicate...

- **Listen** actively
  - **Present** effectively
    - **Expand** vocabulary
      - **Question** appropriately
        - **Engage** constructively

Present an Argument

You will now adapt your argument to create a video presentation for your classmates. You will also listen to their presentations, ask questions to better understand their ideas, and help them improve their work.

SPEAKING AND LISTENING TASK

Go to **Giving a Presentation** in the **Speaking and Listening Studio** to learn more.

1 Adapt Your Argument for Presentation

Use the chart below to guide you as you create a script for a video "news editorial" based on your argument, with you as the speaker.

Presentation Planning Chart	
Title and Introduction	• How will you revise your title and introduction to capture the listener's attention? • Is there a way to state your claim aloud that is more engaging for video?
Audience	• Who is your audience? What do you want them to understand? • Are your tone, word choices, and visual elements or graphics appropriate for persuading this audience?
Effective Language and Organization	• Is your script logically organized? Is it interesting to listen to? Should parts be rearranged or excluded? • Where can you add evidence, persuasive language, or interesting examples to strengthen your argument? • Do you address a counter argument?
Visuals	• What type of media or visual elements will you use? • What type of audio elements will you use? What text will appear on screen?

SPEAKING AND LISTENING STUDIO

What Makes a Dynamic Presentation?

This Speaker was assigned to give an informal demonstration of the verbal and noverbal elements of speech delivery. View each segment of her presentation and respond to the questions.

Question and Respond

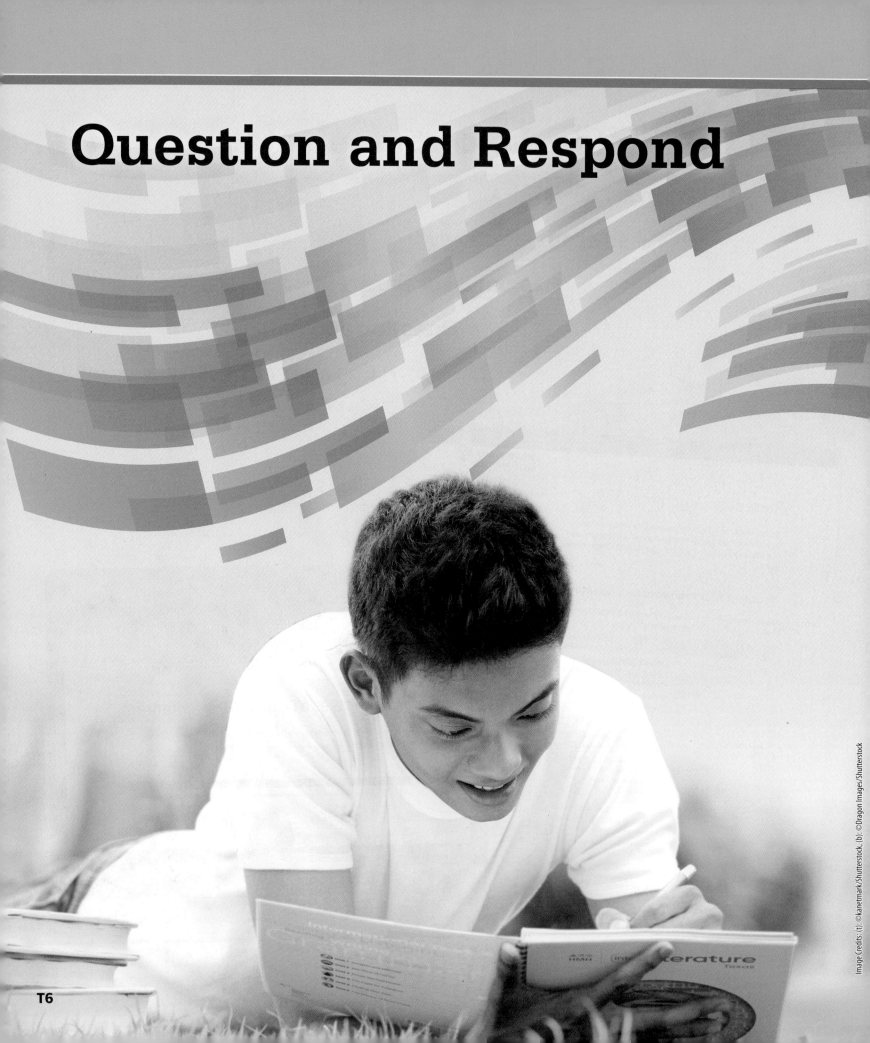

Students who read...

- **Acquire** fluency
- **Choose** independently
- **Monitor** understanding
- **Annotate** and use evidence
- **Write** and discuss within and across texts

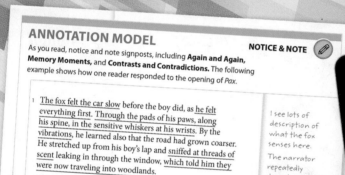

ANNOTATION MODEL

NOTICE & NOTE

As you read, notice and note signposts, including **Again and Again, Memory Moments,** and **Contrasts and Contradictions.** The following example shows how one reader responded to the opening of *Pax*.

1 The fox felt the car slow before the boy did, as he felt everything first. Through the pads of his paws, along his spine, in the sensitive whiskers at his wrists. By the vibrations, he learned also that the road had grown coarser. He stretched up from his boy's lap and sniffed at threads of scent leaking in through the window, which told him they were now traveling into woodlands.

I see lots of description of what the fox senses here.

The narrator repeatedly describes what the fox senses through touch and smell.

HMH DIGITAL LIBRARY

Black Beauty
The Autobiography of a Horse

Anna Sewell

UNIT 2

THROUGH AN ANIMAL'S EYES

? **ESSENTIAL QUESTION:**

What can you learn by seeing the world through an animal's eyes?

> " I have wished that I could . . . look out onto the world through the eyes, with the mind, of a chimpanzee. "
>
> Jane Goodall

ACADEMIC VOCABULARY

Academic Vocabulary words are words you use when you discuss an[...] in this unit, you will learn and practice using five words.

☑ benefit ☐ distinct ☐ environment ☐ illustrate

Study the Word Network to learn more about the word benefit.

SYNONYMS
help, advantage

DEFINITION
something that provides help or improves something else.

ANT[...]
drawback, [...]

benefit
(bĕn´ə-fĭt)
n.

CLARIFYING EXAMPLE
There are many benefits to reading your writing aloud.

WORD [...]
comes from th[...]
benefactum, m[...]
a servi[...]

RELATED WORDS
beneficial, benefitting

Write and Discuss Discuss the completed Word Network with a partner, ma[...] to talk through all of the boxes until you both understand the word, its synon[...] antonyms, and related forms. Then, fill out Word Networks for the remaining fo[...] Use a dictionary or online resource to help you complete the activity.

Go online to access the Word Networks.

RESPOND TO THE ESSENTIAL QUESTION

In this unit, you will explore what can be learned by seeing the world through an animal's eyes. As you read, you will revisit the **Essential Question** and gather your ideas about it in the **Response Log** that appears on page R2. At the end of the unit, you will write an **argument** about what you can learn by seeing the world from an animal's perspective. You will also **present an argument.** Filling out the Response Log will help you prepare for these tasks.

You can also go online to access the Response Log.

Connect
Reading and Writing

ANALYZE & APPLY

GENRE:
Novel

from
PAX

Novel by **Sara Pennypacker**

? ***ESSENTIAL QUESTION:***

What can you learn by seeing the world through an animal's eyes?

GENRE:
Informational Text

ANALYZE

from
ANIMAL SNOOPS: THE WONDROUS WORLD OF WILDLIFE SPIES

Informational Text by **Peter Christie**

? ***ESSENTIAL QUESTION:***

What can you learn by seeing the world through an animal's eyes?

Students who explore genre...

- **Analyze** features

- **Understand** effects of authors' choices

- **Emulate** craft

- **Use** mentor texts

- **Synthesize** ideas

GENRE ELEMENTS: INFORMATIONAL TEXT

- provides factual information

- includes evidence to support ideas

- often contains text features

- includes many forms, such as news articles and essays

- includes science writing, which explains complex scientific topics in language that is easy to understand

QUICK START

Have you ever had a sneaking suspicion that your family pet or the pet of someone you know has been spying on you or listening in on your conversations? Share your experience with the class.

ANALYZE TEXT STRUCTURE

An **anecdote** is a short account of an event that is usually intended to entertain or make a point. Authors use anecdotes to introduce or illustrate important ideas in a way that is easy to understand and remember. As you read the following informational text, note how the author uses anecdotes to structure and present his ideas. Think about how the anecdotes help explain those ideas in a humorous and entertaining way.

DETERMINE KEY IDEAS

To develop and deepen your understanding of what you read, you need to be able to determine key ideas and evaluate details of the text. A **key idea** is a very important idea about a topic in the text. As you read, write down key ideas of the text in the graphic organizer below. Include important details from the text that support each key idea.

KEY IDEA	SUPPORTING DETAILS

Animal Snoops: The Wondrous World of Wildlife Spies 117

Ways to Organize Reasons and Evidence

Every argument must include reasons and evidence to support a claim. There are several effective ways you can organize that support. Check out some of those ways here.

Read the following techniques that will help you achieve cohesion, or coherence, in your writing.

Order of Importance

Least to most important

Claim: Homewood must switch from a volunteer fire

COLLABORATE & COMPARE

POEM
ANIMAL WISDOM
by **Nancy Wood**
pages 133–135

GENRE: Poem

COMPARE THEMES
As you read, focus on discovering themes, or messages about life or human nature, that both poems share. What ideas are communicated by each poem? Which ideas do they have in common?

? ESSENTIAL QUESTION:
What can you learn by seeing the world through an animal's eyes?

POEM
THE LAST WOLF
by **Mary TallMountain**
pages 136–137

Unit 2

Craft and Communicate

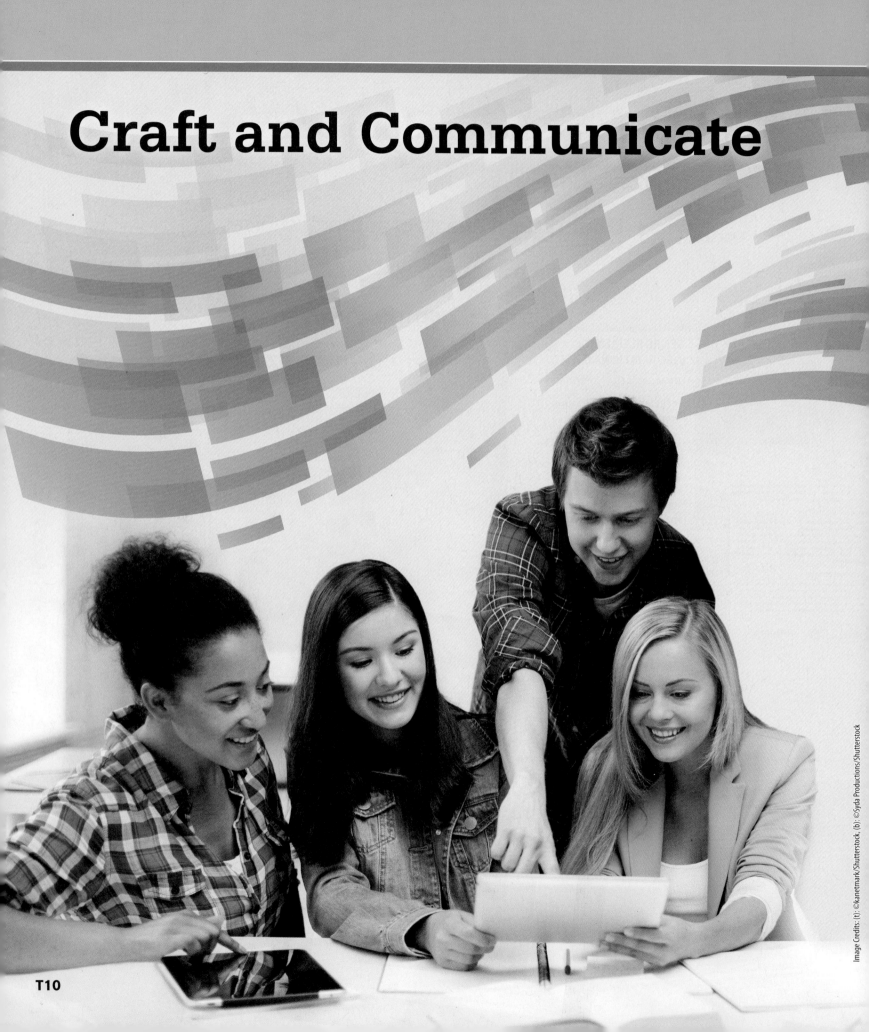

Students who compose...

- **Inform,** argue, and connect
- **Create** in a literary genre
- **Imitate** mentor texts
- **Apply** conventions
- **Use** process and partners

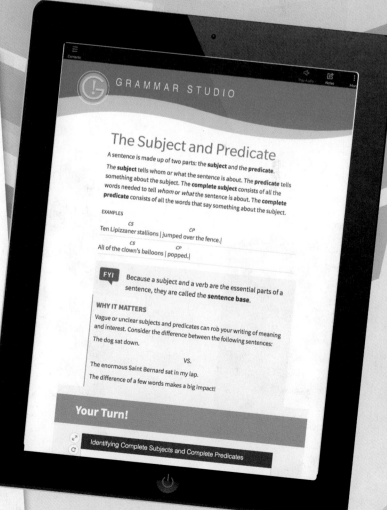

WRITING TASK

Write an Argument

Go to the **Writing Studio** for help writing an argument.

This unit focuses on what we can learn by seeing the world through the eyes of animals. For this writing task, you will write an argumentative essay on a topic related to seeing the world from the perspective of an animal. For examples of arguments that you can use as mentor texts, review "Wild Animals Aren't Pets" and "Let People Own Exotic Animals."

As you write your argument, use the notes from your ___ stud out after reading the texts in this unit.

THROUGH AN ANIMAL'S EYES

This is the topic c___
context for your ___
argument.

This is the Essen___
Question for th___
unit. How woul___
answer this qu___
based on the t___
the unit?

Now mark the ___
that identify e___
what you are ___
asked to prod___

Review these ___
you write an ___
when you fin ___
any needed ___

160   Unit 2

WRITING TASK

Use the Mentor Text

Persuasive Language
Writers use different techniques to persuade readers. Using persuasive language is one technique. Persuasive language includes words with strong negative and positive connotations, which are the ideas and feelings attached to the words.

> Terry Thompson didn't represent the typical responsible owner. He had a criminal record and animal abuse charges. What Thompson did was selfish and insane; we cannot regulate insanity.

The writer of "Let People Own Exotic Animals" uses words with strong negative connotations, like "selfish" and "insane," to make her point that typical exotic animal owners are not like Terry Thompson.

Apply What You've Learned Review your argument for words that you can replace with persuasive language. Consider whether the words you choose have positive or negative connotations.

Author's Craft
Writers often build interest and show the importance of their topic with well-chosen references to familiar stories and events. By citing examples that are relevant to their claims, writers find common ground with their readers—an important step in the process of persuasion.

> But just as a 2007 raid on property owned by football star Michael Vick laid bare the little known and cruel world of dogfighting, a story that unfolded in a small Ohio city recently opened the public's eyes to the little known, distressing world of "exotic" pets.

The writer of "Wild Animals Aren't Pets" builds anticipation and foreshadows a similar sense of public outrage by referring to the 2007 Michael Vick dogfighting story.

Apply What You've Learned To help persuade your readers to agree with your claim, use the strategy of bringing up a well-known story that will influence their reaction to the evidence you cite.

Write an Argument   163

GRAMMAR STUDIO

The Subject and Predicate
A sentence is made up of two parts: the **subject** and the **predicate**. The **subject** tells whom or what the sentence is about. The **predicate** tells something about the subject. The **complete subject** consists of all the words needed to tell *whom* or *what* the sentence is about. The **complete predicate** consists of all the words that say something about the subject.

EXAMPLES

    CS   CP
Ten Lipizzaner stallions | jumped over the fence. |

         CS   CP
All of the clown's balloons | popped. |

FYI Because a subject and a verb are the essential parts of a sentence, they are called the **sentence base.**

WHY IT MATTERS

Vague or unclear subjects and predicates can rob your writing of meaning and interest. Consider the difference between the following sentences:

The dog sat down.

VS.

The enormous Saint Bernard sat in my lap.

The difference of a few words makes a big impact!

Your Turn!

Identifying Complete Subjects and Complete Predicates

Explore and Research

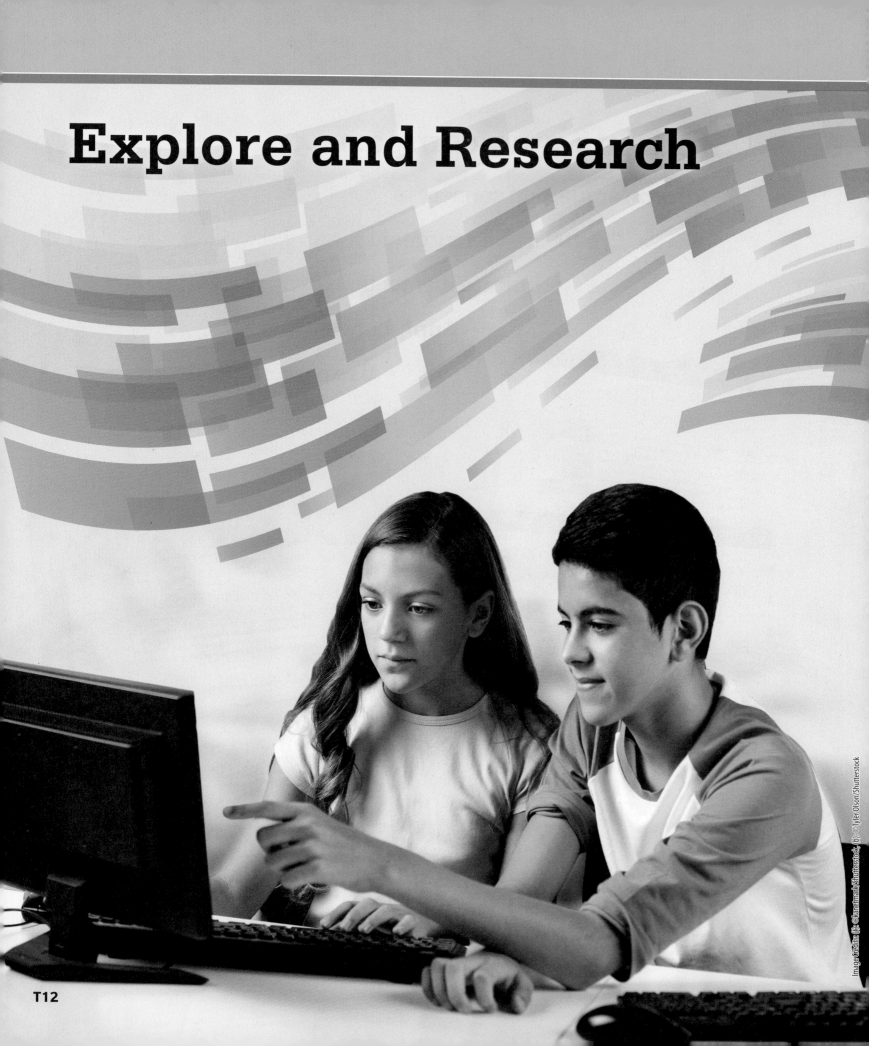

Students who inquire...

- **Generate** questions

- **Plan** and revise

- **Synthesize** information

- **Cite** sources

- **Deliver** results

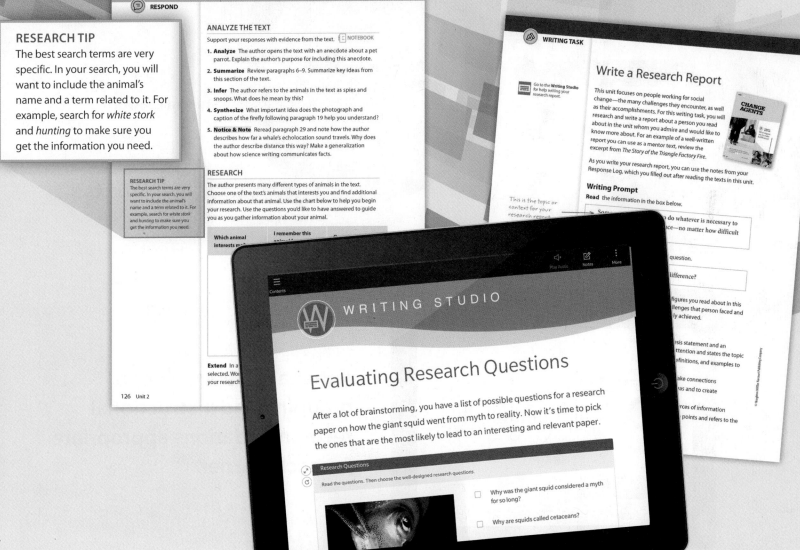

Maximize Growth through Data-Driven Differentiation and Assessment

Ongoing assessment and data reporting provide critical feedback loops to teachers and students, so that each experience encourages self-assessment and reflection, and drives positive learning outcomes for all students.

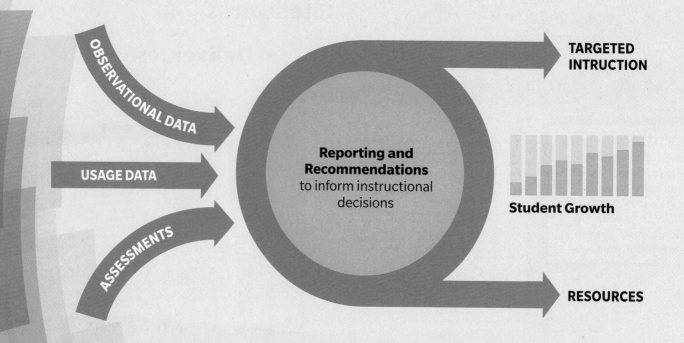

OBSERVATIONAL DATA

USAGE DATA

ASSESSMENTS

Reporting and Recommendations to inform instructional decisions

TARGETED INTRUCTION

Student Growth

RESOURCES

Actionable reports drive grouping and instructional recommendations appropriate for each learner.

Program Assessments

Adaptive Growth Measure

3 times per year

Adaptive Growth Measure allows teachers to gain an understanding of where students are on the learning continuum and identify students in need of intervention or enrichment.

Unit Assessments

6 times per year

Unit Assessments identify mastery of skills covered during the course of the unit across all literacy strands.

Ongoing Feedback from Daily Classroom Activities

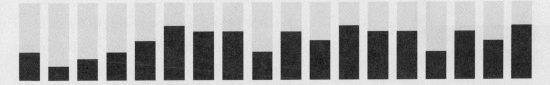

Formative Assessment data is collected across a variety of student activities to help you make informed instructional decisions based on data.

- Check Your Understanding
- Selection Tests
- Writing Tasks
- Independent Reading
- Usage Data
- Online Essay Scoring
- Teacher Observations
- Research Projects

Assessments

HMH Into Literature has a comprehensive suite of assessments to help you determine what your students already know and how they are progressing through the program lessons.

Diagnostic Assessment for Reading is an informal, criterion-referenced assessment designed to diagnose the specific reading comprehension skills that need attention.

Skills-based Diagnostic Assessments will help you quickly gauge a student's mastery of common, grade-level appropriate skills.

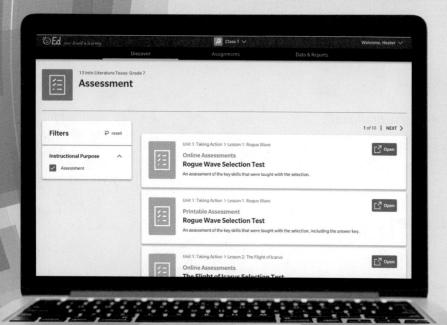

Every selection in the Into Literature program has a corresponding **Selection Test,** focusing on the skills taught in each lesson.
- Analyze & Apply
- Collaborate & Compare, and
- Independent Reading

A **Unit Test** assesses mastery of the skills taught in the entire Unit using new readings aligned with the Unit topic.

The **Diagnostic Screening Test** for Grammar, Usage, and Mechanics provides an assessment of strengths and weaknesses in the conventions of written English.

Each Module in the Grammar Studio has a **Diagnostic Assessment** and a **Summative Assessment,** for before and after instruction.

Foster a Learning Culture

As you encourage a culture of responsibility and collaboration, essential for students' success in the world of work, you will find learning activities that are social, active, and student owned.

Collaborate & Compare Designed to support individual accountability as well as team aptitude, this section requires students to read and annotate texts and compare their responses in small groups.

Peer Review is a critical part of students' creative process. Tools like Checklists for writing and listening and speaking tasks and the Revision Guide with questions, tips, and techniques offer practical support for peer interaction.

Learning Mindset notes and strategies in your Teacher's Edition are designed to help students acquire the attitude of perseverance through learning obstacles. Other resources like ongoing formative assessments, peer evaluation, and Reflect on the Unit questions encourage students to monitor their progress and develop metacognitive ability.

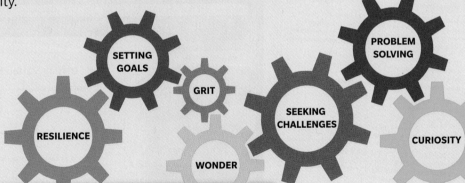

 LEARNING MINDSET

Seeking Challenges Explain that having a growth and learning mindset means taking risks. That involves trying new things and not being afraid to fail (or look silly) in front of friends. Emphasize that trying hard is important, but trying things that are hard is just as important. The brain needs to be stretched and challenged in much the same way as muscles do, and that's the way to think about difficult tasks, as challenges.

Build a Culture of Professional Growth

Embedded and on-going Professional Learning empowers you to develop high-impact learning experiences that provide all your students with opportunities for reading and writing success.

Build agency with purposeful, embedded teacher support and high-impact strategies

- Notice & Note Strategies for Close Reading
- Classroom Videos
- On-Demand Professional Learning Modules

Notice & Note
READING MODEL

ROGUE WAVE

You are about to read the short story "Rogue Wave." In it, you will notice and note signposts that will give you clues about the story's characters and themes. Here are three key signposts to look for as you read this short story and other works of fiction.

For more information on these and other signposts to Notice & Note, visit the **Reading Studio.**

When you read and encounter phrases like these, pause to see if a phrase indicates a **Memory Moment** signpost:

"She remembered that . . ."
"He'd heard of . . ."
"It was just like when . . ."
"Earlier that week . . ."
"as a baby, she'd . . ."

Memory Moment You're sitting on the bench waiting for the coach to post the names of the kids who made the team. As you wait, your mind drifts back to when you started shooting hoops at the neighborhood courts. You were just eight. Others would laugh every time you missed. Not anymore. The coach comes out and you run over to read the list.

Our brains are linking the present to the past almost all of the time . Something—an image, a sound, a smell, an event—will trigger a memory of an earlier time. When an author introduces a memory, it's usually for a good reason. Paying attention to a **Memory Moment** can:

- provide background that relates to the current situation
- reveal details about characters' histories or relationships
- show what motivates or drives a character's actions
- show what leads a character to an "aha moment"

The paragraph below of "Rogue Wave" illustrates a student's annotation of a Memory Moment:

> 5   Below deck Scoot was listening to Big Sandy & His Fly-Rite Boys doing "Swingin' West," and singing along with them while slicing leftover steak from last night's meal. They'd grilled it on a small charcoal ring that was mounted outboard on the starboard side at the stern, trailing sparks into the water. The *Sea Dog* had every blessed thing, including a barbecue pit, she marveled.

Anchor Question
When you notice this signpost, ask: Why might this memory be important?

What memory is introduced?	*the memory of grilling steak the previous night*
Why do you think this memory is important to the story?	*The memory shows that Scoot is impressed by how well equipped the Sea Dog is. It also shows that she and her brother are enjoying this trip.*

2   Unit 1

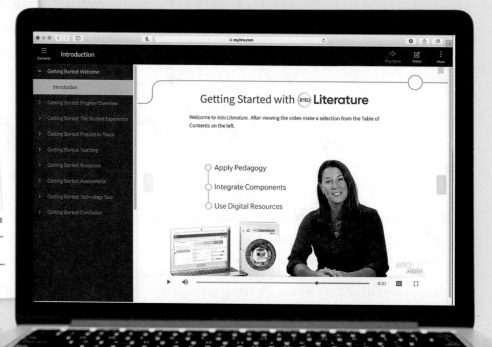

Grow Your Practice with Personalized Blended Professional Learning

- **Getting Started Course and Professional Learning Guide:** Learn the program components, pedagogy, and digital resources to successfully teach with *Into Literature*.

- **Follow-Up:** Choose from relevant instructional topics to create a personalized in-person or online Follow-Up experience to deepen program mastery and enhance teaching practices.

- **Coaching and Modeling:** Experience just-in-time support to ensure continuous professional learning that is student-centered and grounded in data.

- **askHMH:** Get on-demand access to program experts who will answer questions and provide personalized conferencing and digital demonstrations to support implementation.

- **Technical Services:** Plan, prepare, implement, and operate technology with ease.

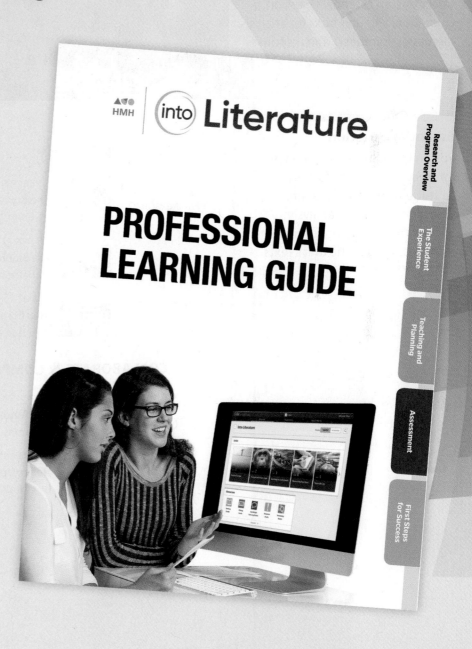

Annotated Student Edition Table of Contents

UNIT ①

GADGETS AND GLITCHES
PAGE 1

Topical Focus

Each unit reflects a topic linking selections, an Essential Question, a Quotation, and unit tasks for analysis, discussion, synthesis, and response.

? **ESSENTIAL QUESTION**

Does technology improve or control our lives?

Essential Question

Posing thought-provoking ideas for discussion and reflection as students read, the Essential Question stimulates analysis and synthesis, leading to a richer understanding of the unit's texts.

ANALYZE & APPLY

COLLABORATE & COMPARE

© Houghton Mifflin Harcourt Publishing Company • Image Credits (t to b): ©Syda Productions/Shutterstock; ©Adam Gault/OJO Images/Getty Images; ©Helene Wiesenhaan/Getty Images; ©Nithid Memanee/Shutterstock; ©Suwin/ Shutterstock; ©Phonlamai Photo/Shutterstock

INDEPENDENT READING

These selections can be accessed through the digital edition.

POEM
If You Go into the Woods You Will Find It Has a Technology
by Heather Christle

SCIENCE FICTION
Hallucination
by Isaac Asimov

SCIENCE FICTION
There Will Come Soft Rains
by Ray Bradbury

NOVEL
from **All the Light We Cannot See**
by Anthony Doerr

Suggested Novel Connection

NOVEL
Singularity
by William Sleator

Additional Novel Connections

• **Brave New World**
by Aldous Huxley

• **The Time Machine**
by H.G. Wells

> **Key Learning Objectives**
> In abbreviated form, each unit's main instructional goals are listed for planning and quick reference.

Key Learning Objectives

• Analyze plot
• Analyze science fiction
• Analyze organization
• Analyze structure
• Analyze irony
• Analyze claim and evidence
• Analyze graphic features
• Evaluate evidence
• Analyze rhetoric and reasoning

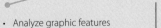 **Visit the Interactive Student Edition for:**

• Unit and Selection Videos
• Media Selections
• Selection Audio Recordings
• Enhanced Digital Instruction

UNIT ②

Instructional Overview and Resources 74A

UNIT ②
THE THRILL OF HORROR
PAGE 74

? ESSENTIAL QUESTION

Why do we sometimes like to feel frightened?

Analyze & Apply

This section of the Table of Contents groups a variety of selections for analysis, annotation, and application of the Notice & Note protocol, as well as standards instruction.

Collaborate & Compare

This section of the Table of Contents provides a comparative analysis of two selections linked by topic but different in genre, craft, or focus. Standards instruction and annotation are also applied.

ANALYZE & APPLY

COLLABORATE & COMPARE

UNIT 2

Independent Reading
Interactive digital texts linked to the unit topic and in a wide range of genres and Lexile levels provide additional resources for students' independent reading, expanding student choice and experience.

INDEPENDENT READING
These selections can be accessed through the digital edition.

POEM
Frankenstein
by Edward Field

POEM
beware: do not read this poem
by Ishmael Reed

SHORT STORY
Blood
by Zdravka Evitmova

SHORT STORY
The Outsider
by H. P. Lovecraft

ESSAY
Scary Tales
by Jackie Torrence

Suggested Novel Connection

NOVEL
Dracula
by Bram Stoker

Additional Novel Connections

- **Frankenstein**
  by Mary Shelley

- **The Strange Case of Dr. Jeckyll and Mr. Hyde**
  by Robert Louis Stevenson

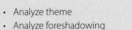

Key Learning Objectives
- Analyze literary criticism
- Make connections
- Analyze rhyme scheme
- Analyze point of view
- Analyze suspense
- Analyze theme
- Analyze foreshadowing
- Evaluate media

Online Ed Visit the Interactive Student Edition for:
- Unit and Selection Videos
- Media Selections
- Selection Audio Recordings
- Enhanced Digital Instruction

© Houghton Mifflin Harcourt Publishing Company • Image Credits (t to b): ©Houghton Mifflin Harcourt; ©Nika Fadul/Moment/Getty Images; ©AlekseySagitov/iStock/Getty Images; ©Elena Dijour/Shutterstock; ©Danomyte/Shutterstock; ©Zacarias Pereira Da Mata/Dreamstime

UNIT (3)
PLACES WE CALL HOME
PAGE 150

? **ESSENTIAL QUESTION**

What are the places that shape who you are?

Notice & Note Reading Model

Using a gradual release model to teach the signposts referred to as Notice & Note, the Reading Model describes two to three signposts and illustrates them in a selection.

ANALYZE & APPLY

COLLABORATE & COMPARE

Mentor Text

This selection exemplifies genre characteristics and craft choices that will be used in end-of-unit writing tasks as models for students.

INDEPENDENT READING

These selections can be accessed through the digital edition.

POEM
My Father and the Figtree
Naomi Shihab Nye

SHORT STORY
Golden Glass
by Alma Luz Villanueva

MEMOIR
from **The Latehomecomer**
by Kao Kalia Yang

RESEARCH STUDY
A Place to Call Home
by Scott Bittle and Jonathan Rochkind

MYTH
Salmon Boy
by Michael J. Caduto and Joseph Bruchac

Suggested Novel Connection

NOVEL
Seedfolks
by Paul Fleischman

Additional Novel Connections

• **Child of the Owl**
  by Laurence Yep

• **The Bean Trees**
  by Barbara Kingsolver

© Houghton Mifflin Harcourt Publishing Company • Image Credits (t to b): ©Valeniker/Shutterstock; ©agsandrew/Shutterstock; ©longtaildog/Shutterstock; ©J. Emilio Flores/Corbis Historical/Getty Images; ©Johann Helgason/Shutterstock; ©Tony Anderson/Digital Vision/Getty Images

Key Learning Objectives

• Analyze plot
• Analyze character
• Analyze narrative structure
• Analyze theme
• Analyze graphical elements
• Analyze literary devices

Online Ed Visit the Interactive
Student Edition for:

• Unit and Selection Videos
• Media Selections
• Selection Audio Recordings
• Enhanced Digital Instruction

Contents FM11

UNIT 4

THE FIGHT FOR FREEDOM
PAGE 238

? **ESSENTIAL QUESTION**

What will people risk to be free?

ANALYZE & APPLY

COLLABORATE & COMPARE

Variety of Genres

Each unit is comprised of different kinds of texts or genres. Essential characteristics of each genre are identified and illustrated. Students then apply those characteristics to their own writing.

Online Ed

INDEPENDENT READING
These selections can be accessed through the digital edition.

POEM
I Saw Old General at Bay
by Walt Whitman

SHORT STORY
A Mystery of Heroism
by Stephen Crane

HISTORY WRITING
from **Bloody Times: The Funeral of Abraham Lincoln
and the Manhunt for Jefferson Davis**
by James L. Swanson

BIOGRAPHY
My Friend Douglass
by Russell Freedman

JOURNAL
Civil War Journal
by Louisa May Alcott

Suggested Novel Connection

NOVEL
The Glory Field
by Walter Dean Myers

Tasks
Each unit concludes with one or two culminating tasks that demonstrate essential understandings, synthesizing ideas and text references in oral and written responses.

Additional Novel Connections

- **North by Night**
  by Katherine Ayres

- **Soldier's Heart**
  by Gary Paulsen

Key Learning Objectives
- Analyze autobiography
- Analyze structure
- Analyze characterization in nonfiction
- Analyze author's craft
- Analyze setting
- Analyze mood
- Analyze figurative language
- Analyze poetry

Online Ed
Visit the Interactive Student Edition for:
- Unit and Selection Videos
- Media Selections
- Selection Audio Recordings
- Enhanced Digital Instruction

UNIT ⑤

FINDING YOUR PATH

PAGE 322

? **ESSENTIAL QUESTION**

How do your teenage years prepare you for adulthood?

ANALYZE & APPLY

COLLABORATE & COMPARE

UNIT (5)

Online Ed

INDEPENDENT READING

These selections can be accessed through the digital edition.

POEM
Teenagers
by Pat Mora

POEM
Identity
by Julio Noboa Polanco

POEM
Hard on the Gas
by Janet S. Wong

SHORT STORY
Marigolds
by Eugenia Collier

ESSAY
My Summer of Scooping Ice Cream
by Shonda Rhimes

Suggested Novel Connection

NOVEL
Cold Sassy Tree
by Olive Ann Burns

> **Suggested Novel Connection**
> One extended text is recommended for its topical and thematic connection to other texts in the unit.

Additional Novel Connections

- **Hitch**
  by Jeanette Ingold

- **Reaching Out**
  by Francisco Jimenez

Unit (5) **Tasks**

Key Learning Objectives

- Analyze structure
- Analyze author's purpose
- Analyze characterization
- Analyze free verse poetry
- Make inferences

- Analyze argument
- Identify counter argument
- Analyze rhetorical devices

Online Ed **Visit the Interactive Student Edition for:**

- Unit and Selection Videos
- Media Selections
- Selection Audio Recordings
- Enhanced Digital Instruction

UNIT (6)

THE LEGACY OF ANNE FRANK
PAGE 404

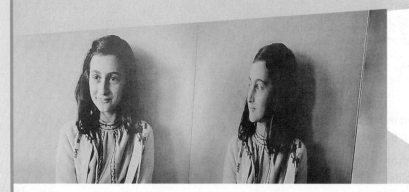

? *ESSENTIAL QUESTION*

What can we learn from
Anne Frank?

ANALYZE & APPLY

COLLABORATE & COMPARE

INDEPENDENT READING

Online Ⓔd

These selections can be accessed through the digital edition.

ESSAY
Peace Can Happen
by Christine Kingery

CHILDREN'S POEMS OF THE HOLOCAUST
The Butterfly
by Pavel Friedmann
On a Sunny Evening
by Anonymous

SHORT STORY
The Singing Women
by Rebecca Makkai

ARTICLE
from **A Tragedy Revealed: A Heroine's Last Days**
by Ernst Schnabel

SPEECH
Nobel Prize Acceptance Speech
by Elie Wiesel

Suggested Novel Connection

NOVEL
Number the Stars
by Lois Lowry

Additional Novel Connections

- **The Book Thief**
  by Mark Zusak

- **Summer of My German Soldier**
  by Bette Greene

Reflection
Students may pause and reflect on their process and understanding of the selections and the themes in each unit.

Key Learning Objectives
- Analyze drama
- Analyze plot development
- Make predictions
- Analyze primary sources
- Make inferences
- Analyze appeals
- Analyze rhetorical devices
- Analyze sound devices
- Analyze figurative language

Online Ⓔd **Visit the Interactive Student Edition for:**
- Unit and Selection Videos
- Media Selections
- Selection Audio Recordings
- Enhanced Digital Instruction

Contents FM17

SELECTIONS BY GENRE

© Houghton Mifflin Harcourt Publishing Company

HMH
Into Literature Dashboard

Easy to use and personalized for your learning.

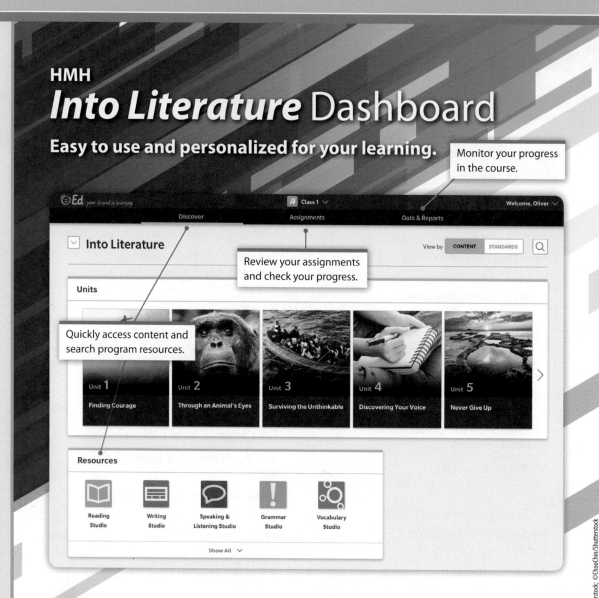

Monitor your progress in the course.

Review your assignments and check your progress.

Quickly access content and search program resources.

Explore Online to Experience the Power of HMH Into Literature

All in One Place
Readings and assignments are supported by a variety of resources to bring literature to life and give you the tools you need to succeed.

Supporting 21st Century Skills
Whether you're working alone or collaborating with others, it takes effort to analyze the complex texts and competing ideas that bombard us in this fast-paced world. What will help you succeed? Staying engaged and organized. The digital tools in this program will help you take charge of your learning.

Ignite Your Investigation

You learn best when you're engaged. The **Stream to Start** videos at the beginning of every unit are designed to spark your interest before you read. Get curious and start reading!

Learn How to Close Read

Close reading effectively is all about examining the details. See how it's done by watching the **Close Read Screencasts** in your eBook. Hear modeled conversations on targeted passages.

Bring the Meaning into Focus

Text in Focus videos dig deeper into complex texts by offering visual explanations for potential stumbling blocks.

 ### Personalized Annotations

My Notes encourages you to take notes as you read and allows you to mark the text in your own customized way. You can easily access annotations to review later as you prepare for exams.

 ### Interactive Graphic Organizers

Graphic organizers help you process, summarize, and keep track of your learning and prepare for end-of-unit writing tasks. **Word Networks** help you learn academic vocabulary, and **Response Logs** help you explore and deepen your understanding of the **Essential Question** in each unit.

 ### No Wi-Fi? No problem!

With HMH *Into Literature,* you always have access: download when you're online and access what you need when you're offline. Work offline and then upload when you're back online.

Communicate "Raise a Hand" to ask or answer questions without having to be in the same room as your teacher.

Collaborate Collaborate with your teacher via chat and work with a classmate to improve your writing.

FM21

HMH
Into Literature
STUDIOS

All the help you need to be successful in your literature class is one click away with the Studios. These digital-only lessons are here to tap into the skills that you already use and help you sharpen those skills for the future.

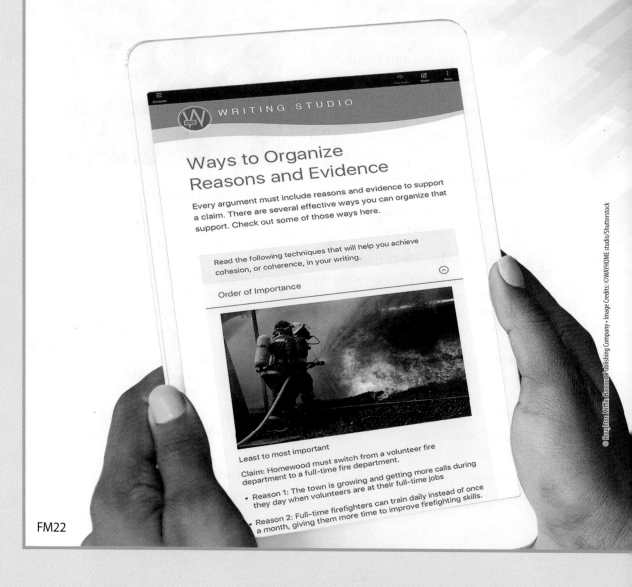

WRITING STUDIO

Ways to Organize Reasons and Evidence

Every argument must include reasons and evidence to support a claim. There are several effective ways you can organize that support. Check out some of those ways here.

Read the following techniques that will help you achieve cohesion, or coherence, in your writing.

Order of Importance

Least to most important

Claim: Homewood must switch from a volunteer fire department to a full-time fire department.

- Reason 1: The town is growing and getting more calls during they day when volunteers are at their full-time jobs
- Reason 2: Full-time firefighters can train daily instead of once a month, giving them more time to improve firefighting skills.

Online

Easy-to-find resources, organized in five separate STUDIOS. On demand and on ED!

Look for links in each lesson to take you to the appropriate Studio.

READING STUDIO

Go beyond the book with the Reading Studio. With over 100 full-length down-loadable titles to choose from, find the right story to continue your journey.

WRITING STUDIO

Being able to write clearly and effectively is a skill that will help you throughout life. The Writing Studio will help you become an expert communicator—in print or online.

SPEAKING & LISTENING STUDIO

Communication is more than just writing. The Speaking & Listening Studio will help you become an effective speaker and a focused listener.

GRAMMAR STUDIO

Go beyond traditional worksheets with the Grammar Studio. These engaging, interactive lessons will sharpen your grammar skills.

VOCABULARY STUDIO

Learn the skills you need to expand your vocabulary. The interactive lessons in the Vocabulary Studio will grow your vocabulary to improve your reading.

FM23

An ABSOLUTELY, POSITIVELY, MUST READ
ESSAY in the FRONT of your Literature Book

YOUR TEACHER AGREES!

BY TWO PEOPLE YOU HAVE NEVER HEARD OF
Dr. Kylene Beers and Dr. Robert E. Probst

If you are reading this essay when we think you are, it's early in the school year. You have this big book in front of you and, for some reason, your teacher has asked you to read these pages by two people you've never met.

Let's begin by telling you something about us.

From Dr. Beers:

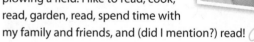

"I've been a teacher all my adult life. I've worked with students at all grades and now I spend most of my time working with teachers, maybe even your teacher! I live in Texas and when I'm not on an airplane flying off to work in a school, I'm on my ranch, plowing a field. I like to read, cook, read, garden, read, spend time with my family and friends, and (did I mention?) read!"

From Dr. Probst:

who are these people ??

"I've also been a teacher all my adult life. When I first started teaching, I taught kids in middle school and high school, and then I spent most of my career teaching people how to be teachers. For many years now, Dr. Beers and I have

written books together, books that are about teaching kids how to be better readers. I live in Florida and when I'm not in schools working with teachers and kids, I enjoy watching my grandkids play soccer and baseball and I love going out on my boat. And, like Dr. Beers, I love reading a great book, too."

So, we're teachers. And we're writers. Specifically, we write books for teachers, books teachers read so that they can help their students become better readers...

. . . and we're going to try to help you become a better reader this year.

We will because we both believe TWO things.

First, we've never met a kid who didn't want to get better at reading. Reading is important for almost everything you do, so doing it well is important.

Second, we believe that reading can change you. Reading something can open up your mind, your thinking, your ideas, your understanding of the world and all the people in it, so that you might choose to change yourself. Reading can help you change yourself.

We think too often it's easy to forget why reading is important. You can come to believe that you need to read better just so your grades will go up, or you need to read better so that you do well on a big state test. Those things are important—you bet—but they aren't as important as reading better so that you can become better. Yes, reading can help you change.

How would that happen—how can reading help you change yourself? Sometimes it is obvious. You read something about the importance of exercise and you start walking a little more.

Or, you read something about energy and the environment and you decide to make sure you always turn off the lights when you leave any room.

Other times, it might be less obvious. You might read *Wonder* and begin to think about what it really means to be a good friend. Maybe you walk over to that person sitting alone in the cafeteria and sit with him or her. Perhaps you'll read *Stella by Starlight* and that book helps you become someone who stands against racism. Or maybe it happens as you read *Mexican Whiteboy* and discover that who you are is more about what you are on the inside than what anyone ever sees on the outside. And when you realize that,

FM25

Note that Beers and Probst list some of the standard reasons students want to be better readers: improve grades and enhance standardized test performance. But they add that reading "can help me change myself."

Ask students to use their consumable book's margins to complete a quick write answering this question:

How has reading led to personal change for you?

Encourage students to be specific.

Ask at least three to five students to share with the group.

perhaps it will give you the courage you need to be truer to yourself, to be the person you really want to be.

Reading gives us moments to think, and as we think we just might discover something about ourselves that we want to change. And that's why we say reading can help us change ourselves.

Finding Important Messages

It sure would be easy to find important messages in the things we read if the authors would just label them and then maybe give us a call.

The reality is, though, that would make the reading less interesting. And it would mean that every reader is supposed to find the same message. Not true! While the author has a message he or she wants to share, the reader—that's you!—has at least three jobs to do:

My Job

1 → **First**, enjoy what you are reading.

2 → **Second,** figure out the message the author wanted to share. Authors write for a reason (no, not to make a lot of money!), and part of that reason is to share something important. That's the author's message, and this year we'll be showing you some ways to really focus in on that.

3 → **Third,** you need to figure out the message that matters most to **YOU.** (YES, WE SAVED THE BEST FOR LAST!!!) Sometimes the author's message and what matters most to you will be the same; sometimes not. For instance, it's obvious that J.K. Rowling wrote the Harry Potter series to show us all the sustaining power of love.

From Dr. Beers:

❝ But when I read these books, what really touched my heart was the importance of standing up to our fears. ❞

From Dr. Probst:

❝ And what mattered most to me was the idea that one person, one small person, can make a huge difference in the world. I think that's a critically important point. ❞

"Hello! I wanted to discuss the Important Message with you!"

Discuss with students the three "jobs" as readers Beers and Probst suggest.

© Houghton Mifflin Harcourt Publishing Company

Understanding the author's message requires you to do some work while you read, work that requires you to read the text closely. No. You don't need a magnifying glass. But you do need to learn how to notice some things in the text we call SIGNPOSTS.

A signpost is simply something the author says in the text that helps you understand how characters are changing, how conflicts are being resolved, and, ultimately, what theme—or lesson—the author is trying to convey.

You can also use signposts to help you figure out the author's purpose when you are reading nonfiction. If you can identify the author's purpose—why she or he wrote that particular piece of nonfiction—then you'll be better able to decide whether or not you agree, and whether you need more information.

We do want you thinking about signposts, but first, as you read, we want you to remember three letters: BHH.

B	Book	As you read, we want you to remember that you have to pay attention to what's in the book (or article).
H	Head	And, you need to think about what you are reading as you read—so you have to think about what's in your head.
H	Heart	And sometimes, maybe as you finish what you're reading, you'll ask yourself what you have taken to heart.

To think carefully about what's in the book and what's in your head, you need to become an alert reader, one who notices things. If you're reading fiction, for instance, you ought to pay attention to how characters act. When a character starts acting in a way you don't expect, something is up! That's as if the author has put up a blinking sign that says "Pay attention here!" Or, if you are reading nonfiction, and the author starts using a lot of numbers, that's the same as the author waving a huge flag that says "Slow down! Pay attention! I'm trying to show you something!"

How do I find the author's message?

So, as I read, I have to think about something called signposts?

Pay attention HERE!

Beers and Probst introduce the concept of **signposts** which will be used throughout *Into Literature*. Ask students to underline this definition in their copy.

Ask students why the term *signpost*, which is used in other contexts, is also a good one for reading. ***Possible answer:*** *Writers give us direction, clues, and insight with their words just as drivers are given vital information with stop signs, yield signs, and school zone warnings.*

Ask students to bracket in their consumable the reference to "BHH." Review each. Provide an example and ask students for additional examples.

Example:

B I read an article in the local newspaper discussing five ways to get involved in my community. One suggestion was to begin volunteering.

H I thought about my personal interests: teaching, animals, and the environment.

H I decided to sign up for a volunteers' orientation at the local animal shelter.

Read aloud the four signposts listed here as examples. Explain that these are only four of the signposts they will be learning while using *Into Literature*. Refer students to the entire list of signposts on Student Edition page FM 29. Ask them to mark this page with a sticky note for easy reference.

Review the "keep reading" challenge. Ask students to discuss if this challenge is one they can accept.

Direct students to complete a three -minute quick write in the margin of their book responding to the quote:

"... reading is something that can help you become the person you most want to be."

Ask a few volunteers to share.

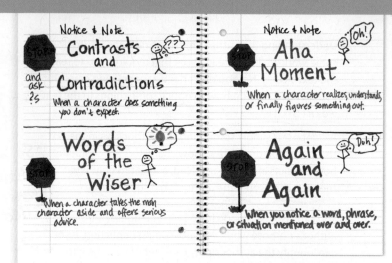

Don't worry about memorizing all the signposts. You'll learn them this year. Your teacher will probably have you make some notes—perhaps as the student above did.

Some of the things you'll read this year, you might not like. (OK—just being honest!) But most of the things we bet you will. What we hope you'll do, throughout this year, is keep reading.

Keep Reading

- » Read every day.
- » Read something hard.
- » Read something easy.
- » Read something you choose.
- » Read what your teachers ask you to read.
- » Read something that makes you laugh.
- » And it's OK if sometimes what you read makes you cry.

One of us LOVES to read scary books while the other much prefers survival books, so don't worry if you like something your best friend doesn't. Read joke books and how-to books and love stories and mysteries and absolutely be sure you read about people who aren't like you. That's the best way to learn about the world around you, about other people, about other ways of thinking. The best way to become a more open person is to live for a while, in the pages of a book, the life of someone you are not.

We hope you have a great year. Stay alert for signposts that you'll be learning throughout this book.

And remember . . .

. . . **reading is something that can help you become the person you most want to be.**

NOTICE & NOTE SIGNPOSTS

Signpost	Definition	Anchor Question(s)
FICTION		
Contrasts and Contradictions	A sharp contrast between what we would expect and what we observe the character doing; behavior that contradicts previous behavior or well-established patterns	Why would the character act (feel) this way?
Aha Moment	A character's realization of something that shifts his actions or understanding of himself, others, or the world around him	How might this change things?
Tough Questions	Questions a character raises that reveal his or her inner struggles	What does this question make me wonder about?
Words of the Wiser	The advice or insight about life that a wiser character, who is usually older, offers to the main character	What is the life lesson, and how might this affect the character?
Again and Again	Events, images, or particular words that recur over a portion of the story	Why might the author bring this up again and again?
Memory Moment	A recollection by a character that interrupts the forward progress of the story	Why might this memory be important?
NONFICTION		
Contrasts and Contradictions	A sharp contrast between what we would expect and what we observe happening. A difference between two or more elements in the text.	What is the difference, and why does it matter?
Extreme or Absolute Language	Language that leaves no doubt about a situation or an event, allows no compromise, or seems to exaggerate or overstate a case.	Why did the author use this language?
Numbers and Stats	Specific quantities or comparisons to depict the amount, size, or scale. Or, the writer is vague and imprecise about numbers when we would expect more precision.	Why did the author use these numbers or amounts?
Quoted Words	Opinions or conclusions of someone who is an expert on the subject, or someone who might be a participant in or a witness to an event. Or, the author might cite other people to provide support for a point.	Why was this person quoted or cited, and what did this add?
Word Gaps	Vocabulary that is unfamiliar to the reader— for example, a word with multiple meanings, a rare or technical word, a discipline-specific word, or one with a far-removed antecedent.	Do I know this word from someplace else? Does it seem like technical talk for this topic? Can I find clues in the sentence to help me understand the word?

FM29

Read the chart on this page noting that it is divided into **Fiction** and **Nonfiction** signposts and includes a definition and an anchor question for each. An **anchor question** helps students identify the signposts as they read by "questioning" the text.

The essay by program consultant Carol Jago is an accessible explanation of **genre** and its importance. Genre has an elevated role in the new standards—both in reading and writing.

Ask students to read the first paragraph and then to write their own definition of genre in the margin of their book.

Ask students to turn to a partner and provide examples of their favorite genre.

If your students need an analogy to better understand **genre**, explain that genre refers to different categories or kinds of texts we read. This is similar to vehicles that we use for transportation. Vehicles transport people and goods but may be trucks, vans, sedans or sports cars—different categories for vehicles—different genres for texts.

READING AND WRITING ACROSS GENRES

by Carol Jago

Reading is a first-class ticket around the world. Not only can you explore other lands and cultures, but you can also travel to the past and future. That journey is sometimes a wild ride. Other books can feel like comfort food, enveloping you in an imaginative landscape full of friends and good times. Making time for reading is making time for life.

Genre

One of the first things readers do when we pick up something to read is notice its genre. You might not think of it exactly in those terms, but consider how you approach a word problem in math class compared to how you read a science fiction story. Readers go to different kinds of text for different purposes. When you need to know how to do or make something, you want a reliable, trusted source of information. When you're in the mood to spend some time in a world of fantasy, you happily suspend your normal disbelief in dragons.

In every unit of *Into Literature,* you'll find a diverse mix of genres all connected by a common theme, allowing you to explore a topic from many different angles.

Writer's Craft

Learning how writers use genre to inform, to explain, to entertain, or to surprise readers will help you better understand—as well as enjoy—your reading. Imitating how professional writers employ the tools of their craft—descriptive language, repetition, sensory images, sentence structure, and a variety of other features—will give you many ideas for making your own writing more lively.

Into Literature provides you with the tools you need to understand the elements of all the critical genres and advice on how to learn from professional texts to improve your own writing in those genres.

GENRE ELEMENTS: SHORT STORY
- is a work of short fiction that centers on a single idea and can be read in one sitting
- usually includes one main conflict that involves the characters and keeps [...] moving
- includes the basic ele[...] of fiction—plot, chara[...] setting, and theme
- may be based on real [...] and historical events

GENRE ELEMENTS: INFORMATIONAL TEXT
- provides factual information
- includes evidence to support ideas
- contains text features
- includes many forms, such as news articles and essays

GENRE ELEMENTS: HISTORICAL FICTION
- includes the basic elements of fiction: setting, character, plot, conflict, and theme
- is set in the past and includes real places and real events of historical importance
- is a type of realistic [...] in which fictional c[...] behave like real pe[...] use human abilities [...] with life's challenge[...]

GENRE ELEMENTS: POETRY
- may use figurative language, including personification
- often includes imagery that appeals to the five senses
- expresses a theme, or a "big idea" message about life

Reading with Independence

Finding a good book can sometimes be a challenge. Like every other reader, you have probably experienced "book desert" when nothing you pick up seems to have what you are looking for (not that it's easy to explain exactly what you are looking for, but whatever it is, "this" isn't it). If you find yourself in this kind of reading funk, bored by everything you pick up, give yourself permission to range more widely, exploring graphic novels, contemporary biographies, books of poetry, historical fiction. And remember that long doesn't necessarily mean boring. My favorite kind of book is one that I never want to end.

Take control over your own reading with *Into Literature's* Reader's Choice selections and the HMH Digital Library. And don't forget: your teacher, librarian, and friends can offer you many more suggestions.

SHORT STORY
Vanquishing the Hungry Chinese Zombie
Claudine Gueh
A girl faces terror to protect her parents and the family store.

POEM
Horrors
Lewis Carroll
What are those terrible things that go bump in the night?

NARRATIVE NONFICTION
Running into Danger on an Alaskan Trail
Cinthia Ritchie
A long-distance runner has a terrifying encounter with a bear.

A Connecticut Yankee in King Arthur's Court
Mark Twain

Twenty Thousand Leagues Under the Sea
Jules Verne

Direct students to read the paragraph under the heading "writer's craft." Ask students to write their own definition of writer's craft in the margin of *Into Literature*. Discuss.

Encourage students to find the Genre Elements chart with each selection in *Into Literature*.

Call students' attention to the **Reader's Choice** selections listed at the end of each unit and show students how to find the **HMH Digital Library** in the **Reading Studio.**

HMH | into Literature™

TEACHER'S EDITION

GRADE 8

Program Consultants:

Kylene Beers

Martha Hougen

Elena Izquierdo

Carol Jago

Erik Palmer

Robert E. Probst

Instructional Overview and Resources

		Instructional Focus	Online **Ed** Resources
	**Unit Instruction** Gadgets and Glitches	**Unit 1 Essential Question** **Unit 1 Academic Vocabulary**	**Stream to Start:** Gadgets and Glitches **Unit 1 Response Log**

ANALYZE & APPLY

	"The Brave Little Toaster" Science Fiction by Cory Doctorow **Lexile 990L** **NOTICE & NOTE** READING MODEL **Signposts** • Again and Again • Contrasts and Contradictions • Aha Moment	**Reading** • Analyze Stories: Plot • Analyze Science Fiction **Writing:** Write a Summary **Speaking and Listening:** Discuss with a Small Group **Vocabulary:** Context Clues **Language Conventions:** The Structure of Sentences	**Audio** **Reading Studio:** Notice & Note **Writing Studio:** Using Textual Evidence **Speaking and Listening Studio:** Participating in Collaborative Discussions **Vocabulary Studio:** Context Clues **Grammar Studio:** Module 1: The Sentence
	Mentor Text *"Are Bionic Superhumans on the Horizon?"* Informational Text by Ramez Naam **Lexile 1110L**	**Reading** • Identify Main Idea and Details • Analyze Organization **Writing:** Write an Informative Essay **Speaking and Listening:** Discuss with a Small Group **Vocabulary:** Synonyms and Antonyms **Language Conventions:** Commonly Confused Words	**Audio** **Text in Focus:** Monitor Comprehension **Reading Studio:** Notice & Note **Writing Studio:** Writing Informative Texts **Speaking and Listening Studio:** Participating in Collaborative Discussions **Vocabulary Studio:** Synonyms and Antonyms **Grammar Studio:** Module 16: Lesson 5: Spelling Words
	"Interflora" Poem by Susan Hamlyn	**Reading** • Analyze Structure • Analyze Irony **Writing:** Write a Sonnet **Speaking and Listening:** Present a Sonnet	**Audio** **Reading Studio:** Notice & Note **Speaking and Listening Studio:** Giving a Presentation

SUGGESTED PACING: 30 DAYS

Unit Introduction 1 | The Brave Little Toaster 2 3 4 5 6 | Are Bionic Superhumans on the Horizon? 7 8 9 10 11 12 | Interflora 13 14 15

English Learner Support	Differentiated Instruction	Online Ed Assessment
• Clarify Vocabulary • Learning Strategies		
• Text X-Ray • Use Graphic Organizers • Use Cognates • Distinguish Formal and Informal Language • Concept Support: Conflict • Gather Evidence • Oral Assessment • Discuss with a Small Group • Language Conventions	**When Students Struggle** • Use Strategies • Make Inferences	**Selection Test**
• Text X-Ray • Understand Directionality • Use Cognates • Understand Idioms and Sayings • Understand Language Structures • Understand Author's Choice • Language Conventions • Oral Assessment • Vocabulary Strategy • Language Conventions	**When Students Struggle** • Main Idea and Details • Reteach: Main Idea and Details **To Challenge Students** • Create an Action Plan	**Selection Test**
• Text X-Ray • Distinguish Rhyming Sounds • Learning Strategies • Oral Assessment • Present a Sonnet	**When Students Struggle** • Reason Inductively • Analyze Sonnet Structure	**Selection Test**

The Automation Paradox/Heads Up, Humans

16 17 18 19 20 21 22 23 24

Independent Reading

25 26

End of Unit

27 28 29 30

UNIT 1 Continued

	Instructional Focus	**Online Ed** Resources

COLLABORATE & COMPARE

"The Automation Paradox"
Argument by James Bessen
Lexile 1140L

Reading
• Analyze Claim and Evidence
• Analyze Graphic Features

Writing: Write a Persuasive Essay

Speaking and Listening: Discuss with a Small Group

Language Conventions: Transitional Words and Phrases

Audio

Close Read Screencast: Modeled Discussions

Reading Studio: Notice & Note

Writing Studio: Writing an Argument

Writing Studio: Writing Informative Texts: Organizing Ideas

Speaking and Listening Studio: Participating in Collaborative Discussions

Vocabulary Studio: Using a Dictionary

"Heads Up, Humans"
Argument by Claudia Alarcón
Lexile 1300L

Reading
• Evaluate Evidence
• Analyze Rhetoric and Reasoning

Writing: Create a Public Service Announcement

Speaking and Listening: Discuss with a Small Group

Language Conventions: Active and Passive Voice

 Audio

Reading Studio: Notice & Note

Writing Studio: Writing Informative Texts

Writing Studio: Writing Informative Texts: Organizing Ideas

Speaking and Listening Studio: Participating in Collaborative Discussions

Vocabulary Studio: Greek Roots

Grammar Studio: Module 3: Lesson 1: The Verb

 Online Ed

Collaborate and Compare

Reading: Compare and Contrast Arguments

Speaking and Listening: Debate

Speaking and Listening Studio: Participating in Collaborative Discussions

INDEPENDENT READING

The Independent Reading selections are only available in the eBook.

 Go to the Reading Studio for more information on Notice & Note.

"If You Go into the Woods You Will Find It Has a Technology"
Poem by Heather Christie

"Hallucination"
Science Fiction by Isaac Asimov
Lexile 790L

END OF UNIT

Writing Task: Write an Informational Essay

Speaking and Listening Task: Present and Respond to an Instructional Speech

Reflect on the Unit

Writing: Write an Informational Essay

Language Conventions: Transitional Words and Phrases

Speaking and Listening: Giving a Presentation

Unit 1 Response Log

Mentor Text: "Are Bionic Superhumans on the Horizon?"

Writing Studio: Writing an Informative Essay

Reading Studio: Notice & Note

Speaking and Listening Studio: Giving a Presentation

English Learner Support	Differentiated Instruction	Online Ed Assessment
• Text X-Ray • Understand Directionality • Use Cognates • Writing Structures • Comparative Adjectives • Figurative Language • Oral Assessment • Vocabulary Strategy • Language Conventions	**When Students Struggle** • Graphic Features **To Challenge Students** • Analyze Graphs	**Selection Test**
• Text X-Ray • Identifying Main Idea • Examining Writer's Evidence • Oral Assessment • Vocabulary Strategy • Comparative Adjectives • Discuss with a Small Group	**When Students Struggle** • Summarize	**Selection Test**
"There Will Come Soft Rains" Science Fiction by Ray Bradbury **Lexile 920L**	from *All the Light We Cannot See* Novel Excerpt by Anthony Doerr **Lexile 880L**	**Selection Tests**
• Language X-Ray • Understand Academic Language • Use Numbers • Adapt the Essay	**When Students Struggle** • Draft the Essay • Use Transitional Words and Phrases • Team Work **To Challenge Students** • Conduct Research	**Unit Test**

GADGETS AND GLITCHES

? Connect to the ESSENTIAL QUESTION

Ask a volunteer to read aloud the Essential Question. Discuss how the images relate to the question. How does technology make life easier? How does it make life more difficult? Ask students to think of real-life examples of how technology impacts our lives.

■ English Learner Support

Clarify Vocabulary Make sure students understand the Essential Question. If necessary, clarify the meaning of the following words:

- *Technology* means "the practical application of science" and often refers to equipment or machines.
- *Improve* means "to make better."
- *Control* means "to have power over."

Help students restate the question in simpler language: Does technology make life better or worse?
SUBSTANTIAL / MODERATE

DISCUSS THE QUOTATION

Tell students that Douglas Adams (1952–2001) was a British author, humorist, dramatist, and visionary who is best known for writing the science fiction classic, *The Hitchhiker's Guide to the Galaxy.*

Ask students to read the quotation. Then discuss what Adams means by "what we really want is just stuff that works." What does Adams imply about technology? Ask students whether they agree with Adams's conclusion, and have them support their opinions with reasons and examples.

? ESSENTIAL QUESTION:

Does technology improve or control our lives?

> " We are stuck with technology when what we really want is just stuff that works. "
>
> Douglas Adams

⚙ LEARNING MINDSET

Growth Mindset Explain that students who believe they can learn and improve their skills are more successful than students who believe they're "just not good at" certain subjects. In order to grow their brain, students must be willing to put forth effort and accept challenges, even if it means making mistakes. This is called having a growth mindset. It is essential to embrace this kind of mindset so students can break out of their comfort zone and reach their full potential.

ACADEMIC VOCABULARY

Academic Vocabulary words are words you use when you discuss and write about texts. In this unit you will practice and learn five words.

☑ commentary ☐ occupation ☐ option ☐ speculate ☐ technology

Study the Word Network to learn more about the word **commentary**.

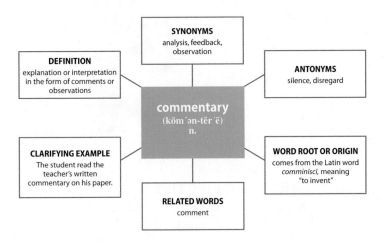

Write and Discuss Discuss the completed Word Network with a partner, making sure to talk through all of the boxes until you both understand the word, its synonyms, antonyms, and related forms. Then, fill out Word Networks for the remaining four words. Use a dictionary or online resource to help you complete the activity.

   Go online to access the Word Networks.

RESPOND TO THE ESSENTIAL QUESTION

In this unit, you will explore how people use and adapt to different forms of technology. As you read, you will revisit the **Essential Question** and gather your ideas about it in the **Response Log** that appears on page R1. At the end of the unit, you will have the opportunity to write an **informational essay** about the future of technology. Filling out the Response Log will help you prepare for this writing task.

   You can also go online to access the Response Log.

ACADEMIC VOCABULARY

As students complete Word Networks for the remaining four vocabulary words, encourage them to include all the categories shown in the completed network if possible, but point out that some words do not have clear synonyms or antonyms. Some words may also function as different parts of speech—for example, *option* may be a noun or a verb.

commentary (kŏm'-ən-tĕr'-ē) *n.* Explanation or interpretation in the form of comments or observations. (Spanish cognate: *comentario*)

occupation (ŏk-yə-pā'-shən) *n.* Principal business of one's life; livelihood. (Spanish cognate: *ocupación*)

option (ŏp'-shən) *n.* Power to choose; something that can be chosen; *v.* to grant or take an option; to acquire rights. (Spanish cognate: *opción*)

speculate (spĕk'-yə-lāt) *v.* To think or wonder about something; to come up with ideas or theories about something. (Spanish cognate: *especular*)

technology (tĕk-nŏl'-ə-jē) *n.* The use of science in solving problems; a method of or machine for doing something that is created by technology. (Spanish cognate: *tecnología*)

RESPOND TO THE ESSENTIAL QUESTION

Direct students to the Unit 1 Response Log. Explain that students will use it to record ideas and details from the selections that help answer the Essential Question. When they work on the writing task at the end of the unit, their Response Logs will help them think about what they have read and make connections between texts.

READING MODEL

THE BRAVE LITTLE TOASTER

Short Story by Cory Doctorow

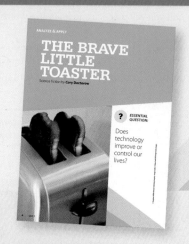

GENRE ELEMENTS
SCIENCE FICTION

Remind students that a **short story** includes all the basic elements of fiction, such as setting, characters, plot, conflict, and theme, but the text is limited in length. **Science fiction** is a genre of fiction that combines real scientific information with imaginary elements. Science fiction often raises questions about issues facing the world today by describing potential outcomes in the future. In this lesson, students will analyze the elements of plot in "The Brave Little Toaster" to draw conclusions about the author's message about technology.

LEARNING OBJECTIVES

- Analyze how a character's motivations influence plot.
- Analyze the characteristics of science fiction.
- Conduct research and synthesize information.
- Write a summary of a short story.
- Collaborate in a group discussion.
- Use context clues to figure out the meaning of unfamiliar words.
- **Language** Discuss causes and effects of character actions.

TEXT COMPLEXITY

Quantitative Measures	The Brave Little Toaster	Lexile: 990L
Qualitative Measure	**Ideas Presented** Much is explicit but moves to some implied meaning. Requires some inferential reasoning.	
	Structure Used Clear, chronological, conventional.	
	Language Used Mostly explicit, some figurative or allusive language. Some dialect and other unconventional language.	
	Knowledge Required Situations and subjects familiar or easily envisioned. Requires no special knowledge.	

RESOURCES

- Unit 1 Response Log

- Selection Audio

- Reading Studio: Notice & Note

- Level Up Tutorial: Making Inferences

- Writing Studio: Using Textual Evidence

- Speaking and Listening Studio: Participating in Collaborative Discussions

- Vocabulary Studio: Context Clues

- Grammar Studio: Module 1: The Sentence

- "The Brave Little Toaster" Selection Test

SUMMARIES

English

Sometime in the near future, most home appliances have been replaced with networked smart machines. Mister Toussaint discovers the downside to such advanced equipment when an energy drink with malicious programming wreaks havoc on his machines' controls. Mister Toussaint struggles to get rid of the clever container until he is rescued by an antique toaster that bravely does exactly what he asks it to do.

Spanish

En un futuro cercano, la mayoría de los electrodomésticos serán reemplazados por máquinas inteligentes interconectadas. El señor Toussaint descubre la desventaja de equipos tan avanzados cuando una bebida energética con programación maliciosa crea caos en los controles de sus máquinas. El señor Toussaint lucha para liberarse del contenedor inteligente, hasta que lo rescata una antigua tostadora, quien valientemente hace exactamente lo que él le pide que haga.

 SMALL-GROUP OPTIONS

Have students work in small groups to read and discuss the selection.

Three-Minute Review

- Pause student activity at any time during reading or discussion, and set a timer for three minutes.
- Direct students to work in pairs to re-read the passage and review their notes to answer the question, "What is the effect of technology?"
- At the end of the three minutes, have each pair write a summary of their review.
- Then ask students, *"What did you notice in your review?"*

Think-Pair-Share

- After students have read and analyzed "The Brave Little Toaster," pose this question: *Who is in control of the technology?*
- Have students think about the question individually and take notes.
- Then have pairs discuss their ideas about the question.
- Finally, ask pairs to share their responses with the class.

Text X-Ray: English Learner Support
for "The Brave Little Toaster"

Use the Text X-Ray and the supports and scaffolds in the Teacher's Edition to help guide students at different proficiency levels through the selection.

INTRODUCE THE SELECTION
DISCUSS TECHNOLOGY

In this lesson, students will need to be able to discuss the functions of different gadgets and technology around the home. Explain that the word *technology* refers to practical ways to use scientific knowledge and solve problems, often in the form of equipment, and that technology is constantly improving and advancing as our knowledge grows. Read paragraphs 1 and 2 with students, and discuss the purpose of the technology in the passage. Point out that the refrigerator in the story is designed not only to store food but also to get rid of spoiled food and to order new groceries. Ask students what they think about these advances in refrigerator technology. Discuss the functions of the following technology around the home:

- microwave
- toaster
- trash can
- dishwasher

Remind students to keep these functions in mind as they discuss the events of the story.

CULTURAL REFERENCES

The following words or phrases may be unfamiliar to students:

- *espresso* (paragraph 8): a strong form of coffee
- *rubbish* (paragraph 9): trash
- *biohazard containment gear* (paragraph 18): suit that protects airways from dangerous materials
- *hazmat* (paragraph 19): hazardous material
- *networked environments* (paragraph 25): areas where devices are connected digitally

LISTENING

Understand Patterns

Explain that authors sometimes repeat images, words, or structures within a text as a way of drawing attention to important points and to reveal character traits.

Have students listen as you read aloud paragraphs 10–15. Use the following supports with students at varying proficiency levels:

- Tell students that you will ask questions about what you just read aloud. Model that they should give a thumbs up if the answer is yes, and a thumbs down for no. For example, ask: *Does the LOONY GOONY always sing in rhymes? (Yes) Are the LOONY GOONY's claims true? (No)* **SUBSTANTIAL**
- Ask: *What do the rhyming songs reveal about the LOONY GOONY's character traits? (**Possible answer:** The LOONY GOONY is not truthful; it is clever.)* **MODERATE**
- After listening to the excerpt read aloud, ask students to work in pairs to identify patterns in the text. **LIGHT**

SPEAKING

Discuss Cause and Effect

Have students discuss the causes and effects of the main character's actions and the relationship to the plot in "The Brave Little Toaster."

Use the following supports with students at varying proficiency levels:

- Display a T-Chart with the headers *Causes* and *Effects*. After reading an action of the main character, ask students: *Is it a cause or an effect?* Write their response in the appropriate column. Guide students to understand that many actions can be a cause and also an effect. **SUBSTANTIAL**

- To help students express their thoughts about causes and effects in the text, display the following sentence frames: *One reason the character _____ is because _____. When the character _____, it causes . One effect of _____ is _____. The main cause of _____ is _____.* **MODERATE**

- Have students discuss with a partner some of the causes and effects of the main character's actions. Ask: *How do the character's actions relate to the plot?* **LIGHT**

READING

Understand Setting and Plot

Tell students that science fiction can seem realistic or farfetched depending on the setting and plot. It is distinguishable from other kinds of fiction, though, by the prominent role of scientific information.

Work with students to read paragraphs 4–9. Use the following supports with students at varying proficiency levels:

- Ask: *How is the refrigerator different from common ones? Do refrigerators talk? Does it throw away food on its own? What do these differences tell you about when the story is set?* Accept single words or phrases. **SUBSTANTIAL**

- Guide students to identify a technology difference in the story that creates conflict. Provide a sentence frame to help students verbalize their analysis: *The refrigerator _____ even though _____.* **MODERATE**

- Have students identify how the technological differences indicate a theme, using this sentence frame: *I think one theme is _____ because _____.* **LIGHT**

WRITING

Write a Summary

Work with students to read the writing assignment on p. 13.

Use the following supports with students at varying proficiency levels:

- Provide an outline with sentence frames that students can use to craft their summaries, such as: *The story "The Brave Little Toaster" is set in_____. Mister Toussaint is _____. He discovers _____.* **SUBSTANTIAL**

- Work with students to create a story map to organize their thoughts as they craft their summaries. Draw a story map. Encourage students to consult their notes and the text to complete the graphic organizer and then use it as an outline for their summaries. **MODERATE**

- Pair students to write their summaries to include at least one example each of simple, compound, complex, and compound-complex sentences. **LIGHT**

EXPLAIN THE SIGNPOSTS

Explain that **NOTICE & NOTE Signposts** are significant moments in the text that help readers understand and analyze works of fiction or nonfiction. Use the instruction on these pages to introduce students to the signposts **Again and Again, Contrasts and Contradictions**, and **Aha Moments**. Then use the selection that follows to have students apply the signposts to a text.

For a full list of the fiction and nonfiction signposts, see p. 62.

▶ AGAIN AND AGAIN

Explain that authors repeat events, images, or particular words **Again and Again** in a story for a reason—the author wants the reader to pay attention to something. The author may be drawing attention to an element, such as the **plot** or the **setting**, or the author may be offering insight into a **character**.

Read aloud the example passage, and ask students what they noticed about LOONY GOONY's speech. Point out that repetitions do not need to be exact, just as **rhyming** is a repetition of sounds but not a duplication of whole words. Explain that the LOONY GOONY's rhyming speech provides insight into the character's personality and motivation. Encourage them to look for different patterns of repetition in the text that add to character development.

Tell students that when they spot an Again and Again signpost, they should pause, mark it in their consumable texts, and ask the anchor question: *Why might the author bring this up again and again?*

READING MODEL

 For more information on these and other signposts to Notice & Note, visit the **Reading Studio**.

When you notice one of the following while reading, pause to see if it's an **Again and Again** signpost:

a word or phrase that rings a bell from earlier in the story

a familiar pattern of events or actions

an object or image that appears more than once

words a character repeats at different points in the story

Anchor Question
When you notice this signpost, ask: Why might the author keep bringing this up?

THE BRAVE LITTLE TOASTER

You are about to read the short story "The Brave Little Toaster." In it, you will notice and note signposts that will give you clues about the story's plot, characters, and themes. Here are three key signposts to look for as you read this short story and other works of fiction.

Again and Again If a friend keeps mentioning the math test that's coming up next week, what might you conclude? Perhaps your friend is nervous about the test and would like some help studying. Or, maybe he's concerned that *you* might need some help studying! Whatever it is, the math test is clearly on his mind.

When an author repeats something, ask yourself if there's a message behind it. Paying attention to something you read **Again and Again** can

- show how different parts of the story are connected
- provide clues to the story's theme or lesson
- reveal a character's traits and personality
- create tension as you wonder how the pattern might change

Read this part of "The Brave Little Toaster" to see a student's annotation of Again and Again:

> . . . "I'm no drink and I'm no <u>meal</u>," LOONY GOONY sang. "I'm a ferrous lump of <u>steel</u>!"
>
> 16   The dishwasher wouldn't wash it ("I don't mean to annoy or <u>chafe</u>, but I'm simply not dishwasher <u>safe</u>!"). The toilet wouldn't flush it ("I don't belong in the <u>bog</u>, because down there I'm sure to <u>clog</u>!"). The windows wouldn't retract their safety screen to let it drop, but that wasn't much of a surprise.

What pattern is repeated?	LOONY GOONY speaks in rhymes.
Why might the author have created this pattern?	The rhymes are funny but also make LOONY GOONY seem kind of annoying.

Contrasts and Contradictions There are some things you expect to be the same every day. The sun will rise. Birds will sing. The neighbor's dog will bark. What if, one day, the birds barked and the dog said, "Good morning"? That would get your attention!

When something happens in a story that goes against your expectations, you'll want to pay attention to it. **Contrasts and Contradictions** often give you a deeper insight into a character or into the story's setting. If a character suddenly does or thinks something unexpected, or a detail about the setting strikes you as surprising, take the time to consider what it means.

The title of the story you're about to read, "The <u>Brave</u> Little <u>Toaster</u>," contains an example of Contrasts and Contradictions.

> **Anchor Question**
> When you notice this signpost, ask: Why did the character act that way?

What contradiction is expressed in the title?	A toaster can't really be brave.
What are some ways the story might explain this contradiction?	A toaster could be a brave character in a science fiction story. Or the title could be meant as a joke.

Aha Moment Some problems or questions can't be resolved quickly. You have to think about them over a period of time. Then, the answer may come to you all at once. In a story, such moments often mark a turning point for the main character. His or her new understanding may take the story's action in a new direction.

A character experiencing an **Aha Moment** may

- finally realize what the real problem is
- understand why another character did or said something
- discover a way to resolve a conflict or solve a problem
- reach a broader understanding about life

In this example, a student underlined the Aha Moment:

> When you see phrases like these, pause to see if it's an **Aha Moment**:
> "All of a sudden . . ."
> "For the first time . . ."
> "Finally she understood . . ."
> "I realized . . ."
> "It all made sense now . . ."

> 6   But the food hadn't been spoiled. Mister Toussaint pored over his refrigerator's diagnostics and logfiles, and soon enough, <u>he had the answer</u>. It was the energy beverage, <u>of course</u>.

> **Anchor Question**
> When you notice this signpost, ask: How might this change things?

What word(s) tell you Mister Toussaint has figured something out?	"he had the answer," "of course"
How might this be connected to the story's conflict?	If Mister Toussaint has figured out what was causing his problem, that might help him resolve the conflict.

WHEN STUDENTS STRUGGLE . . .

Use Strategies Visualizing is important in identifying signposts, especially Aha Moments. If students are struggling to notice a signpost, have them use the Sketch to Stretch strategy to visualize what is happening in a text. Tell students to pick a confusing passage from the selection, reread it, and underline what they find confusing. Then, tell them to sketch what they see happening. Explain that it's acceptable to use stick figures. Finally, have students turn to a partner and share their drawings. To help students understand the importance of visualizing, have them consider how their sketches help them better understand the passage.

CONTRASTS AND CONTRADICTIONS

Explain that **Contrasts and Contradictions** can give readers insight into a **character**, as well as other elements, such as the **setting**.

Read aloud the title "The Brave Little Toaster," and ask students what they think the story will be about. Point out that in our world we would not expect a toaster to be brave. Ask students to consider how this signpost indicates something about the **setting**. Ask, "So what does this contradiction tell us about the world of this story? Where or when is it set?"

Tell students when they spot a Contrast and Contradiction, they should pause, mark it in their consumable text, and ask themselves the anchor question: *What might this mean to the character?*

AHA MOMENT

Explain that **Aha Moments** almost always reveal a change in a **character**, such as a **turning point** in the character's thinking. Point out that some Aha Moments are not so sudden but may be a more gradual realization over time.

Read aloud the example passage and pause at the underlined text, pointing out the phrase *of course*. This clue is significant because it tells readers that the character now understands something important. Ask students to consider what this moment might reveal about Mister Toussaint.

Tell students that when they spot an Aha Moment, they should pause, mark it in their consumable texts, and ask themselves the anchor question: *How might this change things?*

APPLY THE SIGNPOSTS

Have students use the selection that follows as a model text to apply the signposts. As students encounter signposts, prompt them to stop, reread, and ask themselves the anchor questions that will help them understand the story's themes and characters.

Tell students to continue to look for these and other signposts as they read the other selections in the unit.

? Connect to the
ESSENTIAL QUESTION

"The Brave Little Toaster" explores the roles technology might play in our everyday lives in the future. The story raises the question of who should be in control of how technology is used as it describes a series of household malfunctions due to the introduction of a prank energy drink.

THE BRAVE LITTLE TOASTER

Science Fiction by **Cory Doctorow**

? ESSENTIAL QUESTION:

Does technology improve or control our lives?

4   Unit 1

LEARNING MINDSET

Setting Goals Tell students that setting goals is an important part of having a learning mindset. Encourage students to set a goal for reading self-selected texts outside of class; for example, reading for a set time or a specific number of pages a day. Remind students that everyone learns at different speeds. Setting their own personal goals will help them get there eventually.

QUICK START

When you think about technology, you might not think of simple machines like toasters. List some ways a toaster makes your life easier.

ANALYZE STORIES: PLOT

A story's **plot** is a series of events that usually centers on a conflict or problem. The way the main character responds to this conflict depends on his or her **motivations**—what the character wants—as well as the character's traits or qualities. As the character takes action to solve the problem, a series of causes and effects leads to the story's **climax,** or its most intense moment, and to the resolution of the conflict.

As you read, ask yourself what motivates the main character's actions. Use a chart like this one to track causes and effects.

CAUSE	EFFECT/CAUSE
Event that starts the action of the story	

EFFECT/CAUSE	EFFECT
	Climax, when the conflict reaches its peak

ANALYZE SCIENCE FICTION

In **science fiction,** writers explore ways in which science and technology might affect people and the world. The writer combines scientific facts with ideas from his or her imagination to create a believable setting. Science fiction is often set in the future, but it also may describe an alternative past or present. When you read science fiction, you must use details in the text to draw a conclusion about when and where the story takes place.

As you read "The Brave Little Toaster," ask yourself these questions:

- What elements of the story are familiar from today's world? What parts are from the writer's imagination?
- Does the story take place in the future or in an alternative version of the past or present?
- What effect does the technology in the story have on the characters?
- What ideas or messages does the story convey about technology?

GENRE ELEMENTS: SCIENCE FICTION

- includes the basic elements of fiction—setting, characters, plot, conflict, and theme
- combines real scientific facts and theories with imaginative elements
- may comment on the present world by imagining a possible future
- may convey a message about the effects or consequences of technology

---

QUICK START

Have students read the Quick Start prompt, and invite them to share their ideas about toasters. Ask students to think about ways that toasters could be improved in future. What features would they like to see? What do they think other kitchen appliances will be able to do in the future?

ANALYZE STORIES: PLOT

Help students understand the terms and concepts related to **plot** when analyzing a story. Explain that the plot is a sequence of connected events set in motion by a **conflict** or problem. Discuss the concept of **character motivation** (why a character chooses to do something). Point out that the character's choices drive the action of the plot. Every choice has an effect and leads to another event and another choice until the plot reaches a **climax**, which is the peak of the conflict and turning point for the main character. After the climax is the **resolution** of the conflict. Explain that identifying causes and effects in a story can help the reader map and understand the plot.

ANALYZE SCIENCE FICTION

Review that **science fiction** uses real scientific facts but contrasts with the current world in creative ways. Remind them that writers explore possibilities of the future or alternate present or past. Tell students that analyzing science fiction requires the reader to draw conclusions from explicit and implied information to identify elements like setting, theme, and author's message. Suggest that students ask themselves the following questions to help them analyze and annotate the text:

- How is the world of the story different from the present day? How is it alike?
- Where and when is the story set? What does this mean for the characters?
- What message is the author trying to communicate?

 ENGLISH LEARNER SUPPORT

Use Graphic Organizers   Explain that using graphic organizers to note details from the text can enhance comprehension. Review how to use the Cause and Effect chain as students analyze the plot. To read the chain, students should begin at the top left. Tell them to follow the arrows as they write major actions or events of the stories in sequence. Point out that the effect of one action will be the cause of the next. Ask a volunteer to trace with a finger the order that a reader would read the information in the chain. **SUBSTANTIAL**

CRITICAL VOCABULARY

Encourage students to read each question carefully before answering it with a short answer. Remind them to look for context clues for the boldface vocabulary word. Ask students to share their answers. Allow them to use a dictionary to look up words that they do not know.

Answers:

1. *to find the source of a problem*

2. *It would be annoying to hear the same song over and over.*

3. *No, it would extend its claws.*

4. *two or more hours*

5. *It is safer to be together with others.*

6. *an apartment*

7. *Yes, because the noise would scare or startle you.*

8. *No, because the actions were meant to cause harm.*

■ English Learner Support

Use Cognates Tell students that several of the Critical Vocabulary words have Spanish cognates: *diagnostics/ diagnósticos, reintegrate/reintegrar, consternation/ consternación, ample/amplio.* **ALL LEVELS**

LANGUAGE CONVENTIONS

Review the information about sentence structures. Explain that writers use different structures to communicate ideas of different complexities. Display and read aloud each example sentence. Discuss the structure of each sentence. *(Explain how commas and conjunctions connect ideas in the compound and complex sentences.)*

 # ANNOTATION MODEL

Students can review the Reading Model introduction if they have questions about any of the signposts. Suggest that they underline important phrases or circle key words that help them identify signposts. They may want to color-code their annotations by using a different color highlighter for each signpost. Point out that they may follow this suggestion or use their own system for marking up the selections in their write-in texts.

 GET READY

CRITICAL VOCABULARY

diagnostics	retract	reintegrate	consternation
chafe	ample	abode	vindictive

To see how many Critical Vocabulary words you already know, answer these questions.

1. Why might you run a **diagnostics** check on your computer?

2. Why would hearing the same song 50 times **chafe** listeners?

3. If a cat wanted to scratch you, would it **retract** its claws?

4. How many hours would be **ample** time to watch a movie?

5. Why would a lost sheep want to **reintegrate** with its herd?

6. Which is an **abode**—an apartment or a school?

7. If you heard a loud crash, might you feel **consternation**?

8. Would you thank someone who had done something **vindictive**?

LANGUAGE CONVENTIONS

The Structure of Sentences Writers use a variety of sentence structures to express ideas clearly. Note how commas and conjunctions (*so, because*) help connect ideas in these examples.

Simple sentence: My fridge is already full of delicious things.

Compound sentence: My fridge is empty, so I'm going to the grocery to buy food.

Complex sentence: My fridge is full because I went to the grocery store last night.

ANNOTATION MODEL   **NOTICE & NOTE**

As you read, notice and note signposts, including **Again and Again, Contrasts and Contradictions,** and **Aha Moments.** Also note details that help you draw a conclusion about where and when "The Brave Little Toaster" takes place.

1 One day, Mister Toussaint came home to find an extra 300 euros' worth of groceries on his doorstep. So he called up Miz Rousseau, the grocer, and said, "Why have you sent me all this food? My fridge is already full of delicious things. I don't need this stuff and besides, I can't pay for it."

> These details are realistic and modern. The story may be set in the present.

BACKGROUND

Cory Doctorow (b. 1971) is a journalist, a blogger, and the author of many works of science fiction. His young adult novels include Homeland, Pirate Cinema, and the award-winning Little Brother, which was also adapted for the stage. His other works include graphic novels, essays, and short stories. Doctorow was born in Toronto, Canada, and lives in Los Angeles. In addition to his other pursuits, he works for the Electronic Frontier Foundation, which aims to protect freedom in technology law and policies.

THE BRAVE LITTLE TOASTER

Science Fiction by Cory Doctorow

SETTING A PURPOSE

As you read, think about the role that technology plays in this story. Note details about Mister Toussaint's interactions with certain devices and how he is motivated to respond.

1   One day, Mister Toussaint came home to find an extra 300 euros' worth[1] of groceries on his doorstep. So he called up Miz Rousseau, the grocer, and said, "Why have you sent me all this food? My fridge is already full of delicious things. I don't need this stuff and besides, I can't pay for it."

2   But Miz Rousseau told him that he had ordered the food. <u>His refrigerator had sent in the list, and she had the signed order to prove it.</u>

3   Furious, Mister Toussaint confronted his refrigerator. It was mysteriously empty, even though it had been full that morning. Or rather, it was *almost* empty: there was a single pouch of energy drink sitting on a shelf in the back. He'd

---
[1] **euros'** (yŏŏr´ōz) **worth:** valued in euros, the currency of the European Union. 300 euros is about the same as $350 in American currency.

Notice & Note

Use the side margins to notice and note signposts in the text.

CONTRASTS AND CONTRADICTIONS

Notice & Note: Which details in paragraphs 1–5 contrast with your own experiences and expectations? Mark these details.

Draw Conclusions: Based on these details, what do you think is the setting of this story?

BACKGROUND

After students read the Background note, explain that as technology has grown, so has the debate over people's rights and freedom related to the use of technology. Point out that, in addition to being an author, Cory Doctorow works for an organization focused on protecting freedom in technology law and policies. Ask students how they think this background might affect the author's viewpoint.

SETTING A PURPOSE

Direct students to the Setting a Purpose prompt to focus their reading.

▶ CONTRASTS AND CONTRADICTIONS

Remind students that signposts for Contrasts and Contradictions help the reader understand **characters**, **conflicts**, and the relationship of the **setting** to the **plot**. Encourage students to look for contrasts and contradictions between the world of the story and the world of the reader. Remind them to ask themselves, "What might this mean to the character?" (**Possible answer:** *The story is probably set in the near future.*)

 For **reading support** for students at varying proficiency levels, see the **Text X-Ray** on page 2D.

(EL) ENGLISH LEARNER SUPPORT

Distinguish Formal and Informal Language   Explain that some language is acceptable in informal situations but not appropriate to use in formal situations. Point out that informal language will include more personal details, abbreviations, and slang. Ask students to read what Mister Toussaint says to Miz Rousseau in paragraph 1 and note words or details that indicate whether he is using formal or informal language. (**Possible answers:** *fridge; don't; can't; stuff*) Contrast Mister Toussaint's dialogue with the account of Miz Rousseau's response, which is written in language that avoids slang and contractions. Discuss what the differences might mean to the characters. **ALL LEVELS**

ENGLISH LEARNER SUPPORT

Concept Support: Conflict Have students work in pairs to reread this page and identify words and phrases that describe the problem and how Mister Toussaint is feeling in response to it. Then have them practice asking each other the question in the margin and answering the question, using examples from the text.

SUBSTANTIAL/MODERATE

ANALYZE STORIES: PLOT

Explain to students that **plot** may be a series of events in a story, but it is driven by the actions and choices of the **characters** in reaction to a **conflict**. Remind them to look for the actions and choices of the main character as they read to understand the cause-and-effect relationships in the plot. Discuss the causes and effects of Mister Toussaint's actions to identify the conflict of the story. (**Possible answer:** *The conflict is that the energy drink is causing problems in his refrigerator, and he needs to get rid of it.*)

▶ AGAIN AND AGAIN

Remind students that this signpost is often used to reveal patterns of behavior that provide insight into the **character**. Have students identify how Mister Toussaint tries to get rid of the pouch in paragraph 9. Ask them how he tries next to get rid of the pouch in paragraph 15. Discuss what they notice about his repeated attempts. (**Possible answer:** *LOONY GOONY finds a way to survive every time. Each attempt and failure makes me want to see whether Mister Toussaint will ever be able to get rid of it, and how.*)

CRITICAL VOCABULARY

diagnostics: When an electronic machine has an unknown problem, a user can attempt to diagnose, or identify, what is wrong by running diagnostics, which is a computer program that searches for a problem. For example, a mechanic might run a car's diagnostics to find out why a warning light was on.

ASK STUDENTS to discuss diagnostics they have encountered with different devices or equipment and why the diagnostics were necessary. (**Possible answers:** *video games, computers, smartphones, including the reasons why*)

 NOTICE & NOTE

gotten it from an enthusiastically smiling young woman on the metro[2] platform the day before. She'd been giving them to everyone.

4 "Why did you throw away all my food?" he demanded. The refrigerator hummed smugly at him.

5 "It was spoiled," it said.

diagnostics
(dī´əg-nŏs´tĭks) *n. Diagnostics* are tools a computer uses to identify problems.

6 But the food hadn't been spoiled. Mister Toussaint pored over his refrigerator's **diagnostics** and logfiles, and soon enough, he had the answer. It was the energy beverage, of course.

7 "Row, row, row your boat," it sang. "Gently down the stream. Merrily, merrily, merrily, merrily, I'm offgassing ethylene."[3] Mister Toussaint sniffed the pouch suspiciously.

8 "No you're not," he said. The label said that the drink was called LOONY GOONY and it promised ONE TRILLION TIMES MORE POWERFUL THAN ESPRESSO!!!!!ONE11! Mister Toussaint began to suspect that the pouch was some kind of stupid Internet of Things[4] prank. He hated those.

ANALYZE STORIES: PLOT
Annotate: Notice what Mister Toussaint does with LOONY GOONY in paragraph 9. Mark details in paragraphs 6–8 that explain why he does this.

Infer: What conflict is Mister Toussaint facing in this story?

9 He chucked the pouch in the rubbish can and put his new groceries away.

10 The next day, Mister Toussaint came home and discovered that the overflowing rubbish was still sitting in its little bag under the sink. The can had not cycled it through the trapdoor to the chute that ran to the big collection-point at ground level, 104 storeys below.

11 "Why haven't you emptied yourself?" he demanded. The trashcan told him that toxic substances had to be manually sorted. "What toxic substances?"

12 So he took out everything in the bin, one piece at a time. You've probably guessed what the trouble was.

13 "Excuse me if I'm chattery, I do not mean to nattery, but I'm a mercury battery!" LOONY GOONY's singing voice really got on Mister Toussaint's nerves.

AGAIN AND AGAIN
Notice & Note: What pattern do you notice in Mister Toussaint's actions? Underline and circle words that show the pattern.

Analyze: How do Mister Toussaint's repeated actions create tension in the plot, or make you eager to see what will happen next?

14 "No you're not," Mister Toussaint said.

15 Mister Toussaint tried the microwave. Even the cleverest squeezy-pouch couldn't survive a good nuking. But the microwave wouldn't switch on. "I'm no drink and I'm no meal," LOONY GOONY sang. "I'm a ferrous[5] lump of steel!"

---
[2] **metro:** subway.
[3] **offgassing ethylene** (ĕth´ə-lēn´): releasing a flammable gas, C_2H_4.
[4] **Internet of Things:** the network of devices, including "smart" appliances, that are connected to the Internet.
[5] **ferrous** (fĕr´əs): containing iron.

APPLYING ACADEMIC VOCABULARY

☐ commentary ☐ occupation ☒ option ☒ speculate ☒ technology

Write and Discuss Have students turn to a partner to discuss the following questions. Guide students to include the Academic Vocabulary words *option, speculate,* and *technology* in their responses. Ask volunteers to share their responses with the class.

- What **options** do most home appliance have today?
- What would you **speculate** will be common in future **technology**?

16   The dishwasher wouldn't wash it ("I don't mean to annoy or **chafe**, but I'm simply not dishwasher safe!"). The toilet wouldn't flush it ("I don't belong in the bog, because down there I'm sure to clog!"). The windows wouldn't **retract** their safety screen to let it drop, but that wasn't much of a surprise.

17   "I hate you," Mister Toussaint said to LOONY GOONY, and he stuck it in his coat pocket. He'd throw it out in a trash-can on the way to work.

18   They arrested Mister Toussaint at the 678th Street station. They were waiting for him on the platform, and they cuffed him just as soon as he stepped off the train. The entire station had been evacuated and the police wore full biohazard containment gear. They'd even shrinkwrapped their machine-guns.

19   "You'd better wear a breather and you'd better wear a hat, I'm a vial of terrible deadly hazmat," LOONY GOONY sang.

20   When they released Mister Toussaint the next day, they made him take LOONY GOONY home with him. There were lots more people with LOONY GOONYs to process.

21   Mister Toussaint paid the rush-rush fee that the storage depot charged to send over his container. They forklifted it out of the giant warehouse under the desert and zipped it straight to the cargo-bay in Mister Toussaint's building. He put on old, stupid clothes and clipped some lights to his glasses and started sorting.

22   Most of the things in the container were stupid. He'd been throwing away stupid stuff all his life, because the smart stuff

---

NOTICE & NOTE

chafe
(chāf) *v.* To *chafe* is to annoy or bother someone.

retract
(rĭ-trăkt´) *v.* To *retract* is to pull in.

ANALYZE SCIENCE·FICTION

Annotate: Mark details in paragraphs 18–20 that show what happens when Mister Toussaint tries to dispose of LOONY GOONY on the way to work.

Analyze: Why are the police waiting for him at the train station? What ideas about technology are suggested by these events?

The Brave Little Toaster   9

 ## ANALYZE SCIENCE FICTION

Remind students that science fiction describes a possible future or alternate world that results from scientific advances. The author's vision may be positive, negative, or a mix of both. Often the problems explored in science fiction stem from fears about scientific advancements in the present day. Explain that the reader must make inferences about how the problems of the story relate to today's world. Discuss the possible fears people might have about technology. (***Possible answer:*** *LOONY GOONY has communicated the message that it is a "deadly hazmat," so the police respond to the threat. These events suggest that technology can cause trouble.*)

■ English Learner Support

Gather Evidence   Have students work with a partner to discuss possible fears about technology. Each partner can look for clues in the text that indicate why the police were waiting for Mister Toussaint. Have students take turns presenting their evidence to their partner using sentence frames:

- *This shows that* _____.
- *This suggests that* _____.
- *This indicates that* _____.

SUBSTANTIAL/MODERATE

 For **listening support** for students at varying proficiency levels, see the **Text X-Ray** on page 2C.

CRITICAL VOCABULARY

chafe: The word *chafe* also carries a connotation of restriction as the cause of annoyance.

ASK STUDENTS to use the word in a new sentence. (***Possible answer:*** *The extra yard work chafed the brothers who wanted to spend the weekend relaxing.*)

retract: The author uses the word *retract*, which is more specific and has more mechanical connotation than the general phrase *pull in*.

ASK STUDENTS to describe objects that could retract. (***Possible answers:*** *robot's arm; DVD tray; telescope; airplane's landing gear*)

WHEN STUDENTS STRUGGLE . . .

Make Inferences   Remind students that making inferences helps them understand more about the characters, events, and themes in a story.

Clues from the Text	Prior Knowledge	Inference
Mister Toussaint began to suspect that the pouch was some kind of stupid Internet of Things prank.	*I had a computer virus that crashed my computer because of a link I clicked.*	*Technology is vulnerable to malicious programs created by pranksters.*

For additional support, go to the **Reading Studio** and assign the following **Level Up tutorial: Making Inferences.**

AHA MOMENT

Explain that an Aha Moment often marks the **turning point** of the story because the main **character** suddenly understands how to resolve the ongoing conflict. Have students read paragraphs 25–27. What solution is Mister Toussaint attempting in order to get rid of the energy drink? Have students underline the sentences or phrases that explain why he is using this method. Discuss what his actions in paragraph 29 reveal about his plan. (**Answer:** *He realizes that if enough appliances are expressing fear, the quorum-sensor will shut down the toaster. As a result, he unplugs three appliances, so they are not able to "vote."*)

CRITICAL VOCABULARY

ample: This usage of *ample* may be confusing to students because it contrasts with the limited time left to live associated with end of life.

ASK STUDENTS what the narrator's use of the word *ample* reveals about what the character believes about his grandfather. (*It shows that the narrator believes his grandfather had plenty of time to deal with junk but did not do it on purpose.*)

reintegrate: The author uses *reintegrate* to describe a recycling process used in that time period.

ASK STUDENTS to discuss the reasons the narrator would want his grandfather's junk to reintegrate with the material stream. (*His grandfather's junk required storage because it was not able to reintegrate easily.*)

abode: An *abode* is the place where a person lives.

ASK STUDENTS to discuss different types of places that could be an abode. (*house, apartment, cabin, trailer*)

consternation: The word *consternation* includes confusion as part of the feeling of alarm or fear.

ASK STUDENTS to discuss why the appliances would be showing consternation. (*They are both scared and confused by the things the narrator keeps asking them to do because they seem dangerous to their sensors.*)

vindictive: When someone does something harmful as revenge or for spite, it is a *vindictive* act.

ASK STUDENTS to discuss why the fire department would do something vindictive. (*They were angry that he used the toaster to burn the drink pouch.*)

 **NOTICE & NOTE**

was just so much easier. But then his grandpa had died and they'd cleaned out his little room at the pensioner's ward[6] and he'd just shoved it all in the container and sent it out to the desert.

23   From time to time, he'd thought of the eight cubic meters of stupidity he'd inherited and sighed a put-upon sigh. He'd loved Grandpa, but he wished the old man had used some of the **ample** spare time from the tail end of his life to replace his junk with stuff that could more gracefully **reintegrate** with the materials stream.

24   How inconsiderate!

25   The house chattered enthusiastically at the toaster when he plugged it in, but the toaster said nothing back. It couldn't. It was stupid. Its bread-slots were crusted over with carbon residue and it dribbled crumbs from the ill-fitting tray beneath it. It had been designed and built by cavemen who hadn't ever considered the advantages of networked environments.

26   It was stupid, but it was brave. It would do anything Mister Toussaint asked it to do.

27   "It's getting hot and sticky and I'm not playing any games, you'd better get me out before I burst into flames!" LOONY GOONY sang loudly, but the toaster ignored it.

28   "I don't mean to endanger your **abode**, but if you don't let me out, I'm going to explode!" The smart appliances chattered nervously at one another, but the brave little toaster said nothing as Mister Toussaint depressed its lever again.

29   Just as he did, he thought to check in with the flat's diagnostics. Just in time, too! Its quorum-sensors[7] were redlining[8] as it listened in on the appliances' **consternation**. Mister Toussaint unplugged the fridge and the microwave and the dishwasher.

30   The cooker and trash-can were hard-wired, but they didn't represent a quorum.

31   The fire department took away the melted toaster and used their axes to knock huge, **vindictive** holes in Mister Toussaint's walls. "Just looking for embers," they claimed. But he knew that

ample
(ăm´pəl) *adj.* To be *ample* is to be plentiful or enough.

reintegrate
(rē-ĭn´tĭ-grāt´) *v.* To *reintegrate* is to come together, as when similar materials are collected for recycling.

AHA MOMENT

Notice & Note: What words and phrases in paragraph 29 suggest that Mister Toussaint is having an Aha Moment? Mark these words and phrases.

Cause/Effect: What does Mister Toussaint suddenly realize, and how does this affect what he does next?

abode
(ə-bōd´) *n.* An *abode* is a home.

consternation
(kŏn´stər-nā´shən) *n.* *Consternation* is a feeling of alarm or fear.

vindictive
(vĭn-dĭk´tĭv) *adj.* Something is *vindictive* if it is intended to hurt or punish someone.

---

[6] **pensioner's ward:** part of a hospital that provides care for people receiving pensions, or government support for older persons.

[7] **quorum-sensors:** devices that receive input from Mister Toussaint's smart appliances; when a certain number (a quorum) of the appliances signal distress, emergency action is taken.

[8] **redlining:** reaching a limit or maximum; here, approaching the point at which the apartment would take action to stop the toaster.

IMPROVE READING FLUENCY

Targeted Passage Have students work with a partner to read the paragraphs 25–30. Model how to read the different-length sentences in paragraph 25 with appropriate intonation and inflection to create prosody. Have students follow along in their books as you read aloud. Then have each partner choose the role of narrator or LOONY GOONY and read starting with paragraph 26. Remind them to pay attention to punctuation cues. Encourage students to provide feedback. Then, have students switch roles and read the passage again.

 For additional support, go to the **Reading Studio** and assign the following [LEVEL] **Level Up tutorial: Fluency**

they were upset because there was simply no good excuse for sticking a pouch of independently powered computation and sensors and transmitters into an antique toaster and <u>pushing down the lever until oily, toxic smoke filled the whole 104th floor.</u>

32 Mister Toussaint's neighbors weren't happy about it either.

33 But Mister Toussaint didn't mind. It had all been worth it, <u>just to hear LOONY GOONY beg and weep for its life as its edges curled up and blackened.</u>

34 He argued mightily, but the firefighters refused to let him keep the toaster.

ANALYZE STORIES: PLOT

Annotate: Mark details in paragraphs 31–34 that reveal what happens to LOONY GOONY.

Analyze: How do these events resolve the story's main conflict?

CHECK YOUR UNDERSTANDING

Answer these questions before moving on to the **Analyze the Text** section on the following page.

1 Why does Mister Toussaint's refrigerator order more groceries?

A The refrigerator detects that all the food has gone bad.

B Miz Rousseau receives a signed order for more groceries.

C LOONY GOONY tells the refrigerator the food is spoiled.

D The appliances reach a quorum about placing an order.

2 The police arrest Mister Toussaint because —

F they believe the energy beverage is hazardous material

G it is illegal to dispose of smart devices in public

H they are collecting all the energy beverages for disposal

J the train station has been evacuated for no reason

3 The toaster is able to destroy LOONY GOONY because —

A toasters are braver than all other appliances

B the other appliances are afraid of the toaster

C the quorum-sensors approve its actions

D it does not receive messages from other devices

TEACH

ANALYZE STORIES: PLOT

Explain that after the **climax**, or turning point, of the **plot**, there is a **resolution** to the **conflict**. Review the conflict of the story, and discuss the ways Mister Toussaint had tried to get rid of the drink pouch. Ask students to identify the resolution to the conflict. (**Answer:** *By destroying LOONY GOONY, Mister Toussaint stops the destructive prank.*)

CHECK YOUR UNDERSTANDING

Have students answer the questions independently.

Answers:

1. *C*

2. *F*

3. *D*

If they answer any questions incorrectly, have them reread the text to confirm their understanding. Then they may proceed to ANALYZE THE TEXT on p. 12.

 ENGLISH LEARNER SUPPORT

Oral Assessment Use the following questions to assess students' comprehension and speaking skills.

1. Why does the refrigerator order more groceries? (*The LOONY GOONY tells it the food is spoiled.*)

2. Why do the police arrest Mister Toussaint? (*They believe the energy drink is hazardous material.*)

3. Why can the toaster destroy LOONY GOONY? (*It does not receive messages from other devices.*)

SUBSTANTIAL/MODERATE

ANALYZE THE TEXT

Possible answers:

1. **DOK 3:** *The story is set in the near future. Details such as the kinds of appliances Mister Toussaint has (refrigerator, microwave) and the fact that he takes the train to work are similar to today's world. There are also smart devices today, although there is not as much connectivity as in the story (the way "the house chattered enthusiastically" in paragraph 25, the quorum-sensors). The author takes today's technology and imagines how it might evolve in the next few years.*

2. **DOK 2:** *Yes. The prank is that LOONY GOONY creates problems in the house, such as causing the refrigerator to throw away good food and order more, and it cannot be thrown away. It works through the Internet of Things in which smart devices communicate with each other.*

3. **DOK 2:** *Mister Toussaint is motivated by his desire to get rid of LOONY GOONY. This leads him to try many different ways to dispose of the squeezy-pouch, including throwing it in the trash, putting it in the microwave, and flushing it down the toilet. Eventually, he is motivated to get his grandfather's "stupid" toaster out of its storage container.*

4. **DOK 4:** *The climax is when Mister Toussaint is able to destroy LOONY GOONY with the toaster. This scene resolves the story's conflict because he is finally able to defeat the prank.*

5. **DOK 4:** *Each time LOONY GOONY makes a false statement about itself, Mister Toussaint responds, "No you're not." This suggests that people should not blindly follow or believe the machines they have created; human intelligence is always needed.*

RESEARCH

Remind students they should assess the credibility of each source they consult in their research.

Connect Students' discussions may focus on the need for security measures so that networks cannot be hacked by people trying to cause problems.

 RESPOND

ANALYZE THE TEXT

Support your responses with evidence from the text. ☰ NOTEBOOK

1. **Draw Conclusions** Is the story set in the past, the present, or the future? What details in the text help you draw this conclusion?

2. **Interpret** Is LOONY GOONY an "Internet of Things prank," as Mister Toussaint suspects? Explain why.

3. **Cause/Effect** What is Mister Toussaint's main **motivation** throughout the story? How do his goals and desires cause the story's action to unfold?

4. **Analyze** What is the **climax**, or most exciting moment, in the story's plot? How does it lead to the resolution of the main conflict?

5. **Notice & Note** Find the statement that Mister Toussaint repeats in paragraphs 8 and 14. What is he responding to each time? What theme about people and technology does the repetition suggest?

RESEARCH TIP
Remember that you can use quotation marks around a specific phrase to focus your search. For example, searching for "Internet of Things" will weed out search results that are about the Internet in general. If you find that your results are too narrow and you want to see more, just remove the quotation marks.

RESEARCH

How close are we to having refrigerators that automatically order our groceries for us? Do some research about the Internet of Things. Find out what it is today and what it might hold in store for us tomorrow.

QUESTION	ANSWER
What is the Internet of Things?	*It is the network created by both computers and "smart" devices that are connected to the Internet and can communicate with each other.*
What are some examples in today's world?	*a fitness tracker that sends data about your workout to your phone; a thermostat that you can control remotely*
What might the Internet of Things do in the future?	*make farming more productive by connecting sensors on plants to satellite imaging and weather data; create bridges with smart cement that can monitor safety conditions and warn cars of hazards*

Connect Science fiction often conveys a warning about the possible negative effects of technology if people don't use it wisely. With a group, discuss the warning implied by "The Brave Little Toaster." What can people do to gain future benefits from the Internet of Things while also avoiding potential problems?

 LEARNING MINDSET

Belonging Ask students to share and celebrate a mistake. Remind students that we all make mistakes and can learn from each other. You might say, "I make mistakes. Let's learn from each other." Then, model how to reflect on the mistake and learn from it.

CREATE AND DISCUSS

Write a Summary Write a summary of "The Brave Little Toaster." Your summary should briefly retell the most important events of the story in your own words. If you created a cause-and-effect chart to track story events while reading, you may refer to the chart as you write your summary.

❏ Begin by describing the story's setting and introducing the main character, Mister Toussaint.

❏ Next, describe the conflict Mister Toussaint faces and how he responds to it. Tell the main events of the story in the order in which they happened.

❏ Explain how the conflict is resolved at the end of the story.

Discuss with a Small Group What could Mister Toussaint teach his neighbors about dealing with a prank like LOONY GOONY? Work with a group to create a set of helpful tips.

❏ As a group, review the story and note Mister Toussaint's actions in response to LOONY GOONY. Discuss which actions were effective and which were ineffective or destructive, and why.

❏ Brainstorm a list of tips or guidelines that would help someone overcome a similar Internet of Things prank.

❏ Together, organize everyone's ideas into a set of step-by-step instructions for what a person should do if faced with something like LOONY GOONY.

RESPOND TO THE ESSENTIAL QUESTION

? Does technology improve or control our lives?

Gather Information Review your annotations and notes on "The Brave Little Toaster." Then, add relevant details to your Response Log. As you determine which information to include, think about:

• ways in which Mister Toussaint's life is made easier by technology
• ways in which technology causes problems for him
• whether the benefits outweigh the drawbacks

At the end of the unit, you may want to refer to your notes when you write an informational essay.

RESPOND

Go to **Using Textual Evidence** in the **Writing Studio** for more help with writing a summary.

Go to **Participating in Collaborative Discussions** in the **Speaking and Listening Studio** to learn more.

ACADEMIC VOCABULARY
As you write and discuss what you learned from the story, be sure to use the Academic Vocabulary words. Check off each of the words that you use.

❏ **commentary**
❏ **occupation**
❏ **option**
❏ **speculate**
❏ **technology**

APPLY

CREATE AND DISCUSS

Write a Summary Students' summaries should identify the setting (a city in the near future) and the main character, Mister Toussaint, who is the victim of an Internet of Things prank. A "smart" energy drink pouch called LOONY GOONY creates the main conflict when it tells the refrigerator to throw away all of Mister Toussaint's food and order more. Mister Toussaint tries various ways to get rid of LOONY GOONY, such as microwaving it and flushing it down the toilet, but the drink pouch lies to all the other smart appliances to save itself. Finally, Mister Toussaint gets his grandfather's toaster out of storage and uses it to melt LOONY GOONY, which is unable to communicate with a "stupid" appliance.

For **writing support** for students at varying proficiency levels, see the **Text X-Ray** on page 2D.

Discuss with a Small Group Students' instructions may include using some kind of "stupid" technology to destroy a destructive smart device, disabling the network of smart devices so that the quorum-sensor does not intervene, and thinking ahead to avoid consequences like filling the whole building with smoke (such as providing ventilation).

For **speaking and listening support** for students at varying proficiency levels, see the **Text X-Ray** on pages 2C and 2D.

RESPOND TO THE ESSENTIAL QUESTION

Allow time for students to add details from "The Brave Little Toaster" to their Unit 1 Response Logs.

APPLY

CRITICAL VOCABULARY

Answers:

1. *antonyms*
2. *antonyms*
3. *antonyms*
4. *synonyms*
5. *antonyms*
6. *synonyms*
7. *synonyms*
8. *synonyms*

VOCABULARY STRATEGY:
Context Clues

Explain that when faced with an unfamiliar word, a reader should look at the context of the word to try to figure out the meaning. Tell students to look for comparisons and contrasts in the text around a word to understand it better. Encourage them to try substituting the unfamiliar word with possible synonyms to verify the meaning.

WORD BANK
diagnostics
chafe
retract
ample
reintegrate
abode
consternation
vindictive

 Go to the **Vocabulary Studio** to learn more.

CRITICAL VOCABULARY

Practice and Apply Words with similar meanings are called **synonyms**. **Antonyms** are words with opposite meanings. Identify each word pair below as being either synonyms or antonyms.

1. diagnostics/problem
2. chafe/soothe
3. retract/extend
4. ample/plenty
5. reintegrate/explode
6. abode/home
7. consternation/worry
8. vindictive/vengeful

VOCABULARY STRATEGY:
Context Clues

Context clues are words, phrases, and ideas in the surrounding text that help you figure out the meaning of an unfamiliar word or one that could have several different meanings. These clues may appear in the same sentence or paragraph, but sometimes you also need to search in nearby paragraphs. The structure of the sentence in which the word appears can also help you determine its meaning. Find the word *ferrous* in this paragraph from the story:

> 15 Mister Toussaint tried the microwave. Even the cleverest squeezy-pouch couldn't survive a good nuking. But the microwave wouldn't switch on. "I'm no drink and I'm no meal," LOONY GOONY sang. "I'm a ferrous lump of steel!"

Ferrous appears right before *lump*, which is a noun. This helps you determine that the word *ferrous* describes *lump*, and in turn you can tell that it is an adjective. You also know from previous paragraphs that LOONY GOONY pretends to be made of dangerous materials. Microwaving metal is dangerous, and steel contains iron; all of these are clues to the word's meaning, "made of iron."

Practice and Apply Find the words *container* and *stupid* in paragraph 21. Complete the chart for both words.

WORD	POSSIBLE MEANINGS	CONTEXT CLUES	MEANING IN PARAGRAPH 21
container	*small box or jar; very large box for shipping cargo*	*"forklifted it out of the giant warehouse"; "eight cubic meters"*	*very large box for storing household goods*
stupid	*not intelligent; not "cool"*	*"old"; "the smart stuff was just so much easier"*	*not connected to the Internet; unable to communicate with smart devices*

LANGUAGE CONVENTIONS:
The Structure of Sentences

Good writers use a variety of different sentence structures. The simplest structure has one main **clause**, a group of words with a subject and a predicate. Other structures have more than one clause. Study the examples in the chart.

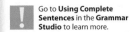 Go to **Using Complete Sentences** in the **Grammar Studio** to learn more.

SENTENCE TYPE	EXAMPLE
A **simple sentence** has one main clause.	The refrigerator hummed smugly at him.
A **compound sentence** has two main clauses joined by a comma and a coordinating conjunction, such as *and, or,* or *but.*	The windows wouldn't retract their safety screen to let it drop, (but) that wasn't much of a surprise.
A **complex sentence** has a main clause and a subordinate clause. The subordinate clause begins with a subordinating conjunction, such as *when, as, after, because,* or *while.*	(When) they released Mister Toussaint the next day, they made him take LOONY GOONY home with him.
A **compound-complex sentence** has at least two main clauses and one subordinate clause.	The smart appliances chattered nervously at one another, (but) the brave little toaster said nothing (as) Mister Toussaint depressed its lever again.

Notice how the conjunctions in the example sentences connect the ideas in the clauses. Without the conjunctions, each sentence would be a **run-on**, or multiple sentences written as if they were one. The writer's meaning would also be less clear without conjunctions.

Run-on: The smart appliances chattered nervously at one another the brave little toaster said nothing Mister Toussaint depressed its lever again.

A common error in writing is to use a comma by itself to join two clauses, instead of using a comma and a conjunction. This error is called a **comma splice**, and it is a type of run-on.

Comma splice: His refrigerator had sent in the list, she had the signed order to prove it.

Correct sentence: His refrigerator had sent in the list, **and** she had the signed order to prove it.

Practice and Apply Write a simple sentence about LOONY GOONY. Then use that sentence to build a compound sentence, a complex sentence, and a compound-complex sentence.

LANGUAGE CONVENTIONS:
The Structure of Sentences

Review the information about sentence structures with students. Remind students that writers use a variety of sentence structures so the text flows naturally and maintains the reader's interest. Explain that understanding sentence structures will help students to understand how ideas are connected.

Point out the circled words in the example sentences, and ask students what they indicate about the ideas in the sentences. (**Answers:** "but" is a coordinating conjunction that shows that the ideas are equal but contrasting; "when" is a subordinating conjunction and introduces a dependent clause or idea; "but" shows contrast between ideas; "as" introduces a dependent clause or idea.)

Practice and Apply Have partners share and discuss how they built their sentences.

(**Sample answer:** LOONY GOONY said it would explode. LOONY GOONY said it would explode, and the other appliances became nervous. LOONY GOONY said it would explode, but the toaster did not get the message because it was not a "smart" toaster. Although LOONY GOONY said it would explode, the toaster continued cooking it, and Mister Toussaint knew he had solved his problem.)

 ENGLISH LEARNER SUPPORT

Language Conventions Use the following supports with students at varying proficiency levels:

- Point out examples of simple and compound sentence structures in "The Brave Little Toaster" and have students copy them. Simple sentence: *Most of the things in the container were stupid.* (paragraph 22) Compound sentence: *It was stupid, but it was brave.* (paragraph 26) **SUBSTANTIAL**

- Have students work with partners to find example sentences in "The Brave Little Toaster" in the simple, compound, and complex sentence structures and then use them as models to write original sentences with the different structures. When they have finished, have them meet with another pair to compare their sentences. **MODERATE**

- Ask students to write original sentences that use simple, compound, complex, and compound-complex sentences. Then have them share their sentences with a partner and explain. **LIGHT**

MENTOR TEXT

ARE BIONIC SUPERHUMANS ON THE HORIZON?

Online Article by Ramez Naam

This article serves as a **mentor text**, a model for students to follow when they come to the Unit 1 Writing Task: Writing an Informational Essay.

GENRE ELEMENTS
INFORMATIONAL TEXT

Remind students that the purpose of **informational text** is to present factual information. An **online article** is an informational text that appears on the Internet and focuses on a narrow topic. The article may use text patterns like main-idea-and-details or question-and-call-to-action. Features, such as headings and captions, also point to main ideas and details. In this lesson, students will use text organization to explore the article "Are Bionic Superhumans on the Horizon?"

LEARNING OBJECTIVES

- Identify the main idea and supporting details.
- Analyze organizational patterns.
- Synthesize information from different sources.
- Discuss opinions of the effect of bionics on the lives of people.
- Write an informative essay about bionic technology.
- Use synonyms and antonyms to determine technical vocabulary.
- **Language** Discuss the text features using the term *subheading*.

TEXT COMPLEXITY

Quantitative Measures	Are Bionic Superhumans on the Horizon?	Lexile: 1110L
Qualitative Measures	**Ideas Presented** Much is explicit but moves to some implied meaning.	
	Structures Used Primarily uses explicit statement of main ideas and details but varies with a call to action at the end.	
	Language Used Mostly explicit. Tier II and III words are defined in context and used sparingly. Sentence structure more complex with perhaps more than one idea presented in a sentence.	
	Knowledge Required Some references to events or people from popular culture. Most of the text deals with common or easily imagined experiences.	

Online

RESOURCES

- Unit 1 Response Log
- Selection Audio
- Text in Focus: Monitor Comprehension
- Reading Studio: Notice & Note
- Writing Studio: Writing Informative Texts
- Speaking and Listening Studio: Participating in Collaborative Discussions
- Vocabulary Studio: Synonyms and Antonyms
- Grammar Studio: Module 12: Lesson 3: Commonly Confused Words
- "Are Bionic Superhumans on the Horizon?" Selection Test
- Level Up Tutorial: Main Idea and Support Details

SUMMARIES

English

Bionic devices, such as cochlear implants, prostheses, and brain stimulators, use technology to help people replace lost function in a body part. Advances in technology are improving the performance of artificial body parts to the point that the bionic devices will be able to surpass the abilities of natural body parts. In the future, technology may be used to enhance the body's abilities, not just restore them.

Spanish

En los artefactos biónicos, como los implantes cocleares, las prótesis y los estimuladores cerebrales, se utiliza la tecnología para reemplazar las funciones que han perdido ciertas personas en una parte del cuerpo. Los avances en la tecnología están mejorando el funcionamiento de partes artificiales del cuerpo hasta tal punto, que los dispositivos biónicos serán capaces de sobrepasar las capacidades de las partes corporales naturales. En el futuro, la tecnología servirá para mejorar las capacidades corporales y no solamente para restaurarlas.

SMALL-GROUP OPTIONS

Have students work in small groups to read and discuss the selection.

Double-Entry Journal

- Have students create two columns on a sheet of paper for notetaking. Have them add the heading "Quotes from the Text" to the left column and "My Notes" to the right column.
- Explain that students that they should record significant, important, or perplexing quotes from the text in the left column as they read.
- Have students write their own interpretations, summaries, questions, and restatements in the right column across from the quotations.
- Then have students compare their notes on the same quotations. Ask students to share and discuss examples in which their views differ.

Three-Minute Review

- Pause student activity at any time during reading or discussion, and set a timer for three minutes.
- Direct students to work independently to re-read the passage and review their notes to answer the question, "What is the effect of technology?"
- At the end of the three minutes, have students write a summary of their review.
- Then ask students, "What did you notice in your review?"

Text X-Ray: English Learner Support
for "Are Bionic Superhumans on the Horizon?"

Use the Text X-Ray and the supports and scaffolds in the Teacher's Edition to help guide students at different proficiency levels through the selection.

INTRODUCE THE SELECTION

DISCUSS ANATOMY

In this lesson, students will need to be able to discuss parts of the human body and use words related to the body. Explain that the word *bionic* refers to having artificial body parts. Read paragraph 2 with students and point out the words *ear*, *cochlear*, and *auditory* in the text and the word *hearing* in the footnote for *auditory*. Provide the following explanations:

- An *ear* is a body part on the side of the head that allows a person to hear.
- The word *cochlear* means "related to an inner canal of the ear."
- *Auditory* means "related to the sense of hearing."
- *Hearing* is a sense that allows a person to understand sound.

Explain to students that parts of the body have different functions and use different senses. By identifying the purpose of the body part, a reader can figure out the meaning of related words in context. Have volunteers discuss the words *teeth* and *skeleton*, explain their uses, and look up related words.

CULTURAL REFERENCES

The following words or phrases may be unfamiliar to students:

- *made a splash* (paragraph 4): gained a lot of attention
- *Iraq war veteran* (paragraph 5): a person who fought in the war in Iraq
- *animal studies* (paragraph 9): scientific experiments using animals
- *the Olympics* (paragraph 15): international competition of amateur athletes

LISTENING

Understand the Central Idea

Draw students' attention to the subheadings in the article. Explain that a subheading shows the beginning of a new section or topic. Direct students' attention to the heading on p. 21, "The Superhuman Frontier." Explain that the subheading of a section can help them figure out the main idea of that section.

Have students listen as you read aloud paragraphs 10–13. Use the following supports with students at varying proficiency levels:

- Tell students you will ask some questions about what they just heard. Model that they should give a thumbs up if the answer is yes, and a thumbs down for no. For example, ask: *Are bionic parts able to do more than what human parts can do?* (Yes) **SUBSTANTIAL**
- Have students identify the central idea of the excerpt. Ask: *How did the subheading help you identify the main idea?* **MODERATE**
- After listening to the excerpt read aloud, ask students to work in pairs to list details that support the central idea. **LIGHT**

SPEAKING

Discuss Text Features

Have student discuss the features of the text using the key term *subheading*. Circulate around the room to make sure students are using the key term correctly.

Use the following supports with students at varying proficiency levels:

- Display and read aloud this sentence: The subheading "From disabled to super-capable" tells me that this section is about how science will be able not only to bring back people's abilities but also to create new abilities. Have students say it aloud back to you and then practice saying it to a partner. **SUBSTANTIAL**
- To help students express their ideas about the subheadings in the article, display the following sentence frames: *Subheadings are one way the author _____. The subheading tells _____.* **MODERATE**
- Have students discuss with a partner how the subheadings can be rephrased as questions. How does rephrasing subheadings into questions help show what the sections will be about? **LIGHT**

READING

Identify Main Idea and Details

Tell students that authors of informational text provide evidence in the form of facts, examples, definitions, direct quotations, and other details to help readers understand the main—or most important—idea.

Work with students to reread paragraphs 14–19. Use the following supports with students at varying proficiency levels:

- Explain that they can identify a main idea in these paragraphs, such as people should think about both the positive and negative effects of advances in bionics in the future. Ask: *What does the author mention as some possible positive effects of advanced bionics in the future? What are some of the negative effects?* Accept single words or phrases. **SUBSTANTIAL**
- Guide students to identify a main idea. Then have students find evidence to support that idea. Supply sentence frames, such as: *According to the text, positive advances in bionics are _____. I think _____ is a possible negative effect.* **MODERATE**
- Have students identify a main idea in the text using this frame: *A main idea in these paragraphs is _____.* Then ask students to identify and share two pieces of evidence to support this main idea. **LIGHT**

WRITING

Write an Informational Essay

Work with students to read the writing assignment on p. 25.

Use the following supports with students at varying proficiency levels:

- Work with students to create a Venn diagram comparing and contrasting bionic technology that heals the human body and bionic technology that makes the human body do things better. Help them list the special features in the outer area of each circle. List the similarities in the space that the circles share. Then use the details to write an informational paragraph on the board. Have students copy the paragraph in their notebooks. **SUBSTANTIAL**
- Provide sentence frames such as the following that students can use to craft their essays: *Bionic technology can _____ and _____. An example of _____ is _____. One way _____ are alike is _____. A difference in _____ and _____ is _____. The effect of _____ is _____. I think _____.* **MODERATE**
- Remind students of the transitions they can use to compare and contrast, such as *both, similarly, in the same way, however, but, unlike,* and *on the other hand.* Have pairs find three places in their essays where they can use a transition. **LIGHT**

? Connect to the
ESSENTIAL QUESTION

"Are Bionic Superhumans on the Horizon?" explores how technology is being used to replace parts of the human body. The article then describes ways people use bionic devices, such as cochlear implants, deep brain implants, and carbon fiber prostheses, to improve physical abilities.

MENTOR TEXT

At the end of the unit, students will be asked to write an informative essay. "Are Bionic Superhumans on the Horizon?" provides a model for how a writer can organize text around a main idea and support the ideas with facts and examples.

ANALYZE & APPLY

ARE BIONIC SUPERHUMANS ON THE HORIZON?

Informational Text by **Ramez Naam**

? **ESSENTIAL QUESTION:**

Does technology improve or control our lives?

16   Unit 1

QUICK START

If a scientist could implant a device inside you that made you smarter, faster, or stronger, would you have the surgery? What if the procedure were risky or expensive? Discuss your reaction with the class.

IDENTIFY MAIN IDEA AND DETAILS

How can you understand a text when you don't know anything about its topic? You can ask questions about the text as you read. You might try re-reading the text. Let the text teach you by doing the following:

- Identify the **main idea**—the most important idea about a topic—of each paragraph or section of text. It may be stated directly at the beginning or end of each paragraph or section.

- Read the **supporting details**, or information about the main idea, to learn more. If the main idea isn't stated, use these details to infer it.

Identifying these elements will help you summarize the text—that is, to briefly retell in your own words the text's main ideas and details.

ANALYZE ORGANIZATION

This article has mostly a **main-idea-and-supporting-details** pattern of organization. Near the end, however, it breaks away from this pattern, filling one paragraph with questions and the next with a call to action. As you read, think about why the author uses both types of organization to convey his **thesis**, or the controlling idea of his entire text. Also pay attention to **text features**, such as headings, subheadings, photos, and captions. These can help you make predictions about the text's main ideas and organizational patterns by making them visually prominent.

TYPE OF ORGANIZATION	EXAMPLE
In **main-idea-and-details organization**, each paragraph or text section introduces a main idea and gives examples or other details about it.	We're in the midst of a bionic revolution, yet most of us don't know it. Around 220,000 people worldwide already walk around with cochlear implants. . . .
In **question-and-call-to-action organization**, the author poses questions and then tells readers what they ought to do.	. . . will only the rich have access to these enhancements? We have a little while to consider these questions, but we ought to start. . . .

GENRE ELEMENTS: INFORMATIONAL TEXT

- provides factual information
- includes evidence to support ideas
- contains text features
- appears in many forms, such as news articles and essays

QUICK START

Have students read the Quick Start question, and invite them to share their opinions about surgical enhancement. (**Possible answers:** *The risk, pain, and expense of having a device implanted would be too great. Implanting a device now could lead to many decades of being smarter, faster, or stronger.*) Discuss the reasons for and against having such surgeries. As a group, make a T-chart comparing reasons for and against surgical enhancement.

IDENTIFY MAIN IDEA AND DETAILS

Help students understand the terms and concepts related to identifying main ideas and details when discussing or analyzing an informational text. Discuss both the concepts of main ideas (the most important ideas about a topic) and of details (words, phrases, and sentences that tell about the main idea). Point out that in a long article, the author might develop several main ideas or topics. Then explain that summarizing is briefly retelling the main ideas and details in a text.

ANALYZE ORGANIZATION

Tell students that analyzing the way an author organizes information in a text will make it easier for them to identify the author's main point, or *thesis*, and purpose for writing. Point out that the article has more than one organization pattern. Review the types of organization in the chart, and discuss how to identify each one, such as looking at the first sentence of a paragraph, looking for questions, or reading headings. Ask students how understanding the organization will help them identify what the author is trying to communicate. Suggest that students use these questions to help them analyze and annotate text features:

- What topics or main ideas do the headings indicate?
- Is there a main idea statement at the beginning of a paragraph or section of text? What details tell more about the statement?
- What questions does the author ask? What does the author want the reader to do?
- What does the organization of information reveal about the author's thesis and purpose for writing?

ENGLISH LEARNER SUPPORT

Understand Directionality Reinforce the directionality of English by reviewing how to read the Analyze Organization chart. Explain that each column heading applies to the text in all the rows beneath it. To read the chart, students should begin at the top left. The top row, left column introduces the first text feature—headings or subheadings. After reading this definition, students should track to the right to see the example of a heading. Then they should move on to the middle row, left column. Ask a volunteer to trace with a finger the order that a reader would read the information in the chart. **SUBSTANTIAL**

TEACH

CRITICAL VOCABULARY

Encourage students to read all the sentences before deciding which word best completes each one. Remind them to look for context clues that match the precise meaning of each word.

Answers:

1. *integrity*

2. *implant*

3. *enhancements*

4. *inert*

■ English Learner Support

Use Cognates Tell students that several of the Critical Vocabulary words have Spanish cognates: *implant/implantar, inert/inerte, integrity/integridad.*
ALL LEVELS

LANGUAGE CONVENTIONS

Review the information about the commonly confused words *its* and *it's*. Explain that *it's* is a contraction of two words—*it* and *is*—and that *its*—without an apostrophe—shows possession. Point out that *'s* is usually needed to show possession for a noun but *its* is an exception to that rule.

Read aloud each example sentence. Ask students which sentence includes the contraction of *it is*. Point out that they can use context to determine whether *its* or *it's* is the correct word by substituting the words *it is* to see whether they make sense in the sentence. If they do, then the contraction *it's* is required. If they do not make sense, then *its* is the correct word.

ANNOTATION MODEL

Remind students to identify main ideas and details discussed on p. 19, which includes looking at headers and the first sentences of paragraphs or sections to find the main ideas and then looking for details about the main ideas in the captions and bodies of paragraphs. Suggest that students circle main ideas and underline details in the text or use their own system for marking up the selection in their write-in text. They may want to color-code their annotations by using highlighters. Their notes in the margin may include questions about ideas that are unclear or topics they want to learn more about.

CRITICAL VOCABULARY

| implant | inert | integrity | enhancements |

To see how many Critical Vocabulary words you already know, use them to complete the sentences.

1. Soccer has no _____ if some players cheat.

2. I broke a tooth, so Dr. Lu will _____ an artificial one in my jaw.

3. These new gadgets are _____ because they save you time.

4. His old artificial hand was _____ ; the fingers did not move.

LANGUAGE CONVENTIONS

Commonly Confused Words In this article, the author uses both *it's* and *its,* two words that even experienced writers sometimes confuse.

It's with an apostrophe is a contraction that means "it is."

What happens when it's possible to improve on the human body and mind?

Its without the apostrophe means "belonging to it."

The technology will sneak its way into our lives.

When you find an *it's* or *its,* consider why it's correct in its sentence.

ANNOTATION MODEL   NOTICE & NOTE

As you read, determine the main ideas and supporting details. You can also mark up the article. Here are one reader's notes.

1 We're in the midst of a bionic revolution, yet most of us don't know it.

2 Around 220,000 people worldwide already walk around with cochlear implants—devices worn around the ear that turn sound waves into electrical impulses shunted directly into the auditory nerve.

3 Tens of thousands of people have been implanted with deep brain stimulators, devices that send an electrode tunneling several inches in the brain. Deep brain stimulators are used to control . . .

First sentence often is main idea. Bionic revolution? What's that?

2nd and 3rd paragraphs give details about devices that help people.

18   Unit 1

---

18   Unit 1

BACKGROUND

*Technology can make our lives better, but it also can change them. In this article, science fiction author **Ramez Naam** shares some science facts about bionic body parts that can now change animal and human capabilities. Bionic body parts are those containing mechanical or electronic elements that improve functioning, and they may be part of your life someday.*

ARE BIONIC SUPERHUMANS ON THE HORIZON?

Informational Text by Ramez Naam

SETTING A PURPOSE

As you read, look for details that reveal what the author means by "bionic superhumans" and how he answers the question posed in the title.

1   We're in the midst of a bionic revolution, yet most of us don't know it.

2   Around 220,000 people worldwide already walk around with cochlear implants—devices worn around the ear that turn sound waves into electrical impulses shunted[1] directly into the auditory[2] nerve.

3   Tens of thousands of people have been **implanted** with deep brain stimulators, devices that send an electrode[3] tunneling several inches in the brain. Deep brain

---

[1] **shunted:** allowed to flow from one pathway to another through surgery.
[2] **auditory** (ô´dĭ-tôr´ē): related to hearing.
[3] **electrode** (ĭ-lĕk´trōd´): a material through which electricity flows.

Notice & Note

Use the side margins to notice and note signposts in the text.

IDENTIFY MAIN IDEA AND DETAILS
Annotate: Circle the main idea of paragraphs 1–4. Underline key details that support this main idea.

Summarize: Write a sentence that summarizes paragraphs 1–4 in your own words.

implant
(ĭm-plănt´) v. To *implant* a device means to place it inside the body through surgery.

ENGLISH LEARNER SUPPORT

Understand Idioms and Sayings Discuss with students the meanings of the following idioms and phrases:

- *superhumans* = "humans with special abilities"
- *on the horizon* = "in the near future"
- *tens of thousands* = "a large estimated number between 20,000 and 99,999"

To confirm understanding, ask students to make up sentences of their own using the words and phrases.   **ALL LEVELS**

TEACH

BACKGROUND

After students read the Background note, explain that scientists are continuously finding new ways to use technology to solve problems and to make life easier or better for people. The article discusses different ways technology is already used in the human body to improve its abilities and health. Discuss that *bionic* means having artificial body parts, especially electromechanical ones.

SETTING A PURPOSE

Direct students to use the Setting a Purpose prompt to focus their reading.

TEXT IN FOCUS

Monitor Comprehension Have students view the **Text in Focus** video on this page of their eBook to learn about using context clues and text features to monitor their comprehension of the ideas presented. Then have students use Text In Focus Practice to apply what they have learned.

IDENTIFY MAIN IDEA AND DETAILS

Remind students that a **main idea** in an informational text is an important topic or idea and key **details** support the main idea by providing examples or specific information as evidence. Explain that stating the main idea and key details in your own words is a way of summarizing a text. (**Possible answer:** *Cochlear implants, deep brain stimulators, and prosthetic limbs are examples of the "bionic revolution" that is changing many people's lives.*)

CRITICAL VOCABULARY

implant: The surgeon will need to *implant* a steel pin in the boy's leg to make sure the broken bone heals correctly.

ASK STUDENTS what are devices or objects a doctor could implant into the human body. (**Possible answers:** *heart pacemaker, insulin pump, false teeth, artificial joints*)

ENGLISH LEARNER SUPPORT

Understand Language Structures Have students locate the sentence in paragraph 3 with em-dashes. Explain that an em-dash indicates a pause in a sentence for an explanation or additional information that the author wants to emphasize. The dashes function similarly to commas but imply more emphasis. They can work in pairs or alone if the explanation is at the end of a sentence.

ASK STUDENTS to discuss with partners why the author put "with encouraging results" between em-dashes. *(The author wanted to emphasize the results.)* Ask students to identify the sentence in paragraph 4 that uses an em-dash and explain what the text after it explains. *(Yet those are a relatively simple technology—a curved piece of slightly springy, super-strong material. It explains the word* those, *which refers to the prostheses in the previous sentence.)* **MODERATE**

WORD GAPS

Explain to students that when words are unfamiliar or confusing, they should reread the paragraph or section to look for **context clues** to guess the meanings of the words. (**Answer:** *Context clues for* **articulating** *include "independently" and "flexing, extending, gripping, and releasing." "Just" and "pressure" are clues for* **mechanically***. Students should make use of the definition provided for* **inert** *and the footnote for* **interface***; they may need to look up* **microprocessor***.)*

CRITICAL VOCABULARY

inert: The toy robot lay *inert* in its box until its power switch was flipped.

ASK STUDENTS to explain the difference between inert protheses and the new digital interface prostheses. (**Possible answer:** *Inert prostheses replaced limbs but could not actively move and interact with the body like a real limb, whereas the new digital prostheses work with the nervous system to function as part of the body.)*

NOTICE & NOTE

stimulators are used to control Parkinson's disease,[4] though lately they've also been tested—with encouraging results—in use against severe depression and obsessive compulsive disorder.

4   The most obvious bionics are those that replace limbs. Olympian "Blade Runner" Oscar Pistorius made a splash with his Cheetah carbon fiber prostheses[5] Yet those are a relatively simple technology—a curved piece of slightly springy, super-strong material. In the digital age, we're seeing more sophisticated limbs.

5   Consider the thought-controlled bionic leg that Zac Vawter used to climb all 103 floors of Chicago's Willis Tower. Or the nerve-controlled bionic hand that Iraq war veteran Glen Lehman had attached after the loss of his original hand.

6   Or the even more sophisticated i-limb Ultra, an artificial hand with five independently articulating artificial fingers. Those limbs don't just react mechanically to pressure. They actually respond to the thoughts and intentions of their owners, flexing, extending, gripping, and releasing on mental command.

7   The age when prostheses were largely inert pieces of wood, metal, and plastic is passing. Advances in microprocessors, in techniques to interface[6] digital technology with the human nervous system, and in battery technology to allow prostheses to pack more power with less weight are turning replacement limbs into active parts of the human body.

8   In some cases, they're not even part of the body at all. Consider the case of Cathy Hutchinson. In 1997, Cathy had a stroke, leaving her without control of her arms. Hutchinson volunteered for an experimental procedure that could one day help millions of people with partial or complete paralysis. She let researchers implant a small device in the part of her brain responsible for motor control. With that device, she is able to control an external robotic arm by thinking about it.

9   That, in turn, brings up an interesting question: If the arm isn't physically attached to her body, how far away could she be and still control it? The answer is at least thousands of miles. In animal studies, scientists have shown that a monkey with a brain implant can control a robot arm 7,000 miles away. The monkey's mental signals were sent over the internet, from Duke University in North Carolina, to the robot arm in Japan. In this day and age, distance is almost irrelevant.

WORD GAPS

Notice & Note: What words in paragraphs 6–7 are unfamiliar or confusing? Mark these words.

Infer: Use context clues to guess the meanings of the words. If you still feel uncertain about any of the words, look them up in a dictionary.

inert
(ĭn-ûrt´) *adj. Inert* means unable to move or act.

---

[4] **Parkinson's disease:** a disease that weakens muscles and causes a person's arms and legs to shake.
[5] **prostheses** (prŏs-thē´sēz): artificial devices that replace injured or missing body parts.
[6] **interface:** to connect or interact smoothly.

WHEN STUDENTS STRUGGLE . . .

Main Idea and Details Have individuals or partners use a chart to note the main idea and details. Remind students that details support or provide evidence of the main idea.

Main Idea	Detail #1	Detail #2	Detail #3
Technology is going to be able to give humans new abilities.	A monkey used mental signals to move a robotic arm 7,000 miles away.	A chip replaced damaged rat brain tissue and repaired memory.	A chip implanted in a monkey's brain increased its intelligence.

For additional support, go to the **Reading Studio** and assign the following **Level Up tutorial: Main Idea and Support Details.**

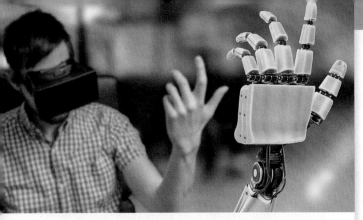

The Superhuman Frontier

10 The 7,000-mile-away prosthetic arm makes an important point: These new prostheses aren't just going to restore missing human abilities. They're going to enhance our abilities, giving us powers we never had before, and augmenting[7] other capabilities we have. While the current generation of prostheses is still primitive, we can already see this taking shape when a monkey moves a robotic arm on the other side of the planet just by thinking about it.

11 Other research is pointing to enhancements to memory and decision making.

12 The hippocampus is a small, seahorse-shaped part of the brain that's essential in forming memories. If it's damaged—by an injury to the head, for example—people start having difficulty forming new long-term memories. In the most extreme cases, this can lead to the complete inability to form new long-term memories, as in the film *Memento*. Working to find a way to repair this sort of brain damage, researchers in 2011 created a "hippocampus chip" that can replace damaged brain tissue. When they implanted it in rats with a damaged hippocampus, they found that not only could their chip repair damaged memory—it could improve the rats' ability to learn new things.

13 Nor is memory the end of it. Another study, in 2012, demonstrated that we can boost intelligence—at least one sort—in monkeys. Scientists at Wake Forest University implanted specialized brain chips in a set of monkeys and trained those monkeys to perform a picture-matching game. When the implant was activated, it raised their scores by an average of 10 points on a 100-point scale. The implant makes monkeys smarter.

---

[7] **augmenting** (ôg-mĕnt´ĭng): increasing or adding to.

ANALYZE ORGANIZATION

Annotate: Circle the heading on this page. Underline details in paragraphs 10–13 that help you understand what the heading means.

Analyze: Does the heading help you predict the main idea of this section? Confirm your prediction by writing the main idea in a sentence.

IDENTIFY MAIN IDEA AND DETAILS

Annotate: Underline the main idea in paragraph 12. Circle key details that give more information about this main idea.

Evaluate: Why do you think the author chose to state the main idea later in the paragraph, instead of in the first sentence?

ANALYZE ORGANIZATION

Remind students that text features, such as headers, help the reader identify the topic of a section and provide a clue to the main idea. (**Answer:** *Yes; a frontier is the farthest point people have reached, and the section describes technology that may take people beyond their current abilities.* **Possible main idea:** *Bionic technology is expanding the limits of what people can do, both physically and mentally.*)

IDENTIFY MAIN IDEA AND DETAILS

Point out that authors often state the main idea of a paragraph in the first sentence, but not always. Explain that an author may choose to state the main idea later in a paragraph for a variety of reasons, such as to transition between ideas, to make connections between concepts, and to create emphasis. (**Answer:** *Understanding the main idea requires readers to know what the hippocampus is, so the author explained the hippocampus first and then stated what researchers had done to fix the problem of a damaged one.*)

EL ENGLISH LEARNER SUPPORT

Understand Author's Choices Help students break down the meaning of the question by asking a series of simpler questions that guide students to think about the author's choices. Ask: *What is the main idea? Where does the author state it? What does the author state in the first sentence? Is this important information for the reader to know? Is it the main idea? Why would the author state it before the main idea?* **SUBSTANTIAL/MODERATE**

 For **listening support** for students at varying proficiency levels, see the **Text X-Ray** on page 16C.

APPLYING ACADEMIC VOCABULARY

❏ **commentary**   ❏ **occupation**   ❏ **option**   ☒ **speculate**   ☒ **technology**

Write and Discuss Have students turn to a partner to discuss the following questions. Guide students to include the Academic Vocabulary words *speculate* and *technology* in their responses. Ask volunteers to share their responses with the class.

- What does the author **speculate** in paragraph 18?
- What role does the author think **technology** will play in our lives in the future?

ANALYZE ORGANIZATION

Remind students that one way to organize information in a text is to pose questions and issue calls to action. Point out that the content and tone of the questions and calls to action help the reader figure out the author's purpose for writing. Ask students to discuss the content and tone of the questions in paragraphs 14–17. (**Answer:** *The questions and the call to action work together because the author asks several questions and then encourages the reader to think about the issue.*)

ENGLISH LEARNER SUPPORT

Language Conventions Remind students that they will usually use *affect* as a verb meaning "to cause a change." Then tell them that they usually will use the word *effect* as a noun meaning "a result." Read the first sentence of paragraph 17 aloud. Invite students to ask for clarification of any unfamiliar words. Then ask if *affect* is an action word in the sentence or a result. (*action word*) Read the second sentence. Ask if *effect* is an action word or a result. (*result*) **MODERATE**

For **reading support** for students at varying proficiency levels, see the **Text X-Ray** on page 16D.

CRITICAL VOCABULARY

integrity: The author uses the word *integrity* to describe the ethical conduct of a group or organization. This usage may be confusing to students if they associate the word with the actions of an individual.

ASK STUDENTS to discuss why the integrity of a group or organization is important. (**Possible answer:** *Groups and organizations consist of many people, so the actions of a group or organization represent the people who belong to it.*)

NOTICE & NOTE

From Disabled to Super-capable

14 Both of those technologies for boosting memory and intelligence are in very early stages, in small animal studies only, and years (or possibly decades) away from wide use in humans. Still, they make us wonder—what happens when it's possible to improve on the human body and mind?

15   The debate has started already, of course. Oscar Pistorius had to fight hard for inclusion in the Olympics. Many objected that his carbon fiber prostheses gave him a competitive advantage. He was able—with the help of doctors and biomedical engineers—to make a compelling case that his Cheetah blades didn't give him any advantage on the field. But how long will that be true? How long until we have prostheses (not to mention drugs and genetic therapies) that make athletes better in their sports?

16   But the issue is much, much wider than professional sports. We may care passionately about the **integrity** of the Olympics or professional cycling or so on, but they only directly affect a very small number of us. In other areas of life—in the workforce in particular—enhancement technology might affect all of us.

ANALYZE ORGANIZATION

Annotate: Underline the questions in the last four paragraphs of the article, and circle the call to action.

Synthesize: How do the questions and the call to action work together?

integrity

(ĭn-tĕg´rĭ-tē) *n. Integrity* is following a strict code of ethical conduct.

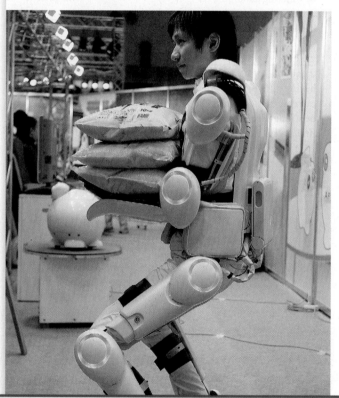

TO CHALLENGE STUDENTS . . .

Create an Action Plan Challenge students to create a response to the call to action at the end of the article. Tell them to review the questions, facts, and examples in the text to identify critical issues and then to brainstorm ideas for next steps in preparing for the future of bionic technology. Ask students to use their analysis and ideas to write a multi-step action plan.

17   When it's possible to make humans smarter, sharper, and faster, how will that affect us? Will the effect be mostly positive, boosting our productivity and the rate of human innovation? Or will it be just another pressure to compete at work? Who will be able to afford these technologies? Will anyone be able to have their body, and more importantly, their brain upgraded? Or will only the rich have access to these **enhancements**?

18   We have a little while to consider these questions, but we ought to start. The technology will sneak its way into our lives, starting with people with disabilities, the injured, and the ill. It'll improve their lives in ways that are unquestionably good. And then, one day, we'll wake up and realize that we're doing more than restoring lost function. We're enhancing it.

19   Superhuman technology is on the horizon. Time to start thinking about what that means for us.

NOTICE & NOTE

LANGUAGE CONVENTIONS
Annotate: The author uses the commonly confused words *affect* and *effect.* Mark them in paragraph 17.

Infer: Use context clues and a dictionary to figure out the words' meanings.

enhancement
(ĕn-hăns´mənt) *n.* An *enhancement* improves or adds to the quality or function of something.

CHECK YOUR UNDERSTANDING

Answer these questions before moving on to the **Analyze the Text** section on the following page.

1 The author included the section "The Superhuman Frontier" to —

  A explain that bionics will do more than replace body parts

  B express his uncertainty about the future of bionics

  C convince readers that bionic body parts are dangerous

  D inform readers which types of bionics they will receive

2 In paragraph 17, the writer includes a series of questions in order to —

  F express his confusion about the issue to readers

  G inform readers about what is certain to happen

  H encourage readers to think deeply about the issue

  J entertain readers with impossible fantasies

3 Which idea is supported by information throughout the selection?

  A Bionics will improve intelligence and memory.

  B Athletes with bionic body parts will perform better.

  C Many people with disabilities already benefit from bionics.

  D Bionics can improve human abilities in many ways.

Are Bionic Superhumans on the Horizon? 23

🖊 LANGUAGE CONVENTIONS

Review the meaning of **affect** (*v.* to influence) and **effect** (*n.* a result) in the text. Point out that although *affect* is usually a verb and *effect* is usually a noun, there are exceptions which cause confusion. Tell students a trick for remembering which word is usually correct: the mnemonic of "a" is for action = *affect* and "e" is for end result = *effect*. Remind them to use context clues to verify meaning. (**Answer:** *Affect is a verb that means "to cause a change in." **Effect** is a noun meaning "result or outcome."*)

🖊 CHECK YOUR UNDERSTANDING

Have students answer the questions independently.

Answers:

1. *A*

2. *H*

3. *D*

If they answer any questions incorrectly, have them reread the text to confirm their understanding. Then they may proceed to ANALYZE THE TEXT on p. 24.

CRITICAL VOCABULARY

enhancement: The article discusses *enhancement* as something that improves a person's physical function or quality of life.

ASK STUDENTS to discuss how the enhancements could also have a negative effect on people's lives in the future. (**Possible answers:** *Not everyone will be able to afford enhancements. They could give unfair advantage to some people.*)

 ENGLISH LEARNER SUPPORT

Oral Assessment Use the following questions to assess students' comprehension and speaking skills:

1. Why does the author include the section "The Superhuman Frontier"? *(The author includes the section to explain that bionics will do more than replace body parts.)*

2. Why does the writer include a series of questions in paragraph 17? *(The author wants to encourage the readers to think deeply about the issue.)*

3. Which idea is supported by information throughout the selection? *(The idea that bionics can improve human abilities in many ways is supported by information throughout the selection.)* **MODERATE/LIGHT**

ANALYZE THE TEXT

Possible answers:

1. **DOK 4:** *Each subhead gives readers a clue to the main idea of the section that follows it. "The Superhuman Frontier" introduces text about expanding the limits of human abilities. The text under "From Disabled to Super-capable" is about using bionic technology not only to help people with disabilities but also to enhance the abilities of people who are not disabled.*

2. **DOK 3:** *Details include Zac Vawter's "thought-controlled bionic leg," Glen Lehman's "nerve-controlled bionic hand," the i-limb Ultra artificial hand, and Cathy Hutchinson's robotic arm, which is controlled remotely by a device in her brain.*

3. **DOK 2:** *The paragraphs describe being able to move a robotic arm from thousands of miles away. If this technology continues to improve, humans might be able to do their jobs from anywhere. They might be able to operate machinery on the other side of the world. They might even be able to control hundreds or thousands of robotic arms at the same time.*

4. **DOK 2:** *Some students will contend that bionics will have an overall positive effect, and they may point to the details about humans becoming smarter, stronger, and faster. Others will predict that bionics will have an overall negative effect, and they are likely to bring up Naam's concern that only the rich will be able to afford bionics.*

5. **DOK 4:** *The bionic revolution refers to all the new technology that not only can replace missing body parts but also may improve people's physical and mental functioning, essentially creating "superhumans."*

RESEARCH

Remind students they should assess the credibility of each source as they search for expert opinions.

Extend Students' responses will depend on which sources they discover. Students should be able to apply reasons they agree or disagree with the sources they found.

 RESPOND

ANALYZE THE TEXT

Support your responses with evidence from the text. 📓 NOTEBOOK

1. **Evaluate** Examine the article's subheadings. In your own words, state the concept or aspect of the main topic that each introduces. Are the subheadings effective? Why or why not?

2. **Cite Evidence** In paragraph 4, the author states, "In the digital age, we're seeing more sophisticated limbs." What details does he provide in support of this main idea?

3. **Interpret** Review paragraphs 9 and 10. What might the author mean by "powers we never had before"?

4. **Predict** Will the effect of bionics on the lives of most people be positive overall or negative overall? Use specific details from the article to support your opinion.

5. **Notice & Note** Now that you have read the article, how would you define the phrase *bionic revolution* (paragraph 1)?

RESEARCH TIP
Most search engines allow you to write your search in the form of a question. For this activity, you might type in the question *When will humans become bionic?*

RESEARCH

Don't just take Ramez Naam's word for it that bionic superhumans will soon be here. Instead, find out what other experts think. Complete this chart with information from classroom resources or reliable websites. Then write a sentence that synthesizes, or combines, the information.

ARTICLE TITLE AND SOURCE	OPINION ABOUT BIONICS
Bionics expert "rewires" humans, Toronto Star newspaper, https://www.thestar.com/news/canada/2016/11/05/new-brunswick-born-bionics-expert-rewires-humans-with-thought-controlled-prosthetics.html	*Dr. Levi Hargrove says that thought-controlled prosthetics are available right now.*
Solar-powered skin for prosthetic limbs, BBC News http://www.bbc.com/news/uk-scotland-39353751	*Dr. Ravinder Dahiya says that completely solar-powered prosthetics will be available in a few years.*

What do the experts think about bionic superhumans?
Dr. Hargrove and Dr. Dahiya agree with Naam that high-technology prosthetics are available now and getting better.

Extend In paragraph 19, Naam states that "superhuman technology is on the horizon." In a small group, discuss the results of your research, and decide whether you agree or disagree with this statement.

WHEN STUDENTS STRUGGLE . . .

Reteach: Main Idea and Details Have students use a chart to note the main idea and details. Remind them that details are examples that provide evidence of the main idea.

Main Idea	Detail #1	Detail #2	Detail #3
In the digital age, we're seeing more sophisticated limbs. (paragraph 4)	*The thought-controlled bionic leg... (paragraph 5)*	*The nerve-controlled bionic hand... (paragraph 5)*	*The i-limb Ultra artificial hand with independently articulating fingers...*

 For additional support, go to the **Reading Studio** and add the following 🔼 **Level Up tutorial: Main Idea and Details.**

CREATE AND DISCUSS

Write an Informational Essay Write a three- to four-paragraph essay in which you compare and contrast bionic technology that repairs damage to the human body and bionic technology that enhances the human body.

❏ Introduce the topic and state your controlling idea about the two kinds of bionic technology.

❏ Then, tell about the similarities and differences between the two kinds of technology, including their effects on people's lives. Use details from the text to support your ideas.

❏ In your final paragraph, state your conclusion about bionic technology and the different ways it can be used.

Discuss with a Small Group Have a discussion about the best ways to distribute bionics fairly. Should people who can pay a lot of money get the best bionics first? Should people with disabilities be first in line? If so, who should pay for those bionics if they are expensive?

❏ As a group, set an agenda and establish clear goals for your discussion. Review the text and decide which information is relevant to the discussion topic. Use the headings to help you locate the information.

❏ Have group members add relevant research findings.

❏ Review the ideas together, listening closely and respectfully to all ideas. Then take a vote on the fairest ways to distribute bionics.

RESPOND TO THE ESSENTIAL QUESTION

 Does technology improve or control our lives?

Gather Information Review your annotations and notes on "Are Bionic Superhumans on the Horizon?" Then, add relevant details to your Response Log. To decide what to include, think about:

• the kinds of bionic advances people want or need
• ways in which advances in bionics may affect individuals and society
• the ethical questions bionic devices may raise

At the end of the unit, you may use your notes to help you write an informational essay.

 Go to **Writing Informative Texts** in the **Writing Studio** to learn more.

Go to **Participating in Collaborative Discussions** in the **Speaking and Listening Studio** for more on having a discussion.

ACADEMIC VOCABULARY
As you write and discuss what you learned from the informational text, be sure to use the Academic Vocabulary words. Check off each of the words that you use.

❏ **commentary**
❏ **occupation**
❏ **option**
❏ **speculate**
❏ **technology**

CREATE AND DISCUSS

Write an Informational Essay Point out that the list on p. 25 can serve as an outline for students' essays. Each item can be one paragraph, or they can have separate paragraphs for similarities and for differences. Students should note examples of both kinds of bionic technology and include reasons for their conclusion.

Discuss with a Small Group Remind students to use the text organization to help them identify important information and then to cite details from the text to support their responses. If students completed the Research activity for this selection, then they should include facts and details from their research in their response. Remind students to listen actively and respectfully as they discuss the topic.

For **writing support** for students at varying proficiency levels, see the Text X-Ray on page 16D.

RESPOND TO THE ESSENTIAL QUESTION

Allow time for students to add details from "Are Bionic Superhumans on the Horizon?" to their Unit 1 Response Logs.

APPLY

CRITICAL VOCABULARY

Answers:

1. *a cube made of solid stone; because it is not moving*

2. *a computer chip in a brain; because it is something placed in the body rather than attached to the body*

3. *new, better features; because they are improvements*

4. *being honest when nobody is watching; because it means a code of honest, ethical conduct*

VOCABULARY STRATEGY:
Synonyms and Antonyms

Answers:

1. *articulating: being able to move*

2. *extracted: removed*

3. *irrelevant: not related*

 RESPOND

WORD BANK
implant
inert
integrity
enhancement

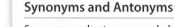 Go to the **Vocabulary Studio** for more on synonyms and antonyms.

26   Unit 1

CRITICAL VOCABULARY

Practice and Apply Choose the correct answer to each question. Then, explain your response.

1. Which of the following is an example of something **inert**?
   a. a cube made of solid stone   **b.** a bionic hand with moving fingers

2. Which of these would a doctor **implant** through surgery?
   a. an artificial leg   **b.** a computer chip in a brain

3. Which of the following could be called an **enhancement**?
   a. an old, persistent problem   **b.** a new, better feature

4. Which of the following is an example of **integrity**?
   a. cheating on a test that you forgot to study for   **b.** being honest when nobody is watching

VOCABULARY STRATEGY:
Synonyms and Antonyms

Synonyms and antonyms can help you understand technical words. A **synonym** is a word with a meaning similar to that of another word. An **antonym** has a meaning opposite that of another word. In paragraph 7, old *inert* artificial limbs are contrasted with newer *active* ones, making *inert* and *active* antonyms. So, if you know that *active* means "able to move," you can infer that *inert* means "not able to move."

Practice and Apply Each sentence includes a pair of words in boldface type. Use context clues to figure out what the words mean and whether they are synonyms or antonyms. Then, in your own words, write the definition of the word indicated below the sentence.

1. Does the prosthetic hand have five **articulating** fingers, or are the fingers part of one **immobile** piece of plastic?

   articulating: _____

2. Soon after researchers **implanted** the device, it malfunctioned, and they quickly **extracted** it.

   extracted: _____

3. "That information is **irrelevant**, so let's get rid of it," Brad said, but I insisted that it was **essential** and needed to stay in the report.

   irrelevant: _____

EL ENGLISH LEARNER SUPPORT

Vocabulary Strategy Explain that prefixes change the meaning of a base word. Share that the prefixes *ir-*, *mal-*, and *im-* can all mean "not" and create antonyms from their base words. Ask: If *irrelevant* means "not related," what does *relevant* mean? If *malfunction* means "not working," what does *function* mean? If *immobile* means "not movable," then what does *mobile* mean? **ALL LEVELS**

LANGUAGE CONVENTIONS:
Commonly Confused Words

English contains so many words that sound alike but are spelled differently that it's easy to get them confused. Ramez Naam's article includes some commonly confused words.

Go to the **Grammar Studio** for more on commonly confused words.

- *It's* (meaning "it is") and *its* (meaning "belonging to it")

  What happens when it's possible to improve on the human body and mind?

  Technology will sneak its way into our lives.

- *Affect* (meaning "to influence") and *effect* (meaning "result")

  When it's possible to make humans smarter, sharper, and faster, how will that affect us? Will the effect be mostly positive?

Here are two other examples.

- *There* (meaning "in that place"), *their* (meaning "belonging to them"), and *they're* (meaning "they are")

  The scientists gave their lecture over there, near the college. They're answering questions now.

- *To* (meaning "toward"), *two* (meaning "a whole number that is more than one and less than three"), and *too* (meaning "also")

  We're going to the lab to see two or three new prosthetics. You can come, too.

Practice and Apply Write your own sentences with commonly misspelled words using the examples above as models. Your sentences might express your opinions about how bionics will affect people. Share your completed sentences with a partner and compare how each of you used the words.

LANGUAGE CONVENTIONS:
Spelling Commonly Confused Words

Review the information about the commonly confused words with students. Explain that words that sound alike when spoken are often confused when written. Remind students to pay attention to which word they are using when writing so they don't create confusing sentences.

Illustrate the importance of choosing the correct word by reading the example sentences aloud and asking students to explain which word is correct in each sentence, and the effect on meaning if the writer uses the wrong spelling.

Practice and Apply Have partners discuss how they used the commonly confused words in their sentences.

Possible answers:

1. *It's amazing to think how much bionics will change before this century reaches its end.*

2. *I believe that bionics will affect nearly all of us, and their effects will be positive.*

3. *Scientists are using their knowledge to improve bionics here, there, and everywhere. They're my heroes.*

4. *We are headed to a future where two or even three bionic implants per person will be possible. I hope that you, too, are excited about this.*

Are Bionic Superhumans on the Horizon?   27

 ENGLISH LEARNER SUPPORT

Language Conventions Use the following supports with students at varying proficiency levels:

- Have students find and circle sentences in "Are Bionic Superhumans on the Horizon?" that use *it's* and *its*, and *there*, *their*, and *they're*. **SUBSTANTIAL**
- Have students work with partners to write original sentences that use *it's/its* and *there/their/they're*. Then have them meet with another pair to compare their sentences. **MODERATE**

- Ask students to write original sentences that use *to/too/two* and *there/their/they're*. Then have them share their sentences with a partner and explain how they used the words. **LIGHT**

INTERFLORA
Poem by Susan Hamlyn

GENRE ELEMENTS
POETRY

Tell students that a sonnet is a form of lyric poetry that expresses thoughts and feelings and has a musical quality. A traditional sonnet, however, contains exactly 14 lines that are the same length and have the same meter, or rhythmic pattern. It also uses one of several possible rhyme schemes, or patterns of end rhymes—such as *abab cdcd efef gg*—to help create its musical effect. In this lesson, students will analyze the structure and use of irony in "Interflora," a humorous love sonnet, to help them understand its message and write their own sonnets.

LEARNING OBJECTIVES

- Analyze the structure and use of irony in a sonnet.
- Conduct research about technology during the 1990s.
- Discuss how changing technologies influence communication.
- Write a sonnet using the characteristics of traditional sonnets and craft.
- Present the sonnet to the class by reading it aloud.
- **Language** Discuss a humorous poem using the key word *detail*.

TEXT COMPLEXITY

Quantitative Measures	Interflora	Lexile: N/A
Qualitative Measures	**Ideas Presented** Multiple levels of meaning involving symbolism and irony.	
	Structure Used Mostly sequential and procedural, with one deviation.	
	Language Used Some figurative, ironic, and formal language with implied meanings.	
	Knowledge Required Relies on familiarity with email; literary references.	

RESOURCES

- Unit 1 Response Log
- Selection Audio
- Reading Studio: Notice & Note
- Level Up Tutorial: Irony
- Level Up Tutorial: Rhyme
- Speaking and Listening Studio: Giving a Presentation
- Writing Studio
- "Interflora" Selection Test

SUMMARIES

English

The 19th-century poet Robert Browning ("Robert B.") emails his wife, Elizabeth Barrett Browning ("E.B.B."), to send her a "virtual bouquet" of flowers in the form of a sonnet. Robert gives Elizabeth instructions on how to "smell" the flowers, read the accompanying tag or card, and unwrap and place the bouquet in a vase. He explains that he sent her virtual flowers because, unlike real flowers, they will last forever. Then he tells her to delete the bouquet if she does not care for it.

Spanish

Robert Browning, el poeta del Siglo XIX, ("Robert B.") le manda un email a su esposa, Elizabeth Barrett Browning ("E.B.B."), para enviarle un "bouquet virtual" de flores en forma de soneto. Robert le da a Elizabeth instrucciones de cómo "oler" las flores, leer la etiqueta o tarjeta que las acompaña, y desenvolver y colocar el bouquet en un envase. Explica que él le manda flores virtuales porque, a diferencia de las flores verdaderas, éstas durarán para siempre. Luego le dice que elimine el bouquet si no le interesa.

SMALL-GROUP OPTIONS

Have students work in small groups to read and discuss the selection.

Contribute to Meaning

- Have small groups read the poem aloud among themselves, taking turns line-by-line.
- Assign each group a different element of the poem, such as situation, structure (line breaks), rhyme/sound devices, tone, word choice, imagery, or figurative language.
- Ask: *How does your assigned element contribute to the poem's meaning?*
- Have students discuss their ideas and collaboratively form a group response.
- Have a student from each group share the group's response with the class.
- Then ask the class to identify connections between the various group responses.

Think-Pair-Share

- Have pairs read the poem aloud to each other, with one partner reading lines 1–8 and the other reading lines 9–14.
- After students have finished, pose this question: *What is the virtual bouquet of flowers in this poem?*
- Have students think about the question individually, identify examples, and take notes.
- Then, have pairs discuss their ideas and examples, and collaboratively form a response.
- Finally, ask pairs to share their responses with the class.

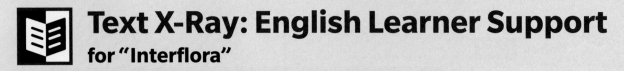

Text X-Ray: English Learner Support
for "Interflora"

Use the Text X-Ray and the supports and scaffolds in the Teacher's Edition to help guide students at different proficiency levels through the selection.

INTRODUCE THE SELECTION
DISCUSS THE CHARACTERISTICS OF LOVE POEMS

In this lesson, students will need to be able to discuss what is expected in a love poem. Point out that the purpose of most love poems is to express love and make a person feel loved. Read aloud line 3 and share these definitions:

- *herewith*: a formal, old-fashioned way of saying "with this"
- *esteem*: respect and admiration or affection

Explain that esteem is not as strong an emotion as love, so it is a less romantic word. However, "herewith as proof of my esteem" suggests that the speaker is not expressing his true feelings because he is being formal. Readers can infer that the poem is a love poem after all.

Ask students to share and contrast examples of other words and images that are romantic and not romantic. Provide the following sentence frames:

- _____ is romantic/unromantic because _____.
- _____ is more/less romantic than _____ because _____.

CULTURAL REFERENCES

Explain that *flora* is the Spanish word for "flower." The following words and phrases may be unfamiliar to students:

- *@ mailexcite dot com (line 1):* the symbol @ is read "at"; the poet uses "dot" in place of a period; "com" in email and website addresses stands for "commercial"
- *uk (line 2):* "uk" stands for "United Kingdom" and shows where E.B.B lives; each letter is read aloud separately
- *virtual* (line 4): existing only on computers or on the Internet; almost something but not in fact that thing
- *cellophane* (line 5): thin, clear wrapping material
- *Encrypt* (line 7): to change information into a secret code (system of numbers, symbols, or letters) to hide it
- *on-line* (line 12): another way of spelling *online*; connected to or done on the Internet

LISTENING

Understand Rhyme Scheme

Help students indentify the rhyme scheme in "Interflora." Explain that it uses some words that rhyme exactly and others that almost rhyme, by ending with a similar vowel or consonant sound. Tell them to mark the last word in each line and listen for repeated sounds.

Have students listen as you read the poem aloud, emphasizing the last word in each line. Then display the poem. Use the following supports with students at varying proficiency levels:

- Tell students that you will ask questions about what you just read aloud. For example, ask: *Do "com" and "uk" rhyme?* (No) Write *a* after *com* and *b* after *uk*. Ask: *Do "com" and "esteem" end with a similar sound?* (Yes) *What letter will show that the words almost rhyme?* (a) . **SUBSTANTIAL**
- After reading, circle *com, uk, press, tag, slime,* and *incomplete.* Help small groups identify which word(s) rhyme or almost rhyme with these. Then label lines 1, 2, 5, 6, 11, and 13 with the letters *a–f*. Have groups share the end rhymes they heard by labeling rhyming lines. **MODERATE**
- Give student pairs the lines written on separate sheets of paper. Repeat just the last words in the lines, then have pairs group lines that end with the same or a similar sound, to create six groups. Ask volunteers to label the displayed lines to show the rhyme scheme. **LIGHT**

SPEAKING

Discuss Humorous Details

Have students discuss details that create humor. Call attention to the image of rotting flowers in lines 10–11. Explain that *stink of mortality's decay* means *smell strongly like something dead and rotten.* Ask students to visualize the flowers.

To help discuss the image in lines 10–11 and other humorous details, give students a T-chart labeled "Not Expected" and "Expected." Use the following supports with students at varying proficiency levels:

- Generate discussion using short-answer questions and the chart. Ask: *Do you expect a love poem to describe flowers that stink?* (No) Write "flowers that stink" in the "Not Expected" column, "flowers that smell" [wol] in the other, and suggest expected adjectives for students to approve. Ask: *Are expected details as funny as unexpected ones?* (No) **SUBSTANTIAL**
- Ask small groups to discuss why the flower image is surprising and funny and complete the chart. Share this sentence frame: *Readers expect _____, not _____, so the image _____.* **MODERATE**
- Have student pairs discuss how the unexpected details in lines 10–11 create humor. Then ask: *Are these details necessary for the speaker to make his point? How do you know?* **LIGHT**

READING

Understand Details

Display lines 5–8 and point out the italicized words. Tell students the italics show the words have a special meaning when discussing computers. Sketch a computer Control (Ctrl) key and a monitor displaying the words *Encrypt, Reverse,* and *Drag.*

Work with students to reread lines 5–8. Point out the *please* in line 5, and explain that the speaker is telling E.B.B. what to do. Use the following supports with students at varying proficiency levels:

- Read aloud line 5 while miming smelling a bouquet, using a computer mouse to click, and pressing the Control key. Have students reread the line with you and copy your motions. Repeat this process with each line. Then have students chorally read all the lines while acting out their meaning. Then ask: *Do you need to do these things with a real bouquet?* (No) **SUBSTANTIAL**
- Give students a T-chart labeled "Do This" and "Why," and help them identify the first command and stated reason. Have small groups complete the chart for lines 6–8 and then use sentence frames to explain the commands, such as: *E.B.B. has to _____ because _____.* **MODERATE**
- Give student pairs a three-column chart labeled "Command," "Speaker's Reason," and "Unexpected Detail." Have them complete the chart and share their findings. **LIGHT**

WRITING

Write a Sonnet

Discuss the sonnet writing assignment on p. 35. Explain that the topic of their poem should be about communicating with technology. Suggest students write a simpler but topical, humorous poem with elements of a sonnet, or an acrostic poem or cinquain.

Display these examples: *Topic: Communicating with Texts, Theme: Technology helps people say what they need to.* Use these supports with students at varying proficiency levels:

- Review that a theme is what the writer wants readers to understand about the topic. Explain that in this example, related words will help show how useful texting is. Create a five W's and How chart, and work with students to add possible words. Then ask how texting can be funny, and allow small groups to use their home language to identify words that add humor. **SUBSTANTIAL**
- Have small groups pick a topic and state a theme using this sentence format: Technology [opinion on technology's usefulness for communication]. Then guide groups to list related details for a poem. **MODERATE**
- Have student pairs pick a topic, write a theme statement, and brainstorm related and humorous details. Ask them to find rhyming words for specific details with common endings. **LIGHT**

Connect to the
? ESSENTIAL QUESTION

"Interflora" uses a traditional poetic form and subject, the love sonnet, to critique a modern form of communication. The speaker's humorous, skeptical attempt to email his wife a virtual bouquet illustrates how this technology comes with rules and limitations that can make personal communication less personal. However, the poem also suggests that ultimately, we can choose to accept or reject what technology offers.

INTERFLORA

Poem by **Susan Hamlyn**

 ESSENTIAL QUESTION:

Does technology improve or control our lives?

QUICK START

In the poem you are about to read, one person communicates with another person through email. What kinds of messages are best conveyed through email? What kinds are not? List your ideas below.

Email is great for . . .	Email is not so great for . . .

ANALYZE STRUCTURE

"Interflora" is a **sonnet,** a 14-line poem with a strictly defined structure and pattern of rhyme. The origins of this traditional form date back to the 1500s. Many famous love poems have been written in the form of the sonnet. One well-known collection of love sonnets is Elizabeth Barrett Browning's *Sonnets from the Portuguese* (1850), which she wrote for her husband, the poet Robert Browning.

In poetry, **meter** is a pattern of stressed and unstressed syllables. Each unit of meter, known as a foot, consists of one stressed syllable and one or two unstressed syllables. Sonnets are written in iambic pentameter, with five feet in each line. Each foot has one unstressed syllable (˘) followed by a stressed syllable (´). The first line of Elizabeth Barrett Browning's Sonnet 43 below has been marked to show the meter. Mark the next three lines to show how the pattern continues.

> ˘ ´ ˘ ´ ˘ ´ ˘ ´ ˘ ´
> How do I love thee? Let me count the ways.   *a*
>
> I love thee to the depth and breadth and height   *b*
>
> My soul can reach, when feeling out of sight   *b*
>
> For the ends of Being and ideal Grace. . . .   *a*

A poem's **rhyme scheme** is its pattern of end rhymes. A rhyme scheme is noted by assigning a letter of the alphabet, beginning with *a*, to each line. Lines that rhyme are given the same letter. The first four lines of Sonnet 43 have been marked to show the rhyme scheme. Notice rhyme scheme and other sonnet characteristics as you read "Interflora."

GENRE ELEMENTS: SONNET

- is a form of lyric poetry that expresses personal thoughts and feelings and has a musical quality
- contains 14 lines
- follows a strict rhyme scheme, or pattern of end rhymes, such as *abbaabba cdcdcd* or *abab cdcd efef gg*
- is a popular form for love poems

QUICK START

Have students read the Quick Start questions. Encourage them to reflect on their own experiences with email to help them list ideas about its uses. If students are having difficulty getting started, help them brainstorm different uses as a class, and create a concept map that they can use as a reference. Ask guiding questions to help students consider the perspectives of both the sender and the receiver, such as, *Would you be disappointed or happy to receive an emailed birthday card?*

ANALYZE STRUCTURE

To help students understand the concept of meter, first point out that stressed and unstressed syllables are a natural part of speech. For example, *hello* is normally pronounced hel**lo**, not **hel**lo. Explain that *hello* contains an unstressed syllable followed by a stressed syllable, so it represents a type of foot called an iamb.

Display this representation of iambic pentameter: iAMB iAMB iAMB iAMB iAMB. Illustrate the rhythm by thumping your chest while saying the line aloud. Repeat the line and have students thump the rhythm with you. Point out that iambic pentameter sounds like a beating heart, which is part of its appeal. Explain that a poet may occasionally reverse the unstressed-stressed pattern in an iamb, however, to create an effect or to add emphasis.

Have students look at the first line of the "Sonnet 43" excerpt while you read the line aloud. Discuss how each one-syllable word forms an iamb with a syllable/word next to it. After students mark the meter in the remaining lines, ask them to share their ideas about how the rhythm and rhyme in these lines are similar to those in a song.

TEACH

ANALYZE IRONY

Tell students that to recognize and appreciate humor created by irony, they need to understand what is being contrasted. Share these examples:

- **Situational irony:** Your friend calls to tell you that she will not be calling you, because she is not allowed to use the phone.

- **Dramatic irony:** A character in a story is waiting for his mother to pick him up and take him to his soccer game. Readers learn that he falls asleep while waiting. When his mother gets home, she thinks he has gotten a ride from a friend. She goes to the game without him, to watch him play.

- **Verbal irony:** After struggling through a difficult test, a student says, "Well, that was easy. All my studying really paid off."

Ask students to explain what contrast or contradiction makes each example ironic. Point out that as students read "Interflora," analyzing unexpected details or exaggeration can help them understand what point the author is making and why it is humorous.

ANNOTATION MODEL

Remind students of the annotation ideas in Analyze Structure on p. 29. Tell students to use those conventions for marking the poem's meter and rhyme scheme. Explain that they also may incorporate their own system for marking up the poem in their write-in text. For example, they may underline uses of irony or other important words and ideas. Students also may find it helpful to use vertical lines to mark the feet in each line, or to color code their annotations by using highlighters. Explain that their notes in the margin may include questions about ideas that are unclear or topics they want to learn more about.

ANALYZE IRONY

Irony is a literary device used to show a special kind of contrast between appearance and reality. Writers often use irony to create humor. There are three types of irony frequently used in literature: situational, dramatic, and verbal. Read the definition of each type in the chart below. Then write how each type could be funny.

TYPE OF IRONY	DEFINITION	WHY THIS COULD BE HUMOROUS
Situational irony	When a character or the reader expects one thing, but something very different happens or is true	
Dramatic irony	When the reader knows something that a character does not know	
Verbal irony	When a character says one thing but means another	

As you read "Interflora," look for examples of irony that create humor.

ANNOTATION MODEL   **NOTICE & NOTE**

As you read, note how the poet uses irony to convey a message or to create humor. This model shows one reader's notes about the beginning of "Interflora."

> From Robert B. @ mailexcite dot com
>
> to E.B.B. @ virgin dot uk:
>
> ⟨Please find herewith as proof of my esteem⟩
>
> a customized, fresh, virtual bouquet.

The sonnet is written like an email message, but line 3 uses old-fashioned language. Is this an example of irony?

BACKGROUND

"Interflora" is a sonnet written as an email. The poem begins with the email addresses of the speaker and the person to whom he is sending a message. Readers familiar with the love sonnets that Elizabeth Barrett Browning wrote to her husband, Robert Browning, may recognize a certain humorous or ironic connection between this sonnet and those earlier works. **Susan Hamlyn** *is a London-based English teacher and writer. Hamlyn has published two collections of poetry,* The Only Thing Untouched *and* Quiet Myth.

INTERFLORA

Poem by Susan Hamlyn

SETTING A PURPOSE

As you read the sonnet, pay attention to details that are surprising or unexpected, and think about how these details create humor.

Notice & Note

Use the side margins to notice and note signposts in the text.

BACKGROUND

Have students read the Background note and information about the author. Tell students that the email addresses that begin "Interflora" include two literary references. Explain that while many people might be named "Robert B.," the author addresses the email to "E.B.B." in the United Kingdom to make readers think of the famous 19th-century British poets discussed on p. 29: Robert Browning and Elizabeth Barrett Browning. Before marrying, they wrote each other hundreds of love letters that have since been published in print and online.

SETTING A PURPOSE

Direct students to use the Setting a Purpose prompt to focus their reading.

Ⓔ ENGLISH LEARNER SUPPORT

LEARNING STRATEGIES   Call students' attention to the selection title, "Interflora." Point out that *Internet* also contains the prefix *inter-*, which means "between." Tell students that what they already know about using email to communicate with others will help them understand the poem. Ask them what someone who has never used a desktop computer before needs to know in order to send an email. Model creating a concept map by writing "Emailing a friend" in a center circle and writing "friend's email address" and "opening the email program" around it. Have students work individually to create their own concept map. Then have volunteers share their ideas with the class. **MODERATE**

TEACH

ANALYZE STRUCTURE

Remind students that a traditional **sonnet** has a specific **meter** that they can mark using a breve (˘) for unstressed syllables and an accent mark (´) for stressed syllables. It also has one of the **rhyme schemes** listed on p. 29 (Elements of a Sonnet). (**Answer:** *"Interflora" does not strictly follow sonnet structure. Most lines are written in iambic pentameter, but the poem ends with three pairs of couplets [bb ee ff] instead of following a traditional rhyme scheme.*)

For **listening support** for students at varying proficiency levels, see the **Text X-Ray** on page 28C.

For **reading support** for students at varying proficiency levels, see the **Text X-Ray** on page 28D.

ANALYZE IRONY

Remind students that humor is often created through **irony**—a contrast between appearances or expectations and reality. Suggest they underline any parts of the poem that seem humorous or ironic and note possible reasons in the margin, instead of immediately looking for specific types of irony. (**Answer:** *The humor is ironic because the poet has Robert say things he doesn't actually mean and that aren't right for the situation. First Robert says he is writing as "proof of my esteem," when he really means "love." Then he ironically calls the virtual bouquet "fresh," knowing that only real bouquets can be fresh, and gives completely unromantic computer instructions in lines 5–8. The poem's ending also contradicts what he led readers to believe about the bouquet.*)

For **speaking support** for students at varying proficiency levels, see the **Text X-Ray** on page 28D.

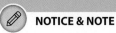

ANALYZE STRUCTURE
Annotate: Use the symbols ˘ and ´ to mark the meter of the sonnet. Use letters of the alphabet to identify and mark the rhyme scheme.

Analyze: Does "Interflora" follow a traditional sonnet rhyme scheme? Explain.

ANALYZE IRONY
Annotate: Mark at least three examples of humor in the sonnet.

Analyze: Explain how the poet uses irony to create humor.

Interflora

From Robert B. @ mailexcite dot com
To E.B.B. @ virgin dot uk:
Please find herewith as proof of my esteem
a customized, fresh, virtual bouquet.
5 For scent please click on cellophane and press
Control. To read the message on the tag
highlight the print, click on *Encrypt Reverse.*
To unwrap blooms and place in vase use *Drag.*
My flowers sent, beloved, in this way,
10 won't fade, stink of mortality's decay.
Petals won't wilt to husks nor leaves to slime;
these on-line flowers for you will outlast Time.
But if, my love, this gift seems incomplete
and does not touch your heart, then press *Delete.*

WHEN STUDENTS STRUGGLE . . .

Reason Inductively Tell students that to identify verbal irony, they need to consider several pieces of information: what the speaker says, what the truth of the situation is, and whether the words match the situation. Explain that if the words and situation do not match, the speaker is saying one thing to make a very different or opposite point. The joke is how ridiculous the speaker's actual words are, once you realize that they do not make sense.

For additional support, go to the **Reading Studio** and assign the following **Level Up tutorial: Irony.**

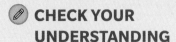 **CHECK YOUR UNDERSTANDING**

Have students answer the questions independently.

Answers:

1. *A*

2. *F*

3. *C*

If they answer any questions incorrectly, have them reread the text to confirm their understanding. Then they may proceed to ANALYZE THE TEXT on page 34.

CHECK YOUR UNDERSTANDING

Answer these questions before moving on to the **Analyze the Text** section on the following page.

1 Which line reveals that the poem's speaker is sending an email?

A *From Robert B. @ mailexcite dot com*

B *Please find herewith as proof of my esteem*

C *To unwrap blooms and place in vase use* Drag

D *Petals won't wilt to husks nor leaves to slime*

2 To smell the flowers, what does the recipient need to do?

F Click on cellophane and press *Control.*

G Highlight the print and click on *Encrypt Reverse.*

H Use *Drag.*

J Press *Delete.*

3 According to the speaker, in what way are the on-line flowers better than real ones?

A They are fresh and virtual.

B They come with a message.

C They will last forever.

D They can easily be deleted.

 ENGLISH LEARNER SUPPORT

Oral Assessment Use the following questions to assess students' comprehension and speaking skills.

1. Which line in the poem shows that the speaker is sending an email? *(Line 1 shows that Robert B. is sending an email and is probably the speaker in the poem.)*

2. What does the person reading the email have to do to smell the flowers? *(The person has to click on the cellophane and press Control.)*

3. Why does the speaker think that the online flowers are better than real ones? *(The online flowers will last forever.)*

SUBSTANTIAL/MODERATE

ANALYZE THE TEXT

Possible answers:

1. **DOK 3:** *Words and phrases that make this a love sonnet include "as proof of my esteem," "beloved," "outlast Time," "my love," and "touch your heart."*

2. **DOK 4:** *The sonnet uses verbal and situational irony. Examples of verbal irony include the contrast between the language and syntax that might appear in a traditional love sonnet (lines 3, 9–12) and the language of computer instructions (lines 5–8). The final couplet represents situational irony because the speaker suddenly says the electronic bouquet and can be deleted with one click. This is surprising after all his effort. It also confirms that he has known all along that the bouquet is of little value.*

3. **DOK 2:** *The last six lines contain three couplets. This breaks the sonnet's form, as traditional sonnets end with just one couplet or six lines that share two rhyming sounds.*

4. **DOK 4:** *The idea that Robert Browning would send Elizabeth a virtual bouquet is humorous because the gesture is so trivial, while their love was so famously profound. A great poet writing a mostly unromantic love poem also is ironic and has a humorous effect, as does imagining how these historical figures might cope with other aspects of modern life.*

5. **DOK 2:** *Answers will vary. Ironically calling the bouquet "fresh" reveals that Hamlyn has a critical point of view about email technology. As she goes through the steps of virtually "smelling" the flowers, removing the cellophane (why would a virtual bouquet need cellophane?), and reading the virtual tag, Hamlyn is pointing out why receiving digital flowers would be an empty experience and suggests the theme that technology cannot replace authentic experiences between people.*

RESEARCH

Remind students that using specific search terms, such as "history long distance communication," will help them research online more efficiently. Point out that including the year 1994 as a search term may be too specific; suggest they use "1990s" to narrow the timeframe first.

Connect Students may note that technologies, such as texting, instant messaging, and video calling via social media or other apps have made it even easier to stay in more constant contact with others. With these tools, conversations may be more fragmented and shorter, consist mainly of photos or images instead of words, or be very close to being in the same room with the other person.

RESPOND

ANALYZE THE TEXT

Support your responses with evidence from the text. 📓 NOTEBOOK

1. **Cite Evidence** Which words and phrases in the poem reveal that it is a love sonnet?

2. **Analyze** Which types of irony are used in the sonnet? Give examples from the poem.

3. **Compare** How are the last six lines of "Interflora" different from the rest of the poem in form? How does this compare to more traditional sonnet forms?

4. **Synthesize** The 19th-century British poets Robert and Elizabeth Barrett Browning shared one of the most famous and passionate romances in the history of literature. How does this fact add to the humor of "Interflora"?

5. **Infer** What theme or message about technology does the poet's use of irony suggest?

RESEARCH TIP
Besides using the Internet, where can you look to find answers to these questions? Consider contacting someone who lived during the time period and ask whether you can conduct an interview about how technology has changed since then.

RESEARCH

"Interflora" was published in 1994. Since then, much has changed about the way people use the Internet in their daily lives. With a partner, research the differences between technologies today and technologies from the time period in which this poem was written.

QUESTION	ANSWER
What devices could people use to connect to the Internet in the mid-1990s?	*Back then, people could only connect to the Internet through computers that had dial-up modems; cellphones were not widely used until the OOs.*
How did people communicate overseas in the 1990s?	*To communicate overseas international calls could be mode, but they were very expensive, Email did improve the way countries communicated and did business together.*
Could you use the Internet to order flowers in 1994?	*Shopping online was still not commonplace. Back then, florists used a wire service. Someone could order a bouquet over the phone to their local florist, then that florist would use the wire service to contact a florist in the town where the flowers were to be delivered.*

Connect In a small group, discuss how technology has changed the way we communicate with other people. How would the people in the poem communicate with each other today? What might Robert B. send to E.B.B. today?

WHEN STUDENTS STRUGGLE . . .

Analyze Sonnet Structure Remind students that a traditional sonnet has a particular rhyme scheme, or pattern of end rhymes. One is *abbaabba cdcdcd*. Another is *abab cdcd efef gg*. Point out that the letters representing the rhyming sounds form a pattern, with some letters/sounds alternating and others repeating. Have students circle the last word in each line of "Interflora." Help them identify and label the rhyme scheme in the first four lines, and ask them to finish the remaining lines with a partner. Explain that they can compare rhyme schemes within a poem and with the ones for traditional sonnets.

 For additional support, go to the **Reading Studio** and assign the following 📖 **Level Up tutorial: Rhyme.**

CREATE AND PRESENT

Write a Sonnet Write a poem in the structure of a sonnet. Review your notes on the Quick Start activity before you begin.

❑ Decide on a topic and theme for your sonnet. Brainstorm some rhyming word pairs related to your topic.

❑ Consider how to include irony and humor in your sonnet.

❑ Write a draft of your sonnet in 14 lines. You might use a rhymed couplet at the end to reveal your theme.

❑ Revise your poem to match the traditional meter of a sonnet and to have a consistent rhyme scheme.

Present a Sonnet Now share your sonnet with the class. When you and your classmates read your sonnets aloud, provide thoughtful feedback to each other.

❑ Practice reading your sonnet. Experiment with stressing different syllables to bring out the musical quality in the text.

❑ Practice making eye contact with your audience, and use facial expressions and natural gestures to convey the meaning of the sonnet.

❑ Finally, read your sonnet aloud to the class.

RESPOND TO THE ESSENTIAL QUESTION

 Does technology improve or control our lives?

Gather Information Review your annotations and notes on "Interflora." Then, add relevant details to your Response Log. As you determine which information to include, think about:

- how people used technology in the past versus today
- whether this has changed for the better or for the worse
- how to keep technology from controlling one's life

At the end of the unit, you may want to refer to your notes when you write an informational essay.

 Go to the **Writing Studio** for more help with writing a poem.

 Go to the **Speaking and Listening Studio** for more on giving a presentation.

ACADEMIC VOCABULARY
As you write and discuss what you learned from the poem, be sure to use the Academic Vocabulary words. Check off each of the words that you use.

❑ **commentary**

❑ **occupation**

❑ **option**

❑ **speculate**

❑ **technology**

CREATE AND PRESENT

Write a Sonnet Encourage students to begin by focusing on just getting their ideas down in 14 lines. Suggest they pause after writing the first line to mark the meter and count the feet, to get a better feel for sonnet line length and rhythm. Remind them that as they revise, they can change and rearrange words as needed—and they may come up with ideas for improvements in the process.

For **writing support** for students at varying proficiency levels, see the **Text X-Ray** on page 28D.

Present a Sonnet Tell students that when reading a sonnet aloud, they should pause only when there is punctuation, not at the end of every line. Explain that doing so can make the poem sound choppy if the lines do not end with a built-in pause. Encourage students to read with meaning and expression.

RESPOND TO THE ESSENTIAL QUESTION

Allow time for students to add details from "Interflora" to their Unit 1 Response Logs.

THE AUTOMATION PARADOX

Argument by James Bessen

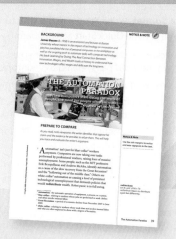

GENRE ELEMENTS
ARGUMENT

Review with students that the goal of an **argument** is to convince a reader to believe or to do a certain thing. Explain that arguments are sometimes called persuasive texts or **opinion** texts because they include an argument or an opinion. In this type of text, the author states an opinion, or a claim, and then provides evidence to support the opinion. This evidence can take on the form of statistical (numerical) data, quotes from experts, or facts; a good argument will usually include some examples of each type of evidence. The text may also use graphic features such as charts, which are present as supporting evidence in "The Automation Paradox."

LEARNING OBJECTIVES

- Identify claims and supporting evidence in an argument.
- Evaluate the effectiveness of facts, statistics, and other evidence in a persuasive essay.
- Identify transitional words and phrases, and explain how they are effective.
- Conduct research about the effect of automation on jobs.
- Write a persuasive essay about automation's impact on employment.
- Analyze graphic features, and explain how they support a claim.
- Become familiar with the meanings of Academic Vocabulary words.
- **Language** Discuss with a partner how graphic features visually represent information.

TEXT COMPLEXITY

Quantitative Measures	The Automation Paradox	Lexile 1140L
Qualitative Measures	**Ideas Presented** Mostly explicit, with some implied meaning.	
	Structures Used Graphic features; compare and contrast a frequent structural feature.	
	Language Used Mostly Tier II and Tier III words with some figurative language.	
	Knowledge Required Basic knowledge of jobs, the economy, and technological innovation.	

Online **Ed**

RESOURCES

- Unit 1 Response Log

- Selection Audio

- Close Read Screencasts: Modeled Discussions

- Reading Studio: Notice & Note

- Writing Studio: Writing Arguments

- Writing Studio: Writing Informative Texts: Organizing Ideas

- Speaking and Listening Studio: Participating in Collaborative Discussions

- Vocabulary Studio: Using a Dictionary

- "Automation Paradox" Selection Test

SUMMARIES

English

Many people believe that increased automation will lead to the loss of jobs as technology becomes faster and cheaper than human beings. The selection argues that this perception is not accurate. While some types of jobs, notably low-skill and low-wage occupations, may indeed lose workers, other jobs are actually expanding. The author explains why this might be the case.

Spanish

Mucha gente cree que el aumento de la automatización llevará a la pérdida de empleos a medida que la tecnología se haga más rápida y barata que los seres humanos. Esta selección sostiene que esta percepción no es acertada. Mientras unos tipos de trabajos, notablemente las ocupaciones de baja capacidad y baja remuneración, puede que ciertamente pierdan trabajadores, otros trabajos están de hecho expandiéndose. El autor explica por qué éste puede ser el caso.

SMALL-GROUP OPTIONS

Have students work in small groups to read and discuss the selection.

Restate and Respond

- Begin by posing a question or other prompt for discussion.
- The first student responds orally to the prompt. Other students are encouraged to take brief notes.
- The second student restates the first student's response ("Lee said–") and then adds his or her own.
- Continue in this way, with each student responsible for a brief summary of the previous student's comments.
- Encourage students to use transitional words and phrases, such as "Jamie said–, but I think–"

Generate Questions

- Have students read the selection independently and generate questions that would be appropriate for a discussion on the article.
- When group members' questions are complete, have them each choose one question for a small group discussion.
- Then have students discuss each question in turn. The asker of the question should participate in the discussion but should also take notes.
- If time permits, repeat with a second question from each student's list.

Text X-Ray: English Learner Support
for "The Automation Paradox"

Use the Text X-Ray and the supports and scaffolds in the Teacher's Edition to help guide students at different proficiency levels through the selection.

INTRODUCE THE SELECTION
DISCUSS JOBS AND THE ECONOMY

To discuss this article, students will need to be familiar with basic vocabulary regarding jobs and economic terms. On the board, write the following words: *occupation, labor, employment.* Read the words aloud, and tell students that these words all refer to jobs and work. Say the following aloud, and have students answer the questions, using sentence frames as needed.

- *My* occupation *is being a teacher. What* occupation *would you like to have?*
- *People who work are doing* labor. *What kind of* labor *do you like or dislike?*
- *When the* employment *rate is high, lots of people have jobs. What happens when the* employment *rate is low?*

CULTURAL REFERENCES

The following words or phrases may be unfamiliar to students:

- *hollowing out* (paragraph 1): reducing the number or importance of something
- *legal industry* (paragraph 3): lawyers and others who work with the law
- *unemployment lines* (paragraph 4): the collection of people without a job
- *basic economics* (paragraph 6): the rules that govern how jobs and businesses work

---

LISTENING

Understand Central Idea

Explain that a persuasive essay always makes a claim and that a claim is an opinion. Tell students that an opinion is not a fact; an opinion is what you believe to be true, but a fact is what everyone agrees is true. Say some opinions, such as *Cats are the best pets,* and some facts, such as *Cats are animals,* and have students identify which are opinions.

Have students listen as you read aloud paragraphs 1–4. Use the following supports with students at varying proficiency levels:

- Tell students that you will ask some questions about what they just heard. Then ask yes/no questions such, as *Are computers better than people at some jobs?* Have them respond to the questions with the words *yes* or *no.* **SUBSTANTIAL**
- Have students identify a fact and an opinion in what they heard. **MODERATE**
- Have students identify a fact in what they heard and tell how they know it is a fact. Then have students identify an opinion in the reading and tell how they know it is an opinion. **LIGHT**

SPEAKING

Discuss Graphic Features

Have students discuss the graphic features of the text. Have them use the terms *graph, bar graph,* and *line graph* as they talk. As you move around the room, be sure that students are on task and showing an understanding of these terms.

Point out the bar graph on p. 40 and the line graph on p. 41. Use the following supports with students at varying proficiency levels:

- Say *A bar graph uses bars to show how many. A line graph uses a line to show changes in how many.* Have students use a sentence frame *This is a _____ graph because _____* to tell a partner about one of the graphs. **SUBSTANTIAL**
- Have students tell a partner at least two things that they notice about the graphs. Be sure they use the terms *bar graph* and *line graph.* **MODERATE**
- Have students tell a partner how the two graphs are alike and different. Be sure they use the terms *bar graph* and *line graph.* **LIGHT**

READING

Read Persuasive Texts

Tell students that people who write persuasive texts use evidence to support their claims or opinions. Give examples of evidence that can sometimes be used, including graphs, numerical data, direct quotations, and facts. Guide students to look for these types of evidence as they read.

Read paragraphs 8–10 with students. Use the following supports with students at varying proficiency levels:

- Call students' attention to paragraph 9. Have them look for a number in the text (5 percent) and read and underline the sentence containing the number. Guide students to understand how the information supports the claim. Ask: *What kind of evidence did the author use here?* (numbers) **SUBSTANTIAL**
- Have students find an example of supporting evidence in these paragraphs. Have them underline the sentence in the text and explain to a partner how they knew it was evidence. **MODERATE**
- Have students find an example of supporting evidence in these paragraphs and explain to a partner how the evidence supports the author's claim. **LIGHT**

WRITING

Write a Persuasive Essay

Work with students to read the writing assignment on p. 47.

Use the following supports with students at varying proficiency levels:

- Guide students to use the graphic organizer on p. 44 as an organizing tool. Have them copy the organizer and write words and short phrases to help them identify their claim, reasons, and evidence. **SUBSTANTIAL**
- Have partners talk about the reasons and evidence that will support their claims. Give them sentence frames, such as *_____ supports my claim because _____.* **MODERATE**
- Have students talk with a partner about the reasons and supports they plan to use to support their claims. Have them explain which reasons they think are most effective and why. **LIGHT**

ARGUMENT

THE AUTOMATION PARADOX

by **James Bessen**
pages 39–43

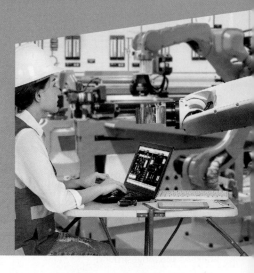

? Connect to the
ESSENTIAL QUESTION

"The Automation Paradox" explores whether the rise in automation in modern society makes life easier or whether it dehumanizes people. The article points out that some people typically view technology as a force that helps people, but argues that the reality may be more complex.

COMPARE AND CONTRAST ARGUMENTS

Point out that both "The Automation Paradox" and "Heads Up, Humans!" are nonfiction and that each is an argumentative text in which the author is trying to persuade readers that his or her perspective is correct. Add, however, that the two texts are very different in their viewpoints. Have students read the texts to identify the different claims made by the authors and the different types of evidence they use to support their arguments.

COMPARE ARGUMENTS

As you read, notice how the claim in each argument is supported by reasons and evidence. Then think about how the arguments relate to each other. After you read both selections, you will collaborate with a group on a final project.

? ESSENTIAL QUESTION:

Does technology improve or control our lives?

ARGUMENT

HEADS UP, HUMANS

by **Claudia Alarcón**
pages 51–55

The Automation Paradox

QUICK START

Early elevators required operators to help passengers ride safely and efficiently. What other once-human jobs are now done by technology? List as many as you can. Then share your list with the class.

ANALYZE CLAIM AND EVIDENCE

In an argument, a **claim** is the writer's position, or opinion, on an issue. Recall the difference between facts and opinions.

- A **fact** is a statement that can be proved, or verified. However, different people may interpret the same fact in different ways.
- An **opinion** is a statement that cannot be proved because it expresses a person's beliefs, feelings, or thoughts.

A strong argument clearly and logically lays out a claim, reasons to accept the claim, and sufficient **evidence**—relevant facts, statistics, quotations, examples, and expert opinions—to support those reasons.

As you read "The Automation Paradox," use a chart like this one to analyze the argument's claims, reasons, and evidence. Is the author's reasoning sound? How you might defend or challenge his claims?

GENRE ELEMENTS: ARGUMENT

- states a claim and reasons to support the claim
- includes facts and other evidence to support reasons
- may note objections to claim and explain why they should be rejected
- takes many forms, such as editorials, feature articles, and essays

ANALYZE GRAPHIC FEATURES

A **graphic feature** is a design element such as a diagram, bar graph, or pie chart that visually represents information. Authors often use graphic features to show patterns and relationships between facts. As you read "The Automation Paradox," examine each graphic feature to see what it emphasizes. Ask yourself the following questions about each graphic feature:

- What information or evidence does the graph provide? What is the author's purpose, or reason, for including this visual?
- What conclusions can be drawn based on the information in the graph?

QUICK START

Have students read the Quick Start question and work in small groups to answer the question. Ask them to make a T-chart listing the job in one column and the technology in the second column for easy reference. Encourage them to estimate when the changeover was made from human labor to machine, paying special attention to which ones they think were within the last two or three decades.

ANALYZE CLAIM AND EVIDENCE

Work with students to help them explain the differences between facts and opinions. Stress that facts are verifiable, while opinions are not; another way to explain the difference may be to tell students that everyone agrees on the truth of facts, while people do not necessarily agree about opinions. Review with students the explanation of what a claim is, and walk students through the different types of evidence listed in the selection. Call students' attention to the Argument list at the side of the main column of text. Point out that the claim generally comes first in an argument and that the reasons and evidence follow, and that they are presented in a logical order. Be sure students understand that one reason may have more than one piece of evidence to support it, as shown on the bottom left part of the graphic at the bottom of the page.

ANALYZE GRAPHIC FEATURES

Ask students what graphic features they have encountered in other texts. Have them describe the features and what they showed; draw out that graphs and charts can often show information in ways that are more compact and more memorable than a block of text. Then have students predict which types of graphic features they may be most likely to encounter in the text they are about to read. Have students use the questions to guide their understanding of the article and to see why the author made use of graphic features.

CRITICAL VOCABULARY

Remind students that they should read through all the sentences before completing them with a word. Tell them that identifying the different parts of speech may help them determine which words go where. For instance, the missing word in the third sentence is most likely a verb, so students should look for verbs in the word list when they reach this sentence.

Answers:

1. *expansive*
2. *collaborate*
3. *redistribute*
4. *predominantly*
5. *relevant*
6. *robustly*

LANGUAGE CONVENTIONS

Review with students the information on transitional words and phrases, calling their attention to the example sentence. Explain that the author of the sentence could have written two separate sentences as follows: *Technology replaces workers. It also creates new jobs.* Ask students how the single sentence using *but* is different from the two sentences, and draw out that the use of *but* connects the two ideas more closely and therefore effectively. Have students generate a list of other transitional words and phrases, such as *because, or,* and *such as*.

ANNOTATION MODEL

Review with students the information about claims, reasons, and evidence on the previous page. Point out that this annotation identifies the sentence that introduces the topic and the sentences that provide evidence for the claim. Remind students that annotations like these can help them keep track of the arguments made in a text and identify the information used to support the arguments.

 GET READY

CRITICAL VOCABULARY

redistribute	robustly	predominantly
relevant	expansive	collaborate

To see how many Critical Vocabulary words you already know, use them to complete the sentences.

1. The topic is too _____ to research, so I'm narrowing it down.

2. If we _____ on the project, we can all share the work.

3. Let's _____ the chores to divide the tasks more fairly.

4. At home, they _____ speak their native language, Spanish.

5. Evidence that is _____ clearly connects to a claim.

6. The vegetables grew _____, so we had a big harvest.

LANGUAGE CONVENTIONS

Transitional Words and Phrases Transitional words and phrases connect ideas and show how they are related. In the example below, the transition *but* connects two ideas and signals a contrast.

Yes, technology replaces workers, <u>but</u> it also creates new jobs.

As you read "The Automation Paradox," note transitional words and phrases that alert you to relationships between ideas.

ANNOTATION MODEL

NOTICE & NOTE

As you read, note how the author presents his claim, reasons, and evidence. In the model, you can see one reader's notes about the introduction to "The Automation Paradox."

1 Automation isn't just for blue-collar workers anymore. Computers are now taking over tasks performed by professional workers, raising fears of massive unemployment. Some people, such as the MIT professors Erik Brynjolfsson and Andrew McAfee, identify automation as a cause of the slow recovery from the Great Recession and the "hollowing out of the middle class." Others see white-collar automation as causing a level of persistent technological unemployment that demands policies that would redistribute wealth. Robot panic is in full swing.

introduces the topic: impact of automation on employment

identifies two points of view that automation causes a negative impact

EL ENGLISH LEARNER SUPPORT

Use Cognates Tell students that some of the Critical Vocabulary words have Spanish cognates: *relevant/relevante* and *expansive/expansivo*. **ALL LEVELS**

BACKGROUND

James Bessen (b. 1958) is an economist and lecturer at Boston University whose interest in the impact of technology on innovation and jobs has paralleled the rise of personal computers in the workplace as well as the ongoing push to automate tasks with computer technology. *His book* Learning by Doing: The Real Connection Between Innovation, Wages, and Wealth *looks at history to understand how new technologies affect wages and skills over the long term.*

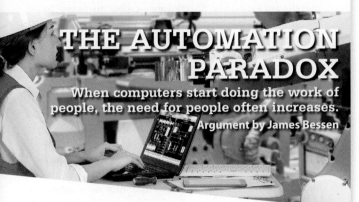

THE AUTOMATION PARADOX

When computers start doing the work of people, the need for people often increases.

Argument by James Bessen

PREPARE TO COMPARE

As you read, note viewpoints the writer identifies that oppose his claim and the evidence he provides to refute them. This will help you trace and evaluate the writer's argument.

1 Automation[1] isn't just for blue-collar[2] workers anymore. Computers are now taking over tasks performed by professional workers, raising fears of massive unemployment. Some people, such as the MIT professors Erik Brynjolfsson and Andrew McAfee, identify automation as a cause of the slow recovery from the Great Recession[3] and the "hollowing out of the middle class." Others see white-collar[4] automation as causing a level of persistent technological unemployment that demands policies that would **redistribute** wealth. Robot panic is in full swing.

---

[1] **automation:** the automatic operation of equipment, a process, or a system.
[2] **blue-collar:** relating to workers whose jobs are performed in work clothes and often involve manual labor.
[3] **Great Recession:** a period of economic decline from December 2007 to June 2009.
[4] **white-collar:** relating to workers whose work does not involve manual labor and who are often expected to dress with a degree of formality.

Notice & Note

Use the side margins to notice and note signposts in the text.

redistribute
(rē´dĭ-strĭb´yōot) *v.* To *redistribute* means to distribute again but differently.

APPLYING ACADEMIC VOCABULARY

❑ **commentary** ☒ **occupation** ❑ **option** ❑ **speculate** ☒ **technology**

Write and Discuss Have students turn to a partner to discuss the following questions. Guide students to include the Academic Vocabulary words *occupation* and *technology* in their responses. Ask volunteers to share their responses with the class.

- What **occupations** are discussed by the author?
- How does the author think **technology** will affect the job market in the future?

BACKGROUND

After students read the Background note, ask them what aspects of Bessen's work make him especially well qualified to write about the issue of technology's impact on the workforce. Have students explain how looking at history can help modern scholars make predictions about the role of technology in the future, and ask them to identify any potential pitfalls in looking to history for guidance on this topic. Close by pointing out that the question of how workers are impacted by new technologies has been around for many decades.

PREPARE TO COMPARE

Direct students to use the Prepare to Compare prompt to focus their reading.

EL ENGLISH LEARNER SUPPORT

Writing Structures Guide students to understand the structure of the article's introduction. Show students that the text begins with compare-and-contrast statements in which one sentence or idea is followed by another that connects with it. Draw students' attention to the contrast of *blue collar* and *white collar* in the first paragraph and to the focus on *some people* and *others* later in the same paragraph. Have students look for similar examples as they read through the text.
MODERATE

CRITICAL VOCABULARY

redistribute: To redistribute is to change the portion of something in a different, and usually fairer, way.

ASK STUDENTS what it means to redistribute wealth. *(It means to transfer wealth, such as money or property, from some people to other people through laws, rules, or other active organized means.)*

ANALYZE CLAIM AND EVIDENCE

Remind students that the claim represents the author's opinion and that the claim usually—though not always—comes early in a paragraph. Review the information about the meaning of the word *paradox,* and discuss what makes the claim seem paradoxical. (**Answer:** *The claim appears in the second sentence: workers whose fields become more computer-dependent will see an increase in their job opportunities. This represents a paradox because it seems counterintuitive: most people would guess that jobs would decline as computers become more important and widespread.*)

NUMBERS AND STATS

Remind students that support for a **claim** can take many different forms. Review that one of these forms is numerical data, which is also known as statistical information. Have students explain how the software study relates to the claim of the article; then have students draw a **conclusion** from the data. (**Answer:** *The data establishes that electronic software is much better than people at finding relevant documents regarding lawsuits. This supports the author's overall claim that technology is becoming more and more common in the workplace, including in some areas—such as the law—where it had not traditionally been widespread. A possible conclusion drawn from the data would be that automation is changing the job market for lawyers and paralegals.*)

ANALYZE GRAPHIC FEATURES

Students should recall that charts and graphs can present a great deal of information in a way that is easy to see and easy to understand. Call students' attention to the graph. Review how bar graphs work as needed; you may want to point out that unlike most bar graphs, this graph does not have a *y*-axis. Then have students answer the questions. (**Answer:** *This information supports the claim by showing that job opportunities in fields with high computer use are expanding more rapidly than in fields with low computer use.*)

NOTICE & NOTE

ANALYZE CLAIM AND EVIDENCE

Annotate: In paragraph 2, mark the statement that best expresses the author's claim, or opinion, about the impact of automation on employment.

Analyze: A **paradox** is a statement that seems to contradict itself but may nonetheless be true. Why is the writer's claim about automation a paradox?

relevant
(rĕl´ə-vənt) *adj.* Something is *relevant* to a topic when it is related or important to that topic.

robustly
(rō-bŭst´lē) *adv. Robustly* means in a strong, healthy way.

NUMBERS AND STATS

Notice & Note: How do the results of the software study relate to the writer's claim? Circle or underline these results in the text.

Draw Conclusions: What conclusion can you draw based on this data?

ANALYZE GRAPHIC FEATURES

Annotate: On this bar graph, mark the text that tells you what, exactly, is represented by the height of each bar.

Analyze: How does the information in the graph support the writer's claim?

2   But these fears are misplaced—what's happening with automation is not so simple or obvious. It turns out that workers will have greater employment opportunities if their occupation undergoes some degree of computer automation. As long as they can learn to use the new tools, automation will be their friend.

3   Take the legal industry as an example. Computers are taking over some of the work of lawyers and paralegals, and they're doing a better job of it. For over a decade, computers have been used to sort through corporate documents to find those that are **relevant** to lawsuits. This process—called "discovery" in the profession—can run up millions of dollars in legal bills, but electronic methods can erase the vast majority of those costs. Moreover, the computers are often more accurate than humans: In one study, software correctly found 95 percent of the relevant documents, while humans identified only 51 percent.

4   But, perhaps surprisingly, electronic discovery software has not thrown paralegals and lawyers into unemployment lines. In fact, employment for paralegals and lawyers has grown **robustly.** While electronic discovery software has become a billion-dollar business since the late 1990s, jobs for paralegals and legal-support workers actually grew faster than the labor force as a whole, adding over 50,000 jobs since 2000, according to data from the U.S. Census Bureau. The number of lawyers increased by a quarter of a million.

5   Something similar happened when ATMs automated the tasks of bank tellers and when barcode scanners automated the work of cashiers: Rather than contributing to unemployment, the number of workers in these occupations grew. These are not special exceptions. On average, since 1980, occupations with above-average computer use have grown substantially faster (0.9 percent per year), as shown in this chart:

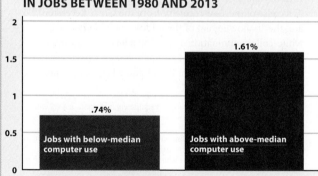

THE AVERAGE ANNUAL PERCENTAGE GROWTH IN JOBS BETWEEN 1980 AND 2013

CRITICAL VOCABULARY

relevant: Another way to think of something as *relevant* is if it is meaningful or has a purpose in the current culture.

ASK STUDENTS what makes some documents relevant to a lawsuit while others are not. (*Relevant documents are on the same topic as the lawsuit or give information about it.*)

robustly: The word *robustly* means strong and vibrant with energy.

ASK STUDENTS to provide examples from their own life of something or a state of being, such as opportunities that have grown robustly. (*Students may cite a garden or a puppy that has grown robustly.*)

6   How can this be? It might seem a sure thing that automating a task would reduce employment in an occupation. But that logic ignores some basic economics: Automation reduces the cost of a product or service, and lower prices tend to attract more customers. Software made it cheaper and faster to trawl through legal documents, so law firms searched more documents and judges allowed more and more **expansive** discovery requests. Likewise, ATMs made it cheaper to operate bank branches, so banks dramatically increased their number of offices. So when demand increases enough in response to lower prices, employment goes up with automation, not down. And this is what has been happening with computer automation overall during the last three decades. It's also what happened during the Industrial Revolution when automation in textiles, steelmaking, and a whole range of other industries led to a major increase in manufacturing jobs.

7   But not all of the news about computer automation is good. Some of that growth in computer-using occupations has come at the expense of other occupations. As depicted in the chart below, desktop publishing systems have meant fewer jobs for typographers,[5] as graphic designers took over their work. Computerized phone lines meant fewer jobs for telephone operators, but more jobs for receptionists. These aren't examples of computers "stealing" jobs; they are cases where computers helped some workers take work from others. Workers with computers frequently substitute for workers in non-computerized jobs.

[5] **typographers:** people who set words into type.

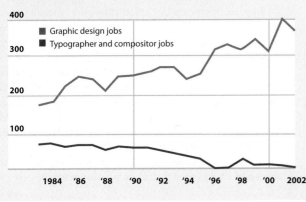

NUMBER OF GRAPHIC DESIGN JOBS VS. TYPOGRAPHER JOBS, IN HUNDREDS OF THOUSANDS

- ■ Graphic design jobs
- ■ Typographer and compositor jobs

NOTICE & NOTE

LANGUAGE CONVENTIONS

Annotate: Transitional words and phrases can signal a comparison or contrast. Mark the transitions in paragraph 6.

Analyze: How does the writer use these transitions to connect ideas?

expansive
(ĭk-spăn´sĭv) *adj.* Expansive means broad in size, range, or degree of openness.

ANALYZE GRAPHIC FEATURES

Annotate: Mark the sentence in paragraph 7 that connects to the information in the graph.

Analyze: What relationship between graphic-design jobs and typographer jobs does the graph show? How does this information relate to the writer's claim?

LANGUAGE CONVENTIONS

Review with students that certain words and phrases serve to combine two or more ideas, often in a single sentence. Draw out or explain that these words and phrases are often called *transitional* and that they help to connect themes and ideas. Then have students mark transitional words and phrases and explain how they connect ideas. (**Answer:** *Some of the transitional words and phrases in this paragraph include likewise, so, but, and also. In the sentence beginning "It's also what happened during the Industrial Revolution" the word also connects ideas by demonstrating that what happened during that period is very much like what happened at a different time already mentioned—in this case, the last thirty years.*)

ANALYZE GRAPHIC FEATURES

Review with students that a line graph is a type of visual feature that is especially well designed for showing changes over time. Explain that this feature is an example of a type of line graph called a double line graph, because it shows and compares the changes in two different pieces of data over the same time period. Have students identify the sentence in the text that refers specifically to the graph and the information it contains. Then have students determine what the graph shows and how that information connects to the claims of the author. (**Answer:** *The graph indicates that the number of jobs for graphic designers more or less doubled between the early 1980s and 2002, while the number of jobs for typographers dropped sharply. The author claims that automation has been problematic for people in certain types of jobs, and the graph clearly shows that typography is a career that has been especially affected by automation.*)

CRITICAL VOCABULARY

expansive: Students may visualize the word *expansive* as increasing in size and in every direction.

ASK STUDENTS What does it mean if discovery requests within the legal system are becoming more expansive? (*The requests are becoming more wide-ranging, so more documents will need to be examined to comply.*)

CLOSE READ SCREENCAST

Modeled Discussion Have students click the *Close Read* icon in their eBooks to access a screencast in which readers discuss and annotate "The Automation Paradox."

As a class, view and discuss the video. Then have students pair up to do an independent close read of the text. Students can record their answers on the Close Read Practice PDF.

 Close Read Practice PDF

ENGLISH LEARNER SUPPORT

Figurative Language Call students' attention to the phrasing "the net effect—is a wash" toward the end of paragraph 8. Explain that "a wash," in this context, does not literally mean that something is being cleaned. Rather, the phrase is figurative and means that the gains on one side are equaled by the gains on the other. Make a T-chart with "it's a wash" in the left-hand column and its meaning in the right-hand side. Have students help you think of other examples of figurative language in which the literal meaning of a word or phrase is not the one intended by the writer. Add them to the chart.
LIGHT

► NUMBERS AND STATS

Remind students that **arguments** and **opinions** always must be backed by supporting **evidence**. Explain that studies carried out by researchers are often used as evidence by writers. Discuss briefly that researchers are generally experts in their fields and are skilled at interpreting data from the studies they carry out; thus, their work is usually widely accepted. Have students discuss the questions with a partner and then share their thinking with another pair or the whole class. Point out that the second part of the question calls for students to evaluate the strength of the evidence. Student **conclusions** may vary, so look closely at the evidence students provide for their perspectives. (**Answer:** *The results of the study suggest that very few jobs are currently at risk of being eliminated because of automation, which matches the author's claim. Students may decide that the evidence is weak because what is true today may not be true in the future; it may not be wise to assume that conditions will always be consistent. Alternatively, they may conclude that the evidence is strong because the argument relies on a study by what is presumably a group of experts.*)

CRITICAL VOCABULARY

predominantly: The author uses *predominantly* to indicate that low-pay, low-skill jobs are mainly—but not exclusively—the ones that get transferred to other occupations.

ASK STUDENTS what it would mean if it were *predominantly* high-paying and high-skilled jobs that were transferred to other occupations. (*It would mean that most, though not all, of the jobs moved in this way were high-paying and high-skilled.*)

 NOTICE & NOTE

8 So, while computers create jobs in some occupations, they also reduce employment in others. The total effect on unemployment depends on which tendency is stronger. Some of my research shows that the net effect, across the economy, is a wash: Computers create about as many jobs as they eliminate. In other words, automation is not causing persistent unemployment.

9 That could change decades into the future, as new generations of software powered by artificial intelligence becomes ever more capable of advanced tasks. But in the near term, the story is much different. A new study by McKinsey & Company took a detailed look at work tasks that are likely to be automated and found that only about 5 percent of jobs are at risk of being completely automated in the near future. The main effect of automation for the time being will not be to eliminate jobs, but to redefine them—changing the tasks and the skills needed to perform them.

10 Even so, this means that automation poses a major challenge. There will be jobs, but workers will only be able to get them if they have the new sets of skills that computers make important. It's not just computer skills that are in demand, because automation can change the nature of jobs. For example, bank tellers have become more like marketing specialists, telling customers about bank loans, CDs, and other financial offerings.

11 Learning new skills is a significant social challenge as well. My research suggests that the jobs that get transferred to other occupations tend to be **predominantly** low-pay, low-skill jobs, so the burdens of automation fall most heavily on those least able and least equipped to deal with it. And often the new

NUMBERS AND STATS

Notice & Note: How do the results of the McKinsey & Company study relate to the writer's argument? Mark these results in the text.

Evaluate: Do you think this data is a strong or weak piece of evidence? Explain.

predominantly
(prĭ-dŏm´ə-nənt-lē) *adv.*
Predominantly refers to the most important, obvious, or typical aspect(s) of something.

TO CHALLENGE STUDENTS

Analyze Graphs Challenge students to sketch double line graphs showing changes in job numbers. Have them graph the following situations:

*one job rises as the other falls
*both jobs rise, but one rises more quickly than the other
*both jobs fall at different rates and then rise again

For each graph, have students write a brief paragraph describing the scenario and explaining what factors might affect the changes over time.

skills need to be learned on the job, so experience matters. To meet this challenge, some community colleges are **collaborating** with local employers to create work-study programs that allow trainees to learn on the job as well as in the classroom. Some trade groups are promoting skill-certification programs, which allow employers to recognize skills acquired through experience. These are the kinds of policies that can help overcome the real burden of automation. They deserve more attention than any panic about a supposed robot apocalypse.

collaborate
(kə-lăb´ə-rāt´) *v.* To *collaborate* means to work together.

CHECK YOUR UNDERSTANDING

Answer these questions before moving on to the **Analyze the Text** section on the following page.

1 Which sentence from the text best supports the writer's claim?

  A *Computers are now taking over tasks performed by professional workers, raising fears of massive unemployment.*

  B *But not all of the news about computer automation is good.*

  C *It might seem a sure thing that automating a task would reduce employment in an occupation.*

  D *It turns out that workers will have greater employment opportunities if their occupation undergoes some degree of computer automation.*

2 Based on the writer's argument, which word best describes the impact of automation on future employment?

  F insignificant

  G transformative

  H limited

  J devastating

3 Which of the following does the writer identify as an effect of automation that will have a positive impact on jobs?

  A more work space

  B slower production

  C increased demand

  D higher prices

 ENGLISH LEARNER SUPPORT

Oral Assessment Use the following to assess students' comprehension and speaking skills.

1. The writer claims automation will be good for workers. Which sentence supports this idea? *(It turns out that workers will have greater employment opportunities...)*

2. Which word tells what the author thinks will be automation's effect on employment? *(limited)*

3. Which of the following has a positive effect on jobs? *(increased demand)*
   MODERATE/LIGHT

CHECK YOUR UNDERSTANDING

Have students answer the questions independently.

Answers:

  1. *D*

  2. *G*

  3. *C*

If students answer any questions incorrectly, have them reread the text to confirm their understanding. Then they may proceed to ANALYZE THE TEXT on page 44.

CRITICAL VOCABULARY

collaborating: In most cases, a *collaboration* is formed to accomplish a common goal. The goal may be general (for example, to make money) or, in this case, specific — to create work-study programs.

ASK STUDENTS to give an example of a time when they were collaborating with others and how that collaboration was helpful. Then have them discuss the value of collaborating in the example given in the text. *(Answers: Responses will vary. The value of collaboration in this example is that many different people and organizations with different perspectives and resources can work on a problem.)*

ANALYZE THE TEXT

Possible answers:

1. **DOK 2:** *One fear is of massive unemployment as automation displaces workers from their jobs. Another is that the middle class will eventually disappear and the only solution will be to institute policies that redistribute wealth in ways many people will not like.*

2. **DOK 2:** *The author's explanation for the increase in jobs in the legal and banking fields is that while automation has taken over some tasks, it has lowered costs and thus allowed clients and customers to expect more. This permits technologically skilled people in displaced jobs to stay in their fields but with new tasks.*

3. **DOK 3:** *The writer cites the fact that as telephone operator jobs decrease, receptionist jobs increase. The writer says that jobs are not disappearing but simply being changed.*

4. **DOK 4:** *The statement in the text supports the author's claim that the effects of automation are not felt by every worker in every industry, but that automation's impact is felt most sharply on workers in a certain type of job.*

5. **DOK 4:** *The writer's use of statistical evidence supports the argument by providing actual evidence about the topic. As the writer points out, there is a great deal of fear and worry surrounding the subject of automation's effects on jobs. It is important to use numbers from studies rather than anecdotal evidence to determine the true effect. For example, readers might be very surprised to know that demand for paralegals has actually increased, not dropped, even after new software was developed to do some of their traditional jobs.*

RESEARCH

Remind students that they need to ensure that the information they find is accurate. They should list their sources and try to find the same evidence in more than one place if possible.

Connect Have students work in small groups to discuss what they found. Have them explore the connections to the article in particular by asking them whether the evidence they found tends to support the author's claim or not. Remind them that the claim recognizes that not all types of workers will benefit from automation, so if they find an example of a job that has been eliminated or greatly reduced through automation, that is not necessarily a refutation of the claim.

(Answers in chart will vary.)

 RESPOND

ANALYZE THE TEXT

Support your responses with evidence from the text. NOTEBOOK

1. **Summarize** Reread paragraphs 1–2. Then, in your own words, restate the two viewpoints on automation that the writer says are fear-based and overly simplistic.

2. **Cause/Effect** Review paragraph 6. What explanation does the writer give to account for the fact that automation seems to have caused an increase in jobs in the legal and banking industries?

3. **Cite Evidence** The writer presents a counter argument to disprove the notion that computers are "stealing" jobs. Cite one piece of evidence from this counter argument. Then note what the writer says is happening instead.

4. **Evaluate** In paragraph 11, the writer states that "the jobs that get transferred to other occupations tend to be predominantly low-pay, low-skill jobs, so the burdens of automation fall most heavily on those least able and least equipped to deal with it." How does this information relate to the writer's claim?

5. **Notice & Note** How does the writer's use of statistical evidence, both in the text and in graphs, impact his argument? Cite evidence from the text to support your answer.

RESEARCH TIP
"The Automation Paradox" cites examples of the impact of automation on jobs in the banking and legal industries and on jobs that are already computerized. To broaden the scope of evidence, you might consider researching the potential impact of automation in other fields, such as the healthcare or service industries.

RESEARCH

Research additional evidence to support the writer's claim in "The Automation Paradox" that automation will create many new jobs. Try to locate different types of evidence, such as facts, statistics, quotations, and examples. Use the chart below to record the evidence and identify its connection to the claim.

EVIDENCE	CONNECTION

Connect Share your evidence with a small group. Discuss which pieces of evidence are most persuasive and why.

WHEN STUDENTS STRUGGLE . . .

Graphic Features Have student pairs look at a graphic feature in the text, such as the double line graph on p. 41. Guide partners to talk about the graphs and what they see, using words like *rise, fall, more, less, higher,* and *lower.* Then show students how the graph tracks the changes in the numbers of available jobs over time. Have them run their index fingers along the paths describing the changes in their own words as they do so. Close by having them tell a partner what they learned.

 For additional support, go to the **Reading Studio** and assign the following LEVEL UP **Level Up tutorial: Reading Graphic Aids.**

CREATE AND DISCUSS

Write a Persuasive Essay Based on the arguments you just read, write a short persuasive essay in which you support a claim of your own about the effects of increased automation on employment.

- ❏ Introduce the topic and state your claim about the impact of automation on future jobs.

- ❏ Give at least two reasons to support your claim. Defend or challenge the writers' claims about automation and cite evidence from the text and your research to support your argument.

- ❏ In your final paragraph, restate your claim. Conclude with a piece of advice or a call to action.

Discuss with a Small Group Have a discussion about ways in which future workers might prepare for changes caused by increased automation. Make sure each group member gets equal time to speak.

- ❏ Review "The Automation Paradox" to identify ways in which the writer suggests automation will change or create future jobs. Take notes during your discussion and list types of skills and training that new or different jobs might require.

- ❏ Discuss steps workers might take to prepare for future changes in the job market and workplace. During the discussion, listen actively to help you ask questions and comment respectfully and thoughtfully on others' ideas.

RESPOND TO THE ESSENTIAL QUESTION

 Does technology improve or control our lives?

Gather Information Review your annotations and notes on "The Automation Paradox." Then, add relevant details to your Response Log. To decide what information to include, think about:

- ways in which automation benefits the economy
- ways in which technology affects various occupations
- what workers will need to do to adapt to changes in job markets

At the end of the unit, you may use your notes to help you write an informational essay.

 Go to **Writing Arguments** in the **Writing Studio** for help writing a persuasive essay.

Go to **Participating in Collaborative Discussions** in the **Speaking and Listening Studio** to learn more.

ACADEMIC VOCABULARY
As you write and discuss what you learned from the argument, be sure to use the Academic Vocabulary words. Check off each of the words that you use.

- ❏ **commentary**
- ❏ **occupation**
- ❏ **option**
- ❏ **speculate**
- ❏ **technology**

CREATE AND DISCUSS

Write a Persuasive Essay Tell students that the list on the student page can serve as a checklist for writing their essays. Explain also that the first paragraph should introduce the topic and that the last should be a conclusion that restates the ideas presented in the body of the text.

Students' essays should meet the following requirements: consist of three to four paragraphs; in the first paragraph, introduce the topic and state their claim about it; in the one or two body paragraphs, give two reasons to accept the claim and provide quotations and other evidence from the selection to support those reasons; in the final paragraph, conclude with a restatement of the claim and a piece of advice to peer readers.

 For **writing** support for students at varying proficiency levels, see the **Text X-Ray** on page **36D**.

Discuss with a Small Group Review with students that they are permitted to disagree with one another, but that these disagreements must be polite and respectful. Provide sentence starters as needed, such as "*I understand your point, but I think _____.*"

RESPOND TO THE ESSENTIAL QUESTION

Allow time for students to add details from "The Automation Paradox" to their Unit 1 Response Logs.

CRITICAL VOCABULARY

Possible answers:

1. *It would help because it allows people to combine their background understanding, their ideas, and their resources, which means that people working together can achieve more than one person on his or her own.*

2. *General search terms produce more expansive results because they will provide more hits; the word expansive means "greater in size."*

3. *Machines have predominantly eliminated low-skilled jobs because people with these jobs often do repetitive and relatively simple tasks that machines can do as well or better.*

4. *Possible reasons include good management, new demand for a product, or developing a reputation for quality.*

5. *You might redistribute items if the package is too heavy on one end.*

6. *If the evidence is relevant, it will support the argument you are trying to make.*

VOCABULARY STRATEGY:
Use a Dictionary

paralegal, noun, definition: a person trained in the law but not qualified as a lawyer

trawl, verb, definition: to engage in a broad search

net, noun, definition: what remains of income after expenses are deducted

persistent, adjective, definition: willing to continue in spite of obstacles

RESPOND

CRITICAL VOCABULARY

Practice and Apply Use your understanding of the Vocabulary words to answer each question.

1. Why would it be helpful to **collaborate** with a partner on a project?

2. What types of search terms produce more **expansive** results? Why?

3. Why have machines **predominantly** eliminated low-skill jobs?

4. What might cause a company's income to grow **robustly**?

5. Why might you want to **redistribute** items in a package?

6. How can you tell if a piece of evidence is **relevant**?

VOCABULARY STRATEGY: Use a Dictionary

 Go to the **Vocabulary Studio** for more on using a dictionary.

A **dictionary** is a reference work that provides information about words. Notice the parts of a dictionary entry:

syllabication	pronunciation	part of speech	forms of the word

rel•e•vant (rĕl´ə-vənt) *adj.* relevance, relevantly

precise meanings of word are numbered —
1. Having a bearing on or connection with the matter at hand. **2.** Meaningful or purposeful in current society or culture: *thought that the traditional male role of breadwinner was no longer relevant.* — example of usage

etymology or word origin —
[Medieval Latin *relevāns, relevant-*, from Latin, present participle of *relevāre*, to relieve, raise up.]

Practice and Apply Use a dictionary to look up the following words from "The Automation Paradox." Then fill out a chart like this one.

WORD	PRONUNCIATION	PART OF SPEECH	GUESSED DEFINITION	DICTIONARY DEFINITION
paralegal	păr′ə-lē′gəl	n.	someone who works with a lawyer	a person who assists a lawyer
trawl	trôl	v.	look	to make an examination of something
net	nĕt	n.	overall	ultimate; final
persistent	pər-sîs′tənt	adj.	continued	existing or remaining in the same state for an indefinitely long time

EL ENGLISH LEARNER SUPPORT

Vocabulary Strategy Have students write the terms *definition, part of speech, pronunciation,* and *forms of the word* on individual cards. Go over the meaning of each of these terms. Write the word *cat,* and have students tell about the word using each of the categories in turn. Have them use full sentences, such as *The part of speech of* cat *is* noun. Have students repeat with other words to ensure that these terms become familiar. **ALL LEVELS**

LANGUAGE CONVENTIONS:
Transitional Words and Phrases

Transitional words and phrases connect ideas and signal how those ideas are related. Transitions are often set off with commas. Read the following sentence from "The Automation Paradox":

Likewise, ATMs made it cheaper to operate bank branches, so banks dramatically increased their number of offices.

The word *likewise* signals a similarity, while the word *so* indicates an effect.

The chart below contains examples of transitional words and phrases based on specific purposes.

RESPOND

Go to **Writing Informative Texts: Organizing Ideas** in the **Writing Studio** for more on using transitional words and phrases.

COMMON TRANSITIONAL WORDS AND PHRASES

Purpose	Examples
compare or contrast ideas	but, however, although, on the other hand, while, similarly, likewise
indicate degree of importance	especially, significantly, most importantly, chiefly, notably, particularly
show time or sequence	first, second, finally, when, initially, next, while, before, after
add information	also, in addition, too, and, furthermore
introduce an example	for example, for instance, such as, this shows
indicate cause or effect	as a result, therefore, consequently, for this reason, so
indicate a conclusion	in conclusion, in summary, overall, to summarize

Practice and Apply Look back at the persuasive essay you wrote to support a claim about the impact of automation. Identify the transitions that you used and revise your essay to add more appropriate or stronger transitions. Then discuss with a partner how these transitions affect the flow of your essay and the connections between ideas.

LANGUAGE CONVENTIONS:
Transitional Words and Phrases

Review the information on transitional words and phrases with students. Emphasize that transitional words and phrases help bring ideas closer together. Explain that when writing lacks these transitions, it often comes across as choppy and poorly organized. Adding transitions provides a connection between ideas and a smooth lead-in from one idea to the next. When students write and read their writing, they should be in the habit of making sure they have used transitional words and phrases.

Have students discuss the role of the word *likewise* in the example sentence. Draw out that the word signals readers that the idea in this sentence will match the previous idea in some important way. Have students read the sentence without *likewise* and *so,* breaking it into two sentences, with the second one beginning "Banks dramatically increased" Point out that the connection between the two sentences is lost without the word *so.*

Have students study the chart. Have them choose one word on each row and write or say a sentence that uses the word in a transitional way. Then discuss how the transitional words and phrases connected the ideas in the sentences.

PRACTICE AND APPLY Have students discuss whether they accurately used transitional words and phrases, and whether there are places where they could be added. Encourage students to make changes as needed. (*Changes will vary.*)

 ENGLISH LEARNER SUPPORT

Language Conventions Use the following supports for students at different proficiency levels.

- Have students find transitional words in "The Automation Paradox" and copy them into their notebooks. Have them underline the transitional words or phrases. Encourage them to use the chart of transitions in the student book to help them identify transitions. **SUBSTANTIAL**

- Have students write two simple sentences and then join them with a transitional word or phrase. Have them use the chart of transitional words in the student book for ideas. **MODERATE**

- Have students write two simple sentences, join them with a transitional word or phrase, and explain to a partner how the resulting sentence is strengthened by the transition. Point out the words and phrases from the chart in the student book, but encourage them to use less familiar terms if possible. **LIGHT**

HEADS UP, HUMANS

Argument by Claudia Alarcón

GENRE ELEMENTS
ARGUMENT

Review with students that the goal of an **argument** is to convince a reader to believe or to do a certain thing. Explain that arguments are sometimes called persuasive texts or **opinion** texts because they include an argument or an opinion. In this type of text, the author states an opinion, or a claim, and then provides **evidence** to support the opinion. This evidence can take on the form of statistical (numerical) data, quotes from experts, or facts; a good argument will usually include some examples of each type of evidence. In this lesson, students will explore how the writer supports the **main idea** in the article "Heads Up, Humans."

LEARNING OBJECTIVES

- Evaluate evidence to support analysis of the text.
- Analyze rhetoric and reasoning.
- Analyze how writers use active and passive voice.
- Research additional evidence to support the writer's claim.
- Create a public service announcement.
- Examine the Greek root *auto*, meaning "self."
- Compare and contrast arguments.
- Conduct a debate on the impact of technology.
- **Language** Discuss with a partner the characteristics of a topic sentence.

TEXT COMPLEXITY

Quantitative Measures	Heads Up, Humans	Lexile: 1300L
Qualitative Measures	**Ideas Presented** Mostly explicit, but the argument is complex.	
	Structures Used Primarily one perspective, no graphics are used.	
	Language Used Mostly Tier II and III words; some rhetorical questions are used.	
	Knowledge Required Explores complex ideas and concerns the future impact of technology.	

RESOURCES

- Unit 1 Response Log
- Selection Audio
- Reading Studio: Notice & Note
- Level Up Tutorial: Summarizing
- Writing Studio:
  Writing Informative Texts
- Speaking and Listening Studio:
  Participating in Collaborative
  Discussions
- Vocabulary Studio:
  Greek Roots
- Grammar Studio:
  Module 3: Lesson 1: Verbs
- "Heads Up, Humans" Selection Test

SUMMARIES

English

Though technology brings fun and convenience, it also creates problems. One of the biggest problems is that technology will eliminate many jobs now held by humans. A report published by a London accounting and consulting firm estimates that 38 percent of U.S. jobs are at great risk of being replaced by robots and automated machines. Even now self-driving trucks and self-driving taxis have begun to replace human drivers. Voices of authority, such as Jerry Kaplan and Stephen Hawking, predict that technology will eliminate many jobs in the future.

Spanish

Aunque la tecnología traiga diversión y conveniencia, también crea problemas. Uno de los problemas más grandes es que la tecnología eliminará muchos de los empleos que ahora ejercen los humanos. Un reporte publicado por una firma de contadores y consultores de Londres estima que el 38% de los empleos de Estados Unidos están en alto riesgo de ser reemplazados por robots o máquinas automatizadas. Incluso ya hay camiones y taxis sin chofer que han empezado a reemplazar a los conductores humanos. Voces de autoridad, como Jerry Kaplan y Stephen Hawking, predicen que la tecnología eliminará muchos trabajos en el futuro.

SMALL-GROUP OPTIONS

Have students work in small groups to read and discuss the selection.

Triple-Entry Journal

- Have students use a notebook for recording Triple-Entry Journal notes.
- Have them divide a notebook page into three columns. The heading for the left column is "Quotes from 'Heads Up, Humans'," and the heading for the middle column is "My Notes."
- Have students record key text passages in the left column.
- Then have students write their own interpretations, summaries, and questions in the middle column and pass the journal to a partner who then responds to the notes in the middle column.

Think-Pair-Share

- Have student pairs read aloud "Heads Up, Humans" to each other, with each partner reading alternating paragraphs.
- After students read and analyze the selection, pose this question: What can our government do to prevent massive job loss as a result of advances in technology?
- Have students think about the question individually, identify examples, and take notes.
- Then have pairs discuss their ideas and examples, and collaboratively form a response.
- Finally, have pairs share their responses with the class.

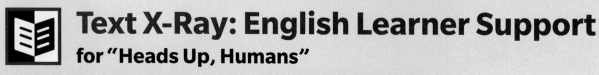

Text X-Ray: English Learner Support
for "Heads Up, Humans"

Use the Text X-Ray and the supports and scaffolds in the Teacher's Edition to help guide students at different proficiency levels through the selection.

INTRODUCE THE SELECTION
DISCUSS ADVANCES IN TECHNOLOGY

In this lesson, students will need to identify advances in technology and consider how they might affect the job market. Read paragraph 1 with students and then ask them to consider some of the advances in technology that add fun and convenience to their lives. Ask students to list examples of technology that were unavailable to their parents when they were growing up.

CULTURAL REFERENCES

The following words or phrases may be unfamiliar to students:

- *phenomenon* (paragraph 2): an occurrence or fact
- *generation* (paragraph 2): people born and living at about the same time
- *displaced* (paragraph 4): let go from a job
- *assembly line* (paragraph 5): an arrangement of workers in which the product being assembled passes from one worker to another until completed

---

LISTENING

Understand the Topic Sentence

Tell students that they should identify the topic sentence of each paragraph. The topic sentence is the sentence that states the main idea of the paragraph. Direct students' attention to the first sentence of paragraph 3 on p. 52. That sentence states the main idea that many jobs now held by humans will be lost to technology. The rest of the paragraph provides statistics that support the topic sentence.

Have students listen as you read aloud paragraphs 3–9. Use the following supports with students at varying proficiency levels:

- Tell students you will ask some questions about what they just heard. Model that they should give a thumbs up if the answer is yes, and a thumbs down for no. For example, ask: *Will many jobs now held by humans be lost to technology in the future?* **SUBSTANTIAL**

- Have students state the main idea of the excerpt. Ask: *What strategy did you use to help you identify the main idea?* **MODERATE**

- After reading the excerpt aloud, ask students to work in pairs to list details that support the main idea. **LIGHT**

SPEAKING

Discuss Key Ideas

Have students discuss the key ideas of the text by rereading each topic sentence, which is generally the first sentence of a paragraph. Circulate around the room to make sure students identify topic sentences correctly.

Use the following supports with students at varying proficiency levels:

- Display and read aloud this sentence from paragraph 3: *There is no argument that many jobs held by humans will be replaced by some form of advanced technology.* Have students say it aloud back to you and then practice saying it to a partner. **SUBSTANTIAL**
- Ask: *How would you state the key idea of paragraph 3? (In the next few years, advances in technology will bring about the loss of many jobs in the U.S., Britain, Germany, and Japan.)* **MODERATE**
- Have pairs of students discuss the key ideas of paragraphs 2–4. Ask: *How would you summarize the author's point of view? (Computer systems have already begun to take over many jobs now held by skilled workers.)* **LIGHT**

READING

Identify Textual Evidence

Tell students that authors of informational texts provide evidence in the form of facts, examples, explanations, definitions, direct quotations, and other details to help readers understand the main idea.

Work with students to reread paragraphs 3–7. Use the following supports with students at varying proficiency levels:

- Read paragraph 4 aloud. Then have students list five words in the paragraph that they consider important. Display the words, and have each student pronounce them correctly. **SUBSTANTIAL**
- Guide students to identify the main idea of paragraph 4. Then have students find evidence to support that idea. Supply sentence frames, such as : *The key idea of the paragraph _____ is that _____.* **MODERATE**
- Have students identify a central idea in paragraph 4 using this frame: *A central idea in this paragraph is _____.* Then, ask students to identify and share two pieces of evidence to support this central idea. **LIGHT**

WRITING

Write a Public Service Announcement

Work with students to read the writing assignment on p. 57.

Use the following supports with students at varying proficiency levels:

- Display the word *technology*, and have students list examples of it. (*Examples might include cell phones, video games, and self-checkout machines.*) Display each example students provide. Then display the sentence: *Technology might bring about the loss of many jobs.* Have students read the sentence aloud, pronouncing each word carefully. **SUBSTANTIAL**
- Provide sentence frames such as the following that students can use to craft their public service announcement. *One of the drawbacks of advanced technology is _____. The number of jobs at risk of being replaced by robots and artificial intelligence is _____.* **MODERATE**
- Remind students of the importance of supporting their message with facts. Then have students identify facts from the text or from their own additional research to support their message. **LIGHT**

ARGUMENT

HEADS UP, HUMANS

by **Claudia Alarcón**

pages 51–55

 Connect to the
ESSENTIAL QUESTION

"Heads Up, Humans" concerns the future impact of advanced technology on employment. The author of the article argues that artificial intelligence and automated machines will eliminate many jobs now held by humans.

COMPARE AND CONTRAST ARGUMENTS

Point out that both "The Automation Paradox" and "Heads Up, Humans" are arguments. The writer of "The Automation Paradox" supports the claim that automation will have a positive Impact on employment. The writer of "Heads Up, Humans" takes a different view of advanced technology and future employment. Ask students to consider which writer makes a more convincing argument about the impact of technology on employment.

COMPARE ARGUMENTS

Now that you've read "The Automation Paradox," read "Heads Up, Humans" to analyze another argument about the future impact of automation on employment. As you read, think about how well the evidence in "Heads Up, Humans" supports the writer's claim. After you are finished, you will collaborate with a group on a final project that involves an analysis of both texts.

 ESSENTIAL QUESTION:

Does technology improve or control our lives?

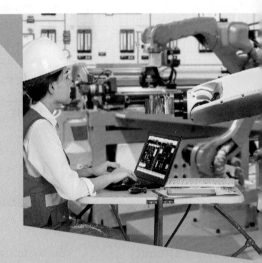

ARGUMENT

THE AUTOMATION PARADOX

by **James Bessen**

pages 39–43

 LEARNING MINDSET

Growth Mindset Remind students that a growth mindset means believing you can get smarter by taking on challenges and pushing yourself. Encourage students to look at comparing two argument selections as an opportunity to set higher goals and stretch past their comfort zone.

Heads Up, Humans

QUICK START

The argument you are about to read makes a claim about the impact of automation. Based on what you already know about the topic, list some effects you think automation will have on jobs and the economy.

EVALUATE EVIDENCE

Evidence is any information that helps prove a claim. Facts, quotations, examples, anecdotes, and statistics can all be used as evidence. When you analyze an author's argument, it's important to **evaluate** the evidence by determining whether it is valid, relevant, and sufficient.

- Valid evidence is based on reliable sources that use sound reasoning. Many texts include **endnotes**, which list sources of information. Credible sources can help you confirm whether the evidence is valid.
- Evidence is relevant if it supports the claim in a logical way. In a strong argument, the way it supports the claim should also be clear.
- Sufficient evidence is enough to support the claim. A thorough and balanced argument includes a convincing amount of information related to the claim, and it addresses opposing viewpoints.

As you read "Heads Up, Humans," identify the main claim and evaluate the evidence the writer uses to support it.

GENRE ELEMENTS: ARGUMENT
- makes a claim
- supports its claim with reasons and evidence
- takes into account other points of view
- for some topics, such as economics, may rely heavily on the analysis and interpretation of data

ANALYZE RHETORIC AND REASONING

Identifying the writer's intended **audience**, or the specific people to whom the argument is addressed, can help you analyze how and why the writer uses certain persuasive techniques, including rhetorical devices and logical fallacies.

Rhetorical devices are techniques writers use to enhance their arguments and communicate more effectively. Here are two examples:

RHETORICAL DEVICE	DEFINITION	EXAMPLE
Direct address	Talking directly to the reader, often using the pronoun *you*	If you're like most young people, you've probably embraced technology.
Rhetorical question	A question that has such an obvious answer that it requires no reply	Will all these people find some other source of employment?

Logical fallacies, such as bandwagon appeals, are misuses of logic or reasoning that can serve persuasive purposes in argumentative texts.

As you analyze "Heads Up, Humans," think about the writer's purposes for using any persuasive techniques you notice.

QUICK START

Have students read the Quick Start activity. To implement the activity, point out that, in the 19th century, blacksmiths were in high demand. People depended on horses for transportation and needed craftsmen to shoe them. Of course, with the appearance of the automobile in the early 20th century, blacksmiths found themselves out of work. Their occupations were obsolete, eliminated by advances in technology. Automobiles became the new means of transportation, and a new industry was born.

EVALUATE EVIDENCE

Help students understand that the argument in "Heads Up, Humans" is supported by facts and statistics. The writer also cites expert opinion to strengthen her central claim. In addition to presenting her own case, the writer acknowledges opposing arguments and contrary evidence.

Help students recall the article "The Automation Paradox." Remind them that the author, James Bessen, provided two key charts to build his case about automation. You might project these charts on a screen for students to examine closely. Then ask students why this technique of contrasting jobs with below-median computer use with those with above-median computer use works so well in supporting the writer's central claim. Have students explain how the charts provide evidence that is valid, relevant, and sufficient to support the writer's argument.

ANALYZE RHETORIC AND REASONING

Remind students that words have not only denotations, or dictionary definitions, but connotations, or emotional suggestions. The word *frightening*, for example, triggers a much stronger negative reaction than would a word like *troubling* or *grim*.

TEACH

CRITICAL VOCABULARY

Encourage students to read all the sentences before deciding which word best completes each one. Remind them to look for context clues that match the precise meaning of each word.

Answers:

1. *renowned*

2. *scrutinize*

3. *exotic*

4. *sector*

LANGUAGE CONVENTIONS

Review the information about active and passive voice. Explain that the original subject in the active voice (*technology*) appears in the passive voice in a prepositional phrase beginning with *by*. The *by* phrase is frequently omitted in passive-voice constructions: *Their jobs were made obsolete.* Tell students that they generally should use the active voice because in most cases they will want to emphasize the actor. The passive voice is appropriate only in those few cases when they want to emphasize the receiver of the action or to minimize the importance of the actor. For example, in the sentence "*The restaurant was closed,*" the use of the passive voice conveys that the actor, or the one who closed the restaurant, is unimportant.

To provide students with additional practice in identifying the voice of verbs, ask students to clip a newspaper or magazine article to bring to class. Students should then circle each verb in a paragraph from the article and label the voice of each verb. Have students share their results in small groups and discuss why the voice of the verb is important in each sentence.

✏ ANNOTATION MODEL

Help students notice that the writer uses a circle to identify the writer's audience and underscoring to highlight important details in the first paragraph. Students' notes in the margin may also include questions about ideas that are unclear or topics they want to explore further.

 GET READY

CRITICAL VOCABULARY

| sector | scrutinize | exotic | renowned |

To see how many Critical Vocabulary words you already know, use them to complete the sentences.

1. _____ scientists are recognized as leading authorities in their fields of study.

2. The inspector will _____ the work to determine whether it has been done correctly.

3. The chef used _____ ingredients that we didn't recognize.

4. While certain positions will be eliminated, the overall demand for jobs in the financial _____ is expected to increase.

LANGUAGE CONVENTIONS

Active and Passive Voice In this lesson, you will learn about active and passive voice. **Active voice** shows that a subject performs the verb's action:

> **New technology made their jobs obsolete.**

Passive voice shows that a subject is being acted upon:

> **Their jobs were made obsolete by new technology.**

As you read "Heads Up, Humans," notice the writer's use of active and passive voice.

ANNOTATION MODEL

NOTICE & NOTE

As you read, mark up the text to trace and evaluate the writer's argument. In the model, you can see one reader's notes about "Heads Up, Humans."

1 If you're like most young people, you've probably embraced technology. You communicate with friends via videos and filters. You have vast numbers of songs and shows within reach. You can get items delivered to your home the same day you ordered them without leaving the house. These benefits of technology are easy to see.

The intended audience is young people.

The writer engages the audience and introduces the topic with examples that relate to young people's daily lives.

BACKGROUND

The potential future impact of automation on employment has been the subject of much heated debate. Such arguments rely on the analysis of historical data as well as economic forecasts that may be influenced by a variety of factors.

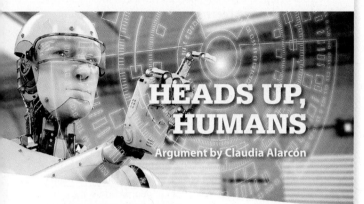

HEADS UP, HUMANS

Argument by Claudia Alarcón

PREPARE TO COMPARE

As you read, note evidence the writer uses to support her claims about the potential impact of automation. This will help you compare this argument with "The Automation Paradox."

1   If (you're) like most young people, (you've) probably embraced technology. (You) communicate with friends via videos and filters. (You) have vast numbers of songs and shows within reach. (You) can get items delivered to your home the same day you ordered them without leaving the house. These benefits of technology are easy to see.

2   Perhaps you take it further, and are one of those who believe that technology does not just add fun and convenience to our lives, but is actually the answer to most of our problems—even problems that are caused by technology itself. In the very near future, one of the biggest of these problems is likely to be that many jobs now held by humans will be done by some combination of artificial intelligence and automated machine. If you're tempted to shrug off concern about this phenomenon because you assume that the wonders of technology will somehow

 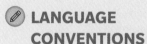

Notice & Note

Use the side margins to notice and note signposts in the text.

LANGUAGE CONVENTIONS
Annotate: Mark instances of the subject *you* in paragraph 1.

Analyze: Does the subject perform or receive the action? How does this use of voice impact the writer's argument?

Heads Up, Humans   51

BACKGROUND

After students read the Background note, explain that this article will help them understand how artificial intelligence and advanced automation might affect employment in the future. The writer describes the effect of automation on employment in the past and predicts its future impact.

PREPARE TO COMPARE

Make sure students understand that as they read they should identify evidence the writer uses to support her claim about the future impact of automation on jobs now held by humans.

LANGUAGE CONVENTIONS

Students should circle *you're* and *you've* in sentence 1 and *You* in sentences 2 and 3. In sentence 4, they should circle *You*. In each of these sentences, the subject *you* performs the action. By using the active voice, the writer connects directly with the reader and emphasizes the subject or actor, who performs the action. The active voice reflects the importance of the subject to the writer's argument. To help students understand the effectiveness of the active voice in this paragraph, have pairs of student work together to recast the verbs from active to passive. Students should then discuss how this change in voice made the writing less direct and concise and far less interesting than the original.

For **speaking support** for students at varying proficiency levels, see the Text X-Ray on page 48D.

 ENGLISH LEARNER SUPPORT

Identifying Main Idea Read paragraph 2 aloud. Invite students to ask for clarification of any words that are unfamiliar. Then help students identify sentence 2 of the paragraph as the sentence that states the writer's main idea. Ask students to paraphrase sentence 2: A big problem in the near future is that many of the jobs humans do will be done by machines.

• Have students paraphrase paragraph 2 of the article. **MODERATE**

• Have students rewrite sentence 2 to change the passive voice "will be done" to the active voice. **LIGHT**

NUMBERS & STATS

Help students note that numbers and statistics are types of **evidence** that help readers understand a work of **nonfiction,** such as this article. In sentences 2 and 3 of paragraph 3, the writer provides specific quantities to depict the scale of future job loss. **(Answer:** *The writer cites the percentage of jobs in the United States, Britain, Germany, and Japan that are at a high risk of being eliminated by technology during the next 15 years. This data supports the writer's claim that automation will replace many jobs now held by humans.)*

✏ ANALYZE RHETORIC AND REASONING

Explain to students that the author draws an analogy between the number of drivers who could lose their jobs and the populations of several cities in Texas. Have students identify the analogy in paragraph 4. **(Answer:** *The analogy does little to strengthen the writer's argument. Because the number of drivers is already identified, the population figures are unnecessary to further qualify the amount.)*

✏ EVALUATE EVIDENCE

Tell students that when they evaluate evidence they should consider the credibility of the source of the evidence. The source should be someone with strong credentials expressing views within his or her field of expertise. **(Answer:** *The writer includes this evidence to provide a voice of authority to strengthen the argument that advances in technology need not result in massive job loss.)*

CRITICAL VOCABULARY

sector: Many *sectors,* or divisions, make up our economy. Health care is one sector; the restaurant industry and the entertainment industry are two other sectors.

ASK STUDENTS to name the three sectors or branches that make up the government of the United States. *(legislative sector, executive sector, judicial sector)*

✏ NOTICE & NOTE

NUMBERS & STATS

Notice & Note: What data does the writer use as evidence in paragraph 3? Mark these details.

Draw Conclusions: How does this data connect to the writer's claim?

ANALYZE RHETORIC AND REASONING

Annotate: An **analogy** is a comparison between two things that are similar in some way but are otherwise dissimilar. Mark the two things the writer compares in paragraph 4.

Evaluate: Does this analogy strengthen the writer's argument? Explain.

sector
(sĕk´tər) *n.* A *sector* is a part or division, as of a city or a national economy.

EVALUATE EVIDENCE

Annotate: Identify the source of the evidence in paragraph 6.

Infer: Why does the writer include this evidence?

create new and better jobs, you should be aware that research tells another story. As part of the generation that will arguably be most affected by these changes, it's in your interest to stay informed rather than simply hope for the best.

3   There is no argument that many jobs now held by humans will be replaced by some form of advanced technology. According to a new report by a multi-national accounting and consulting firm based in London, 38% of U.S. jobs are at high risk of being replaced by robots and artificial intelligence over the next 15 years.[1] The report estimates the percentage of jobs lost to automation in Britain will be 30%, with 35% in Germany, and 21% in Japan.[2]

4   This change is already underway. Shipping companies have made headlines with self-driving trucks carrying cargo across the country. Ride share companies have been testing self-driving taxis in Pennsylvania and Arizona. Once more of our trucks and taxis drive themselves, what will happen to the people who held jobs as drivers? In the U.S., roughly 180,000 taxi drivers, 600,000 ride share drivers, and 3.5 million truck drivers could end up displaced.[3] This number is greater than the population of Houston, San Antonio, Dallas, Austin, and Fort Worth combined. Will all these people find some other source of employment? Or will the numbers of unemployed grow as the out-of-work drivers are joined by the millions of others who have been displaced by artificial intelligence and robots?

5   Technology fans claim that the fears that robots will lead to massive unemployment are unfounded. They say that people who are displaced from jobs will find new and better occupations that will be created by the economic shift. They suggest that a factory worker whose task on the assembly line is now completed by a machine might instead become someone who services the machine, for example. Or that there could be a rise in jobs in **sectors** that are harder to automate, such as healthcare.

6   "The last 200 years, we've had an incredible amount of automation," argues MIT economist David Autor. "We have tractors that do the work that horses and people used to do on farms. We don't dig ditches by hand anymore. We don't pound tools out of wrought iron. We don't do bookkeeping with books! But this has not in net reduced the amount of employment."[4]

7   However, there is plenty of evidence to suggest that it's going to be different going forward. The introduction of the

APPLYING ACADEMIC VOCABULARY

☒ commentary   ☒ occupation   ❑ option   ❑ speculate   ❑ technology

Write and Discuss Have students turn to a partner to discuss the following questions. Guide students to include the Academic Vocabulary words *speculate* and *technology* in their responses. Ask volunteers to share their responses with the class.

- What is the author making a **commentary** about in this selection?
- What does the author mean by "find new and better **occupations**" in paragraph 5?

labor-saving tractor did indeed free up some farmers to plant more crops and others to take on different sorts of work. But the kind of automation combined with artificial intelligence being developed today doesn't just do the physical work of humans. It can do much of the high-level mental work too, faster and more effectively. In the past, newly freed laborers often went on to work in start-up industries that benefited from their availability. Today, the new industries are unlikely to need many human bodies or minds because technology can do the work for less cost.

8   Jerry Kaplan, an artificial intelligence expert who's founded multiple technology startups, has written a book called *Humans Need Not Apply*. In it, he lays out the risks of our new era. He explains what's cutting edge and poised to increase: systems that learn from experience and therefore don't need to be programmed, as we commonly understand the term. Not only will machines be able to do work that we think of as requiring human judgment and skill, such as fixing electrical problems, painting a house, or writing a news story, they will also be able to do work that people simply can't. "Unlike humans who are limited in the scope and scale of experiences they can absorb, these systems can **scrutinize** mountains of instructive examples at blinding speeds. They are capable of comprehending not only the visual, auditory, and written information familiar to us but also the more **exotic** forms of data that stream through computers and networks," he writes.[5]

9   Kaplan is mainly referring to the future he predicts based on his perspective as an expert in the tech world. But already, we can see the consequences. There is no evidence that recent advances in technology have so far offered the majority of workers better pay or positions. In fact, the opposite seems to be true. A report by the National Bureau of Economic Research found that between 1990 and 2007, automation lowered both the number of jobs available and the amount those jobs paid.

ANALYZE RHETORIC AND REASONING

Annotate: In a **juxtaposition**, a writer places two contrasting ideas or examples near each other to highlight the differences between them. Identify the juxtaposition in paragraph 7.

Analyze: How does this juxtaposition impact the writer's argument?

scrutinize
(skrōōt´n-īz´) *v*. To *scrutinize* is to examine or inspect with great care.

exotic
(ĭg-zŏt´ĭk) *adj*. Something that is *exotic* is unusual or different.

Point out to students that juxtaposition is a powerful and concise way to emphasize a key contrast. **(Answer:** *The juxtaposition supports the idea that differences between present and past market conditions make it likely that technology will eliminate many jobs in the future.)*

For **reading support** for students at varying proficiency levels, see the Text X-Ray on page 48D.

CRITICAL VOCABULARY

scrutinize: The author uses the word *scrutinize* to convey to the reader that computer systems can carefully process huge quantities of information at dazzling speeds.

ASK STUDENTS to discuss what the word *scrutinize* suggests about the activity of computer systems. *(The word suggests the pinpoint accuracy of computer systems in handling information. In terms of quantity and quality, computers can significantly outperform humans, making it likely that computers will eventually replace humans in certain jobs.)*

exotic: The adjective *exotic* describes something foreign or excitingly strange, such as birds from a distant country.

ASK STUDENTS what they can conclude about "exotic forms of data that stream through computers and networks." *(These forms of data would likely confuse humans, yet computer networks handle them easily.)*

perspective: The word *perspective* derives from the Latin word *specere*, which means "to look"; so one's perspective is his or her way of looking at a subject or issue.

ASK STUDENTS Why might Jerry Kaplan's perspective be important to consider? *(He is a recognized expert in the field of artificial intelligence and has written on that subject.)*

 ## ENGLISH LEARNER SUPPORT

Examining Writer's Evidence   Read paragraphs 8 and 9 aloud. Invite students to ask for clarification of any words that are unfamiliar. Then ask students what machines of the future will be able to do that humans cannot. If necessary, point out that machines will be able to do high-level mental work and handle vast amounts of data at lightning speed.
ALL LEVELS

EVALUATE EVIDENCE

Have students read aloud the titles of the articles and books listed in the endnotes. Point out that when citing books, the writer provides the name of the author, the title of the work, the place of publication, the name of the publisher, and the year of publication. (**Answer:** *The sources seem current and credible; however, since most are secondary sources, the supporting evidence in each needs careful scrutiny.*)

 NOTICE & NOTE

"We estimate large and robust negative effects of robots on employment and wages," write the authors of the study.[6]

10   **Renowned** theoretical physicist Stephen Hawking is concerned about massive job loss and how that could affect the stability of our society. "The automation of factories has already decimated jobs in traditional manufacturing," says Hawking. "The rise of artificial intelligence is likely to extend this job destruction deep into the middle classes, with only the most caring, creative, or supervisory roles remaining."[7] Hawking emphasizes that we live in a world where financial inequality is growing, not diminishing. He believes that many people can see their standard of living, and their ability to earn a living at all, disappearing.

11   This is a frightening scenario. It's tempting to avoid thinking about it, especially because solutions aren't obvious. But the first step toward avoiding the employment problems we might face is acknowledging them. As someone with your future on the line, don't let anyone tell you that technology is automatically going to create a healthy economy for everyone. If we don't want a bleak future for most of us, we have to prioritize human well-being even as we take advantage of what technology offers.

renowned
(rĭ-nound´) *adj.* Someone or something that is *renowned* is famous.

EVALUATE EVIDENCE
Annotate: Mark important details about the source in each citation.

Evaluate: Do these sources seem credible? Explain.

ENDNOTES

[1] Alanna Petroff, "U.S. workers face higher risk of being replaced by robots. Here's why," *CNNtech* 24 March 2017, 4 Dec. 2017 <http://money.cnn.com/2017/03/24/technology/robots-jobs-us-workers-uk/index.html>.

[2] Samantha Masunaga, "Robots could take over 38% of U.S. jobs within about 15 years, report says," *Los Angeles Times* 24 March 2017, 4 Dec. 2017 <http://http://www.latimes.com/business/la-fi-pwc-robotics-jobs-20170324-story.html>.

CRITICAL VOCABULARY

renowned: The writer uses the word *renowned* to emphasize that Stephen Hawking is respected worldwide as an authority in theoretical physics.

ASK STUDENTS How do people generally respond to the views expressed by someone as renowned as Stephen Hawking? (*They pay attention to what he has to say because he has distinguished himself as a scientist. His views matter to intelligent readers.*)

WHEN STUDENTS STRUGGLE . . .

Summarize Provide students with a graphic organizer to help them distinguish the author's main claim and the supporting details. Have students work in small groups to complete the graphic organizer and then to write a one-sentence summary of "Heads Up, Humans." Remind students that their summaries must state the main idea of the article.

 For additional support, go to the **Reading Studio** and assign the following **Level Up tutorial: Summarizing**

3 David Pogue, "When the robots take over, will there be jobs left for us?," *CBS News* 9 April 2017, 4 Dec. 2017 <https://www.cbsnews.com/news/when-the-robots-take-over-will-there-be-jobs-left-for-us/>.

4 Pogue, "When the robots take over."

5 Jerry Kaplan, *Humans Need Not Apply: A Guide to Wealth and Work in the Age of Artificial Intelligence* (New Haven: Yale University Press, 2015).

6 Daron Acemoglu and Pascual Restrepo, *Robots and Jobs: Evidence from US Labor Markets* (Cambridge, MA: National Bureau of Economic Research, 2017).

7 Rob Price, "Stephen Hawking: This will be the impact of automation and AI on jobs," *World Economic Forum* 6 Dec. 2016, 4 Dec. 2017 <https://www.weforum.org/agenda/2016/12/stephen-hawking-this-will-be-the-impact-of-automation-and-ai-on-jobs>.

CHECK YOUR UNDERSTANDING

Answer these questions before moving on to the **Analyze the Text** section on the following page.

1 The writer supports the claim of the argument by —

   A distinguishing the future of automation from historical trends

   B explaining how machines impacted the farming and manufacturing industries

   C showing how future changes in the job market will mirror past changes

   D providing statistics that relate to many different employment sectors

2 The information in paragraph 4 suggests —

   F a possible impact of automation on people who work as drivers

   G a causal relationship between massive job loss and automation

   H ways in which jobs might change as a result of automation

   J ways in which automation might lead to growth in the shipping industry

3 Based on the text, more automation will cause an increase in —

   A wages

   B inequality

   C the number of unskilled jobs

   D the size of the middle class

CHECK YOUR UNDERSTANDING

Have students answer the questions independently.

Answers:

1. *A*

2. *F*

3. *B*

If they answer any questions incorrectly, have them reread the text to confirm their understanding. Then they may proceed to ANALYZE THE TEXT on page 56.

 ENGLISH LEARNER SUPPORT

Oral Assessment   Use the following questions to assess students' comprehension and speaking skills.

1. How did the writer support the claim of the argument? *(The author supported the claim of the argument by contrasting the future of automation with historical trends.)*

2. What does the information in paragraph 4 suggest? *(The information in paragraph 4 suggests how automation might affect people who work as drivers.)*

3. What will increase because of increased automation? *(Inequality will increase because of increased automation.)* **SUBSTANTIAL/MODERATE**

ANALYZE THE TEXT

Possible answers:

DOK 4: *The writer uses emotional and ethical appeals to address a young audience of future workers. Phrases such as frightening scenario, future on the line, and bleak future in paragraph 11 convey anxiety about the future. The statement that the audience is "part of the generation that will arguably be most affected [by automation]" appeals to the audience's values of civic duty.*

1. **DOK 4:** *The answers to the questions in paragraph 4 are so obvious that a response is not stated, suggesting that the writer's claim that in the future many people will lose their jobs to advanced technology is beyond dispute.*

2. **DOK 2:** *The expert opinions expressed by Jerry Kaplan and Stephen Hawking strengthen and add credibility to the writer's argument. Kaplan is an artificial intelligence expert who wrote a book on the topic, and Stephen Hawking is a renowned British theoretical physicist who has earned international acclaim.*

3. **DOK 3:** *The author argues that in the last 200 years automation in the job market has not resulted in a net loss of jobs. In contrast, Kaplan argues that the "new era" of automation on the horizon will lead to a significant decrease in employment.*

4. **DOK 4:** *The data in paragraph 4 identifies the number of drivers who might someday lose their jobs because of the proliferation of self-driving vehicles. Because the number of drivers represents only a small portion of the job market, the evidence falls short of illustrating that a significant number of people could be left jobless because of automation.*

RESEARCH

Remind students to evaluate the strength of the connection between each piece of evidence and the claim that automation will eliminate many jobs in the future. Students should discard any evidence that seems weak or irrelevant.

Connect Students should rank each piece of evidence according to its relative strength.

(Answers will vary.)

RESPOND

ANALYZE THE TEXT

Support your responses with evidence from the text. NOTEBOOK

1. **Analyze** What persuasive techniques does the writer use to appeal to her intended audience? Cite evidence from the text to support your response.

2. **Critique** What is the purpose of the writer's questions in paragraph 4? How do these questions impact the writer's argument?

3. **Evaluate** Which two pieces of evidence in the argument do you find most convincing? Explain.

4. **Compare** How does the quotation from economist David Autor in paragraph 6 compare with the quotation from artificial intelligence expert Jerry Kaplan in paragraph 8?

5. **Notice & Note** What is the purpose of the data in paragraph 4? How does this evidence impact the writer's argument?

RESEARCH TIP
Web addresses ending in *.gov*, *.edu*, or *.org* often contain reliable information. For example, the National Bureau of Economic Research (nber.org) and the U.S. Bureau of Labor Statistics (bls.gov) gather data related to U.S. jobs and the economy.

RESEARCH

Research additional evidence to support the writer's claim in "Heads Up, Humans" that automation will eliminate many jobs. Try to locate different types of evidence, such as facts, statistics, quotations, and examples. Use the chart below to record the evidence and identify its connection to the claim. You will use the information you gather in a debate on the issue.

EVIDENCE	CONNECTION

Connect Share your evidence with a small group. Discuss the relevance and validity of each piece of evidence.

LEARNING MINDSET

Belonging Remind students that everyone in the classroom is part of a learning community. Everyone belongs, and everyone has something to contribute. Encourage them to take advantage of the different perspectives and suggestions each person can offer that might help them improve their writing. When they receive help and offer help, it gives students a stronger sense of belonging to a learning group or community.

CREATE AND DISCUSS

Create a Public Service Announcement Use ideas from "Heads Up, Humans" to create a public service announcement to build awareness about the potential impact of automation on jobs in the future.

- ❏ Review the text to brainstorm ideas for your announcement. Decide on a slogan or a call to action to focus your message. Identify facts from the text or from additional research to support your message.
- ❏ Choose a format for your announcement, such as a poster or a video. Plan and create your announcement, combining text and visuals to effectively convey your message.

Discuss with a Small Group Have a discussion about how governments and other organizations might prepare for the impact of automation. Make sure all group members are included.

- ❏ Review the text to identify issues and concerns related to the future impact of automation on employment and the economy.
- ❏ Discuss possible ways in which people might solve the problems presented by automation. What steps might government and private organizations take to plan for the future?
- ❏ Listen closely to your group members. Ask questions and respectfully comment on others' ideas. As a group, summarize the key points of the discussion and identify points of agreement.

RESPOND TO THE ESSENTIAL QUESTION

 Does technology improve or control our lives?

Gather Information Review your annotations and notes on "Heads Up, Humans." Then, add relevant details to your Response Log. As you determine which information to include, think about:

- the writer's claim about the impact of technology
- evidence that supports the writer's claim
- best opposing viewpoints the writer addresses

At the end of the unit, you may use your notes to help you write an informational essay.

 Go to the **Writing Studio** for help with creating a public service announcement.

 Go to **Participating in Collaborative Discussions** in the **Speaking and Listening Studio** to learn more.

ACADEMIC VOCABULARY

As you write and discuss what you learned from the argument, be sure to use the Academic Vocabulary words. Check off each of the words that you use.

- ❏ commentary
- ❏ occupation
- ❏ option
- ❏ speculate
- ❏ technology

CREATE AND DISCUSS

Create a Public Service Announcement Students' public service announcements should convey a clear message and accurately reflect information from the text or from their additional research.

📖 For **writing support** for students at varying proficiency levels, see the Text X-Ray on page 48D.

Discuss with a Small Group Students should identify issues and concerns related to the impact of automation and discuss possible ways people might respond to and address the issues. For example, the government and private organizations might provide training programs to educate workers about cutting-edge technologies.

RESPOND TO THE ESSENTIAL QUESTION

Allow time for students to add details from "Heads Up, Humans" to their Unit 1 Response Logs.

APPLY

CRITICAL VOCABULARY

1. *scrutinize; Both* scrutinize *and* examine *relate to careful observation.*

2. *sector; Both* sector *and* division *relate to a part or section of a whole.*

3. *exotic; Both* exotic *and* unusual *describe something that is different from the expected.*

4. *renowned; Both* renowned *and* famous *describe someone or something that is well-known or acclaimed.*

VOCABULARY STRATEGY:
Greek Roots

Possible answers: *autograph, autobiography, automobile. All of the words relate to the self or independent operation.*

RESPOND

WORD BANK
sector
scrutinize
exotic
renowned

 Go to the **Vocabulary Studio** for more on Greek roots.

CRITICAL VOCABULARY

Practice and Apply Use your understanding of the Critical Vocabulary words to answer each question.

1. Which Vocabulary word goes with *examine*? Why?

2. Which Vocabulary word goes with *division*? Why?

3. Which Vocabulary word goes with *unusual*? Why?

4. Which Vocabulary word goes with *famous*? Why?

VOCABULARY STRATEGY:
Greek Roots

A **word root** is a word that forms the basis of a word's meaning. A root is combined with other word parts, such as a prefix or a suffix, to make a word. Many English words have a root that comes from Greek. Identifying word roots can help you understand a word's meaning. Look at this sentence from "Heads Up, Humans":

> As part of the <u>generation</u> that will arguably be most affected by these changes, it's in your interest to stay informed rather than simply hope for the best.

The word *generation* includes the Greek root *gen*, which means "to give birth." This can help you understand that *generation* means "the people born or living at the same time." Another way to use roots to help you determine the meaning of an unfamiliar word is to think of other words that include the same root. For example, *generation* relates to the word *generate*, which means "to come into being."

Practice and Apply Complete the word web with words that share the root *auto*, which means "self." Then tell how the meanings of the words are related.

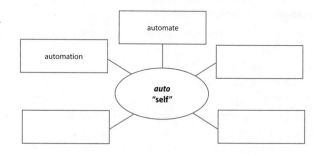

ENGLISH LEARNER SUPPORT

Vocabulary Strategy Give students additional practice in determining the meanings of unfamiliar words. Write the following words on the board: *automaton, autopsy, autonomy*, and *autocrat*. Have pairs of students copy the words, underline the root *auto*, and write definitions. Students may look up each word in a dictionary.

ALL LEVELS

LANGUAGE CONVENTIONS:
Active and Passive Voice

The **voice of a verb** shows whether its subject performs or receives the action expressed by the verb. When the subject performs the action, the verb is in the **active voice**. When the subject is the receiver of the action, the verb is in the **passive voice**. Writers should take care to use active and passive voice consistently and should consider when each voice is most appropriate.

> Go to **Active and Passive Voice** in the **Grammar Studio** to learn more.

	DEFINITION	EXAMPLE	USE TO . . .
Active Voice	• shows that a subject performs an action	• *The robot finished the job.*	• emphasize the subject or actor • keep writing lively
Passive Voice	• shows that a subject is acted upon • uses helping verbs	• *The job was finished.*	• emphasize the action • show that the doer is unknown or unimportant

In this sentence from "Heads Up, Humans," the writer uses the active voice appropriately to emphasize the impact of automation on the audience:

> **But already, we can see the consequences.**

When the sentence is rewritten in the passive voice, the subject becomes unimportant:

> **But already, the consequences can be seen.**

Practice and Apply Identify the voice of the verb in each sentence. Then rewrite the sentence in a different voice.

1. The manufacturing workers were affected by changes in technology.

   _____

2. Automation eliminated their jobs.

   _____

3. The study shows the impact on the healthcare industry.

   _____

4. Your generation will likely be most affected by these changes.

   _____

LANGUAGE CONVENTIONS:
Active and Passive Voice

Remind students that as a rule they should choose an active verb and pair it with a subject that names the person or thing doing the action. Active verbs express meaning more emphatically and concisely than verbs in the passive voice. Verbs in the passive voice lack strength because their subjects receive the action instead of doing it.

1. *passive voice; Changes in technology affected the manufacturing workers.*

2. *active voice; Their jobs were eliminated by automation.*

3. *active voice; The impact on the healthcare industry is shown by the study.*

4. *passive voice; These changes will likely affect your generation the most.*

COMPARE ARGUMENTS

Students should complete the Venn diagram by indicating that "The Automation Paradox" asserts that automation will have a positive effect on jobs; "Heads Up, Humans" supports the opposite view; and both articles contend that automation will transform labor.

ANALYZE THE TEXTS

Possible answers:

1. **DOK 2:** *Both arguments acknowledge that automation will reshape labor and employment markets, and both also state that future workers will need to adapt to the effects of automation.*

2. **DOK 3:** *"The Automation Paradox" cites a study that states that "only about 5 percent of jobs are at risk of being completely automated in the near future." Meanwhile, "Heads Up, Humans" cites another study that states, "38% of U.S. jobs are at high risk of being replaced by robots and artificial intelligence over the next 15 years." Although the statistic cited in "The Automation Paradox," does not identify a time period, the information seems to contradict the study results in the other argument.*

3. **DOK 3:** *Both "The Automation Paradox" and "Heads Up, Humans" include statistical evidence. However, "The Automation Paradox" includes more data and supports some of the data with graphic features. "Heads Up, Humans" relies more heavily on logical reasoning, while the writer of "The Automation Paradox" argues that logical conclusions about the impact of automation do not stand up to basic economic principles. "The Automation Paradox" provides examples of the impact of automation on the legal and financial industries, while "Heads Up, Humans" cites evidence related to transportation and shipping.*

4. **DOK 4:** *Students should support their opinions with evidence from both texts.*

 RESPOND

Respond

Collaborate and Compare

THE AUTOMATION PARADOX
Argument by James Bessen

HEADS UP, HUMANS
Argument by Claudia Alarcón

Collaborate & Compare

COMPARE ARGUMENTS

When you **compare arguments,** you identify similarities and differences between the writers' claims, reasons, and evidence. As you review "The Automation Paradox" and "Heads Up, Humans" to compare the arguments, read carefully to identify each writer's central idea and the facts and interpretations used to support it. Identify where the texts disagree on matters of fact and interpretation.

Also be sure to consider how the two authors use counter arguments to respond to opposing claims. A **counter argument** is an argument made to address an alternative viewpoint or an objection. Good writers anticipate and acknowledge opposing views and objections to their arguments and refute them with counter arguments.

In a small group, complete the Venn diagram with similarities and differences between the two arguments.

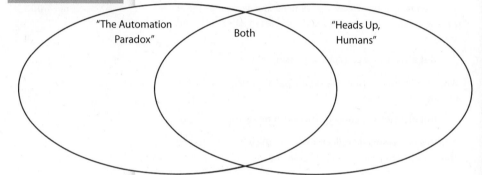

"The Automation Paradox" | Both | "Heads Up, Humans"

ANALYZE THE TEXTS

Discuss these questions in your group.

1. **Compare** What are some points of agreement in both arguments?

2. **Connect** What pieces of evidence in each argument seem to contradict each other?

3. **Identify Patterns** What are some similarities and differences between the types of evidence used in each argument?

4. **Evaluate** Which argument is most convincing to you? Cite evidence from both texts to support your opinion.

DEBATE

Now your group can continue reflecting on the ideas in these texts and your responses to them by debating the impact of automation on employment. Follow these steps:

1. **Choose a Side** Working with a small group, decide which viewpoint you will argue. Will automation have a positive or negative impact on employment?

2. **Gather Information** Review the two arguments and use relevant text evidence to defend or challenge the writers' claims. List reasons from the texts and from your prior research that support your viewpoint.

Reason 1:
Evidence:
Reason 2:
Evidence:

3. **Prepare a Counter Argument**
   Anticipate the opposing team's claim, reasons, and evidence. List reasons and evidence you will cite to argue against the opposing team's position.

Opposing Team's Argument:	Counter Argument:

4. **Conduct the Debate** Debate another group of students who have chosen the opposite position. Each group should be allowed to speak for a set amount of time. Use appropriate eye contact, speaking rate, volume, enunciation, and gestures to communicate your ideas effectively.

RESPOND

Go to the **Speaking and Listening Studio** to learn more about having a debate.

Collaborate & Compare 61

APPLY

DEBATE

Explain that a panel discussion brings together a group of people who know something about a particular topic. During the discussion, each panel member contributes his or her unique knowledge and perspective on the topic.

1. **Choose a Side** To choose a side, students should consider which writer made a more convincing case for the effect of automation on future jobs.

2. **Gather Information** Students should evaluate the strength of their reasons, keeping their strongest reason until last.

3. **Prepare for Counter Arguments** Tell students to anticipate the strongest argument that the opposing side will advance to defend its position.

4. **Conduct the Debate** Encourage students to videotape their performances for future critique.

ENGLISH LEARNER SUPPORT

Comparative Adjectives Speakers of Hmong, Khmer, Korean, and Spanish may have difficulty using the comparative and superlative forms of adjectives. Tell students they will practice comparative adjectives using *-er* for one-syllable words and *more* for longer words:

| old > older | low > lower | hard > harder |
| modern > more modern | positive > more positive | |

Have them practice superlative adjectives using *-est* for short one-syllable words and *most* for longer words:

| old > oldest | low > lowest | hard > hardest |
| modern > most modern | positive > most positive | |

Pair students to practice using comparative and superlative adjectives by interviewing each other about how life is different at school from at home. **SUBSTANTIAL**

Collaborate & Compare **61**

INDEPENDENT READING

READER'S CHOICE

Setting a Purpose Have students review their Unit 1 Response Log and think about what they've already learned about differences between genres and which genres they enjoy most. As they select their Independent Reading selections, encourage them to consider what more they want to know.

NOTICE NOTE

Explain that some selections may contain multiple signposts; others may contain only one. Add that the same type of signpost can occur many times in the same text.

 INDEPENDENT READING

? ESSENTIAL QUESTION:

Does technology improve or control our lives?

Reader's Choice

Setting a Purpose Select one or more of these options from your eBook to continue your exploration of the Essential Question.

- Read the descriptions to see which text grabs your interest.
- Think about which genres you enjoy reading.

Notice & Note

In this unit, you practiced noticing and noting three signposts: **Again and Again**, **Contrasts and Contradictions**, and **Aha Moment**. As you read independently, these signposts and others will aid your understanding. Below are the anchor questions to ask when you read literature and nonfiction.

Reading Literature: Stories, Poems, and Plays		
Signpost	**Anchor Question**	**Lesson**
Contrasts and Contradictions	Why did the character act that way?	p. 3
Aha Moment	How might this change things?	p. 3
Tough Questions	What does this make me wonder about?	p. 152
Words of the Wiser	What's the lesson for the character?	p. 406
Again and Again	Why might the author keep bringing this up?	p. 2
Memory Moment	Why is this memory important?	p. 153

Reading Nonfiction: Essays, Articles, and Arguments		
Signpost	**Anchor Question(s)**	**Lesson**
Big Questions	What surprised me? What did the author think I already knew? What challenged, changed, or confirmed what I already knew?	p. 77
Contrasts and Contradictions	What is the difference, and why does it matter?	p. 241
Extreme or Absolute Language	Why did the author use this language?	p. 76
Numbers and Stats	Why did the author use these numbers or amounts?	p. 325
Quoted Words	Why was this person quoted or cited, and what did this add?	p. 77
Word Gaps	Do I know this word from someplace else? Does it seem like technical talk for this topic? Do clues in the sentence help me understand the word?	p. 240

You can preview these texts in Unit 1 of your eBook.

Then, check off the text or texts that you select to read on your own.

POEM

If You Go into the Woods You Will Find It Has a Technology

Heather Christle

If you look closely, you will see that nature is trying to communicate with us.

SCIENCE FICTION

Hallucination

Isaac Asimov

A boy working in a planetary outpost realizes that things aren't what they seem.

SCIENCE FICTION

There Will Come Soft Rains

Ray Bradbury

A vacant mechanized house is the only thing left standing in a ruined city.

NOVEL

from All the Light We Cannot See

Anthony Doerr

The discovery of a radio brings the power of music to a young boy and girl.

Collaborate and Share   Get with a partner to discuss what you learned from at least one of your independent readings.

- Give a brief synopsis or summary of the text.
- Describe any signposts that you noticed in the text and explain what they revealed to you.
- Describe what you most enjoyed or found most challenging about the text. Give specific examples.
- Decide if you would recommend the text to others. Why or why not?

 Go to the **Reading Studio** for more resources on **Notice & Note.**

MATCHING STUDENTS TO TEXTS

Use the following information to guide students in choosing their texts.

If You Go into the Woods You Will Find It Has a Technology   **Lexile: N/A**
  Genre: poem
  Overall Rating: Accessible

Hallucination   **Lexile: 790L**
  Genre: science fiction
  Overall Rating: Accessible

There Will Come Soft Rains   **Lexile: 920L**
  Genre: science fiction
  Overall Rating: Challenging

***from* All the Light We Cannot See**   **Lexile: 880L**
  Genre: novel excerpt
  Overall Rating: Challenging

Collaborate and Share   To assess how well students read the selections, have partners orally share interesting parts of their discussions.

 for Assessment

- Independent Reading Selection Tests

 Encourage students to visit the **Reading Studio** to download a handy bookmark of **NOTICE & NOTE** signposts.

WHEN STUDENTS STRUGGLE . . .

Keep a Reading Log As students read their selected texts, have them keep a reading log for each selection to note signposts and their thoughts about them. Use their logs to assess how well they are noticing and reflecting on elements of the texts.

Reading Log for (title)		
Page and Paragraph	**Signpost I Noticed**	**My Notes about it**

Shutterstock

UNIT ① Tasks

- **WRITE AN INFORMATIONAL ESSAY**
- **PRESENT AND RESPOND TO AN INSTRUCTIONAL SPEECH**

MENTOR TEXT

ARE BIONIC SUPERHUMANS ON THE HORIZON?

Informational Text by
RAMEZ NAAM

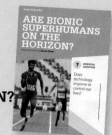

LEARNING OBJECTIVES

Writing Task

- Write an informative essay to explain new technology to someone who is unfamiliar with the technology.
- Use strategies to plan and organize information.
- Develop a focused, structured draft.
- Use the Mentor Text as a model for writing an engaging introduction and integrating details.
- Revise drafts, using feedback from peers.
- Edit drafts, using compound and complex sentences.
- Use a rubric to evaluate writing.
- Publish writing to share it with an audience.
- **Language** Use connecting words.

Speaking Task

- Present an informative essay to an audience.
- Adapt an informative essay for presentation
- Use appropriate verbal and nonverbal techniques.
- Listen actively to a presentation.
- **Language** Share information using the sentence stem *Technology can help people by _____* .

Assign the Writing Task in **Ed.**

RESOURCES

- Unit 1 Response Log
- Writing Studio: Writing an Informative Essay
- Writing Studio: Writing an Informative Essay: Developing a Topic
- Writing Studio: Writing an Informative Essay: Organizing Ideas
- Writing Studio: Writing an Informative Essay: Precise Language and Vocabulary
- Reading Studio: Notice & Note
- Speaking and Listening Studio: Giving a Presentation

Language X-Ray: English Learner Support

Use the instruction below and the supports and scaffolds in the Teacher's Edition to help you guide students of different proficiency levels.

INTRODUCE THE WRITING TASK

Explain that an **informational essay** is a type of writing that presents or explains information and ideas about a topic. Point out that the word *informational* is related to the Spanish adjective *informativo*, which means "providing information." Make sure students understand that informational essays use facts, not personal experiences.

Remind students that the selections in this unit deal with technology and how it can improve, and sometimes control, our lives. Work with students to select a specific new technology to write about. Use sentence frames to help them articulate their ideas. For example: *Some new technologies include _____.*

Brainstorm words and phrases related to the topic, and write them on the board. Then, have students work with a partner to write one sentence about a new technology. Tell students to use their sentences to begin their essays.

WRITING

Use Connecting Words

Tell students that one way to connect ideas in their essays is to combine two related sentences with a **connecting word**, such as *and, but, yet,* or *so*, after a comma.

Use the following supports with students at varying proficiency levels:

- Write one connecting word on the board at a time, and ask students to use it in a sentence at their desk. Ask some students to dictate their sentences to you. **SUBSTANTIAL**
- Use sentence frames to help students practice sentences with connecting words. For example: *Touch-screen menus were once rare, _____ they are common now.* **MODERATE**
- After students complete their first drafts, have them look through their text and see whether they can use connecting words to combine small sentences. **LIGHT**

SPEAKING

Present Information

Provide students with the sentence stem *Technology can help people by _____.* Circulate around the room to make sure students are using the sentence stem correctly.

Use the following supports with students at varying proficiency levels:

- Work with students to complete the sentence stem by discussing different new technologies and how they can benefit people. Have them practice saying the sentence aloud to a partner. **SUBSTANTIAL**
- Have students build on the sentence stem by adding two key ideas they could use in their essays. Encourage them to share their ideas in a conversation with a partner. **MODERATE**
- Have students build on the sentence stem by adding the time words: *now, soon,* or *in the future*, such as *Technology can help people _____ by _____.* Practice with a partner. **LIGHT**

WRITING

WRITE AN INFORMATIONAL ESSAY

Introduce students to the Writing Task by reading the introductory paragraph with them. Remind students to refer to the notes they recorded in the Unit 1 Response Log as they plan and draft their essays. The Response Log should contain ideas about technology from a variety of perspectives. Drawing on these different perspectives will make their own writing more interesting and well informed.

 For **writing support** for students at varying proficiency levels, see the **Language X-Ray** on page 64B.

USE THE MENTOR TEXT

Point out that their essays will be similar to the informational article "Are Bionic Superhumans on the Horizon?" in that they will present interesting new technologies. However, their essays will be shorter than the article and will focus on a less detailed and complicated aspect of the topic of new technology.

WRITING PROMPT

Review the prompt with students. Encourage them to ask questions about any part of the assignment that is unclear. Make sure they understand that the purpose of their essay is to answer the question using facts and examples from the texts they have read.

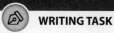 **WRITING TASK**

Write an Informational Essay

 Go to the **Writing Studio** for help writing an informational essay.

This unit focuses on the ways technology can improve—and often control—our lives. For this writing task, you will write a short informational essay. You will tell someone unfamiliar with a new technology how it helped you and how to use it. For an example of a well-written informational text you can use as a mentor text, review "Are Bionic Superhumans on the Horizon?"

As you write your essay, use the notes from your Response Log, which you filled out after reading the texts in this unit.

Writing Prompt

Read the information in the box below.

This is the topic or context for your essay.

> While the overall effects of technology on our lives can be debated, nearly everyone can identify at least one use of technology that makes something in their life easier, faster, better, or more fun.

Think carefully about the following question.

This is the Essential Question for the unit. How would you answer this question, based on the texts in the unit?

> Does technology improve or control our lives?

Write an essay explaining how a new technology helped you. Then explain how to use it to a person unfamiliar with the technology. For example, you might explain how to program a digital watch.

Now mark the words that identify exactly what you are being asked to produce.

Be sure to—

Review these points as you write and again when you finish. Make any needed changes or edits.

- ❑ engage the reader and identify your purpose in your introduction
- ❑ list any necessary tools and materials
- ❑ present steps and details in a logical sequence
- ❑ use appropriate transitions between steps
- ❑ clearly express ideas
- ❑ use formatting to aid comprehension
- ❑ end by summarizing your main points and drawing a conclusion

64   Unit 1

 LEARNING MINDSET

Belonging Ask students to share how someone made them feel welcome in school. Have students discuss some of the changes they faced and why they were glad that they could discuss this with someone. Encourage students to brainstorm with classmates about how they can welcome other new students by explaining how to use technology in the school. Their ideas can potentially be used in the planning or drafting of their essays.

1 Plan

Thorough planning will help you write an effective essay. The first step is to select a genre that is appropriate for your topic, purpose, and audience. For this writing task, you know that the genre will be an informational essay that includes instructions about how to use some type of technology. To identify and narrow your topic, brainstorm about technology with a partner or small group. Next, consider your purpose and audience—to explain a kind of technology to someone unfamiliar with it. As part of your planning process, you also might do some background reading or thinking about personal interests you have that relate to the topic. Use the table below to help you plan your draft.

Informational Essay Planning Table	
Genre	Informational essay with instructions
Topic	How one kind of technology is beneficial and instructions for using it
Purpose	
Audience	
Ideas from discussion with classmates	
Ideas from background reading	
Personal interests related to topic	

Background Reading Review the notes you have taken in your Response Log after reading the texts in this unit. These texts provide background reading that will help you formulate the key ideas you will include in your essay.

Go to **Writing Informative Texts: Developing a Topic** for help planning your essay.

Notice & Note

From Reading to Writing

As you plan your informative essay, apply what you've learned about signposts to your own writing. Remember that writers use common features, called signposts, to help convey their message to readers.

Think about how you can incorporate **Word Gaps** into your essay.

 Go to the **Reading Studio** for more resources on Notice & Note.

Use the notes from your Response Log as you plan your essay.

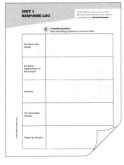

Write an Informational Essay   65

1 PLAN

Allow time for students to discuss the topic with partners or in small groups and then to complete the planning table independently.

■ English Learner Support

Understand Academic Language Make sure students understand words and phrases used in the chart, such as *genre , purpose,* and *audience.* Work with them to fill in the blank sections, providing text that they can copy into their charts as needed. **SUBSTANTIAL**

▶ NOTICE & NOTE

From Reading to Writing Remind students they can use Quoted Words to include the opinions or conclusions of someone who is an expert on the topic. Students can also use Quoted Words to provide support for a point they are trying to make. Remind students to formate direct quotations correctly and to give credit to the source.

Background Reading As they plan their essays, remind students to refer to the notes they took in the Response Log. They may also review the selections to find additional facts and examples to support ideas they want to include in their writing.

TO CHALLENGE STUDENTS . . .

Conduct Research Challenge students to incorporate facts and examples from another text on the topic of technology. They might start by thinking of articles or stories they have already read that connect to the topic in some way. If they cannot think of an appropriate text, they may search online or at the library. Encourage them to add details from their chosen text to the Response Log and think about how these details support their answer to the Essential Question.

WRITING

Organize Your Ideas Tell students that their outlines may have one main section for each paragraph of the essay. Provide the following sample based on the chart:

I. Introduction

II. Description of Chosen Technology

III. How the Technology Has Benefitted You

IV. How to Use the Technology

V. Conclusion

Then point out that they may also outline the body paragraphs by reading the chart from left to right, with one paragraph for each row. In this organizational pattern, a description of the technology, benefits of the technology, and how to use the technology would each be presented in one paragraph. By thinking about the details and examples that they have gathered, students can select the best way to organize their essays.

② DEVELOP A DRAFT

Remind students to follow their outlines as they draft their essays, but point out that they can still make changes to their writing plan during this stage. As they write, they may discover that they need a different example to support an idea or that a particular detail really belongs in a different paragraph.

 **WRITING TASK**

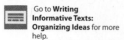 Go to **Writing Informative Texts: Organizing Ideas** for more help.

Organize Your Ideas Once you have identified your topic and other key elements of your essay, you need to organize your information and instructions in a way that will help you draft your essay. You can use the chart below to map out the steps required to use the technology you are describing. However, before you give instructions about how to use the technology, be sure to explain how it has benefited you.

Main Topic: How to Use One Kind of Technology	
Step 1	
Step 2	
Step 3	
Step 4	

You also may want to create an outline of your essay to serve as a kind of map that you can follow as you write. Use a Roman numeral for each paragraph in your essay. Use capital letters beneath each numeral to identify the contents of that paragraph.

② Develop a Draft

 You may prefer to draft your essay online.

Once you have completed planning your informational essay, you will be ready to begin drafting it. As you write your first draft, refer to the chart and outline you have created as well as any notes you took as you studied the unit texts. Be sure to explain how to complete the steps in the correct order. Using a word processor or online writing application makes it easier to move sentences around and make other changes later when you are ready to revise your first draft.

WHEN STUDENTS STRUGGLE . . .

Draft the Essay Even when working from an outline, students may struggle to get started on their drafts. Encourage them to start with the section they feel most confident about—perhaps one of the body paragraphs. Once they are into the writing, they may find that their ideas flow more freely, even for the more difficult sections. Remind students that a first draft is not meant to be perfect. At this stage, they are just getting their ideas down on paper (or on the computer screen). They will have time to revise and edit their writing later.

WRITING TASK

Use the Mentor Text

▶ **Author's Craft**

Your introduction should include a statement or a question to capture the reader's attention. It also should include additional details about your topic to get your reader interested in reading your essay. Note the way the writer captures the reader's attention in "Are Bionic Superhumans on the Horizon?"

> We're in the midst of a bionic revolution, yet most of us don't know it.
>
> Around 220,000 people worldwide already walk around with cochlear implants—devices worn around the ear that turn sound waves into electrical impulses shunted directly into the auditory nerve.

The writer makes an intriguing statement about technology and adds a surprising fact, making the reader want to learn more about the topic.

Apply What You've Learned One way to capture your reader's attention in the introduction is to include a surprising fact or a personal anecdote related to the topic.

▶ **Genre Characteristics**

Supporting details tell more about a central idea. Notice how the author of "Are Bionic Superhumans on the Horizon?" uses the following example to support a key idea about how bionic devices work.

> She let researchers implant a small device in the part of her brain responsible for motor control. With that device, she is able to control an external robotic arm by thinking about it.

The author provides an example as a supporting detail to describe how one type of bionic technology can be used.

Apply What You've Learned The details you include in your own informational essay should be clearly related to your explanation about how technology has benefited you. The step-by-step instructions should clearly show how to perform the task.

Write an Informational Essay   67

WHY THIS MENTOR TEXT?

"Are Bionic Superhumans on the Horizon?" provides a good example of informative writing. Use the instruction below to help students use the mentor text as a model for writing engaging introductions and for integrating facts and details into their informative essays.

USE THE MENTOR TEXT

Author's Craft Ask a volunteer to read aloud the introduction from "Are Bionic Superhumans on the Horizon?" Discuss words and details that make this a vivid description of the possibilities of technology. Then invite students to offer examples of surprising facts, famous quotations, and personal anecdotes that could be used in an introduction. Discuss strategies students might use to search for surprising facts and famous quotations online.

Genre Characteristics To help students understand how the example functions in the article, have them locate paragraph 8 in the text. Note that the content describes how one person benefited from technology and how that same technology could benefit many others. The specific-person detail about how technology benefitted Cathy Hutchinson is an example of a supporting detail that can support the central idea that technology can improve our lives.

 ENGLISH LEARNER SUPPORT

Use the Mentor Text Use the following supports with students at varying proficiency levels:

- To simulate deafness, mouth words to students silently. Then turn around, gesturing toward the back of your ear to indicate a cochlear implant. Face the class and read the first paragraph loudly and with feeling. Discuss the impact of hearing clearly. **SUBSTANTIAL**

- Read the first two paragraphs aloud, and invite students to ask about any words or phrases that are unclear. Ask students whether this text makes them want to read more, and why. **MODERATE**

- Have students read the first two paragraphs and identify words that add to the feeling of excitement. Then ask them to brainstorm other situations that could be used to introduce the topic of amazing advancements in technology. **LIGHT**

WRITING

③ REVISE

Have students answer each question in the chart to determine how they can improve their drafts. Invite volunteers to model their revision techniques.

With a Partner Have students ask peer reviewers to evaluate their supporting evidence by answering the following questions:

- Which pieces of evidence are unclear? Why?
- What questions do you have about my main points?

Encourage students to use the reviewer's feedback to add relevant facts, details, examples, or quotations that further develop their main points.

 **WRITING TASK**

③ Revise

Go to **Writing Informative Texts: Precise Language and Vocabulary** for help revising your essay.

On Your Own Once you have written your draft, you'll want to go back and look for ways to improve your informational essay. Use the Revision Guide to evaluate and revise specific elements of your writing.

Revision Guide		
Ask Yourself	**Tips**	**Revision Techniques**
1. Does my introduction grab the readers' attention?	**Highlight** the introduction.	**Add** an interesting fact or example to illustrate the topic.
2. Does my introduction clearly state the topic?	**Underline** the topic sentence.	**Add** a sentence that clearly states the topic.
3. Are all materials and tools listed in my introduction?	**Draw** a star next to any materials or tools you've noted.	**Add** any missing materials or tools to the list.
4. Are my instructions complete and arranged in a clear and sensible way?	**Underline** the steps and any transitions between them.	**Rearrange** or **add** steps and transitions as needed, being sure to move related details, too.
5. Do supporting details help to clarify the instructions?	**Underline** supporting details.	**Add** supporting details or clarifying prepositional phrases.
6. Does my format help to identify the steps and guide readers through them?	**Highlight** headings, numbers, or bulleted lists. **Circle** words that could be emphasized.	**Add** headings, numbers, or bullets to separate instructions into clear steps or parts.
7. Does my conclusion reinforce the reason(s) I gave for learning this type of technology?	**Highlight** the conclusion. **Underline** the reasons for learning the technology and your final advice to readers.	**Add** any missing reasons or a brief summary of them. **Add** some final advice or **recommend** a particular action.

ACADEMIC VOCABULARY
As you conduct your **peer review,** be sure to use these words.

- ❑ commentary
- ❑ occupation
- ❑ option
- ❑ speculate
- ❑ technology

With a Partner After working through the Revision Guide on your own, exchange papers with a partner and evaluate each other's draft in a **peer review**. Focus on suggesting revisions for at least three of the items mentioned in the chart. Explain why you think your partner's draft should be revised and your specific suggestions for revising it.

When receiving feedback from your partner, listen attentively and ask questions to make sure you fully understand the revision suggestions.

 ## ENGLISH LEARNER SUPPORT

Use Numbers Explain that writers often include impressive numbers in essays as a way to present facts. Have students identify some impressive numbers in this passage:

> Tens of thousands of people have been implanted with deep brain stimulators, devices that send an electrode tunneling several inches in the brain. *(Tens of thousands)*

Encourage students to find opportunities to link ideas with impressive numbers in their essays.
LIGHT

4 Edit

Once you have evaluated the organization, development, and flow of information in your essay and made necessary revisions, one important task remains. Don't let simple mistakes confuse your readers. Edit your final draft for the proper use of standard English conventions and be sure to correct any misspellings or errors in grammar or punctuation.

Language Conventions

Transitional Words and Phrases When explaining how to perform a task with multiple steps, you can use transitional words and phrases to connect ideas and make the process clearer.

The chart below contains commonly used transitions.

Go to **Writing Informative Texts: Organizing Ideas** in the **Writing Studio** for more help with transitional words and phrases.

Type of Transition	Examples
Sequence	*first, second, next, then, finally, when, before, later, while*
Degree of Importance	*mainly, more important, to begin with, then, last*
Compare	*also, and, another, just as, like, likewise, similarly*
Contrast	*although, but, however, yet, on the other hand*

Here are examples of transitions from "Are Bionic Superhumans on the Horizon?"

- **When** the implant was activated, it raised their scores by an average of 10 points on a 100-point scale.
- And **then**, one day, we'll wake up and realize that we're doing more than restoring lost function.

5 Publish

Finalize your essay and choose a way to share it with your audience. Consider these options:

- Produce a brochure for people who will find the instructions useful.
- Present your essay as a speech to the class.
- Post your essay as a blog on a classroom or school website.

WHEN STUDENTS STRUGGLE . . .

Use Transitional Words and Phrases Some students may have difficulty understanding how to use the transition words in the chart. Give them sentence frames for practice, such as this one: _____ *I unlocked my cell phone,* _____ *I checked my text messages, and* _____ *I called my mother back.*

---

4 EDIT

Suggest that students read their drafts aloud to assess how clearly and smoothly they have presented their ideas. If the text sounds choppy in places, or if the connection between certain ideas is unclear, they should consider combining simple sentences into compound or complex sentences.

LANGUAGE CONVENTIONS

Use Transitional Words and Phrases Review the information about transitional words and phrases with students. Then discuss the example sentences below the chart, asking students to identify the effect of each bolded transitional word. To emphasize how transitional words and phrases can improve writing, rewrite the example sentences without transition words, and discuss the differences.

- "The implant was activated, it raised their scores by an average of 10 points on a 100-point scale." (*This versions doesn not provide a time relationship.*)
- "And one day, we'll wake up and realize that we're doing more than restoring lost function." (*The connection between the two ideas is less clear.*)

5 PUBLISH

Students can present their essays as blog posts on a school website. Encourage students to read each others' essays and to write comments about them. Also, encourage authors to respond to the comments.

WRITING

USE THE SCORING GUIDE

Allow students time to read the scoring guide and to ask questions about any words, phrases, or ideas that are unclear. Then have partners exchange final drafts of their informative essays. Ask them to score their partner's essay using the scoring guide. Each student should write a paragraph explaining the reasons for the score he or she awarded in each category.

WRITING TASK

Use the scoring guide to evaluate your essay.

	Writing Task Scoring Guide: Informational Essay		
	Organization/ Progression	Development of Ideas	Use of Language and Conventions
4	• The organization is effective and appropriate for the purpose. • Ideas and steps are presented in a logical sequence. • Transitions clearly show the relationship among ideas and/or steps.	• The introduction catches the reader's attention, identifies the topic, and clearly states a thesis. • All materials, tools, and steps needed to perform the task are included and described in detail. • The thesis is clear and well developed with specific and relevant facts, details, examples, and quotations. • The conclusion summarizes the main points and either offers some final advice or recommends a next step or action.	• Language and word choice is purposeful and precise. • A variety of sentences is used to show how ideas are related. • Spelling, capitalization, and punctuation are correct. • Grammar and usage are correct. • Effective formatting aids comprehension.
3	• The organization is fairly effective and appropriate for the purpose. • Presentation of ideas and steps is logical, with only minor lapses. • A few more transitions are needed to show the relationship among ideas and/or steps.	• The introduction could be more engaging but presents a thesis. • Most materials and tools and all steps needed to perform the task are included. • The thesis is clear and fairly well developed with relevant facts, details, examples, and quotations. • The conclusion summarizes all the main points.	• Language is, for the most part, specific and clear. • Sentences vary somewhat in structure. • Some spelling, capitalization, and punctuation mistakes are present. • Some grammar and usage errors occur. • Some formatting is used to aid comprehension and does so fairly well.
2	• The organization is evident but not always appropriate for the purpose. • Notable gaps occur in the sequence of steps. • More transitions are needed to show the relationship among ideas and/or steps.	• The introduction suggests a topic but the thesis is unclear or missing. • A few key materials, tools, and/or steps needed to perform the task are unclear or missing. • The thesis is minimally and ineffectively developed because the writer uses vague, insufficient, or irrelevant facts, details, examples, and quotations. • The conclusion does not summarize all the main points.	• Language is often vague and general. • There is little variety in sentence structure. • Spelling, capitalization, and punctuation are often incorrect but do not make reading difficult. • Grammar and usage are often incorrect, but the writer's main points are still clear. • There is little formatting to aid comprehension and/or a few formatting inconsistencies or errors are present.
1	• Organization is absent, inconsistent, or not appropriate for purpose. • There is no discernible logical sequence to the ideas or steps presented. • No transitions are used, making the essay difficult to understand.	• The introduction is missing, confusing, or lacking a thesis. • Crucial materials, tools, or steps are omitted. • The development of ideas is weak. Supporting facts, details, examples, or quotations are unreliable, vague, or missing. • The conclusion is missing.	• Language is vague and confusing and, in some cases, inappropriate for the text. • There is no variety in sentence structure. • Many spelling, capitalization, and punctuation errors are present. • Many grammatical and usage errors make the writer's points or steps hard to follow. • Formatting is missing or very confusing.

SPEAKING AND LISTENING TASK

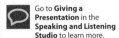

Present and Respond to an Instructional Speech

You will now adapt your informational essay for presentation to your classmates. You will also listen to your classmates' speeches and then give feedback and ask questions that will help them improve their work.

Go to **Giving a Presentation** in the **Speaking and Listening Studio** to learn more.

❶ Adapt Your Essay for Presentation

Review your informational essay and think about how to adapt it for an instructional speech. Keep in mind that listeners may have different needs than readers. How can you adjust the format and organization of your essay to work well as a speech? Use the chart below to guide you as you adapt your essay and create a script and presentation materials.

Presentation Planning Chart		
Title and Introduction	How might you revise your title and introduction to capture your listeners' attention? What do you want listeners to be able to do by the end of your speech?	
Audience	Does your audience already know something about your topic? If so, what information can you exclude? If not, what should you be sure to include or possibly add?	
Effective Language and Organization	Which parts of the instructions in your essay should be simplified? Where can you add transitions to clarify how to progress from one step to another?	
Visuals	What images or graphics would help clarify ideas or add interest? What text should appear on screen?	

Present and Respond to an Instructional Speech 71

SPEAKING AND LISTENING

PRESENT AND RESPOND TO AN INSTRUCTIONAL SPEECH

Introduce students to the Listening and Speaking Task by discussing what makes reading an informational text different from hearing someone speak about the same topic. Point out that readers can adjust their reading rate when the text presents difficult or complicated information. They can also reread passages that they did not understand the first time. Have students consider what a speaker can do to make sure everyone in the audience understands the information.

❶ ADAPT YOUR ESSAY FOR PRESENTATION

Have students read the questions in the chart. Then work with the class to list some general principles for presenting information orally. *(Examples: Use short sentences. Repeat important ideas. Use humor or interesting examples to keep the audience engaged.)* Point out that visuals, such as slides, can serve the same purpose as subheadings in a text. Students can use them to identify the main ideas of their presentations for the audience.

 For **speaking support** for students at varying proficiency levels, see the **Language X-Ray** on page 64B.

 ## ENGLISH LEARNER SUPPORT

Adapt the Essay Use the following supports with students at varying proficiency levels:

- Help students identify several key sentences in their essays. Then have them include these sentences in visuals that illustrate the ideas. **SUBSTANTIAL**
- Review the questions in the chart to ensure students' understanding. Then have students work in pairs to apply the questions to their essays. **MODERATE**
- Have students discuss the questions in the chart with partners before writing their answers independently. **LIGHT**

Present Information **71**

SPEAKING AND LISTENING

② PRACTICE WITH A PARTNER OR GROUP

Review the information and tips with the class, ensuring that all the terms and ideas are clear. Remind students that two purposes of practicing their presentations are to get comfortable speaking in front of a group and to gain useful feedback from their peers. Encourage them to specifically practice enunciating clearly and talking at a pleasant volume, pitch, and rate. Also, emphasize the importance of practicing maintaining eye contact with the audience.

③ DELIVER YOUR PRESENTATION

Set aside time for all students to give their presentations. When everyone has finished, ask students to share their thoughts on how their classmates' feedback helped them improve their performance.

 **SPEAKING AND LISTENING TASK**

As you work to improve your presentations, be sure to follow discussion rules:

- ❑ listen closely to each other
- ❑ don't interrupt
- ❑ stay on topic
- ❑ ask only helpful, relevant questions
- ❑ provide only clear, thoughtful, and direct answers

② Practice with a Partner or Group

Once you've completed a draft of your speech, practice with a partner or group to improve both your presentation and your delivery.

Practice Effective Verbal Techniques

- ❑ **Enunciation** Replace words that you stumble over, and rearrange or restructure sentences to make your delivery easy.
- ❑ **Voice Modulation and Pitch** Use your voice to display enthusiasm and emphasis.
- ❑ **Speaking Rate** Speak slowly enough that listeners understand you. Pause now and then to let them consider important points.
- ❑ **Volume** Remember that listeners at the back of the room need to hear you.

Practice Effective Nonverbal Techniques

- ❑ **Eye Contact** Try to let your eyes rest on each member of the audience at least once.
- ❑ **Facial Expression** Smile, frown, or raise an eyebrow to show your feelings or to emphasize points.
- ❑ **Gestures** Use gestures to emphasize key points or direct attention to visuals.

Provide and Consider Advice for Improvement

As a presenter, listen closely to questions and consider ways to revise your presentation to make sure your points are clear and the steps are logically sequenced. Provide additional information to clarify any misunderstandings. Remember to ask for suggestions about how you might change onscreen text or images to make your presentation clearer and more interesting.

As a listener, pay close attention. Take notes about points you want to remember or questions you want to ask the presenter. Refer to the visuals to help you follow the instructions given by the presenter. Think of ways that presenters can improve their presentations and more effectively use verbal and nonverbal techniques. Paraphrase and summarize each presenter's key ideas and main points to confirm your understanding, and ask questions to clarify any confusing ideas.

③ Deliver Your Presentation

Use the suggestions you received during practice to make final changes to your presentation. Then, using effective verbal and nonverbal techniques, present the speech to your classmates.

WHEN STUDENTS STRUGGLE . . .

Team Work If students have difficulty focusing on all aspects their classmates' presentations, form teams and divide the task between team members. One student may focus on the list of effective verbal techniques, another student may watch for effective nonverbal techniques, and a third may listen for key ideas and supporting details.

Reflect on the Unit

By completing your informational essay, you have created a writing product that pulls together and expresses your thoughts about the reading you have done in this unit. Now is a good time to reflect on what you have learned.

Reflect on the Essential Question

• How does technology improve and control our lives? How has your answer to this question changed since you first considered it at the start of this unit?

• What are some examples from the texts you've read that show how technology can improve and control our lives?

Reflect on Your Reading

• Which selections were the most interesting or surprising to you?

• From which selection did you learn the most about how technology improves and/or controls our lives?

Reflect on the Writing Task

• What difficulties did you encounter while working on your informational essay? How might you avoid them next time?

• Which parts of the essay were the easiest and hardest to write? Why?

• What improvements did you make to your essay as you were revising?

Reflect on the Speaking and Listening Task

• Which parts of your essay did you have to change or adapt for your presentation?

• What aspects of presenting your essay did you find most difficult?

• What are some techniques you could practice to make the task easier?

UNIT 1 SELECTIONS

• "The Brave Little Toaster"
• "Are Bionic Superhumans on the Horizon?"
• "Interflora"
• "The Automation Paradox"
• "Heads Up, Humans"

Reflect on the Unit   73

REFLECT ON THE UNIT

Have students reflect on the questions independently, and write some notes in response to each one. Then have students meet with partners or in small groups to discuss their reflections. Circulate during these discussions to identify the questions that are generating the liveliest conversations. Wrap up with a whole-class discussion focused on these questions.

⚙ LEARNING MINDSET

Self-Reflection Explain to students that an important part of developing a learning mindset is the ability to recognize strengths and weaknesses. As students reflect on the unit, encourage them to ask themselves these questions: *Did I ask questions if I needed help? Did I review my work for possible errors? Am I proud of the work I turned in?*

Instructional Overview and Resources

		Instructional Focus	Online **Ed** **Resources**
	The Thrill of Horror	**Unit 2 Essential Question** **Unit 2 Academic Vocabulary**	**Stream to Start:** The Thrill of Horror **Unit 2 Response Log**

ANALYZE & APPLY

	Mentor Text **"What Is the Horror Genre?"** Literary Criticism by Sharon A. Russell **Lexile 1030L** ▶ **NOTICE & NOTE** READING MODEL **Signposts** • Extreme or Absolute Language • Quoted Words • Big Questions	**Reading** • Analyze Literary Criticism • Paraphrase and Summarize Text **Writing:** Write a Letter **Speaking and Listening:** Discuss with a Small Group **Vocabulary:** Use Suffixes **Language Conventions:** Commas	**Audio** **Text in Focus:** Understanding the Horror Genre **Close Read Screencast:** Modeled Discussions **Reading Studio:** Notice & Note **Speaking and Listening Studio:** Participating in Collaborative Discussions **Vocabulary Studio:** Suffixes **Grammar Studio:** Module 14: Punctuation
	"The Tell-Tale Heart" Short Story by Edgar Allan Poe **Lexile 850L**	**Reading** • Analyze Point of View • Analyze Suspense **Writing:** Write a Scene **Speaking and Listening:** Dramatize a Scene **Vocabulary:** Use a Dictionary **Language Conventions:** Phrases and Clauses	**Audio** **Text in Focus:** Visualizing **Close Read Screencast:** Modeled Discussions **Reading Studio:** Notice & Note **Speaking and Listening Studio:** Participating in Collaborative Discussions **Writing Studio:** Writing Narratives **Vocabulary Studio:** Using a Dictionary **Grammar Studio:** Module 5: The Phrase; Module 6: The Clause
	"The Hollow" Poem by Kelly Deschler	**Reading** • Make Connections • Analyze Rhyme Scheme **Writing:** Write a Poem **Speaking and Listening:** Present a Poem	**Audio** **Reading Studio:** Notice & Note **Speaking and Listening Studio:** Participating in Collaborative Discussions **Writing Studio:** Introduction: Writing as a Process

SUGGESTED PACING: 30 DAYS

Unit Introduction	What Is the Horror Genre?	The Tell-Tale Heart	The Hollow
1	2 3 4 5 6	7 8 9 10 11	12 13 14 15 16

English Learner Support	Differentiated Instruction	Online Ed Assessment
• Clarify Vocabulary		

English Learner Support	Differentiated Instruction	Assessment
• Text X-Ray • Use Cognates • Understand Grammar • Oral Assessment • Write a Letter • Language Conventions	**When Students Struggle** • Analyze Author's Criteria	**Selection Test**
• Text X-Ray • Vocabulay • Use Cognates • Learning Strategies • Compare and Contrast • Oral Reading • Summarize • Oral Assessment • Vocabulary Strategy • Language Conventions	**When Students Struggle** • Analyze Suspense **To Challenge Students** • Analyze Voice	**Selection Test**
• Text X-Ray • Use a Graphic Organizer • Understand Language Structures • Make Connections • Oral Assessment	**When Students Struggle** • Visualize	**Selection Test**

The Monkey's Paw (story)/
The Monkey's Paw (film clip)

Independent Reading   **End of Unit**

17 18 19 20 21 22 23 24 25   26 27   28 29 30

UNIT 2 Continued

Online
Ed Resources

Instructional Focus

COLLABORATE & COMPARE

"The Monkey's Paw"
Short Story by W. W. Jacobs
Lexile 920L

Reading
• Analyze Theme
• Analyze Foreshadowing

Writing: Write a Personal Response

Speaking and Listening: Discuss with a Small Group

Language Conventions: Verb Tenses

🔊 **Audio**

Reading Studio: Short Stories and Novels

Writing Studio: Using Textual Evidence

Speaking and Listening Studio: Participating in Group Discussions

Vocabulary Studio: Latin Roots

Grammar Studio: Module 9: Lesson 3: Verb Tense

"The Monkey's Paw"
Film Clip by Ricky Lewis Jr.

Reading
• Analyze Film

Writing: Create a Public Service Announcement

Speaking and Listening: Discuss with a Small Group

Speaking and Listening Studio: Participating in Collaborative Discussions

Speaking and Listening Studio: Giving a Presentation

Collaborate and Compare

Reading: Compare Versions

Speaking and Listening: Discuss and Present

Speaking and Listening Studio: Participating in Collaborative Discussions

Speaking and Listening Studio: Giving a Presentation

Online
Ed INDEPENDENT READING

The Independent Reading selections are only available in the eBook.

Go to the Reading Studio for more information on **NOTICE & NOTE.**

"Frankenstein"
Poem by Edward Field

"beware: do not read this poem"
Poem by Ishmael Reed

"Blood"
Short story by Zdravka Evitmova
Lexile 660L

END OF UNIT

Writing Task: Write a Literary Analysis

Reflect on the Unit

Writing: Writing a Literary Analysis

Language Conventions: Phrases and Clauses

Unit 2 Response Log
Mentor Text: "What Is the Horror Genre?"

Writing Studio: Writing a Literary Analysis

Grammar Studio: Module 1: Lesson 28: Using Prepositional Phrases

English Learner Support	Differentiated Instruction	Online Assessment

• Text X-Ray • Word Study • Like-Sounding Words • Confirm Understanding • Use Cognates • Understand Pronouns • Understand Language Structures • Oral Assessment • Foreshadowing and Mood • Vocabulary Strategy • Following Foreshadowing Points • Language Conventions	**When Students Struggle** • Determine Theme • Learning Strategy **To Challenge Students** • Mathematics/Economics • Interpret Images	**Selection Test**
• Text X-Ray • Monitor Comprehension • Vocabulary • Listening • Oral Assessment		**Selection Test**
• Use Venn Diagram	**When Students Struggle** • Graphic Organizers **To Challenge Students** • Evaluate Decisions	

"The Outsider"
Short Story by H. P. Lovecraft
Lexile 1270L

"Scary Tales"
Essay by Jackie Torrence
Lexile 730L

Selection Tests

| • Language X-Ray
• Understand Literary Terms
• Provide Text Evidence
• Use Pronouns or Synonyms | **When Students Struggle**
• Read Student Models
• Use an Outline
• Adapt Language Choices
To Challenge Students
• Analyze an Adaptation | **Unit Test** |

THE THRILL OF HORROR

Connect to the
ESSENTIAL QUESTION

? Connect to the
ESSENTIAL QUESTION

Ask a volunteer to read aloud the Essential Question. Discuss how the images on p. 74 relate to the question. Why does seeing red lightening bolts in the man's eyes make someone feel frightened? Ask students how they feel when they see an outstretched hand against the misty night sky and a full moon. Have students discuss times when a book or a movie really frightened them and why they felt that way.

■ English Learner Support

Clarify Vocabulary Make sure that students are clear about the meaning of the adjective *frightened*. Students should understand that frightened means "to be afraid" and that the noun *fright* is sudden intense fear.

Ask students to list some synonyms for *frightened*, such as *scared, fearful, afraid,* or *anxious.*
SUBSTANTIAL

DISCUSS THE QUOTATION

Fredric Brown was a mystery and science fiction writer known for a slick, clever style and often very short densely plotted stories. He won the *Edgar* award from the Mystery Writer's Association of America and was famous for his wit and humor as well as ingenious endings. This quote is the shortest horror story ever written. Have students explain how it contains both setting and characters, and even introduces a plot, all in two sentences.

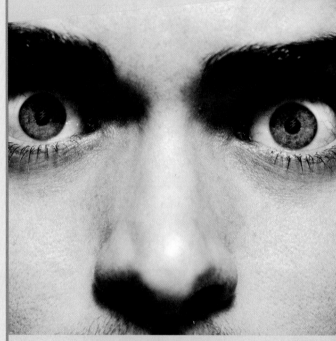

? **ESSENTIAL QUESTION:**

Why do we sometimes like to feel frightened?

" [A] horror story that is only two sentences long: The last man on Earth sat alone in a room. There was a knock at the door. "

Fredric Brown

74   Unit 2

 LEARNING MINDSET

Curiosity Remind students that an important part of being successful in school is being open to changes. Instead of sticking with what someone already knows, students should be open to being challenged by new information. For this to happen, students must be curious enough to ask questions and listen to the responses. Tell students that if they receive information that is hard to believe, then they should dig deeper into the issues. Embracing curiosity may change their perceptions.

ACADEMIC VOCABULARY

Academic Vocabulary words are words you use when you discuss and write about texts. In this unit you will practice and learn five words.

☑ **convention**   ❏ **predict**   ❏ **psychology**   ❏ **summary**   ❏ **technique**

Study the Word Network to learn more about the word **convention**.

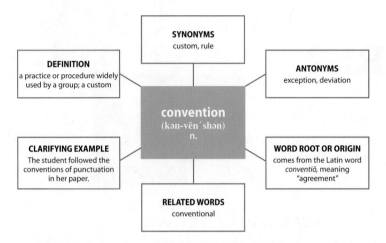

Write and Discuss Discuss the completed Word Network with a partner, making sure to talk through all of the boxes until you both understand the word, its synonyms, antonyms, and related forms. Then, fill out Word Networks for the remaining four words. Use a dictionary or online resource to help you complete the activity.

 Go online to access the Word Networks.

RESPOND TO THE ESSENTIAL QUESTION

In this unit, you will encounter some scary stories and you will think about why so many people enjoy being frightened. As you read, you will revisit the **Essential Question** and gather your ideas about it in the **Response Log** that appears on page R2. At the end of the unit, you will have the opportunity to write a **literary analysis** of one of the stories and explain how it fits into the horror genre. Filling out the Response Log will help you prepare for this writing task.

 You can also go online to access the Response Log.

The Thrill of Horror   75

ACADEMIC VOCABULARY

As students complete Word Networks for the remaining four vocabulary words, encourage them to include all the categories shown in the completed network if possible, but point out that some words do not have clear synonyms or antonyms. Some words may also function as different parts of speech—for example, *predict* can become the noun *prediction* with an added suffix.

> **convention** (kən-vĕn´shən) *n.* A practice or procedure widely used in a group; a custom. (Spanish cognate: *convención*)
>
> **predict** (prĭ-dĭkt´) *v.* To tell about in advance. (Spanish cognate: *predecir*)
>
> **psychology** (sī-kŏl´ə-jē) *n.* The science of mental processes and behavior. (Spanish cognate: *psicología*)
>
> **summary** (sŭm´ə-rē) *n.* A brief statement that mentions the main points of something. (Spanish cognate: *sumario*)
>
> **technique** (tĕk-nēk´) *n.* A basic method of doing something. (Spanish cognate: *técnica*)

RESPOND TO THE ESSENTIAL QUESTION

Direct students to the Unit 2 Response Log. Explain that students will use it to record ideas and details from the selections that help answer the Essential Question. When they work on the writing task at the end of the unit, their Response Logs will help them think about what they have read and make connections between texts.

READING MODEL/MENTOR TEXT

WHAT IS THE HORROR GENRE?

Literary Criticism by Sharon A. Russell

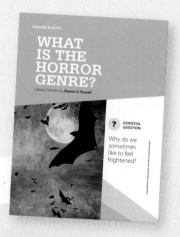

This article serves as a **mentor text**, a model for students to follow when they come to the Unit 2 Writing Task: Write a Literary Analysis.

GENRE ELEMENTS
LITERARY CRITICISM

Remind students that the purpose of **literary criticism** is to influence readers to consider what they read in a new light. It will often comment on more than one piece of literature and usually draws conclusions and discusses trends or shared elements among other works. It will include examples from the literary works as well as other sources to support an argument.

LEARNING OBJECTIVES

- Cite evidence to support analysis of literary criticism and paraphrase and summarize text.
- Conduct research about horror stories and their authors.
- Write about horror story elements.
- Discuss author's purpose and literary references.
- Create different verb tenses using suffixes.
- Analyze how writers use commas.
- **Language** Discuss literary references in a text using appropriate academic language.

TEXT COMPLEXITY

Quantitative Measures	What Is the Horror Genre?	Lexile: 1030L
Qualitative Measures	**Ideas Presented** Complex, subtle arguments, implied meanings. Author's intent may be concealed.	
	Structure Used More complex, multiple perspectives may be presented; more deviation from chronology.	
	Language Used Vocabulary not defined at point of use. Mostly Tier II and III words.	
	Knowledge Required Challenging ideas and unfamiliar experiences. May require specialized knowledge.	

Online Ed

RESOURCES

- Unit 2 Response Log

- Selection Audio

- Text in Focus: Understanding the Horror Genre

- Close Read Screencasts: Modeled Discussions

- Reading Studio: Notice & Note

- Level Up Tutorial: Analyzing Arguments

- Speaking and Listening Studio: Participating in a Discussion

- Vocabulary Studio: Suffixes

- Grammar Studio: Module 14: Punctuation

- "What Is the Horror Genre?" Selection Test

SUMMARIES

English

The author attempts to discover what we consider horror by analyzing what famous horror stories have in common. She concludes that it's not the monsters, creatures, or mad scientists. She argues that the structure and organization of a horror story is its core. The story and setting are a big part of this structure in creating suspense, as well as whether the situation is believable. Last, the source of the horror matters greatly. It can come both from within us and outside us, scaring us both ways.

Spanish

La autora intenta descubrir qué consideramos terror al analizar qué tienen en común las historias de terror. Concluye que no son los monstruos, las criaturas o los científicos locos. Y alega más bien que la estructura y organización de una historia de terror son su centro. La historia y su escenario forman gran parte de esta estructura al crear suspenso. Asimismo, es importante si la situación es creíble o no. Finalmente, la fuente del terror es importantísima. Puede salir tanto de adentro como venir de afuera de nosotros, asustándonos de ambas maneras.

SMALL-GROUP OPTIONS

Have students work in small groups to read and discuss the selection.

Numbered Heads Together

- Students gather in groups of four and then number off 1-2-3-4 within the group.

- Teacher poses a higher-order discussion question to the group or class.

- In groups, students comment on their responses.

- Teacher selects a number from 1-4 then calls it out, and then the student with that number responds for the group.

- For larger classes, groups can choose a nickname like "Aces" or "Badgers" and may wish to stay together.

Double-Entry Journal

- Students take a notebook and draw a line down the center of the page.

- The left-hand column is entitled "Text Quotes" and the right-hand column is called "My Notes."

- Students write down passages from the text that either confuses or intrigue them as they read.

- Students record observations, questions, and comments or notes from discussions.

- Students can create a third column and share their journals with others to record their comments.

Text X-Ray: English Learner Support
for "What Is the Horror Genre?"

Use the Text X-Ray and the supports and scaffolds in the Teacher's Edition to help guide students at different proficiency levels through the selection.

INTRODUCE THE SELECTION
DISCUSS WHAT IS SCARY AND HORRIFYING

In this lesson, students will need to be able to discuss and explore the things that scare them as well as why scary and horrifying things entertain them in the form of stories and films.

Ask students what horror stories they know or have heard of. Make a list as a group. Ask students to explain why these stories are scary. Encourage them to use specific language to describe what they are feeling when they read or view horror stories. Create an emotional word bank from the discussion. Suggest and discuss the meaning of the following word groups: *afraid, scared,* and *terrified; anxious, nervous,* and *jumpy; calm, brave,* and *fearless.*

CULTURAL REFERENCES

The following words and phrases may be unfamiliar to students:

- *suspense as a tactic* (paragraph 2): the author uses anxiety, fear, and nervousness to persuade the reader
- *parallel world* (paragraph 4): a made-up place that is like the real world but different in some way
- *demonic possession* (paragraph 4): some evil force takes hold of a person inside their body
- *forbidden knowledge:* (paragraph 5): something no one should know about

---

LISTENING

Understand the Author's Purpose

Draw students' attention to the reasons why authors write literary criticism. Explain that like persuasive writing, which tries to make an argument, literary criticism discusses books and makes a point about their topic or the type of writing the author uses.

Have students listen as you read aloud paragraphs 1–2. Use the following supports with students at varying proficiency levels:

- Tell students that you will ask questions about what you just read aloud. For example, ask: *Who knows what Frankenstein's monster looks like?* [Answers will vary]. *Which picture in the article shows this monster?* [the first one from left] **SUBSTANTIAL**
- Have students identify the central idea of the excerpt. Ask: *Do you know what these paragraphs were mostly about?* (horror stories) **MODERATE**
- Have students work in pairs to determine the author's first major argument. Ask: *Do you know what the best way is to define horror stories?* (organization or structure) **LIGHT**

SPEAKING

Discuss References

Draw students' attention to the way the author talks about other books or movies to provide examples of what she is saying. Note that this is one way authors refer to the literary works they are discussing.

Use the following supports with students at varying proficiency levels:

- Display and read aloud this sentence: "*In Salem's Lot* Susan approaches the house which is the source of evil." Have students say it aloud back to you and then practice saying it with a partner. **SUBSTANTIAL**
- Have students talk about what part of the sentence is referring to a book. (Salem's Lot) To help students, display the following sentence frames: The author is talking about _____. It is called _____. **MODERATE**
- Have students identify other references the author makes. Help students identify and discuss the specific references. **LIGHT**

READING

Analyze Structure

Draw students' attention to the organization or structure the author uses to help make her argument known. Point out certain sentences that control her argument.

Work with students to read paragraphs 4–5. Use the following supports with students at varying proficiency levels:

- Work with students to have them identify how the author organizes her ideas. Ask: Why is Oz a different world where Dorothy goes in *The Wizard of Oz*? [It is different from our world.] **SUBSTANTIAL**
- Guide students to locate the sentences that help organize the author's ideas Ask: *Which sentence in paragraph 5 talks about categorizing horror?* (the first one) **MODERATE**
- Pair students and have them find how horror can have its greatest effects on us. Identify the sentence that states this. (The last one in paragraph 4) **LIGHT**

WRITING

Write a Letter

Remind students that writing a letter of complaint is a way to express an opinion and also to persuade someone to take action. Discuss with the class what sort of things some people may find offensive and possible solutions to complaints.

Use the following supports with students at varying proficiency levels:

- Provide a letter template with greeting and salutation as well as sentence frames related to the complaints: *I am writing about the (movie/game) called _____. I think the rating for (language/violence/themes) is wrong. I think the rating should be _____.* **SUBSTANTIAL**
- Have students work with a partner to discuss and complete the sentence frames for their main points: *I disagree with the rating because _____. I think you should change _____.* **MODERATE**
- Ask students to discuss their complaints with a partner and to brainstorm suggestions for solutions. **LIGHT**

Notice & Note

READING MODEL

EXPLAIN THE SIGNPOSTS

Explain that **NOTICE & NOTE Signposts** are significant moments in the text that help readers understand and analyze works of fiction or nonfiction. Use the instruction on these pages to introduce students to the signposts **Extreme or Absolute Language, Quoted Words,** and **Big Questions**. Then use the selection that follows to have students apply the signposts to a text.

For a full list of the fiction and nonfiction signposts, see p. 140.

▶ EXTREME OR ABSOLUTE LANGUAGE

Explain that **Extreme or Absolute Language** tends to stand out from the rest of the text because it makes a bold statement without any doubt. These are sweeping observations usually made in nonfiction text. They leave little room for discussion and indicate the author's firm commitment to the points he or she is making.

Absolute language would include exaggerations and overstatements of the opinions or facts the author is expressing. Point to the sentences underlined in the annotated paragraph.

For more information on these and other signposts to Notice & Note, visit the **Reading Studio**.

When you notice one of the following while reading, pause to see if it's an **Extreme or Absolute Language** signpost:

a word or phrase that indicates certainty or completeness, such as *all, none, everyone, no one, always, never, totally*

a phrase that expresses an uncompromising position, such as *We must all agree . . .* or *There's no way that . . .*

Anchor Question
When you notice this signpost, ask: Why did the author use this language?

WHAT IS THE HORROR GENRE?

You are about to read "What Is the Horror Genre?," a work of literary criticism. In it, you will notice and note signposts that will give you clues about the author's purpose. Here are three key signposts to look for as you read this essay and other works of nonfiction.

Extreme or Absolute Language Say your friend wants you to go see a movie, claiming it's "the *best* sci-fi movie *ever*" and "*everyone* is going to see it." Now, your friend may really think you'll love the movie. But she may also simply be trying to convince you to go with her.

Similarly, when authors use **Extreme or Absolute Language**, they usually have a purpose for doing so. Paying attention to Extreme or Absolute Language can

- provide clues to the author's purpose and biases
- point to the main idea the author wants to convey
- help you draw conclusions about the text's main points

The paragraph below shows a student's annotations on "What Is the Horror Genre?" and responses to a Notice and Note signpost.

---

1   Many people define horror by its subjects. <u>We all think of creatures like Frankenstein's monster, Dracula, and the wolfman as monsters in the horror genre.</u> Each one of these creatures has a history and developed over a period of time. But we also know that horror covers more than just these monsters. <u>We could all make long lists of the kind of creatures we identify with horror, especially when we think of films as well as literature.</u> The minute we would start to make such a list we would also realize that not all monsters are alike and that not all horror deals with monsters. The subject approach is not the clearest way to define this genre.

What words or phrases indicate certainty or completeness?	"We all" and "We could all"
Why might the author have used these phrases?	These words create a feeling of agreement between author and readers.

Quoted Words If you were writing a fiction story, you might use quotations to show the words your characters say. In nonfiction, writers often use **Quoted Words** to provide support for a point. Quoted Words might be the conclusions of an expert on a subject or the account of an eyewitness on an event. When you come across quoted words, ask yourself why the words were quoted and what they help you understand about the topic. Consider this example:

> There are good reasons why people flock to horror movies. As psychologist Irene Chen points out, "Like a good roller coaster ride, a scary film offers tremendous thrills, but it also offers safety."

Anchor Question
When you notice this signpost, ask: Why was this person quoted or cited, and what did this add?

What quoted words does the author use?	"Like a good roller coaster ride, a scary film offers tremendous thrills, but it also offers safety."
Why might the author have used this quote?	It gives an example of one good reason people might want to see a horror film.

Big Questions Have you ever listened to a friend tell a story and wondered if you had missed something? Sometimes, people assume you know something or have background knowledge that you don't.

Authors occasionally do the same thing. If you're reading a text and feel lost, stop and ask yourself: **What does the author think I already know?** This can help you clarify the point the author is making and determine what to look for as you continue to read. Here's an example:

When you start to feel lost or confused while reading, pause and ask yourself one or more of these **Big Questions**:

What does the author think I already know?

What surprised me?

What challenged, changed, or confirmed what I already knew?

> 6   We can also look at the kinds of themes common to horror. Many works concentrate on the conflict between good and evil. Works about the fantastic may deal with the search for forbidden knowledge that appears in much horror literature. Such quests are used as a way of examining our attitude toward knowledge. While society may believe that new knowledge is always good, the horror genre may question this assumption, examining how such advances affect the individual and society.

Which words or phrases are confusing?	"the search for forbidden knowledge that appears in much horror literature"
What does the author think I already know?	The author thinks I know some examples of horror works that deal with the search for forbidden knowledge.

WHEN STUDENTS STRUGGLE . . .

Use Strategies Readers tend to remember narrative stories better than expository articles. Use this fact to have your students retell the expository article "What Is the Horror Genre?" as a story that incorporates all of the monsters, as well as the creatures and the mad scientists. Students should skim through the parts that discuss segments of horror stories and remake them into one long horror story of their own narration. This Genre Reformulation will allow students to turn the arguments of this essay into a tale that rivals any horror story.

QUOTED WORDS

Explain that **Quoted Words** can give authority to what the author is saying because he or she is using the exact words that someone else spoke to back up and agree with the author's argument. A quotation is like bringing in another person to back up the author. If the quote comes from an expert or someone with extensive experience and authority, it adds that much more weight to what the author is saying.

BIG QUESTIONS

Discuss with students how authors have to assume that their readers share a certain body of knowledge with them. Therefore, authors can introduce new ideas or refer to things everyone knows in order to make a point. They can assume their readers will follow along.

APPLY THE SIGNPOSTS

Have students use the selection that follows as a model text to apply the signposts. As students encounter the signposts, prompt them to stop, reread, and ask themselves the questions that will help them understand the article's main ideas and details.

Tell students to look for these and other signposts as they read the selections in the unit.

Connect to the
ESSENTIAL QUESTION

In "What Is the Horror Genre?," the author attempts to break down the different ways we feel frightened. She also analyzes the types of horror stories we enjoy, illustrating the joy in fear.

MENTOR TEXT

At the end of the unit, students will be asked to write a literary analysis. "What Is the Horror Genre?" provides a model for an essay that examines and analyzes a literary work.

ANALYZE & APPLY

WHAT IS THE HORROR GENRE?

Literary Criticism by **Sharon A. Russell**

ESSENTIAL QUESTION:

Why do we sometimes like to feel frightened?

78   Unit 2

LEARNING MINDSET

Effort Remind students that they all have the ability to succeed in school, but that an important part of reaching success is realizing that personal growth is a result of honest effort. Effort is shown by consistency and focus—characteristics known simply as hard work. Oftentimes students are measured by a level of being smart. But it is the level of effort that should be used as the students' benchmark. Tell students when you notice their effort and praise them for it by telling them their effort has been observed and appreciated.

QUICK START

Before you read, think about some scary stories you know. What do they have in common? Discuss your ideas with a partner.

ANALYZE LITERARY CRITICISM

Literary criticism is writing that examines, analyzes, and interprets a particular work or an aspect of literature. The **author's purpose**—or reason for writing—is often to inform readers or to persuade them to adopt a particular opinion of the material. This opinion is the **controlling idea** around which the writing is organized. Whether stated directly or implied, the author supports it with evidence.

The chart shows some specific purposes an author might have when writing literary criticism.

PURPOSE	WHAT THE AUTHOR DOES
To define a genre	explains the characteristics of a type of writing using specific examples as evidence
To categorize works of literature	defines and classifies works of literature based on certain **criteria,** or standards
To examine the structure of a work of literature	analyzes the organization of a piece of literature
To analyze an author's technique	explains the effectiveness of literary techniques, such as suspense or flashbacks

As you read, look for clues that help you infer the author's purpose. To whom is she writing? What ideas does she want them to understand?

PARAPHRASE AND SUMMARIZE TEXT

A good way to check your comprehension of a text is to paraphrase or summarize it. These techniques are similar, but not the same.

- When you **paraphrase**, you restate all the information in the text using your own words. Paraphrasing is a helpful way to make sure you understand small, challenging sections of text.

- When you **summarize**, you briefly retell the text's central ideas and most important details in your own words. You must be careful not to change the author's meaning and to present ideas and details in the same order as the text. Summarizing helps you understand a larger section of text or the entire text.

As you read, use paraphrasing and summarizing to understand the author's ideas about the horror genre.

GENRE ELEMENTS:
LITERARY CRITICISM

- often appears in the form of an essay with persuasive elements

- examines one or more works of literature

- contains specific examples and support from the literature and other sources

- may have the purpose of shaping how readers interpret a particular work

QUICK START

Ask students to share some horror stories they know. Point out how many of these stories will have similar elements like something unknown threatening someone who can't escape or fight back. Help students see the ways their stories differ. Ask students whether they know other similar versions of these stories. Encourage students to discuss which aspects of these stories frighten them the most.

ANALYZE LITERARY CRITICISM

Have students focus their understanding of literary criticism on the author's purpose in this selection. Review the definition of *author's purpose* as the author's reason or goal for writing a piece of literature. Then go through the various purposes shown in the chart with the class and discuss ways an author might achieve each of these purposes. Remind students to ask themselves, "Why is the author telling me this? What does the author want me to know?" as they read to help them identify the author's purpose for writing.

PARAPHRASE AND SUMMARIZE TEXT

Remind students that there really isn't a right or a wrong way to paraphrase text other than to retell accurately what they read using language they feel comfortable using. Note that paraphrasing can be wordy as long as all of the author's ideas are expressed. Point out that summarizing is different from paraphrasing because it focuses only on the key points of a text. Ask students how paraphrasing and summarizing could help them better understand a text.

CRITICAL VOCABULARY

Encourage students to read all the sentences before deciding which word best completes each one. Remind them to look for context clues that match the meaning of each word.

Answers:

1. *parallel*
2. *justify*
3. *intensify*
4. *quest*

■ English Learner Support

Use Cognates Tell students that several of the Critical Vocabulary words have Spanish cognates: *parallel/paralelo; justify/justificar.* **ALL LEVELS**

LANGUAGE CONVENTIONS

Tell students that commas are often used to indicate pauses or breaks in a sentence. Have students note where the sample sentences have commas and then read them aloud to hear the pause in their reading.

Have students read the sentences again without the pause, ignoring the commas. Have students explain the difference. (*The sentences can have their meaning confused without a pause to isolate the phrases and expressions.*)

✎ ANNOTATION MODEL

Students can review the Reading Model introduction if they have questions about any of the signposts. Suggest that they underline important phrases or circle key words that help them identify signposts. They may want to color-code their annotation by using a different color highlighter for each signpost. Point out that they may follow this suggestion or use their own system for marking up the selections in their write-in texts.

 GET READY

CRITICAL VOCABULARY

| intensify | justify | parallel | quest |

To see how many Critical Vocabulary words you already know, use them to complete the sentences.

1. I read a science fiction story about a _____ world much like Earth but where computers have enslaved humans.

2. The trip is only two days, so I can't _____ bringing two bags.

3. We watch scary movies in the dark to _____ the experience.

4. How many restaurants have you visited in your _____ to find the perfect hamburger?

LANGUAGE CONVENTIONS

Commas In this lesson, you will learn about the effective use of commas in writing. Commas can make the meaning of sentences clearer by separating certain words, phrases, or clauses. Read aloud these two sentences from the selection and notice where you pause:

She does end up dead in the basement, a victim of the vampire.

This type of hesitation, when we almost believe, falls into the general category of the "fantastic."

How do the commas make the sentences easier to understand? As you read "What Is the Horror Genre?" notice other ways commas are used.

ANNOTATION MODEL   **NOTICE & NOTE**

As you read, notice and note signposts, including **Extreme or Absolute Language** and **Quoted Words**, and ask **Big Questions.** Also note details that help you identify the controlling idea of "What Is the Horror Genre?" Here is how one student annotated the beginning of the selection.

Many people define horror by its subjects. We all think of creatures like Frankenstein's monster, Dracula, and the wolfman as (monsters) in the horror genre. Each one of these creatures has a history and developed over a period of time. But we also know that horror covers more than just these monsters. We could all make long lists of the kind of creatures we identify with horror, especially when we think of films as well as literature. . . .

> "Many people" define horror this way. What does the author think?
>
> subject = monsters
>
> What other kinds of monsters are there?

BACKGROUND

Sharon A. Russell (b. 1941) is a retired professor of Communication and Women's Studies at Indiana State University, where she taught courses on film and television. Russell has published extensively on horror film and literature and detective fiction. She is the author of Stephen King: A Critical Companion, *a book that analyzes several of King's famous horror novels and in which this essay appears.*

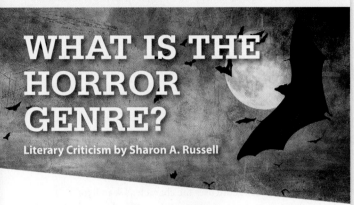

WHAT IS THE HORROR GENRE?

Literary Criticism by Sharon A. Russell

SETTING A PURPOSE

As you read, pay attention to the points the author makes about horror stories. Do her ideas make you think about horror stories in new ways?

1   **M**any people define horror by its subjects. <u>We all think of creatures like Frankenstein's monster, Dracula, and the wolfman[1] as monsters in the horror genre.</u> Each one of these creatures has a history and developed over a period of time. But we also know that horror covers more than just these monsters. We could all make long lists of the kind of creatures we identify with horror, especially when we think of films as well as literature. The minute we would start to make such a list we would also realize that not all monsters are alike and that not all horror deals with monsters. The subject approach is not the clearest way to define this genre.

---

[1] **Frankenstein's monster, Dracula, and the wolfman:** legendary monsters. "Frankenstein's monster" is the creature created by Dr. Victor Frankenstein in Mary Shelley's novel; "Dracula" is the vampire in Bram Stoker's novel; in folklore, the wolfman is a man who can become a wolf.

Notice & Note

Use the side margins to notice and note signposts in the text.

BIG QUESTIONS

Notice & Note: Mark where Russell expects the reader to already know something.

Analyze: Why do you think she expects the reader to know this? Where did you look to get more information?

 Close Read

BACKGROUND

After students read the Background note, tell them that Stephen King is one of the most popular horror story writers in history, and Sharon A. Russell was the first person to write a book for the general public analyzing his work. Russell uses her expertise in the field to analyze how the horror genre works and what makes a good horror story.

SETTING A PURPOSE

Direct students to use the Setting a Purpose prompt to focus their reading.

▶ BIG QUESTIONS

The author begins by assuming readers have sufficient prior knowledge of the horror genre. Point out that the assumption reveals a belief and attitude by the author as well additional information about the assumed knowledge. Ask students what the author's assumption reveals about the author's view of the horror genre. (**Answer:** *These monsters are well known in popular culture. The footnote provides more information about them.*)

TEXT IN FOCUS

Understanding the Horror Genre Have students view the **Text in Focus** video on this page of their eBook to build background that will help them understand the horror genre. Then have students use **Text in Focus Practice** to apply what they have learned.

CLOSE READ SCREENCAST

Modeled Discussions Have students click the Close Read icons in their eBooks to access a screencast in which readers discuss and annotate the key passage:

- Note the rationale for not defining the horror genre by subjects, such as monsters (paragraph 1).

- As a class, view and discuss the video. Then have students work in pairs to do an independent close read of an additional passage— the author's suggestion to categorize works of horror based on the source of the horror (paragraph 5).

 Close Read Practice PDF

ENGLISH LEARNER SUPPORT

Understand Grammar Focus on lines 7–8 of paragraph 2. Underline both instances of the word *they*. Remind students that *they* is a pronoun, and a pronoun must match the number (singular or plural) and gender of the noun it replaces.

- Have students identify the noun or pronoun replaced by *they*. (*characters*)

- Display lines 1–2 of paragraph 2. Highlight each use of the pronoun *it* and ask pairs to identify the two words it stands for. (*it: genre; it: horror story*)

- Have students locate the pronouns in paragraph 3 and identify the words they represent. (*it: horror genre; we/us: readers; them: expectations*)

MODERATE

QUOTED WORDS

Explain to students that **Quoted Words** are used to lend authority through someone who provides proof on a point the author is making. (**Answer:** *This is an example of how horror writers use suspense, because readers of the genre know that characters should not go into dark, creepy places.*)

EXTREME OR ABSOLUTE LANGUAGE

Discuss how an example of **extreme or absolute language** is meant to provoke the reader and grab attention. Because it is an exaggeration, the reader has to think about it and decide whether it is true. (**Answer:** *It is justified because most horror stories involve dark, scary settings. A scene in a "bright, beautiful park" would not create a mood of horror — although an author could have a horrifying event in this setting.*)

CRITICAL VOCABULARY

intensify: When we know what is likely to happen, the suspense we feel grows, or *intensifies*.

ASK STUDENTS what happens when they feel suspense, particularly when it increases. (*Their hearts may race, or they sweat and breathing intensifies in anticipation.*)

justify: Note how in the next sentence Susan is proved right, showing she was *justified* in what she thought.

ASK STUDENTS why we are all looking to have our opinions proven correct. (*When your opinion is justified, you feel positive about your correct choices.*)

 NOTICE & NOTE

QUOTED WORDS

Notice & Note: Mark where Russell uses quoted words in paragraph 2.

Analyze: How does this quote support one of Russell's main ideas?

intensify
(ĭn-tĕn´sə-fī´) *v.* If you *intensify* something, you make it grow in strength.

justify
(jŭs´tə-fī´) *v.* If you *justify* something, you prove it is right or valid.

EXTREME OR ABSOLUTE LANGUAGE

Notice & Note: Mark where Russell makes an absolute statement in paragraph 3.

Evaluate: Is her statement justified, or do you think it is an exaggeration? Why?

2   Some students of this genre find that the best way to examine it is to deal with the way horror fiction is organized or structured. Examining the organization of a horror story shows that it shares certain traits with other types of fiction. Horror stories share the use of suspense as a tactic with many other kinds of literature. The tension we feel when a character goes into the attic, down into the basement, or just into the abandoned house is partially a result of suspense. We don't know what is going to happen. But that suspense is **intensified** by our knowledge of the genre. We know that characters involved in the world of horror always meet something awful when they go where they shouldn't. Part of the tension is created because they are doing something we know is going to get them in trouble. Stephen King refers directly to our anticipation of horror. In *Salem's Lot*[2] Susan approaches the house which is the source of evil. "She found herself thinking of those drive-in horror movie epics where the heroine goes venturing up the narrow attic stairs . . . or down into some dark, cobwebby cellar . . . and she . . . thinking: . . . *I'd never do that!*" Of course Susan's fears are **justified**. She does end up dead in the basement, a victim of the vampire.

3   If the horror genre uses the character's search for information to create suspense, it controls when and where we get our knowledge. Because we are outside of the situation we usually know more than the characters. Our advance knowledge creates suspense because we can anticipate what is going to happen. The author can play with those expectations by either confirming them or surprising us with a different outcome. When suspense is an important element in fiction we may often find that the plot is the most critical part of the story. We care more about what happens next than about who the characters are or where the story is set. But setting is often considered a part of the horror genre. If the genre has traditional monsters, it also has traditional settings. Only authors who want to challenge the tradition place events in bright, beautiful parks. We expect a connection between the setting and the events in this genre. We are not surprised to find old houses, abandoned castles, damp cellars, or dark forests as important elements in the horror story.

---

[2] ***Salem's Lot:*** a horror fiction novel written by Stephen A. King.

82   Unit 2

IMPROVE READING FLUENCY

Targeted Passage Have students work with partners to read from line 26 "In *Salem's Lot* . . . " to the end of the paragraph. Have them pay close attention to the punctuation and ask students how they would pronounce the ellipses (...).

Remind students that when reading a direct quotation, they should pause and distinguish it from other prose by using their speaking voice rather than their reading voice. Have partners take turns and discuss their performance.

 Go to the **Reading Studio** for additional support in developing fluency.

The actor Boris Karloff as the monster in the 1931 film *Frankenstein*, based on the novel

The actor Lon Chaney as a werewolf in the 1941 film *The Wolf Man*

The actor Bela Lugosi as Dracula in the 1931 film by the same name

4   Some people make further distinctions based on how the stories are organized. We can divide stories into different categories based on how we come to believe in the events related and how they are explained to us. Stories that deal with **parallel** worlds expect us to accept those worlds without question. We just believe Dorothy is in Oz; we accept Oz as a parallel world separate from ours. Other times events seem to be supernatural but turn out to have natural explanations: the ghosts turn out to be squirrels in the attic, or things that move mysteriously are part of a plot to drive someone crazy. Sometimes the supernatural is the result of the way the central character sees the world, as in stories told from the point of view of a crazy person. But at times we are not sure, and hesitate about believing in the possibility of the supernatural. When I first read Dracula I seriously considered hanging garlic on my windows because I believed that vampires could exist. This type of hesitation, when we almost believe, falls into the general category of the "fantastic" (Todorov 25).[3] Often horror has its greatest effect on us because we almost believe, or believe while we are reading the book or watching the film, that the events are possible.

---

[3] **Todorov 25:** the author is following MLA style to cite her source for the information just stated: page 25 of a work by an author named Todorov.

parallel
(păr´ə-lĕl´) *adj.* If things are *parallel*, they have comparable or similar parts.

ANALYZE LITERARY CRITICISM
Annotate: Review the purposes for writing literary criticism on page 79. Mark text in paragraph 4 that suggests the author has one of these purposes.

Infer: What is one of the author's purposes for writing this essay, based on the text you marked?

TEACH

ANALYZE LITERARY CRITICISM

Tell students that authors of literary criticism define and classify literature according to certain **criteria**, or purposes. Explain that in paragraph 4, Russell is identifying criteria that helps answer the question she posed in the title: *What is the horror genre? What are some of Russell's purposes in describing horror?* (**Answer:** *One of the author's purposes is to analyze different ways horror stories can be organized to explain events to the reader and make the reader believe in them.*)

For **reading support** for students at varying proficiency levels, see the **Text X-Ray** on page 76D.

WHEN STUDENTS STRUGGLE . . .

Analyze Author's Criteria Students may find it helpful to keep track of the criteria Russell discusses in a graphic organizer. Have them note the criteria along with an example.

CRITERIA	EXAMPLE
parallel world	The *Wizard of Oz*
supernatural, with natural explanations	ghosts turned out to be squirrels in the attic
supernatural	*Dracula*

 For additional support, go to the **Reading Studio** and assign the following **Level Up tutorial: Analyzing Arguments.**

CRITICAL VOCABULARY

parallel: Two things that are *parallel* would be exactly the same but would exist separately.

ASK STUDENTS Do things that are parallel ever change or come together? (*Parallel worlds would be the same but would never change or come together.*)

LANGUAGE CONVENTIONS

Point out that the three sentences on this page that use a comma, do so with a conjunction (*and; and; but*). Remind students that a conjunction is a word that connects two ideas, clauses, or sentences. Explain that the comma helps separate clauses even when the conjunction shows connection. The comma provides a pause and an introduction to the next sentence as an independent clause. (**Answer:** *In all three sentences, the comma separates a cause from its effect. The break or pause helps the reader see two separate events and consider how they are related.*)

PARAPHRASE AND SUMMARIZE

Guide students through the sentences of paragraph 6 on page 85. Ask students to define "a challenging sentence." Ask volunteers: *Which parts of the sentence would challenge them as readers?* (*words whose definitions they are unsure of or they may not know*) The sentences students select will depend on the vocabulary they do not understand. Work through examples, showing students how to paraphrase the meaning of unknown words with synonyms as they summarize that sentence. (**Answer:** *A character's search can help us think about how we feel about knowledge in general.*)

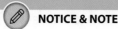

NOTICE & NOTE

LANGUAGE CONVENTIONS
Annotate: Mark the commas used by the author in paragraph 5.

Analyze: How does each comma help you understand the author's meaning in the sentence?

PARAPHRASE AND SUMMARIZE TEXT
Annotate: Underline a challenging sentence in paragraph 6. Circle words in the sentence that could be replaced with simpler ones.

Paraphrase: Restate the sentence in your own words.

5   Yet another way of categorizing works of horror is by the source of the horror. Some horror comes from inside the characters. Something goes wrong inside and a person turns into a monster. Dr. Frankenstein's need for knowledge turns him into the kind of person who creates a monster. Dr. Jekyll also values his desire for information above all else and creates Mr. Hyde.[4] In another kind of horror story the threat to the central character or characters comes from outside. An outside force may invade the character and then force the evil out again. The vampire attacks the victim but then the victim becomes a vampire and attacks others. Stories of ghosts or demonic possession also fall into this category.

---

[4] **Dr. Jekyll . . . and . . . Mr. Hyde:** the good and evil sides of the same character in a novella by Robert Louis Stevenson.

APPLYING ACADEMIC VOCABULARY

❑ convention   ☑ predict   ❑ psychology   ❑ summary   ☑ technique

Write and Discuss Have students turn to a partner to discuss the following questions. Guide students to include the Academic Vocabulary words *predict* and *technique* in their responses. Ask volunteers to share their responses with the class.

• What would you **predict** would happen in a story about a monster on the loose?
• What kind of **technique** would a monster hunter use to stop the terror?

Paragraph 6 body:

6 We can also look at the kinds of themes common to horror. Many works concentrate on the conflict between good and evil. Works about the fantastic may deal with the search for forbidden knowledge that appears in much horror literature. Such quests are used as a way of examining our attitude toward knowledge. While society may believe that new knowledge is always good, the horror genre may question this assumption, examining how such advances affect the individual and society.

NOTICE & NOTE

quest
(kwĕst) n. A *quest* is a search.

ANALYZE LITERARY CRITCISM
Annotate: Mark the first sentence of each paragraph in this selection.

Analyze: Based on these topic sentences, what is the author's controlling idea, or thesis, about the horror genre? What evidence does she provide?

CHECK YOUR UNDERSTANDING

Answer these questions before moving on to the **Analyze the Text** section on the following page.

1 According to the author, what are the limitations of defining horror by its focus on monsters?

A People can think of many different kinds of monsters.

B Some horror stories do not have monsters at all.

C Our ideas about vampires have changed over time.

D The struggle between good and evil is more important.

2 The feeling of suspense in a horror story intensifies when —

F the story takes place in a cheerful setting

G the monsters in the story are unfamiliar to the reader

H the reader expects horrible events to occur

J the characters avoid going into places like basements

3 What is an example of horror that has its source inside a character?

A A woman knows she should not go into a basement but goes anyway.

B A vampire in a story inspires a reader to hang garlic on her windows.

C The squirrels in an attic cause people to think they hear ghosts.

D A scientist desires knowledge so intensely that he creates a monster.

What Is the Horror Genre? 85

TEACH

CHECK YOUR UNDERSTANDING

Have students answer the questions independently.

Answers:

1. *B*

2. *H*

3. *D*

If they answer any questions incorrectly, have them reread the text to confirm their understanding. Then they may proceed to ANALYZE THE TEXT on p. 86

CRITICAL VOCABULARY

quest: A journey is a kind of search or *quest* that is often the theme of horror fiction.

ASK STUDENTS what phrase names the quest that may be the theme of a horror story. (*forbidden knowledge*)

 ENGLISH LEARNER SUPPORT

Oral Assessment Use the following questions to assess students' comprehension and speaking skills.

1. Why aren't horror stories called monster stories? (*Because not all horror stories have monsters.*)

2. When does the feeling of suspense build up in a story? (*When readers expect something to happen at any moment.*)

3. What is an example of a horror that comes from inside a character? (*When a character wants something so much that they do something dangerous like create a monster.*) **SUBSTANTIAL/MODERATE**

What Is the Horror Genre? **85**

ANALYZE THE TEXT

Possible answers:

1. **DOK 2:** *The author's purpose is to define a genre by subjects and organization. In the first paragraph, the author discusses "the clearest way to define genre."*

2. **DOK 4:** *Readers know that awful things happen to characters in horror stories, like when characters go to forbidding places, so when that happens, the readers' tension starts to mount.*

3. **DOK 2:** *Humans are not expected to have "forbidden knowledge," such as how to control life and death like Dr. Frankenstein. The author suggests that "forbidden knowledge" involves evil, as with Dr. Jekyll.*

4. **DOK 2:** *The horror genre refers to scary stories that use certain conventions to increase readers' suspense. The source of the horror may come from either within or outside of the character, and supernatural elements often, but not always, play a role.*

5. **DOK 4:** *The author assumes readers are familiar with the story of the Wizard of Oz and with the idea that garlic keeps vampires away. She is justified in this assumption because the people reading her essay would likely be interested in fantasy and horror literature, and also because these are common examples.*

RESEARCH

Point out to students that they should look up plot descriptions and synopses of well-known horror stories. Compare the plot or review of each to better understand the author's works.

Connect Suggest that students match the stories they find to the categories that Russell describes. For example, "The Lottery" by Shirley Jackson would be an example of a parallel world. Encourage students to create their own categories, too.

(Student answers on the chart will vary.)

 RESPOND

ANALYZE THE TEXT

Support your responses with evidence from the text. ▤ NOTEBOOK

1. **Infer** Reread the first two paragraphs of the essay. What does the opening suggest about the author's purpose in writing this essay?

2. **Connect** In paragraph 2, the author states that in horror stories "suspense is intensified by our knowledge of the genre." What knowledge is the author referring to? Explain why it increases suspense.

3. **Summarize** How does the author answer the question in the title: "What Is the Horror Genre?" To answer, summarize the text.

4. **Analyze** Review the first sentences of each paragraph. How are ideas organized to support the author's controlling idea about the horror genre?

5. **Notice & Note** In paragraph 4, identify two examples of things that the author assumes readers already know. Why might she think her readers would be familiar with these things?

RESEARCH

RESEARCH TIP
The Internet is full of lists of top authors and filmmakers in their genres. If you don't know the names of any famous horror writers or directors, think of a horror story or movie you enjoy, and then look up who made it.

In the selection, Russell discusses the novel *Salem's Lot* by "Master of Horror" Stephen King. Find three other famous Masters of Horror, including writers and directors. In the chart below, record their names and two works by each.

MASTER OF HORROR	TWO WORKS

Connect With a small group, share what you found. Consider whether you want to show images or a movie trailer along with each name. Then, using the categories Russell details in her essay, identify what makes each of the works a good example of the horror genre.

⚙ LEARNING MINDSET

Problem Solving Remind students that everyone runs into problems when learning something new. Tell them that one sure way to keep up their progress is to approach every problem as a challenge, an obstacle that must be overcome. Every individual solves problems in their own unique way; sometimes a different perspective is needed or maybe more information is the key. Solving problems keeps you on the path of progress because every problem has a solution that makes you smarter.

CREATE AND DISCUSS

Write a Letter Have you ever seen a movie or show or played a video game that you thought was either too violent or rated too harshly? Write a three- to four-paragraph letter to the Motion Picture Association of America or to the Entertainment Software Rating Board in which you express a complaint about the rating of a movie, show, or game that includes horror content.

 Go to the **Writing Studio** for more on writing a letter.

❏ Introduce yourself and the title of the movie, show, or game you are writing about.

❏ Explain why you think the rating is too restrictive or not restrictive enough, citing details.

❏ Be sure to keep a professional tone throughout your letter.

Discuss with a Small Group Use the characteristics of the horror genre described in the essay to categorize the horror stories you have read and the horror films you have seen.

Go to the **Speaking and Listening Studio: Participating in Collaborative Discussions** for help.

❏ Work with a small group to create a list of stories and films.

❏ Review the characters, setting, events, structure, and organization of the stories and films. Take notes on each.

❏ Decide how to categorize the stories and films. What creates the suspense in each one? Do they have similar themes or settings? Are the sources of horror alike in some way?

❏ Be prepared to explain your categories as you share your final list with the class or a small group.

RESPOND TO THE ESSENTIAL QUESTION

? Why do we sometimes like to feel frightened?

Gather Information Review your annotations and notes on "What Is the Horror Genre?" Then, add relevant details to your Response Log. As you determine which information to include, think about:

• how we categorize horror

• how our knowledge of the genre shapes how we read it

At the end of the unit, you can use your notes to help you write a literary analysis.

ACADEMIC VOCABULARY

As you write and discuss what you learned from the selection, be sure to use the Academic Vocabulary words. Check off each of the words that you use.

❏ **convention**

❏ **predict**

❏ **psychology**

❏ **summary**

❏ **technique**

CREATE AND DISCUSS

Write a Letter Remind students that they would need to define standards for movies and shows that would regulate their arguments for or against content. Keep in mind that rating agencies use their own standards to apply a rating. Remind students to state their opinions clearly and to offer reasons and evidence to support it.

 For **writing support** for students at varying proficiency levels, see the **Text X-Ray** on page 76D.

Discuss with a Small Group Point out to students that their groups should work together to brainstorm films and their details, but they could also use the Internet to refresh their memories. They should use the questions listed in the text to guide their classifications and categories.

RESPOND TO THE ESSENTIAL QUESTION

Allow time for students to add details from "What Is the Horror Genre?" to their Unit 2 Response Logs.

APPLY

CRITICAL VOCABULARY

Answers:

1. *parallel, because it means "similar or comparable"*

2. *intensify, because it means "to grow in strength"*

3. *quest, because it means "a search"*

4. *justify, because it means "to prove something is right or valid"*

VOCABULARY STRATEGY:
Use Suffixes

Answers:

1. *stopped*

2. *mystified*

3. *glanced*

4. *petrified*

5. *worried*

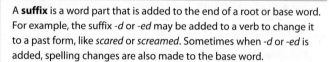

RESPOND

WORD BANK
intensify
justify
parallel
quest

Go to the **Vocabulary Studio** for more on suffixes.

CRITICAL VOCABULARY

Practice and Apply Write the best answer for each question. Then, explain your response.

1. Which Vocabulary word goes with *similar*? Why?

2. Which Vocabulary word goes with *strengthen*? Why?

3. Which Vocabulary word goes with *search*? Why?

4. Which Vocabulary word goes with *defend*? Why?

VOCABULARY STRATEGY:
Use Suffixes

A **suffix** is a word part that is added to the end of a root or base word. For example, the suffix *-d* or *-ed* may be added to a verb to change it to a past form, like *scared* or *screamed*. Sometimes when *-d* or *-ed* is added, spelling changes are also made to the base word.

> But that suspense is <u>intensified</u> by our knowledge of the genre. Of course Susan's fears are <u>justified</u>.

In the two sentences above from "What Is the Horror Genre?," the *y* at the end of each verb form was changed to *i* before the *-ed* suffix was added; that's because in each case, the *y* follows a consonant. This table summarizes patterns that will help you use base words and the suffixes *-d* and *-ed* to identify unfamiliar words:

EXAMPLE	PATTERN TO REMEMBER
abandon**ed**	Add *-ed* to most verbs to create past forms.
reliev<u>e**d**</u>	If a verb ends in *-e*, only *-d* is added.
horrif<u>i**ed**</u>	If a verb ends in consonant + *y*, the *y* is changed to *i*, then *-ed* is added.
occur<u>r**ed**</u>	If a verb ends in a vowel + consonant, the consonant is doubled, then *-ed* is added.

Practice and Apply Read the sentences. Change each verb in parentheses to the past tense by adding *-d* or *-ed*.

1. The main character (stop) for gas in a small town.

2. She was (mystify) when the pump was empty.

3. She (glance) around the town but it was deserted.

4. Suddenly, she heard a scream that (petrify) her.

5. Now, she was (worry) that she was not alone.

88   Unit 2

ENGLISH LEARNER SUPPORT

Vocabulary Strategy Since there are no suffixes or inflections in Khmer, the tendency is to omit them in English. Provide additional practice adding the suffix -ed to the following words: *start, hurry, try, trample, pop*. Have students work with a partner to circle the word endings and use the chart on page 88 to find the pattern for adding the suffix. Then model reading the words and have students repeat them. *(started, hurried, tried, trampled, popped)*
SUBSTANTIAL/MODERATE

LANGUAGE CONVENTIONS:
Commas

A writer's use of punctuation not only helps readers understand the message, but also signals how the writer wants the text to be read. In your writing, you can use commas to signal a break or a pause to the reader. When you write, read your sentences out loud, noticing where you pause. The places where you pause probably need to be punctuated by a comma.

Look at these examples of how Sharon A. Russell uses commas in "What Is the Horror Genre?"

PURPOSE OF COMMA	EXAMPLE
To signal a break in thought or an additional thought	"Often horror has its greatest effect on us because we almost believe, or believe while we are reading the book or watching the film, that the events are possible."
To signal a pause between phrases or clauses	"If the genre has traditional monsters, it also has traditional settings."
To set off a phrase or clause that provides extra information that is not essential to the sentence's meaning	"She does end up dead in the basement, a victim of the vampire."

Practice and Apply These sentences include words, phrases, and clauses that need to be punctuated with commas. Rewrite the sentences, inserting the needed punctuation. If you get stuck, try reading the sentence aloud.

1. Yes I absolutely love horror stories.

2. You know of course that the main purpose of horror stories is to inspire fear and dread.

3. If Frankenstein is frightening he is also sympathetic.

4. The long movie was terrifying so much so that several times I just closed my eyes and blocked my ears.

5. Writing a horror story a big dream of mine will take a lot of thought and hard work.

RESPOND

! Go to the **Grammar Studio: Punctuation** for more on commas.

What Is the Horror Genre?   89

APPLY

LANGUAGE CONVENTIONS:
Commas

Review the information about commas with students, pointing out that comma use can vary greatly from one author to another. Stress that commas are part of a writer's style, and some authors use them to control how their work will be read. Commas also indicate how ideas are organized and how the author wants readers to slow down and take notice of an idea.

Demonstrate the purposes of a comma by having students create examples of their own. They should work with partners to use the example sentences offered as a guide in creating their own sentences.

Practice and Apply

Have partners discuss answers before reviewing with the group.

1. Yes [,] I absolutely love horror stories.

2. You know [,] of course [,] that the main purpose of horror stories is to inspire fear and dread.

3. If Frankenstein is frightening [,] he is also sympathetic.

4. The long movie was terrifying [,] so much so that several times I just closed my eyes and blocked my ears.

5. Writing a horror story [,] a big dream of mine [,] will take a lot of thought and hard work.

 ENGLISH LEARNER SUPPORT

Language Conventions Use the following supports with students at other proficiency levels:

- Have students read through "What Is the Horror Genre?" to locate sentences that use commas. Make sure they have not selected other forms of punctuation. **SUBSTANTIAL**

- Have partners work together in creating their own sentences with commas used as pauses between extended ideas. **MODERATE**

- Have partners work together to create sentences that set off phrases and clauses, which add additional meaning to the sentence. Students should try to use more than one comma in a sentence that demonstrates all three purposes for commas. **LIGHT**

What Is the Horror Genre?   **89**

THE TELL-TALE HEART

Short Story by Edgar Allan Poe

GENRE ELEMENTS
SHORT STORY

Remind students that a **short story** is a work of fiction that is considerably shorter than a novel and which typically can be read in one sitting, but still includes all the basic elements of fiction. Review with students that the action in a short story often takes place in a compressed time frame and not a lot of attention is given to background information or characterization. In this lesson, students will read a classic short story and work of horror, "The Tell-Tale Heart" by the 19th-century American author Edgar Allan Poe.

LEARNING OBJECTIVES

- Cite evidence to support analysis of the story.
- Conduct research about Edgar Allan Poe.
- Determine whether the narrator of a story is reliable or unreliable.
- Identify words and phrases that build suspense in the text.
- Compare and contrast information and ideas in the story.
- Create and act out a dramatization of part of the story.
- **Language** Discuss literary elements of a text using *alike* and *different.*

TEXT COMPLEXITY

Quantitative Measures	The Tell-Tale Heart	Lexile: 850L
Qualitative Measures	**Ideas Presented** Many implied ideas, especially about the narrator's actions and reasons.	
	Structure Used Uses a chronological structure in which ideas are sequential.	
	Language Used Some language is archaic and some word order is unexpected.	
	Knowledge Required The text deals with an unusual situation but one which can easily be imagined.	

RESOURCES

- Unit 2 Response Log
- Selection Audio
- Text In Focus: Visualizing
- Close Read Screencasts: Modeled Discussions
- Reading Studio: Notice & Note
- Level Up Tutorial: Suspense and Foreshadowing
- Writing Studio: Writing Narratives
- Vocabulary Studio: Using a Dictionary
- Grammar Studio: Module 5: The Phrase; Module 6: The Clause
- "The Tell-Tale Heart" Selection Test

SUMMARIES

English

"The Tell-Tale Heart" is narrated by an unbalanced man who kills his neighbor for reasons that seem to make sense to him—but which likely make no sense at all to the reader. After murdering the neighbor, the narrator conceals his work and calmly greets police officers who have been sent to the scene by reports of screams. The narrator deflects the officers' concerns, but soon becomes aware of a sound that he believes is the beating of his dead victim's heart. Though the sound is heard only by him, he confesses his crime.

Spanish

La versión cinematográfica de "La pata de mono" cuenta básicamente la misma historia que el cuento de W.W. Jacobs, sobre la cual se basa. Un hombre recibe una pata de mono disecada y le dicen que ésta puede concederle a su dueño tres deseos. Él se muestra escéptico al principio, pero pide un deseo de todos modos. El deseo se hace realidad, pero resulta en la muerte de su hijo. Un tiempo después su esposa, profundamente afligida, hace que use el segundo deseo para que su hijo vuelva a casa. No obstante, el hijo ya no es humano y el hombre usa su último deseo para que se vaya. Un año después, la esposa muere y el esposo queda enfermísimo.

SMALL-GROUP OPTIONS

Have students work in small groups to read and discuss the selection.

Experts in the Field

- Have each student become an "expert" on a particular aspect of the story: an individual paragraph, the types of phrases used, and so on.
- Form small groups consisting of experts on different materials. For instance, a group might include a student who has looked closely at paragraphs 1–2 and others who have looked closely at other sections of the story.
- Have students take turns sharing what they know while other students take notes.
- Encourage students to build on one another's knowledge.

Developing Questions

- Have students generate questions about the story.
- Tell students to write each question on an index card.
- Ask a volunteer to read one of his or her question cards aloud. Have other students with the same or similar questions join that student to form a group.
- Continue until all students have joined a group.
- Have students discuss the questions and report back to the class.

Text X-Ray: English Learner Support
for "The Tell-Tale Heart"

Use the Text X-Ray and the supports and scaffolds in the Teacher's Edition to help guide students at different proficiency levels through the selection.

INTRODUCE THE SELECTION
DISCUSS STORY NARRATION

In this lesson, students will need to be able to discuss how writers establish an atmosphere of fear in a horror story. One way writers do this is through careful selection of how the story will be narrated. Provide the following information:

- First-person narration is told directly through the eyes of a single person, usually an important character in the story. Words such as *I*, *me*, and *my* are common in this narrative style.
- Third-person narration is told by an outside narrator. Words such as *I* and *me* are absent outside of dialogue.

Explain to students that horror writers often use first-person narration, as Poe does in this story, because it is more immediate: the writer can give the reader a sense of the thoughts and feelings of a character who is narrating the story. Use these sentence frames to help students understand the distinction between the two narrative styles and their importance in horror stories:

- *Words like* I *and* my *are common in* _____.
- *Horror writers might use first-person narration because* _____.

CULTURAL REFERENCES

The following vocabulary terms may be unfamiliar to students:

- *Hearken!* (paragraph 1): Listen!
- *mad* (paragraph 2): insane (rather than angry)
- *lantern* (paragraph 4): a portable light that uses flame rather than electricity
- *chamber* (paragraph 4): room, particularly a bedroom

LISTENING

Understand Characters

Help students explain what they learn about characters in a short story. Remind them that writers carefully choose words and phrases to help readers understand the characters in a fictional text.

Have students listen as you read aloud paragraphs 1–3. Use the following supports with students at varying proficiency levels:

- Tell students that you will ask them questions about what they just heard. Ask questions that can be answered *yes* or *no*. For example, ask: *Did the narrator have good hearing?* (yes) **SUBSTANTIAL**
- Have students answer questions about the main character based on what they heard. For example, ask: *What did the narrator dislike about the old man?* (his eye) **MODERATE**
- Have students use full sentences to answer questions about the main character based on what they heard. For instance, ask: *Why did the narrator decide to kill the old man?* (He did not like the old man's eye.) **LIGHT**

SPEAKING

Discuss Comparing and Contrasting

Point out that the lesson asks students to do a lot of comparing and contrasting. Have students discuss comparisons and contrasts in the text.

Use the following supports with students at varying proficiency levels:

- Have students complete sentence frames to talk about simple comparisons. For example, have students complete the frame *The narrator and the old man are different because _____. They are alike because _____.* **SUBSTANTIAL**
- Have students identify contrasts and comparisons in the text and use simple sentences to talk about them, such as *The narrator hears a sound. The police do not hear the sound.* **MODERATE**
- Have students use complex sentences to talk about contrasts and comparisons in the text, such as *The narrator hears a sound, but the police don't hear it.* **LIGHT**

READING

Analyze Language

Draw students' attention to examples of phrases and clauses. Review with students that a clause includes a subject and a predicate, while a phrase does not. Review the meaning of subject and predicate before beginning.

Work with students to read paragraphs 8–10. Display the first sentence of paragraph 10. Use the following supports with students at varying proficiency levels:

- Underline "wide, wide open" and ask whether it is a phrase or a clause. Model a Think Aloud explaining why this is a phrase: *I know a clause needs a verb. I do not see a verb so I think this is a phrase.* **SUBSTANTIAL**
- Have students underline a phrase and circle a clause in the displayed sentence, and explain orally how each is separated from the rest of its sentence, such as with a comma or with a dash. **MODERATE**
- Have partners work together to underline two phrases and circle two clauses within the section, and then explain how they knew which is which. **LIGHT**

WRITING

Write a Dramatic Scene

Help students read the writing assignment on p. 101. Then guide them to complete the assignment by dramatizing a scene from the story.

Use the following supports with students at varying proficiency levels:

- Take dictation from students as needed to help them record their ideas, or assign a more fluent speaker to help write their ideas down. **SUBSTANTIAL**
- Have students use sentence frames to create dialogue, such as *NARRATOR: I want to kill that man because _____. (I don't like his eye.)* **MODERATE**
- Have students write their ideas in complete sentences without paying excessive attention to grammatical and spelling guidelines. Tell them that once they have created a draft using their ideas, they can make changes to polish the final product. **LIGHT**

Connect to the
ESSENTIAL QUESTION

"The Tell-Tale Heart" is a popular short story by the 19th-century writer Edgar Allan Poe. It is considered to be a classic example of the horror genre. The ending of the story is viewed as especially dramatic and alarming. Ask students why such a frightening story would be popular for so long?

ANALYZE & APPLY

THE TELL-TALE HEART

Short Story by **Edgar Allan Poe**

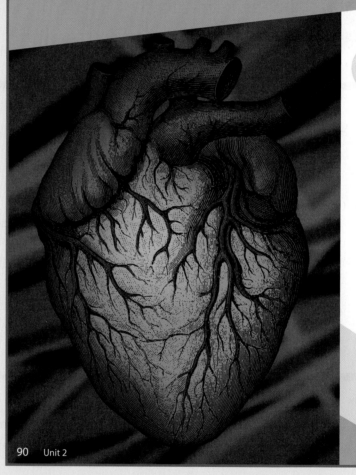

? *ESSENTIAL QUESTION:*

Why do we sometimes like to feel frightened?

QUICK START

How can you tell when someone is nervous? List some of the tell-tale signs, including how the person might act and speak.

ANALYZE POINT OF VIEW

Point of view is the method of narration used in a short story, novel, narrative poem, or work of nonfiction. In a story told from the **third-person point of view,** the **narrator,** or the voice that tells the story, is an outside observer. In a story told from the **first-person point of view,** the narrator is a character and uses the pronouns *I, me,* and *we.*

Just as you can't believe everything everyone tells you, you can't always believe everything you learn from a first-person narrator. An **unreliable narrator** is a narrator whose assessment of events cannot be trusted for some reason—he or she might be purposefully lying, mentally unstable, or too young or unsophisticated to fully understand events. To determine whether or not a narrator is reliable, consider his or her actions, attitudes, and statements, and then decide whether he or she is generally trustworthy.

As you read "The Tell-Tale Heart," look for clues that tell you whether the narrator is reliable or unreliable.

ANALYZE SUSPENSE

Suspense is the sense of growing tension, fear, and excitement felt by the reader. When a story is suspenseful, the reader becomes increasingly curious about what will happen next. Writers use different techniques to create suspense in fiction. Some of these are listed in the chart below. Fill in the chart with examples of these techniques as you read "The Tell-Tale Heart."

TECHNIQUE	EXAMPLE
Describing a character's anxiety or fear	
Using vivid words to describe dramatic sights, sounds, or feelings	
Repeating words, phrases, or characters' actions	

GENRE ELEMENTS: SHORT STORY

- includes the basic elements of fiction—setting, characters, plot, conflict, and theme
- centers on one particular moment or event in the main character's life
- can be read in one sitting

The Tell-Tale Heart   91

QUICK START

Have students read the Quick Start question. Have them make a two-column chart, one showing actions (such as looking down or biting fingernails) and the other showing speech (such as stammering or speaking in an unnaturally high voice). Have students share their lists and reasons for including each item.

ANALYZE POINT OF VIEW

Review with students the differences between a first-person narrator and a third-person narrator. Analyze the following examples together:

- First-person narrator: *I was never kinder to the old man than during the whole week before I killed him.*
- Third-person narrator: *He told himself that he was kind to the old man in the week before he killed him, but it was the delusion of a madman.*

Emphasize that not all first-person narrators are trustworthy. Some narrators are reliable and describe events accurately, but some narrators are unreliable and give a skewed, or false, view of events. For example, should the reader trust a narrator's claim of kindness in the example above? Why? Ask students to think of a time when they told a story involving themselves and did not include all the facts—and why they might have done so.

ANALYZE SUSPENSE

Read the text with students and call their attention to the examples of technique given in the box. Point out that building suspense is a key to writing an effective suspense story. Readers need to feel the tension rising as they read further.

Suggest that students ask these questions to help them analyze how the writer of this text builds suspense:

- Which words are especially effective in establishing a mood or a feeling?
- Which actions of the narrator suggest that he may not be entirely sane?
- Which images does the writer use to create anxiety or fear?

TEACH

CRITICAL VOCABULARY

Encourage students to read all the sentences before deciding which word best completes each one. Remind them to look for context clues that match the meaning of each word.

Answers:

1. *derision*

2. *conceive*

3. *vex*

4. *hypocritical*

5. *audacity*

6. *stifle*

7. *vehemently*

8. *crevice*

■ English Learner Support

Use Cognates Explain that some Critical Vocabulary words have Spanish cognates, such as *conceive/concebir* and *hypocritical/hipocrita*. **ALL LEVELS**

LANGUAGE CONVENTIONS

Remind students that phrases and clauses are parts of sentences and that they are often not the most important parts. Point out that in the example given, the phrases set off by dashes are simply repeating the original idea. Explain that dashes are a common way to set off these clauses. Model reading the sentence so students can hear the longer pauses indicated by the dashes. Discuss how the dashes add to the effectiveness of the sentence. (*Students might note that the piling up of the same idea makes the narrator seem somewhat frantic and overexcited.*)

 ANNOTATION MODEL

Remind students they can use any kind of annotation that works well for them, including underlining, circling, and writing questions.

 GET READY

CRITICAL VOCABULARY

conceive	stifle	audacity	derision
vex	crevice	vehemently	hypocritical

To see how many Critical Vocabulary words you already know, use them to complete the sentences.

1. Expressing an unpopular opinion often leads to _____.

2. It's difficult to _____ that someone could be so cruel.

3. My brother loves to _____ me whenever he gets a chance.

4. A _____ person says one thing and does another.

5. _____ is a characteristic of people who take risks.

6. I wanted to shout out in fear, but I had to _____ my reaction.

7. The convict _____ denied committing the crime.

8. My keys fell into a deep _____ while I was rock climbing.

LANGUAGE CONVENTIONS

Phrases and Clauses In this lesson, you will learn about one way of using phrases and clauses in writing. Edgar Allan Poe often separates a phrase or a clause from the rest of a sentence by using dashes:

You should have seen how wisely I proceeded—with what caution—with what foresight—with what dissimulation I went to work!

As you read, note how Poe uses dashes to set off phrases and clauses.

ANNOTATION MODEL   **NOTICE & NOTE**

As you read, note how the author's use of point of view and suspense builds tension. Also mark up evidence that supports your own ideas. In the model, you can see one reader's notes about "The Tell-Tale Heart."

> 1 True!—nervous—<u>very, very dreadfully nervous</u> I had been and am! but <u>why *will* you say that I am mad?</u> The disease had sharpened my senses—not destroyed—not dulled them. Above all was the sense of hearing acute. I heard all things in the heaven and in the earth. I heard many things in hell. How, then, am I mad? . . .

POV: The person telling the story is very nervous.

I already feel the suspense. Why is he nervous? Who says he is mad?

BACKGROUND

Edgar Allan Poe (1809–1849) was born in Boston to parents who were traveling actors. Orphaned by the time he was three, he moved to Virginia, where friends of his family raised him. As a young man, Poe worked as a journalist while writing the stories and poems that would earn him the title "father of the modern mystery." After his young wife died, Poe fell into despair. He passed away two years later. His dark and sometimes horrifying works perhaps mirror the darkness and sadness of his own short life.

THE TELL-TALE HEART

Short Story by Edgar Allan Poe

SETTING A PURPOSE

As you read, pay attention to the way the narrator describes himself. What makes him unusual?

1 True!—nervous—very, very dreadfully nervous I had been and am! but why *will* you say that I am mad? The disease had sharpened my senses—not destroyed—not dulled them. Above all was the sense of hearing acute. I heard all things in the heaven and in the earth. I heard many things in hell. How, then, am I mad? Hearken! and observe how healthily—how calmly I can tell you the whole story.

2 It is impossible to say how first the idea entered my brain; but once **conceived,** it haunted me day and night. Object there was none. Passion there was none. I loved the old man. He had never wronged me. He had never given me insult. For his gold I had no desire. I think it was his eye! yes, it was this! He had the eye of a vulture—a pale blue eye, with a film over it. Whenever it fell upon me, my blood ran cold; and so by degrees—very gradually—I made up my

Close Read

Notice & Note

Use the side margins to notice and note signposts in the text.

CONTRASTS AND CONTRADICTIONS

Notice & Note: In paragraphs 1–2, mark details that contradict each other or that contrast with your normal expectations.

Critique: Do these details make you want to keep reading, or are they merely confusing? Explain.

conceive
(kən-sēv´) *v.* When you *conceive* an idea, you think of it.

The Tell-Tale Heart 93

BACKGROUND

Have students read the Background note. Tell students that Poe's most famous works, like this short story, tend to be grim and involve death, loss, and fear. Explain that there are good reasons to believe that the tragedies he experienced had an impact on his themes as a writer.

SETTING A PURPOSE

Direct students to use the Setting a Purpose prompt to focus their reading.

▶ CONTRASTS AND CONTRADICTIONS

Authors use **contrasts and contradictions** to highlight traits in their characters. Identifying these signposts helps the reader better understand the character development. As an example of a possible contradiction, point out that students might expect a person who has a disease to have dulled senses, not more acute ones. (***Answer:*** *Students may note that hearing "things in heaven" or in hell is not possible. If students find the details confusing, acknowledge the confusion and remind them that challenging themselves can lead to greater learning.*)

🔵 ENGLISH LEARNER SUPPORT

Learning Strategies Have students create a simple flowchart to list the events of the story in the order they take place. For each event, have them write a sentence about the event and circle it. Then they should draw an arrow pointing to the next event. Have students use their flowcharts as the basis for conversations about the story. They can use the flowcharts to practice time-order words such as *first/next/last* and to discuss the way the suspense builds throughout the story. **LIGHT**

CLOSE READ SCREENCAST

Modeled Discussion Have students click the Close Read icon in their eBooks to access a screencast in which readers discuss and annotate paragraph 1, a key passage that introduces the story.

As a class, view and discuss this video. Then have students work in pairs to do an independent close read of an additional passage—the narrator's description of what he experiences as he speaks with the police officers (paragraph 17).

 Close Read Practice PDF

ENGLISH LEARNER SUPPORT

Compare and Contrast Guide students to compare and contrast events in paragraph 4 that take place during the night with events that take place in the morning. Have them mark each in a separate color.

ASK STUDENTS to discuss how the narrator's actions are different during the different times of day. (**Answer:** *In the morning he is friendly. In the night he seems like he is trying to hurt the old man.*) **LIGHT**

AGAIN AND AGAIN

Point out that much of the story contains **repetition**, or the use of certain words and phrases again and again, but that paragraph 4 is especially repetitive. Explain that repetition is a common device in poetry but is often found in fiction as well. Ask students to describe the effect of repetition in this paragraph. (**Answer:** *It may show that the narrator is not in his right mind or that it is extremely important to him that the reader understand exactly what he has done.*)

ANALYZE POINT OF VIEW

Remind students of the concept of the **unreliable narrator**. Have them look for evidence in paragraph 4 that suggests the unreliability of the narrator. Point out that the narrator claims he "thrust" his head in the door but that it took an hour to do so. Ask students whether this seems realistic. (**Answer:** *"I felt the extent of my own powers—of my sagacity"; "I fairly chuckled at the idea." The narrator seems to have an overly positive view of his own abilities.*)

CRITICAL VOCABULARY

conceive: To *conceive* an idea is to think of it.

ASK STUDENTS whether the narrator is proud of conceiving a single idea or a group of them. (*The narrator is taking pride in conceiving or thinking up a single idea.*)

vex: A person who *vexes* other people annoys them.

ASK STUDENTS who or what is *vexing* the narrator. (*The Evil Eye is what vexes or annoys the narrator.*)

94 Unit 2

AGAIN AND AGAIN

Notice & Note: In paragraph 4, mark details or ideas that the narrator keeps repeating as he tells his story.

Infer: Why do you think the narrator repeats these ideas again and again?

vex

(vĕks) *v.* If you *vex* someone, you annoy that person.

ANALYZE POINT OF VIEW

Annotate: In paragraph 5, mark details that suggest whether the narrator can or cannot be trusted to describe events as they truly are.

Infer: Is the narrator reliable or unreliable? Explain why you think so.

mind to take the life of the old man, and thus rid myself of the eye forever.

3 Now this is the point. You fancy me mad. Madmen know nothing. But you should have seen *me*. You should have seen how wisely I proceeded—with what caution—with what foresight—with what dissimulation¹ I went to work!

4 I was never kinder to the old man than during the whole week before I killed him. And every night, about midnight, I turned the latch of his door and opened it—oh, so gently! And then, when I had made an opening sufficient for my head, I put in a dark lantern, all <u>closed, closed</u>, so that no light shone out, and <u>then I thrust in my head</u>. Oh, you would have laughed to see <u>how cunningly I thrust it in! I moved it slowly—very, very slowly,</u> so that I might not disturb the old man's sleep. It took me an hour to place my whole head within the opening so far that I could see him as he lay upon his bed. Ha!—<u>would a madman have been so wise as this?</u> And then, when my head was well in the room, I undid the lantern <u>cautiously—oh, so cautiously—cautiously</u> (for the hinges creaked)—I undid it just so much that a single thin ray fell upon the vulture eye. And this I did for seven long nights—every night just at midnight—but I found the eye always closed; and so it was impossible to do the work; for it was not the old man who **vexed** me, but his Evil Eye. And every morning, when the day broke, I went boldly into the chamber, and spoke courageously to him, calling him by name in a hearty tone, and inquiring how he had passed the night. So you see he would have been a very profound old man, indeed, to suspect that every night, just at twelve, I looked in upon him while he slept.

5 Upon the eighth night I was more than usually cautious in opening the door. A watch's minute hand moves more quickly than did mine. Never before that night had <u>I *felt* the extent of my own powers—of my sagacity.²</u> <u>I could scarcely contain my feelings of triumph.</u> To think that there I was, opening the door, little by little, and he not even to dream of my secret deeds or thoughts. <u>I fairly chuckled at the idea</u>; and perhaps he heard me; for he moved on the bed suddenly, as if startled. Now you may think that I drew back—but no. His room was as black as pitch

---

¹ **dissimulation** (dĭ-sĭm´yə-lā´shən): a hiding of one's true feelings.
² **sagacity** (sə-găs´ĭ-tē): sound judgment.

with the thick darkness (for the shutters were close fastened, through fear of robbers), and so I knew that he could not see the opening of the door, and I kept pushing it on steadily, steadily.

6   I had my head in, and was about to open the lantern, when my thumb slipped upon the tin fastening, and the old man sprang up in the bed, crying out—"Who's there?"

7   I kept quite still and said nothing. For a whole hour I did not move a muscle, and in the meantime I did not hear him lie down. He was still sitting up in the bed listening,—just as I have done, night after night, hearkening to the death watches[3] in the wall.

8   Presently I heard a slight groan, and I knew it was the groan of mortal terror. It was not a groan of pain or grief—oh, no—it was the low, **stifled** sound that arises from the bottom of the soul when overcharged with awe. I knew the sound well. Many a night, just at midnight, when all the world slept, it has welled up from my own bosom, deepening, with its dreadful echo, the terrors that distracted me. I say I knew it well. I knew what the old man felt, and pitied him, although I chuckled at heart. I knew that he had been lying awake ever since the first slight noise, when he had turned in the bed. His fears had been ever since growing upon him. He had been trying to fancy them causeless, but could not. He had been saying to himself—"It is nothing but the wind in the chimney—it is only a mouse crossing the floor," or "it is merely a cricket which has made a single chirp." Yes, he has been trying to comfort himself with these suppositions; but he had found all in vain. *All in vain;* because Death, in approaching him, had stalked with his black shadow before him, and enveloped the victim. And it was the mournful influence of the unperceived shadow that caused him to feel—although he neither saw nor heard—to *feel* the presence of my head within the room.

9   When I had waited a long time, very patiently, without hearing him lie down, I resolved to open a little—a very, very little **crevice** in the lantern. So I opened it—you cannot imagine how stealthily, stealthily—until, at length, a single dim ray, like the thread of the spider, shot from out the crevice and fell full upon the vulture eye.

---

[3] **death watches**: deathwatch beetles—insects that make a tapping sound with their heads.

stifle
(stī′fəl) *v.* If you *stifle* something, you smother it.

LANGUAGE CONVENTIONS
Annotate: In the first four sentences of paragraph 8, underline each clause (a group of words containing a subject and verb). Circle each phrase set off by commas or dashes.

Evaluate: Does Poe's use of different sentence structures make his writing more interesting to read? Why?

crevice
(krĕv′ĭs) *n.* A *crevice* is a narrow crack.

LANGUAGE CONVENTIONS

Tell students that Poe often uses dashes to set off clauses and phrases. Explain that commas can also set off clauses and phrases, but dashes create more emphasis and drama than commas do. Read paragraph 7 aloud. Ask students to compare the effects of the commas in the paragraph with the dash in the last sentence. Then point out the variety of sentence structures used in this story (clauses and phrases that appear at the beginning, end, and middle of sentences, for example). (**Answer:** *Students should conclude that the varying sentence structures make the writing more interesting; using the same sentence structure can quickly become boring and predictable.*)

For **listening support** for students at varying proficiency levels, see the **Text X-Ray** on page 90C.

APPLYING ACADEMIC VOCABULARY

☐ convention   ☑ predict   ☑ psychology   ☐ summary   ☐ technique

Write and Discuss Have students turn to a partner to discuss the following questions. Guide students to include the vocabulary words *predict* and *psychology* in their responses. Ask students to share their responses with the class.

• What do you **predict** will happen next in the story? Explain.

• How does the **psychology** of the narrator—that is, his thought processes and his mental state—affect his description of events?

CRITICAL VOCABULARY

stifle: To *stifle* something is to strangle or suppress it. A person, an idea, or a sound can all be *stifled.*

ASK STUDENTS to identify who or what is being stifled in the text. (*A sound is being stifled.*)

crevice: A *crevice* is a narrow gap or crack.

ASK STUDENTS to identify the importance of the crevice in this sentence of the text. (*The crevice allows a beam of light to appear from the lantern.*)

ANALYZE SUSPENSE

Explain to students that writers often use especially vivid, sensory words and phrases to build suspense. Remind them that sensory language is related to the five senses: see, smell, taste, touch, and hear. **(Answer:** *These phrases make the situation seem especially frightening or tense; a person who "scarcely breathe[s]," for instance, is probably very nervous. These words and phrases heighten suspense by showing that the narrator might actually go ahead and kill the old man.)*

■ English Learner Support

Oral Reading Read a few sentences from paragraph 12 aloud for students. Use a dramatic voice that fits the tension in the story. Talk with students about how you can change the pitch and speed of your speech to indicate stress or tension. Then have students read a sentence or two aloud using their own dramatic voices. **LIGHT**

TEXT IN FOCUS

Visualizing Have students view the **Text in Focus** video in their eBook to learn how to use descriptive details to visualize the story's characters, setting, and events. Then have students use **Text in Focus Practice** to apply what they have learned.

 NOTICE & NOTE

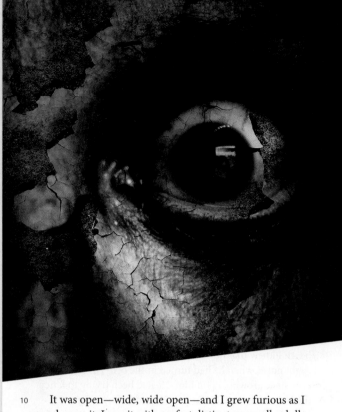

ANALYZE SUSPENSE

Annotate: Mark words and phrases in paragraphs 11–12 that Poe uses to create suspense.

Analyze: Why do these details create suspense?

10 It was open—wide, wide open—and I grew furious as I gazed upon it. I saw it with perfect distinctness—all a dull blue, with a hideous veil over it that chilled the very marrow in my bones; but I could see nothing else of the old man's face or person: for I had directed the ray as if by instinct, precisely upon the damned spot.

11 And now have I not told you that what you mistake for madness is but over-acuteness of the senses?—now, I say, there came to my ears a low, dull, quick sound, such as a watch makes when enveloped in cotton. I knew *that* sound well too. It was the beating of the old man's heart. It increased my fury, as the <u>beating of a drum</u> stimulates the soldier into courage.

12 But even yet I refrained and kept still. I <u>scarcely breathed.</u> I held the lantern motionless. I tried how steadily I could maintain the ray upon the eye. Meantime the <u>hellish tattoo⁴ of the heart</u> increased. It grew quicker and quicker, and louder and louder every instant. The old man's terror *must* have been

⁴ **hellish tattoo:** awful drumming.

WHEN STUDENTS STRUGGLE . . .

Analyze Suspense Have students work independently or in pairs to identify words and phrases that might be used to establish suspense in a story. Read aloud several words and phrases, including suspenseful ones from the story (such as *dreadful* and *shrieked*) and non-suspenseful words (such as *ordinary* and *said*). Have students sort the words and generate more of their own.

For additional support, go to the **Reading Studio** and assign the following **Level Up Tutorial: Suspense and Foreshadowing.**

extreme! It grew louder, I say, louder every moment!—do you mark me well? I have told you that I am nervous: so I am. And now at the dead hour of the night, amid the dreadful silence of that old house, so strange a noise as this excited me to uncontrollable terror. Yet, for some minutes longer I refrained and stood still. But the beating grew louder, louder! I thought the heart must burst. And now a new anxiety seized me—the sound would be heard by a neighbor! The old man's hour had come! With a loud yell, I threw open the lantern and leaped into the room. He shrieked once—once only. In an instant I dragged him to the floor, and pulled the heavy bed over him. I then smiled gaily, to find the deed so far done. But, for many minutes, the heart beat on with a muffled sound. This, however, did not vex me; it would not be heard through the wall. At length it ceased. The old man was dead. I removed the bed and examined the corpse. Yes, he was stone, stone dead. I placed my hand upon the heart and held it there many minutes. There was no pulsation. He was stone dead. His eye would trouble me no more.

13 If still you think me mad, you will think so no longer when I describe the wise precautions I took for the concealment of the body. The night waned, and I worked hastily, but in silence. First of all I dismembered the corpse. I cut off the head and the arms and the legs.

14 I then took up three planks from the flooring of the chamber, and deposited all between the scantlings.[5] I then replaced the boards so cleverly, so cunningly, that no human eye—not even *his*—could have detected anything wrong. There was nothing to wash out—no stain of any kind—no blood-spot whatever. I had been too wary for that. A tub had caught all—ha! ha!

15 When I made an end of these labors, it was four o'clock— still dark as midnight. As the bell sounded the hour, there came a knocking at the street door. I went down to open it with a light heart,—for what had I *now* to fear? There entered three men, who introduced themselves, with perfect suavity,[6] as officers of the police. A shriek had been heard by a neighbor during the night: suspicion of foul play had been aroused; information had been lodged at the police office, and they (the officers) had been deputed to search the premises.

---
[5] **scantlings:** small wooden beams supporting the floor.
[6] **suavity** (swä´vĭ-tē): graceful politeness.

ANALYZE POINT OF VIEW
Annotate: In paragraphs 13–14, mark details that show how the narrator tries to convince readers that he is sane and reliable.

Evaluate: What effect do the narrator's explanations have on the reader?

The Tell-Tale Heart 97

 ANALYZE POINT OF VIEW

Review with students some of the reasons a narrator may not be reliable. For instance, the narrator may wish to portray him- or herself in a more positive light, or the narrator may be out of touch with reality. Ask students to look for examples in paragraph 12 that show that the narrator is perhaps delusional. For example, the narrator's fear that the neighbor will hear his heartbeat is irrational and unrealistic. (**Answer:** *Most readers will not be convinced of the narrator's sanity because of his previous unreliability and because murdering someone—especially for such a reason—is not the act of a sane person.*)

EL ENGLISH LEARNER SUPPORT

Summarize Guide students to summarize this part of the text.

Label the order of events in paragraphs 13 and 14 as *first, next,* and *last*. _____, he chopped up the body. _____, he pulled up the floor boards. _____, he hid the body under the floor. **SUBSTANTIAL**

Focus on paragraphs 13 and 14. Have students complete sentence frames beginning *First, _____; Next _____;* and *Last, _____.* **MODERATE**

Use paragraphs 13, 14, and 15. Have students generate their own sentences to summarize the events described in these paragraphs. **LIGHT**

TEACH

CONTRASTS AND CONTRADICTIONS

Remind students that a **first-person point of view** narrator can be unreliable. Point out the contradiction between the narrator's claims of feeling at ease in paragraph 17 with the physical evidence of his growing anxiety. Have students identify the details that show this contrast and draw conclusions based on what they know about the narrator. (*Answer: Sentences such as "I gasped for breath—and yet the officers heard it not" indicate that the narrator is hearing what sounds like a heartbeat, but the police do not hear anything out of the ordinary. Because we know that the narrator is unreliable and acts peculiarly, it seems likely that the noise is only in his head.*)

CRITICAL VOCABULARY

audacity: This word means fearlessness or exceptional boldness. The implication is that someone ought to be worried or frightened but is not acting in that way.

ASK STUDENTS to explain what about the narrator's actions indicates his audacity. (*He has just killed a man and is having an ordinary conversation with police officers.*)

vehemently: This word means "with intense emotion." The narrator is speaking loudly and with animation.

ASK STUDENTS why the narrator is speaking vehemently. (*He is using his voice to hide the sound from the police.*)

derision: This word implies insult or mockery.

ASK STUDENTS why the narrator assumes the police are treating him with derision. (*He thinks they can hear the sound and are simply pretending they can't to be cruel.*)

hypocritical: This word indicates that someone is behaving in a false or deceptive way, out of line with his or her beliefs.

ASK STUDENTS why the narrator believes the police are smiling hypocritically. (*He thinks they are pretending to be kind but are actually planning to arrest him.*)

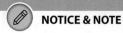

16   I smiled,—for *what* had I to fear? I bade the gentlemen welcome. The shriek, I said, was my own in a dream. The old man, I mentioned, was absent in the country. I took my visitors all over the house. I bade them search—search *well*. I led them, at length, to *his* chamber. I showed them his treasures, secure, undisturbed. In the enthusiasm of my confidence, I brought chairs into the room, and desired them here to rest from their fatigues, while I myself, in the wild **audacity** of my perfect triumph, placed my own seat upon the very spot beneath which reposed the corpse of the victim.

17   The officers were satisfied. My *manner* had convinced them. I was singularly at ease. They sat, and while I answered cheerily, they chatted of familiar things. But, ere long, I felt myself getting pale and wished them gone. My head ached, and I fancied a ringing in my ears: but still they sat and still chatted. The ringing became more distinct:—it continued and became more distinct: I talked more freely to get rid of the feeling: but it continued and gained definitiveness—until at length, I found that the noise was *not* within my ears.

18   No doubt I now grew *very* pale;—but I talked more fluently, and with a heightened voice. Yet the sound increased—and what could I do? It was *a low, dull, quick sound—much such a sound as a watch makes when enveloped in cotton.* I gasped for breath—and yet the officers heard it not. I talked more quickly—more **vehemently**; but the noise steadily increased. I arose and argued about trifles, in a high key and with violent gesticulations,[7] but the noise steadily increased. Why *would* they not be gone? I paced the floor to and fro with heavy strides, as if excited to fury by the observation of the men— but the noise steadily increased. What *could* I do? I foamed— I raved—I swore. I swung the chair upon which I had been sitting, and grated it upon the boards, but the noise arose over all and continually increased. It grew louder—louder—*louder!* And still the men chatted pleasantly, and smiled. Was it possible they heard not?—no, no! They heard!—they suspected!—they *knew!*—they were making a *mockery* of my horror!—this I thought, and this I think. But anything was better than this agony! Anything was more tolerable than this **derision**! I could bear those **hypocritical** smiles no longer! I felt that I must scream or die!—and now—again!—hark! louder! louder! *louder!*—

_____

[7] **gesticulations** (jĕ-stĭk´yə-lā´shəns): energetic gestures of the hands or arms.

audacity
(ô-dăs´ĭ-tē) *n. Audacity* is shameless daring or boldness.

CONTRASTS AND CONTRADICTIONS

Notice & Note: Mark details that show the contrast between the narrator's perception of the noise and the police officers'.

Draw Conclusions: What conclusion can you draw about this noise?

vehemently
(vē´ə-mənt-lē) *adv.* If you do something *vehemently,* you do it with intense emotion.

derision
(dĭ-rĭzh´ən) *n. Derision* is jeering laughter or ridicule.

hypocritical
(hĭp´ə-krĭt´ĭ-kəl) *adj.* If someone is *hypocritical,* the person is false or deceptive.

TO CHALLENGE STUDENTS...

Analyze Voice   Tell students that in literature, the term **voice** has to do with how human personalities appear in texts. Explain that this narrator has an unusually distinctive voice. Have students identify sentence fragments, unusual placements of punctuation, and unconventional word order in "The Tell-Tale Heart" to explore the narrator's personality and voice. Have students describe the voice of the narrator and discuss the effect of Poe's word choices on creating the narrator's voice.

19   "Villains!" I shrieked, "dissemble⁸ no more! I admit the deed!—tear up the planks!—here, here!—it is the beating of his hideous heart!"

_____
⁸ **dissemble:** pretend.

CHECK YOUR UNDERSTANDING

Answer these questions before moving on to the **Analyze the Text** section on the following page.

1 What is the narrator's reason for killing the old man?

   A The old man has insulted the narrator many times.

   B The narrator cannot bear to hear the beating of the old man's heart.

   C The old man's eye reminds the narrator of a vulture's.

   D The narrator hopes to inherit the old man's treasures.

2 To prove he is not mad, the narrator —

   F describes how cunning and cautious he is

   G waits until the eighth night to kill the old man

   H says he pities the old man but laughs in his heart

   J hides the old man's body under the floor boards

3 The police officers cannot hear the old man's heart because —

   A the narrator is talking too loudly

   B they are sitting too far away from the body

   C their senses are not as acute as the narrator's

   D the heart is not actually beating

CHECK YOUR UNDERSTANDING

Have students answer the questions independently.

Answers:

  1. C

  2. F

  3. D

If they answer any questions incorrectly, have them reread the text to confirm their understanding. Then they may proceed to ANALYZE THE TEXT on p.100.

 ENGLISH LEARNER SUPPORT

Oral Assessment Use the following questions to assess students' comprehension and speaking skills. Have students answer in complete sentences if possible. Provide sentence frames as needed.

  1. Why does the narrator kill the old man? (*The narrator killed the old man because he thought that the old man's eye was like a vulture's eye.*)

  2. How does the narrator try to show the reader that he is not insane? (*He tells the reader how cunning and careful he is.*)

  3. Why can't the police officers hear the old man's heart? (*They can't hear the heart because it isn't actually beating.*)
  SUBSTANTIAL/MODERATE

ANALYZE THE TEXT

Possible answers

1. **DOK 2:** *The narrator's statements are immediately suspicious because he mentions "the disease" and its impact on his senses. This suggests that an illness has affected his brain. His further comments about foresight suggest a distorted view of his intelligence.*

2. **DOK 4:** *The narrator waits to kill the old man because he wants the "vulture eye" to be open. Readers sense the narrator's mounting anxiety and feel tension about what will happen when the eye does open.*

3. **DOK 3:** *The narrator claims to hear the old man's heart beating. The murderer describes his own anger at the sound, giving readers an awareness of his thinking and feelings.*

4. **DOK 4:** *Yes. The narrator is mentally ill, so the reader cannot trust his view of events. The reader wonders what really happened and what this unbalanced person is going to do next, which adds to the tension.*

5. **DOK 4:** *The narrator describes the "eye of the vulture" in detail ("a pale, blue eye, with a film over it"). The sense that something very bad is going to happen increases the sense of suspense.*

RESEARCH

Point out to students that they need to be sure the information they find is reliable. That is especially true with online sources, as many people who post information online do not ensure that it is correct.

Extend Remind students to think about their intonation, emphasis, phrasing, and pauses as they practice reading the poems.

ANALYZE THE TEXT

Support your responses with evidence from the text. ☰ NOTEBOOK

1. **Infer** Does the narrator's opinion of himself in paragraphs 1–2 make him seem more reliable, or less? Explain your choice.

2. **Analyze** What prevents the narrator from killing the old man during the first seven nights? Explain how his inaction contributes to the story's suspense.

3. **Draw Conclusions** Reread paragraphs 9–11. What do readers learn from this first-person narration about the narrator's subjective, or personal, experience?

4. **Evaluate** Does the reader's inability to trust the narrator increase the suspense in this story? Explain your answer.

5. **Notice & Note** In what way does the repeated image of the "eye of a vulture" help to create suspense?

RESEARCH TIP
Just as a narrator can be unreliable, so can a website. Be sure to assess the quality of any online sources you use. Personal websites may provide inaccurate information. They may be **biased**, or unfairly slanted toward one side. The websites of museums, universities, and well-known encyclopedias are more likely to be reliable.

RESEARCH

Want to learn more about the writer who created the "very, very dreadfully nervous"—and very murderous—narrator in "The Tell-Tale Heart"? Use various sources to research answers to the following questions about Edgar Allan Poe's career.

QUESTION	ANSWER
What was Poe's first published work?	*Tamerlane and Other Poems (1827)*
What different kinds of writing did Poe do?	*poetry, horror, and mystery*
What are some of Poe's most famous works?	*The Raven," "Annabel Lee," "The Bells," "The Fall of the House of Usher," and "The Murders in the Rue Morgue"*

Extend Locate one of Poe's famous poems. Practice reading it aloud, using your voice to convey the mood or feeling of the poem. Then get together with a partner and read your poems to each other.

CREATE AND DRAMATIZE

Write a Scene Rewrite a scene from "The Tell-Tale Heart" from the point of view of a reliable narrator.

- ❏ Review the story to find a brief scene. Identify specific details that a reliable narrator would describe differently.
- ❏ Decide whether you will write from the first-person or the third-person point of view.
- ❏ Write the scene from the perspective of your reliable narrator.

Dramatize a Scene Working alone or with one or more partners, act out an especially suspenseful scene from "The Tell-Tale Heart."

- ❏ Review your notes to identify a scene in which Poe uses point of view and other literary devices to create suspense.
- ❏ Decide how many characters your scene needs and who will play them. Write dialogue for each character.
- ❏ Practice your scene. Then perform it for the class.

 Go to the **Writing Studio: Writing Narratives** for more on writing a fictional scene.

RESPOND TO THE ESSENTIAL QUESTION

 Why do we sometimes like to feel frightened?

Gather Information Review your annotations and notes on "The Tell-Tale Heart." Then, add relevant details to your Response Log. As you determine which information to include, think about:

- the elements of a classic horror story
- why people might enjoy being spooked by Poe's suspenseful story
- whether Poe's unreliable narrator is like other characters in the unit

At the end of the unit, you can use your notes to help you write a literary analysis.

ACADEMIC VOCABULARY
As you write and discuss what you learned from the story, be sure to use the Academic Vocabulary words. Check off each of the words that you use.

- ❏ **convention**
- ❏ **predict**
- ❏ **psychology**
- ❏ **summary**
- ❏ **technique**

CREATE AND DRAMATIZE

Write a Scene Remind students that they should think about what makes an unreliable narrator unreliable. Review the differences between third- and first-person narration.

For **writing support** for students at varying proficiency levels, see the **Text X-Ray** on page 90D.

Dramatize a Scene Review elements of suspense and dramatic tension with students. Remind them to build a sense of anticipation, or the feeling that something is about to happen, into their scene to create dramatic tension. Note that contrast and contradiction in what characters say and do also creates tension. Review with students which characters will be necessary for a particular scene and work with students to help them use their voices to reflect the growing dramatic tension in the scene.

RESPOND TO THE ESSENTIAL QUESTION

Allow time for students to add details from "The Tell-Tale Heart" to their Unit 2 Response Logs.

APPLY

CRITICAL VOCABULARY

Answers

1. *Yes; people who are deliberately deceptive can be annoying.*

2. *It is extremely bold to show intense emotion while denying something that you actually did.*

3. *I might be able to use tongs or tweezers to retrieve something that had fallen into a small and narrow crack.*

4. *Students can speak up to demand that ridicule stop or can ask adults for help in stopping it.*

VOCABULARY STRATEGY:
Use a Dictionary

Answers

1. **convention:** *A formal meeting of members, representatives, or delegates, as of a political group, fraternal society, profession, or industry; a widely used and accepted device or technique, as in drama, literature, or painting: the theatrical convention of the aside*

2. *verb*

3. *The emotional and behavioral characteristics of an individual, a group, or those engaged in a given activity*

4. *Middle English, from Medieval Latin summarius, of or concerning the sum, from Latin summa, sum*

5. *the second syllable*

 RESPOND

CRITICAL VOCABULARY

WORD BANK
conceive
vex
stifle
crevice
audacity
vehemently
derision
hypocritical

Practice and Apply Use what you know about the Vocabulary words to answer these questions.

1. Would it **vex** you if someone were **hypocritical**? Why?

2. Why does it take **audacity** to **vehemently** deny that you told a lie?

3. What method can you **conceive** to get something out of a **crevice**?

4. What can you do to **stifle derision** of another student?

 Go to the **Vocabulary Studio** for more on using a dictionary.

VOCABULARY STRATEGY:
Use a Dictionary

A **dictionary** is a reference work that provides an alphabetical list of words with their meanings and pronunciations. It also may describe each word's **etymology**, or the history and origin of the word. Some dictionaries are books, while others are electronic or online resources.

Notice the parts of this dictionary entry for the word *wary*.

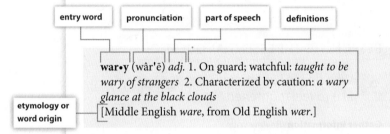

Practice and Apply Use a dictionary to answer these questions about the Academic Vocabulary words for this unit.

1. What are two different meanings for *convention*?

2. What part of speech is *predict*?

3. What definition of *psychology* fits in the sentence *Our track team has a very successful psychology*?

4. What language does *summary* originally come from?

5. Which syllable is stressed when you pronounce the word *technique*?

 ENGLISH LEARNER SUPPORT

Vocabulary Strategy Give students additional practice in using a dictionary to identify the meanings of words. Point out that dictionaries usually give common forms of words in addition to the words themselves. So, the entry for *predict* also includes *predicts*, *prediction*, and other words related to *predict*. Show students how to use this feature and what they know about language to determine the meaning of *predictions* (*more than one prediction*) and *predicted* (*made a prediction in the past*). Continue with other examples as needed. **ALL LEVELS**

LANGUAGE CONVENTIONS:
Phrases and Clauses

Sentences are built from words, phrases, and clauses. A **phrase** is a group of related words that does not contain a subject and a predicate but functions as a single part of speech. A **clause** is a group of words that contains a subject and a predicate.

Both phrases and clauses can be either restrictive or nonrestrictive. A **restrictive** phrase or clause provides information that is necessary to understand the meaning of the sentence. Here is an example of a restrictive phrase from "The Tell-Tale Heart":

> And then, when I had made an opening <u>sufficient for my head</u>, I put in a dark lantern, all closed, closed, so that no light shone out, and then I thrust in my head.

A **nonrestrictive** phrase or clause provides additional information in a sentence whose meaning is already clear. Nonrestrictive phrases and clauses are typically set off from the rest of the sentence with commas. However, Poe often uses dashes instead of commas for dramatic effect, as he does with the following nonrestrictive clause:

> So I opened it—<u>you cannot imagine how stealthily, stealthily</u>—until, at length, a single dim ray, like the thread of the spider, shot from out the crevice and fell full upon the vulture eye.

Practice and Apply In each sentence from "The Tell-Tale Heart" below, identify the underlined text as a phrase or a clause and as restrictive or nonrestrictive.

1. I knew that he had been lying awake <u>ever since the first slight noise</u>, when he had turned in the bed.

2. It was open—<u>wide, wide open</u>—and I grew furious as I gazed upon it.

3. There entered three men, <u>who introduced themselves, with perfect suavity, as officers of the police</u>.

4. . . . I myself, in the wild audacity of my perfect triumph, placed my own seat upon the very spot <u>beneath which reposed the corpse of the victim</u>.

> Go to the **Grammar Studio: The Phrase** and **The Clause** for more on phrases and clauses.

LANGUAGE CONVENTIONS:
Phrases and Clauses

Review the information about phrases and clauses with students, focusing especially on the differences between a phrase and a clause. Have students determine which of the following is a clause and which a phrase: *the person is holding a flashlight* (*clause*) and *George's boat* (*phrase*).

Then focus students' attention on the information about restrictive and nonrestrictive clauses. Emphasize that the distinction involves whether the clause or phrase is essential to understanding the sentence. Point out that students can often determine whether a phrase is restrictive or nonrestrictive by rephrasing the sentence without the clause or phrase to see whether the basic information is still present. In the initial example, for instance, leaving out the underlined phrase changes the meaning of the sentence (it no longer gives an indication of how big the opening is), so the phrase is restrictive.

Practice and Apply

1. *restrictive phrase*

2. *nonrestrictive phrase*

3. *nonrestrictive clause*

4. *restrictive clause*

 ENGLISH LEARNER SUPPORT

Language Conventions Use the following supports with students at varying proficiency levels:

- Read the following excerpts from paragraphs 1 and 2 aloud. Help students to identify whether each statement is a phrase or a clause: "how calmly I can tell you the whole story" (*clause*), "a pale blue eye with a film over it" (*predict*) **SUBSTANTIAL**

- Have students look at paragraphs 1–4 in "The Tell-Tale Heart." Have students identify one phrase and one clause and explain to a partner which is which and how they know. **MODERATE**

- Have students identify two phrases and two clauses from anywhere in "The Tell-Tale Heart." Have students determine whether each phrase or clause is restrictive or nonrestrictive. For each, have students write a sentence explaining how they knew. **LIGHT**

THE HOLLOW

Poem by Kelly Deschler

GENRE ELEMENTS
POETRY

Remind students that poetry takes many forms, but the language is usually condensed to express the emotional intensity of a moment in time. Explain that "The Hollow" is a lyric poem, which is a type of poem that describes a personal viewpoint or experience in a rhythmic pattern with a musical quality to it. To create lyric effects, authors use a variety of literary devices, such as figurative language, allusions, and rhythm and rhyme. These paint a sensory experience for the reader, permitting the reader to imagine a situation from the first-person perspective of the speaker.

LEARNING OBJECTIVES

- Make connections to ideas in other texts.
- Make inferences about the speaker of a poem.
- Demonstrate knowledge of rhyme schemes in poetry.
- Identify and analyze the use of figurative language.
- Compose a lyric poem.
- Identify and gather relevant information from a variety of sources.
- **Language** Discuss connections between a poem and a short story using the key term *connection*.

TEXT COMPLEXITY

Quantitative Measures	The Hollow	Lexile: NA
Qualitative Measures	**Ideas Presented** Multiple levels, use of symbolism, irony, satire. Some ambiguity. Greater demand for inference.	
	Structures Used Unifying rhyming pattern. Narrow perspective with single viewpoint. Conventional structures.	
	Language Used Implied meanings. Allusive and figurative language. Formal verbiage with more complex sentence structures.	
	Knowledge Required Extensive references to events or other texts. Experiences may be less familiar to some.	

Online **Ed**

RESOURCES

- Unit 2 Response Log
- Selection Audio
- Reading Studio: Notice & Note
- LEVELUP Level Up Tutorial: Elements of Literature
- LEVELUP Level Up Tutorial: Elements of Poetry
- Writing Studio: Introduction: Writing as a Process
- "The Hollow" Selection Test

SUMMARIES

English

The poem "The Hollow" is a tribute to the 18th-century horror short story "The Legend of Sleepy Hollow" by Washington Irving. Using a traditional alternate rhyme scheme and vivid sensory language, the poem describes a spooky walk through the woods on an October night, using first-person point of view.

Spanish

El poema "El hueco" es un tributo al cuento de terror "La leyenda de Sleepy Hollow". Con un estilo tradicional de esquema de rima alternativa y lenguaje sensorial vívido, el poema describe una espeluznante caminata a travěs del bosque en una noche de octubre, con un punto de vista en primera persona.

SMALL-GROUP OPTIONS

Have students work in small groups to read and discuss the selection.

Double-Entry Journal

- Have students draw a line down the middle of a sheet of paper to create two columns. Model adding quotes under the heading "Quotes from the Text" on the left side and notes under "My Notes" on the right.
- Explain that they should record important or perplexing quotes as they read "The Hollow."
- Have students write their interpretations, summaries, and questions across from the quotations.
- Then have students discuss their entries with a partner, comparing their interpretations of the same quotations.

Think-Pair-Share

- After students have read and analyzed "The Hollow," pose this question: *How does the imagery contribute to the sense of suspense?*
- Have students think about the question individually and take notes.
- Then, have pairs discuss their ideas about the question.
- Finally, ask pairs to share their responses with the class.

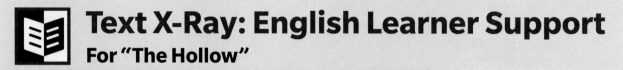

Text X-Ray: English Learner Support
For "The Hollow"

Use the Text X-Ray and the supports and scaffolds in the Teacher's Edition to help guide students at different proficiency levels through the selection.

INTRODUCE THE SELECTION
DISCUSS SENSORY LANGUAGE

In this lesson, students read a poem that appeals to the readers' senses in order to vividly evoke a first-person point of view. Students will need to be able to discuss the sensory language. Explain that sensory language relates to the five senses: sight, hearing, taste, smell, and touch. Read lines 13–16 aloud and ask students to listen for details that relate to the five senses. Point out the following:

- "dark, gnarled thicket" relates to sight
- "I walked through the fallen leaves" relates to the sense of touch
- "chirping of the cricket" and "bullfrogs croak" relate to hearing

Explain to students that using sensory language helps create a stronger first-person perspective by allowing the reader to share an experience through vivid descriptions.

CULTURAL REFERENCES

The following words or phrases may be unfamiliar to students:

- *hollow* (title, line 16): small valley
- *legends* (line 3): myths or stories from the past that are not proven
- *sleepy, little town* (line 4): a small town without much activity
- *harvest moon* (line 10): full moon in October
- *ridge* (line 11): a narrow hilltop
- *thicket* (line 13): dense group of trees or bushes
- *horseman* (line 19): man who rides a horse

LISTENING

Analyze the Rhyme Scheme

Remind students that rhymes are two or more words that share the same end sound. Read the words *cold* and *told*. Ask students what sound the two words share. (/old/) Tell students that a rhyming pattern or rhyme scheme is a way of using sound to create a rhythm or flow in a poem.

Have students listen as you read aloud the poem. Use the following supports with students at varying proficiency levels:

- Tell students you will ask some questions about what they just heard. Model that they should give a thumbs up if the answer is yes, and a thumbs down for no. For example, ask: *Does bridge rhyme with sky?* (No) *Does bridge rhyme with ridge?* (Yes) **SUBSTANTIAL**
- Provide a graphic organizer with 12 boxes labeled *a* to *l*. Direct students to write pairs or groups of rhyming words in each of the boxes as they listen to poem. Have pairs take turns rereading the lines. **MODERATE**
- After listening to the entire poem read aloud, have partners take turns reading each line so that each partner only reads rhyming lines. Ask students to label the rhyme scheme. **LIGHT**

SPEAKING

Discuss Connections

Explain that connecting a text to other texts helps a reader gain a deeper understanding. Remind students that "The Hollow" is based on the short story "The Legend of Sleepy Hollow." Ask students to make connections between the texts.

Use the following supports with students at varying proficiency levels:

- Reread the Background information with students. Ask them to identify the setting of the "The Legend of Sleepy Hollow." (*Sleepy Hollow, NY in 18th century*) Read the title of the poem, and explain that a hollow is the area between two hills. Ask students: *Do you think the poem is about the same hollow? Which words in the first stanza are connected to the short story?* (*legend, sleepy*) **SUBSTANTIAL**

- To help students express their ideas about connections, display the following sentence frames: *The setting of _____ is _____. The story _____ is like _____ because _____. The _____ connects to _____. I had a similar experience as _____ when _____. Because _____, I can infer _____.* **MODERATE**

- Have students discuss with a partner how the two texts are connected. Ask them to infer who is speaking in the poem. **LIGHT**

READING

Develop Fluency

Tell students that developing fluency allows them to read text accurately, quickly, and with expression.

Select a passage from the poem that matches students' reading abilities. Read one stanza aloud while students follow along silently. Use the following supports with students at varying proficiency levels:

- Echo read a stanza with students. Then have the students read the stanza silently several times. Repeat with additional stanzas. **SUBSTANTIAL**

- Have students read and then reread the stanza silently. Ask students to take turns reading the stanza aloud to a partner and to mark errors or hesitations. **MODERATE**

- Allow more fluent readers to select their own stanzas to read aloud. Remind them to experiment to find the natural phrasing as they read to a partner. Check their comprehension by having them summarize orally what they have read. **LIGHT**

WRITING

Write a Poem

Work with students to read the writing assignment on p. 111.

Use the following supports with students at varying proficiency levels:

- Allow students to draw a picture of their subject. Then discuss and cowrite the first few lines of their poem. Allow students to dictate the rest of their poem to a scribe. **SUBSTANTIAL**

- Discuss with students the topic of their poem. Provide a graphic organizer to help them to brainstorm and organize their ideas. Help them create a concept web with the topic in the middle and details surrounding it. For each detail, have students brainstorm associated descriptive words. Point out any rhyming words. Encourage students to use the web as a reference as they write the lines of their poem. **MODERATE**

- Remind students to make connections to the text by including specific details to create allusions. Encourage them to plan out their rhyme scheme. Have them discuss their ideas with a partner. **LIGHT**

Connect to the
? *ESSENTIAL QUESTION*

"The Hollow" falls under the horror genre because it creates a suspenseful mood as it describes a person's walk through the woods. The poem alludes to the frightening things people say about the legend of a headless horseman that haunts the area and points out spooky details in the landscape, yet the situation does not deter the speaker. Ask students to share a time when they decided to do something even though they knew it was supposed to be scary. Discuss reasons people seek out scary situations.

THE HOLLOW

Poem by **Kelly Deschler**

? *ESSENTIAL QUESTION:*

Why do we sometimes like to feel frightened?

104   Unit 2

QUICK START

The poem you are about to read uses **imagery**, a type of figurative language that draws on sensory details, to describe the sights and sounds of a cold October night. Use the graphic organizer below to write or draw about a time when you quietly observed your surroundings and how it made you feel.

What I Saw or Heard	How It Made Me Feel

MAKE CONNECTIONS

When you relate the content of literature to your own experience and prior knowledge, you **make connections** with what you read. Making connections can help you deepen and enrich your understanding of texts and gain insights into your life and the lives of others.

Many written works contain **allusions**, or references to famous people, places, events, or works of literature. The poem "The Hollow," for example, is inspired by the characters and setting of the short story "The Legend of Sleepy Hollow" by Washington Irving. Read this excerpt from the short story.

GENRE ELEMENTS: LYRIC POETRY
- usually short to convey emotional intensity
- written using first-person point of view to express the speaker's thoughts and feelings
- often uses repetition and rhyme to create a melodic quality
- includes many forms, such as sonnets, odes, and elegies

In the dead hush of midnight he could even hear the barking of the watchdog from the opposite shore of the Hudson; but it was so vague and faint as only to give an idea of his distance from this faithful companion of man. Now and then, too, the long-drawn crowing of a cock, accidentally awakened, would sound far, far off, from some farmhouse away in the hills—but it was like a dreaming sound in his ear. No signs of life occurred near him, but occasionally the melancholy chirp of a cricket, or perhaps the guttural twang of a bull-frog from a neighboring marsh, as if sleeping uncomfortably and turning suddenly in his bed.

As you read "The Hollow," make connections between the vivid descriptions in the story and in the poem.

TEACH

QUICK START

Have students read the Quick Start prompt and complete the graphic organizer with their observations and feelings. Challenge them to include specific details related to the senses to create rich, layered descriptions. Ask volunteers to share their experiences.

MAKE CONNECTIONS

Help students understand the concept of connection as ideas being linked like a chain. Point out that authors use allusions purposefully to create connections that add layers of meaning to the text. Remind students to look for these references by identifying similar descriptions of settings or characters and specific words or phrases from the other text.

Read aloud the excerpt from "The Legend of Sleepy Hollow," and ask students which details are sounds they have heard at night. (**Possible answer:** *a barking dog in the distance, crickets chirping, bullfrog croaking.*) Remind them to keep the passage in mind as they read the poem "The Hollow" and to note connections between the texts.

TEACH

ANALYZE RHYME SCHEME

Remind students that rhyme is the repetition of a sound at the end of words. Point out that analyzing the **rhyme scheme** can help readers identify the poem's form because many traditional forms follow specific rhyme schemes. Some examples of traditional forms with their rhyme schemes are:

- alternate rhyme: abab cdcd efef
- couplets: aa bb cc dd
- quatrains: aabb or abcb
- cinquain: ababb
- limerick: aabba
- Shakespearean sonnet: abab cdcd efef gg

✎ ANNOTATION MODEL

Remind students of the ideas to identify connections to other texts discussed on page 105, which include looking at similar descriptions of settings and characters and specific words or phrases used in the other text. Suggest that they underline similar descriptions and circle specific word references. Tell them to write notes in the margin to explain connections they see to other texts or to their own experiences.

 GET READY

ANALYZE RHYME SCHEME

"The Hollow" is a **lyric poem**. In a lyric poem, a single speaker expresses his or her personal ideas and feelings. Lyric poetry has a variety of forms and covers many subjects, from love and death to everyday experiences.

The **rhyme scheme** in any type of poetry is the pattern of rhyming words at the end of a poem's lines. You can use letters to identify a poem's rhyme scheme. Write the letter *a* next to the first rhyming line and all the lines that rhyme with it. Then write the letter *b* next to the second rhyming line, and so on. As you read "The Hollow," note the rhyme scheme and consider its impact on readers.

LINES FROM THE POEM

The October night was dark and cold,	a
As the autumn sun was going down,	b
When I recalled the legends I had been told,	a
About this sleepy, little town.	b
5 There were tales about the haunted woods—	c

ANNOTATION MODEL NOTICE & NOTE

As you read, make notes about connections between the poem and "The Legend of Sleepy Hollow." This model shows one reader's notes about the beginning of "The Hollow."

The October <u>night</u> was <u>dark</u> and <u>cold</u>,

As the autumn sun was going down,

When I recalled the <u>legends</u> I had been told,

About this <u>sleepy</u>, little town.

> The poem's title, "The Hollow," and the words <u>legends</u> and <u>sleepy</u> make it clear that the poem is about "The Legend of Sleepy Hollow."

> The description of the cold, dark night in the poem reminds me of the "dead hush of midnight" in the story.

BACKGROUND

One of the first short stories in American literature and an early example of the horror genre, "The Legend of Sleepy Hollow" by Washington Irving (1783–1859) has inspired numerous adaptations since it was first published in1819. The setting of Sleepy Hollow in 18th-century New York's Hudson River Valley is described in the story as "one of the quietest places in the whole world," where "a drowsy, dreamy influence seems to hang over the land, and pervade the very atmosphere." Tales of a headless horseman who haunts the community both intrigue and terrify main character Ichabod Crane, who arrives from Connecticut for a short-lived stint as the new village schoolmaster.

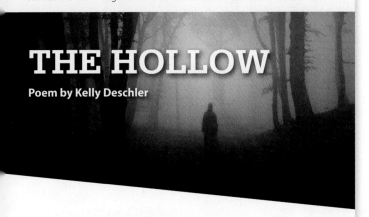

THE HOLLOW
Poem by Kelly Deschler

SETTING A PURPOSE

As you read, make connections between the poem, your own prior knowledge, and what you have learned about "The Legend of Sleepy Hollow" to help you make inferences about the poem's speaker.

The October night was dark and cold,
As the autumn sun was going down,
When I recalled the legends I had been told,
About this sleepy, little town.

5 There were tales about the haunted woods—
They say the wind seems to call your name.
I was going where no one should,
And if I survived, I'd never be the same.

Notice & Note

Use the side margins to notice and note signposts in the text.

MAKE CONNECTIONS

Annotate: In lines 1–12, mark words and phrases that connect to the characters and setting of "The Legend of Sleepy Hollow."

Connect: What can you infer about the poem's speaker based on the details about "The Legend of Sleepy Hollow"?

APPLYING ACADEMIC VOCABULARY

☑ **convention**   ☐ **predict**   ☐ **psychology**   ☐ **summary**   ☑ **technique**

Write and Discuss Have students turn to a partner to discuss the following questions. Guide students to include the Academic Vocabulary words *convention* and *technique* in their responses. Ask volunteers to share their responses with the class.

- How does the poem follow **convention**?
- What **technique** do you use for analyzing the rhyme scheme?

BACKGROUND

After students read the Background note, explain that adapting a literary work means to change it from one genre to another or to another medium. Examples include making a book into a movie or a comic book into a video game, or retelling a short story as a poem. Ask students to consider why "The Legend of Sleepy Hollow" "has inspired numerous adaptations" and if they are familiar with any of its adaptations. (**Answer:** *Adaptations of important works are popular because the original stories have proven literary merit. "The Legend of Sleepy Hollow" was one of the first horror stories. Students will probably mention movies and TV shows based on the story.*)

SETTING A PURPOSE

Direct students to use the Setting a Purpose prompt to focus their reading.

 MAKE CONNECTIONS

Remind students that the poem is based on the short story "The Legend of Sleepy Hollow." Encourage students to revisit the excerpt on p. 105 after reading the first two stanzas of "The Hollow." Explain that making connections to the short story adds a layer of information from outside the poem that helps the reader make inferences about the speaker. (**Possible answer:** *The speaker is walking alone in Sleepy Hollow on a dark October night and thinking about the dangerousness and inadvisability of this action, based on the local legends that the woods are haunted. The speaker is Ichabod Crane.*)

 For **reading support** for students at varying proficiency levels, see the **Text X-Ray** on page 104D.

ENGLISH LEARNER SUPPORT

Understand Language Structures Have students look at the groupings of lines and count how many lines are in each. (*four*) Explain that in poetry, the lines are often organized in stanzas, or groups of lines, which may or may not have a rhyme scheme and regular rhythm. Point out that a stanza groups related thoughts or ideas together in poetry like a paragraph does in prose. Ask students to discuss with partners how the stanzas help organize ideas in the poem. (*Each stanza describes a part of the speaker's walk. Together, they create the impression of moving along the path.*)

MODERATE

ANALYZE RHYME SCHEME

Remind students to note the rhyme scheme by assigning a letter of the alphabet to the end of each line and to repeat the letter when a line ends in the same sound. (**Answer:** *The regular alternate rhyme scheme helps unify and separate each stanza. It creates a sense of predictability that helps build expectations.*)

MAKE CONNECTIONS

Remind students that making a personal connection to a character's actions or perspective will give them a deeper understanding of the text. (**Answer:** *Student responses will vary but should include a personal experience and a reason for their action.*)

For **listening support** for students at varying proficiency levels, see the **Text X-Ray** on page 104C.

 NOTICE & NOTE

ANALYZE RHYME SCHEME
Annotate: Mark the rhyme scheme of the poem.

Analyze: Read several stanzas, or the whole poem, out loud. How does the regular pattern of rhyme affect you as a reader and as a listener?

MAKE CONNECTIONS
Annotate: Underline what the speaker tells herself.

Describe: When have you ever told yourself something similar? What was your motivation for it?

I walked through the covered bridge, *a*
10 As the harvest moon rose into the sky. *b*
I had made it around the darkened ridge, *a*
Just as I heard a lone wolf's cry. *b*

I walked the path of the dark, gnarled thicket, *c*
Through the fallen leaves of maple and oak. *d*
15 I heard the chirping of a cricket, *c*
Near the hollow, where the bullfrogs croak. *d*

Then, I heard the "hoot" of an owl in a tree, *e*
And the "caw" of a raven on its perch. *f*
The headless horseman I hoped not to see, *e*
20 As I passed the graveyard near the church. *f*

I told myself I would be all right, *g*
Just as I heard the hooves of a horse. *h*
But I knew I would make it home tonight, *g*
Because there are no ghosts, of course. *h*

 ## ENGLISH LEARNER SUPPORT

Make Connections Help students locate the words *legends, sleepy, tales,* and *haunted* in the text, and make sure they understand their meanings. Then have students work in pairs to discuss how the words relate to excerpts they have read or heard from "The Legend of Sleepy Hollow." **MODERATE/LIGHT**

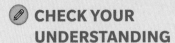 **CHECK YOUR UNDERSTANDING**

Have students answer the questions independently.

Answers:

1. *A*

2. *H*

3. *D*

If they answer any questions incorrectly, have them reread the text to confirm their understanding. Then they may proceed to ANALYZE THE TEXT on p. 110.

CHECK YOUR UNDERSTANDING

Answer these questions before moving on to the **Analyze the Text** section on the following page.

1 Which words from the poem add tension to the mood?

   A *haunted* and *darkened*

   B *autumn* and *harvest*

   C *sleepy* and *little*

   D *maple* and *oak*

2 The sensory language in lines 1–20 helps the reader understand that the speaker is —

   F familiar with the sleepy town

   G enjoying a long walk

   H alone in the dark

   J ready to journey home

3 Lines 21–24 reveal that the speaker —

   A enjoys spending time in nature

   B will not return home that night

   C is uncertain about the future

   D rejects beliefs about the haunted woods

 ENGLISH LEARNER SUPPORT

Oral Assessment Use the following questions to assess students' comprehension and speaking skills:

1. Which words give the poem a scary feeling? (*The words* haunted *and* darkened *make the poem seem scary.*)

2. In lines 1–20, what do the vivid, sensory descriptions tell the reader about the speaker? (*The speaker is alone in the dark.*)

3. What do lines 21–24 reveal about the speaker? (*The speaker does not believe the woods are haunted.*)

   SUBSTANTIAL/MODERATE

APPLY

ANALYZE THE TEXT

Possible answers:

1. **DOK 2:** *Lines 5–8 show that the speaker is thinking about the "tales of the haunted woods," so it sounds as though the speaker is afraid. However, lines 21–24 reveal that the speaker does not believe in the legend and is not afraid.*

2. **DOK 4:** *The Background note says that the stories about the headless horseman "terrify" Ichabod Crane, the story's main character. In contrast, the speaker rejects feelings of fear and belief in the local legend in lines 23–24, saying "I knew I would make It home tonight, / Because there are no ghosts, of course."*

3. **DOK 2:** *The regular pattern of alternate rhyme suggests a lighter mood, but the varying line lengths and dark imagery add tension and contrast with this effect. Overall this contrast hints at the shift in mood in the last stanza.*

4. **DOK 4:** *The last four lines of the poem surprised me. The rest of the poem makes the nighttime walk sound mysterious and scary. In contrast, the last four lines make the speaker sound calm and confident as he or she states, "there are no ghosts, of course."*

5. **DOK 3:** *The details of "the darkened ridge" and "the dark, gnarled thicket" suggest a dangerous or threatening mood and add to the idea that the speaker is alone and isolated.*

RESEARCH

DETAIL	CONNECTION
Point out that students should find connections between the story and the poem.	Remind students that connections could be similar settings, descriptions, events, or other similarities between the two pieces of literature.

Extend Students should cite details from the poem to support their opinions about effective illustrations for "The Hollow."

 RESPOND

ANALYZE THE TEXT

Support your responses with evidence from the text. NOTEBOOK

1. **Infer** Review lines 5–8 and lines 21–24. Based on lines 5–8, what can you infer about the speaker? Do lines 21–24 change your inference, or confirm it? Explain.

2. **Connect** Based on details in the Background note and the poem, how does the speaker of "The Hollow" compare to Ichabod Crane, the main character of "The Legend of Sleepy Hollow"?

3. **Interpret** How does the poem's rhyme scheme affect the **mood,** or the feeling or atmosphere that the poet creates? Cite evidence from the poem to support your interpretation.

4. **Analyze** Trace the poem's shift in mood. Which section of the poem brings a change in mood, and how does the poet accomplish this?

5. **Critique** How do the details about darkness affect the poem's meaning? Use evidence from the poem to support your answer.

RESEARCH TIP
When you research works that have been adapted to many versions, include the full title and author name in your search to locate information about the original version.

RESEARCH

Research "The Legend of Sleepy Hollow" to help you make additional connections between the story and the poem. Use the chart to note details about the story and the connections you make to the poem.

DETAIL	CONNECTION
The horseman "hurried along in the gloom of night, as if on the wings of the wind."	In line 6, the speaker says, "They say the wind seems to call your name." This is probably a reference to the headless horseman.
According to stories, the horseman "tethered his horse nightly among the graves in the churchyard."	Tension builds in lines 19–20 as the speaker hopes to not encounter the horseman at "the graveyard near the church."
Ichabod Crane is knocked off his horse after he sees the headless horseman "hurling his head at him." When Ichabod is missing the following morning, a shattered pumpkin is found next to his hat.	The speaker's assertion that "there are no ghosts, of course" connects with the possible interpretation of the story's ending that Ichabod's vision of the horseman throwing his head was actually just a person throwing a pumpkin.

Extend With your partner, find examples of illustrations of "The Legend of Sleepy Hollow." Share your findings with a small group. Then discuss possible illustrations that might be a good fit for the poem "The Hollow." Support your opinions with details from the poem.

110 Unit 2

WHEN STUDENTS STRUGGLE . . .

Visualize Ask students to close their eyes and listen as you read lines 9–20 aloud. Tell them to pay attention to details that help them create a mental image of the landscape. After reading the passage, ask: *What details stand out? How do the descriptions appeal to the senses? How does this mental image compare to the description in the short story excerpt?*

For additional support, go to the **Reading Studio** and assign the following **Level Up tutorial: Elements of Poetry.**

CREATE AND PRESENT

Write a Poem Write a poem inspired by a favorite story, movie, or character.

- ❏ Consider how the poem will relate to the story, movie, osr character. List details that the poem will include.
- ❏ Decide on a mood for the poem, such as funny or serious.
- ❏ Choose a structure for your poem. If your poem will use rhyme, decide whether you will use an alternate rhyme scheme (*abab*) as in "The Hollow," couplets (*aa bb*), or another rhyme scheme.

Present a Poem Read aloud a poem you wrote or another poem that you choose.

- ❏ Practice reading the poem aloud. Use appropriate volume and rate.
- ❏ Read your poem aloud to the class. Make eye contact with your audience. Use facial expressions and natural gestures to convey the meaning of the poem.

Go to the **Writing Studio** for more on writing a poem.

RESPOND TO THE ESSENTIAL QUESTION

 Why do we sometimes like to feel frightened?

Gather Information Review your annotations and notes on "The Hollow." Then, add relevant details to your Response Log. As you determine which information to include, think about:

- details in the poem
- connections between the poem and "The Legend of Sleepy Hollow"
- your inferences and response to the poem

At the end of the unit, you can use your notes to help you write a literary analysis.

ACADEMIC VOCABULARY

As you write about and discuss your response to the poem, be sure to use the Academic Vocabulary words. Check off each of the words that you use.

- ❏ **convention**
- ❏ **predict**
- ❏ **psychology**
- ❏ **summary**
- ❏ **technique**

CREATE AND PRESENT

Write a Poem Students' poems should convey a particular mood and reflect details about a favorite story, movie, or character. Point out that students do not need to use complete sentences in a poem and that it is their choice how to structure their poem. Encourage them to experiment with different forms such as stanzas and rhyme schemes to find one that suits what they are trying to say.

For **writing support** for students at varying proficiency levels, see the Text X-Ray on page 104D.

Present a Poem Readers should perform at a reasonable, unrushed pace, should make at least occasional eye contact with audience members, and should use facial expressions and natural gestures to help convey the meaning of the poem.

RESPOND TO THE ESSENTIAL QUESTION

Allow time for students to add details from "The Hollow" to their Unit 2 Response Logs.

THE MONKEY'S PAW

Short Story by W. W. Jacobs

GENRE ELEMENTS
SHORT STORY

Remind students that the purpose of a **short story** is to entertain using a plot, characters, setting, and theme. Explain that a **horror story** entertains by inducing feelings of horror or terror and sometimes includes supernatural elements. Make sure they understand that, although not all people find feelings of horror or terror entertaining, people who choose to read horror stories likely enjoy them. Tell students that, as they read "The Monkey's Paw," they can decide for themselves whether they find horror stories entertaining and whether they would likely choose to read horror stories in the future.

LEARNING OBJECTIVES

- Cite evidence to support the identification of a theme.
- Recognize the use of and purpose of foreshadowing.
- Conduct research about the relationship between India and Britain.
- Write personal responses to parts of the story.
- Compare the story to common tales.
- Recognize and use Latin roots to increase understanding.
- Edit text for correct tenses.
- **Language** Discuss with a partner how the author uses present-tense verbs in dialogue but past tense in narration.

TEXT COMPLEXITY

Quantitative Measures	The Monkey's Paw	Lexile: 920L
Qualitative Measures	**Ideas Presented** Multiple levels of symbolism, irony, and allusion. Greater demand for inference.	
	Structures Used Text features clear, chronological order.	
	Language Used Some unconventional language.	
	Knowledge Required Situation includes unfamiliar aspects.	

RESOURCES

- Unit 2 Response Log
- 🔊 Selection Audio
- 📖 Reading Studio: Notice & Note
- Level Up Tutorial: Theme
- Writing Studio: Using Textual Evidence
- 💬 Speaking and Listening Studio: Participating in a Group Discussion
- Vocabulary Studio: Latin Roots
- ❗ Grammar Studio: Module 9: Lesson 3: Verb Tense
- ☑ "The Monkey's Paw" Selection Test

SUMMARIES

English

An old friend, Sergeant-Major Morris, tells the Whites about a monkey's paw that grants three wishes. The Whites use the paw to wish for money, which they get, but as compensation for their son's death. Eventually, Mr. White uses his last wish to end the tragic story.

Spanish

Un viejo amigo, el sargento primero Morris, le cuenta a los White acerca de una pata de mono que concede tres deseos. Los White utilizan la pata para desear dinero, que obtienen, pero como compensación por la muerte de su hijo. Al final, el Sr. White utiliza su último deseo para acabar con la trágica historia.

 SMALL-GROUP OPTIONS

Have students work in small groups to read and discuss the selection.

Double-Entry Journal

- After reading the text, have students draw a line to divide a journal page in half vertically to create two columns.
- Direct students to label the columns as follows:
  - Left column—"Quotes from the Text that Include Old-Fashioned References"
  - Right column—"My Explanations for the Old-Fashioned References"
- Ask volunteers to share some of the old-fashioned references they found as well as their explanations of them.

Numbered Heads Together

- After students have read the text, have them form groups of four.
- Have each group number off 1 – 2 – 3 – 4.
- Tell students to discuss this question within their small groups: If the story were to continue, what do you think would happen next?
- Choose a number, such as #3, and ask all students with that number to share the final answers from their groups.

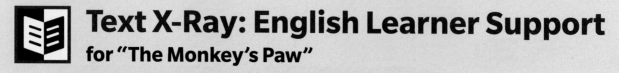

Text X-Ray: English Learner Support
for "The Monkey's Paw"

Use the Text X-Ray and the supports and scaffolds in the Teacher's Edition to help guide students at different proficiency levels through the selection.

INTRODUCE THE SELECTION
DISCUSS FORESHADOWING

In this lesson, students will need to be able to recognize foreshadowing. Read with students the first sentence of the "Prepare to Compare" paragraph that precedes the story. Ask students what is meant by "the different ways the paw affects the members of the White family." After students share their thoughts, explain that this wording is an example of foreshadowing. Guide students to recognize these possible interpretations of the wording:

- Some family members might be happier about the paw than others.
- If the paw is affecting characters, it is likely to be a scary story.

Explain to students that a story with foreshadowing can have one, two, a few, or many incidents of foreshadowing. Have students share tips for recognizing foreshadowing by completing this sentence frame:

- *When a sentence talks about something that _____ has/hasn't happened, it might be foreshadowing.* (*hasn't*)
- *What characters _____ can be a hint about foreshadowing.* (*say/do/think*)

CULTURAL REFERENCES

Words and phrases such as the following may be unfamiliar to students:

- *knowing glance* (paragraph 8): a look of understanding between two people
- *the words died away on his lips* (paragraph 8): decided not to speak
- *slip of a youth* (paragraph 14): an undersized youngster

Help students understand the story's setting.

- Explain that this story takes place in the late 1800s. The home has no electricity; candles and oil lamps provide light and fireplaces provide heat. Laburnum Villa is the name of the house. Many English houses had names instead of numbers.
- Encourage students to read footnotes carefully to understand historical and cultural references. To illustrate 19th-century attitudes toward India, show the video about British imperialism.

LISTENING

Understand Word Choices

Draw students' attention to the author's use of words that relate to fear. Explain that the more fear-related words that are used, the more the sense of fear builds.

Have students listen as you read aloud paragraphs 116–122. Use the following supports with students at varying proficiency levels:

- Tell students you will ask some questions about what they just heard. Model that they should give a thumbs up if the answer is yes, and a thumbs down for no. Stop after the first sentence. Ask: *Do these words relate to fear? darkness* (yes), *parlor* (no), *mantelpiece* (no) **SUBSTANTIAL**
- Ask: *What words in the first sentence have anything to do with fear?* (darkness, felt his way) *What word changes that would make it less frightening.* **MODERATE**
- Ask student pairs to list fear-related words they hear. Ask: *What if the first sentence said "He went downstairs to the mantelpiece in the parlor"? Does that sound as frightening as the original?* (No) Have students discuss other synonyms and the power of word choice. **LIGHT**

SPEAKING

Discuss Old-Fashioned English Words

Draw students' attention to the use of old-fashioned English in the story. Discuss that authors might use such language if they actually lived long ago or if they wanted to set a story in a bygone time.

Use the following supports with students at varying proficiency levels:

- Point out the words *rubicund of visage* in the last sentence in paragraph 10, and tell students this is an old-fashioned term. Read aloud the footnote. Explain that *ruddy* means "red" and *complexion* refers to skin color. Ask: *Would a modern writer use "rubicund of visage"?* (Answers will vary.) *Could a writer use it to make a character or story sound old-fashioned?* (yes) Have partners reword the sentence using *red skin*. **SUBSTANTIAL**
- Direct students to look at the last sentence in paragraph 10. Discuss that the words *rubicund of visage* are not words typically used in modern English. Ask partners to use the footnotes to reword the sentence so it is easier to understand and then share their new sentence with the group. **MODERATE**
- Ask partners to find some words in paragraph 10 that are examples of old-fashioned English and then discuss how to reword some of the sentences using modern English. **LIGHT**

READING

Read Dialogue and Surrounding Text

Draw students' attention to the author's use of present tense verbs within dialogue and past tense in general narration. Discuss that, even when the story takes place in the past or the future, the actual words of dialogue likely will be in present tense.

Work with students to read paragraphs 130–138. Use the following supports with students at varying proficiency levels:

- Ask partners to highlight every present tense verb in one color and every past tense verb in another color. Ask: *Is the dialogue in present tense or past tense?* (present) **SUBSTANTIAL**
- Have partners circle all of the "speaker" words, such as "said." Ask: *In what tense are the speaker words written? Are they in the same tense as the dialogue?* (present; no) **MODERATE**
- As students read paragraphs 130–138, have them emphasize each present-tense verb. Ask: *Did you find any present tense verbs outside of the dialogue? What effect does the use of present tense have on dialogue?* (no; draws the reader in as if it is happening now) **LIGHT**

WRITING

Write to Control Story Direction

Draw students' attention to the fact that the author chose to take the story in an increasingly more horrible direction in order to create a very upsetting horror story. Point out that he could have changed directions.

Use the following supports with students at varying proficiency levels:

- Have students create an idea web that shows "Three wishes" in the center with lines extending to three circles. Have them fill in the circles to show the direction of the story. **SUBSTANTIAL**
- Have students use this sentence frame to suggest a change in direction for the story: *Mr. White's first wish could have been _____, which would have changed the direction of the story because _____.* **MODERATE**
- Have students use this sentence frame to write a new direction for the story: *Mr. White made three wishes right away, and they were _____, _____, and _____.* **LIGHT**

Connect to the
ESSENTIAL QUESTION

"The Monkey's Paw" is a short horror story, and the author wrote it to entertain. Throughout the story, readers are increasingly frightened—and entertained—as the fear level mounts. Discuss with students why and how readers could be frightened and entertained at the same time. Ask them to think of a time when they were frightened but then laughed afterward. Allow volunteers to describe their experiences.

COMPARE VERSIONS

Remind students that the purpose of **short stories** is to entertain using a plot, characters, setting, and theme. Explain that a **horror story** entertains by inducing feelings of horror or terror, and sometimes including supernatural elements. Point out that short stories and horror stories are often presented in both written and video formats and that plots, characters, and settings often vary between the two formats. Tell students that they will first read a written version of "The Monkey's Paw" and will then see some scenes from the video version. Afterwards, they will compare the similarities and differences between the two versions.

COLLABORATE & COMPARE

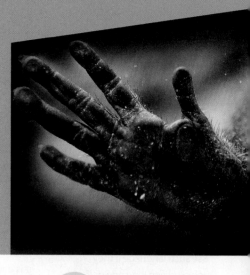

SHORT STORY

THE MONKEY'S PAW

by **W. W. Jacobs**
pages 115–127

COMPARE VERSIONS

As you read, notice key details about the story's characters, setting, and plot events. Then, examine how these elements are adapted in a film version of the story's ending. After you read the story and view the film clip, you will collaborate with a small group on a final project.

ESSENTIAL QUESTION:

Why do we sometimes like to feel frightened?

FILM CLIP

from

THE MONKEY'S PAW

by **Ricky Lewis Jr.**
page 135

LEARNING MINDSET

Persistence Explain to students that it's normal to feel frustrated when reading a difficult text. Even strong readers have trouble completely understanding this short story the first time they read it. Tell students to take a break, and then reread "The Monkey's Paw," this time employing a different strategy, such as using a graphic organizer to track events in the story or to note information about the characters. Say: *It's OK to make mistakes, trying a different strategy may help you learn in a different way.*

The Monkey's Paw

QUICK START

The story you will read is about a monkey's paw that grants wishes. Write a brief paragraph about something you might want to change, and describe the possible effects of having your wish granted.

ANALYZE THEME

One reason people read literature is to learn how to avoid or understand common problems. Literature conveys lessons through **themes,** the messages about life or human nature that writers share with readers.

- In some stories, the theme is **explicit,** or stated directly in the text.

- In most cases, the theme is **implicit,** or not stated directly. Readers must **infer,** or make an educated guess about, the theme based on clues in the text.

- Clues in the text can include the ways that characters interact with each other. For instance, who treats whom lovingly?

- Clues can also include the events in the text. Do the events benefit the characters or harm them? Do the characters do anything to cause the events?

As you read "The Monkey's Paw," pay attention to details that show how the main characters change, and consider the messages about life or human nature that these changes might suggest.

ANALYZE FORESHADOWING

Foreshadowing occurs when a writer provides hints that suggest future events in a story. Writers use this technique to encourage readers to make predictions about what will happen next and to add suspense. Clues about future events may appear in **dialogue** (written conversation between characters), descriptions of events, or **imagery** (descriptive words and phrases that appeal to the senses). Consider how the first example in the chart foreshadows events to come. As you read "The Monkey's Paw," use the chart to note examples of dialogue, events, or imagery that foreshadow what will occur later in the story.

Dialogue	"I did have some idea of selling it, but I don't think I will. It has caused enough mischief already."
Event	
Imagery	

GENRE ELEMENTS: SHORT STORY

- is a work of fiction
- contains a plot, characters, setting, and theme
- is a popular format for horror stories
- if it is a horror story, often includes supernatural elements

---

QUICK START

Discuss with students how having a wish granted could possibly have both positive and negative consequences. Encourage them to think about both the pros and cons that could accompany a granted wish.

ANALYZE THEME

Explain that the theme of a story is the message about life or human nature that an author shares with readers. Tell students that one way an author might reveal a message is through changes in a character.

- Display the following passages: paragraphs 43–54 and paragraphs 96–98.

- Have pairs compare and contrast what the two passages reveal about the characters. (*Before the wish, the Whites are lighthearted, happy, and content; after making the wish, they become heartbroken and isolated.*)

- Have students explain how they think these changes help convey the author's meaning.

ANALYZE FORESHADOWING

Explain that *foreshadowing* means "to point ahead." By hinting about what might happen, authors maintain readers' interest and build suspense.

- Have pairs read paragraphs 17–32.

- Ask them to note details that hint at these events: *The Whites will use the paw to make a wish. Bad things will happen as a result of their wish.*

- Let pairs share their examples of foreshadowing with the class. (*The sergeant-major doesn't want to discuss the monkey's paw; he explains the consequences of the spell; he turns pale when saying he has made wishes; Mrs. White asks whether three people have used their wishes.*)

TEACH

CRITICAL VOCABULARY

Encourage students to read all the sentences before deciding which word best completes each one. Remind them to look for context clues that match the precise meaning of each word.

Answers:

1. *wild animals, poison plants*

2. *sympathetic talking and listening*

3. *dislike*

4. *feels lack of control*

5. *lessen it*

6. *dull, not very memorable*

7. *money*

8. *acceptance*

■ English Learner Support

Use Cognates Tell students that two of the Critical Vocabulary words have Spanish cognates: *peril/peligro, compensation/compensación* **ALL LEVELS**

LANGUAGE CONVENTIONS

Read the following opening sentence from the story to students. Ask them to listen for the words that indicate the story is taking place in the past.

> "Without, the night was cold and wet, but in the small parlor of Laburnum Villa the blinds were drawn and the fire burned brightly." *(was, were drawn, burned)*

Discuss that these words are all verbs in the past tense and that the author consistently uses past tense throughout the story to show that all of the events have already happened.

ANNOTATION MODEL

Point out to students that one way to show contrasting information, such as the setting information where it is cold outside and warm inside, is to box one piece of information and underline the other. Explain that they can use this method or they can use their own techniques, such as different colored highlighters and notes in the margins.

 GET READY

CRITICAL VOCABULARY

| peril | grimace | credulity | compensation |
| condole | fate | prosaic | resignation |

To see how many Critical Vocabulary words you already know, answer these questions.

1. What **perils** might you face while hiking in the forest?

2. How could you **condole** with a friend who lost a pet?

3. What emotion is expressed by a **grimace**?

4. Why might a person believe that **fate** controls his life?

5. What effect might being lied to have on your **credulity**?

6. Why would you be unlikely to remember a **prosaic** day?

7. What **compensation** do people get for doing their jobs?

8. If you met a request with **resignation,** what might you be feeling?

LANGUAGE CONVENTIONS

Verb Tenses This lesson shows how to use **verb tenses** correctly to indicate the time that an action or condition takes place. "The Monkey's Paw" is narrated in the past tense:

There was another knock, and another. The old woman with a sudden wrench broke free and ran from the room.

As you read, note how the author uses verb tenses consistently. The verb tense should change only when an action or condition happens at a different time.

ANNOTATION MODEL

NOTICE & NOTE

As you read, notice details that establish the setting and the mood. You can also mark up evidence that supports your own ideas. In the model, you can see one reader's notes about "The Monkey's Paw."

> 1 Without, the night was cold and wet, but in the small parlor of Laburnum Villa the blinds were drawn and the fire burned brightly. Father and son were at chess; the former, who possessed ideas about the game involving radical changes, putting his king into such sharp and unnecessary perils that it even provoked comment from the white-haired old lady knitting placidly by the fire.

The author contrasts the cold, stormy weather outside with the warm, cozy feeling inside.

BACKGROUND

William Wymark Jacobs (1863–1943) grew up in London near the waterfront wharfs. As a boy, Jacobs absorbed the tales of strange, distant lands told by passing sailors. As a young man, Jacobs worked at a bank—a job that he hated—and wrote stories in his spare time. He eventually became a popular writer of humor. Ironically, his best-known work, "The Monkey's Paw," became a classic of the horror genre.

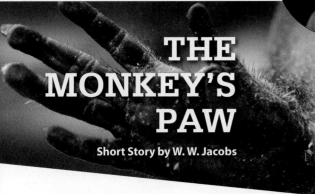

THE MONKEY'S PAW

Short Story by W. W. Jacobs

PREPARE TO COMPARE

As you read, pay attention to the details Sergeant-Major Morris shares about the monkey's paw and the different ways in which the paw affects the members of the White family. This will help you compare the story's ending to a film version of the ending, which you will view after you read the story.

1   Without, the night was cold and wet, but in the small parlor of Laburnum Villa the blinds were drawn and the fire burned brightly. Father and son were at chess; the former, who possessed ideas about the game involving radical changes, putting his king into such sharp and unnecessary perils that it even provoked comment from the white-haired old lady knitting placidly by the fire.

2   "Hark at the wind," said Mr. White, who, having seen a fatal mistake after it was too late, was amiably desirous of preventing his son from seeing it.

3   "I'm listening," said the latter, grimly surveying the board as he stretched out his hand. "Check."

> **Notice & Note**
>
> Use the side margins to notice and note signposts in the text.

ANALYZE FORESHADOWING

Annotate: Mark details in paragraph 1 that reveal the father's personality.

Analyze: What might the details about the father hint about future events in the plot?

peril
(pĕr´əl) *n.* A *peril* is something that is dangerous.

BACKGROUND

Have students read the information about the author. Tell students that William Wymark Jacobs grew up on the rough London waterfront, where his father worked as a wharf manager. Jacobs was fortunate and managed to get a good education. As a young man, Jacobs worked in a bank, and in his leisure time he wrote humorous stories about the sea and sailors. Jacobs began submitting his stories to small magazines, and eventually his stories found interest with publishers. Jacobs became successful enough to focus strictly on writing stories related to his childhood, the sea, and occasionally the supernatural.

PREPARE TO COMPARE

Direct students to use the Prepare to Compare prompt to focus their reading. Discuss that it is usually quite interesting to see how written and film versions compare.

ANALYZE FORESHADOWING

Tell students that **foreshadowing** refers to clues an author gives that hint at what will happen later in the story. Explain that one way authors foreshadow events is through description. (**Answer:** *The father seems like the type of person who might take risks or do dangerous things.*)

CRITICAL VOCABULARY

peril: The author is describing Mr. White's risky method of playing the game of chess.

ASK STUDENTS what can happen in chess or checkers if you put your game piece in peril. (*Your piece may be captured by your opponent.*)

TEACH

EL ENGLISH LEARNER SUPPORT

Understand Language Structures Have students note how many sentences on this page are only narration as opposed to including dialogue. (5 sentences—in paragraphs 8, 10, 12, and 13) Explain that authors often use dialogue to allow the characters to speak for themselves. Ask students to work with partners to make a list of the different words the author uses on this page to indicate that someone is speaking. (said, replied, bawled) **MODERATE**

✐ ANALYZE FORESHADOWING

Explain to students that the author of a horror story may use foreshadowing to prepare the reader for strange and unexpected events. Point out that this technique creates suspense by building the reader's expectations.
(**Possible answer:** *Because the guest is introduced as coming from "distant parts" and having experience with "wild scenes," "wars and plagues," and "strange peoples," readers might expect him to cause something strange or foreboding.*)

CRITICAL VOCABULARY

condole: When Mr. White greets the visitor at the door, he is heard *condoling* with the guest.

ASK STUDENTS what conditions might cause a host to condole with a guest who has just arrived at his door. *(The weather might be very bad, or the guest might have had a long or difficult journey.)*

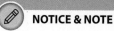

4 "I should hardly think that he'd come tonight," said his father, with his hand poised over the board.

5 "Mate," replied the son.

6 "That's the worst of living so far out," bawled Mr. White, with sudden and unlooked-for violence; "of all the beastly, slushy, out-of-the-way places to live in, this is the worst. Pathway's a bog,[1] and the road's a torrent.[2] I don't know what people are thinking about. I suppose because only two houses in the road are let,[3] they think it doesn't matter."

7 "Never mind, dear," said his wife soothingly; "perhaps you'll win the next one."

8 Mr. White looked up sharply, just in time to intercept a knowing glance between mother and son. The words died away on his lips, and he hid a guilty grin in his thin gray beard.

9 "There he is," said Herbert White, as the gate banged loudly and heavy footsteps came toward the door.

10 The old man rose with hospitable haste, and opening the door, was heard **condoling** with the new arrival. The new arrival also condoled with himself, so that Mrs. White said, "Tut, tut!" and coughed gently as her husband entered the room, followed by a tall, burly man, beady of eye and rubicund of visage.[4]

11 "Sergeant-Major Morris," he said, introducing him.

12 The sergeant-major shook hands, and taking the proffered seat by the fire, watched contentedly while his host brought out drinks and stood a small copper kettle on the fire.

13 He began to talk, the little family circle regarding with eager interest this visitor from distant parts, as he squared his broad shoulders in the chair and spoke of wild scenes and doughty[5] deeds; of wars and plagues and strange peoples.

14 "Twenty-one years of it," said Mr. White, nodding at his wife and son. "When he went away, he was a slip of a youth in the warehouse. Now look at him."

15 "He don't look to have taken much harm," said Mrs. White politely.

16 "I'd like to go to India myself," said the old man, "just to look round a bit, you know."

---

[1] **bog:** a swamp.
[2] **torrent** (tôr´ənt): a swift-flowing stream.
[3] **let:** rented.
[4] **rubicund** (roo´bĭ-kənd) **of visage** (vĭz´ĭj): with a ruddy complexion.
[5] **doughty** (dou´tē): brave.

---

condole
(kən-dōl´) *v.* If you *condole* with someone, you express sympathy or sorrow.

ANALYZE FORESHADOWING
Annotate: Mark details in paragraph 13 that tell about Sergeant-Major Morris.

Analyze: How does this information about the Whites' guest help build suspense?

17 "Better where you are," said the sergeant-major, shaking his head. He put down the empty glass, and sighing softly, shook it again.

18 "I should like to see those old temples and fakirs and jugglers," said the old man. "What was that you started telling me the other day about a monkey's paw or something, Morris?"

19 "Nothing," said the soldier hastily. "Leastways nothing worth hearing."

20 "Monkey's paw?" said Mrs. White curiously.

21 "Well, it's just a bit of what you might call magic, perhaps," said the sergeant-major off-handedly.

22 His three listeners leaned forward eagerly. The visitor absent-mindedly put his empty glass to his lips and then set it down again. His host filled it for him.

23 "To look at," said the sergeant-major, fumbling in his pocket, "it's just an ordinary little paw, dried to a mummy."

24 He took something out of his pocket and proffered it. Mrs. White drew back with a **grimace**, but her son, taking it, examined it curiously.

25 "And what is there special about it?" inquired Mr. White as he took it from his son, and having examined it, placed it upon the table.

26 "It had a spell put on it by an old fakir," said the sergeant-major, "a very holy man. He wanted to show that **fate** ruled people's lives, and that those who interfered with it did so to their sorrow. He put a spell on it so that three separate men could each have three wishes from it."

27 His manner was so impressive that his hearers were conscious that their light laughter jarred somewhat.

28 "Well, why don't you have three, sir?" said Herbert White cleverly.

29 The soldier regarded him in the way that middle age is wont to regard presumptuous youth. "I have," he said quietly, and his blotchy face whitened.

30 "And did you really have the three wishes granted?" asked Mrs. White.

31 "I did," said the sergeant-major, and his glass tapped against his strong teeth.

32 "And has anybody else wished?" persisted the old lady

33 "The first man had his three wishes. Yes," was the reply; "I don't know what the first two were, but the third was for death. That's how I got the paw."

34 His tones were so grave that a hush fell upon the group.

grimace
(grĭm´ĭs) *n.* A *grimace* is a facial expression of pain or disgust.

fate
(fāt) *n. Fate* is a power that is thought to determine the course of events.

ANALYZE THEME

Annotate: In paragraph 26, underline the lesson that the old fakir wanted to teach people.

Infer: What does this lesson suggest about the story's theme?

APPLYING ACADEMIC VOCABULARY

❏ **convention**   ☑ **predict**   ❏ **psychology**   ☑ **summary**   ☑ **technique**

Write and Discuss Have students write a response to the questions below. Then, have them discuss their responses with a partner. Guide students to include the Academic Vocabulary words *predict* and *technique* in both their sentences and their discussions.

- How can you **predict** a story line using foreshadowing?
- What elements might you include in a **summary** of the short story?
- If you were writing a horror story, what **techniques** would you use to build suspense?

 ANALYZE THEME

Explain to students that a **theme** is a message about life or human nature that a writer wants to share with readers. Sometimes, a writer actually states the theme of a story. In other cases, readers must **infer,** or figure out, the theme from details the writer provides. **(Possible answer:** *The old fakir's purpose in putting the spell on the monkey's paw suggests a theme about the dangers of interfering with fate. It also suggests that the family might experience sorrow as a result of trying to change fate.)*

For **reading support** for students at varying proficiency levels, see the **Text X-Ray** on page 112D.

CRITICAL VOCABULARY

grimace: Mrs. White drew back with a grimace when she saw the monkey's paw.

ASK STUDENTS what Mrs. White looked like and what caused her to look that way. (*Her face showed a look of horror and disgust. She was repelled by the appearance of the paw.*)

fate: The Indian fakir wanted to warn people not to interfere with fate.

ASK STUDENTS how having a wish granted would be a way of trying to change fate. (*Having a wish granted would be trying to get something you hadn't worked for or earned or been predetermined to have. It could alter your life's course and change your fate for the worse.*)

ANALYZE THEME

Explain to students that a **universal theme** is a theme found in the literature of different cultures and time periods. Point out that the granting of wishes is a convention used in the literature of many different cultures, such as the *Arabian Nights* and the fairy tales of the Brothers Grimm. The use of granting of wishes suggests a universal theme about interfering with fate. (**Possible answer:** *Family members might develop different points of view about the paw's power, or they might disagree about what to do with the paw. Mr. White's removal of the paw from the fire and his question about how to use the paw suggest that he is eager to make a wish despite the sergeant-major's stern warnings. However, the information about the paw's danger suggests that events might change the Whites' views.*)

▶ WORDS OF THE WISER

Point out to students that, prior to giving actual advice, the sergeant-major repeatedly hinted that wishes would not bring happiness. Encourage students to infer reasons that the sergeant-major would give several hints before giving actual advice about wishes. (**Answer:** *The sergeant-major suggests that the Whites might avoid a horrible outcome by wishing for something sensible. This hints that the Whites will learn that they shouldn't try to change their fate.*)

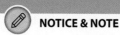

NOTICE & NOTE

ANALYZE THEME

Annotate: Underline evidence in paragraphs 35–44 that suggests the paw will cause the Whites harm.

Predict: How do you think the paw might affect the main characters' relationships? Cite evidence from the text to support your prediction.

WORDS OF THE WISER ◀

Notice & Note: What words of advice about the paw does Sergeant-Major Morris share with the Whites in paragraph 47?

Infer: How does the sergeant-major's advice suggest a lesson the Whites might learn?

35 "If you've had your three wishes, it's no good to you now, then, Morris," said the old man at last. "What do you keep it for?"

36 The soldier shook his head. "Fancy, I suppose," he said slowly. "I did have some idea of selling it, but I don't think I will. It has caused enough mischief already. Besides, people won't buy. They think it's a fairy tale, some of them; and those who do think anything of it want to try it first and pay me afterward."

37 "If you could have another three wishes," said the old man, eyeing him keenly, "would you have them?"

38 "I don't know," said the other. "I don't know."

39 He took the paw, and dangling it between his forefinger and thumb, suddenly threw it upon the fire. White, with a slight cry, stooped down and snatched it off.

40 "Better let it burn," said the soldier solemnly.

41 "If you don't want it, Morris," said the other, "give it to me."

42 "I won't," said his friend doggedly. "I threw it on the fire. If you keep it, don't blame me for what happens. Pitch it on the fire again like a sensible man."

43 The other shook his head and examined his new possession closely. "How do you do it?" he inquired.

44 "Hold it up in your right hand and wish aloud," said the sergeant-major, "but I warn you of the consequences."

45 "Sounds like the *Arabian Nights*,"[6] said Mrs. White, as she rose and began to set the supper. "Don't you think you might wish for four pairs of hands for me?"

46 Her husband drew the talisman[7] from his pocket, and then all three burst into laughter as the sergeant-major, with a look of alarm on his face, caught him by the arm.

47 "If you must wish," he said gruffly, "wish for something sensible."

48 Mr. White dropped it back in his pocket, and placing chairs, motioned his friend to the table. In the business of supper the talisman was partly forgotten, and afterward the three sat listening in an enthralled fashion to a second installment of the soldier's adventures in India.

49 "If the tale about the monkey's paw is not more truthful than those he has been telling us," said Herbert, as the door closed behind their guest, just in time for him to catch the last train, "we shan't make much out of it."

---

[6] *Arabian Nights*: a famous collection of Asian stories.
[7] **talisman** (tăl´ĭs-mən): an object thought to have magical powers.

118 Unit 2

WHEN STUDENTS STRUGGLE . . .

Determine Theme To support students in determining the theme of the story, share these strategies for guided and independent analysis:

- As you read, highlight in yellow the evidence that helps you predict what lesson the characters might learn.
- In notes, jot down what that lesson might be.

  For additional support, go to the **Reading Studio** and assign the following [LEVEL] **Level Up tutorial: Theme.**

50 "Did you give him anything for it, Father?" inquired Mrs. White, regarding her husband closely.

51 "A trifle," said he, coloring slightly. "He didn't want it, but I made him take it. And he pressed me again to throw it away."

52 "Likely," said Herbert, with pretended horror. "Why, we're going to be rich, and famous, and happy. Wish to be an emperor, Father, to begin with; then you can't be henpecked."

53 He darted round the table, pursued by the maligned Mrs. White armed with an antimacassar.[8]

54 Mr. White took the paw from his pocket and eyed it dubiously. "I don't know what to wish for, and that's a fact," he said slowly. "It seems to me I've got all I want."

55 "If you only cleared the house, you'd be quite happy, wouldn't you?" said Herbert, with his hand on his shoulder. "Well, wish for two hundred pounds, then; that'll just do it."

56 His father, smiling shamefacedly at his own **credulity,** held up the talisman, as his son, with a solemn face, somewhat marred by a wink at his mother, sat down at the piano and struck a few impressive chords.

57 "I wish for two hundred pounds," said the old man distinctly.

58 A fine crash from the piano greeted the words, interrupted by a shuddering cry from the old man. His wife and son ran toward him.

59 "It moved," he cried, with a glance of disgust at the object as it lay on the floor. "As I wished, it twisted in my hand like a snake."

60 "Well, I don't see the money," said his son, as he picked it up and placed it on the table, "and I bet I never shall."

61 "It must have been your fancy, father," said his wife, regarding him anxiously.

62 He shook his head. "Never mind, though; there's no harm done, but it gave me a shock all the same."

63 They sat down by the fire again. Outside, the wind was higher than ever, and the old man started nervously at the sound of a door banging upstairs. A silence unusual and depressing settled upon all three, which lasted until the old couple rose to retire for the night.

64 "I expect you'll find the cash tied up in a big bag in the middle of your bed," said Herbert, as he bade them goodnight, "and something horrible squatting up on top of the wardrobe watching you as you pocket your ill-gotten gains."

---

[8] **antimacassar** (ăn´tĭ-mə-kăs´ər): a cloth placed over an arm or the back of a chair.

credulity
(krĭ-dōō´lĭ-tē) *n. Credulity* is a tendency to believe too readily.

ANALYZE THEME

Annotate: Mark details in paragraphs 58–61 that show the main characters' attitudes toward the paw.

Compare: How have the Whites' views of the paw changed? How do you think these changing views relate to the story's theme?

 ANALYZE THEME

Point out that the granting wishes story plot is particularly effective when the recipient is happy and therefore has a lot to lose. Explain that the White family's happiness helps establish the theme of how dangerous it is to play with fate. (**Answer:** *The paw's movement scares Mr. White. Herbert still seems confident that the paw is powerless. Mrs. White is nervous about her husband's reaction but tries to assure him that he imagined the paw's movement. These changes in the characters suggest that they might soon regret not heeding Sergeant-Major Morris's warnings.*)

For **speaking support** for students at varying proficiency levels, see the **Text X-Ray** on page 112D.

TO CHALLENGE STUDENTS . . .

Mathematics/Economics Read paragraph 52 aloud. Make sure students know that the pound is the currency of England, where the story is set. Explain that to understand the value of 200 pounds in American dollars, they need to know the exchange rate. The exchange rate determines how much of one country's money is needed to buy the currency of another country. Explain that exchange rates change frequently, influenced by many factors.

Activity Have small groups look up the value of the dollar against the British pound today. Ask: *What is 200 pounds worth in dollars today?* Have groups present their answers. (*The exact amount will vary.*)

CRITICAL VOCABULARY

credulity: The author explains that Mr. White is ashamed at his own *credulity* in believing the story about the paw.

ASK STUDENTS why credulity might be something to be ashamed of. (*It suggests that a person is gullible or too easily convinced.*)

TEACH

ENGLISH LEARNER SUPPORT

Understand Sequence Encourage students to create a simple graphic organizer to track the sequence of events in the story. For each event, have the students write a short summary of the event and draw a circle around it. Then have them draw an arrow to the next event in the story. Add events in order to create a sequence chain. Encourage students to use the sequence chain during discussions for reference.

MODERATE

CRITICAL VOCABULARY

prosaic: The author is contrasting the exciting atmosphere of the night before with that of the new day.

ASK STUDENTS what makes the house seem prosaic in the morning. *(In the daylight, the room looks as it always does, with its "ordinary breakfast table" and other furnishings.)*

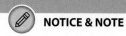

NOTICE & NOTE

65   He sat alone in the darkness, gazing at the dying fire, and seeing faces in it. The last face was so horrible and so simian[9] that he gazed at it in amazement. It got so vivid that, with a little uneasy laugh, he felt on the table for a glass containing a little water to throw over it. His hand grasped the monkey's paw, and with a little shiver he wiped his hand on his coat and went up to bed.

Part II

66   In the brightness of the wintry sun next morning as it streamed over the breakfast table he laughed at his fears. There was an air of **prosaic** wholesomeness about the room which it had lacked on the previous night, and the dirty, shriveled little paw was pitched on the sideboard[10] with a carelessness which betokened no great belief in its virtues.[11]

67   "I suppose all old soldiers are the same," said Mrs. White. "The idea of our listening to such nonsense! How could wishes be granted in these days? And if they could, how could two hundred pounds hurt you, father?"

68   "Might drop on his head from the sky," said the frivolous[12] Herbert.

69   "Morris said the things happened so naturally," said his father, "that you might if you so wished attribute it to coincidence."

70   "Well, don't break into the money before I come back," said Herbert as he rose from the table. "I'm afraid it'll turn you into a mean, avaricious[13] man, and we shall have to disown you."

71   His mother laughed, and following him to the door, watched him down the road; and returning to the breakfast table, was very happy at the expense of her husband's credulity. All of which did not prevent her from scurrying to the door at the postman's knock, when she found that the post brought a tailor's bill.

72   "Herbert will have some more of his funny remarks, I expect, when he comes home," she said, as they sat at dinner.

73   "I dare say," said Mr. White, "but for all that, the thing moved in my hand; that I'll swear to."

74   "You thought it did," said the old lady soothingly.

prosaic
(prō-zā´ĭk) *adj.* If something is *prosaic*, it is dull or ordinary.

---

[9] **simian** (sĭm´ē-ən): monkey- or ape-like.
[10] **sideboard:** a piece of furniture used to store linens and dishes.
[11] **virtues:** powers.
[12] **frivolous** (frĭv´ə-ləs): inappropriately silly.
[13] **avaricious** (ăv´ə-rĭsh´əs): greedy.

IMPROVE READING FLUENCY

Choral Reading   Discuss that, when reading dialogue, readers can more easily understand if they read each speaker's words as a fluent unit. Have students choral read paragraphs 67–69. Remind them to read each speaker's words fluently and then break slightly before reading the next speaker's words fluently.

   Go to the **Reading Studio** for additional support in developing fluency.

75   "I say it did," replied the other. "There was no thought about it; I had just—What's the matter?"

76   His wife made no reply. She was watching the mysterious movements of a man outside, who, peering in an undecided fashion at the house, appeared to be trying to make up his mind to enter. In mental connection with the two hundred pounds, she noticed that the stranger was well dressed, and wore a silk hat of glossy newness. Three times he paused at the gate, and then walked on again. The fourth time he stood with his hand upon it, and then with sudden resolution flung it open and walked up the path. Mrs. White at the same moment placed her hands behind her, and hurriedly unfastening the strings of her apron, put that useful article of apparel beneath the cushion of her chair.

77   She brought the stranger, who seemed ill at ease, into the room. He gazed at her furtively, and listened in a preoccupied fashion as the old lady apologized for the appearance of the room, and her husband's coat, a garment which he usually reserved for the garden. She then waited patiently for him to broach his business, but he was at first strangely silent.

78   "I—was asked to call," he said at last, and stooped and picked a piece of cotton from his trousers. "I come from Maw and Meggins."

79   The old lady started. "Is anything the matter?" she asked breathlessly. "Has anything happened to Herbert? What is it? What is it?"

80   Her husband interposed. "There, there, mother," he said hastily. "Sit down, and don't jump to conclusions. You've not brought bad news, I'm sure, sir;" and he eyed the other wistfully.

81   "I'm sorry—" began the visitor.

82   "Is he hurt?" demanded the mother wildly.

83   The visitor bowed in assent. "Badly hurt," he said quietly, "but he is not in any pain."

84   "Oh!" said the old woman, clasping her hands. "Thank goodness for that! Thank—"

85   She broke off suddenly as the sinister meaning of the assurance dawned upon her and she saw the awful confirmation of her fears in the other's averted face. She caught her breath, and turning to her slower-witted husband, laid her trembling old hand upon his. There was a long silence.

ANALYZE FORESHADOWING

Annotate: Mark details in paragraph 76 that describe the man outside.

Infer: What are some possible causes of the man's behavior? How does this example of foreshadowing propel the story's action?

▶ **AHA MOMENT**

Notice & Note: What "sinister meaning of the assurance" does Mrs. White realize?

Draw Conclusions: What might this realization cause the Whites to believe?

✎ ANALYZE FORESHADOWING

Explain to students that another way writers can foreshadow is through description of a character's behavior. (**Answer:** *The man seems to be putting off the moment when he will enter the house. His reluctance suggests that he has bad news. The man's actions create suspense and suggest that something bad may have happened to Herbert.*)

■ English Learner Support

Foreshadowing and Mood Ask pairs to identify other examples of foreshadowing in paragraph 74 that indicate the man has bad news for the Whites. Have pairs share their examples in small groups and discuss how this foreshadowing affects the mood of the text.
MODERATE/LIGHT

▶ AHA MOMENT

As students encounter the signpost, prompt them to stop, reread, and ask themselves questions that will help them understand the character's realization. (**Answers:** *Mrs. White realizes that the man's assurance that Herbert "is not in any pain" means that her son's suffering ended with his death. The realization will lead them to understand that Herbert's death resulted from Mr. White's wish. They will become grief-stricken about the loss of their son and afraid of the paw's power.*)

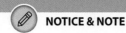

ENGLISH LEARNER SUPPORT

Understanding Dialogue Explain to students that **dialogue,** the words spoken by the characters, can be a very effective technique for communicating plot events. Explain that while narration makes readers feel that they are being told a story, dialogue makes them feel part of the action, as though they are seeing a story unfold. Ask students to closely reread the dialogue in paragraph 90. Ask how these lines move the plot along. (*Through the dialogue between the visitor and Mrs. White, readers realize what has happened to Herbert at the same moment she does.*) **LIGHT**

Dialogue Between Characters Tell students that in paragraph 90 the visitor is speaking in a formal way. Point out that, in the first line of dialogue, the visitor is telling Mr. and Mrs. White difficult news about their son. Ask: *How does the visitor speak in a formal way?* (*He uses complete sentences and polite language.*) Next, ask students to look at the second line of dialogue. Ask: *What phrases does the visitor use to soften his tone?* (*"I beg that you will understand," "only," "merely"*) Have students think of a way the visitor could have used simple, informal language to convey the message, such as "Your son died." If time allows, have students role play the visitor and the Whites using formal and informal statements. Ask students which way they preferred hearing the terrible news. **LIGHT**

86　"He was caught in the machinery," said the visitor at length in a low voice.

87　"Caught in the machinery," repeated Mr. White, in a dazed fashion, "yes."

88　He sat staring blankly out at the window, and taking his wife's hand between his own, pressed it as he had been wont to do in their old courting days nearly forty years before.

89　"He was the only one left to us," he said, turning gently to the visitor. "It is hard."

90　The other coughed, and rising, walked slowly to the window. "The firm wished me to convey their sincere sympathy with you in your great loss," he said, without looking round. "I beg that you will understand I am only their servant and merely obeying orders."

91　There was no reply; the old woman's face was white, her eyes staring, and her breath inaudible; on the husband's face was a look such as his friend the sergeant might have carried into his first action.

92　"I was to say that Maw and Meggins disclaim all responsibility," continued the other. "They admit no liability at all, but in consideration of your son's services, they wish to present you with a certain sum as **compensation**."

93　Mr. White dropped his wife's hand, and rising to his feet, gazed with a look of horror at his visitor. His dry lips shaped the words, "How much?"

94　"Two hundred pounds," was the answer.

95　Unconscious of his wife's shriek, the old man smiled faintly, put out his hands like a sightless man, and dropped, a senseless heap, to the floor.

compensation
(kŏm´pən-sā´shən) *n.*
Compensation is something, such as money, that is received as payment.

CRITICAL VOCABULARY

compensation: The man from Maw and Meggins offers the Whites 200 pounds as *compensation*, or payment.

ASK STUDENTS why the Whites are offered compensation and how they probably feel about it. (*The company offers the money because Herbert died while working at their facility. The Whites probably feel that the money can never compensate for their loss.*)

Part III

96 In the huge new cemetery, some two miles distant, the old people buried their dead, and came back to a house steeped in shadow and silence. It was all over so quickly that at first they could hardly realize it, and remained in a state of expectation as though of something else to happen— something else which was to lighten this load, too heavy for old hearts to bear.

97 But the days passed, and expectation gave place to **resignation**—the hopeless resignation of the old, sometimes miscalled apathy. Sometimes they hardly exchanged a word, for now they had nothing to talk about, and their days were long to weariness.

98 It was about a week after that the old man, waking suddenly in the night, stretched out his hand and found himself alone. The room was in darkness, and the sound of subdued weeping came from the window. He raised himself in bed and listened.

99 "Come back," he said tenderly. "You will be cold."

100 "It is colder for my son," said the old woman, and wept afresh.

101 The sound of her sobs died away on his ears. The bed was warm, and his eyes heavy with sleep. He dozed fitfully, and then slept until a sudden wild cry from his wife awoke him with a start.

102 "*The paw!*" she cried wildly. "The monkey's paw!"

103 He started up in alarm. "Where? Where is it? What's the matter?"

resignation
(rĕz´ĭg-nā´shən) *n. Resignation* is the acceptance of something that is inescapable.

ANALYZE FORESHADOWING

Annotate: Mark details in paragraphs 96–100 that describe the Whites' feelings following their son's burial.

Evaluate: Why do you think the author includes this description? Cite evidence to support your ideas.

ANALYZE FORESHADOWING

Ask volunteers to share the details they marked in paragraphs 96–100 to describe the White's feelings and discuss how to summarize their feelings. *(They are devastated, especially Mrs. White.)* (**Answer:** *The description slows the pacing of the story, suggesting a calm lull before an increase in tension. The details "expectation as though of something else to happen" and "waking suddenly in the night" foreshadow a further complication in the plot.*)

■ English Learner Support

Following Foreshadowing Points Direct students' to paragraphs 96–100. Ask: What does it mean that Mr. White "stretched out his hand and found himself alone"? *(When he awoke, he realized Mrs. White was not in bed.)* What did Mr. and Mrs. White each do after they went back to bed? *(Mr. White fell asleep. Mrs. White continued sobbing until she thought about the monkey's paw and yelled out loudly.)* What does Mrs. White's yelling out foreshadow about the next part of the story? *(She may want to make a wish in relation to her devastation and/or her son.)* **LIGHT**

For **speaking support** for students at varying proficiency levels, see the **Text X-Ray** on page 112D.

CRITICAL VOCABULARY

resignation: The author says that *resignation* is "sometimes miscalled apathy."

ASK STUDENTS how resignation differs from apathy and why it might be mistaken for apathy. *(Apathy means "a lack of caring." When people have become resigned to something, it may appear that they don't care anymore, but this is not true.)*

 ### ENGLISH LEARNER SUPPORT

Word Study Review the following rules for most pronunciations of the letters *c* and *g*.

- If *c* is followed by *e, i,* or *y*, it is generally a soft *c* (pronounced like an *s*). If *c* is followed by any other letter or is at the end of a word, it is generally a hard *c* (pronounced like a *k*).

- A *g* followed by *e, i,* or *y* is usually pronounced like a *j*, or soft *g*. It is a hard *g* when followed by any other letter or is at the end of a word.

Project page 123 on the board. Highlight *cemetery, quickly, expectation, resignation, miscalled, exchanged, long, came, cold, colder, cry, cried.* Pronounce each word and have students repeat it. Then, for each word, ask a volunteer to explain the rule that guides the pronunciation of *c* or *g*. (*cemetery—c followed by e: soft; quickly—c followed by others: hard; expectation—c followed by others: hard; resignation—g followed by others: hard; miscalled—c followed by others: hard; exchanged—g followed by e: soft; long—g at end of word: hard; came, cold, colder, cry, cried—c followed by others: hard,*)
SUBSTANTIAL/MODERATE

AHA MOMENT

Explain that Aha Moments give readers a core piece of a story and that readers can use this new information to predict the next part of the story. After rereading paragraphs 101–111, invite students to share predictions. Discuss how, as you read and learn more details, you can adjust your predictions. Have students reread paragraphs 114–116 and ask for prediction adjustments.

ENGLISH LEARNER SUPPORT

Confirm Understanding Ask students to reread paragraphs 114–116. Explain that a coincidence is when two or more similar or related events happen at the same time, but they are not causes or effects of each other.

- Ask students to explain what Mr. White calls a coincidence. *(wishing for money and getting that exact amount upon the death of their son)*

- Ask how Mr. White would react to his wife's request if he really believed the first wish and his son's death were unrelated. *(He might be willing to make another wish.)*

- Have partners identify words and phrases that show Mr. White's actual reaction. **MODERATE**

For **reading support** for students at varying proficiency levels, see the **Text X-Ray** on page 112D.

LANGUAGE CONVENTIONS

Point out that *had* in paragraph 113 is past tense, but the dialogue is still considered to be present tense because Mrs. White was talking in the present tense while referring to the first wish, which had already happened. (**Answer:** *The characters are experiencing events as they happen, so it makes sense that they would speak about them in the present tense.*)

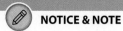

NOTICE & NOTE

104   She came stumbling across the room toward him. "I want it," she said quietly. "You've not destroyed it?"

105   "It's in the parlor, on the bracket," he replied, marveling. "Why?"

106   She cried and laughed together, and bending over, kissed his cheek.

107   "I only just thought of it," she said hysterically. "Why didn't I think of it before? Why didn't *you* think of it?"

108   "Think of what?" he questioned.

109   "The other two wishes," she replied rapidly. "We've only had one."

110   "Was not that enough?" he demanded fiercely.

111   "No," she cried triumphantly; "we'll have one more. Go down and get it quickly, and wish our boy alive again."

112   The man sat up in bed and flung the bedclothes from his quaking limbs. "You are mad!" he cried, aghast.

113   "Get it," she panted; "get it quickly, and wish—Oh, my boy, my boy!"

114   Her husband struck a match and lit the candle. "Get back to bed," he said unsteadily. "You don't know what you are saying."

115   "We had the first wish granted," said the old woman feverishly; "why not the second?"

116   "A coincidence," stammered the old man.

117   "Go and get it and wish," cried his wife, quivering with excitement.

118   He went down in the darkness, and felt his way to the parlor, and then to the mantelpiece. The talisman was in its place, and a horrible fear that the unspoken wish might bring his mutilated son before him ere he could escape from the room seized upon him, and he caught his breath as he found that he had lost the direction of the door. His brow cold with sweat, he felt his way round the table, and groped along the wall until he found himself in the small passage with the unwholesome thing in his hand.

119   Even his wife's face seemed changed as he entered the room. It was white and expectant, and to his fears seemed to have an unnatural look upon it. He was afraid of her.

120   "*Wish!*" she cried, in a strong voice.

121   "It is foolish and wicked," he faltered.

122   "*Wish!*" repeated his wife.

123   He raised his hand. "I wish my son alive again."

124   The talisman fell to the floor, and he regarded it fearfully. Then he sank trembling into a chair as the old woman, with burning eyes, walked to the window and raised the blind.

AHA MOMENT

Notice & Note: What sudden realization causes Mrs. White to become excited in paragraphs 101–111?

Predict: What do you think will happen if Mr. White carries out his wife's orders?

LANGUAGE CONVENTIONS
As in many stories, the events in this story are narrated in the past tense, while the dialogue spoken by the characters is in the present tense. Why does putting dialogue in the present tense make sense?

WHEN STUDENTS STRUGGLE...

Learning Strategy Following the events of the story's conclusion may be difficult because the author presents what Mrs. White is doing only by telling us what Mr. White is hearing. Suggest that students use a graphic organizer to help them keep track of characters' actions.

Action	Character

For additional support, go to the **Reading Studio**.

125　　He sat until he was chilled with the cold, glancing occasionally at the figure of the old woman peering through the window. The candle-end, which had burned below the rim of the china candlestick, was throwing pulsating shadows on the ceiling and walls, until, with a flicker larger than the rest, it expired. The old man, with an unspeakable sense of relief at the failure of the talisman, crept back to his bed, and a minute or two afterward the old woman came silently and apathetically beside him.

126　　Neither spoke, but lay silently listening to the ticking of the clock. A stair creaked, and a squeaky mouse scurried noisily through the wall. The darkness was oppressive, and after lying

 ENGLISH LEARNER SUPPORT

Understand Pronouns Discuss that proper pronoun usage can be confusing because pronouns are handled differently in different languages. Point out that some pronouns are female *(she, her)*; some are male *(he, him, his)*; and some are neutral *(it, they, we)*. Display the pronouns for reference.

One at a time, read to students paragraphs 123 and 124 and ask them to identify each pronoun and indicate whether each is male, female, or neutral. *(He: male; it: neutral; his: male; him: male; his: male; he: male)* Before reading the next sentence, ask students to identify a matching female pronoun for each of the male pronouns. *(He: She; his: her; him: her)*

SUBSTANTIAL/MODERATE

Write these pronoun choices on the board: *she, he, it, they.*

Read each sentence below and ask students to repeat the sentences using correct pronouns.

The wind howled as _____ moved around the house.

Mrs. White thought _____ heard something.

The mice in the house sounded so loud as _____ moved around.

Mr. White was frightened as _____ crept around the house. **LIGHT**

 For **listening support** for students at varying proficiency levels, see the **Text X-Ray** on page 112C.

TO CHALLENGE STUDENTS . . .

Interpret Images Discuss that images are included with the story but their interpretations are left up to the readers. Have students write one-or two-sentence captions to accompany the image on page 125. Make sure that readers understand that there are no right or wrong interpretations but that all interpretations should tie into the story. Ask volunteers to share their captions.

ANALYZE THEME

Remind students that they can determine the theme of a story by asking what lesson(s) the characters learn. (**Answer:** *Mr. White has learned not to try to change fate by making wishes. He is afraid that something terrible will result from his wish. Mrs. White has not learned a lesson. She is still convinced that wishing on the paw has brought her son back to life.*)

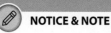

for some time gathering up his courage, he took the box of matches, and striking one, went downstairs for a candle.

127   At the foot of the stairs the match went out, and he paused to strike another; and at the same moment a knock, so quiet and stealthy as to be scarcely audible, sounded on the front door.

128   The matches fell from his hand. He stood motionless, his breath suspended until the knock was repeated. Then he turned and fled swiftly back to his room, and closed the door behind him. A third knock sounded through the house.

129   *"What's that?"* cried the old woman, starting up.

130   "A rat," said the old man in shaking tones—"a rat. It passed me on the stairs."

131   His wife sat up in bed listening. A loud knock resounded through the house.

132   "It's Herbert!" she screamed. "It's Herbert!"

133   She ran to the door, but her husband was before her, and catching her by the arm, held her tightly.

134   "What are you going to do?" he whispered hoarsely.

135   "It's my boy; it's Herbert!" she cried, struggling mechanically. "I forgot it was two miles away. What are you holding me for? Let go. I must open the door."

136   "Don't let it in," cried the old man, trembling.

137   "You're afraid of your own son," she cried, struggling.

138   "Let me go. I'm coming, Herbert; I'm coming."

139   There was another knock, and another. The old woman with a sudden wrench broke free and ran from the room. Her husband followed to the landing, and called after her appealingly as she hurried downstairs. He heard the chain rattle back and the bottom bolt drawn slowly and stiffly from the socket. Then the old woman's voice, strained and panting.

140   "The bolt," she cried loudly. "Come down. I can't reach it."

141   But her husband was on his hands and knees groping wildly on the floor in search of the paw. If he could only find it before the thing outside got in. A perfect fusillade[14] of knocks reverberated through the house, and he heard the scraping of a chair as his wife put it down in the passage against the door. He heard the creaking of the bolt as it came slowly back, and at the same moment he found the monkey's paw, and frantically breathed his third and last wish.

[14] **fusillade** (fyo͞o′sə-läd′): discharge from many guns; a rapid outburst.

ANALYZE THEME

Annotate: In paragraphs 134–138, circle Mr. White's dialogue and underline Mrs. White's.

Infer: What lesson, if any, might each character have learned?

IMPROVE READING FLUENCY

Targeted Passage Discuss that readers often adjust their reading rates based on the nature of the content. Explain that both fear and horror are examples of times when readers might want to read slower or faster. Model reading paragraph 139 slowly and then quickly. Discuss which option best goes with the story. (*Reading slowly will be more haunting.*) Have students slowly and hauntingly read paragraphs 140 and 141.

 Go to the **Reading Studio** for additional support in developing fluency.

142   The knocking ceased suddenly, although the echoes of it were still in the house. He heard the chair drawn back, and the door opened. A cold wind rushed up the staircase, and a long loud wail of disappointment and misery from his wife gave him courage to run down to her side, and then to the gate beyond. The streetlamp flickering opposite shone on a quiet and deserted road.

CHECK YOUR UNDERSTANDING

Answer these questions before moving on to the **Analyze the Text** section on the following page.

1 Mr. White first shows fear of the paw because it —

A makes his friend anxious

B scratches the mantelpiece

C moves in his hand

D has had a spell put on it

2 The dialogue in paragraphs 67–68 indicates that Mrs. White and Herbert are —

F disagreeing about the possible results of their wish

G mocking the idea that the paw is magic

H happy that they wished for something sensible

J nervous about the harm that the paw might cause

3 Based on Mr. White's reaction to the knock on the door in paragraphs 130–136, the reader can conclude that he —

A wants his wife to go downstairs

B realizes he ought to make a third wish

C hopes it will stop if he ignores it

D thinks it is a rat trying to get into his room

The Monkey's Paw   127

✎ CHECK YOUR UNDERSTANDING

Have students answer the questions independently.

Answers:

1. C

2. G

3. C

If they answer any questions incorrectly, have them reread the text to confirm their understanding. Then they may proceed to ANALYZE THE TEXT on p. 128.

 ENGLISH LEARNER SUPPORT

Oral Assessment   Use the following questions to assess students' comprehension and speaking skills.

1. Why did Mr. White first show fear of the paw? (*Mr. White first showed some fear of the paw when the paw moved in his hand right after he made the first wish.*)

2. How does what Mrs. White and Herbert say in paragraphs 64–67 show what they think about the paw and the wish? (*They are mocking the ideas that the paw is magic and that the wish will come true.*)

3. Based on Mr. White's reaction to the knock on the door in paragraphs 130–136, what can the reader conclude about what Mr. White thought about the knocking? (*The knocking will stop if he ignores it.*)
   SUBSTANTIAL/MODERATE

APPLY

ANALYZE THE TEXT

Possible answers:

1. **DOK 4:** *The imagery used to describe the setting suggests potential danger or impending doom. Examples may include "the night was cold and wet" (paragraph 1); "Hark at the wind" (paragraph 2); "of all the beastly, slushy, out-of-the-way places to live in, this is the worst. Pathway's a bog, and the road's a torrent." (paragraph 6).*

2. **DOK 3:** *She refers to Arabian Nights, a collection of fantastical tales, which suggests that she doesn't take the paw seriously or believe its powers are real.*

3. **DOK 3:** *Mr. White's fear of the evil from the monkey's paw deters him from taking a risk. Mrs. White's overpowering love for her son still allows her to hope for a good outcome.*

4. **DOK 4:** *The main message or theme is to be careful what you wish for. Examples of how the theme is developed throughout the story may include that the first man who had the monkey's paw had three wishes granted, but "the third wish was for death"; Morris's desperation to be rid of the paw; and the death of the Whites' son.*

5. **DOK 4:** *When the Whites hear that the amount being offered is 200 pounds, Mrs. White screams and Mr. White faints. They realize that the money is undoubtedly the fulfillment of the wish, meaning they are responsible for their son's death.*

RESEARCH

Point out to students that researching some basic background information about India will help them better understand the references to India in the story.

Connect Students should note in their discussions that the story reflects the British view of Indian culture as exotic but primitive.

ANALYZE THE TEXT

Support your responses with evidence from the text. ☷ NOTEBOOK

1. **Analyze** Review paragraphs 1–6. What details about the setting seem to foreshadow later events?

2. **Draw Conclusions** Reread paragraphs 45–49. Identify the allusion, or reference to a well-known work, that Mrs. White makes. What does the allusion suggest about Mrs. White's view of the paw?

3. **Compare** What do the actions of Mr. and Mrs. White at the end of the story reveal about their different expectations for wishes made on the monkey's paw? Identify what hopes or fears these expectations reveal.

4. **Analyze** What **theme** is suggested by "The Monkey's Paw"? Provide examples that show how the author develops the theme through the characters and plot.

5. **Notice & Note** Review paragraphs 92–95. What do the Whites realize about the two hundred pounds they will receive "as compensation"?

RESEARCH TIP

When you conduct online research, be sure to evaluate the **credibility,** or trustworthiness, of websites. Credible sites are known for not omitting crucial information and for guarding against bias, or preference toward a certain view. Web addresses ending in *.gov, .edu,* or *.org* may have more reliable information than other sites. British government and nonprofit Web addresses often end in *.gov.uk* or *.org.uk,* while academic domains use the ending *.ac.uk.*

RESEARCH

Review paragraphs 13–18. What ideas and attitudes about India are expressed here? Do research to learn more about the historical relationship between Britain and India. Record what you learn in the chart.

QUESTION	ANSWER
What was the British East India Company?	*It was a British merchant company formed in 1600. The British government let it set up trading posts and govern territories in Southeast Asia and the Indian subcontinent.*
How did Britain come to rule India?	*The British East India Company gradually gained power in India as the Mughal Empire declined. The British government took over in 1858 after a rebellion against the company.*
What attitudes did Indians and the British have toward one another during British rule?	*Relations were complex. Many British people discriminated against Indians and viewed Indian culture as exotic but primitive. Many Indians resented British rule.*

Connect With a small group, discuss the ways in which the attitudes in the story reflect the historical context.

 LEARNING MINDSET

Problem Solving Discuss that it is possible that students will run into problems when completing the Analyze the Text questions and the Research work. Point out to students that there are many different ways to solve problems, such as being patient, changing strategies, and asking for help. Make sure they understand that there is no right or wrong way to solve problems and that everyone solves them in their own unique ways. Remind students that everyone runs into problems when learning something new. Emphasize that every problem solved makes you smarter.

CREATE AND DISCUSS

Personal Response Write a personal response to each of the three sections of "The Monkey's Paw." Then write a paragraph that reflects on your responses and connections to the text.

- ❏ Review your annotations and notes about Parts I–III of the story. Write a one-paragraph response to each of the three sections. Cite evidence from the text to support your reactions.

- ❏ Review your responses. Note similarities and differences between your reactions to each section.

- ❏ Write a paragraph that describes how your reactions changed over the course of the story.

Share and Discuss Ideas Are you familiar with the fairy tales "The Three Little Pigs," "Three Billy Goats Gruff," and "The Three Wishes"? These tales and many other traditional stories are structured around three important events or characters. Discuss connections between "The Monkey's Paw" and other familiar stories that follow this "rule of three" pattern.

- ❏ Identify how the "rule of three" structure is used in "The Monkey's Paw" and two other stories with which you are familiar. Note your ideas about the similarities and differences between the stories.

- ❏ Share and discuss your ideas with your group. Ask clarifying questions to make sure you understand others' views.

- ❏ Conclude your discussion by summarizing the main points that were raised and reflecting on new understandings.

RESPOND TO THE ESSENTIAL QUESTION

 Why do we sometimes like to feel frightened?

Gather Information Review your annotations and notes on "The Monkey's Paw." Then, add relevant details to your Response Log. As you determine which information to include, think about:

- the structure of the plot
- supernatural elements of the story
- ways in which the author builds suspense

At the end of the unit, your notes can help you write a literary analysis.

 Go to the **Writing Studio** for help writing a response to literature.

Go to the **Speaking and Listening Studio** to learn more about having a group discussion.

ACADEMIC VOCABULARY
As you write and discuss what you learned from the story, be sure to use the Academic Vocabulary words. Check off each of the words that you use.

- ❏ **convention**
- ❏ **predict**
- ❏ **psychology**
- ❏ **summary**
- ❏ **technique**

The Monkey's Paw 129

CREATE AND DISCUSS

Personal Response Remind students that they should cite evidence from the text to support their response paragraphs to each of the three sections of the story. Also, tell them they should use details from their response paragraphs to describe how their reactions changed over the course of the story.

For **writing support** for students at varying proficiency levels, see the **Text X-Ray** on page 112D.

Share and Discuss Ideas Remind students that they should cite evidence from the text and two other "rule of three" stories to support their ideas about similarities and differences between the stories. Students may discuss the impact of the "rule of three" pattern and note similarities in each story's structure. In contrast to other stories with happy endings, students may point out that "The Monkey's Paw" ending is frightening and tragic.

RESPOND TO THE ESSENTIAL QUESTION

Allow time for students to add details from "The Monkey's Paw" to their Unit 2 Response Logs.

APPLY

CRITICAL VOCABULARY

Answers

1. *Peril and risk both refer to a danger, but a peril is something more serious.*

2. *Both a grimace and a frown are facial expressions. A grimace may show pain or disgust. A frown shows disapproval or displeasure.*

3. *Compensation and wages are types of payment. However, compensation is often money given for some type of loss or suffering.*

4. *Both fate and outcome refer to a future event, but fate suggests an event is determined by an outside power.*

5. *Both credulity and trust have to do with a willingness to believe something, but credulity refers to believing something too readily or easily.*

6. *Resignation and acceptance both refer to deciding to put up with a situation. Resignation suggests that the situation is undesirable and inescapable.*

7. *Both condole and courage suggest supporting another person, but condole suggests a particular type of support through the expression of sympathy.*

8. *Prosaic and dull both mean "ordinary" or "common," but dull has a more negative connotation.*

VOCABULARY STRATEGY
Latin Roots

Answers

1. *incredulous: disbelieving or doubtful, skeptical*

2. *credentials: written evidence that promotes belief or trust*

3. *credence: belief, trust; acceptance as true*

4. *credible: believable*

5. *discredit: to cast doubt on; cause to be distrusted*

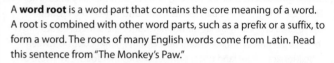 **RESPOND**

WORD BANK

peril	credulity
condole	prosaic
grimace	compensation
fate	resignation

 Go to the **Vocabulary Studio** to learn more about Latin roots.

CRITICAL VOCABULARY

Practice and Apply Explain what is alike and different about the meanings of the words in each pair.

1. peril/risk
2. grimace/frown
3. compensation/wages
4. fate/outcome
5. credulity/trust
6. resignation/acceptance
7. condole/courage
8. prosaic/dull

VOCABULARY STRATEGY:
Latin Roots

A **word root** is a word part that contains the core meaning of a word. A root is combined with other word parts, such as a prefix or a suffix, to form a word. The roots of many English words come from Latin. Read this sentence from "The Monkey's Paw."

His mother laughed, and following him to the door, watched him down the road; and returning to the breakfast table, was very happy at the expense of her husband's credulity.

The word *credulity* includes the Latin root *cred*, which means "believe" or "trust." You can use the meaning of the root *cred* to figure out that *credulity* means "a disposition to believe too readily."

Practice and Apply Find the word in each sentence that includes the Latin root *cred*. Use context and the meaning of the root to help you write the definition of the word. Then verify each of your definitions by finding the word's precise meaning in a print or digital dictionary.

1. Herbert was incredulous when he heard the sergeant-major's tale.

_____

2. A person must have the proper credentials to enter a foreign country.

_____

3. Mrs. White didn't give any credence to the notion that the monkey's paw moved.

_____

4. Were the sergeant-major's stories about India credible?

_____

5. One witness may discredit the story that another person tells.

_____

130 Unit 2

EL **ENGLISH LEARNER SUPPORT**

Vocabulary Strategy Have students locate paragraph 53 and find the vocabulary word *credulity*.

Encourage them to use the following steps:

- Highlight the root and think about its meaning. (*cred*)
- Use the root to define the word.
- Check that the definition makes sense in the context. Use a dictionary to confirm, if necessary. **SUBSTANTIAL/MODERATE**

LANGUAGE CONVENTIONS: Verb Tenses

Correct verb tenses tell the reader when an action happened—in the past, present, or future. As you write, it's important to use the same tense between sentences and across paragraphs to describe actions that take place at the same time and to change tenses when shifting from one time period to another. In general, use the present tense when writing about the action in a story, movie, or book—unless you are describing events that happened before the start of the main action. To describe events that preceded the main action in a story, movie, or book, use the past tense.

RESPOND

Go to **Verb Tenses** in the **Grammar Studio** to learn more.

ORIGINAL	REVISED
Last night I <u>watch</u> a movie about a sea monster that <u>terrorized</u> the people of a small fishing village. In one scene, the monster <u>jumps</u> up and <u>surprised</u> a fisherman. When this <u>happened</u>, I <u>jump</u> up too and <u>spill</u> all of my popcorn. (*The first sentence uses the present tense to describe a past event but uses the past tense to describe the action in a movie. The second and third sentences use the present and past tenses inconsistently.*)	Last night I <u>watched</u> a movie about a sea monster that <u>terrorizes</u> the people of a small fishing village. In one scene, the monster <u>jumps</u> up and <u>surprises</u> a fisherman. When this <u>happened</u>, I <u>jumped</u> up too and <u>spilled</u> all of my popcorn. (*The first sentence uses the present tense to describe the action in the movie but uses the past tense to describe an event that occurred in the past. The second sentence uses the present tense to describe the action of the movie. The third sentence uses the past tense to describe the viewer's reaction.*)

Practice and Apply Read the following paragraph. For each choice in parentheses, choose the verb with the correct tense.

The short story "The Monkey's Paw" by W. W. Jacobs (was, is) set in the English countryside during the late 19th century. At the beginning of the story, Sergeant-Major Morris, a friend of the White family who recently (returned, returns) from India, (arrived, arrives) at the White home for a visit. Morris tells the Whites about a magical monkey's paw that he (obtained, obtains) on his travels. After explaining how the paw (brought, brings) misfortune on himself and another man who (used, uses) it, he reluctantly (gave, gives) the paw to the Whites.

Write a one-paragraph review of "The Monkey's Paw." Tell how the story begins, whether you recommend it, and how you think others will react to it. Then edit your paragraph for appropriate use of verb tenses.

LANGUAGE CONVENTIONS: Verb Tenses

Review the information about verb tenses with students. Explain that using correct verb tenses in your writing helps your readers follow what you are saying. Remind students that every verb has a past, present, and future form. Have students use these three sentence starters to practice identifying all three forms of verbs you call out.

- *Yesterday, I _____.*
- *Today, I _____.*
- *Tomorrow, I _____.*

Practice and Apply The short story "The Monkey's Paw" by W. W. Jacobs is set in the English countryside during the late 19th century. At the beginning of the story, Sergeant-Major Morris, a friend of the White family who recently returned from India, arrives at the White home for a visit. Morris tells the Whites about a magical monkey's paw that he obtained on his travels. After explaining how the paw brought misfortune on himself and another man who used it, he reluctantly gives the paw to the Whites.

Students' reviews should use the present tense to refer to the action in the story and the future tense to describe how they think others will react to it.

 ENGLISH LEARNER SUPPORT

Language Conventions Write these three sentences on the board:

- *Evan told a horror story in class.*
- *Marc will read a horror story for a contest.*
- *Annabelle writes more of her horror story each day.*

Use the following supports with students at varying proficiency levels:

- Have students indicate the tense of each verb. **SUBSTANTIAL**
- Have students revise the sentences so they are all in past tense. **MODERATE**
- Have students write three new sentences that use the same three verbs in the same tenses. **LIGHT**

from THE MONKEY'S PAW

Film Clip by Ricky Lewis Jr.

GENRE ELEMENTS
FILM

Tell students that in this lesson they will watch and discuss a **film clip**. Explain that this clip is the closing part of a movie based on the short story "The Monkey's Paw," which the class recently read. Point out that while the movie is based on the story, the movie doesn't—and can't—replicate the written story in every possible way. Instead, the director made choices that sometimes reflected the original story and sometimes made changes to it. Tell students that after they see the film clip, they will have an opportunity to discuss the differences and similarities between the film and the story.

LEARNING OBJECTIVES

- Identify choices made by a film director.
- Create a storyboard for a film version of a scene from "The Monkey's Paw."
- Compare and contrast a written story with a film based on the story.
- Identify techniques used by filmmakers to build suspense and show emotion.
- Describe how film directors' choices can increase or decrease a film's effectiveness.
- **Language** Discuss with a partner the differences and similarities of film and text using the term *dialogue*.

TEXT COMPLEXITY

Quantitative Measures	The Monkey's Paw: Film clip	Lexile N/A
Qualitative Measures	**Ideas Presented** The existence of magic is assumed, but otherwise the ideas are familiar.	
	Structure Used The film uses time order, including a jump of about a year.	
	Language Used The language is associated with another time and place, but is largely accessible.	
	Knowledge Required Little if any specific background knowledge is necessary to comprehend the clip.	

RESOURCES

- Unit 2 Response Log
- Speaking and Listening Studio: Participating in a Collaborative Discussion
- Speaking and Listening Studio: Giving a Presentation
- "The Monkey's Paw" Selection Test

SUMMARIES

English

The film version of "The Monkey's Paw" tells the same basic story as the W. W. Jacobs short story it's based on. A man is given a dried-up monkey paw and told that it can bring the owner three wishes. He is skeptical but makes a wish anyway. The wish comes true but results in the death of his son. Some time later his wife, deeply grieving, gets him to use the second wish to bring their son home. The son is no longer human, however, and the man uses his final wish to wish him away. A year later; the wife is dead and the husband is very ill.

Spanish

La versión cinematográfica de "La pata de mono" cuenta básicamente la misma historia que el cuento corto de W.W. Jacobs, sobre la cual se basa. Un hombre recibe una pata de mono disecada y le dicen que ésta puede concederle tres deseos. Al principio se muestra escéptico, pero pide un deseo de todos modos. El deseo se hace realidad, pero resulta en la muerte de su hijo. Tiempo después, su esposa, profundamente afligida, hace que use el segundo deseo para que su hijo vuelva a casa. No obstante, el hijo ya no es humano y el hombre usa su último deseo para que se vaya. Un año después, la esposa muere y el esposo queda enfermísimo.

SMALL-GROUP OPTIONS

Have students work in small groups to read and discuss the selection.

Listen and Summarize

- Tell students that it is critical for them to listen closely to other group members.
- Have one student begin with a comment about the topic.
- The next student who wishes to speak must begin by summarizing the first student's comment in a sentence or two.
- If the student can't offer a reasonable summary, remind him or her that the goal is to listen closely to others and suggest that the student try again later.
- Continue the discussion, with each participant summarizing the most recent comment before stating his or her own.

Roles and Tasks

- Create three to five "job titles" for students; try to have one title for every member of a typical small group in your classroom.
- Titles might include Discussion Leader, Note Taker, Summarizer, and Timekeeper, but use roles that make sense to you and your students.
- Each student in a group picks a card to learn his or her role. Explain that roles will vary from one day to the next.
- Tell students that everyone should participate in the discussion by offering ideas, but explain the specific responsibilities for each job title.

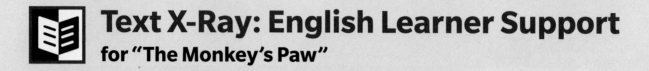

Text X-Ray: English Learner Support
for "The Monkey's Paw"

INTRODUCE THE SELECTION
DISCUSS FILMS AND TEXTS

In this lesson, students will need to be able to compare and contrast a film version of the story "The Monkey's Paw" with the original story. Give students the following explanations of films and texts:

- A film is a movie. Films often show actors moving and speaking on a screen.
- A text is a written document such as a novel, a short story, or an article.

Tell students that films and texts may have a lot in common, but they are different in important ways. For example, a text can only describe a person's facial expression, while a film can show the audience the look on an actor's face. Likewise, the writer of a text can include information about a character's unspoken thoughts, but that is more difficult in a film. Have students use these sentence frames to compare and contrast films and texts:

- *A film/text can show _____, but a text/film _____.*
- *Texts and films are alike because _____.*

CULTURAL REFERENCES

The following references in the film may be unfamiliar to students:

- Western burial customs, including the placing of a headstone to mark a grave.
- The way Mrs. White and her husband express grief over the loss of their son.
- The belief, common in England in the early 1900s, that far-off places, such as India, were exotic and mysterious countries where anything could happen.

LISTENING

Understand Dialogue

Explain that speaking in films is known as dialogue. Point out that students will need to listen very closely to the dialogue in the movie because much of the plot is based on what the characters say.

Have students listen to the dialogue in the film. Use the following supports with students at varying proficiency levels:

- Ask simple *yes* or *no* questions about the dialogue. For example, ask whether a particular line was said by Mr. White or Mrs. White. Pause the film and return to the scene in question to have students listen again and check their answers. **SUBSTANTIAL**
- Ask questions about the dialogue that can be answered in phrases or simple complete sentences. For example, ask students which character spoke a particular line in the scene. **MODERATE**
- Have students recall a line of dialogue from the film that they thought was especially dramatic, sad, or scary. Have them tell a partner the line and explain who said it and what they found interesting about it. **LIGHT**

SPEAKING

Discuss Film Techniques

Remind students that films and texts have different characteristics. Review some of the techniques of effective storytelling in films, such as camera angles and sound effects.

Use the following supports with students at varying proficiency levels:

- Have students act out various techniques while saying their names. For example, have students drum their fingers to imitate a rainstorm while saying the phrase *sound effects*. **SUBSTANTIAL**
- Have students tell a partner what they know about each technique. Have them use phrases and complete sentences, such as *Music can make the film spooky*. **MODERATE**
- Have students tell a partner what they know about each technique. Have them use complex sentences and content vocabulary, such as *When you want to show something scary, you can use a camera filter*. **LIGHT**

READING

Understand Film Techniques

Have students carefully read the information about film techniques and the differences between films and texts.

Have students carefully read the information about film techniques and the information regarding differences between films and texts. Use the following supports with students at varying proficiency levels:

- Ask students to put question marks next to sections they do not understand. Work with students to clear up confusion. Encourage students to help each other to comprehend these sections. **SUBSTANTIAL**
- Ask students to underline individual words and phrases they do not yet know. Work with students to provide simple definitions and examples, and encourage students to ask one another for help with troublesome vocabulary. **MODERATE**
- Have students work with a partner to summarize these sections orally. Have partners share their thinking with another pair. **LIGHT**

WRITING

Write a Storyboard

Tell students that a storyboard does not take the place of a script and will not include all, or even most, of the dialogue in the completed film. Emphasize, though, that students should write as much as is feasible in the space and time they have.

Use the following supports with students at varying proficiency levels:

- Focus on having students write single words and phrases. Model speaking a sentence using the word or phrase they chose. **SUBSTANTIAL**
- Have students write simple complete sentences. Model how you might combine simple sentences to form a more complex sentence. **MODERATE**
- Have students write complex sentences to create dialogue for their scenes. Have them read their sentences aloud using an appropriate voice for the character who will speak that line. **LIGHT**

TEACH

**? Connect to the
ESSENTIAL QUESTION**

In "The Monkey's Paw," a British couple is given a mummified animal paw that allows them to make three wishes. Their wishes come true—but in a horrifying way. Ask students whether this sounds like an enjoyable story. Allow students to offer different opinions. Expect mixed reactions. Ask: *Doesn't being able to make three wishes sound fun? What if we stopped there and the couple was granted three wishes? The end. Would that be a very enjoyable story?* Discuss what makes a story entertaining. Guide the discussion to include the element of surprise.

COMPARE VERSIONS

Point out that film and written words can be very different even when they tell essentially the same story. Discuss with students that visual images can be extremely powerful and that film can show facial expressions and the sounds of people crying or screaming in a way that words on the page cannot convey. On the other hand, readers can make up their own images, which can be powerful as well, and text can also convey interior thoughts and emotions that may be more difficult to portray on the screen. Have students keep this information in mind while discussing differences and similarities between the two versions of the story.

FILM CLIP
from

THE MONKEY'S PAW

by **Ricky Lewis Jr.**
page 135

COMPARE VERSIONS

Now that you've read "The Monkey's Paw," view the film clip based on the short story's ending. As you do, think about similarities and differences between the short story and the film adaptation. After you are finished, you will collaborate with a small group on a final project that involves an analysis of both works.

? ESSENTIAL QUESTION:

Why do we sometimes like to feel frightened?

SHORT STORY

THE MONKEY'S PAW

by **W. W. Jacobs**
pages 115–127

132   Unit 2

from **The Monkey's Paw**

QUICK START

Think back to a suspenseful scene in a movie. How did you feel as you watched the scene? With a partner, describe the scene and your reaction to it.

ANALYZE FILM

Like many movies, the film *The Monkey's Paw* is based on a written work. Writers and directors use different techniques to create suspense and tell a story.

- Writers use words to describe the rising action or the characters' struggles.
- Directors use a combination of visual and sound techniques.

Directors may use different camera shots to convey ideas, to track characters' emotions, or to show a situation from a character's viewpoint.

GENRE ELEMENTS: FILM

- combines images and sound to tell a story or convey information
- uses visual and sound techniques such as camera shots, lighting, music, and sound effects
- often includes actors who play the roles of characters

CAMERA SHOT	WHAT IT IS	WHY IT IS USED
Close-up shot	a shot that focuses on a character's face	to convey a character's emotions or thoughts
Low-angle shot	a shot in which the camera looks up at a subject	to create the impression of height or distance; to make a subject look more menacing
High-angle shot	a shot in which the camera looks down at a subject	to show a character in relation to his or her surroundings; to make a subject look unprotected or exposed
Point-of-view shot	a shot that is filmed from the character's point of view	to show viewers what the character is seeing

The Monkey's Paw   133

QUICK START

Have students read the Quick Start prompt and share their reactions with a partner. Encourage them to note both their physical and emotional reactions as they watched the movie. Provide a checklist of questions to guide their responses: *Did their heart rate speed up or slow down? Did they feel tension in their bodies? If so, where?*

ANALYZE FILM

Help students identify the characteristics of media described. Emphasize the differences in how directors and writers of short stories and novels establish tension. Then go over the various types of camera shots in the chart and the purposes of each. Have students identify the techniques and camera angles that they think are most effective in building suspense and predict which ones they might see in the film clip from "The Monkey's Paw."

TECH

ANALYZE FILM

Explain that film directors have many strategies for setting a mood in a movie and that these techniques can also help instill particular emotions in audience members. Go through the list at the top of the page with students. Have them give brief examples of movies they've seen in which sound effects, lighting, or other techniques have pushed them to feel a certain way. Ask, for example, how slow music played on low strings might establish a different mood than jazzy music played at a fast, upbeat tempo.

Call attention to the chart in the middle of the page. Remind students that different techniques include not only those on this page but the camera angles listed on the previous page as well. Explain that students will fill out the chart as they watch the film clip.

Finally, point out the information at the bottom of the page. Explain that it is usually not possible for a filmmaker to include everything from a novel or even from a short story, and add that it may not be desirable to do so. Tell students that they should watch closely to see what choices the filmmaker made that might be different from those made by the story's author.

■ English Learner Support

Vocabulary Have students read each of the four words or phrases (*lighting, camera filters, sound effects, music*) mentioned at the top of the page. They should write each word on a card and put a definition, description, or drawing on the other side of the card. Have students use the cards to help them talk about the film clip. **MODERATE**

ANALYZE FILM (continued)

Directors may also use other visual and sound techniques to convey mood, to build suspense, and to focus viewers' attention on characters and events.

- **Lighting** can create moods that are gloomy, mysterious, or scary. Suspenseful movies often have minimal lighting with frequent use of shadows.
- **Camera filters** are glass or plastic dishes that are inserted in front of a camera lens. These filters can change the way images appear, making them clearer, brighter, darker, or fuzzier.
- **Sound effects** may include action noises or nature sounds. The sound of a loud bang or heavy rain, for example, might contribute to a threatening or dreary mood.
- **Music** can signal dramatic events or tense moments. Music sometimes foreshadows, or hints at, what is going to happen.

As you view the film clip, use a chart like this to help you analyze the different film techniques the director uses.

TECHNIQUE	PART IN THE FILM	EFFECT
1.		
2.		
3.		
4.		

When a director makes a movie of a written story, he or she has to make choices about how closely to follow the written work. Will the film

- include all of the same characters?
- have the same setting?
- add or cut a scene?

As you view the film clip, think about how the director's choices affect the content of the film version of "The Monkey's Paw."

APPLYING ACADEMIC VOCABULARY

☑ convention ❑ predict ❑ psychology ☑ summary ❑ technique

Write and Discuss Have each student write a response to the questions below. Then, have them discuss their responses with a partner. Guide students to include the Academic Vocabulary words *convention* and *summary* in both their sentences and their discussions.

- What **convention** does a writer use to create a first-person narrative?
- What should you include in **summary** of a short story?

BACKGROUND

The film The Monkey's Paw *is an adaptation of the short story of the same name. The film's writer and director, Ricky Lewis Jr., read the story as a child. He decided to make it into a movie because his "morbid curiosity wanted to see it." While other film adaptations of the story had modernized it, Lewis thought it was important that the film be set in the past, "when odd things were sure to happen." He chose to "let a little darkness" into his film to create its gloomy, sometimes spooky mood.*

PREPARE TO COMPARE

As you view the film clip, note important details about each scene. This will help you identify similarities and differences between the short story and the film adaptation. ▤ **NOTEBOOK**

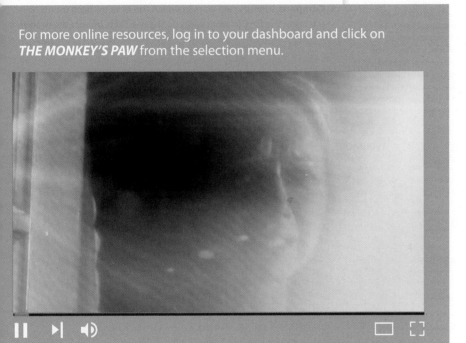

For more online resources, log in to your dashboard and click on ***THE MONKEY'S PAW*** from the selection menu.

As needed, pause the film clip to make notes about each scene. Replay or rewind so that you can analyze techniques and other specific elements of the film.

TEACH

BACKGROUND

Read this section with students. Point out that the filmmaker made several important decisions about how he would present the material in the original story. Ask students to identify these decisions and Lewis's reasons for them. Then ask them what they think about Lewis's decision not to modernize the story.

PREPARE TO COMPARE

Review with students some of the differences between written text and film. Ask students whether they think film or text will prove more effective at conveying different parts of the story, and why. Remind students to take notes as they watch the film clip.

It is a good idea to pause the viewing several times as students watch the film. This allows students a chance to reflect on what they have seen and affords them an opportunity to catch up on their notes. It also permits you to point out particular techniques used by the filmmaker and to identify areas of similarity or difference between the film and book versions.

 ENGLISH LEARNER SUPPORT

Listening Watching a film can be difficult for English learners because they may have difficulty understanding what is being said. Characters may speak with their backs to the viewer, which denies the audience facial cues; the script may require actors to speak some of their lines very softly or even indistinctly; and actors rarely repeat what they say in movies. While viewing the film, be cognizant of potential trouble spots. Stop the film whenever you feel it necessary to repeat a line of dialogue for students or ensure that listeners understood every word. **ALL LEVELS**

ANALYZE MEDIA

Possible answers:

1. **DOK 2:** *Mrs. White realizes there are two remaining wishes in the paw. She begs her husband to wish that Herbert were alive, and he agrees. Herbert returns to the house, but he is not human, and Mr. White uses the third wish to return him to the grave. A year later Mrs. White is dead ,and Mr. White is near death.*

2. **DOK 4:** *The dark lighting creates an ominous feeling when Herbert approaches. The brighter blue lighting when Mr. White makes his third wish is mystical.*

3. **DOK 2:** *The music sounds more threatening and ominous during these scenes. That builds tension and foreshadows the tragic events to come.*

4. **DOK 4:** *The close-up shots of Mrs. White create a desperate mood. The point-of-view shots of Mrs. White from her husband's perspective show her grief. At the cemetery, the angles and filters highlight the cold reality of death.*

5. **DOK 3:** *The sound of a screeching owl contributes to a gloomy mood at the beginning of the film clip. Later, the repeated knocking sound builds tension.*

RESEARCH

Read the prompt with students. Tell students they are likely to find information about this subject on the Internet. Discuss possible search terms and ways to limit searches.

Connect Students might mention the scene showing Mr. White going downstairs to make the second wish is an example of panning. The shot of the grave is an example of zooming. Students should cite details to support their opinions about the effectiveness of these techniques.

 RESPOND

ANALYZE MEDIA

Support your responses with evidence from the film clip. ▤ NOTEBOOK

1. **Summarize** The film clip shows several scenes from the short story "The Monkey's Paw." Summarize the events shown and described in the film.

2. **Analyze** Consider the ways the director uses lighting in the film. What is the effect of the lighting in the scene in which Herbert returns to the house?

3. **Interpret** Why do you think the music changes as Mr. White makes his second and third wishes?

4. **Analyze** How do the camera angles and camera filters that the director uses affect the mood of the film? How do they affect the impact of the final scenes at the cemetery?

5. **Compare** Identify two ways in which the director uses sound effects in the film. In what ways do these effects impact the mood?

RESEARCH TIP
As you begin research, you can start with a general search and use the results to help you narrow your search. For example, you might start with the search terms *filming techniques* or *cinematography*; the results of these searches might lead you to focus your search on particular lighting or camera movement techniques.

RESEARCH

On pp. 133–134, you learned about various film techniques that film directors use to achieve particular effects. Research additional filming techniques to learn more. Record your findings in the chart.

TECHNIQUE	WHAT IT IS
panning	pivoting a movie camera along a horizontal plane in order to follow an object or create a panoramic effect
zooming	simulating movement away from or toward a subject
tracking	moving a camera alongside a subject

Connect With a small group, discuss whether any of the techniques you researched appeared in the film clip. Then discuss effective examples of the techniques in other films. If possible, practice some of the techniques yourself.

EL ENGLISH LEARNER SUPPORT

Oral Assessment To gauge comprehension and speaking skills, conduct an informal assessment. Walk around the class, talking with students and asking questions. Have partners work together to answer the questions and present their answers:

- Which character makes the wishes on the monkey's paw? (*Mr. White*) **SUBSTANTIAL**

- What does Mrs. White beg Mr. White to do? (wish that their son was alive again) **MODERATE**

- How is Mrs. White feeling when she asks her husband to wish their son back to life? How do you know? (Anxious, excited; she speaks quickly and her face looks nervous.) **LIGHT**

CREATE AND DISCUSS

Discuss Ideas Have a group discussion about adapting a scene in "The Monkey's Paw" to create a film version.

❏ Review the story and the film clip. Think about the techniques the film director uses in the adaptation of the story's ending.

❏ Share your ideas about which scene you would choose to adapt to create a film version and why. Cite details from the story and the film clip to support your ideas.

❏ As a group, discuss whether you think a film adaptation should stay true to the text or vary. Support your reasoning with examples.

Create a Storyboard With your group, create a storyboard for a film retelling of a scene from "The Monkey's Paw." A **storyboard** is a device filmmakers use to plan the shooting of a movie. It serves as a map that includes images and descriptions.

❏ Discuss whether you will stay faithful to the text or make changes. Take a vote to determine your path.

❏ Draw a series of several frames. Sketch the characters and scene for each frame.

❏ Underneath each frame, write a description of the shot—such as close-up, medium, or distance shot—and write a line of dialogue or a description of the action.

❏ Decide what kind of music or sound effects you will add, and write where you'll include them.

 Go to the **Speaking and Listening Studio** for help with having a group discussion.

RESPOND TO THE ESSENTIAL QUESTION

 Why do we sometimes like to feel frightened?

Gather Information Review your annotations and notes on the film clip. Then, add relevant details to your Response Log. As you determine which information to include, think about:

• ways in which visual and sound techniques affect the mood of the film

• aspects of the film that elicit a strong reaction

At the end of the unit, you can use your notes to help you write a literary analysis.

ACADEMIC VOCABULARY
As you write and discuss what you learned from the film clip, be sure to use the Academic Vocabulary words. Check off each of the words that you use.

❏ **convention**
❏ **predict**
❏ **psychology**
❏ **summary**
❏ **technique**

CREATE AND DISCUSS

Discuss Ideas Remind students that a film adaptation of a written story is going to be different from the original. Ask students which scenes in the story "The Monkey's Paw" would be most effective if presented in a film version. Have students explain their reasoning. Then guide students to discuss how closely a film version of the scene should adhere to the original. Ask them to consider what might be difficult to get across in a visual image, and what might be added to make the scene more effective.

For **listening support** for students at varying proficiency levels, see the **Text X-Ray** on page 132C.

Create a Storyboard Explain that a storyboard is essentially a detailed outline showing simple images and descriptions for a proposed film. Tell students that they will not be making the movie, but that their storyboard will be detailed enough that other people can understand what the movie would look like. Be sure they understand that characters, music, and camera shots are all important aspects of making a film.

RESPOND TO THE ESSENTIAL QUESTION

Allow time for students to add details from the film version of "The Monkey's Paw" to their Unit 2 Response Logs.

RESPOND

COMPARE VERSIONS

Review with students that films are never exactly the same as the stories they are based on, but point out that films and stories typically have much in common. Have students read the explanation of how filmmakers and directors decide which parts of an original story to include, change, or replace. Be sure students understand the examples given.

Remind students of how a Venn diagram works, if necessary: elements that are specific to the original story go in the left circle, elements specific to the film clip go in the right circle, and the overlapping circle is reserved for elements present in both versions of the tale.

ANALYZE THE TEXT AND FILM CLIP

Possible answers:

1. **DOK 4:** *The clip stays true to the main events and the setting.*

2. **DOK 3:** *The film adds some dialogue, such as Mrs. White's explanation about how disfigured Herbert was when he died. The clip also continues beyond the original story to show that Mrs. White has died and Mr. White will likely die as well.*

3. **DOK 2:** *The story includes more information about Mr. White's reactions to his wife and the paw. The movie has close-up shots of Mrs. White, which effectively show her grief and suffering. Check that students can support their answers.*

4. **DOK 4:** *Answers will vary. Students should cite textual evidence to support their opinions.*

 RESPOND

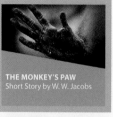

THE MONKEY'S PAW
Short Story by W. W. Jacobs

from **THE MONKEY'S PAW**
Film Clip by Ricky Lewis Jr.

Collaborate & Compare

COMPARE VERSIONS

While authors use language to tell stories, film directors rely on visual and sound techniques to help bring stories to life. When directors decide to make a movie based on a written story or novel, they make choices about what to include and what to omit. For example, they might cut a scene that's hard to portray visually or isn't necessary to move the plot forward. Or they might add a scene to help show what a character is experiencing. In a small group, complete the Venn diagram with similarities and differences between the story's ending and the film clip. Then write a response summarizing your findings.

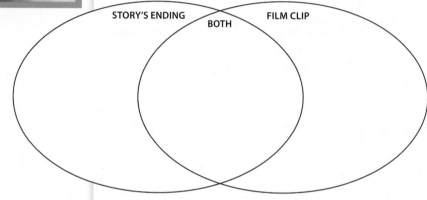

ANALYZE THE TEXT AND FILM CLIP

Discuss these questions in your group.

1. **Connect** In what ways does the film clip stay true to the story?

2. **Contrast** What differences are there between the story's ending and the film clip?

3. **Interpret** Which version helps you better understand how the characters feel? Cite evidence from the versions in your discussion.

4. **Evaluate** Which do you find more frightening, the film version or the story? Which do you find more tragic? Cite evidence to support your ideas.

DISCUSS AND PRESENT

Now, your group can continue comparing the story's ending and the film clip by exploring the reasons for the director's choices and evaluating the advantages of each version.

1. **Decide on the Most Important Details** With your group, review your diagram to identify similarities and differences between the story's ending and the film clip. What are the most important details in each version?

2. **Discuss the Director's Choices** Consider the similarities and differences you identified. Discuss possible reasons why the director might have chosen to stay true to some parts of the story and to tell some parts differently. You can use this chart to record supporting evidence.

 Go to the **Speaking and Listening Studio** for help with having a group discussion and giving a presentation.

	POSSIBLE REASON FOR DIRECTOR'S CHOICE
Setting	The old buildings and the 19th c. English countryside helps the director create an eerie scene.
Characters	Adding details about Herbert's injuries and showing his shadows/footsteps makes audience fearful of his return.
Events	Adding the cemetery scene at the end emphasizes the message that people interfere with fate at their peril.

3. **Evaluate Advantages of Each Version** With your group, discuss advantages of the story and film versions. Record your ideas in the chart.

	ADVANTAGES
Story	The narrator can say what characters are thinking and feeling. Readers can use details to visualize the scene.
Film	Visual and sound effects create a frightening mood for events. Facial expressions, movements, and tone of voice help show what the characters are thinking and feeling.

4. **Present to the Class** Now it is time to share your ideas. Clearly state your inferences about the reasons for the director's choices. Provide examples to support your opinions about the advantages of each version. Adapt the charts you created or create other visuals to help convey your ideas to the class.

DISCUSS AND PRESENT

Guide students through the directions for the entire project before beginning to work. Call students' attention to the chart, and remind them that setting, characters, and events, or plot, are three of the most important elements to a story, whether that story is written or filmed.

Ask students to discuss why the director made the choices he did and whether they agree with those choices. Then have students identify the advantages they perceive for the film and for written text. Though students will discuss this question in small groups, point out that group members do not need to come to the same conclusion.

Finally, point out the presentation guidelines in step 4 and have students use them to explain their ideas to the rest of the class. (Students' presentations should include visuals and text evidence to support their ideas.)

 For **speaking and listening support** for students at varying proficiency levels, see the **Text X-Ray** on pages 132C–132D.

TO CHALLENGE STUDENTS . . .

Evaluate Decisions Have students identify three decisions made by the director of the film clip. These decisions may include filming techniques involving sound, cameras, or lighting, or the decisions may involve what plot and character elements to put into the film version of the story. For each, have students write a short paragraph evaluating how effective the decision was and explaining what made it either effective or ineffective. Before students begin to write, have them consider how the film would be different if the director had made a different decision, and whether an alternative would have been a better choice.

READER'S CHOICE

Setting a Purpose Have students review their Unit 2 Response Log and think about why people sometimes like to feel frightened. As students select their Independent Reading selections, encourage them to consider what more they want to know about the experience of suspense or fear.

NOTICE & NOTE

Explain that some selections may contain multiple signposts; others may contain only one. And the same type of signpost can occur many times in the same text.

LEARNING MINDSET

Curiosity Tell students that curiosity leads to learning. Explain that exploring independent reading selections gives students a chance to develop and satisfy curiosity about new topics. Encourage students to think about ways their reading can help them outside of class.

INDEPENDENT READING

? ESSENTIAL QUESTION:

Why do we sometimes like to feel frightened?

Reader's Choice

Setting a Purpose Select one or more of these options from your eBook to continue your exploration of the Essential Question.

- Read the descriptions to see which text grabs your interest.
- Think about which genres you enjoy reading.

Notice & Note

In this unit, you practiced asking **Big Questions** and noticing and noting two signposts: **Extreme or Absolute Language** and **Quoted Words**. As you read independently, these signposts and others will aid your understanding. Below are the anchor questions to ask when you read literature and nonfiction.

Reading Literature: Stories, Poems, and Plays		
Signpost	**Anchor Question**	Lesson
Contrasts and Contradictions	Why did the character act that way?	p. 3
Aha Moment	How might this change things?	p. 3
Tough Questions	What does this make me wonder about?	p. 152
Words of the Wiser	What's the lesson for the character?	p. 406
Again and Again	Why might the author keep bringing this up?	p. 2
Memory Moment	Why is this memory important?	p. 153

Reading Nonfiction: Essays, Articles, and Arguments		
Signpost	**Anchor Question(s)**	Lesson
Big Questions	What surprised me? What did the author think I already knew? What challenged, changed, or confirmed what I already knew?	p. 77
Contrasts and Contradictions	What is the difference, and why does it matter?	p. 241
Extreme or Absolute Language	Why did the author use this language?	p. 76
Numbers and Stats	Why did the author use these numbers or amounts?	p. 325
Quoted Words	Why was this person quoted or cited, and what did this add?	p. 77
Word Gaps	Do I know this word from someplace else? Does it seem like technical talk for this topic? Do clues in the sentence help me understand the word?	p. 240

ENGLISH LEARNER SUPPORT

Develop Fluency Help students select books of suitable difficulty, content, and interest.

- Have students preview a book by skimming its table of contents, the amount of text on a page, and illustrations.
- Select a passage from a text and read aloud one sentence, and then have students read the sentence back to you. Continue this process for the rest of the passage. **SUBSTANTIAL**
- Have students read and then reread the passage silently. **MODERATE**

- Ask students to read to page 10. They should have to think and clarify some. If not, the book is too easy. If they can't make any sense of it, the book is too hard. **LIGHT**
- Allow more fluent readers to select their own texts. Set a specific time for students to read silently (for example, 15 minutes). Check their comprehension by having them write a summary of what they have read. **LIGHT**

 Go to the **Reading Studio** for additional support in developing fluency.

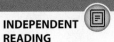

You can preview these texts in Unit 2 of your eBook.

Then, check off the text or texts that you select to read on your own.

POEM

Frankenstein

Edward Field

Frankenstein's monster encounters kindness for the first time.

POEM

beware: do not read this poem

Ishmael Reed

Prepare to be devoured by poetry.

SHORT STORY

Blood

Zdravka Evitmova

A generous impulse has unintended consequences.

SHORT STORY

The Outsider

H. P. Lovecraft

A narrator makes a shocking discovery when he escapes from his home, a dark and lonely castle.

ESSAY

Scary Tales

Jackie Torrence

A storyteller follows in her grandfather's footsteps.

Collaborate and Share Meet with a partner to discuss what you learned from at least one of your independent readings.

- Give a brief synopsis or summary of the text.
- Describe any signposts that you noticed in the text and explain what they revealed to you.
- Describe what you most enjoyed or found most challenging about the text. Give specific examples.
- Decide if you would recommend the text to others. Why or why not?

 Go to the **Reading Studio** for more resources on **Notice & Note**.

INDEPENDENT READING

MATCHING STUDENTS TO TEXTS

Use the following information to guide students in choosing their texts.

Frankenstein
  Genre: poem
  Overall Rating: Accessible

beware: do not read this poem
  Genre: poem
  Overall Rating: Challenging

Blood   Lexile: 660L
  Genre: short story
  Overall Rating: Accessible

The Outsider   Lexile: 1270L
  Genre: short story
  Overall Rating: Challenging

Scary Tales   Lexile: 730L
  Genre: essay
  Overall Rating: Accessible

Collaborate and Share To assess how well students read the selections, walk around the room and listen to their conversations. Encourage students to be focused and specific in their comments.

Online **for Assessment**

- Independent Reading Selection Tests

Encourage students to visit the **Reading Studio** to download a handy bookmark of **NOTICE & NOTE** signposts.

WHEN STUDENT STRUGGLE . . .

Keep a Reading Log As students read their selected texts, have them keep a reading log for each selection to note signposts and their thoughts about them. Use their logs to assess how well they are noticing and reflecting on elements of the texts.

Reading Log for (title)		
Page and Paragraph	**Signpost I Noticed**	**My Notes About It**

UNIT ② Tasks

• WRITE A LITERARY ANALYSIS

MENTOR TEXT

WHAT IS THE HORROR GENRE?

Literary Criticism by
SHARON A. RUSSELL

LEARNING OBJECTIVES

Writing Task

- Write a literary analysis about one of the stories.
- Use strategies to plan and organize your literary analysis.
- Use the Mentor Text as a model for writing an engaging introduction and integrating details.
- Provide an introduction that catches the reader's attention and includes a clear controlling idea.
- Develop support for your controlling idea by including examples and quotations from the story.
- Organize main ideas and supporting evidence.
- Use appropriate transitions to connect ideas.
- Use appropriate word choice and sentence variety.
- End by summarizing or drawing an overall conclusion.
- Revise drafts, incorporating feedback from peers.
- Use a rubric to evaluate writing.
- Present your literary analysis as a speech to the class.
- Post your work as a blog on a classroom website.
- **Language** Use phrases and clauses to add details that help you develop your ideas.

Assign the Writing Task in *Ed.*

Online

RESOURCES

- Unit 2 Response Log
- Writing Studio: Writing as a Process
- Writing Studio: Writing as a Process: Planning and Drafting
- Writing Studio: Writing as a Process: Revising and Editing
- Grammar Studio: Module 5: The Phrase; Module 6: The Clause
- Reading Studio: Notice & Note

Language X-Ray: English Learner Support

Use the instruction below and the supports and scaffolds in the Teacher's Edition to help you guide students of different proficiency levels.

INTRODUCE THE WRITING TASK

Make sure that students understand that a literary analysis uses story details to support the main points a writer wants to make. Remind students that the selections in this unit involve the experience of horror. Have students brainstorm a list of books and movies that come to mind when they think about horror stories.

WRITING

Use Phrases and Clauses

Tell students that one way to add details that help them develop their ideas is to use **phrases and clauses**.

Use the following supports with students at various proficiency levels:

- Review phrases and clauses with students. Provide them with a sample paragraph of literary analysis, and work with them to underline phrases and circle clauses. Ask them to keep a list of ones they can potentially use in their sentences. **SUBSTANTIAL**
- Use sentence frames to help students use phrases and clauses. For example: *Last night I read a story _____ (PHRASE) _____ . This monster mysteriously came to life and terrorized the people _____ (CLAUSE) _____ .* **MODERATE**
- After students have completed their drafts, have them work with a partner to identify phrases and clauses in their own writing. **LIGHT**

WRITING

WRITE A LITERARY ANALYSIS

Introduce students to the Writing Task by reading the introductory paragraph with them. Remind students to refer to the notes they recorded in the Unit 2 Response Log as they plan and draft their analyses. The Response Log should contain their perspectives on different stories and poems they have read in the unit. Drawing on these perspectives will make their own writing more interesting and well-informed.

 For **writing support** for students at varying proficiency levels, see the **Language X-Ray** on page 142B.

USE THE MENTOR TEXT

Point out that their analyses will be similar to the literary analysis article "What Is the Horror Genre?" in that they will present facts and examples related to a topic. However, each student's analysis will be shorter than the article and will focus on a single literary work.

WRITING PROMPT

Review the prompt with students. Encourage them to ask questions about any part of the assignment that is unclear. Make sure they understand that the purpose of writing a literary analysis is to explain how a work from this unit fits into the horror genre. They will use examples from that particular work.

Write a Literary Analysis

 Go to the **Writing Studio** for help writing your literary analysis.

In this unit, you have read some scary stories and you have discussed the horror genre and what makes it enjoyable for many people. For this writing task, you will write a literary analysis in which you analyze and interpret one of the stories in this unit. For an example of a well-written literary analysis you can use as a mentor text, review "What Is the Horror Genre?" You can also use the notes from your Response Log that you recorded after reading the texts in this unit.

Writing Prompt

Read the information in the box below.

This is the topic or context for your literary analysis.

> As Sharon A. Russell points out in "What Is the Horror Genre?," various elements may be used to define and categorize horror stories, including suspense, plot, setting, theme, and the source of threats to the characters.

This is the Essential Question for the unit. Answering this question may offer insights into the horror genre.

Think carefully about the following question.

> Why do we sometimes like to feel frightened?

Now mark the words that identify exactly what you are being asked to produce.

Write a literary analysis of one of the stories in this unit. Refer to the examples given in the selection "What Is the Horror Genre?" to explain how the story fits into the horror genre.

Be sure to —

Review these points as you write and again when you finish. Make any needed changes or edits.

- ❏ provide an introduction that catches the reader's attention and includes a clear controlling idea about the story you are analyzing
- ❏ develop support for your controlling idea by including examples and quotations from the story
- ❏ logically organize main ideas and supporting evidence
- ❏ use appropriate transitions to connect ideas
- ❏ use appropriate word choice and sentence variety
- ❏ end by summarizing ideas or drawing an overall conclusion

142   Unit 2

 LEARNING MINDSET

Asking for Help As they work on their analyses, remind students to ask for help from teachers, peers, or parents as needed. Remind students that asking for help is not a sign of weakness. Rather, it is a way of "trying smarter." Tell students that discussing their work with others may help spark new and fresh ideas.

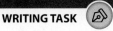

1 Plan

In order to plan the content and organization of your literary analysis, the first thing you need to do is select a story. With a partner, review the stories you read in this unit and identify which elements of horror they include. Use the planning table below to assist you.

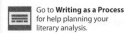 Go to **Writing as a Process** for help planning your literary analysis.

Horror Elements	"The Tell-Tale Heart"	"The Monkey's Paw"	"Blood"	"The Outsider"
Subjects	guilty murderer	normal family	pet-shop owner	normal guy, ghouls
Suspense				
Setting				
Plot				
Supernatural events				
Source of threat				
Theme				

Choose a Story Review the table and decide which story you would like to analyze. Consider how interested you were in the story and also how many elements of the horror genre it will allow you to write about in your literary analysis.

Background Reading Review the notes you took in your Response Log after reading each horror story. They may provide some valuable insights into the story or horror genre that you could include in your literary analysis. You may also wish to reread "What Is the Horror Genre?" to review what Sharon A. Russell wrote about the various elements of horror.

Use the notes from your Response Log as you plan your literary analysis.

1 PLAN

Allow time for students to discuss the topic with partners or in small groups and then to complete the planning table independently.

■ English Learner Support

Understand Literary Terms Ask students to tell you the meaning of some of the basic elements of fiction used in this chart—setting, plot, and theme. Review with students some points of suspense, supernatural events, or a source of threat in any one story to make sure they understand the terms. Work with them to fill in the blank sections, providing text that they can copy into their charts as needed.
SUBSTANTIAL

Choose a Story In considering which work to analyze, tell students to draw upon their own responses. Students should consider which story sent shivers down the spine and what the author did to create the effect of horror.

Background Reading As students plan to write a literary analysis, remind them to refer to the notes they took in the Response Log. Point out to students that when taking notes for their analysis it will be helpful to create a separate file or sheet of paper for each of their criteria listed on the chart. By listing appropriate story details for each criterion, students will be better able to organize their points when getting ready to write.

WRITING

Organize Your Ideas Tell students that their analyses will need to discuss the controlling idea and its related elements. They can use the elements they already have written down, or they can create a chart of their own. Tell them to focus on the examples and quotations that support each element.

▶ NOTICE & NOTE

From Reading to Writing Remind students they can use Quoted Words to include the opinions or conclusions of someone who is an expert on the topic. Students can also use Quoted Words to provide support for a point they are trying to make. Remind students to format direct quotations correctly and to give credit to the source.

② DEVELOP A DRAFT

Remind students to follow their outlines of the points to cover. Point out that they can still make changes to their outlines during this stage. As they write, they may discover that a different example better supports an idea or that particular details should be combined into a paragraph. Tell students to be open to new ideas and strategies that come to them as they are drafting. Encourage them to start with the section they feel most confident about—perhaps one of the body paragraphs. Once they are into the writing, they may find that their ideas flow more freely.

■ English Learner Support

Provide Text Evidence Review the following examples of using quotations to support ideas:

- By repeating the phrase "but the noise steadily increased," Poe builds tension.
- The sergeant-major warns the Whites that the monkey's paw "has caused enough mischief already."

Next, ask pairs to write sentences that contain quotations from their notes and to discuss ways of using them to present text evidence. **MODERATE/LIGHT**

 WRITING TASK

 Go to **Writing as a Process: Planning and Drafting** for help organizing your ideas.

Notice & Note

From Reading to Writing

As you plan your analysis, apply what you learned about signposts to your own writing.

 Go to the **Reading Studio** for more resources on Notice & Note.

Organize Your Ideas After you have selected a story that meets the horror criteria, you will need to come up with a controlling idea for your analysis. Begin by choosing the elements you want to write about. You can draw from those listed in the table on page 143 and include others of your own. Then review the story as well as what you wrote about it in your Response Log. You can use the chart below to collect examples and notes that support your points.

Elements of the Horror Genre in (story title) _____

Horror Elements	Supporting Examples and Quotations from the Story
Element 1:	
Element 2:	
Element 3:	

② Develop a Draft

 You might prefer to draft your essay online.

Once you have completed your planning activities, you will be ready to begin drafting your literary analysis. Refer to your completed chart; it may serve as a kind of map for you to follow as you write. Start with an introduction that includes your controlling idea and previews the elements you'll be talking about. In the body of your analysis, devote a paragraph to each element you previewed. Finish with a conclusion that summarizes your main points.

WHEN STUDENTS STRUGGLE . . .

Read Student Models Allow students to complete the writing task over an extended time. They may benefit from reading examples of other students' drafts to help them consider various approaches to the task. Remind students to use their own ideas and evidence as they write their analyses.

Use the Mentor Text

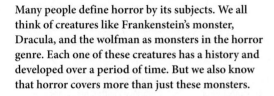

Author's Craft

Your introduction is your first chance to grab the reader's attention. In addition to your controlling idea or thesis statement, your introduction should include something that gets your reader interested in reading your essay. Note the way the writer captures the reader's attention in "What Is the Horror Genre?"

> Many people define horror by its subjects. We all think of creatures like Frankenstein's monster, Dracula, and the wolfman as monsters in the horror genre. Each one of these creatures has a history and developed over a period of time. But we also know that horror covers more than just these monsters.

The writer grabs the reader's attention by naming monsters, then introduces the controlling idea—horror involves other elements besides monsters.

Apply What You've Learned To capture your reader's attention, you might include a surprising fact, a famous quotation, or a personal anecdote related to the topic.

Genre Characteristics

In a literary analysis, each main idea is supported by examples and quotations from the story being analyzed. Notice how the author of "What Is the Horror Genre?" supports a key idea about how Stephen King builds suspense. Also notice how she cites her source.

> . . . Stephen King refers directly to our anticipation of horror. In *Salem's Lot* Susan approaches the house which is the source of evil. "She found herself thinking of those drive-in horror movie epics where the heroine goes venturing up the narrow attic stairs . . . or down into some dark, cobwebby cellar . . . and she . . . thinking: . . . *I'd never do that!*" Of course Susan's fears are justified.

The author provides an example and cites her source. She then includes a quotation to provide more vivid details. The example and quotation support her point that anticipation builds suspense.

Apply What You've Learned Each point you make about an element of the horror genre should be supported by examples and quotations. Be sure to identify the author and title of the story the first time you cite evidence from the story.

Write a Literary Analysis 145

WHY THIS MENTOR TEXT?

"What Is the Horror Genre?" provides a good example of literary analysis. Use the information below to help students use the mentor text as a model for writing effective introductions and for including details in their literary analysis essays.

USE THE MENTOR TEXT

Author's Craft Ask a volunteer to read aloud the introduction from "What Is the Horror Genre?" Then have students identify details that make this introduction appealing to readers. Invite students to offer examples of surprising facts and famous quotations that might make an introduction appealing. Have students discuss strategies they might use to search for famous quotations online.

Genre Characteristics To help students understand how the example functions in the article, have them locate paragraph 2 in the text. Help students understand that the example from *Salem's Lot* provides support for Sharon A. Russell's idea that horror stories not only "share the use of suspense as a tactic with many other kinds of literature," but also for the idea that one's knowledge of the genre intensifies the suspense. Characters in a horror story always have something dreadful happen to them "when they go where they shouldn't."

WHEN STUDENTS STRUGGLE . . .

Use an Outline If students have trouble organizing their evidence, suggest that they work with partners to create outlines showing the main claim, any additional claims, evidence that supports each claim, and reasons that explain the evidence. Let pairs decide whether each piece of evidence is convincing and explain why or why not.

Remind them to suggest ways to make evidence more convincing and/or to revise claims to make them easier to support.

WRITING

3 REVISE

Have students answer each question in the chart to identify how they can improve their drafts. Have volunteers model their revision techniques to the class.

With a Partner Have students ask peer reviewers to evaluate their controlling idea and supporting evidence by answering the following questions:

- What can I do to state my controlling idea more clearly?
- Which pieces of evidence are strong? Which pieces of evidence should be stronger?

Students should use the reviewer's feedback to add relevant examples or quotations to strengthen the development of each main idea.

 **WRITING TASK**

3 Revise

 Go to **Writing as Process: Revising and Editing** for help revising your literary analysis.

On Your Own Once you've written a first draft of your literary analysis, you'll want to go back and look for ways to improve it. As you reread and revise, think about whether you have achieved your purpose. The Revision Guide will help you focus on specific elements to make your writing stronger.

Revision Guide		
Ask Yourself	**Tips**	**Revision Techniques**
1. Does my introduction grab readers' attention?	**Highlight** the introduction.	**Add** an interesting fact, example, or quotation that illustrates the topic.
2. Is my controlling idea clear?	**Underline** the controlling idea.	**Add** a controlling idea or make an existing one clearer.
3. Are ideas organized logically? Is there coherence within and across paragraphs? Do transitions connect ideas?	**Highlight** main ideas. **Underline** the transitional words and phrases that connect them.	**Rearrange** paragraphs or sentences within paragraphs to organize ideas logically and create coherence. **Add** transitions to clarify connections.
4. Do I support each main idea with evidence?	**Underline** each supporting example or quotation.	**Add** more examples or quotations to support ideas.
5. Do I include phrases and clauses to add details and link ideas?	**Circle** phrases that add details. **Underline** clauses that add details or show connections.	**Add** some phrases or clauses if you need more details to develop your ideas.
6. Does my conclusion summarize the topic and support the information presented?	**Underline** the summary, if one is present.	**Add** a statement that summarizes the main ideas.

ACADEMIC VOCABULARY
As you conduct your **peer review,** be sure to use these words.

- ❏ convention
- ❏ predict
- ❏ psychology
- ❏ summary
- ❏ technique

With a Partner Once you have worked through the Revision Guide on your own, exchange papers with a partner and evaluate each other's draft in a **peer review.** Focus on providing revision suggestions for at least three of the items mentioned in the chart. Explain why you think your partner's draft should be revised and what your specific suggestions are.

When receiving feedback from your partner, listen attentively and ask questions to make sure you fully understand the revision suggestions.

 ENGLISH LEARNER SUPPORT

Use Pronouns or Synonyms Explain that using pronouns or synonyms to refer back to nouns can help emphasize and connect ideas. Share the following example:

Not all *horror stories* are intended to scare the reader in a startling way. Many such *tales* focus on building fearful suspense.

Have students create their own pairs of sentences that use synonyms to refer back to nouns. Let pairs exchange sentences and identify each other's original words and synonyms.
LIGHT

4 Edit

Once you have revised your literary analysis, you can address the finer points of your draft. Edit for the proper use of standard English conventions, and make sure to correct any misspellings or grammatical errors.

Language Conventions

Phrases and Clauses You can use phrases and clauses to add details that help you develop your ideas and to create sentence variety.

- A **phrase** is a group of words that functions as a single part of speech. It does not contain a verb and its subject. A phrase often modifies a noun or adjective, adding more detail about it.
- A **clause** is a group of words that contains a verb and its subject. Both phrases and clauses can be either restrictive or nonrestrictive.

A **restrictive** phrase or clause provides information that is necessary to understand the sentence. It is therefore not set off with commas, as shown in these examples from "What Is the Horror Genre?"

- "Stories <u>of ghosts or demonic possession</u> also fall <u>into this category</u>."
- "We don't know <u>what is going to happen</u>."

A **nonrestrictive** phrase or clause provides additional information in a sentence whose meaning is already clear. Nonrestrictive phrases and clauses are typically set off from the rest of the sentence with commas:

- "She does end up dead in the basement, <u>a victim of the vampire</u>."
- "This type of hesitation, <u>when we almost believe</u>, falls into the general category of the 'fantastic' (Todorov 25)."

Review your first draft and check that you have set off nonrestrictive phrases and clauses with commas.

! Go to the **Grammar Studio** to learn more about phrases and clauses.

5 Publish

Finalize your literary analysis and choose a way to share it with your audience. Consider these options:

- Present your literary analysis as a speech to the class.
- Post your literary analysis as a blog on a classroom or school website.

4 EDIT

Have students read their drafts aloud to listen to the flow of their ideas. To help the literary analysis read better, students should strive for a variety of short and longer sentences. Tell students they should have neither all short sentences nor all long ones, but the right mixture of long and short. Too many short sentences creates a choppy effect. Too many long sentences can drain energy from the writing, making it seem monotonous. The right balance of long and short helps keep the reader engaged.

LANGUAGE CONVENTIONS

Phrases and Clauses Review the information about phrases and clauses with students. Then discuss each bulleted sentence with students, making sure that the distinction between nonrestrictive and restrictive elements is clear. Emphasize that a restrictive phrase or clause limits the meaning of the word it modifies and is therefore essential to the meaning of the sentence. A restrictive phrase or clause is not set off with commas.

5 PUBLISH

Encourage other students to read the essays posted as a blog on the school website and to write comments about them. The authors can then respond to the comments.

TO CHALLENGE STUDENTS . . .

Analyze an Adaptation Challenge students to analyze a film or television adaptation of "The Tell-Tale Heart" or "The Monkey's Paw." Let students write a brief review of the adaptation that discusses the criteria they used in their analyses, and compares and contrasts the original text with the adaptation. Invite students to share their reviews with the class.

WRITING

USE THE SCORING GUIDE

Have students use the rubric to evaluate their analyses in each of the three categories. Then have pairs exchange their analyses and discuss whether they agree or disagree with their partner's score. Students should cite specific examples from the analyses and use the language of the rubric to support their opinions. Tell reviewers to provide feedback based on the revision chart. Encourage them to offer suggestions about what details students might add or how a new approach might help clarify or connect ideas.

REFLECT ON THE WRITING PROCESS

Ask students to reflect on the entire writing process as well as their final product. They should consider what they learned and what they might improve in future assignments. Have them write a short response to the following questions:

- *What process did you use to develop your controlling idea?*
- *How did you choose relevant story details for each of your criteria?*
- *What did you learn about the horror genre by writing your analysis?*

WRITING TASK

Use the scoring guide to evaluate your literary analysis.

Writing Task Scoring Guide: Literary Analysis			
	Organization/Progression	**Development of Ideas**	**Use of Language and Conventions**
4	• The organization is very effective and appropriate to the purpose. • The controlling idea is stated very clearly. • Body paragraphs clearly relate to the controlling idea, and ideas within each body paragraph follow a logical order. • There are very clear transitions between paragraphs.	• The introduction grabs the reader's attention and states a compelling controlling idea. • The analysis offers insightful interpretations of the chosen text. • The analysis contains clear main ideas supported by well-chosen examples and quotations. • The conclusion effectively summarizes the analysis.	• Language and word choice is purposeful and precise. • Sources are correctly cited. • Sentences include a variety of phrases and clauses. • Grammar, spelling, capitalization, punctuation, and usage are correct.
3	• The organization is effective and appropriate to the purpose. • The controlling idea is stated clearly. • Body paragraphs relate to the controlling idea, and ideas within each body paragraph are mostly easy to follow. • There are clear transitions between paragraphs.	• The introduction could be more engaging, but it states a controlling idea. • The analysis offers reasonable interpretations of the text. • The analysis is developed with clear main ideas supported by mostly relevant examples and quotations. • The conclusion summarizes the analysis.	• Language and word choice is somewhat purposeful and precise. • Sources are mentioned but may not be correctly cited. • Sentences include a variety of phrases and clauses, and most are punctuated correctly. • Grammar, spelling, capitalization, punctuation, and usage are mostly correct.
2	• The organization is somewhat confusing or lacking in purpose. • The controlling idea is not stated very clearly. • It is unclear how ideas within body paragraphs are related. • More transitions are needed to show connections between paragraphs.	• The introduction is not engaging; the controlling idea is unclear or missing. • The interpretations of the text are unclear or questionable. • The analysis is minimally developed. Main ideas are unclear or lack appropriate examples and quotations to support them. • The conclusion only partially summarizes the analysis.	• Language is often vague and general. • Source(s) are not correctly cited. • Some phrases or clauses are punctuated incorrectly. • There are errors in grammar, spelling, capitalization, punctuation, and usage, but they do not make reading difficult.
1	• The organization is not appropriate to the purpose. • The controlling idea is missing. • The order of paragraphs or ideas within paragraphs is confusing. • There are no transitions between paragraphs.	• The introduction is missing or confusing. • The analysis offers no clear interpretations of the text. • The analysis is poorly developed. Examples and quotations are irrelevant or missing. • The conclusion is missing.	• Language is inappropriate, vague, or confusing. • No source(s) are not mentioned. • Phrases and clauses are punctuated incorrectly. • There are many errors in grammar, usage, and mechanics that make the analysis difficult to follow.

WHEN STUDENTS STRUGGLE . . .

Adapt Language Choices Remind students that a formal, objective tone will help them convince readers that their interpretation is correct. Guide students to recognize the differences between formal and informal language in the following phrases.

- *This seems really important / This is significant because*
- *Lots of people think that / This evidence shows that*

Have students ask a partner to help them identify examples of informal language in their analyses and suggest revisions.

Reflect on the Unit

In the literary analysis you created, you analyzed a story from the unit and explained the elements that make it fit within the horror genre. Now is a good time to reflect on what you have learned in this unit.

Reflect on the Essential Question

• Why do we sometimes like to feel frightened? Has your answer to this question changed since you first considered it when you started this unit? If so, in what way?

• How do authors make stories frightening and enjoyable to read?

Reflect on Your Reading

• Which selections most interested or surprised you?

• From which selection did you learn the most about why people sometimes like to feel frightened?

Reflect on the Writing Task

• What difficulties did you encounter while working on your literary analysis? How might you avoid them next time?

• What parts of the literary analysis were the easiest and hardest to write? Why?

• What improvements did you make to your literary analysis during the revising stage?

UNIT 2 SELECTIONS
• "What Is the Horror Genre?"
• "The Tell-Tale Heart"
• "The Hollow"
• "The Monkey's Paw" (short story)
• from *The Monkey's Paw* (film clip)

REFLECT ON THE UNIT

Have students reflect on the questions independently and write some notes in response to each one. Then have students meet with partners or in small groups to discuss their reflections. Circulate during these discussions to identify the questions that are generating the liveliest conversations. Wrap up with a whole-class discussion focused on these questions.

■ English Learner Support

Spelling Difficult Words Focus on students improving their spelling ability by pointing out the word "frightened." Write the word on the board and underline *gh*. Say: The *gh* in *frightened* is silent. We don't say /g/ or /h/ when we say *frightened*. *Gh* is also special because it makes the vowel or vowels in front of it have a long sound. Point out the letter *i* and say: The *gh* makes this *i* have the /ī/ sound. Say the word again slowly, tracking the letters with your finger, and have students repeat. Ask students for other words that have a silent *gh*, or provide the following words for students to sound out: *light, height, neighbor, dough*.   **MODERATE**

⚙ LEARNING MINDSET

Problem Solving Discuss with students that an important part of developing a learning mindset is to not always depend on others to solve problems for them. Students must believe that they are capable of solving problems on their own and be challenged. Encourage them to develop independence by thinking of how they can solve a problem first before asking for help from the teacher or other students or their families.

UNIT 3

Instructional Overview and Resources

	Instructional Focus	Online **Ed** Resources

Unit Introduction
Places We Call Home

Unit 3 Essential Question
Unit 3 Academic Vocabulary

Stream to Start: Places We Call Home

Unit 3 Response Log

ANALYZE & APPLY

"My Favorite Chaperone"
Short Story by Jean Davies Okimoto
Lexile 790L

NOTICE & NOTE READING MODEL

Signposts
• Tough Questions
• Again and Again
• Memory Moment

Reading
• Analyze Plot
• Analyze Character

Writing: Write a Summary

Speaking and Listening: Discuss with a Small Group

Vocabulary: Context Clues

Language Conventions: Subject-Verb Agreement

🔊 **Audio**

Text in Focus: Understanding Characters

Close Read Screencast: Modeled Discussions

Reading Studio: Notice & Note

Level Up Tutorial: Plot Stages

Writing Studio: Using Textual Evidence

Speaking and Listening Studio: Participate in Collaborative Discussions

Vocabulary Studio: Context Clues

Grammar Studio: Module 8: Agreement

Mentor Text

The Book of Unknown Americans
Novel by Cristina Henriquez
Lexile 870L

Reading
• Analyze Narrative Structure
• Analyze Theme

Writing: Write a Paragraph

Speaking and Listening: Act Out a Scene

Vocabulary: Use a Dictionary

Language Conventions: Pronouns

🔊 **Audio**

Reading Studio: Notice & Note

Level Up Tutorial: Reading for Details

Level Up Tutorial: Make Inferences about Characters

Level Up Tutorial: Theme

Writing Studio: Writing Narratives

Speaking and Listening Studio: Participate in Collaborative Discussions

Vocabulary Studio: Using a Dictionary

Grammar Studio: Module 2: Lesson 3: Pronouns

"The Powwow at the End of the World"
Poem by Sherman Alexie

Reading
• Analyze Line Length
• Analyze Literary Devices

Writing: Write a Poem

Speaking and Listening: Hold a Debate

🔊 **Audio**

Reading Studio: Notice & Note

Writing Studio: Writing Narratives

Speaking and Listening Studio: Participate in Collaborative Discussions

---

**SUGGESTED PACING:
30 DAYS**

Unit Introduction	My Favorite Chaperone								The Book of Unknown Americans					The Powwow at the End of the World	
1	2	3	4	5	6	7	8	9	10	11	12	13	14	15	16

English Learner Support	Differentiated Instruction	Online Ed Assessment
• Sensitive Topics		

• Text X-Ray	• Analyze Character	**When Students Struggle**	**Selection Test**
• Vocabulary Support	• Analyze Tough Questions	• Use Strategies	
• Understand Cohesion	• Confirm Understanding	• Take Notes	
• Analyze Plot	• Understand Environmental Print	• Identify Plot Stages	
• Culturally Responsive Instruction	• Understand Language Choices	**To Challenge Students**	
• Understand Vocabulary	• Analyze Plot	• Analyze Character Choices	
• Tough Questions	• Vocabulary Strategy		
• Understand Punctuation	• Oral Assessment		
• Use Titles	• Vocabulary Strategy		
	• Review Conventions		
• Text X-Ray	• Make Inferences	**When Students Struggle**	**Selection Test**
• Use Cognates	• Oral Assessment	• Use Learning Strategies	
• Demonstrate Comprehension	• Develop Fluency	• Reteaching: Analyze Characters	
• Use Learning Strategies	• Vocabulary Strategy	• Analyze Theme	
• Analyze Narrative Structure	• Language Conventions	**To Challenge Students**	
• Use Contextual Support		• Analyze Language	
• Text X-Ray		**When Students Struggle**	**Selection Test**
• Use Cognates		• Identify Key Details	
• Capitalize Proper Nouns			
• Understand Synonyms			
• Oral Assessment			
• Practice Debate Language			

New Immigrants Share Their Stories / A Common Bond

Independent Reading **End of Unit**

17 > 18 > 19 > 20 > 21 > 22 > 23 > 24 > 25 > 26 > 27 > 28 > 29 > 30

PLAN

| Instructional Focus | **Online Ed** Resources |

COLLABORATE & COMPARE

"New Immigrants Share Their Stories"
Documentary by Lis Gossels

⋯⋯⋯⋯⋯⋯⋯⋯⋯⋯

"A Common Bond"
Informational Text by Brooke Hauser
Lexile 1150L

Reading
• Analyze a Documentary
• Analyze Text Elements

Writing: Write a Letter

Speaking and Listening: Discuss with a Small Group

Vocabulary: Multiple-Meaning Words

Language Conventions: That and Which

🔊 **Audio**

Reading Studio: Notice & Note

Writing Studio: Writing Narratives

Speaking and Listening Studio: Participate in Collaborative Discussions

Vocabulary Studio: Multiple-Meaning Words

Grammar Studio: Module 14: Lesson 5: Restrictive and Nonrestrictive Clauses

---

Collaborate and Compare

Reading:
• Compare Author's Purpose
• Analyze Media and Text

Speaking and Listening: Create and Present

Speaking and Listening Studio: Preparing for Discussion

Online Ed

INDEPENDENT READING

The Independent Reading selections are only available in the eBook.

📖 **Go to the Reading Studio for more information on Notice & Note.**

"My Father and the Figtree"
Poem by Naomi Shihab Nye

"Golden Glass"
Short Story by Alma Luiz Villanueva
Lexile 1010L

END OF UNIT

Writing Task: Write a Short Story

Reflect on the Unit

Writing: Writing a Short Story

Language Conventions: Pronouns and Prepositions

Unit 3 Response Log

Mentor Text: *The Book of Unknown Americans*

Writing Studio: Narrative Structure

Writing Studio: The Language of Narrative

Grammar Studio: Module 10: Lesson 4: Using Pronouns as Objects of Prepositions

English Learner Support	Differentiated Instruction	Online Ed Assessment
• Text X-Ray • Vocab Practice • Determine Meaning • Understand Contrasts • Understand Generalities • Multiple-Meaning Words • Understand a Circle Chart • The Prefix *Bi-* • Reading Graphs • Know What You Know • Oral Assessment • Vocabulary Strategy • That and Which	**When Students Struggle** • Learning Strategy • Reteaching: Common Words with Multiple Meanings **To Challenge Students** • Research Languages	**Selection Test**
• Use a Venn Diagram	**When Students Struggle** • Keep a Reading Log	
from "The Latehomecomer" Memoir by Kao Kalia Yang **Lexile 940L**	"A Place to Call Home" Research Study by Scott Bittle and Jonathan Rochkind **Lexile 1220L** "Salmon Boy" Myth by Michael J. Caduto and Joseph Bruchac **Lexile 700L**	**Selection Tests**
• Language X-Ray • Narrative • Sequence • Use the Mentor Text	**When Students Struggle** • Keep a Reading Log • Draft the Story • Edit for Grammar and Punctuation **To Challenge Students** • Writing Style	**Unit Test**

PLACES WE CALL HOME

? Connect to the
ESSENTIAL QUESTION

Ask a volunteer to read aloud the Essential Question. Discuss how the images on page 150 relate to the question. *Where is the Statue of Liberty? What does it represent? How does the photo of students relate to the places that shape you?* Ask students to think about the cultures and people of the places they and their families have lived.

■ English Learner Support

Sensitive Topics Many of the topics and situations discussed in this unit may be sensitive or triggering for English Learners, especially immigrant students or newcomers.

Teachers should use their best judgment when engaging students in these discussions or topics. They know their students best. **ALL LEVELS**

DISCUSS THE QUOTATION

Tell students that Henning Mankell (1948–2015) was a Swedish mystery writer and social activist. He spent much of his time in Africa where he started a theatre in Mozambique.

Ask students to read the quotation. Discuss what "your roots" usually means. *(your heritage, your background)* Ask students to think about out the imagery of a family tree. Then discuss what Mankell means by "You can carry your roots with you." Ask students whether they agree with Mankell's statement, and have them support their opinions with reasons and examples.

? ESSENTIAL QUESTION:

What are the places that shape who you are?

> " You can have more than one home. You can carry your roots with you, and decide where they grow. "
>
> Henning Mankel

150   Unit 3

⚙ LEARNING MINDSET

Setting Goals Tell students that setting goals is an important part of having a learning mindset. Encourage students to set a goal for reading self-selected texts outside of class. For example, students could choose from selections listed in the Independent Reading section and read for a set time or number of pages a day. Consider setting up a class progress report for students to track their goals.

ACADEMIC VOCABULARY

Academic Vocabulary words are words you use when you discuss and write about texts. In this unit you will practice and learn five words.

☑ contribute ☐ immigrate ☐ reaction ☐ relocate ☐ shifting

Study the Word Network to learn more about the word **contribute**.

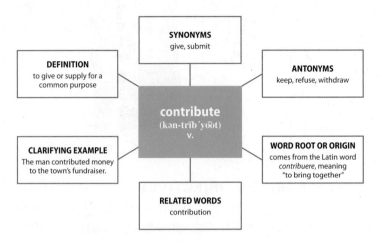

Write and Discuss Discuss the completed Word Network with a partner, making sure to talk through all of the boxes until you both understand the word, its synonyms, antonyms, and related forms. Then, fill out Word Networks for the four remaining words. Use a dictionary or online resource to help you complete the activity.

 Go online to access the Word Networks.

RESPOND TO THE ESSENTIAL QUESTION

In this unit, you will explore how places can shape the way people are. As you read, you will revisit the **Essential Question** and gather your ideas about it in the **Response Log** that appears on page R3. At the end of the unit, you will have the opportunity to write a **short story**. Filling out the Response Log will help you prepare for this writing task.

 You can also go online to access the Response Log.

Places We Call Home 151

ACADEMIC VOCABULARY

As students complete Word Networks for the remaining four vocabulary words, encourage them to include all the categories shown in the completed network if possible, but point out that some words do not have clear synonyms or antonyms. Some words may also function as different parts of speech—for example, *shifting* may also be a noun or a verb without the suffix.

> **contribute** (kən-trĭb´ yo͞ot) *v.* To give or supply for a common purpose (Spanish cognate: *contribuir*)
>
> **immigrate** (ĭm´ ĭ-grāt´) *v.* To enter and settle in a new country (Spanish cognate: *inmigrar*)
>
> **reaction** (rē-ăk´ shən) *n.* A response to something (Spanish cognate: *reacción*)
>
> **relocate** (rē-lō´ kāt) *v.* To move to or establish in a new place (Spanish cognate: *reubicar*)
>
> **shifting** (shĭft´ ĭng) *adj.* Changing attitudes, judgments, or emphases

RESPOND TO THE ESSENTIAL QUESTION

Direct students to the Unit 3 Response Log. Explain that students will use it to record ideas and details from the selections that help answer the Essential Question. When they work on the writing task at the end of the unit, their Response Logs will help them think about what they have read and make connections between texts.

READING MODEL

MY FAVORITE CHAPERONE

Short Story by Jean Davies Okimoto

GENRE ELEMENTS
REALISTIC FICTION

Remind students that **realistic fiction** includes the basic elements of fiction such as setting, characters, plot, and conflict, but the situations and characters seem like real life because they include believable actions and dialogues in realistic settings. A **short story** is a fiction story that can usually be read in one sitting. It typically has a traditional dramatic structure but is simpler than a novel and usually focuses on a single conflict or plot line.

LEARNING OBJECTIVES

- Cite evidence to support analysis of the plot and summarize.
- Analyze how an author uses dialogue to develop characters.
- Research Kazakhstani culture using multiple sources.
- Discuss character relationships and characteristics.
- Use context to clarify meaning of unfamiliar and foreign words.
- Identify subject-verb agreement in complex sentences.
- Write a summary of a short story.
- **Language** Discuss characterization with a partner using the word *feels*.

TEXT COMPLEXITY

Quantitative Measures	**My Favorite Chaperone**	Lexile: 790L
Qualitative Measures	**Ideas Presented** Multiple levels of meaning with multiple themes.	
	Structure Used Less familiar story concepts.	
	Language Used Less straightforward sentence structures.	
	Knowledge Required Experience contains unfamiliar aspects.	

RESOURCES

- Unit 3 Response Log

- Selection Audio

- Understanding Characters

- Close Read Screencasts: Modeled Discussions

- Reading Studio: Notice & Note

- Level Up Tutorial: Plot Stages

- Writing Studio: Using Textual Evidence

- Speaking and Listening Studio: Participating in Collaborative Discussions

- Vocabulary Studio: Context Clues

- Grammar Studio: Module 8: Agreement

- 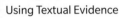 "My Favorite Chaperone" Selection Test

SUMMARIES

English

Maya and her family are immigrants from Kazakhstan. Maya longs for the freedom her classmates have to do things, but she has more responsibilities and restrictions than her peers because of language and cultural differences. Maya is called on to interpret when her brother is suspended for fighting, but her translation to her parents minimizes how much trouble he is in. Her brother returns the favor by convincing their parents to allow Maya to go to a dance with him as a chaperone.

Spanish

Mara y su familia son inmigrantes de Kazakstán. Mara añora la libertad que sus compañeros de clase tienen para hacer cosas, pero ella tiene más responsabilidades y restricciones que sus compañeros debido a sus diferencias culturales y con el idioma. A Mara la llaman para hacer de intérprete cuando a su hermano lo suspenden por pelear; pero al traducirles a sus padres, minimiza la cantidad de problemas en los que está. Su hermano le regresa el favor al convencer a sus padres de que Mara vaya al baile con él como chaperón.

SMALL-GROUP OPTIONS

Have students work in small groups to read and discuss the selection.

Think-Pair-Share

- After students have read and analyzed "My Favorite Chaperone," pose this question: *What challenges do the characters face as immigrants?*

- Have students think about the question individually and take notes.

- Then have pairs discuss their ideas about the question.

- Finally, ask pairs to share their responses with the class.

Three-Minute Review

- Pause student activity at any time during reading or discussion and set a timer for three minutes.

- Direct students to work independently to re-read the passage and review their notes to answer the question: *How do the characters change during the story?*

- At the end of the three minutes, have students write a summary of their review.

- Then ask students, *What did you notice in your review?*

Text X-Ray: English Learner Support
for "My Favorite Chaperone"

INTRODUCE THE SELECTION
DISCUSS CULTURE

In this lesson, students will need to be able to discuss the cultural characteristics of places and their impact on characters. Explain that *culture* refers to shared values, beliefs, attitudes, and social norms.

Read paragraph 1 with students. Point out the lines, "Maybe I just couldn't give up hope. It's like that in America. It's a place where things can change for people, and many people always seem to have hope. At least that's how it seems to me." Ask students to discuss what this reveals about the narrator's view of American culture. Provide the following sentence frames to support discussion:

- *The narrator thinks _____.*
- *_____ is a shared experience.*
- *In America, people seem _____.*

CULTURAL REFERENCES

The following words and phrases may be unfamiliar to students:

- *Kazakhstan* (paragraph 2): a country in Central Asia that was part of the former Soviet Union
- *cab* (paragraph 6): taxi
- *Nordstrom* (paragraph 9): a department store
- *conference* (paragraph 31): a meeting
- *Anne Frank* (paragraph 92): a Jewish girl who kept a diary while hiding from the Nazis during World War II
- *leotards* (paragraph 125): fitted bodysuits worn in gymnastics
- *borscht* (paragraph 131): traditional Russian beet soup
- *kasha* (paragraph 161): a porridge; cooked grains

LISTENING

Understand Point of View

Draw students' attention to the pronouns in paragraph 1. Explain that point of view is the perspective of the narrator. Point out that the narrator's use of the pronoun *I* shows that the narrator is a character in the story and the story is written in first-person point of view, which shapes how the story is told.

Have students listen as you read aloud paragraph 1. Use the following supports with students at varying proficiency levels:

- Tell students that you will ask questions about what you just read aloud. For example, ask: *Do we know the name of who is telling the story? (No, not yet.)* **SUBSTANTIAL**
- Have students identify the narrator. Ask: *What do we know about the narrator? (The narrator is a character in the story. The narrator is a ninth grader in America.)* **MODERATE**
- Pair students to discuss the point of view of the narrator. Ask: *What kind of information do we know about the narrator because of the point of view? (We know the narrator's thoughts about the dance and people in America.)* **LIGHT**

SPEAKING

Discuss Characterization

Tell students that authors reveal the characters' personal traits and motivations through more than just description. Explain that they use what the characters say and do to demonstrate their personalities, beliefs, and feelings.

Work with students to read paragraphs 50–51. Use the following supports with students at varying proficiency levels:

- Display and read aloud: *Maya feels sympathy for her brother. Maya is sympathetic.* Help students to understand the meaning of *sympathy* and *sympathetic.* Have students say the sentences aloud and then practice saying them to a partner. **SUBSTANTIAL**
- To help students express their ideas about characterization, display the following sentence frames: *Maya feels _____ . Maya wants _____ . Maya is _____ .* **MODERATE**
- Pair students to discuss characterization. Ask: *What traits does this passage reveal about Maya?* (*Maya feels bad for her brother and wants to protect him. Maya is sympathetic and protective.*) **LIGHT**

READING

Identify Setting

Tell students that the setting of a story is both a place and a time. Sometimes a story has more than one setting as the characters move from one place to another or with the passage of time, but the main setting is where the action of the plot happens.

Have students read paragraphs 2–7. Use the following supports with students at varying proficiency levels:

- Explain that they can identify the setting of a story by looking for information or clues about the location. Ask: *Where does the family come from? Where is Bob Campbell from? Does the family move to Chicago? Where is Maya when telling the story?* (*Kazakhstan; Seattle; No; Seattle, at school*) **SUBSTANTIAL**
- Guide students to identify the setting. Supply sentence frames, such as: *The family used to live _____ . The family moved _____ . Now Maya lives _____ .* **MODERATE**
- Ask students to identify the setting. (*Part of the story is set in Kazakhstan and part in Seattle.*) **LIGHT**

WRITING

Write a Summary

Point out that a summary is different from a paraphrase of what is written. Explain that a summary captures the most important events or ideas of a text.

Use the following supports with students at varying proficiency levels:

- Work with students to create a story map identifying characters, setting, conflict, major events, climax, and resolution. Help them identify words and phrases in the text to add to the map. Then use the map to write a summary together on the board. Have students copy the paragraph in their notebooks. **SUBSTANTIAL**
- Provide a story map to help students take notes on the important elements of the story. Provide sentence frames for crafting a summary: *The main character is _____ who _____ . The conflict facing _____ is _____ . First, _____ . Then _____ . The turning point, or climax of the story is when _____ . Finally, _____ .* **MODERATE**
- Ask students to work with a partner to complete the story map and discuss which information to include before writing a summary of five to seven sentences. **LIGHT**

EXPLAIN THE SIGNPOSTS

Explain that **NOTICE & NOTE Signposts** are significant moments in the text that help readers understand and analyze works of fiction or nonfiction. Use the instruction on these pages to introduce students to the signposts **Tough Questions, Again and Again,** and **Memory Moment**. Then use the selection that follows to have students apply the signposts to a text.

For a full list of the fiction and nonfiction signposts, see p. 228.

▶ TOUGH QUESTIONS

Explain that **Tough Questions** are the questions we sometimes ask ourselves that seem to not have immediate answers. A person might ask, "What should I do?" when facing a difficult decision, or "Why me?" when something bad happens. In fiction, Tough Questions reveal the inner **conflicts** of the **characters**.

Read aloud the example passage and pause at the underlined text. This question is significant because it reveals the character's thoughts and feelings. Ask students to consider what this reveals about what is bothering the character.

Tell students that when they spot a Tough Question, they should pause, mark it in their consumable texts, and ask themselves the anchor question: *What does this make me wonder about?*

Notice & Note

READING MODEL

MY FAVORITE CHAPERONE

You are about to read the short story "My Favorite Chaperone." In it, you will notice and note signposts that will give you clues about the story's plot, characters, and themes. Here are three key signposts to look for as you read this short story and other works of fiction.

For more information on these and other signposts to Notice & Note, visit the **Reading Studio**.

When you notice one of the following phrases while reading, pause to see if it's a **Tough Questions** signpost:

"What could I possibly do to . . . ?"

"I couldn't imagine how I could cope with . . ."

"Why would she [or he] . . . ?"

Tough Questions If a friend began a sentence with "How in the world will I ever . . . ," you would get the signal that he or she was feeling overwhelmed and was asking for help. So, you would listen closely to what your friend said next.

It's a good idea to take the same approach while reading a story. When characters ask themselves or other characters tough questions, pay attention to what they ask. The question may reveal an important inner struggle, a central conflict, or even a theme. Noticing **Tough Questions** can:

- help you recognize the plot's central conflict
- provide clues to the story's theme or lesson
- reveal a character's traits or motivations

The paragraph below illustrates a student's annotation within "My Favorite Chaperone" and a response to a Tough Questions signpost.

> 1   In homeroom when Mr. Horswill handed out the permission slip for the Spring Fling, the all-school dance, I almost didn't take one. <u>Why should I bother when I was sure the answer would be the same?</u> Even though I'm in ninth grade now, it would still be the same. No. *Nyet* is what they say, and I don't want to hear this again. . . .

Anchor Question
When you notice this signpost, ask: What does this make me wonder about?

What tough question is the character asking herself?	"Why should I bother when I was sure the answer would be the same?"
What clues does the question provide about the character and the plot?	The narrator wants to go to the dance but thinks she won't be allowed. This suggests a conflict between her and her parents.

WHEN STUDENTS STRUGGLE . . .

Use Strategies Have students use the **Somebody Wanted But So** strategy to create one-sentence summaries. Model writing the words of the strategy as heads on a chart.

First, tell students to identify who the *somebody* is that they want to discuss and write the name on the chart. Then tell students to note what the somebody *wanted*. Next, have partners discuss what happened to interfere and write it under *But*. Then have them discuss the result and write It under *So*. Finally, have students use their charts to complete the sentence frame and create a one-sentence summary: _____ wanted _____ but _____ so_____.

Again and Again If a friend mentions someone two or three days in a row, you might start to think there's something significant about that person. Likewise, when an author repeats a phrase, a detail, or an image, take note. Paying attention to something you read **Again and Again** can:

- reveal a symbol, or something that stands for something else
- provide an important insight into a character
- point to a significant idea or theme in the story

Here, a student marked an example of Again and Again.

> 137 ... The door slammed. Papa stood <u>like a huge bull</u> in his dark leather jacket and flung open the back door of the cab.
>
> 141 ... Papa roared in front of me, and as he charged toward the door in his glistening dark leather jacket, <u>he again seemed transformed to a creature that was half man and half bull.</u>

When you notice one of the following while reading, pause to see if it's an **Again and Again** signpost:

a second or third appearance of an object

a word or phrase that you think you may have read earlier in the story

a similar pattern to events or actions

Anchor Question
When you notice this signpost, ask: Why might the author keep bringing this up?

What image is repeated?	the image of Papa looking like a bull
Why might the author have used this image twice?	The author repeats the comparison of Maya's father to a bull as a way of emphasizing that he is angry and threatening.

Memory Moment In life, when a memory suddenly comes to mind, it's usually triggered for a reason. In a story, when the flow of the narrative is interrupted by a memory, there's usually a reason, too. A **Memory Moment** may help reveal:

- what one or more characters are feeling
- why a character is acting or feeling a certain way
- a connection between past and present events
- how the characters came to be in their current situation

In this example, a student marked a Memory Moment.

> 57 ... "That kid Ossie Nishizono was teasing Nurzhan something fierce. Telling him he could never be a real American, making fun of the way he talked." He bent down and picked up a candy wrapper. "<u>Reminded me of how</u> this bully used to treat me when my family came after the revolution."

When you see a phrase like one of these, pause to see if it's signaling a **Memory Moment:**

"I remember when ..."

"That reminds me of ..."

"Once, when I was ..."

"Did I ever tell you about the time ..."

Anchor Question
When you notice this signpost, ask: Why is this memory important?

What word(s) introduce the recollection?	"Reminded me of how"
What does this memory reveal about Ossie and Nurzhan?	Mr. Zabornik's memory suggests that there have always been bullies who pick on kids who are different.

Notice & Note   153

AGAIN AND AGAIN

Explain that when a word, phrase, object, or situation is repeated, the author wants the reader to pay attention to some element of the story. For example, the **Again and Again** signpost might highlight a **theme** or a character's motivation.

Read aloud the example passage and pause at the underlined text. Ask students to identify the repeated **imagery** and discuss how it affects the **characterization** of Papa.

Tell students that when they spot an Again and Again signpost, they should pause, mark it in their consumable texts, and ask the anchor question: *Why might the author keep bringing this up?*

MEMORY MOMENT

Explain that some **Memory Moments** are obvious. The **character** might say something like "I remember when ..." Other Memory Moments are subtle and refer to the memory indirectly.

Read aloud the example passage and pause at the phrase "reminded me of." Model for students how to determine that the phrase is a signpost for a Memory Moment. Point out that this is a subtle signpost and could be easy to miss.

Tell students that when they spot a Memory Moment, they should pause, mark it in their consumable texts, and ask the anchor question: *Why is this memory important?*

APPLY THE SIGNPOSTS

Have students use the selection as a model text to apply the signposts. As students encounter signposts, prompt them to stop, reread, and ask themselves the anchor questions that will help them understand the story's themes and characters.

Tell students to continue to look for these and other signposts as they read the other selections.

Connect to the
ESSENTIAL QUESTION

"My Favorite Chaperone" explores the challenges one family faces after immigrating to the United States from Kazakhstan. The family members struggle to understand and adapt to the social norms in their new country.

MY FAVORITE CHAPERONE

Short Story by **Jean Davies Okimoto**

? **ESSENTIAL QUESTION:**

What are the places that shape who you are?

154   Unit 3

LEARNING MINDSET

Curiosity   Discuss the value of curiosity with your students. Explain that being curious is an important part of having a learning mindset because it is a first step toward taking on the challenges that come with learning new skills. Often, things can be interesting when facing a new situation. Have students think about new situations they may have faced and what they might have been curious to learn about.

QUICK START

In this story, the main character struggles against her parents' rules. With a partner, share rules you must observe and your reactions to them.

ANALYZE PLOT

Most stories contain a **plot,** a series of events that occur in stages of development. Most story plots focus on a **conflict,** or a problem faced by the main character. These are the five stages of plot development:

- **exposition,** which introduces characters, setting, and conflict
- **rising action,** in which the main character takes steps to solve the problem even while complications might be introduced
- **climax,** the point of greatest tension in the story, in which the conflict begins to be resolved
- **falling action,** in which effects of the climax become clear
- **resolution,** in which the final outcome is revealed

Most plots are **linear**—events proceed in chronological order. But some stories have **non-linear** plots—events are told out of order.

ANALYZE CHARACTER

Characterization is the way an author reveals the traits and personalities of characters. Like real people, characters have **motivations**—needs, wants, and impulses that cause them to behave as they do. Authors reveal their characters' motivations through

- direct comments made by the narrator
- the characters' own thoughts, speech, and actions
- the thoughts, speech, and actions of other characters

Characters' motivations and behaviors influence story events and even how the conflict is resolved. Read the following **dialogue,** or conversation. What can you infer about Maya's motivation as she translates the words of Mr. Shanaman, her brother's principal, for Papa?

DIALOGUE	INFERENCES
"We have asked Maya to translate, Mr. Alazova." "Yes." Papa nodded. When he heard my name, he understood what Mr. Shanaman meant. "Your son, Nurzhan, was involved in quite a nasty fight." Papa looked at me, and I said to him in Russian, "Nurzhan was in little fight."	

GENRE ELEMENTS: REALISTIC FICTION

- includes the basic elements of fiction—setting, characters, plot, conflict, and theme
- features events and characters that could exist in real life
- contains natural-sounding dialogue and realistic interactions between characters
- often has a linear plot—story events are presented in chronological order

---

QUICK START

Have students read the Quick Start prompt, and invite them to share their feelings and opinions about the rules they have to follow in different places.

ANALYZE PLOT

Draw a pyramid plot diagram with climax at the peak to focus students' attention on the five stages of plot development. Prompt students to discuss each stage.

Explain to students that to analyze a plot, they should examine the way events and actions in each stage increase or help to resolve the conflict.

 For additional support, go to the **Reading Studio** and assign the following LEVEL UP **Level Up tutorial: Plot Stages.**

ANALYZE CHARACTER

Clarify that characterization can be direct, such as descriptions of a character, or indirect through thoughts, dialogue, actions, and attitudes. Guide students to discuss the bulleted list of indirect characterizations that reveal a character's motivations. Provide examples of each one from familiar stories. Model analyzing the dialogue to infer Maya's motivations. (**Possible inferences:** *Maya doesn't want her father to be too mad at Nurzhan. She is motivated by love and concern for her brother.*)

TEACH

CRITICAL VOCABULARY

Encourage students to read all the sentences before answering the questions. Remind them to look for context clues that match the meaning of each word.

Answers:

1. *Grateful; because the person supported you to join a group*

2. *A special award; because homework is a common occurrence, but awards are often a surprise*

3. *Speak to people; because a dispatcher tells taxi drivers where to pick up people*

4. *Angry; because a scuffle is a fight*

5. *Scared; because a whimper is a cry or a sob*

LANGUAGE CONVENTIONS

Confirm understanding of subject-verb agreement. If necessary, review singular and plural nouns. Point out that when prepositional phrases appear between the subject and verb of a sentence, it can make it tricky to determine the subject-verb agreement. Tell students to ignore or cover up prepositional phrases in order to clarify what is the subject of a sentence.

Read aloud the example sentence. Guide students to identify the two subjects and two verbs. Ask whether the subjects are singular or plural.

 ANNOTATION MODEL

Remind students of the annotation ideas in Notice & Note on pages 152–153, which suggest marking the text when they notice a signpost and then making notes answering its anchor question in the margin. They may want to color-code their annotations for different signposts by using highlighters.

CRITICAL VOCABULARY

sponsor   stun   dispatcher   scuffle   whimper

To see how many Critical Vocabulary words you already know, answer these questions.

1. If someone were to **sponsor** you, would you be annoyed, or grateful? Why?

2. Which would be more likely to **stun** you: getting a homework assignment, or getting a special award? Why?

3. If you were a **dispatcher,** would you need to speak to people, or write to them? Why?

4. Would people be more likely to have a **scuffle** if they were angry, or if they were lost? Why?

5. If you heard someone **whimper,** would you think the person was feeling lucky, or scared? Why?

LANGUAGE CONVENTIONS

Subject-Verb Agreement Verbs must agree with their subjects in number. This is true even when a prepositional phrase (beginning with a preposition such as *at, for, from, in, of, to,* or *with*) lies between the subject and its verb. To determine whether a subject modified by a prepositional phrase is singular or plural, ignore the phrase.

Their parents are unhappy because the punishment for both boys is a two-day suspension.

(This sentence has two subjects and two verbs. The second subject is *punishment*, not *boys*, so the verb needs to be singular: *is*.)

ANNOTATION MODEL   **NOTICE & NOTE**

As you read, note and notice signposts, such as **Tough Questions, Again and Again,** and **Memory Moments.** Here are one reader's notes about the beginning of "My Favorite Chaperone."

1 In homeroom when Mr. Horswill handed out the permission slip for the Spring Fling, the all-school dance, I almost didn't take one. Why should I bother when I was sure the answer would be the same? Even though I'm in ninth grade now, it would still be the same. No. *Nyet* is what they say, and I don't want to hear this again. But I took a permission slip anyway. . . .

> The narrator remembers times in the past when her parents said "nyet." Could be an important clue to their relationship.

BACKGROUND

*In addition to being the author of more than a dozen novels for young adults, **Jean Davies Okimoto** (b. 1942) is a therapist. Perhaps that is why she has such insight into the characters that she portrays. Okimoto typically writes about the everyday problems and challenges faced by teenagers like Maya, the main character in "My Favorite Chaperone." Maya and her family have come to the United States from Kazakhstan, a country in Central Asia that used to be part of the Soviet Union.*

MY FAVORITE CHAPERONE

Short Story by Jean Davies Okimoto

SETTING A PURPOSE

As you read, pay attention to Maya's interactions with her family and her friends. How do these interactions help you to understand the challenges of being an immigrant in a new country?

1   In homeroom when Mr. Horswill handed out the permission slip for the Spring Fling, the all-school dance, <u>I almost didn't take one. Why should I bother when I was sure the answer would be the same?</u> Even though <u>I'm in ninth grade now</u>, it would still be the same. No. <u>*Nyet* is what they say</u>, and <u>I don't want to hear this again</u>. But I took a permission slip anyway. I don't know why I didn't just shake my head when this very popular girl Marcia Egness was handing them out. And even after I took one, I don't know why I didn't throw it away. <u>Maybe I just couldn't give up hope. It's like that in America. It's a place where things can change for people, and many people always seem to have hope. At least that's how it seems to me. Maybe I was beginning to think this way, too, although my hope was very small.</u>

Notice & Note

Use the side margins to notice and note signposts in the text.

ANALYZE CHARACTER

Annotate: In paragraph 1, mark details that reveal something about Maya.

Infer: In a few sentences, summarize what you can infer about Maya from these details.

My Favorite Chaperone   **157**

BACKGROUND

Have students read the background and information about the author. Tell students that when Kazakhstan was part of the Soviet Union, people from outside the region were encouraged to go there to farm. These non-native people eventually outnumbered the natives. When Kazakhstan became an independent country in 1991, the government's policies began to favor native Kazakhs, leading many non-natives to emigrate to other countries.

SETTING A PURPOSE

Direct students to use the Setting a Purpose prompt to focus their reading.

ANALYZE CHARACTER

Point out that the **narrator**, Maya, is a character in the story and that she begins the story by presenting her thoughts and actions in a particular situation.

(**Answer:** *Maya is a foreign-born girl in the ninth grade who has very strict Russian-speaking parents and, although she thinks it's unlikely that they will change, she is beginning to feel some hope that they will.*)

For **listening support** for students at varying proficiency levels, see the **Text X-Ray** on page 152C.

 ### ENGLISH LEARNER SUPPORT

Vocabulary Support   Pronounce the word *chaperone* for students.

- Explain that a *chaperone* is someone, usually an adult, who goes to a school dance to make sure the young people behave properly.
- Point out to students that the word *chaperone* can be used as a noun or as a verb, or action word. Ask students to work with a partner to write a sentence using *chaperone* as a noun and another sentence using it as a verb. **SUBSTANTIAL/MODERATE**

ENGLISH LEARNER SUPPORT

Understand Cohesion Display this sentence from paragraph 3: "The next thing we knew, she had a beautiful photo taken of herself wearing her best outfit, a black dress with a scoop neck and a red silk band around the neck." Underline the words *we*, *she*, *herself*, and *her*. Explain to students that the underlined words are **pronouns**, or words that take the place of nouns or other pronouns. Writers use pronouns to avoid repeating nouns that have already been mentioned.

ASK STUDENTS to work with a partner to identify the nouns to which the pronouns refer. (**Answer:** *The pronouns* she, her, *and* herself *refer to Aunt Madina and* we *refers to the narrator and her family.*)

SUBSTANTIAL/MODERATE

▶ MEMORY MOMENT

Tell students that beginning in paragraph 2, the narrator is describing events from the past that brought her family to America. Remind students to ask themselves the anchor question when they notice signposts: *Why is this memory important?*
(**Answer:** *Students may note that Mama admires her sister and feels protective of her and/or distrustful of men who look for wives in magazines. She was a teacher in Kazakhstan but lost her job when the government ran out of money to pay teachers. She worries a great deal about her sister's well-being, how to feed her family, and so on. Alert readers may infer that Mama likely feels more vulnerable for having recently lost her own mother and then being abandoned by her sister— even though the latter was for a good reason that was not personally motivated.*

The memory explains why the family feels so extremely alone and vulnerable in the United States and why helping one another is so vitally important to them.)

CRITICAL VOCABULARY

sponsor: The narrator is explaining the circumstances that led to her family's move to America.

ASK STUDENTS what is suggested by Aunt Madina's needing to sponsor the narrator's family. (*There is likely to be a law or requirement that someone already living in America must vouch for, or support, any immigrant who wants to come here.*)

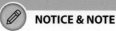

NOTICE & NOTE

MEMORY MOMENT

Notice & Note: Mark the sentences in paragraph 2 that help you realize that Maya is interrupting her story to recall events from an earlier time.

Analyze: What do the events described in paragraphs 2–7 help you understand about Mama and about Maya's family?

2   We came to America through an international dating magazine. I don't mean that our whole family was in the magazine looking for dates, just Madina Zhamejakova, my aunt. Aunt Madina came after Kazakhstan broke away from the Soviet Union and things got very hard. Everyone's pay was cut and the *tenge*, our money, was worth less and less. Then my grandmother died. That was the worst part. She was the head of our family, and without her everything fell apart. That's when Aunt Madina started reading international dating magazines.

3   The next thing we knew, she had a beautiful photo taken of herself wearing her best outfit, a black dress with a scoop neck and a red silk band around the neck. Aunt Madina is very pretty. Mama says she looks like an old American movie star we saw on TV named Natalie Wood, except Aunt Madina looks more Kazakh with her dark, beautiful Asian eyes. She sent the photo to one of these magazines, and in a very short time a man from Seattle saw her picture. He started calling her, and they would talk on the phone for hours. I guess he had plenty of money for these calls, which Aunt Madina thought was a good sign. After about six months, he asked her to marry him.

4   His name was Bob Campbell and he'd been in the navy. He told Aunt Madina he never had a chance to meet anyone because he traveled so much. Maybe that was true, but Mama was worried.

5   "Madina, something must be wrong with this man if he has to find a wife through a magazine."

6   Mama was afraid for her, but Aunt Madina went to America anyway and married Mr. Bob Campbell. She phoned us a lot from America, and Mama admitted she sounded okay. Madina said Bob was a lot older and had less hair than in the picture he had sent her. He was also fatter than in the picture, but he was very nice. She sounded so good, Mama stopped worrying about Aunt Madina, but then things got so bad in Kazakhstan that she worried all the time about us. Papa and Mama lost their teaching jobs because the government was running out of money. Mama had to go to the market and sell many of our things: clothes, dishes, even some furniture. When Aunt Madina asked us to come to America for the hundredth time, we were running out of things to sell and my parents finally agreed. Aunt Madina **sponsored** us, and not long after we got here, Papa got a job driving a cab, and Mama worked cleaning people's houses. It was hard for them not to have the respect they were used to from holding government teaching jobs, but

sponsor
(spŏn´sər) *v.* If you *sponsor* someone, you support his or her admission into a group.

they had high regard for the food they could now easily buy at the store.

7 Six months after we got here, the Boeing Company moved to Chicago and Mr. Bob Campbell got transferred there. When Aunt Madina left with him, it broke Mama's heart. Aunt Madina was the only person we knew from Kazakhstan, and it felt like our family just huddled together on a tiny island in the middle of a great American sea.

8 I looked at the permission slip, wishing there were some special words I could say to get Mama and Papa to sign it. Around me, everyone in my homeroom was talking excitedly about the Spring Fling. Mama says she thinks the school is strange to have parties and events after school when students should be doing their homework. Ever since I've been at Beacon Junior High, the only slip they signed was for the gymnastics team. Papa loves sports. (I think he told Mama that giving permission for this activity was important for my education.) I can't find words to say how grateful I was he signed that slip. The gymnastics team is a fine, good thing in my life. I compete in all the events: vault, beam, floor exercise, and my favorite: the uneven bars. I love to swing up and up, higher and higher, and as I fly through the air, a wonderful thing happens and suddenly I have no worries and no responsibilities. I'm free!

9 But there's another reason why I love gymnastics. Shannon Lui is on the team. We became friends when she was a teaching assistant in my ESL class. We're the same age,

ANALYZE PLOT

Annotate: Mark details in paragraph 8 that reveal the story's main conflict.

Summarize: Describe the story's conflict in one sentence.

ANALYZE CHARACTER

Annotate: Mark the reasons Maya gives in paragraph 8 for loving the gymnastics team.

Infer: What does her description of swinging on the uneven bars reveal about her?

ANALYZE PLOT

Review that most stories begin by introducing **characters**, the people involved in the story, and the **setting**, the time and place of the story. Early in a story, the author also introduces a **conflict**, or problem that has to be solved. (**Answer:** *Maya wants to go to the Spring Fling, but she is sure her parents will not give their permission.*)

■ English Learner Support

Analyze Plot Have students work in pairs to reread the text and identify words and phrases that describe the ongoing problem or conflict Maya faces. Encourage them to use the **Somebody Wants But So** strategy to summarize the conflict with a partner.
SUBSTANTIAL/MODERATE

For **reading support** for students at varying proficiency levels, see the **Text X-Ray** on page 152D.

ANALYZE CHARACTER

Point out that readers learn more about the narrator as she shares her thoughts about being a member of the gymnastics team. (**Answer:** *Maya so cherishes feeling free of worries and responsibilities that it is likely that in her daily life off the uneven bars she feels very trapped by worries and responsibilities.*)

CLOSE READ SCREENCAST

Modeled Discussion Have students click the Close Read icons in their eBooks to access two screencasts in which readers discuss and annotate paragraphs 7—the adjustment Maya's parents must make to provide for the family when they move to America.

As a class, view and discuss the video. Then have students pair up to do an independent close read of paragraph 8. Students can record their answers on the Close Read Practice PDF.

 Close Read Practice PDF

ANALYZE CHARACTER

Tell students that **dialogue** is the written conversation between two or more people in a story. Explain that readers learn new information about the narrator, Maya, through the dialogue in paragraphs 11–17. (**Answer:** *Her feelings suggest that she fears something terrible has happened and is afraid that she might have done something wrong without realizing it. They also suggest that she strives to be good, obedient, and always respects authority figures and the rules.*)

EL ENGLISH LEARNER SUPPORT

Culturally Responsive Instruction Encourage a class discussion to dig deeper into the anecdote Maya relates in paragraph 18.

ASK STUDENTS to describe how Sunstar reacts when Mr. Walsh taps her on the shoulder. *Why did the other children laugh? Why does Maya remember this story when Mr. Walsh comes to find her?* Have students get together with a partner and interview each other about the language(s) they speak. If they speak more than one language, where do they speak each? Then ask students to consider the value of knowing multiple languages. **MODERATE/LIGHT**

CRITICAL VOCABULARY

stun: The narrator is describing her feelings as she is singled out by her school's vice-principal.

ASK STUDENTS to infer why the narrator would feel stunned, based on what they know about her so far. (*The narrator has said that gymnastics makes her feel free, with "no responsibilities." Also, she has mentioned two different permission slips, which implies she usually follows the rules. Readers can infer that she's generally well behaved in school and that having the vice-principal speak to her is very unusual.*)

160 Unit 3

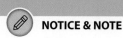

but she says I'm like her little sister. Her grandparents came from China, and her parents speak perfect English. Everything about Shannon's family is very American. Her mother has a red coat with gold buttons from Nordstrom, and her father cooks and sometimes even washes dishes! (I couldn't believe this when I first saw it; no Kazakh man would do kitchen work.) Shannon encouraged me to try out for the gymnastics team, and the team has meant even more to me this year since I got put in the mainstream and had to leave ESL. Since I left ESL, I often feel like I'm in the middle of a game where I don't know the players, the rules, or even the object of the game.

10   In my next class, Language Arts, even though I knew it was foolish, I was dreaming of the Spring Fling. I really like Language Arts. Ms. Coe, our teacher, is also the gymnastics coach, and there's a guy in the class, Daniel Klein, who was my partner for a research project last semester. He encouraged me to talk and listened to what I had to say (he's also a very handsome guy), and I always look forward to this class so I can see him. I was trying to think of some ideas to convince Mama and Papa to give permission (and also sneaking glances at Daniel Klein) when Mr. Walsh, the vice-principal, came into our class. He whispered something to Ms. Coe and she nodded. And then I was **stunned** because she nodded and pointed to me!

11   "Maya, you're wanted in the office," Ms. Coe said. "You can go now with Mr. Walsh."

12   My fingers tingled with fear. What was wrong? What had I done? Mr. Walsh only comes for people when there's trouble.

13   Like a robot, I gathered my books and followed Mr. Walsh. As he closed the classroom door behind us, my heart began to bang and I felt like I needed to go to the bathroom. In the hallway he told me Ms. Johnson, the school counselor, wanted to speak with me.

14   "What is wrong?" My voice came out as a whisper. I felt such terror I could barely speak.

15   "What's that?" Mr. Walsh couldn't hear my whisper.

16   "What is wrong?" I tried to speak more loudly.

17   "She didn't say. She just asked me to find you since I was heading down the hall anyway."

18   I suddenly remembered Sunstar Sysavath, who was in my ESL class last year. Her family came from Cambodia, and on her first day at Beacon she was in the wrong line in the

stun
(stŭn) *v.* To *stun* someone is to make him or her feel shocked or dazed.

ANALYZE CHARACTER

Annotate: Mark words and phrases in paragraphs 11–17 that show how Maya is feeling.

Infer: What do her feelings reveal about her?

160   Unit 3

lunchroom. Mr. Walsh went to help her, and he tapped her on her shoulder to get her attention. When she felt the tap and saw him, she lifted her hands in the air as if she were being arrested and about to be shot. People who saw this in the lunchroom laughed, but it wasn't a joke. Sunstar was filled with terror.

19   I knew I wouldn't be shot, but walking with Mr. Walsh to the office seemed like one of the longest walks of my life. I often fill my mind with nice things, such as imagining myself at the Olympics winning a gold medal for the U.S.A.—especially on days like today, when we have a gymnastics meet after school. But now my mind was filled with nothing. It was empty, like a dry riverbed where there is only cracked, baked earth and nothing lives.

20   I walked into the main office, where Ms. Johnson was waiting for me. "Come with me, Maya." Ms. Johnson smiled at Mr. Walsh. "Thanks, Tom."

21   Like a person made from wood, a puppet, I followed Ms. Johnson through the main office down the hall to her office across from the principal's. She showed me in and closed the door behind us.

22   "Sit down, dear."

23   I sat in a chair across from her desk and clutched my books to my chest. I'd never been in her office before. She had many nice green plants in front of the window and a small fish tank in one corner. I stared at the brightly colored fish swimming back and forth, back and forth. Then Ms. Johnson spoke.

24   "I received a call from Mr. Shanaman, the principal at Evergreen Elementary, and your brother's been suspended for fighting."

25   "Nurzhan?"

26   "Yes. Nurzhan Alazova." She read his name from a pink message slip. "They haven't been able to locate your mother, so they called over here to see if you could help."

27   "Is Nurzhan all right?"

28   "Yes. And I believe the other boy wasn't seriously hurt."

29   "Who did Nurzhan fight?" It was a foolish question—I was sure of the answer. Ms. Johnson hesitated, so I just said, "Ossie Nishizono," and she nodded.

30   "What must I do?" I asked.

31   "The school policy on suspension requires that the parent or guardian must have a conference at school within twenty-four hours of the suspension. Can you help us locate your mother or your father?"

ENGLISH LEARNER SUPPORT

Understand Vocabulary Make sure students understand what *suspension* means. Explain that *suspension* is the noun form of the verb *suspend*, which means "to remove from school for bad behavior." Pronounce both words for students.

ASK STUDENTS to explain why Maya's brother has been suspended from school. (*for fighting*) Then, ask students why the principal is asking for Maya's help. (*The school does not know how to locate her parents to inform them of Nurzhan's suspension.*) **MODERATE**

WHEN STUDENTS STRUGGLE . . .

Take Notes Some students may find it challenging to keep track of events in a longer story like "My Favorite Chaperone." Students may find it helpful to record key events on a graphic organizer, such as a flowchart.

   For additional support, go to the **Reading Studio** and assign the following Level Up tutorial: **Plot Stages.**

ANALYZE PLOT

Explain that in a story's **rising action,** characters encounter issues and complications as they try to resolve a story's conflict. (**Answer:** *Maya has become involved because school officials want her to help locate her parents; she has been asked to act as their translator. Maya's involvement suggests that she is often placed in situations "at the store, at the doctor" in which she must be adult-like as she speaks for her parents.*)

■ English Learner Support

Tough Questions Pair students of different abilities to read the passage and to make a list of the tough questions Maya asks. Then have partners discuss why Maya asks the questions and to speculate on possible answers.
SUBSTANTIAL/MODERATE

For **speaking support** for students at varying proficiency levels, see the **Text X-Ray** on page 152D.

CRITICAL VOCABULARY

dispatcher: The narrator is describing the steps she must take to contact her father.

ASK STUDENTS to explain why having to go through the dispatcher to reach her father adds to Maya's stress. (*Going through the dispatcher adds to Maya's waiting time, and she realizes that she may miss her gymnastics meet.*)

NOTICE & NOTE

ANALYZE PLOT
Annotate: Nurzhan's suspension creates a complication in the plot. Mark the reason that Ms. Johnson wants Maya to attend the meeting about Nurzhan.

Infer: What can you infer about Maya's role in her family?

dispatcher
(dĭs-păch´ər) n. A *dispatcher* is a person who sends out vehicles according to a schedule.

32 "Yes. I can do that."
33 "Do your parents speak English, Maya?"
34 "Just a little."
35 "Then perhaps you could attend the meeting and translate for them."
36 "Yes. I must always do this for my parents—at the store, at the doctor, things like that."
37 "Here's the phone. I'll step out to give you some privacy."
38 Ms. Johnson left the office, quietly closing the door behind her. I looked at the nameplate on her desk. CATHERINE JOHNSON, it said. Outside her window, the sky was gray and it had started to rain. I stared at the phone, wishing I didn't have to be the messenger with this bad news. Then I called the Northwest Cab Company and asked them to contact my father.
39 "Aibek Alazova. Cab 191. I'm his daughter, and there is a family problem I must speak with him about."
40 I stayed on the line while the **dispatcher** radioed Papa. I looked at the clock and felt my heart grow heavy. In a minute the bell would ring, school would be out, and the gymnastics meet would begin.
41 "Maya!" Papa's voice was alarmed. "What is wrong?"
42 "Nurzhan has been in a fight with another boy." Then I explained in Russian what had happened, and Papa said he had to drop his passenger at the Four Seasons Hotel downtown and then he'd come straight to Nurzhan's school. He'd be there about three-thirty.
43 Ms. Johnson came back into the office as I hung up the phone. "Did you get your mother?"
44 "I don't have the number where she works today, but I got my father. He will come to the school."
45 "Good."
46 "Ms. Johnson?"
47 "Yes?"
48 "I will leave now for Evergreen. Will you tell Ms. Coe I have a family problem and I cannot attend the gymnastics meet?"
49 "Of course. And I'll call Mr. Shanaman at Evergreen now and let him know that you and your father will be there."
50 I went to my locker, got my coat, then walked quickly down the hall to the south door that opens onto the play field that joins our school with Evergreen. Poor Nurzhan, getting in such big trouble. I couldn't fault him for fighting with Ossie Nishizono. Such a mean boy—he'd been teasing Nurzhan

---

IMPROVE READING FLUENCY

Targeted Passage Have students work with a partner to read the dialogue in this section. Model for students how to read the dialogue between Ms. Johnson and the narrator starting in paragraph 33. Have students follow along in their books as you read the dialogue aloud. Then have each partner choose a role and continue the dialogue starting in paragraph 43. Encourage students to provide feedback. Then, have students switch roles and read the passage again.

 Go to the **Reading Studio** for additional support in developing fluency.

without mercy for not speaking well and mispronouncing things. I hoped Nurzhan had given him a hard punch. But why did he have to make this fight today! I felt angry that I had to miss the meet because of Nurzhan. <u>Would Ms. Coe still want me on the team? Would she think I wasn't reliable?</u>

51　But as I neared Nurzhan's school—my old school—I only worried about Papa. Even though he didn't shout at me on the phone, that didn't mean he wasn't angry. He had a person in his cab and the dispatcher might have been hearing us. Probably the dispatcher didn't know Russian, but Papa wouldn't show his anger in the cab anyway. But Papa could be very, very angry—not just with Nurzhan but with me, too. He and Mama think it's my duty to watch out for Nurzhan and keep him out of trouble.

52　As I walked up to the front door, Mr. Zabornik, the custodian, waved to me. He was picking up papers and litter around the bushes next to the front walk. It was still raining lightly, and Mr. Zabornik's wet gray hair was pasted against his forehead.

53　"Hi, Maya."

54　"Hello, Mr. Zabornik."

55　"Here about your brother, I suppose."

56　"How did you know?"

57　"I was fixing the drainpipe when it happened." He pointed to the corner of the building by the edge of the play field. "That kid Ossie Nishizono was teasing Nurzhan something fierce. Telling him he could never be a real American, making fun of the way he talked." He bent down and picked up a candy wrapper. "Reminded me of how this bully used to treat me when my family came after the revolution."

58　"Oh." I think Mr. Zabornik could tell I didn't know what revolution this was.

My Favorite Chaperone　163

Understand Punctuation　Point out the dashes in the first sentence of paragraph 51. Explain that dashes signal an interruption or break in thought. Authors use dashes to call special attention to the words that follow it.

Organize students into pairs, and have them take turns punctuating the following sentences with dashes.

- *My brother is graduating tomorrow the same day as my birthday.*
- *Caspar he's the one we met at the football game has become a good friend.*
- *When they sing that song together oh, I have to tell you I get chills.*
- *I saw Sunny and Charles at the mall yesterday in other words, they were not at practice.*

SUBSTANTIAL/MODERATE

▶ **TOUGH QUESTIONS**

Explain that readers gain additional insights into Maya's character as she describes her thoughts and reactions to the news of her brother's fight. Remind students to ask themselves the anchor question when they notice a Tough Question signpost: *What does this make me wonder about?* (**Answer:** *Maya is motivated by a desire to enjoy the gymnastics team experience, to please adults by being dependable, and by a sense of duty to authority figures. Her fear of seeming to be unreliable suggests that she knows adults value reliability—or at least that being unreliable can get you into trouble or result in a loss of something treasured—and so she cultivates this quality in herself.*)

APPLYING ACADEMIC VOCABULARY

☑ contribute ☐ immigrate ☑ reaction ☐ relocate ☐ shifting

Think-Pair-Share　Have students turn to a partner to discuss the following questions. Guide students to include the Academic Vocabulary words *contribute* and *reaction* in their responses. Ask volunteers to share their responses with the class.

- How do Maya's feelings **contribute** to your understanding of Maya as a character?
- Why is Maya worried about her father's **reaction**?

ENGLISH LEARNER SUPPORT

Use Titles Point out that Maya uses the personal titles of the non-family adults she encounters. Note that using a title such as *Mr., Mrs., Ms.,* and *Miss* before a last name is a sign of respect and formality in English.

Explain that the written abbreviations of personal titles should be read as the full words. Read aloud the following list and have students repeat after you. Repeat until students can comfortably read each abbreviation correctly. Call attention to the /s/ and /z/ sounds in the pronunciations of *Mrs., Ms.,* and *Miss,* as well as note that there is no letter *r* in *Misses,* as there is in *Mrs.*

Mr. = Mister

Mrs. = Misses

Ms. = Miz

Miss = Miss

Dr. = Doctor

Discuss when to address someone with each title. Ask volunteers to read aloud examples of dialogue in the text that include personal titles and to tell what each title means.

SUBSTANTIAL/MODERATE

CRITICAL VOCABULARY

scuffle: Mr. Zabornik is explaining to Maya that he witnessed Nurzhan's fight.

ASK STUDENTS what the phrase "this was no scuffle" suggests about the fight. *(Because scuffle usually describes a minor disturbance or fight, the phrase suggests that the fight was fairly serious and could have led to injuries.)*

NOTICE & NOTE

scuffle
(skŭf´əl) *n.* A *scuffle* is a disorderly fight.

59 "The Hungarian revolution, in 1956." He looked out over the play field and folded his arms across his chest. "Guess some things never change."

60 "Nurzhan's going to be suspended."

61 "Sorry to hear that. 'Course, the school can't allow fights, and this was no **scuffle**. But I can sure see how your brother lost his temper." Then he went back to picking up the litter. "Good luck."

62 "Thank you, Mr. Zabornik."

63 I went to the front office, where Ms. Illo, the head secretary, spoke to me in a very kind way. "Maya, Mr. Shanaman is waiting for you in his office. You can go right in."

64 Mr. Shanaman was behind his big desk, and Nurzhan was sitting on a chair in the corner. He looked like a rabbit caught in a trap. He had scrapes on his hands and on his cheek, and his eyes were puffed up. I couldn't tell if that was from crying or being hit.

65 "I understand your father will be coming. Is that right, Maya?"

66 I nodded.

67 "Just take a seat by your brother. Ms. Illo will bring your father in when he gets here."

68 Then Mr. Shanaman read some papers on his desk and I sat down next to Nurzhan and spoke quietly to him in Russian.

69 "*Neechevo, Nurzhan. Ya vas ne veenu.*" It's okay, Nurzhan. I don't blame you, is what I said.

70 Nurzhan's eyes were wet with tears as he nodded to me.

71 I stared out the principal's window. Across the street, the bare branches of the trees were black against the cement gray sky. The rain came down in a steady drizzle, and after a few minutes, I saw Papa's cab turn the corner. His cab is green, the color of a lime, and he always washes and shines it. I watched Papa park and get out of the cab. His shoulders are very broad underneath his brown leather jacket, and Papa has a powerful walk, like a large, strong horse that plows fields. He walked briskly, and as he came up the steps of the school, he removed his driver cap.

72 It seemed like one thousand years, but it was only a minute before Ms. Illo brought Papa into the office. Nurzhan and I stood up when he entered, but he didn't look at us, only at Mr. Shanaman, who shook hands with him and motioned for him to have a seat.

73   Papa sat across the desk from Mr. Shanaman and placed his driver cap in his lap.

74   "We have asked Maya to translate, Mr. Alazova."

75   "Yes." Papa nodded. When he heard my name, he understood what Mr. Shanaman meant.

76   "Your son, Nurzhan, was involved in quite a nasty fight."

77   Papa looked at me, and I said to him in Russian, "Nurzhan was in little fight."

78   Mr. Shanaman continued. "The other boy, Ossie Nishizono, needed two stitches at the hospital."

79   "The other boy, Ossie Nishizono, was a little hurt," I told Papa.

80   <u>Nurzhan's eyes became wide as he listened to my translation.</u>

81   "We have a policy that anyone who fights must be suspended from school. Both boys will receive a two-day suspension."

82   "The other boy, who is very bad," I translated for Papa, "is not allowed to come to school for two days and his parents must punish him. Nurzhan must stay home, too. But he should not be punished so much."

83   Papa nodded.

84   Then Mr. Shanaman said, "We've been told the other boy was teasing your son. We'd like you to help Nurzhan find ways to handle this situation without resorting to violence. We're working with the other boy to help him show respect for all students."

85   I looked at Papa and translated: "The other boy was teasing Nurzhan in a violent manner. This boy will be punished and must learn to respect all students. We understand how Nurzhan became so angry, and we ask that you punish him by not allowing him to watch television."

86   "Yes, I will punish my son as you suggest," Papa said in Russian.

87   I looked at Mr. Shanaman. "My father says he will teach Nurzhan not to fight by giving him a very serious punishment."

88   "We are glad you understand the serious nature of this situation," Mr. Shanaman said. Then I told Papa in Russian the exact words of Mr. Shanaman.

89   Mr. Shanaman held out a form on a clipboard. "We require you to sign this to show that we've discussed the suspension and you'll keep Nurzhan at home until Monday."

ANALYZE CHARACTER

Annotate: Mark the details in paragraphs 76–90 that indicate Nurzhan's reaction to Maya's translations.

Connect: When people react like this, what are they usually thinking and feeling? Why might Nurzhan be having this reaction?

✏ ANALYZE CHARACTER

Remind students that authors use dialogue and the reactions of characters to reveal what characters are like. Draw students' attention to Maya's translation of what Mr. Shanaman says and ask them to think about why she would translate this way. (**Answer:** *When people's eyes get wide but they say nothing, they are usually surprised or even stunned and amazed at what is happening. Nurzhan might be stunned by the unusual fact that his sister is lying to their father and/or that she is attempting to prevent Nurzhan from getting punished too severely. She probably always does the morally correct thing, which in this case would be to translate the statements with full and complete accuracy. Nurzhan might also feel relieved, lucky, and even a little giddy in response to this strange and wonderful turn of events.*)

■ ENGLISH LEARNER SUPPORT

Analyze Character Have students work with a partner to discuss why Maya changes the meaning of her translations. Provide sentence frames to support discussion:

- *The principal says _____, but Maya says _____.*
- *The suggests that _____.*
- *Maya wants _____.*
- *The effect of this is _____.* **MODERATE**

AGAIN AND AGAIN

Explain that readers gain additional insights into Maya's **character** as she describes her thoughts. Remind students to pay attention to repetitions in Maya's reactions and thought processes throughout the story. Encourage students to ask themselves the anchor question when they notice an **Again and Again** signpost: *Why might the author keep bringing this up?* (**Answer:** *She tried to do this when Mr. Walsh called her out of her classroom, but she couldn't. Instead her mind remained blank and empty. Maya has a vivid imagination. She uses her imagination to create pleasant fantasies that make her feel good, but when she's scared her imagination sometimes fails her.*)

MEMORY MOMENT

Point out that authors often use the words *like* and *as* to make **comparisons** between two things in a text. Remind students to ask themselves the anchor question when they notice signposts: *Why is this memory important?* (**Answer:** *Maya might be hoping to justify changing Mr. Shanaman's words because she feels somewhat conflicted about having done something that she has to admit is "like telling lies."*)

ANALYZE CHARACTER

Point out that like their interactions in paragraphs 68–70, the dialogue between Maya and Nurzhan in paragraphs 94–108 gives information about the characters and their relationship. (**Answer:** *Maya is responsible for taking care of her brother. With both parents working, she takes on the role of an adult in his life. The dialogue shows that while she was protective of him during the crisis in the principal's office, she now wants him to realize that she is frustrated, sad, and angry about the sacrifice she had to make for him: "I missed the gymnastics meet because of you!"*)

 NOTICE & NOTE

AGAIN AND AGAIN

Notice & Note: In paragraph 91, mark the details that Maya focuses on and how she tries to calm herself.

Compare: Recall another time when Maya tried to do something similar. What insights into Maya's character can you gain by comparing these instances?

MEMORY MOMENT

Notice & Note: Mark the brief Memory Moment in paragraph 92.

Infer: Why might Maya be recalling this now?

ANALYZE CHARACTER

Annotate: Mark details that indicate the role that Maya plays in Nurzhan's life.

Draw Conclusions: What does Maya want Nurzhan to understand about the events of the day and her feelings about what happened?

---

90   Again, I told Papa exactly what Mr. Shanaman said, and Papa signed the form.

91   We said nothing as we left the school and followed Papa to his cab. Nurzhan and I sat in the back, not daring to speak. There was a small rip in the leather of the seat and I poked my finger in it. The cab smelled of perfume; maybe Papa's last ride was a lady who wore a lot of it. It smelled like some kind of flower, but I couldn't name it. I wished so much I was in a beautiful meadow right then, surrounded by sweet-smelling flowers, lying in the soft grass, looking up at the clouds. I tried to calm myself by thinking about this meadow, but I just kept feeling scared—scared Papa might somehow find out I'd changed what Mr. Shanaman said.

92   Maybe I should've felt bad about changing Mr. Shanaman's words, but I didn't. I only felt afraid. I don't mean that I think changing words like that is okay; I have to admit it's sort of like telling lies. But I think maybe some lies are okay, like in the play we read last semester about Anne Frank and how the people who were hiding her family lied and said no one was in the attic when they really were. They lied to save Anne's family from the Nazis. Maybe I wasn't saving Nurzhan from death, but I was sure scared to death of what Papa might have done if I hadn't changed the words. I stared at the back of Papa's thick neck. It was very red, and he drove in silence until he pulled up in front of our building. Papa shut off the engine. Then he put his arm across the top of the seat and turned his face to us, craning his neck.

93   His dark eyes narrowed and his voice was severe. "I am ashamed of this! To come to this school and find you in trouble, Nurzhan! This does not seem like much punishment to me, this no watching television. You will go to bed tonight without dinner." He clenched his teeth. "I have lost money today because of you. And Maya, you must keep your brother out of trouble!" Then he waved away furiously, like shooing away bugs. "Go now! Go!"

94   We went in the house, and Nurzhan marched straight to the table in the kitchen with his books. He seemed to be in such a hurry to do his work, he didn't even take off his jacket.

95   "Take off your jacket and hang it up, Nurzhan."

96   "Okay."

97   I began peeling potatoes for dinner, while Nurzhan hung up his jacket. Then he sat back down at the table.

98   "Maya, I—"

99   "Don't talk. Do your work."

100 "But I—"

101 "I missed the gymnastics meet because of you!"

102 "Watch the knife!" Nurzhan looked scared.

103 I glanced at my hand. I was holding the knife and I'd been waving it without realizing it.

104 "I wasn't going to stab you, stupid boy."

105 "I was only going to say thank you." Nurzhan looked glumly at his book.

106 I went back to peeling the potatoes. I'd had enough of him and his troubles.

107 "For changing what Mr. Shanaman said when you told Papa," he said in a timid voice, like a little chick peeping.

108 "It's okay, Nurzhan." I sighed. "Just do your work."

109 A few minutes before six, we heard Mama get home. She came straight to the kitchen, and when she saw Nurzhan sitting there doing his work, a smile came over her tired face.

110 "Oh, what a good boy, doing his work."

111 "Not so good, Mama. Nurzhan got in trouble." I didn't mind having to tell her this bad news too much (not like when I had to call Papa). Then I explained about the fight and how Papa had to come to the school.

112 "Oh, my poor little one!" Mama rushed to Nurzhan and examined his hands. Tenderly, she touched his face where it had been cut. Then she turned sharply toward me.

113 "Maya! How could you let this happen?"

114 "Me! I wasn't even there."

115 "On the bus, when this boy is so bad to Nurzhan. You must make this boy stop."

116 "No, Mama," Nurzhan explained. "He would tease me more if my sister spoke for me."

117 "I don't understand this. In Kazakhstan, if someone insults you, they have insulted everyone in the family. And everyone must respond."

118 "It's different here, Mama."

119 Mama looked sad. She sighed deeply. Then the phone rang and she told me to answer it. Mama always wants me to answer because she is shy about speaking English. When her work calls, I always speak on the phone to the women whose houses she cleans and then translate for Mama. (I translate their exact words, not like with Mr. Shanaman.)

120 But it wasn't for Mama. It was Shannon, and her voice was filled with worry.

TOUGH QUESTIONS

Notice & Note: Mark the tough question that prompts the heated dialogue between Mama and her children in paragraphs 113–119.

Analyze: What differences between Kazakh and U.S. culture does this dialogue reveal?

TOUGH QUESTIONS

Explain that while the **dialogue** in paragraphs 113–119 reveals Mama's view of her children, it also shows a **conflict** that the family must deal with as immigrants. Remind students to ask themselves the anchor question when they notice a Tough Question signpost: *What does this make me wonder about?* (**Answer:** *"In Kazakhstan, if someone insults you, they have insulted everyone in the family. And everyone must respond." But, in the United States, if Nurzhan's sister spoke up for him and told the bully to stop, Nurzhan would be teased even more.*)

■ English Learner Support

Tough Questions Direct students to work with a partner to create a Venn diagram comparing Kazakh and U.S. cultures. **MODERATE/LIGHT**

AGAIN AND AGAIN

Remind students that authors often repeat words and descriptions in order to emphasize connections within the text. Encourage students to ask themselves the anchor question when they notice an **Again and Again** signpost: *Why might the author keep bringing this up?* (**Answer:** *The repetition of shy causes me to notice that both Mama and Maya are shy in certain situations. The author might have wanted readers to notice that Mama and Maya have this shyness in common and to start to realize that they may be alike in other ways.)*

ENGLISH LEARNER SUPPORT

Confirm Understanding Use the following supports with students at varying proficiency levels:

- Write *shy* on the board. Pronounce the word several times, with students repeating it after you. Then act out the meaning of *shy* for students. **SUBSTANTIAL**

- Have students pronounce *shy*, and help them understand what it means. (*timid and scared or hesitant*) Prompt them to restate paragraph 127 in their own words. **MODERATE**

- Ask students to pronounce *shy*, correcting them as needed. Then ask them to explain what Maya is feeling and why. **LIGHT**

121 "Maya, why weren't you at the meet? Is everything all right?"

122 "Everything's okay. It was just Nurzhan." Then I explained to her about what had happened. "I hope I can still be on the team."

123 "Ms. Coe is cool. Don't worry, it won't mess anything up."

124 Shannon was right. The next day at practice Ms. Coe was very understanding. Practice was so much fun I forgot all about Nurzhan, and Shannon and I were very excited because Ms. Coe said we were going to get new team leotards.

125 After practice we were waiting for the activity bus, talking about the kind of leotards we wanted, when two guys from the wrestling team joined us. One was David Pfeiffer, a guy who Shannon talked about all the time. She always said he was so cute, that he was "awesome" and "incredible" and things like that. She was often laughing and talking to him after our practice, and I think she really liked him. And today he was with Daniel Klein!

126 "Hey, Maya! How was practice?"

127 "Hi." I smiled at Daniel, but then I glanced away, pretending to look for the bus because talking to guys outside class always made me feel embarrassed and (shy).

128 The guys came right up to us. David smiled at Shannon. "Wrestling practice was great! We worked on takedowns and escapes, and then lifted weights. How was your practice?"

129 "Fun! We spent most of it on the beam."

130 "I'm still pumped from weight training!" David grinned and picked up a metal trash can by the gym door. He paraded around with the can, then set it down with a bang right next to Shannon. Everyone was laughing, and then David bent his knees and bounced up and down on his heels and said, "Check this out, Daniel! Am I strong or what?" The next thing we knew, David had one arm under Shannon's knees and one arm under her back and he scooped her up. Shannon squealed and laughed, and I was laughing watching them, when all of a sudden Daniel scooped me up too!

131 "*Chort!*" I shouted, as he lifted me. I grabbed him around his neck to hang on, and my head was squished against his shoulder. He strutted around in a circle before he let me down. I could feel that my face was the color of borscht, and I flamed

---

AGAIN AND AGAIN

Notice & Note: Do you recall having recently read the word *shy*? Mark the word in paragraph 127 and in the earlier paragraph where it appears.

Analyze: What does this repetition cause you to notice? Why might the author have wanted to draw your attention to this?

---

with excitement and embarrassment and couldn't stop laughing from both joy and nervousness.

132   "That's nothing, man." David crouched like a weight lifter while he was still holding Shannon and lifted her as high as his shoulders.

133   It was exciting and crazy: Daniel and David showing each other how strong they were, first picking up Shannon and me, then putting us down, then picking us up and lifting us higher, as if Shannon and I were weights. After a few times, whenever Daniel picked me up, I was easily putting my arms around his neck, and I loved being his pretend weight, even though Shannon and I were both yelling for them to put us down. (We didn't really mean it. Shannon is a strong girl, and if she didn't like being lifted up and held by David, there was no way it would be happening.) I couldn't believe it, but I began to relax in Daniel's arms, and I laughed each time as he slowly turned in a circle.

134   Then Shannon and I tried to pick them up, and it was hilarious. Every time we tried to grab them, they did wrestling moves on us and we ended up on the grass in a big heap, like a litter of playful puppies. I couldn't remember a time in my life that had been so fun and so exciting. We lay on the grass laughing, and then David and Daniel jumped up and picked Shannon and me up again.

135   But this time when we turned, as my face was pressed against Daniel's shoulder, I saw something coming toward the school that made me tremble with fear.

136   "Daniel, please. Put me down!" My voice cracked as my breath caught in my throat.

137   But Daniel didn't hear. Everyone was shouting and laughing, and he lifted me up even more as the lime green cab came to a halt in front of the school. The door slammed. Papa stood like a huge bull in his dark leather jacket and flung open the back door of the cab.

138   "MAYA ALAZOVA!" His voice roared across the parking lot. He pointed at me the way one might identify a criminal. "*EDEE SUDA!*" he shouted in Russian. COME HERE!

139   Daniel dropped me and I ran to the cab, **whimpering** and trembling inside like a dog caught stealing a chicken.

140   Papa didn't speak. His silence filled every corner of the cab like a dark cloud, slowly suffocating me with its poisonous rage. Papa's neck was deep red, and the skin on the back of my hands tingled with fear. I lay my head back against the seat and closed

ANALYZE CHARACTER

Annotate: A simile is a comparison that uses the word *like* or *as*. Mark the similes that help you visualize the scene that unfolds in paragraphs 137–140.

Analyze: What do these similes reveal about Papa and Maya?

whimper
(hwĭm′pər) *v.* To *whimper* is to sob or let out a soft cry.

ANALYZE CHARACTER

Remind students that a simile is a comparison using the word *like* or *as*. Tell students that such comparisons can help readers make a connection to characters' emotions. (**Answer:** *The similes emphasize Papa's strength and power, and how defenseless Maya feels.*)

CRITICAL VOCABULARY

whimper: Maya is describing her reaction when her father observes Daniel lifting her in the air.

ASK STUDENTS what her whimper reveals about Maya's emotions. (**Answer:** *She is shocked and frightened, and is probably about to cry.*)

TEXT IN FOCUS

Understanding Characters Have students view the **Text in Focus** video on this page of their eBook to learn how the author reveals characters' traits and personalities. Then have students use Text in Focus Practice to apply what they have learned.

ANALYZE PLOT

Remind students that Maya's conflict at the beginning of the story focuses on wanting her parents to sign a permission slip so that she can attend the Spring Fling dance. Discuss how the events in this part of the plot may affect the possibility of resolving that conflict. (**Answer:** *This event and her parents' reactions are likely to make it harder for Maya to resolve her main conflict in the way that she had hoped to resolve it. It seems unlikely that they will sign the permission slip for Maya to go to the dance.*)

my eyes, squeezing them shut, and took myself far away until I was safe on the bars at a beautiful gymnastics meet in the sky. I swung back and forth, higher and higher, and then I released and flew to the next bar through fluffy white clouds as soft as goose feathers, while the air around me was sweet and warm, and my teammates cheered for me, their voices filled with love.

141   We screeched to a stop in front of our building. My head slammed back against the seat. When I struggled from the taxi, it was as though I had fallen from the bars, crashing down onto the street, where I splintered into a million pieces. And as hard as I tried, I couldn't get back on the bars any more than I could stop the hot tears that spilled from my eyes. Papa roared in front of me, and as he charged toward the door in his glistening dark leather jacket, he again seemed transformed to a creature that was half man and half bull.

142   "Gulnara!" He flung open the door, shouting for Mama, his voice filled with anger and blame.

143   "Why are you here? What has happened, Aibek?" Mama came from the kitchen as Nurzhan darted to the doorway and peeked around like a little squirrel.

144   I closed the front door and leaned against it with my wet palms flat against the wood, like a prisoner about to be shot.

145   "Is this how you raise your daughter! Is this what you teach her? Lessons to be a toy for American boys!" Papa spat out the words.

146   The color rose in Mama's face like a flame turned up on the stove, and she spun toward me, her eyes flashing. "What have you done?"

147   "Your daughter was in the arms of an American boy."

148   Mama looked shocked. "When? H-how can this be?" she stammered.

149   "Outside the school as I drove by, I found them at this. Don't you teach her anything?"

ANALYZE PLOT

Annotate: Review paragraphs 137–150. Mark evidence of Maya's parents' reactions to finding her in the arms of an American boy.

Predict: What impact might this complication have on Maya's ability to resolve the story's main conflict?

APPLYING ACADEMIC VOCABULARY

☑ **contribute**   ☐ **immigrate**   ☑ **reaction**   ☐ **relocate**   ☐ **shifting**

Think-Pair-Share Have students turn to a partner to discuss the following question. Guide students to include the Academic Vocabulary words *contribute*, *immigrate*, and *reaction* in their responses. Ask volunteers to share their responses with the class.

- How does the family's decision to move to America **contribute** to Maya's conflict?
- What do the **reactions** of Maya's parents tell the reader about their characters?

150 "Who let her stay after school? Who gives permission for all these things? You are the one, Aibek. If you left it to me, she would come home every day. She would not have this permission!"

151 Mama and Papa didn't notice that I went to the bathroom and locked the door. I huddled by the sink and heard their angry voices rise and fall like the pounding of thunder, and then I heard a bang, so fierce that the light bulb hanging from the ceiling swayed with its force. Papa slamming the front door. Then I heard the engine of the cab and a sharp squeal of tires as he sped away.

152 I imagined running away. I would run like the wind, behind the mini-mart, sailing past the E-Z Dry Cleaner, past the bus stop in an easy gallop through the crosswalk. As I ran, each traffic light I came to would turn green, until there would be a string of green lights glowing like a necklace of emeralds strung all down the street. And then I would be at the Luis' house. Mrs. Lui would greet me in her red Nordstrom coat with the gold buttons. She would hug me and hold me close. Then Mr. Lui would say, "Hi, honey," and make hamburgers. "Want to use the phone, Maya?" Mrs. Lui would say. "Talk as long as you want—we have an extra line for the kids."

153 "Oh, by the way," Mr. Lui would say, "Shannon is having David and some other kids over Friday night for pizza and videos. It's fine if there's a guy you want to invite, too."

154 "Maya! Open this door. Do you want more trouble?" Mama rattled the doorknob so hard I thought she'd rip it off.

155 "I'm coming." My voice caught in my throat. I felt dizzy as I unlocked the door and held my stomach, afraid I would be sick.

156 "You have brought shame to your father and to this family." Mama glared at me.

157 "Mama, it was just kids joking. Guys from the wrestling team pretending some of us were weights."

158 "I don't know this weights."

159 "It was nothing, Mama!"

160 "Do not tell me 'nothing' when your father saw you!" she screamed.

161 The next morning Papa was gone when I woke up. And even though Mama hadn't yet left for work, it was like she was gone, too. She didn't speak to me and didn't even look at me, except once when she came in the kitchen. I was getting *kasha*, and she stared at me like I was a stranger to her. Then she turned

AGAIN AND AGAIN

Notice & Note: Maya imagines nice things time and again during emotionally difficult moments. Mark the fantasy she describes in paragraphs 152–153.

Contrast: What differences between Kazakh and U.S. culture do the details in Maya's fantasy highlight?

▶ AGAIN AND AGAIN

Remind students that Maya's family is adjusting to many cultural differences. Encourage students to analyze Maya's thoughts to determine how the differences affect her. Encourage students to ask themselves the anchor question when they notice an **Again and Again** signpost: *Why might the author keep bringing this up?* (**Answer:** *These details seem to be intended to highlight the following aspects of U.S. culture and to thereby imply that these are different from corresponding aspects of Kazakh culture: In the U.S. women wear bright, expensive clothes; mothers and daughters hug one another closely; fathers talk sweetly and informally to their daughters and cook food; fathers give their daughters permission to make phone calls, talk as long as they want, and socialize with boys; and parents indulge their children with luxuries, such as their own phone line.*)

ENGLISH LEARNER SUPPORT

Understand Environmental Print Encourage students to visualize ideas from the text to make deeper connections. Read paragraph 152 to students. Ask: *How does the author describe where Maya lives?* (by using locations) Tell students that the author only names the locations because the author expects readers to understand what these locations look like. Draw a picture of a basic store front and then say: *Signs help us know what happens at a location. What kinds of signs do you see outside a mini-mart?* (advertisements, signs for ice and ATMs, the mini-mart's phone number) Encourage volunteers to draw the missing signs. Repeat the activity with the dry cleaner, the bus stop, and a street intersection. Read the paragraph again, this time asking students to close their eyes and visualize the town. **MODERATE**

ENGLISH LEARNER SUPPORT

Understand Language Choices Write Mama's response in paragraph 158 on the board: "I don't know this weights." Point out to students that Mama's native language is Russian, not English. The author includes dialogue with non-standard English to help readers get a better understanding of the character.

- Work with students to rewrite the sentence using standard English. **SUBSTANTIAL**

- Have students work with a partner to find examples of dialogue that uses non-standard English. Then, have them rewrite the sentences in standard English. **MODERATE**

- Have students discuss the effect the author creates by using non-standard English in the dialogue for certain characters. **LIGHT**

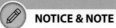

ANALYZE CHARACTER

Explain that the author uses a comparison to describe how Maya's family gets past the crisis brought on by her encounter with Daniel. (**Answer:** *The comparison to being huddled on an island suggests that as new immigrants, Maya and her family are somewhat isolated. She implies that their isolation requires them to rely more on each other, so the family members cannot remain angry at one another.*)

and left. Not only was Mama not speaking to me, but she didn't speak to Nurzhan, either. This never happens. Even when he was punished for the fight with Ossie Nishizono and had to stay home, Mama still spoke to him. But as I was getting dressed in my room, I heard Nurzhan try to talk to her. I put my ear to the door to listen.

162   "It's different here, Mama. I'm sure Maya and those guys were playing. Joking, like in a game."

163   "Quiet, boy! You know nothing of these things!"

164   I was shocked. Mama hardly ever says a harsh word to her precious boy. Then I heard her rush by, and then *bam*! The door slammed. The *kamcha* that hung by the door trembled with the force. We brought our *kamcha* when we came to America. It looks like a riding crop with a carved wooden handle and a leather cord, decorated with some horsehair. It's an old Kazakh tradition to put the *kamcha* inside the house next to the door because it's believed to bring good fortune and happiness. But our *kamcha* was not bringing us good fortune today. Mama left without a word of goodbye to either one of us.

165   I came out of my room and Nurzhan and I just looked at each other. I didn't feel happy that Nurzhan got yelled at; I felt bad about the whole thing.

166   "Did you hear?"

167   I nodded.

168   "She won't listen."

169   "Thank you for trying, Nurzhan."

170   "It did no good," he said with sadness. "They don't know about things here, only their own ways. They are like stone."

ANALYZE CHARACTER

Annotate: In paragraph 171, mark Maya's description of how and why her family's relationships become "almost calm" again.

Analyze: What does this description emphasize about how Maya's family is affected by their being recent immigrants?

171   I wondered how long this tension and anger would stay in our home. I was afraid it might be a long time, because Mama and Papa were so upset. <u>But gradually, in the way that winter becomes spring, there was a slight thaw each day. Perhaps because we huddled together like a tiny Kazakh island in the middle of the great American sea, we couldn't allow our winter to go on and on, and by the next week, things in my family were almost calm.</u>

172   But it was not to last. On Wednesday afternoon of the following week, Mama was waiting to talk to me when I got home from school. I was afraid when I saw her. Her ankle was taped up, and she sat on the couch with her leg up on a chair. Next to it was a pair of crutches!

173   "Mama, what happened?"

174   "I fell at work. Mrs. Hormann took me to the emergency room. I can't work for six weeks until it heals. I must keep my foot up as much as possible."

175   "I'll start dinner." My eyes filled with tears, I felt so bad for her. And I felt bad that I'd made them so upset when my father saw me and Daniel. Even though I knew I hadn't done anything wrong, it still bothered me that I'd been the cause of such trouble in our house.

176   It was decided that I'd take Mama's jobs for her while she couldn't work. I wouldn't go to gymnastics practice; instead, right after school I'd go straight to the houses Mama cleaned. The people Mama worked for agreed to this, and I worked at each house from three-thirty until six-thirty, when Papa came to pick me up. I wasn't able to clean their entire houses in this amount of time, but they told me which rooms were the most important, and I was able to clean those. Bathrooms were on the list at every house.

177   I didn't mind doing Mama's jobs. Although I did get very tired, and I was scared sometimes that I might break something when I dusted (especially at Mrs. Hathaway's house, because she had a lot of glass vases and some small glass birds), but I didn't mind vacuuming, mopping, dusting, cleaning cupboards, counters, stoves, and refrigerators. I didn't even mind cleaning toilets. It was as if all the work I did at Mama's jobs was to make up for the problems I'd caused. And besides, our family needed the money.

178   When I finished working for Mama, as soon as I got home I had to make dinner for everyone. Each day I got more tired, and on Friday, when I was peeling potatoes, I cut my finger. I thought it was just a little cut, so I washed it off and continued to peel.

179   Nurzhan looked up from the table, where he was doing his work. "What's wrong with the potatoes?"

180   "Nothing," I said automatically, with my eyes half-closed.

181   "They're red!"

182   "What?"

183   "The potatoes, Maya. They look like you painted them with red streaks."

184   I looked down and saw my finger bleeding on the potatoes, and it scared me to be so tired that I hadn't seen this. "It's just blood, Nurzhan. I cut myself. It'll wash off."

185   "Oh, yuck."

186   "Quiet, boy! I said I would wash it off."

ANALYZE PLOT

Annotate: Mark the event that results in more responsibilities and sacrifices for Maya.

Analyze: What stage of the plot do this event and its results fall into? Explain why.

ANALYZE PLOT

Focus attention on the ways Mama's injury leads to changes in Maya's life. Have students reread paragraphs 175–179 to identify the ways Maya's life changes as a result of Mama's injury. (**Answer:** *It is part of the rising action because the event and its results further complicate Maya's life and increase the intensity of the story.*)

■ English Learner Support

Analyze Plot Guide students to create a cause-and-effect chain to understand the chain of events in the plot. Write "First: Mama injured" on the board. Ask students what happens because of this. *Who will do Mama's work? (Maya)* Ask students what happens as a result of Maya doing Mama's work. *(Maya quits going to gymnastics.)* Have students work in pairs to continue analyzing the effect of events in the story and complete the chain. **SUBSTANTIAL/MODERATE**

 **NOTICE & NOTE**

ANALYZE CHARACTER

Explain that the dialogue in paragraphs 194 and 195 marks a change in Maya's relationship with Mama. As needed, review earlier evidence of what their relationship was like in paragraphs 112–118 and in paragraphs 154–160. (**Answer:** *Maya is both shocked and grateful.*)

ANALYZE CHARACTER

Remind students that authors present a character's thoughts, speech, and actions to help readers learn what the character is like. (**Answer:** *Nurzhan has developed the ability to look beyond his own needs and feelings to care for others and has become more clever and confident.*)

■ English Learner Support

Analyze Character Tell students that authors do not always use complete sentences in their writing, especially with dialogue. Read aloud paragraphs 189–193. Guide students to identify the sentence fragments that appear in the passage: "Maya!" "The oven!" "Oh, no!" and "Good." Explain that authors deliberately include sentence fragments to draw attention to an important idea or to convey a particular mood and to make interactions sound more natural. **ALL LEVELS**

---

187   That night at dinner, Nurzhan refused to eat the potatoes, even though there was no sign of blood on them, and I wanted to take the whole dish and dump them on his head.

188   The next week I was so tired after going to school and cleaning Mrs. Hathaway's house that I burned the chicken. After I put it in the oven, I sat at the table with Nurzhan to do my homework. I rested my head on my book for just a minute, and the next thing I knew, Nurzhan was pounding on my arm.

189   "Maya! The oven!" he shouted.

190   I woke to see smoke seeping from the oven. "Oh, no!"

191   I leaped up and grabbed a dishtowel and pulled the pan from the oven. The chicken was very dark but not black, although all the juice at the bottom of the pan had burned and was smoking. "It's okay, Nurzhan. We can still eat it."

192   "Good."

193   Nurzhan didn't mind the almost-burned chicken that night, but Papa did.

194   "This tastes like my shoe!" Papa grumbled.

195   "Aibek, I have to keep my foot up, and Maya is doing the best she can. It is not easy. She must go to school, then do my work, then cook for us. She is just a young girl."

196   I looked at Mama and felt tears in my eyes. I couldn't remember another time when Mama spoke on my behalf, and my tears were the kind you have when you know someone is on your side.

197   The next evening as dinner was cooking, I sat with Nurzhan at the kitchen table and helped him with his spelling words. While I waited for him to think how to spell *admire*, I took the permission slip for the Spring Fling from my notebook and stared at it. I'd never thrown it away.

198   "A-D-M-I-E-R."

199   "Almost, Nurzhan. It's this," I said as I wrote the correct spelling on the top of the permission slip and turned it for him to see.

200   "A-D-M-I-R-E," he spelled. Then he looked closely at the slip. "What's this for?"

201   "It's a permission slip for the Spring Fling, the all-school dance, but it is only good for scratch paper to help you with spelling. Papa will never let me go. I don't know why I trouble myself to keep such a thing."

202   Nurzhan took the slip and put it in his notebook.

203   "What are you doing with it?"

204   "Let me try."

ANALYZE CHARACTER
Annotate: In paragraphs 193–196, mark what Mama says and Maya's reaction to it.

Cause/Effect: What is the impact of Mama's statement on Maya?

ANALYZE CHARACTER
Annotate: In the dialogue between Maya and Nurzhan, mark the statements that suggest Nurzhan is going to attempt to resolve the main conflict of the story.

Analyze: What do these statements suggest about how Nurzhan has developed or changed?

WHEN STUDENTS STRUGGLE...

Identify Plot Stages Help students identify the climax of the story and fill it in on the graphic organizer they created at the beginning of the story.

 For additional support, go to the **Reading Studio** and assign the following LEVEL **Level Up tutorial: Plot Stages.**

205 "Try what?"

206 "Let me try to get permission for you from Papa."

207 I laughed. "Oh, Nurzhan. Don't be foolish. You waste your time. Papa will never change his thinking because of you."

208 "I will try anyway. When he comes home tonight, I will speak to him myself. I have a plan."

209 I could only smile a sad smile at the idea of little Nurzhan trying to change the mind of Papa, who is a man like a boulder.

210 After dinner I went to my room to study, leaving Nurzhan to talk with Mama and Papa. I was afraid to really hope that any good thing could come from Nurzhan's plan. To hope and then be disappointed seemed to be worse. It was better not to hope and to live my dreams through Shannon. I could at least hear every little detail of her experience at the dance and be happy for her, giving up the idea that I'd ever be the one who goes to the dance, too.

211 But I comforted myself thinking about the dream in my life that really had come true—the gymnastics team. I still had that, and I was warming my heart with thoughts of the team when Nurzhan burst into the room.

212 "Maya! You can go!" Nurzhan jumped up and down like a little monkey, and I stared at him in disbelief.

213 "Don't joke with me about such a thing, boy!" I snapped.

214 "No! It's true. Look!" He waved the permission slip in front of my face.

215 I stared at the slip, still in disbelief. *Aibek Alazova . . .* Papa's name and Papa's writing. *It was true!* I was still staring at the slip, still afraid to completely believe that such a thing could be true, when Mama and Papa came in.

216 "We give permission for this, Maya, because Nurzhan will go, too," Mama said.

217 "He will not leave your side," Papa announced in a most serious tone. "He is your *capravazhdieuushee*."

218 "Chaperone." I said the English word. I knew this word because the parents who help the teachers supervise the kids at school activities are called this. But I hadn't heard of a little boy being a chaperone.

219 "Thank you, Mama. Thank you, Papa."

220 "It is Nurzhan you must thank," Mama said.

221 I thanked Nurzhan, too, and Mama and Papa left our room. Then I heard the front door close and I knew Papa had left for work.

ANALYZE PLOT

Annotate: Mark the part of the story that appears to be the climax—the point of greatest tension—when the conflict begins to be resolved.

Cite Evidence: What story events and details support your conclusion?

My Favorite Chaperone **175**

 ANALYZE PLOT

Tell students the climax of a story is the point of greatest tension, when the conflict begins to be resolved. Guide students to recall all of the complications that have prevented Maya from even asking her parents to sign the permission slip for the Spring Fling dance. (**Answer:** *Maya's freedom has become more and more constricted by complications in the plot up until this moment. These complicating events have intensified the conflict. At this point in the story, however, Maya's extra responsibilities have been relieved as her mother is once again cooking dinner and Maya has the energy to do her homework and watch over Nurzhan. But the conflict is still unresolved: Maya has not obtained permission to go to the dance so the climax has not yet taken place. Now, as Nurzhan attempts to do for Maya what she cannot do for herself, Maya waits tensely in her room "afraid to really hope that any good thing could come from Nurzhan's plan." While the outcome of the conflict remains uncertain, Maya experiences the greatest tension over her conflict as evidenced by the thoughts that run through her head as she waits. She is trying to stop hoping, to brace herself for disappointment, to imagine being satisfied with the limits that she assumes she will have to accept.*)

IMPROVE READING FLUENCY

Targeted Passage Remind students that in everyday conversation, people often place extra emphasis on certain words in order to make a point or express emotion. Read paragraph 211 aloud. Point out that the dash before "the gymnastics team" tells the reader to pause and emphasize the words that follow. Have students read aloud other sentences with punctuation that helps a reader know what to emphasize. Remind them to be aware of times when they themselves emphasize words in everyday conversations with friends and family members.

 Go to the **Reading Studio** for additional support in developing fluency.

ANALYZE CHARACTER

Point out that this dialogue between Maya and Nurzhan gives evidence of the way he has grown since the beginning of the story. (**Answer:** *When Maya expresses concern about what her friends will think about her having a chaperone, Nurzhan says, "I thought about that problem. You will tell them you must baby-sit for me." The fact that Nurzhan thought about potential problems in advance and came up with a way to address them shows that he is becoming more grownup. The fact that he is willing to present himself as being in need of "babysitting" also reflects his increased confidence because he is not worrying about what other people will think of him as he had earlier in the story. Also, his solution again reveals his understanding of both American and Kazakh cultures.*)

 ANALYZE PLOT

Explain that during the falling action of a story the effects of the climax become clear. In this part of the plot, Maya is attending the dance that she has dreamed about. (**Answer:** *Students should note that Mama's comments reflect the fact that the events of the story have also begun to change Mama's attitudes and ideas. They show that Maya did have reason to hope that "things can change for people."*)

 NOTICE & NOTE

ANALYZE CHARACTER
Annotate: Mark the parts of the whispered conversation between Nurzhan and Maya that best show his growth as a character.

Infer: Based on these details, in what ways has Nurzhan grown?

ANALYZE PLOT
Annotate: The events following a story's climax are the falling action. Mark the most important dialogue that is spoken during the falling action described in paragraphs 230–237.

Connect: Reread the first paragraph of the story. How do Mama's words connect with Maya's earlier thoughts?

222   That night Nurzhan and I whispered in our beds after Mama had gone to sleep.

223   "Nurzhan, what will I tell my friends when you come to the dance?"

224   "Don't worry. I thought about that problem. You will tell them you must baby-sit for me."

225   "But at a dance?"

226   "I think it will work. At least it is better than to say I am your chaperone."

227   "That is true."

228   I watched the orange light of the mini-mart sign blink on and off, and I heard Nurzhan's slow breathing as he fell asleep.

229   "Thank you, Nurzhan," I whispered as I began to dream of the dance.

230   The morning of the dance, Mama came into the kitchen while Nurzhan and I were eating *kasha*. Mama still had a wrap on her ankle, but she was walking without her crutches now. She was happier, and I could tell she felt better. It was better for me, too. When Mama was happier, I didn't feel so worried about her.

231   "Maya, I have something for you." Mama came to the table and put a small package wrapped in tissue paper in front of me. "Open." She pointed at the package.

232   I looked up at her, my face full of surprise.

233   "Open."

234   Carefully, I unfolded the tissue paper and let out a gasp when I saw a small gold bracelet lying on the folds of the thin paper.

235   "You wear this to the dance." Mama patted my shoulder.

236   "Oh, Mama." I wanted to hug her like we hug on the gymnastics team, but I was too shy. We don't hug in our family.

237   "I forget sometimes when there is so much work that you are just a young girl. This bracelet my mother gave to me when

I was sixteen. Girls and boys dance younger here, Maya. So you wear this now."

238   "Thank you, Mama. I will be careful with it."

239   "I know. You're a good girl. And Nurzhan will be right there. Always by your side."

240   "Yes, Mama." Nurzhan nodded.

241   Shannon and I met in the bathroom after school, and she loaned me her peach lip-gloss. I can't remember ever being so excited about anything, and so nervous, too.

242   Nurzhan was waiting by the gym door when we got out of the bathroom. Shannon and I said hi to him, and he followed us into the gym. Nurzhan found a chair next to the door and waved to us while we joined Leslie Shattuck and her sister Tina and Faith Reeves from the gymnastics team. The gym got more and more crowded, and everywhere you looked there were flocks of boys and flocks of girls, but no boys and girls together, as if they were birds that only stayed with their own kind.

243   Then a few ninth-grade guys and girls danced together. They were very cool and everyone watched them, except some seventh-grade boys who were pushing each other around in an empty garbage can.

244   Shannon and I were laughing at those silly boys when Daniel and David came up to us. I was so happy to see Daniel, even though I was embarrassed about my face, which I knew was once again the deepest red, like borscht. But the next thing I knew, Daniel had asked me to dance, and Shannon was dancing with David!

245   Daniel held my hand and put his arm around my waist, and I put my hand on his shoulder just the way Shannon and I had practiced so many times. It was a slow dance, and Mama's bracelet gleamed on my wrist as it lay on Daniel's shoulder.

246   "My little brother's here. I had to baby-sit."

247   "Want to check on him?" Daniel asked.

248   "Sure."

249   We danced over near Nurzhan, who sat on the chair like a tiny mouse in the corner, and I introduced him to Daniel.

250   "Are you doing okay?" I asked Nurzhan.

251   "Yes. It's a little boring though."

252   "I'm sorry you have to be here."

253   "It's not that bad. The boys in the garbage can are fun to watch. I would enjoy doing that if I came to this dance."

LANGUAGE CONVENTIONS

Annotate: In paragraph 253, circle the prepositional phrase that might cause confusion about which noun is the subject of the sentence. Then underline the subject and verb in the sentence.

Evaluate: If the author had left out the prepositional phrase, would the sentence's meaning be more clear, or less so? Why?

LANGUAGE CONVENTIONS

Remind students that a prepositional phrase begins with a preposition such as *at, for, from, in, of,* or *with* and provides information about the subject or verb. Caution students about confusing a noun in the prepositional phrase for the subject when deciding whether the subject is singular or plural. (**Answer:** *The sentence would be less clear. The prepositional phrase "in the garbage can" clarifies which boys are fun to watch.*)

■ English Learner Support

Vocabulary Support   Point out the saying "flocks of boys and flocks of girls" in paragraph 242. Explain to students that author is using figurative language to compare the groups of students to groups of birds that fly together.   **SUBSTANTIAL**

TO CHALLENGE STUDENTS . . .

Analyze Character Choices   Both Maya and Nurzhan do things to deceive their parents as they try to adjust to life in the United States. For example:

- Maya purposely translates the principal's statements incorrectly.
- Nurzhan says he will act as Maya's chaperone, but he leaves the area any time she is dancing with Daniel.

ASK STUDENTS to discuss the choices each young person made to determine whether they seem justified or appropriate for the circumstances. Ask each group to suggest alternatives that might have achieved the same goals without deception.

AGAIN AND AGAIN

Remind students that authors sometimes repeat words to draw attention to something important to the development of the characters or plot. Encourage students to ask themselves the anchor question when they notice an **Again and Again** signpost: *Why might the author keep bringing this up?* (**Answer:** *Students should note that the author may wish to emphasize that Mama's realization is very meaningful to Maya and/or that Maya is heartened to realize that her parents can and do change.*)

254   Then we danced away and danced even more slowly, and Daniel moved a little closer to me. I looked over, afraid that Nurzhan was watching, but all I saw was an empty chair. And then we danced closer.

255   Daniel and I danced four more times that afternoon (two fast and two *very* slow), and each time Nurzhan's chair was empty and he seemed to have disappeared. I didn't think too much about Nurzhan during the rest of the dance, and on the bus going home, while Shannon and I talked and talked, reliving every wonderful moment, I almost forgot he was there.

256   But that night when Nurzhan and I were going to sleep and I was thinking about how that day had been the best day of my life, I thanked him for making it possible for me to go to the dance.

257   "There's just one thing I wondered about," I whispered as the mini-mart sign blinked on and off.

258   "What's that?"

259   "Where did you go when I danced with Daniel?"

260   "To the bathroom."

261   "The bathroom?"

262   "Yes."

263   "You are an excellent chaperone."

264   Nurzhan and I giggled so loud that Mama came in and told us to be quiet. "Shhh, Nurzhan, Maya. Go to sleep!" She spoke sharply to both of us.

265   After she left, Nurzhan fell asleep right away like he usually does. But I lay awake for a while and I looked over at Nurzhan and was struck by how much things had changed. I looked at the table by my bed and saw the gold bracelet shining in the blinking light of the mini-mart sign, and I imagined Mama

AGAIN AND AGAIN

Notice & Note: Mark the statement Maya recalls in paragraph 265.

Analyze: Why might the author have repeated these words?

wearing it when she was sixteen, and I treasured what she'd said as much as the bracelet: "Girls and boys dance younger here, Maya. So you wear this now."

266   And I thought of Daniel, who I think is quite a special boy with a good heart. *Kak horosho.* How wonderful. Thinking of him made me smile inside. Then I closed my eyes, hoping very much that Nurzhan would like to chaperone at the next dance.

CHECK YOUR UNDERSTANDING

Answer these questions before moving on to the **Analyze the Text** section on the following page.

1 What does paragraph 1 reveal about Maya and her conflict?

A She wants to go to the all-school dance, but she isn't sure she should attend because she can't dance.

B She wants to go to the all-school dance, but she thinks her parents are unlikely to give her permission.

C She didn't take a permission slip for the all-school dance, so now she has to figure out how to get one.

D She took a permission slip for the all-school dance, but she will have to confront the popular girl to go.

2 What do Maya's thoughts, feelings, and actions in response to her mother's injury reveal about her traits and motivations?

F She is caring, obedient, and wants to help her family.

G She cares about her brother and wants him to help her out.

H She can't cook and cleans slowly but wants to improve.

J She is self-centered and wants to win in gymnastics.

3 The conflict in the story is resolved when —

A Nurzhan promises to stop fighting Ossie at school

B Maya agrees to quit gymnastics if she can go to the dance

C Nurzhan offers to be Maya's chaperone at the dance

D Maya's father agrees to be her chaperone at the dance

CHECK YOUR UNDERSTANDING

Have students answer the questions independently.

Answers:

1. *B*

2. *F*

3. *C*

If they answer any questions incorrectly, have them reread the text to confirm their understanding. Then they may proceed to ANALYZE THE TEXT on p.180.

 ENGLISH LEARNER SUPPORT

Oral Assessment   Use the following questions to assess students' comprehension and speaking skills:

1. What do we find out about Maya and her conflict in paragraph 1? (*Maya wants to go to the dance, but she does not think her parents will let her go.*)

2. What can we tell about Maya and her motivations based on how she responds to her mother's injury? (*Maya is caring, obedient, and wants to help her family.*)

3. When is the conflict in the story resolved? (*Nurzhan offers to be Maya's chaperone at the dance.*) **SUBSTANTIAL/MODERATE**

ANALYZE THE TEXT

Possible answers:

1. **DOK 2:** *The story shows that immigrants may be affected by harsh experiences in their past. Maya has not had the same experiences Sunstar had, but she is still afraid and nervous about being called to the principal's office.*

2. **DOK 3:** *Maya's changes make the fight sound less severe ("nasty fight" vs. "little fight") and place the blame on the other boy ("teasing" vs. "teasing . . . in a violent manner"). She changes the principal's words to protect her brother from her father's reaction.*

3. **DOK 3:** *The mother feels protective of Nurzhan and blames Maya for not preventing the fight. These lines show that the mother sticks up for Nurzhan and blames Maya.*

4. **DOK 4:** *Nurzhan's motivations affect the resolution of the conflict. He wants to help his sister get what she wants because he is grateful to her for helping him avoid a harsher punishment than he might have gotten and for the sacrifices she makes to look after him and the rest of the family while their mother is injured.*

5. **DOK 4:** *Because doors are literally barriers that open up or close off access to spaces, they might figuratively represent barriers to the freedom Maya wants. Maya's parents and authority figures are the ones who operate most of the doors, suggesting that they are the ones in control of Maya's freedom. In this scene, Mama may be expressing rage at Maya's autonomous act of locking herself in the bathroom and trying to control her boundaries.*

RESEARCH

Remind students that they should make sure their sources are reliable and up-to-date. Encourage them to confirm information with multiple sources.

Connect Point out that social customs are rapidly changing in some places with the spread of global media, so what is considered realistic can change over time.

 RESPOND

ANALYZE THE TEXT

Support your responses with evidence from the text. ☰ NOTEBOOK

1. **Infer** In paragraph 18, Maya tells a story about a student from Cambodia. How does this story enhance the plot's rising action?

2. **Draw Conclusions** Reread paragraph 85. Complete this chart to show how Maya's translation changes the meaning of what the principal says. Why does she make these changes?

PRINCIPAL'S WORDS	MAYA'S TRANSLATION	EFFECT

3. **Compare** Reread the dialogue in paragraphs 109–119. What does this dialogue reveal about how the mother's relationship with Maya differs from her relationship with Nurzhan?

4. **Analyze** A character's motivations can play a role in the resolution of a story's conflict. Whose motivations affect the resolution of this story, and what are those motivations? Support your answer.

RESEARCH TIP
Online encyclopedias are great resources for information about countries and cultures. Also good are sites that are run by the countries themselves or by other credible authorities on culture who do not have a personal bias or agenda.

5. **Notice & Note** Find the reference to a door in paragraph 151, and then review the story for similar references. What ideas might doors represent or symbolize in this story?

RESEARCH

The behavior expected of Maya by her parents reflects their Kazakhstani roots. Learn about Kazakhstani culture by researching answers to these questions.

QUESTION	ANSWER
What roles do gender and age play in Kazakhstani society? Explain.	*It is patriarchal and hierarchical—that is, the father is the leader of the family and everyone shows respect for him and their elders.*
What is one example of a Kazakhstani custom?	*Answers will vary. See http://www.commisceo-global.com/country-guides/kazakhstan-guide for possibilities.*
How free are Kazakhstani young people to choose their marriage partners?	*They are free in some parts of the country. However, in many parts of the country, Kazakhstani young people are still expected to marry partners arranged by their parents.*

Connect Is the author's portrayal of the Alazova family's rules and expectations realistic? Discuss this in a small group.

 LEARNING MINDSET

Try Again Tell students that sometimes they may think they know the answer to a question, but then find out they got it wrong. Remind them that it's not only okay to make mistakes, but making mistakes is a good thing. It's how we learn. Encourage students to share their mistakes and work together to reinvestigate the text and understand the author's message.

CREATE AND DISCUSS

Write a Summary Write a summary of "My Favorite Chaperone." To do this, you will briefly retell the plot of the story in your own words.

❑ Introduce the major characters and state the conflict.

❑ Convey the major events that occur during the rising action. Maintain the author's meaning and the logical order of events.

❑ Identify the climax of the story. Then describe the resolution of the conflict and the story's final outcome.

Discuss with a Small Group Did Maya handle the situation in the principal's office appropriately? Discuss this question with a group.

❑ Reread paragraphs 74–90. Discuss Maya's translations and their outcome. Look for clues as to why she chose to handle the situation in this way.

❑ Discuss what you would have done in Maya's place and whether any of these options would have been better, considering their likely impact on Maya and Nurzhan. Support your ideas.

❑ Together, decide whether Maya's handling of events was appropriate. Be prepared to support your conclusion.

RESPOND TO THE ESSENTIAL QUESTION

 What are the places that shape who you are?

Gather Information Review your annotations and notes on "My Favorite Chaperone." Then, add relevant details to your Response Log. As you determine which details to include, think about:

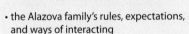

• the Alazova family's rules, expectations, and ways of interacting

• Maya's thoughts, actions, and feelings and what they suggest about her beliefs and values

• the differences Maya notices between the Lui family and hers

At the end of the unit, you can use your notes to help you write a short story.

RESPOND

 Go to **Using Textual Evidence** in the **Writing Studio** for more on writing a summary.

Go to **Participating in Collaborative Discussions** in the **Speaking and Listening Studio** for help.

ACADEMIC VOCABULARY

As you write and discuss what you learned from the story, be sure to use the Academic Vocabulary words. Check off each of the words that you use.

❑ **contribute**

❑ **immigrate**

❑ **reaction**

❑ **relocate**

❑ **shifting**

CREATE AND DISCUSS

Write a Summary Students' summaries should include the following: the major characters; a statement of the story's main conflict; the major events that occur during the rising action; and a description of the climax, how it is resolved, and what the final outcome is to the story.

For **writing support** for students at varying proficiency levels, see the **Text X-Ray** on page 152D.

Discuss with a Small Group Students' discussions should cover the following points:

• her translations minimize the severity of the fight and the principal's statements

• the descriptions of her father in the cab afterwards show that he has a severe temper

• what might have happened if Maya had not changed the principal's statements

• when, if ever, it is okay to alter the truth, and why

RESPOND TO THE ESSENTIAL QUESTION

Allow time for students to add details from "My Favorite Chaperone" to their Unit 3 Response Logs.

APPLY

CRITICAL VOCABULARY

Possible answers:

1. *other friends and family members from Kazakhstan who want to immigrate to the United States*

2. *disappearing while she is dancing with Daniel*

3. *tell him where to pick up his next passenger*

4. *two boys were fighting in the school yard*

5. *fell off the beam and sprained her ankle*

VOCABULARY STRATEGY:
Context Clues

Word	Context Clues	My Guessed Definition	Dictionary Definition
huddled	"only person we knew ... together on tiny island"	be close together	gathered tightly together
mispronouncing	"not speaking well"	saying words incorrectly	to say something incorrectly
drizzle	"rain came down"	a form of rain	light rain

 **RESPOND**

CRITICAL VOCABULARY

WORD BANK
sponsor
stun
dispatcher
scuffle
whimper

 Go to the **Vocabulary Studio** for more on context clues.

Practice and Apply To demonstrate that you understand the Critical Vocabulary words, complete each sentence in a way that makes sense.

1. When Maya becomes a U.S. citizen, she may want to **sponsor** . . .

2. When Nurzhan is Maya's chaperone, he **stuns** her by . . .

3. The cab driver needed to have his **dispatcher** . . .

4. The sounds of a **scuffle** alerted me to the fact that . . .

5. At a gymnastics meet, Maya might **whimper** if she . . .

VOCABULARY STRATEGY: Context Clues

The **context** of a word is made up of the punctuation marks, words, sentences, and paragraphs that surround the word. When you encounter an unfamiliar or ambiguous word or one with multiple meanings, its context may provide you with clues that can help you understand its meaning. Look at the following example:

> Mr. Walsh, the vice-principal, came into our class. He whispered something to Ms. Coe and she nodded. And then I was stunned because she nodded and pointed to me!

The exclamation point suggests that Maya did not expect that Mr. Walsh had come to get her. Feeling stunned probably means feeling surprised or shocked. If you knew the other meaning of *stunned*, "dazed by a blow or a loud noise," this context would help you know that it doesn't apply here.

Practice and Apply Review "My Favorite Chaperone" to find the following words. Then complete this chart.

WORD	CONTEXT CLUES	MY GUESSED DEFINITION	DICTIONARY DEFINITION
huddled (paragraph 7)			
mispronouncing (paragraph 50)			
drizzle (paragraph 71)			

182 Unit 3

ENGLISH LEARNER SUPPORT

Vocabulary Strategy Explain that when faced with an unfamiliar word, a reader should look at the context of the word to try to figure out the meaning. Tell students to look for comparisons and contrasts in the text around a word to understand it better. Encourage them to try substituting the unfamiliar word with possible synonyms to verify the meaning.
ALL LEVELS

LANGUAGE CONVENTIONS:
Subject-Verb Agreement

The subject and verb in a sentence or clause must agree in number. **Agreement** means that if the subject is singular, the verb must also be singular; if the subject is plural, the verb must also be plural. In this sentence from "My Favorite Chaperone," both the subject and the verb are singular.

Nurzhan <u>has been</u> in a fight with another boy.

Notice how the verb changes when the subject is plural:

Nurzhan and Ossie <u>have been</u> in a fight.

Sometimes a **prepositional phrase**—which consists of a preposition, its object, and any modifiers of the object—comes between the subject and the verb. In that case, you must ignore the phrase and identify the sentence's true subject. The subject is never found within a prepositional phrase. In the example below, note how the prepositional phrase *in Maya's class* ends with a singular noun. However, the subject of the sentence is *kids*, which requires the plural noun *were*.

The <u>kids</u> in Maya's class <u>were</u> nice.

The agreement rule is true for all sentence types. Consider the following **complex sentence**, which consists of a main clause and a subordinate clause. The prepositional phrase *on the gymnastics team* ends with a singular noun, but the subject of the clause is *girls*, which requires the plural noun *were*.

While she cleaned houses, the other <u>girls</u> on the gymnastics team <u>were</u> practicing.

Practice and Apply   Choose the verb form that agrees with the subject in each sentence or clause.

1. A stack of permission slips (was, were) lying on the teacher's desk.

2. Students on the gymnastics team (practices, practice) after school.

3. The boys in the fight (shoves, shove) each other hard, while a teacher and a custodian in the yard (runs, run) over to stop them.

4. Boys and girls at the Spring Fling (dances, dance) to the music.

RESPOND

> **!** Go to **Agreement** in the **Grammar Studio** for more on subject-verb agreement.

My Favorite Chaperone   183

APPLY

LANGUAGE CONVENTIONS
Subject-Verb Agreement

Review the information about subject-verb agreement and prepositional phrases with students. Explain that the phrase "agree in number" refers to whether the subject and verb are both singular (one) or both plural (more than one).

Tell students to decide whether the subject of a sentence is singular or plural in order to choose the correct verb form. Encourage them to look for prepositional phrases that might cause confusion and to cover or ignore them to clarify what is the subject of the sentence. Remind students that prepositional phrases begin with a preposition, such as *in, at, for, on,* and *with.*

Display the following examples and work with students to determine the correct answer.

- *Maya [compete, competes] on the gymnastics team. (competes)*

- *She [like, likes] a boy named Daniel. (likes)*

- *Maya and Shannon [is, are] best friends. (are)*

Practice and Apply   Have partners share and discuss how they determined the correct verb form for each sentence.

1. *was*

2. *practice*

3. *shove; run*

4. *dance*

 ENGLISH LEARNER SUPPORT

Review Conventions   Vietnamese- and Arabic-speaking students may struggle with subject-verb agreement. In Vietnamese speakers omit the /s/ in present tense, third-person agreement. In the Arabic language, the verb precedes the subject.

Review with students the rules of **subject-verb agreement**. Then, provide the following examples for students to correct.

- Roger [belong, belongs] to the chess club. (*belongs*)
- She [make, makes] birdhouses from plastic bottles. (*makes*)
- Winston and Yolanda [is, are] the leaders. (*are*)

Have students review the answers with a partner. Then ask students to use the examples as models to write sentences with subject-verb agreement. Have them trade with a partner to verify and discuss their sentences.
SUBSTANTIAL/MODERATE

My Favorite Chaperone   **183**

MENTOR TEXT

THE BOOK OF UNKNOWN AMERICANS

Novel by Cristina Henríquez

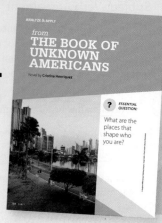

This article serves as a mentor text, a model for students to follow when they come to the Unit Writing Task: Write a Short Story.

GENRE ELEMENTS
NOVEL

Remind students that the purpose of **realistic fiction** is to entertain readers with a story that comes from the writer's imagination, but that also seems as though it could happen in real life. Explain that a **novel** is a longer work of fiction than a short story. Novels allow writers to develop characters and conflict more thoroughly than in a short story. A novel also may contain more than one plot or contain subplots involving minor characters. In this lesson, students will read and analyze an excerpt from a realistic fiction novel that is more self-contained, or able to stand on its own, to analyze narrative structure and the development of themes.

LEARNING OBJECTIVES

- Analyze and explain the narrative structure of a literary text.
- Analyze and use evidence to explain theme development.
- Conduct and discuss research about the history of Panama.
- Write a literary response to a realistic fiction text using craft.
- Write and perform a literary text to demonstrate understanding.
- Use a dictionary to identify part of speech and usage/meaning.
- Use pronouns in prepositional phrases.
- **Language** Describe narrative structure using the key term *pacing*.

TEXT COMPLEXITY

Quantitative Measures	The Book of Unknown Americans	Lexile: 870L
Qualitative Measures	**Ideas Presented** Mostly direct and explicit, with some implied meaning that requires making inferences.	
	Structure Used Primarily chronological and conventional, with a single first-person narrator.	
	Language Used Contemporary language with most Spanish words supported; many complex sentences.	
	Knowledge Required Easily envisioned situations; some historical references rely on outside knowledge.	

Online Ed

RESOURCES

- Unit 3 Response Log
- Selection Audio
- Reading Studio: Notice & Note
- Level Up Tutorial: Reading for Details
- Level Up Tutorial: Make Inferences about Characters
- Level Up Tutorial: Theme
- Writing Studio: Writing Narratives
- Speaking and Listening Studio: Participating in Collaborative Discussions
- Vocabulary Studio: Using a Dictionary
- Grammar Studio: Module 2: Lesson 3: Pronouns
- "The Book of Unknown Americans" Selection Test

SUMMARIES

English

Mayor Toro was a baby when his parents, Rafael and Celia, left Panama for the United States, and he feels more American than Panamanian. Mayor reflects on why his family became U.S. citizens and has never visited Panama, despite two attempts. The family plans their first trip back for Rafael's school reunion, but Rafael cancels it after learning he would be unwelcome there. The next year, they plan another trip but 9/11 prevents them from going. That winter, Rafael tries to ease Celia's homesickness by taking the family to a beach.

Spanish

Mayor Toro era un bebé cuando sus padres, Rafael y Celia, dejaron Panamá para ir a los Estados Unidos y él se siente más americano que panameño. Mayor refleja por qué en su familia se hicieron ciudadanos americanos y nunca han visitado Panamá, a pesar de dos intentos. La familia planea su primer viaje de vuelta para la reunión escolar de Rafael, pero Rafael lo cancela al enterarse de que no sería bienvenido ahí. El año siguiente, planean otro viaje, pero el 11 de Septiembre les impide ir. Ese invierno, Rafael trata de aliviar la añoranza de Celia llevando a la familia a la playa.

 ## SMALL-GROUP OPTIONS

Have students work in small groups to read and discuss the selection.

Numbered Heads Together

- After students have read the selection, have them form small, equal-sized groups and number off within their group.
- Ask groups to explain this sentence in paragraph 27: *And I think we all sensed . . . just how far we were from where we had come, in ways both good and bad.*
- Have students discuss their ideas, identify text evidence to support their views, and collaboratively form a group explanation of what the sentence means.
- For each group, pick a number and have that student share the group's interpretation with the class.

Solving a Problem

- Ask students to consider this question as they read: *What makes a person feel like an "Unknown American"?*
- Divide students into 4 or 8 groups and assign each a different viewpoint: that of Mayor, Celia (his mother), Rafael (his father), or author Cristina Henríquez.
- Have students collaboratively decide how their assigned character or person would answer the question, based on the text, and form a group response.
- Have groups take turns presenting their responses and evidence and answering any questions from the class.

Text X-Ray: English Learner Support
for "The Book of Unknown Americans"

INTRODUCE THE SELECTION
DISCUSS CULTURAL IDENTITY

In this lesson, students will need to understand the concept of cultural identity. Tell students that your *identity* is your sense of yourself, or who you are as a person. Then call attention to this phrase in paragraph 3: *I felt more American than anything.* Explain that the narrator is unsure about his *cultural identity*: his sense or feeling that he is a member of a group with a particular culture. If asked, *What are you?*, he could answer in several ways:

- I'm an American.
- I'm a Panamanian.
- I'm a Panamanian American.

Share other examples to distinguish cultural identity from *nationality*, or the country or nation of which you are a citizen. Point out that the title suggests the narrator is an "unknown" American. Ask students to share ways that people may identify or connect with a culture or place. Provide sentence frames:

- _____ feels like a/an _____ because _____.
- _____ identifies [her/him]self as _____ because _____.

CULTURAL REFERENCES

These words and phrases may be unfamiliar to students:

- *copped to* (paragraph 4): admitted to something
- *broke out* (paragraph 7): suddenly and purposefully began
- *roll out the red carpet* (paragraph 10): make a special effort to welcome and make someone feel important
- *holier-than-thou* (paragraph 21): having the attitude of being a better person than others
- *up-and-coming* (paragraph 22): gaining positive attention and likely to succeed

LISTENING

Understand Implicit Ideas

Explain that in paragraph 9 the narrator says "as I don't know what" because he does not know how to describe how excited Celia is. Instead, he describes what Celia does and says. Readers must use what they already know to decide what these details suggest about her thoughts and feelings.

Have students listen as you read aloud paragraph 9 with expression. Use the following supports with students at varying proficiency levels:

- Tell students that you will ask questions about what you just read aloud, and explain that they may respond by using their hands to indicate amounts. Then ask: *How much does Celia want to go to Panama? (very much) How much does she care about what Rafael says? (not much) How much does Celia think of Panama as her home? (very much)* **SUBSTANTIAL**

- Before reading, tell students to note Celia's actions and words. Then ask inference questions about specific details, such as, *Why does Celia buy a new dress? (to look good in Panama)* Have students use this frame: *I know that _____, so I think that Celia _____.* **MODERATE**

- Have students retell what Celia does and says, and write the details on the board. Then ask what the details suggest about Celia's thoughts and feelings about the trip. **LIGHT**

SPEAKING

Discuss Scenes

For the Act Out a Scene activity on p.197, have students discuss whether scenes would be good to perform. Tell them a Spanish cognate for *scene* is *escena*. Review that a scene is a part of a story in which actions and/or conversations happen in one place and time.

Display paragraph 7 and tell students it is an example of a short scene. Have students read it aloud with you. Then use the following supports with students at varying proficiency levels:

- Say, *A good scene to perform has enough characters for all the actors.* Display sentence frames such as, *There are [wol] characters in this scene. We need ____ actors to play ____. This scene [is/is not] good to perform.* Have small groups use the frames to discuss the scene. **SUBSTANTIAL**
- Have small groups discuss whether to perform the scene. Tell them to discuss the numbers of characters and actors and the scene's importance or meaning to the story. Offer sentence stems: *This scene has/does not have ____. This scene [is/is not] important, because ____.* **MODERATE**
- Have volunteers share what a scene needs for their group to perform it. Add that it should help develop a theme, or message. Have groups discuss whether this scene is a good one. **LIGHT**

READING

Describe Pacing

Tell students *pacing* is the speed with which a story moves forward. Display *Summarizing events = fast pacing* and *Describing events with details = slow pacing.* Model each by walking across the room at different speeds. Explain that pacing shows how important the events are.

Work with students to read paragraphs 10–20. Use the following supports with students at varying proficiency levels:

- After reading, call attention to the displayed information about pacing. Ask: *Does this part of the story describe events with details or summarize them?* (describe) *Does it use fast pacing or slow pacing?* (slow pacing) Have students walk across the room to show the pacing. Then ask: *Is the family going to Panama?* (no) *How important is this?* (very) **SUBSTANTIAL**
- Ask small groups to summarize what happens and estimate how much time the events take. Then have them describe the pacing and the section's importance to the story. Provide sentence frames such as, *The author uses ____ pacing to describe ____, because ____.* **MODERATE**
- Pair students and ask them to describe the pacing of the section and its importance to the plot. Ask: *Why does the author share what everyone says and does for this event?* **LIGHT**

WRITING

Write a Paragraph

Explain that to write from a character's point of view, students should write as though that character is the narrator. They should use a first-person point of view by using mainly the pronouns *I, me,* and *my.* They also should write things that the character would say, based on details in the text.

Have the following supports with students at varying proficiency levels:

- Read aloud the last six sentences in paragraph 19. Then display this example: *My true home will always be Panama, because I miss being there. I miss being able to see my sister Gloria. I miss the gallo pinto at El Trapiche. I even miss the way the air smells there.* Ask: *Whose point of view of this?* (Celia's) Have students copy the sentences. Then help them find the details in paragraphs 19 and 21 that support each sentence, by having them look for key words (*miss, sister, etc.*) **SUBSTANTIAL**
- Have students reread the last sentence in paragraph 1. Ask: *Why might Enrique feel like Panama is his home?* (He has many memories of it.) Have student pairs complete this sentence frame to help them understand the writing task: *Panama may be my home, because I ____.* **MODERATE**
- Ask partners to take turns role playing a character and an interviewer, to form ideas about what place the character feels is home and why. Have them write down what they said. **LIGHT**

Connect to the
ESSENTIAL QUESTION

The narrator in this excerpt from *The Book of Unknown Americans* attributes his confusion over his cultural identity to having been a baby when his family immigrated to the United States from Panama. The difference between where he and his parents have spent most of their lives has given them a different affinity with both their native country and their current home. However, the author suggests that the larger events of 9/11 that the family experiences together in their current home help bridge the gap between their cultural identities and mixed feelings about being Panamanian Americans, at least momentarily.

MENTOR TEXT

At the end of the unit, students will be asked to write a short story. *The Book of Unknown Americans* provides a model for how a writer can use cause-and-effect relationships to structure a narrative, and explicit and implicit details to develop its characters, plot, and theme.

from
THE BOOK OF UNKNOWN AMERICANS

Novel by **Cristina Henríquez**

ESSENTIAL QUESTION:

What are the places that shape who you are?

184   Unit 3

QUICK START

If you moved to another state or country, what would you remember most about where you live now? How would you want to spend your time if you returned for a brief visit? Write down your thoughts.

ANALYZE NARRATIVE STRUCTURE

The **structure** of a work of literature is the way in which it is put together. The excerpt from *The Book of Unknown Americans* spans a stretch of time from the narrator's early childhood until the present, revealing how the characters change over time. Many of these changes occur gradually: One event brings about, or causes, another, and that event in turn causes yet another. Thus, both the short-term and long-term consequences of small events become apparent. As you read the novel excerpt, note these cause-effect relationships between events.

GENRE ELEMENTS: NOVEL

- is a long work of fiction
- tells a story from the writer's imagination
- can develop characters and conflict more thoroughly than a short story
- often develops more than one plot and/or contains subplots

Cause ⟶	Effect
Panama was ravaged by war.	The narrator's family moved to the United States.
Cause ⟶	Effect
Cause ⟶	Effect

ANALYZE THEME

A **theme** is a message about life or human nature that's shared by a writer. Here are some ways to find and analyze themes:

- Look for **explicit** textual statements of the characters' ideas about life or people. Pay particular attention to statements characters make about lessons they have learned over the course of events.

- Look for details that **implicitly** convey, or imply, what a character believes about life or human nature. For instance, how a character reacts to a **conflict,** or problem, and the results of his or her behavior may hold a message the author wants to convey.

One important theme of *The Book of Unknown Americans* is related to the challenges immigrants face in adapting to life in a new culture. As you read the novel excerpt, consider how events in the story affect the characters' sense of their cultural identity. Also consider how details about places in Panama and other settings influence the narrator's values and beliefs about himself.

The Book of Unknown Americans   185

QUICK START

If students struggle with the Quick Start questions, ask them to reflect on or imagine spending an extended period of time away from home—long enough for them to feel homesick or anxious to return. Invite students to share examples of the things they would miss most and look forward to doing again once their trip was over.

ANALYZE NARRATIVE STRUCTURE

Tell students that narrative structure includes all the elements of a story, including the plot. Review that plot is the sequence of events, or what happens. Explain that structure is the overall design: how the writer presents the events, characters, setting, and so on, to make the story unfold in an engaging, meaningful way. Two key aspects of structure are how the writer:

- treats time within the story
- uses cause and effect to link events

Have students read the details in the chart and locate each in the text. Point out that the author introduces the detail about the family moving (paragraph 1) before the detail about the war (paragraph 4) to make readers wonder *why* the family moved. Looking for the cause or reason makes readers more interested in the plot's exposition, or the background information that they need to understand the story. Have students identify two more cause-and-effect relationships in the text to complete the table. If necessary, suggest they start by locating key details and asking themselves *why, how,* or *so what.*

ANALYZE THEME

Explain that novels often have more than one theme, but paying attention to and analyzing details about the main character(s) usually helps readers identify the main theme. Point out that themes are developed throughout a novel, so students must synthesize any explicit or implicit information and draw their own conclusions about what this evidence shows to determine themes.

CRITICAL VOCABULARY

Suggest that students read all the sentences and then begin by completing those with just one word missing.

Answers:

1. *confer, melodrama*

2. *convene, ravage*

3. *assure*

4. *froth*

5. *reminisce*

■ English Learner Support

Use Cognates Tell students that a Spanish cognate for the Critical Vocabulary word *confer* is *conferir*.
ALL LEVELS

LANGUAGE CONVENTIONS

Remind students that subject pronouns include *I, she,* and *they,* and object pronouns include *me, her,* and *them*. Ask students to identify one example of each type of pronoun in paragraph 1 and the word it replaces. (**Possible answer:** *The subject pronoun* I *replaces* Mayor. *The object pronoun* us *replaces* Enrique and me.)

✏ ANNOTATION MODEL

Remind students that in addition to underlining and describing causes and effects, they also should mark explicit statements and clues that appear related to a theme. Suggest they highlight or circle this text evidence, and explain that they may follow these suggestions or use their own system for marking up the selection in their write-in text. They may want to color-code their annotations by using highlighters. Their notes in the margin also may include questions about ideas that are unclear or topics they want to learn more about.

 GET READY

CRITICAL VOCABULARY

reminisce	ravage	froth	convene
assure	melodrama	confer	

To see how many Critical Vocabulary words you already know, use them to complete the sentences.

1. When we met to ___confer___, the _melodrama_ created by people who personally disliked each other interfered with our ability to reach an agreement about the issue.

2. Officials planned to ___convene___ at City Hall to discuss responses for the storm that is expected to ___ravage___ the area.

3. I ___assure___ you that our region is not in the path of the storm.

4. He was in a ___froth___ over the long lines at the store.

5. The two old friends would often ___reminisce___ about their childhood.

LANGUAGE CONVENTIONS

Pronouns A **pronoun** is a word used in place of a noun or another pronoun. In this example, the pronoun *he* refers back to *my dad*:

Besides, my dad never wanted to take time off from his job. He probably could've asked for a few days of vacation time. . . .

As you read the excerpt from *The Book of Unknown Americans,* pay attention to the author's use of pronouns and note how the pronouns differ when they serve as subjects or as objects.

ANNOTATION MODEL   **NOTICE & NOTE**

As you read, note how the characters respond to events. Also mark up evidence that supports your own ideas. In the model, you can see one reader's notes about *The Book of Unknown Americans.*

> 1 I was less than a year old when my parents brought my brother and me to the United States. Enrique was four. He used to tell me things about Panamá that I couldn't possibly have remembered—like about the scorpions in our backyard and the cement utility sink where my mom used to give us baths. He reminisced about walking down the street with my mom to the Super 99, the dust blowing up everywhere, the heat pounding down, and about looking for crabs between the rocks along the bay.

cause: The narrator was brought to the U.S. as a baby.

effect: He does not remember anything about Panama.

BACKGROUND

The *Book of Unknown Americans is told from the points of view of different immigrants who all reside in an apartment building in Delaware. Author* **Cristina Henríquez** *(b. 1977) grew up in Delaware and currently resides in Illinois. Her father emigrated from Panama in 1971, and she spent many childhood summer vacations visiting family there. This excerpt is narrated by Mayor, a boy who came to the United States with his family after the United States invaded Panama in 1989 in order to remove that country's military leader, Manuel Noriega, from power.*

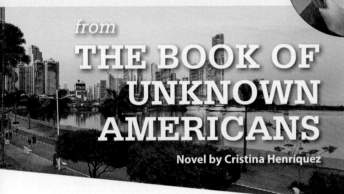

from
THE BOOK OF UNKNOWN AMERICANS

Novel by Cristina Henriquez

SETTING A PURPOSE

As you read, pay attention to details that show how the characters feel about their current home and the home they left.

1   I was less than a year old when my parents brought my brother and me to the United States. Enrique was four. He used to tell me things about Panamá that I couldn't possibly have remembered—like about the scorpions in our backyard and the cement utility sink where my mom used to give us baths. He **reminisced** about walking down the street with my mom to the Super 99, the dust blowing up everywhere, the heat pounding down, and about looking for crabs between the rocks along the bay.

2   "It's in you," my dad **assured** me once. "You were born in Panamá. It's in your bones."

3   I spent a lot of time trying to find it in me, but usually I couldn't. I felt more American than anything, but even that was up for debate according to the kids at school who'd taunted me over the years, asking me if I was related to

Notice & Note

Use the side margins to notice and note signposts in the text.

reminisce
(rĕm´ə-nĭs´) *v.* When you *reminisce,* you think or talk about past experiences.

assure
(ə-shŏŏr´) *v.* To *assure* is to state something positively, so as to remove doubt about it.

BACKGROUND

After students read the Background note, review that Panama is the southernmost country in Central America. It lies on an isthmus, or thin land bridge, between Costa Rica and Colombia, and includes more than 1,600 small islands in the Caribbean Sea and Pacific Ocean. Show students a map of Panama and point out that every place in this tropical country is close to a coast, so there are many beaches and harbors.

Tell students that most Panamanians live in the narrowest, middle section of the country, where Panama City is located and where the United States focused its invasion in 1989. Explain that although "Operation Just Cause" lasted less than a month, hundreds of Panamanian soldiers and civilians died in the fighting, and hundreds more were wounded. Many homes and other buildings around Noriega's military headquarters were destroyed or looted, and the Panamanian government estimated that about 10,000 people were made homeless by the invasion.

SETTING A PURPOSE

Direct students to use the Setting a Purpose prompt to focus their reading.

CRITICAL VOCABULARY

reminisce: Enrique enjoyed thinking about and telling the narrator his memory of walking down the street in Panama.

ASK STUDENTS why Enrique is able to reminisce about being in Panama. *(He lived there until he was four years old, so he can remember some things about it.)*

assure: The narrator's father told him "It's in you," so that he would not worry or be concerned about something.

ASK STUDENTS to infer what the narrator probably had to be assured of, based on his father's next two sentences. *(The narrator probably told his dad that he didn't feel Panamanian.)*

TEACH

✏️ ANALYZE NARRATIVE STRUCTURE

Tell students that part of the **structure** of a story is how the writer provides information about characters' past lives, to help explain their present ones. Have students reread the first sentence in paragraph 4 and ask: *Where is the present story set?* (*in the United States*) *What is the setting for the parents' story about their past?* (*Panama after the invasion*) Tell students to mark words that show time passing in the United States, and consider how the past catches up to the present. (**Answer:** *They did not want to leave Panama and initially thought they would return once the country had recovered. As time passed and they set down roots in the United States, they realized that returning was not worth having to start their lives over again.*)

▶ AGAIN AND AGAIN

Remind students that repeated words can be a signpost for an important idea or **theme**. Point out that the title of the novel is *The Book of Unknown Americans,* and ask students to identify the **explicit** statement in paragraph 5 that refers to the title. ("We became Americans.") Then have them mark the details of this process. Explain that comparing this description to the ideas in paragraph 3 will help students identify an **implicit** idea related to the theme of cultural identity. (**Answer:** *Paragraph 5 shows that one way to be an American is to be officially or legally recognized as a citizen by the government. In paragraph 3, the narrator's confusion over whether he is American or Panamanian is not about nationality or legal status. For him, being American is about feeling like one and being accepted as one by the people in your personal life.*)

CRITICAL VOCABULARY

ravage: Many Panamanian lives and buildings were damaged, or *ravaged*, as a result of the U.S. invasion.

ASK STUDENTS how describing the country as ravaged relates to this statement: "Our hearts kept breaking each time we walked out the door." (*Whenever the narrator's parents went outside, they would see the destroyed buildings and the unhappiness of people who had lost their homes or loved ones, and become upset by the situation.*)

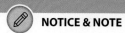

Noriega, telling me to go back through the canal. The truth was that I didn't know which I was. I wasn't allowed to claim the thing I felt and I didn't feel the thing I was supposed to claim.

4 The first time I heard my parents tell the story about leaving Panamá, my mom said, "Our hearts kept breaking each time we walked out the door." They tried to give it time. They assumed conditions would improve. But the country was so **ravaged** that their hearts never stopped breaking. Eventually they sold almost everything they owned and used the money to buy plane tickets to somewhere else, somewhere better, which to them had always meant the United States. A while after I was old enough to understand this story, I pointed out how backwards it was to have fled to the nation that had driven them out of theirs, but they never copped to the irony of it. They needed to believe they'd done the right thing and that it made sense. They were torn between wanting to look back and wanting to exist absolutely in the new life they'd created. At one point, they had planned to return. They'd thought that with enough time, Panamá would be rebuilt and that their hearts, I guess, would heal. But while they waited for that day, they started making friends. My dad got a job as a busboy and then, later on, as a dishwasher. Years passed. Enrique was in school, and I started, too. My dad was promoted to line cook. More years slid by. And before they knew it, we had a life here. They had left their lives once before. They didn't want to do it again.

5 So they applied for U.S. citizenship, sitting up at night reading the Constitution, a dictionary by their side, and studying for the exam. They contacted someone at the Panamanian consulate[1] in Philadelphia who helped them navigate the paperwork. Then they woke up one morning, got dressed in their best clothes, caught a bus to the courthouse, and, while my mom held me in her arms and my dad rested his hand on Enrique's shoulder, took an oath along with a group of other men and women who had made living in the United States a dream. We became Americans.

6 We never went back to Panamá, not even for a visit. It would have taken us forever to save enough money for plane tickets. Besides, my dad never wanted to take time off from his

---

[1] **consulate** (kŏn´sə-lĭt): a representative office of a foreign government located within another nation's borders.

ravage
(răv´ĭj) *v.* To *ravage* is to cause serious damage or destruction.

ANALYZE NARRATIVE STRUCTURE
Annotate: Mark words and phrases in paragraph 4 that show the passage of time.

Interpret: How do the narrator's parents' attitudes about their homeland change as time passes?

AGAIN AND AGAIN
Notice & Note: Mark details in paragraph 5 that tell how the family "became Americans."

Analyze: How does the description of the family becoming Americans in paragraph 5 relate to the ideas the narrator expresses about feeling American in paragraph 3?

APPLYING ACADEMIC VOCABULARY

❏ **contribute**   ☑ **immigrate**   ❏ **reaction**   ☑ **relocate**   ❏ **shifting**

Write and Discuss Have students turn to a partner to discuss the following questions. Guide students to include the Academic Vocabulary words *immigrate* and *relocate* in their responses. Ask volunteers to share their responses with the class.

- Why did the parents think the United States was a good country to **immigrate** to?
- Why would the family need to create a new life if they **relocated** to Panama?

job. He probably could've asked for a few days of vacation time, but even after years of being there, making omelets and flipping pancakes, he knew—we all knew—that he was on the low end of the food chain. He could be replaced in a heartbeat. He didn't want to risk it.

7   Because of that, we'd missed my tía Gloria's wedding, which she'd had on a hillside in Boquete. She told my mom that she'd convinced her new husband, Esteban, to dance and that therefore the whole event was a success. We had my aunt on speakerphone and my mom had said, "Take it from me, hermanita,[2] they dance at the wedding and then they never do it again." My dad had said, "That's what you think?" and clutched my mom by the wrist, sending her into a small spin in the middle of the kitchen. She squealed with delight while he swayed with her for a few beats and then he broke out into some goofy merengue[3] moves, kicking his leg up at the end and shouting "¡Olé!" My aunt started yelling through the phone, "Are you still there? Celia! Rafael!" And my parents laughed

---

[2] **hermanita** (ûr-mə-nē´tə): the Spanish word for "little sister."

[3] **merengue** (mə-rĕng´gā): a dance of Dominican and Haitian folk origin, characterized by a sliding step.

TO CHALLENGE STUDENTS . . .

Analyze Language Point out that many immigrants to the United States are not fluent in English. Ask students whether it is clear that Celia and Rafael are speaking English, or possible that the narrator is translating their words. Ask: *How do you know?* Have students locate text evidence and research other sources to explain and support their answer. (*Students should discover that the test for naturalized U.S. citizenship includes a test in reading, writing, and speaking in English.*) Then ask students how language might relate to the characters' cultural identities, given what they know.

ENGLISH LEARNER SUPPORT

Demonstrate Comprehension Call attention to the first sentence in paragraph 7 and read aloud the phrase, "Because of that, we'd missed my tía Gloria's wedding." Point out that *because* signals a cause-and-effect relationship, as do words and phrases such as *since, as a result, if . . . then,* and *the reason that.*

ASK STUDENTS to explain the cause-and-effect relationship given in the sentence. Use the following supports with students at varying proficiency levels:

- Display a cause-and-effect organizer and rewrite the phrase as, "*We'd missed my tia Gloria's wedding because of that.*" Circle *because* and ask students if missing the wedding is a cause or an effect of something. *(an effect)* Write the phrase and "that" in the organizer. Then ask students the reason, or cause, for the family missing the wedding. *(the father's job, no vacation time, no money)*. If necessary, have students point to words in paragraph 6 that provide the answer, and write the cause below "that." **SUBSTANTIAL**

- Have students work with a partner to rewrite the sentence by replacing *that* with the cause, or reason, the family misses the wedding. If necessary, work with students to reread paragraph 6 and explain any unfamiliar words. **MODERATE**

- Have students explain the meaning of the sentence, and then ask them to identify the longer term or larger effect of the narrator's father's job. (*The family has never visited Panama since they left.*) **LIGHT**

ANALYZE THEME

Remind students that writers develop **themes** using **explicit** or direct statements and/or **implicit** ideas that readers can infer. A main character's feelings about something important often suggest an idea related to the theme.

Review that details such as characters' thoughts, actions, words, and tone are clues to how they are feeling. Tell students to use the details they mark in paragraph 9 to help explain what Celia's feelings suggest about the trip and Panama. (**Answer:** *Celia's excited preparations show that she strongly desires to return to Panama. Her giddy calls show that she is eager to spend time with her sister, so she probably feels as if she is finally going "home." Planning her outfits and insisting that she will check her own bag also reveal that Celia is determined to look her best in Panama. This suggests she cares a great deal about what people there will think of her, possibly because she thinks of herself as Panamanian, too, and wants to fit in with them.*)

For **listening support** for students at varying proficiency levels, see the **Text X-Ray** on page 184C.

LANGUAGE CONVENTIONS

Tell students that the prefix *ante-* means *prior* or *before*, and that another meaning of **antecedent** is a thing that came before and influenced something else. Point out that to find the antecedent for each use of *he* in paragraph 10, they can check the previous words or sentences. (*See answers on pages 190–191.*)

ANALYZE THEME

Annotate: Mark places in paragraph 9 that show Celia's feelings about the trip to Panama.

Infer: What do the narrator's descriptive details suggest about Celia?

LANGUAGE CONVENTIONS

The word or phrase to which a pronoun refers is called its **antecedent**. Circle the uses of the pronoun *he* in paragraph 10 and underline its antecedent in each case.

until my mom dabbed the corners of her eyes with the back of her hand. I'd never seen them so happy with each other, even though it was just for those few seconds.

8 We almost went back for my dad's high school reunion, which my dad somehow got into his head that he didn't want to miss. The reunion was on a Friday, so maybe, he told us, he could fix his work schedule so that he was off on Friday. We could fly there, go to the reunion, and then fly back Saturday night. He was usually off on Sundays, but if he took off Friday instead, he'd have to be back and work Sunday to make up for it. So one night would be the longest we could stay, but one night would be enough. He had decided. And it looked like we were going to try.

9 My mom was as excited about the trip as I don't know what. She went to Sears to buy a new dress and had giddy phone conversations with my aunt about seeing each other again and what they would be able to pack into our eighteen hours on the ground. She started laying out her clothes weeks in advance even though my dad kept telling her she only needed two outfits—one to go and one to come home. "And why do you have ten pairs of shoes here?" he asked, pointing to the sandals and leather high heels my mom had lined up along the baseboard in the bedroom. "Ten!" my mom scoffed. "I don't even own ten pairs of shoes." My father counted them. "Fine. Seven. That's still six too many." He told her that he intended to take only a duffel bag for our things because that would make it easier to get through customs. My mom said, "I'll check my own bag, then." My dad kicked the row of shoes my mom had lined up and sent them flying into the wall. He walked right up to my mom and held his index finger in front of her face. "One bag, Celia. One! For all four of us. Don't talk to me about it again."

10 A few weeks before the reunion, my dad called the number on the invitation to RSVP. The guy who answered had been the class president. He and my dad joked around for a minute and then my dad told the guy we were coming. According to what my dad told us later, the guy said, "We'll roll out the red carpet, then." When my dad asked him what he meant by that, the guy said that my dad would have to forgive him if the party wasn't up to my dad's standards. "We didn't

---

ENGLISH LEARNER SUPPORT

Use Learning Strategies Remind students that they can use organizers to help them understand text details. Have students look at paragraph 8. Clarify that *off* is used to mean "away from work" and that *take off* is an informal way to say *take time off*, or *spend time away from work*. Then give student pairs a blank calendar for one week and have them label it with Rafael's plan for the trip to Panama. Ask students to note both his work schedule and travel plans on the calendar. Then have them explain how important the reunion is to Rafael, based on this information. **MODERATE**

know the gringo[4] royalty was coming. We'll have to get the place repainted before you arrive." When my dad asked again what the guy was talking about, the guy said (he) hoped my dad didn't expect them all to kiss his feet now and reminded my dad how humble Panamá was. It didn't take long for my dad to slam the phone down. (He) stormed over to my mom, who was washing dishes, and said, "We're not going. If that's what they think, then we're not going."

11 My mom said, "What?"

12 "They think we're Americans now. And maybe we are! Maybe we don't belong there anymore after all." My dad went out on the balcony, which he did whenever he was really upset.

13 My mom stood in the kitchen, a soapy pot in her hand, and looked at me, baffled. "What just happened?" she asked.

14 When I told her everything I'd been able to gather, she walked out to the balcony and closed the door behind her. At the commotion, Enrique came out of his room.

15 "We're not going anymore," I told him.

16 "Huh?"

17 "On the trip."

18 "Are you serious?" Enrique asked.

19 My brother and I huddled together, listening through the front door. I heard my mom say, "Please, Rafa. He doesn't know anything about us. We can still go. You'll see. Once we get there . . . All your friends . . . And everyone will love you." I imagined her reaching out to touch his shoulder, the way she did sometimes when she was asking for something. "Don't you miss it?" she asked. "Can't you imagine landing there, being there again? You know how it smells? The air there. And seeing everyone again. Please, Rafa."

20 But my dad wasn't swayed.

21 The following year, we talked about going back, too. My dad's anger over being cast as a holier-than-thou gringo had finally simmered down, and my mom, who couldn't bring herself to return the new dress she'd bought and who hadn't gotten over the disappointment of not being able to see her sister after all, had been dropping hints ever since that she would still like to go even if the trip was only for one night again. She'd become a genius at turning any and every

ANALYZE NARRATIVE STRUCTURE

Annotate: Mark details in paragraph 21 that show the Toros still want to visit Panamá.

Draw Conclusions: How do these details advance the story's plot?

---

[4] **gringo** (grĭng´gō): a foreigner in Latin America, especially an American or English person; the term is often considered offensive.

ANALYZE NARRATIVE STRUCTURE

After students mark the text, remind them that stories contain at least one main **conflict**, or problem for the main character(s) to solve. Point out that most events in a plot involve the characters' attempts to solve or overcome conflict, deal with outcomes, react to complications, and so on, until the conflict is resolved. Explain that in a **linear** plot, this chain of cause-and-effect relationships between events is part of what keeps readers interested in what happens next. Ask students to consider what cause-and-effect relationships link paragraph 21 to the rest of the plot. (**Answer:** *The details advance the plot by skipping ahead in time and introducing future events for readers to look forward to: what will result from the family's continued hope of visiting Panamá. Readers can infer that the family will probably try to plan another trip "the following year," but whether they are able to make the trip happen is less certain.*)

For **reading support** for students at varying proficiency levels, see the **Text X-Ray** on page 184D.

■ English Learner Support

Analyze Narrative Structure Clarify that *advance* means "to move forward," and point out that the family is not going to Rafael's reunion anymore. Explain that paragraph 21 lets readers know that the story is not over yet. It also provides clues to what may happen next. Have students try to predict what happens next and explain what details they used.

SUBSTANTIAL/MODERATE

IMPROVE READING FLUENCY

Targeted Passage Tell students to follow along in the text as they listen to you read aloud paragraphs 21–22. Ask them to circle words or phrases that they hear you read differently than they expected, such as Spanish words or compound adjectives such as *holier-than-thou*. Then read the paragraphs with expression, modeling appropriate phrasing and intonation. Invite students to ask you to reread certain words or sentences. Then pair fluent and less-fluent readers and have partners take turns reading each paragraph aloud to each other. Encourage students to provide helpful feedback with pronunciation and phrasing for longer sentences.

 Go to the **Reading Studio** for additional support in developing fluency.

ANALYZE NARRATIVE STRUCTURE

Explain that writers **structure** time to support the **plot** by pacing events to unfold more quickly or slowly. To keep the plot moving and the reader engaged, less important events or periods of time may be skipped, just briefly mentioned, or summarized. More important events are given more time and attention. They may be expanded into scenes with conversations and descriptions of characters and settings, or writers may focus on actions and keep dialogue short to make an event more exciting with faster pacing.

Tell students that after comparing the passage of time in the two sections, they should consider what happens in each and why the author paced the events that way. (**Answer:** *Both sections explain why a trip was canceled, but they focus on different periods of time. In paragraphs 10–20, the narrator describes everything that happens in the short time it takes for Rafael to make his decision and for the family to react. In paragraphs 23–25, the narrator uses faster pacing to describe several key moments from the whole day of 9/11. The author uses this structure to make 9/11 the climax of the plot. Taking time to describe the first trip cancellation with a full scene helps readers relate to the characters' thoughts and feelings. Then when 9/11 happens, the fast pacing sweeps readers along with the characters' reactions to events. The day is even more upsetting because readers can infer that the Toros probably won't go to Panama as a result.*)

CRITICAL VOCABULARY

melodrama: Celia's words and behavior appear overly emotional and dramatic, like the acting in soap operas.

ASK STUDENTS to give an example of Celia's melodrama. *(Celia's melodrama includes making a big deal over how she misses the mosquito bites she used to get in Panama.)*

froth: Celia is overflowing or bubbling over with excitement.

ASK STUDENTS to describe a mental image of Celia in a froth. *(Celia is probably beaming and gesturing wildly while she talks in an animated voice and rushes around the house.)*

confer: Celia and tía Gloria, her sister, are discussing the trip and making new plans for what they can do together.

ASK STUDENTS what the narrator mentions tía Gloria conferring with Celia over. *(Gloria tries to convince Celia that they should go to the clubs along Calle Uruguay.)*

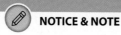 **NOTICE & NOTE**

little thing into a way to talk about Panamá. She would get a mosquito bite on her ankle and point out the welt to us, reminiscing about the bites she used to get in Panamá and wondering aloud "what the mosquitoes there looked like now," as if they were old friends. She would make rice and start talking about the gallo pinto at El Trapiche, which was her favorite restaurant, saying things like "I wonder how Cristóbal—wasn't that the owner's name?—is doing. Wouldn't it be nice to find out?" We would drive over a bridge and suddenly she was talking about the Bridge of the Americas near the canal. "Do you remember, Enrique? That time we took the ferry back from Taboga at night and it was all lit up? It was so beautiful. Mayor, I wish you could have seen it." She sighed. "Maybe one day." And my dad would sometimes shake his head at her **melodrama** and other times would just stay quiet, like he'd fallen into the haze of a particular memory himself.

22 My mom's birthday was September 22, so my dad finally gave in and made plans for us to go to Panamá. The Toro Family! One night only! Put it in lights! My mom worked herself into a **froth** all over again, **conferring** with my tía Gloria on the phone. My aunt apparently said she wanted to take my mom to the new mall and for a drive through Costa del Este, which used to be a garbage dump but now had been transformed into an up-and-coming area of the city, and out for sushi on the causeway, and afterwards they could hit the clubs along Calle Uruguay and yes, she realized they weren't twenty anymore but it would be so much fun! Besides, she and my tío Esteban weren't doing so well, she told my mom. He was never home. He spent the night at friends' apartments. So she could use some distraction and someone to talk to. "Not a divorce!" my mom gasped. To her, there could be nothing worse. "No," my aunt assured her. "Just problems."

23 Then, less than two weeks before we were scheduled to go, two planes flew into the World Trade Center in New York City and another one into the Pentagon in Washington, D.C. The country went into shock and we went right along with it. My dad called my mom from the diner, where, on the television above the counter, he had just seen the second plane hit the second tower. "They're blowing it up!" he apparently told her. "It's just like El Chorrillo.⁵ They're destroying it!" And my mom, in her nightgown, rushed to the set and stood in front of

melodrama
(mĕl´ə-drä´mə) *n. Melodrama* is behavior characterized by exaggerated emotions.

froth
(frôth) *n.* A *froth* is a fit of frustration or excitement.

confer
(kən-fûr´) *v.* To *confer* is to share ideas or make a decision with one or more other people.

ANALYZE NARRATIVE STRUCTURE

Annotate: Mark words and phrases in paragraphs 23–25 that relate to time.

Compare: How does the passage of time in this section of the narrative compare with the passage of time in paragraphs 10–20? What is the impact of this structure on the story's plot?

---

⁵ **El Chorrillo** (ĕl chô-rê´yō): a neighborhood in Panama City that suffered heavy damage during the 1989 U.S. invasion of Panama.

it, watching with her hand over her mouth. I had been eating cereal in the kitchen. I carried my bowl over and stood next to her and kept eating, which, when I thought about it later, seemed kind of messed up, but at the time we didn't know what was happening. The world hadn't stopped—just stopped—like it would later that day and for days after. Everything was still just unfolding in front of our eyes and we had no idea what to make of it.

24   It didn't take long before everyone in our building was knocking on each other's doors and **convening** out on the balcony, standing around stunned and shaking with fear. Nelia Zafón just kept repeating, "What is happening? What is happening? What is happening?" I heard my mom say to someone, "We moved here because it was supposed to be safer! Where can we go after this?" All day long she kept herself no more than an arm's length from me and my brother, hugging us against her and then letting us go, like she wanted to assure herself that we were still there and that we were okay. Enrique, who was old enough by then that he usually squirmed away from my mom's embraces, must have known the situation was serious, because he let her do it. I let her, too, even though every time she did, instead of comforting me, it only made me more scared.

25   By evening, everyone's front doors were open and people were roaming in and out of each other's units, watching each other's televisions as if a different set would deliver different news, checking to see if anyone had heard anything new, getting tedious translations. Benny Quinto led prayer circles in his living room. Micho Alvarez paced up and down the balcony, talking on his cell phone and jotting things in his notebook. Gustavo Milhojas, who was half-Mexican and half-Guatemalan, wrote a letter to the army telling them that as of that day he was 100 percent American and that he was ready to serve the country and kill the cowards who had murdered his fellow paisanos.[6] At the end he wrote, "And here is a list of people who are willing to join me." He drew a few blank lines and spent the afternoon trying to recruit everyone in the building. When my mom saw what it was, she said, "More killing? That's what you want? *More?*" And Gustavo said, "Not killing. Justice."

26   That year around the holidays we were all miserable. Holidays were always bad—my mom in particular got homesick

convene
(kən-vēn´) *v.* To *convene* is to come together for a purpose.

---
[6] **paisanos** (pī-zä´nōs): countrymen.

WHEN STUDENTS STRUGGLE . . .

Use Learning Strategies If students struggle to analyze the passage of time in paragraphs 23–25, give them a flow chart to help them note the main time periods and summarize events. Have partners compare and use the time words they marked to identify when the events described with each paragraph are happening. Tell students to write a description of each time period in a separate box in their chart. Ask: *What is the total period of time described in these three paragraphs? What is the main event?* Have students write their responses at the top of their charts.

 For additional support, go to the **Reading Studio** and assign the following **Level Up** tutorial: Reading for Details.

ENGLISH LEARNER SUPPORT

Use Contextual Support Display this and the next sentence in paragraph 23: *The world hadn't stopped— just stopped—like it would later that day and for days after.* Read both sentences aloud, and have students repeat them. Then display a list of the events of 9/11 involving the four planes and collapsing towers, and point out that these events all occurred in one morning. Use the following supports with students at varying proficiency levels:

• Underline *The world hadn't stopped* and *Everything was still just unfolding*. Explain that the phrases express the same idea: the listed events are happening one after another. Then circle—*just stopped*—and we had no idea what to make of it. Explain that each event would shock and confuse people watching, making time seem to stop as they tried to understand what they were seeing. **SUBSTANTIAL**

• Explain that the second sentence restates the same ideas the narrator expressed in the first sentence, but more clearly. Have students work with a partner to identify the corresponding phrases in the sentences. **MODERATE**

• Ask students to explain what the sentences suggest about the narrator. *Why is it important to him that he explain these thoughts?* **LIGHT**

CRITICAL VOCABULARY

convene: All the residents of the apartment building gather together on the balcony.

ASK STUDENTS why a shocking or frightening event might make people want to convene in a public place. *(Convening can be reassuring, because people can share what they know and feel safer by being with others.)*

ANALYZE THEME

Encourage students to use what they already know about Celia's personality, Panama, and the past events in the story to help them mark clues in the text. Point out that students should use these details to infer the reasons the entire family gets depressed at Christmas. Suggest they consider why Celia's attitude is helpful for understanding the other characters. (**Answer:** *Holidays are times people spend doing traditional things with their families, so being away from family and not able to join in would make most people feel homesick. The situation must be worse for Celia and Rafael because all their relatives are in Panama, and they have not seen them or the place they spent most of their lives for years. They also cannot celebrate Christmas in the United States the same way they would in Panama because the culture and climate are different. Also, while Celia seems to miss Panama the most, her expressive personality causes her moods to affect everyone around her. This makes Christmas depressing for the narrator and Enrique, too, even though their connection to Panama is not as strong as their parents'.*)

ENGLISH LEARNER SUPPORT

Make Inferences Have students mark all uses of the pronoun *we* in the paragraphs.

- Ask: *Who is "we"? (the whole family) Does everyone in the family feel depressed, or sad, at Christmas? (yes)* Tell students that the way Celia acts and her personality help explain why the whole family feels this way every Christmas. **SUBSTANTIAL**

- Call students' attention to Rafael's question, "You want Panama?" Ask them to discuss why Rafael thinks going to the beach is a good idea for both Celia and the rest of them. **MODERATE**

NOTICE & NOTE

ANALYZE THEME

Annotate: Mark places in paragraphs 26–27 that show Celia's attitude toward her home in Panama and her home in the United States.

Infer: Why do you think the holiday season is a particularly difficult time of year for the Toros?

sometimes like it was a genuine illness—but that Christmas was the worst. We were depressed and on edge, still shaken up about September 11, and then re-shaken when someone tried to blow up another plane by hiding a bomb in his shoes two days before Christmas Eve.

27   My aunt called, which cheered my mom up for a while, but once that wore off, she was more down than ever, shuffling around the house in her slippers, no makeup, her hair a disaster. She carried tissues in the pocket of her bathrobe and made a big show of dabbing her nose with them every so often. Eventually, my dad came up with an idea. "You want Panamá?" he said. "A beach is the closest thing you're going to get." He hustled us out the door and down the street, where we took a chain of buses for an hour and a half to Cape Henlopen in southern Delaware. It was snowing when we arrived—Enrique kept complaining that the snow was going to mess up his beloved Adidas sneakers—and everything was so colorless and barren that it looked like the moon. I had to hand it to my dad, though. With the water and the sand, my mom said it almost *was* like a little piece of Panamá. The waves roared in toward us and then silently pulled back again, slipping over the shore. Even with the falling snow, the air had the sting of salt water, and we crunched broken seashells under our shoes. But one beach isn't every beach. And one home isn't every home. And I think we all sensed, standing there, just how far we were from where we had come, in ways both good and bad. "It's beautiful," my mom said, staring out at the ocean. She sighed and shook her head. "This country."

WHEN STUDENTS STRUGGLE . . .

Reteaching: Analyze Characters Have students work with a partner to mark details about Celia and infer why she does or says each thing. Then explain that a character's interactions and relationships with other characters also can be revealing. Ask students to locate the detail in paragraph 27 that explains why Rafael brought the family to the beach. (*You want Panamá? A beach is the closest thing you're going to get.*) Have student pairs brainstorm reasons why going to the beach might make Celia and the rest of the family feel better at Christmas.

   For additional support, go to the **Reading Studio** and assign the following Level Up tutorial: **Making Inferences about Characters.**

CHECK YOUR UNDERSTANDING

Answer these questions before moving on to the **Analyze the Text** section on the following page.

1 Rafa cancels a trip to attend his high school reunion in Panama because he is —

A worried about losing his job if he takes too much time off from work

B afraid that someone tried to blow up a plane two days before he was supposed to leave

C angry about a conversation he had with a former classmate about his plans

D upset that the neighborhood in his home city has been destroyed

2 The novel's title, *The Book of Unknown Americans*, emphasizes the idea in the excerpt that the characters struggle to —

F find out about their past

G locate their other family members

H fit in with their new culture

J return to their former home

3 Which character in the story shows the strongest desire to visit Panama?

A Mayor

B Enrique

C Celia

D Rafa

CHECK YOUR UNDERSTANDING

Have students answer the questions independently.

Answers:

1. *C*

2. *H*

3. *C*

If they answer any questions incorrectly, have them reread the text to confirm their understanding. Then they may proceed to ANALYZE THE TEXT on page 196.

 ENGLISH LEARNER SUPPORT

Oral Assessment Use the following questions to assess students' comprehension and speaking skills:

1. Why does Rafa cancel the trip to attend his high school reunion in Panama? *(He is angry about a conversation with an old classmate about his plans to attend the reunion.)*

2. What does the novel's title, *The Book of Unknown Americans*, emphasize is the main thing that the characters struggle with? *(They struggle to fit in with their new culture.)*

3. Which character in the story most wants to visit Panama? *(Celia)*
SUBSTANTIAL/MODERATE

ANALYZE THE TEXT

Possible answers:

1. **DOK 4:** One theme is that people cannot feel like they belong if they are not accepted or do not feel safe. This is developed through the title, the narrator's stated confusion about his identity, Rafael reconsidering whether he really is Panamanian, and the trip to the beach to reassure Celia after 9/11 that makes them all feel like they are far from home.

2. **DOK 3:** Celia is expressive about her emotions. Other examples include when she "worked herself into a froth" about the second trip (paragraph 22) and then "made a big show of dabbing her nose" (paragraph 27) with tissues after the trip was canceled.

3. **DOK 2:** They help propel the narrative forward. After the first trip is canceled, the author immediately suggests that they will try again. Readers must infer the second cancellation when 9/11 occurs, so they want to keep reading after that climactic event to confirm this.

4. **DOK 4:** In paragraph 3, he feels "more American than anything" but is not accepted as one at school. At home, his family makes him feel like he should identify more with his Panamanian heritage. At the beach, he realizes that they all feel uprooted and in a foreign place, far "from where we had come" (paragraph 27).

5. **DOK 4:** "Maybe we don't belong there anymore" suggests Rafael can be Panamanian or American but not both, and the choice is not completely his. This echoes the idea in paragraph 3 that identity is both "allowed" and something you are "supposed to claim." In contrast, a neighbor feels "100 percent American" (paragraph 25) because his actions are what matter.

RESEARCH

Remind students to also consider a website's purpose. Sites created to inform rather than persuade will be more objective and reliable sources of information.

Connect Students may note that the narrator takes a stark view of a complicated situation. Removing Noriega from power should have benefited both the United States and the people of Panama who wanted a democratic government.

RESPOND

ANALYZE THE TEXT

Support your responses with evidence from the text.   NOTEBOOK

1. **Analyze** State one theme the author develops in this excerpt. Cite evidence from the text to support your analysis.

2. **Draw Conclusions** In paragraph 7, the narrator states, "And my parents laughed until my mom dabbed the corners of her eyes with the back of her hand." What can you conclude about Celia based on this statement? Cite text evidence to support your conclusion.

3. **Cause and Effect** What are the effects of the two canceled trips to Panama on the course of the story?

4. **Analyze** How is the narrator's identity, or sense of himself, affected by his surroundings? Cite text evidence to support your answer.

5. **Notice & Note** How do the statements Rafa makes about being American in paragraph 12 relate to other ideas about American identity expressed elsewhere in the text?

RESEARCH TIP
Some websites are more reliable than others. In your research, try to use websites that have reliable and verified information, such as those of institutions dedicated to fact-checking their information.

RESEARCH

The Book of Unknown Americans references real people, places, and events related to the history of Panama. Conduct research to learn more about Panama's history. Record your findings in the chart.

QUESTION	ANSWER
What is the Panama Canal? When was it built?	*The canal links the Atlantic and Pacific Oceans through the Isthmus of Panama, making international trade easier. The canal was completed in 1914.*
How did the United States gain control of the Panama Canal? When did Panama gain complete control of the canal?	*The United States negotiated treaties to build and control the canal. Panama finally gained control of the canal in 1999.*
Who was Manuel Noriega?	*Noriega was a military leader who made himself ruler of Panama from 1983–1990 and profited from the drug trade.*
Why did the United States invade Panama in 1989?	*The U.S. wanted to protect its interests in Panama, stop the drug trade, and bring Noriega to face criminal charges in the United States.*

Connect In paragraph 4, the narrator says of his parents' decision to emigrate to the United States, "I pointed out how backwards it was to have fled to the nation that had driven them out of theirs, but they never copped to the irony of it." In a small group, discuss how your research about Panama's history helps you understand this statement.

WHEN STUDENTS STRUGGLE . . .

Analyze Theme Review that a theme is the author's message about life or human nature. Have students use a labeled chart to help them synthesize what message is suggested by these elements of a story:

Main Characters	Conflict	What the Ending Shows
Theme:		

For additional support, go to the **Reading Studio** and assign the following LEVEL **Level Up Tutorial: Theme.**

CREATE AND PRESENT

Write a Paragraph Choose a character from *The Book of Unknown Americans* and write a paragraph from that character's point of view explaining how he or she feels about the place(s) he or she calls home.

❑ Review the text for implicit and explicit details that help you make inferences about the character's thoughts and feelings.

❑ Describe the connections the character feels to his or her home(s) and why. Be sure to write from the point of view of the character.

❑ Make sure you include details that clearly identify the character. Convey the voice of the character by using language that allows your reader to "hear" his or her personality.

Act Out a Scene In a small group, choose a scene to act out that's described by the narrator in *The Book of Unknown Americans*.

❑ As a group, review the text and discuss which scenes would be best to perform. Take a vote to decide on a scene. How many actors will you need? How does the scene relate to the themes of the novel excerpt? Take notes to record your group's ideas.

❑ As a group, write a script. Next, cast the characters. Rehearse your scene. Assemble any props you may need.

❑ Finally, perform your scene for the class. Listen attentively as you watch other groups' scenes. Ask questions about the choices each group made in planning and performing their scenes.

 Go to **Writing Narratives** in the **Writing Studio** for more help with writing from a character's point of view.

 Go to **Participating in Collaborative Discussions** in the **Speaking and Listening Studio** for more.

RESPOND TO THE ESSENTIAL QUESTION

 What are the places that shape who you are?

Gather Information Review your annotations and notes on *The Book of Unknown Americans*. Then, add relevant details to your Response Log. To decide what to include, think about:

• where a person calls home after he or she has moved

• why a person can call more than one place home

• how where we live or where we are from affects others' opinions of us

At the end of the unit, you may use your notes to help you write a short story.

UNIT 3 RESPONSE LOG

Essential Question:
What are the places that shape who you are?

My Favorite Chaperone	
from The Book of Unknown Americans	
The Powwow at the End of the World	
New Immigrants Share Their Stories	
A Common Bond Teens Forge Friendships Despite Differences	

ACADEMIC VOCABULARY

As you write and discuss what you learned from the novel, be sure to use the Academic Vocabulary words. Check off each of the words that you use.

❑ **contribute**

❑ **immigrate**

❑ **reaction**

❑ **relocate**

❑ **shifting**

CREATE AND PRESENT

Write a Paragraph Encourage students to create a profile of their selected character, to organize their thoughts and use as a reference while writing. Suggest that students collect and list relevant details and quotes from the text along with what each suggests about their character's thoughts and feelings about "home," personality traits, and voice or manner of speaking.

After students have drafted their paragraph, have them take turns reading it aloud without telling their partner who the character is. Ask students to give each other constructive feedback about how identifiable and accurately portrayed the character is, and then revise and edit their own writing as needed.

For **writing support** for students at varying proficiency levels, see the **Text X-Ray** on page 184D.

Act Out a Scene Briefly review how students can format their scripts to make clear who is speaking, what is happening "onstage," and when any props are needed. If groups cannot find a scene with enough dialogue, consider allowing them to creatively modify scenes. For instance, students could be challenged to smoothly incorporate alter-ego characters who voice their thoughts or remembered words from past conversations. Students also may collaboratively create dialogue from paragraphs with sufficient information, such as paragraphs 4 and 10.

For **speaking support** for students at varying proficiency levels, see the **Text X-Ray** on page 184D.

RESPOND TO THE ESSENTIAL QUESTION

Allow time for students to add details from "The Book of Unknown Americans" to their Unit 3 Response Logs.

APPLY

CRITICAL VOCABULARY

Possible Answers:

1. *I like to reminisce about fun times I had at summer camp when I was ten.*

2. *The whole island was ravaged by the hurricane.*

3. *Crying and saying that someone hates you because of a minor insult is an example of melodrama.*

4. *She was in a froth about the plans for the party.*

5. *Two people might confer about their plans for a project.*

6. *My teacher might assure me that studying will help me improve my grades.*

7. *Teachers might convene to discuss school policies.*

VOCABULARY STRATEGY:
Use a Dictionary

Remind students that some words have multiple meanings and can be different parts of speech depending on how they are used, so they need to check each definition against how the word is used in the text.

CRITICAL VOCABULARY

WORD BANK
reminisce
assure
ravage
melodrama
froth
confer
convene

Practice and Apply Write a short answer to show that you understand each of the Critical Vocabulary words.

1. Write about a time in your life you like to **reminisce** about.

2. Write a sentence using the word **ravage**.

3. Share an example of a **melodrama**.

4. Write a sentence using the word **froth**.

5. Describe something two people might **confer** about.

6. Describe how someone might **assure** you of something.

7. Give a reason why a group of people might **convene**.

VOCABULARY STRATEGY:
Use a Dictionary

Go to the **Vocabulary Studio** for more on using a dictionary.

While you can use online search engines to look up a word's spelling or meaning, it is important to evaluate the source you use. A reliable print or online dictionary will tell you not only a word's correct spelling and definition but also its pronunciation, syllabication, part of speech, and word origin. Note the word *copped* in paragraph 4 of the excerpt from *The Book of Unknown Americans*. You can use context, or the words and sentences around the word, to infer its meaning. If you look the word up in the dictionary to confirm its precise meaning, you might find these definitions for the transitive verb form of *cop*:

> **cop** (kŏp) *tr. v.* *Slang* **1.** To get hold of; gain or win. **2.** To take unlawfully or without permission; steal. **3.** To plead guilty; admit. [Probably variant of *cap*, to catch, from Old French *caper*, from Latin *capere*.]

Definition **3** best matches the meaning of *copped* in the sentence.

Practice and Apply Find the words below in the excerpt from *The Book of Unknown Americans*. Use a print or online dictionary to identify the definition that matches the word's meaning in context and its part of speech. Then use the pronunciation to say the word.

WORD	PART OF SPEECH	MEANING
utility (paragraph 1)	adjective	Designed for heavy-duty practical use
taunted (paragraph 3)	transitive verb	To mock or ridicule
recruit (paragraph 25)	transitive verb	To enlist someone in military service

---

🔵 ENGLISH LEARNER SUPPORT

Vocabulary Strategy Give students additional practice in recognizing and correctly pronouncing the Critical Vocabulary words. For each word, ask: *What paragraph is the word [word] used in?* Ask students to respond by telling you the word and its location in a complete sentence. Display this sentence frame for students to use, if needed: *The word [word] is used in paragraph ___.* Read aloud the given definition and have students repeat it after you. For the verbs, ask students what tense is used in the text. Read aloud the sentences containing the verbs, and have students practice reading them to a partner. **SUBSTANTIAL/MODERATE**

LANGUAGE CONVENTIONS: Pronouns

It's important to know how to use subject pronouns and object pronouns correctly in formal writing and speech. A **subject pronoun** is used as a subject in a sentence. An **object pronoun** is used as a direct object, an indirect object, or the object of a preposition.

SUBJECT PRONOUNS	OBJECT PRONOUNS
I, we	me, us
you	you
he, she, it, they	him, her, it, them

```
        SUBJECT    OBJECT
           ↓          ↓
        We will give them to her.
                           ↑
              OBJECT OF PREPOSITION
```

Sometimes a pronoun is part of a **compound,** which means that more than one subject or object is joined by the conjunction *or* or *and.* Study these examples from *The Book of Unknown Americans:*

> **My brother and I** huddled together, listening through the front door.

In this sentence, notice how "I huddled" still sounds correct without the compound part *My brother and,* but "me huddled" would not sound correct.

> All day long she kept herself no more than an arm's length from <u>me and my brother</u>.

In this sentence, the preposition *from* and the compound object *me and my brother* form a **prepositional phrase.** Note that "an arm's length from me" sounds correct, but "an arm's length from I" would not.

Practice and Apply Choose the correct personal pronoun in each sentence.

1. You should give the paper to him or (her/she).

2. My teacher asked my classmate and (me/I) to help hand out papers.

3. When they are finished, you and (I/me) will take a turn.

4. After we present our work, (they/them) will give their presentation.

RESPOND 💬

! Go to **Using Pronouns Correctly** in the **Grammar Studio** for more on pronouns.

LANGUAGE CONVENTIONS: Pronouns

Review the information about personal pronouns with students. Point out that whether the subject of a sentence is a single pronoun or a compound subject consisting of a pronoun and one or more nouns, the job of the pronoun is the same—to replace a noun as a subject—so a subject pronoun should be used. The same is true in the case of pronouns in compound objects.

Demonstrate by displaying the following sentence and changing it to have a compound subject or object:

He would tell me things about his relatives.

- *<u>He and Joe</u> would tell me things about his relatives.*

- *He would tell <u>me and my friend</u> things about his relatives.*

Point out that *about* is a preposition, so *about his relatives* is a prepositional phrase. Review that a preposition relates the noun or pronoun after it to other words in the sentence. This makes the noun or pronoun the *object* of the preposition, so any pronoun that follows a preposition should be an object pronoun.

Ask students what pronoun could be used in place of *his relatives.* (*them*)

- *He would tell me things about **them**.*

Answers:

1. *her*

2. *me*

3. *I*

4. *they*

🗨 ENGLISH LEARNER SUPPORT

Language Conventions Help students develop an ear for correct pronouns by practicing in small groups. Give each group index cards with a simple sentence with an underlined noun or proper noun printed on one side, and the same sentence rewritten with an underlined pronoun on the other side. Ask students to take turns holding up a card and reading aloud the sentence on the front; then the rest of the group should read aloud the sentence on the back of the card. Vietnamese-speaking students may struggle with pronouns as the Vietnamese language often omits pronouns when they are subject of a sentence. **SUBSTANTIAL**

Increase the difficulty level by using sentences containing compound subjects, compound objects, and prepositional phrases. **MODERATE**

THE POWWOW AT THE END OF THE OF THE WORLD

Poem by Sherman Alexie

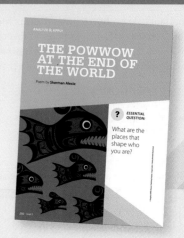

GENRE ELEMENTS
POETRY

Remind students that the language of **poetry** is full of opportunities for students to interpret and gain insights about the writer's message. In this lesson, students will read Sherman Alexie's poem, "The Powwow at the End of the World." Students will focus on his use of imagery, allusion, and irony. Students will then make inferences about the deeper meaning of the poem and the culture it reflects.

LEARNING OBJECTIVES

- Analyze line length and literary devices, such as imagery, allusion, and irony.
- Conduct research on the Grand Coulee Dam and its effects.
- Write a free-verse poem, using strong imagery.
- Hold a debate about the benefits and drawbacks of dams.
- Determine meanings of words and phrases.
- Analyze how a modern work draws on traditional stories.
- Make inferences to determine the poem's subject and tone.
- **Language** Answer questions about how details contribute to the tone of the poem.

TEXT COMPLEXITY

Quantitative Measures	The Powwow at the End of the World		
Qualitative Measures	**Ideas Presented** Single level of complex meaning.		
	Structures Used Free verse, no particular patterns.		
	Language Used More complex descriptions.		
	Knowledge Required Increased amount of cultural and literary knowledge useful.		

Online Ed

RESOURCES

- Unit 3 Response Log
- 🔊 Selection Audio
- 📖 Reading Studio: Notice & Note
- 📰 Writing Studio: Writing Narratives
- 💬 Speakin and Listening Studio: Participating in Collaborative Discussions
- ✅ "The Powwow at the End of the World" Selection Test

SUMMARIES

English

The speaker tells unidentified listeners that he shall do what they demand: that is, forgive those who have permanently damaged his tribe's way of life. However, he then goes on to describe several events that must occur before he forgives, each of which is impossible. For example, the first event is that a Native American woman will topple the Grand Coulee Dam by leaning her shoulder into it. The speaker goes on to describe an apocalyptic powwow in which a salmon will provide his tribe with joy and wisdom.

Spanish

El orador les comenta a oyentes no identificados que él hará todo lo que ellos le piden; eso significa, perdonar a todos los que han dañado el estilo de vida de su tribu permanentemente. Sin embargo, luego describe varios eventos que deben ocurrir antes de perdonarlos. Y cada uno de ellos parece imposible. Por ejemple, el primer evento es que una mujer india derribe la presa Grand Coulee empujándola con el hombro. El orador pasa a describir cómo un Pow Wow apocalíptico traerá a su tribu alegría y sabiduría.

SMALL-GROUP OPTIONS

Have students work in small groups to read and discuss the selection.

Think-Pair-Share

Explain that powwows are gatherings at which Native Americans celebrate by singing, dancing, and feasting. Have students read and analyze "The Powwow at the End of the World." Then, ask: *What will happen during "The Powwow at the End of the World"?*

- Have students think about the question individually and take notes.
- Then, have pairs discuss their ideas about the question.
- Finally, have pairs share their responses with the class.

KWL

- Have students work in groups to create a three-column chart about Native American culture labeled "K (know)," "W (want to know)," and "L (learned)."
- In the first column, ask students to write words, terms, and phrases they associate with the culture.
- In the second column, have students list questions they want to learn from the poem.
- During or after students have read the poem, have them complete the third column by writing what they learned from the poem. Discuss the information that students learned.

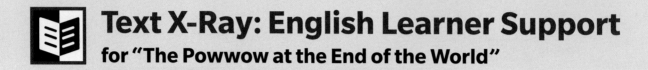

Text X-Ray: English Learner Support
for "The Powwow at the End of the World"

INTRODUCE THE SELECTION
TOPICAL POETRY

Explain to students that **poetry** may comment on a current social topic, expressing **opinions** or criticisms about enduring concerns and dominant forces in society. In this poem, students will examine how the speaker of the poem conveys his ideas about how government policy has forever damaged the place that shaped him and other members of his Native Ameican tribe. Before reading, ask volunteers to share their knowledge about Native American cultures and history. What do they know about modern Native American cultures and society? Encourage students to draw upon studies and research to make valid generalizations by asking questions:

- *What associations to ancient culture still endure within Native Americans cultures?*
- *How important is tribal identity to modern-day Native Americans?*

CULTURAL REFERENCES

The following words and phrases may be unfamiliar to students:

- *successive* (line 4): one after another
- *mouth* (line 7): the part of a river that empties into a larger body of water
- *reservation* (line 16): a piece of land set apart for the use of Native American people
- *powwow* (line 27): a council or meeting of Native Americans

LISTENING

Understand Tone

Explain to students that poetry is a type of writing that uses language in creative ways to describe an experience, an event, or feelings about these things. A poem's tone is reflected in the speaker's attitude toward the poem's subject.

Have students listen as you read aloud lines 1–10 of the poem. Use the following supports with students at varying proficiency levels:

- Tell students that you will ask questions about details of what you just read aloud that affect the tone. Model that students should give a thumbs up if the answer is *yes*, and a thumbs down for *no*. For example, ask: *Does the speaker think the Grand Coulee Dam was good for his people? (No)* **SUBSTANTIAL**
- Have students reread lines 1–10 of the poem. Then ask them to describe the tone, or the speaker's attitude, toward the subject. *(anger, sarcasm)* **MODERATE**
- Ask: *What details in lines 1–10 help you understand the tone of the poem? (The speaker says that he will forgive but only when the dams are destroyed, an event that is unlikely to happen.)* **LIGHT**

SPEAKING

Discuss Free Verse

Have students discuss the basic elements of free verse poetry. Make sure students understand that unlike verse poems, free verse poems have neither a rhyme scheme nor a regular metrical pattern.

Use the following supports with students at varying proficiency levels:

- Display the poem. Ask students what they notice about the arrangement of the lines. (*The lines are not the same length.*) **SUBSTANTIAL**
- Have students highlight punctuation in the poem. Ask: *Where does the punctuation most often occur?* (*within lines of the poem*) **MODERATE**
- Pair students and have them take turns reading each sentence of the poem. Ask: *What effect does the poet create by arranging the poem in sentences?* (*The poem sounds natural and conversational because of this arrangement.*) **LIGHT**

READING

Make Inferences

Tell students that readers need to make inferences, or educated guesses, about what the poet is saying. Tell students to pay close attention to the details in the poem, and then use those details and their own prior knowledge to figure out what the poet implies but does not directly say.

Have students read lines 1–16. Use the following supports with students at varying proficiency levels:

- Write the word *salmon* on the board. Then pronounce the word and have students repeat the word, making sure they do not pronounce the silent *l*. Ask: *What is a salmon?* (*a fish*) *How do you know?* (*it is in the water, swimming*) *Which lines of the poem tell what the salmon does?* (*lines 9–16*) **SUBSTANTIAL**
- Have students complete the following sentence frame: *The salmon swims not downstream, but _____.* (*upstream*) Explain that swimming upstream implies struggle. If the salmon represents the Indians, what might the salmon's effort represent to the speaker? (*The salmon might represent the struggles of Native Americans against the changes to their way of life.*) **MODERATE**
- Explain that *abandoned* means "deserted, or left behind." Pair students. Ask: *What adjectives in the poem helps you infer the speaker's feelings about the environment?* (*flooded cities, broken dams, abandoned reactors*) *What do these adjectives imply?* (*destruction and desertion*) **LIGHT**

WRITING

Write a Poem

Remind students that a free verse poem has language that sounds like natural speech and focuses on imagery.

Reread the poem aloud. Use the following supports with students at varying proficiency levels:

- Have students write down the phrase: *"I am told . . . that I must forgive ..."* Point out that the poet is not ready to forgive or not be upset by the dam. Ask students to think of something that upsets them and add it to the phrase. Accept one-word answers and visual depictions. **SUBSTANTIAL**
- Provide a sentence frame: *I am told by ____ that I must forgive ____ and so I shall after____.* Tell students to complete the frame with their own ideas about something that upsets them. **MODERATE**
- Have students pick a section of the poem and rewrite it to fit their own thoughts, feelings, or situation. Tell them to pay attention to where the lines break and adjust to shape the rhythm of their poem. **LIGHT**

THE POWWOW AT THE END OF THE WORLD

Poem by **Sherman Alexie**

? Connect to the
ESSENTIAL QUESTION

"The Powwow at the End of the World" concerns one of the places that shaped the speaker's identity. Like countless other Native Americans in the Washington area, the speaker criticizes the wholesale destruction of salmon in the Columbia River, which was caused by the construction of the Grand Coulee Dam and other dams. The dams not only destroyed the salmon population but also changed the way of life and damaged the cultural identity of an entire people.

? ESSENTIAL QUESTION:

What are the places that shape who you are?

200   Unit 3

IMPROVE READING FLUENCY

Oral Reading   Divide students into small groups. Have one member of the group read the first sentence, beginning with "I am told by many of you that I must forgive and so I shall." Then have the second member read the second sentence. Continue until different students have read all eight sentences. Then have students read the entire eight sentences again for increased fluency and emphasis.

 Go to the **Reading Studio** for additional support in developing fluency.

GET READY

TEACH

QUICK START

The poem you are about to read is about a place that helped make the poet who he is. Make notes about a place that has helped to shape your character, personality, likes, or dislikes. It can be a place you have visited regularly or only once.

Description of Place	How It Has Affected Me

ANALYZE LINE LENGTH

The **form** of a poem is the way it is laid out on the page. A **line** is the core unit of a poem. The place where a line ends is called a **line break**. Sometimes a complete line as written by the poet cannot fit on the page or screen. When that happens, the words that spill over to the next line are indented, or pushed in slightly to the right. Notice the line breaks in these five lines from "The Powwow at the End of the World."

> I am told by many of you that I must forgive and so I shall
> after an Indian woman puts her shoulder to the Grand
>   Coulee Dam
> and topples it. I am told by many of you that I must forgive
> and so I shall after the floodwaters burst each successive
>   dam
> 5 downriver from the Grand Coulee. . . .

Line length is an essential element of a poem's meaning and rhythm. What else do you need to know about line breaks?

- They do not always signal the end of a sentence or thought.
- A line break can occur in the middle of a sentence or phrase to create a meaningful pause or emphasis.
- Poets use a variety of line breaks to convey a wide range of effects, such as pace, mood, rhythm, and tone.

As you read the poem, think about why the poet breaks lines where he does. Is it to create a dramatic pause, to encourage the reader to stop and think, to focus on a particular word, or for some other reason?

GENRE ELEMENTS: POETRY

- can convey emotional intensity in relatively few words
- is sometimes written using first-person point of view to express the speaker's thoughts and feelings
- often uses repetition to emphasize important ideas
- may include rhyming words or may be written in free verse, with no regular pattern of rhyme

QUICK START

Encourage students to recall a special place where they had fun with their family and friends or a vacation spot where they learned something new or had a new experience that helped influence who they are today. Have students create a T-chart to organize their answers. Then, ask for volunteers to share what they wrote.

Sample answer:

Description of Place	How It Has Affected Me
- my grandmother's apartment	- spend time with Nana
- lots of family photos	- we both love corny jokes
- have to help clean for her	- learned about my family history
	- makes me more responsible

ANALYZE LINE LENGTH

To help students understand the structure of Alexie's free-verse poem, bring in several copies of traditional poems for comparison. Point out that some traditional poems are written in stanzas and have a rhyme scheme and a regular rhythm created by the alternation of stressed and unstressed syllables. Explain that other poems are arranged in cantos or books. Have a volunteer read the first stanza of a traditional poem such as Walt Whitman's "O Captain! My Captain!" to illustrate the difference between a free-verse and structured poem. Then, have another volunteer read aloud the first twelve lines of "The Powwow at the End of the World." Help students notice that a free-verse poem does not contain a regular pattern of rhyme and meter.

The Powwow at the End of the World   **201**

TEACH

ANALYZE LITERARY DEVICES

Point out to students that poets use imagery, allusion, and irony to create meaning and enhance the reader's experiences.

Overall Meaning and Effect

Allusion: *"Floodwaters burst" suggests a wild, destructive force that cannot be controlled, like the anger surging within the speaker.*

Imagery: *The leaping salmon is displaying a mythical quality as it prepares to become the spiritual leader of the tribe.*

Students should notice the speaker's use of verbal irony in the phrase "I must forgive." The speaker says one thing and means another: he says that he must forgive but makes that forgiveness conditional on impossible occurrences.

■ English Learner Support

Use Cognates Tell students that some of the words in Alexie's poem have Spanish cognates: *abandoned/abandonado, arrive/arribar, reservation/reserva.*
ALL LEVELS

ANNOTATION MODEL

Have students read the notes in the margin that accompany the opening lines of the poem. Point out to students that margin notes are a good way to take a snapshot of what they are thinking while responding to certain lines in the poem. The notes may include questions about topics, unfamiliar vocabulary, or ideas that are unclear. Notes should also include responses to striking images the text creates and the implications of the speaker's words.

 GET READY

ANALYZE LITERARY DEVICES

Each word in a poem contributes to its overall meaning and effect. One way poets create meaning is through the use of **imagery,** descriptions that appeal to the senses of sight, hearing, smell, taste, and touch and help a reader create mental images.

Poets also convey meaning through **allusions,** which are connections to ideas in other texts and society. Alexie makes connections to the culture of Northwest Native Americans by alluding to characters and places that are important in their history. The poem contains references to dams that have affected how Northwest Coast peoples make a living. As you read the poem, use a chart like this one to help you analyze imagery and allusions.

EXAMPLE OF IMAGERY OR ALLUSION	OVERALL MEANING AND EFFECT
Allusion: "the floodwaters burst each successive dam / downriver from the Grand Coulee"	*Where is the Grand Coulee? Why is it important to the speaker?*
Imagery: "that salmon leaps into the night air above the water"	*Why did the poet chosse to write about a salmon?*

The poet also uses **irony,** which is a contrast between appearance and reality. As you read, notice how the speaker uses the phrase "I must forgive," and then consider the terms of his forgiveness.

ANNOTATION MODEL   **NOTICE & NOTE**

As you read, notice the allusions and imagery in the poem, and think about the poet's use of irony. This model shows one reader's notes about the beginning of "The Powwow at the End of the World."

I am told by many of you that <u>I must forgive</u> and so I shall
after an Indian woman puts her shoulder to the Grand
    Coulee Dam
<u>and topples it</u>. I am told by many of you that I must forgive
and so I shall after the floodwaters burst each successive
    dam

What's the Grand Coulee Dam?

strong image of a woman toppling a dam

Is the speaker really forgiving?

BACKGROUND

Award-winning author and poet **Sherman Alexie** (b. 1966) was born on the Spokane Indian Reservation in the state of Washington. Salmon have long played an important role in the economic and spiritual life of Native Americans in the Washington area. The building of dams in the 20th century destroyed the population of the once plentiful salmon and the way of life of the people who depended upon them. Many of Alexie's poems and stories deal with how the Native American community has been affected by this destruction.

THE POWWOW AT THE END OF THE WORLD

Poem by Sherman Alexie

SETTING A PURPOSE

As you read, pay attention to the details Alexie presents about the river and salmon. How do these details show his feelings about the dams and their effects on the lives of Native Americans?

I am told by many of you that I must forgive and so I <u>shall</u>
after an Indian woman puts her shoulder to the Grand
    Coulee <u>Dam</u>[1]
and topples it. I am told by many of you that I must <u>forgive</u>
and so I shall after the floodwaters burst each successive
    <u>dam</u>
5 downriver from the Grand Coulee. I am told by many of
    <u>you</u>
that I must forgive and so I shall after the floodwaters <u>find</u>
their way to the mouth of the Columbia River as it enters
    the <u>Pacific</u>
and causes all of it to rise. I am told by many of you that I
    must <u>forgive</u>

---

[1] **Grand Coulee Dam:** a dam built across the Columbia River in the 1930s to provide hydroelectric power and irrigation.

Notice & Note

Use the side margins to notice and note signposts in the text.

ANALYZE LINE LENGTH
Annotate: Mark the line breaks in lines 1–8. Notice any patterns in where the line breaks occur in each sentence.

Analyze: How do the line breaks mirror the subject of these lines, the floodwaters bursting from dams?

BACKGROUND

Have students read the background and information about the poet. Tell them that the building of the Grand Coulee Dam was one of President Franklin D. Roosevelt's New Deal projects. Explain that the New Deal was a set of programs and policies designed to promote economic recovery and social reform introduced during the 1930s. The intent of building the Grand Coulee Dam was to help farmers by irrigating farmland. However, little consideration was given to the changes it would bring to the Columbia River and the impact on Native Americans whose lives revolved around it.

SETTING A PURPOSE

Direct students to use the Setting a Purpose question to focus their reading. Tell students to write any additional questions they generate during reading.

ANALYZE LINE LENGTH

Students may note that these line breaks occur at different points in sentences that all begin with the same words. Like the water tumbling from a toppled dam, the lines break in an unpredictable pattern throughout the poem.

For **reading support** for students at varying proficiency levels, see the **Text X-ray** on page 200D.

ENGLISH LEARNER SUPPORT

Capitalize Proper Nouns Provide students with a video or photos of these key terms and images from the poem: the Grand Coulee Dam, Columbia River, Hanford (nuclear facility in Washington state), and Native Americans (Spokane tribe). Write sentences on the board using each of these terms without capitalization. Ask volunteers to explain what is wrong with each sentence. Explain that the names of places and groups are proper nouns and should be capitalized. Have students write a sentence about each term based on the information.
SUBSTANTIAL/MODERATE

TEACH

ENGLISH LEARNER SUPPORT

Understand Synonyms Explain that synonyms are words that have similar meanings and that not all synonyms will produce the same effect as the original word choice. Display line 12 and highlight *abandoned*. Discuss feelings and ideas associated with the word (*deserted, useless, obsolete, discarded*). Then replace *abandoned* with a synonym, such as *empty*. Discuss how changing the word also changes the line's impact.

LIGHT

For **listening support** for students at varying proficiency levels, see the **Text X-Ray** on page 200C.

 **ANALYZE LITERARY DEVICES**

Remind students that an allusion is an indirect reference to another literary work or to a famous person, place, or event.

Students may say that all the allusions relate to places near the Grand Coulee Dam in Washington state. Have students go online to research some of the places Alexie alludes to in the poem.

CONTRASTS AND CONTRADICTIONS

Explain to students that this signpost is often used to set up a **compare-and-contrast** pattern of organization. The repeated words at the beginning of each sentence state that the speaker "shall" forgive, but the speaker then says it will happen "after" something impossible happens. The contrast between the speaker's stated willingness to forgive and the impossible conditions for that forgiveness create the irony.

 NOTICE & NOTE

ANALYZE LITERARY DEVICES

Annotate: Mark examples of allusions in lines 8–15.

Compare: What do all these allusions have in common? How could you find out more about them?

CONTRASTS AND CONTRADICTIONS

Notice & Note: In lines 1–16, circle the repeated words about forgiveness. Underline other text that contradicts or contrasts with those words.

Analyze: What is ironic, or contradictory, about the speaker's statements about forgiveness?

and so I shall after the first drop of floodwater is swallowed
    by that salmon
10 waiting in the Pacific. I am told by many of you that I must
    forgive and so I shall
    after that salmon swims upstream, through the mouth of the
    Columbia
    and then past the flooded cities, broken dams and abandoned
    reactors
    of Hanford,² I am told by many of you that I must forgive and
    so I shall
    after that salmon swims through the mouth of the Spokane
    River
15 as it meets the Columbia, then upstream, until it arrives
    in the shallows of a secret bay on the reservation where I wait
    alone.
    I am told by many of you that I must forgive and so I shall after
    that salmon leaps into the night air above the water, throws
    a lightning bolt at the brush near my feet, and starts the fire
20 which will lead all of the lost Indians home. I am told
    by many of you that I must forgive and so I shall
    after we Indians have gathered around the fire with that salmon
    who has three stories it must tell before sunrise: one story will
        teach us
    how to pray; another story will make us laugh for hours;
25 the third story will give us reason to dance. I am told by many
    of you that I must forgive and so I shall when I am dancing
    with my tribe during the powwow at the end of the world.

² **reactors of Hanford:** a series of abandoned nuclear reactors along the Columbia River.

204   Unit 3

APPLYING ACADEMIC VOCABULARY

❏ contribute   ❏ immigrate   ☑ reaction   ❏ relocate   ☑ shifting

THINK-PAIR-SHARE Have students turn to a partner and discuss the questions below. Encourage students to include the Academic Vocabulary words *reaction* and *shifting* in their responses. Ask for volunteers to share their answers with the class.

- What is the speaker's **reaction** to being told to forgive?
- What **shifting** occurred in the Native American economy after the Grand Coulee Dam was built?

CHECK YOUR UNDERSTANDING

Answer these questions before moving on to the **Analyze the Text** section on the following page.

1 The speaker most likely repeats the words "I am told by many of you that I must forgive and so I shall" to —

 A stress that he or she forgives everything

 B emphasize the irony in the poem

 C joke about how difficult forgiveness can be

 D explain that building the dams was not that important

2 The lines "I must forgive and so I shall when I am dancing / with my tribe during the powwow at the end of the world" emphasize that the speaker is —

 F never going to forgive the dam builders

 G willing to forgive the people who built the dams

 H going to dance at a party very soon

 J confused about when the tribe will reunite

3 Which of the following is an important idea in the poem?

 A How technology can improve lives

 B The impossibility of forgiving great wrongs

 C How problems can bring changes

 D The power of business and commerce

The Powwow at the End of the World   205

CHECK YOUR UNDERSTANDING

Have students answer the questions independently.

Answers:

 1. *B*

 2. *F*

 3. *B*

If they answer any questions incorrectly, have them reread the text to confirm their understanding. Then they may proceed to ANALYZE THE TEXT on page 206.

 ## ENGLISH LEARNER SUPPORT

Oral Assessment Use the following questions to assess students' comprehension and speaking skills:

1. Why did the speaker repeat the phrase "I am told by many of you that I must forgive and so I shall"? *(to emphasize the irony in the poem)*

2. What do the following lines emphasize about the speaker: "I must forgive and so I shall when I am dancing / with my tribe during the powwow at the end of the world"? *(These words emphasize that the speaker is never going to forgive the dam builders.)*

3. Which idea is an important idea in the poem? *(the impossibility of forgiving great wrongs)* **SUBSTANTIAL/MODERATE**

ANALYZE THE TEXT

Possible answers:

1. **DOK 2:** *To the speaker, the dam has caused great harm and must be destroyed. The image of an Indian woman putting her shoulder to the Grand Coulee Dam and making it topple suggests the speaker's anger toward the dam.*

2. **DOK 3:** *The image appeals to the sense of touch, sound, and sight. The power of the floodwaters breaking through each dam is similar to the powerful feelings the poet has for it to be destroyed.*

3. **DOK 3:** *Possible answer:* *The line breaks call attention to the irony in the poem. The repetition of "so I shall / after" emphasizes that even though others are pressuring the speaker to forgive the dam builders, the speaker won't do so until many impossible things happen—which implies he will never forgive.*

4. **DOK 3:** *The speaker will never show forgiveness until impossible things happen, such as the Grand Coulee being toppled by a Native American woman and a salmon throwing a lightning bolt to start a signal fire. The speaker will only forgive after all wrongs have been righted in the future.*

5. **DOK 4:** *The irony becomes more intense at the end of the poem as the conditions for forgiveness become more fantastic. The speaker describes a gathering of Native Americans who have lost their homes and way of life convened by a magical salmon who tells wonderful stories at the powwow. Healing the damage inflicted on the speaker's people is as likely as this "powwow at the end of the world."*

RESEARCH

Remind students that when they read an article, they need to decide whether the information is accurate and reliable. Tell them that a writer's viewpoint, or bias, can influence his or her choice of what to report and how to report it. Tell students that they should consider the source of the article and whether they expect it to be fair and balanced.

Connect Even though the dam helped many people by making electricity, it made it impossible for native peoples to catch the salmon that were important to their economy and culture.

 RESPOND

ANALYZE THE TEXT

Support your responses with evidence from the text. ☷ NOTEBOOK

1. **Infer** The poem begins with an allusion to the Grand Coulee Dam, built on the Columbia River in the mid-20th century and widely considered to be an engineering marvel. Reread lines 1–3. What is the speaker's view of the mighty dam? Tell what image helps you understand the speaker's feelings about the dam.

2. **Interpret** Identify the imagery in lines 4–5. To what senses does it appeal? Explain what this imagery suggests about the intensity of the speaker's feelings.

3. **Evaluate** Read aloud lines 10–16. Notice that the line breaks do not always come at the ends of sentences. What effect do the line breaks have on the poem's rhythm, mood, or tone? Why do you think the poet chooses to break the lines where he does?

4. **Draw Conclusions** When will the speaker show forgiveness? Identify the lines in the poem that help you answer.

5. **Notice & Note** Reread lines 17–27. Does the speaker's irony become more intense at the end of the poem? Explain.

RESEARCH TIP
When you research online, think about possible biases that the sites' creators may have. For instance, a site designed to encourage people to visit the Grand Coulee Dam will most likely discuss it positively. A site created by an affected Native American group, such as the Colville or the Spokane, may view the dam negatively.

RESEARCH

With a partner, research the Grand Coulee Dam and its effects on the environment and on the Native American cultures in the Pacific Northwest. Use what you learn to answer these questions.

QUESTION	ANSWER
How do people use the power that the dam generates?	*to make electricity*
What effect has the dam had on the salmon population?	*The salmon could no longer breed, so they no longer exist in that area.*
Flooding from the dam left some towns permanently underwater. What were the names of some of those towns?	*Inchelium, Kettle Falls*

Connect In a small group, present your results. Discuss how your research affected your understanding of the poem. What long-lasting effects did the building of the Grand Coulee Dam have?

WHEN STUDENTS STRUGGLE . . .

Identify Key Details Have students create a chart that describes what the salmon does in the poem. Then have students write what they infer about the salmon based on these details.

What salmon does	Inference
swallows the first drop of floodwater	
swims though the mouth of the Spokane River	
leaps into the night air above the water	

CREATE AND DEBATE

Write a Poem Write a poem that includes the line repeated in Alexie's poem: "I am told by many of you that I must forgive and so I shall." Use these guidelines to help you plan and draft your poem.

- ❏ Decide if you want your poem to be serious or funny.
- ❏ Use a free-verse structure, and think about where you will break lines and why.
- ❏ Use strong imagery that creates clear mental pictures for your reader.

Hold a Debate Research how dams affect people and wildlife. Then hold a debate in which half the class argues that dams are helpful and the other half argues that dams are harmful.

- ❏ Research the benefits and drawbacks of dams. Use at least three sources. Look for sources that have opposing viewpoints.
- ❏ Set time limits for each speaker to make sure everyone who wants to contribute to the debate gets equal time.
- ❏ When it's your turn to present your side's argument, make eye contact with audience members, speak at an appropriate volume and at an appropriate rate, enunciate your words clearly, and make natural hand gestures to emphasize your points.

RESPOND TO THE ESSENTIAL QUESTION

 What are the places that shape who you are?

Gather Information Review your annotations and notes on "The Powwow at the End of the World." Then, add relevant details to your Response Log. As you determine which information to include, think about:

- how allusions to a real-life place can enrich a poem
- how vivid imagery can capture a reader's attention
- why people often feel attached to the places that shaped them

At the end of the unit, you may use your notes to help you write a short story.

 Go to the **Writing Studio** for more on writing a poem.

 Go to the **Speaking and Listening Studio** for more on holding a debate.

ACADEMIC VOCABULARY
As you write and discuss what you learned from the poem, be sure to use the Academic Vocabulary words. Check off each of the words that you use.

- ❏ **contribute**
- ❏ **immigrate**
- ❏ **reaction**
- ❏ **relocate**
- ❏ **shifting**

CREATE AND DEBATE

Write a Poem Student poems should use a line from the Alexie poem but apply it to a different situation. Poems should be free verse and contain purposeful line breaks and imagery. Students should be able to explain why they broke the lines as they did.

 For **writing support** for students at varying proficiency levels, see the **Text X-Ray** on page 200D.

Hold a Debate Debate presentations should be based on evidence and clearly present the advantages and drawbacks of dams. Presenters should make eye contact with audience members, enunciate, speak clearly and at an appropriate volume, and use natural hand gestures. Presenters should also finish within the time limit allotted. Students who are not presenting should take notes and ask thoughtful, respectful questions about the other side's presentation.

■ English Learner Support

Practice Debate Language Prepare students for participating in a debate by introducing them to appropriate debate language. Have students practice these phrases.

- **Stating an Opinion:** *In my opinion . . . , As far as I'm concerned . . . , It seems to me that . . . ,*
- **Introducing a Point:** *First of all, I'd like to say . . . , The main point I have to raise is this . . . ,*
- **Disagreeing:** *I'm sorry, but I don't agree . . . , It is not always true that . . . , I beg to differ. . . ,*
- **Interrupting:** *About your point, may I just add . . . , Excuse me, but . . . ,*
- **Clarifying:** *Would you say that . . . , If that is true, then what about . . . .* **ALL LEVELS**

For **speaking support** for students at varying proficiency levels, see the **Text X-Ray** on page 200D.

RESPOND TO THE ESSENTIAL QUESTION

Allow time for students to add details from "The Powwow at the End of the World" to their Unit 5 Response Logs.

COLLABORATE AND COMPARE

NEW IMMIGRANTS SHARE THEIR STORIES
Documentary directed by Lisa Gossels

A COMMON BOND
Informational Text by Brooke Hauser

GENRE ELEMENTS
DOCUMENTARY AND INFORMATIONAL TEXT

Remind students that the purpose of both **documentaries and informational text** is to present facts and information. Point out that the two genres differ in the ratio of verbal to visual content. Explain that documentaries use film techniques to provide key information verbally, but a greater amount of information is typically provided visually. Tell them that, informational text, on the other hand, typically provides the greater amount of information verbally as text and might elaborate on the text with some additional visual content.

LEARNING OBJECTIVES

- Analyze and compare features of documentaries and informational text.
- Research to find high schools that serve recent immigrants.
- Write a letter requesting information.
- Determine meanings of multiple-meaning words
- Conduct and record interviews.
- **Language** Discuss with a partner the use of quotations as a way to add interest and credibility to a text.

TEXT COMPLEXITY

Quantitative Measures	A Common Bond	Lexile: 1150L
Qualitative Measures	**Ideas Presented** Text is simple, literal, and direct.	
	Structure Used Text is direct and builds on ideas supported through subheads.	
	Language Used Mostly literal, familiar language.	
	Knowledge Required Relies on outside knowledge about countries, religions, customs, and schools.	

Online **Ed**

RESOURCES

- Unit 3 Response Log
- 🔊 Selection Audio
- 📖 Reading Studio: Notice & Note
- 📰 Writing Studio: Writing Narratives
- 💬 Speaking and Listening Studio: Participating in Collaborative Discussions
- Vocabulary Studio: Multiple-Meaning Words
- ❗ Grammar Studio: Module 14: Lesson 5: Restrictive and Nonrestrictive Clauses
- ✅ "A Common Bond" Selection Test

SUMMARIES

English

"New Immigrants Share Their Stories" Documentary:

In New York City, St. Luke's Middle School students interview Newcomer's High School students about being immigrants. In addition, some teachers share ideas and some students share their thoughts in video diaries.

"A Common Bond" Selection:

Newcomer's High School in New York City is a second home to new-immigrant students. It helps these students find an American identity and provides students with a global perspective.

Spanish

Documental "Los nuevos inmigrantes comparten sus historias":

En la ciudad de Nueva York, los estudiantes de la escuela media San Luke entrevistan a los estudiantes de la escuela secundaria de los "Newcomer" acerca de ser inmigrantes. Adicionalmente, algunos profesores comparten ideas y algunos estudiantes comparten sus pensamientos en video diarios.

"Un Vínculo Común" Selección

La escuela secundaria de los "Newcomer", en la ciudad de Nueva York es una segunda casa para los estudiantes inmigrantes nuevos; ayuda a estos estudiantes a encontrar una identidad americana y provee a sus estudiantes con una perspectiva global.

SMALL-GROUP OPTIONS

Have students work in small groups to read and discuss the selection.

Reciprocal Teaching

Have students watch the documentary. Then, ask them to use these question stems to write three to five questions about the documentary:

- *Why did the middle school students . . . ?*
- *How can the teachers . . . ?*
- *Why would the immigrant students . . . ?*
- *Why do the students seem to . . . ?*

Make sure students understand that they can ask questions without knowing the answer.

Have students discuss question answers in small groups, decide by consensus on the best answer, and find text evidence to support it.

Pinwheel Discussion

Have students arrange their chairs forming inner and outer circles. Inner circle chairs should face out with backs not quite touching. Outer circle chairs should each face one inner circle chair creating a discussion pair.

Allowing two to three minutes per question, ask students to discuss questions such as in the following list. Have students in the outer circle rotate one chair before starting each question.

- *Is it a good idea for immigrant children to go to a separate school?*
- *How can teachers handle 30–60 different languages?*

Text X-Ray: English Learner Support
for *New Immigrants Share Their Stories and "A Common Bond"*

Use the Text X-Ray and the supports and scaffolds in the Teacher's Edition to help guide students at different proficiency levels through the selection.

INTRODUCE THE SELECTION
DISCUSS THE IMMIGRANT STUDENT EXPERIENCE

In this lesson, students will need to explore how a home-like school setting can help shape the lives of children who are new immigrants to the United States. Read paragraph 6 with students and then have students individually complete each of the following sentences. Ask volunteers who are new immigrants to share their personal experiences related to these questions.

- *The hardest part about not speaking the language of the country in which I live would be _____.*
- *When trying to learn a new language, I think I would _____.*
- *A part of my culture that I would want to keep even if I were living in a different country would be _____.*
- *If I had to suddenly move to a new country and leave my extended family and friends, one thing I would try to do to handle it all would be to _____.*
- *One priority of mine that would probably change if I was suddenly forced to move for my family's safety would be _____.*
- *When I see someone who is clearly from another culture, I _____.*

CULTURAL REFERENCES

The following words and phrases may be unfamiliar to students:

- *rising senior* (paragraph 5): a student who will soon be a senior
- *biculturalism* (paragraph 18): the presence of two different cultures
- *global perspective* (paragraph 20): an understanding or mental view of cultures around the world

LISTENING

Understand the Building Bridges Project

Draw students' attention to the point about 2:15 into the video in which the narrator describes the Building Bridges project. Discuss that this project exists between these two schools because two teachers decided it would be a good learning experience.

Have students listen to the description of the Building Bridges project (2:15–2:48). Use the following supports with students at varying proficiency levels:

- Tell students you will ask questions about what they just heard. Model that they should give a thumbs up for yes and a thumbs down for no. Ask: *Is an immigrant story something immigrants have to write to get into the U.S.?* (no) **SUBSTANTIAL**
- Discuss that each immigrant story is a little or a lot different from others. Ask: *What is it that makes each immigrant story different?* (reasons/situations) **MODERATE**
- Discuss that the video indicates the name of the project is "Building Bridges" and why they might have chosen that name. Ask: *What are the students planning to build bridges between?* (each other) **LIGHT**

SPEAKING

Discuss Film Features

Draw students' attention to the fact that film and text handle content differently. Point out that one of the main differences is that viewers rarely have to assume what something looks like in film.

Use the following supports with students at varying proficiency levels:

- Tell students that you will ask questions about the film they have just watched. For example, ask: *What can you learn about the people in the video that you cannot know from reading the information?* (**Possible answer:** *their looks and actions.*)   **SUBSTANTIAL**
- Discuss that a feature called "video diary" (0:58–1:41) showed some individuals' thoughts. Ask: *What types of photos were included in the video diaries?* (*personal ones*)   **MODERATE**
- Pair students to discuss film features. Ask: *How is what you learn from a video diary different from what you learn from an interview?* (*An interview is answering others' questions and a video diary is talking about what you want to talk about.*)   **LIGHT**

READING

Understand Quotations

Draw students' attention to the many quotations in the "A Common Bond" selection. Discuss that including quotations from others is a way for the author to add interest and credibility by including others' ideas and opinions.

- Work with students to read paragraph 7. Use the following supports with students at varying proficiency levels:
- Tell students that you will ask questions about what you just read aloud. For example, ask: *Whose words are quoted at the end of the paragraph?* (*Principal Nedda de Castro*)   **SUBSTANTIAL**
- Have students reread the quoted text. Ask: *Is this quoted information opinion or fact?* (*opinion*)   **MODERATE**
- Pair students to discuss why the author chose to use the quotations. Ask: *How would the text be different if the author, rather than quoting the principal, simply told you the same information in her own words?* (*It would not be as powerful because readers know that the principal really knows what goes on in the school and the author does not.*)   **LIGHT**

WRITING

Write a Letter of Request

Remind students to keep the audience in mind as they write their request letters and to be specific about what they are requesting and why.

Work with students to read the writing assignment on p. 223. Use the following supports with students at varying proficiency levels:

- Work with students to create a Venn Diagram comparing and contrasting school situations that would and would not be helpful to immigrant students. Then use the Venn Diagram to write a paragraph on the board. Have students copy the paragraph.   **SUBSTANTIAL**
- Provide sentence frames such as the following that students can use to write their letters. *Immigrant students benefit when _____. One thing that makes school hard for immigrant students is _____. Both immigrant students and native students could benefit from _____.*   **MODERATE**
- Remind students of the importance of being diplomatic when requesting information. Have student pairs think of something negative that some schools might do and write a question that diplomatically asks about the situation.   **LIGHT**

? Connect to the
ESSENTIAL QUESTION

The documentary *New Immigrants Share Their Stories* shows that, for immigrant students, high school can be a place that helps shape a new you in a new country.

COMPARE PURPOSES

Encourage students to discuss the purposes the authors likely had for creating their works. Ask: *Do you think the director and author want to inform, entertain, persuade, or express feelings or opinions? Have you ever watched a film based on a book that you read? How was your perception of the story different seeing it on-screen rather than in text on a page? How do you think what a director or author includes reflects their purpose? Why would a director or author only include positive information?*

DOCUMENTARY
NEW IMMIGRANTS SHARE THEIR STORIES

directed by **Lisa Gossels**
page 211

COMPARE PURPOSES

As you view the documentary and read the text that follows it, think about how each author achieves her purpose by using the unique elements of film or text to convey ideas. After you view and read the selections, you will collaborate with a group on a final project.

? **ESSENTIAL QUESTION:**

What are the places that shape who you are?

INFORMATIONAL TEXT
A COMMON BOND

Teens Forge Friendships Despite Differences

by **Brooke Hauser**
pages 212–221

LEARNING MINDSET

Effort Remind students that effort, such as working hard to compare a documentary and informational text, is necessary for growth. Emphasize that hard work leads to success. Make sure to praise students for their effort rather than for being "smart." Offer feedback on a specific situation for a specific student, such as "I noticed you put a lot of effort into your reading today. When you stumbled on *documentary*, you stopped, took a breath, and tried to sound the word out again."

QUICK START

Many families have dramatic stories to tell about how and why the first family members came to the United States. In a small group, take turns sharing immigration stories about your own family or someone else's.

ANALYZE A DOCUMENTARY

New Immigrants Share Their Stories is a **documentary,** a nonfiction film that presents, or documents, information about people or events. A documentary's **purpose** is the reason it is made: to inform, entertain, persuade, or express feelings or opinions. The opinion, claim, or idea a filmmaker wants to convey is the film's **message.** Documentary filmmakers usually have a **motive,** or a reason why they feel the story is worth telling. Here are some examples of motives and clues that can help you identify a motive based on the film's emphasis, or focus:

MOTIVE	FOCUS OF FILM / CLUES TO MOTIVE
Social	human interactions, changing behaviors or attitudes
Commercial	a product that viewers are encouraged to buy
Political	support for or opposition to government or laws

Documentary filmmakers combine visual and sound techniques to present information. These techniques can include:

- **Voice-over**—the voice of an unseen commentator or narrator. The narrator explains or clarifies images and provides important new information. *New Immigrants Share Their Stories* uses several narrators, including a commentator, teachers, and students.
- **Stills**—images that are motionless, such as illustrations or photographs. In this film, the students' video diaries include photographs from their years growing up in other countries.
- **Animation**—images that appear to move and seem alive. For example, *New Immigrants Share Their Stories* includes an animated graphic of travel across the globe.

To **evaluate** a documentary, you examine its techniques and content to judge its impact. Ask yourself these questions:

- How well does the film achieve its main purpose?
- What is the film's main message, and is it conveyed effectively?
- What techniques caught my interest? Why?
- What kind of motive did the filmmaker most likely have?

GENRE ELEMENTS: DOCUMENTARY

- provides factual information
- may investigate or tell a true story
- employs the basic elements of film, such as live footage, narration, music, animation, and on-screen text
- often includes interviews with experts or other people involved with the topic

---

QUICK START

For any students who do not know the story about how their families first came to the United States, encourage them to see if their parents or grandparents know. Make sure students understand that, because he United States is only about 250 years old, the families of most people who live in the United States has a fairly recent immigration story. As a group, brainstorm a list of reasons that families have immigrated to the United States.

ANALYZE A DOCUMENTARY

Explain to students that in this documentary, the director includes interviews, or conversations in which one speaker asks specific questions of another.

The director also includes video diaries, which are video recordings that share a person's personal views and on-the-spot reactions over a period of time.

Ask students to watch the documentary to identify how the interviews and the video diaries are alike and different. *(They both tell about the lives of the students; interviews have the students answer questions about their lives; the students make video diaries to tell about their own lives; video diaries may include maps and photographs.)* Prompt students to discuss the filmmaker's purpose for including both types of footage. Ask: *How do the two formats together present a more complete story? (***Possible answer:** *By their nature, video diaries present personal ideas and information that an individual finds important. The interviews reflect what someone else wants to know about the subject. Together, the formats provide a more complete view of the students.)*

For **speaking support** for students at varying proficiency levels, see the **Text X-Ray** on page 208D.

APPLY

ANALYZE TEXT ELEMENTS

Have students look through the selection and find examples of each text element that is listed in the table.

CRITICAL VOCABULARY

Encourage students to make sure they know the meanings of all of the vocabulary words before beginning to answer the questions.

Answers:

1. *Happy because being qualified to receive an award is a pleasant and exciting thing.*
2. *They would more likely need to learn to speak English to assimilate into U.S. culture.*
3. *I would be wearing it often because to embrace means to use and promote.*
4. *Yes, they should want to capitalize on their strengths because doing so would mean they were making the most of them.*
5. *It would make me anxious because unrest would mean there could be riots or violence.*

LANGUAGE CONVENTIONS:
Semicolons, Colons, and Parentheses

Have students look at the two sentences in the Language Conventions information. Ask: *Do these two sentences have restrictive or nonrestrictive clauses?* (They both have nonrestrictive clauses.) Ask: *Should punctuation be used with restrictive and/or nonrestrictive clauses and what punctuation?* (*A comma should be used with nonrestrictive clauses.*)

 GET READY

- provides factual information
- often includes graphic features
- typically makes use of text elements such as subheadings, boldfacing, sidebars, and footnotes

ANALYZE TEXT ELEMENTS

Text elements are print and graphic features that authors use to structure texts. As you read "A Common Bond," notice how these elements help guide your reading and achieve specific purposes.

TEXT ELEMENT	EXAMPLE
A **heading** is a text's title. A **subtitle** may follow the title and give more detail about the topic. **Subheadings** within the text introduce new topics or sections.	**A COMMON BOND** **Teens Forge Friendships** **Despite Differences** Part 1: A Second Home
Graphic features include graphs, charts, diagrams, photographs, and other visuals. Graphs present statistical information and show numerical relationships.	NY 4% FL 5% TX 18% CA 29% All others 44%
Footnotes are numbered notes that explain selected words or phrases in the text.	[1] **under the umbrella:** part of a larger organization.

CRITICAL VOCABULARY

eligible	assimilate	embrace	capitalize	unrest

To see how many Critical Vocabulary words you already know, answer each question and explain your answer.

1. If you were **eligible** for an award, would you be happy or scared?
2. To **assimilate** into U.S. culture, would immigrants more likely need to learn to speak English or become good at sports?
3. If you **embraced** a new fashion, would you wear it often or rarely?
4. Should people want to **capitalize** on their strengths?
5. Would **unrest** in your hometown make you sleepy or anxious?

LANGUAGE CONVENTIONS:
Semicolons, Colons, and Parentheses

In this lesson, you will learn how to correctly use semicolons, colons, and parentheses to punctuate sentences. For example, notice how the author uses a **semicolon** to separate two clauses in a compound sentence or a **colon** to introduce a list. **Parentheses** set off extra information that does not change the overall meaning of a sentence.

 ENGLISH LEARNER SUPPORT

Use All Text Features Discuss that text features provide an opportunity to gain meaning from text even if you cannot read it all. Explain that, for this reason, English learners should always pay close attention to text features. Ask: *What are some text features that could help you understand text?* (Some examples: photos, maps, diagrams, graphs, charts, headings, subheadings, underlining, bold, italics)   **MODERATE**

BACKGROUND

The Building Bridges project is a collaboration between two very different New York schools. Through letter writing, video diaries, and interviews, the English language learners from Newcomers High School in Queens, New York, tell their personal immigration stories to their "buddies" from St. Luke's, a private middle school in Manhattan. Together, students from both schools hope to change stereotyped ideas about immigrants. The documentary New Immigrants Share Their Stories *chronicles the students' project.*

PREPARE TO COMPARE

As you view the film, pay attention to the interviews between the immigrant students and their "buddies." Listen to the questions asked and the answers given. Also watch the facial expressions and gestures of the individuals. Think about what you learn about the two groups from these conversations. Write down any questions you have as you view the film. NOTEBOOK

GET READY

For more online resources, log in to your dashboard and click on **"NEW IMMIGRANTS SHARE THEIR STORIES"** from the selection menu.

As needed, pause the video to make notes about what impresses you or about ideas you might want to talk about later. Replay or rewind so that you can clarify anything you do not understand.

New Immigrants Share Their Stories / A Common Bond   211

TEACH

BACKGROUND

Have students read the background about the Building Bridges project. Tell students that the documentary was made by Not in Our Town, an organization based in Oakland, California. For almost 20 years, its mission has been to guide, support, and inspire people and communities to work together to build safe, inclusive environments for all. Not in Our Town has completed many projects in an effort to achieve this goal. The documentary about the Building Bridges project was filmed in 2010.

PREPARE TO COMPARE

Direct students to use the Prepare to Compare prompt to focus their reading. Suggest that they keep a sheet of paper handy so that they can make quick notes to help them remember questions they want to ask and ideas they want to discuss. Also, make sure students know how to pause, rewind, and replay.

 For **listening support** for students at varying proficiency levels, see the **Text X-Ray** on page 208C.

ENGLISH LEARNER SUPPORT

Determine Meaning Guide students to recognize that *newcomer* is a **compound word,** one formed by combining two words. Explain that they can often define a compound word by using the meanings of the smaller words.

ASK STUDENTS to define *newcomer* using the meaning of the two words it contains. Is Newcomers High School an appropriate name for the school that is the subject of the documentary? Why or why not?   **MODERATE**

BACKGROUND

Have students read the background information about Brooke Hauser. Tell students that Brooke Hauser published *The New Kids: Big Dreams and Brave Journeys at a High School for Immigrant Teens* in 2011 after spending a year at Newcomers High School in Queens. As an adult book that appeals to teens, Ms. Hauser's book won the American Library Association's Alex Award. The book is used in middle school through college curriculums.

PREPARE TO COMPARE

Make sure students understand that "individuals you get to hear from" in the text refers to quotations. Also, encourage them, while they are reading, to look for ways that the informational text is similar to and different from the video they watched.

✎ ANALYZE TEXT ELEMENTS

Discuss that **subheadings** provide a means for writers to organize their text and for readers to more easily understand and use the text. (**Answer:** *The article will be divided into at least two parts with subheadings introducing themes.*)

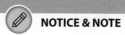

NOTICE & NOTE

BACKGROUND

*Longtime journalist **Brooke Hauser** has profiled a wide array of subjects, from Chinese beauty queens to former U.S. Secretary of State Colin Powell. However, in her first book, The New Kids: Big Dreams and Brave Journeys at a High School for Immigrant Teens, she chronicled the experiences of people who don't normally take center stage: recent immigrants who attend the International High School at Prospect Heights. The following text is informed by what she learned and whom she got to know while writing that award-winning book.*

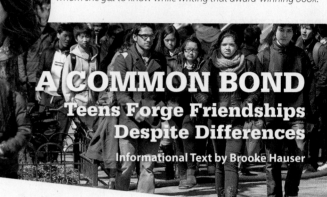

A COMMON BOND
Teens Forge Friendships Despite Differences
Informational Text by Brooke Hauser

Notice & Note

Use the side margins to notice and note signposts in the text.

ANALYZE TEXT ELEMENTS
Annotate: Mark the first subheading in the article.

Infer: Based on this subheading, what can you infer about the overall structure of the article?

PREPARE TO COMPARE

As you read this article, take note of the surprising facts and statistics you learn about students who have recently immigrated to the United States. Also keep track of all the individuals you get to hear from.

Part 1: A Second Home

1   Have you ever been the new kid at school? Or maybe you've known the new kid at school? Either way, if you answered yes, then you might have a little glimpse into the experiences of the students at the International High School at Prospect Heights in Brooklyn, New York. Started in 2004, the school serves recent immigrants and refugees to the United States. How recent? Well, some of the students come to America just months or weeks before the first day of school in September each year.

2   According to a book about the school written by the author of this article, *The New Kids: Big Dreams and Brave Journeys at a High School for Immigrant Teens*, the students hail from 40-plus different countries and speak nearly 30

APPLYING ACADEMIC VOCABULARY

❏ **contribute**   ☑ **immigrate**   ❏ **reaction**   ☑ **relocate**   ❏ **shifting**

Write and Discuss   Have students discuss with a partner the following questions. Guide students to include the Academic Vocabulary words *immigrate* and *relocate* in their responses. Ask volunteers to share their responses with the class.

- Why do you think that people who **immigrate** almost always have an interesting story to tell?
- Would you like to **relocate** to a city five states away?

languages: Spanish, Creole, Arabic, Fulani, and Tibetan, to name just a few. Imagine walking down those halls: They're noisy! In many ways, they're also a reflection of our country and what's special about America, which has always been home to newcomers.

3   Spend a few hours at the International High School, and you'll quickly realize that students here represent a range of backgrounds and beliefs. Some are Christian or Jewish, others Buddhist or Muslim. But despite their differences, all of the students share one very important thing in common: They are all learning English together. In fact, to be **eligible** for enrollment, students must have failed an English language assessment test and be relatively new to the country, says Joe Luft, Executive Director of the Internationals Network for Public Schools, which oversees the school in Prospect Heights and others like it around New York City, and beyond: "All of the students in our schools are recently arrived immigrant youth who are new to learning English. Generally, they've been in this country for less than four years, although the majority have been here for less than a year or two."

4   Maybe you've heard the term ESL, which stands for "English as a second language." The funny thing is, for many of these students, English isn't their second language: In some cases, it's their third, fourth, or fifth.

5   Take Nourou Sow, a rising senior at the International High School who immigrated from Guinea in West Africa when she was 12, along with her mother, older brother, and little sister. In her native country, Nourou grew up speaking Fulani, as well as Susu and Mandinka. So technically, English is her *fourth* language, but we don't have a term for that, like "EFL." The better term for these students is "ELL" for English language learner.

6   Learning a new language is hard enough, but English is just one part of what these students must conquer as new immigrants in America. They are adapting to a new way of life, too. Every once in a while, there's a student who has never been to *any* school before the International High School. Some students have fled from their homes in countries damaged by war, political strife, or famine. Some have spent time in refugee camps, where a formal education isn't an option. Many students grew up in rural places, such as on farms or in the mountains, and they can experience major culture shock when they arrive in New York City: They have to take a bus or subway to school, navigating new routes through the city, which can be a scary

eligible
(ĕl´ĭ-jə-bəl) *adj. Eligible* means qualified to be selected.

TO CHALLENGE STUDENTS . . .

Research Languages Challenge students to research where the languages mentioned in the text are predominantly spoken. Encourage them to create a color-coded map of the world representing the languages spoken by students at the school.

■ English Learner Support

Understand Contrasts Help students locate the words *differences, common, rural,* and *city* in the text, and make sure they understand the meanings. Then have students take turns calling out one of the four words to complete sentences you say, such as the following examples.

Chocolate cake and white cake have many _____, but they have sweetness in _____.

I live on a farm, so I live in a _____ area, not in a _____.
MODERATE

CRITICAL VOCABULARY

eligible: To be accepted into the school, students have to have low English skills.

ASK STUDENTS whether they think they would be eligible to attend Newcomers International High School. *(Only new English language learners could be eligible.)*

ENGLISH LEARNER SUPPORT

Understand Generalities Use the following supports with students at varying proficiency levels:

Have students look at the photo. Tell them that you are going to ask them some questions. Model that they should give a thumbs up for yes and a thumbs down for no. Ask: *Are these people in a building? (no) Do you think these people are having fun? (no) Do you think these people want to be here? (yes)* **SUBSTANTIAL**

Working in small groups, have students look at the photo and, in English, orally count the people. *(about 30)* Have groups compare their counts. **MODERATE**

Discuss the title of the selection, "A Common Bond." Explain that the students at Newcomers High School have a common bond because they are all trying to learn English and to find their way in America. Ask: *In what way do the people in this photo have a common bond? (They are all participating in a mundane trip on a crowded subway.)* **LIGHT**

Have students look at the photo, choose one person, and, in English, make up a short story about where that person is going and why.

WHEN STUDENTS STRUGGLE . . .

Learning Strategy If students struggle with numbers in English, have them create a 10-row, 10-column table like the one started below.

one	eleven	twenty-one	thirty-one	forty-one	fifty-one	sixty-one	seventy-one	eighty-one	ninety-one
two	twelve	twenty-two	thirty-two	forty-two	fifty-two	sixty-two	seventy-two	eighty-two	ninety-two

For additional support, go to the **Reading Studio** and assign the following Level **Level Up tutorial: Informational Text.**

prospect when you don't speak the language. A good number of students also work after school, some in restaurants or nail salons, to help provide for their families. Others help out with housework and childcare, cooking and cleaning, and looking after younger siblings.

7   For many students, the International High School at Prospect Heights is kind of like a second home in the city. "<u>What makes our school a welcoming place and feel like home is in the importance we put on relationships: You can only develop a relationship with a people if you spend time with them and do things together</u>," says the school principal, Nedda de Castro. Students and teachers get to know each other in small groups and different settings both inside and outside of school, on field trips, for instance. "<u>Even though they come from all over the world and may be very different from each other</u>," she says, "<u>they are all in the same boat and have much in common in their journey to becoming a new American</u>."

8   You may have heard the term "melting pot" to describe America as a place where people from different cultures and backgrounds mix together and **assimilate** into the whole, to create a new culture. At the International High Schools, there's another metaphor that students **embrace**, according to Luft. "The thing that I hear more than any other idea is the school as a family, in all its complexity," he says. "Everybody doesn't always get along, but ultimately they feel this very strong connection to each other and care about each other."

Part 2: A New Identity

9   Indeed, most of the students are learning a new culture, all the while honoring traditions from their home countries. When the school's first-ever graduating class wanted to organize their senior prom, first they had to figure out exactly what a prom *was*. The prom committee, made up of mostly African and Haitian girls, watched Hollywood prom movies as research. When the big night arrived, the girls and boys who went embraced many American prom customs, like buying corsages for their dates and getting their hair done at the beauty salon, but they also incorporated their own international touches. For instance, a girl from Bangladesh opted to wear a sari as her prom dress, and all the students danced to music from around the world.

10   For Lobsang Jampa, who's originally from Tibet, that was the best part: "<u>The disco</u>," he says and laughs. "The teachers

> **QUOTED WORDS**
>
> **Notice & Note:** Mark the quoted words in paragraph 7.
>
> **Evaluate:** The author could have paraphrased what the principal said, or restated the ideas in her own words. What is the effect of including the principal's exact words?

assimilate
(ə-sĭm´ə-lāt´) *v.* To *assimilate* means to blend into or become similar to the prevailing culture.

embrace
(ĕm-brās´) *v.* To *embrace* an idea means to accept and support it.

> **QUOTED WORDS**
>
> **Notice & Note:** Mark the quoted words in paragraph 10.
>
> **Evaluate:** Is the quotation essential to understanding the main ideas of the text? Why do you think the author included it?

 ENGLISH LEARNER SUPPORT

Multiple-Meaning Words Address some of the multiple-meaning words in paragraph 9:

Have students highlight the word *dates*. On the board, write yesterday and today's dates, draw a dried-prune date, and draw two stick figures holding hands. Say sentences using each of the different meanings of *dates*, and ask students to point to the correct meanings. **SUBSTANTIAL**

Read the words *customs*, *dates*, *touches*, and *wear*. Then say definitions for different meanings of the words, and ask students to identify the words.   **MODERATE**

Have students highlight at least six words in paragraph 9 that have multiple meanings and tell each other sentences using the different meanings. (**Examples:** *figure, customs, dates, done, touches, wear.*) **LIGHT**

 QUOTED WORDS

Have students reread paragraph 7. Ask: *How do they make the school a welcoming place? (They develop relationships with them.)* Discuss that **quotations** are only meaningful if readers understand who is being quoted and why. Then have students answer the question to address the effect of including the principal's exact words. (**Answer:** *Using the principal's exact words makes the paragraph both more interesting and more credible.*)

For **reading support** for students at varying proficiency levels, see the **Text X-Ray** on page 208D.

QUOTED WORDS

Discuss that **quotations** can be useful from both experts and non-experts. Then have students answer the question to address whether the quotation is essential and why the author included it. (**Answer:** *No; to add a personal touch to which readers can relate.*)

CRITICAL VOCABULARY

assimilate: America is a "melting pot" because people from many cultures blend together.

ASK STUDENTS how they would assimilate into a new high school if they moved. (**Possible answer:** *I would join a couple clubs and the volleyball team.*)

embrace: Students at Newcomers International High School support the idea that they are a family.

ASK STUDENTS to identify a holiday-related idea that they embrace. (**Possible answer:** *I like hiding Easter eggs for my little cousins.*)

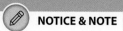 ANALYZE TEXT ELEMENTS

Discuss that the author included this **footnote** because she thought readers might not know the phrase "under the umbrella," and she did not want to define it within the text. Also, explain that whenever students see an superscript number following a word, they should always search on the page for a matching number followed by a description. (**Answer:** *The footnote explains that the phrase means "part of a larger organization" and helps readers understand that the International High School is part of a network of similar schools.*)

---

also danced, and they showed some funny moves that I had never seen, never expected."

11   While every culture has its specific traits, being a teenager can be challenging whether you're from Tibet or Texas. And as Nedda de Castro points out, an American teenager from another part of the country might actually share more in common with one of her immigrant students than with a native New Yorker. "For instance, a young person who lives on a farm in the United States could have more in common with one of my immigrant students who came from a farming community in their native country," she says. "You may not speak the same language, wear the same clothes, or even have the same religion, but there may be ways in which you understand each other very well and have the same values."

12   Like most kids, International High School students worry about what to wear on the first day of school and where to sit in the cafeteria and how to talk to someone they have a crush on. They also worry about getting good grades and getting into college. Nourou, the girl from Guinea, dreams of being a doctor.

13   Her classmate Daniel Coradin, a rising senior originally from the Dominican Republic, wants to be a professional baseball player like his idol, Derek Jeter. "My dream since I was 11 years is to sign with the Yankees," says Daniel, who moved to New York when he was ten.

14   Finally, Lobsang is determined to become a film director. His favorite movie? *"Forrest Gump,"* says Lobsang, who recently graduated high school and plans to study theater at college in the fall. "I love the story. It's not just one story, there's many different stories."

15   The same could be said about the high school. It's amazing how many different stories are inside of one school—around 415, in fact.

16   The International High School at Prospect Heights in Brooklyn is one of many schools of its kind popping up around the nation, from Bowling Green, Kentucky, to San Francisco, California. Many are <u>under the umbrella</u>[1] of the Internationals Network of Public Schools, which oversees 27 schools and academies with more than 9,000 students. In New York City alone, there are around 15 of these schools, serving newcomers who are learning English. At last count, the New York schools, combined, had students representing nearly 120 countries and more than 90 different languages.

ANALYZE TEXT ELEMENTS
Annotate: Mark the phrase in paragraph 16 that has a footnote.

Infer: What does the footnote help you understand about the International High School at Prospect Heights?

---

[1] **under the umbrella:** part of a larger organization.

IMPROVE READING FLUENCY

Paired Oral Reading   Model reading informational text with quotations by reading paragraph 10 aloud to students. Discuss that the goal is to read so that the content makes sense to you as you read and so that listeners can easily follow the meaning. Ask partners to take turns reading aloud to each other. Have students read paragraphs 11–16 in order, with Student A reading paragraphs 11, 13, and 15 and Student B reading paragraphs 12, 14, and 16.

   Go to the **Reading Studio** for additional support in developing fluency.

PERCENTAGE OF ENGLISH LANGUAGE LEARNERS IN PUBLIC SCHOOLS ACROSS THE UNITED STATES

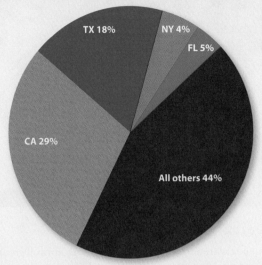

In 2014–15, there were nearly 5 million students who were English language learners (ELLs) in public schools across the United States. That's approximately 1 in 10 students. Most of these students live in five states, although every state has some population of students who participate in language assistance programs. Note: Not all ELLs are immigrants (some students born here grew up speaking a different primary language at home), just as not all immigrants are ELLs (many newcomers from England or Jamaica, for example, speak English as their native language).

17   New York City is very diverse. Any public high school is likely to have some newcomers, so some people wonder why there is a high school just for immigrants learning English in the first place. Wouldn't they be better off mixing with other students born here? But one idea behind these "international" schools and academies is that English language learners (ELLs) benefit from incorporating their native cultures and languages into the classroom.

18   "Biculturalism is something that we celebrate because when our students arrive in this country, they immediately begin a process of developing a new identity," says the principal, Nedda de Castro. "They bring all of the richness of their languages and culture from their own countries, and then, as soon as they arrive, they begin to develop an identity <u>that includes the new experiences they have in the United States</u>.

19   "Coming to a new place changes you," she adds, "but it does not mean that you leave everything behind or erase your past."

LANGUAGE CONVENTIONS

Annotate: In paragraph 17, mark the use of parentheses.

Analyze: Does the sentence make sense without the parenthetical information? Why do you think the author included it?

 **ENGLISH LEARNER SUPPORT**

Understand a Circle Chart Review with students how to read a circle chart. Discuss that the chart represents a whole — in this case, the percentage of English language learners, or ELLs, in U.S. public schools. Some sections are titled with an abbreviation of a state. Ask students to name the state represented by each abbreviation. Explain that each section of the chart represents the percentage of ELLs going to school in that state or area. The percentages in each section, when totaled, equal 100% of all ELL students in the United States. Encourage students to talk about which states have the largest section. Discuss what percentage of ELLs are in just five states (56%). Then have students work in pairs to write two or three questions about the information in the chart. Have volunteers ask and answer these question in a class discussion. **ALL LEVELS**

✐ LANGUAGE CONVENTIONS

If some students choose the first sentence, which has the word that in it, explain that the word *that* is used as a simple preposition in that situation.

Remind students that they do not place a comma before a restrictive clause. Add that the word which begins a nonrestrictive phrase and that a comma is needed before a nonrestrictive phrase. *(Answer: If that clause weren't present, the sentence would convey the incorrect notion that their identities didn't even begin to form until they arrived in the United States. Its absence would also fail to make clear that the author is referring to a reshaping of identity that happens when U.S. experiences blend with earlier ones.)*

 ENGLISH LEARNER SUPPORT

The Prefix *Bi-* Explain that the prefix *bi-* can mean both "twice" or "two." Provide this example: *Biweekly* could mean "twice each week" or "every two weeks." Direct students' attention to the word *"biculturalism"* in paragraph 18. Ask: *In this paragraph, does it make sense that the bi- in biculturalism means for "culture of every two people"? (no) Does it makes sense that, in this paragraph, the bi- in biculturalism means "two cultures for each person"? (yes)*
SUBSTANTIAL/MODERATE

ANALYZE TEXT ELEMENTS

Point out that, if you study the **graph** thoroughly, you will see that it provides quite a bit of information. Along with looking at the bars, encourage students to read the title, row and column labels, and the caption before responding. (**Answer:** *The dramatic difference in the bars' heights helps the author to emphasize what a huge positive benefit the International High School model clearly has on student outcomes.*)

■ English Learner Support

Reading Graphs Discuss that numbers and bar graphs are part of a universal language, but that titles, captions, and column labels are rarely in a universal language. Point out that you can miss or misinterpret critical information by not getting an understanding of the parts of a graph that are not in a universal language. Ask: *What does the 31% on the graph mean?* Make sure to use both the graph title and the column label before answering. (*The number of ELL students who graduate in New York City schools in 2016.*)
MODERATE/LIGHT

CRITICAL VOCABULARY

capitalize: Teachers look for ways for students to use their life experiences from their home countries as they learn to live in the United States.

ASK STUDENTS for examples of life experiences that they could capitalize on if they were learning to be film directors? (*their experiences watching and reacting to films*) Do you think that you would be able to capitalize on those experiences if you grew up in a country other than the United States? (*of course*)

NOTICE & NOTE

Part 3: A Global Perspective

20 In the classroom, students frequently work in small groups, along with students who speak other languages. Sometimes, students are paired together with friends from their home country who speak the same native language and are able to translate words and ideas into English. All of the students mingle with classmates from a range of other countries throughout the day, whether they're learning math, playing basketball in the gym, eating lunch in the cafeteria, or attending a meeting of one of the many after-school clubs. ("I was in chess club, photography club, magazine club, dance club, and fashion club," says Lobsang. "I was a male model.") In the process, they learn English in addition to picking up bits and pieces of other languages and cultures.

21 "Our belief is that language and content cannot be separated and therefore you have to teach them together," says Luft. "There's a myth that students can't learn meaningful content until they learn English, and we think that's not true. Teenage immigrants know a lot about life and academics from their home country. We should think about ways to **capitalize** on that."

22 This approach shows positive results: According to a recent study looking at English language learners over four years in New York City, International High School students graduate at a higher percentage than ELL students at other schools in the area (74% compared to approximately 31%).

ANALYZE TEXT ELEMENTS
Annotate: In paragraph 22, mark the information that is also represented by the bar graph.

Analyze: What does showing this information graphically help the author to emphasize? Explain.

capitalize
(kǎp´ǐ-tl-īz´) v. To *capitalize* on something means to use it to one's advantage.

WHEN STUDENTS STRUGGLE...

Reteaching: Common Words with Multiple Meanings In paragraph 20, have students locate the words *work* (1st sentence) and *range* (3rd sentence). Explain that both of these common words have multiple meanings. Have students create a table for these and other multiple-meaning words.

Word	Meaning 1	Meaning 2	Meaning 3
work	Noun: Place to earn money	Verb: to put out effort	Verb: to meet needs

 For additional support, go to the **Reading Studio** and assign the following **Level Up** tutorial: **Informational Text.**

23 "You want students to use all of the tools they have; that's part of what education should teach you, how to use every tool and source at your disposal," Luft says. "Think of a carpenter trying to bang in a nail," he adds: "You wouldn't tell a carpenter to build something and take the hammer away, and say, 'OK, do the job without your most important tool.' So the whole idea of telling a student, 'Don't use your language,' or that it's not important… It's how they think, and it's often a part of how they express their emotions. It's an integral part of who they are as a person. You should always try to capitalize on all aspects of who you are as a person and extend that into learning."

NOTICE & NOTE

BIG QUESTIONS

Notice & Note: One question you should ask yourself when reading nonfiction text is "What challenged, changed, or confirmed what I already knew?" Mark any details in the bar graph that help you answer this question.

Summarize: How does the information in the graph connect with what you already knew or believed to be true about graduation rates?

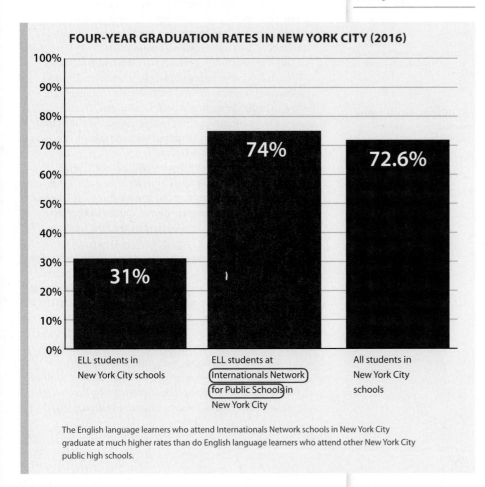

FOUR-YEAR GRADUATION RATES IN NEW YORK CITY (2016)

- ELL students in New York City schools: 31%
- ELL students at Internationals Network for Public Schools in New York City: 74%
- All students in New York City schools: 72.6%

The English language learners who attend Internationals Network schools in New York City graduate at much higher rates than do English language learners who attend other New York City public high schools.

BIG QUESTIONS

Discuss that most people have some prior knowledge and previous ideas about many topics. Explain that, when exposed to some information, it sometimes helps to sort things out if you **summarize** both your prior knowledge/ideas and new information. (***Possible answer:*** *I would have thought that ELLs would have a below-average graduation rate simply because of the challenge of learning English. The graph shows that with effective support, they graduate at a slightly above-average rate compared to the general student population.*)

EL ENGLISH LEARNER SUPPORT

Know What You Know Help students explore what they already think or know about ELL graduation rates.

Tell students to answer *yes* or *no* to each question. Ask: *Did you think most non-ELL students graduated? Did you think ELL students could graduate at a higher rate than non-ELL students?* **SUBSTANTIAL**

Have students complete these sentence frames: *I thought _____ non-ELL students would graduate. Compared to non-ELL students, I thought _____ ELL students would graduate.* **MODERATE**

Ask students to each make a verbal statement indicating what they thought about ELL graduation rates before seeing this graph. Also, ask them to explain whether their thoughts had more in common with the 31% bar or the 74% bar. **LIGHT**

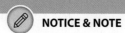 LANGUAGE CONVENTIONS

Explain to students that a **semicolon** is needed to link together two clauses that are closely related in thought, especially if the two clauses together express a contrast or clarify information. Semicolons also are used between two independent clauses that are joined by conjunctive adverbs or transitional phrases, such as *for example, of course,* or *in fact.* Phrases like these aid the semicolon in carrying the idea between the clauses. Semicolons signify a more definite break and a longer pause in reading than a comma does but less of a break than a period does. (***Answer:*** *A semicolon is used in this sentence to emphasize the relationship between the two independent clauses. The first clause says the mangú is like the plaintain, and the second clause makes clear in what way the mangú and plantain are similar. Linking the two statements with a semicolon makes a stronger statement than two sentences would make because it links the ideas.*)

CRITICAL VOCABULARY

unrest: One of the students is referring to political and safety issues in her home country.

ASK STUDENTS why it is not a good idea to visit a country where there is a lot of unrest. (*A country with a lot of unrest would likely be a dangerous place for visitors.*)

220   Unit 3

---

24   For some students, their native language *is* their identity. Take Lobsang, for example. His family left Tibet because they weren't allowed to live freely there under Chinese rule. Before coming to the U.S., he says, "We had to immigrate to Nepal to live the way we want." In America, Lobsang and his family are free to speak their language and honor their culture in a variety of ways. "Right now, I live in Queens, so I think of myself as an American New Yorker," says Lobsang, who embraces his Tibetan identity at the same time. "We still practice celebrations like the Tibetan New Year," he says. Nourou, from Guinea, honors her culture by attending West African weddings in the city. She also celebrates religious holidays such as Eid al-Fitr, which marks the end of Ramadan, when Muslims fast for a month. It's important to honor her culture here, she says, partly because **unrest** in her country has made her nervous about returning. "I can't remember a lot from there."

25   Another way students connect to their home countries is through food. The International High School at Prospect Heights sometimes hosts food festivals, where students are invited to bring dishes that reflect their culture. Daniel, from the Dominican Republic, brings mangú. "It's like green plantain; you mash it, and then put on some salami, egg, onions and cheese," he says. "It's delicious."

26   Meanwhile, Lobsang and many of the other Tibetan students enjoy *momo*, a kind of Tibetan dumpling. "In Queens, there's a lot of Tibetan restaurants, and we also cook Tibetan food," he says. "Even though the pizza and the burger taste delicious, we still eat traditional food to keep the tradition alive."

27   Now that he has graduated, Lobsang is looking forward to college and his dream of becoming a filmmaker. But he also took some time to look back at the past four years and all that he accomplished and experienced at the International High School.

28   "I made a lot of friends from different countries: Yemen, Mexico, Pakistan, I have African friends," Lobsang says. "It's kind of like a family; a family with different races."

29   When he was still a student at the school, he says, some of his friends from the neighborhood who grew up here would laugh about the fact that he went to an International High

unrest
(ŭn-rĕst´) *n. Unrest* refers to an unstable or turbulent condition that is often marked by protests or riots.

LANGUAGE CONVENTIONS
Annotate: In paragraph 25, mark the sentence that uses a semicolon.

Analyze: Explain why a semicolon is needed in this sentence instead of a comma.

IMPROVE READING FLUENCY

Echo Reading   Tell students that you are going to fluently read sentences from a paragraph and you want them to then practice reading fluency using the same sentences. Echo read Paragraph 24 by reading one sentence at a time and having students read the sentence back to you. Repeat once or twice to give students a chance to improve their fluency.

   Go to the **Reading Studio** for additional support in developing fluency.

School. "They called it 'immigrant high school,'" he says, "but they don't know how helpful the school is.

30   "If you are in a school with people from different countries, they share their problems, and it gives you more information to understand the world better," he continues. "If everyone is from same country and go to same school, then they don't have a lot of stories to share. Here, there are a lot of interesting stories."

CHECK YOUR UNDERSTANDING

Answer these questions before moving on to the **Analyze Media and Text** section on the following page.

1 Which of the following best expresses the focus of Part 2 of the text?

  A The purpose and organization of international schools

  B How and why immigrant students form new identities

  C Who benefits from going to international schools and why

  D The origins of most immigrants and the languages they speak

2 Which claim from the text does the bar graph best support?

  F *International High School students graduate at a higher percentage than ELL students at other schools in the area.*

  G *There's a myth that students can't learn meaningful content until they learn English, and we think that's not true.*

  H *Indeed, most of the students are learning a new culture, all the while honoring traditions from their home countries.*

  J *For many students, the International High School at Prospect Heights is kind of like a second home in the city.*

3 About which person do you learn the most from the text?

  A Nourou Sow

  B Nedda de Castro

  C Daniel Coradin

  D Lobsang Jampa

TEACH

CHECK YOUR UNDERSTANDING

Have students answer the questions independently.

Answers:

  1. *B*

  2. *F*

  3. *D*

If they answer any questions incorrectly, have them reread the text to confirm their understanding. Then they may proceed to ANALYZE THE TEXT on page 222.

 ## ENGLISH LEARNER SUPPORT

Oral Assessment   Use the following questions to assess students' comprehension and speaking skills:

  1. What is the focus of Part 2 of the text? *(The focus of Part 2 is how and why immigrant students form new identities.)*

  2. Which of the claims from the text is supported by the bar graph? *(International High School students graduate at a higher percentage than ELL students at other schools in the area.)*

  3. In the text, do you learn the most from Nourou Sow, Nedda de Castro, Daniel Coradin, or Lobsang Jampa? *(Lobsang Jampa)*
  SUBSTANTIAL/MODERATE

APPLY

ANALYZE THE TEXT

Possible answers:

1. **DOK 2:** *Students should note that ELL students may have to adapt to going to school because they may have come from refugee camps where they couldn't receive any formal education; deal with major culture shock when they arrive in New York City because they have spent all their lives in rural places; learn how to take a bus or subway to school because they are new to public transportation and to NYC; work after school because they have to help provide for their families; and help out with housework and childcare because their parents are too busy to do those things.*

2. **DOK 4:** *The scenes students choose will vary; accept reasonable choices. The voice-over narration provides background and general information throughout. The stills capture a moment-in-time of the students' lives. The animation of the globe shows the route one immigrant traveled to get to New York.*

3. **DOK 4:** *Students should note that the subheads introduce each new focus or subtopic, reveal the organization of the information, and help readers recognize the shifts in focus.*

4. **DOK 4:** *The circle chart shows that, in 2014–2015, most ELL students in the United States live in five states. The bar graph supports the author's claim that "International High School students graduate at a higher percentage than ELL students at other schools in the area." Both graphic aids also contribute to the article by adding visual interest and focusing the reader's attention on the statistical information they represent.*

5. **DOK 4:** *The author quotes Joe Luft, who is "Executive Director of the Internationals Network for Public Schools." His expert opinion about the connection between learning English and learning new content allows the author to make a strong point about why the school is effective.*

RESEARCH

Point out that students may opt to research facts and statistics similar to those presented in the two selections. Remind students they should confirm any information they find by checking multiple websites and assessing the credibility of each one.

Connect Students' discussions should highlight the similarities and differences that impressed them as being unusual, significant, and/or in sync with—or in opposition to—information presented in the documentary and text.

 RESPOND

ANALYZE MEDIA AND TEXT

Support your responses with evidence from the documentary and the text. NOTEBOOK

1. **Summarize** Reread paragraph 6. Then, briefly restate the challenges many immigrants must deal with besides learning English and why they may face these difficulties.

2. **Analyze** Identify an example from the documentary of each technique in the chart and note what it emphasizes.

TECHNIQUE	SCENE FROM FILM	WHAT IT EMPHASIZES
Voice-over		
Stills		
Animation		

RESEARCH TIP
To begin your research, review *New Immigrants Share Their Stories* and "A Common Bond" to identify useful search terms such as school names and locations as well as the names of organizations, experts, and administrators. Use these as starting points for online research. Then, follow links from your results to discover other similar schools and related information.

3. **Analyze** Review the subheadings in the text. What purposes do they serve?

4. **Synthesize** Choose one of the two graphic features from the informational text and explain what it contributes to the text.

5. **Notice & Note** What is the author's purpose for including quoted words in paragraph 21?

RESEARCH

Research high schools that specifically serve recent immigrants. Use the chart below to record what you learn.

HIGH SCHOOL	FACTS & STATISTICS	SIGNIFICANT SIMILARITIES	SIGNIFICANT DIFFERENCES

Connect Share your discoveries with a small group. Discuss which similarities and differences are most significant and why.

 LEARNING MINDSET

Try Again Point out to students that it is normal to find some or all parts of the Analyze Media and Text and Research tasks difficult, and that making mistakes is okay and expected. Encourage students to learn from mistakes and try again in a different way. Have students share mistakes they made and describe what they learned from them. As much as possible, make the classroom a "risk-free" zone where students feel free to take risks, make mistakes, and learn from them.

CREATE AND DISCUSS

Write a Letter Write a three- to four-paragraph letter to one of the high schools you discovered in your research. In your letter, request information that will help you determine whether the school is one that you would recommend to recent immigrants.

❏ Provide the date, your return address, the name and address of the recipient, and a salutation in correct letter format.

❏ Begin the body of your letter by explaining who you are and why you are writing. Then ask for the information you are seeking.

❏ Thank the recipient for his or her time. End with an appropriate closing, such as "Sincerely," or "Yours truly," and your signature.

Discuss with a Small Group Have a discussion about what makes you feel welcome at your school and what gives you a sense of belonging there.

❏ Review the text to identify ways in which the students form bonds with one another. Then consider whether you do anything similar.

❏ Identify school-sponsored activities at your school that help foster a sense of school spirit, unity, and belonging. During the discussion, listen actively to ask questions and comment respectfully on others' ideas.

RESPOND TO THE ESSENTIAL QUESTION

 What are the places that shape who you are?

Gather Information Review your notes on the two selections. Then, add relevant details to your Response Log. As you determine which information to include, think about:

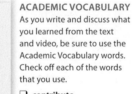

- factors that shaped the students' early identities
- current challenges students face and how these affect them
- what the students themselves say about identity

At the end of the unit, you can use your notes to help you write a short story.

 Go to the **Writing Studio** for help with writing a letter.

Go to **Participating in Collaborative Discussions** in the **Speaking and Listening Studio** for more.

ACADEMIC VOCABULARY
As you write and discuss what you learned from the text and video, be sure to use the Academic Vocabulary words. Check off each of the words that you use.

❏ **contribute**

❏ **immigrate**

❏ **reaction**

❏ **relocate**

❏ **shifting**

CREATE AND DISCUSS

Write a Letter Point out to students that they can use details in the documentary and informational text to come up with ideas that they think schools should implement. Explain that they could present each idea in a separate paragraph or combine related ideas within one paragraph.

For **writing support** for students at varying proficiency levels, see the **Text X-Ray** on page 208D.

Discuss with a Small Group Explain to students that forming bonds sometimes requires a willingness to take risks, such as offering your true opinions even when you do not know how others will react. Encourage them to offer their opinions freely and diplomatically.

RESPOND TO THE ESSENTIAL QUESTION

Allow time for students to add details from *New Immigrants Share Their Stories* and "A Common Bond" to their Unit 3 Response Logs.

APPLY

CRITICAL VOCABULARY

Answers:

1. *B*
2. *A*
3. *A*
4. *B*
5. *A*

VOCABULARY STRATEGY:
Multiple-Meaning Words

Answers:

1. *B*
2. *A*

 RESPOND

CRITICAL VOCABULARY

WORD BANK
eligible
assimilate
embrace
capitalize
unrest

Practice and Apply Select the best answer to each question. Then explain your response. If a word has more than one meaning, use the meaning that it has in the selection.

1. Which of the following would be a sign of **unrest**?
   a. a cold
   b. a rebellion

2. Which should make a baseball player **eligible** to play on the team?
   a. showing up to every practice
   b. showering every day

3. Which is a way to **capitalize** on hot weather?
   a. selling misting fans
   b. closing a store early

4. What is one reason to try to **assimilate**?
   a. to honor old traditions
   b. to connect with others

5. Which would you be more likely to **embrace**?
   a. more free time
   b. extra chores

VOCABULARY STRATEGY:
Multiple-Meaning Words

 Go to the **Vocabulary Studio** for more on multiple-meaning words.

Many words have more than one meaning. To determine the meaning of a **multiple-meaning word**, you can use clues from its **context**— the words, sentences, paragraphs, and punctuation surrounding it. In the example below from "A Common Bond," learning a language is identified as something new immigrants conquer. One meaning of *conquer* is "to defeat in war," but the context helps you understand that the intended meaning in this sentence is "to overcome."

> Learning a new language is hard enough, but English is just one part of what these students must conquer as new immigrants in America.

Practice and Apply Select the best meaning of each boldfaced word.

1. Lederhosen and dirndls are perfect clothes to wear in Switzerland, but to **assimilate** here, you will need to wear blue jeans.
   a. to absorb into the mind
   b. to blend into the main group

2. Ellie's friends all wanted to **capitalize** on her new job at the ice cream parlor by getting her to give them extra toppings.
   a. take advantage of
   b. invest funds in

224   Unit 3

🔵 ENGLISH LEARNER SUPPORT

Vocabulary Strategy Give students extra practice recognizing the correct meanings for multiple-meaning words. One at a time, call out the following words and meanings, and ask students to use them in sentences:

embrace: to hug a person

embrace: to accept and support an idea

capitalize: to use an uppercase letter

capitalize: to use to one's advantage   **SUBSTANTIAL/MODERATE**

224   Unit 3

LANGUAGE CONVENTIONS:
Semicolons, Colons, and Parentheses

Writers use punctuation to make the meaning of a sentence clear. Some punctuation marks, such as periods and exclamation points, indicate the end of a sentence and the end of a complete thought. Other marks occur in the middle of a sentence and help separate one idea from the next. The chart explains how semicolons (;), colons (:), and parentheses are used.

RESPOND

 Go to **Punctuation** in the **Grammar Studio** for more on semicolons, colons, and parentheses.

PUNCTUATION MARK	WHAT IT DOES	EXAMPLES
Semicolon	separates parts of a compound sentence with no coordinating conjunction	"You want students to use all of the tools they have**;** that's part of what education should teach you, how to use every tool and source at your disposal."
	separates items in a series that contain commas	There are schools for recent immigrants in Brooklyn, New York**;** Bowling Green, Kentucky**;** and San Francisco, California.
Colon	introduces a list	"I made a lot of friends from different countries**:** Yemen, Mexico, Pakistan. . . ."
	introduces a long quotation	Joe Luft explained that eligible students must have failed an English language assessment test**:** "All of the students in our schools are recently arrived immigrant youth who are new to learning English."
	follows the salutation of a business letter	To Whom It May Concern**:** Dear Mr. Luft**:**
Parentheses	set off extra information that explains or expands upon an idea in the sentence	"International High School students graduate at a higher rate than ELL students at other schools in the area **(**74% compared with approximately 31%**)**."

Practice and Apply With the help of a partner, review the letter you wrote. Look for sentences that could be improved or clarified by using one of the punctuation marks in the chart. Consider the following:

- ❏ Can I use a semicolon to combine two simple sentences with closely related meanings?
- ❏ Can I use a colon to add a list of examples or introduce a quotation from "A Common Bond"?
- ❏ Can I use parentheses to add an extra detail about one of my ideas?

LANGUAGE CONVENTIONS:
That and Which

Discuss with students that, when they read the rule that **nonrestrictive clauses** do not change the meaning of sentences, it doesn't mean that the clauses do not add additional information. Rather, it is only the core meaning of the sentence that does not change. Write the examples below on the board. Have students each re-create the chart that follows the question. As a group, work through the sentences and have students complete their charts.

- The living room, which has two open windows, is quite cool and breezy.
- The students need backpacks, which they will use every day.
- Tuesday, which is a day I can't miss school, is pizza day in the cafeteria.
- The show, which is on at 5:00, has my favorite actress in it.

Sentence	Core Meaning of Sentence	Meaning Added by Nonrestrictive Clause

Practice and Apply Point out that, when editing to exchange *which* and *that*, it is easy to leave commas in place that need to be eliminated. Make sure partners remember to set their clauses off with commas when using *which* but not when using *that*.

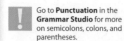 ENGLISH LEARNER SUPPORT

That* and *Which Help students understand how incorrect usage of *that* and *which* can change the meaning of a sentence. Write these two sentences on the board:

- *The store, which has a yellow sign, is on Main Street.*
- *The store that has a yellow sign is on Main Street.*

Explain to students that the first sentence says that there is one store on Main Street and it has a yellow sign.

Tell students that the other sentence means there is more than one store, and the one with the yellow sign is on Main Street.

Have students write their own sentences, using these clauses. Have them tell how each clause is used.

which I got from my mother

that I saw in the window   **SUBSTANTIAL/MODERATE**

APPLY

COMPARE PURPOSES

Before groups work on the Venn diagram, emphasize that they are comparing not only what they learned from the two genres, but also how the information was presented. By recognizing comparisons and contrasts, students connect ideas and elements that are similar and different, which helps them better understand how each of the sources are organized.

ANALYZE MEDIA AND TEXT

Discussions about the five questions should cover the following.

1. **DOK 2:** *The documentary and the text share similarities between the recent immigrants' personal stories about the challenges they faced.*

2. **DOK 2:** *The documentary focuses mostly on interviews between the teen immigrants and their middle-school "buddies" as well as the filmmakers' interviews with those buddies, which suggests that the documentarians had a social motive for filming this documentary.*

3. **DOK 3:** *While both clearly want to inform, just what they want to inform their audiences about is different: The documentary focuses on sharing a great program for encouraging and supporting immigrants and enlightening more sheltered students; the text focuses on sharing a new model for schooling recent immigrants that results in great success for them and why this may be.*

4. **DOK 4:** *Many immigrant teens experienced profound traumas and hardships as children and continue to face serious challenges that can make their lives in the United States much more difficult than it is for the average U.S. citizen.*

 RESPOND

Collaborate & Compare

NEW IMMIGRANTS SHARE THEIR STORIES
Documentary directed by Lisa Gossels

A COMMON BOND
Informational Text by Brooke Hauser

COMPARE PURPOSES

When you compare the information in two or more sources on the same topic, you also synthesize that information, making connections, expanding on key ideas, and even developing new questions. In a small group, compare and contrast the purposes of *New Immigrants Share Their Stories* and "A Common Bond." Remember, each selection may have been made to fulfill one or more of the following purposes: to inform, to entertain, to persuade, or to express the feelings or opinions of its creator. Complete the Venn diagram with similarities and differences in each selection's purpose and how effectively you think the purpose is achieved. One example is completed for you.

New Immigrants Share Their Stories   Both   "A Common Bond"

To inform viewers about a great system for encouraging and supporting immigrants and enlightening more sheltered students

To inform people about challenges immigrants face
To persuade people to have more sympathy and respect for immigrants

To inform people about a new model for schooling that results in more positive outcomes for recent immigrants and why this may be

ANALYZE MEDIA AND TEXT

Discuss these questions in your group.

1. **Connect** What similarities do you see between the immigrants' stories in the documentary and those mentioned in the text?

2. **Infer** Based on the focus of the documentary, what possible motives did the filmmakers have in creating it?

3. **Contrast** In what ways do the filmmakers' purpose and the writer's purpose differ?

4. **Synthesize** What do both sources reveal about the challenges recent teen immigrants face and how best to overcome them?

 ENGLISH LEARNER SUPPORT

Use a Venn Diagram Make sure students understand how to use a Venn diagram. Draw two-overlapping circles Venn diagram on the board. Add these labels: Left only: "Joe"; Center: "Both"; Right only: "Darva." Share this simple story and ask students to fill in the Venn diagram: Joe and Darva both like to play soccer. Joe scored a winning goal in a game, and Darva was awarded team captain. (*Answer: Joe—scored a winning goal; Both: Like to play soccer; Darva: was awarded captain.*) If time allows, add to the story and diagram.
SUBSTANTIAL/MODERATE

CREATE AND PRESENT

Now your group can continue unearthing the kinds of stories and information you learned about in the documentary and the informational text. Follow these steps:

1. **Choose a brief personal story to tell.** In your group, tell a brief personal story that you would feel comfortable sharing in an interview. The story you share might be a family immigration story, or it could be a story about another important event in your life.

2. **Choose a "buddy" to interview.** After everyone has shared a story, choose a "buddy" in the group whose story interests you.

3. **Prepare for the interview.** Use the chart to jot down details or aspects of the story that sparked your interest. Then list questions that can help you learn more. Use the interview questions from *New Immigrants Share Their Stories* as a guide. Keep your questions general and open-ended.

INTERESTING DETAIL OR ASPECT OF STORY	INTERVIEW QUESTION ABOUT IT

4. **Record your interviews.** Modeling the techniques you saw used in the documentary, take turns interviewing your buddies and recording one another's interviews.

RESPOND 🗩

Go to the **Speaking and Listening Studio** for more on conducting an interview.

VIDEOGRAPHY TIP

If you can use more than one camera angle to record each interview, that will give you the best opportunity to create an effective film. With different camera angles you can capture

- both people together from a middle distance
- the interviewee's facial reactions and verbal responses to questions
- the interviewer's reactions to what he or she hears and sees

Collaborate & Compare   227

CREATE AND PRESENT

Discuss that interviews can be both fun and enlightening. Have students gather in small groups. If possible, make sure each group has an even number of students.

1. **Choose a brief personal story to tell.** As group members share their personal stories, circulate among the groups and check that the stories are appropriate for telling in interviews. The stories should not reveal information that is too personal that could infringe on anyone else's privacy.

2. **Choose a "buddy" to interview.** Discuss that we all have personal preferences, so it is logical that each student would be more interested in some personal stories than others. If it appears that the buddy-choosing process will result in hard feelings, assign buddies rather than having students choose. In addition, if a group has an uneven number of members, have one group of three students do three sets of two people interviewing one person.

3. **Prepare for the interview.** Discuss that some people think that they can come up with interview questions "off the cuff." Explain that the best interview questions are brainstormed, written, and revised.

WHEN STUDENTS STRUGGLE . . .

Keep a Reading Log As students read their selected texts, have them keep a reading log for each selection to note signposts and their thoughts about them. Use their logs to assess how well they are noticing and reflecting on elements of the texts.

Reading Log for "A Common Bond"		
Location	Signpost I Noticed	My Notes about It

INDEPENDENT READING

READER'S CHOICE

Setting a Purpose Have students review their Unit 3 Response Log and think about what they've already learned about how places can affect people. As they choose their Independent Reading selections, ask them to consider what more they want to know.

NOTICE NOTE

Explain that some selections may contain multiple signposts; others may contain only one. Tell students that the same type of signpost may occur many times in the same text.

 INDEPENDENT READING

 ESSENTIAL QUESTION:

What are the places that shape who you are?

Reader's Choice

Setting a Purpose Select one or more of these options from your eBook to continue your exploration of the Essential Question.

- Read the descriptions to see which text grabs your interest.
- Think about which genres you enjoy reading.

Notice & Note

In this unit, you practiced noticing and noting three signposts: **Tough Questions, Again and Again,** and **Memory Moments.** As you read independently, these signposts and others will aid your understanding. Below are the anchor questions to ask when you read literature and nonfiction.

Reading Literature: Stories, Poems, and Plays		
Signpost	**Anchor Question**	**Lesson**
Contrasts and Contradictions	Why did the character act that way?	p. 3
Aha Moment	How might this change things?	p. 3
Tough Questions	What does this make me wonder about?	p. 152
Words of the Wiser	What's the lesson for the character?	p. 406
Again and Again	Why might the author keep bringing this up?	p. 2
Memory Moment	Why is this memory important?	p. 153

Reading Nonfiction: Essays, Articles, and Arguments		
Signpost	**Anchor Question(s)**	**Lesson**
Big Questions	What surprised me? What did the author think I already knew? What challenged, changed, or confirmed what I already knew?	p. 77
Contrasts and Contradictions	What is the difference, and why does it matter?	p. 241
Extreme or Absolute Language	Why did the author use this language?	p. 76
Numbers and Stats	Why did the author use these numbers or amounts?	p. 325
Quoted Words	Why was this person quoted or cited, and what did this add?	p. 77
Word Gaps	Do I know this word from someplace else? Does it seem like technical talk for this topic? Do clues in the sentence help me understand the word?	p. 240

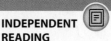
You can preview these texts in Unit 3 of your eBook.

Then, check off the text or texts that you select to read on your own.

POEM

My Father and the Figtree

Naomi Shihab Nye

For one girl's father, no house could truly be a home without a figtree growing in the yard.

SHORT STORY

Golden Glass

Alma Luz Villanueva

How can sleeping in a fort in the woods help heal a broken heart?

MEMOIR

from **The Latehomecomer**

Kao Kalia Yang

An immigrant family from a war-torn country adapts to American life, while a daughter struggles to survive.

RESEARCH STUDY

A Place to Call Home

Scott Bittle and
Jonathan Rochkind

Life in America is not the way many immigrants imagined it would be.

MYTH

Salmon Boy

Michael J. Caduto and
Joseph Bruchac

A young boy who does not respect the ways of his people pays a high price.

Collaborate and Share   With a partner, discuss what you learned from at least one of your independent readings.

- Give a brief synopsis or summary of the text.
- Describe any signposts that you noticed in the text and explain what they revealed to you.
- Describe what you most enjoyed or found most challenging about the text. Give specific examples.
- Decide if you would recommend the text to others. Why or why not?

 Go to the **Reading Studio** for more resources on **Notice & Note**.

INDEPENDENT READING

MATCHING STUDENTS TO TEXTS

Use the following information to guide students in choosing their texts.

My Father and the Figtree
  Genre: poem
  Overall Rating: Accessible

Golden Glass   Lexile 1010L
  Genre: short story
  Overall Rating: Challenging

from **The Latehomecomer**   Lexile 940L
  Genre: memoir
  Overall Rating: Challenging

A Place to Call Home   Lexile 1220L
  Genre: research study
  Overall Rating: Challenging

Salmon Boy   Lexile 700L
  Genre: myth
  Overall Rating: Accessible

Collaborate and Share   To assess how well students read the selections, walk around the room and listen to their conversations. Encourage students to be focused and specific in their comments.

 for Assessment

- Independent Reading Selection Tests

 Encourage students to visit the **Reading Studio** to download a handy bookmark of **NOTICE & NOTE** signposts.

WHEN STUDENTS STRUGGLE...

Keep a Reading Log As students read their selected texts, have them keep a reading log for each selection to note signposts and their thoughts about them. Use their logs to assess how well they are noticing and reflecting on elements of the texts.

Reading Log for (title)		
Page and Paragraph	**Signpost I Noticed**	**My Notes About It**

UNIT ③ Tasks

- **WRITE A SHORT STORY**

MENTOR TEXT

THE BOOK OF UNKNOWN AMERICANS

Novel by

CRISTINA HENRIQUEZ

LEARNING OBJECTIVES

Writing Task

- Write a short story about a person affected by a place.
- Use a graphic organizer to organize and plan writing.
- Focus on character, plot, setting, and conflict.
- Use a plot diagram to develop a clear and structured draft.
- Write using dialogue and descriptive details.
- Use the Mentor Text as a guide or model.
- Revise a short story based on narrative flow and on meaning.
- Revise based on partner feedback.
- Edit for spelling, punctuation, and grammar.
- Use a rubric to evaluate the revised and edited story.
- **Language** Write using transitions and transitional words.

Assign the Writing Task in *Ed.*

Online
Ed

RESOURCES

- Unit 3 Response Log

- Writing Studio: Narrative Structure

- Writing Studio: The Language of Narrative

- Grammar Studio: Module 10: Lesson 4: Using Pronouns as Objects of Prepositions

Language X-Ray: English Learner Support

Use the instruction below and the supports and scaffolds in the Teacher's Edition to help you guide students of different proficiency levels.

INTRODUCE THE WRITING TASK

Explain that a **short story** is a focused narrative that typically can be read in one sitting. Point out that the word *short* can have several meanings, mostly referring to a small size, and in this case *short* refers to length. Point out also that the Spanish word *corto* is similar to *short*. Be sure students understand that a short story is not just shorter than a longer narrative, such as a novel, but that it is more tightly written, with fewer scenes, fewer characters, and a plot that is addressed with few if any diversions.

Remind students that this unit focused on how places shape people: visiting a desert may be very different from visiting a city, and living in a large apartment can be quite different from living in a small house. Review with students that people are often shaped by places. Tell students that their stories will deal with people who are impacted by a place. Have students write sentences about a possible character, using sentence frames such as _____ *lived in (a/n)* _____. *He/she liked it because* _____. Have students use these sentences as a starting point for their stories.

WRITING

Use Transitions

Tell students that they can connect ideas and sentences in their stories by using transition words and phrases such as *then, later, in fact, but,* and *moreover*.

Use the following supports with students at varying proficiency levels:

- Use a paragraph or other selection from the Mentor Text or some other text students have read. Help students identify and mark transition words in the text. Have them work as a group to write pairs of short sentences that use these words. **SUBSTANTIAL**
- Use a paragraph or other selection from the Mentor Text or some other text students have read. Have students identify and mark transition words in the text. Have them work with a partner to write pairs of sentences that use these words. **MODERATE**
- Have students generate transition words. Have them work independently to write pairs of sentences that use these words. **LIGHT**

GRAMMAR

Pronouns and Prepositions

Draw students' attention to how pronouns are used after prepositions. Point out that the pronouns appearing after prepositions are not usually the same as the pronouns that appear at the beginning of a sentence: We would say *We are hungry,* but *Give the food to us.*

Use the following supports with students at varying proficiency levels:

- Present students with simple incomplete sentences in which a pronoun follows a preposition, such as *Friends gave the pictures to* _____. Have students choose the correct pronoun from a choice of two, such as *I* and *me.* (*me*) **SUBSTANTIAL**
- Have students write a correct pronoun to complete sentences in which a pronoun follows a preposition. For example, students can complete *Dad's dog took a walk with* _____ . (**Possible answers:** *me, him, them*) **MODERATE**
- Have students create sentences in which a pronoun follows a preposition. **LIGHT**

WRITING

WRITE A SHORT STORY

Introduce students to the Writing Task by reading the introductory paragraph with them. Remind students to refer to the notes they recorded in the Unit 3 Response Log as they plan and draft their stories. The Response Log should contain ideas about the connections between places and people. Drawing on these relationships will make students' stories more vivid and interesting.

 For writing support for students at various proficiency levels, see the **Language X-Ray** on page 230B.

USE THE MENTOR TEXT

Point out that students can use the excerpt from *The Book of Unknown Americans* to help them organize and tell a story, and explain that the language of the excerpt can be a good model for students as they write their own stories. Remind students, however, that they need to develop their own themes and events, along with an original writer's voice.

WRITING PROMPT

Review the instructions with students, making sure they understand each step of the process. Encourage them to ask questions they may have about the assignment. Make sure they understand that the story must include a conflict, a structured plot, and other features listed at the bottom of the page. Check that students have circled *how a character is shaped by an important place*.

 Go to the **Writing Studio** for help writing your short story.

Write a Short Story

In this unit, you read about how places shape people's lives. For this writing task, you will write a short story about a character who is struggling with an obstacle in relation to a place. For an example of a well-written story you can use as a mentor text, review the excerpt from *The Book of Unknown Americans*.

As you write your short story, you can use the notes from your Response Log, which you filled out after reading and viewing the selections in this unit.

Writing Prompt

Read the information in the box below.

This is the context for your short story.

> Where we come from affects who we are. Everything about a place—people and their culture, land, and history—contributes to our identity, our relationships, and our choices.

Think carefully about the following question.

This is the Essential Question for the unit. How might some of the people and characters from the unit answer it?

> What are the places that shape who you are?

Now circle the word or words that tell what your short story should be about.

Write a short story about how a character is shaped by an important place.

Be sure to—

Review these points as you write and again when you finish. Make any needed changes or edits.

- ❑ establish, develop, and resolve a conflict
- ❑ introduce and develop characters and a setting
- ❑ create a plot with a well-structured sequence of events
- ❑ use transitions to show sequence
- ❑ use dialogue, pacing, descriptive details, and reflection to develop characters and events
- ❑ provide a resolution that reflects a theme, or message, about life or human nature

---

 LEARNING MINDSET

Seeking Challenges Explain to students that having a growth mindset means taking risks, trying new things, and even, on occasion, failing. Trying things that are hard, and being willing to risk failure, helps a person grow. Experiencing challenges can help students gain strength. Encourage students to show persistence as they work. Model positive self-talk: "If I keep working on this part, I know I will make it better." Review with students that writers are constantly revising; fixing mistakes is a crucial part of the process. Emphasize that challenges are a part of learning.

① Plan

Short stories include made-up characters and events, many of which could exist or happen in real life. Before you start writing, plan how you want your story to be structured and what its main events will be.

Writers of novels, short stories, and narratives consider the following elements of fiction as they plan their work. Think about these questions as you begin planning your story.

Short Story Planning Table	
Characters Who is your main character, and what is he or she like? Who are the other characters in the story?	
Point of View Who tells the story? Decide if it will be a character in the story (first-person point of view) or a voice outside the story (third-person point of view).	
Setting What place is important to the character? What details can you use to describe the place vividly?	
Conflict What does the main character want? What obstacles does he or she need to overcome to achieve that goal?	

Background Reading Review the notes you have taken in your Response Log after reading the texts in this unit. These texts provide background reading that may give you some ideas you can use when planning your short story.

 Go to **Writing Narratives** for help planning your short story.

Notice & Note

From Reading to Writing

As you plan your short story, apply what you've learned about signposts to your own writing. Remember that writers use common features, called signposts, to help convey their message to readers.

Think about how you can incorporate **Tough Questions** into your story.

Go to the **Reading Studio** for more resources on Notice & Note.

Use the notes from your Response Log as you plan your short story.

UNIT 3
RESPONSE LOG

① PLAN

Allow time for students to read through the introductory paragraph and the Planning Table. Review with students that all four lines of the table are important, but remind them that this lesson's writing prompt calls for them to focus on a character and on a place. Thus, students need to be sure they are clear about who the main character is and what the setting will be.

■ English Language Support

Narrative Work with students to explore the differences between first- and third-person narration. Say: *I am drawing a picture* as you act out drawing; explain that the *I* indicates first-person narration. Then have another student pretend to draw and say: *He/She is drawing a picture.* Explain that this is third person. Have students practice these sentence structures. **SUBSTANTIAL**

▶ NOTICE & NOTE

From Reading to Writing Remind students that they can use **Tough Questions** to incorporate into their story.

Background Reading As they plan their short stories, remind students to refer to the notes they took in the Response Log. They may also review the selections to find additional information about the connections between people and places to give them further ideas for their writing.

TO CHALLENGE STUDENTS...

Writing Style Review with students that every writer has a particular writing style. Ask students to think about the writing style used by Cristina Henriquez in *The Book of Unknown Americans*. Have them generate words and phrases that describe Henriquez's style. As students write their own short stories, have them pay attention to the similarities and differences between Henriquez's writing style and theirs. Close by having students read each other's stories and generate words and phrases to describe other students' styles.

WRITING

Organize Your Ideas Tell students that making a plot diagram is a good way to ensure that a story has all the elements it needs. Review the diagram with students, focusing especially on the rise and fall of the action.

Have students begin by filling in the box on the lower left with information about character and setting as well as describing briefly what the conflict will be. Have students follow as you move into the next box above and to the right, where they should describe the initial events that create the conflict. Have students continue filling in the boxes independently. Remind them that they can use the Mentor Text as a model for how a plot can be structured. Tell them that they should use bulleted notes; this is not a time for writing full sentences or dialogue between characters.

Once students are finished, have them reread the ideas in the boxes to ensure that the plot makes sense and follows the structure shown.

2 DEVELOP A DRAFT

Explain to students that as they write, they may discover that they need to make changes to the plot structure they planned at the top of the page. As long as the changes are not enormous, this is fine. Explain that the draft fleshes out the outline by adding description, dialogue, and other story elements.

■ English Learner Support

Sequence Use the list of tasks in the Develop a Draft section to have students practice using time-order words such as *first, next,* and *last.* Encourage them to use some of these words in their stories as appropriate. **SUBSTANTIAL**

Go to **Writing Narratives: Narrative Structure** for help organizing your short story.

Organize Your Ideas Before drafting your short story, you need to organize all the ideas you have generated about your characters, point of view, setting, and conflict. Placing the main events of your story on a plot diagram will help you see the "big picture."

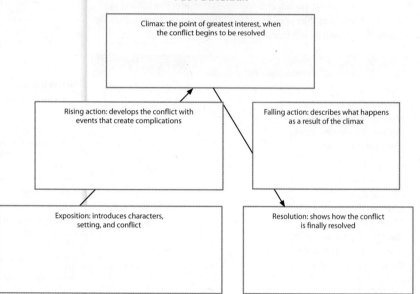

PLOT DIAGRAM

Climax: the point of greatest interest, when the conflict begins to be resolved

Rising action: develops the conflict with events that create complications

Falling action: describes what happens as a result of the climax

Exposition: introduces characters, setting, and conflict

Resolution: shows how the conflict is finally resolved

2 Develop a Draft

 You might prefer to draft your story online.

Once you have completed your planning activities, you are ready to begin drafting your short story. Refer to your Planning Table and the plot diagram you created, as well as any notes you took as you studied the texts in the unit.

- Introduce the main character, setting, and conflict.
- Establish the point of view.
- Create a sequence of events, using transition words.
- Use precise words and sensory language to create vivid pictures.
- Build tension as your story approaches its climax.
- Tell how the conflict is resolved.
- Leave the reader with a theme on which to reflect.

Using a word processor or online writing application makes it easier to make changes later, when you are ready to revise your first draft.

WHEN STUDENTS STRUGGLE...

Draft the Story Students may become frustrated because they are having difficulty translating their outline into story form. Write a brief description of a scene as it might appear in an outline, such as *Thomas argues with his friend.* Then model turning it into a paragraph with full sentences. A possible beginning might be *Thomas jammed his hands into his pockets. He was furious.* Do a Think-Aloud if possible to show students the process you are using.

Use the Mentor Text

Author's Craft

Your task in the exposition is to capture the reader's attention. Your first paragraph should include something intriguing, such as dialogue or a description, that gets your reader interested in reading your short story. Note the way the writer captures the reader's attention in this paragraph from *The Book of Unknown Americans*.

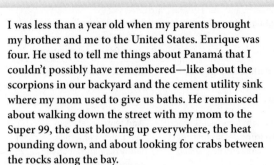

I was less than a year old when my parents brought my brother and me to the United States. Enrique was four. He used to tell me things about Panamá that I couldn't possibly have remembered—like about the scorpions in our backyard and the cement utility sink where my mom used to give us baths. He reminisced about walking down the street with my mom to the Super 99, the dust blowing up everywhere, the heat pounding down, and about looking for crabs between the rocks along the bay.

> The reader knows right away that the story will be told by a first-person narrator. The narrator provides vivid sensory details that describe an important setting.

Apply What You've Learned To capture your reader's attention, you might include details of setting, introduce an interesting character, or establish the point of view with a distinctive voice.

Genre Characteristics

Fiction writers give information about characters by describing what they say and how they act. Notice how the author of *The Book of Unknown Americans* describes a character's words and actions.

She'd become a genius at turning any and every little thing into a way to talk about Panamá. She would get a mosquito bite on her ankle and point out the welt to us, reminiscing about the bites she used to get in Panamá and wondering aloud "what the mosquitoes there looked like now," as if they were old friends.

> The narrator's mother attempts to persuade her husband to visit Panamá by evoking memories of their life there. Sensory details contribute to our understanding of this character.

Apply What You've Learned The descriptions of important characters in your story should include how they speak and act. Dialogue and sensory details make the characters seem real.

WHY THIS MENTOR TEXT?

The excerpt from *The Book of Unknown Americans* is a good model for the writing of a short story in which place is especially significant. Though the Mentor Text is a novel rather than a short story, the excerpt is structured similarly to a shorter work, and the setting is very important. Use the instruction below to guide students to use the mentor text as a guide for writing their short stories.

USE THE MENTOR TEXT

Author's Craft Have a volunteer read aloud the information in the introductory paragraph. Focus students' attention on the idea that the first paragraph of a story should draw the reader in. Have students identify vivid language and memorable details (such as *dust blowing up everywhere*) in the excerpt from the Mentor Text. Discuss with students how they might begin their stories in a way that will make readers want to continue reading them.

Genre Characteristics Point out that readers learn about characters in different ways, including through dialogue and through description of their physical features and emotional lives. Ask students to read the introductory text on their own. Then have them read the excerpt at the bottom of the page and discuss how the author reveals the character of the mother. Have students jot down specific details and snatches of dialogue that might reveal information about the characters in their own stories.

 ENGLISH LEARNER SUPPORT

Use the Mentor Text Use the following supports with students at varying proficiency levels. Begin by reading the first excerpt from the mentor text with students.

- Have students act out some of the activities mentioned, such as looking for crabs. Have classmates use full sentences to guess what they are doing. **SUBSTANTIAL**

- Have students underline words and phrases they do not understand. Have students ask partners for assistance in defining the words. **MODERATE**

- Have students summarize the information with a partner. Have partners compare their summaries with another pair. **LIGHT**

WRITING

③ REVISE

Have students go through the items in the chart one by one to see which parts of their story need revision. Remind students that virtually all first drafts benefit from careful editing and revision; leaving a first draft unchanged is not an option. Ask students to discuss the revision suggestions and techniques that were most effective for them.

With a Partner Have students ask peer reviewers to evaluate their stories by answering the following questions.

- Does the beginning of my story make you want to read on?
- Have I described the conflict clearly?
- Do my characters reveal themselves in details and in dialogue?
- What sections are unclear, if any? How are they unclear?

Have students use feedback from the peer review to add or delete details, events, or dialogue or to make changes in the story's organization as necessary. Remind them that the goal is to have a story that is as clear and as interesting as possible.

 WRITING TASK

 Go to **Writing Narratives: The Language of Narrative** for help revising your short story.

③ Revise

On Your Own Once you have written your draft, you'll want to go back and look for ways to improve your short story. As you reread and revise, think about whether you have achieved your purpose. The Revision Guide will help you focus on specific elements to make your writing stronger.

Revision Guide		
Ask Yourself	**Tips**	**Revision Techniques**
1. Does my exposition grab my readers' attention?	**Highlight** the exposition.	**Introduce** a character. **Add** dialogue and specific, vivid details of the setting.
2. Are my characters believable and well-developed?	**Underline** examples of characters' authentic speech and actions.	**Add** speech and actions that are original and unique to the characters.
3. How well does the setting affect characters and help shape the plot?	**Highlight** details of setting. **Underline** details that affect characters and help shape the plot.	**Add** sensory details to descriptions of setting. **Show** their impact on the characters and story events.
4. Is the conflict in the story clear? Do events build to a climax?	**Circle** details about the conflict. **Highlight** the climax.	**Add** details that make it clear how the conflict is developing. **Add** a strong climax.
5. Does the pacing keep the action moving, building interest and suspense?	**Underline** events that build interest and suspense.	**Delete** any unnecessary events. **Add** some foreshadowing.
6. Does my resolution reflect a theme, or message, about life or human nature?	**Highlight** the resolution. **Underline** phrases or sentences that reflect the theme.	**Insert** phrases or sentences that clearly reflect and/or state the theme.

ACADEMIC VOCABULARY
As you conduct your **peer review,** be sure to use these words.

- ❑ contribute
- ❑ immigrate
- ❑ reaction
- ❑ relocate
- ❑ shifting

With a Partner Once you and your partner have worked through the Revision Guide on your own, exchange drafts and evaluate each other's stories in a **peer review.** Focus on providing revision suggestions for at least three of the items mentioned in the guide. Explain why you think your partner's draft should be revised and what your specific suggestions are.

When receiving feedback from your partner, listen attentively and ask questions to make sure you fully understand the revision suggestions.

④ Edit

Once you have made the necessary revisions to your short story, you can consider how to improve the language in your draft. Edit for the proper use of standard English conventions, and make sure to correct any misspellings or grammatical errors.

Language Conventions

Pronouns and Prepositions A **pronoun** is a word used in place of one or more nouns. Personal pronouns change their form to express person, number, gender, and case. A **subject pronoun** is used as the subject of a sentence. An **object pronoun** is used as the object of a verb or of a preposition.

	Subject Pronouns	Object Pronouns
Singular		
First Person	I	me
Second Person	you	you
Third Person	she, he, it	her, him, it
Plural		
First Person	we	us
Second Person	you	you
Third Person	they	them

In your writing, make sure to use the objective case in prepositional phrases. In other words, use only object pronouns as the objects of prepositions.

> **INCORRECT:** Keep this a secret <u>between **you and I.**</u>
> **CORRECT:** Keep this a secret <u>between **you and me.**</u>

To check whether to use *I* or *me* in a sentence like the one above, try reading the preposition with each pronoun separately. "Between you" and "between me" sound correct. "Between I" does not.

⑤ Publish

Finalize your short story and choose a way to share it with your audience. Consider these options:

- Read your story aloud to the class.
- Post your short story on a classroom or school website.

> ! Go to **Using Pronouns as Objects of Prepositions** in the **Grammar Studio** to learn more.

---

④ EDIT

Tell students that it is often a good idea to read drafts aloud; sometimes writers catch errors when they hear the words even when they do not see the errors on the page or the screen. Review important aspects of punctuation and grammar, such as the proper use of commas and the need for subject-verb agreement.

LANGUAGE CONVENTIONS

Pronouns Point out that pronouns are used in place of a noun. Have students study the pronouns given in the text. Read several sentences aloud with nouns and then have students replace the noun with the correct pronoun. Examples might include *The girl gave the guinea pig some food/_____ gave the guinea pig some food* (*she*) and *The high waves threatened to destroy the ships/The high waves threatened to destroy _____* (*them*). Review the material on when to use the objective case. Ask students which of *She invited him and me to the party/She invited he and I to the party* is correct (*the first*).

⑤ PUBLISH

Students may choose either option for publication, assuming that time and technology permit. If students choose to read their stories aloud, encourage them to use a dramatic voice as they approach the climax of the story and to experiment with slightly different voices for different characters.

WHEN STUDENTS STRUGGLE . . .

Edit for Grammar and Punctuation Students who are not confident in their writing may have particular difficulty with the editing component in a writing project. It can seem to them that there are simply too many things to check, from appropriate use of pronouns to the correct placement of question marks. These students may benefit from being asked to check for a few specific issues in their stories. For example, if a student's story includes many sentence fragments, assign that student to seek out sentence fragments and fix them. Give each student a list with three to four items to check.

WRITING

USE THE SCORING GUIDE

Have students read the scoring guide carefully and assign themselves a score for each of the three items at the top of the chart: organization/progression, development of ideas, and use of language and conventions.

Point out that students' work will ideally earn a 4 in each category, but remind them to score according to the actual quality of the work, not what they wish the score would be. Explain as well that a lesser score can indicate areas for students to work on as they continue to write. You may have students rate each other's work in addition to their own. In this case, be sure to remind them to be kind and respectful as they score their partner's story.

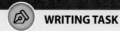
WRITING TASK

Use the scoring guide to evaluate your short story.

Writing Task Scoring Guide: Short Story			
	Organization/Progression	**Development of Ideas**	**Use of Language and Conventions**
4	• The event sequence is smooth and well structured, building to a satisfying climax and resolution. • The pacing is effective. • Transitions clearly signal shifts between settings. • The resolution clearly reflects a theme, or message, about life.	• A conflict is skillfully introduced, developed, and resolved. • A vividly described setting shapes the characters and plot. • Characters are well developed, compelling, and believable. • Dialogue and descriptions are used successfully.	• A consistent point of view is maintained. • Vivid, precise words and sensory language describe the setting and the characters. • Spelling, capitalization, and punctuation are correct. • Grammar and usage are correct.
3	• The event sequence is well structured, but it includes some extraneous events. • Pacing is somewhat uneven and confusing. • Transition words are used sporadically. • The resolution does not present the theme clearly.	• A conflict is introduced, developed, and resolved. • The setting somewhat affects the characters and the conflict. • Characters are interesting and have some believable traits. • Dialogue and descriptions are not consistently effective.	• The point of view is mostly consistent. • Some descriptive words and phrases are used, but there could be more sensory details. • Spelling, capitalization, and punctuation are correct. • Some grammatical and usage errors occur in the story.
2	• Some of the story's events are out of order or structured poorly, making the plot hard to follow at times. • Pacing is choppy or distracting. • Transition words are used ineffectively, if at all. • The resolution does not reflect a theme about life.	• The conflict is introduced but not developed or resolved. • The setting is not clearly established and does not impact the story. • Characters are not adequately developed. • The story lacks sufficient dialogue and descriptions.	• The point of view is inconsistent. • The story lacks precise words and sensory language. • Spelling, capitalization, and punctuation are unreliable. • There are some grammar and usage errors, but the ideas are still clear.
1	• The story does not have a clear sequence of events or plot. • There is no evidence of pacing. • Transition words are not used. • The resolution is inappropriate to the story or missing.	• The story has no identifiable conflict. • The setting is vague. • Characters are underdeveloped or not believable. • Dialogue and descriptions are missing.	• A clear point of view is not established. • The language is vague. • Many spelling, capitalization, and punctuation errors occur. • Many grammatical and usage errors obscure the meaning.

Reflect on the Unit

By completing your short story, you have created a writing product that expresses ideas related to those you have read about in this unit. Now is a good time to reflect on what you have learned.

Reflect on the Essential Question

- What are the places that shape who you are? How has your answer to this question changed since you first considered it when you started this unit?

- What are some examples from the texts you've read about the way places shape people?

Reflect on Your Reading

- Which selections were the most interesting or surprising to you?

- From which selection did you learn the most about how people interact with places—both new places and places from their past?

Reflect on the Writing Task

- What challenges did you encounter while working on your short story? How might you deal with them next time?

- How did analyzing the mentor text help you craft your own story?

- Which part of your short story was the easiest to write? Which was the hardest? Why?

- How did you improve your short story as you were revising?

UNIT 3 SELECTIONS

- "My Favorite Chaperone"
- *The Book of Unknown Americans*
- "The Powwow at the End of the World"
- *New Immigrants Share Their Stories*
- "A Common Bond: Teens Forge Friendships Despite Differences"

REFLECT

REFLECT ON THE UNIT

Have students reflect on the questions independently and write some notes in response to each one. Then have students meet with partners or in small groups to discuss their reflections. Circulate during these discussions to identify the questions that are generating the liveliest conversations. Wrap up with a whole-class discussion focused on these questions.

 LEARNING MINDSET

Self-Reflection It is important for students to develop the ability to reflect on their work. This capacity for self-reflection allows students to identify their strengths and their weaknesses and gives them a realistic indication of where they stand. Explain that developing this capacity is part of building a growth mindset in which students feel confident about their ability to learn. Have students ask themselves questions, such as *Did I put in my best effort?* and *What could I do differently next time to produce even better work?*

UNIT (4)

Instructional Overview and Resources

	Instructional Focus	**Online Ed Resources**

**Unit Introduction
The Fight for Freedom**

Instructional Focus

Unit 4 Essential Question
Unit 4 Academic Vocabulary

Resources

Stream to Start: The Fight for Freedom

Unit 4 Response Log

ANALYZE & APPLY

from **"Narrative of the Life of Frederick Douglass, An American Slave"**
Autobiography by Frederick Douglass
Lexile 1010L

> **NOTICE & NOTE** READING MODEL
>
> **Signposts**
> • Word Gaps
> • Contrasts and Contradictions
> • Big Questions

Reading
• Analyze Autobiography
• Analyze Structure

Writing: Write a Literary Analysis

Speaking and Listening: Discuss with a Small Group

Vocabulary: Latin Roots

Language Conventions: Pronoun-Antecedent Agreement

🔊 **Audio**

Text in Focus: Analyzing Language

Close Read Screencast: Modeled Discussions

Reading Studio: Notice & Note

Writing Studio: Writing Informative Texts

Speaking and Listening Studio: Participating in Collaborative Discussions

Vocabulary Studio: Latin Roots

Grammar Studio: Module 8: Lesson 8: Correct Pronoun-Antecedent Agreement

---

from **"Harriet Tubman: Conductor on the Underground Railroad"**
Biography by Ann Petry
Lexile 1010L

Reading
• Analyze Characterization
• Analyze Author's Craft

Writing: Write a Speech

Speaking and Listening: Present a Speech

Vocabulary: Latin Roots

Language Conventions: Run-On Sentences

🔊 **Audio**

Reading Studio: Notice & Note

Writing Studio: Writing Arguments

Speaking and Listening Studio: Giving a Presentation

Vocabulary Studio: Latin Roots

Grammar Studio: Module 1: Lesson 2: Run-on Sentences

"The Drummer Boy of Shiloh"
Historical Fiction by Ray Bradbury
Lexile 990L

Reading
• Analyze Setting
• Analyze Mood

Writing: Write a Report

Speaking and Listening: Dramatize a Scene

Vocabulary: Interpret Figures of Speech

Language Conventions: Sentence Fragments

🔊 **Audio**

Text in Focus: Visualizing

Close Read Screencast: Modeled Discussions

Reading Studio: Notice & Note

Writing Studio: Conducting Research

Writing Studio: Writing Informative Texts

Speaking and Listening Studio: Giving a Presentation

Vocabulary Studio: Figures of Speech

Grammar Studio: Module 1: Lesson 2: Run-on Sentences

SUGGESTED PACING: 30 DAYS	**Unit Introduction**	*from* **Narrative of the Life of Frederick Douglass**	*from* **Harriet Tubman**	**The Drummer Boy of Shiloh**	**O Captain! My Captain!**
	1	2　3　4　5	6　7　8　9　10	11　12　13　14	15　16

Online Ed Assessment

English Learner Support	Differentiated Instruction	Assessment
• Understand U.S. History		

English Learner Support	Differentiated Instruction	Assessment
• Text X-Ray • Use Cognates • Read Closely • Create a Table • Oral Assessment • Vocabulary Strategy • Pronoun-Antecedent Agreement	**When Students Struggle** • Open Your Mind to Signposts • Practice Reading Long, Complex Sentences **To Challenge Students** • View Government Documents	Selection Test
• Text X-Ray • Use Cognates • Learning Strategies • Analyze Characterization • Understand Text Structure • Analyze Author's Craft • Big Questions • Confirm Understanding • Draw Conclusions • Understand Visuals • Understand Vocabulary • Oral Assessment • Present a Speech • Language Conventions	**When Students Struggle** • Analyze Characterization **To Challenge Students** • Use Visuals • Analyze Visuals	Selection Test
• Text X-Ray • Vocabulary Support • Sentence Structure • Oral Language • Recognize Metaphor • Understand Dialogue • Oral Assessment • Read a Dramatic Scene • Vocabulary Strategy • Language Conventions	**When Students Struggle** • Make a Bulleted List	Selection Test

Not My Bones / Fortune's Bones
17 18 19 20 21 22 23 24 25

Independent Reading
26 27

End of Unit
28 29 30

PLAN

Instructional Focus

Online
Ed Resources

"O Captain! My Captain!"
Poem by Walt Whitman

Reading
• Analyze Figurative Language
• Analyze Genre: Poetry

Writing: Write a Poem

Speaking and Listening: Choral Reading

 Audio

Reading Studio: Notice & Note

Writing Studio: Writing Narratives

Speaking and Listening Studio: Giving a Presentation

COLLABORATE & COMPARE

"Not My Bones"
Poem by Marilyn Nelson

Reading
• Paraphrase Poetry
• Analyze Chronological Structure

Speaking and Listening:
Express Ideas Visually, Recite a Poem

 Audio

Reading Studio: Notice & Note

Speaking and Listening Studio: Participating in Collaborative Discussions

Speaking and Listening Studio: Giving a Presentation

Mentor Text

from **"Fortune's Bones"**
History Writing by Pamela Espeland
Lexile 790L
Collaborate and Compare

Reading:
• Compare Treatments
• Analyze the Texts

Speaking and Listening: Decide and Discuss

Audio

Reading Studio: Notice & Note

Speaking and Listening Studio: Participating in Collaborative Discussions

Speaking and Listening Studio: Giving a Presentation

Online
Ed

INDEPENDENT READING

The independent Reading selections are only available in the eBook.

 Go to the Reading Studio for more information on NOTICE & NOTE.

"I Saw Old General at Bay"
Poem by Walt Whitman

"A Mystery of Heroism"
Short Story by Stephen Crane
Lexile 1010L

END OF UNIT

Writing Task: Write a Research Report

Reflect on the Unit

Writing: Writing a Research Report

Language Conventions: Run-On Sentences

Speaking and Listening: Participate in a Collaborative Discussion

Unit 4 Response Log

Mentor Text: "Fortune's Bones"

Reading Studio: Notice & Note

Writing Studio: Writing Informative Texts

Writing Studio: Conducting Research

Speaking and Listening Studio: Participating in Collaborative Discussions

Grammar Studio: Module 1: Lesson 2: Run-On Sentences

English Learner Support	Differentiated Instruction	Online Ed Assessment
• Text X-Ray • Understand Poetic Forms • Use Vocabulary Support • Write a Prose Summary • Oral Assessment • Listen for Narrative Shifts • Prewrite for a Poem	**When Students Struggle** • Find Extended Metaphors	**Selection Test**
• Text X-ray • Use Visual Support • Use Language Support • Demonstrate Comprehension • Employ Analytical Skills • Oral Assessment	**When Students Struggle** • Reteaching: Paraphrasing **To Challenge Students** • Analyze Imagery and Theme	**Selection Test**
• Use Prereading Supports • Comprehend Language Structures • Oral Assessment • Use Support from Teachers and Peers	**When Students Struggle** • Summarize **When Students Struggle** • Reteaching: Comparing Treatment	**Selection Test**

from "Bloody Times: The Funeral of Abraham Lincoln and the Manhunt for Jefferson Davis" History Writing by James L. Swanson
Lexile 980L

"My Friend Douglass" Biography by Russell Freedman
Lexile 1180L

"Civil War Journal" Journal by Louisa May Alcott
Lexile 1480L

Selection Tests

• Language X-Ray • Adapt Writing • Condense Ideas • Explaining with Specificity and Detail • Plan a Collaborative Discussion	**When Students Struggle** • Add Quotations • Extend the Completion Time • Practice Speaking Techniques **To Challenge Students** • Create an Exhibit	**Unit Test**

THE FIGHT FOR FREEDOM

 Connect to the
ESSENTIAL QUESTION

Ask a volunteer to read aloud the Essential Question. Discuss how the images on page 238 relate to the question. Ask students to think of other ways, besides fighting in a war, to take risks to be free.

■ English Learner Support

Understand U.S. History Draw students' attention to the title of the unit: The Fight for Freedom. Tell students that this title refers to the Civil War, which was a war fought in the United States between the North, or the Union, and the South, or the Confederacy. Explain that this war is a key factor in U.S. history. Ask: *Do you know which side won the war? Do you know the name of the U.S. president during that war?* Discuss that two key aspects of this war were the North wanting to free the African Americans who were enslaved in the South and the South wanting to be freed from the Union so they could make their own decisions. Ask: *What were the soldiers in this war willing to risk for freedom?*
ALL LEVELS

DISCUSS THE QUOTATION

Tell students that Harriet Tubman was born an American slave in Maryland around 1820 and began working as a house servant around age five or six. Explain that after working as a slave for about 25 years, she decided to escape even though she knew she could be severely punished or even killed if she were caught. Add that she cleverly found her way to a Northern non-slave state without being caught and that she then returned to Maryland nineteen different times to lead other slaves to freedom. Direct students to read the quotation. Ask: *What do you think Harriet Tubman meant by "fight for liberty"? (She meant to fight to free enslaved African Americans.)* Ask: *Why do you think Harriet Tubman referred to her strength lasting? (Helping slaves run away without getting caught was dangerous and hard work.)*

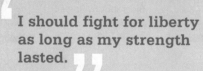 **ESSENTIAL QUESTION:**

What will people risk to be free?

" I should fight for liberty as long as my strength lasted. "

Harriet Tubman

238   Unit 4

 LEARNING MINDSET

Effort Remind students that effort is necessary for growth. Emphasize that hard work leads to success. Make sure to praise students for effort, rather than for being "smart." When possible, provide specific feedback that encourages effort, such as, "I noticed you put a lot of effort into your reading/writing today. When you got stuck, you stopped, took a breath, and kept going."

ACADEMIC VOCABULARY

Academic Vocabulary words are words you use when you discuss and write about texts. In this unit you will practice and learn five words.

☑ **access**   ☐ **civil**   ☐ **demonstrate**   ☐ **document**   ☐ **symbolize**

Study the Word Network to learn more about the word **access**.

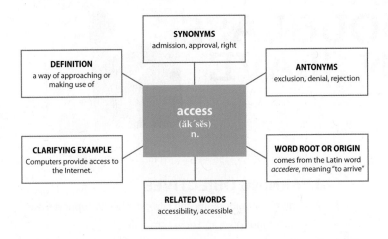

Write and Discuss Discuss the completed Word Network with a partner, making sure to talk through all of the boxes until you both understand the word and its synonyms, antonyms, and related forms. Then, fill out Word Networks for the remaining four words. Use a dictionary or online resource to help you complete the activity.

 Go online to access the Word Networks.

RESPOND TO THE ESSENTIAL QUESTION

In this unit, you will meet people who sacrificed for freedom. As you read, you will revisit the **Essential Question** and gather your ideas about it in the **Response Log** that appears on page R4. At the end of the unit, you will have the opportunity to write a **research report** on a topic related to the abolition movement in the United States. Filling out the Response Log will help you prepare for this writing task.

 You can also go online to access the Response Log.

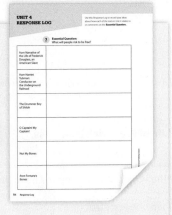

ACADEMIC VOCABULARY

As students complete Word Networks for the remaining four vocabulary words, encourage them to include all the categories shown in the completed network if possible. Point out that some words do not have clear synonyms or antonyms. Explain that some words may also function as different parts of speech—for example, *document* may be a noun or a verb.

access (ăk´sĕs) *n.* a way of approaching or making use of (Spanish cognate: *accessar/acceso*)

civil (sĭv´əl) *adj.* of, or related to, citizens and their relations with each other and the state (Spanish cognate: *civil*)

demonstrate (dĕm´ ən-strāt´) *v.* to show clearly and deliberately (Spanish cognate: *demostrar*)

document (dŏk´yə-mənt) *n.* written or printed paper that provides evidence or information (Spanish cognate: *documento*)

symbolize (sĭm´bə-līz´) *v.* to serve as a symbol of, or represent something else (Spanish cognate: *simbolizar*)

RESPOND TO THE ESSENTIAL QUESTION

Direct students to the Unit 4 Response Log. Explain that students will use it to record ideas and details from the selections that help answer the Essential Question. When they work on the writing task at the end of the unit, their Response Logs will help them think about what they have read and make connections between texts.

READING MODEL

from NARRATIVE OF THE LIFE OF FREDERICK DOUGLASS, AN AMERICAN SLAVE

Autobiography by Frederick Douglass

GENRE ELEMENTS
AUTOBIOGRAPHY

Remind students that the purpose of an **autobiography** is to present a first-hand account of a person's life. Explain that students will encounter autobiographies, which are first-person historical accounts, and other primary sources as they continue to study history and literature. Point out that this lesson will help students learn to understand the unique perspective such first-person accounts provide.

LEARNING OBJECTIVES

- Analyze autobiography and cite evidence to support ideas.
- Understand cause and effect structure.
- Conduct research about Frederick Douglass's life.
- Discuss Douglass's assertion that learning to read has disadvantages.
- Use Latin roots to help define words.
- **Language** Discuss Frederic Douglass's life and feelings using the word *frustrated*.

TEXT COMPLEXITY

Quantitative Measures	*from* Narrative of the Life of Frederick Douglass, An American Slave	Lexile: 1010L
Qualitative Measures	**Ideas Presented** More than one purpose; implied meanings, but easily identified from context.	
	Structure Used More than one text structure.	
	Language Used Some unfamiliar language; some complex sentence structure.	
	Knowledge Required Some references to difficult historical concepts.	

RESOURCES

- Unit 4 Response Log
- Selection Audio
- Analyzing Language
- Close Read Screencasts: Modeled Discussions
- Reading Studio: Notice & Note
- Writing Studio: Writing Informative Texts
- Speaking and Listening Studio: Participating in Collaborative Discussions
- Vocabulary Studio: Latin Roots
- Grammar Studio: Module 8: Lesson 8: Correct Pronoun-Antecedent Agreement
- from "Narrative of the Life of Frederick Douglass, An American Slave" Selection Test

SUMMARIES

English

In this excerpt from his autobiography, Frederick Douglass describes his great efforts to learn to read. At first, the mistress of the house was teaching him, but she then joined her husband in believing that slaves should not learn to read. Determined, Douglass started to take reading lessons from children he encountered in town. He goes on to discuss the types of materials he read and his internal conflict surrounding how learning to read made him acutely aware of the intolerable state of being enslaved.

Spanish

En este pasaje de su autobiografía, Frederick Douglass describe sus grandes esfuerzos para aprender a leer. Al principio, la señora de la casa le enseñaba, pero ella luego se plegó a la creencia de su esposo de que los esclavos no deberían aprender a leer. Decidido, Douglass empezó a tomar lecciones de lectura de los niños que encontraba en el pueblo. Luego discute los tipos de materiales que leía y su conflicto interno respecto a cómo al aprender a leer se había hecho sumamente consciente del estado intolerable que significaba estar esclavizado.

SMALL-GROUP OPTIONS

Have students work in small groups to read and discuss the selection.

Think-Pair-Share

Present this background and question to students:

Why do you think slave owners did not want their slaves to learn to read?

- Have students individually think about the question and make notes.
- Then, pair students and have them listen, discuss, and formulate a common response.
- Finally, have students share responses with the class.

Double-Entry Journal

Have students divide a notebook page in half by drawing a line from top to bottom to create two columns.

In the left column, ask students to list frustrations that Frederick Douglass describes and how he handled them.

In the right column, ask students to write how they think they would have reacted if they had been in the same situation.

Text X-Ray: English Learner Support

for *from* "Narrative of the Life of Frederick Douglass, an American Slave"

Use the Text X-Ray and the supports and scaffolds in the Teacher's Edition to help guide students at different proficiency levels through the section.

INTRODUCE THE SELECTION
DISCUSS THE CAUSES AND EFFECTS OF CHOICES

In this lesson, students will need to be able to understand the thought processes behind extreme choices people made so that they and others could be free. Explain that it would have been much easier for young Frederick Douglass to have given up on the idea of learning to read, but he was not willing to take the easy way out because he had an inner drive to have a better life. Point out that, even though young Frederick Douglass might not have realized it at the time, his desire to read—despite adversity—was the beginning of his fight for freedom from slavery despite facing extreme risks.

Supply the following sentence frames:

- *One reason that _____ was because _____.*
- *The possible choices were _____.*
- *_____ chose to _____ and the effect was _____.*

CULTURAL REFERENCES

The following words and phrases may be unfamiliar to students:

- *Master and Mistress* (paragraph 1): It was customary for slaves to refer to their owners as Master and Mistress.
- *little white boys whom I met in the street* (paragraph 4): It was common at the time for young boys to gather in the streets to play and talk.
- *gave tongue* (paragraph 6): discussed

LISTENING

Understand the Pronouns in an Autobiography

Draw students' attention to the pronouns used in the first paragraph. Point out that the use of *I*, *me*, and *my* show that the author is the speaker, which is typical for autobiographies. Also, point out that the use of *she* and *her* are part of his descriptions of his mistress.

Have students listen as you read aloud the title, author line, and paragraph 1. Use the following supports with students at varying proficiency levels:

- Tell students that you will ask questions about what you just read and they should show thumbs up for "yes" and thumbs down for "no." Ask: *Is I in this selection the mistress?* (no) *Is I in this selection Frederick Douglass?* (yes) **SUBSTANTIAL**
- Have small groups count the number of times the words *I*, *my*, or *me* are used. (I: 5; my: 3; me: 2) Ask: *Who is I or me in this selection?* (Frederick Douglass) **MODERATE**
- Ask students to complete this sentence frame: *Since you hear the words _____, _____, and _____ throughout the first paragraph, you can guess that this whole selection will be about _____.* (*I, me, my,* Frederick Douglass) **LIGHT**

SPEAKING

Discuss Douglass's Frustrations

Draw students' attention to Frederick Douglass's frustrations with learning to think. Circulate to make sure students understand that he wants to think deeply, but that doing so causes him grief because he is enslaved.

Read the second half of paragraph 6, beginning with "I preferred the condition of the meanest reptile to my own." Use the following supports with students at varying proficiency levels:

- Ask students to discuss the first sentence you just read aloud. Reread the sentence. Begin the discussion by asking: *Is Frederick Douglass happy when he compares himself to a reptile?* (no) **SUBSTANTIAL**
- Begin a discussion by asking: *Why is Frederick Douglass frustrated about thinking?* (*He thinks about being free, but he is not free.*) **MODERATE**
- Pair students and have them discuss why Frederick Douglass is frustrated about thinking. **LIGHT**

READING

Understand Personal Details

Draw students' attention to Frederick Douglass's reading of "The Columbian Orator" in relation to his concerns about being enslaved for life. Explain that in their autobiographies, authors often share intimate, personal details.

Work with students to read paragraph 5. Use the following supports with students at varying proficiency levels:

- Read one sentence at a time and have students repeat it. After each sentence, ask yes/no questions to confirm and clarify understanding. For example, after the first sentence, ask: *Does Douglass feel sad?* (*yes*) **SUBSTANTIAL**
- After students finish reading the paragraph, ask: *What does Frederick Douglass share that makes him sad?* (*the idea of being a slave for life*) **MODERATE**
- After they finish reading, pair students and ask: *What does the dialogue in "The Columbian Orator" have to do with Douglass's concerns about being a slave for life?* (*The idea of thinking and talking his way out of slavery appealed to Douglass.*) **LIGHT**

WRITING

Write a Literary Analysis

Draw students' attention to the writing assignment on p. 251. Read and discuss each part.

Use the following supports with students at varying proficiency levels:

- Work with students to understand the meaning of "tone." Explain that negative words show a negative or frustrated tone. Create a word web on the board, and ask students to look on p. 248 for negative words to add to the web. **SUBSTANTIAL**
- Have students work in small groups to look for and list words on p. 248 that suggest an attitude, or tone, of frustration. **MODERATE**
- Pair students and ask them to make a list of words from p. 248 that suggest Douglass's feelings. Then, ask them to identify an overall attitude, or tone, that relates to all of the words on their lists. **LIGHT**

EXPLAIN THE SIGNPOSTS

Explain that **NOTICE & NOTE Signposts** are significant moments in the text that help readers understand and analyze works of fiction or nonfiction. Use the instruction on these pages to introduce students to the signposts **Word Gaps, Contrasts and Contradictions,** and **Big Questions.** Then use the selection that follows to have students apply the signposts to a text.

For a full list of the fiction and nonfiction signposts, see p. 310.

▶ WORD GAPS

Explain that **Word Gaps** are words and phrases that are unfamiliar because they are not commonly used today in American English.

Read aloud the example passage and ask: *Have you ever used the words "gave tongue to" when you were talking about interesting thoughts?* Model for students the thought process to use when they first come upon Word Gaps. Say: *I don't know what that means, but I know that this selection was written over 170 years ago, so it could easily be that "gave tongue to" was a phrase that was commonly used then.*

Tell students that when they suspect à Word Gap, they should look at the **context clues** within the sentence or paragraph and try to figure out what it means.

For more information on these and other signposts to Notice & Note, visit the **Reading Studio.**

When you notice one of the following while reading, pause to see if it's a **Word Gaps** signpost:

unfamiliar vocabulary

familiar words used in unexpected ways

phrases that seem awkward or unclear

words in italic or boldfaced type, which may be specialized or technical terms

Anchor Question
When you notice this signpost, ask: Do clues in the sentence help me understand the word or phrase?

---

from

NARRATIVE OF THE LIFE OF FREDERICK DOUGLASS, AN AMERICAN SLAVE

You are about to read an excerpt from the autobiography of Frederick Douglass. As you read it, you will ask questions and notice and note signposts that will help you analyze the author's purpose and message. Here are two key signposts and a Big Question to look for as you read this autobiography and other works of nonfiction.

Word Gaps Because Douglass wrote his autobiography more than 170 years ago, some of his language can be challenging for modern readers. Some words might be unfamiliar because they had different meanings in the past than they do now. You may also encounter phrases that seem clumsy or unclear, as in this example:

> They <u>gave tongue to</u> interesting thoughts of my own soul, which had frequently flashed through my mind, and died away <u>for want of utterance.</u>

The underlined phrases may seem strange to you. We usually think of *tongue* as the thing that helps us eat and *want* as desire; however, in this context, those words have other meanings. Context clues can help us figure that out: *thoughts* and *flashed through my mind* suggest that both underlined phrases have to do with expressing ideas, or speaking. In this example a student underlined a Word Gap:

> 1   I lived in Master Hugh's family about seven years. During this time, I succeeded in learning to read and write. In accomplishing this, I was <u>compelled to resort to various stratagems.</u> I had no regular teacher. My mistress, who had kindly commenced to instruct me, had, in compliance with the advice and direction of her husband, not only ceased to instruct, but had set her face against my being instructed by any one else. . . .

What does the phrase "compelled to resort to various stratagems" mean? What clues help you find the meaning?

> Stratagems looks like the word strategy. The context reveals that Douglass wanted to learn to read and write. He didn't have a real teacher, so he had to figure out another way to learn.

TO CHALLENGE STUDENTS . . .

View Government Documents Have students look at government documents from the 1700s, such as the U.S. Constitution, and search for Word Gaps. Have them make a list of Word Gaps they find and explain the meaning of each one.

Contrasts and Contradictions When something unexpected happens, our first reaction is usually surprise. Upon further reflection, however, we might ask ourselves whether the event was truly unusual or our expectations were just unrealistic.

Noticing similar **Contrasts and Contradictions** while reading can help deepen your understanding of the topic you are reading about. An author might point out an interesting contrast, using signal words and phrases such as *however* and *on the other hand*. Or, something you read might contradict your own expectations. If the latter is the case, pause to see how the new information fits in with your previous knowledge. The following sentence from *Narrative of the Life of Frederick Douglass* could be an example of Contrasts and Contradictions:

> **Slavery proved as injurious to her as it did to me.**

Anchor Question
When you notice this signpost, ask: What is the difference, and why does it matter?

What expectation does this sentence contradict?	The sentence suggests that slavery can cause harm to both slaveholders and enslaved people. This contradicts the expectation that slavery is harmful only to the people who are enslaved.

Big Questions Suppose you watch a TV show about a foreign country. What will you share with your friends the next day? Most likely, you'll talk about the things that surprised you—such as strange foods and unusual clothing. They are the most interesting new facts you learned.

When you read a nonfiction text, pause now and then to ask yourself: **What surprised me?** This question can help you identify the new information you are learning. It can also help you recognize any incorrect ideas you had before you read the text.

Notice how a student answered Big Questions about the following passage:

Remember to ask **Big Questions** when you read nonfiction text. Pause to ask yourself these questions:

- What surprised me?
- Why was it surprising?
- Does the new information challenge my previous ideas or beliefs about the topic?

> 2   Nothing seemed to make her more angry than to see me with a newspaper. She seemed to think that here lay the danger. I have had her rush at me with a face made all up of fury, and snatch from me a newspaper, in a manner that fully revealed her apprehension [fear].

What surprised you in this passage?	Douglass's mistress seems to be angry when she sees him with a newspaper, but she's actually afraid.
What new information did you learn?	Slaveholders were afraid of what would happen if enslaved children learned to read.

CONTRASTS AND CONTRADICTIONS

Make sure students understand that **Contrasts and Contradictions** can be tools authors use or reactions by readers.

When it is a tool the author uses, there will be signal words indicating that a Contrasts and Contradictions is taking place. Authors use Contrasts and Contradictions to highlight dramatic points.

When it is a reaction by the reader, there are no signal words. Rather, the reader is reading along and encounters something unexpected.

Whether Contrasts and Contradictions are tools the author is using or reactions by readers, they can involve people, places, things, situations, or ideas. The points can be **opposite situations, unexpected happenings** or **changes,** or simply **different views.**

BIG QUESTIONS

Explain that **Big Questions** are readers' thoughts rather than ideas authors provide. Make sure students realize that there are no right or wrong Big Questions or responses to them because the basis for Big Questions are individual responses by readers.

Explain that strong readers ask themselves Big Questions because it helps them sort out **key details** in informational text and helps them check to see if their **prior information** was correct.

APPLY THE SIGNPOSTS

Have students use this selection to practice applying the signposts. Encourage students to handle signposts by stopping, rereading, and asking themselves questions that will help them understand the text.

Tell students to continue to look for these and other signposts as they read the other selections in the unit.

WHEN STUDENTS STRUGGLE . . .

Open Your Mind to Signposts Point out to students who are struggling with using **signposts** that they are meant to be helpful, not stressful. Tell them that, when they come to text that is confusing, they should try opening their minds to a possible signpost to help clarify the confusion. Ask: *Which signpost can help make sense of information if you read something other than what you think is true?* (Big Questions) *Which signpost can help if a text includes words you know but are used in a way you've never heard before?* (Word Gaps) *Which signpost can help if the author describes something unexpected?* (Contrasts and Contradictions)

Connect to the
ESSENTIAL QUESTION

In this excerpt from his autobiography, Frederick Douglass describes the great lengths he went to in order to have the freedom to learn to read. Even though he was only a child, he was willing to risk punishment to have reading lessons.

from
NARRATIVE OF THE LIFE OF FREDERICK DOUGLASS, AN AMERICAN SLAVE

Autobiography by **Frederick Douglass**

ESSENTIAL QUESTION:

What will people risk to be free?

242   Unit 4

LEARNING MINDSET

Seeking Challenges Explain that seeking challenges means taking risks, trying new things, and not being afraid to fail or look silly in front of others. Emphasize that trying hard is important, but trying things that *are* hard is just as important. Encourage students to think of difficult texts and tasks as a challenge. Discuss that Frederick Douglass is an example of a person who was always seeking challenges.

QUICK START

How did you learn to read? In what ways would your life be different if you couldn't read? Discuss these questions with your classmates.

ANALYZE AUTOBIOGRAPHY

Narrative of the Life of Frederick Douglass, an American Slave is an **autobiography,** which is an account of the writer's own life.

Authors of autobiography often have a **purpose,** or reason for writing, beyond informing readers about events in their own lives. For example, writers might also want to shed light on the time period in which they have lived, or share a message about an issue that has shaped their lives as well as the lives of others. Sometimes writers state their purpose directly, but often you must infer it from the details the author chooses to share and comment on.

As you read, try to identify Frederick Douglass's main purpose in this section of his autobiography.

ANALYZE STRUCTURE

In an autobiography, authors often choose to focus on events that are related by **cause and effect,** which means that one event brings about another event or creates a change in attitude. Paragraphs may be structured to show these cause-and-effect relationships, even in narratives told in chronological order.

For example, Douglass states that his mistress was "a kind and tender-hearted woman," and he gives examples to support his statement. Then he explains how slavery caused her to change. "Under its influence, the tender heart became stone, and the lamblike disposition gave way to one of tigerlike fierceness." He supports this description of slavery's effects by giving examples: "I have had her rush at me with a face made all up of fury, and snatch from me a newspaper."

As you read, note how the cause-and-effect structure helps Douglass achieve his purpose. Use a chart like this.

CAUSE		EFFECT
Slavery	▶	A kind woman turns angry and cruel.

GENRE ELEMENTS: AUTOBIOGRAPHY

- gives an account of the writer's own life, told from the first-person point of view
- describes events in chronological order
- provides interesting details and anecdotes
- has a tone that reveals the author's attitude toward people and events

Narrative of the Life of Frederick Douglass, an American Slave   243

QUICK START

Have students read the Quick Start questions and share their responses. As a group, brainstorm some daily activities that involve reading. Make sure to include a range of tasks, such as recording a TV show, finding a product online and buying it, and reading a book for pleasure. Discuss that Frederick Douglass lived in a very different time, but that reading was also important then.

ANALYZE AUTOBIOGRAPHY

Discuss that autobiographers' purposes might range greatly, such as the following possibilities:

- Making sense of their lives
- Sharing a personal statement about life
- Giving credit to important people in their lives
- Reconciling past actions
- Warning others not to make the mistakes they made
- Explaining or justifying actions in their lives
- Making money
- Telling their part in important happenings
- Healing from past trauma

ANALYZE STRUCTURE

Tell students that practice will help them recognize cause and effect. Have students read this last sentence from paragraph 3:

"Mistress, in teaching me the alphabet, had given me the inch, and no precaution could prevent me from taking the ell."

Explain that an "ell" is a measurement of about 45 inches, so he was saying that she gave him an inch, so he was going to take more than she offered. Then, ask students to identify the cause and effect in the sentence. *(Cause: Mistress taught him the alphabet; Effect: nothing could stop him from learning to read)*

CRITICAL VOCABULARY

Encourage students to read all the sentences before deciding which word best completes each one. Remind them to look for context clues that indicate the meaning of each word.

Answers:

1. *apprehension*

2. *unabated*

3. *vindication*

4. *commence*

5. *prudence*

6. *denunciation*

■ English Learner Support

Use Cognates Tell students that two of the Critical Vocabulary words have Spanish cognates: *commence/ comenzar, prudence/predencia.* **ALL LEVELS**

LANGUAGE CONVENTIONS

Explain that pronoun-antecedent agreement has four components:

- A pronoun must have an antecedent, which is a noun that it is replacing.
- A pronoun must agree in gender with the noun it is replacing: male (Joey/he), female (Mrs. Jones/she), or gender-neutral (house/it).
- A pronoun must agree in number with the noun it is replacing: plural (dogs/they) or singular (girl/her).
- A pronoun must agree in person with the noun it is replacing: first person/talking about yourself (the speaker/I, me, we, us), second person/talking to someone (person or group talking to/you), or third person/(talking about someone (Ricardo/he).

Have partners write cloze passage sentences using pronouns. Then, have them exchange their work with another group to complete the passages.

ANNOTATION MODEL

Encourage students to review the information about signposts on pp. 240-241. Suggest that they underline important phrases or circle key words that help them identify signposts. Suggest they color-code their annotations by using a different color highlighter for each signpost or use their own system for marking up the selections.

 GET READY

CRITICAL VOCABULARY

commence	prudence	denunciation
apprehension	unabated	vindication

To see how many Critical Vocabulary words you already know, use them to complete the sentences.

1. You might feel _____ about moving to another country.

2. The fierce argument continued _____ for hours.

3. The convict received _____ of his innocence and was freed.

4. Did you _____ watching the TV series with the first episode, or did you start watching it later?

5. Saving some of your money instead of spending it all is an example of _____.

6. The entire school united in its _____ of the arsonist who burned down the library.

LANGUAGE CONVENTIONS

Pronoun-Antecedent Agreement In this lesson, you will learn how writers use pronouns to refer to their antecedents correctly. In the following sentence, notice how Douglass uses the plural pronoun *they* to refer back to a plural antecedent, *fellows*.

It is enough to say of the dear little <u>fellows,</u> that <u>they</u> lived on Philpot Street. . . .

ANNOTATION MODEL   **NOTICE & NOTE**

As you read, notice and note signposts, such as **Word Gaps** and **Contrasts and Contradictions,** and pause to ask yourself **Big Questions.** In the model, you can see one reader's notes about *Narrative of the Life of Frederick Douglass, an American Slave.*

> 1 I lived in Master Hugh's family about seven years. During this time, I succeeded in learning to read and write. In accomplishing this, I was compelled to resort to various stratagems. I had no regular teacher. <u>My mistress, who had kindly commenced to instruct me,</u> had, in compliance with the advice and direction of her husband, not only ceased to instruct, but <u>had set her face against my being instructed by any one else</u>. . . .

It's surprising that Douglass's mistress started to teach him but later made sure no one did. Was it just her husband that changed her?

IMPROVE READING FLUENCY

Targeted Passage Use echo reading to practice pausing for commas. One sentence at a time, read the Background paragraph, modeling how to fluently read while briefly pausing for commas. Have students repeat each sentence imitating fluent reading while pausing for commas.

Go to the **Reading Studio** for additional support in developing fluency.

BACKGROUND

Frederick Douglass (1818–1895) was born into enslavement in Maryland at a time when slavery was still legal in many states in the Union. As Douglass grew up, he tried to escape several times. Finally, in 1838, he succeeded. Douglass went on to become a famous speaker and writer, fighting to abolish, or end, slavery. His autobiography, Narrative of the Life of Frederick Douglass, an American Slave, *became a best seller in the United States and Europe.*

from
NARRATIVE OF THE LIFE OF FREDERICK DOUGLASS, AN AMERICAN SLAVE

Autobiography by Frederick Douglass

SETTING A PURPOSE

As you read, consider why Frederick Douglass chose these particular events to write about. Think about what his focus on these events reveals about his character and his struggle for freedom.

1   I lived in Master Hugh's family about seven years. During this time, I succeeded in learning to read and write. In accomplishing this, I was compelled to resort to various stratagems. I had no regular teacher. My mistress, who had kindly commenced to instruct me, had, in compliance with the advice and direction of her husband, not only ceased to instruct, but had set her face against my being instructed by any one else. It is due, however, to my mistress to say of her, that she did not adopt this course of treatment immediately. She at first lacked the depravity[1] indispensable to shutting me up in mental darkness. It was at least necessary for her to have some training in the exercise of irresponsible power, to make her equal to the task of treating me as though I were a brute.

 Close Read

---
[1] **depravity** (dĭ-prăv´ĭ-tē): moral corruption.

NOTICE & NOTE

Notice & Note

Use the side margins to notice and note signposts in the text.

LANGUAGE CONVENTIONS

Annotate: Mark the antecedent of the pronoun *her* in the fifth sentence of paragraph 1.

Analyze: How does correct pronoun-antecedent agreement make the meaning of this sentence clear?

TEACH

ANALYZE AUTOBIOGRAPHY

Point out that Douglass writes a long paragraph about his mistress. He begins by praising her, but then describes how her behavior changed because of her husband's influence and slavery itself. (**Answer:** *Douglass's mistress had a big influence on him; she was one of the two people who were completely in control of his life. Describing the change in her behavior helps readers understand the effects that slavery had on slave owners, as well as on the enslaved people themselves.*)

 ENGLISH LEARNER SUPPORT

Read Closely Display the first sentence in paragraph 2. Highlight the commas in yellow and the semicolon in blue.

- Tell students that the phrases and clauses enclosed in commas add information but do not change the meaning of the sentence. Work with them to understand what information the phrases add. (*that Douglass already described his mistress earlier; that she was kind when he first lived with her*) **MODERATE**

BIG QUESTIONS

Discuss that texts from many years ago will almost always include surprising and different ideas compared to today's world. (**Answer:** *It's surprising that the people Douglass lived with were so determined to make sure he didn't learn to read. By contrast, most young people today are strongly encouraged by parents and teachers to read.*)

CRITICAL VOCABULARY

commence: Douglass describes the nature of his mistress's early behavior.

ASK STUDENTS why it is significant that the mistress commenced to treat Douglass kindly. (*Her behavior in the beginning is in stark contrast to the way she treated him later. Douglass blames slavery for the terrible change in her.*)

apprehension: The mistress seems to fear the sight of Douglass with a newspaper.

ASK STUDENTS what Douglass implies by saying that the mistress showed apprehension about his reading. (*He implies that she feared what might happen if slaves were to become literate and educated.*)

246 Unit 4

 **NOTICE & NOTE**

commence
(kə-měns´) v. When things *commence*, they begin or start.

ANALYZE AUTOBIOGRAPHY
Annotate: Mark details in paragraph 2 that describe Douglass's mistress.

Infer: What might Douglass's purpose be in devoting so much space to describing his mistress?

BIG QUESTIONS

Notice & Note: Mark details in paragraphs 2–3 that are surprising when compared to the lives of most young people today.

Synthesize: What is surprising about these details of Douglass's life?

apprehension
(ăp´rĭ-hĕn´shən) n. *Apprehension* is the fear or dread of the future.

2   My mistress was, as I have said, a kind and tender-hearted woman; and in the simplicity of her soul she **commenced,** when I first went to live with her, to treat me as she supposed one human being ought to treat another. In entering upon the duties of a slaveholder, she did not seem to perceive that I sustained to her the relation of a mere chattel,[2] and that for her to treat me as a human being was not only wrong, but dangerously so. Slavery proved as injurious to her as it did to me. When I went there, she was a pious, warm, and tender-hearted woman. There was no sorrow or suffering for which she had not a tear. She had bread for the hungry, clothes for the naked, and comfort for every mourner that came within her reach. Slavery soon proved its ability to divest her of these heavenly qualities. Under its influence, the tender heart became stone, and the lamblike disposition gave way to one of tigerlike fierceness. The first step in her downward course was in her ceasing to instruct me. She now commenced to practise her husband's precepts.[3] She finally became even more violent in her opposition than her husband himself. She was not satisfied with simply doing as well as he had commanded; she seemed anxious to do better. Nothing seemed to make her more angry than to see me with a newspaper. She seemed to think that here lay the danger. I have had her rush at me with a face made all up of fury, and snatch from me a newspaper, in a manner that fully revealed her **apprehension.** She was an apt woman; and a little experience soon demonstrated, to her satisfaction, that education and slavery were incompatible with each other.

3   From this time I was most narrowly watched. If I was in a separate room any considerable length of time, I was sure to be suspected of having a book, and was at once called to give an account of myself. All this, however, was too late. The first step had been taken. Mistress, in teaching me the alphabet, had given me the inch, and no precaution could prevent me from taking the *ell.* 📹 Text in FOCUS

4   The plan which I adopted, and the one by which I was most successful, was that of making friends of all the little white boys whom I met in the street. As many of these as I could, I converted into teachers. With their kindly aid, obtained at different times and in different places, I finally succeeded in learning to read. When I was sent of errands, I always took my book with me, and by going one part of my errand quickly,

---

[2] **chattel** (chăt´l): a property or slave.
[3] **precepts** (prē´sĕpts´): rules or principles regarding action or conduct.

246   Unit 4

I found time to get a lesson before my return. I used also to carry bread with me, enough of which was always in the house, and to which I was always welcome; for I was much better off in this regard than many of the poor white children in our neighborhood. This bread I used to bestow upon the hungry little urchins, who, in return, would give me that more valuable bread of knowledge. I am strongly tempted to give the names of two or three of those little boys, as a testimonial of the <u>gratitude</u> and <u>affection</u> I bear them; but **prudence** forbids;—not that it would injure me, but it might embarrass them; for it is almost an unpardonable offence to teach slaves to read in this Christian country. It is enough to say of the <u>dear little fellows</u>, that they lived on Philpot Street, very near <u>Durgin and Bailey's</u> ship-yard. I used to talk this matter of slavery over with them. I would sometimes say to them, I wished I could be as free as they would be when they got to be men. "You will be free as soon as you are twenty-one, *but I am a slave for life!* Have not I as good a right to be free as you have?" These words used to trouble them; they would express for me (the liveliest sympathy), and console me with the hope that something would occur by which I might be free.

5   I was now about twelve years old, and the thought of being *a slave for life* began to bear heavily upon my heart. Just about this time, I got hold of a book entitled "The Columbian Orator."[4] Every opportunity I got, I used to read this book. Among much of other interesting matter, I found in it a dialogue between a master and his slave. The slave was represented as having run away from his master three times. The dialogue represented the conversation which took place between them, when the slave was retaken the third time. In this dialogue, the whole argument in behalf of slavery was brought forward by the master, all of which was disposed of by the slave. <u>The slave was made to say some very smart as well as impressive things in reply to his master</u>—things which had the desired though unexpected effect; for the conversation resulted in the voluntary emancipation of the slave on the part of the master.

6   In the same book, I met with one of Sheridan's mighty speeches on and in behalf of Catholic emancipation.[5] These were choice documents to me. I read them over and over

---

[4] **"The Columbian Orator":** a collection of political essays, poems, and dialogues that were used to teach reading and speaking at the beginning of the 19th century.

[5] **one of Sheridan's mighty speeches on and in behalf of Catholic emancipation:** Richard Brinsley Sheridan (1751–1816) was an Irish playwright and politician who made speeches about the rights of Roman Catholics in Britain and Ireland.

NOTICE & NOTE

ANALYZE AUTOBIOGRAPHY
Annotate: In paragraph 4, circle words and phrases that describe the boys' attitude toward Douglass. Underline text that tells how Douglass feels about them.

Infer: What message about people does Douglass convey by describing his interactions with these boys?

prudence
(pro͞od´ns) *n.* Prudence is the wise handling of practical matters.

ANALYZE STRUCTURE
Annotate: In paragraphs 5 and 6, mark details about the texts Douglass read at age 12 that were especially important to him.

Cause/Effect: What effect did reading these texts have on Douglass?

TEACH

 TEXT IN FOCUS

Analyzing Language Have students view the **Text in Focus** video in their eBook to analyze an expression Douglass uses in his autobiography in paragraph 3. Then, have students use **Text in Focus Practice** to apply what they have learned.

✏ ANALYZE AUTOBIOGRAPHY

Point out that, at the time he was talking to the boys, Frederick Douglass was a child between the ages of seven and twelve, so he and the boys who helped him read were probably about the same age. (**Answer:** *The boys' attitude toward Douglass is very different from his master's and mistress's. Douglass's message is that the adults' treatment and attitude towards him as chattel is not natural. The children he encounters see him as a fellow human being.*)

📖 For **reading support** for students at varying proficiency levels, see the **Text X-Ray** on page 240D.

✏ ANALYZE STRUCTURE

Encourage students to try to think and feel like Frederick Douglass. (**Answer:** *The dialogue gave Douglass the idea that there was a way out of slavery and that freedom was possible. The Sheridan speech showed him that there were logical arguments against slavery and in favor of human rights. Both texts helped him understand and express ideas that had been mainly feelings or instincts.*)

APPLYING ACADEMIC VOCABULARY

☑ **access**   ☐ **civil**   ☑ **demonstrate**   ☐ **document**   ☐ **symbolize**

Think-Pair-Share Have students turn to a partner to discuss the following questions. Guide students to include the Academic Vocabulary words *access* and *demonstrate* in their responses. Ask volunteers to share their responses.

- Think about the changes that Douglass describes in his mistress. Which of her actions **demonstrate** how slavery affected her?
- Discuss the process of Douglass's self-education. How did having **access** to various types of reading materials affect Douglass's ideas and development?

CRITICAL VOCABULARY

prudence: Out of prudence, Douglass declines to name the boys who helped him.

ASK STUDENTS why it was prudent for Douglass not to name the boys. (*Because it was an "unpardonable offence" to teach slaves to read, Douglass doesn't want the boys to suffer any consequences for helping him.*)

CONTRASTS AND CONTRADICTIONS

Explain that the **Contrasts and Contradictions** signpost is that Douglass did not foresee that learning to read would be anything but positive. *(He had sought freedom, but learning to read had only shown him how enslaved he was. It gave him more pain and not freedom.)*

■ English Learner Support

Create a Table Discuss that keeping track all of the Contrasts and Contradictions and Word Gaps can get confusing. Suggest students create a table to help keep them organized. **LIGHT**

WORD GAPS

Tell students that, sometimes when they are reading older texts and see words or phrases that do not make sense, they won't be able to figure out the meaning and will need to ask for help. **(Answer:** *Today,* meanest *would usually mean "most cruel," but Douglass uses it to mean "low in value or rank."* Trump *is short for trumpet, an instrument that makes a loud sound. The association here is with a trumpet being blown to announce the arrival of an important person or of an important event.)*

 For **speaking support** for students at varying proficiency levels, see the **Text X-Ray** on page 240D.

CRITICAL VOCABULARY

unabated: Douglass reads Sheridan's speeches over and over without tiring of them.

ASK STUDENTS to explain why Douglass's interest in these speeches was unabated. *(The more he read them, the more they helped him understand and express his own thoughts about slavery.)*

denunciation: In his reading, Douglass is glad to find a *denunciation* of slavery.

ASK STUDENTS where in the text Douglass made a denunciation of his own against slavery. *(When Douglass talked with the white boys, he denounced slavery by saying "Have not I as good a right to be free as you have?")*

vindication: Douglass finds powerful *vindication* for human rights in Sheridan's speeches.

ASK STUDENTS what the speeches might have said as a vindication of human rights. *(Most likely, the speeches expressed ideas similar to Douglass's—that it was wrong to "own" a person, and that it was right to treat all human beings with respect.)*

 NOTICE & NOTE

unabated
(ŭn´ə-bā´tĭd) *adj.* If something is *unabated,* it keeps its full force without decreasing.

denunciation
(dĭ-nŭn´sē-ā´shən) *n.* A *denunciation* is the public condemnation of something as wrong or evil.

vindication
(vĭn´dĭ-kā´shən) *n. Vindication* is the evidence or proof that someone's claim is correct.

CONTRASTS AND CONTRADICTIONS

Notice & Note: Douglass went to great lengths to teach himself how to read. In paragraph 6, mark the feelings he had after learning to read.

Infer: Why did Douglass feel that learning to read was "a curse rather than a blessing"?

WORD GAPS

Notice & Note: Mark words and phrases on this page that signal the fact that Douglass was writing in the 1800s rather than today.

Infer: Use context clues to infer the meanings of the words and phrases you marked.

again with **unabated** interest. They gave tongue to interesting thoughts of my own soul, which had frequently flashed through my mind, and died away for want of utterance. The moral which I gained from the dialogue was the power of truth over the conscience of even a slaveholder. What I got from Sheridan was a bold **denunciation** of slavery, and a powerful **vindication** of human rights. The reading of these documents enabled me to utter my thoughts, and to meet the arguments brought forward to sustain slavery; but while they relieved me of one difficulty, they brought on another even more painful than the one of which I was relieved. The more I read, the more I was led to abhor and detest my enslavers. I could regard them in no other light than a band of successful robbers, who had left their homes, and gone to Africa, and stolen us from our homes, and in a strange land reduced us to slavery. I loathed them as being the meanest as well as the most wicked of men. As I read and contemplated the subject, behold! that very discontentment which Master Hugh had predicted would follow my learning to read had already come, to torment and sting my soul to unutterable anguish. As I writhed under it, I would at times feel that learning to read had been a curse rather than a blessing. It had given me a view of my wretched condition, without the remedy. It opened my eyes to the horrible pit, but to no ladder upon which to get out. In moments of agony, I envied my fellow-slaves for their stupidity. I have often wished myself a beast. I preferred the condition of the meanest reptile to my own. Anything, no matter what, to get rid of thinking! It was this everlasting thinking of my condition that tormented me. There was no getting rid of it. It was pressed upon me by every object within sight or hearing, animate or inanimate. The silver trump of freedom had roused my soul to eternal wakefulness. Freedom now appeared, to disappear no more forever. It was heard in every sound, and seen in every thing. It was ever present to torment me with a sense of my wretched condition. I saw nothing without seeing it, I heard nothing without hearing it, and felt nothing without feeling it. It looked from every star, it smiled in every calm, breathed in every wind, and moved in every storm.

WHEN STUDENTS STRUGGLE . . .

Practice Reading Long, Complex Sentences Listening to fluently read text will help students understand long and complex sentences. Project sentences 1–7 of paragraph 6.

- Model reading the lines aloud with appropriate pacing, intonation, and expression. Demonstrate how to use punctuation as a guide to phrasing.

- Have students reread to a partner while you monitor.

 For additional support, go to the **Reading Studio** and assign the following **Level Up Tutorial: Biographies and Autobiographies.**

 **CHECK YOUR UNDERSTANDING**

Have students answer the questions independently.

Answers:

1. *C*

2. *G*

3. *A*

If they answer any questions incorrectly, have them reread the text to confirm their understanding. Then they may proceed to ANALYZE THE TEXT on p. 250.

CHECK YOUR UNDERSTANDING

Answer these questions before moving on to the **Analyze the Text** section on the following page.

1 Through the experiences described in this excerpt, Douglass gained —

  A gratitude for his master's and mistress's actions

  B a belief that people are not to be trusted

  C more knowledge about the problem of slavery

  D pleasure in spending time with his white friends

2 Which sentence from the excerpt best demonstrates Douglass's feelings about reading after he learned about slavery?

  F *In the same book, I met with one of Sheridan's mighty speeches on and in behalf of Catholic emancipation.*

  G *In moments of agony, I envied my fellow-slaves for their stupidity.*

  H *It was pressed upon me by every object within sight or hearing, animate or inanimate.*

  J *I heard nothing without hearing it, and felt nothing without feeling it.*

3 Why does Douglass first describe his mistress as "a kind and tender-hearted woman"?

  A To contrast with her later, cruel behavior

  B To show how much he wanted to learn to read

  C To prove that some slaveholders were caring

  D To emphasize his good fortune

 ENGLISH LEARNER SUPPORT

Oral Assessment Use the following questions to assess students' comprehension and speaking skills:

1. What did Douglass gain through the experiences described in the excerpt? (*He gained more knowledge about the problem of slavery.*)

2. Which sentence from the excerpt best explains Douglass's feelings after learning more about slavery from reading? (*In moments of agony, I envied my fellow-slaves for their stupidity.*)

3. Why does Douglass say that first his mistress was "a kind and tender-hearted woman"? (*He used this wording to contrast with her later, cruel behavior.*) **SUBSTANTIAL/MODERATE**

ANALYZE THE TEXT

Possible answers:

1. **DOK 2:** *The mistress's initial kindness had a greater effect because it was during that time that she taught Douglass to read, an event that had enormous impact on his life. He acknowledges this when he says, "Mistress, in teaching me the alphabet, had given me the inch, and no precaution could prevent me from taking the ell."*

2. **DOK 2:** *People are fed and sustained not only by food, but also by ideas and understanding.*

3. **DOK 3:** *He regards slaveholders as "a band of successful robbers" and as "the meanest as well as the most wicked of men."*

4. **DOK 4:** *Douglass's purpose is to express his thoughts and feelings about being enslaved and about the effects of literacy. He relates three events that help him achieve his goal: his mistress teaching him to read, his further pursuit of instruction from "all the little white boys," and the acquisition of certain reading materials that encouraged his own thoughts and feelings about slavery.*

5. **DOK 4: Possible response:** *He thinks that if he were an animal, he wouldn't have the ability to think and worry about his circumstances. Now that he can read, Douglass is tormented by his constant thoughts about being enslaved and the impossibility of freedom.*

RESEARCH

Childhood: *Douglass's parents were an enslaved mother and an unknown white man. As a young child, he was often cold and hungry and saw other slaves treated badly. His mother died when he was seven, and he was sent to live in Baltimore a year later. After seven years in Baltimore, he was hired out to a brutal slave owner who beat and starved him.*

Freedom: *Douglass planned to escape in 1836, but he was found out and jailed. He tried again in 1838, and succeeded in reaching New York, then Massachusetts.*

The Fight Against Slavery: *Douglass became an abolitionist, writing and speaking against slavery. He published his autobiography in 1845. During the Civil War, he recruited African American troops to the Union Army and spoke with Abraham Lincoln. After the war, he fought against segregation.*

Extend Students may find the events of Douglass's life upsetting and difficult to read. Be sensitive to students' emotions as they read the passages and encourage them to identify what they are feeling.

 RESPOND

ANALYZE THE TEXT

Support your responses with evidence from the text. NOTEBOOK

1. **Cause/Effect** Reread paragraphs 2 and 3. Did the mistress's initial kindness or her eventual cruelty have a greater effect on Frederick Douglass? Explain.

2. **Interpret** When describing how he paid his child tutors, Douglass says, "This bread I used to bestow upon the hungry little urchins, who, in return, would give me that more valuable bread of knowledge." In what way is knowledge "bread"?

3. **Evaluate** Reread paragraph 6. What words reveal Douglass's perspective on, or view of, slaveholders?

4. **Analyze** What is Douglass's purpose for writing? Identify three passages that help him achieve his goal, and explain why.

5. **Notice & Note** In paragraph 6, Douglass says, "I have often wished myself a beast." What does the word *beast* mean in other contexts? What point do you think Douglass is making when he uses it here?

RESEARCH TIP

The best search terms are very specific. Along with the name Frederick Douglass, you will want to include a word such as *slavery* or *abolitionist* to make sure you get the information you need.

RESEARCH

You have read about how Frederick Douglass learned to read in spite of the limitations placed upon him as an enslaved person. Research more details about the significant events in Douglass's life. You might focus on what his life was like as an enslaved person, how he gained his freedom, and how he fought for an end to slavery. Record what you learn in the chart. Then share what you learn with a small group.

PARTS OF DOUGLASS'S LIFE	HIS EXPERIENCES
Childhood	
Freedom	
The Fight Against Slavery	

Extend Find another passage from Douglass's autobiography. Take turns reading it aloud with members of a small group. Discuss the feelings and ideas stirred by Douglass's language and the events he describes.

LEARNING MINDSET

Asking for Help Encourage students to ask others for help—such as peers, teachers, or family—when they get stuck on a problem. Explain that asking for help from others can help students get "unstuck" and move forward. Reinforce that asking for help does not equal failure. Clarify that seeking help is a way of "trying smarter."

CREATE AND DISCUSS

Write a Literary Analysis In one to three paragraphs, explain how the tone of Douglass's autobiography helps him achieve his purpose and communicate his message.

❑ Think about the author's purpose for writing.

❑ Identify the **tone**—the writer's attitude toward his subject. Find examples where Douglass's choice of words helps establish the tone.

❑ When you write, begin by stating your view. Then support that view with evidence from the text.

Discuss with a Small Group In paragraph 6, Douglass says, "I would at times feel that learning to read had been a curse rather than a blessing."

❑ With a small group, discuss Douglass's statement and examine whether people today might share his attitude.

❑ Be sure to support your views with evidence from the autobiography.

❑ During your discussion, listen closely and respectfully to all ideas.

 Go to the **Writing Studio** for more on writing a literary analysis.

 Go to the **Speaking and Listening Studio** for help with having a group discussion.

RESPOND TO THE ESSENTIAL QUESTION

 What will people risk to be free?

Gather Information Review your annotations and notes on the excerpt from *Narrative of the Life of Frederick Douglass, an American Slave*. Then, add relevant details to your Response Log. As you determine which information to include, think about:

• the obstacles that Douglass faced

• the risks he took to learn how to read

• how knowledge both liberated and frightened him

At the end of the unit, you can use your notes to help you write a research report.

ACADEMIC VOCABULARY

As you write and discuss what you learned from the autobiography, be sure to use the Academic Vocabulary words. Check off each of the words that you use.

❑ **access**

❑ **civil**

❑ **demonstrate**

❑ **document**

❑ **symbolize**

CREATE AND DISCUSS

Write a Literary Analysis Suggest to students that they think about their views and then write them down. Tell them to then read what they wrote and look for ways to make it clearer and more precisely what they mean. Discuss that good writers rarely go with the first version of a core sentence.

For **writing support** for students at varying proficiency levels, see the **Text X-Ray** on page 240D.

Discuss with a Small Group Remind students that listening "closely and respectfully" means to pay attention and to accept what others say without making negative comments or dismissing their ideas. Explain that making suggestions that build on other ideas is a technique that both accepts others ideas and puts your ideas out there. Give students this example: "I think Corinne's idea that Frederick Douglass was upset at his situation is exactly right. I also believe that the ability to think thoroughly about his situation made him feel cursed."

RESPOND TO THE ESSENTIAL QUESTION

Allow time for students to add details from "*from* Narrative of the Life of Frederick Douglass, An American Slave" to their Unit 4 Response Logs.

TEACH

CRITICAL VOCABULARY

Answers:

1. *relieved*

2. *studying a little each day*

3. *study the recipe*

4. *criticism*

5. *taking a test*

6. *many books*

VOCABULARY STRATEGY:
Latin Roots

Answers:

1. *dictionary/ a reference source with an alphabetical list of words and their meanings*

2. *dictator/ an absolute ruler*

3. *contradict/ to assert or express the opposite of a statement*

4. *dictate/ to say or read aloud to be recorded or written by another; to control or command*

5. *verdict/ the finding of a jury in a trial; a judgment or an opinion*

 RESPOND

CRITICAL VOCABULARY

WORD BANK
commence
apprehension
prudence
unabated
denunciation
vindication

Practice and Apply Use what you know about the vocabulary words to answer the following questions.

1. If an innocent convict receives **vindication,** will he feel relieved or upset?

2. Which demonstrates **prudence,** studying a little each day or waiting until the night before the test to begin studying?

3. To **commence** baking a cake, would you stir the batter or study the recipe?

4. Which is a type of **denunciation,** praise or criticism?

5. Would you feel **apprehension** about taking a test or getting an A?

6. If your interest in Frederick Douglass is **unabated,** will you read many books about him or just one?

 Go to the **Vocabulary Studio** for more on Latin roots.

VOCABULARY STRATEGY: Latin Roots

A **word root** is a word part that contains the core meaning of a word. A root is combined with other word parts, such as a prefix or a suffix, to form a word. The roots of many English words come from Latin. Read this sentence from Frederick Douglass's autobiography.

> **She was not satisfied with simply doing as well as he had underlined{commanded}; she seemed anxious to do better.**

The word *commanded* includes the Latin root *mand,* which means "to entrust." You can use the meaning of the root *mand* as a clue to figure out that *commanded* means "entrusted someone to carry out an order."

Practice and Apply Find the word in each sentence that includes the Latin root *dict,* which means "to say." Use context and the meaning of the root to help you write a definition of the word. Then verify each of your definitions by finding the word's precise meaning in a print or digital dictionary.

1. Douglass probably did not have access to a dictionary as he learned how to read.

2. Douglass's cruel master and mistress were like dictators.

3. He did not contradict his master's view of the dangers of reading.

4. No one could dictate to him not to follow his desires.

5. The verdict for Douglass's "crime" of reading is "not guilty."

ⓔⓛ **ENGLISH LEARNER SUPPORT**

Vocabulary Strategy Give students additional practice in determining the meanings of unfamiliar words. Write the following words on the board: *disappear, inanimate, unutterable, incompatible, precaution.* Have pairs of students copy the words, underline the prefixes, and write definitions. Tell them to confirm their definitions by looking up each word in a dictionary.
LIGHT

LANGUAGE CONVENTIONS:
Pronoun-Antecedent Agreement

A **pronoun** is a word used in place of a noun or another pronoun. The word or phrase to which the pronoun refers is called its **antecedent.** For example, in the following sentence, the pronoun *their* refers to the antecedent *they*: **They** took **their** *seats at the restaurant.*

For **agreement in number,** use singular pronouns with singular antecedents and plural pronouns with plural antecedents.

• *Incorrect:* <u>Douglass</u> was grateful to **their** friends for teaching **them** how to read.
• *Revised:* <u>Douglass</u> was grateful to **his** friends for teaching **him** how to read.

For **agreement in gender,** masculine pronouns (*he, his, him*) refer to male antecedents, and feminine pronouns (*she, her*) refer to female antecedents.

• *Incorrect:* <u>Douglass</u> was grateful to **her** friends.
• *Revised:* <u>Douglass</u> was grateful to **his** friends.

For **agreement in person,** a pronoun in the first-, second-, or third-person form must match the person of its antecedent.

• *Incorrect:* <u>You</u> were grateful to **their** friends.
• *Revised:* <u>You</u> were grateful to **your** friends.

Practice and Apply Rewrite each sentence to correct the pronoun-antecedent error.

1. Following his husband's example, Douglass's mistress became cruel.

2. The boys taught her friend Douglass how to read.

3. I want to acquire another book by Douglass for your library.

4. Douglass was angry when they read about slavery.

5. Douglass gave many speeches about their experiences with slavery.

> Go to the **Grammar Studio** for more on pronoun-antecedent agreement.

LANGUAGE CONVENTIONS:
Pronoun-Antecedent Agreement

Review the information about pronouns and antecedents with students. Explain that pronoun-antecedent errors are an issue both in writing and speaking. Point out that people can misinterpret what you write or say if you use incorrect pronouns and antecedents. Tell students that, on the other hand, correct pronouns can be helpful when they are reading. Provide these two examples:

• Understanding pronouns can help readers interpret complex sentences.
• Comparing pronouns and antecedents can help readers determine whether an unfamiliar name is that of a male or female.

Call on students to create sentences that use the following combinations of pronoun features:

• Person: Third; Number: Singular; Gender: Female
• Person: First; Number: Plural; Gender: Male
• Person: Second; Number: Plural; Gender: Female
• Person: Third; Number: Plural; Gender: Neutral
• Person: First; Number: Singular; Gender: Male

Practice and Apply

1. *Following her husband's example, Douglass's mistress became cruel.*
2. *The boys taught their friend Douglass how to read.*
3. *I want to acquire another book by Douglass for my library.*
4. *Douglass was angry when he read about slavery.*
5. *Douglass gave many speeches about his experiences with slavery.*

 ENGLISH LEARNER SUPPORT

Pronoun-Antecedent Agreement Tell students that, until they are comfortable with English pronouns, it would likely be helpful to create a pronoun chart to which they can refer when confused. Have students each create this table and work together to fill it in. Review how pronouns can change depending on the usage in a sentence. Provide example sentences for each pronoun. **SUBSTANTIAL/MODERATE**

	First Person			Second Person			Third Person		
	Male	Female	Neutral	Male	Female	Neutral	Male	Female	Neutral
Singular									
Plural									

from HARRIET TUBMAN: CONDUCTOR ON THE UNDERGROUND RAILROAD

Biography by Ann Petry

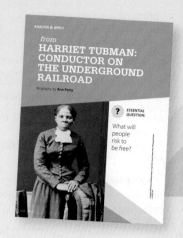

GENRE ELEMENTS
BIOGRAPHY

A good way to learn about a historical figure is to read a biography, a true and balanced account of a person's life told by someone other than the subject, usually in the third-person point of view. Biographers thoroughly research the people they write about. They then use the research to give readers access to their subjects through one or more methods of characterization, techniques that reveal a person's qualities and personality.

LEARNING OBJECTIVES

- Examine the author's use of characterization.
- Analyze structure of a biography.
- Use academic and general vocabulary in writing and speaking.
- Evaluate word choice and sentence structure to create mood and convey meaning.
- Recognize and correct run-on sentences.
- **Language** Discuss the author's word choices with a partner or in groups using the word *repetition*.

TEXT COMPLEXITY

		Lexile: 1010L
Quantitative Measures	*from* Harriet Tubman: Conductor on the Underground Railroad	
Qualitative Measures	**Ideas Presented** Multiple levels of meaning; greater demand for inference.	
	Structure Used No major shifts in chronology; occasional use of flashback.	
	Language Used Mostly explicit; some figurative language.	
	Knowledge Required Distinctly unfamiliar experiences for students.	

Online Ed

RESOURCES

- Unit 4 Response Log
- Selection Audio
- Reading Studio: Notice & Note
- Level Up Tutorial: Biographies and Autobiographies
- Level Up Tutorial: Character Traits
- Level Up Tutorial: Synthesizing Information
- Level Up Tutorial: Analyzing Visuals
- Writing Studio: Writing Arguments
- Speaking and Listening Studio: Giving a Presentation
- Vocabulary Studio: Latin Roots
- Grammar Studio: Module 1: Lesson 2: Run-on Sentences
- "Harriet Tubman: Conductor on the Underground Railroad" Selection Test

SUMMARIES

English

Harriet Tubman was a famous conductor on the Underground Railroad. She quietly slipped into slave-held areas and then helped groups of fugitive slaves find their way north to Canada where they could be free.

Spanish

Harriet Tubman fue una famosa conductora del ferrocarril subterráneo. Ella calladamente entraba en áreas con esclavos y ayudaba a grupos de esclavos fugitivos a encontrar su camino a Canadá, donde podían ser libres.

SMALL-GROUP OPTIONS

Have students work in small groups to read and discuss the selection.

Double-Entry Journal

- Have students create two columns for notetaking. Model heading the first column "Quotes from the Text" and "My Notes" on the right column.
- Explain to students that they should record significant, important, or perplexing quotes from the text in the left column as they read.
- Have students write their own interpretations, summaries, questions, and restatements in the right column across from the quotations.
- Then have students discuss their entries with a partner, comparing their interpretations of the same quotations.

Think-Pair-Share

- After students have read and analyzed "Harriet Tubman," pose this question: *What were the people in the story risking to be free? What does this say about their values?*
- Have students think about the question individually and take notes.
- Then have pairs discuss their ideas about the question.
- Finally, ask pairs to share their responses with the class.

Text X-Ray: English Learner Support
for "Harriet Tubman: Conductor on the Underground Railroad"

Use the Text X-Ray and the supports and scaffolds in the Teacher's Edition to help guide students at different proficiency levels through the section.

INTRODUCE THE SELECTION
DISCUSS SLAVERY

In this lesson, students will need to be able to discuss events and people in a historical context. Students will need to understand historical terms specific to the pre-Civil War era. Explain that slavery is the practice of one human claiming ownership over another person. Tell students that slavery has existed throughout human history but came to the United States during the colonial period and lasted until the Civil War.

Read paragraphs 1 and 2. Review words associated with slavery that may be unfamiliar to students:

- *masters:* slave owners
- *slaves:* people under the total control of another person
- *capture:* to catch and lock up
- *plantation:* a large farm or estate
- *overseer:* person in charge of supervising work

CULTURAL REFERENCES

The following words and phrases may be unfamiliar to students:

- *man named Moses* (paragraph 1): allusion to biblical character Moses who led group of slaves out of Egypt
- *taken to their heels* (paragraph 3): run away
- *camp meetings* (paragraph 4): a type of church service
- *spiritual* (paragraph 7): religious song
- *rheumatism* (paragraph 34): arthritis
- *frame house* (paragraph 54): house made of wood
- *colony* (paragraph 56): community

LISTENING

Understand the Author's Craft

Explain that the author's craft is a broad label that refers to the many ways that an author uses literary techniques to create mood, tone, and a sense of voice in their writing. They can do this through word choice, sentence structures, syntax, and parallelism, to name a few techniques.

Have students listen as you read aloud paragraph 44. Use the following supports with students at varying proficiency levels:

- Tell students that you will ask questions about what you just read aloud. For example, ask: *Does the author use repetition?* (yes) *What word does the narrator keep repeating?* (sometimes)   **SUBSTANTIAL**
- Explain that repetition can create structure in a text. Ask: *What follows each time the narrator uses the word "sometimes"?* (*The narrator describes something Tubman does to keep the fugitives going.*)   **MODERATE**
- Pair students to discuss the use of repetition in the text. Ask: *What are examples of repetition or parallelism in the passage? How do they affect the mood or tone?* (*The narrator describes actions ending in -ing and begins descriptions with sometimes. It creates a mood of perseverance as she keeps doing things and doesn't give up.*)   **LIGHT**

SPEAKING

Discuss Characterization

Tell students that authors reveal the characters' personal traits through more than just description. Explain that they use what the characters say and do, and also the way other characters react.

Work with students to read paragraphs 20–22. Use the following supports with students at varying proficiency levels:

- Display and read aloud: *Thomas Garrett is kind. He is a big man and strong, but would not harm anyone.* Have students practice saying the sentence to a partner. **SUBSTANTIAL**
- To help students express their ideas about characterization, display the following sentence frame: *Thomas Garrett is a _____ man. He is _____.* **MODERATE**
- Pair students to discuss characterization. Ask: *How does the author characterize Thomas Garrett?* (*He is a kind, big man, who chooses to use his strength to help people instead of hurt them.*) **LIGHT**

READING

Analyze Word Choice

Explain that authors choose their words carefully to create layers of meaning in the text and to create mood, tone, and voice.

Work with students to read paragraph 4. Use the following supports with students at varying proficiency levels:

- Draw attention to the phrase "four-footed game." Explain that the word *"game"* refers to something that is hunted by hunters. Ask: *What does this phrase mean or refer to?* (animals) *Does the author's use of phrase help you understand that these men treat enslaved people like animals?* (yes) **SUBSTANTIAL**
- Point out the phrase "four-footed game" and ask what it means and why the author would include it. *The phrase means _____. The phrase reminds me of _____. The effect of the word choice is _____.* **MODERATE**
- Ask students to explain why the author uses the phrase "four-footed game." (*The author was making a comparison to the way they hunt fugitive slaves, treating them like animals.*) **LIGHT**

WRITING

Write a Speech

Draw students' attention to the writing assignment on p. 271. Read the prompt and questions aloud. Make an outline of the important points of their speeches.

Use the following supports with students at varying proficiency levels:

- Work with students to create outlines with an introduction, body, and conclusion. Provide a sentence frame to get them started: *Harriet Tubman was _____.* Guide them to create visuals illustrating the points they would like to make and to caption each drawing with a word or phrase. **SUBSTANTIAL**
- Help students create outlines for their speeches with an introduction, body, and conclusion. Provide sentence frames but emphasize that students should alter the frames to fit their topic and voice: *Harriet Tubman was _____. She is a hero because _____. I think _____. Finally, _____.* **MODERATE**
- Ask students to work with a partner to outline their speeches. Discuss which information to include before writing a short speech explaining why Tubman is a hero. Encourage students to focus on one of the bullet points. **LIGHT**

Connect to the
? ESSENTIAL QUESTION

The accounts of Harriet Tubman and the people she helped escape slavery remind us of what people were willing to do and to risk in order to be free.

from

HARRIET TUBMAN: CONDUCTOR ON THE UNDERGROUND RAILROAD

Biography by **Ann Petry**

? ESSENTIAL QUESTION:

What will people risk to be free?

254   Unit 4

LEARNING MINDSET

Seeking Challenges Remind students that in order to grow, we need to challenge ourselves. It's important to try to do things that are hard. We might fail, but that's okay. Failing is part of learning.

QUICK START

Imagine being led on a difficult or dangerous journey. What qualities would you want the leader of this journey to have? List the top three.

ANALYZE CHARACTERIZATION

A **biography** is a form of nonfiction in which a writer provides a true account of another person's life. In a strong biography, the writer not only recounts the most significant events of the subject's life but also provides insights about the subject's traits and motivations. The way a biographer creates and develops the subject's character is called **characterization.** There are four main methods of characterization. As you read Petry's biography of Tubman, look for the following:

- Direct comments about Tubman—what the author states about Tubman's hopes, thoughts, and worries
- Descriptions of Tubman's physical appearance
- Tubman's own thoughts, speech, and actions and her possible **motivations,** or reasons for her actions
- How others behave toward Tubman and what you can infer about her from their thoughts, speech, and actions toward her

ANALYZE AUTHOR'S CRAFT

Author's craft refers to how an author uses literary techniques and narrative elements. **Mood** is the feeling or atmosphere that an author creates for the reader. **Tone** is the author's attitude toward his or her subject. **Voice** refers to the author's unique use of language that allows a reader to "hear" the author's personality behind the words. Study the examples below to see how Petry uses literary techniques to convey Tubman's story and establish mood, tone, and voice. Then, as you read, look for additional examples of each technique.

TECHNIQUE	DEFINITION	EXAMPLES
word choice	the author's use of specific words	The man who stood in the doorway looked at her coldly, looked with <u>unconcealed astonishment and fear</u>. . . .
sentence variety; punctuation variations	variations in sentence length; use of punctuation for dramatic effect	She had never used it—except as a threat.
parallelism	the use of similar grammatical constructions to express ideas that are related or equal in importance	When she knocked on the door of a farmhouse, a place where she and her parties of runaways had <u>always been welcome, always been given shelter</u>. . . .
syntax	the arrangement of words and phrases in sentences	Sometimes the masters thought <u>they had heard the cry of a hoot owl, repeated,</u> . . .

GENRE ELEMENTS: BIOGRAPHY

- presents a true and balanced account of a person's life
- is based on multiple credible sources
- is told from the third-person point of view

Harriet Tubman: Conductor on the Underground Railroad **255**

QUICK START

Have students read the Quick Start prompt, and invite them to share their lists. Discuss why they feel different leadership qualities are important.

ANALYZE CHARACTERIZATION

Discuss what makes a biography different from other nonfiction works and from fiction. Point out that, just as fiction writers use characterization techniques, biographers also try to show their subject's qualities and motivations. For each bulleted characterization technique, ask students to find an example in the text, explaining what they learn about Tubman from each one.

For additional support, go to the **Reading Studio** and assign the following Level Up Tutorial: Biographies and Autobiographies.

ANALYZE AUTHOR'S CRAFT

Tell students that author's craft refers to the methods authors use to make their writing lively and vivid. Discuss what it means to make writing "come alive." Guide students to understand that this biography is an example of literary nonfiction, in which the author has carefully chosen words, constructed sentences, and structured paragraphs and details so that meaning, sound, and feeling are conveyed.

After reviewing the four examples in the chart, have students identify additional examples. Discuss the effects on the reader.

TEACH

CRITICAL VOCABULARY

Encourage students to read all the sentences before answering the questions. Remind them to look for context clues that match the meaning of each word.

Answers:

1. *You might not want to stay at a party if you were the only guest not dressed nicely.*

2. *It might be possible to teach someone to speak in an eloquent way, but it would likely take a long time.*

3. *Someone might say or do something to hurt a person's feelings to evoke a sullen response.*

4. *Yes; you could try to coax a friend out of a bad mood with gentle suggestions or humor.*

■ English Learner Support

Use Cognates Tell students that two of the Critical Vocabulary words have Spanish cognates: *eloquence/ elocuencia, evoke/evocar.* **ALL LEVELS**

LANGUAGE CONVENTIONS

Review the information about run-on sentences. Point out the terms *conjunction* and *compound sentence* in the lesson. Explain that a *conjunction* is a word that can join two words or two phrases or two sentences. Work with students to create a list of conjunctions to display: *and, but, or, so,* and others that students suggest. Remind them that the two halves of a compound sentence can be joined together by a conjunction or a semicolon, and writing compound sentences is only one way to avoid run-ons.

Read aloud the example on page 256, pausing at the conjunction. Ask students to identify each independent clause in the compound sentence. Encourage them to look for similar structures as they read.

✏ ANNOTATION MODEL

Remind students of the four methods of characterization introduced on page 255. Tell students to look for and underline or highlight examples of these methods as they read. Suggest using different colors to mark the different methods. Encourage students to write notes in the margin about the author's craft, noting any signposts they see in the text.

 GET READY

CRITICAL VOCABULARY

disheveled	dispel	sullen	cajole
instill	linger	eloquence	evoke

To see how many Critical Vocabulary words you already know, answer the following questions.

1. Would you **linger** at a party if you were **disheveled**? Why or why not?

2. Could someone **instill eloquence** in you? Why or why not?

3. What might someone do to **evoke** a **sullen** response?

4. Would you **cajole** a friend to **dispel** a bad mood? Why or why not?

LANGUAGE CONVENTIONS

Run-on Sentences In this lesson, you will learn about run-on sentences and how to avoid them. A run-on sentence is made up of two or more **independent clauses**—a group of words that contains a subject and predicate and that can stand alone as a sentence—that are run together as a single sentence. In the sentence below, the author uses a comma and the conjunction *but* to create a **compound sentence** and avoid a run-on.

He was a big man and strong, <u>but</u> he had never used his strength to harm anyone, always to help people.

Throughout *Harriet Tubman: Conductor on the Underground Railroad,* notice the way the author uses punctuation and conjunctions to avoid run-on sentences.

ANNOTATION MODEL   **NOTICE & NOTE**

As you read, pay attention to the author's characterization of Harriet Tubman and the techniques she uses in her writing. You can also mark up evidence that supports your own ideas. In the model, you can see one reader's notes about *Harriet Tubman: Conductor on the Underground Railroad.*

5   Harriet Tubman could have told them that there was <u>far more involved</u> in this matter of running off slaves <u>than</u> signaling the would-be runaways by imitating the call of a whippoorwill, or a hoot owl, <u>far more involved than</u> a matter of waiting for a clear night when the North Star was visible.

> The author's use of parallelism emphasizes the idea that Tubman's work was difficult and involved careful preparations.

256   Unit 4

BACKGROUND

Ann Lane Petry (1908–1997) grew up in a small town in Connecticut, where she and her family were the only African American residents. Much of her writing focuses on the important contributions of African Americans. Before the Civil War, many enslaved people fled north to freedom along the Underground Railroad, a secret network of safe houses. One of the Underground Railroad's most famous "conductors" was Harriet Tubman.

from
HARRIET TUBMAN: CONDUCTOR ON THE UNDERGROUND RAILROAD

Biography by Ann Petry

SETTING A PURPOSE

As you read, look for clues about the kind of person Harriet Tubman was.

The Railroad Runs to Canada

1   Along the Eastern Shore of Maryland, in Dorchester County, in Caroline County, the masters kept hearing whispers about the man named Moses, who was running off slaves. At first they did not believe in his existence. The stories about him were fantastic, unbelievable. Yet they watched for him. They offered rewards for his capture.

2   They never saw him. Now and then they heard whispered rumors to the effect that he was in the neighborhood. The woods were searched. The roads were watched. There was never anything to indicate his whereabouts. But a few days afterward, a goodly number of slaves would be gone from the plantation. Neither the master nor the overseer had heard or seen anything unusual

Notice & Note

Use the side margins to notice and note signposts in the text.

ANALYZE AUTHOR'S CRAFT
Annotate: A **simple sentence** contains a single independent clause. In paragraph 2, mark two simple sentences with very similar structures that appear in a row.

Analyze: What effect does the author create by expressing these two ideas in separate but parallel sentences?

Harriet Tubman: Conductor on the Underground Railroad 257

BACKGROUND

Have students read the Background and information about the author. Clarify that the word *underground* means "secret or hidden" in this context and not literally underground. Also, clarify the Biblical allusion: The subject of this biography had the nickname Moses because, like the biblical Moses, she led enslaved people to freedom. Share additional historical information about Harriet Tubman's background:

Born around 1820 in Maryland, Tubman was sent to work in the fields when she was about 12. She was injured in the head as she tried to protect another field hand from an angry overseer. This injury caused the sudden bouts of sleep mentioned in the text. She escaped in 1849, following the North Star to Philadelphia. On her first trips back into Maryland, she rescued family members, including her 70-year-old parents.

SETTING A PURPOSE

Direct students to use the Setting a Purpose prompt to focus their reading.

✏ ANALYZE AUTHOR'S CRAFT

Remind students that author's craft refers to the methods authors use to create mood, tone, and voice, and to convey meaning through word choice, word order, and sentence structures. (**Answer:** *The author may have chosen to use simple sentences to create a convey a mood of mystery about "the man named Moses."*)

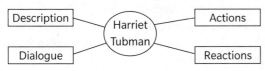

ANALYZE CHARACTERIZATION

Remind students that authors use a technique called characterization to reveal what a person is like. Explain that characterization can be shown through the traits and actions of the person or through how the person is seen by others. Point out that the author's characterization of Harriet Tubman shifts from the viewpoint of the masters to the viewpoint of Tubman herself: her actions reveal her qualities. (**Answer:** *The information in the preceding paragraphs is told from the viewpoint of masters, but the viewpoint shifts to Tubman's in paragraph 7. The author may have relied on sources from the plantations for the first section and first-hand accounts of the escapes for Tubman's viewpoint.*)

■ English Learner Support

Analyze Characterization Guide students to add details from paragraphs 6–8 to the "Actions" and "Reactions" sections of their characterization organizers. Model for students how to think about what these actions and reactions reveal about Tubman. (**Actions:** *planned trip for days; carefully selected slaves to take with her; sang forbidden spiritual; Tubman was a careful planner but unafraid.* **Reactions:** *people whispered, "Moses is here"; People saw her as a leader.*) **MODERATE/LIGHT**

 For **reading support** for students at varying proficiency levels, see the **Text X-Ray** on page 254D.

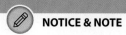
in the quarter.[1] Sometimes one or the other would vaguely remember having heard a whippoorwill call somewhere in the woods, close by, late at night. Though it was the wrong season for whippoorwills.

3 Sometimes the masters thought they had heard the cry of a hoot owl, repeated, and would remember having thought that the intervals between the low moaning cry were wrong, that it had been repeated four times in succession instead of three. There was never anything more than that to suggest that all was not well in the quarter. Yet when morning came, they invariably discovered that a group of the finest slaves had taken to their heels.

4 Unfortunately, the discovery was almost always made on a Sunday. Thus a whole day was lost before the machinery of pursuit could be set in motion. The posters offering rewards for the fugitives could not be printed until Monday. The men who made a living hunting for runaway slaves were out of reach, off in the woods with their dogs and their guns, in pursuit of four-footed game, or they were in camp meetings saying their prayers with their wives and families beside them.

ANALYZE CHARACTERIZATION

Annotate: Mark details in paragraphs 5–7 that reveal Harriet Tubman's character.

Draw Conclusions: How does the information in these paragraphs differ from the details about "the man named Moses" in paragraphs 1–4? What do these differences suggest about the sources each may have been based on?

5 Harriet Tubman could have told them that there was far more involved in this matter of running off slaves than signaling the would-be runaways by <u>imitating the call of a whippoorwill</u>, or a hoot owl, far more involved than a matter of <u>waiting for a clear night</u> when the North Star was visible.

6 In December, 1851, when she started out with the band of fugitives that she planned to take to Canada, <u>she had been in the vicinity of the plantation for days, planning the trip, carefully selecting the slaves that she would take with her</u>.

7 She had announced her arrival in the quarter by singing the forbidden spiritual—"Go down, Moses, 'way down to Egypt Land"[2]—<u>singing it softly</u> outside the door of a slave cabin, late at night. The <u>husky voice</u> was beautiful even when it was barely more than a murmur borne[3] on the wind.

8 Once she had made her presence known, word of her coming spread from cabin to cabin. The slaves whispered to each other, ear to mouth, mouth to ear, "Moses is here." "Moses has come." "Get ready. Moses is back again." The ones who had agreed to go North with her put ashcake and salt herring in

---

[1] **quarter:** the area in which enslaved people lived.
[2] **"Go down, Moses, 'way down to Egypt Land":** a line from an African American folk song. In the Bible, Moses led the Israelite slaves in Egypt to freedom.
[3] **borne:** carried.

APPLYING ACADEMIC VOCABULARY

☑ access   ☐ civil   ☐ demonstrate   ☐ document   ☑ symbolize

THINK-PAIR-SHARE Have students turn to a partner to discuss the following questions. Guide students to include the Academic Vocabulary words *access* and *symbolize* in their responses. Ask volunteers to share their responses.

- Point out the references to Moses and Canada as well as Tubman's singing of the forbidden spiritual. What do these ideas and actions **symbolize** to the enslaved people to whom Harriet Tubman is signaling?
- How did Tubman gain **access** to the enslaved people she fought to free?

an old bandanna, hastily tied it into a bundle, and then waited patiently for the signal that meant it was time to start.

9   There were eleven in this party, including one of her brothers and his wife. It was the largest group that she had ever conducted, but she was determined that more and more slaves should know what freedom was like.

10   She had to take them all the way to Canada. The Fugitive Slave Law[4] was no longer a great many incomprehensible words written down on the country's lawbooks. The new law had become a reality. It was Thomas Sims, a boy, picked up on the streets of Boston at night and shipped back to Georgia. It was Jerry and Shadrach, arrested and jailed with no warning.

11   She had never been in Canada. The route beyond Philadelphia was strange to her. But she could not let the runaways who accompanied her know this. As they walked along she told them stories of her own first flight, she kept painting vivid word pictures of what it would be like to be free.

12   But there were so many of them this time. She knew moments of doubt when she was half-afraid, and kept looking back over her shoulder, imagining that she heard the sound of pursuit. They would certainly be pursued. Eleven of them. Eleven thousand dollars' worth of flesh and bone and muscle that belonged to Maryland planters. If they were caught, the eleven runaways would be whipped and sold South, but she— she would probably be hanged.

13   They tried to sleep during the day but they never could wholly relax into sleep. She could tell by the positions they assumed, by their restless movements. And they walked at night. Their progress was slow. It took them three nights of walking to reach the first stop. She had told them about the place where they would stay, promising warmth and good food, holding these things out to them as an incentive to keep going.

14   When she knocked on the door of a farmhouse, a place where she and her parties of runaways had always been welcome, always been given shelter and plenty to eat, there was no answer. She knocked again, softly. A voice from within said, "Who is it?" There was fear in the voice.

15   She knew instantly from the sound of the voice that there was something wrong. She said, "A friend with friends," the password on the Underground Railroad.

16   The door opened, slowly. The man who stood in the doorway looked at her coldly, looked with unconcealed

---

[4] **Fugitive Slave Law:** a law by which enslaved people who escaped could be recovered by their owners.

ANALYZE AUTHOR'S CRAFT

Annotate: Mark the language the author uses to describe the effects of the Fugitive Slave Law in paragraph 10.

Interpret: What does the author's word choice and syntax help her convey about the law?

ANALYZE AUTHOR'S CRAFT

Tell students that syntax is the arrangement of words, phrases, and clauses within sentences. Explain that because there are many correct ways to shape a sentence, an author's choices reflect his or her craft and style. (**Answer:** *It shows how the law threatened people and prevented them from feeling safe even after they had escaped slavery.*)

 ENGLISH LEARNER SUPPORT

Understand Text Structure   Tell students that biographies are often told in chronological order, or the order that events happened. Explain that these events may be related to each other as causes and effects. In many cases, readers must infer the cause-and-effect relationships between events.

- Read the following statement: *Escaped slaves had to go to Canada to be free because of the Fugitive Slave Law.* Ask students whether the Fugitive Slave Law is a cause or effect in the sentence. *(cause)*   **SUBSTANTIAL**

- Have students complete this sentence frame identifying the cause-and-effect relationship in paragraph 10: *Because of the Fugitive Slave Law, _____. (escaped slaves had to go all the way to Canada)*   **MODERATE**

- Have students write a sentence explaining the effect of the Fugitive Slave Law on Harriet Tubman's route.   **LIGHT**

TEACH

ANALYZE AUTHOR'S CRAFT

Tell students that repeated grammatical constructions are called **parallelism**. Point out that authors may use parallelism to create rhythm and emphasize similar ideas. (**Answer:** *The first and second list are oppositional, emphasizing the stark contrast between what the band expected and what they would receive. Similarly, the third list, refrains the good things that were promised to them.*)

■ English Learner Support

Analyze Author's Craft Make sure students understand the concept of parallelism. Write out the second sentence of paragraph 17 on two lines so the words "food and rest and warmth" are stacked above "hunger and cold and more walking" to visually support the concept. Draw arrows or circle parallel words if additional support is needed to make the connections. **MODERATE**

ANALYZE CHARACTERIZATION

Tell students that characterization in a biography includes information about the subject's thoughts and feelings. (**Answer:** *The author wants to show that Tubman admired others for their kindness, generosity, and cleverness.*)

For **speaking support** for students at varying proficiency levels, see the **Text X-Ray** on page 254D.

CRITICAL VOCABULARY

disheveled: The author is explaining how the fugitives look after three nights of walking.

ASK STUDENTS to describe how the disheveled people might look. (*Their clothes are wrinkled and spotted with dirt,*)

instill: Harriet Tubman wants to build courage in the people she is leading.

ASK STUDENTS why Tubman needs to instill courage. (*They are facing a frightening and unfamiliar situation.*)

dispel: Harriet Tubman is trying to keep the runaways calm.

ASK STUDENTS why it is important for Tubman to dispel their fears. (*If they are afraid, they might panic and run or make noise.*)

260   Unit 4

---

disheveled
(dĭ-shĕv´əld) *adj.* When something is *disheveled*, it is messy or untidy.

ANALYZE AUTHOR'S CRAFT
Annotate: Find and mark an example of parallelism in paragraph 17.

Evaluate: Explain the effect of that technique in the example.

instill
(ĭn-stĭl´) *v.* When you *instill* something, you establish or implant it gradually.

dispel
(dĭ-spĕl´) *v.* When you *dispel* something, you drive it away.

ANALYZE CHARACTERIZATION
Annotate: Mark details the author uses to show Tubman's view of Thomas Garrett in paragraphs 20–21.

Predict: Why might the author have included this information?

astonishment and fear at the eleven **disheveled** runaways who were standing near her. Then he shouted, "Too many, too many. It's not safe. My place was searched last week. It's not safe!" and slammed the door in her face.

17   She turned away from the house, frowning. She had promised her passengers <u>food and rest and warmth</u>, and instead of that, there would be <u>hunger and cold and more walking</u> over the frozen ground. Somehow she would have to **instill** courage into these eleven people, most of them strangers, would have to feed them on hope and bright dreams of freedom instead of the <u>fried pork and corn bread and milk</u> she had promised them.

18   They stumbled along behind her, half-dead for sleep, and she urged them on, though she was as tired and as discouraged as they were. She had never been in Canada but she kept painting wondrous word pictures of what it would be like. She managed to **dispel** their fear of pursuit, so that they would not become hysterical, panic-stricken. Then she had to bring some of the fear back, so that they would stay awake and keep walking though they drooped with sleep.

19   Yet during the day, when they lay down deep in a thicket, they never really slept, because if a twig snapped or the wind sighed in the branches of a pine tree, they jumped to their feet, afraid of their own shadows, shivering and shaking. It was very cold, but they dared not make fires because someone would see the smoke and wonder about it.

20   She kept thinking, eleven of them. Eleven thousand dollars' worth of slaves. And she had to take them all the way to Canada. Sometimes she told them about Thomas Garrett, in Wilmington. She said he was their friend even though he did not know them. He was <u>the friend of all fugitives</u>. He called them God's poor. <u>He was a Quaker[5] and his speech was a little different</u> from that of other people. His clothing was different, too. He wore the wide-brimmed hat that the Quakers wear.

21   She said that <u>he had thick white hair, soft, almost like a baby's</u>, and <u>the kindest eyes she had ever seen</u>. He was a <u>big man and strong, but he had never used his strength to harm anyone, always to help people</u>. <u>He would give all of them a new pair of shoes</u>. Everybody. He always did. Once they reached his house in Wilmington, they would be safe. He would see to it that they were.

22   She described the house where he lived, told them about the store where he sold shoes. She said he kept a pail of milk and a loaf of bread in the drawer of his desk so that he would have

---
[5] **Quaker:** a member of a religious group called the Society of Friends.

260   Unit 4

food ready at hand for any of God's poor who should suddenly appear before him, fainting with hunger. There was a hidden room in the store. A whole wall swung open, and behind it was a room where he could hide fugitives. On the wall there were shelves filled with small boxes—boxes of shoes—so that you would never guess that the wall actually opened.

23   While she talked, she kept watching them. They did not believe her. She could tell by their expressions. They were thinking, New shoes, Thomas Garrett, Quaker, Wilmington— what foolishness was this? Who knew if she told the truth? Where was she taking them anyway?

24   That night they reached the next stop—a farm that belonged to a German. She made the runaways take shelter behind trees at the edge of the fields before she knocked at the door. She hesitated before she approached the door, thinking, suppose that he, too, should refuse shelter, suppose— Then she thought, Lord, I'm going to hold steady on to You and You've got to see me through—and knocked softly.

25   She heard the familiar guttural voice say, "Who's there?"

26   She answered quickly, "A friend with friends."

27   He opened the door and greeted her warmly. "How many this time?" he asked.

28   "Eleven," she said and waited, doubting, wondering.

29   He said, "Good. Bring them in."

30   He and his wife fed them in the lamplit kitchen, their faces glowing, as they offered food and more food, urging them to eat, saying there was plenty for everybody, have more milk, have more bread, have more meat.

LANGUAGE CONVENTIONS
Annotate: Mark the author's use of dashes in paragraphs 22–24.

Analyze: Which sentences would become run-ons if the dashes were not used?

LANGUAGE CONVENTIONS

Remind students that a run-on sentence has two or more independent clauses run together. Tell students that run-ons should be avoided in order to clarify ideas. (**Answer:** *All of the sentences would be run-ons without the dashes. The use of dashes builds tension and helps convey a mood of suspense.*)

A stop on the Underground Railroad

Harriet Tubman: Conductor on the Underground Railroad   261

IMPROVE READING FLUENCY

Targeted Passage Have students work with a partner to read this section. Point out that the narration frequently shifts from a third-person point of view to revealing the inner thoughts of Harriet Tubman. Explain that the inner dialogue is often fragmented like the way people speak. Model for students how to read the shift from narration to inner dialogue in paragraph 23. Have students follow along in their books as you read aloud. Then have each partner take turns reading paragraphs 24–30. Encourage students to provide feedback.

ANALYZE AUTHOR'S CRAFT

Remind students that authors use **grammatical constructions** and **word choice** for effect to shape mood and tone. Read aloud paragraphs 33–36. Point out the repeated use of the phrases "No one" and "She told," and discuss how the repetition creates a mood of fatigue. (**Answer:** *The words describing unpleasant feelings followed by "too long" help the reader understand the difficulty of the journey and the desperation the people must have felt.*)

■ English Learner Support

Analyze Author's Craft Support student analysis and discussion of the word choice and sentence structures by providing the following sentence frames: *The phrase _____ is used _____ times. The effect of _____ on the reader is _____. I think the author included _____ because _____.*
MODERATE

CRITICAL VOCABULARY

linger: The author is describing how people's feelings continued after they spent the night in a safe kitchen.

ASK STUDENTS to describe the feelings that lingered on. (*The warm, peaceful feelings they had inside the kitchen stayed with them.*)

sullen: Harriet Tubman sees sullen looks on the people's faces.

ASK STUDENTS to explain why sullen feelings are a problem for Harriet Tubman. (*She fears the people might give up or even turn against her.*)

eloquence: The author is describing Tubman's stories about the abolitionist Frederick Douglass.

ASK STUDENTS why eloquence might make a person famous. (*When someone speaks with eloquence, he or she can persuade and inspire others.*)

evoke: Harriet Tubman shares a painful memory of her miserable childhood.

ASK STUDENTS why telling a painful story might evoke a memory. (*It brings the pain back to mind.*)

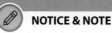

31   They spent the night in the warm kitchen. They really slept, all that night and until dusk the next day. When they left, it was with reluctance. They had all been warm and safe and well-fed. It was hard to exchange the security offered by that clean warm kitchen for the darkness and the cold of a December night.

"Go On or Die"

32   Harriet had found it hard to leave the warmth and friendliness, too. But she urged them on. For a while, as they walked, they seemed to carry in them a measure of contentment; some of the serenity and the cleanliness of that big warm kitchen **lingered** on inside them. But as they walked farther and farther away from the warmth and the light, the cold and the darkness entered into them. They fell silent, **sullen**, suspicious. She waited for the moment when some one of them would turn mutinous. It did not happen that night.

33   Two nights later she was aware that the feet behind her were moving slower and slower. She heard the irritability in their voices, knew that soon someone would refuse to go on.

34   She started talking about William Still and the Philadelphia Vigilance Committee.[6] No one commented. No one asked any questions. She told them the story of William and Ellen Craft and how they escaped from Georgia. Ellen was so fair that she looked as though she were white, and so she dressed up in a man's clothing and she looked like a wealthy young planter. Her husband, William, who was dark, played the role of her slave. Thus they traveled from Macon, Georgia, to Philadelphia, riding on the trains, staying at the finest hotels. Ellen pretended to be very ill—her right arm was in a sling, and her right hand was bandaged, because she was supposed to have rheumatism. Thus she avoided having to sign the register at the hotels for she could not read or write. They finally arrived safely in Philadelphia, and then went on to Boston.

35   No one said anything. Not one of them seemed to have heard her.

36   She told them about Frederick Douglass, the most famous of the escaped slaves, of his **eloquence**, of his magnificent appearance. Then she told them of her own first vain effort at running away, **evoking** the memory of that miserable life she had led as a child, reliving it for a moment in the telling.

37   But they had been tired too long, hungry too long, afraid too long, footsore too long. One of them suddenly cried out in

---

[6] **Philadelphia Vigilance Committee:** a fundraising organization that helped people who had escaped enslavement.

linger
(lǐng´gər) *v.* To *linger* is to remain or stay longer.

sullen
(sŭl´ən) *adj. Sullen* people show silent resentment.

ANALYZE AUTHOR'S CRAFT
Annotate: Mark the author's use of parallelism in paragraph 37.

Interpret: What words are repeated? Explain the effects of this repeated grammatical construction and word choice.

eloquence
(ĕl´ə-kwəns) *n. Eloquence* is the ability to speak powerfully and persuasively.

evoke
(ĭ-vōk´) *v.* When you *evoke* something, you bring it to mind.

despair, "Let me go back. It is better to be a slave than to suffer like this in order to be free."

38   She carried a gun with her on these trips. She had never used it—except as a threat. Now as she aimed it, she experienced a feeling of guilt, remembering that time, years ago, when she had prayed for the death of Edward Brodas, the Master, and then not too long afterward had heard that great wailing cry that came from the throats of the field hands, and knew from the sound that the Master was dead.

39   One of the runaways said, again, "Let me go back. Let me go back," and stood still, and then turned around and said, over his shoulder, "I am going back."

40   She lifted the gun, aimed it at the despairing slave. She said, "Go on with us or die." The husky low-pitched voice was grim.

41   He hesitated for a moment and then he joined the others. They started walking again. She tried to explain to them why none of them could go back to the plantation. If a runaway returned, he would turn traitor, the master and the overseer would force him to turn traitor. The returned slave would disclose the stopping places, the hiding places, the cornstacks they had used with the full knowledge of the owner of the farm, the name of the German farmer who had fed them and sheltered them. These people who had risked their own security to help runaways would be ruined, fined, imprisoned.

42   She said, "We got to go free or die. And freedom's not bought with dust."

43   This time she told them about the long agony of the Middle Passage[7] on the old slave ships, about the black horror of the holds, about the chains and the whips. They too knew these stories. But she wanted to remind them of the long hard way they had come, about the long hard way they had yet to go. She told them about Thomas Sims, the boy picked up on the streets of Boston and sent back to Georgia. She said when they got him back to Savannah, got him in prison there, they whipped him until a doctor who was standing by watching said, "You will kill him if you strike him again!" His master said, "Let him die!"

44   Thus she forced them to go on. Sometimes she thought she had become nothing but a voice speaking in the darkness, **cajoling**, urging, threatening. Sometimes she told them things to make them laugh, sometimes she sang to them, and heard the eleven voices behind her blending softly with hers, and then she knew that for the moment all was well with them.

---

[7] **Middle Passage:** a sea route along which enslaved Africans were transported to the Americas.

NOTICE & NOTE

BIG QUESTIONS

Notice & Note: Mark anything that surprises you in paragraph 38. If nothing surprises you, mark details that confirm what you already knew.

Analyze: Why might the author have included the facts you marked?

cajole
(kə-jōl´) *v.* When you *cajole*, you coax or urge gently.

BIG QUESTIONS

Remind students to note anything that makes them think, "Really?" Point out that this could be something they did not know or do not believe; it could also be something that helps them understand or presents a different **perspective**. Model answering the Big Question, "What surprised me?" Draw attention to paragraph 40. Say, *"I was surprised she would aim the gun at the slave she was trying to help free and would be so harsh and unsympathetic. I wonder why she would act this way."* (**Answer:** *Responses will vary depending on student experience and understanding of the text.*)

■ English Learner Support

Big Questions   Clarify any words that are confusing. Make sure students understand the concept of surprise. Act out the meaning if necessary. Provide sentence frames to support analysis and discussion: *I was surprised by _____ because _____.*   **SUBSTANTIAL/MODERATE**

For **listening support** for students at varying proficiency levels, see the **Text X-Ray** on page 254C.

CRITICAL VOCABULARY

cajole: THE author uses three verbs—*cajoles, urges, threatens*—to show what Harriet Tubman does to keep her followers from giving up.

ASK STUDENTS for ideas about why the author puts *cajole* first in the list. (*Cajoling is the mildest form of urging. Cajoles is followed by the stronger verb, urges, and then the strongest, threatens.*)

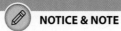

ANALYZE CHARACTERIZATION

Explain that the reaction of others to a character is an important part of **characterization**. Point out that, after the incident in which Tubman threatens to shoot the runaway, the group seems to have changed its view of her. (**Answer:** *Tubman's strong character and leadership have helped her gain the trust and respect of the people in her group.*)

■ English Learner Support

Analyze Characterization Have students discuss with a partner which details to add to their characterization organizers. Ask students to identify words that describe Tubman in paragraph 45. *(short, muscular, indomitable)* Then have them identify one sentence in paragraph 46 that explains the slaves' reactions to her. *(They had come to trust her implicitly, totally.)* **SUBSTANTIAL/MODERATE**

NOTICE & NOTE

ANALYZE CHARACTERIZATION

Annotate: Mark details in paragraph 46 that tell how the people in Tubman's group felt about her.

Infer: What do the details about the group members' actions suggest about Tubman?

45 She gave the impression of being a short, muscular, indomitable woman who could never be defeated. Yet at any moment she was liable to be seized by one of those curious fits of sleep, which might last for a few minutes or for hours.

46 Even on this trip, she suddenly fell asleep in the woods. The runaways, ragged, dirty, hungry, cold, did not steal the gun as they might have, and set off by themselves, or turn back. They sat on the ground near her and waited patiently until she awakened. They had come to trust her implicitly, totally. They, too, had come to believe her repeated statement, "We got to go free or die." She was leading them into freedom, and so they waited until she was ready to go on.

47 Finally, they reached Thomas Garrett's house in Wilmington, Delaware. Just as Harriet had promised, Garrett gave them all new shoes, and provided carriages to take them on to the next stop.

48 By slow stages they reached Philadelphia, where William Still hastily recorded their names, and the plantations whence

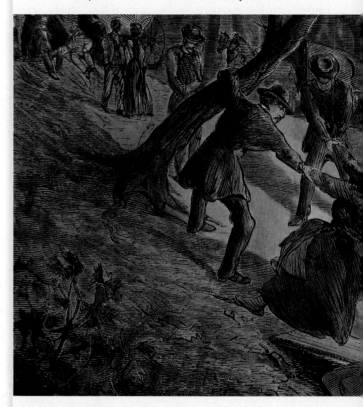

WHEN STUDENTS STRUGGLE . . .

Analyze Characterization Have individuals or partners use a chart to analyze the characterizations in the text.

Character	Description of the character	Actions by the character	Reactions to the character	What does this tell me about the character?
Harriet Tubman	short, muscular, indomitable	She sleeps in the woods.	Runaways wait while she sleeps.	They trust her completely.

 For additional support, go to the **Reading Studio** and assign the following [LEVEL] **Level Up tutorial: Character Traits.**

they had come, and something of the life they had led in slavery. Then he carefully hid what he had written, for fear it might be discovered. In 1872 he published this record in book form and called it *The Underground Railroad*. In the foreword to his book he said: "While I knew the danger of keeping strict records, and while I did not then dream that in my day slavery would be blotted out, or that the time would come when I could publish these records, it used to afford me great satisfaction to take them down, fresh from the lips of fugitives on the way to freedom, and to preserve them as they had given them."

49   William Still, who was familiar with all the station stops on the Underground Railroad, supplied Harriet with money and sent her and her eleven fugitives on to Burlington, New Jersey.

50   Harriet felt safer now, though there were danger spots ahead. But the biggest part of her job was over. As they went farther and farther north, it grew colder; she was aware of the wind on the Jersey ferry and aware of the cold damp in New

ENGLISH LEARNER SUPPORT

Confirm Understanding Use the following supports with students at varying proficiency levels:

• Write *station* on the board, and read it aloud several times, with students repeating it after you. Point out that *-tion* is pronounced /shun/ and explain that the ending comes from Greek. Clarify that a *station* is a place along a railroad where a train stops so passengers can get on and off safely. Ask students *yes/no* questions to confirm their understanding of the paragraphs 48–50, such as: *Are the stations on the Underground Railroad along real railroad tracks? (no) Do the stations on the Underground Railroad sell tickets? (no)* **SUBSTANTIAL**

• Ask students to pronounce *station*, correcting them as needed. Then ask them how the stations along the Underground Railroad are alike and different from the stations of an actual railroad. **MODERATE**

• Have students pronounce *station*, correcting them as needed. Then ask them to explain whether the name Underground Railroad is fitting. **LIGHT**

TO CHALLENGE STUDENTS . . .

Use Visuals Point out that what is called the Underground Railroad is really a variety of secret paths from Southern slave-holding states to free states or Canada in the north. Ask students to locate the places mentioned in the text on a map and trace the path taken by Tubman and the eleven fugitives. Ask students to find Canada on the map and to use the map tools to measure how far the fugitives need to travel. Encourage students to research other common paths along the Underground Railroad.

 For additional support, go to the **Reading Studio** and assign the following [LEVEL] **Level Up tutorial: Synthesizing Information.**

QUOTED WORDS

Remind students to ask themselves, "Why did the author quote or cite this person?" whenever they notice a **quotation**. Point out that the answer will help them think about the author's point of view, purpose, bias, and conclusions. (**Answer:** *Douglass described what it was like to be a host to fugitives on the Underground Railroad.*)

ANALYZE CHARACTERIZATION

Explain that readers use what the biographer tells and shows, along with what they can figure out, to answer the question, "What is this person like?" (**Answer:** *She was hardworking, generous, strong, encouraging, and independent.*)

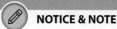

NOTICE & NOTE

QUOTED WORDS

Notice & Note: Mark the details that the author uses to introduce the quotation in paragraph 52.

Connect: How does the information in the quote relate to the information the author provides about Douglass? Why might the author have chosen to include this quote?

ANALYZE CHARACTERIZATION

Annotate: Mark details in paragraph 54 that describe Tubman's actions after she arrives in Canada.

Infer: What do these details reveal about Tubman's character?

York. From New York they went on to Syracuse, where the temperature was even lower.

51   In Syracuse she met the Reverend J. W. Loguen, known as "Jarm" Loguen. This was the beginning of a lifelong friendship. Both Harriet and Jarm Loguen were to become friends and supporters of Old John Brown.[8]

52   From Syracuse they went north again, into a colder, snowier city—Rochester. Here they almost certainly stayed with Frederick Douglass, for he wrote in his autobiography:

> On one occasion I had eleven fugitives at the same time under my roof, and it was necessary for them to remain with me until I could collect sufficient money to get them to Canada. It was the largest number I ever had at any one time, and I had some difficulty in providing so many with food and shelter, but, as may well be imagined, they were not very fastidious in either direction, and were well content with very plain food, and a strip of carpet on the floor for a bed, or a place on the straw in the barnloft.

53   Late in December, 1851, Harriet arrived in St. Catharines, Canada West (now Ontario), with the eleven fugitives. It had taken almost a month to complete this journey; most of the time had been spent getting out of Maryland.

54   That first winter in St. Catharines was a terrible one. Canada was a strange frozen land, snow everywhere, ice everywhere, and a bone-biting cold the like of which none of them had ever experienced before. Harriet rented a small frame house in the town and set to work to make a home. The fugitives boarded with her. They worked in the forests, felling trees, and so did she. Sometimes she took other jobs, cooking or cleaning house for people in the town. She cheered on these newly arrived fugitives, working herself, finding work for them, finding food for them, praying for them, sometimes begging for them.

55   Often she found herself thinking of the beauty of Maryland, the mellowness of the soil, the richness of the plant life there.

---

[8] **Old John Brown:** an anti-slavery leader who was executed.

266   Unit 4

 ENGLISH LEARNER SUPPORT

Draw Conclusions Remind students that a *conclusion* is a judgment or belief based on details in a text and a person's prior knowledge and experience. Read paragraph 52 aloud.

- Point out that the phrase "almost certainly" tells readers that the author is drawing a conclusion; in other words, she did not find this idea stated directly in any source.
- Ask students what the author must have known from her previous research in order to draw this conclusion. (*She must have known that*

Harriet Tubman went to Rochester from Syracuse and that Frederick Douglass lived there at the same time that Tubman was passing through.)

- What details from Douglass's writing help the author draw this conclusion by connecting his story to Tubman's? (*He speaks of "eleven fugitives" staying with him on their way "to Canada.*")
- Point out that the final part of a nonfiction piece of writing is called the "conclusion." Make sure that students understand the difference between the two meanings of "conclusion." **MODERATE/LIGHT**

Harriet Tubman is honored in this bronze statue, titled *Step on Board*, by sculptor Fern Cunningham. Located at the entrance to Harriet Tubman Park in Boston, Massachusetts, the statue shows Tubman holding a Bible as she leads a group northward to freedom.

ENGLISH LEARNER SUPPORT

Understand Visuals   Read the caption aloud. Explain that the statue of Harriet Tubman and escaped slaves is located in Boston, Massachusetts, an important stop on the path of the Underground Railroad. Have students locate Boston on a map. Ask partners to discuss what characteristics are represented in the statue and why the people of Boston would erect it. Provide sentence frames to support discussion:

- *Harriet Tubman looks _____.*
- *I see that _____.*
- *The statue shows _____.*
- *The people look _____.*
- *I think the way _____ creates the effect of _____.*
- *Perhaps the people wanted _____.*
- *The Underground Railroad was _____ to Boston.*

MODERATE/LIGHT

TO CHALLENGE STUDENTS . . .

Analyze Visuals   Ask students to add St. Catharines to the maps they created on page 265. Challenge students to research other locations on their maps that may have erected statues, monuments, or memorials to Harriet Tubman or the Underground Railroad and add this info to their maps.

Ask students   to analyze which characteristics these monuments focus on honoring. Have students brainstorm ideas for new monuments. Encourage them to share their ideas.

 For additional support, go to the **Reading Studio** and assign the following **Level Up tutorial: Analyzing Visuals.**

ENGLISH LEARNER SUPPORT

Understand Vocabulary Make sure students understand what *climate* means. Explain that *climate* refers to long-standing weather and temperature patterns for an area. Point out that the farther north you go, the colder the climate becomes. Pronounce *climate* for students, and have them repeat it several times.

ASK STUDENTS to compare the climates of Maryland and St. Catharines, Canada, described in the text. *(Maryland was mellow and warm, while St. Catharines was extremely cold and bleak.)*

LIGHT

The climate itself made for an ease of living that could never be duplicated in this bleak, barren countryside.

56   In spite of the severe cold, the hard work, she came to love St. Catharines, and the other towns and cities in Canada where black men lived. She discovered that freedom meant more than the right to change jobs at will, more than the right to keep the money that one earned. It was the right to vote and to sit on juries. It was the right to be elected to office. In Canada there were black men who were county officials and members of school boards. St. Catharines had a large colony of ex-slaves, and they owned their own homes, kept them neat and clean and in good repair. They lived in whatever part of town they chose and sent their children to the schools.

57   When spring came she decided that she would make this small Canadian city her home—as much as any place could be said to be home to a woman who traveled from Canada to the Eastern Shore of Maryland as often as she did.

58   In the spring of 1852, she went back to Cape May, New Jersey. She spent the summer there, cooking in a hotel. That fall she returned, as usual, to Dorchester County, and brought out nine more slaves, conducting them all the way to St. Catharines, in Canada West, to the bone-biting cold, the snow-covered forests—and freedom.

59   She continued to live in this fashion, spending the winter in Canada, and the spring and summer working in Cape May, New Jersey, or in Philadelphia. She made two trips a year into slave territory, one in the fall and another in the spring. She now had a definite crystallized purpose, and in carrying it out, her life fell into a pattern which remained unchanged for the next six years.

CHECK YOUR UNDERSTANDING

Answer these questions before moving on to the **Analyze the Text** section on the following page.

1 What was significant about the group Tubman led to escape slavery in December 1851?

A It was the largest number of people she had ever taken.

B It traveled deeper into the swamp than ever before.

C It journeyed farther south than previous groups.

D It included eleven members of the same family.

2 Read this sentence from paragraph 12.

> If they were caught, the eleven runaways would be whipped and sold South, but she—she would probably be hanged.

The author includes this sentence most likely to emphasize that Tubman —

F felt that she needed to look out for herself more than others

G thought that the risks of danger on her journey were unlikely

H wanted to turn back and lead the travelers into slavery again

J continued bravely despite her own fears and doubts

3 What can you conclude about the travelers based on the details in paragraph 19?

A They were afraid of getting caught.

B They were thankful to be journeying north.

C They slept a lot to restore their energy.

D They knew the most difficult part of the journey was over.

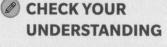 **CHECK YOUR UNDERSTANDING**

Have students answer the questions independently.

Answers:

1. *A*

2. *J*

3. *A*

If they answer any questions incorrectly, have them reread the text to confirm their understanding. Then they may proceed to ANALYZE THE TEXT on page 270.

 ENGLISH LEARNER SUPPORT

Oral Assessment Use the following questions to assess students' comprehension and speaking skills:

1. What was special about the group Tubman led in December 1851? *(It was the largest group she had ever taken.)*

2. Listen to this sentence from paragraph 12: "If they were caught, the eleven runaways would be whipped and sold South, but she—she would probably be hanged." What was the author trying to emphasize about Tubman? *(that Tubman was brave and continued despite her fears)*

3. What do the details in paragraph 19 imply about the travelers? *(They were afraid of getting caught.)* **SUBSTANTIAL/MODERATE**

TEACH

ANALYZE THE TEXT

Possible answers:

1. **DOK 2:** *The description gives the impression that Moses is more clever and powerful than any of the plantation owners. No one can figure out who or where he is: "The stories about him were fantastic, unbelievable. Yet they watched for him."*

2. **DOK 2:** *The parallelism in "ear to mouth, mouth to ear" lets readers hear and visualize how the messages were shared.*

3. **DOK 2:** *Although Tubman is worried and afraid herself, she keeps up a brave front, indicating that she is a strong, selfless, and determined person.*

4. **DOK 4:** *Parallelism: The list of adjectives after "runaways"—"ragged, dirty, hungry, cold"—emphasizes their desperate condition. Word Choice: "short, muscular, indomitable" helps readers picture Tubman's physical appearance and inner strength. Syntax: The word order in the sentence that begins with "The runaways" points out the contrast between the actions they did not take and their decision to remain with Tubman.*

5. **DOK 4:** *Tubman tells her group stories about life in the North, other people who have escaped, and what lies ahead on their journey. In addition to encouraging the group to continue, the stories likely also help the members of the party develop a growing sense of trust in and respect for Tubman.*

RESEARCH

Remind students to verify information by checking multiple websites and assessing the credibility of each one.

Extend research by having students interpret their research to form an opinion and then present it to the group. Remind them to state their opinion and to give specific reasons to support it based on their research.

 RESPOND

ANALYZE THE TEXT

Support your responses with evidence from the text. NOTEBOOK

1. **Infer** Reread paragraphs 1–2. What does the description suggest about the qualities of the person called Moses?

2. **Interpret** Identify the parallelism in paragraph 8. What does this technique help to evoke?

3. **Infer** In paragraphs 10–11, the author describes the difficulty of the task facing Harriet Tubman. What is Tubman's response? Explain what her words and actions reveal about her.

4. **Analyze** Why might the author have included details from the stories Tubman likely told while leading the slaves to freedom?

5. **Notice & Note** Identify a fact or detail in this selection that surprised or impressed you. Then explain why it was surprising or impressive and how it affected your view of Harriet Tubman.

RESEARCH TIP
Instead of searching for each question individually, try finding a short biographical summary of each subject's life. Searching for both individuals might help you find out about ways in which the two leaders interacted.

RESEARCH

In this selection, not only does Tubman tell her band of fugitives about Frederick Douglass, they eventually meet him. Conduct research to learn more about Tubman and Douglass. Record what you learn below.

QUESTION	ANSWER
What did Tubman and Douglass have in common?	*Both were born into slavery around 1820 in Maryland and eventually gained freedom. Both fought against slavery.*
How did Tubman and Douglass differ in their fight against slavery?	*Douglass wrote and spoke publicly to support the abolition movement. Tubman worked directly to help people escape slavery. During the Civil War, Tubman worked as a spy for the Union army, while Douglass became a consultant to President Lincoln.*
What interactions did the two leaders have with each other?	*Douglass supported Tubman by hosting her "passengers" in his home in Rochester, New York. He also wrote her a letter in 1868 praising her efforts.*

Extend Tubman and Douglass took different approaches to winning slaves' freedom. Was one approach better or more necessary than the other? Take a position on this matter and present it to a small group, using evidence from your research to back up your claim.

LEARNING MINDSET

Asking for Help Encourage students to ask peers/teachers/parents for help. Explain that asking for help from others can help students get "unstuck" and move forward. Reinforce that asking for help does not equal failure. Rather, seeking help is a way of "trying smarter."

CREATE AND PRESENT

Write a Speech Prepare a persuasive speech to convince the board of a museum that Harriet Tubman should be included in a "Heroes Hall of Fame" exhibit. The following tips will help you.

❏ Remember, this speech is an argument. Form a claim, and state it in early in your speech, along with an attention-grabbing example of Tubman's heroism.

❏ Support your claim with reasons, and each reason with strong, relevant evidence. Consider quoting an historian's opinion of Tubman's impact on the quest for freedom prior to the Civil War.

❏ Use transitional words and phrases to help listeners follow how your claim, reasons, and evidence are related.

❏ Utilize persuasive devices to be as convincing as possible.

❏ Close by summarizing your main points.

Present a Speech Practice delivering your speech with the following in mind:

❏ Mark the points you want to emphasize and try out different ways of emphasizing them. For instance, you might pause to scan faces, raise your volume, slow your pace, or pound your fist.

❏ Speak clearly, and talk at a pace your audience can follow.

❏ If you have planned to include charts, graphs, or other visual aids, practice showing these items until you can do so smoothly.

 Go to the **Writing Studio** for more on writing an argument.

Go to the **Speaking and Listening Studio** for help with giving a presentation.

RESPOND TO THE ESSENTIAL QUESTION

 What will people risk to be free?

Gather Information Review your annotations and notes on *Harriet Tubman: Conductor on the Underground Railroad*. Then, add relevant details to your Response Log. To determine which information to include, think about:

• what people have risked to be free

• what it means to be free

• what kinds of qualities a person would need to be willing to risk her life to obtain freedom for others

At the end of the unit, you can use your notes to help you write a research report.

UNIT 4 RESPONSE LOG

ACADEMIC VOCABULARY
As you write and discuss what you learned from the biography, be sure to use the Academic Vocabulary words. Check off each of the words that you use.

❏ **access**

❏ **civil**

❏ **demonstrate**

❏ **document**

❏ **symbolize**

TEACH

CREATE AND PRESENT

Write a Speech Remind students to create a structure for their speeches that begins with an introduction and ends with a conclusion. Encourage them to choose their words and sentence structures to create a persuasive voice and tone for the audience. Remind them that one effective technique is parallelism.

For **writing support** for students at varying proficiency levels, see the **Text X-Ray** on page 254D.

Present a Speech Point out that a speech is meant to be heard. Encourage students:

• to practice their speeches aloud with a partner before presenting to the group

• to revise as necessary to improve verbal flow

• to include visuals, such as photos or maps, to add interest

RESPOND TO THE ESSENTIAL QUESTION

Allow time for students to add details from "Harriet Tubman: Conductor on the Underground Railroad" to their Unit 4 Response Logs.

🔵 ENGLISH LEARNER SUPPORT

Present a Speech Before students begin planning their presentations, remind them that visual support can include photos, drawings, charts or graphs, and videos. If necessary, help them brainstorm ideas. Provide the following sentence frames: *My idea is _____. I think that _____. In my presentation, I will show _____ because _____.*

SUBSTANTIAL/MODERATE

CRITICAL VOCABULARY

Answers:

1. *a*
2. *b*
3. *b*
4. *b*
5. *a*
6. *b*
7. *a*
8. *b*

VOCABULARY STRATEGY:

Latin Roots

Answers:

1. *aqueduct: a channel designed to transport water from a remote source*

2. *induct: to place in a position; to admit as a member*

3. *abduct: to carry off by force*

4. *deduct: to take away from another*

 RESPOND

WORD BANK
disheveled
instill
dispel
linger
sullen
eloquence
evoke
cajole

CRITICAL VOCABULARY

Practice and Apply Circle the letter of the best answer to each question. Then, explain your response.

1. Which of the following would **instill** a sense of responsibility?
   a. having a child care for a plant   **b.** giving a child fresh flowers

2. Which of the following would be **disheveled**?
   a. a car that was just washed   **b.** a person who just woke up

3. Which of the following would require **eloquence**?
   a. cheering at a football game   **b.** giving a speech

4. Which of the following exemplifies what it means to **cajole**?
   a. worrying about losing   **b.** giving someone a pep talk

5. Which of the following exemplifies what it means to **evoke**?
   a. getting sympathy from others by looking sad   **b.** getting removed from someone else's property

6. Which of the following exemplifies what it means to **dispel**?
   a. walking off into the sunset   **b.** proving a rumor isn't true

7. Which of the following exemplifies what it means to **linger**?
   a. staying seated after a movie to watch the credits   **b.** making eye contact as you walk down the street

8. Which of the following would you describe as **sullen**?
   a. an angry mob   **b.** an unhappy loser

 Go to the **Vocabulary Studio** for more on Latin roots.

VOCABULARY STRATEGY: Latin Roots

Recognizing **word roots** can help you determine the meanings of unfamiliar words. For example, the word *conducted* includes the Latin root *duc* or *duct*, which means "to lead." This information can help you infer that *conducted* in the sentence below means "led or guided together." Similarly, a *conductor* is "a person who leads."

> It was the largest group that she had ever <u>conducted</u>, but she was determined that more and more slaves should know what freedom was like.

Practice and Apply Use online or print resources to find four additional examples of words that use the Latin root *duc* or *duct*. Use your knowledge of the root's meaning to write a definition for each word. Then consult a dictionary to confirm each word's meaning.

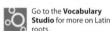 **ENGLISH LEARNER SUPPORT**

Cognates Explain to students that cognates are words in two languages that share similar meaning, pronunciation, and spelling. Tell them that 30-40 percent of all words in English have a cognate in Spanish due to common Latin roots. Point out that several words include the Latin root *duc* or *duct* and have English/Spanish cognates: *produce/producir, conduct/conducta, deduct/deductive, reduce/reducer*. Encourage Spanish-speaking students to look for cognates as a way to expand their English vocabulary. **SUBSTANTIAL/MODERATE**

LANGUAGE CONVENTIONS:
Run-on Sentences

A **run-on sentence** is made up of two or more sentences written as though they were one. Knowing how to construct and punctuate different types of sentences can help you avoid run-ons. For example, to join the two independent clauses that make up a **compound sentence,** you could use a comma and a coordinating conjunction such as *and, but, or, for, so, yet,* or *nor.*

> **Run-on:** They were too tired to walk any farther they stopped to rest.

> **Correct:** They were too tired to walk any farther, so they stopped to rest.

Similarly, in a complex sentence you would use a comma between the independent and subordinate clauses. As you may recall, a **complex sentence** is a sentence made up of an independent clause—that is, one that could stand alone as a sentence—and one or more subordinate clauses. **Subordinate clauses** express incomplete thoughts and contain subordinating conjunctions such as *although, after, while,* or *because.* Here is a complex sentence from the selection.

> **While she talked,** <u>she kept watching them.</u>

The underlined part of the sentence is an independent clause. The part in boldface type is a subordinate clause. Without the comma, the sentence would not be a run-on, but the meaning would be less clear.

In a **compound-complex sentence,** which is one that has at least one subordinate clause and at least two independent clauses, you would also use commas and conjunctions to avoid creating a run-on. For example, look at this sentence from the selection.

> <u>They stumbled along behind her, half-dead for sleep, and she urged them on,</u> **though she was as tired and as discouraged as they were.**

The underlined part consists of two independent clauses joined by a comma and the coordinating conjunction *and.* The part in boldface type is a subordinate clause. If a comma and *and* did not separate the two independent clauses, this sentence would be a run-on.

Practice and Apply Write three sentences about a journey. Make one sentence complex, another compound, and another compound-complex. Be sure to use commas and conjunctions appropriately to avoid creating run-ons.

> **!** Go to the **Grammar Studio** for more on run-on sentences.

Harriet Tubman: Conductor on the Underground Railroad   273

LANGUAGE CONVENTIONS:
Run-On Sentences

Review the information about run-on sentences with students. Explain that a run-on sentence is made up of two or more sentences written as though they were one. Note that some run-ons have no punctuation within them, but others may have only commas where conjunctions or stronger punctuation marks are necessary.

Summarize the different ways students can correct run-on sentences:

- If the thoughts are not closely connected, change a run-on into two sentences.
- If the thoughts are closely related but equal, change the run-on into a compound sentence by adding a semicolon or a conjunction.
- If the thoughts are closely related but have a more complex relationship, change the run-on into a complex sentence by revising the verbiage and/or adding punctuation such as commas or dashes.

Practice correcting sample run-ons with students until they can choose an appropriate correction strategy independently.

EL ENGLISH LEARNER SUPPORT

Language Conventions   Use the following supports with students at varying proficiency levels:

- Have students work in mixed proficiency pairs to write three sentences about a journey. Ask them to illustrate each sentence in a storyboard sequence.

- Provide sentence frames to support sentence structures if needed:

  _____ *went to* _____, *but* _____ *was* _____. *While* _____ *was* _____, *they* _____. *Though* _____ *and* _____, *they knew* _____, *so they* _____ *and* _____.

- When complete, ask volunteers to share their storyboards. Ask them whether each sentence is a run-on, and if it is, discuss how to correct it. **ALL LEVELS**

THE DRUMMER BOY OF SHILOH

Historical Fiction by Ray Bradbury

GENRE ELEMENTS
HISTORICAL FICTION

Remind students that the purpose of **historical fiction** is to present a novel or short story within a historical context. Historical fiction is always set in a particular era of the past (such as World War I, the days of the Roman Empire, or the 1980s) and in a specific place (such as Chicago, the Sahara, or a village in China). Some characters and many places mentioned in the story may actually exist, while others are the invention of the story's author. In this story, author Ray Bradbury creates fictional characters who would have been much like those who fought during the Civil War.

LEARNING OBJECTIVES

- Analyze the setting of the story and how it draws the reader in.
- Determine how the author uses language to create a mood.
- Identify changes in the emotions of the main character.
- Carry out research on the actual Battle of Shiloh.
- Dramatize a scene from the story.
- Write a report about the connection between the historical period and the character of the General.
- **Language** Discuss two characters, comparing and contrasting characteristics of each with a partner or in a group.

TEXT COMPLEXITY

Quantitative Measures	The Drummer Boy of Shiloh	Lexile: 990L
Qualitative Measures	**Ideas Presented** Much is explicit but moves to implied meanings.	
	Structure Used Clear, chronological third-person narrative.	
	Language Used Meanings are often implied but support is offered.	
	Knowledge Required Some knowledge of armies and the Civil War.	

Online

RESOURCES

- Unit 4 Response Log

- 🔊 Selection Audio

- Visualizing

- ▶ Close Read Screencasts: Modeled Discussions

- 📖 Reading Studio: Notice & Note

- Writing Studio: Conducting Research

- Writing Studio: Writing Informative Texts

- 💬 Speaking and Listening Studio: Participating in a Discussion

- Vocabulary Studio: Figures of Speech

- ❗ Grammar Studio: Module 1: Lesson 2: Run-on Sentences

- ✓ "The Drummer Boy of Shiloh" Selection Test

SUMMARIES

English

"The Drummer Boy of Shiloh" is a work of historical fiction. A boy has run away to become a drummer boy in an army during the Civil War. The boy knows that there will be a big battle near Shiloh Church in Tennessee the next day; he is worried and homesick. His general speaks to him, confessing some of his own fears and assuring the boy that the work of a drummer sets the tone for the soldiers: he is the "heart" of the army. The General's words lighten the boy's mood, and he is able to approach the next day's events with more courage.

Spanish

"El baterista de Shiloh" es una obra de ficción histórica. Un niño ha huido para convertirse en baterista del ejército durante la Guerra Civil. El niño sabe que habrá una gran batalla cerca de la iglesia de Shiloh en Tennessee el siguiente día; está preocupado y añora su hogar. Su general le habla, confesando sus propios miedos y asegurándole al niño que el trabajo de un baterista marca el tono para los soldados: él es el "corazón" del ejercito. Las palabras del general alivianan el humor del niño, y es capaz de aproximarse a los sucesos del día siguiente con más valor.

👥 SMALL-GROUP OPTIONS

Have students work in small groups to read and discuss the selection.

Repeat After Me

- Remind students that they need to listen closely to one another during discussions.

- Give students a topic to discuss. The first student makes a comment while others listen.

- The second student rephrases the first student's comment before adding his or her own contribution to the discussion. If the student can't summarize the first comment, he or she must wait until later in the discussion.

- The third student begins by rephrasing the second student's comment, and so on. This encourages students to listen to each other.

Signs

Small group conversations can quickly become noisy as students talk over each other. To help, teach students a group of simple signs, each with its own meaning, and have students use the signs to indicate agreement, confusion, and so on, instead of speaking out of turn. Some sample signs follow.

- Thumbs up: "I agree with you."

- Curled index finger: "I'm not sure what you mean."

- Upraised forefinger: "I have something to add to your point."

- Palms together: "I have a question."

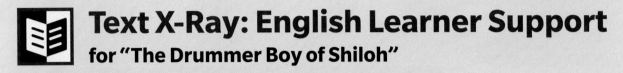

Text X-Ray: English Learner Support
for "The Drummer Boy of Shiloh"

Use the Text X-Ray and the supports and scaffolds in the Teacher's Edition to help guide students at different proficiency levels through the selection.

INTRODUCE THE SELECTION
DISCUSS SETTING AND MOOD

In this lesson, students will need to be able to identify the setting and the mood of a story and how these story elements help readers learn about characters. Write the words *setting* and *mood* on the board, and provide the following explanations of their meanings:

- The setting is where and when a story takes place.
- The mood of a story describes the prevailing emotions of the story.

Tell students that a long work of fiction, such as a novel or a play, may have several settings or moods, but a short story may only have one. Tell students that, for example, a story may take place in Germany in 1989, when the Berlin Wall came down, and that the emotions of the story's characters are mostly joyful. Have students complete the sentence frames using the example:

- *The setting of the story is _____ in the year _____.*
- *The mood of the story is _____ or _____.*

CULTURAL REFERENCES

The following words and phrases may be unfamiliar to students:

- *bayonet* (paragraph 10): a knife-like weapon common in the 19th century that could be fitted to the end of a rifle
- *shield* (paragraphs 11): a large piece of strong material, like metal, carried by someone as protection from people or objects during battle
- *"a head put on hind side front"* (paragraph 37): an expression implying "all wrong" or "backward" (*hind* means "back")

LISTENING

Understand Sequence

Tell students that many stories are told sequentially: that is, they use time order, with the events of the story happening one after the other. Direct students' attention to paragraphs 15 through 26, where Joby meets the General. Ask them to identify the sequence of events.

Have students listen as you read aloud paragraphs 15–26. Use the following supports with students at varying proficiency levels:

- Tell students that you will ask questions about what you just read aloud. Tell them to show one finger for the first choice, two for the second. For example, ask: *Which happens first: the General hears Joby crying, or Joby tells theGeneral his name?* (*one finger*) **SUBSTANTIAL**
- Have students identify two events in the excerpt. Ask: *Which of these events comes first?* **MODERATE**
- Have students identify three events in the excerpt and order them using the time-order words *first, next,* and *last.* **LIGHT**

SPEAKING

Discuss Characters

Remind students that "The Drummer Boy of Shiloh" reveals important information about Joby and the General in different ways. Have them use text evidence to talk about these two people.

Use the following supports with students at varying proficiency levels:

- Have students complete simple sentence frames by inserting either *Joby* or *The General*. For instance, _____ *is a drummer boy* (Joby) or _____ *smells like horse.* (the General) **SUBSTANTIAL**
- Have students generate simple sentences about the two characters, such as "*Joby ran away from home*" or "*The General is an old man and an experienced soldier.*" **MODERATE**
- Have students generate complex sentences that tell about one character, such as "*Joby is a drummer boy who ran away to join the army and feels lost*" or "*The General is an old man who is experienced in war and who is honest and kind.*" **LIGHT**

READING

Identify Sentence Fragments

Tell students that a sentence fragment expresses only a partial thought because it lacks a subject, a verb, or both. Explain that authors sometimes use sentence fragments to replicate the way people actually talk.

Work with students to read paragraphs 22–32. Use the following supports with students at varying proficiency levels:

- Point out sentences that are missing subjects, such as "Run off from home" Have students repeat the sentences with the subject added. ("Did you run off from home") **SUBSTANTIAL**
- Help students identify sentences that are missing subjects. Have students supply the missing subjects and say the sentences aloud. **MODERATE**
- Help students identify sentence fragments and explain how they know the fragments are not complete sentences. **LIGHT**

WRITING

Write a Report

Work with students to read the writing assignment on page 285.

Use the following supports with students at varying proficiency levels:

- Have students begin by writing individual words that describe the General, such as *old, brave,* and *kind.* **SUBSTANTIAL**
- Have students begin by writing short sentences about the General, such as *The General is an older man. He cares about his army. He likes the drummer boy.* **MODERATE**
- Have students begin by making a two-column chart listing the General's characteristics on the left and how they match his time and place on the right. **LIGHT**

ANALYZE & APPLY

THE DRUMMER BOY OF SHILOH

Historical Fiction by **Ray Bradbury**

? Connect to the
ESSENTIAL QUESTION

Have a student read aloud the Essential Question. Ask students what the image on page 274 makes them think about. Discuss with students that a drummer boy was a member of an army who usually did not fight but who filled other roles that helped soldiers. Then ask how the image relates to the Essential Question.

? ESSENTIAL QUESTION:

What will people risk to be free?

274   Unit 4

 LEARNING MINDSET

Questioning Reinforce with students that questioning, or asking for information and ideas, is central to learning. Set up your classroom expectations and guidelines to encourage students to ask questions as often as they feel they need. Compliment students on the questions they ask, and use student questions as an opportunity to mention that asking questions shows curiosity, drive, and a desire to learn. Explain that self-questioning can be a good strategy, too. It can be very easy to get bogged down while working on an assignment, and questions like "Can I try this another way?" can get students going again.

QUICK START

What do you know about drummer boys in the Civil War? For example, how old were they? What role did they play in battles? Discuss your ideas with a partner.

ANALYZE SETTING

Every story has a **setting,** the time and place in which the action occurs. In historical fiction such as "The Drummer Boy of Shiloh," the setting is usually a key aspect of the work.

Historical fiction is set in the past and includes real places and events from the time period. Like other works of historical fiction, Ray Bradbury's story involves characters that may be based on real people, plot developments that reflect real events, and details that are historically accurate. The story feels realistic because his characters hold beliefs and values that real people in the historical period would have had.

As you read, pay attention to details about the setting, and consider how the setting influences the characters' beliefs and values.

ANALYZE MOOD

When you get a general sense of anxiety, sadness, giddiness, or some other emotion as you read a story, you are responding to the work's **mood,** the feeling or atmosphere that the author creates for readers. Writers use language and literary elements to create a mood.

GENRE ELEMENTS: HISTORICAL FICTION

- includes the basic elements of fiction—setting, characters, plot, conflict, and theme
- is set in the past
- includes real places and historical events, along with events from the author's imagination
- has characters based on real people from history

ELEMENTS	HOW THEY CREATE MOOD
Setting, where and when the events take place	The writer's choice of setting and the words he or she uses to describe it can create a mood.
Imagery, language that appeals to the five senses	What we see, hear, or otherwise sense can make us feel frightened, cheerful, or many other things.
Symbol, a person, place, object, or activity that stands for something beyond itself	The emotions evoked by a symbol or what happens to it can affect the overall feeling of a piece. For example, a wounded bird might contribute to a mood of vulnerability.
Allusion, or reference to a famous person, place, event, or work of literature	An allusion to a serious person can help set a somber mood, just as an allusion to a fanciful place can contribute to a whimsical mood.

Look for language and literary elements that help create different moods in "The Drummer Boy of Shiloh."

TEACH

QUICK START

Have students discuss the questions. You may wish to explain that drummer boys were attached to many regiments (military divisions) during the Civil War, but are not a feature of modern warfare.

ANALYZE SETTING

Review the information on setting with students; stress that setting includes both place and time. Have students briefly identify the setting of other works of fiction they have read. Emphasize that setting is especially important in historical fiction, which tells of past times, perhaps of a distant past and of places unfamiliar as well. Then review the genre elements of historical fiction in the right column of p. 275.

Tell students to look for ways that the setting of this story seems especially realistic, and point out that while the characters, dialogue, and other aspects of the story may not be real, they are based on historical truth.

ANALYZE MOOD

Have students summarize the information on mood and what it means to a story. Have them predict the overall mood of the selection based simply on the title and their knowledge of drummer boys and the Civil War. Then call students' attention to the table at the bottom of p. 275. Ask students to predict which of these four elements will have the greatest effect on mood in the story they will be reading. Remind students to check the accuracy of their predictions as they read.

CRITICAL VOCABULARY

Encourage students to read both of the answer choices carefully before deciding which word represents the correct definition. Remind them to look for context clues that match the meaning of each word.

Answers:

1. *A*
2. *B*
3. *A*
4. *A*
5. *A*
6. *B*

LANGUAGE CONVENTIONS

Have students read the information about sentence fragments. Explain that sentences include both subjects and predicates, and tell students that sentence fragments often lack one or both of these features. Tell students that fragments are not generally acceptable in formal writing, but stress that they are common in everyday speech and so are frequently found in fiction.

■ English Learner Support

Vocabulary Support Explain that a *fragment* is a part of a thing. Guide students to use the word *fragment* in sentences.
SUBSTANTIAL

ANNOTATION MODEL

Point out that the underlined phrases and margin notes in the model can help students keep track of important information about mood and setting. Tell students that they can use the strategies given in the model or develop others that they find more helpful.

 GET READY

CRITICAL VOCABULARY

solemn	strew	resolute
askew	legitimately	muted

To see how many Critical Vocabulary words you already know, answer these questions.

1. Which of these is a **solemn** occasion?
   a. a funeral
   b. a birthday party

2. Which could you describe as **askew**?
   a. a door shut tight
   b. a picture hanging crookedly

3. What might you **strew** across a front yard?
   a. grass seeds
   b. a rake

4. Which action is done **legitimately**?
   a. registering to vote
   b. stealing a pack of gum

5. Which gesture makes someone appear **resolute**?
   a. standing up straight
   b. shrugging the shoulders

6. What makes a **muted** sound?
   a. a car's horn
   b. a kitten under a blanket

LANGUAGE CONVENTIONS

Sentence Fragments In this lesson, you will learn about complete sentences and fragments. The story's dialogue includes fragments because people often use them in speaking. As you read, observe how Ray Bradbury uses fragments to create realistic-sounding dialogue.

God's truth. Thinking of everything ahead. Both sides figuring the other side will just give up, and soon, and the war done. . . .

ANNOTATION MODEL   **NOTICE & NOTE**

As you read, note how the author describes the setting and creates mood. You can also mark up evidence to support your own ideas. The model shows one reader's notes about "The Drummer Boy of Shiloh."

1   In the April night, more than once, blossoms fell from the <u>orchard trees</u> and lit with rustling taps on the drumskin. <u>At midnight</u> a peach stone left miraculously on a branch through winter, flicked by a bird, fell swift and unseen, <u>struck once</u>, <u>like panic</u>, which jerked the boy upright. . . .

setting—in an orchard during the spring

mood—a little spooky, since it's midnight. Will the boy be safe?

BACKGROUND

*Though **Ray Bradbury** (1920–2012) is best known as a science fiction writer, he's also written plays, mysteries, fantasies, realistic stories, and novels. In this story, Bradbury tells about a drummer boy on the night before the Battle of Shiloh in the Civil War. This two-day battle began on April 6, 1862, near the southwestern Tennessee church from which the bloody clash takes its name. More than 23,000 soldiers died during those two days. At that time, it was the bloodiest battle in American history.*

THE DRUMMER BOY OF SHILOH

Historical Fiction by Ray Bradbury

SETTING A PURPOSE

As you read, pay attention to the details the author provides about the scene of the battle and about the men who were preparing to fight. What do the details suggest about the realities of war?

1 In the April night, more than once, blossoms fell from the orchard trees and lit with rustling taps on the drumskin. At midnight a peach stone left miraculously on a branch through winter, flicked by a bird, fell swift and unseen, struck once, like panic, which jerked the boy upright. In silence he listened to his own heart ruffle away, away, at last gone from his ears and back in his chest again.

2 After that, he turned the drum on its side, where its great lunar[1] face peered at him whenever he opened his eyes.

3 His face, alert or at rest, was **solemn**. It was indeed a solemn time and a solemn night for a boy just turned fourteen in the peach field near the Owl Creek not far from the church at Shiloh.

---

[1] **lunar** (loo´nər): of or relating to the moon.

Notice & Note

Use the side margins to notice and note signposts in the text.

ANALYZE SETTING
Annotate: Mark words the author uses to describe the story's setting in paragraphs 1–3.

Compare: How do these details compare or contrast with what you already know about the historical setting of this story?

solemn
(sŏl´əm) *adj.* If an event is *solemn*, it is deeply serious.

The Drummer Boy of Shiloh 277

BACKGROUND

Have students read the Background note. Emphasize that historical fiction is not the genre Bradbury is best known for, but that he was a versatile writer comfortable with many different types of writing. Review the information on the Battle of Shiloh, and be sure students understand that both sides suffered tremendous losses during the fighting.

SETTING A PURPOSE

Direct students to use the Setting a Purpose prompt to guide their reading.

 ANALYZE SETTING

Remind students that they can use evidence in the text to identify the setting of the story. Review that **setting** encompasses both place and time. Point out that in these opening paragraphs, the year is not named, but the text does give the month and the time of day. Have students determine what information about the setting Bradbury does provide in the opening paragraphs; then have students look back to the Background note to find more information. (**Answer:** *The details make the orchard seem quiet and peaceful, which contrasts with the battle scene that will unfold the next day.*)

ENGLISH LEARNER SUPPORT

Sentence Structure The sentences in paragraph 1 can be difficult for students to unpack. Take students through the sentences one clause at a time. Then connect the pieces through careful questioning, such as *What did the peach stone do? (It fell.) When did it fall? (at midnight) Why did it fall? (It was struck by a bird.)* Then help students work as a group to summarize each sentence by breaking it into smaller parts: *It was midnight. A bird hit a peach stone. The stone fell. It fell fast . . .* Remind students that they can make longer sentences easier to understand by breaking them down. **SUBSTANTIAL**

CRITICAL VOCABULARY

solemn: This word implies seriousness, often involving some sort of formal event.

ASK STUDENTS when they might have a solemn face, and why. (**Possible Answer:** *When attempting a difficult task or hearing potentially bad news.*)

TEACH

✏ ANALYZE MOOD

Remind students that authors of fiction choose words and phrases carefully to establish a mood for their work. Tell students to look for words that show the soldiers are thinking about life and death and to think about the effect on the mood of the passage. (**Answer:** *These details help create the mood of muffled tension or foreboding.*)

✏ ANALYZE SETTING

Tell students that the setting, or the time and place, is especially important to understanding this story. Review the Background information about the setting. Ask students to think about how knowing that it is the night before a battle provides context for the narrator's descriptions. (**Answer:** *Soldiers were inspired by family and patriotism. People on both sides were so passionate about their side that many men and even boys joined the army, and families were proud to send their men to fight despite the dangers.*)

■ English Learner Support

Oral Language Have students use simple sentence frames to respond to the analyzing questions on page 278:

- *The words _____ create a mood of _____.*
- *The values of _____ inspired the men and boys.*
- *The values of _____ were _____ during the Civil War.*
SUBSTANTIAL

CRITICAL VOCABULARY

askew: This word means *crooked* or *off-center*. If something is *askew*, the implication is a lack of order or care.

ASK STUDENTS whether the description of the army as askew suggests that the soldiers are organized and how they know. (*No; we would not use* askew *to describe organization.*)

strew: The word *strew* suggests that something has carelessly been thrown around.

ASK STUDENTS to describe how the words *strew* and *askew* each fit the description of the army. (*Both words imply a lack of order and arrangement; both imply randomness.*)

✏ NOTICE & NOTE

askew
(ə-skyōō´) *adj.* When something is *askew*, it is off center.

strew
(strōō) *v.* If you *strew* something, you spread it here and there, or scatter it.

ANALYZE MOOD
Annotate: Mark language in paragraphs 7–10 that reveals the atmosphere in the camp on the night before the battle.

Analyze: What mood do these details create?

ANALYZE SETTING
Annotate: Mark text in paragraph 12 that describes what the young men and boys did before their first battle.

Infer: What values inspired these men and boys, and how do those values reflect the story's Civil War setting?

---

4   ". . . thirty-one, thirty-two, thirty-three . . ."

5   Unable to see, he stopped counting.

6   Beyond the thirty-three familiar shadows, forty thousand men, exhausted by nervous expectation, unable to sleep for romantic dreams of battles yet unfought, lay crazily **askew** in their uniforms. A mile yet farther on, another army was **strewn** helter-skelter, turning slow, basting themselves with the thought of what they would do when the time came: a leap, a yell, a blind plunge their strategy, raw youth their protection and benediction.[2]

7   Now and again the boy heard a vast wind come up, that gently stirred the air. But he knew what it was, the army here, the army there, whispering to itself in the dark. Some men talking to others, others murmuring to themselves, and all so quiet it was like a natural element arisen from south or north with the motion of the earth toward dawn.

8   What the men whispered the boy could only guess, and he guessed that it was: Me, I'm the one, I'm the one of all the rest won't die. I'll live through it. I'll go home. The band will play. And I'll be there to hear it.

9   Yes, thought the boy, that's all very well for them, they can give as good as they get!

10   For with the careless bones of the young men harvested by night and bindled[3] around campfires were the similarly strewn steel bones of their rifles, with bayonets fixed like eternal lightning lost in the orchard grass.

11   Me, thought the boy, I got only a drum, two sticks to beat it, and no shield.

12   There wasn't a man-boy on this ground tonight did not have a shield he cast, riveted or carved himself on his way to his first attack, compounded of remote but nonetheless firm and fiery family devotion, flag-blown patriotism and cocksure immortality strengthened by the touchstone of very real gunpowder, ramrod, minnieball and flint.[4] But without these last the boy felt his family move yet farther off away in the dark, as if one of those great prairie-burning trains had chanted them away never to return, leaving him with this drum which was worse than a toy in the game to be played tomorrow or some day much too soon.

13   The boy turned on his side. A moth brushed his face, but it was peach blossom. A peach blossom flicked him, but it was a

---

[2] **benediction** (bĕn´ĭ-dĭk´shən): a blessing.
[3] **bindled:** fastened or wrapped by encircling, as with a belt.
[4] **ramrod, minnieball, and flint:** items used to fire a rifle.

moth. Nothing stayed put. Nothing had a name. Nothing was as it once was.

14   If he lay very still, when the dawn came up and the soldiers put on their bravery with their caps, perhaps they might go away, the war with them, and not notice him lying small here, no more than a toy himself.

15   "Well, by God, now," said a voice.

16   The boy shut up his eyes, to hide inside himself, but it was too late. Someone, walking by in the night, stood over him.

17   "Well," said the voice quietly, "here's a soldier crying *before* the fight. Good. Get it over. Won't be time once it all starts."

18   And the voice was about to move on when the boy, startled, touched the drum at his elbow. The man above, hearing this, stopped. The boy could feel his eyes, sense him slowly bending near. A hand must have come down out of the night, for there was a little rat-tat as the fingernails brushed and the man's breath fanned his face.

19   "Why, it's the drummer boy, isn't it?"

20   The boy nodded, not knowing if his nod was seen. "Sir, is that *you?*" he said.

21   "I assume it is." The man's knees cracked as he bent still closer.

22   He smelled as all fathers should smell, of salt sweat, ginger tobacco, horse and boot leather, and the earth he walked upon. He had many eyes. No, not eyes, brass buttons that watched the boy.

23   He could only be, and was, the General.

24   "What's your name, boy?" he asked.

25   "Joby," whispered the boy, starting to sit up.

26   "All right, Joby, don't stir." A hand pressed his chest gently, and the boy relaxed. "How long you been with us, Joby?"

27   "Three weeks, sir."

28   "Run off from home or joined **legitimately,** boy?"

29   Silence.

30   "Damn-fool question," said the General. "Do you shave yet, boy? Even more of a damn-fool. There's your cheek, fell right off the tree overhead. And the others here not much older. Raw, raw, damn raw, the lot of you. You ready for tomorrow or the next day, Joby?"

31   "I think so, sir."

32   "You want to cry some more, go on ahead. I did the same last night."

33   "*You,* sir?"

The Drummer Boy of Shiloh   279

APPLYING ACADEMIC VOCABULARY

☐ **access**   ☑ **civil**   ☑ **demonstrate**   ☐ **document**   ☐ **symbolize**

Write and Discuss   Have students turn to a partner to discuss the following questions. Guide students to include the Academic Vocabulary words *civil* and *demonstrate* in their responses. Ask volunteers to share their responses with the class.

- What made the Civil War a **civil** war?
- How can you **demonstrate** the role of a drummer boy in the battles?

LANGUAGE CONVENTIONS

Review with students that sentence fragments typically lack either subject or predicate, and may lack both. Have students identify and underline the sentence fragments and explain how they know that these are fragments. (**Answer:** *The dialogue sounds more realistic because real people often do speak in fragments, especially in less formal situations or when tense or worried.*)

■ English Learner Support

Recognize Metaphor   Point out that the mention of eyes in paragraph 22 is a way of referring to the buttons on the officer's coat. Explain that this is an example of figurative language.   **ALL LEVELS**

   For **listening support** for students at varying proficiency levels, see the **Text X-Ray** on page 274C.

   For **reading support** for students at varying proficiency levels, see the **Text X-Ray** on page 274D.

CRITICAL VOCABULARY

legitimately: Something done *legitimately* is done in a way consistent with the law or with custom.

ASK STUDENTS what the man means when he asks Joby if he joined *legitimately*. (*He is asking whether he signed up properly with the full knowledge of his parents, as opposed to defying regulations and running away from home.*)

ENGLISH LEARNER SUPPORT

Understand Dialogue Point out to students that reading dialogue aloud can help students determine which words to stress in a sentence. That in turn can assist students in understanding individual words in context and in deciding on the meaning of a sentence. Have students read aloud parts of the General's speech in paragraph 37 and critique each other's reading.

LIGHT

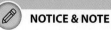 **NOTICE & NOTE**

34   "God's truth. Thinking of everything ahead. Both sides figuring the other side will just give up, and soon, and the war done in weeks, and us all home. Well, that's not how it's going to be. And maybe that's why I cried."

35   "Yes, sir," said Joby.

36   The General must have taken out a cigar now, for the dark was suddenly filled with the Indian smell of tobacco unlit as yet, but chewed as the man thought what next to say.

37   "It's going to be a crazy time," said the General. "Counting both sides, there's a hundred thousand men, give or take a few thousand out there tonight, not one as can spit a sparrow off a tree, or knows a horse clod from a minnieball. Stand up, bare the breast, ask to be a target, thank them and sit down, that's us, that's them. We should turn tail and train four months, they should do the same. But here we are, taken with spring fever and thinking it blood lust, taking our sulphur

WHEN STUDENTS STRUGGLE . . .

Make a Bulleted List Help students identify the General's main points in paragraphs 34 and 37 and write them in a bulleted list. For example:

- The General knows the war will not be over soon.
- He thinks that many soldiers are not prepared to fight.
- He thinks the armies need more training.

 For additional support, go to the **Reading Studio** and assign the following [LEVEL UP] **Level Up tutorial: Methods of Characterization.**

with cannons instead of with molasses[5] as it should be, going to be a hero, going to live forever. And I can see all of them over there nodding agreement, save the other way around. It's wrong, boy, it's wrong as a head put on hind side front and a man marching backward through life. It will be a double massacre if one of their itchy generals decides to picnic his lads on our grass. More innocents will get shot out of pure Cherokee enthusiasm than ever got shot before. Owl Creek was full of boys splashing around in the noonday sun just a few hours ago. I fear it will be full of boys again, just floating, at sundown tomorrow, not caring where the tide takes them."

38   The General stopped and made a little pile of winter leaves and twigs in the darkness, as if he might at any moment strike fire to them to see his way through the coming days when the sun might not show its face because of what was happening here and just beyond.

39   The boy watched the hand stirring the leaves and opened his lips to say something, but did not say it. The General heard the boy's breath and spoke himself.

40   "Why am I telling you this? That's what you wanted to ask, eh? Well, when you got a bunch of wild horses on a loose rein somewhere, somehow you got to bring order, rein them in. These lads, fresh out of the milkshed, don't know what I know, and I can't tell them: men actually die, in war. So each is his own army. I got to make *one* army of them. And for that, boy, I need you."

41   "Me!" The boy's lips barely twitched.

42   "Now, boy," said the General quietly, "you are the heart of the army. Think of that. You're the heart of the army. Listen, now."

43   And, lying there, Joby listened.

44   And the General spoke on.

45   If he, Joby, beat slow tomorrow, the heart would beat slow in the men. They would lag by the wayside.[6] They would drowse in the fields on their muskets. They would sleep forever, after that, in those same fields, their hearts slowed by a drummer boy and stopped by enemy lead.

46   But if he beat a sure, steady, ever faster rhythm, then, then their knees would come up in a long line down over that hill, one knee after the other, like a wave on the ocean shore! Had

---
[5] **taking our sulphur with cannons instead of with molasses:** Sulphur was an ingredient in gunpowder that was used to fire cannons; at that time sulphur was also used as a tonic or medical treatment. Molasses is a thick, brown syrup, used to mask the unpleasant taste of medicines.
[6] **lag by the wayside:** fall behind.

NOTICE & NOTE

ANALYZE MOOD
Annotate: In paragraph 38, mark the thing that may be a symbol, standing for something beyond itself.
Synthesize: What might this object symbolize?

WORDS OF THE WISER
Notice & Note: Read paragraphs 42–52. Then mark the main ideas in the advice that the General gives Joby.
Analyze: How does the General's advice help Joby overcome a problem?

The Drummer Boy of Shiloh   281

TEACH

ANALYZE MOOD
Remind students that symbols are often present in fiction and that a symbol can help underscore the themes of the book. An object or an image can help reveal the thinking of a character, for example, or remind the reader of a situation described directly in the story. Have students underline the symbol and explain it in their own words. (**Answer:** *The pile may symbolize the guidance the General is seeking. Set afire, the twigs and leaves could help him see how to win the battle and save his soldiers' lives. This symbol emphasizes the darkness and uncertainty the General feels about the coming battle.*)

WORDS OF THE WISER
Tell students that in paragraphs 42–52 the General is trying to make a particular point to Joby. Have students read the prompt and determine what the **main ideas** are. They should mark these main ideas and answer the question. (**Answer:** *When the General explains how important his job is and tells him exactly how he should do it, Joby no longer feels alone and afraid. He has the courage and the will to do his job in battle.*)

CLOSE READ SCREENCAST
Modeled Discussion Have students click the Close-Read icon in their eBook to access a screencast in which readers discuss and annotate paragraphs 12–14, a passage from the section in which the unarmed drummer boy compares himself to the armed soldiers, and paragraphs 45–46, when the General describes the different rhythms of the drumbeat.

As a class, view and discuss the video. Then have students pair up to do an independent close read of these paragraphs. Students can record their answers on the Close Read Practice PDF.

 Close Read Practice PDF

ANALYZE MOOD

Tell students that the discussion with the General has changed Joby's perspective on the war and his role in it and that while he remains apprehensive about what will happen the next day, he is no longer as frightened and alone as he was at the start of the story. Explain that the author of the story has chosen words and images that reflect that change in Joby's mood. Have students read the prompt, mark the appropriate words and phrases, and answer the question. (**Answer:** *The mood reflects the way Joby feels after listening to the General's inspiring words—hopeful and heroic.*)

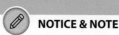 **TEXT IN FOCUS**

Visualizing Have students view the **Text in Focus** video on this page of their eBook to learn how to use story details to visualize a key scene. Then have students use **Text in Focus Practice** to apply what they have learned.

CRITICAL VOCABULARY

resolute: If you are *resolute*, you are sure of your opinion and purpose.

ASK STUDENTS to hold their jaws in a position that might be considered resolute. (*Students should hold their jaws up high and keep them stiff and unmoving.*)

 NOTICE & NOTE

he seen the ocean ever? Seen the waves rolling in like a well-ordered cavalry charge to the sand? Well, that was it, that's what he wanted, that's what was needed! Joby was his right hand and his left. He gave the orders, but Joby set the pace!

47 So bring the right knee up and the right foot out and the left knee up and the left foot out. One following the other in good time, in brisk time. Move the blood up the body and make the head proud and the spine stiff and the jaw **resolute.** Focus the eye and set the teeth, flare the nostrils and tighten the hands, put steel armor all over the men, for blood moving fast in them does indeed make men feel as if they'd put on steel. He must keep at it, at it! Long and steady, steady and long! Then, even though shot or torn, those wounds got in hot blood—in blood he'd helped stir—would feel less pain. If their blood was cold, it would be more than slaughter, it would be murderous nightmare and pain best not told and no one to guess.

resolute
(rĕz´ə-lōot´) *adj.* If you are *resolute*, you are firm or determined.

48 The General spoke and stopped, letting his breath slack off. Then, after a moment, he said, "So there you are, that's it. Will you do that, boy? Do you know now you're general of the army when the General's left behind?"

49 The boy nodded mutely.

50 "You'll run them through for me then, boy?"

51 "Yes, sir."

52 "Good. And, God willing, many nights from tonight, many years from now, when you're as old or far much older than me, when they ask you what you did in this awful time, you will tell them—one part humble and one part proud— 'I was the drummer boy at the battle of Owl Creek,' or the Tennessee River, or maybe they'll just name it after the church there. 'I was the drummer boy at Shiloh.' Good grief, that has a beat and sound to it fitting for Mr. Longfellow. 'I was the drummer boy at Shiloh.' Who will ever hear those words and not know you, boy, or what you thought this night, or what you'll think tomorrow or the next day when we must get up on our legs and *move!*"

53 The general stood up. "Well, then. God bless you, boy. Good night."

54 "Good night, sir."

55 And, tobacco, brass, boot polish, salt sweat and leather, the man moved away through the grass.

56 Joby lay for a moment, staring but unable to see where the man had gone.

57 He swallowed. He wiped his eyes. He cleared his throat. He settled himself. Then, at last, very slowly and firmly, he turned the drum so that it faced up toward the sky.

ANALYZE MOOD

Annotate: Read paragraphs 56–58. Mark words and phrases that indicate a change in the mood compared to the beginning of the story.

Analyze: How would you describe the mood at the end of the story?

IMPROVE READING FLUENCY

Targeted Passage Have students work in pairs to read paragraph 47 aloud. Point out that these are the summarized words of the General, even though they do not appear in quotation marks. Encourage students to think about what the General is saying and adjust their voices accordingly. For instance, because the General is speaking about the need for Joby to keep drumming no matter what, it would make sense for them to read the sentences in a quick rhythmic way.

Go to the **Reading Studio** for additional support in developing fluency.

58   He lay next to it, his arm around it, feeling the tremor, the touch, the **muted** thunder as, all the rest of the April night in the year 1862, near the Tennessee River, not far from the Owl Creek, very close to the church named Shiloh, the peach blossoms fell on the drum.

muted
(myo͞o´tĭd) *adj.* When something is *muted,* it is softened or muffled.

CHECK YOUR UNDERSTANDING

Answer these questions before moving on to the **Analyze the Text** section on the following page.

1 The "vast wind" that Joby hears in paragraph 7 indicates that —

   A April weather in Tennessee is windy and cold

   B Joby is frightened to be alone in the darkness

   C the battle is likely to begin at any moment

   D the two armies are camped very close together

2 The General says Joby is "the heart of the army" because —

   F Joby has more training than the other soldiers

   G Joby's drumbeat sets the pace for the battle

   H Joby gives the orders for the soldiers to march

   J Joby's battle position is in the middle of the action

3 How does Joby feel at the end of the story?

   A He misses his father even more than before.

   B He feels ready to face the next battle.

   C He is overwhelmed by the task before him.

   D He is confident that he is the most important soldier.

The Drummer Boy of Shiloh   283

TEACH

✎ CHECK YOUR UNDERSTANDING

Have students answer the questions independently.

Answers:

   1. *D*

   2. *G*

   3. *B*

If they answer any questions incorrectly, have them reread the text to confirm their understanding. Then they may proceed to ANALYZE THE TEXT on page 284.

CRITICAL VOCABULARY

muted: This word suggests softening or muffling. *Muted* is often an antonym of *bright* or *loud.*

ASK STUDENTS to give an example of a *muted* sound in the classroom. (*Possible Answers: the hum of an electronic device or the muffled squeak of a marker on the whiteboard*)

 ENGLISH LEARNER SUPPORT

Oral Assessment   Use the following questions to assess students' comprehension and speaking skills:

1. In paragraph 7, the author writes that Joby hears a "vast wind." What does this image tell the reader? (*That the two armies are camped very close to one another, and each can be heard from the other's camp.*)

2. The General says that Joby is "the heart of the army." What does he mean when he says this? (*That Joby's drumbeat sets the pace for the army in the battle.*)

3. At the start of the story, Joby is lonely and frightened. How does he feel at the end of the story? (*He is feeling ready to face the challenges of the next day.*)   **SUBSTANTIAL/MODERATE**

ANALYZE THE TEXT

Possible answers:

1. **DOK 3:** *The author mentions the smells of tobacco, sweat, horse, and leather. These details are all smells that an army officer of the time might have: he would ride a horse, wear leather boots, smoke cigars, and not bathe often.*

2. **DOK 2:** *Joby's silence suggests that he has run away without his parents' knowledge or consent, and that he is too young to join the army legitimately. This suggests that Joby values fighting for his cause and his side.*

3. **DOK 2:** *The falling of the peach blossoms takes place in the late spring and symbolizes loss of youth and innocence associated with the upcoming battle. They contribute to the overall mood of sadness in the story.*

4. **DOK 4:** *"that has a beat and sound to it fitting for Mr. Longfellow"; the idea that an author would immortalize the battle adds to a mood of seriousness and heroism.*

5. **DOK 4:** *The General's advice helps Joby understand his role in the battle and the importance of what he will be doing. Joby is no longer so frightened, homesick, or alone, but determined to do his job well.*

RESEARCH

Point out to students that they should be sure their research sources are legitimate. Have them read the information in the Research Tip to help them understand how to use online encyclopedias.

Extend Students may want visit the website at https://www.nps.gov/shil/planyourvisit/things2do.htm to find out about the special events that take place throughout the year.

 RESPOND

ANALYZE THE TEXT

Support your responses with evidence from the text.   NOTEBOOK

1. **Cite Evidence** What descriptive details does the author provide about the General in paragraph 22? What is the effect of such details in a work of historical fiction?

2. **Infer** The General asks Joby if he has "run off from home or joined legitimately." What is the answer to this question, and what do Joby's actions reveal about his values?

3. **Interpret** What do the peach blossoms symbolize in this story? Explain how this symbol contributes to the overall mood.

4. **Analyze** Henry Wadsworth Longfellow was a popular American author who wrote "Paul Revere's Ride" and other works immortalizing early American history. Locate the allusion to him in paragraph 52. What mood does this allusion help create?

5. **Notice & Note** How does the General's advice to Joby about his role in the next day's battle affect Joby?

RESEARCH TIP
Online encyclopedias can be a great place to start your research. The first paragraph of an article often gives a summary of the topic. If you need more in-depth information, scan the headings in the rest of the article to zero in on the precise facts you need.

RESEARCH

Want to learn more about the historical events that inspired Ray Bradbury to write "The Drummer Boy of Shiloh"? Research the Battle of Shiloh and its historical importance.

QUESTION	ANSWER
What did the Union army hope to achieve by fighting this battle in Tennessee?	*The Union army hoped to cut off Southern rail lines that the Confederate army used.*
Why did the battle begin sooner than the army expected?	*Confederate General A. S. Johnson attacked while the Union camp was waiting for reinforcements.*
How were the Union and Confederate armies affected by the battle's outcome?	*Both suffered heavy casualties. The Confederate army was seriously weakened, and Union General U. S. Grant began an important campaign to capture Vicksburg, Mississippi.*

Extend Plan a visit to the Shiloh National Military Park. Find out what there is to see and do, and create a schedule of your activities. Then ask some friends to join you, either by writing to them, talking to them, or showing them some images. Choose the method you think will convince them.

LEARNING MINDSET

Asking for Help Point out that students sometimes may feel reluctant to ask for assistance, especially in front of a large group of their peers. Explain that students may worry that they will be teased or embarrassed if they admit to not knowing an answer or understanding a concept or direction. Emphasize that students should always feel justified in asking questions, and that it is never acceptable for others to try to make students feel bad for asking for help. Tell students that many of the world's most successful people asked for help again and again, and that effective learning is much more difficult if students do not ask for help when they need it.

CREATE AND DRAMATIZE

Write a Report Use your research about the Battle of Shiloh to write a report about how the General's beliefs and values would have been influenced by the historical setting in which he lived.

- ❏ Review your research notes and conduct additional research as needed about soldiers' experiences fighting battles during the Civil War.
- ❏ Make inferences about how the General's beliefs and values would have been affected by his experiences.
- ❏ Write a report that combines historical facts with your inferences about the General.

Dramatize a Scene Working with a partner, act out the scene in which the General discusses Joby's fears and his role in the coming battle.

- ❏ Discuss the General's motivation for the conversation, and draw conclusions about how that might affect the way he speaks.
- ❏ Make a script with the dialogue each character will speak. Note movements, gestures, and facial expressions that will bring the scene to life.
- ❏ Practice your scene. Then perform it for the class.

RESPOND TO THE ESSENTIAL QUESTION

 What will people risk to be free?

Gather Information Review your annotations and notes on "The Drummer Boy of Shiloh." Then, add relevant details to your Response Log. As you determine which information to include, think about:

- elements of the story that make it historical fiction
- how the setting influences the characters' beliefs and values
- details that contribute to the story's mood

At the end of the unit, you can use your notes to help you write a research report.

 Go to the **Writing Studio** for more on conducting research and writing informative texts.

 Go to the **Speaking and Listening Studio** for help with performing a scene.

ACADEMIC VOCABULARY

As you write and discuss what you learned from the story, be sure to use the Academic Vocabulary words. Check off each of the words that you use.

- ❏ **access**
- ❏ **civil**
- ❏ **demonstrate**
- ❏ **document**
- ❏ **symbolize**

CREATE AND DRAMATIZE

Write a Report Remind students that they will be producing a work of nonfiction, but that they can use textual evidence about the General's character from "The Drummer Boy of Shiloh." Point out to students that the General's time was different from our own in some important ways.

For **writing support** for students at varying proficiency levels, see the **Text X-Ray** on page 274D.

Dramatize a Scene Remind students that they need to begin by discussing the scene and its role in the narrative; after that, they should begin the process of dramatizing it. Emphasize that drama is much more than just words and intonation, though speaking with expression is important; facial expressions, gestures, and changes in posture are all part of creating a dramatic scene as well.

RESPOND TO THE ESSENTIAL QUESTION

Allow time for students to add details from "The Drummer Boy of Shiloh" to their Unit 4 Response Logs.

ENGLISH LEARNER SUPPORT

Read a Dramatic Scene Guide students to speak their lines with confidence and understanding. You may wish to pair an English learner with a fluent English speaker to model reading with fluency and assist the English learner in the process of reading a scene. As students practice reading their lines, guide them to speak clearly and with expression; help them see which words should be emphasized and where a fluent English speaker might raise or lower his or her voice. It may also help to combine the speaking of lines with an action or other movement to help ensure that students understand the meaning of the words. **SUBSTANTIAL/MODERATE**

CRITICAL VOCABULARY

Answers:

1. *when I had to write a report on a weekend*

2. *when I returned some unopened batteries to a store and asked for a refund*

3. *when I tossed my books on my bedroom floor because I was glad it was Friday*

4. *when I was attending a sad event, such as a funeral*

5. *when I didn't care about the news, such as when I learned about a team winning a championship in a sport I don't follow*

6. *when my older brother tipped it in fun*

VOCABULARY STRATEGY:
Interpret Figures of Speech

Answers:

1. *"they can give as good as they get!"* **Explanation:** *The soldiers on both sides have weapons that make them roughly equal.* **Context Clues:** *"I only got a drum, two sticks to beat it, and no shield."*

2. *"not one as can spit a sparrow off a tree, or knows a horse clod from a minnieball"* **Explanation:** *The soldiers are untrained and inexperienced.* **Context Clues:** *"should turn tail and train."*

3. *"sun might not show its face"* **Explanation:** *gloomy or depressing stretches of time;* **Context Clues:** *"the coming days"*

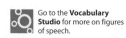

RESPOND

WORD BANK
solemn
askew
strew
legitimately
resolute
muted

Go to the **Vocabulary Studio** for more on figures of speech.

CRITICAL VOCABULARY

Practice and Apply Use what you know about the Vocabulary words to answer these questions.

1. When did you have to act in a **resolute** way to face a challenge?

2. When did you **legitimately** claim that someone owed you something?

3. When might you **strew** things across a room? Why might you do that?

4. When would you need to be **solemn** in a group of people?

5. When has your response to news been **muted?**

6. When has your hat been **askew** on your head?

VOCABULARY STRATEGY:
Interpret Figures of Speech

A **figure of speech** is a word or phrase that communicates meanings beyond the literal definition of the words. **Idioms,** or expressions in which the entire phrase means something different from the words in it, are one kind of figure of speech. Consider this idiom from the story.

> These lads, <u>fresh out of the milkshed</u>, don't know what I know, and I can't tell them.

You can use nearby words and phrases, or **context,** to help you understand that "fresh out of the milkshed" implies that not long ago these lads were farm hands milking cows. The phrase "don't know what I know" helps you understand that the General is using a figure of speech to express concern that his soldiers lack battle experience.

Practice and Apply Use context to explain the meaning of each underlined figure of speech below.

1. "Yes, thought the boy, that's all very well for them, <u>they can give as good as they get</u>! . . . Me, thought the boy, I got only a drum, two sticks to beat it, and no shield."

2. "There's a hundred thousand men, . . . <u>not one as can spit a sparrow off a tree, or knows a horse clod from a minnieball</u>. . . . We should turn tail and train four months."

3. "He might at any moment strike fire to them to see his way through the coming days when the <u>sun might not show its face</u>."

EL ENGLISH LEARNER SUPPORT

Vocabulary Strategy Tell students that when they read fiction such as this short story, they should always look for the possibility that words do not reflect their literal meaning. Point out that all languages make use of figurative language and that English is no exception. Give examples from the text as well as expressions such as "a horse of a different color" to mean "something unexpected," and have students practice interpreting these phrases in context. You may wish to have students create a chart of figures of speech they know.
ALL LEVELS

LANGUAGE CONVENTIONS:
Sentence Fragments

A **complete sentence** contains a subject and a predicate. The **subject** is a noun, pronoun, or noun phrase—all the words that identify the person, place, thing, or idea that the sentence is about. The **predicate** includes a verb and all the words that tell about the subject.

He could only be, and was, the General.

[subject] [predicate]

Writers usually use complete sentences to make their meaning clear. However, they may sometimes include **fragments,** or incomplete sentences that lack either a subject or a predicate. Fragments may be used to create a particular style of writing or to imitate the way people speak. Notice the underlined fragments in the following dialogue:

> "<u>Damn-fool question</u>," said the General. "Do you shave yet, boy? <u>Even more of a damn-fool.</u> There's your cheek, fell right off the tree overhead. <u>And the others here not much older. Raw, raw, damn raw, the lot of you.</u> . . ."

Practice and Apply For each fragment, identify whether the subject or predicate is missing. Then rewrite the fragment as a complete sentence.

FRAGMENT	MISSING PART	COMPLETE SENTENCE
1. Gathered around the campfire.		
2. Joby, a drummer boy.		
3. Thousands of soldiers, dreaming of glory in battle.		
4. Inspired Joby by telling him about his important role in the battle.		

> ! Go to the **Grammar Studio** for more on sentence fragments.

The Drummer Boy of Shiloh 287

LANGUAGE CONVENTIONS:
Sentence Fragments

Read the information in the text with students. Review the differences between complete sentences and sentence fragments. Remind students that sentence fragments are often found in fiction, especially where dialogue is concerned. They are much less common in nonfiction, and they are almost nonexistent in formal academic styles.

Practice and Apply

Have students fill out the chart by identifying the missing part of the sentence and rewriting the fragment with subject and predicate included.

1. *Subject; Thirty-three soldiers gathered around the campfire, exhausted by nervous expectation.*

2. *Predicate; Joby, a drummer boy, lay awake in the peach orchard at midnight.*

3. *Predicate: Thousands of soldiers camped around the orchard, dreaming of glory in battle.*

4. *Subject: The General inspired Joby by telling him about his important role in the battle.*

 **ENGLISH LEARNER SUPPORT**

Language Conventions Use the following supports with students at varying proficiency levels:

- Give students sentences that include both subjects and predicates. Have pairs identify each subject and each predicate. Then have students cover up each part of the sentence in turn and read the resulting fragment. **SUBSTANTIAL**

- Have students sort sentences from the text into two groups: those that are fragments and those that are complete sentences. Have them identify the missing part of speech in the fragments. **MODERATE**

- Have students explain to a partner how to distinguish a complete sentence from a sentence fragment. **LIGHT**

O CAPTAIN! MY CAPTAIN!

Poem by Walt Whitman

GENRE ELEMENTS
LYRIC POETRY

Remind students that the purpose of **lyric poetry** is to convey strong emotions. It usually uses first-person point of view to express a speaker's thoughts and feelings. It is often melodic, created by repetition and rhyme. An **elegy** like "O Captain! My Captain!" is usually a tribute or commemoration of a worthy person or event that reflects on death. It may also express sorrow and grief or praise for the person who has died by providing comforting thoughts or ideas.

LEARNING OBJECTIVES

- Cite evidence to support analysis of the poem and of the use of figurative language in an elegy.
- Conduct research about events surrounding the Civil War.
- Write a poem of tribute.
- Recite poetry as a choral reading.
- **Language** Discuss the structure of a poem with a partner or in a group using the words *chorus* and *lines*.

TEXT COMPLEXITY

Quantitative Measures	O Captain! My Captain!	
Qualitative Measures	**Ideas Presented** Subtle arguments; implied meanings; author's intent may be concealed; difficult ideas, evidence hard to assess; main idea must be inferred across many lines.	
	Structure Used Complex, multiple perspectives, deviates from chronological order.	
	Language Used Implied meanings, figurative language, complex poetic structures.	
	Knowledge Required Explores complex ideas, may require specialized knowledge.	

Online **Ed**

RESOURCES

- Unit 4 Response Log
- Selection Audio
- Reading Studio: Notice & Note
- Level Up Tutorial: Figurative Language
- Writing Studio: Writing Narratives
- Speaking and Listening Studio: Giving a Presentation
- "O Captain! My Captain!" Selection Test

SUMMARIES

English

"O Captain! My Captain!" laments the death of President Abraham Lincoln, portraying him as the fallen captain of a ship that has weathered the storm of the Civil War.

Spanish

"¡O capitán! ¡mi capitán!" lamenta la muerte del presidente Abraham Lincoln, retratándolo como el capitán caído de un barco que ha capeado el temporal de la Guerra Civil.

SMALL-GROUP OPTIONS

Have students work in small groups to read and discuss the selection.

Pinwheel Discussion

- Have four students sit in a circle facing out
- Have another four students sit facing them, forming an outer circle.
- Students in the inner circle remain stationary throughout the discussion.
- Students in the outer circle move to their right for each rotation.
- Provide discussion questions for each rotation, and determine when it is time to rotate on to the next question.

Reciprocal Teaching

- After a brief lecture, assign a reading passage or conduct a discussion.
- Provide general question stems.
- Have students use the stems to write questions about the reading or the lecture.
- Group students into teams, and have each team offer two questions for discussion.
- Then have each group locate text evidence for their answers and form a consensus.

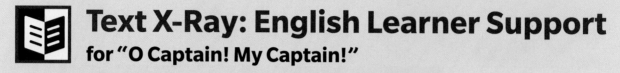

Text X-Ray: English Learner Support
for "O Captain! My Captain!"

Use the Text X-Ray and the supports and scaffolds in the Teacher's Edition to help guide students at different proficiency levels through the selection.

INTRODUCE THE SELECTION
DISCUSS THE COST OF FREEDOM

In this lesson, students will need to be able to understand and discuss the sacrifice someone has to make in order to have the majority of the people enjoy freedom. The theme of this unit uses the word *risk* and students have to understand that:

- Freedom comes with a cost, and freedom can be lost.

Explain to students that before President Lincoln's death when he was assassinated, millions of soldiers on both sides of the Civil War lost their lives because their leaders sent them into combat for what they perceived as freedom. Have students discuss this issue.

- What different freedoms did the South and North fight to preserve?

Point out that the North fought to preserve the Union and its ideal of freedom for all people, but the South fought to preserve its society and the right of white people to own slaves.

CULTURAL REFERENCES

The following words and phrases may be unfamiliar to students:

- *The ship has weather'd every rack* (line 2): On the open ocean, a storm could sink a sailing ship.
- *For you bouquets and ribbon'd wreaths* (line 11): These recall decorations for returning heroes or sailors.
- *The ship is anchor'd safe and sound* (line 19): In port, the ship would drop a heavy anchor to keep it from drifting.
- *Exult O shores, and ring O bells* (line 21): A crowd would gather on the dock to welcome sailors returning from a long voyage at sea.

LISTENING

Understand the Elegy Genre

Draw students' attention to the emotional tribute of the poem. Explain that the poet is trying to make the reader feel the emotions he feels and honor the memory of the fallen leader by focusing on the sorrow of what has been lost.

Have students listen as you read aloud lines 1–8. Use the following supports with students at varying proficiency levels:

- Tell students that you will ask questions about what you just read aloud. For example, ask: *Is this the beginning of a journey or the end? Where is the ship? Who is dead?* (end; near the port; the captain of the ship) **SUBSTANTIAL**
- Tell students the ship is a metaphor for our country, and the poet describes the emotional experience of the country by describing the ship's journey. Ask: *What kind of trip has the ship been on? What happened? What is the emotion or mood on the ship?* (a fearful trip; storms, the captain died; grim and daring) **MODERATE**
- Pair students to discuss words the poet uses to as metaphor for America and the Civil War, such as *prize* and *port*. Ask: *What do these words symbolize?* (victory, peace) **LIGHT**

SPEAKING

Discuss a Chorus

Draw students' attention to the cries of, "O Heart! heart! heart!" in the chorus of the poem. Ask why this part is indented and how it is different from the rest of the poem? Explain that it is like a chorus spoken out loud.

Use the following supports with students at varying proficiency levels:

- Tell students that you will ask questions about the chorus you just read aloud. For example, ask: *How is the first line of the chorus like the first line of the poem?* (*It is a cry using O and exclamation points.*) **SUBSTANTIAL**
- Have pairs decide how this chorus would be spoken. Ask: *How would you read this chorus to make it sound like it was written?* (*with emotion*) **MODERATE**
- Have small groups discuss the similarities and differences of the first four lines and the second four lines. Ask different volunteers to read aloud the first four lines and the chorus. Ask the class to discuss what they heard. **LIGHT**

READING

Read a Stanza

Draw students' attention to the beginning of the second stanza. Have students read it to themselves and focus on the scene that the poet is describing. Have students particularly describe the emotions or tributes contained in these lines.

Work with students to read lines 9–13. Use the following supports with students at varying proficiency levels:

- Read the sentences aloud and have students repeat them. Ask: *Why are people ringing bells, flying flags, and blowing on horns?* (*They are celebrating.*) **SUBSTANTIAL**
- Have students discuss who the poet is telling to rise up. Ask: *Why is the author describing this celebration to Lincoln?* (*He wants him to see it.*) **MODERATE**
- Have pairs describe how the poet is urging Lincoln to rise and view the celebration even though he is dead. Ask: *Why does he talk to Lincoln if he's dead?* (*to show he's loved*) Have students volunteers read lines that illustrate a celebration. **LIGHT**

WRITING

Write a Poem

Work with students to read the writing assignment on page 295.

Use the following supports with students at varying proficiency levels:

- Work with students to create a word web to organize sensory details that belong to the person they are writing about. Have them write their topic in the center of the web and then brainstorm and list details about the person that appeal to each of the five senses. **SUBSTANTIAL**
- Ask students to describe what it is like to be in this person's presence. Explain that simile is a comparison of two things using *like* or *as*. Help them find similes to get them thinking of figurative language. **MODERATE**
- Have students list sensory details and similes that describe the person they wish to write about. Then have them freewrite, using these the best details that lets the reader experience the person. **LIGHT**

Connect to the
ESSENTIAL QUESTION

"O Captain! My Captain!" considers the high cost of freedom and the sacrifice made by those like President Abraham Lincoln who gave their lives for a moral cause. Have students note that Lincoln took huge political risks and was assassinated as a result, but preserving the Union mattered to him greatly.

O CAPTAIN! MY CAPTAIN!

Poem by **Walt Whitman**

ESSENTIAL QUESTION:

What will people risk to be free?

288 Unit 4

QUICK START

The poem you are about to read mourns the passing of a great leader. Make notes about people who inspire you—either real or fictional—and their admirable qualities. After you read the poem, you'll write your own poem about someone you admire.

Person or Character	Admirable Qualities

ANALYZE FIGURATIVE LANGUAGE

One way poets can help readers understand things in new ways is by using **figurative language,** or imaginative descriptions that are not literally true. A **metaphor** is a type of figurative language in which an author compares two things that are basically dissimilar but have some quality or qualities in common. Unlike a simile, a metaphor does not use the word *like* or *as*. In an **extended metaphor,** this comparison between two things is developed at some length and in different ways.

An extended metaphor may continue, or extend, through several lines or stanzas or throughout the entire poem. In "O Captain! My Captain!" Whitman uses an extended metaphor to express his feelings about President Lincoln and the Civil War.

Read the poem to determine what is being compared. Also consider the poet's purpose in using the extended metaphor. Use a chart like this to record your ideas.

GENRE ELEMENTS: LYRIC POETRY

- is usually short and conveys strong emotions
- uses first-person point of view to express the speaker's thoughts and feelings
- often uses repetition and rhyme to create a melodic quality
- includes many forms, such as sonnets, odes, and elegies

QUESTIONS	ANSWERS AND TEXT EVIDENCE
What two things are compared in the extended metaphor?	
What effect does the extended metaphor have?	

IMPROVE READING FLUENCY

Targeted Passage Have students work with partners to read from lines 17–20 "My Captain does not answer . . . ". Have them pay close attention to the rhythm of the meter and stress in these lines. Ask students how they would pronounce the back-and-forth, on-and-off beat of these lines.

Remind students that this is lyric poetry and can be read like the lines of a song. Have volunteers sing these lines to any sort of music. Encourage students to take turns reading with pauses that indicate the stress and non-stressed words of each lines.

QUICK START

Encourage students to include both famous people they have heard about and people in the community they know well. Students can choose both living and deceased individuals. Help students provide rounded portraits of those they chose by asking about the work they have done as well as their effects on others.

ANALYZE FIGURATIVE LANGUAGE

Ask volunteers to help define why language that extends the meanings of the words is called figurative. Help students realize that describing something in imaginative ways that may not be true is like creating a figure or a solid thing out of an intangible or invisible idea. Use examples like someone being "madder than a wet hornet" to show that this is describing anger which doesn't exist as a thing, but everyone can imagine how a hornet will act if you spray his nest with a hose. Work with students to discuss that authors use extended metaphors to help readers clearly visualize details.

ANALYZE GENRE: POETRY

Have students try to answer the question, "Why does the poet discuss Lincoln by depicting him as a captain of a ship, instead of talking about him directly?" Help students realize that Whitman's technique of writing an elegy about a lost captain helps the reader see the president in a different way. Show how he uses the elements of an elegy: grief, praise, comfort, as well as formal tone to praise a leader of the ship of state. Note that this technique allows readers to be part of the crew along with the narrator, as though all Americans have been through the long voyage of the Civil War and now mourn the leader who guided them through safely, only to give up his own life.

■ English Learner Support

Understand Poetic Forms Ask students to mention things that people would say to praise someone. Students should give examples and discuss when they would be likely to praise someone. Accept simple words and phrases as answers, according to proficiency level. **ALL LEVELS**

✎ ANNOTATION MODEL

Have students go over the words that are underlined and circled, and then explain how they relate to a ship, as well as how they relate to the extended metaphor of America as a ship that is commanded by the president. Have volunteers advance interpretations of what a "steady keel" might mean and help them recognize that a ship's captain tries to make the voyage through rough seas as smooth as possible. Have groups discuss how a vessel could be "grim and daring" and how this describes Lincoln as well. Encourage students to underline other elements of an elegy they come across as they read.

GET READY

ANALYZE GENRE: POETRY

Certain forms of poetry are associated with particular topics. For example, sonnets are often associated with love, and limericks are often associated with humor. "O Captain! My Captain!" is an elegy. An **elegy** is a poem in which the speaker reflects on death. In contrast to other forms of poetry, elegies often pay tribute to people who have recently died.

Most elegies use formal, dignified language that contributes to a serious **tone,** which is the writer's attitude toward the subject. Elegies may also express

- sorrow and grief
- praise for the person who has died
- comforting thoughts or ideas

Punctuation, such as exclamation points, can help communicate emotion and tone. In these lines from "O Captain! My Captain!" Whitman expresses his shock and sorrow.

> But O heart! heart! heart!
>   O the bleeding drops of red,
>   Where on the deck my Captain lies,
>   Fallen cold and dead.

As you read "O Captain! My Captain!," identify words, phrases, and punctuation that pay tribute to Lincoln's greatness and express emotions related to his death.

ANNOTATION MODEL

NOTICE & NOTE

As you read, note details that develop an extended metaphor involving Abraham Lincoln, as well as language that expresses the speaker's tone. You can also record your own thoughts on the poem. This model shows one reader's notes about the beginning of "O Captain! My Captain!"

O Captain! my Captain! our <u>fearful trip</u> is done,

The <u>ship</u> has weather'd every rack, the prize we sought is won,

The <u>port</u> is near, the ⟨bells⟩ I hear, the people all ⟨exulting,⟩

While follow eyes the <u>steady keel</u>, the <u>vessel grim and daring</u>:

Is the poem really about a ship? What could be compared to a "fearful trip"?

"bells" and "exulting" sound like a celebration

APPLYING ACADEMIC VOCABULARY

☐ access   ☐ civil   ☑ demonstrate ☑ document   ☐ symbolize

Write and Discuss Have students turn to a partner to discuss the following questions. Guide students to include the Academic Vocabulary words *demonstrate* and *document* in their responses. Ask volunteers to share their responses with the class.

- How could you **demonstrate** that you believe in the exercise of freedom?
- What kind of a **document** would you need to make sure you live in a free country?

BACKGROUND

On April 14, 1865, only five days after the Civil War ended, President Abraham Lincoln was assassinated at the Ford Theater in Washington, D.C., where he was watching a performance. Lincoln was shot by John Wilkes Booth, a famous actor and a Confederate sympathizer. Although Booth initially escaped, he was discovered days later by Union soldiers. Booth was killed while trying to avoid capture.

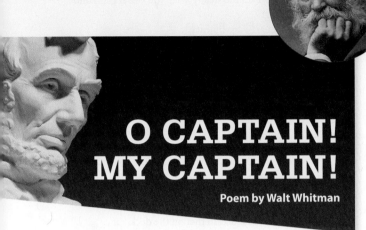

O CAPTAIN! MY CAPTAIN!

Poem by Walt Whitman

Walt Whitman (1819–1892) was a great admirer of President Lincoln. After the president was assassinated, Whitman wrote "O Captain! My Captain!" to capture the sense of tragedy that descended upon the country. Largely unknown to the public when he wrote this poem, Whitman eventually gained a reputation as one of the greatest American writers. "O Captain! My Captain!" is among his most famous works, and his book of poems, Leaves of Grass, *is considered one of the masterpieces of American literature.*

SETTING A PURPOSE

As you read, look for evidence of Whitman's feelings about Abraham Lincoln. Do others seem to share his feelings? Write down any questions you have as you read.

Notice & Note

Use the side margins to notice and note signposts in the text.

BACKGROUND

After students read the Background note, make sure they understand the basic issues surrounding the Civil War. Explain that Lincoln was elected before the war began and his stance against slavery caused many Southern states to call for ceding from the Union. The bitter feelings on both sides came to a head with his assassination. Whitman, like many Americans in the North, saw Lincoln as their leader and a brave reformer who brought them through a horrible time. Ask students what they know about the Civil War, slavery, Lincoln's assassination, and Walt Whitman.

SETTING A PURPOSE

Direct students to use the Setting a Purpose prompt to focus their reading. As they read "O Captain! My Captain!" ask students to think about the historical context in which Lincoln lived.

ENGLISH LEARNER SUPPORT

Use Vocabulary Support Have students use a dictionary to help them define these words:

- *port* (line 3), "place where ships anchor or find shelter"
- *exulting* (line 3), "rejoicing, celebrating"
- *vessel* (line 4), "ship"
- *pulse* (line 18), "rhythmic throbbing of blood in the arteries caused by heart contractions; sign of life"
- *victor* (line 20), "winner"   **SUBSTANTIAL**

ANALYZE GENRE: POETRY

Ask students to review the elements of an **elegy** and discuss how the poet uses words and phrases to stimulate the emotions of sorrow or joy, as well as strong feelings. Go through the lines of the poem, and select some examples like "bleeding drops of red" and "the people all exulting." (**Answer:** *"Prize we sought is won" and "people all exulting" give a feeling of excitement, which is quickly overshadowed by the sadness in "fallen cold and dead." The contrast makes the poem more emotionally powerful.*)

For **listening support** for students at varying proficiency levels, see the **Text X-Ray** on page 288C.

For **reading support** for students at varying proficiency levels, see the **Text X-Ray** on page 288D.

ANALYZE FIGURATIVE LANGUAGE

Review with students how an **extended metaphor** is carried out over a series of lines and with different words all related to the first metaphor or larger metaphor. Have students discuss how these words and phrases are related to the idea of a ship's captain and a voyage. (**Answer:** *The "Captain" is Abraham Lincoln, and the "fearful trip" is the Civil War.*)

■ English Learner Support

Write a Prose Summary Have students work with a partner to write a prose summary of the scene described in the first four lines of the second stanza. Encourage them to describe in greater detail the visual images that Whitman uses. **LIGHT**

NOTICE & NOTE

ANALYZE GENRE: POETRY

Annotate: In lines 1–16, underline words and phrases that evoke either sorrow or joy. Circle punctuation that conveys strong emotion.

Analyze: What is the overall effect on the reader of the language in this elegy?

ANALYZE FIGURATIVE LANGUAGE

Annotate: After reading the poem once, go back and mark details in lines 17–24 that are part of the extended metaphor of a ship's voyage and return.

Draw Conclusions: In the extended metaphor, who is the "Captain," and what is the "fearful trip"?

O Captain! My Captain!

O Captain! my Captain! our fearful trip is done,
The ship has weather'd every rack,[1] the prize we sought[2] is
    won,
The port is near, the bells I hear, the people all exulting,
While follow eyes the steady keel,[3] the vessel grim and
    daring:
5   But O heart! heart! heart!
      O the bleeding drops of red,
        Where on the deck my Captain lies,
          Fallen cold and dead.

O Captain! my Captain! rise up and hear the bells;
10 Rise up—for you the flag is flung[4]—for you the bugle trills,
For you bouquets and ribbon'd wreaths—for you the shores
    a-crowding,
For you they call, the swaying mass, their eager faces
    turning;
    Here Captain! dear father!
    This arm beneath your head!
15   It is some dream that on the deck,
        You've fallen cold and dead.

My Captain does not answer, his lips are pale and still,
My father does not feel my arm, he has no pulse nor will,
The ship is anchor'd safe and sound, its voyage closed and
    done,
20 From fearful trip the victor ship comes in with object won;
    Exult O shores, and ring O bells!
    But I with mournful tread,[5]
      Walk the deck my Captain lies,
        Fallen cold and dead.

---

[1] **rack:** a mass of wind-driven clouds.
[2] **sought** (sôt): searched for; tried to gain.
[3] **keel:** the main part of a ship's structure.
[4] **flung:** suddenly put out.
[5] **tread** (trĕd): footsteps.

WHEN STUDENTS STRUGGLE . . .

Find Extended Metaphors Have students read lines 17–20. In the first column, have them list the extended metaphors that relate to Lincoln. In the second column, list the other extended metaphors and what they mean.

Lincoln Metaphors	Other Metaphors
My Captain	The ship is anchor'd safe and sound (the Union is preserved)
My father	fearful trip (Civil War)
	victor ship (the country)

For additional support, go to the **Reading Studio** and assign the following **Level Up** tutorial: Figurative Language.

The funeral procession of President Abraham Lincoln

CHECK YOUR UNDERSTANDING

Answer these questions before moving on to the **Analyze the Text** section on the following page.

1 Why are the people "all exulting" in line 3?

A The ship has returned with "the prize . . . won."

B The ringing of the bells signals a celebration.

C They don't see that the ship is "grim and daring."

D They are relieved that the Captain is dead.

2 In the poem's extended metaphor, the "fearful trip" is —

F the speaker's grief

G the Captain's death

H the Civil War

J the election of Abraham Lincoln

3 In lines 13 and 18, the speaker calls the Captain his "father" most likely to —

A suggest that the poem is really about Whitman's father

B reveal that the speaker is the Captain's son

C create doubt about the poem's subject

D show the speaker's respect and love for the Captain

O Captain! My Captain!   293

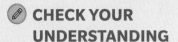 CHECK YOUR UNDERSTANDING

Have students answer the questions independently.

Answers:

1. *A*

2. *H*

3. *D*

If they answer any questions incorrectly, have them reread the text to confirm their understanding. Then they may proceed to ANALYZE THE TEXT on p. 294.

 ENGLISH LEARNER SUPPORT

Oral Assessment Use the following questions to assess students' comprehension and speaking skills:

1. For what reason are the people "all exulting" in line 3? (*The ship has returned with "the prize . . . won."*)

2. What is the "fearful trip" in the poem's extended metaphor? (*The "fearful trip" is the Civil War.*)

3. Why does the speaker call the Captain his "father" in lines 13 and 18? (*He wants to show the speaker's respect and love for the Captain.*)

SUBSTANTIAL/MODERATE

APPLY

ANALYZE THE TEXT

Possible answers:

1. **DOK 2:** *The "fearful trip" is the Civil War. The "ship" is the United States, and the "prize" is the preservation of the Union. The "port" is the peace that will follow the war.*

2. **DOK 2:** *People are "exulting." They are ringing bells, waving flags, and playing bugles. The crowds have brought flowers and wreaths for Lincoln. They are celebrating the end of the Civil War.*

3. **DOK 3:** *Readers would expect the people to be sad as they mourn the death of President Lincoln, but the people are also celebrating the end of the Civil War.*

4. **DOK 3:** *He cries "But O heart! heart! heart!" upon learning of his death. He calls to Lincoln to "rise up" from death and speaks of his passing as "some dream." In the last stanza, he cannot join in celebrating the end of the war because Lincoln has died.*

5. **DOK 4:** *Though the United States has survived the Civil War and is now "safe and sound," its leader, Lincoln, is dead. The mission of preserving the Union has been accomplished.*

RESEARCH

Remind students that they should double-check dates with at least two different sources. They should also be careful to make sure their sources are trustworthy.

Connect Students should see that Whitman wrote the poem not long after Lincoln's assassination. Have students discuss how would this affects his writing.

 RESPOND

ANALYZE THE TEXT

Support your responses with evidence from the text. NOTEBOOK

1. **Interpret** Reread lines 1–3. In Whitman's metaphor, what are the "fearful trip," the "ship," and the "prize" that was won? What is the "port"? Express your response in a chart like the one shown.

ELEMENT	WHAT IT REPRESENTS
fearful trip	
ship	
prize	
port	

2. **Summarize** Describe the grand celebration that Whitman tells about in lines 3–12. Why are the crowds rejoicing?

3. **Evaluate** When there is a contrast between appearance and reality, **irony** results. Why is it ironic that the crowds in this poem are celebrating?

4. **Cite Evidence** How does Whitman express his own grief about Lincoln's death? Cite three specific examples from the poem.

5. **Analyze** Reread lines 19–20. What is the meaning of these lines in terms of Whitman's extended metaphor?

RESEARCH

RESEARCH TIP
Timelines are a popular visual aid in reference books as well as on educational websites. In addition to the events listed in the chart, try to find information about other significant events that happened during the same time period. You might be surprised how this will expand your understanding of history.

Walt Whitman's "O Captain! My Captain!" was first published the year Abraham Lincoln was assassinated. Use a variety of sources to research significant events of this period and use them to construct a timeline.

EVENT	DATE
End of the Civil War	May 9, 1865;
Assassination of Abraham Lincoln	April 14, 1865;
Lincoln's funeral and burial	April 18-May 4, 1865;
Publication of "O Captain! My Captain!"	November, 1865

Connect Get together with a partner and compare your timelines. Then review the poem and discuss whether knowing more about the historical context affects the poem's impact on you.

 ENGLISH LEARNER SUPPORT

Listen for Narrative Shifts Read parts of the poem aloud, and encourage students to listen carefully.

1. As you read, place particular emphasis on any part with an exclamation point. Explain that these parts are the poet speaking to President Lincoln with great emotion.

2. Have listeners give a thumbs-up when you add emphasis for the parts with exclamation points. **ALL LEVELS**

CREATE AND RECITE

Write a Poem Write a poem in which you pay tribute to someone you respect or admire, either real or imaginary. Review your notes from the Quick Start activity before you begin.

❏ Decide if you want your poem to be an elegy, a limerick, a sonnet, or some other form.

❏ Consider creating an extended metaphor that connects to your subject in multiple ways.

❏ Draft your poem and then read it aloud to find places where you can sharpen the language or improve the rhythm.

Choral Reading Work with a small group to present a choral reading of "O Captain! My Captain!"

❏ Reread the poem carefully. As a group, decide how each line should be read. Do the words express sorrow? praise? comfort?

❏ Decide who will read each line or part of a line. Should some words be read by one speaker? two speakers? the entire group?

❏ The choices you make should reflect your analysis of the poem. Be prepared to explain your choices.

 Go to the **Writing Studio** for more on writing a poem.

 Go to the **Speaking and Listening Studio** for more on presenting a choral reading.

RESPOND TO THE ESSENTIAL QUESTION

 What will people risk to be free?

Gather Information Review your annotations and notes on "O Captain! My Captain!" Then, add relevant details to your Response Log. As you determine which information to include, think about:

• what Abraham Lincoln and others risked during the Civil War

• the role of heroes and leaders in the fight for freedom

• what this poem says about sacrifice

At the end of the unit, you can use your notes to help you write a research report.

ACADEMIC VOCABULARY

As you write and discuss what you learned from the poem, be sure to use the Academic Vocabulary words. Check off each of the words that you use.

❏ **access**
❏ **civil**
❏ **demonstrate**
❏ **document**
❏ **symbolize**

CREATE AND RECITE

Write a Poem Point out to students that they could use some of the basic elements of an elegy like Whitman used to help structure their poems. Suggest that their extended metaphor should be broad enough so as to allow for a variety of ways to extend it. Note that comparing something well known to the person they are paying tribute to will provide for a variety of metaphors.

For **writing support** for students at varying proficiency levels, see the **Text X-Ray** on page 288D.

Choral Reading Remind students that they can try a variety of different ways to recite the poem. Have them experiment with individuals reading each line or having groups act as various choruses to recite the indented choral cries.

RESPOND TO THE ESSENTIAL QUESTION

Allow time for students to add details from "O Captain! My Captain!" to their Unit 4 Response Logs.

 ## ENGLISH LEARNER SUPPORT

Prewrite for a Poem Explain to students that during prewriting, writers narrow their topic and organize their ideas. Help students focus their ideas with simple questions they can answer to get an idea or perhaps a first line.

• How do you feel when you think about someone you love or admire?

• What word or phrase comes into your mind when you think about this person?

Help students focus their thoughts and ideas about what they like about this person, using graphic organizers such has lists, three-column charts, and webs. Then have students meet with a partner and tell each other about the person you want to write about. Finally, encourage them to help each other express their feelings in lines of a poem. **SUBSTANTIAL/MODERATE**

NOT MY BONES

Poem by Marilyn Nelson

MENTOR TEXT

from **FORTUNE'S BONES**

History Writing by Pamela Espeland

> This article serves as a mentor text, a model for students to follow when they come to the Unit Writing Task: Write a Research Report.

GENRE ELEMENTS
HISTORY WRITING

Remind students that the purpose of **history writing** is to relate facts about events or individuals from the past. To help readers understand the sequence of past events, history writing uses a chronological text structure. It also may include unfamiliar words that have a specific meaning in the given context. In this lesson, students will analyze and compare how a poem and its accompanying historical notes treat the same topic, considering the purpose and effect of each genre.

LEARNING OBJECTIVES

- Paraphrase a poem to explain its language and meaning.
- Annotate and analyze the structure of an informational text.
- Conduct research about the history of slavery in the North.
- Create mental images and visual illustrations of ideas.
- Collaboratively recite a poem for the class.
- Compare and discuss texts from different genres and collaboratively present ideas supported by text evidence.
- **Language** Rephrase lines of poetry with a partner using teacher and peer support.

TEXT COMPLEXITY

Quantitative Measures	Fortune's Bones	Lexile: 790L
Qualitative Measures	**Ideas Presented** Mostly explicit; implied meaning requires inferences about tone.	
	Structure Used Mostly chronological, but deviations are supported with dates.	
	Language Used Largely explicit, with some academic/content-area vocabulary and complex sentences.	
	Knowledge Required Some historical context and references rely on outside knowledge.	

Online

RESOURCES

- Unit 4 Response Log
- Selection Audio
- Reading Studio: Notice & Note
- Level Up Tutorial: Chronological Order
- Level Up Tutorial: Paraphrasing
- Level Up Tutorial: Synthesizing Information
- Speaking and Listening Studio: Participating in Collaborative Discussions
- "Not My Bones" / "Fortune's Bones" Selection Test

SUMMARIES

English

"Not My Bones": The speaker, Fortune, says that his body was just a physical form he inhabited in life. He rejoices that the free parts of him (his mind and soul, or essence) are now fully free of his body and he can rest in peace.

"Fortune's Bones": Fortune was a slave who died in 1798. His master, a doctor, preserved his bones to study human anatomy. Fortune's skull was labeled "Larry" before his skeleton was given to a museum to display in 1933. In the 1990s, researchers identified Fortune's bones and how he died.

Spanish

"No mis huesos": La voz narrativa, Fortuna, dice que su cuerpo era solo una forma física que habitó en la vida. Se regocija de que sus partes libres (su mente y alma, o esencia) ahora son completamente libres de su cuerpo y ahora puede descansar en paz.

"Los huesos de Fortuna": Fortuna fue un esclavo que murió en 1798. Su amo, un doctor, preservó su cuerpo para estudiar la anatomía humana. El cráneo de Fortuna fue llamado "Larry" antes de que su esqueleto fuese entregado a un museo para la exhibición en 1933. En los años 90, investigadores identificaron los huesos de Fortuna y cómo murió.

SMALL-GROUP OPTIONS

Have students work in small groups to read and discuss the selection.

Pinwheel Discussion ("Not My Bones")

- Have small groups sit in circles and face outwards. Have other students each sit facing a person in a circle.
- Explain that groups should read aloud two stanzas at a time, with each member reading two lines. After each set, partners will discuss a given question. Then those sitting on the outside move to their right.
- Provide these questions: Lines 1–16: *Where is the speaker?* Lines 17–32: *Why does the speaker think your body is different from the rest of you?* Lines 33–48: *How are lines 33–40 related to 37–48?*
- Have groups discuss the whole poem.

Jigsaw with Experts ("Fortune's Bones")

- Have students read the selection.
- Ask students to count off from 1–6 and join the others with the same number.
- Assign groups these sections of the text by number order: paragraphs 1–4, 5–8, 9–11, 12–15, 16–18, and 19–21.
- Tell groups to discuss their section and identify the period of time it addresses.
- Have students form new groups with one person from each numbered group.
- Explain that each person should tell their group about their assigned section.
- Then the groups should discuss the whole selection.

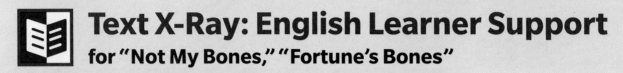

Text X-Ray: English Learner Support
for "Not My Bones," "Fortune's Bones"

Use the Text X-Ray and the supports and scaffolds in the Teacher's Edition to help guide students at different proficiency levels through the selection.

INTRODUCE THE SELECTION
DISCUSS RESPECT FOR THE DEAD

To appreciate Fortune's story, students need to be familiar with and able to discuss the customs and etiquette surrounding death and human remains. Review that a *skeleton* is a person's bones arranged as they are inside the body. Explain that *bones* and *skeleton* are neutral words, but more general words for a dead body can have positive or negative connotations.

- *Corpse* is a formal, more dignified word for a dead body.
- *Remains* is a more caring, respectful word that reminds us the body once belonged to a person. ("Fortune's Bones," paragraph 19)

Point out that language is not the only way people show that they respect, or value and care for, a dead person. Tell students that the person discussed in the texts was a Christian, so it would have been respectful to bury his remains. Have volunteers share other ways of showing respect and disrespect to the dead. Provide these stems and ask what other words could be used:

- *It is respectful/disrespectful to _____ because_____ .*
- *_____ show respect/disrespect by _____ .*

CULTURAL REFERENCES

The following words and phrases may be unfamiliar to students.

In "Not My Bones":

- *longing* (line 37): a strong desire for something
- *itty-bitty* (line 38): very small or tiny
- *glory hallelujah* (line 47): praise the Lord

In "Fortune's Bones":

- *estate* (paragraph 5): all the property a person owns at the time of his or her death
- *bonesetter* (paragraph 10): a person who sets, or puts back into place, bones that are broken or out of place
- *anthropologists* (paragraph 20): people who study the development of human bodies, societies, and cultures
- *giving up* (paragraph 20): releasing or letting go of

LISTENING

Understand Sound Devices

Tell students that the poem uses repetition and rhyme to make it musical, or like a song, and help give it meaning. Have them look at lines 37–40 in "Not My Bones." Explain that *essential* means "having the qualities that give something its true identity" or "necessary for being."

Have students listen as you read aloud lines 37–40. Use the following supports with students at varying proficiency levels:

- Tell students that you will ask questions about what you just read aloud. For example, ask: *Which lines use repetition?* (lines 39 and 40) *Which words are repeated?* (*You are not your body.*) Allow students to point to the lines to give answers. **SUBSTANTIAL**
- Have student pairs identify the repetition and rhyme in the lines. Then ask: *Why does the speaker repeat these words? How do the rhyme and repetition make the poem musical?* **MODERATE**
- Ask students to identify the repetition and two uses of rhyme. Then ask them to explain how these devices add meaning to the lines. **LIGHT**

SPEAKING

Discuss Opinions about Texts

Encourage students to ask questions and participate in an open class discussion. Give them time to practice phrasing their opinions and using new words, so they will be more confident when sharing.

Display lines 17–24 of "Not My Bones." Demonstrate creating discussion notes. Ask students to think about what was most important to Fortune. Use the following supports with students at varying proficiency levels:

- Model writing notes for a discussion: *Fortune valued his life. In line 22, he says, "Life's the best thing that can happen to you." He probably would not have risked his life to escape. For other slaves, freedom was worth the risk.* Read the model aloud and have students repeat each sentence. **SUBSTANTIAL**
- Have small groups practice presenting and discussing their opinions. Provide sentence frames that they can use to offer/respond to opinions and ask/answer questions: *I think _____ because _____. I agree with your point that _____. In my opinion, _____ was most important to Fortune.* **MODERATE**
- Ask student pairs to take turns presenting and discussing their opinions, as well as playing "devil's advocate" by asking their partner to clarify or explain a statement. **LIGHT**

READING

Paraphrase Poetry

Tell students that every word in a poem is important. Define *respirators* ("living things that breathe"). Have students watch you take a deep breath in and let it out slowly, and then copy you. Explain other words in lines 9–12 of "Not My Bones" as needed.

Ask volunteers to name who the *We* is in lines 9–12. *Who is the speaker talking about?* (*people*) Then work with students to paraphrase the lines, using the following supports for varying proficiency levels:

- Ask small groups to sketch a picture illustrating each line and think of a word or words to describe what they drew. Then read each line aloud and ask, *What are we?* Have groups show you their sketch for that line and tell you their description (accept single words or phrases). **SUBSTANTIAL**
- Assign lines 9–10 and 11–12 to small groups to paraphrase. Have the groups assigned the same lines compare their work and collaboratively write a new paraphrase that is more accurate. Ask representatives to read aloud the final paraphrase of each pair of lines. **MODERATE**
- Have each student in a pair paraphrase lines 9–10 or 11–12. Ask partners to exchange their paraphrases, offer suggestions for improvement, and then collaboratively produce a final paraphrase of all four lines. **LIGHT**

WRITING

Write a Theme Statement

Remind students that a theme statement expresses what a work says about a central topic. Ask them to think about topics common to both "Not My Bones" and "Fortune's Bones."

Ask: *What are the two works about? What do the works say about the topic?* Use the following supports with students at varying proficiency levels:

- Ask students *yes/no* questions to confirm and guide their understanding. For example: *Are both works about human bones? Do the bones belong to Fortune? Does Fortune think he is his body?* **SUBSTANTIAL**
- Provide sentence frames to support discussion: *A theme in _____ is _____. The bones belong to _____. The bones are important because_____. The works tell us_____ about _____.* **MODERATE**
- Ask students to outline the main points about the topic and their ideas for their response. Have them use their outlines to write a response. Challenge them to include one complex sentence. **LIGHT**

TEACH

? Connect to the
ESSENTIAL QUESTION

"Not My Bones" and "Fortune's Bones" both tell the story of an enslaved man in Connecticut who died a slave in 1798. The selections offer different perspectives on what freedom is, inviting students to consider varying ways that slavery denies people their basic human rights and dignity. They also raise the question of whether there are levels of freedom that apply to a person's body, mind, soul or spirit, and memory.

COMPARE TREATMENTS

Point out that "Not My Bones" is a poem that is inspired by the life of a real person, while the "Fortune's Bones" excerpt is history writing that relates facts about the person. Ask students what they expect to learn about the topic from each selection. Then use the following questions to discuss how the selections may complement each other: *Has a poem, novel, or movie about a historical figure ever made you curious about the facts of that person's life? Has a biography or documentary about a person ever made you imagine what she or he may have thought or felt in different situations? Why might someone want to read both a literary and an informational text about a real person?*

COLLABORATE & COMPARE

POEM
NOT MY BONES
by **Marilyn Nelson**
pages 299–301

COMPARE TREATMENTS

The poem and nonfiction text you are about to read share the same topic. As you read, notice how each writer uses the elements of her chosen genre to explore the topic, and how each treatment helps you understand different aspects of the topic. After reading, you will collaborate with a small group on a final project.

 ESSENTIAL QUESTION:

What will people risk to be free?

HISTORY WRITING
from
FORTUNE'S BONES
by **Pamela Espeland**
pages 302–305

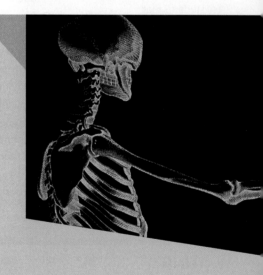

296   Unit 4

QUICK START

What makes you *you*? Is it your physical body or something inside you that determines the person you are? Write down your thoughts. Then share them with a partner or a small group.

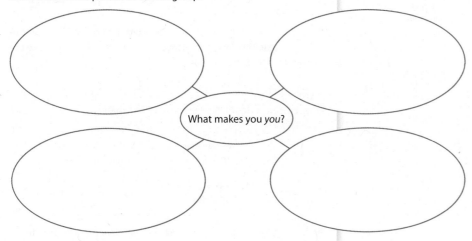

PARAPHRASE POETRY

As you read, make sure you **monitor your comprehension,** or notice how well you understand the meaning of the poem or text. One way to do so is to see if you can **paraphrase** a passage, or restate it in your own words. A paraphrase should be about as long as the original text. It should use simpler language and explain any figurative language in more literal terms.

If you find you don't understand a passage well enough to paraphrase it, go back and reread it. Annotate the parts that are confusing to you, and ask questions as needed. You can seek answers by asking others, using reference sources, or drawing on your own background knowledge until you have a better understanding. Then try to paraphrase the passage again. It should be easier this time.

Monitor your comprehension of "Not My Bones" by paraphrasing the sections that are hard to understand. The chart shows an example of how two lines from the first stanza can be paraphrased.

ORIGINAL	PARAPHRASE
Elementary molecules converged for a breath, / then danced on beyond my individual death.	While I was alive, my body was composed of tiny particles, but when I died, these elements were released from my body.

GENRE ELEMENTS: POETRY

- uses imagery and figurative language to convey meaning and mood
- uses sound devices such as rhythm and repetition to unify the poem and create emphasis
- expresses a theme, or a message about life or human nature
- includes a speaker who "talks" to the reader, like a narrator in fiction; the speaker is not necessarily the poet

TEACH

QUICK START

Have students read the Quick Start questions and explain that physical aspects of one's identity might include being athletic, having red hair, or being the oldest child in a family. Internal sources of identity could include things such things as loves, beliefs, or values. Suggest that students write sentences beginning with the phrase *I am*, and then use symbols to note which characteristics are physical and which are internal.

PARAPHRASE POETRY

Help students understand that paraphrasing is not summarizing. Explain that a summary briefly states just the main ideas in a text, but a paraphrase restates all the ideas in a simpler way, without changing or adding meaning. By paraphrasing a poem, readers put what the speaker is literally saying—or implying with figurative language—into plain words and sentences. Share these steps for paraphrasing:

- Look up any unfamiliar words or phrases.
- Think about what the poet is literally saying, and infer what the figurative language is comparing.
- Find your own words to express the same ideas with sentences.
- Use the speaker's point of view.

Read aloud lines 1–6 from "Not My Bones." Have volunteers define *elementary molecules* and *converged* or read aloud the definitions on p. 299, and ask students how lines 5–6 relate to the previous lines. (*They build on the idea that the speaker's body is a temporary home.*) Work with students to relate the original and paraphrased lines, such as by linking "elementary molecules" to "tiny particles." Then share this second example: *The particles that make up everything in the universe briefly came together to create my body, and then were freed to move on when I died.* Discuss which paraphrase more closely conveys the meaning of the original lines.

APPLY

ANALYZE CHRONOLOGICAL STRUCTURE

Review the transition words and clues about time in the table, and ask students to share other examples of words or phrases that indicate when events took place. (**Possible answers:** *later, during, meanwhile, today, last June, that winter, as a child*) Tell students that as they read, it can be helpful to use the evidence in the text to sketch a timeline of events for their own reference. Explain that clues like *for 25 years* require readers to look at previous text to determine the fixed date or event from which the 25 years began. Point out that readers are able to do this because the author used a chronological structure to present the information.

■ English Learner Support

Use Visual Support Model placing the examples on a timeline with labels, such as *1784: Law is passed* and *1798: Fortune died*. Ask questions about the timeline to have students use time-order words. For example, point to 1784 and ask whether Fortune died before or after the law was passed. (*after*) **SUBSTANTIAL**

ANNOTATION MODEL

Explain the annotation ideas in the model: placing brackets around lines students paraphrase, underlining imagery or figurative language, circling key words, and writing paraphrases and notes in the side margin. Point out that they can apply these suggestions to the second selection, such as by circling transitions and clues that signal the time and sequence of events. Tell students that they also may use their own system for marking up the selection. They may want to color-code their annotations by using highlighters. Their notes in the margin may include questions about ideas that are unclear or topics they want to learn more about.

**GENRE ELEMENTS:
HISTORY WRITING**

- uses chronological structure
- relates facts about important events from history or from an individual's life
- is most often written to inform or teach
- may include domain-specific vocabulary (e.g., words about slavery)

ANALYZE CHRONOLOGICAL STRUCTURE

Chronological structure is the arrangement of events by their order of occurrence, or the order in which they happen. This organizational pattern is used in biography, autobiography, and other history writing, such as the notes you will read from *Fortune's Bones*. It is also often used in fiction.

Writers use textual clues and transition words to make a chronological structure clear. This chart summarizes some ways that writers make the time and order of events clear:

TYPES OF TRANSITION WORDS	HOW THEY'RE USED	EXAMPLES
Order words	to show the order or sequence of events	*before, first, afterward, then, during, finally*
Time words	to specify a date, a time, or a period of time	*in 1784, the late 1700s, between 1798 and 1933, for 25 years, over the years*

As you read the history writing from *Fortune's Bones* that follows the poem "Not My Bones," note the words and phrases the author uses to signal the order of events and when events take place. Consider how the chronological structure helps the author achieve her purpose.

ANNOTATION MODEL   NOTICE & NOTE

As you read, you can paraphrase difficult passages in the side margin. The model shows one reader's notes about the first stanza of "Not My Bones."

I was not this body,
I was not these bones.
This skeleton was just my
temporary home.
5   Elementary molecules converged for a breath,
then danced on beyond my individual death.
And I am not my body,
I am not my body.

Paraphrase: This body and these bones weren't all I was. My physical body was just a shelter for my being.

great image—like molecules gathered for a meeting

"danced" is a happy word

ENGLISH LEARNER SUPPORT

Use Language Support Tell students to ask for help understanding unfamiliar words.

- Ask students to raise their hands if they do not understand words in lines 5–6. Share these Spanish cognates and use illustrations to help define the words as needed: *elementary/elemental, molecules/moléculas, converge/convergir, individual/individual.* **SUBSTANTIAL**

- Provide these sentence stems: *I don't understand ___. Does this word mean ___?* If students need help, share the given cognates and read aloud and discuss the definitions provided on p. 299. **MODERATE**

BACKGROUND

The poem "Not My Bones" comes from the book Fortune's Bones: The Manumission Requiem. *The author,* **Marilyn Nelson,** *is a former poet laureate of Connecticut and the winner of many awards, including the Newbery Honor and the Coretta Scott King Honor. She wrote Fortune's Bones to honor the memory of Fortune, an enslaved person who died in 1798. Nelson was commissioned to write the book by the Mattatuck Museum of Connecticut, where Fortune's skeleton had been displayed after descendants of the man who owned Fortune donated it to the museum.*

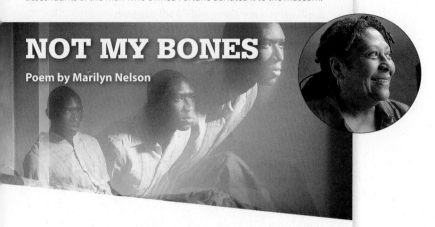

NOT MY BONES

Poem by Marilyn Nelson

PREPARE TO COMPARE

As you read the poem, look for how the poet uses language to create images, communicate ideas, and convey mood.

I was not this body,
I was not these bones.
This skeleton was just my
temporary home.
5 Elementary molecules[1] converged[2] for a breath,
then danced on beyond my individual death.
And I am not my body,
I am not my body.

We are brief incarnations,[3]
10 we are clouds in clothes.
We are water respirators,
we are how earth knows.

---

[1] **elementary molecules:** the smallest, most basic particles of substances.
[2] **converged:** came together in one place; met.
[3] **incarnations:** bodily forms.

Notice & Note

Use the side margins to notice and note signposts in the text.

PARAPHRASE POETRY
Annotate: Circle the word *incarnations* in the poem. Underline its definition in the footnotes.

Interpret: Restate lines 9–12 in your own words. Do not quote directly from the text in your paraphrase.

BACKGROUND

Have students read the Background note, and point out that the title "Not My Bones" suggests that Fortune is the speaker in the poem. Then call students' attention to the title of the book containing the poem, *Fortune's Bones: The Manumission Requiem.* Explain that the word *manumission* means freeing or being freed from slavery. A requiem is a piece of music written to mourn, praise, or honor the dead. Requiems are traditionally played at funerals and religious services for the dead, but they may have uplifting as well as somber moments. Encourage students to consider how the musical qualities of the poem may support the words and imagery, and help create the poem's mood and theme.

PREPARE TO COMPARE

Direct students to use the Prepare to Compare prompt to focus their reading.

PARAPHRASE POETRY

Remind students that before they **paraphrase** a poem, they should look up the meaning of any unfamiliar words. This will help them determine what the writer is literally saying and implying with each sentence. Then students can restate the ideas in each line using different words. (***Possible answer:*** *All of us exist in our physical bodies for only a short time, as we are just bunches of molecules wearing clothing. All of us breathe in water vapor from the air, and because we are thinking beings, we make the earth aware of itself.*)

For **reading support** for students at varying proficiency levels, see the **Text X-Ray** on page 296D.

ENGLISH LEARNER SUPPORT

Demonstrate Comprehension After students have paraphrased lines 9–12, give them a main-idea-and-details organizer, and ask them to identify the main idea of the lines. Ask guiding questions.

- Ask yes/no questions, such as: *Who is "we"?* (everyone/people) *Are brief incarnations, clouds in clothes, water respirators, and earth all made of molecules?* (yes) *Are they all a part of nature?* (yes) *Are people a part of nature?* (yes) **MODERATE**

- Ask partners to discuss and prepare responses to these questions: *What is the speaker saying about our relationship with nature? How do the images support this idea?* Share these sentence frames: *The speaker wants readers to understand that _____. The image of _____ make readers think that _____.* **LIGHT**

PARAPHRASE POETRY

Remind students that figurative language expresses a meaning that is different from the literal meaning of words, usually by comparing one thing to another. Tell students that they can **paraphrase** metaphors, similes, personification, and other figurative language by clarifying what is being compared and restating the comparisons in their own words. (**Possible answer:** *Like people, a dream or desire can be killed, and a strong belief or trust in something can be beaten down and weakened. But these things also are like plants that are hard to get rid of and that grow without being planted. Hope and faith always return.*)

■ English Learner Support

Employ Analytical Skills Tell students that *restate* is another word for *paraphrase*. Point out that in lines 29–30, the poet makes several comparisons using personification and a simile. Explain that students should identify the things being compared and how they are alike, to help them make the same comparisons with different words. Give students Venn diagrams and demonstrate how they can use them.

- Have students look at line 29. Write "hope" in one circle and "can be murdered" in the intersection. Ask: *Can hope really be murdered?* (no) *What is hope compared to?* (people) Write "people" in the other circle. Have students work in small groups to identify all the comparisons.

- Have students look at line 30. Write "weeds and wildflowers" in one circle, and ask what they think *they* refers to. Have students work with a partner to identify all the comparisons. **LIGHT**

 For **speaking support** for students at varying proficiency levels, see the **Text X-Ray** on page 296D.

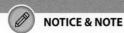
NOTICE & NOTE

> I bore[4] light passed on from an original flame;
> while it was in my hands it was called by my name.
> 15 But I am not my body,
> I am not my body.
>
> You can own a man's body,
> but you can't own his mind.
> That's like making a bridle
> 20 to ride on the wind.
> I will tell you one thing, and I'll tell you true:
> Life's the best thing that can happen to you.
> But you are not your body,
> you are not your body.
>
> 25 You can own someone's body,
> but the soul runs free.
> It roams the night sky's
> mute geometry.
> You can murder hope, you can pound faith flat,
> 30 but like weeds and wildflowers, they grow right back.
> For you are not your body,
> you are not your body.
>
> You are not your body,
> you are not your bones.
> 35 What's essential[5] about you

PARAPHRASE POETRY
Annotate: Reread lines 29–30. Mark examples of figurative language.

Interpret: Restate those lines in your own words.

---

[4] **bore:** carried; transported.
[5] **essential:** having the qualities that give something its true identity.

TO CHALLENGE STUDENTS . . .

Analyze Imagery and Theme Explain that *essential* comes from the Latin root *esse*, meaning "to be." Ask students to analyze how the writer uses imagery to help readers understand everything that is essential to a person's being and develop the poem's theme. Remind students that visual imagery is just one type of imagery, and encourage them to look for other types. Then have them discuss their ideas with others and share their findings with the class.

is what can't be owned.
What's essential in you is your longing to raise
your itty-bitty voice in the cosmic[6] praise.
For you are not your body,
40 you are not your body.

Well, I woke up this morning just so glad to be free,
glad to be free, glad to be free.
I woke up this morning in restful peace.
For I am not my body,
45 I am not my bones.
I am not my body,
glory hallelujah, not my bones,
I am not my bones.

---
[6] **cosmic:** universal; infinitely large.

CHECK YOUR UNDERSTANDING

Answer these questions about "Not My Bones" before moving on to the next selection.

1 The speaker in the poem is most likely —

A the author of the poem, Marilyn Nelson

B one of Dr. Porter's descendants

C Fortune or another formerly enslaved person

D one of Fortune's ancestors or descendants

2 Which of the following is an example of personification?

F *You can murder hope*

G *you can pound faith flat*

H *We are water respirators*

J *You can own someone's body*

3 The primary message in "Not My Bones" is that —

A a person's most important qualities can't be owned

B a person's remains should be treated with respect

C Dr. Porter's descendants were wrong to use Fortune's skeleton

D people should not own or control other people

PARAPHRASE POETRY

Annotate: In the last stanza, mark the lines that describe how the speaker felt upon waking.

Interpret: Paraphrase those lines. What idea might they be conveying?

PARAPHRASE POETRY

Point out to students that there are two parts to the Interpret task: paraphrasing the lines they marked about the speaker's feelings when waking and answering the question about what idea the lines convey.

Tell students that when they paraphrase poems with repetition, they should use repetition in the same way as the original lines. Explain that the repetition in a poem contributes to voice and mood, so it also influences the poem's meaning and should be kept. (**Possible answer:** *Paraphrase; Anyway, this morning I awoke overjoyed, just so pleased with my freedom, pleased with my freedom, pleased with my freedom. This morning I awoke contented, with my mind and soul at ease. Answer; The speaker, who is probably Fortune, didn't literally wake up. Instead, he feels awake and alive because death has at last freed him from slavery. He is happy to discover that his soul is free, and this knowledge gives him a sense of peace.*)

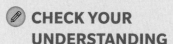 For **listening support** for students at varying proficiency levels, see the **Text X-Ray** on page 296C.

CHECK YOUR UNDERSTANDING

Have students answer the questions independently.

Answers:

1. *C*

2. *F*

3. *A*

If they answer any questions incorrectly, have them reread the text to confirm their understanding. Then they may proceed to "Fortune's Bones" on p. 302.

 ENGLISH LEARNER SUPPORT

Oral Assessment   Use the following questions to assess students' comprehension and speaking skills:

1. Who is probably the speaker in the poem? (*The speaker is probably Fortune or another person who was a slave.*)

2. Which is an example of personification, or the act of treating an object or idea like it is a person. (*You can murder hope.*)

3. What is the primary, or main, message in "Not My Bones"? (*A person's most important qualities can't be owned.*) **SUBSTANTIAL/MODERATE**

BACKGROUND

Have students read the Background note and call their attention to the fact that the selection is from the same book as the poem, *Fortune's Bones: The Manumission Requiem*. Remind students that the book was written at the request of the museum that had displayed Fortune's skeleton. Tell students that attitudes about what is proper to display in museums have changed in recent years, so it is unlikely that any museum would treat human remains in the same way today.

MENTOR TEXT

At the end of the unit, students will be asked to write a research report. "Fortune's Bones" provides a model for how a writer can research a topic and support ideas with facts and examples.

PREPARE TO COMPARE

Direct students to use the Prepare to Compare prompt to focus their reading.

ANALYZE CHRONOLOGICAL STRUCTURE

Remind students that writers use order and time words or phrases, such as *first*, *today*, and *in 2001*, to make the sequence and timing of the events they are describing clear to readers. Paying attention to these clues helps readers recognize when a text is organized with a **chronological structure**. (**Answer:** *It emphasizes who Fortune was when he was alive, so most likely that's the part of his history the author will explain first. The sentence also suggests that Fortune's life is just as important as what happened after his death, so if the author uses a chronological structure, readers may not learn more about how his bones ended up in a museum until much later.*)

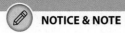 **NOTICE & NOTE**

BACKGROUND

Along with "Not My Bones" and five other poems by Marilyn Nelson, Fortune's Bones includes history writing and primary source documents and illustrations that tell Fortune's story. Some of the historical notes written by Pamela Espeland are included here. Read these notes to learn facts and additional information about Fortune's life and about what happened to his bones after he died.

from
FORTUNE'S BONES
History Writing by Pamela Espeland

PREPARE TO COMPARE

As you read this history writing, think about how the writer uses a chronological structure to relate key moments during and after Fortune's life. Think about how this selection compares to the poem "Not My Bones" and how it adds to your understanding of the topic.

ANALYZE CHRONOLOGICAL STRUCTURE

Annotate: Mark the word that signals sequence in the first paragraph.

Predict: What does this first sentence tell you about how the text will be organized?

1   Before Fortune was bones in a Connecticut museum, he was a husband, a father, a baptized Christian, and a slave.

2   His wife's name was Dinah. His sons were Africa and Jacob. His daughters were Mira and Roxa. He was baptized in an Episcopal church, which did not make him free. His master was Dr. Preserved Porter, a physician who specialized in setting broken bones.

3   They lived in Waterbury, Connecticut, in the late 1700s. Dr. Porter had a 75-acre farm, which Fortune probably ran. He planted and harvested corn, rye, potatoes, onions, apples, buckwheat, oats, and hay. He cared for the cattle and hogs.

 ENGLISH LEARNER SUPPORT

Use Prereading Supports Give students a sequence-of-events organizer with six sections labeled with paragraph numbers: "1–4," "5–8," "9–11," "12–15," "16–18," and "19–21." Explain that in each section, students should note the period of time discussed in the paragraphs, the main event(s)/facts, and key time-order words.

• Demonstrate what students should record by completing the first section. Read the notes aloud, and have students name or indicate which paragraph the information is from. Allow students to sketch pictures instead writing notes, as needed. **SUBSTANTIAL**

• Have students work with a partner to complete the first section for paragraphs 1–4. Have volunteers share what they recorded. **MODERATE**

4   Unlike many slaves, who owned little or nothing and were often separated from their families, Fortune owned a small house near Dr. Porter's home. He and Dinah and their children lived together.

5   When Dr. Porter died in 1803, he left an estate that was worth about $7,000—a lot of money for the time. The estate included Fortune's widow, Dinah, and their son Jacob. Fortune had died in 1798.

6   According to Connecticut's Act of Gradual Emancipation, children born to enslaved parents after March 1, 1784, were to be freed when they reached age 21. Jacob was 18. By law, he could be enslaved for another three years.

7   In Dr. Porter's will, he left Dinah to his wife, Lydia. He gave Jacob to his daughter Hannah.

8   No one knows what happened to Africa, Mira, and Roxa.

9   Most slaves who died in Waterbury in the 1700s were buried in one of the town's cemeteries. When Fortune died, he wasn't buried. Instead, Dr. Porter preserved Fortune's skeleton to further the study of human anatomy.[1]

10   Dr. Porter had been a bonesetter for many years, but he'd never had a skeleton to study. He had two sons who were also doctors. They could learn from the skeleton, too.

11   Fortune was about 60 at the time of his death and, in spite of his injuries, in relatively good health. His skeleton was sturdy and complete.

12   Four more generations of Porters became physicians, and the skeleton stayed in the family. Porter children, grandchildren, and great-grandchildren used it to learn the names of the bones. This was their earliest medical training.

13   Sally Porter Law McGlannan, the last Porter doctor, remembered playing with the skeleton as a young girl. . . . Another family member, Leander Law, once brought part of Fortune's skeleton to a college physiology class.

14   At some point—no one knows exactly when—"Larry" was written on the skull. Fortune's name was forgotten for nearly a century.

15   Over the years, the skeleton was lost and found. It was boarded up[2] in an attic, then discovered by a crew of workers hired to renovate an old building.

16   In 1933, Sally Porter Law McGlannan gave the bones to the Mattatuck Museum. The museum sent the bones to Europe

---

[1] **anatomy:** the structure and parts of the body.
[2] **boarded up:** packed away.

ANALYZE CHRONOLOGICAL STRUCTURE

Annotate: Mark the time words in paragraphs 5–8.

Draw Conclusions: In what year was Fortune's son Jacob probably emancipated?

CONTRASTS AND CONTRADICTIONS

Notice & Note: Review paragraphs 12–14. Underline how the Porter family made use of Fortune's skeleton. Circle the name someone gave it.

Interpret: What is ironic and perhaps shocking about this contradiction?

✎ ANALYZE CHRONOLOGICAL STRUCTURE

Remind students that writers may name a specific date for an event or describe its timing in relation to another event. Explain that time-order words help readers identify relationships between events and draw conclusions to determine unstated facts. (**Answer:** *He probably was emancipated in 1806 because that's when he would have turned 21.*)

▶ CONTRASTS AND CONTRADICTIONS

Tell students that this signpost will help them infer the author's purpose for sharing these details. Remind them that **irony** is a contrast between appearances or expectations and reality, so something ironic is the opposite of what is expected. Writers use irony to create humor, emphasize the sadness or tragedy of a situation, or make a point about what the contradiction shows. (**Answer:** *The fact that four generations learned the names of the many bones but not Fortune's name is both sadly ironic and shocking. The author probably wants to emphasize that the family thought of the skeleton as just as an object, with no respect for the person's humanity.*)

WHEN STUDENTS STRUGGLE . . .

Summarize Explain that sometimes writers will discuss certain events out of time order, even when using a chronological structure. Have students draw a box around paragraphs 9–11 and summarize the main idea of the section. Then have them locate the year that Fortune died (paragraph 5). Have students draw another box around paragraphs 5–8. Ask: *Why do you think the writer discussed Dr. Porter's death before explaining what he did with Fortune's body?* (Paragraphs 5–8 explain what happened to Fortune's children. Because they were part of his life, this information should come after paragraph 4.)

 For additional support, go to the **Reading Studio** and assign the following [LEVEL UP] **Level Up tutorial: Chronological Order.**

ANALYZE CHRONOLOGICAL STRUCTURE

Explain that some references to time are used to make a point, not to establish timing or order. Tell students that as they read paragraphs 12–16, they should mark only those time-order words that help them understand what happened to Fortune's skeleton. (*Answer: The skeleton was used as a learning tool for several generations, labeled with someone else's name, and then stored in an attic and forgotten. It was discovered years later during some building renovations, sometime before 1933.*)

ENGLISH LEARNER SUPPORT

Comprehend Language Structures Have students look at the first sentence in paragraph 19. Explain that writers may interrupt a sentence to add a word or phrase that provides extra information but is not necessary to the basic meaning of the sentence. This word or phrase usually comes right after the word it describes or explains, and it is set off from the rest of the sentence with commas.

ASK STUDENTS to underline the phrase "still called Larry." Ask: *Who or what is still called Larry?* (the skeleton) Have students circle the answer in the sentence. *What was "taken out of its case and put into storage"?* (the skeleton) **SUBSTANTIAL**

Ask students these guiding questions: *What was "taken out of its case and put into storage"?* (the skeleton) *Which word or phrase in the sentence is not needed to answer this question?* ("still called Larry") Have students discuss with a partner why the author adds this information, and then tell you their idea. (*to show that people still do not know that it's Fortune's skeleton*) **MODERATE**

A sculptor used information about Fortune's bones to create this reconstruction of Fortune's face.

ANALYZE CHRONOLOGICAL STRUCTURE

Annotate: In paragraphs 12–16, mark time and order words that help you follow what happened to Fortune's skeleton.

Summarize: What had become of Fortune's skeleton before Sally Porter Law McGlannan gave it to the Mattatuck Museum?

to be assembled for display. The skeleton hung in a glass case in the museum for decades, fascinating adults and frightening children.

17 Many stories were invented about the skeleton. Some said that "Larry" was a Revolutionary War hero—maybe even George Washington. Some said he fell to his death. Some said he drowned. Some said he was killed trying to escape. Some thought he had been hanged.

18 One Waterbury resident remembers, "Larry was the thing to see when you go to the museum. I don't think anybody ever envisioned[3] that this was truly a human being."

19 In 1970, the skeleton, still called "Larry," was taken out of its case and put into storage. Times had changed. The museum now believed that displaying the skeleton was disrespectful. It wasn't just a bunch of bones. It was the remains of someone's son, maybe someone's father.

---

[3] **envisioned:** imagined.

APPLYING ACADEMIC VOCABULARY

❏ **access** ☑ **civil** ❏ **demonstrate** ☑ **document** ❏ **symbolize**

Write and Discuss Have students discuss the following questions with a partner. Guide students to include the Academic Vocabulary words *civil* and *document* in their responses. Ask volunteers to share their responses with the class.

- How were Fortune's **civil** rights violated or broken by the use of his skeleton?
- What kinds of historical **documents** provide facts about people's lives? What kinds of documents might exist for someone who was a slave?

20   The skeleton rested for more than 25 years. Then, in the 1990s, historians searched local records and found a slave named Fortune. Archaeologists and anthropologists studied the bones, which started giving up their secrets. <u>The bones told how Fortune labored, suffered, and died: A quick, sudden injury, like whiplash, may have snapped a vertebra[4] in his neck.</u> He did not drown or fall from a cliff. He was not hanged.

21   But he was free.

_____
[4] **vertebra:** a piece of bone that makes up the spinal column.

BIG QUESTIONS

Notice & Note: In paragraph 20, mark a fact that raises the question of whether or not Fortune's death was accidental.

Analyze: What does the author expect you to know or to wonder about whiplash? Where could you look to get more information?

CHECK YOUR UNDERSTANDING

Answer these questions before moving on to the **Analyze the Text** section on the following page.

1 Which of the following is not one of the reasons we know about Fortune today?

   A Historians searched local records and found information about him.

   B Archaeologists and anthropologists studied his bones.

   C Marilyn Nelson was commissioned to write poems about him.

   D Sally Porter Law McGlannan asked the museum to research his bones.

2 For what period of time were Fortune's bones displayed in the Mattatuck Museum?

   F From 1798 to 1970

   G From 1803 to 1970

   H From 1933 to 1970

   J From 1933 to the 1990s

3 The last line, "But he was free," emphasizes that —

   A Fortune and his family were freed after Dr. Porter died

   B Fortune managed to escape from slavery before he died

   C Fortune's family reclaimed his bones from the museum

   D Fortune could no longer be owned after his death

Not My Bones / Fortune's Bones   305

BIG QUESTIONS

After students mark the detail in paragraph 20, ask them to consider why the author specifically mentions whiplash as a possible cause of Fortune's death. Point out that the author may want readers to both wonder about this detail and to infer particular ideas from it. Encourage students to reflect on the **author's purpose** and what information they need to infer this. (**Possible answer:** *The author wants readers to wonder whether whiplash is what broke Fortune's neck and, if so, what caused it. The author also expects readers to know what whiplash is. She mentions it because she wants readers to visualize a person's head and neck being violently jerked back and forth. Whiplash also is the blow of a whip. Both images make readers think about how people would whip and physically abuse slaves, so the possibility of him dying from an accident seems less likely. Curious readers might wonder whether Fortune was beaten and killed while trying to escape, as suggested in paragraph 17. An encyclopedia entry and health website are two sources of more information.*)

CHECK YOUR UNDERSTANDING

Have students answer the questions independently.

Answers:

   1. *D*

   2. *H*

   3. *D*

If they answer any questions incorrectly, have them reread the text to confirm their understanding. Then they may proceed to ANALYZE THE TEXT on page 306.

 ENGLISH LEARNER SUPPORT

Oral Assessment Use the following questions to assess students' comprehension and speaking skills:

   1. What are some reasons we know about Fortune today? (*Historians searched local records and found information about him, archaeologists and anthropologists studied his bones, and the museum asked Marilyn Nelson to write poems about him.*)

   2. When were Fortune's bones displayed in the Mattatuck Museum? (*His bones were displayed from 1933 to 1970.*)

   3. What idea is emphasized by the last sentence in the selection, "But he was free"? (*Fortune could no longer be owned after his death.*)
   SUBSTANTIAL/MODERATE

ANALYZE THE TEXT

Possible answers:

1. **DOK 2:** *"I am not my body" (lines 7, 8, 15, 16, 44, 46) and "you are not your body" (lines 23, 24, 31, 32, 33, 39, 40) are the most repeated. The repetition emphasizes the idea that we are all much more than our physical bodies; our bodies do not define us.*

2. **DOK 4:** *A person's physical shell can be controlled, but not the essential part of a person. That is free to travel throughout the silent universe, from star to star or to infinity. This silent, free movement contrasts with the imagery of a voice joining and rising with others in a choir, but both ideas suggest that the soul is boundless, like the universe, and transcends the body.*

3. **DOK 4:** *Calling Fortune's skeleton "the thing to see" suggests that the resident and people who invented stories about "Larry" thought of him just an object and a spectacle. This is confirmed by the comment that no one imagined the skeleton as a human being.*

4. **DOK 4:** *The author's primary purpose was to inform readers of Fortune's personal history. Using a chronological structure helps make this history clear by organizing information in time order and signaling key events with time and sequence words.*

5. **DOK 4:** *By the 1970s, people had become more sensitive to the need to treat all people equally and with respect. In contrast, in 1933, the skeleton was seen as an oddity, like a sideshow attraction, not a person.*

RESEARCH

Remind students to check websites' "About" page to help evaluate whether the publisher/author is a credible source.

Extend Students may note that passing state abolition laws did not immediately end slavery in those states. Most states took partial steps like gradual emancipation and banning the importation of slaves.

ANALYZE THE TEXTS

Support your responses with evidence from the texts. **NOTEBOOK**

1. **Identify Patterns** Review "Not My Bones." Which lines in the poem are most often repeated? How might that repetition help underscore the message of the poem?

2. **Connect** Paraphrase lines 25–28 of "Not My Bones." How is this idea related to the imagery in lines 37–38?

3. **Analyze** Reread paragraph 18 of the notes from *Fortune's Bones*. What do the Waterbury resident's observations reveal about people's feelings and behavior toward Fortune? Cite evidence in your response.

4. **Evaluate** How does the chronological structure of the history writing from *Fortune's Bones* help the author achieve her purpose?

5. **Notice & Note** State in your own words why the museum put Fortune's skeleton in storage. How does this attitude contrast with the attitude of the museum and its visitors in 1933?

RESEARCH TIP

Remember that when you do research, you need to keep track of where you find information. For print sources, make a note of the title, author, publisher, publication date, and page number. For online sources, make a note of the website, URL, article title, author, and access date. Keep in mind that it's often wise to verify each fact you find in a second source. For example, if you used an online encyclopedia to find out which northern states were free states in 1861, then you might confirm that information by looking in a second online source, or in a print encyclopedia or history book.

RESEARCH

The man called Fortune was held in slavery on a farm in Connecticut until his death in 1798. After reading these selections, what do you know want to know about slavery in the northern states? With your group, note research questions in the chart below. One question has been provided for you. Research to find the answers.

QUESTION	ANSWER
In what year did Connecticut abolish slavery?	*It officially abolished slavery in 1848.*
Possible questions: What were the first northern states to abolish slavery?	*Vermont (1777), Pennsylvania (1780), Massachusetts and New Hampshire (1783), Connecticut and Rhode Island (1784), New York (1799), New Jersey (1804)*
How did most northern states abolish slavery?	*They freed the slaves in the state and made the sale and purchase of slaves illegal, but most did this gradually. Some northern states also passed laws to protect fugitive slaves from the South from their owners and slave catchers.*

Extend With your group, share your research findings with the class. Then discuss what surprised you or what you found most interesting or noteworthy. Identify one or two questions that you still have that you would like to explore.

WHEN STUDENTS STRUGGLE . . .

Reteaching: Paraphrasing Remind students that paraphrasing is restating details and ideas with different words. Explain that readers often must infer ideas from the details in a poem. Clarify any confusing words in the lines. Then have partners discuss the meaning of lines 27–28. Ask: *What do you see and hear when you imagine something "roaming" through the night sky? How might this movement make someone think of geometry?*

For additional support, go to the **Reading Studio** and assign the following **LEVEL UP** **Level Up tutorial: Paraphrasing.**

CREATE AND RECITE

Express Ideas Visually Create a visual work of some kind—such as a painting, drawing, or video—that is inspired by details you learned about Fortune's life.

❑ As a group, decide what kind of visual work you will create.

❑ Reread the poem and the history notes. Draw on imagery in the poem and details in the history writing to form mental images about Fortune's story.

❑ Create your part of the group's work.

❑ As a group, present your work. Explain the aspects of Fortune's life or story that it focuses on or was inspired by.

Recite a Poem With your group, recite part of "Not My Bones" aloud for the class.

❑ Work with your group to select one stanza of the poem.

❑ Discuss how you will recite it. Will you recite it together chorally? Will you sing it like a song? Will different members of your group speak different lines? Will you accompany the words with movements or gestures?

❑ Memorize your lines and rehearse them a few times with your group.

❑ Present the poem to the class, using appropriate volume, phrasing, and expression.

RESPOND TO THE ESSENTIAL QUESTION

 What will people risk to be free?

Gather Information Review your annotations and notes on "Not My Bones" and *Fortune's Bones*. Then, add relevant details to your Response Log. As you determine which information to include, think about:

• information you learned about Fortune and what became of his bones

• what it means to be free

• how each writer treats the topic of freedom

At the end of the unit, you can use your notes to help you write a research report.

ACADEMIC VOCABULARY

As you write and discuss what you learned from the two selections, be sure to use the Academic Vocabulary words. Check off each of the words that you use.

❑ **access**

❑ **civil**

❑ **demonstrate**

❑ **document**

❑ **symbolize**

CREATE AND RECITE

Express Ideas Visually Encourage groups to collaboratively write a theme statement while planning their visual work. Explain that having a common theme will help give their group's work a focus and unity, while still allowing them to visually interpret and represent the poem in creative ways.

For **writing support** for students at varying proficiency levels, see the **Text X-Ray** on page 296D.

Recite a Poem Remind students that to read a poem with expression, they should try to convey its meaning and emotions with their voices. Students can emphasize different words and adjust their phrasing, intonation, and pacing, in addition to their volume. As students plan how they will read their stanza, encourage them to discuss the emotion the speaker is conveying with each line.

RESPOND TO THE ESSENTIAL QUESTION

Allow time for students to add details from "Not My Bones" and "Fortune's Bones" to their Unit 4 Response Logs.

APPLY

COMPARE TREATMENTS

Explain that a writer's **treatment** is his or her approach to the topic, which is indicated by the form used, purpose for writing, the text's tone, and other characteristics. Students can describe the writing in each selection by identifying the elements of the genre that the writer uses.

ANALYZE THE TEXTS

Possible answers:

1. **DOK 3:** *"Not My Bones" used more of these elements to express ideas in surprising ways and move readers' emotions. Examples include metaphors like "we are clouds in clothes" (line 10), the personification of molecules that "danced on" (lines 5–6), and imagery of the soul traveling freely from star to star (lines 26–27).*

2. **DOK 4:** *A book combining these two treatments would present a multidimensional look at the man. The poem gives a voice to the thoughts and feelings Fortune might have had, to communicate an emotional truth about slavery. The historical writing presents facts about Fortune's life and explains his personal history in the context of the history of slavery in the United States.*

3. **DOK 4:** *The poem allows more freedom because of the purpose and characteristics of each treatment. History writing is meant to inform, so writers are limited by the need to clearly relate facts about real people and events. Poems attempt to make readers feel something, and there are many ways to do that with imagery, sound, language, and varied structures.*

4. **DOK 4:** *The title of the book is a good one. Both writings "free" Fortune by addressing his humanity, granting his memory the dignity and respect he was denied. The poem's repetition and rhyme give it musical qualities, so it is like a requiem honoring Fortune as much more than a body that labored for another man or a skeleton on display. The historical notes also honor Fortune's life by telling the facts of his experience of slavery and unjust treatment.*

NOT MY BONES
Poem by Marilyn Nelson

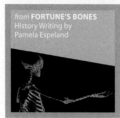

from **FORTUNE'S BONES**
History Writing by
Pamela Espeland

Collaborate & Compare

COMPARE TREATMENTS

Marilyn Nelson and Pamela Espeland both wrote on the same topic—Fortune's bones—but they handled the topic differently. The way a topic is handled is called its **treatment.** In order to identify a writer's treatment, ask yourself the following questions:

❏ What form does the writing take? For example, is it a poem, a biography, a blog post, or a newspaper article?

❏ For what primary purpose was the selection written? Was it mostly written to entertain, to express ideas and feelings, to inform, or to persuade?

❏ What is the writer's **tone,** or attitude toward the subject?

In a small group, identify similarities and differences in the treatment of each selection. Record your thoughts in the chart.

	"Not My Bones"	from *Fortune's Bones*
Form of writing	*poem*	*history writing*
Primary purpose	*to express thoughts*	*to inform*
Tone	*respectful, joyful*	*rmatter-of-fact, serious*
Description of the writing	*uses figurative language; stanzas*	*factual descriptions; uses chronological structure*

ANALYZE THE TEXTS

Discuss these questions in your group.

1. **Connect** Which text uses more figurative language and imagery? Cite examples. What purpose does it serve?

2. **Synthesize** Think about the understanding of Fortune that you get from "Not My Bones" and from the *Fortune's Bones* historical notes. What might be the strengths of a book that combines poems with historical notes?

3. **Evaluate** Think about how the poem and the historical notes were written. Which type of writing allows more freedom in its treatment? Why do you think that is?

4. **Critique** The full title of Marilyn Nelson's book is *Fortune's Bones: The Manumission Requiem.* (*Manumission* means being freed from slavery, and a *requiem* is music written to honor the dead.) Do you think that is a good title for the book? Why? Draw on information from both selections to support your answer.

WHEN STUDENTS STRUGGLE . . .

Reteaching: Comparing Treatment To help students to connect form and treatment, ask how the discovery of Fortune's identity might be treated in a news article. (To inform readers, the writer would use factual details and photographs.) Ask: *If the article was read aloud, what tone of voice would be used?* (*a matter-of-fact tone*) Point out that "Fortune's Bones" is both an informational text and history writing, and have students use the list of Genre Elements on p. 298 to help them complete the column for this selection.

For additional support, go to the **Reading Studio** and assign the following LEVEL **Level Up tutorial: Synthesizing Information.**

DECIDE AND DISCUSS

Now, you can continue exploring the ideas in these texts by discussing with classmates which treatment of Fortune's life and death is more effective. Follow these steps:

1. **Choose a Position** Decide for yourself which treatment of Fortune's is the most effective or powerful. Ask:
   - ❑ Which treats the topic more comprehensively, or fully?
   - ❑ Which gives readers a better sense of the man and the issue of slavery in the United States?
   - ❑ Which evokes stronger feelings?
   - ❑ Which conveys a more universal message?

2. **Gather Information** Form a group with others who share the same opinion. Working together, support that opinion with examples from the text.

What I Learned or Understood Better	Support from the Text
Fortune valued his life, so he probably would not have risked losing it by running away. Slaves who did try to escape slavery must have thought freedom was worth the risk.	*I will tell you one thing, and I'll tell you true:* *Life's the best thing that can happen to you.* *"Not My Bones," lines 21–22*

3. **Select Information** As a group, select three of the strongest examples to present to the class.

4. **Share Your Views** With your group, present your views to the class. Cite text evidence from both the poem and the historical notes to support your ideas. Listen to what others have to say, ask questions to request and clarify information, and build on the ideas of others as you discuss this topic.

Collaborate & Compare 309

RESPOND

Go to the **Speaking and Listening Studio** for more on participating in a collaborative discussion and on giving a presentation.

APPLY

DECIDE AND DISCUSS

Explain to students that this discussion is an opportunity for them to develop and share their opinions on both texts, as well as to refine or possibly adjust their opinions based on the insights and evidence presented by others.

1. **Choose a Position** Encourage students to use a two-column chart and record the reasons for their responses to the given questions. Explain that this will help them give equal consideration to both texts. If students have trouble making a decision, suggest they pretend that someone with no knowledge of slaves' experiences asked them to recommend one text.

2. **Gather Information** Remind students to note the location of each piece of evidence or example in the text, so they can easily refer others to it when supporting their opinions. Tell students to also identify a few examples of how the other text is less effective than their chosen text, for contrast.

   Circulate around the room and use guiding questions to help students locate evidence. Consider allowing students to change groups if they realize that their opinion is unsupported.

3. **Select Information** Ask students to make sure that everyone has a say in which examples the group will present. Point out that if students feel strongly about a less popular choice, making a case for it will give them practice in presenting opinions to the class.

4. **Share Your Views** Ask students to wait until a group has finished presenting before asking questions. If possible, be ready to display either text to help groups clarify information. After all groups have presented, have an open discussion and invite students to share whether they changed any of their opinions and why.

ENGLISH LEARNER SUPPORT

Use Support from Teachers and Peers To help students understand the listed questions and choose their position, share and read aloud the following versions:

- Which text is better at telling the whole story of Fortune's life and death?
- Which text made you care and feel more strongly about slavery in the United States?
- Which text has a message that is meaningful to more people in more places?

Have students discuss the questions with a partner and note their answers.

SUBSTANTIAL/MODERATE

READER'S CHOICE

Setting a Purpose Have students review their Unit 4 Response Log and think about what they've already learned about what people will risk to be free. As they select their Independent Reading selections, encourage them to consider what more they want to know.

NOTICE NOTE

Explain that some selections may contain multiple signposts; others may contain only one. The same type of signpost can occur many times in the same text.

 LEARNING MINDSET

Persistence Encourage students to stick with challenges and not give up when tasks seem hard. Explain that all people have more strength and intelligence than they suspect. Tell them that sticking with a challenge and putting in effort has unexpected rewards and yields breakthroughs. Model positive self-talk: "If I stay with this task and give it more time, I know I can figure it out."

 INDEPENDENT READING

? **ESSENTIAL QUESTION:**

What will people risk to be free?

Reader's Choice

Setting a Purpose Select one or more of these options from your eBook to continue your exploration of the Essential Question.

- Read the descriptions to see which text grabs your interest.
- Think about which genres you enjoy reading.

Notice **&** Note

In this unit, you practiced asking **Big Questions** and noticing and noting two signposts: **Word Gaps** and **Contrasts and Contradictions**. As you read independently, these signposts and others will aid your understanding. Below are the anchor questions to ask when you read literature and nonfiction.

Reading Literature: Stories, Poems, and Plays		
Signpost	Anchor Question	Lesson
Contrasts and Contradictions	Why did the character act that way?	p. 3
Aha Moment	How might this change things?	p. 3
Tough Questions	What does this make me wonder about?	p. 152
Words of the Wiser	What's the lesson for the character?	p. 406
Again and Again	Why might the author keep bringing this up?	p. 2
Memory Moment	Why is this memory important?	p. 153

Reading Nonfiction: Essays, Articles, and Arguments		
Signpost	Anchor Question(s)	Lesson
Big Questions	What surprised me? What did the author think I already knew? What challenged, changed, or confirmed what I already knew?	p. 77
Contrasts and Contradictions	What is the difference, and why does it matter?	p. 241
Extreme or Absolute Language	Why did the author use this language?	p. 76
Numbers and Stats	Why did the author use these numbers or amounts?	p. 325
Quoted Words	Why was this person quoted or cited, and what did this add?	p. 77
Word Gaps	Do I know this word from someplace else? Does it seem like technical talk for this topic? Do clues in the sentence help me understand the word?	p. 240

 ENGLISH LEARNER SUPPORT

Setting Expectations for Independent Reading Clear expectations will help students nurture good reading habits.

- Establish definite time for students to read independently.
- Work with students to create rules for silent reading time. Post the rules where they can be seen.
- Ask students to think about questions that will help their understanding.

- Enlist parents' help to encourage students to read each day. Have them read to their students and give them a progress report to fill out.
- Work with school and public librarians to help students select books.
  ALL LEVELS

You can preview these texts in Unit 4 of your eBook.

Then, check off the text or texts that you select to read on your own.

POEM

I Saw Old General at Bay
Walt Whitman

What kind of leader makes soldiers feel honored to risk their lives?

SHORT STORY

A Mystery of Heroism
Stephen Crane

A soldier struggles with the true meaning of heroism.

HISTORY WRITING

***from* Bloody Times: The Funeral of Abraham Lincoln and the Manhunt for Jefferson Davis**   James L. Swanson

As the city of Richmond burns, one president escapes while another is welcomed like a king.

BIOGRAPHY

My Friend Douglass
Russell Freedman

Discover why Abraham Lincoln was so eager to speak with Frederick Douglass after his second inauguration.

JOURNAL

Civil War Journal
Louisa May Alcott

Alcott reflects on her experiences as a nurse during the Civil War.

Collaborate and Share   With a partner, discuss what you learned from at least one of your independent readings.

- Give a brief synopsis or summary of the text.
- Describe any signposts that you noticed in the text and explain what they revealed to you.
- Describe what you most enjoyed or found most challenging about the text. Give specific examples.
- Decide if you would recommend the text to others. Why or why not?

 Go to the **Reading Studio** for more resources on **Notice & Note.**

WHEN STUDENTS STRUGGLE . . .

Keep a Reading Log   As students read their selected texts, have them keep a reading log for each selection to note signposts and their thoughts about them. Use their logs to assess how well they are noticing and reflecting on elements of the texts.

Reading Log for (title)		
Page and Paragraph	**Signpost I Noticed**	**My Notes About It**

MATCHING STUDENTS TO TEXTS

Use the following information to guide students in choosing their texts.

I Saw Old General at Bay
Genre: poem
Overall Rating: Accessible

A Mystery of Heroism   **Lexile: 1010L**
Genre: short story
Overall Rating: Challenging

from Bloody Times:
The Funeral of Abraham Lincoln and
the Manhunt for Jefferson Davis   **Lexile: 980L**
Genre: history writing
Overall Rating: Accessible

My Friend Douglass   **Lexile: 1180L**
Genre: biography
Overall Rating: Challenging

Civil War Journal   **Lexile: 1480L**
Genre: journal
Overall Rating: Challenging

Collaborate and Share   To assess how well students read the selections, walk around the room and listen to their conversations. Encourage students to be focused and specific in their comments.

 Online **Ed** **for Assessment**

- Independent Reading Selection Tests

Encourage students to visit the **Reading Studio** to download a handy bookmark of **NOTICE & NOTE** signposts.

UNIT ④ Tasks

- **WRITE A RESEARCH REPORT**
- **PARTICIPATE IN A COLLABORATIVE DISCUSSION**

MENTOR TEXT
FORTUNE'S BONES
History writing by PAMELA ESPELAND

LEARNING OBJECTIVES

Writing Task

- Write a research report about an aspect of the abolition movement in the United States.
- Use strategies to plan and develop your research report.
- Use the Mentor Text as a model for writing an engaging introduction and including quotations, facts, and examples from sources.
- Revise draft, working with a partner in a peer review.
- Edit draft to eliminate misspellings and grammatical errors and correct run-on sentences.
- Use a rubric to evaluate writing.
- Publish writing to share it with an audience.
- **Language** Use precise language and vocabulary in a research report; avoid run-on sentences.

Speaking and Listening Task

- Plan a series of panel discussions that honor the abolition movement and those who took part in it.
- Choose roles and discussion subtopics.
- Hold the panel discussion, using effective verbal and nonverbal techniques.
- **Language** Use formal English, enunciate clearly, and speak slowly and at an appropriate volume.

Assign the writing Task in *Ed*.

RESOURCES

- Unit 4 Response Log

- 📖 Reading Studio: Notice & Note

- 🖥 Writing Studio: Writing Informative Texts

- 🖥 Writing Studio: Conducting Research

- 💬 Speaking and Listening Studio: Participating in Collaborative Discussions

- ❗ Grammar Studio: Module 1: Lesson 2: Run-on sentences

Language X-Ray: English Language Support

Use the instruction below and the supports and scaffolds in the Teacher's Edition to help you guide students of different proficiency levels.

INTRODUCE THE WRITING TASK

Make sure students understand that a **research report** uses both print and digital sources to investigate a topic and defend a thesis. To create a research report, students synthesize information from credible sources to support their conclusions.

A research report presents facts and ideas gathered from various primary and secondary sources about a specific topic or issue. A primary source is one that provides a firsthand account of events. A

secondary source is a source created after an event and is often based upon primary sources.

Tell students that they may need to revise their initial thesis as they uncover information during their research. Remind students to analyze a variety of perspectives and to be aware of bias in their sources.

WRITING

Avoid Run-On Sentences

Tell students that they can make their research reports clearer by correcting run-on sentences, which are two or more sentences written as though they were a single sentence.

Use the following supports with students at varying proficiency levels:

- Show students several several examples of run-on sentences. Explain why each is a run-on sentence and how to correct it. **SUBSTANTIAL**
- Give students this run-on sentence. *The story tells about a runaway slave, he hid his identity for years*. Ask students to correct the run-on sentence. **MODERATE**
- After students have completed their drafts, have them work in a group to identify run-on sentences to correct. **LIGHT**

SPEAKING

Present Information

After students have completed their drafts, give them this sentence stem: *By completing my research report, I learned that the abolition movement _____.*

Use the following supports with students at varying proficiency levels:

- Work with students to complete the sentence stem by stating a key idea in their research report. Have them practice saying the sentence aloud to a partner. **SUBSTANTIAL**
- Have students state two key ideas from their research reports. Then have them present their information in a conversation with a partner. **MODERATE**
- Have students complete the sentence stem by stating three or more key ideas and then adding a transition word or phrase, such as *for example, furthermore,* or *on the other hand*. Have students read their completed sentence aloud to a partner. **LIGHT**

WRITING

WRITE A RESEARCH REPORT

Introduce students to the Writing Task by reading the introductory paragraph with them. Remind students to refer to the notes they recorded in the Unit 4 Response Log as they plan and draft their research reports. The Response Log should contain ideas about the abolition movement in the United States. Drawing on these different perspectives will make their own writing more interesting and well informed

 For **writing support** for students at varying proficiency levels, see the **Language X-Ray** on p. 312B.

USE THE MENTOR TEXT

Point out that their research reports will be similar to the informational article "Fortune's Bones" by Pamela Espeland in that they will present facts, quotations, and examples to support a thesis, or conclusion. However, their research reports will be shorter than the article and will focus on a specific aspect of the abolition movement in the United States.

WRITING PROMPT

Review the prompt with students. Encourage them to ask questions about any part of the assignment that is unclear. Make sure they understand that the purpose of their research report is to explore an aspect of the abolition movement in the United States.

 **WRITING TASK**

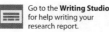 Go to the **Writing Studio** for help writing your research report.

Write a Research Report

This unit focuses on the struggle against slavery before, during, and after the Civil War. For this writing task, you will research and write a report about an aspect of the abolition movement in the United States. A research report is a type of informational text that uses information from a variety of sources to support a thesis or answer a question. For an example of a well-written informational text that you can use as a mentor text, review *Fortune's Bones*. As you plan your report, you can also use any relevant notes from your Response Log.

Writing Prompt

Read the information in the box below.

This is the context for your research report. →

> The movement to end slavery in the United States was a long process that took many years.

Think carefully about the following question.

This is the Essential Question for the unit. How would you answer this question, based on the texts in the unit? →

> What will people risk to be free?

Research and write a report about an aspect of the abolition movement in the United States.

Be sure to —

Review these points as you write and again when you finish. Make any needed changes and edits.

- ❑ provide an engaging introduction that catches the reader's attention, clearly states the topic, and includes a thesis statement
- ❑ develop the topic and support the thesis by synthesizing facts, definitions, and examples from multiple sources
- ❑ accurately quote and paraphrase source material and document each source of information
- ❑ clearly organize ideas and use transitions to connect ideas
- ❑ create coherence within and across paragraphs
- ❑ provide a conclusion that summarizes main points and restates the thesis or answers the original question

---

 LEARNING MINDSET

Belonging   Talk to students about the importance of community. A community is ideally a group in which everyone is encouraged, everyone belongs, and everyone contributes in their own way. Tell students that the classroom is a community. All students belong and can help each other. Encourage them to feel comfortable asking for and giving assistance. Help students understand that when everyone actively participates, the classroom becomes more engaging and real learning happens.

1 Plan

Go to **Conducting Research: Starting Your Research** for more help.

The first thing you need to do is take the broad topic of abolition and narrow it. Will you discuss the efforts of one abolitionist? Will you trace milestones in the movement to end slavery?

Develop Research Questions A good way to narrow a topic is to ask questions about it. For example, you might begin by asking "Who were famous abolitionists?" Based on your preliminary research, you may realize that you need to refine, or change, your research questions in order to narrow your topic further or find something more interesting to write about. For example, a question that begins with *how* or *why* will usually generate more write about than one that begins with *who* or *where*. Use the table below, or one like it, to record questions and take notes that will help you narrow or refine your topic.

Preliminary and Refined Research Questions	
(initial question) Who started the abolition movement in the U.S.?	William Lloyd Garrison founded the American Anti-Slavery Society in 1833. (<u>Encyclopædia Britannica</u>)
(refined question) How did the abolition movement grow and spread?	

Research Your Report Once you've refined your question, search for both digital and print sources to help you answer it. Your report will be more interesting if you include **primary sources**—materials that were created by people who witnessed events, such as the autobiography *Narrative of the Life of Frederick Douglass*. Also consult **secondary sources,** which are those created by people who were not involved with the event, such as the biography *Harriet Tubman: Conductor on the Underground Railroad.* Take notes on what you learn. As you research, you might find that you want to revise your plan in response to the information you're finding. If that happens, follow your interests.

Evaluate and Document Your Sources Evaluate the sources you locate—particularly online sources—to ensure that they are reliable, credible, unbiased, and do not include loaded language or faulty reasoning. Avoid commercial, political, and personal websites. Keep a list of your sources; this will make them easier to cite and document later.

Use any relevant notes from your Response Log as you plan your report.

Write a Research Report 313

1 PLAN

Allow time for students to discuss the topic with partners or in small groups and then to refine their research questions independently. Tell students that when conducting online research they should look for author and publication information for each website or sponsoring organization to help them determine whether the source is credible. Remind students that the most reliable websites usually have the extensions *.gov, .org,* and *.edu.* Point out that if students have concerns they should look for more reliable sources.

▶ NOTICE & NOTE

From Reading to Writing Remind students that they can use **Quoted Words** to include the opinions or conclusions of someone who is an expert on the topic. Students can also use **Quoted Words** to provide support for a point they are trying to make. Remind students to format direct quotations correctly and to give credit to the source.

Background Reading As students plan their research reports, remind them to refer to the notes they took in the Response Log. They may also review the selections to find additional facts and examples to support ideas.

TO CHALLENGE STUDENTS . . .

Create an Exhibit Challenge students to adapt their research reports for an informative exhibit about people's experience during the abolition movement. Encourage students to include various types of audio and visual elements in their displays.

WRITING

Organize Your Ideas Notice that the student's thesis is a key part of the outline. Everything else in the outline supports it, directly or indirectly. Note the following guidelines:

1. Put the thesis at the top.

2. Make items at the same level of generality as parallel as possible.

3. Always use at least two subdivisions for a category.

4. Limit the number of major sections in the outline.

5. Be prepared to modify your outline as your research report evolves.

② DEVELOP A DRAFT

As students begin their first drafts, point out that each main idea should be supported by relevant details and evidence. Suggest that students keep their outlines nearby, checking off details and facts as they write. Remind students to include only one main idea in each paragraph.

■ English Learner Support

Adapt Writing Explain that students should use formal English in their research reports. Give them some simple examples and discuss. Then guide students to recognize differences between formal and informal English in the following example: *The team had a bad awful time yesterday/ The team performed poorly yesterday.*

SUBSTANTIAL/MODERATE

 Go to **Writing Informational Texts: Organizing Ideas** for help with creating an outline.

Notice & Note
From Reading to Writing

As you draft your research report, apply what you've learned about signposts to your own writing.

Think about how you can incorporate **Quoted Words** into your essay.

 Go to the **Reading Studio** for more resources on Notice & Note.

You might prefer to draft your research report online.

Go to **Conducting Research: Summarizing, Paraphrasing, and Quoting** for help.

Organize Your Ideas The answer to your research question is likely to be your thesis. To support it thoroughly, you will need to **synthesize,** or combine information from multiple sources. Create an outline to guide your writing. For each paragraph of the body, group related ideas together and organize them by central ideas and supporting information. This will help create coherence within paragraphs. Also, check that all paragraphs support your thesis statement; this will help create coherence across paragraphs. This example outline shows you how you might group your ideas:

Outline for Research Report
I.   Introduction with thesis statement
II. Body
A.   Subtopic
1.   Supporting facts and details
2.   Supporting facts and details
B.   Subtopic
1.   Supporting facts and details
2.   Supporting facts and details
II. Conclusion with summary and reworded thesis statement

② Develop a Draft

Refer to your outline as you draft your report.

- State your thesis clearly in your introduction. Include a fact, quote, or anecdote to interest the reader in your topic.
- Group your ideas and information into paragraphs. Support each point with relevant and specific details, facts, and examples. These may include quotations, paraphrases, or summaries of source material.
- Create a formal style by using complete sentences with precise language. Avoid contractions and pronouns such as *I* and *you*.
- Include transition words and phrases such as *because, also, in addition,* and *finally* to clarify the relationships between ideas.
- Write a conclusion that follows from and supports your thesis.

Cite Your Sources As you write, be careful to avoid plagiarizing your sources. **Plagiarizing** means using other people's words or ideas without giving them credit. One way to avoid plagiarizing is to place the source's exact words in quotation marks. Another way is to write a good **paraphrase,** in which you restate the author's ideas in your own words. In either case, you should always identify the author and the title of the work you are quoting or paraphrasing.

WHEN STUDENTS STRUGGLE . . .

Add Quotations Provide the following example sentence frames to help students add quotations to their research:

- *He said the conditions were "."*
- *They summarized their experiences as, "."*
- *"," she complained.*

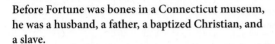

Use the Mentor Text

Author's Craft

In the introduction of your research report, you should express your thesis statement, or controlling idea. You should also include something that gets your reader interested in reading your report. Notice the way the writer captures the reader's attention in this opening sentence from *Fortune's Bones*.

> Before Fortune was bones in a Connecticut museum, he was a husband, a father, a baptized Christian, and a slave.

The writer grabs the audience's attention by making a connection between a real person and his remains in a museum.

Apply What You've Learned To capture your reader's attention, you might include a surprising fact, a famous quotation, or an anecdote related to the topic.

Genre Characteristics

Writers of informational texts often include quotations to provide supporting evidence for their main points—and if they do so, they must cite their sources. In this example, notice how the writer uses a quotation and cites her source to support an idea in *Fortune's Bones*. In this case, the person quoted may have preferred to be unnamed.

> One Waterbury resident remembers, "Larry was the thing to see when you go to the museum. I don't think anybody ever envisioned that this was truly a human being."

The writer provides a quotation to support her idea that the display of Fortune's bones was dehumanizing. She cites the source of her quote.

Apply What You've Learned To develop and support your ideas, you will want to include quotations, facts, and examples from sources. Cite each source of information so readers know where it came from.

WHY THIS MENTOR TEXT?

"Fortune's Bones" serves as a mentor text for a research report because it is history writing that includes primary source documents. The writer uses a chronological structure and provides quotations and commentary on a research topic.

USE THE MENTOR TEXT

Author's Craft Tell students that an effective strategy for writing an introduction is to open the paragraph with a few sentences that engage the reader, establish your purpose for writing, and conclude with a main point, or thesis. The sentences leading to the thesis should hook the reader, perhaps by using one of the following techniques:

- a startling statistic, an unusual fact, or a striking example
- a paradoxical statement
- a quotation
- a question
- an analogy
- an anecdote

Genre Characteristics Tell students that writers of research reports must cite all direct quotations, as in the example from "Fortune's Bones." Writers must also cite any ideas or opinions borrowed from a source, summaries and paraphrases, and statistics and other specific facts that are not common knowledge.

ENGLISH LEARNER SUPPORT

Condense Ideas Model how to condense ideas using embedded clauses. Make sure students understand the function of the relative pronouns *who* and *that* in the examples.

- *The story tells about the abolitionist John Brown. He led an attack on Harper's Ferry. (The story tells about the abolitionist John Brown, who led an attack on Harper's Ferry.)*

- *They shared a room. It had one window. It had no furniture. (They shared a room that had one window and no furniture.)*

Encourage students to use these strategies to create precise and detailed sentences in their drafts. **LIGHT**

WRITING

③ REVISE

Remind students that revising is a multi-step process. Tell students to pay attention to larger issues first—focus, purpose, organization, and overall strategy. Later, they can concentrate on the finer points: improvements in sentence structure and word choice.

With a Partner When students read each other's research reports, they may benefit from their partner's expertise or knowledge about a topic. To help students draw upon each other's strengths, post all students' topics and pair students with strong backgrounds in each other's topics.

③ Revise

 Go to **Writing Informative Texts: Precise Language and Vocabulary** for help revising your research report.

On Your Own Once you have written your draft, you'll want to go back and look for ways to improve your report. As you reread and revise, think about whether you have achieved your purpose. The Revision Guide will help you focus on specific elements to make your writing stronger.

Revision Guide		
Ask Yourself	**Tips**	**Revision Techniques**
1. Is the thesis statement clear?	**Underline** the thesis statement.	**Add** a thesis statement. **Revise** a vague thesis to make it stronger.
2. Does each paragraph have a main point related to the thesis?	**Highlight** the main point of each paragraph.	**Add** a main point if one is missing. **Rewrite** any main points that are unclear.
3. Are there relevant supporting details for each point?	**Underline** facts, statistics, examples, and quotations that support your points.	**Delete** unrelated ideas. **Add** more facts, statistics, examples, and quotations from your notes.
4. Are ideas organized logically? Do transitions clearly connect ideas? Is there coherence within and across paragraphs?	**Highlight** transitional words and phrases within and between paragraphs.	**Rearrange** sentences and paragraphs to organize ideas logically. **Add** transitions to connect ideas and create coherence.
5. Is information gathered from a variety of sources, and are those sources cited correctly?	**Underline** references to sources.	**Add** more sources for variety. **Cite** all sources correctly.
6. Does the conclusion summarize the topic and support the information presented?	**Underline** the summary. **Highlight** sentences that support information in the report.	**Add** a statement that summarizes the main ideas. **Insert** supporting sentences.

ACADEMIC VOCABULARY
As you conduct your **peer review,** be sure to use these words.

❑ access
❑ civil
❑ demonstrate
❑ document
❑ symbolize

With a Partner After working through the Revision Guide on your own, exchange papers with a partner and evaluate each other's drafts in a **peer review**. Take turns reading or listening to each other's reports and use the Revision Guide to offer suggestions to make the reports more effective. Provide revision suggestions for any points mentioned in the chart that might improve your partner's report. Remember to be positive and respectful. When receiving feedback from your partner, listen attentively and ask questions to make sure you fully understand the revision suggestions.

ⓔⓛ ENGLISH LEARNER SUPPORT

Explaining with Specificity and Detail Tell students that as they write, they should work to add an increasing layer of complexity to their explanations. Model the process for students by having them listen to a brief news video, about two minutes, such as from an Internet news site. Have students listen for any specifics by jotting down notes on cards. Ask students to discuss which details they think helped enhance understanding of the news article and whether the speaker's voice and intonation helped them remember.
LIGHT

4 Edit

Once you have addressed the organization, development, and flow of ideas in your research report, you can improve the language of your draft. Edit for the proper use of standard English conventions, such as correct punctuation. Be sure to correct any misspellings or grammatical errors.

Language Conventions

Run-On Sentences A **run-on sentence** is made up of two or more sentences that have been run together as if they were one thought. This can be confusing to readers, especially in informational texts that contain many facts and examples. Consider the following example of a run-on sentence. The corrected sentence is from *Fortune's Bones:*

EXAMPLE:

> **Run-on sentence:** The museum now believed that displaying the skeleton was <u>disrespectful it</u> wasn't just a bunch of <u>bones it</u> was the remains of someone's son, maybe someone's father.

> **Corrected example:** The museum now believed that displaying the skeleton was <u>disrespectful. It</u> wasn't just a bunch of <u>bones. It</u> was the remains of someone's son, maybe someone's father.

To correct run-on sentences, do the following:

- Divide the sentence into separate sentences. Mark the end of each idea with a period (as in the above example), a question mark, or an exclamation point. Begin each sentence with a capital letter.
- If the two sentences are very closely related, use a conjunction, such as *and* or *but* (and a comma, if necessary) to combine them into a compound or complex sentence. Or, you may use a semicolon to join the two sentences.

> ! Go to the **Grammar Studio** to learn more about run-on sentences.

5 Publish

Create a final version of your research report and choose a way to share it with your audience. Consider these options:

- Present your report as a speech to the class.
- Post your report on a school website.
- Produce a multi-modal presentation of your report.

4 EDIT

Tell students to proofread their work several times. First, students should focus on errors in structure and reasoning; then, on grammar; finally, on spelling and punctuation.

LANGUAGE CONVENTIONS

Run-on Sentences Tell students to be on the alert for the comma splice: two or more independent clauses joined by a comma without a coordinating conjunction. For example, *Everyone huddled together, we were terrified.* In other comma splices, the comma is accompanied by a word that is not a coordinating conjunction. For example, *We ran as fast as we could, however, we could not catch the train.* Give students the following seven coordinating conjunctions: *and, but, or, nor, for, so,* and *yet.*

5 PUBLISH

Remind students that visual aids can deepen a reader's understanding of ideas. Suggest that students add visuals, such as photographs, charts, graphs, or illustrations to their research reports. Tell students that the visuals should appear near the text that they support.

WHEN STUDENTS STRUGGLE . . .

Extend the Completion Time Allow students to break their work into manageable chunks to complete the task over an extended period. For example, students may investigate the answers to one research question at a time. Consider modifying students' schedules to allow them to work on the task at a time of day when they work productively, such as at the beginning of the day or directly after an activity period.

WRITING

USE THE SCORING GUIDE

Have students use the rubric to score their own research reports. Then have partners evaluate each other's score. Students should use the language of the rubric to provide feedback in each category.

 **WRITING TASK**

Use the scoring guide to evaluate your research report.

Writing Task Scoring Guide: Research Report		
Organization/Progression	**Development of Ideas**	**Use of Language and Conventions**
4 • The organization is effective and logical throughout the report. • Transitions clearly show the relationship among ideas from one paragraph to another. • There is very strong coherence within and across paragraphs.	• The thesis statement is clear, and the introduction is appealing and informative. • The topic is well developed with relevant facts, concrete details, interesting quotations, and examples from reliable sources. • The conclusion effectively summarizes the information presented and repeats the thesis statement.	• The writing maintains a formal style throughout. • Language is strong and precise. • Ideas have been combined to create detailed sentences. • Spelling, grammar, usage, and mechanics are correct. • Research sources are cited correctly.
3 • The organization is mostly effective and logical but may be confusing in a couple places. • A few more transitions are needed to connect related ideas. • There is coherence within and across paragraphs.	• The introduction contains a thesis statement, but the introduction does not create interest in the topic. • Some key points need more support from relevant facts, concrete details, quotations, and examples from reliable sources. • The conclusion summarizes the information presented and includes the thesis statement.	• The style is inconsistent in a few places. • Language is not always precise. • Some ideas have been combined to add detail to sentences; there may be one or two run-ons. • There are a few errors in spelling, grammar, usage, and mechanics. • Sources are not cited consistently.
2 • The organization is logical in some places but often doesn't follow a pattern. • More transitions are needed throughout to connect ideas. • There is little coherence within and across paragraphs.	• The thesis statement is confusing. The introduction is not very informative or engaging. • The development of ideas is minimal. The writer uses facts, details, and examples that are inappropriate or ineffectively presented. • The conclusion does not include a complete summary or a rewording of the thesis statement.	• The style is informal in many places. • The language is often overly general. • There are several run-on sentences. • There are many spelling, grammar, usage, and mechanics errors, but they do not obscure meaning. • Only one or two research sources are cited, and the format is incorrect.
1 • A logical organization is not used; information is presented randomly. • Transitions are not used, making the writing difficult to understand. • There is no coherence within and across paragraphs.	• The thesis statement is missing. The introduction is not engaging and does not prepare the reader for the content of the report. • There are few, if any, facts, details, quotations, and examples. Or, they are from unreliable sources. • There is no conclusion.	• The style is inappropriate for the report. • Language is too general to convey meaningful information. • There are many run-on sentences. • There are many errors in spelling, grammar, usage, and mechanics that obscure meaning. • Research sources are not cited.

Participate in a Collaborative Discussion

This unit, "The Fight for Freedom," focuses on the Civil War and the struggle against slavery. Imagine you are invited to design a new unit that addresses the same essential question: "What will people risk to be free?" Work collaboratively with group members to choose a topic for such a unit, select materials you would use to teach it, and then present your ideas to the class.

1 Make a Plan

Brainstorm With your group, assign a notetaker and moderator. Then brainstorm a list of other fights for freedom you know about. Consider these types of struggles:

- periods of war or unrest, such as the Revolutionary War
- political movements, such as the fight for civil rights or the fight against apartheid
- efforts to escape oppression or preserve democracy

Vote Discuss the pros and cons of designing a Fight for Freedom unit around each idea on your list. Then vote on which topic to focus on. You can vote by a show of hands, or by a secret ballot.

Set an Agenda and Identify Action Items With group members, analyze the task and create an **agenda,** or a list of things the group must discuss, agree upon, and do in order to design a unit to present to the class. One item on your agenda should be to create a list of **action items,** or tasks that must be done before the next meeting. Decide together who will do each one.

Create a Schedule Keeping in mind the final deadline date, set progress deadlines by which each task must be completed. Make sure deadlines are realistic; for example, researching a topic will require more time than practicing for the final presentation. You may find it helpful to use an online calendar and collaborative workspace to help keep everyone on track. Reconvene as necessary to report on progress and make adjustments to your plan.

SPEAKING AND LISTENING TASK

 Go to the **Speaking and Listening Studio** for help conducting your collaborative discussion.

As you work collaboratively, follow these rules of polite discussion:

- ❏ listen closely to one another
- ❏ value contributions of all group members
- ❏ stay on topic
- ❏ express disagreement politely and respectfully
- ❏ ask only helpful, relevant questions
- ❏ provide only clear, thoughtful, and direct answers

Participate in a Collaborative Discussion **319**

SPEAKING AND LISTENING

PARTICIPATE IN A COLLABORATIVE DISCUSSION

Introduce students to the Speaking and Listening Task by reading the introductory paragraph with them. Remind students that participants in an effective panel discussion use text evidence to support their ideas and to respond to the ideas of others.

1 PLAN THE CONFERENCE

When organizing panels and selecting possible panel topics for discussion, groups should focus on the most important aspects of their subject to present and explain to their audience. Remind students that the role of the moderator will be to ask thought-provoking questions and to elicit well-supported responses.

For **speaking support** for students at varying proficiency levels, see the **Language X-Ray** on page 312B.

ENGLISH LEARNER SUPPORT

Plan a Collaborative Discussion Explain that students will draw upon evidence from texts in the unit to support conclusions about responses to the abolition movement's struggle against slavery. Have two members of each group review one half of the texts while a second pair reviews the other. Ask pairs to say aloud or write summaries of the texts they review, using the following sentence frames to share information: *[Text title] is about _____. In this text, abolitionists respond to slavery by _____. I think we [should, should not] discuss this text because _____.* Groups can use ideas from these conversations to gather information.

MODERATE/LIGHT

Participate in a Collaborative Discussion **319**

SPEAKING AND LISTENING TASK

② PREPARE FOR YOUR PANEL DISCUSSION

Encourage students to make thorough and detailed outlines and to include support for their main points. Advise students to organize their outlines in a way that lets them quickly locate information. Explain that during the discussion, they can refer to their outlines as a general guide, but they might not have the time or opportunity to present all their evidence.

- List reasons and evidence in logical order.
- Highlight the strongest pieces of evidence to help remember and refer to them easily.

③ HOLD THE CONFERENCE

When presenting, panelists should speak with appropriate volume, speak clearly, and remember to maintain eye contact with the moderator, panelists, and audience members as they address them. When not speaking, panelists should model good listening behavior and direct their full attention to the person talking.

② Prepare to Present

Once you have decided what your unit will focus on and include, prepare to present your proposal to the class. Everyone in the group should have a role. Practice for each other to improve your performance. Below are some other guidelines on presenting and giving feedback.

Provide and Consider Advice for Improvement

As a presenter, use the techniques below to help make your points clear. Then, listen to feedback and consider ways to revise your work.

- Effective **verbal techniques** include clearly enunciating words, speaking slowly enough so that listeners can understand you, and speaking at an appropriate volume.
- Effective **nonverbal techniques** include making eye contact, varying facial expressions, and using meaningful gestures.

As a listener, pay close attention. Suggest ways that presenters can improve their presentations. Ask questions to clarify any confusing ideas and provide feedback.

③ Present the Unit

Based on the practice session, make any final changes as you get ready for your presentation. Then, groups should take turns presenting their units to the whole class:

- As group members present their unit, they may refer briefly to their notes to recall main points, but they should speak directly to the audience.
- Audience members should listen closely and take notes.
- After each presentation, groups should invite the audience to ask questions about their unit.

WHEN STUDENTS STRUGGLE . . .

Practice Speaking Techniques Give students an opportunity to view a video of a panel discussion. Pause the video to discuss examples of strong speaking techniques. Point out examples of maintaining eye contact and using facial expressions, gestures, and voice modulation and inflection. Then let students practice the techniques to emphasize points they want to make.

Reflect on the Unit

By completing your research report and engaging in a collaborative discussion, you have expressed your thoughts about the reading you have done in this unit as well as the information you discovered in your research. Now is a good time to reflect on what you have learned.

Reflect on the Essential Question

• What will people risk to be free? How has your answer changed since you first considered this question at the beginning of the unit?

• What are some examples you've read in the unit, and in other sources, of people taking risks to be free?

Reflect on Your Reading

• Which selections were the most interesting or surprising to you?

• Which selection or selections made you want to learn more about the topic?

• From which selection did you learn the most about what people will risk to be free?

Reflect on the Writing Task

• What difficulties did you encounter while working on your research report? How might you avoid them next time?

• Which part of the report was the easiest to write? Which was the hardest? Why?

• What improvements did you make to your report as you were revising?

Reflect on the Speaking and Listening Task

• What did you learn from creating and presenting your unit?

• In what ways was your collaboration on developing and presenting the material successful? How could you improve the process the next time?

UNIT 4 SELECTIONS

• *Narrative of the Life of Frederick Douglass, an American Slave*

• *Harriet Tubman: Conductor on the Underground Railroad*

• "The Drummer Boy of Shiloh"

• "O Captain! My Captain!"

• "Not My Bones"

• *Fortune's Bones*

Reflect on the Unit **321**

REFLECT ON THE UNIT

Have students reflect on the questions independently and write some notes in response to each one. Then have students meet with partners or in small groups to discuss their reflections. Circulate during these discussions to identify the questions that are generating the liveliest conversations. Wrap up with a whole-class discussion focused on these questions.

 ENGLISH LEARNER SUPPORT

Spell Correctly Focus on students improving their spelling ability by pointing out the word "question." Write the word "quest" on the board and read it aloud, enunciating the /t/ sound. Say: This word ends in a t, and we say the /t/ sound when we say the word. But, what happens when we add *–ion* to the end of the word? Write the letters ion to form the word "question," and underline *tion*. Encourage students to try to read the word aloud. Say: *The letters tion make the /ch[schwa]n/ sound in this word.* Model saying the word correctly, tracking the letters with your finger, and have students repeat. Ask students for other words that end in -*tion*, or provide the following words for students to sound out: *attention, suggestion, invention, and convention.* **MODERATE**

 LEARNING MINDSET

Try Again Explain to students that many successful people have experienced failure, but what sets them apart is their willingness to learn from mistakes and try again. Let students know that mistakes will happen and that is expected and okay. You may wish to provide an example of a time you made a mistake and tell what you learned.

UNIT 5

Instructional Overview and Resources

		Online
	Instructional Focus	**Ed Resources**

Unit Introduction
Finding Your Path

Unit 5 Essential Question
Unit 5 Academic Vocabulary

Stream to Start: Finding Your Path

Unit 5 Response Log

ANALYZE & APPLY

"The Debt We Owe to the Adolescent Brain"
Informational Text by Jeanne Miller
Lexile 1010L

NOTICE & NOTE READING MODEL

Signposts
• Contrasts and Contradictions
• Big Questions
• Numbers and Stats

Reading
• Analyze Structure
• Analyze Author's Purpose

Writing: Write a Letter

Speaking and Listening: Discuss with a Small Group

Vocabulary: Use Resources

Language Conventions: Pronoun-Antecedent Agreement

 Audio

Reading Studio: Notice & Note

Writing Studio: Writing Informative Texts

Speaking and Listening Studio: Participating in Collaborative Discussions

Vocabulary Studio: Using Resources

Grammar Studio: Module 8: Agreement

Bronx Masquerade
Novel by Nikki Grimes
Lexile 710L

Reading
• Analyze Structure
• Analyze Characterization

Writing: Write a Poem

Speaking and Listening: Present a Poem

Vocabulary: Use Context Clues

Language Conventions: Modifiers

Audio

Close Read Screencast: Modeled Discussions

Reading Studio: Notice & Note

Writing Studio: Writing Narratives

Speaking and Listening Studio: Giving a Presentation

Vocabulary Studio: Using Context Clues

Grammar Studio: Module 11: Using Modifiers Correctly

COLLABORATE & COMPARE

"Hanging Fire"
Poem by Audre Lorde

· ·

"Summer of His Fourteenth Year"
Poem by Gloria Amescua

Reading
• Analyze Free Verse Poetry
• Make Inferences

Writing: Write a Response to Literature

Speaking and Listening: Give a Dramatic Reading

Audio

Reading Studio: Making Inferences About Characters

Writing Studio: Writing a Response to Literature

Speaking and Listening Studio: Giving a Presentation; Participating in Collaborative Discussions

---

Collaborate and Compare

Reading:
• Compare Poems
• Analyze the Texts

Speaking and Listening: Create and Present

Speaking and Listening Studio: Participating in Collaborative Discussions

---

SUGGESTED PACING: 30 DAYS	Unit Introduction	The Debt We Owe to the Adolescent Brain	Bronx Masquerade	Hanging Fire/Summer of His Fourteenth Year
	1	2 3 4 5 6	7 8 9 10 11	12 13 14 15 16

English Learner Support		Differentiated Instruction	Online **Ed** Assessment
• Vocabulary			

English Learner Support		Differentiated Instruction	Assessment
• Text X-Ray	• Adjectives	**When Students Struggle**	**Selection Test**
• Vocabulary	• Oral Assessment	• Use Strategies	
• Use Cognates	• Dictation	• Identify Main Idea and Details	
• Pronouns	• Vocabulary Strategy	**To Challenge Students**	
• Quotation Marks	• Language Conventions	• Structure	
• Word Forms			

English Learner Support		Differentiated Instruction	Assessment
• Text X-Ray	• Visual Support	**When Students Struggle**	**Selection Test**
• Understand Directionality	• Narrate and Describe	• KWL 2.0	
• Comparative and Superlative Forms in Spanish	• Oral Assessment		
• Use Prereading Supports	• Write and Present a Poem		
	• Language Differences		

English Learner Support		Differentiated Instruction	Assessment
• Text X-Ray	• Suffix -ly	**When Students Struggle**	**Selection Test**
• Analyze Free Verse Poetry	• Oral Assessment	• Take Notes	
• Make Inferences	• Give a Dramatic Reading	**To Challenge Students**	
• Inside/Outside Circles		• Analyze Multiple Viewpoints	
• Support Arguments			

The Social Lives of Networked Teens / Outsmart Your Smartphone

17 **18** **19** **20** **21** **22** **23** **24** **25**

Independent Reading

26 **27**

End of Unit

28 **29** **30**

UNIT 5 Continued

| | **Instructional Focus** | **Online** **Resources** |

COLLABORATE & COMPARE

MENTOR TEXT

from "It's Complicated: The Social Lives of Networked Teens"

Argument by danah boyd

Lexile 1080L

Reading
• Analyze Claim and Evidence
• Identify Counter Argument
Writing: Write an Opinion Piece

Speaking and Listening: Advocate a Position

Vocabulary: Context Clues

Language Conventions: Compound Sentences

 Audio

Text in Focus: Compare Arguments

Reading Studio: Notice & Note

Writing Studio: Writing Arguments

Speaking and Listening Studio: Using Media in a Presentation

Grammar Studio: Module 1: The Sentence

"Outsmart Your Smartphone"

Argument by Catherine Steiner-Adair

Lexile 1110L

Reading
• Analyze Structure
• Analyze Rhetorical Devices

Writing: Write a Letter

Speaking and Listening: Critique as a Class

Vocabulary: Word Families

Language Conventions: Correct Capitalization

 Audio

Reading Studio: Notice & Note

Writing Studio: Writing Arguments

Speaking and Listening Studio: Participating in Collaborative Discussions

Vocabulary Studio: Word Families

Grammar Studio: Module 13: Capital Letters

Collaborate and Compare

Reading
• Compare Arguments
• Analyze the Texts
Speaking and Listening: Create and Present

Speaking and Listening Studio: Participating in Collaborative Discussions

---

INDEPENDENT READING

The independent Reading selections are only available in the eBook.

 Go to the Reading Studio for more information on NOTICE & NOTE.

"Teenagers"
Poem by Pat Mora

"Identity"
Poem by Julio Noboa Polanco

END OF UNIT

Writing Task: Write an Argument

Speaking and Listening Task: Present an Argument

Reflect on the Unit

Writing: Writing an Argument

Language Conventions: Modifiers

Speaking and Listening: Present an Argument

Unit 5 Response Log

Mentor Text: "It's Complicated: The Social Lives of Networked Teens"

Writing Studio: Writing Arguments

Speaking and Listening Studio: Giving a Presentation

Grammar Studio: Module 11: Using Modifiers Correctly

English Learner Support	Differentiated Instruction	Online Ed Assessment

- Text X-Ray
- Claims, Arguments, and Counter Arguments
- Use Cognates
- Clarify Terms
- Conjunctions
- Slang
- Oral Assessment
- Advocate a Position
- Vocabulary Strategy
- Language Conventions

When Students Struggle
- Context Clues

Selection Test

- Text X-Ray
- Recognize Sounds
- Use Cognates
- Use Support
- Demonstrate Understanding

- Oral Assessment
- Express Opinions
- Distinguish Sounds
- Understand Language Structures

When Students Struggle
- Learning Strategies

Selection Test

- Explain with Detail

When Students Struggle
- Reteaching: Analyze Rhetorical Devices

To Challenge Students
- Use Rhetorical Devices

"Hard on the Gas"
Poem by Janet S. Wong

"Marigolds"
Short Story by Eugenia Collier
Lexile 1140L

"My Summer of Scooping Ice Cream"
Essay by Shonda Rhimes
Lexile 810L

Selection Tests

- Language X-Ray
- Plan an Argument
- Connect Ideas
- Edit Draft
- Plan an Argument Presentation

When Students Struggle
- Vary Word Choice in Drafting
- Edit Drafts

To Challenge Students
- Adapt the Argument
- Reflect on the Process

Unit Test

Connect to the
ESSENTIAL QUESTION

Ask a volunteer to read aloud the Essential Question. Discuss how the images on page 322 relate to the question. What is the woman doing with the microphone, and how does that activity relate to adolescence and adulthood? How are the five people in the lower photo preparing themselves to be adults? Have students discuss ways they and other teenagers they know are moving toward adulthood.

■ English Learner Support

Vocabulary Point out the parts of the words *teenage* (*teen + age*) and *adulthood* (*adult + hood*) in the Essential Question. Write the words on the board, and underline the parts. Explain that *teenage* refers to a period of life, also known as adolescence, in which a person is a teenager. Add that *adulthood* means "the period of being an adult, or a grownup." Have students use these words and their forms and synonyms to discuss the Essential Question.

MODERATE

DISCUSS THE QUOTATION

Tell students that Gail Carson Levine is an author of young adult literature. Explain that she is perhaps best known for her award-winning novel *Ella Enchanted,* which was named a Newbery Honor book in 1997. Tell students that Levine's interest in writing for young adults has helped her take a particular interest in what adolescence is like. Read the quotation with students. Ask what common object or activity the quote compares to becoming a teenager (*a bridge, specifically crossing a bridge*). Have students explain what lies ahead of teenagers on this bridge (*adulthood*) and what lies behind them (*childhood*). Discuss with students whether the image of adolescence as a bridge works for them, and have them explain why or why not.

FINDING YOUR PATH

 ESSENTIAL QUESTION:

How do your teenage years prepare you for adulthood?

" When you become a teenager, you step onto a bridge. . . . The opposite shore is adulthood. "

Gail Carson Levine

⚙ LEARNING MINDSET

Plan Remind students that to grow involves planning. Planning can help them complete their work efficiently and exceptionally. As they move through the unit, encourage them plan out how to complete their assignments. This may involve creating a schedule that will allow them to prioritize their time appropriately.

ACADEMIC VOCABULARY

Academic Vocabulary words are words you use when you discuss and write about texts. In this unit you will practice and learn five words.

☑ debate   ☐ deduce   ☐ license   ☐ sufficient   ☐ trend

Study the Word Network to learn more about the word **debate.**

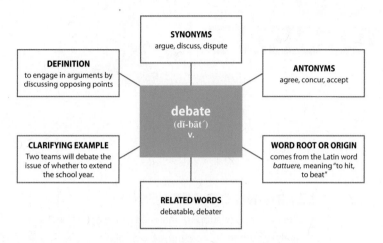

Write and Discuss Discuss the completed Word Network with a partner, making sure to talk through all of the boxes until you both understand the word, its synonyms, antonyms, and related forms. Then, fill out Word Networks for each of the remaining four words. Use a dictionary or online resource to help you complete the activity.

 Go online to access the Word Networks.

RESPOND TO THE ESSENTIAL QUESTION

In this unit, you will explore the teenage years as a unique stage of life between childhood and adulthood. As you read, you will revisit the **Essential Question** and gather your ideas about it in the **Response Log** that appears on page R5. At the end of the unit, you will have the opportunity to write an **argument** about the impact of technology on teen friendships. Filling out the Response Log will help you prepare for this writing task.

 You can also go online to access the Response Log.

ACADEMIC VOCABULARY

As students complete Word Networks for the remaining four vocabulary words, encourage them to include all the categories shown in the completed network if possible, but point out that some words do not have clear synonyms or antonyms. Some words may also function as different parts of speech—for example, *debate,* the word introduced on page 323, is listed as a verb but can also be used as a noun.

debate (dǐ-bāt´) *v.* to engage in arguments by discussing opposing points (Spanish cognate: *debatir*)

deduce (dǐ-dōōs´) *v.* to determine through logical reasoning (Spanish cognate: *deducir*)

license (lī´-səns) *n.* permission or authority (Spanish cognate: *licencia*)

sufficient (sə-fǐsh´ənt) *adj.* enough or adequate (Spanish cognate: *suficiente*)

trend (trěnd) *n.* a general tendency or course of events

RESPOND TO THE ESSENTIAL QUESTION

Direct students to the Unit 5 Response Log. Explain that students will use it to record ideas and details from the selections that help answer the Essential Question. When they work on the writing task at the end of the unit, their Response Logs will help them think about what they have read and make connections between texts.

READING MODEL

THE DEBT WE OWE TO THE ADOLESCENT BRAIN

Informational Text by Jeanne Miller

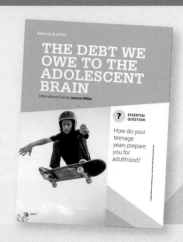

GENRE ELEMENTS
INFORMATIONAL TEXT

Remind students that the purpose of **informational text** is to present facts and information. Unlike persuasive writing, another form of nonfiction, informational text typically does not try to convince an audience to do or believe something; instead, it simply provides information for the reader. Tell students that informational text is usually structured in one of a few ways, including compare/contrast and main idea and details, and that it often includes supporting evidence in the form of quotations from experts in the field. Have students look for these features as they read the article.

LEARNING OBJECTIVES

- Cite evidence to support analysis of an informational text.
- Analyze author's purpose and message.
- Identify the structure(s) of an informational text.
- Do further research into the features of the teenage brain.
- Write a letter explaining common teenage behavior in terms of the information learned in the text.
- Accurately connect pronouns with their antecedents.
- **Language** Discuss with a partner the features of the text using the key term *headings*.

TEXT COMPLEXITY

Quantitative Measures	The Debt We Owe to the Adolescent Brain	Lexile: 1010L
Qualitative Measures	**Ideas Presented** Mostly explicit, but moves to some implied meaning.	
	Structure Used Compare/contrast and main idea/details.	
	Language Used Mostly familiar, non-technical words, with a few exceptions.	
	Knowledge Required Some knowledge of the brain and of the animal kingdom.	

Online Ed

RESOURCES

- Unit 5 Response Log
- Selection Audio
- Reading Studio: Notice & Note
- Writing Studio:
  Writing Informative Texts
- Speaking and Listening Studio:
  Participating in Collaborative
  Discussions
- Vocabulary Studio:
  Using Resources
- Grammar Studio: Module 8:
  Agreement
- "The Debt We Owe to the Adolescent
  Brain" Selection Test

SUMMARIES

English

The article describes the features of teenagers' brains and their role in allowing humans to become creative, risk-taking, and most of all adaptable. The author makes the point that humans have a much longer period of adolescence than other species, including closely related ones, such as Neanderthals, and notes that the adolescent brain seeks out risk and challenge. The article concludes that this long period, in which the brain is still developing, allows humans to practice problem solving and become more able to use their curiosity.

Spanish

Este artículo describe las características de los cerebros adolescentes y la función que cumplen al permitir que los humanos se conviertan en seres creativos, corredores de riesgo y, sobre todo, adaptables. El autor afirma que los humanos tienen un período de adolescencia mucho mayor al de otras especies, incluyendo a parientes cercanos, como el hombre de Neandertal, y observa que el cerebro adolescente busca riesgos y retos. El artículo concluye que este largo período, en el que el cerebro se desarrolla, les permite a los humanos practicar sus capacidades de resolución de problemas y los hace más aptos para utilizar su curiosidad.

SMALL-GROUP OPTIONS

Have students work in small groups to read and discuss the selection.

Assigned Roles

Assign each student a role to play to further the discussion. For example, you might have

- a timekeeper, who keeps track of the length of time each student speaks and limits it;
- a summarizer, who restates the most important points of each person's comments;
- a facilitator, who ensures that everyone has an opportunity to speak.

Other roles are possible as well. The goal is to ensure that students do not talk over one another as they discuss their ideas.

Hand Signals

Encourage students to listen without talking over each other by using simple hand signals to indicate agreement, confusion, and desire to interrupt or add to the discussion. Some sample signals could be:

- thumbs up: "I agree with you."
- curled index finger: "I'm not sure what you mean."
- upraised forefinger: "I have something to add to your point."
- palms together: "I have a question."

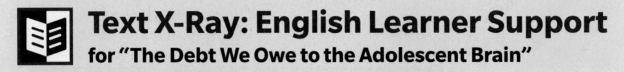

Text X-Ray: English Learner Support
for "The Debt We Owe to the Adolescent Brain"

Use the Text X-Ray and the supports and scaffolds in the Teacher's Edition to help guide students at different proficiency levels through the selection.

INTRODUCE THE SELECTION
DISCUSS TEENAGE YEARS AND ADULTHOOD

In this lesson, students will need to be able to think about the teenage years and adulthood. This article includes important pieces of information about these two stages of life, especially regarding the differences between the brains of people in these two groups. Write the following on the board and read it aloud:

- *The teenage years are also known as adolescence.*
- *The teenage years begin about age 13 and end around age 18 or 19.*
- *Adulthood begins after adolescence.*

Tell students that they will need to look in the text to see how adults and teenagers are alike, and especially how they are different. Provide them with sentence frames such as the following:

- *Adults and teenagers are alike because ____.*
- *Adults and teenagers are different because ____.*
- *Teenagers are (have) ____, but adults are (have) ____.*

CULTURAL REFERENCES

The following words and phrases may be unfamiliar to students:

- *golden age* (paragraph 4): a period of time in which things are better than they are before or afterward
- *hang out with* (paragraph 6): spend time together
- *hallmarks* (paragraph 6): central features
- *push-pull tension* (paragraph 7): factors that move people first in one direction and then in another

LISTENING

Understand Contrast

Draw students' attention to the use of contrast in the text. Tell students that there are many ways for a writer to show that two things are different and that writers often use certain words and phrases to signal these contrasts or differences. Explain that these words include *but* and *by contrast*.

Have students listen as you read aloud paragraphs 1–2. Use the following supports with students at varying proficiency levels:

- Tell students that you will ask questions about what you just read aloud. Then ask questions with yes or no answers. For example, ask: *Can polar bears live above the Arctic Circle? (yes) Can they live at the equator? (no)* Point out the language structure using *but*.   **SUBSTANTIAL**
- Ask questions about what you just read. Have students respond with phrases or simple sentences: For example, ask: *Which animals can live at the equator? (gorillas)* Point out the sentence structure with *but*.   **MODERATE**
- Have students raise their hands when you read aloud a signal word such as *but* or *by contrast*. Have them tell each other what is being contrasted.   **LIGHT**

SPEAKING

Discuss in Small Groups

Guide students to participate fully in small-group discussion by providing them with sentence frames and giving them a sense of the give-and-take of a collaborative conversation.

Use the following supports with students at varying proficiency levels:

- Have students use simple sentence frames to ask and answer questions of others in a small group. For example, have students say: *I think _____. What do you think?* **SUBSTANTIAL**
- Have students use the word *because* to explain their thinking, using sentence frames such as: *I think _____ because _____.* **MODERATE**
- Have students go around the circle in a small group. Have each student summarize the previous student's idea before expressing a new idea of his or her own. **LIGHT**

READING

Use Headings

Draw students' attention to the headings in the text. Remind them that the headings help organize the material in the article and make it easier to follow the author's points.

Work with students to read paragraphs 3–5, "Brain Under Construction." Use the following supports with students at varying proficiency levels:

- Have students read the heading. Explain the meaning of the phrase "under construction," and have students connect the use of the phrase here to the construction of buildings. **SUBSTANTIAL**
- Have students read the heading and the text. Explain the meaning of "under construction," and have students predict what the section will mostly be about based on that information. **MODERATE**
- Have students read the heading and the text. Ask them to explain how the heading fits the information in the paragraphs below it. **LIGHT**

WRITING

Write a Letter

Draw students' attention to the assignment on writing a letter on p. 335.

Use the following supports with students at varying proficiency levels:

- Have students complete sentence frames to write about adolescent brains, such as: *Brains are _____.* **SUBSTANTIAL**
- Have students make a list of behaviors that adolescents might engage in. Have them talk about their lists with a partner. **MODERATE**
- Talk with students about cause-and-effect words such as *because* and how they help connect ideas. Explain that good writing makes use of these connections. Have students use these words to write sentences describing how brain research connects to early adolescent behaviors. **LIGHT**

EXPLAIN THE SIGNPOSTS

Explain that **NOTICE & NOTE Signposts** are significant moments in the text that help readers understand and analyze works of fiction or nonfiction. Use the instruction on these pages to introduce students to the signposts **Contrasts and Contradictions, Big Questions,** and **Numbers and Stats**. Then use the selection that follows to have students apply the signposts to a text.

For a full list of the fiction and nonfiction signposts, see p. 392.

CONTRASTS AND CONTRADICTIONS

Explain that **Contrasts and Contradictions** are a common way of structuring a nonfiction article. Review with students that **contrasts** tell how two or more ideas or objects are different. Then explain that a **contradiction** is a sharp contrast which uses surprise to make a point. Tell students that a contradiction is unexpected as though they were to ask a football player what sport he liked best and he replied "Baseball."

Read aloud the sample passage, emphasizing the rhythm of *polar bears/gorillas can . . . but they can't . . .* Explain that there are contrasts within these sentences (what polar bears or gorillas can or cannot do) and a larger contrast within the paragraph: a distinction between human adaptability and the adaptability of other animals.

Call students' attention to the words and phrases that mark contrasts. Explain that when students see this language, they should recognize that the author is contrasting two or more things or ideas, and they should ask themselves the anchor question *"What is the difference, and why does it matter?"*

THE DEBT WE OWE TO THE ADOLESCENT BRAIN

For more information on these and other signposts to Notice & Note, visit the **Reading Studio**.

You are about to read the informational text "The Debt We Owe to the Adolescent Brain." In it, you will ask questions and notice and note signposts that will help you analyze the author's purpose and the organizational structure she uses to support her main ideas. Here are two key signposts and a Big Question to look for as you read this magazine article and other works of nonfiction.

When you read and encounter phrases like these, pause to see if it's a **Contrasts and Contradictions** signpost:

"on the other hand, . . ."

"by contrast, . . ."

"however, . . ."

"another viewpoint . . ."

Contrasts and Contradictions If you ask an older student to tell you about the classes he is taking, he might contrast his classes with those in your grade by naming ways they are more difficult. If he said that one of his classes was much easier than yours, however, you might be surprised by this contradiction in what you expected to hear.

In nonfiction texts, **Contrasts and Contradictions** can help you better understand main ideas and supporting details. Contrasts can reveal the unique qualities of a subject in comparison to others that seemed to be similar. Contradictions may highlight sharp or startling contrasts between what we expect and what we observe.

Read this paragraph from "The Debt We Owe to the Adolescent Brain" to see a student's annotation of Contrasts and Contradictions:

> 1 Polar bears can live above the Arctic Circle but they can't live at the Equator. Gorillas can live at the Equator but they can't live above the Arctic Circle. Humans, however, can live in the Arctic or they can live in the tropics. Why is our species so adaptable? We can thank our long period of adolescence for that.

Anchor Question
When you notice this signpost, ask: What is the difference, and why does it matter?

What does the author contrast in the example?	The author contrasts the adaptability of humans with that of polar bears and gorillas.
Why does the author point out this contrast?	The author wants to emphasize that humans are unusual by contrasting them with other animals.

Big Questions When you tell a friend about a movie that only you have seen, you might share some basic information about the plot and your overall reaction. When you and a friend talk about a movie you've both seen, you might discuss details about specific parts of the movie.

Authors have an intended audience when they write. Asking the Big Question **What does the author think I already know?** can help you make inferences about the author's reasons for including or leaving out certain facts, details, and examples. Here's an example of a student identifying and marking this Big Question in the text:

> 3   Dr. Jay Giedd, professor of psychiatry at the University of California at San Diego, says, "Nothing is even close to humans in terms of <u>how long we're dependent on caregivers.</u>"

What does the author think I already know about animals?	*Animals are more independent from their parents at younger ages than humans.*
Why doesn't the author provide more details about the differences between humans and animals?	*She thinks her audience knows enough to understand her point: that humans depend on their parents for an unusually long time.*

Numbers and Stats For what purposes might you count or measure something? Authors often use **Numbers and Stats** as evidence to support their main ideas. They might cite, track, or compare specific quantities or sizes to support an idea, identify a pattern, or point out a change over time. Paying attention to Numbers and Stats can help you:

- analyze an author's use of evidence
- understand an author's message and purpose
- identify author bias or faulty reasoning

Here's an example of a student underlining some Numbers and Stats:

> 13   . . . It's a sad paradox that, relative to children, people in their late adolescence, who are generally the strongest and healthiest they'll ever be, face a <u>200 percent increase</u> in the chance of dying.

How does the author use numbers to compare children and adolescents?	*The risk of death in adolescence is 200 percent higher than in childhood.*
Why might this number be important to the author's message?	*There might be something about the adolescent brain that increases the risk of death.*

Remember to apply the **Big Questions** strategy when you read nonfiction text. Pause to ask yourself these questions:

- Who is the author's intended audience?
- What prior knowledge does the author think the audience has?
- What experiences does the author think the audience can relate to?

When you see words and phrases like these, pause to see if it's a **Numbers and Stats** signpost:

"amount"

"increase"

"greater/less than"

"60 percent"

"three times as many as"

"one out of every four"

Anchor Question
When you notice this signpost, ask: Do these numbers help prove a point?

Notice & Note   325

BIG QUESTIONS

Explain that asking **Big Questions** can help students determine what the author most wants them to know or to learn. Point out that asking Big Questions can help students identify an **author's message** or **purpose in writing**. Have students look at the example from the text. Point out that authors think about their audience and tailor their writing to those readers. Give an example like a student writing about video games for an audience of fellow gamers as opposed to their grandparents.

Tell students that when they spot a Big Question they should mark it and ask themselves the anchor question, "*What does the author think I already know?*"

NUMBERS AND STATS

Explain that **Numbers and Stats** help readers understand key ideas. Using numbers can help writers explain a pattern, provide a contrast, or highlight changes over time. Review with students the list of words and phrases associated with Numbers and Stats. Guide students to read the list of how paying attention to Numbers and Stats can help them. Walk students through the example. Point out the phrase "300 percent increase." Ask students what they learned from this number and why the author used it.

Tell students that when they see numbers or statistics, they should stop and ask themselves the anchor question, "*Do these numbers help prove a point?*"

APPLY THE SIGNPOSTS

Have students use the selection that follows as a model text to apply the signposts. As students encounter signposts, prompt them to stop, reread, and ask themselves the anchor questions that will help them understand the article. Tell students to continue to look for signposts as they read the other selections in the unit.

WHEN STUDENTS STRUGGLE . . .

Use Strategies Call students' attention to the key words that indicate the signposts on the student pages, especially those which indicate contrasts and contradictions. Have students make simple posters with a chart that lists some or all of these words and phrases. Then have them share their posters with others, and display their poster in an easily accessible place. The act of making the posters can help focus students on the words they need to look for, and the charts will also provide a handy reference for students as they read.

ANALYZE & APPLY

THE DEBT WE OWE TO THE ADOLESCENT BRAIN

Informational Text by **Jeanne Miller**

326   Unit 5

Connect to the
ESSENTIAL QUESTION

Teenagers are not children, and yet they are not quite adults, either. Most notably, the adolescent brain is more sophisticated than the child's brain, but is not as fully formed as an adult brain. This difference can make teenagers behave differently than grown-ups.

In this article, author Jeanne Miller argues that teenagers' brains make adulthood possible. Without a long period of learning, Miller asserts, adult humans would be much less adaptable than they actually are.

? ESSENTIAL QUESTION:

How do your teenage years prepare you for adulthood?

LEARNING MINDSET

Grit A person who has grit is persistent even in the face of adversity. Many students believe that learning should come easily, but in fact learning can often be hard work. Thus, students who are willing to put in effort are likely to experience the most academic success. Point out to students that the brain is essentially a muscle, and like other muscles it must be exercised to be at its most effective. Encourage students to see difficult assignments not as barriers, but as challenges to be overcome; explain that students with grit are always looking for new ways to solve problems. When you can, offer praise for hard work rather than for right answers.

QUICK START

What might be special about the brains of teenagers? Make a list of questions about the adolescent brain that you'd like the text to answer.

ANALYZE STRUCTURE

The **structure** of a text is the way in which it is put together. In "The Debt We Owe to the Adolescent Brain," the author uses **headings** to divide the article into sections. Previewing the article by skimming the headings can help you predict the text's structure and its **pattern(s) of organization,** or arrangement of ideas and information.

Pattern	What It Highlights	Signal Words
main-idea-and-details order	evidence that supports a key idea	*for example, experts say, others agree that*
cause-and-effect order	relationships between causes and effects	*because, so, as a result, therefore*
compare-and-contrast order	ways in which subjects are alike and different	*all, most, similarly, by contrast, but, however*

A pattern of organization may be used to organize an entire piece of writing or single paragraphs or sections within a work. As you read, note the pattern of organization in each section of the article.

ANALYZE AUTHOR'S PURPOSE

An **author's purpose** is his or her main reason for writing. In an informational text, the author's purpose is usually to inform or explain. An author's **message** is the main idea he or she wants to convey. To analyze how the author of this article achieves her purpose and to infer what her message is, complete the chart below as you read.

SECTION	KEY IDEAS
Introduction (paragraphs 1–2)	
"Brain Under Construction" (paragraphs 3–5)	
"Moving On from Childhood" (paragraphs 6–11)	
"Stone Age Impulses in the Modern World" (paragraphs 12–14)	
Author's Purpose and Message:	

GENRE ELEMENTS: INFORMATIONAL TEXT

- provides factual information
- may include headings and subheadings to help readers navigate the text
- uses organizational patterns such as main idea and details to present information clearly
- may appear in a variety of formats, including magazine articles—brief pieces that report on current events or topics

The Debt We Owe to the Adolescent Brain   327

QUICK START

Have students work in pairs to generate a list of questions. If needed, begin the process by asking *How are adolescent brains different from adult brains?* or *What are the best features of teenagers' brains?* Tell students that the class will try to answer as many of these questions as possible during this unit.

ANALYZE STRUCTURE

Review the information in the paragraph and the table with students. Tell students that headings are a common way to organize a text; the heading usually tells what the next few paragraphs will be about.

Point out that the table shows three organizing patterns, or organizing structures, and explain that these three are among the most commonly used patterns in nonfiction. Emphasize that a single article may use more than one of these patterns. Look over the signal words in the third column with students and encourage students to look for these words and phrases as they read the text.

ANALYZE AUTHOR'S PURPOSE

Discuss the concepts of author's purpose and author's message with students, and have them explore how the two ideas are alike and different. Remind them that this article is divided into sections, each with its own heading, and that each section focuses on a specific message. Have students read the text with an eye toward determining the author's message and purpose, and remind them to fill in the table as they complete each section of the text.

(EL) ENGLISH LEARNER SUPPORT

Vocabulary   Review with students the list of signal words in the table. Have students identify words they already know and words that are not yet familiar. You may wish to make students "experts" on particular words, giving them the opportunity to display their knowledge for classmates and help others understand the meanings of those words. For words that are less familiar, give students model sentences using the words to get them used to the structure of sentences with the words. Then have students practice pronouncing the words before generating similar sentences.   **MODERATE**

TEACH

CRITICAL VOCABULARY

Encourage students to read all the sentences before deciding which word best completes each one. Remind them to look for context clues that match the meaning of each word.

Answers:

1. *deplete*
2. *lethal*
3. *dependent*
4. *insulate*
5. *paradox*
6. *adaptable*

■ English Learner Support

Use Cognates Tell students that some Critical Vocabulary words have Spanish cognates, such as *paradox/paradoja* and *dependent/dependiente*.   **ALL LEVELS**

LANGUAGE CONVENTIONS

Tell students that pronouns, such as *her, they,* and *we,* are words that stand for nouns, and that antecedents are the nouns the pronouns stand for. Call students' attention to the boldfaced example, and explain that the pronoun *they* refers to the antecedent *adolescents.* Emphasize that *adolescents* is in the plural form, so the pronoun that refers to it (*they*) must also be plural. Have students replace *they* in the sentence with *I, she,* or *it* to help them recognize that a singular pronoun with *adolescents* neither sounds nor looks correct.

 ANNOTATION MODEL

Remind students that annotating can help them keep track of important ideas. Point out that students can use annotation strategies other than the one shown here.

CRITICAL VOCABULARY

adaptable	insulate	lethal
dependent	deplete	paradox

To see how many Critical Vocabulary words you already know, use them to complete these sentences.

1. Due to the dry conditions, too much water use will _____ the town's supply of water.

2. Certain bacteria can cause _____ illness.

3. Infants are _____ on caregivers to feed and clothe them.

4. An extra layer of clothing helps _____ you from the cold.

5. It felt like a _____ that the team scored only one goal but still won the game.

6. A highly _____ species is able to grow and thrive in extreme conditions.

LANGUAGE CONVENTIONS

Pronoun-Antecedent Agreement In this lesson, you will see that pronouns agree with their antecedents and learn how to check them in your own writing. In this example, note that the speaker uses the plural pronoun *they* to refer back to a plural antecedent, *adolescents*:

"Adolescents are dealing with a lot," Casey says, "but they should remember they have greater potential for change now than at any other time."

As you read the text, notice the author's correct use of pronouns.

ANNOTATION MODEL   **NOTICE & NOTE**

As you read, notice and note signposts, such as **Contrasts and Contradictions** and **Numbers and Stats,** and pause to ask yourself **Big Questions.** In the model, you can see one reader's notes about "The Debt We Owe to the Adolescent Brain."

> 2   Most mammals have a period of adolescence. But as soon as they're able to reproduce, they begin bearing and caring for children. By contrast, humans, under the protection of their families, take many years to develop and grow into adulthood.

Difference: other mammals have a shorter period of adolescence than humans.

 ENGLISH LEARNER SUPPORT

Pronouns It can be helpful for students to see a list of pronouns to assist them in identifying pronouns in the text. Help them create a chart that shows pronouns as subjects, objects, and possessives. Then have students practice pronouncing the pronouns.

I	you	he	she	it	we	they
me	you	him	her	it	us	them
my	your	his	her	its	our	their
mine	yours	his	hers	its	ours	theirs

Display the chart where it is easily accessible. **ALL LEVELS**

BACKGROUND

Jeanne Miller grew up in northwestern Pennsylvania but later settled in Berkeley, California. She writes children's and young adult magazine articles on a variety of science topics. Her book Food Science *informs young readers about food chemistry, the movement to promote local and traditional foods, and the future of food.*

THE DEBT WE OWE TO THE ADOLESCENT BRAIN

Informational Text by Jeanne Miller

SETTING A PURPOSE

As you read, pay attention to details that reveal the author's purpose and message.

1   Polar bears can live above the Arctic Circle <u>but</u> they can't live at the Equator. Gorillas can live at the Equator <u>but</u> they can't live above the Arctic Circle. Humans, <u>however</u>, can live in the Arctic or they can live in the tropics. Why is our species so **adaptable**? We can thank our long period of adolescence for that.

2   Most (mammals) have a period of adolescence. <u>But</u> as soon as they're able to reproduce, they begin bearing and caring for children. <u>By contrast,</u> (humans) under the protection of <u>their</u> families, take many years to develop and grow into adulthood.

Notice & Note

Use the side margins to notice and note signposts in the text.

adaptable
(ə-dăp´tə-bəl) *adj. Adaptable* means able to survive under certain conditions.

LANGUAGE CONVENTIONS
Annotate: In paragraph 2, underline all the pronouns. Then circle the two antecedents—the nouns to which the pronouns refer.

Analyze: Could the author have used the pronoun *our* instead of *their* in the last sentence? Explain.

The Debt We Owe to the Adolescent Brain   329

BACKGROUND

Read the Background information with students. Point out that the author's science writing experience is highlighted, which gives her credibility when it comes to writing about scientific matters such as the human brain.

SETTING A PURPOSE

Remind students that they should try to determine the author's purpose and author's message as they read the text. Ask students to reread the title of the article along with the subtitle (Utterly Unique, Very Valuable). Have students predict what the author's perspective on the adolescent brain will be, based on the title and subtitle, and ask students whether they think the author's opinion about the brain is largely positive or mainly negative. Then ask students to predict the author's purpose and message.

✏ LANGUAGE CONVENTIONS

Remind students of the function and use of pronouns, and review with them that all pronouns refer to a noun mentioned earlier in the text. Have students carry out the activity. (**Answer:** *The pronouns are* they're, they, *and* their. *The first two refer to the antecedent* mammals. *The final one refers to the antecedent* humans. *Yes, the author could have used* our *instead of* their *because she and all her readers are included under the heading of* humans. *You may wish to point out that the author used both* they *and* our *to refer to the antecedent* humans *in the first paragraph.*)

📖   For **listening support** for students at varying proficiency levels, see the **Text X-Ray** on page 324C.

TO CHALLENGE STUDENTS . . .

Structure Remind students that there are several different ways of structuring a nonfiction text, such as cause and effect and compare and contrast. Point out that three of these ways are specified in this lesson. Have students look through the article and determine which structure is used for each paragraph. Then have students write a brief explanation of what makes each of these organizational patterns effective, along with a recommendation of when each one should be used.

CRITICAL VOCABULARY

adaptable: The first three sentences provide context clues to help readers understand the meaning of the term.

ASK STUDENTS to identify an animal, other than human, that is adaptable and explain how they know. (**Possible answers:** *mice, because they can live in many different kinds of places.*)

ENGLISH LEARNER SUPPORT

Quotation Marks Point out to students that several parts of page 330 are enclosed inside quotation marks, and that the words inside the quotation marks were not originally spoken or written by the author of the article but by someone else—in this case, a doctor. Write simple sentences with quotation marks, such as *"Look at the cat," said Milaura*, and have students identify which words were first spoken or written by someone other than the writer. Arabic students may be used to guillemets (« and ») or parentheses rather than quotation marks. **SUBSTANTIAL**

 ANALYZE STRUCTURE

Remind students that signal words connect writing more closely together. Have students find the words in question and discuss how the words help make for a more cohesive narrative. Then ask them to determine the primary organizational pattern of this section of the text. (**Answer:** *The author is using a compare-and-contrast structure. This organization helps the author introduce and develop the idea that humans are unique in their adaptability and in their extended period of adolescent development. Relating these ideas shows that adolescence is an important developmental period.*)

 For **reading support** for students at varying proficiency levels, see the **Text X-Ray** on page 326D.

CRITICAL VOCABULARY

dependent: A *dependent* person or animal relies on some other human or animal for support.

ASK STUDENTS who they are dependent on. (**Possible answers:** *parents, teachers, neighbors.*)

insulate: to protect with a layer of extra material, especially against cold, sound, or electricity

ASK STUDENTS what it means that myelin forms an *insulating sheath*. (*It covers and protects nerve fibers.*)

 NOTICE & NOTE

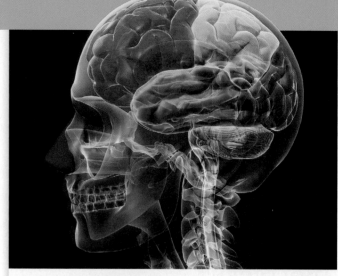

dependent
(dĭ-pĕnˊdənt) *adj.* Dependent means relying on or requiring the aid or support of another.

ANALYZE STRUCTURE
Annotate: Mark signal words and phrases that show relationships between ideas in paragraphs 1–3.

Analyze: What is the author's pattern of organization in these paragraphs? How does this pattern help the author introduce and develop main ideas?

insulate
(ĭnˊsə-lātˊ) *v.* To *insulate* means to surround or cover to prevent the passage of heat, electricity, or sound.

Brain Under Construction

3 Dr. Jay Giedd, professor of psychiatry[1] at the University of California at San Diego, says, "Nothing is even close to humans in terms of how long we're **dependent** on caregivers." He points out that in their early teens, Neanderthals[2] already had children of their own. Neanderthals died out, but our ancestors, *Homo sapiens*, thrived. A large part of that success comes from our brain's taking a long time to mature. This extended period of development lets us build exactly the brain we need in our circumstances. Giedd says, "All the brain's parts have their periods of rapid explosive growth and then rapid pruning back. You have overproduction—more connections than can possibly survive—and then they fight it out. The ones that are used and lead to positive outcomes stay, and those that aren't used, or are used and lead to bad outcomes, are eliminated."

4 We lose "gray matter" and gain "white matter": myelin, which forms an **insulating** sheath around nerve fibers. "We get more and more myelin, which speeds up the communication between nerve cells, as we go through adolescence," says Giedd. "We learn what we need to do and be good at and then the process streamlines that." But the price we pay is that, as myelin is laid down, flexibility diminishes. Adolescence is a kind of golden age when, as Giedd puts it, "You're asking your brain, 'What do I need to be good at? What do I need to do to make it in this world?' Every choice you make trains your brain."

---

[1] **psychiatry** (sī-kīˊə-trē): the branch of medicine that deals with the diagnosis, treatment, and prevention of mental and emotional disorders.
[2] **Neanderthals** (nē-ănˊdər-thôlzˊ): an extinct human species or subspecies.

IMPROVE READING FLUENCY

Targeted Passage Read aloud a section of the text, modeling appropriate speed and phrasing. Emphasize that you are not reading the text as quickly as possible. Demonstrate what it sounds like when you go at a rapid rate of speed, and point out that it is difficult for you to sustain the pace—and even more difficult for your listeners to hear and understand every word. Then model reading all or part of the same section again, but this time too slowly. Have students work with partners to read the section you just read at an appropriate rate of speed.

5   This lets us adjust to our surroundings. Giedd points out, "We all had ancestors that were good at adapting to change. Neanderthals had brains that were about (13 percent bigger) than ours and they lived in pretty tough conditions and harsh climates, but they didn't adapt."

Moving On from Childhood

6   Dr. B. J. Casey is a professor of psychology at Weill Cornell Medical College. Her focus on adolescent brains includes those of humans and mice. "There is evidence," she says, "that even adolescent rodents tend to hang out with same-aged peers and tend to have more fights with their parents." Sound familiar? These behaviors—sensitivity to influence from peers, taking risks, and pulling away from parents—are hallmarks of human adolescence. They have their roots in the hunter-gatherer world of our early ancestors, where success meant surviving and reproducing.

7   Finding a mate and passing on your genes means leaving the comfort of your home. Casey says, "If you're getting all your needs met, why in the world would you leave? There needs to be some push-pull tension in evolution to get you to leave that home. Otherwise you'll **deplete** all the resources and it will be difficult to find a mate to partner with."

8   Going out into the world can involve risks, but the adolescent brain is wired for that. Giedd points out that "high risk equals high reward at times." And, compared to children or adults, teens are much more sensitive to rewards.

9   A study in Casey's lab demonstrated that fact when researchers put teenagers in a brain-scanning machine and asked them to complete a simple task. Successfully completing it earned them a lot of money. The resulting brain scans showed

---

NUMBERS AND STATS

Notice & Note: In paragraph 5, what comparison does the author make using a percentage number? Circle this statistic in the text.

Infer: What purpose does this number serve in this context?

BIG QUESTIONS

Notice & Note: A **rhetorical question** has such an obvious answer that it does not require a reply. Underline the rhetorical question in paragraph 6. Why do you think the author poses this question?

Infer: What prior knowledge or experience does the author's rhetorical question assume?

---

deplete
(dĭ-plēt´) v. To *deplete* means to use up or to reduce to a very small amount.

CONTRASTS AND CONTRADICTIONS

Notice & Note: What evidence does the author provide in paragraphs 8–9 to contrast adolescents with children and adults? Mark these details.

Analyze: Why does the author point out these differences?

TEACH

NUMBERS AND STATS

Review with students that using numbers can be very useful in an informational text. Explain that numbers and **statistics**, such as percentages, can often make a case more quickly and simply than words. Have students answer the question. (**Answer:** *The author uses the percentage to compare the sizes of Neanderthal and human brains. She links brain size to ability to adapt to underscore her point that brain size helped human adaptation.*)

BIG QUESTIONS

Have students discuss why they might ask a question to which they already know the answer. Then have them answer the questions. (**Answer:** *Asking the question helps the author connect with her audience. It also helps pave the way for the notion that the behavior of adolescent mice is similar to the behavior of adolescent humans. The author assumes that the audience will relate to hanging out with friends, taking risks, and seeking independence from parents.*)

CONTRASTS AND CONTRADICTIONS

Have students read the prompt and answer the questions. (**Answer:** *The author cites expert opinion and a research study to show that adolescent brains are more sensitive to rewards. The contrast illustrates a way that adolescent brains are different from those of children and adults.*)

■ **English Learner Support**

Word Forms List with students different forms of common words in the article, such as *adapt/adapting/adapted/adaptation.*   **MODERATE**

APPLYING ACADEMIC VOCABULARY

❑ **debate**   ☑ **deduce**   ❑ **license**   ☑ **sufficient**   ❑ **trend**

Write and Discuss Have students turn to a partner to discuss the following questions. Guide students to include the Academic Vocabulary words *deduce* and *sufficient* in their responses. Ask volunteers to share their responses with the class.

- What can you **deduce** about the weather if people are wearing heavy coats?
- If you wake up at 6:30 a.m., will you have **sufficient** time to get to school? Explain.

CRITICAL VOCABULARY

deplete: to reduce a resource to a very small amount or to eliminate it

ASK STUDENTS to describe a time when they felt that their energy was *depleted*. (**Possible answer:** *after running a long race.*)

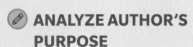

ANALYZE AUTHOR'S PURPOSE

Review with students that each section of the text has its own **heading**. Tell students that the author had a reason, or a purpose, for using the heading "Stone Age Impulses in the Modern World." Have students read the prompt and answer the questions. (**Answer:** *The heading refers to types of risk-taking that teenagers often engage in today. Underscores for pay off, lethal, innovation and creativity, reckless driving, dangerous behaviors opportunities, and potential for mastering new skills. Just as in hunter-gatherer societies, teenage risk-taking today still involves danger but has great potential for rewards.*)

■ English Learner Support

Adjectives Point out the words *strongest* and *healthiest* in paragraph 13. Show students how they can use the ending *-est* to form some superlative forms of adjectives. Have students create the superlative forms of *large, warm,* and *loud* and use them in sentences. (*largest, warmest, loudest*)

SUBSTANTIAL

CRITICAL VOCABULARY

lethal: Something that is lethal is dangerous enough to cause death.

ASK STUDENTS to name some things in modern society that can be lethal. (***Possible answers:*** *gun violence, disease, drunk driving.*)

paradox: This word is used to describe a situation that seems self-contradictory, or impossible on the surface.

ASK STUDENTS to reread the sentence that uses the word *paradox* in paragraph 13 and describe what makes that situation paradoxical. (*It would seem that strong and healthy people would be less likely to die, but in fact teens make choices that make them more likely to die.*)

NOTICE & NOTE

ANALYZE AUTHOR'S PURPOSE

Annotate: Circle the heading of the last section. Consider its meaning and make a prediction about how this section helps the author achieve her purpose. Then, underline possible effects of "Stone Age impulses in the modern world" in paragraphs 12–14.

Analyze: After reading the last section, confirm or correct the prediction you made previously. What overall message does the information in this section help support?

lethal
(lē´thəl) *adj.* Lethal means causing or capable of causing death.

paradox
(păr´ə-dŏks´) *n.* A paradox is a person, thing, or situation that is contradictory.

an exaggerated response in the reward center of the teens' brains, but only a moderate response in children and adults.

10   Sometimes the reward might be approval by their peers, who will be important to a teenager's future. In another study, Casey's group showed that, unlike children and adults, adolescents found smiling faces to be almost irresistible. She says, "When your peers are smiling it means they're accepting you."

11   Giedd says, "The peer group is the one that will help protect you, who will be your teammates, and who will supply resources. Job one for adolescents is navigating their social world."

Stone Age Impulses in the Modern World

12   In hunter-gatherer societies, success in a risk-taking activity might result in a supply of food, in securing a mate, or in finding new territory. Of course, it can sometimes result in being killed by a predator. Taking certain risks can also pay off for modern teens. Giedd says, "As long as it's not **lethal**—as in the case of foolish risk-taking—it can lead to innovation and creativity."

13   The dangers today's teens face are different from those our early ancestors faced. It's a sad **paradox** that, relative to children, people in their late adolescence, who are generally the strongest and healthiest they'll ever be, face a 200 percent increase in the chance of dying. The main cause is accidents, with one-third of those being automobile crashes. Reckless driving and other dangerous behaviors put teenagers at risk, but young people also face threats to their health from the considerable stresses of growing up in the 21st century. "Adolescents are dealing with a lot," Casey says, "but they

---

WHEN STUDENTS STRUGGLE . . .

Identify Main Idea and Details Use a web organizer to help students find the main idea and details in each paragraph. Review that main ideas often appear in the first sentence or two of a paragraph, though this is not always the case. Model finding a main idea, and then ask yourself, *Is this what the paragraph is mostly about?* Then help students identify main ideas and details, put them in the web, and discuss how they function in the paragraph.

     For additional support, go to the **Reading Studio** and assign the following LEVEL UP **Level Up Tutorial: Main Idea and Supporting Details.**

should remember they have greater potential for change now than at any other time. There will be many opportunities for them to change behaviors that they don't want to engage in and to become what they want to be."

14   Giedd agrees. "The challenges adolescents present to their brains now will have effects for decades," he says. The potential for mastering new skills and honing their abilities is phenomenal. "We never lose it completely," Giedd says, "but it's never going to be as good as it is when we're adolescents."

 CHECK YOUR UNDERSTANDING

Have students answer the questions independently.

Answers:

1. *D*

2. *J*

3. *C*

If they answer any questions incorrectly, have them reread the text to confirm their understanding. Then they may proceed to ANALYZE THE TEXT on p. 334.

CHECK YOUR UNDERSTANDING

Answer these questions before moving on to the **Analyze the Text** section on the following page.

1 The word pruning in paragraph 3 means —

  A connecting

  B overproducing

  C growing

  D eliminating

2 What idea does the evidence in paragraph 9 support?

  F The adolescent brain is highly efficient in completing simple tasks.

  G The adolescent brain is wired to seek safety.

  H Adolescents do not want to leave home if all of their needs are met.

  J Adolescents are more sensitive to rewards than children or adults.

3 What is the author's main purpose in "The Debt We Owe to the Adolescent Brain"?

  A to entertain

  B to persuade

  C to inform or explain

  D to express thoughts or feelings

ENGLISH LEARNER SUPPORT

Oral Assessment   Use the following questions to assess students' comprehension and speaking skills:

1. Look at paragraph 3. Find the word *pruning*. What is the meaning of this word? *(eliminating)*

2. Reread paragraph 9. Look for the evidence given in this paragraph. This evidence supports an idea. What is the idea? *(Teenagers are more likely than children or adults to be motivated by rewards.)*

3. Authors have different reasons for writing. What is the main purpose for writing "The Debt We Owe to the Adolescent Brain?" *(to inform or explain)* **SUBSTANTIAL/MODERATE**

APPLY

ANALYZE THE TEXT

Possible answers

1. **DOK 4:** *The author wants to inform readers that our species has benefited from a long adolescence. She compares humans and other species, presents causal relationships to show adolescent brains are wired to take risks, and provides expert opinions to show that adolescence is crucial for developing skills.*

2. **DOK 2:** *The comparison shows humans are unique in their ability to adapt and supports the idea that an extended adolescence has helped humans survive, in contrast to Neanderthals.*

3. **DOK 2:** *Risk-taking was necessary for survival in hunter-gatherer societies, so people became wired for risk-taking. This relates to the idea that risk-taking is a uniquely sensitive period of development.*

4. **DOK 4:** *The author relies on quotations from experts to support the idea that adolescence is crucial for development.*

5. **DOK 4:** *The paradox is that adolescents face increased risk of death even as they become stronger and healthier. The paradox supports the idea that adolescents face challenges but can overcome them.*

RESEARCH

Call students' attention to the research prompt and the Research Tip feature. Explain that just as numbers and statistics can help readers make sense of complex information, graphs and tables also make complex information easier to grasp.

Connect Students should have an informed discussion, citing facts, expert's opinions, and other evidence. They may note that older sources seem less relevant, and discuss details that prove a source is credible and current.

 RESPOND

ANALYZE THE TEXT

Support your responses with evidence from the text. 📖 NOTEBOOK

1. **Analyze** What is the author's main purpose for writing this article? How do the text's structure, headings, and patterns of organization help the author to achieve this purpose?

2. **Infer** Why does the author compare humans to Neanderthals? Cite evidence to support your answer.

3. **Cause/Effect** What cause-effect relationship does the author identify in the section "Moving On from Childhood"? How does this information relate to the author's main message?

4. **Analyze** What patterns of organization does the author use to convey information in this article? For each pattern you identify, cite an example and give a reason why she might have used it.

5. **Notice & Note** What paradox does the author point out in paragraph 13? How does this contradiction relate to the author's message?

RESEARCH TIP
When you research science topics, look for sources that include diagrams and charts to help you interpret complex information.

RESEARCH

In "The Debt We Owe to the Adolescent Brain," you learned about ways in which adolescents' brains are unique. Conduct research to find out more about the brain's structure and characteristics. Record what you learn in the chart.

QUESTION	ANSWER
What is the cerebral cortex?	*The cerebral cortex is the outer layer of the brain, responsible for sensation, reasoning, and memory.*
What is the function of each lobe of the cerebral cortex?	*The parietal lobe governs sensory processing and movement; the frontal lobe, motor function, speech, and reasoning; the occipital lobe, visual processing; the temporal lobe, auditory processing.*
What is the difference between the cerebral cortex of an adult and that of an adolescent?	*The frontal lobe doesn't fully develop till adulthood.*

Connect Consider what you have learned from your research about the brain. How does this information help support key ideas in "The Debt We Owe to the Adolescent Brain"? Discuss your ideas with a partner.

⚙ LEARNING MINDSET

Questioning Tell students that asking questions is one of the best strategies they can use to improve their ability to learn. Remind students that asking questions is all about being open to new ideas and trying new things. Encourage students to feel comfortable asking questions, and try to compliment them when they do ask.

- Encourage students to question how they arrived at their answer.
- Have students ask themselves whether they can try a different strategy.
- Remind students that asking questions is a sign of curiosity.
- Tell students that asking questions leads to learning new information.

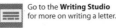
CREATE AND DISCUSS

Write a Letter Write a friendly letter to an adult in your life using research on the adolescent brain to explain the evolutionary purpose of some aspect of your behavior.

- ❏ Format your letter with an appropriate heading, a salutation, and a closing.
- ❏ Identify an aspect of your behavior that might be explained by current research on brain changes that occur during adolescence.
- ❏ Cite evidence from the text to support your ideas about the evolutionary purpose of your behavior.

Discuss with a Small Group Have a discussion about how information in "The Debt We Owe to the Adolescent Brain" can help you navigate school and life.

- ❏ With a small group, discuss practical ways in which your understanding of adolescent brain changes might influence choices you make or goals that you set at school and at home.
- ❏ Be sure to support your views with evidence from the article.
- ❏ During your discussion, listen closely and respectfully to all ideas.

 Go to the **Writing Studio** for more on writing a letter.

 Go to **Participating in Collaborative Discussions** in the **Speaking and Listening Studio** for more help.

RESPOND TO THE ESSENTIAL QUESTION

? How do your teenage years prepare you for adulthood?

Gather Information Review your annotations and notes on "The Debt We Owe to the Adolescent Brain." Then, add relevant details to your Response Log. As you determine which information to include, think about:

- brain changes that happen during adolescence
- ways in which the adolescent brain is unique
- dangers today's teens face

At the end of the unit, you can use your notes to help you write an argument.

ACADEMIC VOCABULARY

As you write and discuss what you learned from the article, be sure to use the Academic Vocabulary words. Check off each of the words that you use.

- ❏ debate
- ❏ deduce
- ❏ license
- ❏ sufficient
- ❏ trend

CREATE AND DISCUSS

Write a Letter Remind students that they need to use evidence from the text to support the ideas in their letters. Review the information about the parts of a letter and what it means to write a friendly letter. You might want to begin by asking students to think about something they do that adults might find exasperating.

For **writing support** for students at varying proficiency levels, see the **Text X-Ray** on page 324D.

Discuss with a Small Group Remind students of the guidelines you have set up in your classroom for small group work. Consider having a member of each group record the group's conclusions and report on them to the class as a whole.

For **speaking support** for students at varying proficiency levels, see the **Text X-Ray** on page 324D.

RESPOND TO THE ESSENTIAL QUESTION

Allow time for students to add details from "The Debt We Owe to the Adolescent Brain" to their Unit 5 Response Logs.

APPLY

CRITICAL VOCABULARY

Possible answers:

1. *No, I do my homework independently.*

2. *A wetsuit would insulate a swimmer because it protects from cold water and air temperatures.*

3. *A long soccer practice might deplete energy because it would be tiring.*

4. *A paradox would represent a contradiction; a corroboration would support or affirm.*

5. *No; an adaptable species would not be likely to die in a new environment but would make changes to allow it to continue to thrive.*

VOCABULARY STRATEGY:
Use Resources

Answers (precise meanings; guessed definitions will vary):

1. **Nerve cell:** *an impulse-conducting cell that is part of the brain, spinal column, or nerves*

2. **Psychology:** *the science that deals with mental processes*

3. **Gene:** *a hereditary unit consisting of DNA and occupying a specific location on a chromosome*

 RESPOND

WORD BANK
adaptable
dependent
insulate
deplete
lethal
paradox

 Go to the **Vocabulary Studio** for more on using resources.

CRITICAL VOCABULARY

Practice and Apply Use what you know about the Vocabulary words to answer the following questions.

1. Are you **dependent** on anyone for help with your homework? Why or why not?

2. What would **insulate** a swimmer, a wetsuit or a life jacket? Why?

3. What might **deplete** your energy, a good night's rest or a long soccer practice? Why?

4. Is a **paradox** more of a contradiction or an affirmation? Why?

5. If a species is highly **adaptable**, will a change in its environment likely be **lethal**? Why or why not?

VOCABULARY STRATEGY: Use Resources

When reading an informational text such as a science article, looking up technical or cross-curricular terms in print or digital resources such as dictionaries or glossaries can help you better understand the ideas.

Read this passage from "The Debt We Owe to the Adolescent Brain."

> We lose "gray matter" and gain "white matter": myelin, which forms an insulating sheath around nerve fibers. "We get more and more myelin, which speeds up the communication between nerve cells, as we go through adolescence," says Giedd.

In that passage, you can determine the meaning of the technical term *myelin* from the context clues "white matter," "forms an insulating sheath around nerve fibers," and "speeds up communication between nerve cells." However, you can also look up the word *myelin* in a dictionary to confirm its meaning and determine its pronunciation. Consulting another resource, such as a science reference book, will further deepen your understanding.

Practice and Apply Use context clues to define the following terms from "The Debt We Owe to the Adolescent Brain." Then use a resource such as a dictionary, glossary, or science reference book to confirm that your definition is correct.

TERM	GUESSED DEFINITION	RESOURCE DEFINITION
nerve cell (paragraph 4)		
psychology (paragraph 6)		
gene (paragraph 7)		

EL ENGLISH LEARNER SUPPORT

Vocabulary Strategy Point out that this activity asks students to learn about meanings of words in two different ways. Students whose native language is not English may be reluctant to try to use context clues to guess at meanings, or may not know how. Model with students how to use context clues by writing a simple sentence that uses one unfamiliar word, such as *She runs as fast as a gazelle.* Point out the words *she* and *fast* and point out that the sentence is saying that a certain person is a fast runner. Then do a brief think-aloud to determine that a gazelle is something that is fast, such as a fast animal, and how you know.
MODERATE

LANGUAGE CONVENTIONS:
Pronoun-Antecedent Agreement

A pronoun must agree with its antecedent in number, gender, and person.

- A **pronoun** is a word used in the place of one or more nouns or pronouns.
- An **antecedent** is the noun or pronoun to which a pronoun refers.

Read these sentences from "The Debt We Owe to the Adolescent Brain":

> **Dr. B. J. Casey is a professor of psychology at Weill Cornell Medical College. Her focus on adolescent brains includes those of humans and mice.**

The third-person singular pronoun *her* agrees with the antecedent *Dr. B. J. Casey*. Since the author used a feminine pronoun, readers can assume that Casey's gender must be female.

Indefinite pronouns do not refer to specific persons or things. The chart explains how to use indefinite pronouns and antecedents.

> ! Go to **Agreement** in the **Grammar Studio** for more on pronoun-antecedent agreement.

IF THE ANTECEDENT IS …	THE PRONOUN SHOULD BE …	EXAMPLE
a singular indefinite pronoun such as *each, either*, or *everything*	singular	Either is fine; just make sure you identify **it** in your notes.
a plural indefinite pronoun such as *both, many, several*, or *few*	plural	Both of the sources were relevant, but **they** didn't seem reliable.
an indefinite pronoun such as *all, some, none*, or *most* modified by a **prepositional phrase**, when the object of the preposition refers to a quantity or one part of something	singular	I thought I put all of my homework in my folder, but **it** isn't there now.
an indefinite pronoun such as *all, some, none*, or *most* modified by a **prepositional phrase**, when the object of the preposition refers to numbers of individual things	plural	Some of my library books are overdue, so I need to return **them** immediately.

Practice and Apply Correct the pronoun-antecedent error in each sentence and, where necessary, revise the verb to match in number.

1. All of the teens showed that she could adapt.

2. I dropped my phone, and now they won't work.

3. Everything is served and ready, but now they are getting cold.

4. I knew that all of the research was valid because they came from a reliable source.

 ENGLISH LEARNER SUPPORT

Language Conventions Give students a number of words, including pronouns, proper nouns, and common nouns, and have them identify which are pronouns; for example, of *carpenter, Sheila,* and *she,* the pronoun is *she.* Then have students write the correct missing pronoun in sentence frames in which a pronoun is clearly linked to an antecedent, such as *I clapped for Sheila after ___ sang.* **MODERATE**

LANGUAGE CONVENTIONS:
Pronoun-Antecedent Agreement

Review the information on pronouns and antecedents with students. Remind students that pronouns usually take the place of a common noun (such as *carpenter, athletes, butterfly*) or proper nouns (like *Henry, Ms. Dyrud,* or *the Cougars*). Be sure they understand, however, that possessive pronouns such as *his, their,* and *ours* can be used as well. Be sure students understand that antecedents must agree with pronouns not just in number, but in gender and person as well: we would not write *he* or *his* to refer to a woman or a girl.

Review the information about indefinite pronouns with students. Tell students that if they are uncertain whether to use a plural or singular pronoun, they may be able to determine which one to use by checking the verb after the antecedent. We would say *Many people are tall,* for example, so it would make sense to use a plural pronoun such as *they* to refer to *many people.*

Go through the examples with students. Have students explain why each pronoun is used. Then have students complete the Practice and Apply section.

Answers

1. *All of the teens showed that they could adapt.*

2. *I dropped my phone, and now it won't work.*

3. *Everything is served and ready, but now it is getting cold.*

4. *I knew that all of the research was valid because it came from a reliable source.*

BRONX MASQUERADE
Novel by Nikki Grimes

GENRE ELEMENTS
NOVEL

Remind students that the purpose of a **novel** is to entertain. Its plot is focused on a conflict that characters try to solve. It may have a variety of settings and have different types of action taking place at a variety of times that involves the characters, who will change over time and develop as the plot is carried out. Novels will often feature a theme or convey a message about life that readers will learn from the events of and characters in the novel.

LEARNING OBJECTIVES

- Cite evidence to support analysis of the text's structure and characters.
- Research the psychological effects of writing poetry.
- Write a poem.
- Discuss the story connects different character perspectives.
- Identify context clues to determine meaning of new terms.
- Analyze the use of comparative and superlative modifiers.
- **Language** Discuss with a partner narration and narrator's point of view.

TEXT COMPLEXITY

Quantitative Measures	Bronx Masquerade	Lexile: 710L
Qualitative Measures	**Ideas Presented** Multiple levels, subtle and implied meanings.	
	Structure Used Complex, deviates from chronological or sequential.	
	Language Used More figurative or ironic language, inference demanded.	
	Knowledge Required More complex theme of self-identity with cultural demands.	

RESOURCES

- Unit 5 Response Log

- Selection Audio

- Close Read Screencasts:
  Modeled Discussions

- Reading Studio:
  Notice & Note

- Writing Studio:
  Writing Narratives

- Speaking and Listening Studio:
  Giving a Presentation

- Vocabulary Studio:
  Using Context Clues

- Grammar Studio: Module 11:
  Using Modifiers Correctly

- "Bronx Masquerade" Selection Test

SUMMARIES

English

Different characters who are classmates speak in their own distinctive first-person narrative monologues about both how they are perceived by other students as well as how they see themselves. They discuss their roles in the arts and sports and a nonlinear plot follows their interactions. The author stresses the importance of resisting stereotypes and the value of self-discovery and expression.

Spanish

Diferentes personajes, que son compañeros de clase, hablan en sus propios monólogos narrativos en primera persona sobre cómo los perciben los otros estudiantes y cómo se ven a sí mismos. Discuten sus papeles en las artes y deportes mientras una trama no lineal sigue sus interacciones. El autor enfatiza la importancia de resistir los estereotipos y el valor del autodescubrimiento y la autoexpresión.

SMALL-GROUP OPTIONS

Have students work in small groups to read and discuss the selection.

Three-Minute Review

- While reading a passage, lecturing, or in the middle of a discussion, declare a pause in the action.
- Set a timer to three minutes.
- Have students read back over material already covered or look through their notes. They can also write questions to clarify what they have learned.
- After the time is up, ask students to report what they have learned in their review. Encourage students to discuss the information reported and ask clarifying questions.

Jigsaw with Experts

- Divide the passage up into smaller parts or sections.
- Assign small groups of students to read and take notes on a given section.
- The ask groups to discuss and become "experts" on this segment of the text.
- Have each group send one representative to a composite group, which then discusses the whole work, with each representative serving as the expert on his or her section.

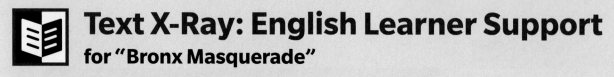

Text X-Ray: English Learner Support
for "Bronx Masquerade"

Use the Text X-Ray and the supports and scaffolds in the Teacher's Edition to help guide students at different proficiency levels through the selection.

INTRODUCE THE SELECTION
DISCUSS TEENS' PURSUIT OF IDENTITY

In this lesson, students will discuss the effects of peer expectations on teens and why these expectations are relevant to the lives of the characters in the selection. Explain that the characters in the selection are forming their adult personalities. Their attitudes toward their schoolwork and their talents aid in defining them. Discuss how the young adults in this selection:

- form opinions of others based on appearance.
- search for ways to disguise, validate, and express their talents.
- look for ways to distinguish themselves among their peers.

Explain to students that members of a school's basketball team often hold a prominent social status, whereas those with artistic pursuits sometimes are considered difficult to understand generally by their teen peers. Students should be aware that social roles have a strong effect on teens, who seek their true identity as they pursue a social identity. Appearance, attitude, and the groups they join all play a part in this pursuit.

CULTURAL REFERENCES

The following words and phrases may be unfamiliar to students:

- *Jolly Green Giant* (paragraph 4): a cartoon giant from an advertisement
- *Jump Shot* (paragraph 13): the term used in basketball for a movement in which the player shoots the ball while jumping. It is used here as a character's nickname.
- *gangsta in sheep's clothing* (paragraph 15) a slang term for a criminal, or gangster, who pretends to obey the law
- *Langston Hughes, Claude McCay* (paragraph 18): poets from the Harlem Renaissance
- *The Panther & the Lash* (paragraph 19): a book by Hughes

LISTENING

Understand Context Through Narrative

Explain that the story is narrated from a first-person point of view. Tell students that the context, or situation around the events and feelings, are from the narrator. First-person narrative can be used to give the reader a sense of closeness to the character.

Have students listen as you read aloud paragraphs 4–5. Use the following supports with students at varying proficiency levels:

- Tell students you will ask some questions about what they just heard. Model that they should give a thumbs up if the answer is yes, and a thumbs down for no. For example, ask: *Is Diondra angry at herself? (no) Does she think others don't know her? (yes)* **SUBSTANTIAL**
- Have students identify in paragraph 4 what Diondra knows about herself. (*I am an artist.*) Ask: *What does Diondra want to show others about herself?* **MODERATE**
- After listening to the excerpt read aloud, ask students to work in pairs to compare how Diondra sees herself and how she says other students see her. **LIGHT**

SPEAKING

Discuss Narration and Point of View

Have students discuss the author's device of telling the story from the point of view of three different narrators. The narrators reveal information from the first person, which means they tell about their own experiences and feelings.

Use the following supports with students at varying proficiency levels:

- Display and read aloud this sentence: *Each part of the story is told by a different narrator. The narrator tells only what the narrator thinks and feels.* Have students say it aloud back to you and then practice saying it to a partner. **SUBSTANTIAL**
- To help students express their ideas about first-person narration in the article, display the following sentence frame: *First-person is one way the author helps you understand what the _____ (narrator) feels about _____ (characters and events).* **MODERATE**
- Have students discuss with a partner how a first-person narrator helps you to understand the setting of the story. Ask: *How would you describe Devon's feelings about how basketball fits into his life?* **LIGHT**

READING

Use Informal Language

Tell students that authors choose how a character speaks to reveal something about that character's personality and relationship to others.

Work with students to read paragraphs 10–12. Use the following supports with students at varying proficiency levels:

- Tell students that you want them to think about the kind of person Tyrone is. Model that they should give a thumbs up if the answer is *yes,* and a thumbs down for *no.* For example, ask: *Do you think Tyrone is a funny guy? Do you think he is mean? Why or why not?* **SUBSTANTIAL**
- Guide students to discuss Tyrone's relationship to Diondra. Ask: *How does Tyrone describe Diondra reading her poem aloud? What does Tyrone say to Diondra to make her smile?* Accept single words or phrases. **MODERATE**
- Have students discuss Tyrone's feelings for Diondra. Ask: *Do you think Tyrone's comment was intended to make Diondra smile? If Tyrone had spoken to Diondra more formally, do you think she would have smiled?* **LIGHT**

WRITING

Write a Poem

Work with students to read the writing assignment on p. 349.

Use the following supports with students at varying proficiency levels:

- Help students form a statement that uses simple language that could be used in a poem. For example, ask: *What is a word that has something to do with happiness?* Use this frame: *_____ makes me happy. I like to _____.* **SUBSTANTIAL**
- Have students think of words that describe things that make them happy Ask: *Can you tell me what makes you happy? Can you make two sentences about these things?* Fill in these frames: *I'm happy when I_____. The best thing is _____.* **MODERATE**
- Remind students that a poem uses words to observe something clever or interesting about its subject. Ask: *What can you say about your favorite activity that is unlike other things that have been said about it?* **LIGHT**

Connect to the
ESSENTIAL QUESTION

In *Bronx Masquerade* different teenagers try to cope with how others try to define who they are based on how they look, think, or act without taking the time to know and understand them as a person. Their hope is to control that process and define themselves as adults.

from

BRONX MASQUERADE

Novel by **Nikki Grimes**

? ESSENTIAL QUESTION:

How do your teenage years prepare you for adulthood?

LEARNING MINDSET

Grit Remind students that if something seems hard to understand, continued efforts to make sense of it will work eventually. To train a muscle to lift a heavy weight requires repeated efforts. The same is true of deeper thinking. Repeated efforts to understand ideas will produce results.

QUICK START

Have you ever taken part in or attended a poetry reading? Discuss with your group what you do or do not like about reading, writing, or listening to poetry.

ANALYZE STRUCTURE

In a novel, **structure** involves the writer's arrangement of plot elements to tell a story. A **linear plot structure** tells the story in chronological order, following one or more protagonists, or main characters, as they deal with conflict. Some realistic fiction uses a **non-linear plot structure** in which the narrative jumps back and forth in time, using multiple protagonists, flashbacks, foreshadowing, parallel plot structures, or subplots. *Bronx Masquerade* has a non-linear plot structure and multiple first-person narrators. It includes both poetry and prose. The narration proceeds along parallel lines, with some time jumps. As you read, notice how each narrator provides his or her unique point of view.

ANALYZE CHARACTERIZATION

The way a writer creates and develops characters is known as **characterization.** In *Bronx Masquerade*, the school setting influences the characters' values and beliefs and has an important effect on their growth and development. The characters are encouraged to see and understand one another in new ways and to examine their own goals and aspirations.

To understand the characters' conflicts, challenges, and goals, pay attention to the clues the author provides about them. Here are some examples from *Bronx Masquerade*.

GENRE ELEMENTS: NOVEL

- is a long work of fiction
- has a plot, or series of events, centered on a conflict that characters try to solve
- has a setting, or time and place of the action, that may affect the characters
- depicts characters who develop and change over time
- develops one or more themes, or messages about life

CHARACTER CLUES	EXAMPLE
A character's own thoughts, speech, and actions	I refuse to give them new reasons to laugh at me. The Jolly Green Giant jokes are bad enough.
Thoughts, speech, and actions of other characters	Talk about nervous! Diondra's hands were shaking the whole time she was holding that poem. She sure spooks easy for somebody so tall. "Yo!" I said. "Take a deep breath. Ain't nobody going to hurt you here."
Description of a character's physical appearance	I've got good height and good hands, and that's a fact.

As you read *Bronx Masquerade*, think about ways in which the author uses characterization to convey meaning.

QUICK START

If students have not had the experience of a poetry reading, select some famous poetry appropriate to their age group and read it aloud. Ask for volunteers to share their reactions to the poem. Explain to students that they may also have experienced poetry in song lyrics. Ask students to share lyrics from a song that speaks to who they are as a person, and discuss the different reactions to the lyrics shared.

ANALYZE STRUCTURE

Help students break down the terms *linear* and *nonlinear* by using a timeline that they will fill in with the events of their day since they woke up. Note that this would form a linear plot and jot down some sample entries such as "eat breakfast" or "wait for bus." Then, create a nonlinear plot line in which these events are presented outside of the order in which they occurred in their day. Have them note how a nonlinear plot brings out things that happened in the future as well as the plot. Explain that this affects the reader's appreciation of what is happening at any given time in the story.

ANALYZE CHARACTERIZATION

Point out that authors provide details about their characters as a way of describing them. Stress that good fiction "shows not tells." Readers make their own decisions about who characters are based on details provided by the author. Some character clues are:

- Thoughts, speech, and actions are indicators of personality.
- Physical appearance also informs readers.

 ENGLISH LEARNER SUPPORT

Understand Directionality   Reinforce the directionality of English by reviewing how to read the Analyze Characterization chart. Explain that each column heading applies to the text in all the rows beneath it. To read the chart, students should begin at the top left. The top row, left column introduces the first character clue—a character's thoughts, speech, and actions. Students should track to the right to see the example of a character's thoughts. Then they should move on to the middle row, left column. Ask a volunteer to trace with a finger the order that a reader would read the information in the chart. **SUBSTANTIAL/MODERATE**

TEACH

CRITICAL VOCABULARY

Encourage students to refer back to the definition of words provided in the text.

Answers:

1. *confide*
2. *snicker*
3. *tirade*
4. *hunker*

LANGUAGE CONVENTIONS

Have students identify the spelling differences for comparative and superlative forms of modifiers. Remind students that some modifiers like *good* (*better* and *best*) undergo spelling changes for comparative and superlative forms. **LIGHT**

 ## ANNOTATION MODEL

Point out to students that first-person narration not only tells readers something about the world of the narrator and the people she or he is discussing but that it also gives us information about the narrator themselves, such as an experience that shaped how he or she thinks and feels.

CRITICAL VOCABULARY

| tirade | hunker | snicker | confide |

To see how many Critical Vocabulary words you already know, use them to complete the sentences.

1. When you _____ in a trusted friend, he or she can often help you understand how to deal with problems.

2. When I finished reading my poem, I was afraid that instead of applause, I would hear a _____ coming from the audience.

3. When Coach caught us making fun of the other team, she launched into a long _____ about sportsmanship.

4. If you want to be successful at something, you need to _____ down and work at it.

LANGUAGE CONVENTIONS

Modifiers Adjectives and adverbs are **modifiers** that can be used to show comparisons. Modifiers have **comparative** and **superlative** forms. The **comparative form** is used to compare two things, groups, or actions. The **superlative form** is used to compare more than two things, groups, or actions. Study these examples from *Bronx Masquerade*.

Comparative: "It's not much <u>better</u> at home."

Superlative: "I hate always being the <u>tallest</u> girl in school."

As you read, note how Nikki Grimes uses modifiers to show comparisons.

ANNOTATION MODEL   **NOTICE & NOTE**

As you read *Bronx Masquerade*, note how the author uses different first-person points of view to reveal characters' conflicts, goals, relationships, and values. Also note your observations about characters, events, and setting. In the model, you can see one reader's notes about *Bronx Masquerade*.

> 1   <u>If only I was as bold as Raul</u>. The other day, he left one of his paintings out on Mr. Ward's desk where anybody could see it. Which was the point. He sometimes works at Mr. Ward's desk during lunch. The wet paintbrushes sticking up out of the jar are always a sign that he's been at it again. <u>So of course, anybody who glances over in that direction will be tempted to stop by and look.</u>

Diondra admires Raul's confidence. Is she jealous of his artistic talent?

 ## ENGLISH LEARNER SUPPORT

Comparative and Superlative Forms in Spanish

Point out that modifiers in Spanish form their comparative and superlative forms in much the same way they do in English. Guide students to see that in Spanish, *más* ("more") is the comparative, and rather than add the suffix –*er*, the definite article *el* ("the") is added to the modifier to create the superlative and *el más*. Point out that this is similar to certain modifiers in English, which use *more* for the comparative and *most* for the superlative.
SUBSTANTIAL/MODERATE

BACKGROUND

Nikki Grimes (b. 1950) was born in Harlem and spent some of her younger years in foster homes. At age 13, she gave her first public poetry reading at a local library named after the poet Countee Cullen. She was already steeped in the works of Cullen and other black poets of the era known as the Harlem Renaissance. These poets, she says, have been the primary influences in her work. Grimes has written prose and poetry for adults, children, and young adults, winning many honors and awards for her work.

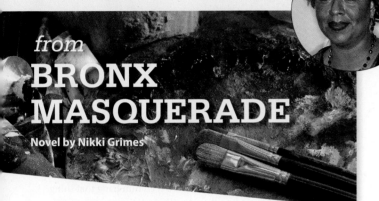

from
BRONX MASQUERADE

Novel by Nikki Grimes

SETTING A PURPOSE

As you read, pay attention to ways in which the novel's setting influences the characters.

Diondra Jordan

1   If only I was as bold as Raul. The other day, he left one of his paintings out on Mr. Ward's desk where anybody could see it. Which was the point. He sometimes works at Mr. Ward's desk during lunch. The wet paintbrushes sticking up out of the jar are always a sign that he's been at it again. So of course, anybody who glances over in that direction will be tempted to stop by and look.

2   This particular painting was rough, but anyone could tell it was Raul. A self-portrait. He'll probably hang it in class. Back in September, Mr. Ward covered two of the classroom walls with black construction paper and then scattered paper frames up and down the walls, each one a different size and color. Now half the room looks sort of like an art gallery, which was the idea. We're supposed to use the paper frames for our work. Whether we put up poems or photographs or even paintings is up to us, so

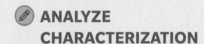

Notice & Note

Use the side margins to notice and note signposts in the text.

ANALYZE CHARACTERIZATION

Annotate: Mark the words and phrases in paragraphs 1–2 that suggest Diondra's view of Raul.

Infer: What is Diondra's opinion of Raul?

BACKGROUND

After reading Nikki Grimes, ask students what they know about the Harlem Renaissance and the poet Countee Cullen. Elicit from the students any expectations they may have as readers approaching a selection from a novel written by a poet. Ask what kind of language might they expect from her.

SETTING A PURPOSE

Have students discuss ways setting has had effects on other characters they know from literature. Have students consider how characters have to cope or make the most of their surroundings.

ANALYZE CHARACTERIZATION

Work with the class to identify **character clues** that reveal who Diondra and Raul are as characters. Go through Diondra's thoughts and Raul's actions and words that she describes, and determine what the author wants her readers to know about her characters. (***Answer:*** *Diondra admires Raul's talent, admitting that his self-portrait is good. But she wishes she had his self-confidence and felt secure enough to show her artwork.*)

ENGLISH LEARNER SUPPORT

Use Prereading Supports   Point out that the word *character* has two meanings. Explain that either definition could be used for discussion about story, and then model the use of each (Raul is a character, or a person, in the story. But the chart will list details about Raul's character, or personality.) Create a chart similar to the one used on p. 337 but focus on Raul and what we know about this character from this page. Model defining Raul's character from what we read on the page that Diondra narrates:

I see that Raul is bold – I will write that as a clue to his character and an example in the chart. I also see that criticism and likes to have just his way. I will enter these in the chart as well.   **LIGHT**

TEACH

ANALYZE CHARACTERIZATION

Go through paragraphs 3 and 4 and as students identify details that give you clues to Diondra's **character,** have volunteers suggest what each of these statements tells you about her and why the author included them. (**Answer:** *Diondra's father and her schoolmates expect her to be a good basketball player because she's tall. But she's not a good player and she feels that her father, whose approval she craves, is disappointed in her. He does not like her art, and no one at home "ever mentions it," so she puts no value on it. Her schoolmates already make jokes about her height, and she's afraid if they knew about her art, they would laugh at it.*)

tirade
(tī´rād) *n.* A *tirade* is a long, angry speech.

ANALYZE CHARACTERIZATION

Annotate: Mark details in paragraphs 3–4 that help you understand Diondra's character.

Interpret: Why doesn't Diondra want her schoolmates to know about the art she creates?

long as the work is ours and we can tie it in with our study of the Harlem Renaissance.[1] I guess Raul's self-portrait fits, since we've been talking a lot about identity. He'll probably put it up next to his poem. You should have seen him hang that thing. You'd think he was handling a million-dollar masterpiece the way he took his time placing it just so. If you look close, you can see the smudges where he erased a word or two and rewrote it. Mr. Ward must be in shock. He can never get Raul to rewrite a lick of homework or anything else. And don't even talk to him about checking his spelling! He'll launch into a **tirade** on you in a minute. "What?" he'll snap. "You think Puerto Ricans can't spell?" Forget it. Anyway, I dare you to find one misspelled word in that poem of his! Maybe it's a visual thing. Maybe he wants his poem to look as good as his self-portrait. And it is good.

3   I've never tried doing a self-portrait, but why not? I could maybe do one in charcoal. I like drawing faces in charcoal. I've been drawing since I can't remember when. Not that anyone here knows that, except Tanisha, and she found out by accident when she came to my house to study once and saw a couple of drawings hanging in my room. Mom loves my watercolors and she hung one in the living room, but it isn't signed. Nobody

---

[1] **Harlem Renaissance:** Between the end of World War I and the 1930s, black writers, artists, scholars, and musicians fled the repression of the Jim Crow South and moved to Harlem in New York City. The influential literary and cultural movement that began there is known as the Harlem Renaissance.

CRITICAL VOCABULARY

tirade: The author uses the word *tirade* to add emphasis to the lines she has Raul saying. It could be read as a simple question but she's suggesting that he would say a lot more and be very angry or excited if anyone challenged his work.

ASK STUDENTS to discuss whether they know someone like Raul who doesn't take criticism very well. Ask them to try to explain why someone like Raul acts this way. (*He always has to be right because he's unable to accept helpful criticism of his work.*)

ever mentions it, especially not my father. He's not too wild about my art. Mostly, he's disappointed, first off that I wasn't born a boy, and second that I won't play ball like one. I'm six feet tall, almost as tall as he, and he figures the height is wasted on me since I don't share his dreams of me going to the WNBA. I keep telling him not to hold his breath.

4   I hate always being the tallest girl in school. Everybody expects me to play basketball, so they pick me for their team, throw me the ball, and wait for me to shoot. Big mistake. I fumble it every time. Then they have the nerve to get mad at me, like I did it on purpose! But basketball is not my game. I have no game. I'm an artist, like Raul. The difference is, I don't tell anybody. I refuse to give them new reasons to laugh at me. The Jolly Green Giant jokes are bad enough.

5   Yeah, it's definitely time to try a self-portrait. I think I'll paint myself in front of an easel. With a basketball jersey sticking up out of the trash. Then I could hang it in Mr. Ward's class. See if anybody notices.

LANGUAGE CONVENTIONS

Annotate: Mark the superlative modifier in paragraph 4 that shows a comparison.

Analyze: How does the modifier help explain why Diondra resents the expectations people have of her?

APPLYING ACADEMIC VOCABULARY

☑ **debate**   ☐ **deduce**   ☑ **license**   ☐ **sufficient**   ☐ **trend**

Write and Discuss Have students turn to a partner to discuss the following questions. Guide students to include the Academic Vocabulary words *debate* and *license* in their responses. Ask volunteers to share their responses with the class.

- What would be involved in a **debate** between two groups discussing a serious issue they face?

- What types of things would someone need a **license** to do correctly and safely?

LANGUAGE CONVENTIONS

After students identify the **superlative modifier** discuss with students how she chooses to describe herself as *the tallest girl in the school* relative to the height of other girls. Have students note that because of her height, people expect her to be a good basketball player and she is not. (**Answer:** *The superlative modifier "tallest" indicates that no one else in her class is as tall as she is. People often stereotype others based on appearance, and Diondra feels that it's unfair of people to expect her to be good at basketball just because of her height.*)

■ English Learner Support

Visual Support Create visual demonstrations of modifiers like *tall*. Have students of various heights stand beside each other and form *taller* and *tallest*. Repeat with objects in the room for *big, bigger, biggest* or *new, newer, newest*. Ask students to suggest other adjectives from the page or ones of their own choosing and give the various forms. (*mad, madder, maddest*) **SUBSTANTIAL/MODERATE**

For **listening support** for students at varying proficiency levels, see the **Text X-Ray** on page 338C.

TEACH

ANALYZE STRUCTURE

Have students discuss how **repetition** with subtle variations from line to line places emphasis on those variations. Point out how the phrase begins with "would you laugh" and ends with "out loud," "still laugh," "at me," and "then" from line to line. Note how the reader is forced to consider the different conditions that relate to the repeated "If."

(**Answer:** *The repetition of the word If emphasizes Diondra's hesitancy about expressing her true self. The repetition of the words "would you" shows Diondra wonders about what other people think.*)

■ English Learner Support

Narrate and Describe Have students mimic the same structure used in each stanza of this poem. Students can start with "If" then add something they would do, and then conclude with "would you" and then describe a reaction. Students should express their feelings about something they always wanted to do. **MODERATE**

 For **speaking support** for students at varying proficiency levels, see the **Text X-Ray** on page 338D.

ANALYZE CHARACTERIZATION

Point out that Tyrone only mentions one thing he actually did in this scene ("I only had to tell one of them to loosen up.") But have students point out all of his opinions, and have them discuss how his opinions tell you something about who he is.

(**Answer:** *Tyrone's comment that Diondra "sure spooks easy for someone so tall" confirms that Diondra is correct in feeling that people have certain expectations about her because of her height. Diondra is nervous because she is reading her poem "If" aloud for the class.*)

For **reading support** for students at varying proficiency levels, see the **Text X-Ray** on page 338D.

 NOTICE & NOTE

ANALYZE STRUCTURE
Annotate: Mark the repeated words and phrases in the poem.
Analyze: How does repetition in the poem emphasize the feelings Diondra described about poetry and art as a narrator?

OPEN MIKE

[If]

By Diondra Jordan

6 [*If*]*I stood on tiptoe*
reached up and sculpted
mountains from clouds
would you laugh out loud?

7 [*If*]*I dipped my brush in starlight*
painted a ribbon of night
on your windowsill
would you still laugh?

8 [*If*]*I drew you adrift*
in a pen and ink sea
in a raging storm
would you laugh at me?

9 [*If*]*I planted watercolor roses*
in your garden
would you laugh then?
Or would you breathe deep
to sample their scent?
I wonder.

Tyrone

ANALYZE CHARACTERIZATION
Annotate: Mark the words and phrases that show what Tyrone thinks about the readers.
Draw Conclusions: What do Tyrone's comments about Diondra and the other readers reveal about his personality?

10 If the sista read any faster, I'd be looking for her Supergirl cape. Talk about nervous! Diondra's hands were shaking the whole time she was holding that poem. She sure spooks easy for somebody so tall.

11 "Yo!" I said. "Take a deep breath. Ain't nobody going to hurt you here." She smiled a little and tried to slow down. But I swear that girl burned rubber getting back to her seat when she was through. I guess she's not exactly used to the limelight.

12 She's got plenty of company. Four more kids read their poetry for the first time today. They were shaking in their boots, but it was all good. I only had to tell one of them to loosen up. Guess you could call that progress!

WHEN STUDENTS STRUGGLE . . .

KWL 2.0 Create a chart for students to use for both a prereading and postreading exercise when approaching the poem. Use the following headings:

What Do I Know?	What Do I Want to Know?	What Answers Did I Learn?	What Did I Learn That's New?

 For additional support, go to the **Reading Studio** and assign the following Level Up tutorial: **Making Predictions.**

NOTICE & NOTE

Devon Hope

13 Jump Shot. What kind of name is that? Not mine, but try telling that to the brothers at school. That's all they ever call me.

14 You'd think it was written somewhere. Tall guys must be jocks. No. Make that tall *people,* 'cause Diondra's got the same problem. Everybody expects her to shoot hoops. The difference is, she's got no talent in that direction. Ask me, she's got no business playing b-ball. That's my game.

15 I've got good height and good hands, and that's a fact. But what about the rest of me? Forget who I really am, who I really want to be. The law is be cool, be tough, play ball, and use books for weight training—not reading. Otherwise, everybody gives you grief. Don't ask me why I care, especially when the grief is coming from a punk like Wesley. Judging from the company he keeps, he's a gangsta in sheep's clothing. I don't even know why he and Tyrone bother coming to school. It's clear they don't take it seriously, although maybe they're starting to. That's according to Sterling, who believes in praying for everybody and giving them the benefit of the doubt. I love the preacher-man, but I think he may be giving these brothers too much credit. Anyway, when I hang around after school and any of the guys ask me: "Yo, Devon, where you going?" I tell them I'm heading for the gym to meet Coach and work on my layup. Then once they're out the door, I cut upstairs to the library to sneak a read.

ANALYZE STRUCTURE

Annotate: Mark thoughts and ideas Devon expresses in paragraphs 13–15 that are similar to those that Diondra expresses.

Analyze: How is Devon's comparison of his situation with Diondra's an example of parallel plot structure?

Bronx Masquerade 345

IMPROVE READING FLUENCY

Targeted Passage Have students work with partners to read Diondra's poem "If" on p. 344.

Have partners take turns performing echo readings of each line. Have students focus on:

- the pacing and emphasis of the *if* lines
- the emphasis on the use of rhyming in the last words of the lines
- the colorful expression of her emotion and questioning

 Go to the **Reading Studio** for additional support in developing fluency.

TEACH

ANALYZE STRUCTURE

As students point out the parallel elements of construction, have them also determine the nonlinear structure of Devon's thoughts and comments. Have students discuss when the events occurred that he mentions, such as the afterschool incident when he sneaks away to the library. (**Answer:** *Like Diondra, Devon is struggling with issues of identity and self-image. He, too, is tall and plays basketball. Although he enjoys basketball and is good at it, he hides his real passion because his friends would give tease him if they knew he loved poetry.*)

TEACH

ANALYZE CHARACTERIZATION

To appreciate the effects of the **setting** in this scene, have students discuss how Janelle and Devon would speak to each other if they were not in the library and were in the gym or the hall instead. Encourage students to see how their thoughts, words, and actions are affected by their surroundings. (**Answer:** *Devon reveals that he enjoys reading poetry on his own, but that he still needs the excuse of having homework to explain that he carries his poetry books around. His experience in the library leaves him thinking that it may be time to show his true self.*)

AHA MOMENT

Remind students that the **Aha Moment** is a signpost that shows when a character comes to a realization about something important. Discuss what Devon has learned about Janelle and what change in behavior this realization would cause in the way he relates to her in the future. (**Answer:** *Knowing that there are others, like Janelle, who share his interests will give Devon the courage and confidence to be himself.*)

CRITICAL VOCABULARY

hunker: The author wants readers to see the image of this tall, lanky basketball player hunched down around a book.

ASK STUDENTS what effect this image has on the reader. (*It shows he is just like anyone else.*)

snicker: The author doesn't use the word *laughs* because there is something mocking and embarrassing in the meaning of the word *snicker*.

ASK STUDENTS to describe the difference between a laugh and a snicker. (*Snickers are more hidden   and mocking.*)

346   Unit 5

ANALYZE CHARACTERIZATION

Annotate: Mark details about setting in paragraph 19.

Infer: What do the descriptions of the library and the books of poetry reveal about Devon's character?

hunker

(hŭng´kər) *v.* To *hunker* down means to stay in a place and focus on a task for a period of time.

snicker

(snĭk´ər) *n.* A *snicker* is a superior, partially suppressed laugh.

AHA MOMENT

Notice & Note: In paragraphs 19–20, mark words and phrases that show a change in Devon's attitude.

Predict: How might this realization change things for Devon?

---

16   It's not much better at home. My older brother's always after me to hit the streets with him, calls me a girly man for loving books and jazz.

17   Don't get me wrong. B-ball is all right. Girls like you, for one thing. But <u>it's not *you* they like. It's Mr. Basketball. And if that's not who you are inside, then it's not you they're liking.</u> So what's the point? Still, I don't mind playing, just not all the time.

18   This year is looking better. My English teacher has got us studying the Harlem Renaissance, which means we have to read a lot of poetry. That suits me just fine, gives me a reason to drag around my beat-up volumes of Langston Hughes and Claude McKay. Whenever anybody bugs me about it, all I have to say is "Homework." Even so, I'd rather the brothers not catch me with my head in a book.

19   The other day, I duck into the library, snare a corner table, and **hunker** down with *3000 Years of Black Poetry*. Raynard sees me, but it's not like he's going to tell anybody. He hardly speaks, and he never hangs with any of the brothers I know. So I breathe easy. I'm sure no one else has spotted me until a head pops up from behind the stacks. It's Janelle Battle from my English class. I freeze and wait for the **snickers** I'm used to. Wait for her to say something like: "What? Coach got you *reading* now? Afraid you're gonna flunk out and drop off the team?" But all she does is smile and wave. Like it's no big deal for me to be in a library reading. Like I have a right to be there if I want. Then she pads over, slips a copy of *The Panther & the Lash* on my table, and walks away without saying a word. It's one of my favorite books by Langston Hughes. How could she know? Seems like she's noticed me in the library more often than I thought.

20   Janelle is all right. So what if she's a little plump? At least when you turn the light on upstairs, somebody's at home. <u>She's smart, and she doesn't try hiding it. Which gets me thinking. Maybe it's time I quit sneaking in and out of the library</u> like some thief. Maybe it's time I just started being who I am.

346   Unit 5

CLOSE READ SCREENCAST

Modeled Discussion   Have students click the *Close Read* icon in their eBook to access a screencast in which readers discuss and annotate paragraph 19, a passage from the section where Devon Hope speaks.

As a class, view and discuss the video. Then have students pair up to do an independent close read of paragraphs 19–20. Students can record their answers on the Close Read Practice PDF.

   Close Read Practice PDF

OPEN MIKE
Bronx Masquerade
By Devon Hope

21 *I woke up this morning*
exhausted from hiding
the me of me
*so I stand here **confiding***
there's more to Devon
than jump shot and rim.
I'm more than tall
and lengthy of limb.
I dare you to peep
behind these eyes,
discover the poet
in tough-guy disguise.
Don't call me Jump Shot.
My name is Surprise.

NOTICE & NOTE

confide
(kən-fīd′) *v.* To *confide* means to share private or secret information.

CHECK YOUR UNDERSTANDING

Answer these questions before moving on to the **Analyze the Text** section on the following page.

1 Diondra secretly —

  A is excited to present her poem

  B is proud of her basketball skills

  C sees herself as an artist

  D enjoys being very tall

2 Devon secretly —

  F hates being tall

  G loves reading poetry

  H feels jealous of Wesley

  J wants to be friends with Tyrone

3 When Devon first sees Janelle Battle, he —

  A worries she will tease him

  B encourages her to read his poem

  C reminds her they are in a class together

  D feels relieved she does not recognize him

Bronx Masquerade 347

CHECK YOUR UNDERSTANDING

Have students answer the questions independently.

Answers:

  1. C

  2. G

  3. A

If they answer any questions incorrectly, have them reread the text to confirm their understanding. Then they may proceed to ANALYZE THE TEXT on p. 348.

CRITICAL VOCABULARY

confide: If someone is *confiding*, they are sharing a secret, yet the author has Devon confiding to himself.

ASK STUDENTS what effect this use of this word has on the reader. *(It shows that Devon is learning something about himself and he is telling himself something he has been reluctant to admit. He has been "hiding the me of me.")*

ENGLISH LEARNER SUPPORT

Oral Assessment Use the following questions to assess students' comprehension and speaking skills:

  1. What does Diondra keep a secret? *(She sees herself as an artist.)*

  2. What does Devon secretly keep a secret? *(He loves reading poetry.)*

  3. What does Devon feel when he first sees Janelle Battle? *(He fears that she will tease him about being in the library and wanting to read poetry rather than play basketball.)* **SUBSTANTIAL/MODERATE**

APPLY

ANALYZE THE TEXT

Possible answers:

1. **DOK 2:** *The setting of the school emphasizes that Diondra resents being stereotyped because of her physical traits and being teased for not living up to the expectations of her father and her schoolmates. Her plan to paint herself "in front of an easel with a basketball jersey sticking up out of the trash" suggests that she wants to face her fear of being laughed at and acknowledge that art—not basketball— is her passion.*

2. **DOK 4:** *Like its title, Diondra's poem "If" is tentative. She wants people to appreciate her paintings, but she's still afraid people will laugh at her efforts. Devon's poem, "Bronx Masquerade," shows that he has a more determined attitude and feels confident about letting people "discover the poet" behind this "tough-guy."*

3. **DOK 4:** *Unlike Diondra and Devon, Tyrone does not appear to be struggling with inner conflict. His speech pattern suggests that he cultivates a street-smart image. Devon uses the words punk and gangsta in describing Tyrone and his friends, yet his attempt to reassure Diondra and other students during their poetry readings suggests that beneath his image, he has sympathy for them.*

4. **DOK 4:** *The image of a masquerade is used in the title of the novel and Devon's poem. The title Bronx Masquerade suggests that hiding behind masks is a central theme in the novel. The three main characters are all hiding behind facades, or masks, an idea that is reinforced when Devon titles his poem "Bronx Masquerade." The image helps connect the different perspectives in the story.*

5. **DOK 4:** *The classroom project prompts students to think about and express their true identity. They realize they're not alone in wanting to drop their masks, and they're reassured by observing how others have the courage to express their true selves. Diondra admires Raul's work and it inspires her to follow her own artistic impulses. When Janelle shows that she understands his interest in poetry, Devon realizes that meeting the tough-guy expectations of "the brothers" may not be as important as following his own interests.*

RESEARCH

Point out to students that when researching the connection between poetry and health, it is best to stick to well-documented sites that use scientific principles rather than personal opinion or unverified statements.

Extend Tell students they should compare their research to their personal experiences writing poetry, determining how it made them feel.

 RESPOND

ANALYZE THE TEXT

Support your responses with evidence from the text. NOTEBOOK

1. **Evaluate** What do the various settings reveal about the characters? How do the settings influence the values and beliefs of the characters?

2. **Analyze** Reread Diondra's poem "If" and Devon's poem "Bronx Masquerade." What does the tone, or attitude, of each poem reveal about its writer's search for identity?

3. **Critique** What does Tyrone's perspective add to the plot development? Explain.

4. **Analyze** A masquerade is a costume party at which people wear masks. How does the author use the idea of a masquerade to pull together the different perspectives in the story?

5. **Notice & Note** What does the classroom project help Diondra and Devon realize about themselves and others in their struggle for self-expression? Cite examples to support your answer.

RESEARCH TIP
Be sure to assess the quality of any online sources you use. Personal websites may provide inaccurate or misleading information. The websites of museums, universities, and well-known encyclopedias are more likely to be reliable.

RESEARCH

Can writing to express your deepest feelings impact your physical and mental health? Research answers to the following questions about the relationship between expressive writing and health. Record what you learn in the chart.

QUESTION	ANSWER
How can expressive writing impact health?	*Expressive writing can have a positive impact on emotional and physical health.*
What are some specific possible effects of expressive writing?	*Possible benefits include improved sleep and immune function, relief of chronic disease symptoms, and reduced anxiety.*

Extend In *Bronx Masquerade*, the students who share their writing experience social benefits as well as emotional benefits. Discuss with your group how poetry readings can help create understanding and a sense of community.

⚙ LEARNING MINDSET

Questioning Remind students that the first part of appreciating what they are learning is to ask questions. The simple act of questioning will not only produce answers for what may confuse them, but the very act of formulating questions requires students to think about what they do understand and pinpoint what needs clarification.

CREATE AND PRESENT

Write a Poem Write a poem about identity or the search for identity that you might perform at a poetry reading.

❏ Review the poems in the story for inspiration, and decide on the message you want to convey in your own poem.

❏ Think about the form and tone that will best suit your message.

❏ Consider using repetition to emphasize the most important idea.

❏ Have a partner read your poem and give you feedback. Make revisions, if necessary.

Present a Poem Recite your poem aloud for the class.

❏ With a partner, rehearse reading your poem aloud.

❏ Decide whether you will accompany the words with movement or gestures.

❏ Present your poem to the class, using appropriate volume, phrasing, and expression.

RESPOND TO THE ESSENTIAL QUESTION

 How do your teenage years prepare you for adulthood?

Gather Information Review your annotations and notes on *Bronx Masquerade*. Then add relevant details to your Response Log. As you determine which information to include, think about:

• elements of *Bronx Masquerade* that make it realistic fiction
• how the story connects the perspectives of different characters
• the importance of resisting stereotypes and the value of self-expression

At the end of the unit, you may use your notes to help you write an argument.

 Go to the **Writing Studio** for more on writing a poem.

 Go to the **Speaking and Listening Studio** for help with presenting a poem.

ACADEMIC VOCABULARY

As you write and discuss what you learned from the selection, be sure to use the Academic Vocabulary words. Check off each of the words that you use.

❏ **debate**
❏ **deduce**
❏ **license**
❏ **sufficient**
❏ **trend**

CREATE AND PRESENT

Write a Poem Discuss with the class what a search for identity involves. Have students review the poems as a class or in small groups. Ask students to isolate parts of the poems that deal with searching for one's identity. Have volunteers point out the structures used by the student poets. Pair students to review and provide feedback on their own poems.

📖 For **writing support** for students at varying proficiency levels, see the **Text X-Ray** on page 338D.

Present a Poem Ask volunteers to provide examples of proper reading technique in front of the class. Others can also suggest movements or gestures that would enhance the presentation of their poem. Remind students to be kind listeners who will want the same respect when they read their poems.

RESPOND TO THE ESSENTIAL QUESTION

Allow time for students to add details from *Bronx Masquerade* to their Unit 5 Response Logs.

EL ENGLISH LEARNER SUPPORT

Write and Present a Poem Have students use sentence frames to write lines that examine identity. Help students by completing the first frame, using Think Alouds to portray your thought process. Then have students fill in the frames with their own words or phrases.

When I ___, the world feels like ___.

In my mind I see ___ but it is really ___.

If I look in the mirror I feel ___ and this makes me want to ___.

When I am older I want to ___ but first I have to ___. **SUBSTANTIAL/MODERATE**

APPLY

CRITICAL VOCABULARY

Remind students to read the sentence stem carefully and think about how to apply the meaning of the word in that context before completing each item.

VOCABULARY STRATEGY:
Use Context Clues

Remind students that context clues can appear before and after a word.

WORD BANK
tirade
hunker
snicker
confide

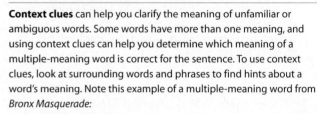
Go to the **Vocabulary Studio** for more on using context clues.

CRITICAL VOCABULARY

Practice and Apply Use your understanding of the Vocabulary words to complete each sentence.

1. A basketball fan might launch into a **tirade** if . . .

2. A serious writer hates to hear **snickers** from the audience during a poetry reading because . . .

3. If you **confide** in a trusted friend, you are . . .

4. When you **hunker** down with a good book, you are . . .

VOCABULARY STRATEGY: Use Context Clues

Context clues can help you clarify the meaning of unfamiliar or ambiguous words. Some words have more than one meaning, and using context clues can help you determine which meaning of a multiple-meaning word is correct for the sentence. To use context clues, look at surrounding words and phrases to find hints about a word's meaning. Note this example of a multiple-meaning word from *Bronx Masquerade*:

> So of course, anybody who glances over in that direction will be tempted to stop by and look.
> This particular painting was <u>rough</u>, but anyone could tell it was Raul. A self-portrait. He'll probably hang it in class.

The context clues help you understand that the narrator is referring to what the painting looks like, not how it feels. You can tell from the context that *rough* means "unpolished," not "coarse to the touch."

Practice and Apply Find the following words in paragraphs 2, 4, and 15 of *Bronx Masquerade*. Identify context clues to each word's meaning, and write your guessed definition in the chart. Then look up each word in a dictionary to check your definition.

WORD	CONTEXT CLUES	GUESSED DEFINITION
gallery	*Like an art gallery*	*Answers will vary.*
smudge	*Where he erased a word or two*	*Answers will vary.*
launch	*he'll launch into a tirade*	*Answers will vary.*
fumble	*Big mistake.*	*Answers will vary.*
credit	*he may be giving these brothers too much credit*	*Answers will vary.*

350   Unit 5

LANGUAGE CONVENTIONS: Modifiers

Modifiers are words or groups of words that change or limit the meanings of other words. Adjectives and adverbs are common modifiers. Modifiers can be used to compare two or more things. The form of a modifier shows the degree of comparison.

• The **comparative form** is used to compare two things, groups, or actions.

• The **superlative form** is used to compare more than two things, groups, or actions.

Regular forms of comparative modifiers are often preceded by the word "more" or "less" or end in -er. Superlative modifiers are often preceded by the word "most" or "least" or end in -est. There are also some irregular forms of comparative and superlative modifiers.

The chart shows some examples of each kind of modifier.

TYPE OF MODIFIER	EXAMPLE	COMPARATIVE FORM	SUPERLATIVE FORM
One syllable	tall fast	taller faster	tallest fastest
More than one syllable	graceful happy	more graceful happier	most graceful happiest
Irregular	good bad	better worse	best worst

Practice and Apply In their search for identity, the characters in *Bronx Masquerade* often compare themselves to others or to the expectations of others. Write a paragraph using the first-person point of view that describes the thoughts and feelings of a narrator. Use at least one comparative and one superlative modifier.

RESPOND

> ! Go to **Using Modifiers Correctly** in the **Grammar Studio** for more help.

LANGUAGE CONVENTIONS: Modifiers

Point out to students that modifiers change the meaning of other words. Review the two types of modifiers, *comparative* and *superlative*.

Write the following sentences on the board: *Janelle is smart. Diondra is smart*. Have students note that both women are smart but without a way to distinguish any difference between the two of them, you would either have to add "also" or use another modifier. Have students explain how to use a comparative or superlative suffix or a spelling change to show the difference between comparing only two things versus comparing many things. *(The addition of -er, or -est makes a distinction although for some adjectives a spelling change is required.)*

Have students go through the chart and make specific note of spelling changes and syllable counts to determine the use of *more* or *most* with certain words. Encourage students to listen to how an adjective like *serious* would sound with an -er ending, which is why it uses *more* or *most*.

Practice and Apply Help students identify the parts of *Bronx Masquerade* that demonstrate how characters compare themselves to others or the expectations of others. Remind students that comparative and superlative modifiers can take different forms.

 ENGLISH LEARNER SUPPORT

Language Differences Vietnamese students may struggle with the use of both definite and indefinite articles and may often use *one* for *a*, depending on the context. (*He is one teacher.*) These speakers may also struggle with gerunds or infinitive verb forms using –ing. (*Stop walk; I want go there.*) In Vietnamese, the subject may be omitted, particularly if it is a pronoun. *There is/are* may also not be used.

Arabic-speaking students may need particular review of using articles with days, months, places, or with idioms. They may omit *be* forms with verbs, and verbs may precede the subject.

ALL LEVELS

HANGING FIRE
Poem by Audre Lorde

SUMMER OF HIS FOURTEENTH YEAR
Poem by Gloria Amescua

GENRE ELEMENTS
FREE VERSE

Remind students that **poetry** is a condensed form of literature that uses sounds and imagery to create meaning and capture the mood of a moment in time. Explain that **free verse** is a poetic form that sounds like a person speaking. Point out that it may use sound devices such as rhythm and repetition but lacks the rigid structure of other forms and does not have regular pattern of rhyme. Free verse relies on imagery and figurative language to convey meaning and express a theme.

LEARNING OBJECTIVES

- Identify the elements of free verse poetry and evaluate their effect on meaning.
- Conduct research on the causes of teen mood swings and ways to cope with them.
- Freewrite in response to literature and personal experience.
- Collaborate with a group to present analysis of free verse poems.
- Analyze multiple points of view of a shared topic.
- **Language** Discuss connections between poems and personal connections to poems with a partner.

TEXT COMPLEXITY

Quantitative Measures	Hanging Fire/Summer of His Fourteenth Year		
Qualitative Measures	**Ideas Presented** Complex meanings.		
	Structures Used Free verse, no patterns of rhythm or rhyme.		
	Language Used Some figurative language and unconventional structures.		
	Knowledge Required Familiar and unfamiliar perspectives.		

Online Ed

RESOURCES

- Unit 5 Response Log
- Selection Audio
- Reading Studio: Making Inferences About Characters
- Writing Studio: Writing Narratives
- Speaking and Listening Studio: Giving a Presentation
- "Hanging Fire" and "Summer of His Fourteenth Year" Selection Tests

SUMMARIES

English

The poem "Hanging Fire" expresses the concerns of a teenage girl who feels isolated and overlooked by the adults in her life.

The poem "Summer of His Fourteenth Year" presents the perspective of the mother of a teenage boy as she witnesses his growing independence in everyday actions.

Spanish

El poema "El fuego que pende" expresa las preocupaciones de una adolescente que se siente aislada e ignorada por los adultos de su vida.

El poema "El verano de sus catorce años" presenta la perspectiva de la madre de un adolescente mientras es testigo de la creciente independencia en las acciones cotidianas de su hijo.

 ## SMALL-GROUP OPTIONS

Have students work in small groups to read and discuss the selection.

Think-Pair-Share

- After students have read and analyzed both poems, pose this question: *How are the perspectives of the teenagers and   adults different?*
- Have students think about the question individually and take notes.
- Then have pairs discuss their ideas about the question.
- Finally, ask pairs to share their responses with the class.

Double-Entry Journal

- Model how to draw a line down the middle of a sheet of paper to create two columns for notetaking. Add the heading "Quotes from the Text" on the left and "My Notes" on the right.
- Explain that students should record important or perplexing quotes from the text on the left.
- Tell them to write their interpretations, summaries, questions, and restatements of the quotes on the right side.
- Have partners compare and discuss their interpretations of the same quotations. Ask students to share their views with the class.

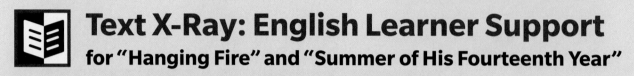

Text X-Ray: English Learner Support
for "Hanging Fire" and "Summer of His Fourteenth Year"

Use the Text X-Ray and the supports and scaffolds in the Teacher's Edition to help guide students at different proficiency levels through the selection.

INTRODUCE THE SELECTION
DISCUSS EMOTIONS

In this lesson, students will need to be able to discuss emotions. "Hanging Fire" presents the point of view of a teenage girl who feels overwhelmed by typical teen problems, while "Summer of His Fourteenth Year," told by a parent of a teenage son, shows what teenage struggles look like from the point of view of a concerned observer.

Create an emotion word wall to display words related to feelings and emotions. Add to the wall throughout the lesson as deeper, more complex emotions are discussed. Consider using a web formation to show the relationships of various words. Start by discussing the meaning of the following words and adding them to the wall:

- *happy*
- *sad*
- *angry*
- *afraid*
- *disappointed*

CULTURAL REFERENCES

Discuss the following words and phrases which, may be unfamiliar to students:

"Hanging Fire":

- *ashy* (line 7): having light discoloration from dry skin
- *my side of it* (line 25): my perspective or opinion
- *my marks* (line 27): grades or scores
- *braces* (line 30): sets of wires attached to teeth to make them straighter

"Summer of His Fourteenth Year":

- *Coke cans* (line 11): soda cans
- *cocoon* (line 15): protective enclosure
- *recess* (line 16): space that is set back
- *chores* (line 21): jobs

LISTENING

Analyze Pronouns

Draw students' attention to the pronouns in the first stanza of "Hanging Fire." Point out that the use of *I*, *me*, and *my* show that the author is the speaker, which is typical of the first-person point of view of many free verse poems. Have students listen as you read aloud the first stanza.

Use the following supports with students at varying proficiency levels:

- Tell students that you will ask questions about what you just read and they should show thumbs up for yes and thumbs down for no. *Is I the speaker of the poem?* (yes) Ask: *Is I momma?* (no) *Is the speaker 14 years old?* (yes) **SUBSTANTIAL**

- Have small groups count the number of times the words *I*, *my*, or *me* are used. (I: 3; my: 2; me: 1) Ask: *Who is 14 in the poem?* (the speaker) *What has betrayed the speaker?* (the speaker's skin) *Whose knees are ashy?* (the speaker's) **MODERATE**

- Ask students to complete this sentence frame: *Since you hear the words _____, _____, and _____ throughout the first stanza, you can guess that this poem shows the perspective of _____.* (I, me, my, the 14-year-old speaker) **LIGHT**

SPEAKING

Discuss Connections

Explain that connecting a text to other texts and to personal experiences helps a reader gain a deeper understanding and make inferences about the content of a text. Ask students to make connections between the two poems and to their personal experiences.

Work with students to read the first stanzas of "Hanging Fire" and "Summer of His Fourteenth Year." Use the following supports with students at varying proficiency levels:

- Point out that the speaker asks some questions in "Hanging Fire." Ask: *Which words or phrases signal the beginning of a question? (how, what) Do you think the questions show the speaker is scared, angry, or worried? (Responses will vary.) Do you ever ask yourself questions? (Answers will vary.)* **SUBSTANTIAL**
- Ask students to discuss how the speakers are alike and different. To help students discuss the speakers, display the following sentence frames: *Both speakers are talking about _____. The speaker in _____ is worried about _____ but the speaker in _____ is worried about _____.* **MODERATE**
- Pair students to discuss connections between the poems. Ask: *What do the poems have in common? (Both poems are about teens even though from different perspectives.)* **LIGHT**

READING

Identify Figurative Language

Explain that poets use figurative language to create images and associations that create layers of meaning. Draw students' attention to the phrase "my skin has betrayed me" in "Hanging Fire." Explain why this is an example of personification.

Work with students to read lines 15–18 of "Summer of His Fourteenth Year." Use the following supports with students at varying proficiency levels:

- Read aloud the phrase, "Wailing guitars weave a cocoon." Ask students to give a thumbs up if they have seen a guitar, and then a cocoon. Show photos if students are unfamiliar with the words *guitar* or *cocoon*. Ask: *Would you expect a guitar to make a cocoon? (no)* **SUBSTANTIAL**
- Ask students to identify figurative language. Ask: *What is an example of personification?* Supply sentence frames, such as: *An example of personification is _____ playing on a muted keyboard. It is personification because _____. (his teeming emotions; emotions cannot play a keyboard)* **MODERATE**
- Ask students to explain an example of figurative language. *("Wailing guitars weave a cocoon" means that he uses loud music to keep others out and to create a private space.)* **LIGHT**

WRITING

Write a Response

Explain that freewriting means writing freely about whatever comes to mind without stopping and thinking. Tell students that writers freewrite to connect their thoughts with the process of writing.

Use the following supports with students at varying proficiency levels:

- Ask students to draw a picture or graphic that captures the emotions in the two poems. Work with students to label the emotions in the image. Provide a word bank of emotions: *scared, angry, hurt, worried, confused, sad, happy, hopeful, joyful, relaxed.* **SUBSTANTIAL**
- Provide sentence frames to support student freewrites: *I like/dislike being a teenager because _____. I agree/disagree with the speaker in _____ because _____. I think the poem _____ showed _____ in teens _____.* **MODERATE**
- Ask students to describe what it feels like to be a teenager. **LIGHT**

Connect to the
ESSENTIAL QUESTION

Both "Hanging Fire" and "Summer of His Fourteenth Year" deal with the difficulties facing teenagers as they gain independence and prepare for adulthood.

COMPARE POEMS

Point out that the poems "Hanging Fire" and "Summer of His Fourteenth Year" both describe the changes and anxiety of the transition to adulthood but from different perspectives. The speaker in "Hanging Fire" feels the weight of her growing need to be self-reliant, while the speaker of "Summer of His Fourteenth Year" recognizes the need of her son to break away from her.

POEM
HANGING FIRE

by **Audre Lorde**
pages 355–357

COMPARE POEMS

The free verse poems you are about to read share the same topic. As you read, notice how each writer uses the elements of poetry to express the speaker's thoughts and feelings. After reading, you will collaborate with a small group on a final project.

ESSENTIAL QUESTION:

How do your teenage years prepare you for adulthood?

POEM
SUMMER OF HIS FOURTEENTH YEAR

by **Gloria Amescua**
pages 358–359

352　Unit 5

QUICK START

What pressures, emotions, and concerns make the teenage years challenging? Think about your own experience and write down your thoughts. Then share them with a partner or a small group.

ANALYZE FREE VERSE POETRY

Free verse is poetry that does not have regular patterns of rhythm or rhyme. The lines in free verse often flow more naturally than lines in rhymed, metrical poems; they may have a rhythm more like that of everyday speech. Although free verse does not have conventional meter, it may contain a variety of rhythmic and sound effects, such as repetition of syllables or words.

In free verse poetry, poets often create different effects by using a variety of line lengths and unexpected line breaks, playing with sense, grammar, and syntax. Line length is an essential element of the poem's meaning and rhythm. Lines may or may not break, or end, at the ends of sentences or grammatical units. A line break in the middle of a grammatical unit can create a meaningful pause or provide emphasis. Punctuation (such as dashes) or a lack of punctuation within or at the ends of sentences can help to convey the speaker's state of mind or emotions.

This chart summarizes some elements of free verse poetry:

ELEMENT	FREE VERSE	EFFECT
Meter	Lacks conventional meter	Flows like everyday speech
Line length	Uses a variety of line lengths; may follow no set pattern	Suggests pauses or emphasis; creates rhythm, drama, or other effects
Punctuation	May be omitted or used for emphasis	Omission of commas or periods suggests anxiety or fear; use of dashes provides emphasis

As you read "Hanging Fire" and "Summer of His Fourteenth Year," analyze how the poets use meter, line breaks, and punctuation to convey each speaker's feelings.

GENRE ELEMENTS: FREE VERSE

- like other poetic forms, uses imagery and figurative language to convey meaning and mood
- may use sound devices such as rhythm and repetition
- sounds like everyday speech, with no regular patterns of rhythm or rhyme
- expresses a theme, or a message about life
- includes a speaker who "talks" to the reader

QUICK START

After students share their thoughts about the challenges of the teen years, ask them to compare their lists to identify the most common concerns. Challenge them to state their analysis in a sentence explaining the teenage experience to adults.

ANALYZE FREE VERSE POETRY

Review the characteristics and elements of free verse poetry. Point out that free verse does not use a rhyme scheme or rigid meter like many of the poems they have heard, so it sounds more natural. Explain that free verse relies on imagery, metaphor, personification, and other literary elements to create meaning. Then, discuss how stanzas, line length, and punctuation can also be used in unexpected ways in free verse poetry. Ask students to think about how these elements could affect the meaning of the poem. Encourage students to pay attention to how the poet uses these elements as they read "Hanging Fire" and "Summer of My Fourteenth Year" and to note the effect on the poem.

■ English Learner Support

Analyze Free Verse Poetry Review the meanings of the literary elements mentioned and give examples using familiar texts: rhyme scheme, meter, imagery, metaphor, personification, stanzas, line length, and punctuation. Have students confirm understanding by having them paraphrase explanations of the literary elements. **LIGHT**

TEACH

MAKE INFERENCES

Make sure students understand that making inferences is a way of figuring out things that are not directly stated. Ask volunteers to provide examples of inferences they make, or provide one yourself, such as seeing someone laughing and inferring that he or she is happy. Then review the chart. Walk through the steps with students to make an inference about who the speaker of each poem is.

■ English Learner Support

Make Inferences Point out that the word *inference* is a noun that means "a logical guess," but the word *infer* is a verb that means "to make a logical guess." So inferring is an action, but an inference is the end result of that action. **LIGHT**

ANNOTATION MODEL

Review the definition of speaker. Emphasize that the speaker is not necessarily the poet, so students will need to make inferences to determine who is speaking. Encourage them to underline evidence in the text that will help them make inferences about the speaker. Remind students of other elements of free verse poetry discussed on p. 353, and encourage them to note punctuation and line breaks to evaluate their effect on meaning.

 GET READY

MAKE INFERENCES

Both "Hanging Fire" and "Summer of His Fourteenth Year" are poems about adolescence, but they offer starkly different points of view—in part because the speakers in the poems are quite different. In poetry, the **speaker** is the voice that "talks" to the reader and shares his or her point of view, similar to the narrator in a story. A poem's speaker may or may not be the poet.

Often readers must make an **inference,** or logical guess based on clues and their own knowledge and experience, in order to identify a poem's speaker. For example, text clues in "Hanging Fire" help readers figure out that the speaker is a teenager, and text clues in "Summer of His Fourteenth Year" help readers figure out that the speaker is an adult.

TEXT CLUES	WHAT YOU KNOW FROM EXPERIENCE	INFERENCE ABOUT THE SPEAKER
I am fourteen / and my skin has betrayed me / . . . and momma's in the bedroom / with the door closed. —from "Hanging Fire"	Many teens are dissatisfied with their appearance and feel they can't communicate with their parents.	a teen who feels unsettled and would like to be reassured by her mother
He tears at the seams / that hold us together / and sees in mother only ties to childhood —from "Summer of His Fourteenth Year"	Teens often challenge their parents as they begin to assert their independence.	a mother who is struggling with her son's growth into adulthood

As you read the two poems, think about what text-based inferences you can make about each speaker and her point of view.

ANNOTATION MODEL
NOTICE & NOTE

As you read each poem, you can mark details and make notes about the speaker in the side margin. The model shows one reader's notes about the first few lines of "Hanging Fire."

> I am fourteen
> and my skin has betrayed me
> <u>the boy I cannot live without</u>
> <u>still sucks his thumb</u>
> 5 in secret

I'm fourteen too, and my skin is breaking out.

This detail shows that the speaker feels more mature than the boy she likes.

BACKGROUND

Audre Lorde (1934–1992) was born in New York City and found early success as a poet. One of her poems was published in a popular magazine while she was still in high school. In addition to poetry, Lorde went on to write acclaimed essays and novels. She won many important awards for her writing and worked to support several social causes close to her heart. Toward the end of her life, Lorde took the African name Gamba Adisa, which is believed to mean "she who makes her meaning clear."

HANGING FIRE

Poem by Audre Lorde

PREPARE TO COMPARE

As you read the poem, look for details that help you understand the speaker's point of view.

I am fourteen
and my skin has betrayed me.
the boy I cannot live without
still sucks his thumb
5 in secret.
how come my knees are
always so ashy?
what if I die
before morning?
10 and momma's in the bedroom
with the door closed.

ANALYZE FREE VERSE POETRY
Annotate: Mark the first stanza with punctuation to show each separate thought.

Analyze: What effect does the poet create by omitting punctuation throughout the poem?

APPLYING ACADEMIC VOCABULARY

❑ debate   ☑ deduce   ❑ license   ☑ sufficient   ❑ trend

Think-Pair-Share Have partners answer and discuss the questions below. Encourage them to include the Academic Vocabulary words *deduce* and *sufficient* in their discussion. Ask volunteers to share their responses with the class.

- What can you **deduce** about being a teenager from reading this poem?
- Do you have **sufficient** details to identify the speaker or to infer what the speaker is feeling in "Hanging Fire"? Why or why not?

BACKGROUND

After students read the Background note, point out that Audre Lorde demonstrates pride in her cultural heritage by taking the African name Gamba Adisa. Discuss the meaning of the name and why it is fitting for a poet.

PREPARE TO COMPARE

Direct students to use the Prepare to Compare prompt to focus their reading.

ANALYZE FREE VERSE POETRY

Remind students that poets use elements like **punctuation** and **line length** to shape the flow and rhythm of a free verse poetry. Point out that sometimes poets use a lack of punctuation to shape the flow of thoughts. Discuss the challenge for the reader to identify separate thoughts when there is no punctuation. Ask students to think about and discuss why a poet would not clearly separate thoughts. (**Answer:** *The run-on stream-of-consciousness style conveys the speaker's anxiety and confusion.*)

■ English Learner Support

Analyze Free Verse Poetry Point out the **question words** in lines 6 and 8 (*how come* and *what if*). Explain that *how come* is an informal way of asking why. *What if* is used when asking what would happen in a specific situation. Draw a chart to show the definitions of and differences between *How/How come* and *What/What if*. Then explain that English questions usually begin with a question word and end with a question mark, but the rules do not apply in poetry. Ask students to identify the questions being asked and to write them in their notes. (*How come my knees are always so ashy? What if I die before morning?*) **SUBSTANTIAL/MODERATE**

 For **listening support** for students at varying proficiency levels, see the **Text X-Ray** on page 352C.

ENGLISH LEARNER SUPPORT

Inside/Outside Circles Encourage discussion by placing students in two concentric circles facing each other.

ASK STUDENTS to think about the speaker's complaints or concerns. Have students share with the person facing them one way they can relate to her complaints or understand her concerns. Then have the inner circle shift to the right to form new partners. Again, have students share an experience or something they know that helps them understand one of the speaker's complaints. Continue rotating until students are back to their original partner. **LIGHT**

For **speaking support** for students at varying proficiency levels, see the **Text X-Ray** on page 352D.

 MAKE INFERENCES

Review that the **speaker** in a poem is the voice that talks to readers. Note that the poem does not say directly who is speaking, but there are many clues about the speaker in the details. Read aloud lines 12–23. Point out the word *graduation* in line 15, and explain that it helps you infer the speaker is either in high school or college because you know those are times in life when someone would be thinking about graduation. Remind students to combine what they know with the details in the poem to make inferences about the speaker. (**Answer:** *Based on the evidence of complaints 1–5, the speaker seems overly dramatic and sees herself as persecuted and misunderstood. Complaints 6 and 7 reveal that she feels vulnerable and in need of her mother's support.*)

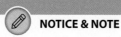 **NOTICE & NOTE**

I have to learn how to dance
in time for the next party
my room is too small for me
15 suppose I die before graduation
they will sing sad melodies
but finally
tell the truth about me
There is nothing I want to do
20 and too much
that has to be done
and momma's in the bedroom
with the door closed.

MAKE INFERENCES

Annotate: In the last stanza, mark the phrases that describe the speaker's complaints. Then number the complaints.

Infer: What can you infer about the speaker based on the complaints she expresses?

Nobody even stops to think
25 about my side of it ①
I should have been on Math Team ②
my marks were better than his
why do I have to be ③
the one
30 wearing braces ④
I have nothing to wear tomorrow ⑤
will I live long enough
to grow up ⑥
and momma's in the bedroom
35 with the door closed. ⑦

TO CHALLENGE STUDENTS...

Analyze Multiple Viewpoints Discuss perspectives and opinions on any issue. Discuss how the research questions could lead to conflicting answers. Then discuss the benefits of examining an issue from different viewpoints.

ASK STUDENTS to use multiple sources to answer the questions and to find at least two viewpoints for each answer. Have students share their research with the class and explain whther they agree more with one viewpoint than another.

CHECK YOUR UNDERSTANDING

Have students answer the questions independently.

Answers:

1. *B*

2. *F*

3. *C*

If they answer any questions incorrectly, have them reread the text to confirm their understanding. Then they may proceed to ANALYZE THE TEXT on p. 358.

CHECK YOUR UNDERSTANDING

Answer these questions about "Hanging Fire" before moving on to the next selection.

1 The speaker in the poem feels —

A proud to be a teenager

B dissatisfied with many aspects of her life

C optimistic about her future

D annoyed by her mother's strict rules

2 Which of the following is an example of personification?

F *my skin has betrayed me*

G *my room is too small for me*

H *they will sing sad melodies*

J *I should have been on Math Team*

3 The image of the closed bedroom door suggests that the speaker —

A is determined to be independent

B feels frustrated by her math scores

C craves attention from her mother

D has closed the door on her problems

 ENGLISH LEARNER SUPPORT

Oral Assessment Use the following questions to assess students' comprehension and speaking skills:

1. What does the speaker in the poem feel? (*The speaker feels unhappy with her life.*)

2. Which is an example of personification, or saying a thing acts like a person? (*my skin has betrayed me*)

3. What does the image of the closed bedroom door tell us about the speaker? (*She craves attention from her mother.*)
   SUBSTANTIAL/MODERATE

BACKGROUND

After students read the Background note, ask students how Gloria Amescua honors her Mexican American heritage with her work. Guide them to identify her work with Canto Mundo and her themes of family and community.

PREPARE TO COMPARE

Direct students to use the Prepare to Compare prompt to focus their reading.

ANALYZE FREE VERSE POETRY

Remind students that poets sometimes use the **line lengths** to create specific effects. Explain that, in addition to changing the flow of the text, poets sometimes use the **visual space** to create an added layer of meaning or to provide a sense of structure. Give examples, such as a poem about recycling that is written in the shape of a tree or a poem that is organized in **stanzas** but lacks a **rhyme scheme** or **meter**. (*Answer: The appearance of the poem on the page gives an impression of imbalance and struggle. The contrast of long and short lines in the first stanza suggests the ups and downs of emotions, building to a peak in the second stanza. The uneven line breaks continue to the last two stanzas, in which regular, short lines seem to suggest a resolution to the turmoil and conflict. The short lines at the end of the poem may represent the closed door of childhood.*)

For **reading support** for students at varying proficiency levels, see the **Text X-Ray** on page 352D.

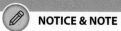

BACKGROUND

Gloria Amescua has been writing poems and stories since she was a child. Born in Austin, Texas, of Mexican American heritage, she became an inaugural member of Canto Mundo, a national Latino poetry community. Amescua has received numerous awards for her work, including the 2016 New Voices Award Honor. Much of her poetry revolves around the importance of family and community.

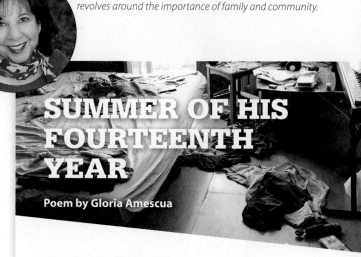

SUMMER OF HIS FOURTEENTH YEAR

Poem by Gloria Amescua

Notice & Note

Use the side margins to notice and note signposts in the text.

ANALYZE FREE VERSE POETRY

Annotate: Mark the end of the longest line. Notice that from this point the stanzas taper down to the shortest lines at the end of the poem.

Analyze: What does the shape of the poem on the page suggest about the boy's turbulent journey through adolescence to adulthood?

PREPARE TO COMPARE

As you read the poem, look for details that help you understand the speaker's point of view.

A deep, resonant voice answers when I call home.
My child is gone—
In his place is someone who resembles him,
only taller, size ten shoes.

5 Empty sneakers and dirty socks mark his passage down vacant halls.
He wanders aimlessly, flexing against walls grown too narrow,
as tensely strung as the tennis racket he grips,
as easily punctured as the deflated hand of the batting glove—
his passions are flung across the hours.

10 He leaves a trail of teenage hunger—
half empty Coke cans, stale chips in an unclosed bag.
Intermittent impulses, quickly sated,
rarely fill his emptiness,
never end his searching.

 ENGLISH LEARNER SUPPORT

Suffix -ly Point out examples of words with the suffix -ly lines 6–13 (*aimlessly, tensely, easily, quickly,* and *rarely*), and identify the base words. Have students say the words after you several times. Write the words on the board, and draw a vertical line between syllables if students have difficulty with correct syllabification. Explain that adding the suffix -ly to an adjective creates an adverb. Review the difference between an adjective and an adverb if needed. Challenge students to create new words by adding the suffix -ly to adjectives. **SUBSTANTIAL/MODERATE**

15 Wailing guitars weave a cocoon
   as he sits cross legged in a recess of his room,
   his teeming emotions playing on a muted keyboard.

   He tears at the seams
   that hold <u>us</u> together
20 and sees in mother only ties to childhood
   Choking him with nagging chores,
   Cloying protection,
   Closed doors.

   Surliness is his knife
25 Cutting away the bonds.

   Silence is his distance
   Murmuring goodbye.

> **WORDS OF THE WISER**
>
> **Notice & Note:** In lines 18–23, mark a comment that reveals an important insight about the teen's behavior.
>
> **Analyze:** What does this comment suggest the speaker understands about her son?

CHECK YOUR UNDERSTANDING

Answer these questions about "Summer of His Fourteenth Year" before moving on to the **Analyze the Text** section on the following page.

1 In "Summer of His Fourteenth Year," the speaker —

   A is angry because her son misbehaves

   B doesn't understand why her son is so restless

   C is filled with grief because her son has died

   D accepts that change is part of growing up

2 Which of the following is an example of simile?

   F *as tensely strung as the tennis racket he grips*

   G *Intermittent impulses, quickly sated*

   H *Wailing guitars weave a cocoon*

   J *Surliness is his knife*

3 An important message in "Summer of His Fourteenth Year" is that —

   A teenagers are messy and inconsiderate

   B it's impossible to communicate with a surly teenager

   C leaving childhood behind is hard for parents and teens

   D parents of teens are too nagging and protective

WORDS OF THE WISER

Remind students that **Words of the Wiser** are words of insight, understanding or advice offered by an older or wiser character and that the signpost often suggests a **theme** in a piece of literature. (**Answer:** *The comment shows that the speaker understands that her son is struggling to cut his "ties to childhood" and part of that struggle involves separating himself from dependence on his mother.*)

CHECK YOUR UNDERSTANDING

Have students answer the questions independently.

Answers:

1. D

2. F

3. C

If they answer any questions incorrectly, have them reread the text to confirm their understanding. Then they may proceed to ANALYZE THE TEXT on p. 360.

ENGLISH LEARNER SUPPORT

Oral Assessment Use the following questions to assess students' comprehension and speaking skills:

1. What does the speaker in the poem feel or know? (*The speaker knows that change is a part of growing up.*)

2. Which is an example of simile, or saying how two different things are alike? (*as tensely strung as the tennis racket he grips*)

3. What is an important message in "Summer of His Fourteenth Year"? (*Growing up is hard for both parents and teens.*)
    SUBSTANTIAL/MODERATE

APPLY

ANALYZE THE TEXT

Possible answers

1. **DOK 2:** The speaker's use of personification shows that she is unhappy about her appearance. Her word choice suggests that she is creative and dramatic.

2. **DOK 4:** The repetition of these lines, with the image of momma "in the bedroom/with the door closed" emphasizes the theme of leaving childhood behind. It puts a focus on the speaker's feelings of isolation and need for parental understanding and support.

3. **DOK 4:** The dashes indicate longer pauses, suggesting the speaker is reflecting on an unfamiliar situation. The dashes create a dramatic effect and emphasize the speaker's insights.

4. **DOK 4:** The poet uses alliteration in lines 10–12: "a **t**rail of **t**eenage hunger . . . / **C**oke **c**ans . . . / **I**ntermittent **i**mpulses," and lines 15–16 contain alliteration and rhyme: "**W**ailing guitars **w**eave a **c**o**c**oon / as he sits **c**ross legged in a recess of his **r**oom." The repetition lends dramatic emphasis and creates a rhythm that suggests the behavior being described is repetitive.

5. **DOK 4:** The speaker's comment that her son "sees in mother only ties to childhood" in the context of how he uses "surliness" and "silence" to distance himself from her suggests that she understands that creating distance from his mother is a necessary stage in the transition to adulthood.

RESEARCH

Remind students to make sure their sources are reliable and up-to-date. Point out that they can find academic journals and other periodicals online or at the library. Explain that such sources undergo editorial and peer review, so their information is the most credible.

Extend Point out that opinions will vary, so students will need to compromise when choosing a topic.

ANALYZE THE TEXT

Support your responses with evidence from the texts. 📓 NOTEBOOK

1. **Infer** The figure of speech in which human qualities are given to an object, idea, or animal is called **personification.** What does the speaker's use of personification in the first stanza of "Hanging Fire" reveal about her self-image and her personality?

2. **Analyze** How does the use of repetition at the end of each stanza in "Hanging Fire" relate to the message of the poem?

3. **Analyze** Read stanzas 1–3 of "Summer of His Fourteenth Year" aloud. What effect does the author create by using dashes in these stanzas?

4. **Analyze** Reread lines 10–17 of "Summer of His Fourteenth Year." What effect is created by the poet's use of alliteration and rhyme in these two stanzas?

5. **Notice & Note** Reread lines 18–27 of "Summer of His Fourteenth Year." What does the insight in line 20 suggest about the mother's point of view on her son's "surliness" and "silence"?

RESEARCH TIP

Remember that when you do research, you need to keep track of where you find information. For print sources, make a note of the title, author, publisher, publication date, and page number. For online sources, make a note of the website, URL, article title, author, and access date. Keep in mind that it's often wise to verify each fact you find in a second source. For example, if you used an online health website for teens, then you might confirm that information by looking in a second online source or in a print book.

RESEARCH

The teens in both poems suffer from mood swings and anxiety that are common during adolescence. Work in small groups to research causes of teenage mood swings and ways to cope with them. Locate the answers to the questions below and generate other questions to research and answer with your group.

QUESTION	ANSWER
What causes teenage mood swings?	*Dealing with constant change and pressure; struggling with identity and self-image; hormones*
Does exercise help to prevent mood swings? If so, how?	
What are some good coping techniques for teens?	
How do sleep patterns affect mood?	

Extend With your group, select an appropriate method of sharing your research findings with the class. Then discuss what surprised you or what you found most interesting or noteworthy. Present the highlights of your research to the class.

WHEN STUDENTS STRUGGLE . . .

Take Notes Some students may find it challenging to keep track of text clues. Provide a simple chart for students to jot down notes about clues and then a space for what a student knows. Finally, include a space for students to make an inference. Provide guiding questions if needed to focus student notes:

- Who is the speaker? What is the speaker like?

- What does the speaker talk about? What is important to the speaker?

 For additional support, go to the **Reading Studio** and assign the following [LEVEL] **Level Up Tutorial: Making Inferences about Characters.**

CREATE AND PRESENT

Write a Response to Literature How do the poems connect to your own experiences? Capture your thoughts and feelings by freewriting about being a teenager. Then use ideas from your writing to decide what feelings and emotions you want to convey in a dramatic reading of one of the poems.

❏ Set a time limit of 10 or 15 minutes for your writing.

❏ Write without stopping to check spelling or grammar.

❏ At the end of your time limit, read what you wrote and underline all the ideas you would like to convey in a dramatic poetry reading.

❏ If your freewriting doesn't yield any useful ideas, try another session.

Give a Dramatic Reading Work with a partner to create a dramatic reading of one of the poems.

❏ Begin by discussing the impact of the poet's word choices.

❏ Practice reading each line of your chosen poem in a way that conveys your personal connection to the poem's meaning.

❏ Consider how you will accompany the words with movements or gestures.

❏ Take turns rehearsing with a partner, giving and receiving feedback.

❏ Present your dramatic reading to the class, using appropriate volume, phrasing, and expression.

RESPOND TO THE ESSENTIAL QUESTION

? How do your teenage years prepare you for adulthood?

Gather Information Review your annotations and notes on "Hanging Fire" and "Summer of His Fourteenth Year." Then add relevant details to your Response Log. As you determine which information to include, think about:

• the fears and challenges that seem to overwhelm the teens in the poems

• what it means to become an adult

• how each writer treats the topic of adolescence

At the end of the unit, you can use your notes to help you write an argument.

Go to the **Writing Studio** for more on writing a response to literature.

Go to the **Speaking and Listening Studio** for more on reciting a poem.

ACADEMIC VOCABULARY
As you write and discuss what you learned from the two poems, be sure to use the Academic Vocabulary words. Check off each of the words that you use.

❏ debate
❏ deduce
❏ license
❏ sufficient
❏ trend

CREATE AND PRESENT

Write a Response to Literature Tell students to follow the list of steps on p. 361 to freewrite about their feelings about being a teenager. Explain that freewriting is a way to overcome inhibitions and uncover subconscious ideas and thoughts about a topic. Remind students:

• write whatever comes to mind about being a teenager
• don't worry about the wording, spelling, grammar, or structure
• focus on ideas and emotions

For **writing support** for students at varying proficiency levels, see the **Text X-Ray** on page 352D.

Give a Dramatic Reading Explain that a dramatic reading is more than just reading aloud. Point out that the reader interprets the poem as an actor playing the role of the poem's speaker. Encourage students to think about the meaning of the lines in order to make a personal connection to the poem.

RESPOND TO THE ESSENTIAL QUESTION

Allow time for students to add details from "Hanging Fire" and "Summer of His Fourteenth Year" to their Unit 5 Response Logs.

ENGLISH LEARNER SUPPORT

Give a Dramatic Reading Pair students of mixed English proficiencies to prepare for the dramatic readings. Explain that getting feedback from a partner is important when preparing for an audience. Explain that feedback should offer helpful suggestions or opinions, not bluntly stated judgments. Encourage students to use the following scripts to ask for and provide feedback:

Ask for feedback: *Should I change the way I read _____? Should I speed up? Slow down? Which way sounds better? How would you say _____? Do my hands/gestures/movement fit _____? What do you think of _____?*

Provide feedback: *I like how you _____. I think the_____ way was _____. Could you try _____? Another way to say that would be _____. Why did you _____? What does _____ mean to you? Perhaps you could _____.* **ALL LEVELS**

COMPARE POEMS

Tell students that the two poems have many elements in common but also have significant differences. Remind them to look beyond the different viewpoints and examine the literary elements and styles each poet uses to create their poems and the effects on the poems.

ANALYZE THE TEXTS

Possible answers:

1. **DOK 3:** *"Summer of His Fourteenth Year" includes more figurative language and imagery. It includes similes such as "as tensely strung as the tennis racket he grips" (line 7), personification, such as "Wailing guitars weave a cocoon" (line 15), and metaphors such as "Surliness is his knife" (line 24). "Hanging Fire," in contrast, uses more natural language, typical of what a teen speaker would use.*

2. **DOK 4:** *"Hanging Fire" puts readers in the shoes of a teen who feels overwhelmed by her struggle with new questions about self-image, identity, independence, self-worth, and even mortality. "Summer of His Fourteenth Year" shows readers what teen struggles look like from the outside, and serves as a reminder that living with a teen who is going through adolescence can be painful and overwhelming for parents as well as teens.*

3. **DOK 3:** *In "Hanging Fire," the speaker mentions her mother's closed bedroom door at the end of each stanza. This emphasis suggests that she wishes her mother would open the door and communicate with her. In "Summer of His Fourteenth Year," the teen's mother refers to "closed doors" (line 23) in the context of describing how her son seems to be actively trying to sever the ties between them. This seems to suggest that the son associates closed doors with the restrictions of childhood.*

4. **DOK 4:** *In "Hanging Fire," the quotation "There is nothing I want to do / and too much that has to be done" sums up a feeling of a lack of goals along with pressure to get things done. The poem also connects with concerns about what others think about me. In "Summer of His Fourteenth Year," the images of sneakers and dirty socks, junk food, escaping into music, and disputes with parents are similar to my experiences. Making connections between the poems and my own experience helps me understand that everyone goes through life problems and makes me realize that I am not alone.*

⊜ **RESPOND**

HANGING FIRE
Poem by Audre Lorde

SUMMER OF HIS FOURTEENTH YEAR
Poem by Gloria Amescua

Collaborate & Compare

COMPARE POEMS

Both "Hanging Fire" and "Summer of His Fourteenth Year" are free verse poems about the problems and changes teenagers are going through. Although the poems are about the same topic, they differ in a number of ways. Ask yourself the following questions to compare the poems.

❏ How does the speaker's point of view affect the poem's theme?

❏ What effect does the form of the poem, or the arrangement of lines on the page, create for the reader?

❏ What do style elements such as word choice, syntax, and imagery contribute to the overall mood or tone?

In a small group, identify similarities and differences between the two poems. Record your thoughts in the chart.

	"Hanging Fire"	**"Summer of His Fourteenth Year"**
Point of View	*teenage girl*	*mother of teenage boy*
Form	*free verse poem*	*free verse poem*
Impact of Style Elements	*Possible response: anxious and depressed tone*	*Possible response: frustrated but empathetic tone*

ANALYZE THE TEXTS

Discuss these questions in your group.

1. **Compare** Which poem makes more effective use of figurative language and imagery? Cite text evidence in your discussion.

2. **Synthesize** Think about the different points of view in the poems. How do these different perspectives help the reader form a fuller understanding of the trials of adolescence?

3. **Cite Evidence** Both poems include the image of a closed door. Discuss what the closed door represents to the teen in each poem. Cite text evidence in your discussion.

4. **Connect** Discuss quotations or images from each poem that reflect feelings, worries, or problems that you have experienced or have observed in others. How does making these connections add to your understanding and appreciation of the poems?

CREATE AND PRESENT

Now your group can continue exploring these poems by comparing their styles and considering how each poem appeals to teen readers.

1. **Decide on the Most Important Style Elements** Think about the elements of each poem that appeal to you. Ask:
   - ❏ Which evokes stronger feelings?
   - ❏ Which style elements best connect with the reader?
   - ❏ What insights does each speaker offer?
   - ❏ What message about teenage years does each poem convey?

2. **Gather Information** With your group, discuss and list the examples of the most important style elements of each poem.

"Hanging Fire"	"Summer of His Fourteenth Year"

3. **Compare Styles** As a group, select two of the strongest style examples for each poem. Discuss how each style choice helps to convey the message of the poem.

4. **Present to the Class** Now present your views to the class. Cite text evidence from the poems to support your ideas. Discuss what each poem adds to your understanding about why teenage years can be so difficult. You may use charts or other visuals to help convey information to the class.

RESPOND

Go to the **Speaking and Listening Studio** for more on participating in a collaborative discussion and on making a presentation.

CREATE AND PRESENT

Explain that a group presentation requires cooperation between different people with differing viewpoints, but the result can be a richer, more complex understanding because each member contributes his or her unique knowledge and perspective on the topic.

1. **Decide on the Most Important Style Elements** Remind students to review their notes and the charts they completed comparing the poems to consider the style elements in each poem. Encourage them to evaluate each style element using the bulleted list.

2. **Gather Information** As groups discuss the style elements and decide which ones are the most important, encourage students to use evidence from the text to support their opinions. Remind them to use quotation marks for exact quotes and to note the line locations.

3. **Compare Styles** Point out that group members may not agree on which two styles are the most important. Encourage them to listen and consider everybody's opinion before voting or choosing styles.

4. **Present to the Class** Tell students, as a group, to create an outline of points to present to the class and to decide who will present which points. Have students practice their presentation in private before presenting to the class.

ENGLISH LEARNER SUPPORT

Support Arguments Before students begin their discussions, provide the following sentence stems:

- *I would like to point out, however, that _____.*
- *I disagree with that conclusion because _____.*
- *I think _____ is more important than _____ because _____.*
- *The poem _____ has a good example of _____ in line _____.*
- *A stronger example is _____.*
  SUBSTANTIAL/MODERATE

MENTOR TEXT

from IT'S COMPLICATED: The Social Lives of Networked Teens

Argument by danah boyd

This article serves as a mentor text, a model for students to follow when they come to the Unit Writing Task: Write an Argument.

GENRE ELEMENTS
ARGUMENT

Remind students that the purpose of **argument** is to present and support the author's opinion. Explain that it is important in argument text to make sure to include support that is solid and meaningful in order to give credence to the opinion. Point out that, in other words, if an author were to simply say, "Here's what I think," without any support as to why he or she has that opinion, the opinion would seem to be unimportant or, perhaps, without substance.

LEARNING OBJECTIVES

- Cite evidence to support analysis of the text and analyze argument claims.
- Conduct research about the amount of time teens and adults spend online and any resulting effects.
- Write an opinion piece about social media use at school.
- Create a multimodal presentation to accompany your opinion piece and advocate position.
- Use context clues to define unfamiliar words.
- **Language** Express opinions, ideas, and feelings in discussions.

TEXT COMPLEXITY

Quantitative Measures	*from* It's Complicated: The Social Lives of Networked Teens	Lexile: 1080L
Qualitative Measures	**Ideas Presented** Mostly explicit, but moves to some implied meaning.	
	Structure Used Somewhat chronological, largely conventional.	
	Language Used A combination of common-talk and technical wording.	
	Knowledge Required Some reference to outside events and knowledge.	

Online Ed

RESOURCES

- Unit 5 Response Log

- 🔊 Selection Audio

- **Text in FOCUS** Compare Arguments

- 📖 Reading Studio: Notice & Note

- 📃 Writing Studio: Writing Arguments

- 💬 Speaking and Listening Studio: Using Media in a Presentation

- ❗ Grammar Studio: Module 1: The Sentence

- ✅ *from* "It's Complicated: The Social Lives of Networked Teens" Selection Test

SUMMARIES

English

The author argues that teens' obsession with being connected on social media is driven by their desire for social connection. She asserts that parents' should let up on their concerns about the amount of time teens spend online because, for most teens, this time is simply a way to meet their social needs. The author also claims that teens look to adults to understand growing up, but that teens also want to make their own choices, which social media helps them to do.

Spanish

La autora expresa que la obsesión de los adolescentes con estar conectados a redes sociales es impulsada por el deseo de formar conexiones sociales. Asegura que los padres deberían dejar de preocuparse acerca del tiempo que sus hijos adolescentes pasan en línea debido a que, para la mayoría de los adolescentes, este tiempo es sencillamente una manera de satisfacer sus necesidades sociales. La autora también afirma que los adolescentes buscan guía en los adultos para entender el crecimiento, pero que también les conviene tomar sus propias decisiones, cosa que las redes sociales les permite.

 SMALL-GROUP OPTIONS

Have students work in small groups to read and discuss the selection.

Activating Academic Vocabulary

Write the Unit 5 Academic Vocabulary words on the board: *debate, deduce, license, sufficient,* and *trend*.

Ask volunteers to use at least one of the words when answering these questions:

- Does the author sufficiently supports her claim that teens' obsession with social media is okay?

- With your friends, what social media option is the top current trend?

- From reading the argument about networked teens, what do you deduce about the author's opinion of parents?

Silent Sustained Reading

- Assure that every student has a book at the appropriate reading level and that he or she can read for 30 minutes.

- Provide a chart, such as the one in the Reader/ Writer Notebook, in which students can record the title, date, and number of pages read.

- Have students read for 30 sustained minutes each day.

- Have students record new vocabulary words and give brief oral overviews of the content they read.

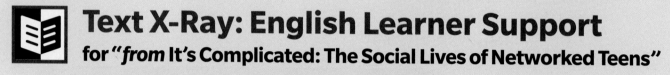

Text X-Ray: English Learner Support
for "*from* It's Complicated: The Social Lives of Networked Teens"

Use the Text X-Ray and the supports and scaffolds in the Teacher's Edition to help guide students at different proficiency levels through the selection.

INTRODUCE THE SELECTION

USING SOCIAL MEDIA TO FIND A PATH TO ADULTHOOD

In this lesson, students will need to think about the amount of time teens spend on social media and whether it is a positive or negative situation. They also must evaluate the claims made by the author of the selection suggesting that the use of social media is part of teens' paths to adulthood and part of their social development. Students will need to use the text and their own prior knowledge to decide for themselves whether they think the author's claims are sound.

Make sure students understand the following points about reading argumentative text:

- The claims authors make in argumentative text are opinions, not facts.
- Readers of argumentative text must decide whther they agree or disagree with some or all of the author's claims.
- Even if a reader agrees with the author's claims, they are still just opinions. Others might not agree.

CULTURAL REFERENCES

The following words and phrases may be unfamiliar to students:

- *underlying social motivations* (paragraph 3): unseen social reasons
- *media narratives/broader narratives* (paragraph 5): TV and movie stories/actual daily life
- *messages of adulthood* (paragraph 6): examples of adult choices

---

LISTENING

Understand the Readers' Choices

Draw students' attention to paragraph 2. Help them find the two claims the author makes. Explain that these claims are opinions and readers should only accept them if they agree with them.

Have students listen as you read aloud paragraph 2. Use the following supports with students at varying proficiency levels:

- Write the word *fact* on the board. In his or her home language, assist each student in writing a word that means *fact*. As a group, work together to answer these questions in English: *What is a fact?* (information that can be proven to be true) *Should you assume that everything that is written in the text is a fact?* (no) **SUBSTANTIAL**

- After reading the paragraph to students, assist each student in writing words that mean *fact* and *opinion*. As a group, work together to decide whether it is *a fact or opinion that "the fears that surround teens' use of social media overlook this fundamental desire for social connection"?* (opinion) **MODERATE**

- Pair students, and have them discuss the meanings of *fact* and *opinion*. Ask: *Can you find a sentence in the selection that is a claim, or opinion?* (sentence 2 or 3) **LIGHT**

SPEAKING

Discuss Your Stand

Draw students' attention to paragraph 1. Discuss that the four sentences are a combination of opinion and fact and that they are all worded or slanted to support the author's position.

Use the following supports with students at varying proficiency levels:

- Read sentences 1 and 2 with students. Write the word *stand* on the board, and circle it. Extend rays out to *take a stand, stand up,* and *fruit stand.* Discuss the meaning of each use of *stand.* Ask which meaning relates to whether you agree that friendships are important to growing up. **SUBSTANTIAL**
- Read paragraph 1 with students. Write the words *stand* and *slanted* on the board. Discuss different meanings of each word. Have students work in small groups to take a stand on whether friendships are important to growing up. Have each group complete this frame: *Our stand (is, is not) slanted because ___.* **MODERATE**
- Pair students and have them read paragraph 1 together. Then have them pairs complete this sentence frame: *I think the author slanted ___.* **LIGHT**

READING

Use Context Clues

Draw students' attention to the background information about the author. Point out that you can learn about a person by considering their choices and preferences. Tell students that they will learn about the author and that they can use context clues to figure out some of the details.

Work with students to read the author's background information. Use the following supports with students at varying proficiency levels:

- Write the word *background* on the board. Ask a volunteer to draw a line between the two small words that make up *background.* Discuss different meanings of *back* and *ground* including "belonging to the past," and "subject for discussion." **SUBSTANTIAL**
- In small groups, discuss the meaning of the term *background information.* Ask: *Why is the background information not part of the story?* (*It is about the author.*) **MODERATE**
- Pair students and have them read the background information. Ask: *How is danah boyd's name different from most English proper nouns?* (*It does not start with capital letters.*) **LIGHT**

WRITING

Write an Opinion Piece

Work with students to read the writing assignment on p. 373.

Use the following supports with students at varying proficiency levels:

- Work with students to each write an opinion they have about social media. Have them begin with this sentence frame: *I think that social media _____.* **SUBSTANTIAL**
- Provide sentence frames such as the following that students can use when writing their opinion pieces: *In regards to the use of social media use at school, I think _____ because _____. Some people would disagree with me because they think _____.* **MODERATE**
- Tell students to begin by writing these two pieces: a position statement stating how they feel about social media use at school and a statement about a viewpoint that is different from theirs. Tell them to work in pairs to check each other's English to make sure their base statements make sense. **LIGHT**

TEACH

Connect to the
ESSENTIAL QUESTION

In *"from It's Complicated: The Social Lives of Networked Teens"* and *"Outsmart Your Smartphone,"* the authors offer opposite stands on the value of social networking in preparing students for adulthood. Each contends that her stand is critical to preparing teens for adulthood.

COMPARE ARGUMENTS

Point out that both authors are professionals who have stated claims and supported them. Tell students that they, the readers, must decide where they stand on the issue. Explain that the decision process involves comparing the arguments and evidence to support the arguments.

ENGLISH LEARNER SUPPORT

Claims, Arguments, and Counter Arguments Explain that *claims* and *arguments* are sometimes used as synonyms. Then, using the classroom clock, show students clockwise and counterclockwise, and discuss that *counter* means "opposite." Point out that claims and counter claims are also opposites. Say: *Assume that you believe that schools should teach grade school students to swim.* Ask: *How could you word a claim supporting that belief? (I claim that schools should teach grade school students to swim.) How could you word a counter claim? (I claim that parents should be responsible for teaching children to swim.)*
MODERATE

COLLABORATE & COMPARE

ARGUMENT

from

IT'S COMPLICATED:
The Social Lives of Networked Teens

by **danah boyd**
pages 367–371

COMPARE ARGUMENTS

As you read the next two selections, look for the main claim in each argument and the reasons and evidence given to support it. Then, consider whether your opinion of teens' media use has changed at all as a consequence of reading these arguments. After you read both selections, you will collaborate on a final project.

ESSENTIAL QUESTION:

How do your teenage years prepare you for adulthood?

ARGUMENT

OUTSMART YOUR SMARTPHONE

by **Catherine Steiner-Adair**
pages 379–385

LEARNING MINDSET

Grit Explain to students that our brains are muscles and that the more you work them the stronger they become. Also, remind them that hard work and flexible thinking patterns lead to success. Point out that flexible people can turn problems into opportunities. Make sure to offer praise for student effort and strategy use rather than for getting something right.

It's Complicated

QUICK START

Poll a small group of friends or classmates to find out how many belong to social media networks. Discuss whether using social media creates a "complicated" social life, and why.

ANALYZE CLAIM AND EVIDENCE

A strong argument clearly states a **claim,** or position on an issue, and reasons to accept the claim. It provides sufficient relevant evidence to support those reasons. **Evidence** consists of the specific facts, examples, statistics, and expert opinions that support a claim.

Evidence is **relevant** if it supports the claim in a logical way. If it isn't based on sound reasoning and isn't clearly connected to the claim, then it is irrelevant. When you analyze an argument, watch out for irrelevant facts that don't actually support the claim.

Also watch out for **opinions,** or personal beliefs, that are stated without proof or facts to support them. The author should provide **citations**—references to research studies, books, and other sources—to back up his or her assertions. A citation may be provided directly in the text where the assertion is made. In other cases, the author may use numbered **footnotes** that cite sources at the bottom of each page, or **endnotes** that list sources at the end of the text.

IDENTIFY COUNTER ARGUMENT

A **counter argument** is an argument made to oppose another argument. Good writers understand the viewpoints of their intended audience or reader, and anticipate possible objections and alternative viewpoints and provide counter arguments for them. By doing so, they can show how weak an opposing viewpoint is, and they can clear the way for the reader to accept their position without reservations.

In the selection from *It's Complicated,* the author first introduces common parental concerns about teens' media use. Then she presents her own counter argument: she explains why adults really don't need to worry so much about these things. As you read, notice how the author does this and note relevant examples in a chart like this one.

PARENTS' CONCERNS ABOUT SOCIAL MEDIA USE	THE AUTHOR'S COUNTER ARGUMENTS
"Why are my kids tethered to their cell phones or perpetually texting with friends even when they are in the same room?"	"Most teens are not compelled by gadgetry as such—they are compelled by friendship."

GENRE ELEMENTS: ARGUMENT

- states a claim and reasons to support the claim
- includes facts and other evidence to support reasons
- may note objections to the claim or alternative viewpoints and explain why they should be dismissed
- takes many forms, such as editorials, feature articles, and essays

QUICK START

After discussing whether social media creates complicated social lives, challenge students to individually make general statements indicating how it would affect their social lives if they stopped using social media.

ANALYZE CLAIM AND EVIDENCE

Help students to understand the types of details that can serve as evidence to support a claim. As a group, brainstorm some sources, such as those listed below, that could support a claim that social media does or does not create a complicated social life.

- quotations from teens
- quotations from parents
- studies by psychologists or teachers
- police statistics
- think Tank studies
- government agency studies and reports
- American Academy of Pediatrics studies and reports

IDENTIFY COUNTER ARGUMENT

Review the concept of and reasons for counter arguments. Present the following argument ideas, and ask volunteers to suggest some counter argument ideas:

- People who own pets are happier than those who do not have pets.
- Students should not watch TV while doing homework.
- Eighth-Graders should be in a separate building from high school students.
- Ballroom dancing is a good social skill for students to learn at a young age.

CRITICAL VOCABULARY

Encourage students to read all the sentences before deciding which word best completes each one. Remind them to look for context clues that match the meaning of each word.

Answers:

1. *dynamic*

2. *intimacy*

3. *appease*

4. *relish*

■ English Learner Support

Use Cognates Tell students that two of the Critical Vocabulary words have Spanish cognates: *dynamic/dinámico, intimacy/ intimidad.* **ALL LEVELS**

LANGUAGE CONVENTIONS

Review the information about compound sentences. Explain that both of the clauses in a compound sentence must be independent clauses, which means that they could be their own sentences.

Direct students' attention to the last sentence in paragraph 4. Ask: *Is this sentence a compound sentence? Explain why or why not. (Yes. Both clauses are independent.)* Direct students' attention to the last sentence in paragraph 6. Ask: *Is this sentence a compound sentence? Explain why or why not. (No. The second clause is not independent.)*

 ANNOTATION MODEL

Discuss that the combination of marking the text and taking notes can be quite effective because it ties the reader's ideas to specific words in the text. Point out that students can use this method or some other method that works well for them.

 GET READY

CRITICAL VOCABULARY

relish   dynamic   appease   intimacy

To see how many Critical Vocabulary words you already know, use them to complete the sentences.

1. The family _____ can make for some tense car rides.

2. Spending time alone with someone can create a feeling of _____.

3. After a fight with his sister, Jamie had to _____ her by letting her choose the movie.

4. Ana loves to travel, so she will _____ her upcoming trip.

LANGUAGE CONVENTIONS

Compound Sentences In a compound sentence like the following one, the clauses are joined with a conjunction to avoid producing a run-on sentence, and a comma is placed before the conjunction.

Some teens may reject the messages of adulthood that they hear or see, <u>but</u> they still learn from all of the signals around them.

As you read *It's Complicated,* notice other compound sentences in which the author uses a conjunction preceded by a comma.

ANNOTATION MODEL   **NOTICE & NOTE**

As you read, note the main claim on which the author's argument is based and how she supports it. In the model, you can see the notes one reader made while reading the first paragraph.

1 Developing meaningful friendships is a key component of the <u>coming of age process</u>. Friends offer many things—advice, support, entertainment, and a connection that combats loneliness. And in doing so, they <u>enable the transition to adulthood</u> by providing a context beyond that of family and home. Though family is still important, many teens relish the opportunity to create relationships that are not simply given but chosen.

"coming of age" = the transition to adulthood

I can relate to this. My friends are very important to me.

BACKGROUND

When **danah boyd** (b. 1977) was born, her mother named her "danah michele mattas." Her name was later changed and properly capitalized. As an adult, however, she legally renamed herself "danah boyd," taking her grandfather's last name, honoring her mother's original lowercase spelling, and satisfying her own "political irritation at the importance of capitalization." A Principal Researcher at Microsoft Research and a visiting professor at New York University, she has spent years researching how young people use social media.

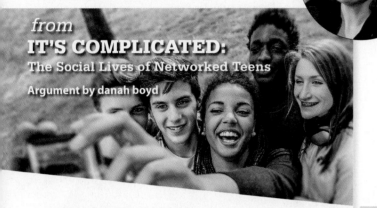

from
IT'S COMPLICATED:
The Social Lives of Networked Teens

Argument by danah boyd

PREPARE TO COMPARE

As you read boyd's argument, notice her tone, choice of language, and way of expressing herself to readers. Paying attention to these aspects of her writing will allow you to compare her style to that of Catherine Steiner-Adair, the author of the second argument.

Text in FOCUS

1   Developing meaningful friendships is a key component of the coming of age process. Friends offer many things—advice, support, entertainment, and a connection that combats loneliness. And in doing so, they enable the transition to adulthood by providing a context[1] beyond that of family and home. Though family is still important, many teens **relish** the opportunity to create relationships that are not simply given but chosen.

2   The importance of friends in social and moral development is well documented. But the fears that surround teens' use of social media overlook this fundamental desire for social connection. All too often,

[1] **context:** setting or environment.

Notice & Note

Use the side margins to notice and note signposts in the text.

relish
(rĕl´ĭsh) *v.* To *relish* is to take great joy or pleasure in something.

ANALYZE CLAIM AND EVIDENCE

Annotate: In paragraph 2, mark the sentence that summarizes the main idea of this paragraph.

Infer: Might this be boyd's claim? If so, what should the rest of the argument show or prove?

It's Complicated: The Social Lives of Networked Teens   **367**

BACKGROUND

Point out that the *It's Complicated* book has 281 pages, so danah boyd clearly has quite a bit to say about the social lives of teens! Also, share that Ms. boyd has a computer science degree from Brown, a master's in sociable media from MIT, and a Ph.D. in Information from Berkeley.

 For **speaking support** for students at varying proficiency levels, see the **Text X-Ray** on page 364D.

PREPARE TO COMPARE

Direct students to use the Prepare to Compare prompt to focus their reading.

Text in FOCUS   TEXT IN FOCUS

Compare Arguments   Have students view the Text in Focus video on this page of their eBook to learn about the arguments about the positive and negative effects of social media use on teens. Then have students use Text in Focus Practice to apply what they have learned.

✎ ANALYZE CLAIM AND EVIDENCE

Point out that authors often place their main claims near the beginning of the text and then use the rest of the text to support the claim. (***Answer**: Students should note that this might be the claim. They should then predict that the rest of the argument should prove that the primary motivation for using social media is the desire for social connection and nothing more worrisome.*)

For **reading support** for students at varying proficiency levels, see the **Text X-Ray** on page 364D.

IMPROVE READING FLUENCY

Targeted Passage   Have partners take turns reading the first paragraph aloud to each other. Point out that, the more familiar you are with a text, the easier it is to read it fluently. Suggest that students each read the paragraph at least three times, and then discuss if they feel their fluency improved with each reading.

 Go to the **Reading Studio** for additional support in developing fluency.

CRITICAL VOCABULARY

relish: Many teens take great pleasure in the relationships that they are free to choose.

ASK STUDENTS if teens can relish both their families and their friends. (*yes*)

ENGLISH LEARNER SUPPORT

Clarify Terms Help students understand the words *gadgets* and *gadgetry*.

ASK STUDENTS to locate the words *gadgets* and *gadgetry* in paragraph 3. Explain that the two words are both nouns and can be used somewhat interchangeably, but that *gadgets* can be used with an article (*a* or *the*) while *gadgetry* is not used with an article. Tell them that any mechanical device can be considered a gadget. Ask volunteers to identify some gadgets. (**Some examples:** *cell phone, Bluetooth ear plug, remote control.*) **SUBSTANTIAL/MODERATE**

IDENTIFY COUNTER ARGUMENT

Remind students that, even though the author is an expert in this field, she is simply sharing her opinions and they should read her ideas and then form their own opinions. (**Answer**: *Accept all well-supported answers. Students who say "yes" may note that she responds to each question with a reasonable alternate viewpoint that minimizes or even totally deflates the concern. They may also point out that she is an expert so a worried parent could take her opinions as evidence that answers his or her concerns. Students who say "no" may note that she's only voicing her alternate perspective but isn't providing any evidence to back it up.*)

 For **listening support** for students at varying proficiency levels, see the **Text X-Ray** on page 364C.

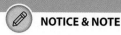

NOTICE & NOTE

parents project their values onto their children, failing to recognize that school is often not the most pressing concern for most teens. Many parents wonder: Why are my kids tethered to their cell phones or perpetually texting with friends even when they are in the same room? Why do they seem compelled to check Facebook hundreds of times a day? Are they addicted to technology or simply wasting time? How will they get into college if they are constantly distracted? I encounter these questions from concerned adults whenever I give public lectures, and these attitudes figure prominently in parenting guides and in journalistic accounts of teens' engagement with social media.

3   Yet these questions seem far less urgent and difficult when we acknowledge teens' underlying social motivations. Most teens are not compelled by gadgetry as such—they are compelled by friendship. The gadgets are interesting to them primarily as a means to a social end. Furthermore, social interactions may be a distraction from school, but they are

IDENTIFY COUNTER ARGUMENT

Annotate: In paragraph 3, mark all the statements that address the worries the author noted in paragraph 2.

Evaluate: Might a worried parent reading paragraph 3 be convinced by what she says here? Explain.

often not a distraction from learning. Keeping this basic social **dynamic** firmly in view makes networked teens suddenly much less worrisome and strange.

4   Consider, for example, the widespread concern over internet addiction. Are there teens who have an unhealthy relationship with technology? Certainly. But most of those who are "addicted" to their phones or computers are actually focused on staying connected to friends in a culture where getting together in person is highly constrained.[2] Teens' preoccupation[3] with their friends dovetails[4] with their desire to enter the public spaces that are freely accessible[5] to adults. The ability to access public spaces for sociable purposes is a critical component of the coming of age process, and yet many of the public spaces where adults gather—bars, clubs, and restaurants—are inaccessible to teens.

[2] **constrained:** limited.
[3] **preoccupation:** mental absorption or sole focus of attention.
[4] **dovetails:** fits together well, unites, or joins.
[5] **accessible:** open and available.

dynamic
(dī-năm´ĭk) *n.* A *dynamic* is a system in which conflicting or competing forces are at work.

LANGUAGE CONVENTIONS
Annotate: Mark the compound sentence in paragraph 4 that is joined by two conjunctions preceded by a comma.

Analyze: Is the word *and* necessary in this sentence? Explain what it adds, if anything.

It's Complicated: The Social Lives of Networked Teens   369

APPLYING ACADEMIC VOCABULARY

❏ debate   ❏ deduce   ☑ **license**   ❏ sufficient   ☑ **trend**

Write and Discuss   Have students turn to a partner to discuss the following questions. Guide students to include the Academic Vocabulary words *license* and *trend* in their responses. Ask volunteers to share their responses with the class.

- Why are social media rules necessary for people using a driver's **license**?
- Do you think the **trend** in social media engagement will continue for teens as they transition into adulthood?

LANGUAGE CONVENTIONS

Discuss that, rather than always using completely formal formats, writers sometimes choose to use more casual wording to better reach their audience. (**Answer**: *"And" might be unnecessary because she only needed to insert a comma and the conjunction "yet" to avoid a run-on sentence and convey the same idea she conveys with the conjunction "and" added. The "and" makes the sentence sound more like natural conversation.*)

■ English Learner Support

Conjunctions   Make sure students understand that the word *conjunctions* refers to the words that join independent clauses in compound sentences. Point out that compound sentences typically have only one conjunction. Ask: *What is the conjunction used in the last sentence in paragraph 4? (and)* In this sentence, *yet* is not a conjunction; it is an adverb used to mean "nevertheless" or "even so."   **SUBSTANTIAL**

CRITICAL VOCABULARY

dynamic: Teens' social system often includes being distracted from school by social interactions.

ASK STUDENTS how tech gadgets contribute to teens' social **dynamics**. (*Gadgets are a tool teens use to form friendships.*)

IDENTIFY COUNTER ARGUMENT

Point out that addressing possible counter arguments is one method of providing support for the main claim. (**Answer**: *Students should write some version of the question, "Why does my teenager need to 'follow' [or track every move of] celebrities like Kanye West and Kim Kardashian online?")*

▶ CONTRASTS AND CONTRADICTIONS

Remind students that, as a writer, it is important to know your audience and to know what might or might not surprise them. (**Answer**: *Someone unfamiliar with the "networked publics" that exist on the Internet would not already know this. Because boyd thinks her readers will be surprised by learning that there is more privacy available online than at home, she is probably writing for parents who are unfamiliar with the fact that social networks can be manipulated to be more private than they seem to be.)*

■ English Learner Support

Slang Point out to students that the word *nosy* does not refer to "having a lot of nose," but rather, it is a slang term that refers to "people who are overly curious about other people's business." Explain to students that "nosy" is similar to the phrase "to stick your nose in." Ask: *In paragraph 7, with what are the nosy adults interfering? (teens' privacy)*
ALL LEVELS

CRITICAL VOCABULARY

appease: TV shows suggest that some young adults do not need to make concessions for parents and teachers.

ASK STUDENTS what they would do with their cell phones at the dinner table that would most appease adults. *(put it away)*

intimacy: Teens want personal closeness within their social situations.

ASK STUDENTS how using social media can provide **intimacy** for teens. *(It gives them a chance to talk without those around them hearing.)*

IDENTIFY COUNTER ARGUMENT
Annotate: In paragraph 5, mark the clues that help reveal what concern boyd is answering here.

Infer: Use these clues to infer the concern she is addressing in this paragraph. Then write this concern in the form of a question posed by a concerned parent.

appease
(ə-pēz´) *v.* To *appease* means to pacify or lessen the anger of, usually by making concessions.

CONTRASTS AND CONTRADICTIONS

Notice & Note: Mark the word in paragraph 7 that suggests the information boyd is about to share may come as a surprise to her readers.

Infer: Who would not already know this? What does this suggest about who boyd's intended readers are?

intimacy
(ĭn´tə-mə-sē) *n. Intimacy* refers to a state of personal closeness that is usually experienced in privacy.

5   As teens transition from childhood, they try to understand how they fit into the larger world. They want to inhabit public spaces, but they also look to adults, including public figures, to understand what it means to be grown-up. They watch their parents and other adults in their communities for models of adulthood. But they also track celebrities like Kanye West and Kim Kardashian to imagine the freedoms they would have if they were famous. For better or worse, media narratives also help construct broader narratives for how public life works. "Reality" TV shows like *Jersey Shore* signal the potential fun that can be had by young adults who don't need to **appease** parents and teachers.

6   Some teens may reject the messages of adulthood that they hear or see, but they still learn from all of the signals around them. As they start to envision themselves as young adults, they begin experimenting with the boundaries of various freedoms, pushing for access to cars or later curfews. Teens' determination to set their own agenda can be nerve-racking for some parents, particularly those who want to protect their children from every possible danger. Coming of age is rife with self-determination, risk taking, and tough decision-making.

7   Teens often want to be with friends on their own terms, without adult supervision, and in public. Paradoxically, the networked publics they inhabit allow them a measure of privacy and autonomy that is not possible at home where parents and siblings are often listening in. Recognizing this is important to understanding teens' relationship to social media. Although many adults think otherwise, teens' engagement with public life through social media is not a rejection of privacy. Teens may wish to enjoy the benefits of participating in public, but they also relish **intimacy** and the ability to have control over their social situation. Their ability to achieve privacy is often undermined by nosy adults—notably their parents and teachers—but teens go to great lengths to develop innovative strategies for managing privacy in networked publics.

8   Social media enables a type of youth-centric[6] public space that is often otherwise inaccessible. But because that space is highly visible, it can often provoke concerns among adults who are watching teens as they try to find their way.

---
[6] **youth-centric:** focused on young people's needs, concerns, and interests.

WHEN STUDENTS STRUGGLE . . .

Context Clues Remind students to use context clues to understand unfamiliar words while they are reading. Ask: *In the first sentence in paragraph 5, which words and thought processes can help you figure out the meaning of transition? (The sentence suggest that "teens" are doing something "from childhood," so that they can figure out how to "fit into the larger world," so it seems that "transition" must refer to teens moving on from childhood.)*

  For additional support, go to the **Reading Studio** and assign the following [LEVEL UP] **Level Up tutorial: Using Context Clues.**

CHECK YOUR UNDERSTANDING

Answer these questions before moving on to the **Analyze the Text** section on the following page.

1 What is the author's main claim in paragraph 1?

  A Coming of age is a lonely and difficult process.

  B Friends offer one another advice, support, and fun.

  C Teens have a profound need to make deep friendships.

  D Family members become unimportant to teenagers.

2 In paragraph 7, the author encourages readers to recognize that —

  F teens reject privacy in favor of socializing with their friends in a public space

  G social media sites offer teens more privacy and autonomy than their homes do

  H the nosiness of adults and siblings at home forces teens to rebel

  J teens are better at using and manipulating social media than adults are

3 Which statement best characterizes the author's main message to people who worry about teens' use of social media?

  A Instead of worrying about your teens, you should worry about developing your own life more fully.

  B You need to recognize that it's safer for teens to meet online than it is to get together in person these days.

  C Teens' use of social media is not so worrisome if you take into account how much they need friends at this age.

  D The real danger of teens using social media is that it makes them want to live like celebrities who have lots of freedom.

It's Complicated: The Social Lives of Networked Teens   371

 CHECK YOUR UNDERSTANDING

Have students answer the questions independently.

Answers:

  1. *C*

  2. *G*

  3. *C*

If they answer any questions incorrectly, have them reread the text to confirm their understanding. Then they may proceed to ANALYZE THE TEXT on p. 372.

 ENGLISH LEARNER SUPPORT

Oral Assessment Use the following questions to assess the students' comprehension and speaking skills:

  1. What is the main claim the author makes in paragraph 1? *(Teens have a profound need to make deep friendships.)*

  2. What does the author encourage readers to recognize in paragraph 7? *(Social media sites offer teens more privacy and autonomy than their homes do.)*

  3. What is one of the author's main messages? *(Teens' use of social media is not so worrisome if you take into account how much they need friends at this age.)* **SUBSTANTIAL/MODERATE**

APPLY

ANALYZE THE TEXT

Possible answers:

1. **DOK 2:** *She suggests that it's the public nature of being on social media that makes parents concerned about their teenagers' use of it—especially because that means any misstep at such a precarious time would be public as well.*

2. **DOK 4:** *The author might have chosen to provide these observations about some teens' behavior to help parents see social media use as just another arena for teens' typical behavior and also to better understand their own reactions to seeing their children act this way. Accept all well-reasoned conclusions. Some students may say that it is relevant because it offers readers another reason why they shouldn't worry so much about their teens' behavior. Others may say that it isn't relevant because it does not support her claim that teens' extreme need to develop meaningful social relationships is the force behind their social media use.*

3. **DOK 4:** *It does not help to prove the author's claim because her claim is not about "reality" TV, teens' TV watching habits, or the risk of teens being enticed to behave in disobedient ways.*

4. **DOK 3:** *Students who say that she doesn't may note that she relies primarily on one basic notion accepted about childhood development to make all her points. She does not offer much, if any, evidence to back up her reasoning. Students who say that she does may note that she is an expert in her field and so needs no additional evidence to prove her point; her opinions are evidence enough.*

5. **DOK 4:** *She points out that virtual public spaces actually offer teenagers' more privacy than they get at home or elsewhere in the physical world. She also points out that teens actually go to great lengths to develop strategies for managing their privacy online than adults realize. The first fact contradicts the assumption that teens would have more privacy if they met at home rather than online. The second contradicts the notion that teens' preference for meeting online means that they don't value privacy.*

RESEARCH

Check that students' research yielded different types of evidence. Also, make sure their research is relevant to the topics proposed. Finally, if their research supports or contradicts boyd's argument, make sure that is noted.

Extend Point out to students that their discussions should reach into assessing the credibility of sources, currency of information, and relevance of evidence.

372   Unit 5

 RESPOND

ANALYZE THE TEXT

Support your responses with evidence from the text.   NOTEBOOK

1. **Interpret** In paragraph 8, what reason does boyd give to explain why adults may be so worried about teenagers' use of social media?

2. **Analyze** Review paragraph 6. Why might the author have chosen to provide this information? Is it relevant to her argument or not? Explain.

3. **Analyze** Reread the last sentence in paragraph 5. Is this statement relevant to the author's argument? Explain.

4. **Evaluate** Does boyd provide sufficient relevant reasons and evidence to support her position? Cite evidence to support your response.

5. **Notice & Note** In paragraph 7, identify the two seemingly contradictory things that teens want. How does this idea counter the assumption that many adults make about social media use?

RESEARCH

RESEARCH TIP
When investigating a field of study such as psychology, in which ongoing research constantly prompts experts to revise older ideas and propose new ones, only the most recent information may be currently accepted as true. Therefore, when doing such research, check the date of your sources to make sure they are as current as possible.

Research social media use to learn more about the amount of time teens and adults spend online and the effects of doing so, if any. Try to locate different types of evidence, such as facts, statistics, research studies, and quotes from experts. Use the chart below to record the evidence and, if it's related to boyd's argument, explain whether it supports or contradicts her argument.

EVIDENCE	SUPPORTS OR CONTRADICTS BOYD'S ARGUMENT?

Extend Share your evidence with a small group. Discuss which pieces of evidence are the most persuasive and why. Then, develop a claim about social media use that you could support with this evidence.

LEARNING MINDSET

Questioning Reinforce that asking questions is about being open to new ideas and trying new things. Encourage students to always feel comfortable asking questions. Suggest that, when they get stuck, they should ask themselves, "Can I try this in a different way?" Make sure to compliment students' questions and to mention how asking questions shows curiosity and leads to learning new things.

CREATE AND PRESENT

Write an Opinion Piece Write a one- or two-paragraph opinion piece in which you take a position regarding social media use at school. Use evidence from *It's Complicated* and your own research to support your points.

❏ Introduce the topic, state your position on it, and give one good reason to accept your viewpoint. Also state an opposing viewpoint and make a strong counter argument.

❏ Alternatively, begin by introducing the topic and the prevailing viewpoint that differs from your own. Present a reason to reject or modify that viewpoint, and conclude by stating your position.

❏ Use facts, quotations, and other relevant evidence from the text and your research to support your opinions.

❏ In your conclusion, tell readers what you think they should believe, why they should believe it, and what to do because they now hold this belief.

Advocate a Position Deliver a multimodal presentation of your argument to the class by adding an illustration, a poster, a software demonstration, or sound effects to more effectively convey your message. Use appropriate eye contact, speaking rate, volume, enunciation, and gestures to communicate your argument effectively. After giving your presentation, respond to any questions or comments your classmates may have.

RESPOND TO THE ESSENTIAL QUESTION

 How do your teenage years prepare you for adulthood?

Gather Information Review your annotations and notes on *It's Complicated*. Then, add relevant details to your Response Log. To decide what to include, think about:

• the author's information about how teens develop into adults

• what the author says matters most to teens and why

• what you have learned about the process of "coming of age" through research and firsthand observation

At the end of the unit, use your notes to help you write an argument.

 Go to **Writing Arguments** in the **Writing Studio** for help with writing an opinion piece.

 Go to **Using Media in a Presentation** in the **Speaking and Listening Studio** for more help.

ACADEMIC VOCABULARY
As you write and discuss what you learned from the argument, be sure to use the Academic Vocabulary words. Check off each of the words that you use.

❏ **debate**
❏ **deduce**
❏ **license**
❏ **sufficient**
❏ **trend**

CREATE AND PRESENT

Write an Opinion Piece Point out that the list on p. 373 can serve as an outline for students' opinion pieces. Explain that they would need to expand the points into one or two paragraphs and exhibit the following:

• a clear position regarding social media use at school

• at least one good reason to accept this opinion as sound

• evidence from the selection and their research to support their claim

• a call to action in the conclusion

 For **writing support** for students at varying proficiency levels, see the **Text X-Ray** on page 364D.

Advocate a Position Remind students that the point in advocating a position is to persuade others to agree with you. Point out that they should, therefore, prepare their presentation from the point of view of persuading others.

RESPOND TO THE ESSENTIAL QUESTION

Allow time for students to add details from *from It's Complicated: The Social Lives of Networked Teens* to their Unit 5 Response Logs.

🅔🅛 ENGLISH LEARNER SUPPORT

Advocate a Position Make sure students understand that *multimodal* means more than one mode of presentation, such as combining speaking and a poster. Point out that they can build in English clues within their presentation materials so it is easier for them to speak in front of the class. Help students build in English clues by including key words in both English and the student's home language, using icons or pictures that remind students of difficult English words, and including known English words as part of the visual presentation.

SUBSTANTIAL/MODERATE

CRITICAL VOCABULARY

Answers:

1. *Showing up early would be more likely to appease a coach's irritation because it would reduce that irritation, whereas coming late would increase it.*

2. *If I relish a song I would want to learn it because I'd love it and want to remember it.*

3. *She thinks parents ought to keep in mind the fact that teens are highly motivated to make meaningful friendships and social connections outside their immediate family.*

4. *Intimacy would be more likely to strengthen a relationship because that state of personal closeness would foster communication and affection between people.*

VOCABULARY STRATEGY:
Context Clues

Answers:

Students should provide four sentences that explain something about social media or smartphones. Each sentence should contain a synonym or an antonym to help clarify the meaning of a difficult word. Accept all clear examples. Sentences do not have to be based on the frames provided in the lesson.

 RESPOND

CRITICAL VOCABULARY

WORD BANK
relish
dynamic
appease
intimacy

Practice and Apply Demonstrate your understanding of the Critical Vocabulary words by answering the following questions.

1. What would be more likely to **appease** a coach's irritation with you, showing up to practice sessions early or arriving late? Why?

2. If you **relish** a song, are you more likely to want to learn it or forget it? Why?

3. What **dynamic** does boyd think parents ought to keep in mind when evaluating their teens' use of social media? Why?

4. Would **intimacy** be more or less likely to strengthen a relationship? Why?

VOCABULARY STRATEGY: Context Clues

Go to the **Vocabulary Studio** for more on using context clues.

You know that a word's **context,** or the text that comes before and after it, can help you figure out its meaning. But did you know that some of the clearest context clues are **synonyms**—words with the same meaning as the unfamiliar word—and **antonyms**—words with the opposite meaning? When one of these turns up in a sentence, it can immediately help you clarify the meaning of a word that is unfamiliar or that has multiple meanings. The chart shows an example.

Any of the following words can be a clue to the presence of a synonym: *similarly, as, like, or.* These words and phrases can signal the presence of an antonym: *but actually, whereas, on the other hand, by contrast.*

CONTEXT SENTENCE	ANALYSIS
Teens may wish to enjoy the benefits of participating in public, but they also relish intimacy and the ability to have control over their social situation.	*In public* and *intimacy* are antonyms, as signaled by the word *but.* Since *in public* means "open to the knowledge or judgment of all," you can infer that *intimacy* is the opposite of that, and means something like "privacy."

Practice and Apply Imagine you need to explain social media and smartphones to a younger person unfamiliar with the technology. Write four sentences that you might use in your explanation. In each sentence, use a synonym or an antonym to clarify the meaning of one unfamiliar or difficult word. You may use these sentence frames if you like:

❑ The [unfamiliar word], or [synonym], is something that _____.

❑ You might think that [clause containing unfamiliar word], but actually [clause containing antonym of unfamiliar word].

374   Unit 5

 ## ENGLISH LEARNER SUPPORT

Vocabulary Strategy Give students additional practice using context clues. Write the following sentences on the board and tell them to use context clues to fill the blanks.

1. *Moses is a _____ boy, but his sister is quiet and shy.*

2. *When Janice saw the new ____ Toni posted on Facebook, she was glad she had worn her best outfit.*

3. *Dana's nose turned red and her ____came out like puffs of steam in the ____ air.*

SUBSTANTIAL/MODERATE

LANGUAGE CONVENTIONS:
Compound Sentences

A **clause** is a group of words that contains a subject and a predicate. A **compound sentence** consists of two or more **independent clauses,** or clauses that can each stand alone as a sentence. There are two ways to correctly form and punctuate a compound sentence.

You may join independent clauses by using a coordinating conjunction (*and, but, or, nor, yet, for,* or *so*) preceded by a comma (,).

> **Furthermore, social interactions may be a distraction from school, <u>but</u> they are often not a distraction from learning.**

You may also join two independent clauses with a semicolon (;).

> **Furthermore, social interactions may be a distraction from school; they are often not a distraction from learning.**

If you do not join clauses correctly, you will have a **run-on sentence,** which is a grammatical error. Using only a comma between the two clauses, without a coordinating conjunction, creates a run-on error called a **comma splice.**

Practice and Apply Rewrite the following sentences to correct run-ons and add any missing punctuation. Then look back at the opinion piece you wrote to find and fix any comma splices and run-on sentences you may have created.

1. You may be preoccupied by social media but you aren't necessarily addicted to it.

2. The sleek smartphones are alluring, they glow, *ping*, and provide access to movies, music, games, and friends.

3. The two friends were constantly connected on social media they even stayed connected while they were asleep.

4. Theresa's mother watches TV all the time but she criticizes Theresa for being online for more than an hour.

5. Raj keeps his social network open on his computer he hides it with the screen containing his homework.

! Go to **The Sentence** in the **Grammar Studio** for more on punctuating compound sentences.

LANGUAGE CONVENTIONS:
Compound Sentences

Make sure students understand that **compound sentences** always have two **independent clauses**, that could be complete sentences. Also, make sure they understand that they cannot simply put the two clauses together with a comma because compound sentences require **conjunctions**.

Practice and Apply Accept all properly punctuated sentences but don't require students to have submitted more than one option. The following are correct options with the likeliest or best correction first. But accept all properly punctuated responses.

1. *You may be preoccupied by social media, but you aren't necessarily addicted to it. You may be preoccupied by social media; you aren't necessarily addicted to it.*

2. *The sleek smartphones are alluring; they glow, ping, and provide access to movies, music, games, and friends. The sleek smartphones are alluring, for they glow, ping, and provide access to movies, music, games, and friends.*

3. *The two friends were constantly connected on social media; they stayed connected even while they were asleep. The two friends were constantly connected on social media, so they stayed connected even while they were asleep.*

4. *Theresa's mother watches TV all the time, but she criticizes Theresa for being online for more than an hour. Theresa's mother watches TV all the time; she criticizes Theresa for being online for more than an hour.*

5. *Raj keeps his social network open on his computer, but he hides it with the screen containing his homework. Raj keeps his social network open on his computer; he hides it with the screen containing his homework.*

 ENGLISH LEARNER SUPPORT

Language Conventions Write the word Conjunctions on the board and list these words under it: *and, but, for, nor , yet, or, so.* Add the word *because* and then put an *X* over it. Explain that the use of *because* makes any clause that follows it dependent on the first clause, so even if it appears to be an independent clause that could be a stand-alone sentence, it is not functioning as an independent clause in the sentence. Therefore, the word *because* is not a conjunction and should not have a comma before it. **LIGHT**

OUTSMART YOUR SMARTPHONE
Article by Catherine Steiner-Adair

GENRE ELEMENTS
ARGUMENT

Remind students that the purpose of an **argument** is to present and persuade others to agree with the writer's position about an issue. Writers introduce their position by making a claim. They then support this claim by explaining their reasons and relevant evidence. Strong evidence for topics researched by scientists, such as trends in society or human behavior, includes statistics and other findings from scientific studies. To strengthen their argument, writers also discuss counter claims, or opposing viewpoints, and disprove them with counter arguments. In this lesson, students will analyze and compare an argument to another they have read on the same topic.

LEARNING OBJECTIVES

- Analyze and use evidence to explain the structure and rhetorical devices used to develop an argument.
- Conduct research about smartphones and social media.
- Write a letter to register a formal complaint.
- Compare the characteristics and strength of two arguments.
- Collaboratively develop and present an argument and counter argument through role-playing.
- Correctly capitalize proper nouns and hyphenated words.
- **Language** Describe evidence using the key term *relevant*.

TEXT COMPLEXITY

Quantitative Measures	Outsmart Your Smartphone	Lexile: 1110L
Qualitative Measures	**Ideas Presented** Mostly explicit but challenging ideas; argument requires higher-order reasoning.	
	Structure Used Clear cause-and-effect structure, with supporting ideas signaled with key words.	
	Language Used Explicit, contemporary language, but includes many Tier Two and Tier Three words.	
	Knowledge Required Relies on first-hand knowledge of social media; contexts are familiar.	

RESOURCES

- Unit 5 Response Log
- 🔊 Selection Audio
- 📖 Reading Studio: Notice & Note
- 📋 Writing Studio: Writing Arguments
- 💬 Speaking and Listening Studio: Participating in Collaborative Discussions
- ⚛ Vocabulary Studio: Word Families
- ❗ Grammar Studio: Module 13: Capital Letters
- ☑ "Outsmart Your Smartphone" Selection Test

SUMMARIES

English

Research shows that overusing social media can harm a teenager's well-being. Its addictive effect on the brain can lead to behavior that one regrets. It can take time away from real communication, prevent the development of skills needed for meaningful friendships, and cause anxiety that reduces self-esteem. Multitasking on social media can impair one's ability to focus and learn. Social media also promotes negative social behavior that can change one's personality. Teens can protect themselves by using social media less often.

Spanish

Estudios muestran que el uso excesivo de las redes sociales puede perjudicar el bienestar de los adolescentes. Su efecto adictivo en el cerebro lleva a comportamientos de los cuales uno se arrepiente. Pueden restar tiempo para comunicaciones reales, frustrar el desarrollo de capacidades necesarias para formar amistades significativas, así como causar ansiedad y reducir la autoestima. Las multitareas en las redes sociales reducen la capacidad de concentración y entendimiento. Las redes sociales promueven comportamientos sociales negativos que le cambian a uno la personalidad. Los adolescentes pueden protegerse al utilizar redes sociales con menos frecuencia.

 ## SMALL-GROUP OPTIONS

Have students work in small groups to read and discuss the selection.

Reciprocal Teaching

- Have students read the selection.
- Give students these question stems:
  Why does the author _____?
  Is the author saying that _____?
  What causes _____?
  How does _____ affect ...?
  How does _____ support ...?
- Ask students to use each stem to write a question they have about the selection.
- Have students form small groups, take turns asking a question, and discuss the answer to each using text evidence.
- Ask groups to share a question and their answer with the class.

Think-Pair-Share

- Have students read paragraphs 1–7.
- Pose this question: *Why does the author begin her argument this way?*
- Have student pairs think about the question individually, find evidence to support their response, and take notes.
- Tell pairs to discuss their responses and evidence and form a shared response.
- Have pairs tell you their response and then finish reading the selection.
- Ask pairs to repeat the process for this new question: *What is the most convincing reason to be cautious about social media? Why do you think so?*

Text X-Ray: English Learner Support
for "Outsmart Your Smartphone"

Use the Text X-Ray and the supports and scaffolds in the Teacher's Edition to help guide students at different proficiency levels through the selection.

INTRODUCE THE SELECTION
DISCUSS ONLINE CONNECTIONS

In this lesson, students will need to be able to discuss connections in terms of the Internet and relationships. Tell students that the verb *connect* has several meanings, and display and read aloud these definitions and examples:

Connect: To join or become joined through a phone or computer	**Connect**: To have or share feelings of affection and understanding
People can **connect** online by using Facebook and other social media to communicate.	People feel like they **connect** when they laugh together or have a good conversation.

Have small groups collaboratively make a concept map of ways they connect in either context: by communicating through smartphones or by having relationships. Provide these sentence stems help students think of, map, and share their examples with the class:

- *You can use a smartphone to connect by _____.*
- *You connect with someone when you _____.*

CULTURAL REFERENCES

The following words and phrases may be unfamiliar to students:

- *adolescence* (paragraph 1): the time of life when a child develops into an adult; the teenage years
- *antsy* (paragraph 6): not able to wait or keep still
- *went viral* (paragraph 7): became very popular or spread very quickly on the Internet
- *snarky* (paragraph 10): ironic or saying the opposite of what you mean, to be funny or hurtful

LISTENING

Understand the Main Ideas

Draw students' attention to the word *Fifth* in paragraph 17, and ask how many reasons the author gives to support her claim. (*five*) Explain that the author discusses her last reason in paragraphs 17–18, and invite students to ask for clarification of any words in the paragraphs.

Have students listen as you read aloud paragraphs 17–18. Use the following supports with students at varying proficiency levels:

- Tell students that you will ask questions about what you just read aloud. For example, after reading paragraph 17, ask: *Are people always nice to each other on social media?* (*no*) *Does the author think social media makes people act less friendly?* (*no*) Continue asking *yes/no* questions to help students recognize the main idea of both paragraphs. **SUBSTANTIAL**

- For each paragraph, have students share words or phrases that they think describe the main idea. Then ask students to listen as you offer several different summaries of the author's fifth reason, and tell you which they think is correct. **MODERATE**

- Tell students that you will ask them to identify the main idea of the paragraphs, and allow them to take notes as they listen. Have student pairs work together to state the main idea. **LIGHT**

SPEAKING

Discuss Viewpoints

Help students prepare for the role-playing activity on p. 391. Display expressions for disagreeing (*I disagree; I don't agree; Yes, but; The problem is that*) and persuading (*Don't you think/agree that; We know that; Isn't it true that*).

Use the following supports with students at varying proficiency levels:

- Display this sample conversation: [Teen] *I think social media helps people make friends.* [Adult] *I disagree, because people also use it to be mean to others.* [Teen] *Yes, but not everyone acts like a bully.* [Adult] *Don't you think social media makes it easier to be a bully?* Have students chorally read the conversation with you and then take turns playing each role with a partner. **SUBSTANTIAL**

- Display and have students chorally read aloud the sample conversation with you. Call attention to the expressions used to introduce each point (e.g., *I disagree, because*). Then underline the point made in each sentence (e.g., *social media helps people make friends*). Have student pairs use the sample as a model to frame their viewpoints and practice role-playing. **MODERATE**

- Have students prepare note cards for making points, disagreeing with possible opposing points, and persuading their partner to agree with them. Ask pairs to practice role-playing. **LIGHT**

READING

Evaluate Evidence

Have students evaluate and describe the evidence in paragraphs 15–16 using the key term *relevant*. Tell students a Spanish cognate for *relevant* is *relevante*. Review that *relevant evidence* helps explain a reason or support a claim.

Work with students to read paragraphs 15–16, and have them take notes in their Reason, Evidence, and What It Shows charts. Use the following supports with students at varying proficiency levels:

- Ask questions such as, *Do students who use social media do worse on tests?* (yes) *Does this help explain that social media hurts your grades?* (yes) *Is this relevant evidence?* Have them respond with *It is/is not relevant* or with a thumbs up/down. **SUBSTANTIAL**

- Have student pairs respond to guiding questions such as, *Does taking longer to do homework mean that you are not learning?* (no) *Does it help explain that social media makes learning harder?* (yes) *Why is this relevant evidence?* Provide this stem: *It is/is not relevant because _____.* **MODERATE**

- Have student pairs use their notes to help them answer these questions: *Which evidence do you think is the strongest? How relevant is it to the point the author is making?* **LIGHT**

WRITING

Write a Letter

Create and use a letter outline to explain the writing assignment on p. 387. Explain that the social media site may agree that the problem needs to be fixed, if students' reasoning is clear. Display a variety of expressions they may use. read the words/phrases aloud. Have students repeat them.

Use the following supports with students at varying proficiency levels:

- Display and read aloud a sample paragraph, such as: *I'm writing to complain about a mean person on your site. You should know that this person is a bully. She said mean things to my friends every day. As a result, we do not use your site anymore.* Work with students to brainstorm or locate other words in the text for *mean*. Have students replace the word and copy the sentences. **SUBSTANTIAL**

- Display cloze sentences, and have small groups use the displayed expressions to complete them. For example: *_____ complain about person on your site. _____ this person is a bully who makes fun of people and scares them away. _____ many of my friends have stopped using the site. _____ you warn her to act nicely, _____ she may listen.* Tell groups to use them as a model to write a shared letter. **MODERATE**

- Discuss possible uses of the displayed expressions, such as stating a claim, giving reasons and evidence, and offering suggestions. Then have pairs work together to draft a letter. **LIGHT**

Connect to the
ESSENTIAL QUESTION

"Outsmart Your Smartphone" argues that excessive use of social media can impair teenagers' social, emotional, and academic development, stunting the personal growth necessary to become healthy adults. "Life online" can be particularly damaging to teens because they are in the process of defining themselves, how they relate to others, and how the world works—and the online world is not the same as the real one.

COMPARE ARGUMENTS

Point out to students that reading an opposing argument will help them consider both sides of the issue—and that if evidence in "Outsmart Your Smartphone" causes them to question what they read in *It's Complicated*, it is a sign that it was well presented or chosen. On the other hand, students may find some of Steiner-Adair's evidence or reasoning unconvincing. Explain that noting both instances will help them compare the texts, decide whether one position was better argued than the other, and determine why that is the case. Then students can try out the techniques they found effective when they make their own argument later.

ARGUMENT

OUTSMART YOUR SMARTPHONE

by **Catherine Steiner-Adair**
pages 379–385

COMPARE ARGUMENTS

Now that you've read *It's Complicated,* read an argument that takes the opposite position. As you read, pay attention to how well the evidence in "Outsmart Your Smartphone" supports the writer's claim. Also notice whether the evidence ever causes you to question your opinion on this matter. After you are finished, you will collaborate on a final project that involves analyzing both texts.

ESSENTIAL QUESTION:

How do your teenage years prepare you for adulthood?

ARGUMENT

from

IT'S COMPLICATED:
The Social Lives of Networked Teens

by **danah boyd**
pages 367–371

376   Unit 5

Outsmart Your Smartphone

QUICK START

Do you ever feel that technology and social media are having a negative impact on your life? Make a list of some possible drawbacks.

ANALYZE STRUCTURE

All arguments take a position on an issue—that is, they make a **claim.** Writers almost always state their claims early in their arguments. However, they may present their reasons and evidence to support the claim in a variety of ways. In "Outsmart Your Smartphone," the author uses a cause-effect structure. Specifically, she tries to convince readers that five kinds of effects result from social media use. She introduces each with a transition such as *first, second,* and *third.* As you read, look for these transitions and the cause-effect relationships they introduce.

GENRE ELEMENTS: ARGUMENT

• makes a claim

• supports claim with reasons and evidence

• notes counter claims and provides counter arguments to disprove them

• for topics involving society or psychology, may cite scientific studies as evidence

ANALYZE RHETORICAL DEVICES

Rhetorical devices are techniques writers use to enhance their arguments and communicate effectively. Several of these techniques are defined in the chart. As you read "Outsmart Your Smartphone," add more examples from the text. Then consider why the author might have used these devices. What audience is she trying to reach?
Possible examples:

RHETORICAL DEVICE	DEFINITION	EXAMPLE
Analogy	A point-by-point comparison between two things that are alike in some respect	Paragraph 11: The author compares learning conversation skills to learning to drive.
Direct address	Talking directly to the reader, often using the pronoun *you*	Paragraph 2: "You can use smartphones and social media to build healthy relationships and a sense of belonging."
Juxtaposition	The placement of two or more things side by side to show their similarities and/or differences	*Paragraph 1: "At first, people took sides on this issue based on their own gut feelings. Now...it's possible to hold a more informed perspective on the effects of engaging with social media and life online."*
Rhetorical question	A question that has such an obvious answer that it requires no reply	*Paragraph 1: "But was the technology itself significantly changing the landscape of teen life?"*

Being aware of rhetorical devices helps you recognize how the author is trying to persuade you. Watching out for **logical fallacies,** or misuses of logic, helps you decide whether the argument is sound. One kind of fallacy is **circular reasoning,** which is supporting a statement simply by repeating it in different words.

Outsmart Your Smartphone   377

QUICK START

Explain that students also may list complaints they have heard or personally have about other people's use of smartphones and social media. Have them share some of the drawbacks and categorize them. Ask: *What parts of life are negatively affected? How serious is this issue?*

ANALYZE STRUCTURE

Remind students that a claim is a stated position on an issue. Point out that the claim is introduced early in an argument because it is the main idea being developed. Ask students what the title "Outsmart Your Smartphone" suggests is the author's claim. (Your smartphone will get the better of you in some way if you are not careful.)

Explain that identifying the cause-and-effect structure in the text will help students analyze the author's reasoning. One way to identify logical fallacies is to analyze whether a stated effect of something actually is an effect or result.

ANALYZE RHETORICAL DEVICES

Point out that people also use rhetorical devices in everyday speech, sometimes in combination. Share these examples, and ask students to identify the effect of each:

- **analog:** Alex is like a fish in the water; he can swim faster and farther than anyone. He's more at home in the water than out. (It explains how well he swims.)
- **direct address:** You can imagine what a mess her room was after that. (It makes you imagine the mess.)
- **juxtaposition:** After dinner, I have to put the dishes in the dishwasher. My brother gets to go to his room to do homework. (The difference points out the unfairness.)
- **rhetorical question:** That's a great idea for a gift. Who doesn't like chocolate? (It shows how great the idea is.)

Tell students paragraph 11 uses two rhetorical devices and ask them to identify the second (direct address).

 ENGLISH LEARNER SUPPORT

Recognize Sounds Remind students that concentrating on syllables can help them read and pronounce longer words correctly. Call students' attention to the rhetorical devices in the table, and point out that the *h* in *rhetoric* is silent. Tell students to listen carefully for each syllable in each word as you read the terms aloud. Repeat them while clapping your hands to mark syllables. Then have students say the terms with you. Ask student pairs to practice pronouncing the words, and circulate around the room to assist by clapping out syllables, pronouncing the words, or helping students with specific sounds, like the *j* in *juxtaposition.*
ALL LEVELS

TEACH

CRITICAL VOCABULARY

Remind students to look for context clues about the meaning of the word in each question.

Answers:

1. *It means I want to know that person's opinion or viewpoint on the topic because perspective means "point of view."*

2. *A stimulant like coffee makes you more alert, so you would be less likely to fall asleep.*

3. *A deliberate comment is worse because it would be made after considering the consequences, which means it was intended to be hurtful. An impulsive comment is made spontaneously and without thinking, so it could be unintentional.*

4. *To be anonymous is to remain unknown or be unidentifiable, so a likely reaction would be anger that your name was revealed against your wishes.*

5. *A stern look would be more inhibiting, or restraining, because it could be interpreted as a warning not to act or behave a certain way.*

■ English Learner Support

Use Cognates Tell students that three of the Critical Vocabulary words have Spanish cognates: *perspective/ perspectiva, anonymous/anónimo,* and *inhibit/inhibir.*
ALL LEVELS

LANGUAGE CONVENTIONS

Explain that *twenty* does not need to be capitalized if the sentence is rewritten: *According to a 2015 study by the Pew Research Center, twenty-four percent of them say they are online "almost constantly."*

✎ ANNOTATION MODEL

Ask students to note the elements listed on p. 377. Suggest underlining them and using the margin to note their ideas or questions, as shown. Also suggest circling transition words that signal a cause-and-effect structure. Point out that students may use their own system for marking up the selection in their write-in text. They may want to color-code their annotations for rhetorical devices by using highlighters. Their notes in the margin may include definitions of unfamiliar words.

 GET READY

CRITICAL VOCABULARY

perspective	deliberate	impulsive
stimulant	anonymous	inhibited

To see how many Critical Vocabulary words you already know, answer the following questions.

1. What does asking for someone's **perspective** on a topic mean you want to know? Why?

2. If someone took a **stimulant,** would he or she be likely to fall asleep immediately? Why?

3. Why might a **deliberate** comment that's hurtful be worse than an **impulsive** one?

4. If you wanted to be an **anonymous** source for a news article, how might you react to seeing your full name in the article? Why?

5. Which is more likely to make you feel **inhibited:** a stern look from your teacher or a kind smile? Why?

LANGUAGE CONVENTIONS

Correct Capitalization In this lesson, you will learn to correctly capitalize proper nouns, such as the names of organizations, and hyphenated words that begin sentences. The author models proper capitalization in sentences such as this one:

Twenty-four percent of them say they are online "almost constantly," according to a 2015 study by the **Pew Research Center**.

ANNOTATION MODEL

NOTICE & NOTE

As you read "Outsmart Your Smartphone," mark the text to trace the writer's argument. This model shows one reader's notes.

1   Adolescence has always been a hero's journey of growing independence, exploration, and self-discovery. When smartphones swept onto the scene in 2008, teenagers used them for familiar purposes—to connect to each other and share interests out of adults' view. [But was the technology itself significantly changing the landscape of teen life?] At first, <u>people took sides on this issue based on their own gut feelings</u>. Now with more than a decade of experience, <u>it's possible to hold a more informed perspective</u> on the effects of engaging with social media and life online. . . .

Will the argument give the author's answer to this question?

She may provide scientific evidence to replace "gut feelings."

BACKGROUND

Catherine Steiner-Adair is an internationally recognized clinical psychologist, consultant, and speaker and the author of the award-winning book The Big Disconnect. *She has a different perspective on teenagers and technology than danah boyd in* It's Complicated. *In this argument, Steiner-Adair explores problems associated with teenagers' use of social media and smartphones.*

OUTSMART YOUR SMARTPHONE

Argument by Catherine Steiner-Adair

PREPARE TO COMPARE

As you read, analyze both the author's style and the argument she makes. Do all the reasons given by the author support her claim? Is there sufficient relevant evidence to support her position?

1 Adolescence has always been a hero's journey of growing independence, exploration, and self-discovery. When smartphones swept onto the scene in 2008, teenagers used them for familiar purposes—to connect to each other and share interests out of adults' view. But was the technology itself significantly changing the landscape of teen life? At first, people took sides on this issue based on their own gut feelings. Now with more than a decade of experience, it's possible to hold a more informed **perspective** on the effects of engaging with social media and life online. In writing my book *The Big Disconnect: Protecting Childhood and Family Relationships in the Digital Age,* I studied the current research and interviewed hundreds of teenagers around the country. I can say without hesitation that though social media is a useful and enticing tool, it poses unique risks to adolescent well-being.

Notice & Note

Use the side margins to notice and note signposts in the text.

ANALYZE RHETORICAL DEVICES

Annotate: In paragraph 1, mark two ways the author identifies for arriving at an opinion on an issue.

Infer: What might be the author's purpose for using this juxtaposition?

perspective
(pər-spĕk′tĭv) *n.* A *perspective* is a viewpoint on or understanding of something.

Outsmart Your Smartphone **379**

BACKGROUND

After students read the Background information, explain that a clinical psychologist is a person who has an advanced degree in *psychology*, or the study of the mind and how it affects human behavior. Clinical psychologists help people identify the causes of their behavior and deal with the problems that result from their actions.

PREPARE TO COMPARE

Direct students to use the Prepare to Compare prompt to focus their reading.

ANALYZE RHETORICAL DEVICES

Remind students that a **juxtaposition** is a **rhetorical device** that places one or more things close together to call attention to their similarities or differences. (***Answer:*** *The author probably juxtaposes these methods to point out that there is an old way and a new way of thinking about this issue, to convince readers that the new viewpoint she is about to present is better. The phrase "At first, people" suggests that all the early viewpoints and popular opinions were based on gut feelings. Juxtaposing them with the "more informed perspective" possible "now," which is based on study results and other evidence that wasn't available before, automatically makes the earlier views seem out-of-date and inferior compared to the author's. It also may imply that people who still hold these views—including readers—need to change them to stay up-to-date and become better informed themselves.)*

 ENGLISH LEARNER SUPPORT

Use Support Remind students that time and transition words can help them understand the relationship between ideas in nearby sentences. Call their attention to the phrase *At first* in paragraph 1. Have students scan the rest of the paragraph for another time word (*Now*). Explain that these contrasting time words suggest that the sentences provide contrasting ideas or information about changes over time. **MODERATE**

ANALYZE STRUCTURE

Encourage students to identify the author's main **claim** before responding to the question. Remind them that the purpose of an argument is to convince readers that a claim is true or correct. (**Answer**: *By acknowledging these benefits, the author shows that she has considered the opposite viewpoint, or counter claim, to her claim that social media poses risks to teens' well-being. This can make readers think that her argument is reasonable and be more willing to accept it.*)

▶ CONTRASTS AND CONTRADICTIONS

Remind students that words such as *however* and *although* can signal meaningful **contrasts or contradictions**. Have them look for a word signaling a contrast in paragraph 3 and then consider why the information it introduces is familiar. (**Answer**: *The author is echoing the juxtaposition in paragraph 1 between old views based on gut feelings and new views based on evidence, to expand on the idea that the old views based on gut feelings are wrong. She does this by suggesting that one such view is the belief that "social media is just a new version of what's always been," and then stating that this view is not supported by studies.*)

NOTICE & NOTE

ANALYZE STRUCTURE

Annotate: Mark all the positive effects of using social media listed in paragraph 2.

Infer: How might identifying these benefits at the beginning of her argument help the author achieve her purpose?

◀ **CONTRASTS AND CONTRADICTIONS**

Notice & Note: Mark the two sentences in paragraph 3 that introduce a sharp contrast or contradiction.

Connect: What earlier juxtaposition is the author echoing and expanding upon here? Explain.

---

2   The benefits of social media are obvious. You can use smartphones and social media to build healthy relationships and a sense of belonging. You can partner with others to help, share, volunteer, collaborate. Never before have middle school students been able to take a class with students in China. You can get in touch with total strangers who like the same rock band, write fan fiction together with people anywhere in the world, or join an online gaming group. Texting and social networking sites make it easier to connect with kids right where you are, too. Social networking lets you get together with friends where your parents aren't around. Expressing yourself, figuring out who you are and developing a sense of self and identity that's separate from your parents and family are important parts of adolescent development.

3   But there's more to the story. While it's tempting to believe that social media is just a new version of what's always been, with the same dangers and benefits, studies suggest that's just not true. A growing body of scientific evidence and everyday experience show that social media is not simply a natural and healthy extension of teens' social lives and development. It can negatively affect the brain and behavior in ways that mimic addiction, adversely affect learning, distort normal aspects of social and emotional development, and increase anxiety. There is too much research and too much everyday evidence now for us to ignore the risks. You have to approach social media with restraint and caution if you want to avoid harm.

4   How and how often you use social media matters. Ninety-two percent of teens report going online daily. Twenty-four percent of them say they are online "almost constantly," according to a 2015 study by the Pew Research Center. More than half (fifty-six percent) of teens, ages thirteen to seventeen, go online several times a day. Most use mobile devices and three-quarters of the teens say they have access to a smartphone. The more time you spend texting or online, the greater the risks of harm. This is especially concerning in

ENGLISH LEARNER SUPPORT

Demonstrate Understanding   Point out the word *While* in paragraph 3. Explain that it can mean "at the same time" or "although," and tell students to use context clues to identify its meaning in the sentence. Ask students to identify the meaning of *while* and tell you the clue they used. *(although; But)* **MODERATE**

adolescence. It's a critical window of time for brain growth, physical development, and social and emotional development.

5   Social media is a **stimulant** to the brain. Texting and other use triggers release of dopamine, a natural chemical that produces a pleasurable sensation that most brains crave to repeat. But the more you use social media, the more you want to use it, and that impulse can override the **deliberate** decision-making activity of the part of the brain called the prefrontal cortex. It also creates a sense of urgency. You feel compelled to react or respond right away and hit send.

6   The combination of the stimulants to the brain and the fact that you feel **anonymous** or at a distance from the person you're communicating with can lead you to behave differently than you would face to face. You become **impulsive,** quick to act and react, even when it carries a risk. You feel less **inhibited,** more likely to say mean or careless things without a thought to the impact of your words, or the consequences. It's easy to say things you later wish you hadn't. On the receiving (or waiting) end, you feel anxious when someone doesn't respond right away, or you feel antsy or bored when there's a lull in communication. Every ping, buzz, or text you send or receive keeps you hooked.

7   A false sense of privacy can trick you into thinking it's safe to share anything—or text or post private or inflammatory[1] things. Plenty of teens have found themselves entangled in social drama made worse when posts went viral. At the most tragic extreme, social media has provided a platform for cyberbullying. In a study of teens and social media use, nine out of ten teens reported that they had seen bullying online.

8   Bullying gets a lot of attention and for good reason, but let's look at other common social media behaviors or beliefs with negative consequences.

9   First, texting is easier than talking and seems like the same thing, but it isn't. Social media is no substitute for face-to-face conversation or hanging out, a handshake or comforting hug, shared laughter or even shared quiet time. Texting, tweeting, email and other text-only forms of messaging eliminate two essential aspects of human communication: the power of voice and the ability to see the impact of your words.

10   Tone of voice gives meaning to our words. You might use the phrase "I hate you!" jokingly to mean "I'm so jealous of you!" but what if that's not clear? Even a simple text like "sorry" can be difficult to decipher—are you being snarky or sincere?

---

[1] **inflammatory:** provocative; likely to provoke a strong reaction.

NOTICE & NOTE

stimulant
(stĭm´yə-lənt) *n*. A *stimulant* is an agent that excites or temporarily speeds up mental and/or physical functions.

deliberate
(dĭ-lĭb´ər-ĭt) *adj*. *Deliberate* decision-making activity is the process of making a choice only after carefully considering its likely effects.

anonymous
(ə-nŏn´ə-məs) *adj*. To be *anonymous* means to be unknown or unidentified by name.

impulsive
(ĭm-pŭl´sĭv) *adj*. To be *impulsive* means to act quickly, before thinking about the consequences.

inhibited
(ĭn-hĭb´ĭt-əd) *adj*. If you feel *inhibited,* you feel restrained, held back, or self-conscious.

ANALYZE RHETORICAL DEVICES

Annotate: Review paragraphs 5 and 6. Mark the sentences in which the author uses direct address.

Analyze: What is the impact of using direct address to convey this particular information?

✏ ANALYZE RHETORICAL DEVICES

Remind students that **direct address** is a **rhetorical device** in which the author talks directly to the reader, usually using the pronouns *you* and *your*. (**Answer**: *The author conveys to the reader, in effect, "I know how you feel and think when you use social media, and I understand." This helps her establish a relationship with the reader, so they are more likely to believe what she is saying. Also, by directly telling readers what they think and feel, the author is compelling them to relive or imagine the experience, as though she is giving them directions.*)

CRITICAL VOCABULARY

stimulant: Using social media is a *stimulant* because it excites the brain and makes it more active.

ASK STUDENTS what a brain stimulated by using social media does that creates a pleasurable feeling. (*The brain releases the chemical dopamine.*)

deliberate: Decision making is a *deliberate* activity when choices and their effects are carefully thought out.

ASK STUDENTS how the desire to use social media makes decision making a less deliberate activity. (*It makes you rush through decisions to take action.*)

anonymous: People may be or feel *anonymous* online if their user name is not their real name or they do not have a profile picture.

ASK STUDENTS why an anonymous social media user is more likely to make mean comments. (*If people do not know who you really are, you probably will care less about what they think of you.*)

impulsive: Saying the first thing that comes to mind is *impulsive*.

ASK STUDENTS what could result from an impulsive comment. (*You might reveal a secret or say something that you regret later.*)

inhibited: People who are not *inhibited* by rules of acceptable social behavior are more likely to be rude to others.

ASK STUDENTS what could make someone inhibited online. (*You might be inhibited if all your classmates know your user name.*)

ENGLISH LEARNER SUPPORT

Spell Vowel Patterns   Explain to students that different vowel patterns can create a similar sounds, such as *au, augh, al,* and *aw*.

Write the following words on the board: *because, taught, walk,* and *draw*. Have volunteers identify and underline the letters that form the same sound in each word: *bec<u>au</u>se; t<u>augh</u>t; w<u>al</u>k; dr<u>aw</u>*. Then have students work in small groups to write sentences using each word.

SUBSTANTIAL/MODERATE

Write the following on the board *bec_ _se, t_ _t, w_ _k,* and *dr_ _*. Have students complete the correct vowel pattern for each word. **LIGHT**

ANALYZE RHETORICAL DEVICES

Remind students that an **analogy** is a comparison between two things that are alike in some way. (**Answer:** *The author is most likely writing for a teenage audience, because these would be the readers for whom learning to drive would be a fresh and recent experience.*)

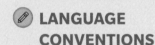

ANALYZE STRUCTURE

Tell students to consider both the author's reasoning and supporting evidence. Remind them to look out for **logical fallacies**, or misuses of logic. (**Answer**: *These relationships do not fully support the third reason for the author's claim. Dependence "can" occur and, if online access isn't available, anxiety "can" result for "some" teens, but these issues are not certain to occur. She has not proven that constant connectivity may cause dependence in the first place.*)

LANGUAGE CONVENTIONS

Point out that the purpose of capitalizing **proper nouns** is to name specific people, places, or things. (*Only the truly important words in institution names should be capitalized. Articles such as "of" are not as important as the words that specify the kind of institution [University] and its location [Cologne].*)

NOTICE & NOTE

ANALYZE RHETORICAL DEVICES

Annotate: Mark the analogy in paragraph 11.

Infer: Think about who would be able to relate to this analogy. For what audience is the author most likely writing? Explain.

ANALYZE STRUCTURE

Annotate: In paragraph 13, underline the effect of "constant connectivity," according to the author. Then circle what that, in turn, can cause.

Evaluate: Does this cause-effect relationship help the author support her argument? Explain.

LANGUAGE CONVENTIONS

Annotate: Mark the capitalized proper nouns in paragraph 14.

Infer: Why is it incorrect to capitalize words such as *of* in the name of an institution?

Distanced from the impact your words have on others, you can't see their reaction or correct a misunderstanding.

11   Also, when texting takes the place of face-to-face talking, you don't get the real-time practice of conversation skills and the confidence that goes with it. You can't get a driver's license just by passing an online test. You have to log hours of actual driving time to develop the real-time, real life skills to drive. The same in-real-life practice is required for the social and emotional skills you need to navigate life. Direct communication is one of the most important.

12   Second, social media expands social networks, but not necessarily the deeper stuff of meaningful friendship. Research and life experience tell us that "likes" and casual online "friends" are no substitute for friendship. Friendship includes a deeper knowing of one another, shared respect and trust, and acceptance. It's easy to think that your "street smarts"—your ability to assess if someone is trustworthy or not—work just as well on social media sites as in real life, but research tells us that we tend to trust too easily online. Social media was designed to be a way to connect people. But it also has put a crimp in teens' ability to connect in deep and meaningful ways. Some find it harder to be emotionally vulnerable and emotionally honest with one another. Emotional growth and learning how to be a partner in relationship are hard work, and part of natural development that emerges in adolescence. But it takes time and practice to develop that natural capacity. The default text of *hey what's up?* mutes those moments for more textured conversations. You might find it easier to say things that are serious and important to you by texting, where you don't feel as vulnerable as you might face to face. Ultimately, though, it's important in life to be able to say directly to people what's on your mind and what's in your heart, and have difficult conversations. That takes practice.

13   Third, the "everywhere, always on" presence of social media and life online creates new kinds of psychological issues. The constant connectivity can create psychological dependence. This can cause anxiety when you're separated from your phone or unable to go online. Some teens experience a form of separation anxiety if they don't have their phone, or if an adult takes it away.

14   If you are "always on," the fear of missing out often creates anxiety with no relief. On social media, like never before, you can see every party, every event, every "inside joke" that you are not a part of. You see the endless stream of nasty comments or trending gossip and might start to quietly fear you'll become

---

WHEN STUDENTS STRUGGLE . . .

Learning Strategy Tell students that there are two levels at which they should analyze the text: the reasons supporting the main claim, and the evidence supporting each reason. Have students individually use a chart to help them identify these elements.

Main Claim	
Reason	**Supporting Evidence**

For additional support, go to the **Reading Studio** and assign the following **Level Up tutorial: Analyzing Arguments.**

the target of it. A growing number of studies have also found that looking at "perfect" photos of other people may increase anxiety and make people feel bad about themselves. A 2016 study by researchers at the University of Cologne in Germany described so-called Facebook envy and depression as a serious concern, echoing other studies of social media's negative effects on mental health. Students often tell me that class outings or summer camp where cell phones weren't allowed were "the best ever." Why? Because after a short withdrawal period, classmates enjoyed the freedom from the pressures of social media and the fun of being together.

15   Fourth, social media distraction has a negative effect on learning and on grades. When you multitask on different devices or online activities your brain makes you feel really powerful. It makes you think you can multitask

effectively. That's one reason it's so hard to listen to teachers or parents when they say don't do it. But actually, in your brain, multitasking on digital devices takes away from your attention to any one thing with a continuous stream of mini-interruptions.

16   Studies show that multitasking with social media makes homework take longer. It also weakens short-term and long-term memory. Students who used social networking scored twenty percent lower on tests, and had lower grades compared to those that stayed off social media until their work was done. Even when users just go on social media for a "quick" break, the average amount of time off their task is typically twenty to twenty-five minutes. That increases the time it takes to complete a two-hour task by thirty percent. A study conducted by scientists at University of Texas-Austin in 2017 found that just having your smartphone nearby reduces cognitive performance—how well your brain can think and learn—even when the phone is silent or out of sight.

ANALYZE STRUCTURE

Annotate: In paragraph 14, mark the sentences that present scholarly research.

Analyze: Which point does this evidence support?

ANALYZE RHETORICAL DEVICES

Annotate: Underline the effect the author introduces in paragraph 15, and circle the information she provides to support it.

Analyze: Has the author provided sufficient evidence to support her point, or does the paragraph use circular reasoning? Explain.

Outsmart Your Smartphone   **383**

ANALYZE STRUCTURE

Discuss that, rather than always using completely formal formats, writers sometimes choose to use more casual wording to better reach their audience. (**Answer**: *The only cause-effect relationship that is supported by scholarly evidence is "looking at 'perfect' photos of other people may increase anxiety and make people feel bad about themselves."*)

ANALYZE RHETORICAL DEVICES

Have students read the Annotate note. Point out that each effect of using social media that the author lists is another claim that needs to be supported. After students mark the text, remind them that **circular reasoning** is an attempt to support a point by restating it in another way, as if the point is already known to be true. (**Answer**: *Paragraph 15 uses circular reasoning. Instead of providing evidence that social media distraction interferes with learning, the author talks around this point by explaining how social media is a distraction (you multitask when you use it). The last sentence then restates the main point in terms of multitasking, assuming that it is understood that the "one thing" is learning.*)

For **reading support** for students at varying proficiency levels, see the **Text X-Ray** on page 376D.

APPLYING ACADEMIC VOCABULARY

☑ **debate**   ☐ **deduce**   ☐ **license**   ☐ **sufficient**   ☑ **trend**

Write and Discuss Have students turn to a partner to discuss the following questions. Guide students to include the Academic Vocabulary words *debate* and *trend* in their responses. Ask volunteers to share their responses with the class.

- Why might schools **debate** allowing students to carry smartphones with them?
- What negative **trends** in teens' social media use does the author discuss?

ANALYZE RHETORICAL DEVICES

Point out that the subject of an imperative sentence, or a command, is often implied instead of stated. **(Answer:** *These are all examples of direct address, because the author is directly telling the reader to do these things.)*

For **listening support** for students at varying proficiency levels, see the **Text X-Ray** on page 376C.

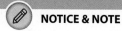

17   Fifth, the distraction of social media can pull you away from your best self, drawing you into the online culture where it's cool to be cruel or disingenuous,[2] and where snarky, mean posts get lots of "likes." This dark side of social networking is not just about meanness. It's that social media cultivates an image-based value system that creates unrealistic expectations and rewards shallowness. As shaming, hate-talk, and other destructive behaviors online get worse, social media becomes increasingly antisocial.

18   A generation ago, parents worried about their kids watching too much TV, which was also seen as spreading poor values. Today's "screen time" is even more problematic. While TV and online entertainment both use screens, our brains don't connect with them in the same ways. TV is at a distance, compared to the close-up visual stimulation on a smartphone or computer screen. Think of how different it feels to binge-watch on the big TV screen versus on your smartphone. TV also tends to be a more social activity. You watch with other people, share the experience, and perhaps talk as you do so.

19   All of this does not mean we must abandon social media entirely, along with those prosocial benefits it does have. But you need self-awareness so that you use this tool to be your best self, make the most of your education, and protect your brain and your own well being. It's important not to let any new app, virtual reality, or whatever the next tech innovation is delete what science has told us for years and still stands true: As a species, we thrive in the context of healthy relationships. We need to manage our use of social media to create supportive connections for learning and life.

20   For example, you don't have to be part of every social media stream your friends are. Be conscious of how much time you're online and limit yourself. Take breaks. Take off one day a week or at mealtimes. Even when it seems easier to stay home and text with your friends, make an effort to get together somewhere and see them instead. If your school allows

ANALYZE RHETORICAL DEVICES

Annotate: An imperative sentence is a direct command, instruction, or request. Mark the imperative sentences In paragraph 20.

Analyze: What rhetorical device are these sentences examples of?

---

[2] **disingenuous** (dĭs´ĭn-jĕn´yoo-əs): insincere, false.

IMPROVE READING FLUENCY

Targeted Passage   Use choral reading to have students read aloud paragraphs 18–20. First, ask students to follow along in their books as you model fluent reading, reading the text aloud with appropriate phrasing, rate, and expression. Then, have the class read aloud the paragraphs in unison with you, and at least once again on their own. Encourage students to note words they have difficulty pronouncing or sentences they stumbled over, and to practice them with a partner.

Go to the **Reading Studio** for additional support in developing fluency.

students to use phones, exercise restraint. Resist the temptation to multitask when you need to have singular focus on your homework. Educate your peers—remember that just having your phone on your desk or in your backpack interferes with your attention.

21   Adolescents have always been the pioneers in evolving cultures, and today's teens are, too. Given the information and education needed to make sound choices, you'll learn to master the social media tool and be able to share tips with the generations before you and after you, as well.

CHECK YOUR UNDERSTANDING

Answer these questions before moving on to the **Analyze the Text** section on the following page.

1 Which is the writer's main claim in "Outsmart Your Smartphone"?

  A *As a species, we thrive in the context of healthy relationships.*

  B *Social media . . . poses unique risks to adolescent well-being.*

  C *The constant connectivity can create psychological dependence.*

  D *You might find it easier to say things that are serious . . . by texting.*

2 The author uses the statistics in paragraph 4 to suggest that —

  F almost all teens use or have access to social media in their daily lives and are therefore affected by it

  G adolescence is a time when people develop mentally, physically, socially, and emotionally

  H a significant percentage of teenagers overestimate the amount of time they spend online each day

  J teens can become physically addicted to social media because it triggers the release of dopamine

3 In paragraph 18, the author suggests that although TV and online entertainment both use screens —

  A watching TV is a more dangerous habit than going online

  B going online doesn't result in the acquisition of poor values

  C dramas on big screens feel more real than those on smartphones

  D watching TV is not as engaging or as isolating as being online

Outsmart Your Smartphone   385

CHECK YOUR UNDERSTANDING

Have students answer the questions independently.

Answers:

  1. *B*

  2. *F*

  3. *D*

If they answer any questions incorrectly, have them reread the text to confirm their understanding. Then they may proceed to ANALYZE THE TEXT on p. 386.

EL ENGLISH LEARNER SUPPORT

Oral Assessment   Use the following questions to assess students' comprehension and speaking skills:

  1. What is the author's main claim in "Outsmart Your Smartphone"? In your response, use the words in the text that state the main idea the author is trying to prove. (*Social media "poses unique risks to adolescent well-being."*)

  2. What does the author suggest with the statistics, or research data, in paragraph 4? (*The author suggests that almost all teens use social media in their daily lives, so they are affected by it.*)

  3. In paragraph 18, what does the author suggest is the difference between watching TV and going online? (*Watching TV is not as stimulating as being online, and online is more social.*) **SUBSTANTIAL/MODERATE**

ANALYZE THE TEXT

Possible answers:

1. **DOK 1:** *Her main claim is that social media "poses unique risks to adolescent well-being." In paragraph 2, the author presents a counter claim that social media has obvious benefits, so she may then show how these pros are outweighed by the risks.*

2. **DOK 4:** *The claim is that "The more time you spend texting or online, the greater the risks of harm." The statistics are not completely relevant because they only prove that many teens go online frequently, not that this results in harm or that they are at greater risk of it.*

3. **DOK 2:** *Certain activities on social media make the brain release dopamine, a chemical that causes you to feel pleasure and want to experience that pleasure again. So, the more you use social media, the more you want to use it. The strength of this craving can be hard to resist long enough to think through decisions and their consequences before you take actions.*

4. **DOK 3:** *In paragraphs 5–6, the author uses direct address to suggest she understands readers' feelings and sympathizes. In paragraph 20, she makes her instructions in how to use social media sound more like advice, so readers will be more accepting of the rules.*

5. **DOK 4:** *The author explores the reasons you can have many online friends but few real friends among them. By contrasting superficial connections online and real friendships in person, she develops her counter argument about the benefits of social media. She also supports her claim that social media interferes with teens' social and emotional development.*

RESEARCH

Point out that wikis and more reliable, credible sources often list their own sources, which students can look up to find relevant information and more details.

Connect Students should have an informed discussion, citing facts, expert's opinions, and other evidence. They may note that older sources seem less relevant, and discuss details that prove a source is credible and current.

 RESPOND

ANALYZE THE TEXT

Support your responses with evidence from the text. 📓 NOTEBOOK

1. **Identify** What is the author's main claim about social media? How does the information in paragraph 2 relate to the claim?

2. **Analyze** Are the statistics in paragraph 4 relevant to the author's claim? Explain.

3. **Cause/Effect** In your own words, explain the cause-effect relationship the author describes in paragraph 5.

4. **Compare** How does the author's use of direct address in paragraphs 5–6 differ from her use of that same rhetorical device in paragraph 20?

5. **Notice & Note** What contradiction does the author explore in paragraph 12, and why is it important?

RESEARCH TIP

When researching online, you may quickly find information on a wiki—a website published collaboratively by online users. While it may be a place to begin exploring a subject, a wiki is not a source you should rely upon. It is not credible because anyone can write or edit the articles there—including people with a bias or personal agenda, vandals with malicious intent, and individuals who lack accurate information. Always verify information in multiple credible sources before accepting it as true.

RESEARCH

What topics mentioned in this argument intrigued you? Smartphones, social media sites, the effects of social network addiction? Research one of these or a related topic. Use the chart to note your findings. Be sure to use credible sources and note those sources for your records. *Possible examples:*

TOPIC	FACTS	SOURCES
Smartphones	• *First smartphone was the Simon Personal Computer by IBM in 1992* • *Often thought to be the first: iPhone by Apple 2007*	*Sources will vary.*
Social Networking Sites	• *First recognizable site: Sixdegrees.com, opened 1997 and closed 2000* • *Site shut down because there were not enough people online to make it fun or useful*	*Sources will vary.*
Social Network Addiction	• *This is not an official disease or disorder.* • *A condition attributed to people who spend so much time on social media sites and/or the Internet that they fail to attend properly to their daily life activities* • *Negative effects: withdrawal from actual social community, relationship problems, decline in academic achievement*	*Sources will vary.*

Connect In a small group, share what you've learned from your research. If group members' facts conflict, use the credibility of sources to decide which facts to believe. As you discuss, note what you learn for later use in a critique of the argument.

WHEN STUDENTS STRUGGLE...

Reteaching: Analyze Rhetorical Devices Have students use a chart to analyze the effect of direct address. Read aloud the first three sentences of paragraph 14. Tell students to pay attention to how they feel about the author, her attitude, and the information, and make notes in the chart. Read the sentences again, but replace each *you* with *teenagers* or *they*. Have partners discuss the differences they observed.

 For additional support, go to the **Reading Studio** and assign the following 🔼 **Level Up Tutorial: Persuasive Techniques.**

CREATE AND DISCUSS

Write a Letter Write a letter to the owner or administrator of a social media site that you believe has negatively affected you or someone you know.

❏ Provide the date, your address, the name and address of the recipient, and a salutation in correct letter format.

❏ In the body of your letter, explain the nature of the negative impact that you have experienced or witnessed. Be sure to support your position with facts, examples, or other relevant evidence.

❏ In your final paragraph, make a constructive suggestion for how the site owners might help prevent this problem from occurring again. Close with "Sincerely," and your signature.

Critique as a Class Critique the argument presented in "Outsmart Your Smartphone" to decide whether it is convincing enough to accept as valid.

❏ Review the text and your notes to identify flaws or fallacies, such as circular reasoning. Also look for strengths, such as well-used rhetorical devices. Discuss your observations.

❏ Share what you learned about the topic from your research. Discuss how this information confirms or contradicts Steiner-Adair's evidence and conclusions.

❏ As a class, identify points of agreement and draw a conclusion about the effectiveness and soundness of the author's argument.

RESPOND TO THE ESSENTIAL QUESTION

 How do your teenage years prepare you for adulthood?

Gather Information Review your annotations and notes on "Outsmart Your Smartphone." Then, add relevant details to your Response Log. To decide what to include, think about:

- the writer's main points
- her recommendations and the reasons she gives for them
- what you have learned from your research and discussions

At the end of the unit, use your notes to help you write an argument.

 Go to the **Writing Studio** for help with writing a letter.

Go to **Participating in Collaborative Discussions** in the **Speaking and Listening Studio** for more help.

ACADEMIC VOCABULARY
As you write and discuss what you learned from the argument, be sure to use the Academic Vocabulary words. Check off each of the words that you use.

❏ debate
❏ deduce
❏ license
❏ sufficient
❏ trend

CREATE AND DISCUSS

Write a Letter Tell students that social media sites will sometimes will remove offensive posts or ban specific users if problems are brought to their attention. However, they must be convinced that the problem is a serious one. Point out that the listed requirements for the letter provide an outline that students can use to help them structure and write their letter.

For **writing support** for students at varying proficiency levels, see the **Text X-Ray** on page 376D.

Critique as a Class Remind students that they should use text evidence to support their opinions about the strengths and weaknesses of the text. Suggest that students use an organizer to note evidence of each as they review the text and their notes, so they can easily refer to this information in their group discussion.

To moderate the class discussion, have students share their observations regarding a particular aspect of the text, such as its strengths, and take a vote to identify points of agreement before moving on to a different aspect. Record and display students' main points as they make them, or have the students or a representative from each group add them to the board.

RESPOND TO THE ESSENTIAL QUESTION

Allow time for students to add details from "Outsmart Your Smartphone" to their Unit 5 Response Logs.

 ## ENGLISH LEARNER SUPPORT

Express Opinions Use the Pinwheel Discussion routine to have students discuss the argument. Arrange students into two concentric circles, with up to five students in the inner circle facing a partner in the outer circle. Explain that they will discuss how well the author supports each of her reasons with evidence, and provide sentence frames such as, *In my opinion, this _____ proven, because the evidence _____.* Have students silently review their notes and prepare their responses. Then pose this question: *Does the author prove*

that texting is harmful? Have facing pairs briefly discuss their responses, and then ask students in the outer circle to move one chair to the right. For each rotation, ask students the same question about a different reason given in the text. Continue the process until all of the author's reasons have been discussed. Finally, ask students to share what they have learned and whether their perspectives have changed.

MODERATE/LIGHT

CRITICAL VOCABULARY

Answers:

1. *Both are agents or drugs but a stimulant excites and speeds up mental and bodily functions, whereas a sedative calms and slows them down. So, they are similar things with opposite functions.*

2. *A perspective is a viewpoint or understanding of something, which can be fair or biased. A bias is a preference for something or someone that can unfairly influence one's perspective.*

3. *These are opposite ways of acting. To be inhibited is to be restrained in speech or action, but to be impulsive is to speak or act quickly and without restraint.*

4. *These adjectives are antonyms. A deliberate act is an action taken only after carefully contemplating the options available and their possible results. A thoughtless act is one done in haste, without any thought at all to the consequences.*

5. *These are opposite states of being. To be anonymous is to be unknown, while to be renowned is to be known far and wide. However, the word renowned also has favorable connotations, such as being respected.*

VOCABULARY STRATEGY:
Word Families

Possible Answers:

- *duct: A duct is a channel or passageway for conveying a liquid or gas, such as an air duct.*
- *induct: To induct is to formally or ceremoniously place in an office or position.*
- *conduct: To conduct is to lead, manage, or control. It also may mean to control your behavior in order to act in a certain way, or to act as a medium for transmitting something.*

In the sentence, conducted *means that "the scientists managed every aspect of the study, including planning and doing the research and evaluating the findings."*

RESPOND

WORD BANK
perspective
stimulant
deliberate
anonymous
impulsive
inhibited

Go to the **Vocabulary Studio** for more on word families.

CRITICAL VOCABULARY

Practice and Apply Explain how the meanings of the words in each pair are related.

1. stimulant/sedative
2. perspective/bias
3. inhibited/impulsive
4. deliberate/thoughtless
5. anonymous/renowned

VOCABULARY STRATEGY: Word Families

You can use word families to figure out the meanings of unfamiliar words. A **word family** consists of words that have the same root and, thus, related meanings. However, their meanings may be altered by different **affixes**—word parts that are attached before or after the root. For example, the word *perspective* is derived from the Latin root *specere*, meaning "to look at," and the prefix *per-*, meaning "through." Can you see how the meanings of words with this root are similar?

LATIN ROOT	WORD FAMILY
specere: to look at	**inspect:** to examine carefully **perspective:** a viewpoint on or understanding of something **speculate:** to engage in reasoning based on incomplete evidence

Practice and Apply Complete the word web with words that share the Latin root *ductus*, meaning "to lead." Define each related word. Then infer the meaning of *conducted* as it is used in this sentence from the selection:

> A study <u>conducted</u> by scientists at University of Texas-Austin in 2017 found that just having your smartphone nearby reduces cognitive performance—how well your brain can think and learn—even when the phone is silent or out of sight.

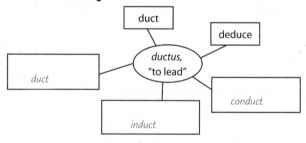

ENGLISH LEARNER SUPPORT

Distinguish Sounds Speakers of Spanish and Vietnamese may have difficulty pronouncing the short *i* sounds in these Critical Vocabulary words: ĭnhĭbited, ĭmpulsĭve, deliberate (dĭ-lĭb´ər-ĭt), stĭmulant, perspectĭve. To practice the short *i* sound, read aloud words such as *sit, hit, did, hid, big,* and *pig,* and have students repeat them. Then tell them to raise their hand when they hear words that have a different sound. Read aloud more short *i* words mixed with words with long-e vowel sounds such as in *seat* and *heat.* Confirm which words were different, then ask students to repeat the Critical Vocabulary words after you. Give students a list of short *i* words, and have them work with a partner to highlight this sound in the vocabulary words and produce it by reading the words aloud. **ALL LEVELS**

LANGUAGE CONVENTIONS:
Correct Capitalization

Capitalize the first letters of all the important words in the names of organizations and institutions. However, do not capitalize words such as *hospital, school, college, university, center,* or even *research center* when they are not used as parts of the official names.

Incorrect:	Studies conducted by the <u>Pew research center</u> show that many teens are online frequently.
Correct:	Studies conducted by the <u>Pew Research Center</u> show that many teens are online frequently.
Incorrect:	Psychologists at the <u>Research Center</u> conduct studies daily.
Correct:	Psychologists at the research center conduct studies daily.

The first word in a sentence is always capitalized. However, when a hyphenated word begins a sentence, capitalize only the first word in the compound—that is, the one that comes before the first hyphen.

Incorrect:	<u>Ninety-Two</u> percent of teens report going online daily.
Correct:	<u>Ninety-two</u> percent of teens report going online daily.

Practice and Apply Review the letter you wrote to the owner or administrator of a social media site, checking it for errors in capitalization. Then trade letters with a classmate and peer edit one another's work. Discuss the reasons for any recommended corrections to capitalization before fixing those errors.

Go to **Capital Letters** in the **Grammar Studio** for more on the rules of capitalization.

LANGUAGE CONVENTIONS:
Correct Capitalization

Review the rules for capitalization and given examples with students. Point out that the official names of organizations are proper nouns that name a specific organization, so even if the official name contains what are usually common nouns or adjectives—such as "research center" in Pew Research Center—each word in the name (excepting articles) should begin with a capital letter.

Explain that in the second incorrect example, "Research Center" is not capitalized because the sentence refers to the center that the psychologists work at in general terms, or with a generic label.

Point out that many Internet and technology companies, including social media sites and websites, may not follow standard rules of capitalization in their official names. Tell students to check the official names of Internet-related organizations by looking at the "About" page of their websites. Share these examples:

- WhatsApp
- eBay

When reviewing the rules for hyphenated words, point out that they do not apply if the hyphenated words are names or part of a name, as with this example:

- University of Texas-Austin is a fine school.

Practice and Apply Have partners refer to the given rules for correct capitalization when explaining why they think a correction is needed. Remind students to double-check the official names of Internet-related organizations.

 ENGLISH LEARNER SUPPORT

Understand Language Structures Call students' attention to the definite article *the* in front of *Pew Research Center.* Use images or demonstrations to review that *the* refers to specific or particular nouns and *a/an* refers to nonspecific nouns. Then have students locate the name of a country and the name of a company in paragraph 14 (*Germany, Facebook*). Read the sentence aloud, and have students repeat after you. Point out that aside from the United States, the official names for places such as countries, cities, and states usually do not have a *the* in front of them. The names of companies also usually do not have a *the* in front. Have students review their letters to a social media company (or provide new sample sentences) to check that they used *the* correctly in these two cases. **MODERATE**

COMPARE ARGUMENTS

Review students' options for the type of comparison they may do. Explain that they should use the chart to help them consider the same characteristics of each text, record brief descriptions for each, and then describe what the texts have in common in the "Both" column. Then students should locate text evidence of the similarities and differences they identified. Suggest students add their text evidence to the chart.

Point out that the given chart shows how students might begin a comparison that focuses on evidence, with an "Evidence" heading and aspects of evidence (credibility, relevancy, etc.) listed in the left column.

ANALYZE THE TEXTS

Possible answers:

1. **DOK 2:** *Both arguments include counter arguments and are mostly based on the expert opinions and observations of their authors.*

2. **DOK 4:** *It's Complicated seems to be written to a well-educated audience of parents and teachers. "Outsmart Your Smartphone" is clearly written for a teenage audience. The adult audience results in a focus on parents' viewpoints and a more formal tone and style. The teen audience results in a more conversational style that uses a lot of direct address.*

3. **DOK 4:** *Steiner-Adair relies mostly on her own opinions as an expert to persuade and a few research studies. boyd also relies heavily on her own opinions as an expert, as well as upon commonly accepted theories and accepted facts.*

4. **DOK 4:** *Answers will vary, but students' opinions should refer to each author's style of writing, use of rhetorical devices, and logic.*

 RESPOND

Collaborate & Compare

from IT'S COMPLICATED: THE SOCIAL LIVES OF NETWORKED TEENS
Argument by danah boyd

OUTSMART YOUR SMARTPHONE
Argument by Catherine Steiner-Adair

COMPARE ARGUMENTS

When you **compare arguments,** you identify similarities and differences between important aspects of each, using examples from the texts to make your points. You might compare and contrast the claims, reasons, and evidence in each. Alternatively, you might focus more deeply on an analysis of one of the following:

❏ **Evidence:** Is the evidence relevant, credible, current, sufficient, impressive, and/or accurate?

❏ **Use of facts and opinions:** Does the argument depend mostly on facts or on opinions? What are the sources of each?

❏ **Audience:** Whom is the piece meant to persuade? How does the intended audience affect the argument?

❏ **Objections and/or differing viewpoints:** Are the most important or popular objections raised and addressed?

❏ **Counter arguments:** Are opposing claims disproved with effective reasons and evidence?

❏ **Overall quality of writing:** Are rhetorical devices used effectively? Does the writing contain any logical fallacies?

In a small group, choose what you would like to focus on as you compare. Complete a chart like this one, adjusting the headings in the left column as necessary to reflect your particular focus. Then, review the texts to find examples of each similarity and difference you note.

Evidence	*It's Complicated*	**Both**	"Outsmart Your Smartphone"
Credibility	• *Interprets conclusions*	• *Are credible*	• *Cites findings of studies*
Relevancy	• *Includes her opinions*	• *Offer expert opinions*	• *Includes expert opinions*
Currency	• *Notes counterargument*	• *Include counterargument*	• *Lists counterargument*
	• *Examples mostly relevant*	• *Mostly relevant*	• *Variety of examples*
	• *Mentions older example*		• *Data from recent studies*

ANALYZE THE TEXTS

Discuss these questions in your group.

1. **Compare** What do both arguments have in common?

2. **Connect** For what audience is each piece written, and how does this affect each argument?

3. **Analyze** What kind of support does each author rely upon most?

4. **Critique** Which argument exhibits the best overall quality of writing? Cite evidence from both texts to support your opinion.

 ENGLISH LEARNER SUPPORT

Explain with Detail Provide sentence frames that students can use to compare the texts. Remind them that they can refer to their organizers and other notes to help them give detailed responses.

• *Both texts have/use _____, but neither _____.*

• *_____ is similar to _____ because _____.*

• *One significant similarity/difference is _____ because _____.*

• *Unlike _____, _____ has/uses _____.*

• *_____ is more effective at _____, because _____.* **MODERATE/LIGHT**

CREATE AND PRESENT

With a partner, play the role of an adult and a teenager in a discussion about social media use. The adult may be a parent, a teacher, or someone who is an expert on the topic. However, the adult and teen should take opposing viewpoints. Follow these steps:

1. **Choose a Role and a Position** With your partner, decide who will play the adult and who will play the teenager. Also choose the viewpoint you each plan to promote. This may mean that one of you must adopt a viewpoint that does not match your own.

2. **Gather Information** List reasons and evidence from the texts and from your prior research that support your chosen viewpoint.

Reason 1:
Evidence:
Reason 2:
Evidence:

3. **Prepare Your Counter Argument** Anticipate the other person's claim as well as his or her objections to your points. List reasons and evidence you will cite to challenge the opposing viewpoint.

Other's Claims and/or Objections	Your Counter Argument

4. **Role-play the Discussion** In your chosen roles, have a conversation with your partner in which each of you tries to convince the other to adopt your position. Be on the lookout for errors in one another's reasoning, and point them out as appropriate. Also, as your partner presents evidence to support his or her position, reflect on your own argument and think about how you might adjust your approach to the issue in response. Consider beginning your argument by acknowledging the other's position and its merits and then countering it.

TO CHALLENGE STUDENTS . . .

Use Rhetorical Devices Tell students that *rhetorical* devices are part of *rhetoric*, or the art of persuasive speaking and writing. Encourage them to think of and plan ways to incorporate rhetorical devices into their conversation. Point out that metaphors and similes, for example, are two types of analogy that students can use to make factual evidence, such as statistics from scientific studies, more understandable and impressive. Students also may be able to incorporate juxtapositions by summarizing their partner's last point before offering a counter claim.

CREATE AND PRESENT

Tell students that the purpose of the role-playing is to apply what they learned to create, present, and defend an argument about social media use to a specific audience.

1. **Choose a Role and Position** Explain that in addition to taking opposing positions, each student's position should reflect the role he or she is playing. Point out that the perspective, interests, and concerns of an adult are different from those of a teenager. Encourage students to adopt a perspective different from their own, so they may look at the issues in a new way.

2. **Gather Information** Point out that both texts include counter arguments, so students may find useful information in each. Emphasize that their arguments should not be just a restatement of the texts, however. Tell students to develop their own arguments by

   • synthesizing reasons and evidence from the texts and their own research, to determine what will best support their position;

   • deciding how they will make their points and evidence convincing to their partner.

3. **Prepare Your Counter Argument** Explain that students will be able to challenge their partner's argument as well as defend their own. Reflecting on what they found ineffective or questioned in the texts, such as irrelevant evidence and logical fallacies, can help them look critically at their own arguments and anticipate counter arguments.

4. **Role-Play the Discussion** Remind students that just as in regular conversation, they should allow their partner to finish his or her point before raising an objection or asking a question. Consider having them take turns presenting their full argument before debating points, with the person listening jotting down notes of points that they want to address later.

 For **speaking support** for students at varying proficiency levels, see the **Text X-Ray** on page 376D.

READER'S CHOICE

Setting a Purpose Have students review their Unit 5 Response Log and think about what they've already learned about how their teenage years helped prepare them for adulthood. As they select their Independent Reading selections, encourage them to consider what more they want to know.

NOTICE NOTE

Explain that some selections may contain multiple signposts; others may contain only one. And the same type of signpost can occur many times in the same text.

LEARNING MINDSET

Seeking Challenges Tell students that those with a learning mindset look forward to the next challenge and make long-range plans for new challenges. Point out that reading independently gives students an opportunity to develop this characteristic. Each of the independent readings poses a distinct challenge. Help students plan how to meet these challenges.

 INDEPENDENT READING

? ESSENTIAL QUESTION:

How do your teenage years prepare you for adulthood?

Reader's Choice

Setting a Purpose Select one or more of these options from your eBook to continue your exploration of the Essential Question.

- Read the descriptions to see which text grabs your interest.
- Think about which genres you enjoy reading.

Notice **&** Note

In this unit, you practiced asking **Big Questions** and noticing and noting two signposts: **Contrasts and Contradictions** and **Numbers and Stats.** As you read independently, these signposts and others will aid your understanding. Below are the anchor questions to ask when you read literature and nonfiction.

Reading Literature: Stories, Poems, and Plays		
Signpost	**Anchor Question**	**Lesson**
Contrasts and Contradictions	Why did the character act that way?	p. 3
Aha Moment	How might this change things?	p. 3
Tough Questions	What does this make me wonder about?	p. 152
Words of the Wiser	What's the lesson for the character?	p. 406
Again and Again	Why might the author keep bringing this up?	p. 2
Memory Moment	Why is this memory important?	p. 153

Reading Nonfiction: Essays, Articles, and Arguments		
Signpost	**Anchor Question(s)**	**Lesson**
Big Questions	What surprised me? What did the author think I already knew? What challenged, changed, or confirmed what I already knew?	p. 77
Contrasts and Contradictions	What is the difference, and why does it matter?	p. 241
Extreme or Absolute Language	Why did the author use this language?	p. 76
Numbers and Stats	Why did the author use these numbers or amounts?	p. 325
Quoted Words	Why was this person quoted or cited, and what did this add?	p. 77
Word Gaps	Do I know this word from someplace else? Does it seem like technical talk for this topic? Do clues in the sentence help me understand the word?	p. 240

 ENGLISH LEARNER SUPPORT

Think Aloud This strategy helps students think about how they make meaning from texts:

- Model the strategy using an Independent Reading text.
- Tell students, *"As I read aloud, I will be stopping to voice my thinking about the text."*
- Read a short section, stopping frequently to talk about what you are visualizing, predicting, questioning, comparing, or identifying as cause or effect.

- Have students practice the strategy with a partner.
  SUBSTANTIAL / MODERATE

  Go to the **Reading Studio** for additional support in developing fluency.

You can preview these texts in Unit 5 of your eBook.

Then, check off the text or texts that you select to read on your own.

POEM

Teenagers

Pat Mora

Parents and teenagers living in the same house feel like strangers behind closed doors.

POEM

Identity

Julio Noboa Polanco

A young poet imagines being free from society's rules.

POEM

Hard on the Gas

Janet S. Wong

Doing things his own way, a grandfather challenges a teen's expectations.

SHORT STORY

Marigolds

Eugenia Collier

The impulsive actions of a young girl change her life forever.

ESSAY

My Summer of Scooping Ice Cream

Shonda Rhimes

A teenager gets more than a paycheck from her summer job.

Collaborate and Share   With a partner, discuss what you learned from at least one of your independent readings.

- Share a brief synopsis or summary of the text.
- Describe any signposts that you noticed in the text and explain what they revealed to you.
- Describe what you most enjoyed or found most challenging about the text. Give specific examples.
- Decide if you would recommend the text to others. Why or why not?

 Go to the **Reading Studio** for more resources on **Notice & Note.**

INDEPENDENT READING

MATCHING STUDENTS TO TEXTS

Use the following information to guide students in choosing their texts.

Teenagers
  Genre: poem
  Overall Rating: Accessible

Identity
  Genre: poem
  Overall Rating: Challenging

Hard on the Gas
  Genre: poem
  Overall Rating: Accessible

Marigolds   **Lexile: 1140L**
  Genre: short story
  Overall Rating: Challenging

My Summer of Scooping Ice Cream **Lexile: 810L**
  Genre: essay
  Overall Rating: Accessible

Collaborate and Share   To assess how well students read the selections, walk around the room and listen to their conversations. Encourage students to be focused and specific in their comments.

Online
Ed **for Assessment**

- Independent Reading Selection Tests

 Encourage students to visit the **Reading Studio** to download a handy bookmark of **NOTICE & NOTE** signposts.

WHEN STUDENTS STRUGGLE . . .

Keep a Reading Log As students read their selected texts, have them keep a reading log for each selection to note signposts and their thoughts about them. Use their logs to assess how well they are noticing and reflecting on elements of the texts.

Reading Log for (title)		
Page and Paragraph	**Signpost I Noticed**	**My Notes About It**

UNIT ⑤ Tasks

- WRITE AN ARGUMENT
- PRESENT AN ARGUMENT

MENTOR TEXT

IT'S COMPLICATED: THE SOCIAL LIVES OF NETWORKED TEENS

Argument by DANAH BOYD

LEARNING OBJECTIVES

Writing Task

- Write an argument about whether technology and social media are obstacles to friendship.
- Use strategies to plan and develop your argument.
- Use the Mentor Text as a model for writing an appealing introduction and using reasons and evidence to support a claim.
- Revise your draft, working with a partner in a peer review.
- Edit drafts using standard English conventions, correcting misspellings and grammatical errors.
- Publish your argument to share it with an audience.
- Use the scoring guide to evaluate your argument.
- **Language** Use the correct form of modifiers to show the comparative and superlative degrees.

Speaking and Listening Task

- Adapt your argument for presentation.
- Practice with a partner or group, using effective verbal and nonverbal techniques, and providing and considering advice for improvement
- Deliver your presentation.
- **Language** Use transitions to better connect your claim with reasons and evidence.

Assign the Writing Task in **Ed.**

Online
Ed

RESOURCES

- Unit 5 Response Log
- Reading Studio: Notice & Note
- Writing Studio: Writing Arguments
- Speaking and Listening Studio: Giving a Presentation
- Grammar Studio : Module 11: Using Modifiers Correctly

Language X-Ray: English Learner Support

Use the instruction below and the supports and scaffolds in the Teacher's Edition to help you guide students of different proficiency levels.

INTRODUCE THE WRITING TASK

Explain that an argument is a type of writing that presents a claim and the reasons and evidence that support it. Point out that a successful argument contains an engaging introduction that states the claim, supports the claim with credible reasons and evidence, establishes and maintains a formal style, and includes a conclusion that follows from the argument. Emphasize that students must support an argument with reasons and facts. Appealing to emotion alone usually does not convince an audience to embrace a particular claim. Tell students that to write a convincing argument they often must do some research to uncover the factual information to support a claim.

WRITING

Use Modifiers Correctly

Tell students that they can make their arguments stronger and clearer by using modifiers correctly to show the degree of comparison, either two things (comparative degree) or more than two (superlative degree).

Use the following supports with students at varying proficiency levels:

- Read aloud several sentences that contain modifiers, either adjectives or adverbs. Have students raise their hand each time they hear a modifier. **SUBSTANTIAL**
- Give students these sentences: *Elizabeth is a better writer than her sister. Elizabeth is the best writer in our school.* Ask students how many people are compared in the first sentence (*two*) and then in the second sentence. (*three or more*) **MODERATE**
- After students have completed their drafts, have them circle all modifiers. Have students change one modifier to the comparative or the superlative degree. **LIGHT**

SPEAKING

Present Information

After students have completed their drafts, have them identify the claim and the reasons and facts that support it.

Use the following supports with students at varying proficiency levels:

- Have students state their claim to a partner. **SUBSTANTIAL**
- Have students state their claim and one supporting reason to a small group. **MODERATE**
- Have students state their claim, two or more reasons, and the facts that support it to a small group. **LIGHT**

WRITING

WRITE AN ARGUMENT

Introduce students to the Writing Task by reading the introductory paragraph with them and reviewing the criteria for what makes a good argument. Explain that a written argument is not a conflict or disagreement. Review that an argument is a carefully stated claim that is supported by reasons and evidence. Remind students to refer to the notes they recorded in the Unit 5 Response Log as they plan and draft their arguments. The Response Log should contain their perspectives on different selections they have read in the unit. Drawing on these different perspectives will make their own writing more interesting and well informed.

 For **writing support** for students at varying proficiency levels, see the **Language X-Ray** on page 394B.

USE THE MENTOR TEXT

Point out to students that their arguments will be similar to danah boyd's essay "It's Complicated: The Social Lives of Networked Teens" in that they will state a claim and support it with reasons and facts. However, their arguments will be shorter than the essay and will focus on the effects of technology and social media on friendship.

WRITING PROMPT

Review the prompt with students. Encourage them to ask questions about any part of the assignment that is unclear. Make sure they understand that the purpose of their argument is to state a claim about whether or not technology and social media help or harm friendship and then use reasons and facts to support the claim.

 **WRITING TASK**

Write an Argument

 Go to the **Writing Studio** for help writing an argument.

This unit focuses on the challenges faced by teenagers as they move toward adulthood. For this writing task, you will write an argument on a topic related to teenagers. In a writing context, an argument is not a conflict or disagreement. It is a carefully stated claim that is supported by reasons and evidence. For a well-written argument you can use as a mentor text, review the selection from *It's Complicated: The Social Lives of Networked Teens*.

As you write your argument, you can use the notes from your Response Log, which you filled out after reading the texts in this unit.

Writing Prompt

Read the information in the box below.

This is the topic or context for your argument.

> As they move toward being adults, teenagers encounter many obstacles in their struggles for identity and independence.

Think carefully about the following question.

This is the Essential Question for the unit. How would you answer this question based on the texts in the unit?

> How do your teenage years prepare you for adulthood?

Now mark the words that identify exactly what you are being asked to produce.

Write an argument about whether or not technology and social media are obstacles to friendship.

Be sure to —

Review these points as you write and again when you finish. Make any needed changes or edits.

- ❑ provide an engaging introduction that establishes your claim
- ❑ support the claim with valid reasons and evidence, including facts, details, and examples from credible sources
- ❑ logically organize your reasons and evidence
- ❑ use transitional words and phrases to clarify relationships among your claim, reasons, and evidence
- ❑ establish and maintain a formal style
- ❑ summarize your main points in an effective conclusion

 LEARNING MINDSET

Try Again As students work on their arguments, remind them not to worry about making mistakes. Making mistakes is a sign that they are willing to take risks and try new ways of conveying ideas. Remind them to regard mistakes as temporary setbacks, easy to correct. Tell students that they can learn much from mistakes, reflect on what they have learned, and apply it to create a stronger piece of writing.

1 Plan

Before you start writing, you need to plan your argument. The first step is to choose a position you can defend. Use a range of strategies as you identify your position in response to the prompt. Begin by reviewing the notes you have taken in your Response Log for this unit. What other reading have you done about this topic? Think about this background reading as you formulate the key ideas you will include in your argument. Discuss the topic with your classmates and consider any personal interests you have that relate to the topic.

Use the table below as you determine your position in response to the prompt.

Go to **Writing Arguments: Developing a Topic** for help planning your argument.

Argument Planning Table	
Topic	
Ideas from background reading	
Discussion with classmates	
Personal interest in the topic	
Position/Claim	

Gather Support Once you have determined your position and stated your claim, the next step is to gather support. Consider the reasons you have for your position. Then conduct research online and in print sources to gather evidence—facts, statistics, and examples—that backs up these reasons. Next, anticipate alternative or opposing views and consider how you might refute them. Incorporating counter arguments to disprove opposing views will make your own argument stronger.

Consider Your Purpose and Audience Keep your purpose and audience in mind. Do you want to persuade your classmates? Your friends? A group of adults? The reasons and evidence you will use to support your claim—and the tone you will use to convey your argument—may vary according to who that audience is.

Use the notes from your Response Log as you plan your argument.

UNIT 5
RESPONSE LOG

Write an Argument **395**

1 PLAN

Allow time for students to discuss the topic with partners or in small groups and then to complete the Argument Planning Table independently.

■ English Learner Support

Plan an Argument Explain that students can better support a claim when they understand both sides of an argument. Have students work with an English-proficient partner to list evidence that supports arguments for and against technology and social media as obstacles to friendship. Have each pair use the following sentence frames and question to discuss their plans:

I think technology and social media (are/are not) obstacles to friendship because _____.

I agree that _____ ; however, I still think that _____ because _____.

I want to find examples of technology and social media that show _____.

What other evidence do you think I should find?
LIGHT

Gather Support As they plan their arguments, remind students to refer to the notes they took in the Response Log. They may also review the selections to find additional facts and examples to support ideas in their writing.

Consider Your Purpose and Audience Remind students that they should always take their audience into account when choosing the tone to use in persuasive writing. For example, using a humorous tone may strike the wrong note if they are trying to persuade a group of serious-minded adults to agree to a particular claim. Remind students to choose words carefully to convey the appropriate tone, which may range from formal to casual.

TO CHALLENGE STUDENTS . . .

Adapt the Argument Challenge students to adapt their arguments for an opinion letter to a school newspaper. Students' letters should focus on how the issue of technology and social media affects the community. Encourage students to research additional evidence to support their arguments.

WRITING

Organize Your Ideas Tell students to make an outline to organize the reasons and evidence for their arguments. The introduction should describe the issue (technology and social media as helpful or harmful to friendship) and state a claim, or position. Each body paragraph should include a reason and supporting evidence. The conclusion should summarize the argument and leave the reader with a parting thought.

I. Introduction

II. Body Paragraph(s)

III. Conclusion

2 DEVELOP A DRAFT

Remind students that the purpose of an argument is to convince others that a claim is valid. Suggest that students deliver their arguments in their heads as they write. Students should ask themselves whether the points they are making would be convincing to their audience. Tell students that they should strive to get all their ideas on paper during the drafting stage. They will be able to refine and reorganize their argument when they revise their writing.

WRITING TASK

 Go to **Writing Arguments** in the **Writing Studio** for help organizing your ideas.

Notice & Note

From Reading to Writing

Remember that writers use common features, called signposts, to help convey their message to readers.

 Go to the **Reading Studio** for more resources on Notice & Note.

Organize Your Ideas After you have gathered ideas and evidence, you need to organize the information in a way that will help you draft your argument. You can use this graphic organizer to make an outline of your argument. Place your claim in the top box, your reasons in the next row of boxes, and your evidence in the bottom row.

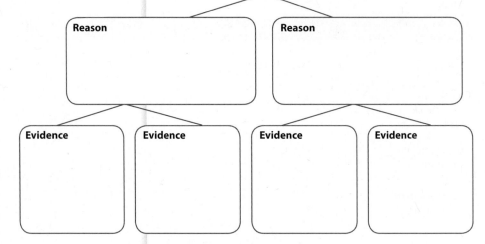

2 Develop a Draft

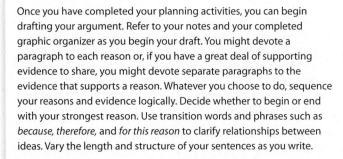 You might prefer to draft your argument online.

Once you have completed your planning activities, you can begin drafting your argument. Refer to your notes and your completed graphic organizer as you begin your draft. You might devote a paragraph to each reason or, if you have a great deal of supporting evidence to share, you might devote separate paragraphs to the evidence that supports a reason. Whatever you choose to do, sequence your reasons and evidence logically. Decide whether to begin or end with your strongest reason. Use transition words and phrases such as *because, therefore,* and *for this reason* to clarify relationships between ideas. Vary the length and structure of your sentences as you write.

Using a word processor or online writing application makes it easier to make changes or move sentences around later when you are ready to revise your first draft.

WHEN STUDENTS STRUGGLE...

Vary Word Choice in Drafting Have partners check each other's draft for frequently repeated words. Ask partners to highlight overused words and to help each other look up appropriate synonyms for each one in a thesaurus.

 For additional support, go to the **Reading Studio** and assign the following **Level Up tutorial: Revising for Word Choice.**

Use the Mentor Text

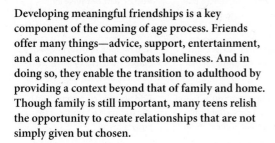

Author's Craft

Use your introduction to get your reader interested in your topic. Sometimes you can do this by making a bold statement. Another way is to begin with an accepted idea upon which you can build your argument. Note the way the writer begins the excerpt from *It's Complicated: The Social Lives of Networked Teens.*

> Developing meaningful friendships is a key component of the coming of age process. Friends offer many things—advice, support, entertainment, and a connection that combats loneliness. And in doing so, they enable the transition to adulthood by providing a context beyond that of family and home. Though family is still important, many teens relish the opportunity to create relationships that are not simply given but chosen.

The first sentence states an accepted idea and proceeds to develop that idea into the claim that teens want to develop social relationships in their own way.

Apply What You've Learned To lay the foundation for your argument, you might begin with some facts or ideas that your audience is likely to agree with. Then you can state your claim within this shared context.

Genre Characteristics

An argument uses reasons and evidence to support a claim and to argue against anticipated objections and opposing views. Evidence can include facts, statistics, and examples. Notice how the author of *It's Complicated* uses the following example to support her claim.

> Most teens are not compelled by gadgetry as such—they are compelled by friendship. The gadgets are interesting to them primarily as a means to a social end.

The author provides an example to support her claim: most teens use their phones to nurture their relationships with others.

Apply What You've Learned The evidence you include to support your argument should be clearly related to your claim. Some types of details you can use to support your ideas are facts, examples, and statistics.

WHY THIS MENTOR TEXT?

"It's Complicated: The Social Lives of Networked Teens" provides a good example of argument. Use the information below to help students use the mentor text as a model for writing an effective introduction, for using evidence to support the claim, and for treating counterarguments.

USE THE MENTOR TEXT

Author's Craft Ask a volunteer to read aloud the introduction from "It's Complicated: The Social Lives of Networked Teens." Then have students analyze the paragraph to determine what makes it appealing to the audience. Help students notice that the paragraph proceeds from general to specific. Invite students to offer examples of accepted ideas that might introduce their arguments about the impact of technology and social media on friendship.

Genre Characteristics To help students understand how the example functions in the article, have them locate paragraph 3 in the text. Have students note that the context of the example is "teens' underlying social motivations." The author emphasizes that to understand teenagers, one should remember that social interactions and friendships are important to them, not the gadgets that they use. The gadgets serve as a means to an end—increased social interaction—not an end in themselves.

WRITING

③ REVISE

After students finish writing their arguments, have them wait a day or two before revising. By taking a short time away from their writing, they will approach their drafts with fresh eyes and renewed enthusiasm. Then have students answer each question in the chart to determine how they can improve their drafts. Have volunteers model their revision techniques.

With a Partner Have students ask peer reviewers to evaluate their reasons and supporting evidence by answering the following questions:

- Is there a strong connection between the reasons and the claim they support?
- What might I do to strengthen the structure of the argument, particularly the organization of my main points?
- Which piece of evidence seems the strongest? The least convincing?

Students should use the reviewer's feedback to improve the organization and to strengthen the evidence, if necessary.

 ENGLISH LEARNER SUPPORT

Connect Ideas Model how to combine clauses to create new sentences.

- Each clause in a compound sentence has a subject and is joined by a conjunction (*and, but, or, yet*). *Technology helps students communicate. It helps manage their time. = Technology helps students communicate, and it helps manage their time.*
- A complex sentence has an independent clause and a dependent clause with a connecting word (*after, since, unless, when*). *When students are busy. Social media can interfere. = When students are busy, social media can interfere.* **MODERATE**

 WRITING TASK

 Go to the **Writing Studio** for help revising your argument.

③ Revise

On Your Own Once you have written your draft, you'll want to go back and look for ways to improve your argument. As you reread and revise, think about whether you have achieved your purpose. The Revision Guide will help you focus on specific elements to make your writing stronger.

Revision Guide		
Ask Yourself	**Tips**	**Revision Techniques**
1. Does my introduction contain a clear claim?	**Highlight** the sentences that state the issue and the claim.	**Add** a claim, or **revise** an existing claim for clarity.
2. Is my claim supported by solid reasons and evidence?	**Highlight** each reason, and **underline** the evidence that supports it.	**Add** reasons, or **insert** evidence. **Elaborate** to clarify evidence or how it relates to a given reason.
3. Do I address counter claims?	**Underline** where you mention opposing claims. **Highlight** sentences that address them.	**Add** possible opposing claims and persuasive responses to answer them.
4. Do I use and maintain a formal style?	**Highlight** contractions, slang, or informal language.	**Reword** contractions and **replace** informal language with precise, formal vocabulary.
5. Does the conclusion restate my claim?	**Underline** the restatement of the claim.	**Add** a sentence that restates the claim.

ACADEMIC VOCABULARY
As you conduct your **peer review,** be sure to use these words.

- ❏ debate
- ❏ deduce
- ❏ license
- ❏ sufficient
- ❏ trend

With a Partner Once you and your partner have worked through the Revision Guide on your own, exchange papers and evaluate each other's draft in a **peer review**. Focus on providing revision suggestions for at least three of the items mentioned in the chart. Explain why you think your partner's draft should be revised and what your specific suggestions are.

When receiving feedback from your partner, listen attentively and ask questions to make sure you fully understand the revision suggestions.

398   Unit 5

4 Edit

Once you are satisfied with your argument, you'll want to proofread and edit it to find and correct any errors in grammar, usage, or mechanics.

Language Conventions

Modifiers A modifier gives information about another word. When a modifier is used in a comparison, the form of the modifier shows the degree of comparison—that is, whether it is comparative or superlative.

The **comparative** form compares two things, groups, or actions.

> Most teenagers are **more skilled** than adults, who have been **slower** to use social media.

The **superlative** form compares more than two things, groups, or actions.

> The **most popular** smartphones have the **newest** features.

To form comparatives and superlatives of most one- and some two-syllable modifiers, add -*er* and -*est*. To properly use most two-syllable and all three-syllable modifiers in comparisons, just add *more* or *most*.

REGULAR COMPARISONS		
Modifier	Comparative	Superlative
tall	taller	tallest
curious	more curious	most curious

IRREGULAR COMPARISONS		
Modifier	Comparative	Superlative
bad	worse	worst
much	more	most

> Go to **Using Modifiers Correctly** in the **Grammar Studio** to learn more.

5 Publish

Finalize your argument and choose a way to share it with your audience. Consider these options:

- Adapt your argument as an opinion letter to a local newspaper.
- Post your argument as a blog on a classroom or school website.
- Hold a debate with someone with an opposing position.

WRITING

4 EDIT

Have students read their arguments aloud to listen to the flow and rhythm of their sentences and to detect anything that doesn't sound quite right. After students edit their own work, have them exchange their drafts with a partner. Then have students check each other's writing for errors in grammar, punctuation, and spelling.

LANGUAGE CONVENTIONS

Modifiers Emphasize that when a modifier is used in a comparison, its form changes to reflect the number of things being compared. With two things, students should use the comparative form; with more than two things, the superlative form.

■ English Learner Support

Edit Draft Pair English learners with native English speakers. Have English learners read their arguments aloud to their partners. English speakers should pay particular attention to the modifiers used in comparisons. Have English speakers explain each change they make so English learners understand the language convention that dictates the change. **SUBSTANTIAL/MODERATE**

5 PUBLISH

Tell students that after revising and editing they are ready to prepare the final manuscript for publication. To make sure that the final manuscript is free of errors, students must take the time to proofread meticulously. Share with students these tips: proofread your manuscript out loud, and proofread your sentences in reverse order.

WHEN STUDENTS STRUGGLE . . .

Edit Drafts Have students make audio recordings of their drafts. Then have partners listen to their recordings and discuss ways they might improve their arguments. Students should revise their drafts and then make a recording of the revised version.

 For additional support, go to the **Reading Studio** and assign the following Level Up tutorial: **Revising for Unity, Coherence, and Organization.**

WRITING

USE THE SCORING GUIDE

Have students use the scoring guide to evaluate their own arguments. Then ask partners to assess each other's score. Students should use the language of the scoring guide to provide feedback for each category.

WRITING TASK

Use the scoring guide to evaluate your argument.

	Writing Task Scoring Guide: Argument		
	Organization/Progression	**Development of Ideas**	**Use of Language and Conventions**
4	• Reasons and evidence are organized logically and consistently throughout the argument. • Transitions effectively connect reasons and evidence to the writer's claim.	• The introduction is attention-getting and states the writer's position. • Logical reasons and relevant evidence support the writer's claim. • Opposing or alternate claims are acknowledged and addressed. • The conclusion effectively summarizes the claim.	• A formal style is maintained. • Sentence variety creates a rhythmic flow. • Comparative and superlative modifiers are formed and used correctly. • Spelling, grammar, mechanics, and usage are correct.
3	• The organization of reasons and evidence is confusing in a few places. • A few more transitions are needed to connect reasons and evidence to the writer's claim.	• The introduction could be more engaging; the claim states a position. • Reasons and evidence support the claim, but they could be stronger. • Opposing or alternate claims are acknowledged, but the responses need to be better developed. • The conclusion restates the claim.	• The style becomes informal in a few places. • There could be more sentence variety. • Most comparative and superlative modifiers are used correctly. • Some errors in spelling, grammar, mechanics, and usage are made.
2	• The organization of reasons and evidence is logical in some places, but the writing lacks focus. • Many more transitions are needed to connect reasons and evidence to the writer's claim.	• The introduction is uninteresting; the introduction identifies an issue, but the writer's position is not clearly stated. • Reasons and evidence are not always logical or relevant. • Opposing or alternate claims are acknowledged but not always addressed or countered logically. • The conclusion provides an incomplete summary of the claim.	• The style becomes informal in many places. • There is little or no sentence variety. • There are a few errors with comparative and superlative modifiers. • Spelling, grammar, mechanics, and usage errors are distracting to the reader.
1	• The organization is not logical. Reasons and evidence are presented randomly. • The lack of any transitions makes the argument difficult to understand.	• The introduction is confusing; no claim is made. • Reasons are unconvincing and the evidence is not relevant. • Opposing or alternate claims are neither acknowledged nor addressed. • The conclusion is missing.	• The style is informal and inappropriate. • Poorly or incorrectly formed sentences make the argument hard to follow. • Modifiers are missing or used incorrectly. • Spelling, grammar, mechanics, and usage errors obscure the writer's meaning.

Present an Argument

You will now adapt your argument for presentation to your classmates. You also will listen to their presentations, ask questions to better understand their ideas, and make suggestions to help them improve their work.

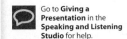 Go to **Giving a Presentation** in the **Speaking and Listening Studio** for help.

① Adapt Your Argument for Presentation

Use the chart below to plan how you will adapt the key elements of your argument in order to create a script and other presentation materials.

Presentation Planning Chart		
Title and Introduction	How will you revise your title and introduction to capture the listener's attention? Is there a more concise way to state your claim?	
Audience	What tone will be most persuasive in an oral presentation? To what specific vocabulary will your audience respond most positively?	
Effective Language and Organization	Which parts of your argument could be clearer? Where can you add transitions to better connect reasons and evidence back to your claim?	
Visuals	What images or graphics would help clarify your claim, reasons, and evidence? How can you add interest? What text should appear on screen?	

PRESENT AN ARGUMENT

Introduce students to the Speaking and Listening Task by reading the introductory paragraph with them. Remind students that a good argument needs to be written well, but that the delivery of the speech is also important.

① ADAPT YOUR ARGUMENT FOR PRESENTATION

Tell students as they adapt their arguments for presentation they should keep their audience in mind. Emphasize that the reasons and evidence they use to support their claims may vary according to who that audience is. Adapting the vocabulary for a particular audience will strengthen the force of an argument. Point out to students that the careful use of transitions will help the audience connect what the speaker has said to the point about to be made.

 For **speaking support** for students at varying proficiency levels, see the **Language X-Ray** on page 394B.

(EL) ENGLISH LEARNER SUPPORT

Plan an Argument Presentation Have students discuss their argumentation presentation plans with a partner. Ask them to say aloud the sentence frames and questions below:

- *I agree that social media may hurt a friendship, but I also think that _____ .*
- *I heard you say _____, and that is a good point. However, I still think that _____is also true.*
- *Would you please repeat that? Did you mean _____, or _____?*

ALL LEVELS

SPEAKING AND LISTENING

2 PRACTICE WITH A PARTNER OR GROUP

As students practice delivering their presentations, remind them to consider where they might use transitions to link ideas and make their arguments stronger. Provide examples of cause-and-effect transition words such as *as a result* and *therefore*, and transition words that reinforce ideas, such as *further* and *in addition*. If students make recordings of themselves, have them use the recording to analyze the content and delivery of the argument.

3 DELIVER YOUR PRESENTATION

If desired, pairs of students can present opposing views in a debate. After students listen to each other's arguments, allow time for them to question each other regarding their points of view. Remind students to be respectful when questioning the points of view of others.

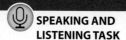 **SPEAKING AND LISTENING TASK**

As you work to improve your presentations, be sure to follow discussion rules:

- ❏ listen closely to each other
- ❏ don't interrupt
- ❏ stay on topic
- ❏ ask only helpful, relevant questions
- ❏ provide only clear, thoughtful, and direct answers

2 Practice with a Partner or Group

Once you've completed your draft, practice with a partner or group to improve both the presentation and your delivery. Keep in mind that even when an argument is well written, an oral presentation of the argument won't be as effective if the delivery is weak.

Practice Effective Verbal Techniques

- ❏ **Enunciation** Replace words that you stumble over, and rearrange sentences so that your delivery is smooth.
- ❏ **Voice Modulation and Pitch** Use your voice to display enthusiasm and emphasis.
- ❏ **Speaking Rate** Speak slowly enough that listeners understand you. Pause now and then to let them consider important points.
- ❏ **Volume** Remember that listeners at the back of the room need to hear you.

Practice Effective Nonverbal Techniques

- ❏ **Eye Contact** Try to let your eyes rest on each member of the audience at least once.
- ❏ **Facial Expression** Smile, frown, or raise an eyebrow to show your feelings or to emphasize points.
- ❏ **Gestures** Stand tall and relaxed, and use natural gestures—shrugs, nods, or shakes of your head—to add meaning and interest to your presentation.

Provide and Consider Advice for Improvement

As a listener, pay close attention. Take notes about ways that presenters can improve their presentations and more effectively use verbal and nonverbal techniques. Paraphrase and summarize each presenter's claim and reasons to confirm your understanding, and ask questions to clarify any confusing ideas.

As a presenter, listen closely to questions and consider ways to revise your presentation to make sure your points are clear and logically sequenced. Remember to ask for suggestions about how you might change onscreen text or images to make your presentation clearer and more interesting.

3 Deliver Your Presentation

Use the advice you received during practice to make final changes to your presentation. Then, using effective verbal and nonverbal techniques, present it to your classmates.

TO CHALLENGE STUDENTS . . .

Reflect on the Process Tell students that taking time to reflect on their process in writing and delivering their arguments will help them apply what they learned and improve their skills. Have them answer the following questions:

- How could you have made your argument more convincing?
- How did presenting counter arguments help you understand opposing views?
- Which piece of evidence do you think was your most persuasive?

Reflect on the Unit

In writing your argument, you have formulated and expressed your thoughts about the reading you have done in this unit. Now is a good time to reflect on what you have learned.

Reflect on the Essential Question

• How do your teenage years prepare you for adulthood? How has your answer to this question changed since you first considered it when you started this unit?

• What are some examples from the texts you read that show how teens can prepare for the transition into adulthood?

Reflect on Your Reading

• Which selections were the most interesting or surprising to you?

• From which selection did you learn the most about the challenges teenagers face as they move toward becoming adults?

Reflect on the Writing Task

• Which part of the argument was the easiest to write? Which was the hardest? Why?

• How could you have made your argument more convincing?

Reflect on the Speaking and Listening Task

• Did your delivery make your argument more effective? Why or why not?

• What kinds of ideas about how to revise your presentation did your listeners' reactions and feedback give you?

UNIT 5 SELECTIONS
• "The Debt We Owe to the Adolescent Brain"
• *Bronx Masquerade*
• "Hanging Fire"
• "Summer of His Fourteenth Year"
• *It's Complicated: The Social Lives of Networked Teens*
• "Outsmart Your Smartphone"

Reflect on the Unit   403

REFLECT ON THE UNIT

Have students reflect on the questions independently and write some notes in response to each one. Then have students meet with partners or in small groups to discuss their reflections. Circulate during these discussions to identify the questions that are generating the liveliest conversations. Wrap up with a whole-class discussion focused on these questions.

 LEARNING MINDSET

Questioning Tell students that asking specific questions is a sure sign that you are developing a learning mindset. You ask questions about the claim you support, the reasons and evidence you present, and the response of your audience to different parts of your argument. You realize the value of open-ended questions and their power to promote discussions and stimulate thinking.

Instructional Overview and Resources

		Instructional Focus	**Online Ed Resources**
	**Unit Introduction** **The Legacy of Anne Frank**	**Unit 6 Essential Question** **Unit 6 Academic Vocabulary**	**Stream to Start:** The Legacy of Anne Frank **Unit 6 Response Log**

ANALYZE & APPLY

	"The Diary of Anne Frank" Drama by Frances Goodrich and Albert Hackett **NOTICE & NOTE** READING MODEL **Signposts** • Words of the Wiser • Memory Moment • Contrasts and Contradictions	**Reading** • Analyze Drama • Analyze Plot Development **Writing:** Make a Poster **Speaking and Listening:** Dramatize a Relationship **Vocabulary:** Use Prefixes **Language Conventions:** Correct Capitalization	🔊 **Audio** **Close Read Screencast:** Modeled Discussions **Reading Studio:** Notice & Note **Vocabulary Studio:** Using Prefixes **Grammar Studio:** Module 13: Lessons 1–6: Capital Letters
	Mentor Text *from* **"The Diary of a Young Girl"** Diary by Anne Frank	**Reading** • Analyze a Primary Source • Make Inferences **Writing:** Create a Comic **Speaking and Listening:** Discuss with a Partner **Vocabulary:** Connotation and Denotation **Language Conventions:** Parentheses	🔊 **Audio** **Reading Studio:** Making Inferences About Characters **Writing Studio:** Planning a Story **Speaking and Listening Studio:** Discussing with a Partner **Vocabulary Studio:** Connotation and Denotation **Grammar Studio:** Module 14: Lesson 2: Other Marks of Punctuation

SUGGESTED PACING:
30 DAYS

Unit Introduction	The Diary of Anne Frank	The Diary of a Young Girl
1	2 3 4 5 6 7 8 9 10 11 12	13 14 15 16

English Learner Support	Differentiated Instruction	Online Ed Assessment
• Learn New Vocabulary • Learning Strategies		

English Learner Support		Differentiated Instruction	Assessment
• Text X-Ray • Use Cognates • Take Notes • Act Out Contrasts • Use Language Support • Practice Speaking • Use Language Support • Understand Idioms • Formative Oral Assessment • Read Closely • Write Summaries • Analyze Language • Conduct Word Study • Analyze Character • Support Comprehension	• Exchange Ideas • Understand Text Structure • Oral Assessment • Use Nouns and Verbs • Analyze Drama • Confirm Understanding • Understand Cohesion • Use Helping Verbs • Culturally Responsive Instruction • Use Verbs • Analyze Words of the Wiser • Analyze Plot Development • Use Prefixes • Language Conventions	**When Students Struggle** • Use Strategies • Genre Reformulation • Identifying Details • Learning Strategy • Compare and Contrast • Chart Outcomes **To Challenge Students** • Respond to the Drama • Analyze Motivation • Analyze the Impact of Perspective • Debate Issues • Impact of Setting	**Selection Test**
• Text X-Ray • Identify Cognates • Use Cognates • Use Learning Strategies • Comprehend Language Structures	• Use Reading Strategies • Oral Assessment • Create a Comic • Language Conventions	**When Students Struggle** • Learning Strategy	**Selection Test**

After Auschwitz
17 18 19

There But for the Grace / Days
20 21 22 23 24 25

Independent Reading
26 27

End of Unit
28 29 30

	Instructional Focus	**Online** **Ed** **Resources**

ANALYZE & APPLY

| **"After Auschwitz"** Speech by Elie Wiesel | **Reading** • Analyze Appeals • Analyze Rhetorical Devices **Writing:** Make a Poster **Speaking and Listening:** Discuss with a Group | **Audio** **Reading Studio:** Notice & Note **Speaking and Listening Studio:** Giving a Presentation; Particpating in a Collaborative Discussion |

COLLABORATE AND COMPARE

| **"There But for the Grace"** Poem by Wislawa Szymborska .... **"Days"** Poem by Billy Collins | **Reading** • Analyze Sound Devices • Analyze Figurative Language **Writing:** Illustrate Figurative Language **Speaking and Listening:** Recite a Poem | **Audio** **Text in Focus:** Compare Arguments **Reading Studio:** Elements of Poetry |
| **Collaborate and Compare** | **Reading** • Compare Themes • Analyze the Texts **Speaking and Listening:** Create and Present | **Speaking and Listening Studio:** Having a Collaborative Discussion |

Online **Ed** INDEPENDENT READING

| The independent Reading selections are only available in the eBook. **Go to the Reading Studio for more information on Notice & Note.** | **"Peace Can Happen"** Diary by Christine Kingery **Lexile 720L** | **"The Butterfly"** Poem by Pavel Friedman **"On a Sunny Evening"** Poem by Anonymous |

END OF UNIT

| **Writing Task:** Write a Personal Narrative **Reflect on the Unit** | **Writing:** Writing a Personal Narrative **Language Conventions:** Correct Capitalizations | **Unit 6 Response Log** **Mentor Text:** *from* "The Diary of a Young Girl" **Reading Studio:** Notice & Note **Writing Studio:** Writing Narratives; Writing as a Process **Grammar Studio:** Module 13: Lessons 1–6: Capital Letters |

English Learner Support		Differentiated Instruction	Online Ed Assessment
• Text X-Ray • Use Articles • Identify Suffixes • Learn Argument Terms	• Analyze Word Choice • Summarize Main Ideas • Oral Assessment • Understand Special Phrases	**When Students Struggle** • Use Learning Strategy **To Challenge Students** • Analyze the Speaker	**Selection Test**
• Text X-Ray • Understand Directionality • Use Cognates • Repetition • Oral Assessment • Vowel Sounds • Syllabication • Discuss Theme		**When Students Struggle** • Graphic Support	**Selection Tests**

"The Singing Women"
Short Story by Rebecca Makkai
Lexile

"A Tragedy Revealed: A Heroine's Last Days"
Article by Ernst Schnabel
Lexile 990L

"Nobel Prize Acceptance Speech"
Essay by Elie Wiesel
Lexile 790L

Selection Tests

English Learner Support	Differentiated Instruction	Assessment
• Language X-Ray • Link Events • Recognize Formal and Informal Language • Use Modal Expressions	**When Students Struggle** • Organize Details • Visualize Details **To Challenge Students** • Structure Your Narrative	**Unit Test**

THE LEGACY OF ANNE FRANK

? Connect to the ESSENTIAL QUESTION

Ask a volunteer to read aloud the Essential Question. Ask students what they know about Anne Frank. Explain that Anne Frank was a young girl living in Holland during the Holocaust, a very dark time in the 1940s in which millions of Jewish people were killed. To avoid being captured, Anne and her family went into hiding in an upstairs annex above her father's business. During that time, Anne kept a diary. Unfortunately, Anne and her family were discovered and captured, and Anne did not survive. Her diary lives on as a memoir of her thoughts and experiences. It reveals that despite difficult circumstances, Anne tried to live a normal life and remain positive. Even today, people can learn a lot from Anne Frank.

■ English Learner Support

Learn New Vocabulary Make sure students understand the Essential Question. If necessary, explain the following ideas, using pictorial support as necessary:

- Anne Frank (pictured on page 404) was a young girl who lived from 1929 to 1945. She was hiding above her father's business and kept a diary.
- A diary is a book in which somebody records thoughts. We can learn from Anne Frank because of her diary.
  SUBSTANTIAL/MODERATE

DISCUSS THE QUOTATION

Read the quotation with students. In her diary, Anne Frank says she doesn't want to have lived in vain, which means she wanted her life to have a purpose. She says she wants to go on living after she dies. Tell students that her diary has been published in more than 60 languages and read by millions. Discuss with students how Anne was able to go on living after her death by sharing her experiences with so many people.

? ESSENTIAL QUESTION:

What can we learn from Anne Frank?

> " I don't want to have lived in vain like most people . . . I want to go on living even after my death! "
>
> Anne Frank

404   Unit 6

 LEARNING MINDSET

Growth Mindset Remind students that a *growth mindset* means believing you can improve by taking on challenges and pushing yourself. Acknowledge the power of *yet*. Students may not understand the text/concept yet, but if they keep trying, eventually they will succeed.

ACADEMIC VOCABULARY

Academic Vocabulary words are words you use when you discuss and write about texts. In this unit you will practice and learn five words.

☑ communicate ☐ draft ☐ liberation ☐ philosophy ☐ publish

Study the Word Network to learn more about the word **communicate**.

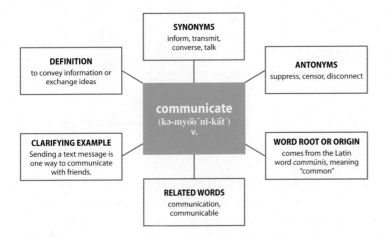

Write and Discuss Discuss the completed Word Network with a partner, making sure to talk through all of the boxes until you both understand the word and its synonyms, antonyms, and related forms. Then, fill out Word Networks for the remaining four words. Use a dictionary or online resource to help you complete the activity.

 Go online to access the Word Networks.

RESPOND TO THE ESSENTIAL QUESTION

In this unit, you will consider the lessons to be learned from tragic events such as the Holocaust. As you read, you will revisit the **Essential Question** and gather your ideas about it in the **Response Log** that appears on page R6. At the end of the unit, you will have the opportunity to write a **personal narrative** similar to the diary entries written by Anne Frank. Filling out the Response Log will help you prepare for this writing task.

 You can also go online to access the Response Log.

ACADEMIC VOCABULARY

As students complete Word Networks for the remaining four vocabulary words, encourage them to include all the categories shown in the completed network if possible, but point out that some words do not have clear synonyms or antonyms. Some words may also function as different parts of speech—for example, *draft* may be a noun or a verb.

communicate (kə-myōō′ nĭ-kāt′) *v.* to convey information or to exchange ideas (Spanish cognate: *comunicar*)

draft (drăft) *n.* any of various versions or stages of a written document or plan

liberation (lĭb′ə-rā′shən) *n.* the act of freeing or the state of being free

philosophy (fĭ-lŏs′ə-fē) *n.* the study of the underlying theory or set of ideas related to life as a whole based on logical reasoning (Spanish cognate: *filosofía*)

publish (pŭb′lĭsh) *v.* to prepare and issue a book or other material to the public (Spanish cognate: *publicar*)

RESPOND TO THE ESSENTIAL QUESTION

Direct students to the Unit 6 Response Log. Explain that students will use it to record ideas and details from the selections that help answer the Essential Question. When they work on the writing task at the end of the unit, their Response Logs will help them think about what they have read and make connections between texts.

 ENGLISH LEARNER SUPPORT

Learning Strategies Use this strategy to help students understand the Anne Frank quote:

- Write the following sentences: *To "have lived in vain" means to die without doing anything important in your life. Anne wants to make sure she does something important that will make a difference even after she dies.* Have students read the sentences out loud and copy them into their notebooks.
- Have students complete the sentence frame in writing: *One way not to live in vain would be to _____.* Have them illustrate their sentences.

- Ask students the following questions: *Did Anne Frank live in vain? What did Anne Frank do so that she lived on after her death?* Accept single words or simple phrases as answers.
- Have students draw an illustration of one personal goal they have so that they do not live in vain. Have them complete the sentence frame in writing under their illustrations: *So that I don't live in vain, I want to _____.* Make sure they write the whole sentence.

MODERATE

READING MODEL

THE DIARY OF ANNE FRANK

Drama by Frances Goodrich and Albert Hackett

GENRE ELEMENTS
DRAMA

Remind students that a **drama** is a play. The text is written in the form of a script to be performed by actors in front of an audience. A drama tells a story through characters' words and actions. Remind students that the script for a drama also contains stage directions that are not to be read by the actors but that give important details that explain what is happening in the drama. Dramas are divided into acts. Acts are further divided into scenes, which change when the time or place of the action of the drama change.

LEARNING OBJECTIVES

- Analyze drama, including analysis of plot development.
- Make, correct, and confirm predictions.
- Conduct research about the Nazi campaign against the Jews.
- Create a poster about the influence of setting on characters.
- Discuss and dramatize a subplot.
- Use prefixes to determine meaning of unfamiliar words.
- Understand conventions of correct capitalization.
- **Language** Discuss with a partner the features of the text using the key term *plot*.

TEXT COMPLEXITY

Quantitative Measures	The Diary of Anne Frank	Lexile N/A
Quantitative Measures	**Ideas Presented** Much is explicit but moves to some implied meaning.	
	Structure Used Primarily explicit but varies from simple chronological order.	
	Language Used Mostly explicit, some dialect used.	
	Knowledge Required Cultural or historical references make heavier demands.	

RESOURCES

- Unit 6 Response Log
- Selection Audio
- Understanding Setting
- Close Read Screencasts: Modeled Discussions
- Reading Studio: Notice & Note
- Vocabulary Studio: Using Prefixes
- Grammar Studio: Module 13: Capital Letters
- "The Diary of Anne Frank" Selection Test

SUMMARIES

English

In 1942 Amsterdam, the Jewish Frank family, fearful of being captured by the Nazis and sent to a concentration camp, decides to go into hiding in an annex above Mr. Frank's business. The Franks and a few others must remain in the annex at all times, and must keep silent during the day. Young Anne Frank uses her diary to keep an account of their time in the annex, which proves to be an important resource for future generations to learn about the Holocaust. Readers can also learn a lot from Anne's indomitable spirit and zest for life.

Spanish

En Ámsterdam en 1942, una la familia judía, los Frank, deciden esconderse en un anexo encima del negocio del Sr. Frank, por miedo a ser capturados por los nazis y llevados a un campo de concentración. Los Frank y otros deben permanecer en el anexo a toda hora y deben guardar silencio durante el día. La joven Ana Frank relata en su diario su estancia en el anexo; el diario se convierte en una fuente importante de conocimiento sobre el Holocausto para las futuras generaciones. Los lectores también pueden aprender mucho del indomable espíritu de Ana y su entusiasmo por la vida.

 ## SMALL-GROUP OPTIONS

Have students work in small groups to read and discuss the selection.

Readers' Theater

- Divide the class into groups, and assign each group a portion of the script to perform.
- Tell students to designate roles for each group member, either randomly or based on volunteers. Some scenes may require a student to play multiple characters.
- Have students rehearse their scenes several times, including acting out the stage directions. Emphasize that students do not have to memorize their scripts.
- If you prefer, students may create or bring costumes to wear during the reading.

Reciprocal Teaching

- Present students with a list of generic question stems.
- Have students use the stems to independently write three to five questions about the text. They do not have to be able to answer the questions.
- Put students in groups of three. Each student should ask at least two questions to the group, without duplicating another student's questions.
- The group should reach consensus on how to answer the question and find text evidence to support their answers.

Text X-Ray: English Learner Support
for "The Diary of Anne Frank"

Use the Text X-Ray and the supports and scaffolds in the Teacher's Edition to help guide students at different proficiency levels through the selection.

INTRODUCE THE SELECTION
DISCUSS ANNE FRANK

In this lesson, students will need some background knowledge about Anne Frank and the historical context in which she lived. Write down bullet points such as:

- Anne Frank (1929–1945)
- Anne was born in Germany and moved to Amsterdam.
- Nazi soldiers from Germany were capturing Jewish people and sending them to death camps.
- Anne and her family hid above Anne's father's office with another family for two years. They couldn't leave or make much noise.
- Anne kept a diary about her time in hiding.

Give students these sentence frames to help them discuss the selection:

- Anne Frank and her family did not want to be caught by the Nazis, so they hid in _____.
- We know about Anne's time in hiding because she _____.

CULTURAL REFERENCES

The following words and phrases may be unfamiliar to students:

- *Jewish* (Background note): describes a person who follows the religion of Judaism
- *Adolf Hitler* (Background note): a cruel German leader who wanted to take over the world and kill all Jewish people
- *annex* (Background note): an area added on to a building
- *Amsterdam* (paragraph 3): the capital of the country of the Netherlands, located in the region of Holland
- *diary* (paragraph 31): a book in which a person writes down his or her private thoughts
- *Dutch capitulation* (paragraph 33): an event in 1940 in which Nazi soldiers invaded the Netherlands and the Dutch soldiers there had to give up control of the country to the Nazis

LISTENING

Understand Background

Draw students' attention to Scene 1. Tell students that this scene takes place in 1945, after Anne has died and her father finds her diary. At the end of this scene, the action of the play goes back to 1942, as Anne's father reads about that year in the diary and Anne's voice joins in.

Have students listen as you read aloud paragraphs 31–35. Use the following supports with students at varying proficiency levels:

- Tell students that you will ask questions about what you just read aloud. They should answer with a yes or no. *Was Anne's family safe in Holland? Were the German rules for Jews fair? Did Anne's family hide from the Germans?* **SUBSTANTIAL**
- Have students complete the following sentence frames: *When the Germans took over Holland, they made a lot of unfair rules for the Jewish people, like they couldn't _____ or _____. Anne's family was not safe anymore, so they _____.* **MODERATE**
- Have students answer the following questions in complete sentences. *Why was life difficult for the Franks and other Jewish people? Why did the Franks decide to hide? Where did they hide?* **LIGHT**

SPEAKING

Discuss Plot

Remind students that the *plot* of a story is the series of events that happen in a story. Point out that in this drama, the plot is not told in order, because it starts and ends in 1945 but most of it takes place before then.

Guide students to discuss the story, and make sure they use the term *plot* correctly. Use the following supports with students at varying proficiency levels:

- Write the following sentences on the board: *The plot of this play starts in 1945 when Mr. Frank finds Anne's diary. Most of the plot tells about their time in hiding. The plot ends back in 1945 when Mr. Frank says he knows Anne is dead.* Have students chorally read the sentences three times. **SUBSTANTIAL**
- Provide students with these sentence frames to discuss plot: *The plot begins in the year ____. Mr. Frank has found Anne's ____. Most of the plot tells about ____. The ____ ends in 1945 after Anne's death.* **MODERATE**
- Have student pairs discuss the following questions: *When does the plot begin? What is most of the plot about? What happens at the end of the plot?* **LIGHT**

READING

Understand Setting

Draw students' attention to paragraphs 76–86, in which the Franks and the Van Daans talk about the rules for noise. Tell students it is important to understand how dangerous the Franks' and Van Daans' situation was and why they had to be so careful.

Work with students to read paragraphs 76–86. Use the following supports with students at varying proficiency levels:

- Draw a rough sketch of the secret annex and its inhabitants. Show factory workers below and say, "If they talk or walk loudly, or run water, the factory workers will hear them." **SUBSTANTIAL**
- Work with students to draw their own individual sketches of the annex and the factory below. Make sure they draw the inhabitants of the annex and the people below. Discuss why they must be quiet during the day. **MODERATE**
- Ask students to answer the following questions to demonstrate comprehension: *What rules must the Franks and Van Daans follow during the day? Why must they follow these rules?* **LIGHT**

WRITING

Make a Poster

Draw students' attention to the assignment on p. 497 to make a poster conveying how the characters were affected by the setting.

Use the following supports with students at varying proficiency levels:

- Work with students in a group. Select three characters you will depict. Ask students questions about how each character behaved, felt, and changed. Write down students' ideas, and have them incorporate the ideas into a pictorial group poster. **SUBSTANTIAL**
- Have students work with a partner and choose three characters. Have them write the following for each character on their posters: *name, how character felt, what character did, how character changed.* They should create accompanying illustrations. **MODERATE**
- Have students make a poster with the following information about each of three characters: how they behaved, what they thought, and how the annex changed them. **LIGHT**

Notice & Note

EXPLAIN THE SIGNPOSTS

Explain that **NOTICE & NOTE Signposts** are significant moments in the text that help readers understand and analyze works of fiction or nonfiction. Use the instruction on these pages to introduce students to the signposts **Words of the Wiser, Memory Moment,** and **Contrasts and Contradictions**. Then use the selection that follows to have students apply the signposts to a text

For a full list of the fiction and nonfiction signposts, see p. 534.

WORDS OF THE WISER

Explain that **Words of the Wiser** are the advice or insight a wiser character offers about life to the main character. The wiser character is often older than the main character. The wiser figure shares wisdom or advice to help the main character with a problem or decision. Recognizing a **Words of the Wiser** signpost can help a reader understand a text's theme or explain a character's development.

Draw students' attention to the sample passage. The student annotated Mr. Frank's words to Anne when she is struggling with the idea of going into hiding. Mr. Frank tells Anne that "there are no walls, there are no bolts, no locks that anyone can put on your mind." That is an important lesson for Anne, one that perhaps inspires her to keep up her studies and write in her diary.

Explain to students that, while there are no specific words to indicate a **Words of the Wiser** signpost, it usually occurs when an older person is having a serious discussion with a younger person about his or her problems. When students spot a **Words of the Wiser** signpost, they should ask themselves the anchor question: *What's the lesson for the character?*

For more information on these and other signposts to Notice & Note, visit the **Reading Studio**.

THE DIARY OF ANNE FRANK

You are about to read a drama called *The Diary of Anne Frank*. In it, you will notice and note signposts that will give you clues about the play's characters and themes. Here are three key signposts to look for as you read this drama and other works of fiction.

Words of the Wiser To whom do you turn when you need help figuring something out? As in real life, characters in literature sometimes benefit from the wisdom and guidance of another—often a character who is older and wiser than they are.

When a character speaks helpful or inspiring words, stop and think. Paying attention to **Words of the Wiser** can:

- highlight something a character needs to learn
- reveal a solution to a problem a character is facing
- explain or provide insight into a situation
- hint at the theme or lesson of the story

The passage below illustrates a student's annotation in *The Diary of Anne Frank* and a response to a Words of the Wiser signpost.

---

165 **Mr. Frank.** Never. I am sorry, Anneke. It isn't safe. No, you must never go beyond that door.

166 *(For the first time Anne realizes what "going into hiding" means.)*

167 **Anne.** I see.

168 **Mr. Frank.** It'll be hard, I know. But always remember this, Anneke. There are no walls, there are no bolts, no locks that anyone can put on your mind.

Anchor Question
When you notice this signpost, ask: What's the life lesson, and how might it affect the character?

What wise words does Mr. Frank share with his daughter?	He says that her mind will always be free—even if she must live in hiding for a time.
Why might Mr. Frank want Anne to know this?	He wants her to remember something encouraging even if life becomes very difficult in their small space.

Memory Moment When a character recalls events from the past, the author is likely sharing important information. Paying attention to a **Memory Moment** can:

- provide historical context for a story or play
- provide background that relates to the current situation
- reveal details about characters' lives or relationships
- show what motivates or drives a character's actions

Here, a student marked a Memory Moment.

> 31 **Mr. Frank** (*quietly*). Anne's diary. (*He opens the diary and begins to read.*) "<u>Monday, the sixth of July, nineteen forty-two.</u>" (*to* Miep) Nineteen forty-two. Is it possible, Miep? . . . <u>Only three years ago</u>. . . .

When you encounter a phrase like these while reading, pause to see if it's a **Memory Moment** signpost:

"Only three years ago . . ."

"that reminded him of . . ."

"It was just like when . . ."

"I remember when . . ."

"when we were little . . ."

Anchor Question
When you notice this signpost, ask: Why might this memory be important?

What memory is introduced at the beginning of the play?	the memory of his daughter Anne, writing in the diary three years earlier
Why might this memory be important to the story?	It provides a transition into the three-year-old story, which focuses on Anne.

Contrasts and Contradictions When a character acts in a way that clashes with what you would expect, take the time to figure out what it means. **Contrasts and Contradictions** often give you a deeper insight into a character or a situation. In this example, a student underlined details that show Contrasts and Contradictions.

> 19 **Miep.** Mr. Frank, you can't leave here! This is your home! <u>Amsterdam is your home. Your business is here, waiting for you . . . You're needed here</u> . . . Now that the war is over, there are things that . . .
>
> 20 **Mr. Frank.** <u>I can't stay in Amsterdam, Miep. It has too many memories for me.</u>

Anchor Question
When you notice this signpost, ask: Why did the character act (or feel) that way?

What makes Mr. Frank's choice an unexpected one?	It's surprising that he wants to leave his home, a place where he has a business.
Why might Mr. Frank wish to leave a place with many memories?	The memories are of sad events in that place and of loved ones who now are dead.

WHEN STUDENTS STRUGGLE . . .

Use Strategies A story that flashes back like this one piques a reader's curiosity, providing an opportunity for a **KWL Chart.** Make a large poster with three columns, labeled **Know, Want to Know,** and **Learned.** At the beginning of the story, have students share what they already know about Anne Frank or the Holocaust. Then have them share what they want to know. During reading you should pause periodically and check to see whether any questions have been answered, or whether students have anything new to add to what they know or want to know. Update the chart as needed.

MEMORY MOMENT

Tell students that a **Memory Moment** is when a character has a sudden memory of the past. Authors usually include these memories to share important information. That information might be historical context for a story, explanation of background related to the current situation, details about a character's life, or an explanation of what motivates a character's actions.

Review the sample selection with students. Note that the student annotated a **Memory Moment** in which Mr. Frank sees a date and begins to recall that time in the past.

Some **Memory Moments** signposts are obvious because they begin with, "I remember when" or similar wording. Other times they may not be as clearly introduced. When students encounter a **Memory Moment**, they should ask themselves the anchor question: *Why is this memory important?*

CONTRASTS AND CONTRADICTIONS

Explain that **Contrasts and Contradictions** signposts occur when a character acts in a way that is different (that is, *in contrast*) to his or her usual or expected behavior. A character behaving in this *contradictory* way usually gives a reader insight into the character and also the story's conflict. For example, in the sample passage, Mr. Frank says he has to leave Amsterdam, even though Miep says it is his home and he is needed there. A reader should take note of a **Contrast and Contradiction** signpost and ask the anchor question: *Why did the character act or feel that way?*

APPLY THE SIGNPOSTS

Have students use the selection that follows as a model text to apply the signposts. As students encounter signposts, prompt them to stop, reread, and ask themselves the anchor questions that will help them understand the text. Tell students to continue to look for these and other signposts as they read the other selections in the unit.

THE DIARY OF ANNE FRANK

Drama by **Frances Goodrich** and **Albert Hackett**

? Connect to the
ESSENTIAL QUESTION

This selection is a drama based on real events. Anne Frank was a real person who was born in Germany in 1929. When Hitler came to power and Jewish people were persecuted in Germany, Anne and her family moved to Amsterdam, Holland. Soon, however, Hitler's Nazis took control of Amsterdam, as well, and enforced all kinds of unfair policies against the Jewish community. Soon it became clear that the Nazis were rounding up Jewish people and sending them to concentration camps. To avoid being caught, Anne and her family went into hiding in a secret annex above her father's business. Anne's family and the others who lived in the annex were never allowed outside and had to remain silent during the day. Anne kept a diary the entire time she was in the annex. The residents of the annex were discovered and caught in 1944. Anne was sent to a concentration camp, where she died. Her father found her diary after her death and had it published. The diary demonstrated that despite the horrors she experienced, Anne had an optimistic spirit and a desire to make the world better. Future generations can learn a lot from Anne Frank.

? ESSENTIAL QUESTION:

What can we learn from Anne Frank?

408 Unit 6

 LEARNING MINDSET

Plan Tell students that planning is often a hallmark of a strong student. Explain that planning ahead can help a student complete work efficiently and exceptionally. Encourage students to make a plan for completing this longer selection, including mapping out the steps. Ask them what they already know about Anne Frank and what they would like to learn.

QUICK START

Do you agree or disagree with the view that most people are basically good at heart? Briefly share your views and reasons with a partner.

ANALYZE DRAMA

A **drama,** or play, is a form of literature meant to be performed by actors for an audience. The author is called a **playwright,** and the text of the drama is the **script.** The script includes these elements:

- The **cast of characters** is a list of all the characters in the play.
- **Stage directions,** which often are italicized and in parentheses, are mostly instructions about how to perform the drama. Some stage directions describe the setting and the characters.
- **Dialogue** is the written conversation between characters.
- A drama is often divided into acts and scenes. An **act** is a major division within a play, similar to a chapter in a book. Each act may be divided into smaller sections, called **scenes.**

As you read Act One of this drama, note differences between Scene 1 and Scene 2. What do these differences help you understand?

SCENE	WHERE?	WHEN?	KEY EVENTS
Scene 1			
Scene 2			

ANALYZE PLOT DEVELOPMENT

Each scene in a drama presents an episode of the play's **plot,** or story line. To analyze a drama's plot development, consider these factors:

- Most plays have a **linear plot,** with events presented in the order in which they occur. However, some plays have a **nonlinear plot,** in which events are told out of order.
- The plot may include one or more subplots. A **subplot** is an additional, or secondary, plot that contains its own conflict.
- When an author interrupts the chronological order by describing something that took place at an earlier time, it is called a **flashback.** A flashback can help readers better understand a current situation.
- The playwright may provide hints to suggest future events. This is called **foreshadowing.** Foreshadowing creates suspense and makes readers eager to find out what will happen.

As you analyze the plot of *The Diary of Anne Frank,* think about how certain events cause others to happen. Also note the playwrights' use of subplot, flashback, and foreshadowing.

GENRE ELEMENTS: DRAMA

- is written to be performed by actors in front of an audience
- tells a story through characters' words and actions
- includes stage directions with important details that explain what's happening
- may be divided into acts, which are in turn divided into scenes
- may show that the time or place of the action has changed by starting a new act or scene

QUICK START

Have students read the Quick Start question, and then share their responses with a partner. Tell students that Anne Frank, despite having witnessed some of the worst human behavior from the Nazis, still believed most people were good at heart. Remind students to include their reasoning during their partner discussions. If time permits, you may have students share their views and reasons with the class.

ANALYZE DRAMA

After reviewing the information on drama, tell students that *The Diary of Anne Frank* is a script based on real events. The real Anne Frank wrote a diary—which they will read selections from later in the unit—and her father had it published. Two playwrights, Frances Goodrich and Albert Hackett, adapted Anne's story and her diary into a script for a play and later a movie.

During this selection, students will analyze how playwrights develop dramatic action throughout the play, so it is important that they know the key terms for discussing drama. They need to know that a drama is divided into acts, which are large portions of a play that often have a break, or intermission, in between. Acts are then broken into scenes, which change whenever the action in the play changes locations or times. Point out the chart students need to complete about Scene 1 and Scene 2. Students also need to know that scripts consist of dialogue, or the words the characters actually say, and stage direction, which are words describing scenery or characters' behavior.

ANALYZE PLOT DEVELOPMENT

Students will probably already know that a plot is a play's story line. They may be unfamiliar with some of the other terms related to plot. Have students work in small groups to discuss each of the bullet points. Ask them to cite an example of each dramatic factor from some familiar form of media they've seen or read recently. Then have each group present their examples as part of a class discussion. Tell students to ask themselves these questions as they read:

- Is this plot linear or nonlinear?
- Do I see examples of flashbacks or foreshadowing?
- Are there any subplots?

TEACH

CRITICAL VOCABULARY

Encourage students to read all the sentences before deciding which word best completes each one. Remind them to look for context clues that match the meaning of each word.

Answers:

1. *indignantly*

2. *conspicuous*

3. *ostentatiously*

4. *loathe*

5. *inarticulate*

6. *appalled*

■ English Learner Support

Use Cognates Tell students that some of the Critical Vocabulary words have Spanish cognates: *indignantly/ con indignación, conspicuous/conspicuo, ostentatiously/ ostentosamente.* **ALL LEVELS**

LANGUAGE CONVENTIONS

Review the information about correct capitalization with students. Ask student why each word is capitalized in the example sentence. (*Jewish* is a religion/ethnicity, *Holland* is the name of a place, and *Hitler* is a last name.) Ask students to help you generate a list of other categories of words that are capitalized. For example, the list may include capitalizing the first word in a sentence, the first word in a direct quotation, and the pronoun *I*. Remind them to note which words the playwrights capitalized in *The Diary of Anne Frank* and to consider why they capitalized these words.

 ANNOTATION MODEL

Point out the annotation model, which demonstrates how one student annotated Notice & Note signposts. This student used underlining, circling, and margin notes, but students are free to use whatever annotation style works best for them.

 GET READY

CRITICAL VOCABULARY

conspicuous	indignantly	appalled
loathe	ostentatiously	inarticulate

To see how many Critical Vocabulary words you already know, use them to complete the sentences.

1. Maya _____ washed the dishes that her brother had left in the sink.

2. The bicyclist was _____ with her bright yellow reflectors.

3. The mayor arrived _____ in a long black limousine.

4. Binh used to _____ math, but now he loves it.

5. She was shy and _____ around strangers but very talkative among friends.

6. People were _____ by all the storm damage.

LANGUAGE CONVENTIONS

Correct Capitalization In this lesson, you will learn which types of words need to be capitalized.

As my family is Jewish, we emigrated to Holland when Hitler came to power.

In the above example, words that name an ethnicity, a country, and a person are capitalized. As you read *The Diary of Anne Frank*, note which words the playwrights capitalized, and why they did so.

ANNOTATION MODEL   **NOTICE & NOTE**

As you read, notice and note signposts, including **Words of the Wiser, Memory Moments,** and **Contrasts and Contradictions.** In the model, you can see one reader's notes about *The Diary of Anne Frank*.

33 **Mr. Frank and Anne.** "My father started a business, importing spice and herbs. Things went well for us until nineteen forty. Then the war came, and the Dutch capitulation, followed by the arrival of the Germans. Then things got very bad for the Jews."	*memories of life before hiding*
34 (Mr. Frank's Voice *dies out.* Anne's Voice *continues alone. The lights dim slowly to darkness. The curtain falls on the scene.*)	
35 **Anne's Voice.** You could not do this and you could not do that. They forced Father out of his business. We had to wear yellow stars. I had to turn in my bike. I couldn't go to a Dutch school any more. . . .	*This contradicts what decent people would do.*

Frances Goodrich (1890–1984) and *Albert Hackett* (1900–1995) were a married couple who worked together to write screenplays for movies. They wrote the play called The Diary of Anne Frank based on Anne's actual diary entries. Although the play differs from the diary in many ways, Anne's father, who survived the Holocaust, believed that it captured the essence of his daughter's diary. The play won the 1956 Pulitzer Prize for drama. It was later made into an Oscar-winning movie, for which Goodrich and Hackett also wrote the screenplay.

THE DIARY OF ANNE FRANK

Drama by Frances Goodrich and Albert Hackett

BACKGROUND

Anne Frank and her family were Jewish citizens of Germany. After the Nazi Party, led by Adolf Hitler, came to power in 1933, the Franks moved to the Netherlands to escape persecution. However, the Nazis invaded that country in 1940. In order to survive, Anne's family went into hiding when she was 13 years old. They hid in attic rooms behind Mr. Frank's office, and several other Jews joined them. In this "Secret Annex," Anne kept a diary about her life in hiding. More than two years later, the group's worst fears came true when the Nazis found them. Everyone who had been living there was sent to concentration camps. Anne's diary was discovered later.

SETTING A PURPOSE

As you read, think about what the play reveals about Anne Frank's philosophy of life. How are her thoughts communicated?

Notice & Note

Use the side margins to notice and note signposts in the text.

BACKGROUND

Have students read the Background information about Anne Frank and her family. Explain that after the Nazis found the Franks' hiding place the family was sent to the Auschwitz concentration camp in Poland. At the camp, the men and women were separated, and Mr. Frank never saw his wife and daughters again. Anne and her sister were eventually transferred to another concentration camp, Bergen-Belsen.

After the war, Mr. Frank returned to Amsterdam and discovered Anne's diary, which had been found and saved by a friend. The diary, originally published in Dutch in 1947, has now been printed in many other languages. This has allowed millions of people around the world to read Anne's words.

SETTING A PURPOSE

Direct students to use the Setting a Purpose prompt to focus their reading.

▶ ## NOTICE & NOTE

Remind students of the prompt to indicate signposts in the margin. This lesson asks students to look for **Words of the Wiser, Memory Moments,** and **Contrasts and Contradictions.**

TEACH

 ## ANALYZE DRAMA

Tell the students that Anne Frank and her family are going to hide out in the secret annex with a family that Anne has never met. Despite being virtual strangers, they will have to remain in a very small space and follow difficult rules together. Clarify that Mr. Dussel is an elderly dentist who arrives at the annex later. (**Answer:** *The Frank family and the Van Daan family live in the secret annex. There are three other characters in the play: a man named Mr. Dussel who also lives in the annex and two people who work for Mr. Frank's business, Miep Gies and Mr. Kraler.*)

■ English Learner Support

Take Notes Before reading, help students make notes about each character in or near the Cast of Characters box. For Anne, they can write "young girl," and for Margot they can write "older sister." They can label Mr. and Mrs. Frank as Mom and Dad. They should already have underlined the three Van Daans, and they can further label them as mom, dad, and son. Mr. Dussel can be labeled as "dentist who comes later." Have students indicate that Miep Gies is a young female employee at Mr. Frank's business and Mr. Kraler is a male employee.   **MODERATE**

 ## ANALYZE DRAMA

Remind students that the whole play takes place in one scene, the secret annex. The play starts in 1945 with Mr. Frank visiting the annex and finding Anne's diary. From there the play flashes back to the time they all lived in the annex from 1942 to 1944. The play will end with Mr. Frank in the annex in 1945 again. (**Answer:** *The sounds make the whole scene more realistic. The sounds remind the readers [and the audience] that there is a whole world outside the secret annex. Also, because the residents can't go outside, the sounds they hear are very important. They remind readers that these sounds are one of the few sources of information the residents have about the outside world. The church bells tell the time. The "marching feet" are a constant reminder that German soldiers are close by.*)

 NOTICE & NOTE

ANALYZE DRAMA
Annotate: Review the cast of characters. Circle four members of one family. Underline three members of another.

Analyze: What two families live in the Secret Annex? What other characters are in the play?

ANALYZE DRAMA
Annotate: In paragraphs 3–5, mark details that describe what this scene looks like and sounds like.

Analyze: Why do you think the stage directions include a description of the sounds outside the Annex?

CHARACTERS

SECRET ANNEX RESIDENTS

Anne Frank	Peter Van Daan
Margot Frank	Mr. Van Daan
Mr. Frank	Mrs. Van Daan
Mrs. Frank	Mr. Dussel

WORKERS IN MR. FRANK'S BUSINESS

Miep Gies (mēp gēs)   Mr. Kraler (krä´lər)

1 **The Time.** *July 1942–August 1944, November 1945*

2 **The Place.** *Amsterdam, the Netherlands*

3 *The scene remains the same throughout the play. It is the top floor of a warehouse and office building in Amsterdam, Holland. The sharply peaked roof of the building is outlined against a sea of other rooftops, stretching away into the distance. Nearby is the belfry of a church tower, the Westertoren, whose carillon rings out the hours. Occasionally faint sounds float up from below: the voices of children playing in the street, the tramp of marching feet, a boat whistle from the canal.*

4   *The three rooms of the top floor and a small attic space above are exposed to our view. The largest of the rooms is in the center, with two small rooms, slightly raised, on either side. On the right is a bathroom, out of sight. A narrow steep flight of stairs at the back leads up to the attic. The rooms are sparsely furnished with a few chairs, cots, a table or two. The windows are painted over, or covered with makeshift blackout curtains. In the main room there is a sink, a gas ring for cooking and a wood-burning stove for warmth.*

---

5 *The room on the left is hardly more than a closet. There is a skylight in the sloping ceiling. Directly under this room is a small steep stairwell, with steps leading down to a door. This is the only entrance from the building below. When the door is opened we see that it has been concealed on the outer side by a bookcase attached to it.*

ACT ONE
Scene 1

6 *The curtain rises on an empty stage. It is late afternoon November, 1945.*

7 *The rooms are dusty, the curtains in rags. Chairs and tables are overturned.*

8 *The door at the foot of the small stairwell swings open. Mr. Frank comes up the steps into view. He is a gentle, cultured European in his middle years. There is still a trace of a German accent in his speech.*

9 *He stands looking slowly around, making a supreme effort at self-control. He is weak, ill. His clothes are threadbare.*

10 *After a second he drops his rucksack on the couch and moves slowly about. He opens the door to one of the smaller rooms, and then abruptly closes it again, turning away. He goes to the window at the back, looking off at the Westertoren as its carillon strikes the hour of six, then he moves restlessly on.*

11 *From the street below we hear the sound of a barrel organ and children's voices at play. There is a many-colored scarf hanging from a nail. Mr. Frank takes it, putting it around his neck. As he starts back for his rucksack, his eye is caught by something lying on the floor. It is a woman's white glove. He holds it in his hand and suddenly all of his self-control is gone. He breaks down, crying.*

12 *We hear footsteps on the stairs. Miep Gies comes up, looking for* Mr. Frank. Miep *is a Dutch girl of about twenty-two. She wears a coat and hat, ready to go home. She is pregnant. Her attitude toward* Mr. Frank *is protective, compassionate.*

13 **Miep.** Are you all right, Mr. Frank?

14 **Mr. Frank** (*quickly controlling himself*). Yes, Miep, yes.

15 **Miep.** Everyone in the office has gone home . . . It's after six. (*then pleading*) Don't stay up here, Mr. Frank. What's the use of torturing yourself like this?

ANALYZE DRAMA

Annotate: In paragraphs 8–9, mark details that describe the character of Mr. Frank.

Infer: What details do the stage directions provide about Mr. Frank? What does the description suggest about him?

ANALYZE DRAMA

Annotate: Review the stage directions in paragraphs 11–12 and the first lines of dialogue in paragraphs 13–16. Mark the lines that describe how seeing the glove affects Mr. Frank.

Analyze: Why has Mr. Frank returned to the Secret Annex? Why does he have that reaction to the glove?

The Diary of Anne Frank: Act One   413

ANALYZE DRAMA

Remind students that stage directions are italicized and explain what a character does, not what a character says. Dialogue is not italicized and shows the actual words a character says. Students need to understand the distinction in order to complete this annotation. (**Answer:** *He has returned to the secret annex to say goodbye. He is leaving Amsterdam. The glove probably belonged to someone he loved, and the glove reminds him of that person.*)

ANALYZE DRAMA

Remind students that in a drama, the only way playwrights can develop characters is through the characters' actions and dialogue, and through stage directions. They can't tell you what a character thinks, so readers have to draw inferences about the characters' personalities. (**Answer:** *The directions tell Mr. Frank's age and manner; they explain how he looks, sounds, feels, and moves. They suggest that he has been through a very difficult time.*)

TEACH

CONTRASTS AND CONTRADICTIONS

Remind students that a **Contrast-and-Contradiction** signpost is when a character's behavior seems completely different from his previous behavior. Mr. Frank's reactions to the glove and the papers seem to be in contrast with one another. (**Answer:** *He puts the glove in his rucksack but he wants Miep to destroy the papers. The glove represents a part of his former life that is still meaningful to him; he thinks the papers do not.*)

■ English Learner Support

Act Out Contrasts Have volunteers act out paragraphs 10–28 to make Mr. Frank's contradictory behaviors clear to English learners. Include the props of a glove and a stack of papers and make sure Mr. Frank's reactions to the two are portrayed as totally opposite.
SUBSTANTIAL/MODERATE

 For **listening support** for students at varying proficiency levels, see the **Text X-Ray** on page 406C.

---

16 **Mr. Frank.** I've come to say goodbye . . . I'm leaving here, Miep.

17 **Miep.** What do you mean? Where are you going? Where?

18 **Mr. Frank.** I don't know yet. I haven't decided.

19 **Miep.** Mr. Frank, you can't leave here! This is your home! Amsterdam is your home. Your business is here, waiting for you . . . You're needed here . . . Now that the war is over, there are things that . . .

20 **Mr. Frank.** I can't stay in Amsterdam, Miep. It has too many memories for me. Everywhere there's something . . . the house we lived in . . . the school . . . that street organ playing out there . . . I'm not the person you used to know, Miep. I'm a bitter old man. (*breaking off*) Forgive me. I shouldn't speak to you like this . . . after all that you did for us . . . the suffering . . .

21 **Miep.** No. No. It wasn't suffering. You can't say we suffered. (*As she speaks, she straightens a chair which is overturned.*)

22 **Mr. Frank.** I know what you went through, you and Mr. Kraler. I'll remember it as long as I live. (*He gives one last look around.*) Come, Miep.

23 (*He starts for the steps, then remembers his rucksack, going back to get it.*)

24 **Miep** (*hurrying up to a cupboard*). Mr. Frank, did you see? There are some of your papers here. (*She brings a bundle of papers to him.*) We found them in a heap of rubbish on the floor after . . . after you left.

25 **Mr. Frank.** Burn them.

26 (*He opens his rucksack to put the glove in it.*)

27 **Miep.** But, Mr. Frank, there are letters, notes . . .

28 **Mr. Frank.** Burn them. All of them.

29 **Miep.** Burn *this?*

30 (*She hands him a paperbound notebook.*)

31 **Mr. Frank** (*quietly*). Anne's diary. (*He opens the diary and begins to read.*) "Monday, the sixth of July, nineteen forty-two." (*to* Miep) Nineteen forty-two. Is it possible, Miep? . . . Only three years ago. (*As he continues his reading, he sits down on the couch.*) "Dear Diary, since you and I are going to be great friends, I will start by telling you about myself. My name is Anne Frank. I am thirteen years old. I was born in Germany the twelfth of June, nineteen twenty-nine. As my family is Jewish, we emigrated to Holland when Hitler came to power."

CONTRASTS AND CONTRADICTIONS

Notice & Note: Mark what Mr. Frank tells Miep to do with the papers she brings to him.

Compare: Recall what Mr. Frank did with the glove he found. How do his actions contrast with his words about the papers? What might explain his behavior?

414 Unit 6

WHEN STUDENTS STRUGGLE . . .

Genre Reformulation If students are struggling to comprehend the drama, help them retell the events of the play as a traditional story. Pause periodically while reading to have students retell the story of what they just read.

 For additional support, go to the **Reading Studio** and assign the following LEVEL **Level Up tutorial: Elements of Drama.**

Close Read

32 (*As Mr. Frank reads on, another voice joins his, as if coming from the air. It is Anne's Voice.*)

33 **Mr. Frank and Anne.** "My father started a business, importing spice and herbs. Things went well for us until nineteen forty. Then the war came, and the Dutch capitulation, followed by the arrival of the Germans. Then things got very bad for the Jews."

34 (*Mr. Frank's Voice dies out. Anne's Voice continues alone. The lights dim slowly to darkness. The curtain falls on the scene.*)

35 **Anne's Voice.** You could not do this and you could not do that. They forced Father out of his business. We had to wear yellow stars.[1] I had to turn in my bike. I couldn't go to a Dutch school any more. I couldn't go to the movies, or ride in an automobile, or even on a streetcar, and a million other things. But somehow we children still managed to have fun. Yesterday Father told me we were going into hiding. Where, he wouldn't say. At five o'clock this morning Mother woke me and told me to hurry and get dressed. I was to be put on as many clothes as I could. It would look too suspicious if we walked along carrying suitcases. It wasn't until we were on our way that I learned where we were going. Our hiding place was to be upstairs in the building where

---

[1] **yellow stars:** the six-pointed Stars of David that the Nazis ordered all Jews to wear for identification.

MEMORY MOMENT

Notice & Note: In paragraphs 31–35, mark time words that indicate this is a Memory Moment.

Infer: What information do these memories provide? Why might the playwrights have chosen to include them?

ANALYZE DRAMA

Annotate: Mark details in paragraphs 32–34 that describe how the speech shifts from Mr. Frank's voice to Anne's voice.

Interpret: Why might the playwrights have written the stage directions in this way? How might this affect the mood?

▶ **MEMORY MOMENT**

Remind students that a **Memory Moment** signpost is when a character suddenly has an important memory. Here Mr. Frank remembers back to 1942, and Anne remembers back to the previous 24 hours when they left their house. Tell students that when they see a Memory Moment, they should always ask themselves why this memory (or memories) is included in the story. (***Answer:*** *The memories provide a brief history of Anne Frank and her family. They explain why the Franks emigrated to Holland and then they describe how life got harsher after the Germans took control of the country. The playwrights probably included this information because they wanted to provide readers with background information to understand the events of the play.*)

✐ **ANALYZE DRAMA**

Remind students that this play's plot is **nonlinear** because it starts at a later time and then contains a **flashback** to an earlier time. This moment where Mr. Frank and Anne read together, then the voice transitions to just Anne's, marks the beginning of the flashback. (***Answer:*** *The playwrights wanted to emphasize that there is a shift in time from the present as Mr. Frank is reading Anne's diary, to the past moment when Anne wrote those words in her diary. The mood changes from one of sadness, when Mr. Frank speaks, to a more hopeful one, as Anne speaks.*)

CLOSE READ SCREENCAST

Modeled Discussions Have students click the Close Read icon in their eBook to access two screencasts in which readers discuss the following key passages:

- The audience hears Anne's voice join Mr. Frank's as he reads from her diary (Act One: paragraph 32).
- Residents of the annex fear their hiding place has been discovered (Act One: paragraph 721).

As a class, view and discuss one of these videos. Then have students pair up to do an independent close read of an additional passage—Mr. Frank's description of the events after he was released from the camp (Act Two: paragraph 465). Students can record their answers on the Close Read Practice PDF.

 Close Read Practice PDF

ANALYZE PLOT DEVELOPMENT

Have students mark the date in Scene 2. Ask them to clarify how this date differs from the date in paragraph 6. Ask a volunteer to remind the class what this plot device is called and whether this is a linear or nonlinear plot. (**Answer:** *Scene 1 took place in 1945 [the present time of the play], and Scene 2 takes place in 1942, so this scene is a flashback. The rooms [in 1942] are "clean and orderly." In Scene 1 [1945], the rooms are described as dusty and the furniture is overturned. The rooms are probably neater and cleaner in 1942 because people have been there to take care of them.*)

ANALYZE PLOT DEVELOPMENT

Emphasize to students what a frightening time the characters in the play are living in. They are Jewish, and the Nazi soldiers are rounding up Jewish people and sending them to concentration camps. Under these conditions, it is natural that Mrs. Van Daan's fear would be heightened. (**Answer:** *She is afraid that the Franks have been arrested by the Nazis; if they have, then the Van Daan's may also be in danger.*)

CRITICAL VOCABULARY

conspicuous: The yellow Star of David, which all Jewish people were forced to wear, is very easy to see on the Van Daan's clothes.

ASK STUDENTS why wearing a conspicuous yellow star would make Jewish people nervous. (*The star makes the Jewish people very easy to be spotted by the Nazis, who might mistreat or arrest them.*)

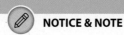

NOTICE & NOTE

Father used to have his business. Three other people were coming in with us . . . the Van Daans and their son Peter . . . Father knew the Van Daans but we had never met them . . .

36 (*During the last lines the curtain rises on the scene. The lights dim on. Anne's Voice fades out.*)

Scene 2

ANALYZE PLOT DEVELOPMENT

Annotate: Mark the new date indicated in Scene 2. Then look back at paragraph 6.

Analyze: What indicates that this is a flashback? How does this flashback affect the mood of what is happening on the stage? What questions does this change raise for the audience?

conspicuous
(kən-spĭk´yōō-əs) *adj.*
Something *conspicuous* is obvious or very easy to see.

ANALYZE PLOT DEVELOPMENT

Annotate: Mark details in paragraphs 42–47 that indicate that Mrs. Van Daan is worried about something.

Draw Conclusions: What is she worried about?

37 *It is early morning, July, 1942. The rooms are bare, as before, but they are now clean and orderly.*

38 Mr. Van Daan, *a tall, portly man in his late forties, is in the main room, pacing up and down, nervously smoking a cigarette. His clothes and overcoat are expensive and well cut.*

39 Mrs. Van Daan *sits on the couch, clutching her possessions, a hatbox, bags, etc. She is a pretty woman in her early forties. She wears a fur coat over her other clothes.*

40 Peter Van Daan *is standing at the window of the room on the right, looking down at the street below. He is a shy, awkward boy of sixteen. He wears a cap, a raincoat, and long Dutch trousers, like "plus fours." At his feet is a black case, a carrier for his cat.*

41 *The yellow Star of David is* **conspicuous** *on all of their clothes.*

42 **Mrs. Van Daan** (*rising, nervous, excited*). Something's happened to them! I know it!

43 **Mr. Van Daan.** Now, Kerli!

44 **Mrs. Van Daan.** Mr. Frank said they'd be here at seven o'clock. He said . . .

45 **Mr. Van Daan.** They have two miles to walk. You can't expect . . .

46 **Mrs. Van Daan.** They've been picked up. That's what's happened. They've been taken . . .

47 (Mr. Van Daan *indicates that he hears someone coming.*)

48 **Mr. Van Daan.** You see?

49 (Peter *takes up his carrier and his schoolbag, etc., and goes into the main room as* Mr. Frank *comes up the stairwell from below.* Mr. Frank *looks much younger now. His movements are brisk, his manner confident. He wears an overcoat and carries his hat and a small cardboard box. He crosses to the Van Daans, shaking hands with each of them.*)

50 **Mr. Frank.** Mrs. Van Daan, Mr. Van Daan, Peter. (*then, in explanation of their lateness*) There were too many of the Green Police[2] on the streets . . . we had to take the long way around.

51 (*Up the steps come Margot Frank, Mrs. Frank, Miep [not pregnant now] and Mr. Kraler. All of them carry bags, packages, and so forth. The Star of David is conspicuous on all of the Franks' clothing. Margot is eighteen, beautiful, quiet, shy. Mrs. Frank is a young mother, gently bred, reserved. She, like Mr. Frank, has a slight German accent. Mr. Kraler is a Dutchman, dependable, kindly.*

52 *As Mr. Kraler and Miep go upstage to put down their parcels, Mrs. Frank turns back to call Anne.*)

53 **Mrs. Frank.** Anne?

54 (*Anne comes running up the stairs. She is thirteen, quick in her movements, interested in everything, mercurial in her emotions. She wears a cape, long wool socks and carries a schoolbag.*)

55 **Mr. Frank** (*introducing them*). My wife, Edith. Mr. and Mrs. Van Daan (*Mrs. Frank hurries over, shaking hands with them.*) . . . their son, Peter . . . my daughters, Margot and Anne.

56 (*Anne gives a polite little curtsy as she shakes Mr. Van Daan's hand. Then she immediately starts off on a tour of investigation of her new home, going upstairs to the attic room. Miep and Mr. Kraler are putting the various things they have brought on the shelves.*)

57 **Mr. Kraler.** I'm sorry there is still so much confusion.

58 **Mr. Frank.** Please. Don't think of it. After all, we'll have plenty of leisure to arrange everything ourselves.

59 **Miep** (*to Mrs. Frank*). We put the stores of food you sent in here. Your drugs are here . . . soap, linen here.

60 **Mrs. Frank.** Thank you, Miep.

61 **Miep.** I made up the beds . . . the way Mr. Frank and Mr. Kraler said. (*She starts out.*) Forgive me. I have to hurry. I've got to go to the other side of town to get some ration books[3] for you.

62 **Mrs. Van Daan.** Ration books? If they see our names on ration books, they'll know we're here.

---

[2] **Green Police:** the Nazi police, who wore green uniforms.

[3] **ration books:** books of stamps or coupons issued by the government in wartime. With these coupons, people could purchase scarce items, such as food, clothing, and gasoline.

LANGUAGE CONVENTIONS

Annotate: The first word in a sentence always begins with a capital letter, as do people's names (such as Margot or Mr. Frank). Mark other words that are capitalized in paragraphs 50–51.

Analyze: What other words are capitalized? Why?

TEACH

LANGUAGE CONVENTIONS

One term students will underline is *Star of David*. Explain to students that the Star of David is an important religious symbol of Judaism, but that the yellow Star of David was also a badge that the Nazis made Jewish people sew onto their clothing so they could be easily identified. (**Answer:** *The words German and Dutchman are capitalized because they are nationalities. "Star of David" is capitalized because it's the name of a religious symbol. "Green Police" is capitalized because it's the name of a particular organization or group.*)

■ English Learner Support

Use Language Support In Vietnamese, there is no equivalent of *there is* or *there are*. Vietnamese-speaking students may struggle to use sentences containing *there is* or *there are*. Give them practice using this language structure. Write the following sentences on the board:

- *There is a flashback to 1942 in the play.*
- *There are soldiers arresting Jewish people.*
- *There is a secret annex above Mr. Frank's old business.*
- *There are people living in the secret annex.*

Read these sentences out loud to students, emphasizing *there is* or *there are*. Then have students chorally repeat the sentences twice as a group and once to a partner.
SUBSTANTIAL

APPLYING ACADEMIC VOCABULARY

❏ **communicate** ❏ **draft**   ❏ **liberation** ☑ **philosophy** ☑ **publish**

Write and Discuss Have students turn to a partner to discuss the following questions. Guide students to include the Academic Vocabulary words *philosophy* and *publish* in their responses. Ask volunteers to share their responses with the class.

- How would you describe Anne's **philosophy** of life?
- Why do you think Mr. Frank decided to **publish** Anne's diary?

ANALYZE DRAMA

Direct students' attention to the footnote on the previous page that explains ration books. When a country is at war, it needs foods like sugar, meat, and coffee to feed soldiers. That means there is less of these items for everybody else. In order to divide supplies up fairly, each person was issued ration books that included coupons that could be exchanged for an item. Once you used up all your ration coupons for one particular item, you could not buy that item again until your next ration book was issued. Shoes, meat, oil, typewriters, and gasoline were among the many items rationed during World War II. (**Answer:** *The stage directions indicate that Mr. Kraler and Miep both say their lines at the same time. The playwrights may have had them speak the lines this way because this is how people talk in real life and also because the characters may both be rushing to explain that there is no problem.*)

For **reading support** for students at varying proficiency levels, see the **Text X-Ray** on page 406D.

 NOTICE & NOTE

ANALYZE DRAMA

Annotate: Mark the stage directions that reveal how Mr. Kraler and Miep respond to Mrs. Van Daan's comment about the ration books.

Interpret: What does that stage direction mean? Why might the playwrights have used it?

---

63 **Mr. Kraler.** There isn't anything . . .

64 **Miep.** Don't worry. Your names won't be on them. (*as she hurries out*) I'll be up later.

 Together

65 **Mr. Frank.** Thank you, Miep.

66 **Mrs. Frank** (*to Mr. Kraler*). It's illegal, then, the ration books? We've never done anything illegal.

67 **Mr. Frank.** We won't be living here exactly according to regulations. (*As Mr. Kraler reassures Mrs. Frank, he takes various small things, such as matches, soap, etc., from his pockets, handing them to her.*)

68 **Mr. Kraler.** This isn't the black market,[4] Mrs. Frank. This is what we call the white market . . . helping all of the hundreds and hundreds who are hiding out in Amsterdam.

69 (*The carillon is heard playing the quarter-hour before eight. Mr. Kraler looks at his watch. Anne stops at the window as she comes down the stairs.*)

70 **Anne.** It's the Westertoren!

71 **Mr. Kraler.** I must go. I must be out of here and downstairs in the office before the workmen get here. (*He starts for the stairs leading out.*) Miep or I, or both of us, will be up each day to bring you food and news and find out what your needs are. Tomorrow I'll get you a better bolt for the door at the foot of the stairs. It needs a bolt that you can throw yourself and open only at our signal. (*to Mr. Frank*) Oh . . . You'll tell them about the noise?

72 **Mr. Frank.** I'll tell them.

73 **Mr. Kraler.** Good-bye then for the moment. I'll come up again, after the workmen leave.

74 **Mr. Frank.** Good-bye, Mr. Kraler.

75 **Mrs. Frank** (*shaking his hand*). How can we thank you? (*The others murmur their good-byes.*)

76 **Mrs. Kraler.** I never thought I'd live to see the day when a man like Mr. Frank would have to go into hiding. When you think— (*He breaks off, going out. Mr. Frank follows him down the steps, bolting the door after him. In the interval before he returns, Peter goes over to Margot, shaking hands with her. As Mr. Frank comes back up the steps, Mrs. Frank questions him anxiously.*)

77 **Mrs. Frank.** What did he mean, about the noise?

---

[4] **black market:** a system for selling goods illegally, in violation of rationing and other restrictions.

TO CHALLENGE STUDENTS . . .

Respond to the Drama   Remind students that meaning in drama is expressed through a combination of sight and sound. To be fully involved and have a personal reaction to the play, the audience must visualize the setting and imagine the characters in action as the moments take place between them. Ask students to discuss these questions to help them discover their personal reaction to the play.

- What is the most memorable scene in the play so far? Why?
- To which of the characters do you feel closer?
- What aspects of life do you think the playwrights are trying to dramatize?
- Do you agree or disagree with the playwrights' point of view about life or human nature?

78 **Mr. Frank.** First let us take off some of these clothes. (*They all start to take off garment after garment. On each of their coats, sweaters, blouses, suits, dresses, is another yellow Star of David. Mr. and Mrs. Frank are underdressed quite simply. The others wear several things, sweaters, extra dresses, bathrobes, aprons, nightgowns, etc.*)

79 **Mr. Van Daan.** It's a wonder we weren't arrested, walking along the streets . . . Petronella with a fur coat in July . . . and that cat of Peter's crying all the way.

80 **Anne** (*as she is removing a pair of panties*). A cat?

81 **Mrs. Frank.** (*shocked*). Anne, please!

82 **Anne.** It's all right. I've got on three more. (*She pulls off two more. Finally, as they have all removed their surplus clothes, they look to Mr. Frank, waiting for him to speak.*)

83 **Mr. Frank.** Now. About the noise. While the men are in the building below, we must have complete quiet. Every sound can be heard down there, not only in the workrooms, but in the offices too. The men come at about eight-thirty, and leave at about five-thirty. So, to be perfectly safe, from eight in the morning until six in the evening we must move only when it is necessary, and then in stockinged feet. We must not speak above a whisper. We must not run any water. We cannot use the sink, or even, forgive me, the w.c.[5] The pipes go down through the workrooms. It would be heard. No trash . . . (*Mr. Frank stops abruptly as he hears the sound of marching feet from the street below. Everyone is motionless, paralyzed with fear. Mr. Frank goes quietly into the room on the right to look down out of the window. Anne runs after him, peering out with him. The tramping feet pass without stopping. The tension is relieved. Mr. Frank, followed by Anne, returns to the main room and resumes his instructions to the group.*) . . . No trash must ever be thrown out which might reveal that someone is living up here . . . not even a potato paring. We must burn everything in the stove at night. This is the way we must live until it is over, if we are to survive.

84 (*There is silence for a second.*)

85 **Mrs. Frank.** Until it is over.

86 **Mr. Frank** (*reassuringly*). After six we can move about . . . we can talk and laugh and have our supper and read and play games . . . just as we would at home. (*He looks at his watch.*) And now I think it would be wise if we all went to our rooms,

---

[5] **w.c.:** water closet; toilet.

Annotate: Mark details in paragraphs 83–84 about how the residents of the Secret Annex must behave in order to survive.

Interpret: What is the main conflict, or problem, in the plot? How do Mr. Frank's words add tension, or suspense, to the plot?

🖉 ANALYZE PLOT DEVELOPMENT

Have volunteers share which one of the rules they think would be the hardest to follow and why. (**Answer:** *The main problem in the plot is that the Franks and the Van Daans must avoid being captured by the Nazis—they must hide in the secret annex and not be found. The fact that they must not make a sound adds a great deal of tension to the plot because it makes clear how dangerous their situation is.*)

■ English Learner Support

Practice Speaking To scaffold student understanding of the play's plot and provide practice speaking in English, write the following sentence frames on the board:

- *The secret annex is a hiding place above Mr. Frank's _____.*

- *_____ and _____, two people who work in the office below the annex, are helping the Franks and Van Daans hide.*

- *During the day, the people in the secret annex are not allowed to _____ or _____ because people working below them might hear them.*

- *They can only _____ and _____ at night.*

After reading through paragraph 86, have students complete the sentence frames and repeat the entire sentences to a partner. **MODERATE**

TEACH

MEMORY MOMENT

Remind students that a **Memory Moment** signpost is when a character suddenly has an important memory. Here Mr. Frank remembers how Mr. Van Daan helped him when he first moved to Amsterdam. Remind students that when they see a Memory Moment signpost, they should annotate it and ask themselves, *Why is this memory important?* (**Answer:** *Mr. Frank's memory establishes the relationship between the two families. It suggests that Mr. Van Daan was generous to Mr. Frank when the Franks were newly arrived in Holland. It also reveals that Mr. Frank is an honorable person who does not forget those who have helped him in the past, and who tries to repay kindnesses.*)

and were settled before eight o'clock. Mrs. Van Daan, you and your husband will be upstairs. I regret that there's no place up there for Peter. But he will be here, near us. This will be our common room, where we'll meet to talk and eat and read, like one family.

87 **Mr. Van Daan.** And where do you and Mrs. Frank sleep?

88 **Mr. Frank.** This room is also our bedroom.

89 **Mrs. Van Daan.** That isn't right. We'll sleep here and you take the room upstairs

90 **Mrs. Van Daan.** It's your place. } *Together*

91 **Mr. Frank.** Please. I've thought this out for weeks. It's the best arrangement. The only arrangement.

92 **Mrs. Van Daan** (*to* Mr. Frank). Never, never can we thank you. (*then to* Mrs. Frank) I don't know what would have happened to us, if it hadn't been for Mr. Frank.

MEMORY MOMENT

Notice & Note: Review paragraphs 92–93. Mark what Mr. Frank recalls when Mrs. Van Daan tries to thank him for taking her family into the Annex.

Analyze: What does this Memory Moment reveal about the characters?

---

93 **Mr. Frank.** You don't know how your husband helped me when I came to this country . . . knowing no one . . . not able to speak the language. I can never repay him for that. (*going to* Van Daan) May I help you with your things?

94 **Mr. Van Daan.** No. No. (*to* Mrs. Van Daan) Come along, *liefje*.[6]

95 **Mrs. Van Daan.** You'll be all right, Peter? You're not afraid?

96 **Peter** (*embarrassed*). Please, Mother.

97 (*They start up the stairs to the attic room above.* Mr. Frank *turns to* Mrs. Frank.)

98 **Mr. Frank.** You too must have some rest, Edith. You didn't close your eyes last night. Nor you, Margot.

99 **Anne.** I slept, Father. Wasn't that funny? I knew it was the last night in my own bed, and yet I slept soundly.

100 **Mr. Frank.** I'm glad, Anne. Now you'll be able to help me straighten things in here. (*to* Mrs. Frank *and* Margot) Come with me . . . You and Margot rest in this room for the time being. (*He picks up their clothes, starting for the room on the right.*)

101 **Mrs. Frank.** You're sure . . . ? I could help . . . And Anne hasn't had her milk . . .

102 **Mr. Frank.** I'll give it to her. (*to* Anne *and* Peter) Anne, Peter . . . it's best that you take off your shoes now, before you forget. (*He leads the way to the room, followed by* Margot.)

103 **Mrs. Frank.** You're sure you're not tired, Anne?

---

[6] **liefje** (lĕf´yə) *Dutch:* little darling.

104 **Anne.** I feel fine. I'm going to help Father.

105 **Mrs. Frank.** Peter, I'm glad you are to be with us.

106 **Peter.** Yes, Mrs. Frank.

107 (Mrs. Frank *goes to join* Mr. Frank *and* Margot.)

108 *During the following scene* Mr. Frank *helps* Margot *and* Mrs. Frank *to hang up their clothes. Then he persuades them both to lie down and rest. The* Van Daans *in their room above settle themselves. In the main room* Anne *and* Peter *remove their shoes.* Peter *takes his cat out of the carrier.*)

109 **Anne.** What's your cat's name?

110 **Peter.** Mouschi.[7]

111 **Anne.** Mouschi! Mouschi! Mouschi! (*She picks up the cat, walking away with it. To* Peter.) I love cats. I have one . . . a darling little cat. But they made me leave her behind. I left some food and a note for the neighbors to take care of her . . . I'm going to miss her terribly. What is yours? A him or a her?

112 **Peter.** He's a tom. He doesn't like strangers.

113 (*He takes the cat from her, putting it back in its carrier.*)

114 **Anne** (*unabashed*). Then I'll have to stop being a stranger, won't I? Is he fixed?

115 **Peter** (*startled*). Huh?

116 **Anne.** Did you have him fixed?

117 **Peter.** No.

118 **Anne.** Oh, you ought to have him fixed—to keep him from— you know, fighting. Where did you go to school?

---
[7] **Mouschi** (mōō´shē)

IMPROVE READING FLUENCY

Targeted Passage Have student partners read the parts of Anne and Peter in paragraphs 109–139. Use paragraph 135 to model how to read dramatic text with appropriate emotions and pausing. Point out that ellipses indicate a longer pause in the dialogue, as though the character were thinking. Remind students to read slowly and clearly to help the listener understand what is being said. Then, have partners work together to read aloud the two characters' lines in the paragraphs. Encourage students to provide feedback and support for any challenging words, and to encourage each other to read with appropriate speed and phrasing.

 Go to the **Reading Studio** for additional support in developing fluency.

ANALYZE PLOT DEVELOPMENT

Discuss with students how Anne and Peter are different. Have students predict what plot developments they think will happen between Anne and Peter. (**Answer:** *Peter means that he is someone who prefers to take action and be on his own. While Anne is very social and enjoys being with others, Peter prefers being alone.*)

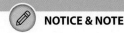 **NOTICE & NOTE**

ANALYZE PLOT DEVELOPMENT

Annotate: In paragraphs 121–125, underline details that describe Anne. Circle details that describe Peter.

Compare: What does Peter mean when he says he is "a lone wolf"? What contrast do the playwrights reveal between the two characters?

119 **Peter.** Jewish Secondary.

120 **Anne.** But that's where Margot and I go! I never saw you around.

121 **Peter.** I used to see you . . . sometimes . . .

122 **Anne.** You did?

123 **Peter.** . . . in the school yard. You were always in the middle of a bunch of kids. (*He takes a penknife from his pocket.*)

124 **Anne.** Why didn't you ever come over?

125 **Peter.** I'm sort of a lone wolf. (*He starts to rip off his Star of David.*)

126 **Anne.** What are you doing?

127 **Peter.** Taking it off.

128 **Anne.** But you can't do that. They'll arrest you if you go out without your star.

129 (*He tosses his knife on the table.*)

130 **Peter.** Who's going out?

131 **Anne.** Why, of course! You're right! Of course we don't need them any more. (*She picks up his knife and starts to take her star off.*) I wonder what our friends will think when we don't show up today?

132 **Peter.** I didn't have any dates with anyone.

133 **Anne.** Oh, I did. I had a date with Jopie to go and play ping-pong at her house. Do you know Jopie de Waal?[8]

134 **Peter.** No.

135 **Anne.** Jopie's my best friend. I wonder what she'll think when she telephones and there's no answer? . . . Probably she'll go over to the house . . . I wonder what she'll think . . . we left everything as if we'd suddenly been called away . . . breakfast dishes in the sink . . . beds not made . . . (*As she pulls off her star, the cloth underneath shows clearly the color and form of the star.*) Look! It's still there! (Peter *goes over to the stove with his star.*) What're you going to do with yours?

136 **Peter.** Burn it.

137 **Anne** (*She starts to throw hers in, and cannot.*) It's funny, I can't throw mine away. I don't know why.

138 **Peter.** You can't throw . . . ? Something they branded you with . . . ? That they made you wear so they could spit on you?

---

[8] **Jopie de Waal** (yō′pē də väl′)

 ENGLISH LEARNER SUPPORT

Spell Homophones Explain to students that some words sound alike but have different spellings and meanings. Help students identify and spell familiar homophones, such as *way/weigh, here/hear, write/right, rode/road,* and *mist/missed.*

Have students work in small groups to draw pictures or write definitions of each word pair. Then have students practice writing the correct word to complete sentence frames such as: The girl found a new _____ to get to school. (*way*) Some chefs _____ ingredients instead of using measuring cups. (*weigh*) **ALL LEVELS**

139 **Anne.** I know. I know. But after all, it is the Star of David, isn't it?

140 (*In the bedroom, right,* Margot *and* Mrs. Frank *are lying down.* Mr. Frank *starts quietly out.*)

141 **Peter.** Maybe it's different for a girl.

142 (Mr. Frank *comes into the main room.*)

143 **Mr. Frank.** Forgive me, Peter. Now let me see. We must find a bed for your cat. (*He goes to a cupboard.*) I'm glad you brought your cat. Anne was feeling so badly about hers. (*getting a used small washtub*) Here we are. Will it be comfortable in that?

144 **Peter** (*gathering up his things*). Thanks.

145 **Mr. Frank** (*opening the door of the room on the left*). And here is your room. But I warn you, Peter, you can't grow any more. Not an inch, or you'll have to sleep with your feet out of the skylight. Are you hungry?

146 **Peter.** No.

147 **Mr. Frank.** We have some bread and butter.

148 **Peter.** No, thank you.

149 **Mr. Frank.** You can have it for luncheon then. And tonight we will have a real supper . . . our first supper together.

150 **Peter.** Thanks. Thanks.

151 (*He goes into his room. During the following scene he arranges his possessions in his new room.*)

152 **Mr. Frank.** That's a nice boy, Peter.

153 **Anne.** He's awfully shy, isn't he?

154 **Mr. Frank.** You'll like him, I know.

155 **Anne.** I certainly hope so, since he's the only boy I'm likely to see for months and months.

156 (Mr. Frank *sits down, taking off his shoes.*)

157 **Mr. Frank.** Annele,[9] there's a box there. Will you open it? (*He indicates a carton on the couch.* Anne *brings it to the center table. In the street below there is the sound of children playing.*)

158 **Anne** (*as she opens the carton*). You know the way I'm going to think of it here? I'm going to think of it as a boarding house. A very peculiar summer boarding house, like the one that we—(*She breaks off as she pulls out some photographs.*) Father! My movie stars! I was wondering where they were! I

---

[9] **Annele/Anneke:** a nickname for Anne.

 ENGLISH LEARNER SUPPORT

Understand Idioms Read the sentence "He's awfully shy, isn't he?" Explain that the word *awful* is an adjective that means "bad," but when the suffix *-ly* is added to make it an adverb, the meaning changes to "very." Point out that the word *awfully* is usually reserved for informal language. Review the difference between adjectives and adverbs as needed to clarify. **MODERATE**

TEACH

ANALYZE PLOT DEVELOPMENT

Discuss with students how having something special from home would make time in a frightening, unfamiliar place easier. Ask students to turn to a partner and say which small item they would most like to bring with them if they had to go away for a long period of time. (**Answer:** *He is an understanding father who wants his daughter to thrive in a difficult situation. Mr. Frank may already be aware that Anne is a talented writer, but he also wants his energetic daughter to have something meaningful to do while in hiding.*)

WORDS OF THE WISER

Remind students that a **Words of the Wiser** signpost is when a wiser (and usually older) person gives the main character some important words of wisdom when the main character is struggling with a problem or decision. This wisdom can help drive the plot. When students encounter a **Words of the Wiser** signpost, they should ask, *What is the lesson for the character?* (**Answer:** *Mr. Frank sees that Anne now realizes what it will be like to live in hiding. He understands that it will be a great hardship for his active daughter to occupy a small space and not have many things to do. So he gently teases her to lighten her mood. He thinks of things that she hates doing and he points out that she won't have to do those things while they're in hiding.*)

NOTICE & NOTE

ANALYZE PLOT DEVELOPMENT

Annotate: In paragraphs 158–160, mark the gifts that Mr. Frank gives Anne.

Interpret: What do these gifts reveal about Mr. Frank? How does the diary tie to the events in Scene 1?

WORDS OF THE WISER

Notice & Note: Review paragraphs 168–169. Mark the advantages to living in the Secret Annex that Mr. Frank points out to Anne.

Interpret: How does Mr. Frank probably think Anne is feeling in paragraphs 164–167? How does Mr. Frank use what he knows about his daughter to comfort her?

---

was looking for them this morning . . . and Queen Wilhelmina! How wonderful!

159 **Mr. Frank.** There's something more. Go on. Look further. (*He goes over to the sink, pouring a glass of milk from a thermos bottle.*)

160 **Anne** (*pulling out a pasteboard-bound book*). A diary! (*She throws her arms around her father.*) I've never had a diary. And I've always longed for one. (*She looks around the room.*) Pencil, pencil, pencil, pencil. (*She starts down the stairs.*) I'm going down to the office to get a pencil.

161 **Mr. Frank.** Anne! No! (*He goes after her, catching her by the arm and pulling her back.*)

162 **Anne** (*startled*). But there's no one in the building now.

163 **Mr. Frank.** It doesn't matter. I don't want you ever to go beyond that door.

164 **Anne** (*sobered*). Never . . . ? Not even at nighttime, when everyone is gone? Or on Sundays? Can't I go down to listen to the radio?

165 **Mr. Frank.** Never. I am sorry, Anneke. It isn't safe. No, you must never go beyond that door.

166 (*For the first time* Anne *realizes what "going into hiding" means.*)

167 **Anne.** I see.

168 **Mr. Frank.** It'll be hard, I know. But always remember this, Anneke. There are no walls, there are no bolts, no locks that anyone can put on your mind. Miep will bring us books. We will read history, poetry, mythology. (*He gives her the glass of milk.*) Here's your milk. (*With his arm about her, they go over to the couch, sitting down side by side.*) As a matter of fact, between us, Anne, being here has certain advantages for you. For instance, you remember the battle you had with your mother the other day on the subject of overshoes? You said you'd rather die than wear overshoes. But in the end you had to wear them? Well now, you see, for as long as we are here you will never have to wear overshoes! Isn't that good? And the coat that you inherited from Margot, you won't have to wear that any more. And the piano! You won't have to practice on the piano. I tell you, this is going to be a fine life for you!

169 (Anne's *panic is gone.* Peter *appears in the doorway of his room, with a saucer in his hand. He is carrying his cat.*)

170 **Peter.** I . . . I . . . I thought I'd better get some water for Mouschi before . . .

171 **Mr. Frank.** Of course.

172 (*As he starts toward the sink the carillon begins to chime the hour of eight. He tiptoes to the window at the back and looks down at the street below. He turns to Peter, indicating in pantomime that it is too late. Peter starts back for his room. He steps on a creaking board. The three of them are frozen for a minute in fear. As Peter starts away again, Anne tiptoes over to him and pours some of the milk from her glass into the saucer for the cat. Peter squats on the floor, putting the milk before the cat. Mr. Frank gives Anne his fountain pen, and then goes into the room at the right. For a second Anne watches the cat, then she goes over to the center table, and opens her diary.*

173 *In the room at the right, Mrs. Frank has sat up quickly at the sound of the carillon. Mr. Frank comes in and sits down beside her on the settee, his arm comfortingly around her.*

174 *Upstairs, in the attic room, Mr. and Mrs. Van Daan have hung their clothes in the closet and are now seated on the iron bed. Mrs. Van Daan leans back exhausted. Mr. Van Daan fans her with a newspaper.*

175 *Anne starts to write in her diary. The lights dim out, the curtain falls.*

176 *In the darkness Anne's Voice comes to us again, faintly at first, and then with growing strength.*)

177 **Anne's Voice.** I expect I should be describing what it feels like to go into hiding. But I really don't know yet myself. I only know it's funny never to be able to go outdoors . . . never to breathe fresh air . . . never to run and shout and jump. It's the silence in the nights that frightens me most. Every time I hear a creak in the house, or a step on the street outside, I'm sure they're coming for us. The days aren't so bad. At least we know that Miep and Mr. Kraler are down there below us in the office. Our protectors, we call them. I asked Father what would happen to them if the Nazis found out they were hiding us. Pim said that they would suffer the same fate that we would . . . Imagine! They know this, and yet when they come up here, they're always cheerful and gay as if there were nothing in the world to bother them . . . Friday, the twenty-first of August, nineteen forty-two. Today I'm going to tell you our general news. Mother is unbearable. She insists on treating me like a baby, which I **loathe.** Otherwise things are going better. The weather is . . .

178 (*As Anne's Voice is fading out, the curtain rises on the scene.*)

loathe
(lōth) *v.* To *loathe* something is to dislike it very much.

 ENGLISH LEARNER SUPPORT

Formative Oral Assessment To check student comprehension of the play so far, ask the following questions:

• What two gifts does Anne's dad give her?

• What does Anne's father say to cheer her up when she is sad that she can't leave the secret annex?

• Why is Anne frightened at night? **MODERATE**

For **speaking support** for students at varying proficiency levels, see the **Text X-Ray** on page 406D.

CRITICAL VOCABULARY

loathe: Anne thinks her mother treats her like a baby, and she dislikes that very much.

ASK STUDENTS to name some reasons Anne loathes being treated like a baby. (*She thinks she is mature and doesn't need to be treated like a baby. She is the youngest person in the annex and she wants to seem older and more mature to the others, especially to her older sister and Peter.*)

ENGLISH LEARNER SUPPORT

Read Closely Tell students that one way playwrights create realistic characters is by having them change. Have students work in pairs to reread paragraphs 178–197. Ask them to write two or three sentences explaining which characters seem different and why. Have them highlight details in their eBooks or use sticky notes to label lines that support their views. Then discuss these questions as a class, inviting students to share their evidence as support:

- How has Mr. Frank's role changed since the group went in hiding?
- How have two months in hiding affected Anne?
- What is the relationship between Anne and Peter? Is it the same or different from the way it was at the beginning? **MODERATE/LIGHT**

ANALYZE PLOT DEVELOPMENT

Remind students that a plot is more than a series of events. An author crafts the events so the tension in the story builds. Point out that tensions had been building between characters in Scene 2. Ask students to think about how those tensions probably continued to build in the the time between scenes and what else might have happened to the people living in the annex. (**Possible answer:** *The people are probably even more annoyed with each other because they have been living in small space. They may have started to fight over food or who is in charge. The conflicts over food or how people act could create subplots in addition to the main story about the family hiding from the Nazis.*)

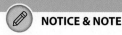 NOTICE & NOTE

Scene 3

ANALYZE PLOT DEVELOPMENT

Annotate: Mark the stage direction that tells you how much time has passed since the end of Scene 2.

Predict: During that time, what kinds of tensions do you think have grown among the residents of the Secret Annex, and why? How might those tensions create subplots in this drama?

179   *It is a little after six o'clock in the evening, two months later.*

180   Margot *is in the bedroom at the right, studying.* Mr. Van Daan *is lying down in the attic room above.*

181   *The rest of the "family" is in the main room.* Anne *and* Peter *sit opposite each other at the center table, where they have been doing their lessons.* Mrs. Frank *is on the couch.* Mrs. Van Daan *is seated with her fur coat, on which she has been sewing, in her lap. None of them are wearing their shoes.*

182   *Their eyes are on* Mr. Frank, *waiting for him to give them the signal which will release them from their day-long quiet.* Mr. Frank, *his shoes in his hand, stands looking down out of the window at the back, watching to be sure that all of the workmen have left the building below.*

183   *After a few seconds of motionless silence,* Mr. Frank *turns from the window.*

184 **Mr. Frank** (*quietly, to the group*). It's safe now. The last workman has left. (*There is an immediate stir of relief.*)

185 **Anne** (*Her pent-up energy explodes*). WHEE!

186 **Mrs. Frank** (*startled, amused*). Anne!

187 **Mrs. Van Daan.** I'm first for the w.c. (*She hurries off to the bathroom.* Mrs. Frank *puts on her shoes and starts up to the sink to prepare supper.* Anne *sneaks* Peter's *shoes from under the table and hides them behind her back.* Mr. Frank *goes in to* Margot's *room.*)

188 **Mr. Frank** (*to* Margot). Six o'clock. School's over.

189 (Margot *gets up, stretching.* Mr. Frank *sits down to put on his shoes. In the main room* Peter *tries to find his.*)

190 **Peter** (*to* Anne). Have you seen my shoes?

191 **Anne** (*innocently*). Your shoes?

192 **Peter.** You've taken them, haven't you?

193 **Anne.** I don't know what you're talking about.

194 **Peter.** You're going to be sorry!

195 **Anne.** Am I? (Peter *goes after her.* Anne, *with his shoes in her hand, runs from him, dodging behind her mother.*)

196 **Mrs. Frank** (*protesting*). Anne, dear!

197 **Peter.** Wait till I get you!

APPLYING ACADEMIC VOCABULARY

☑ **communicate**   ☐ **draft**   ☑ **liberation**   ☐ **philosophy**   ☐ **publish**

Write and Discuss Have students turn to a partner to discuss the following questions. Guide students to include the Academic Vocabulary words *communicate* and *liberation* in their responses. Ask volunteers to share their responses with the class.

- How do the residents of the annex feel about their **liberation** each evening after the workers in the rooms below go home?
- How does the arrival of evening change the way the "family" members are able to **communicate** with each other?

198 **Anne.** I'm waiting! (Peter *makes a lunge for her. They both fall to the floor.* Peter *pins her down, wrestling with her to get the shoes.*) Don't! Don't! Peter, stop it. Ouch!

199 **Mrs. Frank.** Anne! . . . Peter! (*Suddenly* Peter *becomes self-conscious. He grabs his shoes roughly and starts for his room.*)

200 **Anne** (*following him*). Peter, where are you going? Come dance with me.

201 **Peter.** I tell you I don't know how.

202 **Anne.** I'll teach you.

203 **Peter.** I'm going to give Mouschi his dinner.

204 **Anne.** Can I watch?

205 **Peter.** He doesn't like people around while he eats.

206 **Anne.** Peter, please.

207 **Peter.** No! (*He goes into his room.* Anne *slams his door after him.*)

208 **Mrs. Frank.** Anne, dear, I think you shouldn't play like that with Peter. It's not dignified.

209 **Anne.** Who cares if it's dignified? I don't want to be dignified.

210 (Mr. Frank *and* Margot *come from the room on the right.* Margot *goes to help her mother.* Mr. Frank *starts for the center table to correct* Margot's *school papers.*)

211 **Mrs. Frank** (*to* Anne). You complain that I don't treat you like a grownup. But when I do, you resent it.

212 **Anne.** I only want some fun . . . someone to laugh and clown with . . . After you've sat still all day and hardly moved, you've got to have some fun. I don't know what's the matter with that boy.

213 **Mr. Frank.** He isn't used to girls. Give him a little time.

214 **Anne.** Time? Isn't two months time? I could cry. (*catching hold of* Margot) Come on, Margot . . . dance with me. Come on, please.

215 **Margot.** I have to help with supper.

216 **Anne.** You know we're going to forget how to dance . . . When we get out we won't remember a thing.

217 (*She starts to sing and dance by herself.* Mr. Frank *takes her in his arms, waltzing with her.* Mrs. Van Daan *comes in from the bathroom.*)

218 **Mrs. Van Daan.** Next? (*She looks around as she starts putting on her shoes.*) Where's Peter?

CONTRASTS AND CONTRADICTIONS

Notice & Note: In paragraphs 208–212, underline how Anne feels when her mother doesn't treat her like a grownup. Circle how she feels when her mother *does* treat her like a grownup.

Infer: What does this contradiction reveal about Anne? What does it reveal about her relationship with her mother?

CONTRASTS AND CONTRADICTIONS

Explain to students that this signpost is often used to set up a **compare-and-contrast** pattern of organization. Remind students that many words have both a dictionary definition and a connotation, or feelings associated with them.

Point out the word *dignified* in paragraph 208 and note the **contrast,** or disparity, between how Mrs. Frank and Anne use the word. Have students use context clues to explain what Mrs. Frank means by the use of this word. (*Mrs. Frank uses the word as it is defined in the dictionary, which means "being worthy of respect," such as behaving in a mature, ladylike way.*) Explain what Anne's comments in paragraph 209 show about the way she interprets the word *dignified*. (*Anne thinks being dignified is the same as "boring."*)

(**Answer:** *The contradiction in Anne's behavior suggests that Anne is transitioning from being a child to being an adult. She is no longer fully one or the other. This stage in her life shows clashes between her and her mother. She also has a strong will, so when her mother gives her advice, she doesn't want to take it. She talks back and that hurts her mother.*)

 ENGLISH LEARNER SUPPORT

Write Summaries Remind students that a summary tells only the most important events that happen.

- Have pairs take turns reading Scene 3 aloud, pausing every two pages to discuss what has happened. They should take notes about the most important events. When they finish the scene, help them as needed to write a summary using complete sentences. **MODERATE**

- As pairs read Scene 3 aloud, have them pause every three or four pages to write a sentence summarizing what has happened. When they finish, have them combine their sentences and edit them to form a concise summary. **MODERATE/LIGHT**

- Have students write a summary of Scene 3 after reading it aloud. Encourage them to use key words from the text to express ideas clearly. Then have partners exchange summaries and give each other feedback to make the writing more concise. **LIGHT**

ENGLISH LEARNER SUPPORT

Analyze Language To help students understand exaggeration, display this statement: *My book bag weighs a million pounds.* Read it aloud and guide students to understand that the weight is exaggerated, or described as greater than it actually is. Have pairs state the same idea without exaggeration. (*My book bag is very heavy.*) Then display paragraph 220. Work with students to identify the exaggeration in the statement and the reason Mrs. Van Daan states it.

MODERATE/LIGHT

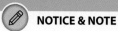

219 **Anne** (*as they are dancing*). Where would he be!

220 **Mrs. Van Daan.** He hasn't finished his lessons, has he? His father'll kill him if he catches him in there with that cat and his work not done.

221 (*Mr. Frank and Anne finish their dance. They bow to each other with extravagant formality.*) Anne, get him out of there, will you?

222 **Anne** (*at Peter's door*). Peter? Peter?

223 **Peter** (*opening the door a crack*). What is it?

224 **Anne.** Your mother says to come out.

225 **Peter.** I'm giving Mouschi his dinner.

226 **Mrs. Van Daan.** You know what your father says. (*She sits on the couch, sewing on the lining of her fur coat.*)

227 **Peter.** For heaven's sake, I haven't even looked at him since lunch.

228 **Mrs. Van Daan.** I'm just telling you, that's all.

229 **Anne.** I'll feed him.

230 **Peter.** I don't want you in there.

231 **Mrs. Van Daan.** Peter!

232 **Peter** (*to* Anne). Then give him his dinner and come right out, you hear? (*He comes back to the table.* Anne *shuts the door of* Peter's *room after her and disappears behind the curtain covering his closet.*)

233 **Mrs. Van Daan** (*to* Peter). Now is that any way to talk to your little girl friend?

234 **Peter.** Mother . . . for heaven's sake . . . will you please stop saying that?

235 **Mrs. Van Daan.** Look at him blush! Look at him!

236 **Peter.** Please! I'm not . . . anyway . . . let me alone, will you?

237 **Mrs. Van Daan.** He acts like it was something to be ashamed of. It's nothing to be ashamed of, to have a little girl friend.

238 **Peter.** You're crazy. She's only thirteen.

239 **Mrs. Van Daan.** So what? And you're sixteen. Just perfect. Your father's ten years older than I am. (*to* Mr. Frank) I warn you, Mr. Frank, if this war lasts much longer, we're going to be related and then . . .

240 **Mr. Frank.** *Mazeltov!*[10]

---

[10] *Mazeltov!* (mä´zəl-tôf´) *Hebrew:* Congratulations!

241 **Mrs. Frank** (*deliberately changing the conversation*). I wonder where Miep is. She's usually so prompt. (*Suddenly everything else is forgotten as they hear the sound of an automobile coming to a screeching stop in the street below. They are tense, motionless in their terror. The car starts away. A wave of relief sweeps over them. They pick up their occupations again.* Anne *flings open the door of* Peter's *room, making a dramatic entrance.* <u>She is dressed in Peter's clothes.</u> Peter *looks at her in fury. The others are amused.*)

242 **Anne.** Good evening, everyone. Forgive me if I don't stay. (*She jumps up on a chair.*) I have a friend waiting for me in there. My friend Tom. Tom Cat. <u>Some people say that we look alike. But Tom has the most beautiful whiskers, and I have only a little fuzz.</u> I am hoping . . . in time . . .

243 **Peter.** All right, Mrs. Quack Quack!

244 **Anne** (*outraged—jumping down*). Peter!

245 **Peter.** I heard about you . . . How you talked so much in class they called you Mrs. Quack Quack. How Mr. Smitter made you write a composition . . . "'Quack, quack,' said Mrs. Quack Quack."

246 **Anne.** Well, go on. Tell them the rest. How it was so good he read it out loud to the class and then read it to all his other classes!

247 **Peter.** Quack! Quack! Quack . . . Quack . . . Quack . . .

248 (Anne *pulls off the coat and trousers.*)

249 **Anne.** You are the most intolerable, insufferable boy I've ever met!

250 (*She throws the clothes down the stairwell.* Peter *goes down after them.*)

251 **Peter.** Quack, quack, quack!

252 **Mrs. Van Daan** (*to* Anne). That's right, Anneke! Give it to him!

253 **Anne.** With all the boys in the world . . . Why I had to get locked up with one like you! . . .

254 **Peter.** Quack, quack, quack, and from now on stay out of my room!

255 (*As* Peter *passes her,* Anne *puts out her foot, tripping him. He picks himself up, and goes on into his room.*)

256 **Mrs. Frank** (*quietly*). Anne, dear . . . your hair. (*She feels* Anne's *forehead.*) You're warm. Are you feeling all right?

ANALYZE PLOT DEVELOPMENT

Annotate: In paragraphs 241–249, underline details that show how Anne teases Peter. Circle what Peter says about Anne.

Draw Conclusions: What do Anne and Peter tease each other about? What conclusions can you draw about Anne and Peter based on their actions, their speech, and the descriptions provided by the playwrights?

 ANALYZE PLOT DEVELOPMENT

Remind students that playwrights develop characters through **dialogue** and the characters' actions. Students can determine what characters are like by what they see as well as by direct comments playwrights add in the **stage directions.**

Paragraphs 241–249 reveal the contrasts between Anne and Peter. The friction between them—after living in close proximity for months—stems from their different personalities. Anne is enthusiastic, clever, and talkative by nature, while Peter is a shy and private person. (**Answer:** *Anne wears Peter's clothes and pretends to be him; she teases Peter about the moustache that's starting to grow, saying that his cat has more whiskers than Peter does. Peter teases Anne about being called "Mrs. Quack Quack Quack" by one of the teachers at school because Anne is always chattering. These clues suggest that Anne is high-spirited and enjoys teasing people for the sake of humor. Peter is more withdrawn and quick to take offense. Neither likes to be teased and both lack sensitivity to the other's feelings.*)

Conduct Word Study Display the words *intolerable* and *insufferable* from paragraph 249. Explain that they are synonyms meaning "impossible to bear or tolerate." Highlight the word parts *in-* and *–able* in both. Elicit from students that *in-* is a prefix that means "not." Then tell students that *-able* means "capable of" or "having a certain quality."

- Display these words and define them: *excuse, describe, support, escape.*

- Have small groups add the prefix *in-* and the suffix *-able* to each word. Remind students to drop the silent *e* for some words. As a class, define the terms.

- Then have groups write a sentence about an element of the play using each word. Have groups share their sentences with the class.
  MODERATE

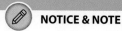

ENGLISH LEARNER SUPPORT

Read Closely Read aloud paragraph 267. Discuss with students what Mr. Frank means by his remarks. *(Anne is just sick of being cooped up inside; she misses her friends and her old life.)* Then remind students that dialogue often provides insight into the characters who speak it. Ask students to discuss in small groups what Mr. Frank's comments reveal about his relationship with Anne and what his role in the group seems to be. *(He looks out for Anne and understands that she is still just a young girl; he seems to realize that this situation is harder for her in some ways than for the others. As the group's leader and Anne's father, he is the one who keeps calm and tries to solve problems.)* **MODERATE/LIGHT**

257 **Anne.** Please, Mother. (*She goes over to the center table, slipping into her shoes.*)

258 **Mrs. Frank** (*following her*). You haven't a fever, have you?

259 **Anne** (*pulling away*). No. No.

260 **Mrs. Frank.** You know we can't call a doctor here, ever. There's only one thing to do . . . watch carefully. Prevent an illness before it comes. Let me see your tongue.

261 **Anne.** Mother, this is perfectly absurd.

262 **Mrs. Frank.** Anne, dear, don't be such a baby. Let me see your tongue. (*As Anne refuses, Mrs. Frank appeals to Mr. Frank.*) Otto . . . ?

263 **Mr. Frank.** You hear your mother, Anne. (*Anne flicks out her tongue for a second, then turns away.*)

264 **Mrs. Frank.** Come on—open up! (*as Anne opens her mouth very wide*) You seem all right . . . but perhaps an aspirin . . .

265 **Mrs. Van Daan.** For heaven's sake, don't give that child any pills. I waited for fifteen minutes this morning for her to come out of the w.c.

266 **Anne.** I was washing my hair!

267 **Mr. Frank.** I think there's nothing the matter with our Anne that a ride on her bike, or a visit with her friend Jopie de Waal wouldn't cure. Isn't that so, Anne?

268 (*Mr. Van Daan comes down into the room. From outside we hear faint sounds of bombers going over and a burst of ack-ack.*)

269 **Mr. Van Daan.** Miep not come yet?

270 **Mrs. Van Daan.** The workmen just left, a little while ago.

271 **Mr. Van Daan.** What's for dinner tonight?

272 **Mrs. Van Daan.** Beans.

273 **Mr. Van Daan.** Not again!

274 **Mrs. Van Daan.** Poor Putti! I know. But what can we do? That's all that Miep brought us.

275 (*Mr. Van Daan starts to pace, his hands behind his back. Anne follows behind him, imitating him.*)

276 **Anne.** We are now in what is known as the "bean cycle." Beans boiled, beans en casserole, beans with strings, beans without strings . . .

277 (*Peter has come out of his room. He slides into his place at the table, becoming immediately absorbed in his studies.*)

278 **Mr. Van Daan** (*to* Peter). I saw you . . . in there, playing with your cat.

279 **Mrs. Van Daan.** He just went in for a second, putting his coat away. He's been out here all the time, doing his lessons.

280 **Mr. Frank** (*looking up from the papers*). Anne, you got an excellent in your history paper today . . . and very good in Latin.

281 **Anne** (*sitting beside him*). How about algebra?

282 **Mr. Frank.** I'll have to make a confession. Up until now I've managed to stay ahead of you in algebra. Today you caught up with me. We'll leave it to Margot to correct.

283 **Anne.** Isn't algebra *vile*, Pim!

284 **Mr. Frank.** Vile!

285 **Margot** (*to* Mr. Frank). How did I do?

286 **Anne** (*getting up*). Excellent, excellent, excellent, excellent!

287 **Mr. Frank** (*to* Margot). You should have used the subjunctive here . . .

288 **Margot.** Should I? . . . I thought . . . look here . . . I didn't use it here . . . (*The two become absorbed in the papers.*)

289 **Anne.** Mrs. Van Daan, may I try on your coat?

290 **Mrs. Frank.** No, Anne.

291 **Mrs. Van Daan** (*giving it to* Anne). It's all right . . . but careful with it. (Anne *puts it on and struts with it.*) My father gave me that the year before he died. He always bought the best that money could buy.

292 **Anne.** Mrs. Van Daan, did you have a lot of boy friends before you were married?

293 **Mrs. Frank.** Anne, that's a personal question. It's not courteous to ask personal questions.

294 **Mrs. Van Daan.** Oh I don't mind. (*to* Anne) Our house was always swarming with boys. When I was a girl we had . . .

295 **Mr. Van Daan.** Oh, God. Not again!

296 **Mrs. Van Daan** (*good-humored*). Shut up! (*Without a pause,* to Anne. Mr. Van Daan *mimics* Mrs. Van Daan, *speaking the first few words in unison with her.*) One summer we had a big house in Hilversum. The boys came buzzing round like bees around a jam pot. And when I was sixteen! . . . We were wearing our skirts very short those days and I had good-looking legs. (*She pulls up her skirt, going to* Mr. Frank.) I still have 'em. I may not be as pretty as I used to be, but I still have my legs. How about it, Mr. Frank?

> **MEMORY MOMENT**
>
> **Notice & Note:** In paragraphs 294–296, mark the words that signal that Mrs. Van Daan is about to share a memory with Anne.
>
> **Interpret:** How does Mr. Van Daan react when his wife begins to share her memory? Why does he react that way?

MEMORY MOMENT

Explain that some **Memory Moments** are obvious. In this case, a grown woman begins to tell a story, "When I was a girl . . ." that her husband has clearly heard many times. This memory reveals important information about the **characters** of Mrs. and Mr. Van Daan. (**Answer:** *He says, "Oh, God. Not again!" He probably says that because his wife has told the same story many times before. He is tired of hearing it.*)

ENGLISH LEARNER SUPPORT

Analyze Language Remind students that playwrights might use figurative language to describe something vividly. Figurative expressions have a meaning other than what the words say and often compare two different things.

• Display paragraph 294 and highlight the word *swarming*. Tell students that it usually refers to the movement of bees or other insects. Discuss what the use of this word is saying about Mrs. Van Daan. (*She was surrounded by many admirers.*)

• Display paragraph 296 and highlight the sentence "The boys came buzzing round like bees around a jam pot." Have pairs explain the comparison implied by this simile. (*Mrs. Van Daan is the "jam pot" that attracts many bees, or admirers.*) Ask students why they think Mrs. Van Daan is sharing this memory with the others. (*She is remembering happier times and how popular she was.*) **LIGHT**

AGAIN AND AGAIN

Explain to students that the **Again and Again** signpost is often used to draw attention to a recurring theme in a piece of literature. In this case, the playwrights are echoing the **theme** about how women are expected to behave in that time. Ask students to identify where else they have heard this theme come up. (*In paragraph 208, Anne's mother tells her that she's not acting dignified.*)

(**Answer:** *The playwrights might have had Anne repeat the words for comic effect, or they may have wanted to show that Anne is trying to remember those words for use later—or possibly to suggest that she wants to write them down in her diary, as Mr. Van Daan implies.*)

NOTICE & NOTE

AGAIN AND AGAIN

Notice & Note: In paragraphs 300–302, mark the words that Mrs. Van Daan's father told her to tell boys who got "fresh." Then mark the same words where Anne repeats them.

Interpret: Why might the playwrights have made Anne repeat those lines?

297 **Mr. Van Daan.** All right. All right. We see them.

298 **Mrs. Van Daan.** I'm not asking you. I'm asking Mr. Frank.

299 **Peter.** Mother, for heaven's sake.

300 **Mrs. Van Daan.** Oh, I embarrass you, do I? Well, I just hope the girl you marry has as good. (*then to* Anne) My father used to worry about me, with so many boys hanging round. He told me, if any of them gets fresh, you say to him . . . "Remember, Mr. So-and-So, remember I'm a lady."

301 **Anne.** "Remember, Mr. So-and-So, remember I'm a lady." (*She gives* Mrs. Van Daan *her coat.*)

302 **Mr. Van Daan.** Look at you, talking that way in front of her! Don't you know she puts it all down in that diary?

303 **Mrs. Van Daan.** So, if she does? I'm only telling the truth!

304 (Anne *stretches out, putting her ear to the floor, listening to what is going on below. The sound of the bombers fades away.*)

305 **Mrs. Frank** (*setting the table*). Would you mind, Peter, if I moved you over to the couch?

306 **Anne** (*listening*). Miep must have the radio on.

307 (Peter *picks up his papers, going over to the couch beside* Mrs. Van Daan.)

308 **Mr. Van Daan** (*accusingly, to* Peter). Haven't you finished yet?

309 **Peter.** No.

310 **Mr. Van Daan.** You ought to be ashamed of yourself.

311 **Peter.** All right. All right. I'm a dunce. I'm a hopeless case. Why do I go on?

312 **Mrs. Van Daan.** You're not hopeless. Don't talk that way. It's just that you haven't anyone to help you, like the girls have. (*to* Mr. Frank) Maybe you could help him, Mr. Frank?

313 **Mr. Frank.** I'm sure that his father . . . ?

314 **Mr. Van Daan.** Not me. I can't do anything with him. He won't listen to me. You go ahead . . . if you want.

315 **Mr. Frank** (*going to* Peter). What about it, Peter? Shall we make our school coeducational?

316 **Mrs. Van Daan** (*kissing* Mr. Frank). You're an angel, Mr. Frank. An angel. I don't know why I didn't meet you before I met that one there.

317 Here, sit down, Mr. Frank . . . (*She forces him down on the couch beside* Peter.) Now, Peter, you listen to Mr. Frank.

318 **Mr. Frank.** It might be better for us to go into Peter's room. (Peter *jumps up eagerly, leading the way.*)

319 **Mrs. Van Daan.** That's right. You go in there, Peter. You listen to Mr. Frank. Mr. Frank is a highly educated man. (*As Mr. Frank is about to follow* Peter *into his room,* Mrs. Frank *stops him and wipes the lipstick from his lips. Then she closes the door after them.*)

320 **Anne** (*on the floor, listening*). Shh! I can hear a man's voice talking.

321 **Mr. Van Daan** (*to* Anne). Isn't it bad enough here without your sprawling all over the place? (Anne *sits up.*)

322 **Mrs. Van Daan** (*to* Mr. Van Daan). If you didn't smoke so much, you wouldn't be so bad-tempered.

323 **Mr. Van Daan.** Am I smoking? Do you see me smoking?

324 **Mrs. Van Daan.** Don't tell me you've used up all those cigarettes.

325 **Mr. Van Daan.** One package. Miep only brought me one package.

326 **Mrs. Van Daan.** It's a filthy habit anyway. It's a good time to break yourself.

327 **Mr. Van Daan.** Oh, stop it, please.

328 **Mrs. Van Daan.** You're smoking up all our money. You know that, don't you?

329 **Mr. Van Daan.** Will you shut up? (*During this,* Mrs. Frank *and* Margot *have studiously kept their eyes down. But* Anne, *seated on the floor, has been following the discussion interestedly.* Mr. Van Daan *turns to see her staring up at him.*) And what are you staring at?

330 **Anne.** I never heard grownups quarrel before. I thought only children quarreled.

331 **Mr. Van Daan.** This isn't a quarrel! It's a discussion. And I never heard children so rude before.

332 **Anne** (*rising, indignantly*). I, rude!

333 **Mr. Van Daan.** Yes!

334 **Mrs. Frank** (*quickly*). Anne, will you get me my knitting? (Anne *goes to get it.*) I must remember, when Miep comes, to ask her to bring me some more wool.

335 **Margot** (*going to her room*). I need some hairpins and some soap. I made a list. (*She goes into her bedroom to get the list.*)

indignantly
(ĭn-dĭg′nənt-lē) *adv.* Someone who does something *indignantly* acts in a way that shows anger or shock over something that is unjust or unfair.

The Diary of Anne Frank: Act One **433**

ENGLISH LEARNER SUPPORT

Read Closely Remind students that the major conflict in a work of fiction often leads to other conflicts that increase the tension and suspense.

- Have students read paragraphs 321–330. Ask them what is happening, based on the dialogue between the three characters. (*Mr. Van Daan is annoyed with Anne on a minor issue. This leads Mrs. Van Daan to argue with him on why he's bad-tempered.*)
- Work with students to make inferences about how living in hiding is affecting Mr. Van Daan. (*He is feeling the strain of the living situation. He is stressed and irritable.*)

MODERATE/LIGHT

CRITICAL VOCABULARY

indignantly: Anne is angrily responding to Mr. Van Daan's mean remark about her being rude.

ASK STUDENTS why Anne responds indignantly to Mr. Van Daan calling her "rude." (**Possible answer:** *He has called her rude, and she does not think she is. She thinks she has the right to make an observation about adults quarreling. She thinks the Van Daans are arguing like children and being rude to one another.*)

ANALYZE PLOT DEVELOPMENT

Remind students that they can learn something about what **characters** in a play are like by examining their **dialogue**, or their conversation. In paragraph 353, Mr. Van Daan reveals his narrow ideas about what women should be like.

(**Answer:** *Mr. Van Daan has traditional values about how girls and women should behave—he thinks they should be quiet and focus their attention on cooking, sewing, and keeping house. Anne is idealistic and independent; she wants to have her own career. She is ambitious and expects to do something "remarkable" and "wonderful" with her life.*)

 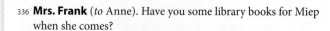

336 **Mrs. Frank** (*to* Anne). Have you some library books for Miep when she comes?

337 **Anne.** It's a wonder that Miep has a life of her own, the way we make her run errands for us. Please, Miep, get me some starch. Please take my hair out and have it cut. Tell me all the latest news, Miep.

338 (*She goes over, kneeling on the couch beside* Mrs. Van Daan.) Did you know she was engaged? His name is Dirk, and Miep's afraid the Nazis will ship him off to Germany to work in one of their war plants. That's what they're doing with some of the young Dutchmen . . . they pick them up off the streets—

339 **Mr. Van Daan** (*interrupting*). Don't you ever get tired of talking? Suppose you try keeping still for five minutes. Just five minutes. (*He starts to pace again. Again* Anne *follows him, mimicking him.* Mrs. Frank *jumps up and takes her by the arm up to the sink, and gives her a glass of milk.*)

340 **Mrs. Frank.** Come here, Anne. It's time for your glass of milk.

341 **Mr. Van Daan.** Talk, talk, talk. I never heard such a child. Where is my . . . ? Every evening it's the same, talk, talk, talk. (*He looks around.*) Where is my . . . ?

342 **Mrs. Van Daan.** What're you looking for?

343 **Mr. Van Daan.** My pipe. Have you seen my pipe?

344 **Mrs. Van Daan.** What good's a pipe? You haven't got any tobacco.

345 **Mr. Van Daan.** At least I'll have something to hold in my mouth! (*opening Margot's bedroom door*) Margot, have you seen my pipe?

346 **Margot.** It was on the table last night.

347 (Anne *puts her glass of milk on the table and picks up his pipe, hiding it behind her back.*)

ANALYZE PLOT DEVELOPMENT

Annotate: In paragraphs 348–358, underline details that show how Mr. Van Daan expects girls and women to behave. Circle what Anne wants for herself.

Compare: How do these differences highlight the conflict in values between Mr. Van Daan and Anne?

348 **Mr. Van Daan.** I know. I know. Anne, did you see my pipe? . . . Anne!

349 **Mrs. Frank.** Anne, Mr. Van Daan is speaking to you.

350 **Anne.** Am I allowed to talk now?

351 **Mr. Van Daan.** You're the most aggravating . . . The trouble with you is, you've been spoiled. What you need is a good old-fashioned spanking.

352 **Anne** (*mimicking* Mrs. Van Daan). "Remember, Mr. So-and-So, remember I'm a lady." (*She thrusts the pipe into his mouth, then picks up her glass of milk.*)

353 **Mr. Van Daan** (*restraining himself with difficulty*). Why aren't you nice and quiet like your sister Margot? Why do you have to show off all the time? Let me give you a little advice, young lady. Men don't like that kind of thing in a girl. You know that? A man likes a girl who'll listen to him once in a while . . . a domestic girl, who'll keep her house shining for her husband . . . who loves to cook and sew and . . .

354 **Anne.** I'd cut my throat first! I'd open my veins! I'm going to be remarkable! I'm going to Paris . . .

355 **Mr. Van Daan** (*scoffingly*). Paris!

356 **Anne.** . . to study music and art.

357 **Mr. Van Daan.** Yeah! Yeah!

358 **Anne.** I'm going to be a famous dancer or singer . . . or something wonderful. (*She makes a wide gesture, spilling the glass of milk on the fur coat in* Mrs. Van Daan's *lap.* Margot *rushes quickly over with a towel.* Anne *tries to brush the milk off with her skirt.*)

359 **Mrs. Van Daan.** Now look what you've done . . . you clumsy little fool! My beautiful fur coat my father gave me . . .

360 **Anne.** I'm so sorry.

361 **Mrs. Van Daan.** What do you care? It isn't yours . . . So go on, ruin it! Do you know what that coat cost? Do you? And now look at it! Look at it!

362 **Anne.** I'm very, very sorry.

363 **Mrs. Van Daan.** I could kill you for this. I could just kill you! (Mrs. Van Daan *goes up the stairs, clutching the coat.* Mr. Van Daan *starts after her.*)

364 **Mr. Van Daan.** Petronella . . . *liefje! Liefje!* . . . Come back . . . the supper . . . come back!

365 **Mrs. Frank.** Anne, you must not behave in that way.

366 **Anne.** It was an accident. Anyone can have an accident.

367 **Mrs. Frank.** I don't mean that. I mean the answering back. You must not answer back. They are our guests. We must always show the greatest courtesy to them. We're all living under terrible tension. (*She stops as* Margot *indicates that* Van Daan *can hear. When he is gone, she continues.*) That's why we must control ourselves . . . You don't hear Margot getting into arguments with them, do you? Watch Margot. She's always courteous with them. Never familiar. She keeps her distance. And they respect her for it. Try to be like Margot.

► WORDS OF THE WISER

Notice & Note: Mark the reason that Mrs. Frank gives for why Anne must not answer back or behave rudely to the Van Daans.

Infer: What does Mrs. Frank understand about people that Anne has yet to learn?

WORDS OF THE WISER

Explain to students that the **Words of the Wiser** signpost is often used to highlight a moment in which a supporting character shares wisdom or advice with the main character. In paragraph 367, Mrs. Frank tries to get Anne to understand why it is important to always be courteous to their guests in the annex. (**Answer:** *She understands that stressful situations can cause people to lose patience and behave badly. That's why she tells Anne they need to make allowances for the Van Daans and control their behavior towards them, using Margot's actions as an example.*)

 ENGLISH LEARNER SUPPORT

Analyze Character   Explain that one way playwrights develop their characters is through contrast.

• Write the names *Anne* and *Margot* on the board. Display paragraphs 353 and 367. Work with students to record details that these passages reveal about each character. Then have pairs complete this sentence: *Unlike Margot, Anne is___*. Have them share their comparisons. **SUBSTANTIAL**

• Have pairs reread paragraphs 348 to 377. Ask one student to note details about Margot and the other to note details about Anne. Have them share and discuss their notes with each other. Ask them to collaborate to write two sentences that compare Margot and Anne. **MODERATE**

• Have pairs reread paragraphs 371 to 385 and discuss the ways that Anne and Margot are the same and different. Have them present their comparisons in a Venn diagram. **LIGHT**

TEACH

ENGLISH LEARNER SUPPORT

Analyze Language Remind students that idiomatic expressions help make dialogue sound more natural. Highlight these phrases: "Make something of myself" (paragraph 370); "she flies at me" (paragraph 376); "my heart stops" (paragraph 381). Have students work in mixed-ability groups to define these phrases, using context clues or a dictionary as needed. Have them rewrite the paragraphs using clearer phrases. Ask them to describe how the substitutions affect their impressions of the characters.

MODERATE/LIGHT

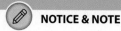

368 **Anne.** And have them walk all over me, the way they do her? No, thanks!

369 **Mrs. Frank.** I'm not afraid that anyone is going to walk all over you, Anne. I'm afraid for other people, that you'll walk on them. I don't know what happens to you, Anne. You are wild, self-willed. If I had ever talked to my mother as you talk to me . . .

370 **Anne.** Things have changed. People aren't like that any more. "Yes, Mother." "No, Mother." "Anything you say, Mother." I've got to fight things out for myself! Make something of myself!

371 **Mrs. Frank.** It isn't necessary to fight to do it. Margot doesn't fight, and isn't she . . . ?

372 **Anne** (*violently rebellious*). Margot! Margot! Margot! That's all I hear from everyone . . . how wonderful Margot is . . . "Why aren't you like Margot?"

373 **Margot** (*protesting*). Oh, come on, Anne, don't be so . . .

374 **Anne** (*paying no attention*). Everything she does is right, and everything I do is wrong! I'm the goat around here! . . . You're all against me! . . . And you worst of all!

375 (*She rushes off into her room and throws herself down on the settee, stifling her sobs.* Mrs. Frank *sighs and starts toward the stove.*)

376 **Mrs. Frank** (*to* Margot). Let's put the soup on the stove . . . if there's anyone who cares to eat. Margot, will you take the bread out? (Margot *gets the bread from the cupboard.*) I don't know how we can go on living this way . . . I can't say a word to Anne . . . she flies at me . . .

377 **Margot.** You know Anne. In half an hour she'll be out here, laughing and joking.

378 **Mrs. Frank.** And . . . (*She makes a motion upwards, indicating the* Van Daans.) . . . I told your father it wouldn't work . . . but no . . . no . . . he had to ask them, he said . . . he owed it to him, he said. Well, he knows now that I was right! These quarrels! . . . This bickering!

379 **Margot** (*with a warning look*). Shush. Shush.

380 (*The buzzer for the door sounds.* Mrs. Frank *gasps, startled.*)

381 **Mrs. Frank.** Every time I hear that sound, my heart stops!

382 **Margot** (*starting for* Peter's *door*). It's Miep. (*She knocks at the door.*) Father?

383 (Mr. Frank *comes quickly from* Peter's *room.*)

---

384 **Mr. Frank.** Thank you, Margot. (*as he goes down the steps to open the outer door*) Has everyone his list?

385 **Margot.** I'll get my books. (*giving her mother a list*) Here's your list.

386 (Margot *goes into her and* Anne's *bedroom on the right.* Anne *sits up, hiding her tears, as* Margot *comes in.*) Miep's here.

387 (Margot *picks up her books and goes back.* Anne *hurries over to the mirror, smoothing her hair.*)

388 **Mr. Van Daan** (*coming down the stairs*). Is it Miep?

389 **Margot.** Yes. Father's gone down to let her in.

390 **Mr. Van Daan.** At last I'll have some cigarettes!

391 **Mrs. Frank** (*to* Mr. Van Daan). I can't tell you how unhappy I am about Mrs. Van Daan's coat. Anne should never have touched it.

392 **Mr. Van Daan.** She'll be all right.

393 **Mrs. Frank.** Is there anything I can do?

394 **Mr. Van Daan.** Don't worry.

395 (*He turns to meet* Miep. *But it is not* Miep *who comes up the steps. It is* Mr. Kraler, *followed by* Mr. Frank. *Their faces are grave.* Anne *comes from the bedroom.* Peter *comes from his room.*)

396 **Mrs. Frank.** Mr. Kraler!

397 **Mr. Van Daan.** How are you, Mr. Kraler?

398 **Margot.** This is a surprise.

399 **Mrs. Frank.** When Mr. Kraler comes, the sun begins to shine.

400 **Mr. Van Daan.** Miep is coming?

401 **Mr. Kraler.** Not tonight.

402 (Kraler *goes to* Margot *and* Mrs. Frank *and* Anne, *shaking hands with them.*)

403 **Mrs. Frank.** Wouldn't you like a cup of coffee? . . . Or, better still, will you have supper with us?

404 **Mr. Frank.** Mr. Kraler has something to talk over with us. Something has happened, he says, which demands an immediate decision.

405 **Mrs. Frank** (*fearful*). What is it?

406 (Mr. Kraler *sits down on the couch. As he talks he takes bread, cabbages, milk, etc., from his briefcase, giving them to* Margot *and* Anne *to put away.*)

 ENGLISH LEARNER SUPPORT

Support Comprehension Have students read aloud paragraph 399. Point out that the statement "the sun begins to shine" is an example of figurative language. Ask students to describe what the playwrights mean by that statement. (*The arrival of Mr. Kraler is always a good thing because he brings supplies and news of the outside world. He is their protector.*)

SUBSTANTIAL/MODERATE

ANALYZE PLOT DEVELOPMENT

Remind students that they can learn something about what **characters** in a play are like by examining the words they say. In this **subplot,** the addition of another person to the annex creates a new source of conflict among the characters.

(**Answer:** *Bringing a new person into the secret annex creates tension among the people there. The Van Daans do not welcome him. Mr. Van Daan doesn't want to share limited food supplies with an additional person.*)

NOTICE & NOTE

ANALYZE PLOT DEVELOPMENT

Annotate: In paragraphs 407–419, mark the request that Mr. Kraler makes of Mr. Frank and the others.

Interpret: Remember that a subplot can add a new conflict to a main plot. How does Mr. Kraler's request create a new problem for the residents of the Secret Annex?

407 **Mr. Kraler.** Usually, when I come up here, I try to bring you some bit of good news. What's the use of telling you the bad news when there's nothing that you can do about it? But today something has happened . . . Dirk . . . Miep's Dirk, you know, came to me just now. He tells me that he has a Jewish friend living near him. A dentist. He says he's in trouble. He begged me, could I do anything for this man? Could I find him a hiding place? . . . So I've come to you . . . I know it's a terrible thing to ask of you, living as you are, but would you take him in with you?

408 **Mr. Frank.** Of course we will.

409 **Mr. Kraler** (*rising*). It'll be just for a night or two . . . until I find some other place. This happened so suddenly that I didn't know where to turn.

410 **Mr. Frank.** Where is he?

411 **Mr. Kraler.** Downstairs in the office.

412 **Mr. Frank.** Good. Bring him up.

413 **Mr. Kraler.** His name is Dussel . . . Jan Dussel.

414 **Mr. Frank.** Dussel . . . I think I know him.

415 **Mr. Kraler.** I'll get him. (*He goes quickly down the steps and out. Mr. Frank suddenly becomes conscious of the others.*)

416 **Mr. Frank.** Forgive me. I spoke without consulting you. But I knew you'd feel as I do.

417 **Mr. Van Daan.** There's no reason for you to consult anyone. This is your place. You have a right to do exactly as you please. The only thing I feel . . . there's so little food as it is . . . and to take in another person . . .

418 (Peter *turns away, ashamed of his father.*)

419 **Mr. Frank.** We can stretch the food a little. It's only for a few days.

420 **Mr. Van Daan.** You want to make a bet?

421 **Mrs. Frank.** I think it's fine to have him. But, Otto, where are you going to put him? Where?

422 **Peter.** He can have my bed. I can sleep on the floor. I wouldn't mind.

423 **Mr. Frank.** That's good of you, Peter. But your room's too small . . . even for *you.*

424 **Anne.** I have a much better idea. I'll come in here with you and Mother, and Margot can take Peter's room and Peter can go in our room with Mr. Dussel.

TO CHALLENGE STUDENTS . . .

Analyze Motivation Remind students that characters have motivations, or reasons, for their actions. Draw attention to Mr. Frank's words and actions in paragraphs 408–416, and tell students to consider Mr. Frank's motivations.

Ask students to consider the following:

- Mr. Frank acted on instinct, and he did not think to discuss his decision with the others.
- Mr. Frank feared the others would not agree to have Dussel join them, and so he made the choice without consulting anyone.

Prompt them to cite evidence from the text to support their opinions.

425 **Margot.** That's right. We could do that.

426 **Mr. Frank.** No, Margot. You mustn't sleep in that room . . . neither you nor Anne. Mouschi has caught some rats in there. Peter's brave. He doesn't mind.

427 **Anne.** Then how about *this?* I'll come in here with you and Mother, and Mr. Dussel can have my bed.

428 **Mrs. Frank.** No. No. *No!* Margot will come in here with us and he can have her bed. It's the only way. Margot, bring your things in here. Help her, Anne.

429 (Margot *hurries into her room to get her things.*)

430 **Anne** (*to her mother*). Why Margot? Why can't I come in here?

431 **Mrs. Frank.** Because it wouldn't be proper for Margot to sleep with a . . . Please, Anne. Don't argue. Please. (Anne *starts slowly away.*)

432 **Mr. Frank.** (*to* Anne). You don't mind sharing your room with Mr. Dussel, do you, Anne?

433 **Anne.** No. No, of course not.

434 **Mr. Frank.** Good. (Anne *goes off into her bedroom, helping* Margot. Mr. Frank *starts to search in the cupboards.*) Where's the cognac?

435 **Mrs. Frank.** It's there. But, Otto, I was saving it in case of illness.

436 **Mr. Frank.** I think we couldn't find a better time to use it. Peter, will you get five glasses for me?

437 (Peter *goes for the glasses.* Margot *comes out of her bedroom, carrying her possessions, which she hangs behind a curtain in the main room.* Mr. Frank *finds the cognac and pours it into the five glasses that* Peter *brings him.* Mr. Van Daan *stands looking on sourly.* Mrs. Van Daan *comes downstairs and looks around at all the bustle.*)

438 **Mrs. Van Daan.** What's happening? What's going on?

439 **Mr. Van Daan.** Someone's moving in with us.

440 **Mrs. Van Daan.** In here? You're joking.

441 **Margot.** It's only for a night or two . . . until Mr. Kraler finds him another place.

442 **Mr. Van Daan.** Yeah! Yeah!

443 (Mr. Frank *hurries over as* Mr. Kraler *and* Dussel *come up.* Dussel *is a man in his late fifties, meticulous, finicky . . . bewildered now. He wears a raincoat. He carries a briefcase, stuffed full, and a small medicine case.*)

The Diary of Anne Frank: Act One **439**

ENGLISH LEARNER SUPPORT

Read Closely Guide students to understand the conversation in paragraphs 427–433. Note the cultural differences of what was considered acceptable in that time but not today, and acknowledge student discomfort with the reasoning of times past.

- Have students explain what solution Anne proposes to the problem of where to put Mr. Dussel. (*She says that she will share the main room with her parents; she suggests Margot can share a room with Mr. Dussel.*)

- Read aloud Mrs. Frank's reaction in paragraph 428. Ask students to describe the way she sounds about Anne's idea. (*She sounds horrified.*) Make sure students understand why she has this reaction. Tell them that because Margot is eighteen, it is not appropriate for her to share a room with a grown man. At that time, because Anne is younger, it was considered more appropriate for her to share a room with Mr. Dussel.

- Then have students reread paragraph 430. Point out that Anne doesn't understand why her mother is against her suggestion. Ask them how Anne might interpret her mother's response. (*She most likely feels rejected by her mother; it appears that her mother prefers to share her room with Margot than share it with Anne.*)

MODERATE/LIGHT

444 **Mr. Frank.** Come in, Mr. Dussel.

445 **Mr. Kraler.** This is Mr. Frank.

446 **Dussel.** Mr. Otto Frank?

447 **Mr. Frank.** Yes. Let me take your things. (*He takes the hat and briefcase, but* Dussel *clings to his medicine case.*) This is my wife Edith . . . Mr. and Mrs. Van Daan . . . their son, Peter . . . and my daughters, Margot and Anne.

448 (Dussel *shakes hands with everyone.*)

449 **Mr. Kraler.** Thank you, Mr. Frank. Thank you all. Mr. Dussel, I leave you in good hands. Oh . . . Dirk's coat.

450 (Dussel *hurriedly takes off the raincoat, giving it to Mr. Kraler. Underneath is his white dentist's jacket, with a yellow Star of David on it.*)

451 **Dussel** (*to Mr. Kraler*). What can I say to thank you . . .?

452 **Mrs. Frank** (*to Dussel*). Mr. Kraler and Miep . . . They're our life line. Without them we couldn't live.

453 **Mr. Kraler.** Please. Please. You make us seem very heroic. It isn't that at all. We simply don't like the Nazis. (*to Mr. Frank, who offers him a drink*) No, thanks. (*then going on*) We don't like their methods. We don't like . . .

454 **Mr. Frank** (*smiling*). I know. I know. "No one's going to tell us Dutchmen what to do with our damn Jews!"

455 **Mr. Kraler** (*to Dussel*). Pay no attention to Mr. Frank. I'll be up tomorrow to see that they're treating you right. (*to Mr. Frank*) Don't trouble to come down again. Peter will bolt the door after me, won't you, Peter?

456 **Peter.** Yes, sir.

457 **Mr. Frank.** Thank you, Peter. I'll do it.

458 **Mr. Kraler.** Good night. Good night.

459 **Group.** Good night, Mr. Kraler. We'll see you tomorrow, (*etc., etc.*)

460 (Mr. Kraler *goes out with* Mr. Frank. Mrs. Frank *gives each one of the "grownups" a glass of cognac.*)

461 **Mrs. Frank.** Please, Mr. Dussel, sit down.

462 (Mr. Dussel *sinks into a chair.* Mrs. Frank *gives him a glass of cognac.*)

463 **Dussel.** I'm dreaming. I know it. I can't believe my eyes. Mr. Otto Frank here! (*to Mrs. Frank*) You're not in Switzerland

ENGLISH LEARNER SUPPORT

Read Closely Review the steps for defining idiomatic expressions: first, use context to understand meaning; then, analyze the image suggested by the phrase.

- Point out the phrase "leave you in good hands" in paragraph 449. Guide students to understand it by asking what is happening. (*Someone new is coming to stay.*) Then ask what this person might want. (*to feel welcomed; to have an ally*) Elicit from students that in this

context, Mr. Kraler's remark suggests that Mr. Frank is his ally and will take good care of Mr. Dussel.

- Have students work in pairs to identify two idiomatic or figurative expressions in paragraphs 446–463. (**Possible responses:** *"They're our life line"* in paragraph 452; *"I can't believe my eyes"* in paragraph 463.) List them on the board. Encourage students to use contex to define the expressions they found. **MODERATE/LIGHT**

then? A woman told me . . . She said she'd gone to your house . . . the door was open, everything was in disorder, dishes in the sink. She said she found a piece of paper in the wastebasket with an address scribbled on it . . . an address in Zurich. She said you must have escaped to Zurich.

464 **Anne.** Father put that there purposely . . . just so people would think that very thing!

465 **Dussel.** And you've been here all the time?

466 **Mrs. Frank.** All the time . . . ever since July.

467 (Anne *speaks to her father as he comes back.*)

468 **Anne.** It worked, Pim . . . the address you left! Mr. Dussel says that people believe we escaped to Switzerland.

469 **Mr. Frank.** I'm glad . . . And now let's have a little drink to welcome Mr. Dussel. (*Before they can drink,* Mr. Dussel *bolts his drink.* Mr. Frank *smiles and raises his glass.*) To Mr. Dussel. Welcome. We're very honored to have you with us.

470 **Mrs. Frank.** To Mr. Dussel, welcome.

471 (*The* Van Daans *murmur a welcome. The "grown-ups" drink.*)

472 **Mrs. Van Daan.** Um. That was good.

473 **Mr. Van Daan.** Did Mr. Kraler warn you that you won't get much to eat here? You can imagine . . . three ration books among the seven of us . . . and now you make eight.

474 (Peter *walks away, humiliated. Outside a street organ is heard dimly.*)

475 **Dussel** (*rising*). Mr. Van Daan, you don't realize what is happening outside that you should warn me of a thing like that. You don't realize what's going on . . . (*As* Mr. Van Daan *starts his characteristic pacing,* Dussel *turns to speak to the others.*) Right here in Amsterdam every day hundreds of Jews disappear . . . They surround a block and search house by house. Children come home from school to find their parents gone. Hundreds are being deported . . . people that you and I know . . . the Hallensteins . . . the Wessels . . .

476 **Mrs. Frank** (*in tears*). Oh, no. No!

477 **Dussel.** They get their call-up notice . . . come to the Jewish theatre on such and such a day and hour . . . bring only what you can carry in a rucksack. And if you refuse the call-up notice, then they come and drag you from your home and ship you off to Mauthausen.[11] The death camp!

---

[11] **Mauthausen** (mout´hou´zən): a Nazi concentration camp in Austria.

CONTRASTS AND CONTRADICTIONS

Notice & Note: In paragraphs 473–474, mark how Peter reacts to his father's words to Mr. Dussel.

Compare: What causes Peter's embarrassment? How does Mr. Van Daan's behavior contrast with how we would expect a person to behave?

CONTRASTS AND CONTRADICTIONS

Explain to students that the **Contrasts and Contradictions** signpost is often used to signal a moment when a character's behavior **contrasts,** or differs, from generally expected behavior.

Ask students to contrast how Mr. Frank and Mr. Kraler act toward Mr. Dussel with what Mr. Van Daan implies with his comment, "Did Mr. Kraler warn you that you won't get much to eat here?"

(**Answer:** *Peter is embarrassed by his father's lack of generosity. Mr. Dussel has just come to the annex because he had nowhere else to go. Mr. Van Daan implies that he will be taking food away from the rest of the residents. This contrasts with how we expect a good person to behave—we would expect people to empathize with Mr. Dussel, as Mr. Frank and Mr. Kraler do.*)

IMPROVE READING FLUENCY

Targeted Passage Organize students into groups with six members to perform a readers' theater of paragraphs 463–477.

- Have group members decide who will play each role. Explain that they will act out the stage directions instead of reading them.
- Go over how to read the lines on this page. Have students echo read some of the more dramatic passages, such as paragraph 463.

- Give groups time to rehearse. Circulate to check their progress.
- Have students perform their readers' theater. Ask listening students to comment on the strengths of each group's reading.

 Go to the **Reading Studio** for additional support in developing fluency.

478 **Mrs. Frank.** We didn't know that things had got so much worse.

479 **Dussel.** Forgive me for speaking so.

480 **Anne** (*coming to* Dussel). Do you know the de Waals? . . . What's become of them? Their daughter Jopie and I are in the same class. Jopie's my best friend.

481 **Dussel.** They are gone.

482 **Anne.** Gone?

483 **Dussel.** With all the others.

484 **Anne.** Oh, no. Not Jopie!

485 (*She turns away, in tears.* Mrs. Frank *motions to* Margot *to comfort her.* Margot *goes to* Anne, *putting her arms comfortingly around her.*)

486 **Mrs. Van Daan.** There were some people called Wagner. They lived near us . . . ?

487 **Mr. Frank** (*interrupting, with a glance at* Anne). I think we should put this off until later. We all have many questions we want to ask . . . But I'm sure that Mr. Dussel would like to get settled before supper.

488 **Dussel.** Thank you. I would. I brought very little with me.

489 **Mr. Frank** (*giving him his hat and briefcase*). I'm sorry we can't give you a room alone. But I hope you won't be too uncomfortable. We've had to make strict rules here . . . a schedule of hours . . . We'll tell you after supper. Anne, would you like to take Mr. Dussel to his room?

490 **Anne** (*controlling her tears*). If you'll come with me, Mr. Dussel? (*She starts for her room.*)

491 **Dussel** (*shaking hands with each in turn*). Forgive me if I haven't really expressed my gratitude to all of you. This has been such a shock to me. I'd always thought of myself as Dutch. I was born in Holland. My father was born in Holland, and my grandfather. And now . . . after all these years . . . (*He breaks off.*) If you'll excuse me.

492 (Dussel *gives a little bow and hurries off after* Anne. Mr. Frank *and the others are subdued.*)

493 **Anne** (*turning on the light*). Well, here we are.

494 (Dussel *looks around the room. In the main room* Margot *speaks to her mother.*)

495 **Margot.** The news sounds pretty bad, doesn't it? It's so different from what Mr. Kraler tells us. Mr. Kraler says things are improving.

WHEN STUDENTS STRUGGLE . . .

Identifying Details Display a flow chart graphic organizer like the one shown. Encourage pairs to complete the frame for Scene 3. Review what they have written, and then ask students to predict what they think might happen in Scene 4. Record their predictions on the board, and adjust or confirm them as the class reads the next scene.

 For additional support, go to the **Reading Studio** and assign the following ▣ **Level Up tutorial: Reading for Details.**

Scene 1: November 1945
Mr. Frank returns to the annex. He is given Anne's diary and begins to read it.

↓

Scene 2: July 1942
The Van Daans and the Franks arrive at the annex to start their life in hiding.

↓

Scene 3: September 1942

496 **Mr. Van Daan.** I like it better the way Kraler tells it.

497 (*They resume their occupations, quietly.* Peter *goes off into his room. In* Anne's *room,* Anne *turns to* Dussel.)

498 **Anne.** You're going to share the room with me.

499 **Dussel.** I'm a man who's always lived alone. I haven't had to adjust myself to others. I hope you'll bear with me until I learn.

500 **Anne.** Let me help you. (*She takes his briefcase.*) Do you always live all alone? Have you no family at all?

501 **Dussel.** No one. (*He opens his medicine case and spreads his bottles on the dressing table.*)

502 **Anne.** How dreadful. You must be terribly lonely.

503 **Dussel.** I'm used to it.

504 **Anne.** I don't think I could ever get used to it. Didn't you even have a pet? A cat, or a dog?

505 **Dussel.** I have an allergy for fur-bearing animals. They give me asthma.

506 **Anne.** Oh, dear. Peter has a cat.

507 **Dussel.** Here? He has it here?

508 **Anne.** Yes. But we hardly ever see it. He keeps it in his room all the time. I'm sure it will be all right.

509 **Dussel.** Let us hope so.

510 (*He takes some pills to fortify himself.*)

511 **Anne.** That's Margot's bed, where you're going to sleep. I sleep on the sofa there. (*indicating the clothes hooks on the wall*) We cleared these off for your things. (*She goes over to the window.*) The best part about this room . . . you can look down and see a bit of the street and the canal. There's a houseboat . . . you can see the end of it . . . a bargeman lives there with his family . . . They have a baby and he's just beginning to walk and I'm so afraid he's going to fall into the canal some day. I watch him . . .

512 **Dussel** (*interrupting*). Your father spoke of a schedule.

513 **Anne** (*coming away from the window*). Oh, yes. It's mostly about the times we have to be quiet. And times for the w.c. You can use it now if you like.

514 **Dussel** (*stiffly*). No, thank you.

515 **Anne.** I suppose you think it's awful, my talking about a thing like that. But you don't know how important it can get to be, especially when you're frightened . . . About this room, the

ENGLISH LEARNER SUPPORT

Read Closely Display paragraphs 502–523. Work with students to highlight details that reveal Mr. Dussel's character and personality.

- Model for students how to make inferences from the details in paragraphs 505 and 509–510. Say: "Mr. Dussel's first comments and actions concern his health. He does not ask Anne any questions about herself. I would infer that he is quite focused on himself."

- Have pairs use a similar strategy to make inferences based on the remaining details.
MODERATE

CONTRASTS AND CONTRADICTIONS

Explain to students that the **Contrasts and Contradictions** signpost is often used to highlight a passage where a character's behavior is **contradicted** by his or her actions. In this case, Mr. Dussel's claim that he gets along well with children is contradicted by the subsequent narrative by Anne, in which she says he criticizes her constantly.

(**Answer:** *There are several possible explanations for this contradiction: Dussel may have been overly boastful about how well he got along with children to persuade Anne that he belongs in the group; Anne may be particularly difficult to get along with, perhaps because she's transitioning from being a child to being an adult; the close confines of the annex may have frayed everyone's nerves, so that both Mr. Dussel and Anne have less patience than they would in normal circumstances.*)

CONTRASTS AND
CONTRADICTIONS

Notice & Note: In paragraphs 525–529, mark lines that show a surprising contrast between how Mr. Dussel and Anne expect to get along and how they actually get along.

Interpret: What might explain this contradiction?

way Margot and I did . . . she had it to herself in the afternoons for studying, reading . . . lessons, you know . . . and I took the mornings. Would that be all right with you?

516 **Dussel.** I'm not at my best in the morning.

517 **Anne.** You stay here in the mornings then. I'll take the room in the afternoons.

518 **Dussel.** Tell me, when you're in here, what happens to me? Where am I spending my time? In there, with all the people?

519 **Anne.** Yes.

520 **Dussel.** I see. I see.

521 **Anne.** We have supper at half past six.

522 **Dussel** (*going over to the sofa*). Then, if you don't mind . . . I like to lie down quietly for ten minutes before eating. I find it helps the digestion.

523 **Anne.** Of course. I hope I'm not going to be too much of a bother to you. I seem to be able to get everyone's back up.

524 (Dussel *lies down on the sofa, curled up, his back to her.*)

525 **Dussel.** I always get along very well with children. My patients all bring their children to me, because they know I get on well with them. So don't you worry about that.

526 (Anne *leans over him, taking his hand and shaking it gratefully.*)

527 **Anne.** Thank you. Thank you, Mr. Dussel.

528 (*The lights dim to darkness. The curtain falls on the scene. Anne's Voice comes to us faintly at first, and then with increasing power.*)

529 **Anne's Voice.** . . . And yesterday I finished Cissy Van Marxvelt's latest book. I think she is a first-class writer. I shall definitely let my children read her. Monday the twenty-first of September, nineteen forty-two. Mr. Dussel and I had another battle yesterday. Yes, Mr. Dussel! According to him, nothing, I repeat . . . nothing, is right about me . . . my appearance, my character, my manners. While he was going on at me I thought . . . sometime I'll give you such a smack that you'll fly right up to the ceiling! Why is it that every grownup thinks he knows the way to bring up children? Particularly the grownups that never had any. I keep wishing that Peter was a girl instead of a boy. Then I would have someone to talk to. Margot's a darling, but she takes everything too seriously. To

pause for a moment on the subject of Mrs. Van Daan. I must tell you that her attempts to flirt with Father are getting her nowhere. Pim, thank goodness, won't play.

530 (*As she is saying the last lines, the curtain rises on the darkened scene.* Anne's Voice *fades out.*)

Scene 4
⊷═══⟨═⊷

531 *It is the middle of the night, several months later. The stage is dark except for a little light which comes through the skylight in Peter's room.*

532 *Everyone is in bed. Mr. and Mrs. Frank lie on the couch in the main room, which has been pulled out to serve as a makeshift double bed.*

533 *Margot is sleeping on a mattress on the floor in the main room, behind a curtain stretched across for privacy. The others are all in their accustomed rooms.*

534 *From outside we hear two drunken soldiers singing "Lili Marlene." A girl's high giggle is heard. The sound of running feet is heard coming closer and then fading in the distance. Throughout the scene there is the distant sound of airplanes passing overhead.*

535 *A match suddenly flares up in the attic. We dimly see Mr. Van Daan. He is getting his bearings. He comes quickly down the stairs, and goes to the cupboard where the food is stored. Again the match flares up, and is as quickly blown out. The dim figure is seen to steal back up the stairs.*

536 *There is quiet for a second or two, broken only by the sound of airplanes, and running feet on the street below.*

537 *Suddenly, out of the silence and the dark, we hear* Anne *scream.*

538 **Anne** (*screaming*). No! No! Don't . . . don't take me!

539 (*She moans, tossing and crying in her sleep. The other people wake, terrified.* Dussel *sits up in bed, furious.*)

540 **Dussel.** Shush! Anne! Anne, for God's sake, shush!

541 **Anne** (*still in her nightmare*). Save me! Save me!

542 (*She screams and screams.* Dussel *gets out of bed, going over to her, trying to wake her.*)

543 **Dussel.** For God's sake! Quiet! Quiet! You want someone to hear?

NOTICE & NOTE

ANALYZE PLOT DEVELOPMENT

Annotate: In paragraphs 531–535, mark where Mr. Van Daan goes in the dark.

Predict: What do you think Mr. Van Daan is doing? How might his action cause trouble in the future?

ANALYZE PLOT DEVELOPMENT

Remind students that they can learn something about what **characters** in a play are like by their actions as well as by their words. In this scene, Mr. Van Daan—who earlier implied that the addition of Mr. Dussel would strain their food resources—shows his hypocrisy by sneaking food at night.

(**Answer:** *Mr. Van Daan is going to the food cupboard in the dark, most likely stealing food. This may cause trouble because he may be discovered or because the group will run out of food earlier than they expect.*)

EL ENGLISH LEARNER SUPPORT

Exchange Ideas Read aloud paragraph 535. Explain that the word *steal* has more than one meaning. It can be defined as "take what doesn't belong to you" or "move silently or sneakily."

- Ask students which meaning fits the context. (*to move silently or sneakily*) Then ask why Mr. Van Daan is creeping around. (*He doesn't want anyone to know he is taking or stealing food.*)
- Have pairs of students use both meanings of the word in sentences.

MODERATE

544 (*In the main room* Mrs. Frank *grabs a shawl and pulls it around her. She rushes in to* Anne, *taking her in her arms.* Mr. Frank *hurriedly gets up, putting on his overcoat.* Margot *sits up, terrified.* Peter's *light goes on in his room.*)

545 **Mrs. Frank** (*to* Anne, *in her room*). Hush, darling, hush. It's all right. It's all right. (*over her shoulder to* Dussel) Will you be kind enough to turn on the light, Mr. Dussel? (*back to* Anne) It's nothing, my darling. It was just a dream.

546 (Dussel *turns on the light in the bedroom.* Mrs. Frank *holds* Anne *in her arms. Gradually* Anne *comes out of her nightmare, still trembling with horror.* Mr. Frank *comes into the room, and goes quickly to the window, looking out to be sure that no one outside had heard* Anne's *screams.* Mrs. Frank *holds* Anne, *talking softly to her. In the main room* Margot *stands on a chair, turning on the center hanging lamp. A light goes on in the* Van Daans' *room overhead.* Peter *puts his robe on, coming out of his room.*)

547 **Dussel** (*to* Mrs. Frank, *blowing his nose*). Something must be done about that child, Mrs. Frank. Yelling like that! Who knows but there's somebody on the streets? She's endangering all our lives.

548 **Mrs. Frank.** Anne, darling.

549 **Dussel.** Every night she twists and turns. I don't sleep. I spend half my night shushing her. And now it's nightmares!

550 (Margot *comes to the door of* Anne's *room, followed by* Peter. Mr. Frank *goes to them, indicating that everything is all right.* Peter *takes* Margot *back.*)

551 **Mrs. Frank** (*to* Anne). You're here, safe, you see? Nothing has happened. (*to* Dussel) Please, Mr. Dussel, go back to bed. She'll be herself in a minute or two. Won't you, Anne?

552 **Dussel** (*picking up a book and a pillow*). Thank you, but I'm going to the w.c. The one place where there's peace! (*He stalks out.* Mr. Van Daan, *in underwear and trousers, comes down the stairs.*)

553 **Mr. Van Daan** (*to* Dussel). What is it? What happened?

554 **Dussel.** A nightmare. She was having a nightmare!

555 **Mr. Van Daan.** I thought someone was murdering her.

556 **Dussel.** Unfortunately, no.

557 (*He goes into the bathroom.* Mr. Van Daan *goes back up the stairs.* Mr. Frank, *in the main room, sends* Peter *back to his own bedroom.*)

558 **Mr. Frank.** Thank you, Peter. Go back to bed.

© Houghton Mifflin Harcourt Publishing Company

ENGLISH LEARNER SUPPORT

Analyze Character Remind students that how the characters react to Anne's nightmare may reveal something about them.

- Project paragraphs 545–552. Highlight Dussel's lines and read them aloud. Guide students to hear his lack of sympathy. Then have pairs complete this sentence: *Dussel's reaction shows that he is ___.* Discuss students' responses. **SUBSTANTIAL**

- Have small groups find details that describe how Dussel reacts and then use the details to make inferences about his character. Ask them to share their inferences and supporting evidence. **MODERATE**

- Have pairs describe Dussel's character based on what he says and does in response to Anne's nightmare. Ask them to discuss how his arrival has affected the group: has he been a positive, negative, or neutral presence? Ask pairs to share their views. **LIGHT**

559 (Peter *goes back to his room.* Mr. Frank *follows him, turning out the light and looking out the window. Then he goes back to the main room, and gets up on a chair, turning out the center hanging lamp.*)

560 **Mrs. Frank** (*to* Anne). Would you like some water? (Anne *shakes her head.*) Was it a very bad dream? Perhaps if you told me . . . ?

561 **Anne.** I'd rather not talk about it.

562 **Mrs. Frank.** Poor darling. Try to sleep then. I'll sit right here beside you until you fall asleep.

563 (*She brings a stool over, sitting* there.)

564 **Anne.** You don't have to.

565 **Mrs. Frank.** But I'd like to stay with you . . . very much. Really.

566 **Anne.** I'd rather you didn't.

567 **Mrs. Frank.** Good night, then. (*She leans down to kiss* Anne. Anne *throws her arm up over her face, turning away.* Mrs. Frank, *hiding her hurt, kisses* Anne's *arm.*) You'll be all right? There's nothing that you want?

568 **Anne.** Will you please ask Father to come.

569 **Mrs. Frank** (*after a second*). Of course, Anne dear. (*She hurries out into the other room.* Mr. Frank *comes to her as she comes in.*) *Sie verlangt nach Dir!*[12]

570 **Mr. Frank** (*sensing her hurt*). Edith, *Liebe, schau* . . .[13]

571 **Mrs. Frank.** *Es macht nichts! Ich danke dem lieben Herrgott, dass sie sich wenigstens an Dich wendet, wenn sie Trost braucht! Geh hinein, Otto, sie ist ganz hysterisch vor Angst.*[14] (*as* Mr. Frank *hesitates*) *Geh zu ihr.*[15] (*He looks at her for a second and then goes to get a cup of water for* Anne. Mrs. Frank *sinks down on the bed, her face in her hands, trying to keep from sobbing aloud.* Margot *comes over to her, putting her arms around her.*) She wants nothing of me. She pulled away when I leaned down to kiss her.

572 **Margot.** It's a phase . . . You heard Father . . . Most girls go through it . . . they turn to their fathers at this age . . . they give all their love to their fathers.

---

[12] *Sie verlangt nach Dir* (zē fer-längt´näкн dîr) *German*: She is asking for you.

[13] *Liebe, schau* (lē´bə shou´) *German*: Dear, look.

[14] *Es macht . . . vor Angst* (ĕs mäкнt´ nĭкнts´! ĭкн dängk´ə däm lē´bən hĕr´gôt´, däs zē zĭкн´ vān ĭкнshtənz än dĭкн´ vĕn´dət, vĕn zē trôst´ brouкht´! gä hĭn-īn´, ôt´tô; zē ĭst gänts hüstĕr´ĭsh fôr ängst´) *German*: It's all right. I thank dear God that at least she turns to you when she needs comfort. Go in, Otto; she is hysterical with fear.

[15] *Geh zu ihr* (gä´ tsoō îr´) *German*: Go to her.

ANALYZE DRAMA

Annotate: In paragraphs 569–571, notice the lines that Mr. and Mrs. Frank speak in German. Mark the English translations in the footnotes.

Infer: Why might the playwrights have chosen to have the characters speak German in this part of the script?

 ANALYZE DRAMA

Point out that although most of the play is written in English, here the playwrights present parts of the **dialogue** in German. Remind students that they earlier learned that the Franks had left Germany when Hitler came to power.

(**Answer:** *People who speak more than one language may revert to the one they feel most comfortable with in times of stress. Because the play is written in English, the playwrights may be emphasizing that Mr. and Mrs. Frank are under extreme stress. Or, sometimes parents speak a language that their children don't understand to privately make a point about something.*)

ENGLISH LEARNER SUPPORT

Read Closely Remind students that *Pim* (paragraph 575) is Anne's nickname for her father. In paragraph 584, he calls her *Annele*, which is one of his special names for her. Have small groups discuss these questions:

- What do these nicknames show about the relationship between Anne and her father?
- Do you have a nickname for any family members? How do nicknames get started? **MODERATE**

▶ TOUGH QUESTIONS

Explain to students that the **Tough Questions** signpost is often used to highlight a character's realization or understanding about herself or himself. In her dialogue, paragraphs 583–591, Anne recognizes that her behavior toward her mother is wrong but feels powerless to stop herself.

(**Answer:** *Anne asks her father to tell her "what's the matter" with her. The question reveals that Anne is conflicted about her behavior toward her mother. She wants to understand how she can sometimes behave cruelly to her mother even though she knows it's wrong.*)

 NOTICE & NOTE

573 **Mrs. Frank.** You weren't like this. You didn't shut me out.

574 **Margot.** She'll get over it . . . (*She smooths the bed for* Mrs. Frank *and sits beside her a moment as* Mrs. Frank *lies down. In* Anne's *room* Mr. Frank *comes in, sitting down by* Anne. Anne *flings her arms around him, clinging to him. In the distance we hear the sound of ack-ack.*)

575 **Anne.** Oh, Pim. I dreamed that they came to get us! The Green Police! They broke down the door and grabbed me and started to drag me out the way they did Jopie.

576 **Mr. Frank.** I want you to take this pill.

577 **Anne.** What is it?

578 **Mr. Frank.** Something to quiet you.

579 (*She takes it and drinks the water. In the main room* Margot *turns out the light and goes back to her bed.*)

580 **Mr. Frank** (*to* Anne). Do you want me to read to you for a while?

581 **Anne.** No. Just sit with me for a minute. Was I awful? Did I yell terribly loud? Do you think anyone outside could have heard?

582 **Mr. Frank.** No. No. Lie quietly now. Try to sleep.

583 **Anne.** I'm a terrible coward. I'm so disappointed in myself. I think I've conquered my fear . . . I think I'm really grown-up . . . and then something happens . . . and I run to you like a baby . . . I love you, Father. I don't love anyone but you.

584 **Mr. Frank** (*reproachfully*). Annele!

585 **Anne.** It's true. I've been thinking about it for a long time. You're the only one I love.

586 **Mr. Frank.** It's fine to hear you tell me that you love me. But I'd be happier if you said you loved your mother as well . . . She needs your help so much . . . your love . . .

587 **Anne.** We have nothing in common. She doesn't understand me. Whenever I try to explain my views on life to her she asks me if I'm constipated.

588 **Mr. Frank.** You hurt her very much just now. She's crying. She's in there crying.

589 **Anne.** I can't help it. I only told the truth. I didn't want her here . . . (*then, with sudden change*) Oh, Pim, I was horrible, wasn't I? And the worst of it is, I can stand off and look at myself doing it and know it's cruel and yet I can't stop doing it. What's the matter with me? Tell me. Don't say it's just a phase! Help me.

◀ TOUGH QUESTIONS

Notice & Note: Mark how Anne describes her behavior toward her mother.

Interpret: What question does Anne ask her father? What internal conflict does this question reveal?

590 **Mr. Frank.** There is so little that we parents can do to help our children. We can only try to set a good example . . . point the way. The rest you must do yourself. You must build your own character.

591 **Anne.** I'm trying. Really I am. Every night I think back over all of the things I did that day that were wrong . . . like putting the wet mop in Mr. Dussel's bed . . . and this thing now with Mother. I say to myself, that was wrong. I make up my mind, I'm never going to do *that* again. Never! Of course I may do something worse . . . but at least I'll never do that again! . . . I have a nicer side, Father . . . a sweeter, nicer side. But I'm scared to show it. I'm afraid that people are going to laugh at me if I'm serious. So the mean Anne comes to the outside and the good Anne stays on the inside, and I keep on trying to switch them around and have the good Anne outside and the bad Anne inside and be what I'd like to be . . . and might be . . . if only . . . only . . . (*She is asleep.* Mr. Frank *watches her for a moment and then turns off the light, and starts out. The lights dim out. The curtain falls on the scene.* Anne's Voice *is heard dimly at first, and then with growing strength.*)

592 **Anne's Voice.** . . . The air raids are getting worse. They come over day and night. The noise is terrifying. Pim says it should be music to our ears. The more planes, the sooner will come the end of the war. Mrs. Van Daan pretends to be a fatalist. What will be, will be. But when the planes come over, who is the most frightened? No one else but Petronella! . . . Monday, the ninth of November, nineteen forty-two. Wonderful news! The Allies have landed in Africa. Pim says that we can look for an early finish to the war. Just for fun he asked each of us what was the first thing we wanted to do when we got out of here. Mrs. Van Daan longs to be home with her own things, her needle-point chairs, the Beckstein piano her father gave her . . . the best that money could buy. Peter would like to go to a movie. Mr. Dussel wants to get back to his dentist's drill. He's afraid he is losing his touch. For myself, there are so many things . . . to ride a bike again . . . to laugh till my belly aches . . . to have new clothes from the skin out . . . to have a hot tub filled to overflowing and wallow in it for hours . . . to be back in school with my friends . . .

593 (*As the last lines are being said, the curtain rises on the scene. The lights dim on as* Anne's Voice *fades away.*)

ENGLISH LEARNER SUPPORT

Read Closely Encourage students to use context clues to understand the ideas in Anne's monologue in paragraph 592.

- Direct students' attention to the word *fatalist*. Then read the sentence that follows: "What will be, will be." Guide students to recognize that a fatalist is someone who accepts that all events are predetermined and therefore unalterable.
- Ask students whether Mrs. Van Daan really is a fatalist. Why or why not? (*She is not a fatalist, or else she would not be the most frightened of them all when the planes fly over.*)
- Have students work in mixed-ability groups to define these words and expressions using context clues: "music to our ears," "losing his touch," and "wallow." **LIGHT**

LANGUAGE CONVENTIONS

Remind students that proper nouns are *always* capitalized. Proper nouns are specific people, places, and things and may include religions, religious holidays, major religious symbols, and sacred texts.

(**Answer:** Hanukkah *is capitalized because it is an important Jewish holiday, and* Menorah *and* Shamos *are capitalized because they are important Hanukkah symbols or artifacts. The words* Thou, Lord, God, Ruler, *and* Thy *are capitalized because they refer to the Jewish god.)*

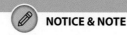

LANGUAGE CONVENTIONS

Annotate: To use correct capitalization, you need to capitalize the names of religions, religious texts, and important symbols or artifacts. Review paragraph 594 and mark three words that are capitalized.

Identify: Into which category, or group, does each word fall? Note that many religions also capitalize words to show respect for their deity. What other words are capitalized in paragraph 595?

Scene 5

594   *It is the first night of the* Hanukkah[16] *celebration. Mr. Frank is standing at the head of the table on which is the* Menorah.[17] *He lights the* Shamos, *or servant candle, and holds it as he says the blessing. Seated listening is all of the "family," dressed in their best. The men wear hats,* Peter *wears his cap.*

595   **Mr. Frank** (*reading from a prayer book*). "Praised be Thou, oh Lord our God, Ruler of the universe, who has sanctified us with Thy commandments and bidden us kindle the Hanukkah lights. Praised be Thou, oh Lord our God, Ruler of the universe, who has wrought wondrous deliverances for our fathers in days of old. Praised be Thou, oh Lord our God, Ruler of the universe, that Thou has given us life and sustenance and brought us to this happy season." (*Mr. Frank lights the one candle of the Menorah as he continues.*) "We kindle this Hanukkah light to celebrate the great and wonderful deeds wrought through the zeal with which God filled the hearts of the heroic Maccabees, two thousand years ago. They fought against indifference, against tyranny and oppression, and they restored our Temple to us. May these lights remind us that we should ever look to God, whence cometh our help." Amen. [Pronounced O-mayn.]

596   **All.** Amen.

597   (Mr. Frank *hands* Mrs. Frank *the prayer book.*)

598   **Mrs. Frank** (*reading*). "I lift up mine eyes unto the mountains, from whence cometh my help. My help cometh from the Lord who made heaven and earth. He will not suffer thy foot to be moved. He that keepeth thee will not slumber. He that keepeth Israel doth neither slumber nor sleep. The Lord is thy keeper. The Lord is thy shade upon thy right hand. The sun shall not smite thee by day, nor the moon by night. The Lord shall keep thee from all evil. He shall keep thy soul. The Lord shall guard thy going out and thy coming in, from this time forth and forevermore." Amen.

599   **All.** Amen.

600   (Mrs. Frank *puts down the prayer book and goes to get the food and wine.* Margot *helps her.* Mr. Frank *takes the men's hats and puts them aside.*)

---

[16] **Hanukkah** (hä´nə-kə): a Jewish holiday, celebrated in December and lasting eight days.

[17] **Menorah** (mə-nôr´ə): a candleholder with nine branches, used in the celebration of Hanukkah.

601 **Dussel** (*rising*). That was very moving.

602 **Anne** (*pulling him back*). It isn't over yet!

603 **Mrs. Van Daan.** Sit down! Sit down!

604 **Anne.** There's a lot more, songs and presents.

605 **Dussel.** Presents?

606 **Mrs. Frank.** Not this year, unfortunately.

607 **Mrs. Van Daan.** But always on Hanukkah everyone gives presents . . . everyone!

608 **Dussel.** Like our St. Nicholas's Day.[18] (*There is a chorus of "no's" from the group.*)

609 **Mrs. Van Daan.** No! Not like St. Nicholas! What kind of a Jew are you that you don't know Hanukkah?

610 **Mrs. Frank** (*as she brings the food*). I remember particularly the candles . . . First one, as we have tonight. Then the second night you light two candles, the next night three . . . and so on until you have eight candles burning. When there are eight candles it is truly beautiful.

611 **Mrs. Van Daan.** And the potato pancakes.

612 **Mr. Van Daan.** Don't talk about them!

613 **Mrs. Van Daan.** I make the best *latkes*[19] you ever tasted!

614 **Mrs. Frank.** Invite us all next year . . . in your own home.

615 **Mr. Frank.** God willing!

[18]**St. Nicholas's Day:** December 6, the day that Christian children in the Netherlands receive gifts.
[19]*latkes* (lät´kəz): potato pancakes.

TO CHALLENGE STUDENTS . . .

Analyze the Impact of Perspective Remind students that Frances Goodrich and Albert Hackett wrote their play based on Anne's diary. Have students form small groups to create diary entries that one of the other characters might have written about the Hanukkah celebration. You may wish to assign a specific character to each group.

Ask students to review the main events of the celebration and to consider what they have learned about each character. How would that character describe the celebration differently? In what ways would the character's description be similar to what the play presents? Have groups share their diary entries with the class.

MEMORY MOMENT

Explain to students that the **Memory Moments** signpost is used here to highlight the contrast between the **characters'** lives before they moved into the annex, their situation now, and how Anne tries to continue holiday traditions from that time.

(**Answer:** *Anne also remembers the presents they used to exchange at Hanukkah, and she announces that she has presents for the residents of the annex.*)

ENGLISH LEARNER SUPPORT

Analyze Language Guide students to use context clues to help them understand the meaning of *cross* in Anne's poem in paragraph 628. Point out the phrases "never lost your temper" and "But if you should" to lead them to define *cross* as "annoyed." Then show students a sample of a crossword puzzle to make sure they understand Anne's play on words.

SUBSTANTIAL/MODERATE

NOTICE & NOTE

MEMORY MOMENT

Notice & Note: Review paragraphs 610–622. Mark the Memory Moment that Margo has.

Connect: How does Margot's memory relate to what Anne does next in the play?

616 **Mrs. Van Daan.** God willing.

617 **Margot.** What I remember best is the presents we used to get when we were little . . . eight days of presents . . . and each day they got better and better.

618 **Mrs. Frank** (*sitting down*). We are all here, alive. That is present enough.

619 **Anne.** No, it isn't. I've got something . . .

620 (*She rushes into her room, hurriedly puts on a little hat improvised from the lamp shade, grabs a satchel bulging with parcels and comes running back.*)

621 **Mrs. Frank.** What is it?

622 **Anne.** Presents!

623 **Mrs. Van Daan.** Presents!

624 **Dussel.** Look!

625 **Mr. Van Daan.** What's she got on her head?

626 **Peter.** A lamp shade!

627 **Anne** (*She picks out one at random*). This is for Margot. (*She hands it to Margot, pulling her to her feet.*) Read it out loud.

628 **Margot** (*reading*).
"You have never lost your temper.
You never will, I fear,
You are so good.
But if you should,
Put all your cross words here."
(*She tears open the package.*)
A new crossword puzzle book!
Where did you get it?

629 **Anne.** It isn't new. It's one that you've done. But I rubbed it all out, and if you wait a little and forget, you can do it all over again.

630 **Margot** (*sitting*). It's wonderful, Anne. Thank you. You'd never know it wasn't new.

631 (*From outside we hear the sound of a streetcar passing.*)

632 **Anne** (*with another gift*). Mrs. Van Daan.

633 **Mrs. Van Daan** (*taking it*). This is awful . . . I haven't anything for anyone . . . I never thought . . .

634 **Mr. Frank.** This is all Anne's idea.

635 **Mrs. Van Daan** (*holding up a bottle*). What is it?

452   Unit 6

636 **Anne.** It's hair shampoo. I took all the odds and ends of soap and mixed them with the last of my toilet water.

637 **Mrs. Van Daan.** Oh, Anneke!

638 **Anne.** I wanted to write a poem for all of them, but I didn't have time. (*offering a large box to* Mr. Van Daan) Yours, Mr. Van Daan, is really something . . . something you want more than anything. (*as she waits for him to open it*) Look! Cigarettes!

639 **Mr. Van Daan.** Cigarettes!

640 **Anne.** Two of them! Pim found some old pipe tobacco in the pocket lining of his coat . . . and we made them . . . or rather, Pim did.

641 **Mrs. Van Daan.** Let me see . . . Well, look at that! Light it, Putti! Light it.

642 (Mr. Van Daan *hesitates.*)

643 **Anne.** It's tobacco, really it is! There's a little fluff in it, but not much.

644 (*Everyone watches intently as* Mr. Van Daan *cautiously lights it. The cigarette flares up. Everyone laughs.*)

645 **Peter.** It works!

646 **Mrs. Van Daan.** Look at him.

647 **Mr. Van Daan** (*spluttering*). Thank you, Anne. Thank you.

648 (Anne *rushes back to her satchel for another present.*)

649 **Anne** (*handing her mother a piece of paper*). For Mother, Hanukkah greeting. (*She pulls her mother to her feet.*)

650 **Mrs. Frank** (*She reads.*) "Here's an I.O.U. that I promise to pay. Ten hours of doing whatever you say. Signed, Anne Frank." (Mrs. Frank, *touched, takes* Anne *in her arms, holding her close.*)

651 **Dussel** (*to* Anne). Ten hours of doing what you're told? *Anything* you're told?

652 **Anne.** That's right.

653 **Dussel.** You wouldn't want to sell that, Mrs. Frank?

654 **Mrs. Frank.** Never! This is the most precious gift I've ever had!

655 (*She sits, showing her present to the others.* Anne *hurries back to the satchel and pulls out a scarf, the scarf that* Mr. Frank *found in the first scene.*)

656 **Anne** (*offering it to her father*). For Pim.

657 **Mr. Frank.** Anneke . . . I wasn't supposed to have a present! (*He takes it, unfolding it and showing it to the others.*)

ANALYZE DRAMA

Annotate: In the stage directions, mark the gift that Anne gives her father.

Connect: How is the scarf connected to Act One, Scene 1? Why is it important for the audience to make this connection?

EL **ENGLISH LEARNER SUPPORT**

Read Closely Help students make the connection by directing them to turn to paragraph 11 of Scene 1. Ask what Mr. Frank does in this part of the scene. (*takes the scarf hanging from the nail and wraps it around his neck*) Then read paragraphs 657–659 to students. Have them complete this statement: *The _____ in Scene 1 is the one that _____ gives _____ for a present.* (*scarf; Anne; Mr. Frank*) **MODERATE**

ANALYZE DRAMA

Point out that **stage directions** can provide important information that links scenes in a play. Have students reread the stage directions in paragraph 11 of Scene 1, and discuss the significance of the scarf in the play.

(**Answer:** *The handmade scarf that Anne gives to her father for Hanukkah in Scene 3 is the same scarf that Mr. Frank puts around his neck in Scene 1. It explains why the scarf is meaningful to Mr. Frank after the war and why he saves it when he returns to the annex.*)

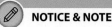

658 **Anne.** It's a muffler . . . to put round your neck . . . like an ascot, you know. I made it myself out of odds and ends . . . I knitted it in the dark each night, after I'd gone to bed. I'm afraid it looks better in the dark!

659 **Mr. Frank** (*putting it on*). It's fine. It fits me perfectly. Thank you, Annele.

660 (*Anne hands Peter a ball of paper, with a string attached to it.*)

661 **Anne.** That's for Mouschi.

662 **Peter** (*rising to bow*). On behalf of Mouschi, I thank you.

663 **Anne** (*hesitant, handing him a gift*). And . . . this is yours . . . from Mrs. Quack Quack. (*as he holds it gingerly in his hands*) Well . . . open it . . . Aren't you going to open it?

664 **Peter.** I'm scared to. I know something's going to jump out and hit me.

665 **Anne.** No. It's nothing like that, really.

666 **Mrs. Van Daan** (*as he is opening it*). What is it, Peter? Go on. Show it.

667 **Anne** (*excitedly*). It's a safety razor!

668 **Dussel.** A what?

669 **Anne.** A razor!

670 **Mrs. Van Daan** (*looking at it*). You didn't make that out of odds and ends.

671 **Anne** (*to Peter*). Miep got it for me. It's not new. It's second-hand. But you really do need a razor now.

672 **Dussel.** For what?

673 **Anne.** Look on his upper lip . . . you can see the beginning of a mustache.

674 **Dussel.** He wants to get rid of that? Put a little milk on it and let the cat lick it off.

675 **Peter** (*starting for his room*). Think you're funny, don't you.

676 **Dussel.** Look! He can't wait! He's going in to try it!

677 **Peter.** I'm going to give Mouschi his present! (*He goes into his room, slamming the door behind him.*)

678 **Mr. Van Daan** (*disgustedly*). Mouschi, Mouschi, Mouschi.

679 (*In the distance we hear a dog persistently barking. Anne brings a gift to Dussel.*)

680 **Anne.** And last but never least, my roommate, Mr. Dussel.

 ENGLISH LEARNER SUPPORT

Analyze Language Display paragraph 663. Highlight *hesitant* and *gingerly*.

- Tell students that *hesitant* means "uncertain" or "slow to act." Demonstrate Anne being hesitant about giving the package to Peter. Work with students to identify reasons why she might feel this way. **SUBSTANTIAL**

- Read the lines aloud. Explain the definitions of *hesitant* ("uncertain" or "slow to act") and *gingerly* ("cautiously, with great care").

Ask volunteers to act out the parts. Then have students write a sentence explaining why they both act this way. **MODERATE**

- Remind students that words with the same meaning may have different connotations. Define *hesitant* and *gingerly*. Then ask pairs to replace *hesitant* with *doubtful* and *gingerly* with *carefully*. Ask them to discuss how the changes affect their understanding of Anne's and Peter's actions. (**Possible response:** *Doubtful is more negative than hesitant. Carefully is more positive than gingerly.*) **LIGHT**

681 **Dussel.** For me? You have something for me? (*He opens the small box she gives him.*)

682 **Anne.** I made them myself.

683 **Dussel** (*puzzled*). Capsules! Two capsules!

684 **Anne.** They're ear-plugs!

685 **Dussel.** Ear-plugs?

686 **Anne.** To put in your ears so you won't hear me when I thrash around at night. I saw them advertised in a magazine. They're not real ones . . . I made them out of cotton and candle wax. Try them . . . See if they don't work . . . see if you can hear me talk . . .

687 **Dussel** (*putting them in his ears*). Wait now until I get them in . . . so.

688 **Anne.** Are you ready?

689 **Dussel.** Huh?

690 **Anne.** Are you ready?

691 **Dussel.** Good God! They've gone inside! I can't get them out! (*They laugh as* Mr. Dussel *jumps about, trying to shake the plugs out of his ears. Finally he gets them out. Putting them away.*) Thank you, Anne! Thank you!

692 **Mr. Van Daan.** A real Hanukkah! ⎫
693 **Mrs. Van Daan.** Wasn't it cute of her? ⎬ *Together*
694 **Mrs. Frank.** I don't know when she did it. ⎟
695 **Margot.** I love my present. ⎭

696 **Anne** (*sitting at the table*). And now let's have the song, Father . . . please . . . (*to* Dussel) Have you heard the Hanukkah song, Mr. Dussel? The song is the whole thing! (*She sings.*) "Oh, Hanukkah! Oh Hanukkah! The sweet celebration . . ."

697 **Mr. Frank** (*quieting her*). I'm afraid, Anne, we shouldn't sing that song tonight. (*to* Dussel) It's a song of jubilation, of rejoicing. One is apt to become too enthusiastic.

698 **Anne.** Oh, please, please. Let's sing the song. I promise not to shout!

699 **Mr. Frank.** Very well. But quietly now . . . I'll keep an eye on you and when . . .

700 (*As* Anne *starts to sing, she is interrupted by* Dussel, *who is snorting and wheezing.*)

701 **Dussel** (*pointing to* Peter). You . . . You! (Peter *is coming from his bedroom,* **ostentatiously** *holding a bulge in his coat as if he*

ostentatiously
(ŏs′tĕn-tā′shəs-lē) *adv.*
Someone who does something *ostentatiously* acts in an exaggerated way in order to attract attention.

The Diary of Anne Frank: Act One   455

TEACH

CRITICAL VOCABULARY

ostentatiously: Peter is coming from his bedroom, very obviously holding a bulge in his coat as if he were holding his cat, and dangling Anne's present before it.

ASK STUDENTS why Peter ostentatiously pretends that he is holding his cat. (*He is playing a joke on everyone.*)

ENGLISH LEARNER SUPPORT

Read Closely Have students reread paragraphs 704–716 to draw conclusions about Mr. Van Daan. Ask what they can infer about Mr. Van Daan from the words he speaks to Peter and to Mr. Dussel. (**Possible answer:** *Mr. Van Daan is very direct and isn't afraid to say just what he thinks. His thoughts can be based more on emotion than on facts and logic: "Don't tell me! He gets fatter every day! Damn cat looks better than any of us." His threat to get rid of Peter's cat and to allow Peter himself to leave show that he is not an understanding or supportive parent.*)

LIGHT

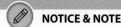

were holding his cat, and dangling Anne's *present before it.*) How many times . . . I told you . . . Out! Out!

702 **Mr. Van Daan** (*going to* Peter). What's the matter with you? Haven't you any sense? Get that cat out of here.

703 **Peter** (*innocently*). Cat?

704 **Mr. Van Daan.** You heard me. Get it out of here!

705 **Peter.** I have no cat. (*Delighted with his joke, he opens his coat and pulls out a bath towel. The group at the table laugh, enjoying the joke.*)

706 **Dussel** (*still wheezing*). It doesn't need to be the cat . . . his clothes are enough . . . when he comes out of that room . . .

707 **Mr. Van Daan.** Don't worry. You won't be bothered any more. We're getting rid of it.

708 **Dussel.** At last you listen to me. (*He goes off into his bedroom.*)

709 **Mr. Van Daan** (*calling after him*). I'm not doing it for you. That's all in your mind . . . all of it! (*He starts back to his place at the table.*) I'm doing it because I'm sick of seeing that cat eat all our food.

710 **Peter.** That's not true! I only give him bones . . . scraps . . .

711 **Mr. Van Daan.** Don't tell me! He gets fatter every day! Damn cat looks better than any of us. Out he goes tonight!

712 **Peter.** No! No!

713 **Anne.** Mr. Van Daan, you can't do that! That's Peter's cat.

714 **Mrs. Frank** (*quietly*). Anne.

715 **Peter** (*to* Mr. Van Daan). If he goes, I go.

716 **Mr. Van Daan.** Go! Go!

717 **Mrs. Van Daan.** You're not going and the cat's not going! Now please . . . this is Hanukkah . . . Hanukkah . . . this is the time to celebrate . . . What's the matter with all of you? Come on, Anne. Let's have the song.

718 **Anne** (*singing*). "Oh, Hanukkah! Oh, Hanukkah! The sweet celebration."

719 **Mr. Frank** (*rising*). I think we should first blow out the candle . . . then we'll have something for tomorrow night.

720 **Margot.** But, Father, you're supposed to let it burn itself out.

721 **Mr. Frank.** I'm sure that God understands shortages. (*before*

blowing it out) "Praised be Thou, oh Lord our God, who hast sustained us and permitted us to celebrate this joyous festival."

722 (*He is about to blow out the candle when* <u>suddenly there is a crash of something falling below.</u> *They all freeze in horror, motionless. For a few seconds there is complete silence. Mr. Frank* slips off his shoes. *The others noiselessly follow his example. Mr. Frank* turns out a light near him. He motions to Peter *to turn off the center lamp. Peter* tries to reach it, realizes he cannot and gets up on a chair. Just as he is touching the lamp he loses his balance. The chair goes out from under him. He falls. The iron lamp shade crashes to the floor. *There is a sound of feet below, running down the stairs.*)

723 **Mr. Van Daan** (*under his breath*). God Almighty! (*The only light left comes from the Hanukkah candle. Dussel* comes from his room. *Mr. Frank* creeps over to the stairwell and stands listening. The dog is heard barking excitedly.) Do you hear anything?

724 **Mr. Frank** (*in a whisper*). No. I think they've gone.

725 **Mrs. Van Daan.** It's the Green Police. They've found us.

726 **Mr. Frank.** If they had, they wouldn't have left. They'd be up here by now.

727 **Mrs. Van Daan.** I know it's the Green Police. They've gone to get help. That's all. They'll be back!

728 **Mr. Van Daan.** Or it may have been the Gestapo,[20] looking for papers . . .

729 **Mr. Frank** (*interrupting*). Or a thief, looking for money.

730 **Mrs. Van Daan.** We've got to do something . . . Quick! Quick! Before they come back.

731 **Mr. Van Daan.** There isn't anything to do. Just wait.

732 (*Mr. Frank* holds up his hand for them to be quiet. He is listening intently. There is complete silence as they all strain to hear any sound from below. Suddenly Anne *begins to sway. With a low cry she falls to the floor in a faint. Mrs. Frank* goes to her quickly, sitting beside her on the floor and taking her in her arms.)

733 **Mrs. Frank.** Get some water, please! Get some water!

734 (*Margot starts for the sink.*)

735 **Mr. Van Daan** (*grabbing* Margot). No! No! No one's going to run water!

736 **Mr. Frank.** If they've found us, they've found us. Get the water.

---

[20]**Gestapo** (gə-stä´pō): the Nazi secret police force, known for its terrorism and brutality.

ANALYZE PLOT DEVELOPMENT

Annotate: Reread the stage directions in paragraph 722 and identify two key events—one downstairs and one in the Annex. Underline details describing the sounds downstairs and circle details about what causes noise in the Annex.

Cause and Effect: What has just happened? What effects could these events have on future events in the plot?

ANALYZE PLOT DEVELOPMENT

Remind students that the series of events in a story or play is called the **plot**. Explain that **stage directions** in a play may describe a key event in the plot. (**Answer:** *The residents of the annex suddenly hear a crashing noise downstairs, although nobody should be there. Immediately afterward, Peter falls off a chair and knocks over a lamp shade as he's turning off the center lamp. The residents then hear the sound of running feet below. They fear that someone downstairs has heard the noise that could potentially lead to future discovery and arrest.*)

ENGLISH LEARNER SUPPORT

Understand Text Structure Explain that identifying cause-and-effect relationships can clarify the plot or help predict what might occur.

- Draw a cause-and-effect chain on the board. Work with students to record the events in paragraph 722. Ask students whether each event is a cause, an effect, or both. (*Cause: The residents hear a crash below; effect/cause: Peter tries to turn off the light; effect/cause: He knocks over the lamp shade, making a loud noise; effect: whoever is below now knows that there are people upstairs.*) **SUBSTANTIAL**

- Have pairs write four sentences explaining the causes and effects in paragraph 722. Encourage them to think of longer-term effects by using words such as *because, as a result of,* and *consequently* to show the relationships among events. Have them share their sentences in small groups. **MODERATE**

- Have students reread paragraph 722 and write sentences explaining how the events will create or affect conflicts. Ask them to read their sentences aloud. **LIGHT**

TEACH

ENGLISH LEARNER SUPPORT

Read Closely Have students reread paragraphs 750–755 with a partner.

- Ask them why Mr. Frank has gone downstairs into the office. *(to find out who made the noise as they have no idea if someone has discovered their hiding place or if it's an isolated event)*

- Have students then explain what Mr. Van Daan is doing while Mr. Frank investigates. *(He pushes his wife and Peter out of the way and yells at them and Anne. He has no intention of going downstairs.)*

- Discuss how the contrast in the behaviors of Mr. Frank and Mr. Van Daan helps define their characters more clearly. *(Mr. Frank is courageous and concerned for others. He is a natural leader. Mr. Van Daan is concerned only for himself. He is too selfish to put himself in danger for the sake of the group.)* **LIGHT**

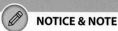

NOTICE & NOTE

(Margot *starts again for the sink.* Mr. Frank, *getting a flashlight*) I'm going down.

737 (Margot *rushes to him, clinging to him.* Anne *struggles to consciousness.*)

738 **Margot.** No, Father, no! There may be someone there, waiting . . . It may be a trap!

739 **Mr. Frank.** This is Saturday. There is no way for us to know what has happened until Miep or Mr. Kraler comes on Monday morning. We cannot live with this uncertainty.

740 **Margot.** Don't go, Father!

741 **Mrs. Frank.** Hush, darling, hush. (Mr. Frank *slips quietly out, down the steps and out through the door below.*) Margot! Stay
742 close to me.

743 (Margot *goes to her mother.*)

744 **Mr. Van Daan.** Shush! Shush!

745 (Mrs. Frank *whispers to* Margot *to get the water.* Margot *goes for it.*)

746 **Mrs. Van Daan.** Putti, where's our money? Get our money. I hear you can buy the Green Police off, so much a head. Go upstairs quick! Get the money!

747 **Mr. Van Daan.** Keep still!

748 **Mrs. Van Daan** (*kneeling before him, pleading*). Do you want to be dragged off to a concentration camp? Are you going to stand there and wait for them to come up and get you? Do something, I tell you!

749 **Mr. Van Daan** (*pushing her aside*). Will you keep still! (He goes over to the stairwell to listen. Peter *goes to his mother, helping her up onto the sofa. There is a second of silence, then* Anne *can stand it no longer.*)

750 **Anne.** Someone go after Father! Make Father come back!

751 **Peter** (*starting for the door*). I'll go.

752 **Mr. Van Daan.** Haven't you done enough?

753 (He pushes Peter *roughly away. In his anger against his father* Peter *grabs a chair as if to hit him with it, then puts it down, burying his face in his hands.* Mrs. Frank *begins to pray softly.*)

754 **Anne.** Please, please, Mr. Van Daan. Get Father.

755 **Mr. Van Daan.** Quiet! Quiet!

756 (Anne *is shocked into silence.* Mrs. Frank *pulls her closer, holding her protectively in her arms.*)

458   Unit 6

IMPROVE READING FLUENCY

Targeted Passage Project paragraphs 749–755. Read the dialogue and the stage directions aloud and discuss what the stage directions reveal about the characters' actions and the way in which the lines should be spoken.

- Organize students into groups of three. Ask them to decide on a passage to read aloud that is about 15 to 20 lines long and has three parts. Tell them that they will each read a character's part, following any stage directions.

- Have each group practice its passage as you listen. Help students work on pronunciation and expression as well as pace.

- Then have groups do their readings for the class.

- As a class, discuss how hearing the lines read aloud helps them better understand the characters and the events.

 Go to the **Reading Studio** for additional support in developing fluency.

757 **Mrs. Frank** (*softly, praying*). "I lift up mine eyes unto the mountains, from whence cometh my help. My help cometh from the Lord who made heaven and earth. He will not suffer thy foot to be moved . . . He that keepeth thee will not slumber . . ." (*She stops as she hears someone coming. They all watch the door tensely.* Mr. Frank *comes quietly in.* Anne *rushes to him, holding him tight.*)

758 **Mr. Frank.** It was a thief. That noise must have scared him away.

759 **Mrs. Van Daan.** Thank God.

760 **Mr. Frank.** He took the cash box. And the radio. He ran away in such a hurry that he didn't stop to shut the street door. It was swinging wide open. (*A breath of relief sweeps over them.*) I think it would be good to have some light.

761 **Margot.** Are you sure it's all right?

762 **Mr. Frank.** The danger has passed. (Margot *goes to light the small lamp.*) Don't be so terrified, Anne. We're safe.

763 **Dussel.** Who says the danger has passed? Don't you realize we are in greater danger than ever?

764 **Mr. Frank.** Mr. Dussel, will you be still!

765 (Mr. Frank *takes* Anne *back to the table, making her sit down with him, trying to calm her.*)

766 **Dussel** (*pointing to* Peter). Thanks to this clumsy fool, there's someone now who knows we're up here! Someone now knows we're up here, hiding!

767 **Mrs. Van Daan** (*going to* Dussel). Someone knows we're here, yes. But who is the someone? A thief! A thief! You think a thief is going to go to the Green Police and say . . . I was robbing a place the other night and I heard a noise up over my head? You think a thief is going to do that?

768 **Dussel.** Yes. I think he will.

769 **Mrs. Van Daan** (*hysterically*). You're crazy! (*She stumbles back to her seat at the table.* Peter *follows protectively, pushing* Dussel *aside.*)

770 **Dussel.** I think some day he'll be caught and then he'll make a bargain with the Green Police . . . if they'll let him off, he'll tell them where some Jews are hiding!

771 (*He goes off into the bedroom. There is a second of* **appalled** *silence.*)

772 **Mr. Van Daan.** He's right.

ANALYZE PLOT DEVELOPMENT

Annotate: In paragraphs 758–768, underline Mr. Frank's explanation for what caused the noise downstairs. Circle Mr. Dussel's fears about what will happen as a result of this.

Predict: Remember that when a writer hints at future events, it is called foreshadowing. Do you think the playwrights are foreshadowing what will actually happen in the future—that the Annex residents will be caught because of the thief? Explain your prediction.

appalled
(ə-pôld´) *adj.* To be *appalled* is to feel horror and shock about something.

ANALYZE PLOT DEVELOPMENT

Remind students that **foreshadowing** is when a writer provides hints of future events. In this scene, foreshadowing creates suspense and makes readers eager to find out whether the characters will be discovered hiding in the annex. (**Possible answer:** *The playwrights may be foreshadowing what will actually happen—after all, someone probably discovers the people in the annex; that would explain why Mr. Frank returns by himself several years later. On the other hand, it's also possible that the thief will never be caught. It could be that the playwrights just want to create tension in the plot.*)

CRITICAL VOCABULARY

appalled: There is a second of shocked and stunned silence as everyone realizes the danger they face.

ASK STUDENTS why the characters would be appalled at this moment of the play. (*They realize that Mr. Dussel may be correct—that they are now in great danger.*)

ANALYZE DRAMA

Remind students again of the importance of reading the **stage directions** while reading a play. Dialogue alone will not convey the mood or significance of a scene. The stage directions explain the emotions of the characters, as well as their physical actions on stage. (**Answer:** *When Mr. Frank and Anne begin singing, Anne's voice is very quiet. The others join in, and it's clear from their voices that they're very afraid. But gradually the characters "sing on with growing courage." The playwrights do this to suggest that the characters are recovering from their fear. They are gaining comfort and courage from one another and from the song they are singing.*)

ANALYZE DRAMA

Annotate: Review paragraphs 776–785. Mark details in the stage directions that reveal how the characters sing the Hanukkah song.

Interpret: How does the gradual change in the way the characters are singing reveal their feelings? How does this change affect the mood, or emotional atmosphere, at the end of Act One?

773 **Anne.** Father, let's get out of here! We can't stay here now . . . Let's go . . .

774 **Mr. Van Daan.** Go! Where?

775 **Mrs. Frank** (*sinking into her chair at the table*). Yes. Where?

776 **Mr. Frank** (*rising, to them all*). Have we lost all faith? All courage? A moment ago we thought that they'd come for us. We were sure it was the end. But it wasn't the end. We're alive, safe. (Mr. Van Daan *goes to the table and sits.* Mr. Frank *prays.*) "We thank Thee, oh Lord our God, that in Thy infinite mercy Thou hast again seen fit to spare us." (*He blows out the candle, then turns to* Anne.) Come on, Anne. The song! Let's have the song! (*He starts to sing.* Anne *finally starts falteringly to sing, as* Mr. Frank *urges her on. Her voice is hardly audible at first.*)

777 **Anne** (*singing*). "Oh, Hanukkah! Oh, Hanukkah! The sweet . . . celebration . . . " (*As she goes on singing, the others gradually join in, their voices still shaking with fear.* Mrs. Van Daan *sobs as she sings.*)

778 **Group.** "Around the feast . . . we . . . gather
In complete . . . jubilation . . .
Happiest of sea . . . sons
Now is here. Many are the reasons for good cheer."

779 (Dussel *comes from the bedroom. He comes over to the table, standing beside* Margot, *listening to them as they sing.*)

780 "Together
We'll weather
Whatever tomorrow may bring."

781 (*As they sing on with growing courage, the lights start to dim.*)

782 "So hear us rejoicing
And merrily voicing
The Hanukkah song that we sing.
Hoy!"

783 (*The lights are out. The curtain starts slowly to fall.*)

784 "Hear us rejoicing
And merrily voicing
The Hanukkah song that we sing."

785 (*They are still singing, as the curtain falls.*)

786 *The Curtain Falls.*

CHECK YOUR UNDERSTANDING

Answer these questions before moving on to the **Analyze the Text** section on the following page.

1 A major difference in Mr. Frank between Scene 1 and Scene 2 is that in Scene 1, —

A he feels gratitude for the help provided by Miep Gies

B he is overwhelmed by a mix of grief and bitterness

C he wishes that he had taken his family out of Amsterdam

D he is haunted by memories of life in a concentration camp

2 In Act One, the dialogue between Anne and Peter reveals that —

F they have a number of things in common

G they did not have many friends when they were at school

H Anne looks up to Peter because he is a few years older

J Anne is lively and sociable, but Peter is shy and awkward

3 The arrival of Mr. Dussel increases tension because —

A the Annex residents do not trust strangers

B Dussel insists on having his own room

C Dussel is not used to being around children

D there is barely enough food for everyone

The Diary of Anne Frank: Act One 461

CHECK YOUR UNDERSTANDING

1. *D*

2. *J*

3. *D*

If they answer any questions incorrectly, have them reread the text to confirm their understanding. Then they may proceed to ANALYZE THE TEXT on page 462.

 ENGLISH LEARNER SUPPORT

Oral Assessment Use the following questions to assess students' comprehension and speaking skills:

1. How is Mr. Frank different in Scene 1 than he was in Scene 2? (*In Scene 1, he is haunted by memories of life in a concentration camp.*)

2. In Act One, what does the dialogue between Anne and Peter reveal? (*Anne is lively and sociable, but Peter is shy and awkward.*)

3. Why does the arrival of Mr. Dussel increase tension? (*There is barely enough food for everyone.*)

ALL LEVELS

ANALYZE THE TEXT

Possible answers:

1. **DOK 2:** *There are five scenes in Act One. They began a new scene because the time has changed, and they are going to tell about a new episode in the plot.*

2. **DOK 3:** *Mr. Van Daan is narrow-minded and traditional in his views. Anne is idealistic, hopeful, and forward thinking. Mrs. Van Daan is materialistic.*

3. **DOK 4:** *Students may identify one or more of the following subplots: the relationship between Anne and Peter (conflict arises due to their different personalities); how Mr. Dussel will fit in with the others at the annex (conflict arises between Mr. Van Daan and Mr. Dussel due to food rations); whether Anne and Mr. Dussel can get along (conflict arises due to their different ages and personalities); what will become of Peter's cat (conflict arises because Mr. Van Daan doesn't like the cat and threatens to get rid of it).*

4. **DOK 2:** *The arrival of Mr. Dussel heightens the tension in the annex, causing additional strains on food and space. Mr. Dussel explains that Jews in Amsterdam are disappearing. He is a loner who has difficulty adjusting to living with children and other adults. He is allergic to Peter's cat.*

5. **DOK 4:** *Many people act in contradictory ways—it is part of human nature. In addition, Anne is in between being a child and a woman. Her mother tries to teach her things, but Anne has opinions of her own and the two often argue. Anne is learning to balance her own will with the feelings of others.*

MAKE PREDICTIONS

Tell students that making predictions involves thinking about what will happen next. It involves making an educated guess based on what has occurred thus far. To help students make their predictions, ask them to consider the major plot points in Act One and what they already know about this era in history.

RESPOND

ANALYZE THE TEXT

Support your responses with evidence from the text. 📓 NOTEBOOK

1. **Identify Patterns** How many scenes are there in Act One of this play? Why might the playwrights have begun a new scene after paragraph 178?

2. **Draw Conclusions** Examine paragraphs 351–363. What do the stage directions and dialogue reveal about the characters?

3. **Analyze** What subplot or subplots have the playwrights introduced in Act One? For each subplot you identify, what is the conflict?

4. **Cause/Effect** Plot events are often related by cause and effect; that is, one event causes something else to happen. How does the arrival of Mr. Dussel affect life in the Annex?

5. **Notice & Note** Review paragraph 589. What might explain the contradictions in Anne's feelings and behavior toward her mother?

MAKE PREDICTIONS

Predicting is a reading strategy that involves using text clues to make a reasonable guess about what will happen next in a story. To make predictions, think about what events have already taken place. Also consider how the plot is developing. What events, if any, have been foreshadowed? Is there rising tension between characters? Are there certain actions or events—either in the main plot or in a subplot—that you predict will have certain effects, or consequences?

Based on what you have read, make predictions about what will happen in Act Two. Record your predictions in the chart. Then, as you read Act Two, note which predictions are confirmed by the text, and correct those predictions that did not come true.

MY PREDICTION	WHAT HAPPENS

ENGLISH LEARNER SUPPORT

Exchange Ideas Adapt the collection opener strategy, Think-Write-Pair-Share, to help students review Act One before beginning Act Two.

First, tell students that they are going to summarize Act One. Review that a summary includes only the most important events and details.

Then, have students review Act One and take notes about characters, plot, and setting. Have them outline their summaries.

Next, have students share their outlines with partners, asking clarifying questions as they discuss organization and content. **Then have pairs collaborate on a summary that reflects both of their inputs.**

Finally, have students share their summaries with the entire class. **MODERATE/LIGHT**

ACT TWO
Scene 1

1 *In the darkness we hear* Anne's Voice, *again reading from the diary.*

2 **Anne's Voice.** <u>Saturday, the first of January, nineteen forty-four.</u> Another new year has begun and we find ourselves still in our hiding place. We have been here now for one year, five months and twenty-five days. It seems that our life is at a standstill.

3 *The curtain rises on the scene. It is late afternoon. Everyone is bundled up against the cold. In the main room* Mrs. Frank *is taking down the laundry which is hung across the back.* Mr. Frank *sits in the chair down left, reading.* Margot *is lying on the couch with a blanket over her and the many-colored knitted scarf around her throat.* Anne *is seated at the center table, writing in her diary.* Peter, Mr. *and* Mrs. Van Daan, *and* Dussel *are all in their own rooms, reading or lying down.*

4 *As the lights dim on,* Anne's Voice *continues, without a break.*

5 **Anne's Voice.** We are all a little thinner. The Van Daans' "discussions" are as violent as ever. Mother still does not understand me. But then I don't understand her either. There is one great change, however. A change in myself. I read somewhere that girls of my age don't feel quite certain of themselves. That they become quiet within and begin to think of the miracle that is taking place in their bodies. I think that what is happening to me is so wonderful . . . not only what can be seen, but what is taking place inside. Each time it has happened I have a feeling that I have a sweet secret. (*We hear the chimes and then a hymn being played on the carillon outside.*) And in spite of any pain, I long for the time when I shall feel that secret within me again.

6 (*The buzzer of the door below suddenly sounds. Everyone is startled,* Mr. Frank *tiptoes cautiously to the top of the steps and listens. Again the buzzer sounds, in* Miep's *V-for-Victory signal.*)

7 **Mr. Frank.** It's Miep! (*He goes quickly down the steps to unbolt the door.* Mrs. Frank *calls upstairs to the* Van Daans *and then to* Peter.)

8 **Mrs. Frank.** Wake up, everyone! Miep is here! (Anne *quickly puts her diary away.* Margot *sits up, pulling the blanket around her shoulders.* Mr. Dussel *sits on the edge of his bed, listening, disgruntled.* Miep *comes up the steps, followed by* Mr. Kraler.

ANALYZE DRAMA

Annotate: Mark the date of Anne's diary entry at the beginning of Act Two, Scene 1.

Draw Conclusions: How much time has passed between the end of Act One and the beginning of Act Two? What does this suggest about the suspected thief who may have heard noise from the Annex?

ANALYZE DRAMA

Remind students that plays are divided into **acts**, which are large sections of the plot in the story, and **scenes** are smaller parts of the plot that take place in a specific time and place. Point out that a new act and scene begin at this point, signaling a change in the time of the action. (**Answer:** *The residents celebrated their first Hanukkah in in the annex in December 1942, and now it is January 1944. Just over a year has passed between the end of Act One and the beginning of Act Two. This suggests that if there was a thief, he or she has not revealed to police that there was noise upstairs.*)

TEXT IN FOCUS

Understanding Setting Have students view the **Text in Focus** video on this page of their eBook to learn how to understand setting. Then have students use the Text in Focus Practice to apply what they have learned.

EL ENGLISH LEARNER SUPPORT

Read Closely Tell students that adverbs modify, or describe, verbs. Point out that adverbs ending in *-ly* tell how something is done; this kind of adverb is often found in stage directions. Work with students to highlight *-ly* adverbs and the verbs they modify. Make sure students understand the meaning of each.
SUBSTANTIAL

⚙ LEARNING MINDSET

Persistence Remind students that they will grow as learners if they have a "stick to it" attitude and don't give up on challenging tasks. They should find enough stamina to complete even the most difficult assignment, and they shouldn't quit until they have finished the assignment.

They bring flowers, books, newspapers, etc. Anne *rushes to* Miep, *throwing her arms affectionately around her.*) Miep . . . *and* Mr. Kraler . . . What a delightful surprise!

9 **Mr. Kraler.** We came to bring you New Year's greetings.

10 **Mrs. Frank.** You shouldn't . . . you should have at least one day to yourselves. (*She goes quickly to the stove and brings down teacups and tea for all of them.*)

11 **Anne.** Don't say that, it's so wonderful to see them! (*sniffing at* Miep's *coat*) I can smell the wind and the cold on your clothes.

12 **Miep** (*giving her the flowers*). There you are. (*then to* Margot, *feeling her forehead*) How are you, Margot? . . . Feeling any better?

13 **Margot.** I'm all right.

14 **Anne.** We filled her full of every kind of pill so she won't cough and make a noise. (*She runs into her room to put the flowers in water.* Mr. *and* Mrs. Van Daan *come from upstairs. Outside there is the sound of a band playing.*)

15 **Mrs. Van Daan.** Well, hello, Miep. Mr. Kraler.

16 **Mr. Kraler** (*giving a bouquet of flowers to* Mrs. Van Daan). With my hope for peace in the New Year.

17 **Peter** (*anxiously*). Miep, have you seen Mouschi? Have you seen him anywhere around?

18 **Miep.** I'm sorry, Peter. I asked everyone in the neighborhood had they seen a gray cat. But they said no.

19 (Mrs. Frank *gives* Miep *a cup of tea.* Mr. Frank *comes up the steps, carrying a small cake on a plate.*)

20 **Mr. Frank.** Look what Miep's brought for us!

21 **Mrs. Frank** (*taking it*). A cake!

22 **Mr. Van Daan.** A cake! (*He pinches* Miep's *cheeks gaily and hurries up to the cupboard.*) I'll get some plates.

23 (Dussel, *in his room, hastily puts a coat on and starts out to join the others.*)

24 **Mrs. Frank.** Thank you, Miepia. You shouldn't have done it. You must have used all of your sugar ration for weeks. (*giving it to* Mrs. Van Daan) It's beautiful, isn't it?

25 **Mrs. Van Daan.** It's been ages since I even saw a cake. Not since you brought us one last year. (*without looking at the cake, to* Miep) Remember? Don't you remember, you gave us one on New Year's Day? Just this time last year? I'll never forget it

ENGLISH LEARNER SUPPORT

Use Nouns and Verbs Tell students that some words can function as either a noun or a verb. Point out the word *ration* in paragraph 24. Explain that it is a noun in this sentence and means "a fixed or specific amount." Write these words from the play on the board: *smell, ration, cough.* Explain that they can be used as nouns or as verbs. Ask pairs of students to write sentences for each function of the three words. **SUBSTANTIAL/MODERATE**

because you had "Peace in nineteen forty-three" on it. (*She looks at the cake and reads.*) "Peace in nineteen forty-four!"

26 **Miep.** Well, it has to come sometime, you know. (*as Dussel comes from his room*) Hello, Mr. Dussel.

27 **Mr. Kraler.** How are you?

28 **Mr. Van Daan** (*bringing plates and a knife*). Here's the knife, *liefje*. Now, how many of us are there?

29 **Miep.** None for me, thank you.

30 **Mr. Frank.** Oh, please. You must.

31 **Miep.** I couldn't.

32 **Mr. Van Daan.** Good! That leaves one . . . two . . . three . . . seven of us.

33 **Dussel.** Eight! Eight! It's the same number as it always is!

34 **Mr. Van Daan.** I left Margot out. I take it for granted Margot won't eat any.

35 **Anne.** Why wouldn't she!

36 **Mrs. Frank.** I think it won't harm her.

37 **Mr. Van Daan.** All right! All right! I just didn't want her to start coughing again, that's all.

38 **Dussel.** And please, Mrs. Frank should cut the cake.

39 **Mr. Van Daan.** What's the difference? ⎫
40 **Mrs. Van Daan.** It's not Mrs. Frank's cake, is it, Miep? It's for all of us. ⎬ *Together*
 ⎭

41 **Dussel.** Mrs. Frank divides things better.

42 **Mrs. Van Daan** (*going to Dussel*). What are you trying to say? ⎫
 ⎬ *Together*
43 **Mr. Van Daan.** Oh, come on! Stop wasting time! ⎭

44 **Mrs. Van Daan** (*to Dussel*). Don't I always give everybody exactly the same? Don't I?

45 **Mr. Van Daan.** Forget it, Kerli.

46 **Mrs. Van Daan.** No. I want an answer! Don't I?

47 **Dussel.** Yes. Yes. Everybody gets exactly the same . . . except Mr. Van Daan always gets a little bit more.

48 (Mr. Van Daan *advances on Dussel, the knife still in his hand.*)

49 **Mr. Van Daan.** That's a lie!

50 (Dussel *retreats before the onslaught of the* Van Daans.)

ANALYZE DRAMA

Annotate: Review paragraphs 38–51. Mark the lines that reveal who Mr. Dussel thinks should cut the cake and why.

Interpret: Think about Mr. and Mrs. Van Daan's reaction to Dussel's comments, and what Mr. Frank says. What does the characters' dialogue reveal about them?

ANALYZE DRAMA

Remind students that the story in a play is told mainly through **dialogue** and that the words characters say and the way they say them helps readers analyze the characters throughout the story. (**Answer:** *Mr. Van Daan says, "That's a lie!"; he is self-centered and has a temper. Mrs. Van Daan says, "Don't I always give everybody exactly the same? Don't I?"; she is petty and defensive. Mr. Frank says, "You see what a little sugar cake does to us?" because he is a peacemaker; he doesn't want to lay guilt at anyone's door.*)

■ English Learner Support

Analyze Drama Have students work with a partner to complete the activity above. Have them highlight each character's comments and then take turns describing him or her based on the dialogue. Encourage students to ask each other clarifying questions and present their inferences using these sentence frames:

- *Mr. Van Daan's comments suggest that he ___.*
- *Mrs. Van Daan's reaction suggests that she ___.*
- *Mr. Frank's remarks suggest that he ___.*

EL ENGLISH LEARNER SUPPORT

Understand Text Structure Remind students that conflict is the struggle between two forces. Explain that characters may struggle with their own feelings or with someone or something else.

Have students explain the conflicts they find on pages 464–465. Ask them which are new conflicts and which are continued from Act One. Then have them discuss how these conflicts relate to the characters' main conflict. **LIGHT**

NOTICE & NOTE

51 **Mr. Frank.** Please, please! (*then to* Miep) You see what a little sugar cake does to us? It goes right to our heads!

52 **Mr. Van Daan** (*handing* Mrs. Frank *the knife*). Here you are, Mrs. Frank.

53 **Mrs. Frank.** Thank you. (*then to* Miep *as she goes to the table to cut the cake*) Are you sure you won't have some?

54 **Miep** (*drinking her tea*). No, really, I have to go in a minute.

55 (*The sound of the band fades out in the distance.*)

56 **Peter** (*to* Miep). Maybe Mouschi went back to our house . . . they say that cats . . . Do you ever get over there . . . ? I mean . . . do you suppose you could . . . ?

57 **Miep.** I'll try, Peter. The first minute I get I'll try. But I'm afraid, with him gone a week . . .

58 **Dussel.** Make up your mind, already someone has had a nice big dinner from that cat!

inarticulate
(ĭn´är-tĭk´yə-lĭt) *adj.* Someone who is *inarticulate* is unable to speak in a clear way.

59 (Peter *is furious,* **inarticulate**. *He starts toward* Dussel *as if to hit him.* Mr. Frank *stops him.* Mrs. Frank *speaks quickly to ease the situation.*)

60 **Mrs. Frank** (*to* Miep). This is delicious, Miep!

61 **Mrs. Van Daan** (*eating hers*). Delicious!

62 **Mr. Van Daan** (*finishing it in one gulp*). Dirk's in luck to get a girl who can bake like this!

63 **Miep** (*putting down her empty teacup*). I have to run. Dirk's taking me to a party tonight.

64 **Anne.** How heavenly! Remember now what everyone is wearing, and what you have to eat and everything, so you can tell us tomorrow.

65 **Miep.** I'll give you a full report! Good-bye, everyone!

66 **Mr. Van Daan** (*to* Miep). Just a minute. There's something I'd like you to do for me. (*He hurries off up the stairs to his room.*)

67 **Mrs. Van Daan** (*sharply*). Putti, where are you going? (*She rushes up the stairs after him, calling hysterically.*) What do you want? Putti, what are you going to do?

68 **Miep** (*to* Peter). What's wrong?

69 **Peter** (*his sympathy is with his mother*). Father says he's going to sell her fur coat. She's crazy about that old fur coat.

70 **Dussel.** Is it possible? Is it possible that anyone is so silly as to worry about a fur coat in times like this?

CRITICAL VOCABULARY

inarticulate: Peter is so angry with Mr. Dussel, he is unable to speak.

ASK STUDENTS what Mr. Dussel says that causes Peter to be unable to speak in a clear way. (*Mr. Dussel says that Peter's lost cat has probably been eaten.*)

71 **Peter.** It's none of your darn business . . . and if you say one more thing . . . I'll, I'll take you and I'll . . . I mean it . . . I'll . . .

72 (*There is a piercing scream from* Mrs. Van Daan *above. She grabs at the fur coat as* Mr. Van Daan *is starting downstairs with it.*)

73 **Mrs. Van Daan.** No! No! No! Don't you dare take that! You hear? It's mine! (*Downstairs* Peter *turns away, embarrassed, miserable.*) My father gave me that! You didn't give it to me. You have no right. Let go of it . . . you hear?

74 (Mr. Van Daan *pulls the coat from her hands and hurries downstairs.* Mrs. Van Daan *sinks to the floor, sobbing. As* Mr. Van Daan *comes into the main room the others look away, embarrassed for him.*)

75 **Mr. Van Daan** (*to* Mr. Kraler). Just a little—discussion over the advisability of selling this coat. As I have often reminded Mrs. Van Daan, it's very selfish of her to keep it when people outside are in such desperate need of clothing . . . (*He gives the coat to* Miep.) So if you will please to sell it for us? It should fetch a good price. And by the way, will you get me cigarettes. I don't care what kind they are . . . get all you can.

76 **Miep.** It's terribly difficult to get them, Mr. Van Daan. But I'll try. Good-bye.

77 (*She goes.* Mr. Frank *follows her down the steps to bolt the door after her.* Mrs. Frank *gives* Mr. Kraler *a cup of tea.*)

78 **Mrs. Frank.** Are you sure you won't have some cake, Mr. Kraler?

79 **Mr. Kraler.** I'd better not.

80 **Mr. Van Daan.** You're still feeling badly? What does your doctor say?

81 **Mr. Kraler.** I haven't been to him.

82 **Mrs. Frank.** Now, Mr. Kraler! . . .

83 **Mr. Kraler** (*sitting at the table*). Oh, I tried. But you can't get near a doctor these days . . . they're so busy. After weeks I finally managed to get one on the telephone. I told him I'd like an appointment . . . I wasn't feeling very well. You know what he answers . . . over the telephone . . . Stick out your tongue! (*They laugh. He turns to* Mr. Frank *as* Mr. Frank *comes back.*) I have some contracts here . . . I wonder if you'd look over them with me . . .

84 **Mr. Frank** (*putting out his hand*). Of course.

85 **Mr. Kraler** (*He rises*). If we could go downstairs . . . (Mr. Frank *starts ahead,* Mr. Kraler *speaks to the others.*) Will you forgive

---

AGAIN AND AGAIN

Notice & Note: In paragraph 75, mark the word that Mr. Van Daan uses to refer to the quarrel he and his family have been having. Then look back at paragraph 331 from Act One.

Interpret: What have the Van Daans been arguing about? What is the impact of Mr. Van Daan's using the word *discussion* again rather than *quarrel*?

AGAIN AND AGAIN

Explain to students that this signpost is often used to emphasize ideas or reveal **character traits**. Have students identify the word Mr. Van Daan uses again and again to describe his quarrels. (***Answer:*** *Mr. and Mrs. Van Daan have been arguing about whether they should sell her fur coat. Mr. Van Daan tries to make the situation seem better than it is by calling it a discussion. His repetition of the word discussion shows that this is how Mr. and Mrs. Van Daan usually handle disagreements—they quarrel.*)

EL ENGLISH LEARNER SUPPORT

Read Closely Explain to students that symbols are objects that stand for something more than what they actually are.

- Tell students that Mrs. Van Daan's fur coat is a symbol. Remind them that her father gave it to her. Work with them to state what it represents to her. (*a time when she felt happy, safe, and secure*) **SUBSTANTIAL**

- Have small groups discuss the symbolism of the fur coat to Mrs. Van Daan. Have them share their ideas with the class. **MODERATE**

- Have students discuss what the fur coat symbolizes to Mrs. Van Daan. Then ask them to consider what the selling of it represents. (***Possible response:*** *The coat's loss symbolizes all that the Nazis took from those they persecuted—homes, possessions, security, and happiness.*). **LIGHT**

ANALYZE PLOT DEVELOPMENT

Guide students to understand that dialogue can propel the action in a play, moving the plot forward. Point out that sometimes dialogue increases tension and forces characters to make a decision. (**Answer:** *If Carl knows the Franks are hiding in the loft, he could report them. He may ask for more and more money to stay quiet. This problem complicates their situation. They do not know whether they have been discovered, and Mr. Frank will have to decide whether or not to pay Carl more money. The residents also have to figure out whether Carl is trying to blackmail them.*)

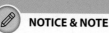

ENGLISH LEARNER SUPPORT

Confirm Understanding Tell students that blackmail is the practice of demanding money in exchange for keeping a secret. Guide students to identify the secret that Carl may know. (*that the Franks are living upstairs in the annex*) Work with them to underline the details that explain why Mr. Kraler thinks that Carl knows this information. **ALL LEVELS**

NOTICE & NOTE

us? I won't keep him but a minute. (*He starts to follow* Mr. Frank *down the steps.*)

86 **Margot** (*with sudden foreboding*). What's happened? Something's happened! Hasn't it, Mr. Kraler?

87 (Mr. Kraler *stops and comes back, trying to reassure* Margot *with a pretense of casualness.*)

88 **Mr. Kraler.** No, really. I want your father's advice . . .

89 **Margot.** Something's gone wrong! I know it!

90 **Mr. Frank** (*coming back, to* Mr. Kraler). If it's something that concerns us here, it's better that we all hear it.

91 **Mr. Kraler** (*turning to him, quietly*). But . . . the children . . . ?

92 **Mr. Frank.** What they'd imagine would be worse than any reality.

93 (As Mr. Kraler *speaks, they all listen with intense apprehension.* Mrs. Van Daan *comes down the stairs and sits on the bottom step.*)

94 **Mr. Kraler.** It's a man in the storeroom . . . I don't know whether or not you remember him . . . Carl, about fifty, heavy-set, near-sighted . . . He came with us just before you left.

95 **Mr. Frank.** He was from Utrecht?

96 **Mr. Kraler.** That's the man. A couple of weeks ago, when I was in the storeroom, he closed the door and asked me . . . how's Mr. Frank? What do you hear from Mr. Frank? I told him I only knew there was a rumor that you were in Switzerland. He said he'd heard that rumor too, but he thought I might know something more. I didn't pay any attention to it . . . but then a thing happened yesterday . . . He'd brought some invoices to the office for me to sign. As I was going through them, I looked up. He was standing staring at the bookcase . . . your bookcase. He said he thought he remembered a door there . . . Wasn't there a door there that used to go up to the loft? Then he told me he wanted more money. Twenty guilders[1] more a week.

97 **Mr. Van Daan.** Blackmail!

98 **Mr. Frank.** Twenty guilders? Very modest blackmail.

99 **Mr. Van Daan.** That's just the beginning.

100 **Dussel** (*coming to* Mr. Frank). You know what I think? He was the thief who was down there that night. That's how he knows we're here.

ANALYZE PLOT DEVELOPMENT

Annotate: Mark the problem that Mr. Kraler tells the group about in paragraphs 94–96.

Analyze: How does this problem affect the plot?

---

[1] **guilders** (gĭl´dərz): the basic monetary unit of the Netherlands at the time.

WHEN STUDENTS STRUGGLE . . .

Learning Strategy Help students understand the conflict experienced by the characters as a result of the possible blackmail. Prompt them to use a cause-and-effect diagram like this one to examine the consequences of each of Mr. Frank's possible decisions.

Cause	Effect/Cause	Effect
Mr. Frank pays Carl	*He keeps their secret.*	*They are safe.*
Mr. Frank does not pay Carl	*He tells the authorities.*	*The residents are caught and sent to concentration camps.*

 For additional support, go to the **Reading Studio** and assign the following [LEVEL UP] **Level Up tutorial: Conflict.**

101 **Mr. Frank** (*to* Mr. Kraler). How was it left? What did you tell him?

102 **Mr. Kraler.** I said I had to think about it. What shall I do? Pay him the money? . . Take a chance on firing him . . . or what? I don't know.

103 **Dussel** (*frantic*). For God's sake don't fire him! Pay him what he asks . . . keep him here where you can have your eye on him.

104 **Mr. Frank.** Is it so much that he's asking? What are they paying nowadays?

105 **Mr. Kraler.** He could get it in a war plant. But this isn't a war plant. Mind you, I don't know if he really knows . . . or if he doesn't know.

106 **Mr. Frank.** Offer him half. Then we'll soon find out if it's blackmail or not.

107 **Dussel.** And if it is? We've got to pay it, haven't we? Anything he asks we've got to pay!

108 **Mr. Frank.** Let's decide that when the time comes.

109 **Mr. Kraler.** This may be all my imagination. You get to a point, these days, where you suspect everyone and everything. Again and again . . . on some simple look or word, I've found myself . . . (*The telephone rings in the office below.*)

110 **Mrs. Van Daan** (*hurrying to* Mr. Kraler). There's the telephone! What does that mean, the telephone ringing on a holiday?

111 **Mr. Kraler.** That's my wife. I told her I had to go over some papers in my office . . . to call me there when she got out of church. (*He starts out.*) I'll offer him half then. Good-bye . . . we'll hope for the best!

112 (*The group call their good-byes half-heartedly.* Mr. Frank *follows* Mr. Kraler, *to bolt the door below. During the following scene,* Mr. Frank *comes back up and stands listening, disturbed.*)

113 **Dussel** (*to* Mr. Van Daan). You can thank your son for this . . . smashing the light! I tell you, it's just a question of time now. (*He goes to the window at the back and stands looking out.*)

114 **Margot.** Sometimes I wish the end would come . . . whatever it is.

115 **Mrs. Frank** (*shocked*). Margot!

116 (Anne *goes to* Margot, *sitting beside her on the couch with her arms around her.*)

117 **Margot.** Then at least we'd know where we were.

 ENGLISH LEARNER SUPPORT

Exchange Ideas To help students understand Mr. Frank's and Mr. Kraler's dilemma more clearly, have students work in small groups to discuss these questions:

- What is Mr. Dussel's theory in paragraph 100 about how Carl would know about them? (*Carl may have been the thief the year before.*)
- Reread paragraphs 101–105. What makes the decision harder for Mr. Kraler and Mr. Frank? (*They cannot be certain that Carl knows anything at all.*)
- Why might paying Carl the full amount he asks for be the wrong decision? (*It might confirm his suspicions that the Franks are living in the annex.*)
- Reread paragraph 106. What is Mr. Frank's solution? (*to pay him half the amount he has asked for*) What does Mr. Frank think will happen next if Carl has actual knowledge of the annex? (*He will demand the full amount and reveal that he knows their secret.*)
- Would you make the same decision as Mr. Frank? Why or why not?

LIGHT

TO CHALLENGE STUDENTS . . .

Debate Issues Draw attention to the characters' discussion of the potential blackmail situation described in paragraphs 94–109. Tell students to reread the section and note the questions, concerns, and suggestions that each character describes. Have students form two groups to conduct an debate about an appropriate response to the blackmail situation. Remind students to use text evidence as well as logic and reasoning to present their arguments.

ANALYZE DRAMA

Review that playwrights can reveal what characters are like through their speech, thoughts, and actions. (**Answer:** *Peter cares about Anne—he knows she's upset, so he brings her cake and praises the way she is able to speak and clearly express her feelings to adults.*)

■ **English Learner Support**

Analyze Drama Help students identify changes in Peter and Anne's relationship.

• Read aloud paragraphs 245–251 from Act One, Scene 3. Work with students to complete this sentence: *In the beginning, Anne and Peter thought the other was ___.* (annoying)

• Then display paragraphs 125–135 from Act Two, Scene 1. Highlight the details that show the way Peter feels about Anne now. Work with students to complete this second sentence: *After being in hiding for more than a year, Peter and Anne ___.* (have become friends)

MODERATE

 NOTICE & NOTE

118 **Mrs. Frank.** You should be ashamed of yourself! Talking that way! Think how lucky we are! Think of the thousands dying in the war, every day. Think of the people in concentration camps.

119 **Anne** (*interrupting*). What's the good of that? What's the good of thinking of misery when you're already miserable? That's stupid!

120 **Mrs. Frank.** Anne!

121 (*As Anne goes on raging at her mother, Mrs. Frank tries to break in, in an effort to quiet her.*)

122 **Anne.** We're young, Margot and Peter and I! You grownups have had your chance! But look at us . . . If we begin thinking of all the horror in the world, we're lost! We're trying to hold onto some kind of ideals . . . when everything . . . ideals, hopes . . . everything, are being destroyed! It isn't our fault that the world is in such a mess! We weren't around when all this started! So don't try to take it out on us!

123 (*She rushes off to her room, slamming the door after her. She picks up a brush from the chest and hurls it to the floor. Then she sits on the settee, trying to control her anger.*)

124 **Mr. Van Daan.** She talks as if we started the war! Did we start the war? (*He spots Anne's cake. As he starts to take it, Peter anticipates him.*)

125 **Peter.** She left her cake. (*He starts for Anne's room with the cake. There is silence in the main room. Mrs. Van Daan goes up to her room, followed by Van Daan. Dussel stays looking out the window. Mr. Frank brings Mrs. Frank her cake. She eats it slowly, without relish. Mr. Frank takes his cake to Margot and sits quietly on the sofa beside her.* Peter *stands in the doorway of Anne's darkened room, looking at her, then makes a little movement to let her know he is there. Anne sits up, quickly, trying to hide the signs of her tears.* Peter *holds out the cake to her.*) You left this.

126 **Anne** (*dully*). Thanks.

127 (Peter *starts to go out, then comes back.*)

128 **Peter.** I thought you were fine just now. You know just how to talk to them. You know just how to say it. I'm no good . . . I never can think . . . especially when I'm mad . . . That Dussel . . . when he said that about Mouschi . . . someone eating him . . . all I could think is . . . I wanted to hit him. I wanted to give him such a . . . a . . . that he'd . . . That's what I used to do when there was an argument at school . . . That's the way I . . . but here . . . And an old man like that . . . it wouldn't be so good.

ANALYZE DRAMA

Annotate: In paragraphs 125–128, mark details in the stage directions and dialogue that reveal Peter's changing feelings toward Anne.

Infer: What do you infer from Peter's actions and words?

129 **Anne.** You're making a big mistake about me. I do it all wrong. I say too much. I go too far. I hurt people's feelings . . .

130 (Dussel *leaves the window, going to his room.*)

131 **Peter.** I think you're just fine . . . What I want to say . . . if it wasn't for you around here, I don't know. What I mean . . .

132 (Peter *is interrupted by* Dussel's *turning on the light.* Dussel *stands in the doorway, startled to see* Peter. Peter *advances toward him forbiddingly.* Dussel *backs out of the room.* Peter *closes the door on him.*)

133 **Anne.** Do you mean it, Peter? Do you really mean it?

134 **Peter.** I said it, didn't I?

135 **Anne.** Thank you, Peter!

136 (*In the main room* Mr. *and* Mrs. Frank *collect the dishes and take them to the sink, washing them.* Margot *lies down again on*

 ENGLISH LEARNER SUPPORT

Understand Cohesion Remind students that ellipses are used to indicate missing words. Explain that the playwrights include enough words so the audience understands the intended meaning.

- Read paragraphs 128–129 aloud, demonstrating how to indicate through your voice where the ellipses occur. Then have students take turns reading the passage to a partner. **SUBSTANTIAL**

- Have students work with a partner to list words to replace the ellipses in paragraph 128. Have pairs compare their words and decide which ones are most fitting. Then, have them recite the speeches with the missing words inserted. Ask them how each version differs. **MODERATE**

- Have students work with a partner to rewrite paragraph 128 with the missing words. Have pairs read aloud their lines and the actual dialogue. Ask students how their version affects their understanding of Peter's emotion. **LIGHT**

ANALYZE DRAMA

Tell students that part of analyzing drama is analyzing the relationships between characters. One way to do that is to look at what a character says about another character when that character cannot hear him or her. (**Answer:** *She has different relationships with her mother and her father because she only feels comfortable talking about serious topics with her father. She feels that her mother does not understand her so she avoids telling her anything important. Anne may have different relationships because her parents treat her differently. Her mother may be trying to shape Anne's behavior and character by telling her what to do, whereas her father listens more and tries to teach by example. She is also in a transitional period of her life, so this may complicate her relationships and make her less patient with her mother than she may have been when she was younger.*)

NOTICE & NOTE

the couch. Dussel, *lost, wanders into* Peter's *room and takes up a book, starting to read.*)

137 **Peter** (*looking at the photographs on the wall*). You've got quite a collection.

138 **Anne.** Wouldn't you like some in your room? I could give you some. Heaven knows you spend enough time in there . . . doing heaven knows what . . .

139 **Peter.** It's easier. A fight starts, or an argument . . . I duck in there.

140 **Anne.** You're lucky, having a room to go to. His lordship is always here . . . I hardly ever get a minute alone. When they start in on me, I can't duck away. I have to stand there and take it.

141 **Peter.** You gave some of it back just now.

142 **Anne.** I get so mad. They've formed their opinions . . . about everything . . . but we . . . we're still trying to find out . . . We have problems here that no other people our age have ever had. And just as you think you've solved them, something comes along and bang! You have to start all over again.

143 **Peter.** At least you've got someone you can talk to.

144 **Anne.** Not really. Mother . . . I never discuss anything serious with her. She doesn't understand. Father's all right. We can talk about everything . . . everything but one thing. Mother. He simply won't talk about her. I don't think you can be really intimate with anyone if he holds something back, do you?

145 **Peter.** I think your father's fine.

146 **Anne.** Oh, he is, Peter! He is! He's the only one who's ever given me the feeling that I have any sense. But anyway, nothing can take the place of school and play and friends of your own age . . . or near your age . . . can it?

147 **Peter.** I suppose you miss your friends and all.

148 **Anne.** It isn't just . . . (*She breaks off, staring up at him for a second.*) Isn't it funny, you and I? Here we've been seeing each other every minute for almost a year and a half, and this is the first time we've ever really talked. It helps a lot to have someone to talk to, don't you think? It helps you to let off steam.

149 **Peter** (*going to the door*). Well, any time you want to let off steam, you can come into my room.

150 **Anne** (*following him*). I can get up an awful lot of steam. You'll have to be careful how you say that.

ANALYZE DRAMA

Annotate: In paragraphs 143–146, underline details in the dialogue that reveal Anne's relationship with her mother. Circle details that reveal her relationship with her father.

Compare: Contrast these two relationships. Why do you think Anne has such different relationships with her father and mother?

ENGLISH LEARNER SUPPORT

Read Closely Have pairs of students use context clues to define the expressions "duck in" and "duck away" in paragraphs 139 and 140. (*"hide in or escape into"; "escape or run off"*) Ask students to discuss why the playwrights use these less formal phrases in the two characters' dialogue. How does their language contribute to the audience's understanding of their character? (*The language shows that Peter is not as trapped as Anne because he has somewhere to go when conflicts arise and Anne does not. She has to stay and listen to it all.*)

LIGHT

151 **Peter.** It's all right with me.

152 **Anne.** Do you mean it?

153 **Peter.** I said it, didn't I?

154 (*He goes out.* Anne *stands in her doorway looking after him. As* Peter *gets to his door he stands for a minute looking back at her. Then he goes into his room.* Dussel *rises as he comes in, and quickly passes him, going out. He starts across for his room.* Anne *sees him coming, and pulls her door shut.* Dussel *turns back toward* Peter's *room.* Peter *pulls his door shut.* Dussel *stands there, bewildered, forlorn.*

155 *The scene slowly dims out. The curtain falls on the scene.* Anne's Voice *comes over in the darkness . . . faintly at first, and then with growing strength.*)

156 **Anne's Voice.** We've had bad news. The people from whom Miep got our ration books have been arrested. So we have had to cut down on our food. Our stomachs are so empty that they rumble and make strange noises, all in different keys. Mr. Van Daan's is deep and low, like a bass fiddle. Mine is high, whistling like a flute. As we all sit around waiting for supper, it's like an orchestra tuning up. It only needs Toscanini[2] to raise his baton and we'd be off in the Ride of the Valkyries.[3] Monday, the sixth of March, nineteen forty-four. Mr. Kraler is in the hospital. It seems he has ulcers. Pim says we are his ulcers. Miep has to run the business and us too. The Americans have landed on the southern tip of Italy. Father looks for a quick finish to the war. Mr. Dussel is waiting every day for the warehouse man to demand more money. Have I been skipping too much from one subject to another? I can't help it. I feel that spring is coming. I feel it in my whole body and soul. I feel utterly confused. I am longing . . . so longing . . . for everything . . . for friends . . . for someone to talk to . . . someone who understands . . . someone young, who feels as I do . . .

157 (*As these last lines are being said, the curtain rises on the scene. The lights dim on.* Anne's Voice *fades out.*)

---

[2] **Toscanini** (tŏs'kə-nē'nē): Arturo Toscanini, a famous Italian orchestral conductor.
[3] **Ride of the Valkyries** (văl-kîr'əz): an exciting passage from an opera by Richard Wagner, a German composer.

IMPROVE READING FLUENCY

Targeted Passage Direct students' attention to paragraph 156. Explain that Anne's tone changes from matter-of-fact to exuberant to wistful at the end. Read the lines aloud, using voice expression to convey each of these attitudes.

Have students rehearse the passage with a partner, striving to convey the same emotions. Have them offer feedback about pace, pronunciation, and tone. Invite volunteers to read the monologue aloud for the class.

 Go to the **Reading Studio** for additional support in developing fluency.

ANALYZE DRAMA

Remind students that the **stage directions** are in italics. The stage directions help set the scene for readers so they picture what the characters are doing before the dialogue starts. (**Answer:** *These stage directions suggest that Anne and Peter will visit together. The playwrights included these details about Peter and Anne so the reader knows that they are both nervous about the visit. They want to impress each other.*)

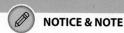
NOTICE & NOTE

Scene 2

158   *It is evening, after supper. From outside we hear the sound of children playing. The "grownups," with the exception of Mr. Van Daan, are all in the main room. Mrs. Frank is doing some mending, Mrs. Van Daan is reading a fashion magazine. Mr. Frank is going over business accounts. Dussel, in his dentist's jacket, is pacing up and down, impatient to get into his bedroom. Mr. Van Daan is upstairs working on a piece of embroidery in an embroidery frame.*

ANALYZE DRAMA

Annotate: Mark details in paragraphs 159–161 that reveal what Peter and Anne are doing at the beginning of Scene 2.

Predict: What do these stage directions suggest will happen next? Why did the playwrights choose to include those details about Peter and Anne?

159   *In his room* Peter *is sitting before the mirror, smoothing his hair. As the scene goes on, he puts on his tie, brushes his coat and puts it on, preparing himself meticulously for a visit from* Anne. *On his wall are now hung some of Anne's motion picture stars.*

160   *In her room* Anne *too is getting dressed. She stands before the mirror in her slip, trying various ways of dressing her hair.* Margot *is seated on the sofa, hemming a skirt for* Anne *to wear.*

161   *In the main room* Dussel *can stand it no longer. He comes over, rapping sharply on the door of his and* Anne's *bedroom.*

162   **Anne** (*calling to him*). No, no, Mr. Dussel! I am not dressed yet. (Dussel *walks away, furious, sitting down and burying his head in his hands.* Anne *turns to* Margot.) How is that? How does that look?

163   **Margot** (*glancing at her briefly*). Fine.

164   **Anne.** You didn't even look.

165   **Margot.** Of course I did. It's fine.

166   **Anne.** Margot, tell me, am I terribly ugly?

167   **Margot.** Oh, stop fishing.

168   **Anne.** No. No. Tell me.

169   **Margot.** Of course you're not. You've got nice eyes . . . and a lot of animation, and . . .

170   **Anne.** A little vague, aren't you?

171   (*She reaches over and takes a brassière out of* Margot's *sewing basket. She holds it up to herself, studying the effect in the mirror. Outside,* Mrs. Frank, *feeling sorry for* Dussel, *comes over, knocking at the girls' door.*)

172   **Mrs. Frank** (*outside*). May I come in?

173   **Margot.** Come in, Mother.

ENGLISH LEARNER SUPPORT

Use Helping Verbs   Remind students that verbs sometimes may require a helping verb. Display these lines from the play:

- "Mr. Frank is going over business accounts." (paragraph 158) "How does that look? (paragraph 162)

- "But you've already spent a great deal of time in there today." (paragraph 178)

Say them aloud and have students repeat them. Then ask pairs to identify the helping verb in each sentence. (*is, does, have*) Have them write sentences using these helping and main verbs: *is going, does look, have spent.* Ask pairs to take turns reading their sentences aloud.
MODERATE

174 **Mrs. Frank** (*shutting the door behind her*). Mr. Dussel's impatient to get in here.

175 **Anne** (*still with the brassière*). Heavens, he takes the room for himself the entire day.

176 **Mrs. Frank** (*gently*). Anne, dear, you're not going in again tonight to see Peter?

177 **Anne** (*dignified*). That is my intention.

178 **Mrs. Frank.** But you've already spent a great deal of time in there today.

179 **Anne.** I was in there exactly twice. Once to get the dictionary, and then three-quarters of an hour before supper.

180 **Mrs. Frank.** Aren't you afraid you're disturbing him?

181 **Anne.** Mother, I have some intuition.

182 **Mrs. Frank.** Then may I ask you this much, Anne. Please don't shut the door when you go in.

183 **Anne.** You sound like Mrs. Van Daan! (*She throws the brassière back in* Margot's *sewing basket and picks up her blouse, putting it on.*)

184 **Mrs. Frank.** No. No. I don't mean to suggest anything wrong. I only wish that you wouldn't expose yourself to criticism . . . that you wouldn't give Mrs. Van Daan the opportunity to be unpleasant.

185 **Anne.** Mrs. Van Daan doesn't need an opportunity to be unpleasant!

186 **Mrs. Frank.** Everyone's on edge, worried about Mr. Kraler. This is one more thing . . .

187 **Anne.** I'm sorry, Mother. I'm going to Peter's room. I'm not going to let Petronella Van Daan spoil our friendship.

188 (Mrs. Frank *hesitates for a second, then goes out, closing the door after her. She gets a pack of playing cards and sits at the center table, playing solitaire. In* Anne's *room* Margot *hands the finished skirt to* Anne. *As* Anne *is putting it on,* Margot *takes off her high-heeled shoes and stuffs paper in the toes so that* Anne *can wear them.*)

189 **Margot** (*to* Anne). Why don't you two talk in the main room? It'd save a lot of trouble. It's hard on Mother, having to listen to those remarks from Mrs. Van Daan and not say a word.

190 **Anne.** Why doesn't she say a word? I think it's ridiculous to take it and take it.

ENGLISH LEARNER SUPPORT

Conduct Word Study Tell students that the ending of a word often indicates its part of speech. Explain that the -*ous* suffix is added to words to form adjectives, words that describe nouns or pronouns. Ask pairs of students to look for an adjective on this page that has the -*ous* suffix. (*ridiculous*) Discuss the meaning of the word and what it is used to describe in paragraph 190. Then have pairs of students write a sentence using the word. Call on pairs to read their sentences aloud.

MODERATE

WORDS OF THE WISER

Explain to students that this signpost is sometimes used to reveal details about **characters**. Have students identify the reason Margot gives Anne for why Mrs. Frank does not respond to Mrs. Van Daan's remarks. (**Answer:** *Margot understands that not all people are the same—that Mrs. Frank and Anne are fundamentally different and that because they are so different, Anne is having trouble understanding and accepting her mother's behavior.*)

NOTICE & NOTE

Notice & Note: In paragraphs 189–191, mark the explanation Margot gives Anne for why Mrs. Frank doesn't react to Mrs. Van Daan's remarks.

Infer: What wisdom do Margot's words reveal?

191 **Margot.** You don't understand Mother at all, do you? She can't talk back. She's not like you. It's just not in her nature to fight back.

192 **Anne.** Anyway . . . the only one I worry about is you. I feel awfully guilty about you.

193 (*She sits on the stool near* Margot, *putting on* Margot's *high-heeled shoes.*)

194 **Margot.** What about?

195 **Anne.** I mean, every time I go into Peter's room, I have a feeling I may be hurting you. (Margot *shakes her head.*) I know if it were me, I'd be wild. I'd be desperately jealous, if it were me.

196 **Margot.** Well, I'm not.

197 **Anne.** You don't feel badly? Really? Truly? You're not jealous?

198 **Margot.** Of course I'm jealous . . . jealous that you've got something to get up in the morning for . . . But jealous of you and Peter? No.

199 (Anne *goes back to the mirror.*)

200 **Anne.** Maybe there's nothing to be jealous of. Maybe he doesn't really like me. Maybe I'm just taking the place of his cat . . . (*She picks up a pair of short white gloves, putting them on.*) Wouldn't you like to come in with us?

201 **Margot.** I have a book.

202 (*The sound of the children playing outside fades out. In the main room* Dussel *can stand it no longer. He jumps up, going to the bedroom door and knocking sharply.*)

203 **Dussel.** Will you please let me in my room!

204 **Anne.** Just a minute, dear, dear Mr. Dussel. (*She picks up her Mother's pink stole and adjusts it elegantly over her shoulders, then gives a last look in the mirror.*) Well, here I go . . . to run the gauntlet.[4] (*She starts out, followed by* Margot.)

205 **Dussel** (*as she appears—sarcastic*). Thank you so much.

206 (Dussel *goes into his room.* Anne *goes toward* Peter's *room, passing* Mrs. Van Daan *and her parents at the center table.*)

207 **Mrs. Van Daan.** My God, look at her! (Anne *pays no attention. She knocks at* Peter's *door.*) I don't know what good it is to have a son. I never see him. He wouldn't care if I killed myself. (Peter *opens the door and stands aside for* Anne *to come in.*) Just

---

[4] **to run the gauntlet:** to endure a series of troubles or difficulties.

a minute, Anne. (*She goes to them at the door.*) I'd like to say a few words to my son. Do you mind? (*Peter and Anne stand waiting.*) Peter, I don't want you staying up till all hours tonight. You've got to have your sleep. You're a growing boy. You hear?

208 **Mrs. Frank.** Anne won't stay late. She's going to bed promptly at nine. Aren't you, Anne?

209 **Anne.** Yes, Mother . . . (*to Mrs. Van Daan*) May we go now?

210 **Mrs. Van Daan.** Are you asking me? I didn't know I had anything to say about it.

211 **Mrs. Frank.** Listen for the chimes, Anne dear.

212 (*The two young people go off into* Peter's *room, shutting the door after them.*)

213 **Mrs. Van Daan** (*to Mrs. Frank*). In my day it was the boys who called on the girls. Not the girls on the boys.

214 **Mrs. Frank.** You know how young people like to feel that they have secrets. Peter's room is the only place where they can talk.

215 **Mrs. Van Daan.** Talk! That's not what they called it when I was young.

216 (Mrs. Van Daan *goes off to the bathroom.* Margot *settles down to read her book.* Mr. Frank *puts his papers away and brings a chess game to the center table. He and* Mrs. Frank *start to play. In* Peter's *room,* Anne *speaks to* Peter, *indignant, humiliated.*)

217 **Anne.** Aren't they awful? Aren't they impossible? Treating us as if we were still in the nursery.

218 (*She sits on the cot.* Peter *gets a bottle of pop and two glasses.*)

219 **Peter.** Don't let it bother you. It doesn't bother me.

220 **Anne.** I suppose you can't really blame them . . . they think back to what *they* were like at our age. They don't realize how much more advanced we are . . . When you think what wonderful discussions we've had! . . . Oh, I forgot. I was going to bring you some more pictures.

221 **Peter.** Oh, these are fine, thanks.

222 **Anne.** Don't you want some more? Miep just brought me some new ones.

223 **Peter.** Maybe later. (*He gives her a glass of pop and, taking some for himself, sits down facing her.*)

EL **ENGLISH LEARNER SUPPORT**

Analyze Language Explain that in a play a character's tone is the attitude he or she expresses toward a subject or another character. To help students hear Mrs. Van Daan's tone, read paragraph 207 sarcastically and bitterly. Ask them how they would describe her attitude toward Anne and Peter based on the expression they hear in her voice and the words she says. Have students practice reading the lines in a similar tone. **ALL LEVELS**

TEACH

MEMORY MOMENT

Explain to students that this signpost is often used to reveal more about a **character**. It is also used to contrast the character's past experiences with his or her current situation. (**Answer:** *Anne feels that she is more serious now and is focused on writing and becoming a journalist. She thinks playing games and being silly would bore her now.*)

EL ENGLISH LEARNER SUPPORT

Understand Cohesion Tell students that the pronoun used in a comparison depends on whether it acts as the subject or the object of a verb. Display these examples:

- "You're much better than I am in dozens of things." (paragraph 228) Explain that in this comparison, the subject pronoun *I* is used because it is the subject of the verb *am*.

- "Right from the start you liked her, liked her much better than [you liked] me." (paragraph 228) Tell students that the object pronoun *me* is used because it is the object of the verb *liked*. Explain that the phrase in brackets is understood by readers to be part of the sentence.

- Have students work together to choose the correct pronoun for each of the following sentences. Discuss their choices.
  - Peter is better at math than (she, her) is. (*she*)
  - Mr. Dussel finds Anne more annoying than (he, him). (*him*) **ALL LEVELS**

NOTICE & NOTE

MEMORY MOMENT

Notice & Note: Mark the memories that Anne has as she looks at the photos that Miep brought her.

Interpret: How does Anne feel that she's changed since the days when she played ping-pong with her friends?

---

224 **Anne** (*looking up at one of the photographs*). I remember when I got that . . . I won it. I bet Jopie that I could eat five ice-cream cones. We'd all been playing ping-pong . . . We used to have heavenly times . . . we'd finish up with ice cream at the Delphi, or the Oasis, where Jews were allowed . . . there'd always be a lot of boys . . . we'd laugh and joke . . . I'd like to go back to it for a few days or a week. But after that I know I'd be bored to death. I think more seriously about life now. I want to be a journalist . . . or something. I love to write. What do you want to do?

225 **Peter.** I thought I might go off some place . . . work on a farm or something . . . some job that doesn't take much brains.

226 **Anne.** You shouldn't talk that way. You've got the most awful inferiority complex.

227 **Peter.** I know I'm not smart.

228 **Anne.** That isn't true. You're much better than I am in dozens of things . . . arithmetic and algebra and . . . well, you're a million times better than I am in algebra. (*with sudden directness*) You like Margot, don't you? Right from the start you liked her, liked her much better than me.

229 **Peter** (*uncomfortably*). Oh, I don't know.

230 (*In the main room* Mrs. Van Daan *comes from the bathroom and goes over to the sink, polishing a coffee pot.*)

231 **Anne.** It's all right. Everyone feels that way. Margot's so good. She's sweet and bright and beautiful and I'm not.

232 **Peter.** I wouldn't say that.

233 **Anne.** Oh, no, I'm not. I know that. I know quite well that I'm not a beauty. I never have been and never shall be.

234 **Peter.** I don't agree at all. I think you're pretty.

235 **Anne.** That's not true!

236 **Peter.** And another thing. You've changed . . . from at first, I mean.

237 **Anne.** I have?

238 **Peter.** I used to think you were awful noisy.

239 **Anne.** And what do you think now, Peter? How have I changed?

240 **Peter.** Well . . . er . . . you're . . . quieter.

241 (*In his room* Dussel *takes his pajamas and toilet articles and goes into the bathroom to change.*)

478   Unit 6

242 **Anne.** I'm glad you don't just hate me.

243 **Peter.** I never said that.

244 **Anne.** I bet when you get out of here you'll never think of me again.

245 **Peter.** That's crazy.

246 **Anne.** When you get back with all of your friends, you're going to say . . . now what did I ever see in that Mrs. Quack Quack.

247 **Peter.** I haven't got any friends.

248 **Anne.** Oh, Peter, of course you have. Everyone has friends.

249 **Peter.** Not me. I don't want any. I get along all right without them.

250 **Anne.** Does that mean you can get along without me? I think of myself as your friend.

251 **Peter.** No. If they were all like you, it'd be different.

252 (*He takes the glasses and the bottle and puts them away. There is a second's silence and then* Anne *speaks, hesitantly, shyly.*)

253 **Anne.** Peter, did you ever kiss a girl?

254 **Peter.** Yes. Once.

255 **Anne** (*to cover her feelings*). That picture's crooked. (Peter *goes over, straightening the photograph.*) Was she pretty?

256 **Peter.** Huh?

257 **Anne.** The girl that you kissed.

258 **Peter.** I don't know. I was blindfolded. (*He comes back and sits down again.*) It was at a party. One of those kissing games.

259 **Anne** (*relieved*). Oh. I don't suppose that really counts, does it?

260 **Peter.** It didn't with me.

261 **Anne.** I've been kissed twice. Once a man I'd never seen before kissed me on the cheek when he picked me up off the ice and I was crying. And the other was Mr. Koophuis, a friend of Father's who kissed my hand. You wouldn't say those counted, would you?

262 **Peter.** I wouldn't say so.

263 **Anne.** I know almost for certain that Margot would never kiss anyone unless she was engaged to them. And I'm sure too that Mother never touched a man before Pim. But I don't know . . . things are so different now . . . What do you think? Do you think a girl shouldn't kiss anyone except if she's engaged or

ENGLISH LEARNER SUPPORT

Culturally Responsive Instruction Read aloud paragraph 263. Remind students that this conversation is taking place in the early 1940s in a culture in which young girls were strictly supervised to make sure their behavior was proper. Tell students that this expectation for girls is one of the reasons that Mrs. Frank is unhappy with Anne's visiting Peter in his room without an adult present. Ask students how Anne's culture differs from modern American culture. Then have them discuss in small groups the importance of codes of behavior imposed by different cultures.
LIGHT

NOTICE & NOTE

WHEN STUDENTS STRUGGLE...

Compare and Contrast   Provide support for students to analyze the changes in the relationship between Anne and Peter in Act One and in Act Two. Prompt students to compare and contrast the relationships using a chart like the one shown.

	Act One	Act Two
What Anne Thinks of Peter		
What Peter Thinks of Anne		

 For additional support, go to the **Reading Studio** and assign the following ᴸᴱⱽᴱᴸ **Level Up tutorial: Making Inferences About Characters.**

something? It's so hard to try to think what to do, when here we are with the whole world falling around our ears and you think . . . well . . . you don't know what's going to happen tomorrow and . . . What do you think?

264 **Peter.** I suppose it'd depend on the girl. Some girls, anything they do's wrong. But others . . . well . . . it wouldn't necessarily be wrong with them. (*The carillon starts to strike nine o'clock.*) I've always thought that when two people . . .

265 **Anne.** Nine o'clock. I have to go.

266 **Peter.** That's right.

267 **Anne** (*without moving*). Good night.

268 (*There is a second's pause, then* Peter *gets up and moves toward the door.*)

269 **Peter.** You won't let them stop you coming?

270 **Anne.** No. (*She rises and starts for the door.*) Sometime I might bring my diary. There are so many things in it that I want to talk over with you. There's a lot about you.

271 **Peter.** What kind of things?

272 **Anne.** I wouldn't want you to see some of it. I thought you were a nothing, just the way you thought about me.

273 **Peter.** Did you change your mind, the way I changed my mind about you?

274 **Anne.** Well . . . You'll see . . .

275 (*For a second* Anne *stands looking up at* Peter, *longing for him to kiss her. As he makes no move she turns away. Then suddenly* Peter *grabs her awkwardly in his arms, kissing her on the cheek.* Anne *walks out dazed. She stands for a minute, her back to the people in the main room. As she regains her poise she goes to her mother and father and* Margot, *silently kissing them. They murmur their good nights to her. As she is about to open her bedroom door, she catches sight of* Mrs. Van Daan. *She goes quickly to her, taking her face in her hands and kissing her first on one cheek and then on the other. Then she hurries off into her room.* Mrs. Van Daan *looks after her, and then looks over at* Peter's *room. Her suspicions are confirmed.*)

276 **Mrs. Van Daan** (*She knows*). Ah hah!

277 (*The lights dim out. The curtain falls on the scene. In the darkness* Anne's Voice *comes faintly at first and then with growing strength.*)

 ENGLISH LEARNER SUPPORT

Use Verbs Display paragraph 270 and highlight "talk over." Explain to students that "talk over" is a phrasal verb—a verb followed by a preposition or adverb that acts as one unit and has its own meaning.

- Guide students to use context clues to define *talk over* as "discuss thoroughly, consider." Work together to write sentences using *talk over, talked over,* and *will talk over.* **SUBSTANTIAL**

- Ask pairs to use context clues to define *talk over.* Then, have them write one sentence using the phrase and another sentence using *is/are talking over* or *has/have talked over.* **MODERATE**

- Have pairs define these phrasal verbs from the play: "*gets up*" (paragraph 268), "*talk over*" (paragraph 270), "*turns away*" (paragraph 275). Then have them use each in a sentence. Challenge them to use different moods, as in *Anne wishes that she and Peter ___,* or *It is important to Anne that ___.* **LIGHT**

ENGLISH LEARNER SUPPORT

Understand Text Structure Point out to students that Anne's monologue ends each scene. Discuss how this part of the scene often contains important information about outside events, such as the progress of the war, as well as developments in the annex. It also reveals Anne's inner thoughts. Explain that the playwrights use Anne's diary as a way to summarize necessary details and prepare the audience for the next scene.

Call on a volunteer to read aloud sentences 1–6 of paragraph 278. Ask them to write a sentence making an inference about what is happening to the food in the annex. Have them share their statements with a partner to compare their inferences. Discuss what they predict might happen in the next scene.

MODERATE/LIGHT

 **ANALYZE PLOT DEVELOPMENT**

Review that dialogue in a play, along with the stage directions, may establish a conflict that the characters must then resolve. (**Answer:** Mr. Van Daan is discovered as he tries to steal bread from the food safe. The characters must decide what to do about his betrayal of trust. This event was foreshadowed earlier in the play when the stage directions described Mr. Van Daan standing near the bread safe in the dark.)

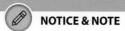 **NOTICE & NOTE**

278 **Anne's Voice.** By this time we all know each other so well that if anyone starts to tell a story, the rest can finish it for him. We're having to cut down still further on our meals. What makes it worse, the rats have been at work again. They've carried off some of our precious food. Even Mr. Dussel wishes now that Mouschi was here. Thursday, the twentieth of April, nineteen forty-four. Invasion fever is mounting every day. Miep tells us that people outside talk of nothing else. For myself, life has become much more pleasant. I often go to Peter's room after supper. Oh, don't think I'm in love, because I'm not. But it does make life more bearable to have someone with whom you can exchange views. No more tonight. P.S. . . . I must be honest. I must confess that I actually live for the next meeting. Is there anything lovelier than to sit under the skylight and feel the sun on your cheeks and have a darling boy in your arms? I admit now that I'm glad the Van Daans had a son and not a daughter. I've outgrown another dress. That's the third. I'm having to wear Margot's clothes after all. I'm working hard on my French and am now reading *La Belle Nivernaise.*

279 (*As she is saying the last lines—the curtain rises on the scene. The lights dim on, as* Anne's Voice *fades out.*)

Scene 3

ANALYZE PLOT DEVELOPMENT

Annotate: In paragraphs 280–299, mark details in the stage directions and dialogue that introduce a new conflict to the drama.

Connect: What conflict arises in this scene? What event earlier in the play foreshadowed this conflict?

280 *It is night, a few weeks later. Everyone is in bed. There is complete quiet. In the Van Daans' room a match flares up for a moment and then is quickly put out.* Mr. Van Daan, *in bare feet, dressed in underwear and trousers, is dimly seen coming stealthily down the stairs and into the main room, where* Mr. *and* Mrs. Frank *and* Margot *are sleeping. He goes to the food safe and again lights a match. Then he cautiously opens the safe, taking out a half-loaf of bread. As he closes the safe, it creaks. He stands rigid.* Mrs. Frank *sits up in bed. She sees him.*

281 **Mrs. Frank** (*screaming*). Otto! Otto! *Komme schnell!*[5]

282 (*The rest of the people wake, hurriedly getting up.*)

283 **Mr. Frank.** *Was ist los? Was ist passiert?*[6]

284 (Dussel, *followed by* Anne, *comes from his room.*)

285 **Mrs. Frank** (*as she rushes over to* Mr. Van Daan). *Er stiehlt das Essen!*[7]

---

[5] *Komme schnell!* (kôm´e shnĕl´) *German:* Come quickly!

[6] *Was ist los? Was ist passiert?* (väs ĭst lôs´? väs ĭst pä-sērt´?) *German:* What's the matter? What has happened?

[7] *Er stiehlt das Essen!* (ĕr shtēlt´ däs ĕs´ən) *German:* He is stealing food!

286 **Dussel** (*grabbing* Mr. Van Daan). You! You! Give me that.

287 **Mrs. Van Daan** (*coming down the stairs*). Putti . . . Putti . . . what is it?

288 **Dussel** (*his hands on* Van Daan's *neck*). You dirty thief . . . stealing food . . . you good-for-nothing . . .

289 **Mr. Frank.** Mr. Dussel! For God's sake! Help me, Peter!

290 (Peter *comes over, trying, with* Mr. Frank, *to separate the two struggling men.*)

291 **Peter.** Let him go! Let go!

292 (Dussel *drops* Mr. Van Daan, *pushing him away. He shows them the end of a loaf of bread that he has taken from* Van Daan.)

293 **Dussel.** You greedy, selfish . . . !

294 (Margot *turns on the lights.*)

295 **Mrs. Van Daan.** Putti . . . what is it?

296 (*All of* Mrs. Frank's *gentleness, her self-control, is gone. She is outraged, in a frenzy of indignation.*)

297 **Mrs. Frank.** The bread! He was stealing the bread!

298 **Dussel.** It was you, and all the time we thought it was the rats!

299 **Mr. Frank.** Mr. Van Daan, how could you!

300 **Mr. Van Daan.** I'm hungry.

301 **Mrs. Frank.** We're all of us hungry! I see the children getting thinner and thinner. Your own son Peter . . . I've heard him moan in his sleep, he's so hungry. And you come in the night and steal food that should go to them . . . to the children!

302 **Mrs. Van Daan** (*going to* Mr. Van Daan *protectively*). He needs more food than the rest of us. He's used to more. He's a big man.

303 (Mr. Van Daan *breaks away, going over and sitting on the couch.*)

304 **Mrs. Frank** (*turning on* Mrs. Van Daan). And you . . . you're worse than he is! You're a mother, and yet you sacrifice your child to this man . . . this . . . this . . .

305 **Mr. Frank.** Edith! Edith!

306 (Margot *picks up the pink woolen stole, putting it over her mother's shoulders.*)

307 **Mrs. Frank** (*paying no attention, going on to* Mrs. Van Daan). Don't think I haven't seen you! Always saving the choicest bits

---

CONTRASTS AND CONTRADICTIONS

Notice & Note: Mark details in paragraphs 301–313 that reveal how Mrs. Frank feels about the theft and what she wants to happen as a result of it.

Analyze: How does Mrs. Frank's behavior contradict what you would expect of her? Do you think she would have reacted the same way at the beginning of the play? Explain.

CONTRASTS AND CONTRADICTIONS

This signpost is often used to challenge readers' previous notions about a topic or character. (**Answer:** *Mrs. Frank doesn't usually fight back. She probably would not have reacted the same way at the beginning of the play because she did not know everyone well then. At this point in the play, their situation is dire and she is fed up with Mr. and Mrs. Van Daan's behavior. Also, it is possible that she is more angry now because she is a protective mother and she feels that Mr. Van Daan has taken food that belongs to the children.*)

■ English Learner Support

Understand Text Structure Display a flow chart on the board to help students clarify the sequence of events in paragraphs 281–290. Work with students to fill in the first box of the flow chart: *Mr. Van Daan creeps down the stairs to the kitchen.* Then have them work with a partner to record the remaining events through paragraph 290. Have pairs compare their flow charts in small groups. **MODERATE**

ENGLISH LEARNER SUPPORT

Read Closely Tell students that realistic characters have reasons for acting as they do. These reasons are called motives. Ask students why Mrs. Frank is so upset about Mr. Van Daan's actions. (*She is horrified that he has been taking food away from the children, including his own son.*) **ALL LEVELS**

MAKE PREDICTIONS

Remind students that readers should look at the personal traits and actions of characters to determine their motivations and predict future actions. (**Possible response:** *The Franks will forgive Mr. Van Daan for taking the food and let him stay in the annex.*)

MAKE PREDICTIONS

Annotate: As you read this scene, mark details that match predictions you made at the end of Act One. In the chart on page 462, describe what actually happens.

Predict: Make a new prediction about what will happen as a result of Mr. Van Daan's being caught stealing food. Use details from the play to support your prediction.

for him! I've watched you day after day and I've held my tongue. But not any longer! Not after this! Now I want him to go! I want him to get out of here!

308 **Mr. Frank.** Edith!

309 **Mr. Van Daan.** Get out of here? } *Together*

310 **Mrs. Van Daan.** What do you mean?

311 **Mrs. Frank.** Just that! Take your things and get out!

312 **Mr. Frank** (*to Mrs. Frank*). You're speaking in anger. You cannot mean what you are saying.

313 **Mrs. Frank.** I mean exactly that!

314 (Mrs. Van Daan *takes a cover from the* Franks' *bed, pulling it about her.*)

315 **Mr. Frank.** For two long years we have lived here, side by side. We have respected each other's rights . . . we have managed to live in peace. Are we now going to throw it all away? I know this will never happen again, will it, Mr. Van Daan?

316 **Mr. Van Daan.** No. No.

317 **Mrs. Frank.** He steals once! He'll steal again!

318 (Mr. Van Daan, *holding his stomach, starts for the bathroom.* Anne *puts her arms around him, helping him up the step.*)

319 **Mr. Frank.** Edith, please. Let us be calm. We'll all go to our rooms . . . and afterwards we'll sit down quietly and talk this out . . . we'll find some way . . .

320 **Mrs. Frank.** No! No! No more talk! I want them to leave!

321 **Mrs. Van Daan.** You'd put us out, on the streets?

322 **Mrs. Frank.** There are other hiding places.

323 **Mrs. Van Daan.** A cellar . . . a closet. I know. And we have no money left even to pay for that.

324 **Mrs. Frank.** I'll give you money. Out of my own pocket I'll give it gladly. (*She gets her purse from a shelf and comes back with it.*)

325 **Mrs. Van Daan.** Mr. Frank, you told Putti you'd never forget what he'd done for you when you came to Amsterdam. You said you could never repay him, that you . . .

326 **Mrs. Frank** (*counting out money*). If my husband had any obligation to you, he's paid it, over and over.

WHEN STUDENTS STRUGGLE . . .

Chart Outcomes Help students understand how Mr. Van Daan's actions have created a complex situation. Have them chart the possible negative consequences if the Van Daans leave the annex.

For additional support, go to the **Reading Studio** and assign the following **Level Up** tutorial: Conflict.

Action
The Van Daans leave the annex

↓

Possible Consequences		
They are caught	They reveal the annex and others are captured	Mrs. Frank lives with burden of guilt

327 **Mr. Frank.** Edith, I've never seen you like this before. I don't know you.

328 **Mrs. Frank.** I should have spoken out long ago.

329 **Dussel.** You can't be nice to some people.

330 **Mrs. Van Daan** (*turning on* Dussel). There would have been plenty for all of us, if you hadn't come in here!

331 **Mr. Frank.** <u>We don't need the Nazis to destroy us. We're destroying ourselves.</u>

332 (*He sits down, with his head in his hands.* Mrs. Frank *goes to* Mrs. Van Daan.)

333 **Mrs. Frank** (*giving* Mrs. Van Daan *some money*). Give this to Miep. She'll find you a place.

334 **Anne.** Mother, you're not putting *Peter* out. Peter hasn't done anything.

335 **Mrs. Frank.** He'll stay, of course. When I say I must protect the children, I mean Peter too.

336 (Peter *rises from the steps where he has been sitting.*)

337 **Peter.** I'd have to go if Father goes.

338 (Mr. Van Daan *comes from the bathroom.* Mrs. Van Daan *hurries to him and takes him to the couch. Then she gets water from the sink to bathe his face.*)

339 **Mrs. Frank** (*while this is going on*). He's no father to you . . . that man! He doesn't know what it is to be a father!

340 **Peter** (*starting for his room*). I wouldn't feel right. I couldn't stay.

341 **Mrs. Frank.** Very well, then. I'm sorry.

342 **Anne** (*rushing over to* Peter). No, Peter! No! (Peter *goes into his room, closing the door after him.* Anne *turns back to her mother, crying.*) I don't care about the food. They can have mine! I don't want it! Only don't send them away. It'll be daylight soon. They'll be caught . . .

343 **Margot** (*putting her arms comfortingly around* Anne). Please, Mother!

344 **Mrs. Frank.** They're not going now. They'll stay here until Miep finds them a place. (*to* Mrs. Van Daan) But one thing I insist on! He must never come down here again! He must never come to this room where the food is stored! We'll divide what we

WORDS OF THE WISER

Notice & Note: Mark the lines of dialogue that reveal what Mr. Frank believes is destroying the group in the Annex.

Infer: What does Mr. Frank mean?

TEACH

The Diary of Anne Frank: Act Two **485**

WORDS OF THE WISER

Explain that this signpost is often used to convey the author or playwright's message. (**Answer:** *Mr. Frank means that their behavior, stealing and fighting, will destroy them.*)

■ English Learner Support

Analyze Words of the Wiser Help students infer what Mr. Frank means by his statement in paragraph 331. Read the lines in a tone that sounds tired and discouraged. Guide students in a discussion about how the residents in the annex might destroy themselves. **ALL LEVELS**

ANALYZE PLOT DEVELOPMENT

Guide students to understand the significance of the invasion and its impact on the plot. (**Answer:** *The news that the Allies have landed in Normandy leads them to believe that the Nazis will soon be defeated, and they will finally be free.*)

■ English Learner Support

Analyze Plot Development Explain that the invasion that Miep refers to occurred on June 6, 1944. Western Allies landed on the beaches of Normandy in France and began to push German troops out of the countries they had occupied. Discuss why this development in the war gives the residents of the annex hope.

Have volunteers take the roles of the characters and act out paragraph 369. Ask students what their actions show they are feeling. **LIGHT**

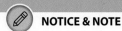 **NOTICE & NOTE**

have . . . an equal share for each! (Dussel *hurries over to get a sack of potatoes from the food safe.* Mrs. Frank *goes on, to* Mrs. Van Daan.) You can cook it here and take it up to him.

345 (Dussel *brings the sack of potatoes back to the center table.*)

346 **Margot.** Oh, no. No. We haven't sunk so far that we're going to fight over a handful of rotten potatoes.

347 **Dussel** (*dividing the potatoes into piles*). Mrs. Frank, Mr. Frank, Margot, Anne, Peter, Mrs. Van Daan, Mr. Van Daan, myself . . . Mrs. Frank . . .

348 (*The buzzer sounds in Miep's signal.*)

349 **Mr. Frank.** It's Miep! (*He hurries over, getting his overcoat and putting it on.*)

350 **Margot.** At this hour?

351 **Mrs. Frank.** It is trouble.

352 **Mr. Frank** (*as he starts down to unbolt the door*). I beg you, don't let her see a thing like this!

353 **Mr. Dussel** (*counting without stopping*). . . . Anne, Peter, Mrs. Van Daan, Mr. Van Daan, myself . . .

354 **Margot** (*to Dussel*). Stop it! Stop it!

355 **Dussel.** . . . Mr. Frank, Margot, Anne, Peter, Mrs. Van Daan, Mr. Van Daan, myself, Mrs. Frank . . .

356 **Mrs. Van Daan.** You're keeping the big ones for yourself! All the big ones . . . Look at the size of that! . . . And that! . . .

357 (Dussel *continues on with his dividing.* Peter, *with his shirt and trousers on, comes from his room.*)

358 **Margot.** Stop it! Stop it!

359 (*We hear* Miep's *excited voice speaking to Mr. Frank below.*)

ANALYZE PLOT DEVELOPMENT

Annotate: In paragraphs 360–373, mark details that reveal what Miep has come to tell everyone about.

Summarize: Why do the residents of the Annex go "crazy" and have a "wild demonstration"?

360 **Miep.** Mr. Frank . . . the most wonderful news! . . . The invasion has begun!

361 **Mr. Frank.** Go on, tell them! Tell them!

362 (Miep *comes running up the steps, ahead of* Mr. Frank. *She has a man's raincoat on over her nightclothes and a bunch of orange-colored flowers in her hand.*)

363 **Miep.** Did you hear that, everybody? Did you hear what I said? The invasion has begun! The invasion!

364 (*They all stare at* Miep, *unable to grasp what she is telling them.* Peter *is the first to recover his wits.*)

365 **Peter.** Where?

366 **Mrs. Van Daan.** When? When, Miep?

367 **Miep.** It began early this morning . . .

368 (*As she talks on, the realization of what she has said begins to dawn on them. Everyone goes crazy. A wild demonstration takes place.* Mrs. Frank *hugs* Mr. Van Daan.)

369 **Mrs. Frank.** Oh, Mr. Van Daan, did you hear that? (Dussel *embraces* Mrs. Van Daan. Peter *grabs a frying pan and parades around the room, beating on it, singing the Dutch National Anthem.* Anne *and* Margot *follow him, singing, weaving in and out among the excited grownups.* Margot *breaks away to take the flowers from* Miep *and distribute them to everyone. While this pandemonium is going on* Mrs. Frank *tries to make herself heard above the excitement.*)

370 **Mrs. Frank** (*to* Miep). How do you know?

371 **Miep.** The radio . . . The B.B.C.! They said they landed on the coast of Normandy!

372 **Peter.** The British?

373 **Miep.** British, Americans, French, Dutch, Poles, Norwegians . . . all of them! More than four thousand ships! Churchill spoke, and General Eisenhower! D-Day they call it!

374 **Mr. Frank.** Thank God, it's come!

375 **Mrs. Van Daan.** At last!

376 **Miep** (*starting out*). I'm going to tell Mr. Kraler. This'll be better than any blood transfusion.

377 **Mr. Frank** (*stopping her*). What part of Normandy did they land, did they say?

378 **Miep.** Normandy . . . that's all I know now . . . I'll be up the minute I hear some more! (*She goes hurriedly out.*)

379 **Mr. Frank** (*to* Mrs. Frank). What did I tell you? What did I tell you?

380 (Mrs. Frank *indicates that he has forgotten to bolt the door after* Miep. *He hurries down the steps.* Mr. Van Daan, *sitting on the couch, suddenly breaks into a convulsive sob. Everybody looks at him, bewildered.*)

381 **Mrs. Van Daan** (*hurrying to him*). Putti! Putti! What is it? What happened?

382 **Mr. Van Daan.** Please. I'm so ashamed.

 ENGLISH LEARNER SUPPORT

Read Closely Have students work with a partner to reread paragraphs 377–382 and summarize the important ideas using these sentence frames:

- *After hearing the news of the invasion, the characters are ___.* (overjoyed and hopeful)
- *But then, Mr. Van Daan ___.* (becomes very upset)
- *Mr. Van Daan feels ___.* (ashamed for stealing food)

MODERATE

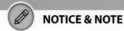 **NOTICE & NOTE**

383 (Mr. Frank *comes back up the steps.*)

384 **Dussel.** Oh, for God's sake!

385 **Mrs. Van Daan.** Don't, Putti.

386 **Margot.** It doesn't matter now!

387 **Mr. Frank** (*going to* Mr. Van Daan). Didn't you hear what Miep said? The invasion has come! We're going to be liberated! This is a time to celebrate!

388 (*He embraces* Mrs. Frank *and then hurries to the cupboard and gets the cognac and a glass.*)

389 **Mr. Van Daan.** To steal bread from children!

390 **Mrs. Frank.** We've all done things that we're ashamed of.

391 **Anne.** Look at me, the way I've treated Mother . . . so mean and horrid to her.

392 **Mrs. Frank.** No, Anneke, no.

393 (Anne *runs to her mother, putting her arms around her.*)

394 **Anne.** Oh, Mother, I was. I was awful.

395 **Mr. Van Daan.** Not like me. No one is as bad as me!

396 **Dussel** (*to* Mr. Van Daan). Stop it now! Let's be happy!

397 **Mr. Frank** (*giving* Mr. Van Daan *a glass of cognac*). Here! Here! *Schnapps! L'chaim!*[8] (Van Daan *takes the cognac. They all watch him. He gives them a feeble smile.* Anne *puts up her fingers in a V-for-Victory sign. As* Van Daan *gives an answering V-sign, they are startled to hear a loud sob from behind them. It is* Mrs. Frank, *stricken with remorse. She is sitting on the other side of the room.*)

398 **Mrs. Frank** (*through her sobs*). When I think of the terrible things I said . . .

399 (Mr. Frank, Anne, *and* Margot *hurry to her, trying to comfort her.* Mr. Van Daan *brings her his glass of cognac.*)

400 **Mr. Van Daan.** No! No! You were right!

401 **Mrs. Frank.** That I should speak that way to you! . . . Our friends! . . . Our guests! (*She starts to cry again.*)

402 **Dussel.** Stop it, you're spoiling the whole invasion!

403 (*As they are comforting her, the lights dim out. The curtain falls.*)

---

[8] *Schnapps!* (shnäps) *German:* Brandy!
L'chaim! (lə khä´yĭm) *Hebrew:* To life!

TO CHALLENGE STUDENTS . . .

Impact of Setting   Point out that the residents of the secret annex had to rely on Miep and Mr. Kraler for most of their information about the outside world. Prompt students to recall that the residents spend the majority of their time in silence, unable to speak more than a whisper.

Have students meet in a small group to consider how the characters' sense of isolation might have impacted the tensions in the annex. Remind students to use text evidence as well as logic and reasoning in their discussions.

404 Anne's Voice (*faintly at first and then with growing strength*). We're all in much better spirits these days. There's still excellent news of the invasion. The best part about it is that I have a feeling that friends are coming. Who knows? Maybe I'll be back in school by fall. Ha, ha! The joke is on us! The warehouse man doesn't know a thing and we are paying him all that money! . . . Wednesday, the second of July, nineteen forty-four. The invasion seems temporarily to be bogged down. Mr. Kraler has to have an operation, which looks bad. The Gestapo have found the radio that was stolen. Mr. Dussel says they'll trace it back and back to the thief, and then, it's just a matter of time till they get to us. Everyone is low. Even poor Pim can't raise their spirits. I have often been downcast myself . . . but never in despair. I can shake off everything if I write. But . . . and that is the great question . . . will I ever be able to write well? I want to so much. I want to go on living even after my death. Another birthday has gone by, so now I am fifteen. Already I know what I want. I have a goal, an opinion.

405 (*As this is being said—the curtain rises on the scene, the lights dim on, and* Anne's Voice *fades out.*)

Scene 4

406 *It is an afternoon a few weeks later . . . Everyone but* Margot *is in the main room. There is a sense of great tension.*

407 *Both* Mrs. Frank *and* Mr. Van Daan *are nervously pacing back and forth,* Dussel *is standing at the window, looking down fixedly at the street below.* Peter *is at the center table, trying to do his lessons.* Anne *sits opposite him, writing in her diary.* Mrs. Van Daan *is seated on the couch, her eyes on* Mr. Frank *as he sits reading.*

408 *The sound of a telephone ringing comes from the office below. They all are rigid, listening tensely.* Mr. Dussel *rushes down to* Mr. Frank.

409 Dussel. There it goes again, the telephone! Mr. Frank, do you hear?

410 Mr. Frank (*quietly*). Yes. I hear.

411 Dussel (*pleading, insistent*). But this is the third time, Mr. Frank! The third time in quick succession! It's a signal! I tell you it's Miep, trying to get us! For some reason she can't come to us and she's trying to warn us of something!

ANALYZE DRAMA

Annotate: In paragraph 404, mark details that show how the mood in the Annex changes immediately after the residents learn about D-Day (the Allied invasion on June 6, 1944) and a month later.

Interpret: What has happened in the month since D-Day? How has this affected people's spirits?

⬤ ANALYZE DRAMA

Point out that the passage from Anne's diary covers more than just one day. The playwrights include excerpts from different entries to show a change among the residents. (**Answer:** *At first, the residents of the annex believe that the war will end soon and their lives will return to normal. But then a series of events remind them of the dangers they still face. Mr. Kraler's condition has worsened and may require surgery. Also, the Gestapo have found the radio that was stolen from them. Everyone is worried, even Anne's father. This causes the mood to become darker.*)

■ English Learner Support

Analyze Language Display paragraphs 406–408 on the board. Remind students that the playwrights describe the scene in a way that will produce a particular effect on the audience.

- Highlight the word *tension* in paragraph 406. Discuss its meaning with students. Then work with them to find other words in the stage directions that reinforce the same feeling or mood. ("*nervously pacing back and forth," "rigid," "tensely"*) **SUBSTANTIAL**

- Have students read the lines with a partner and describe the mood of this scene. Ask them to identify words that contribute to this feeling. Discuss and define these words together. **MODERATE**

- Have students identify the mood of this passage and the words that convey this feeling. Ask pairs to group words that share a similar definition and then explain how they reinforce the same feeling.
  LIGHT

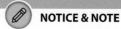

412 **Mr. Frank.** Please. Please.

413 **Mr. Van Daan** (*to* Dussel). You're wasting your breath.

414 **Dussel.** Something has happened, Mr. Frank. For three days now Miep hasn't been to see us! And today not a man has come to work. There hasn't been a sound in the building!

415 **Mrs. Frank.** Perhaps it's Sunday. We may have lost track of the days.

416 **Mr. Van Daan** (*to* Anne). You with the diary there. What day is it?

417 **Dussel** (*going to* Mrs. Frank). I don't lose track of the days! I know exactly what day it is! It's Friday, the fourth of August. Friday, and not a man at work. (*He rushes back to* Mr. Frank, *pleading with him, almost in tears.*) I tell you Mr. Kraler's dead. That's the only explanation. He's dead and they've closed down the building, and Miep's trying to tell us!

418 **Mr. Frank.** She'd never telephone us.

419 **Dussel** (*frantic*). Mr. Frank, answer that! I beg you, answer it!

420 **Mr. Frank.** No.

421 **Mr. Van Daan.** Just pick it up and listen. You don't have to speak. Just listen and see if it's Miep.

422 **Dussel** (*speaking at the same time*). For God's sake . . . I ask you.

423 **Mr. Frank.** No. I've told you, no. I'll do nothing that might let anyone know we're in the building.

424 **Peter.** Mr. Frank's right.

425 **Mr. Van Daan.** There's no need to tell us what side you're on.

426 **Mr. Frank.** If we wait patiently, quietly, I believe that help will come.

427 (*There is silence for a minute as they all listen to the telephone ringing.*)

428 **Dussel.** I'm going down. (*He rushes down the steps.* Mr. Frank *tries ineffectually to hold him.* Dussel *runs to the lower door, unbolting it. The telephone stops ringing.* Dussel *bolts the door and comes slowly back up the steps.*) Too late. (Mr. Frank *goes to* Margot *in* Anne's *bedroom.*)

429 **Mr. Van Daan.** So we just wait here until we die.

430 **Mrs. Van Daan** (*hysterically*). I can't stand it! I'll kill myself! I'll kill myself!

ENGLISH LEARNER SUPPORT

Understand Text Structure Draw a plot diagram on the board. Explain that the events up to this point are all leading to the climax of the play. Tell students that the climax is the point of greatest tension, after which the conflict will be resolved.

- Work with students to record the significant events from Act One and Act Two on the plot diagram. (*The Franks and Van Daans move into the annex; Mr. Dussel arrives; the thief hears them; Carl seems to be blackmailing Mr. Kraler; Mr. Kraler undergoes surgery; the ration book suppliers are arrested; Mr. Van Daan is found stealing food; the invasion begins; Miep is gone for three days; the warehouse is deserted.*)
SUBSTANTIAL

- Ask students to list the events they think belong on the plot diagram. Have them compare their lists with a partner and resolve discrepancies by reviewing the text. Call on pairs to take turns recording their details on the class diagram. **MODERATE**

- Have pairs of students complete their own plot diagrams. Then, ask them to predict what the climactic event will be.
LIGHT

431 **Mr. Van Daan.** For God's sake, stop it!

432 (*In the distance, a German military band is heard playing a Viennese waltz.*)

433 **Mrs. Van Daan.** I think you'd be glad if I did! I think you want me to die!

434 **Mr. Van Daan.** Whose fault is it we're here? (*Mrs. Van Daan starts for her room. He follows, talking at her.*) We could've been safe somewhere . . . in America or Switzerland. But no! No! You wouldn't leave when I wanted to. You couldn't leave your things. You couldn't leave your precious furniture.

435 **Mrs. Van Daan.** Don't touch me!

436 (*She hurries up the stairs, followed by* Mr. Van Daan. Peter, *unable to bear it, goes to his room.* Anne *looks after him, deeply concerned.* Dussel *returns to his post at the window.* Mr. Frank *comes back into the main room and takes a book, trying to read.* Mrs. Frank *sits near the sink, starting to peel some potatoes.* Anne *quietly goes to* Peter's *room, closing the door after her.* Peter *is lying face down on the cot.* Anne *leans over him, holding him in her arms, trying to bring him out of his despair.*)

437 **Anne.** Look, Peter, the sky. (*She looks up through the skylight.*) What a lovely, lovely day! Aren't the clouds beautiful? You know what I do when it seems as if I couldn't stand being cooped up for one more minute? I *think* myself out. I think myself on a walk in the park where I used to go with Pim. Where the jonquils and the crocus and the violets grow down the slopes. You know the most wonderful part about *thinking* yourself out? You can have it any way you like. You can have roses and violets and chrysanthemums all blooming at the same time . . . It's funny . . . I used to take it all for granted . . . and now I've gone crazy about everything to do with nature. Haven't you?

438 **Peter.** I've just gone crazy. I think if something doesn't happen soon . . . if we don't get out of here . . . I can't stand much more of it!

439 **Anne** (*softly*). I wish you had a religion, Peter.

440 **Peter.** No, thanks! Not me!

441 **Anne.** Oh, I don't mean you have to be Orthodox[9] . . . or believe in heaven and hell and purgatory and things . . . I just mean some religion . . . it doesn't matter what. Just to believe in something! When I think of all that's out there . . . the

---

[9] **Orthodox:** Orthodox Jews who strictly observe Jewish laws and traditions.

IMPROVE READING FLUENCY

Targeted Passage Tell students that paragraphs 337 and 441 help the audience appreciate Anne's perspective on life even after years of living in hiding. By reading them aloud, students will be able to hear her expression as well as focus on her words more closely.

Explain that students are going to choral read each paragraph. Model by reading the first paragraph aloud with a student. Stop and provide feedback about the student's pronunciation and expression. Then have partners follow the same steps. Encourage them to pause with each paragraph to review pronunciation, expression, and pace.

 Go to the **Reading Studio** for additional support in developing fluency.

TEACH

CONTRASTS AND CONTRADICTIONS

Explain to students that this signpost is often used to reveal how characters change over time. (**Answer:** *These lines reveal a contrast between Anne's previous opinion about the value of thinking of others who are suffering. When her mother said something similar in paragraphs 118–119, Anne responded impatiently, saying, "What's the good of thinking of misery when you're already miserable?" Now Anne is somewhat in agreement with what her mother said earlier. This shows that she is growing in wisdom. Her mother's words are having an effect on her, and she's also struggling to form her own point of view.*)

ENGLISH LEARNER SUPPORT

Read Closely Remind students that the climax of the play is the event that creates the greatest tension. Display paragraphs 447–453 on the board.

- Work with students to highlight words and phrases that describe what the characters hear. Ask students what mood is created by these sound effects. **SUBSTANTIAL**

- Using a different color, highlight the characters' reactions to what is happening. Discuss with students why the characters are calm. What do they understand? **MODERATE**

 NOTICE & NOTE

trees . . . and flowers . . . and seagulls . . . when I think of the dearness of you, Peter . . . and the goodness of the people we know . . . Mr. Kraler, Miep, Dirk, the vegetable man, all risking their lives for us every day . . . When I think of these good things, I'm not afraid any more . . . I find myself, and God, and I . . . (Peter *interrupts, getting up and walking away.*)

442 **Peter.** That's fine! But when I begin to think, I get mad! Look at us, hiding out for two years. Not able to move! Caught here like . . . waiting for them to come and get us . . . and all for what?

443 **Anne.** We're not the only people that've had to suffer. There've always been people that've had to . . . sometimes one race . . . sometimes another . . . and yet . . .

444 **Peter.** That doesn't make me feel any better!

CONTRASTS AND CONTRADICTIONS

Notice & Note: Mark what Anne says to Peter in paragraph 443. Then look back at the dialogue between Anne and her mother in paragraphs 118–119 of Act Two.

Interpret: What contrast do these lines reveal? What does this contrast reveal about Anne?

445 **Anne** (*going to him*). I know it's terrible, trying to have any faith . . . when people are doing such horrible . . . But you know what I sometimes think? I think the world may be going through a phase, the way I was with Mother. It'll pass, maybe not for hundreds of years, but some day . . . I still believe, in spite of everything, that people are really good at heart.

446 **Peter.** I want to see something now . . . Not a thousand years from now! (*He goes over, sitting down again on the cot.*)

447 **Anne.** But, Peter, if you'd only look at it as part of a great pattern . . . that we're just a little minute in the life . . . (*She breaks off.*) Listen to us, going at each other like a couple of stupid grownups! Look at the sky now. Isn't it lovely? (*She holds out her hand to him. Peter takes it and rises, standing with her at the window looking out, his arms around her.*) Some day, when we're outside again, I'm going to . . .

448 (*She breaks off as she hears the sound of a car, its brakes squealing as it comes to a sudden stop. The people in the other rooms also become aware of the sound. They listen tensely. Another car roars up to a screeching stop. Anne and Peter come from Peter's room. Mr. and Mrs. Van Daan creep down the stairs. Dussel comes out from his room. Everyone is listening, hardly breathing. A doorbell clangs again and again in the building below. Mr. Frank starts quietly down the steps to the door. Dussel and Peter follow him. The others stand rigid, waiting, terrified.*)

449 In a few seconds Dussel *comes stumbling back up the steps. He shakes off* Peter's *help and goes to his room.* Mr. Frank *bolts the door below, and comes slowly back up the steps. Their eyes are all*

492 Unit 6

*on him as he stands there for a minute. They realize that what
they feared has happened. Mrs. Van Daan starts to whimper.
Mr. Van Daan puts her gently in a chair, and then hurries off
up the stairs to their room to collect their things. Peter goes to
comfort his mother. There is a sound of violent pounding on a
door below.)*

450 **Mr. Frank** (*quietly*). <u>For the past two years we have lived in fear.
Now we can live in hope.</u>

451 (*The pounding below becomes more insistent. There are muffled
sounds of voices, shouting commands.*)

452 **Men's Voices.** *Auf machen! Da drinnen! Auf machen! Schnell!
Schnell! Schnell! etc., etc.*[10]

453 (*The street door below is forced open. We hear the heavy tread
of footsteps coming up.* Mr. Frank *gets two school bags from the
shelves, and gives one to* Anne *and the other to* Margot. *He goes
to get a bag for* Mrs. Frank. *The sound of feet coming up grows
louder.* Peter *comes to* Anne, *kissing her good-bye, then he goes
to his room to collect his things. The buzzer of their door starts
to ring.* Mr. Frank *brings* Mrs. Frank *a bag. They stand together,
waiting. We hear the thud of gun butts on the door, trying to
break it down.*

454 Anne *stands, holding her school satchel, looking over at her
father and mother with a soft, reassuring smile. She is no longer a
child, but a woman with courage to meet whatever lies ahead.*

455 *The lights dim out. The curtain falls on the scene. We hear a
mighty crash as the door is shattered. After a second* Anne's Voice
is heard.)

456 **Anne's Voice.** And so it seems our stay here is over. They are
waiting for us now. They've allowed us five minutes to get our
things. We can each take a bag and whatever it will hold of
clothing. Nothing else. So, dear Diary, that means I must leave
you behind. Good-bye for a while. P.S. Please, please, Miep, or
Mr. Kraler, or anyone else. If you should find this diary, will you
please keep it safe for me, because some day I hope . . .

457 (*Her voice stops abruptly. There is silence. After a second the
curtain rises.*)

---

[10] *Auf machen! . . . Schnell!* (ouf´ mäкн´ən! dä drĭn´ən! ouf´ mäкн´ən! shnĕl! shnĕl!
shnĕl!) *German:* Open up! Inside there! Open up! Quick! Quick! Quick!

WORDS OF THE WISER

Notice & Note: Mark what
Mr. Frank tells the group after
they hear pounding on the
door downstairs.

Interpret: What does Mr. Frank
mean?

TEACH

▶ **WORDS OF THE WISER**

This signpost is often used to reveal how characters respond
to adversity. (**Answer:** *Mr. Frank means that every day for the
past two years everyone in the annex has been afraid of being
caught by the Nazis. Now they have been caught; therefore,
they must hold onto the hope that they will one day be freed.*)

ANALYZE PLOT DEVELOPMENT

Remind students that stage directions provide information about the time and place of the action in a play. (**Answer:** *The play has returned to its starting point—Act One begins in 1945 and Act Two ends there. Everything that happens in between is a long flashback. Events during that period are told in chronological order, or time order.*)

■ English Learner Support

Analyze Plot Development Remind students of the structure of the play: the majority of the play takes place in the flashback. Have partners reread paragraphs 456–459 and identify where the flashback ends and where the action returns to the present. As needed, provide a circle diagram with 1945 at the top and the intervening years shown in a clockwise position to illustrate how the play begins and ends in the same place. **ALL LEVELS**

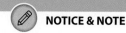

NOTICE & NOTE

ANALYZE PLOT DEVELOPMENT

Annotate: Mark details in the stage directions at the opening of Scene 5 that reveal the time and place of that scene.

Interpret: How does the setting of Scene 5 complete the structure of the play?

Scene 5

458   *It is again the afternoon in November, 1945. The rooms are as we saw them in the first scene. Mr. Kraler has joined Miep and Mr. Frank. There are coffee cups on the table. We see a great change in Mr. Frank. He is calm now. His bitterness is gone. He slowly turns a few pages of the diary. They are blank.*

459 **Mr. Frank.** No more. (*He closes the diary and puts it down on the couch beside him.*)

460 **Miep.** I'd gone to the country to find food. When I got back the block was surrounded by police . . .

461 **Mr. Kraler.** We made it our business to learn how they knew. It was the thief . . . the thief who told them.

462 (Miep *goes up to the gas burner, bringing back a pot of coffee.*)

463 **Mr. Frank** (*after a pause*). It seems strange to say this, that anyone could be happy in a concentration camp. But Anne was happy in the camp in Holland where they first took us. After two years of being shut up in these rooms, she could be out . . . out in the sunshine and the fresh air that she loved.

464 **Miep** (*offering the coffee to* Mr. Frank). A little more?

465 **Mr. Frank** (*holding out his cup to her*). The news of the war was good. The British and Americans were sweeping through France. We felt sure that they would get to us in time. In September we were told that we were to be shipped to Poland . . . The men to one camp. The women to another. I was sent to Auschwitz. They went to Belsen. In January we were freed, the few of us who were left. The war wasn't yet over, so it took us a long time to get home. We'd be sent here and there behind the lines where we'd be safe. Each time our train would stop . . . at a siding, or a crossing . . . we'd all get out and go from group to group . . . Where were you? Were you at Belsen? At Buchenwald? At Mauthausen? Is it possible that you knew my wife? Did you ever see my husband? My son? My daughter? That's how I found out about my wife's death . . . of Margot, the Van Daans . . . Dussel. But Anne . . . I still hoped . . . Yesterday I went to Rotterdam. I'd heard of a woman there . . . She'd been in Belsen with Anne . . . I know now.

APPLYING ACADEMIC VOCABULARY

❏ **communication**   ☑ **draft**   ☑ **liberation**   ❏ **philosophy** ❏ **publish**

Write and Discuss Have partners discuss the following questions. Guide students to include the Academic Vocabulary words *draft* and *liberation* in their responses.

- If Anne survived, do you think she would have wanted to publish her diary? If so, do you think she would have made any changes to her original **draft?** Explain?

- How is the timing of the **liberation** connected to the events in Scene 5? How might the events be different if the liberation had come earlier or much later?

466 (*He picks up the diary again, and turns the pages back to find a certain passage. As he finds it we hear* Anne's Voice.)

467 **Anne's Voice.** In spite of everything, I still believe that people are really good at heart.

468 (Mr. Frank *slowly closes the diary.*)

469 **Mr. Frank.** She puts me to shame. (*They are silent.*)

470 *The Curtain Falls.*

NOTICE & NOTE

ANALYZE PLOT DEVELOPMENT

Annotate: Mark the lines that cause Mr. Frank to say that Anne "puts [him] to shame."

Analyze: What does Mr. Frank mean? Why might the playwrights have chosen to end the play with this line?

CHECK YOUR UNDERSTANDING

Answer these questions before moving on to the **Analyze the Text** section on the following page.

1 Which of the following scenes take place after WWII has ended?

 A Act One, Scenes 1 and 2

 B Act One, Scenes 2–5 and Act Two, Scenes 1–4

 C Act One, Scenes 1–5

 D Act One, Scene 1 and Act Two, Scene 5

2 Reread paragraph 86 of Act Two.

> **Margot** (*with sudden foreboding*). What's happened? Something's happened! Hasn't it, Mr. Kraler?

 The playwrights include these lines to suggest that —

 F Margot doesn't trust Mr. Kraler any longer

 G Margot is afraid that Mr. Kraler has informed on them

 H Margot fears that a thief has broken into the office

 J Margot senses that Mr. Kraler has bad news

3 In Act Two, what results in a temporary easing of the tensions in the Annex?

 A Mr. Kraler's release from his hospitalization

 B News that the Allies have landed in Normandy

 C The sharing of Miep's cake on New Year's Day

 D The Franks' promise that they will take care of Peter

TEACH

ANALYZE PLOT DEVELOPMENT

Have students think about the mood and tone of the last lines and how they contribute to the playwrights' message. (**Answer:** *Knowing that his family and so many friends have died in the concentration camps, Mr. Frank is probably finding it very difficult to believe that "people are really good at heart." But, Mr. Frank believes that it is better to believe as Anne did; that's why he feels shame at not being able to. The playwrights might have chosen to end with this line because they wanted to send the message that, as hard as it is, people need to keep faith in others in order to keep on living their lives.*)

CHECK YOUR UNDERSTANDING

Have students answer the questions independently.

Answers

 1. *D*

 2. *J*

 3. *B*

If they answer any questions incorrectly, have them reread the text to confirm their understanding. Then they may proceed to ANALYZE THE TEXT on p. 496.

ENGLISH LEARNER SUPPORT

Oral Assessment Use the following questions to assess students' comprehension and speaking skills:

1. Which scenes happen in 1945 after WWII? (*Act One, Scene 1 and Act Two, Scene 5*)

2. In paragraph 86 of Act Two, Margot says with fear, "What's happened? Something's happened! Hasn't it, Mr. Kraler?" What do Margot's words tell you about how she feels? (*Margot worries that Mr. Kraler has   bad news.*)

3. In Act Two, what causes the residents to stop fighting for a short time? (*The residents hear news that the Allies have landed in Normandy.*)

 SUBSTANTIAL/MODERATE

APPLY

ANALYZE THE TEXT

Possible answers:

1. **DOK 4:** *In Act One, the families had just moved in together and are getting used to each other. Personal relationships and conflicts were just beginning. In Act Two the residents had lived together for years. Personal relationships and conflicts were solidly in place as well as tested. These relationships and events create the action that moved the plot towards the climax and resolution.*

2. **DOK 2:** *Students may have correctly predicted this outcome based on what happened in paragraphs 746–760 of Act One. Or, they may have needed to correct a prediction they made based on paragraphs 94–109 of Act Two.*

3. **DOK 2:** *This is the event that finally causes Mrs. Frank to lose her temper, and she expresses feelings that she has so far kept to herself. She insists that Mr. Van Daan leave. This event precipitates a long discussion about whether the Van Daans should be allowed to stay.*

4. **DOK 4:** *Students should note that the first and last scenes take place in the present and that the rest of the play is a flashback. They may point out that seeing Mr. Frank in the first scene adds to the play's impact by showing him as an essentially broken man; it is a stark contrast to his portrayal in the flashback.*

5. **DOK 4:** *When the Franks first arrived at the annex, Mr. Frank told Anne that no one could imprison her mind. Now we learn that she has indeed roamed freely in her mind and that this has been a comfort to her. The playwrights may want readers to know that Anne has grown in wisdom. They may also want readers to take comfort in the fact that Anne has been able to transcend her imprisonment in the annex. This may be a theme or message that they want to share—that our freedom of thought is our most important freedom.*

RESEARCH

Remind students that they should check multiple, credible websites to gather information about key events in the rise of the Nazi regime and the effects those events had on Jewish people.

Extend Point out to students that they should do some fact checking to determine whether a source provides valid information, weighted opinions, or both. Instruct them to search for the same facts across multiple sources including at least one appearance in information found on an .edu or .gov site.

496   Unit 6

RESPOND

ANALYZE THE TEXT

Support your responses with evidence from the text.   NOTEBOOK

1. **Analyze** Briefly summarize Act One and then Act Two, identifying the main focus of each. How do the two acts work together to develop the action in this drama?

2. **Predict** In Scene 5, Mr. Kraler reveals who told the police about the Franks' hiding place. Did this outcome confirm or contradict a prediction you had made? Explain.

3. **Cause/Effect** Examine the dialogue in paragraphs 281–307 that describes the aftermath of Mr. Van Daan's theft. Explain the effect of this event and how it propels the action of the story.

4. **Evaluate** How do the playwrights use a flashback to tell the story of life in the Annex? Does the use of a nonlinear plot add to or detract from the impact of this play? Note how the play would be different if it had a linear plot as you explain your opinion.

5. **Notice & Note** How do Anne's wise words in paragraph 437 relate to what her father told her in Act One, Scene 2? Why might the playwrights have had Anne speak these words to Peter in Act Two?

RESEARCH TIP
You will be able to find many World War II timelines online. However, each may have a different focus, and much of the information may not be relevant. To find events that focus on the Nazi regime and its effects on Jews in Europe, you might try search terms such as "Nazi rise to power timeline," "the rise of the Nazi party," or "Holocaust timeline."

RESEARCH

Most of the events in *The Diary of Anne Frank* focus on a two-year period toward the end of the Second World War. World War II began in 1939, but the Nazis' rise to power had begun 20 years earlier. Using several sources, research key events in the rise of the Nazi regime and the effects those events had on Jewish people. Present your findings in a timeline. Each date or year entry should include a detailed caption to make its significance clear. As you research, record your notes in this chart, continuing on a separate sheet of paper as necessary.

DATE	EVENT

Extend With a partner or group, create a parallel timeline of key events in Anne Frank's life. Then discuss how the events taking place in Europe impacted her and her family.

496   Unit 6

 LEARNING MINDSET

Problem Solving Remind students there are many different ways to solve problems (being patient; changing strategies; asking for help, etc.) Everyone solves problems in their own unique way. Remind students that everyone runs into problems when learning something new. Every problem solved makes you smarter.

CREATE AND DRAMATIZE

Make a Poster Setting influences character development in literature just as people's surroundings affect their values, beliefs, and actions in real life. Create a poster to convey how the characters in the drama were affected by their time in the Secret Annex during World War II.

❏ As a group, choose three Annex residents to depict.

❏ Analyze how the conditions in the Annex affected each character. Explain each character's motivations, actions, and reactions in relation to others and to the historical context. Cite details from the text to support your analysis.

❏ Create a poster to show the effects of setting on each character, and how these effects change or remain the same over time. As a group, present your poster to the class.

Dramatize a Relationship Act out (or do a dramatic reading of) two sections of the drama to demonstrate how a relationship between two characters changes over time.

❏ As a group, discuss how the subplot of Anne's relationship with Peter develops throughout the play. How does each character's personality affect the way the relationship develops?

❏ Choose two short sections of the play that show how Anne and Peter's relationship changes over time. Rehearse the lines. Then act them out for the class.

RESPOND TO THE ESSENTIAL QUESTION

? What can we learn from Anne Frank?

Gather Information Review your annotations and notes on *The Diary of Anne Frank*. Then, add relevant details to your Response Log. As you determine which information to include, think about:

- the types of conflicts Anne had with others
- the ways in which her relationships changed over time
- the wisdom Anne gained through her interactions and experiences

At the end of the unit, you may use your notes to help you write a personal narrative.

ACADEMIC VOCABULARY

As you write and discuss what you learned from the drama, be sure to use the Academic Vocabulary words. Check off each of the words that you use.

❏ **communicate**

❏ **draft**

❏ **liberation**

❏ **philosophy**

❏ **publish**

CREATE AND DRAMATIZE

Make a Poster Remind students that they should create a three-column chart for each chosen character to note the setting's effects on his or her motivations, actions, and reactions.

 For **writing support** for students at varying proficiency levels, see the **Text X-Ray** on page 406D.

Dramatize a Relationship Remind students to refer back to their **NOTICE & NOTE** responses that pertain to Anne and Peter's personalities and relationship.

RESPOND TO THE ESSENTIAL QUESTION

Allow time for students to add details from "The Diary of Anne Frank" to their Unit 6 Response Logs.

CRITICAL VOCABULARY

Answers:

1. If you wanted to be conspicuous in a crowd you might wear a large, colorful hat.

2. My friends loathe that TV show because the plot is predictable and the jokes aren't funny.

3. The player spoke indignantly to the coach when she benched him unjustly.

4. The pop star dressed ostentatiously because he wanted his performance to go viral.

5. The hostess of the party was appalled when her guests spilled food on her new carpet.

6. The politician suddenly became inarticulate because he didn't want to give a clear answer to the reporter's question.

VOCABULARY STRATEGY:
Use Prefixes

Answers:

1. **review:** I need to review my notes before the test.

2. **prearrange:** She asked that I prearrange her flight home.

3. **recommitted:** I recommitted to maintaining an A average this term.

4. **impulse:** I bought that shirt on impulse.

 RESPOND

WORD BANK
conspicuous
loathe
indignantly
ostentatiously
appalled
inarticulate

 Go to the **Vocabulary Studio** for more on using prefixes.

CRITICAL VOCABULARY

Practice and Apply Complete each sentence in a way that shows the meaning of the Critical Vocabulary word.

1. If you wanted to be **conspicuous** in a crowd, you might . . .

2. My friends **loathe** that TV show because . . .

3. The player spoke **indignantly** to the coach when . . .

4. The pop star dressed **ostentatiously** because . . .

5. The hostess of the party was **appalled** when . . .

6. The politician suddenly became **inarticulate** because . . .

VOCABULARY STRATEGY:
Use Prefixes

A **prefix** is a word part that has been added to the beginning of a base word to form a new word. You can sometimes use prefixes to figure out the meanings of unfamiliar words. Imagine, for example, that aren't sure what *inarticulate* means but you know that someone who is articulate speaks clearly and you know that the prefix *in-* means "not." Then you can figure out that someone who is inarticulate does not speak clearly. Here are some common prefixes and their meanings:

PREFIX	MEANING
dis-, in-, im-, non-, un-	not
pre-	before
re-	back or again

Practice and Apply Choose a prefix to add to each of these base words. (In each case, more than one prefix is possible.) Then, use each new word in an original sentence.

1. view

2. arrange

3. committed

4. pulse

 ENGLISH LEARNER SUPPORT

Use Prefixes Give students additional practice in determining the meanings of unfamiliar words. Write the following words on the board: *disadvantage, preowned, recalculate, unaware.* Have pairs of students copy the words, underline the prefix, and write the definition. Then have them use each word in a sentence. **ALL LEVELS**

LANGUAGE CONVENTIONS:
Correct Capitalization

You already know a lot about correct capitalization. For example, you know that the first word in a sentence is always capitalized. You also know that certain proper nouns, such as a person's name and the city in which you live, are always capitalized. But there are other types of words—many having to do with government and culture—that also need to be capitalized. The chart lists types of words to capitalize, along with examples.

TYPES OF WORDS TO CAPITALIZE	EXAMPLES
Languages	English, Spanish, German, Japanese
Countries and continents	Holland (the Netherlands), Mexico; Europe, North America
Nationalities and regional affiliations	American, Dutch, Chinese; European, Asian
Ethnicities	Hispanic, Native American, Jewish, Asian
Political parties	Democrats, Republicans, Nazis, Socialists
Religions	Judaism, Islam, Christianity, Buddhism
Religious words (texts, symbols, and words referring to a deity)	Bible, Koran; Menorah, Star of David; Thou, God, Ruler

Practice and Apply Rewrite the following sentences, correcting any errors in capitalization. A sentence may contain more than one error.

1. Not all germans wanted the nazis to be in control.

2. For many europeans, it was dangerous to practice judaism.

3. Because they were jewish, the Franks fled to holland to escape persecution.

4. Anne Frank's diary was translated into many languages, including english.

5. The first Country that Hitler's army invaded was Poland.

When you have finished, share your sentences with a partner and compare your use of capitalization.

Go to the **Grammar Studio: Capital Letters** for more on correct capitalization.

The Diary of Anne Frank   499

LANGUAGE CONVENTIONS:
Correct Capitalization

Review the information about capitalization with students. Explain that the types of words that need to be capitalized are proper nouns, which name a specific person, place, thing, or idea. The words in the chart about government and culture name specific things, such as a specific language or a specific religion.

Re-create the chart on the board, keeping the examples column blank. Ask volunteers to think of other examples, not listed in their books, for each category in the chart. Write their ideas on the board.

Practice and Apply Have partners review their capitalizations. Have them discuss and correct any discrepancies.

Answers:

1. *Germans; Nazis*

2. *Europeans; Judaism*

3. *Jewish; Holland*

4. *English*

5. *country*

ENGLISH LEARNER SUPPORT

Language Conventions Use the following supports with students at varying proficiency levels:

• Have students find proper nouns in *The Diary of Anne Frank* and copy them in their notebooks. **SUBSTANTIAL**

• Have students work with partners to correct the capitalizations in each sentence. Then have them meet with another pair to compare their corrections. **MODERATE**

• Have students write several sentences that use examples from the capitalization chart. **LIGHT**

MENTOR TEXT

THE DIARY OF A YOUNG GIRL

Diary by Anne Frank

This diary excerpt serves as a **mentor text**, a model for students to follow when they come to the Unit Writing Task: Write a Personal Narrative.

GENRE ELEMENTS
DIARY

Remind students that a diary is a day-to-day account of events and feelings kept by a single person. Explain that diaries are often thought of as private, but that some diaries have been published—including the one excerpted in this text. Review with students that diaries can be intensely personal or can simply be matter-of-fact discussions of what happened to the diarist on any given day. Tell students that diaries can be very useful sources for historians because they give a clear picture of what life was like for the diarist.

LEARNING OBJECTIVES

- Analyze elements of a diary entry.
- Make and support inferences about a text.
- Conduct research about Anne Frank's diary.
- Illustrate an event in Anne Frank's life.
- Discuss the value and characteristics of primary sources.
- Distinguish between connotative and denotative text.
- Analyze how writers use parentheses.
- **Language** Discuss with a partner how first-person narrative differs from third-person narrative using Academic Vocabulary.

TEXT COMPLEXITY

Quantitative Measures	The Diary of a Young Girl	
Qualitative Measures	**Ideas Presented** Ideas are clear, with some need for making inferences.	
	Structure Used Events are described in chronological order.	
	Language Used Language is accessible; a few words may be unfamiliar.	
	Knowledge Required Basic understanding of World War II and the Holocaust.	

Online **Ed**

RESOURCES

- Unit 6 Response Log
- Selection Audio
- Reading Studio: Making Inferences About Characters
- Writing Studio: Planning a Story
- Speaking and Listening Studio: Discussing with a Partner
- Vocabulary Studio: Connotation and Denotation
- Grammar Studio: Module 14: Lesson 2: Other Marks of Punctuation
- "The Diary of a Young Girl" Selection Test

SUMMARIES

English

Anne Frank, a young Jewish girl originally from Germany, fled to the Netherlands with her family when World War II began. The family went into hiding when the Nazis conquered the Netherlands. While confined to her hiding place, Anne wrote a diary. She was eventually caught and taken to a concentration camp, where she died. The diary was published by her father following Anne's death. Anne's insight into her situation, her feelings, and her description of living in hiding still resonate with audiences today.

Spanish

Ana Frank, una joven judía de origen alemán, huyó a Holanda con su familia cuando comenzó la Segunda Guerra Mundial. Su familia se escondió cuando los nazis conquistaron Holanda. Mientras estuvo confinada en su escondite, Ana escribió un diario. Luego fue capturada y llevada a un campo de concentración, donde murió. El diario fue publicado por su padre luego de la muerte de Ana. La visión de Ana sobre su situación, sus sentimientos y su descripción acerca de vivir escondida aún resuena en los lectores de hoy en día.

SMALL-GROUP OPTIONS

Have students work in small groups to read and discuss the selection.

Repeat It

Students are sometimes more interested in speaking than in listening during group discussion. To help, require students to begin their contribution to a discussion by repeating or summarizing what a previous speaker has said.

- Students should not repeat a comment if someone else has just said it, and students may not cite the same comment twice.
- If students cannot cite an earlier comment, or if they can cite only the one that has just been mentioned, they may not contribute to the discussion. Encourage these students to listen closely so they too may participate.

Questions

Before students begin their discussions, have them write one to two open-ended questions they have about the text or the assignment on index cards. Then have students place their cards in the middle of the table face down and mix them.

- Each student draws a card in turn, reads the question aloud, and answers it if possible.
- If the student cannot answer the question, he or she should get help from the next student in the circle.
- Continue until all questions have been answered.

Text X-Ray: English Learner Support
for "The Diary of a Young Girl"

Use the Text X-Ray and the supports and scaffolds in the Teacher's Edition to help guide students at different proficiency levels through the selection.

INTRODUCE THE SELECTION
DISCUSS PURPOSE OF A DIARY

In this lesson, students will need to be able to understand reasons that people might keep diaries. Tell students that a diary is a kind of record book in which people can write down information about their day, including what they are thinking and feeling. Explain that many teenagers keep diaries to help them make sense of their thoughts and feelings throughout the day and that these diaries are usually private. Tell students that they will read several excerpts from the diary of Anne Frank, a Jewish girl who was killed by the Nazis during World War II. Have students complete the following sentences about diaries:

- A diary tells about _____.
- If I wrote a diary, my entry for today would tell about _____.
- People like to keep diaries because _____.

CULTURAL REFERENCES

The following words and phrases may be unfamiliar to students:

- *at odds with* (paragraph 18): in conflict with
- *do without* (paragraph 18): not have any of something
- *dungeon* (paragraph 2): a dark, unpleasant cell in a jail or prison
- *fountain pen* (paragraph 7): a type of ink pen
- *gravy boat* (paragraph 18): a container for sauce
- *preaching* (paragraph 21): in this context, telling other people what they should do as a minister might in a sermon

LISTENING

Understand Emotional Language

Tell students that diaries often use vivid descriptions of how the writer is feeling about certain things.

Have students listen as you read aloud paragraph 1. Use the following supports with students at varying proficiency levels:

- Tell students that you will ask questions about what you just read aloud. Focus the questions on what Anne says about her emotional life. Questions should only require one or two words to answer. For example, ask *Does Anne say she is happy or afraid? (afraid)* **SUBSTANTIAL**
- Have students raise their hands when they identify a description of a feeling in the paragraph, such as *depression* and *afraid*. Stop and discuss the feeling each time someone raises their hand. **MODERATE**
- After listening to the paragraph, have students work in pairs to write short sentences that restate Anne's feelings. **LIGHT**

SPEAKING

Discuss Comparisons

Comparing helps the reader recognize the significance of details and relationships in a story. Tell students it is important to analyze how things are alike and different as they read.

Use the following supports with students at varying proficiency levels:

- Introduce the terms *alike* and *different* by holding up two similar objects and describing how they are alike, then two objects that are very different and saying *different*. Have students analyze pairs of objects and say if they are *alike* or *different*. **SUBSTANTIAL**
- Have students describe pairs of objects using sentence frames such as: *A ____ and a ___ are alike/ different because _____.* **MODERATE**
- Have students generate their own sentences to tell a partner whether two objects are *alike* or *different* and how they know. **LIGHT**

READING

Identify Figurative Language

Explain that authors use figurative language to create mental images that explain concepts or connections in the text. Discuss examples of figurative language, such as similes, metaphors, and personification.

Work with students to read paragraph 5. Use the following supports with students at varying proficiency levels:

- Have students underline "the eight of us" and "patch of blue sky surrounded by menacing black clouds" and circle "as if we were." Then ask them to repeat after you: *This is figurative language. Anne is comparing two things that are not alike.* **SUBSTANTIAL**
- Have students discuss how Anne uses figurative language in this excerpt. Have them use sentence starters such as: *Anne uses the blue sky to mean ____* or *The black clouds show _____.* **MODERATE**
- Have students talk with a partner about figurative language in this paragraph. Ask them to explain the importance of the sky and the clouds. **LIGHT**

WRITING

Write in First and Third Person

Draw students' attention to the fact that Anne's diary uses pronouns like *I, me,* and *my.* Explain that these words indicate that the diary is in first person, or told directly by the writer. Tell students that third person is also a narrative point of view used by many writers.

Use the following supports with students at varying proficiency levels:

- Write a simple sentence with *I, she, he,* and *it* on the board, such as *I like to eat fruit* and *She runs fast.* Circle the pronouns. Guide students to sort the sentences into first and third person. **SUBSTANTIAL**
- Give students simple sentence frames with first- and third-person pronouns, and have students complete them in writing. Sample sentences include: *I have _____. / She has _____.* **MODERATE**
- Have students write their own sentences with first- and third-person pronouns. Be sure they use the correct verb form as appropriate. **LIGHT**

from

THE DIARY OF A YOUNG GIRL

Diary by **Anne Frank**

? Connect to the ESSENTIAL QUESTION

Review with students that Anne Frank was a young Jewish teenager who lost her life to the Nazis during World War II. Explain that Anne is known today for the diary that she wrote in which she described what it was like for her family to be in hiding. Emphasize that Anne's diary describes painful and frightening situations, but is not unrelievedly negative; Anne was able to find some hope, beauty, and goodness in her life even as her world was falling apart. Relate this information to the Essential Question and have students discuss what lessons they might take from Anne Frank's experience.

MENTOR TEXT

At the end of the unit, students will be asked to write a personal narrative. "The Diary of a Young Girl" provides a model of how writers can discuss their personal responses to significant events in their lives.

? ESSENTIAL QUESTION:

What can we learn from Anne Frank?

500   Unit 6

QUICK START

Asking questions before you read a selection can help you realize what you'd like to learn from it and what you think you already know. What questions do you have about Anne's diary? Jot them down.

ANALYZE A PRIMARY SOURCE

A source is anything that supplies information. **Secondary sources,** such as encyclopedia articles, are those produced by people who have learned about an event through research. **Primary sources** are those created by people who witnessed or took part in the event. Diaries are primary sources.

A **diary** is a record of its author's thoughts and feelings during a particular time. They often contain headings and salutations, as shown below. As you read Anne Frank's diary, notice what you learn about life during World War Two.

MONDAY EVENING, NOVEMBER 8, 1943 ←

Dearest Kitty, ←

If you were to read all my letters in one sitting, you'd be struck by the fact that they were written in a variety of moods.

The **heading** contains the date on which the entry was made.

The **salutation** reveals to whom the entry has been addressed.

GENRE ELEMENTS: DIARY

- is a type of autobiographical writing
- uses first-person point of view
- includes a daily record of a writer's thoughts, experiences, and feelings
- uses date headings—text features that help to structure and organize the writing

MAKE INFERENCES

Since Anne does not explain everything she writes about, readers must fill in gaps in their understanding by making **inferences,** or logical guesses, from clues in the text and their prior knowledge. For example, in this passage, readers must infer why the doorbell frightens Anne:

This evening, when Bep was still here, the doorbell rang long and loud. I instantly turned white, my stomach churned, and my heart beat wildly—and all because I was afraid.

| What the text says: The doorbell rang. | + | What I know: The Franks are hiding from the Nazis. | = | Inference: Anne is afraid they have been discovered. |

As you read and analyze *The Diary of a Young Girl,* use clues in the text and your knowledge of the Franks' situation as well as what it's like to be a teenager to make inferences about events and experiences that Anne does not fully explain.

The Diary of a Young Girl 501

QUICK START

Have students read the prompt. Encourage students to think of specific events or ideas they might write about in a diary entry: would they write about something that made them happy, something sad, something that made them angry? Tell students that nearly all of what we know about Anne Frank's outlook on life comes from what she wrote in her diary. Have students share what they think their own diary entries would reveal about them.

ANALYZE A PRIMARY SOURCE

Read the information about primary and secondary sources with students. Have them identify whether the following are primary or secondary sources: an account of a baseball game written by someone who played in it (primary), an account of a presidential election written 100 years after the voting (secondary), a journal entry describing a circus attended by the writer (primary).

Have students study the information on diary entries. Explain that Anne Frank wrote her diary entries as though they were letters, but not all diarists use this convention. Emphasize that the most important feature of a diary is that it gives a direct account of the writer's experiences.

MAKE INFERENCES

Tell students that writers often leave information out for the reader to fill in. Have students look closely at the example given in the text. Point out that the reader must use background knowledge, information from earlier in the text, and logic to determine why the ringing of the doorbell caused such a dramatic reaction in Anne; stress that Anne does not tell us directly why she responds as she does.

ENGLISH LEARNER SUPPORT

Identify Cognates Help students connect the terms *primary* and *secondary sources* to cognates in familiar languages. Read the words aloud, and have students repeat the words. Point out the similarities in pronunciation with different cognates.

Spanish: *primario / secundario*

French: *primaire / secundaire*

Portuguese: *primário / secundário* **LIGHT**

TEACH

CRITICAL VOCABULARY

Encourage students to read all the sentences before deciding which word best completes each one. Remind them to look for context clues that match the meaning of each word.

Answers:

1. *splendid*

2. *conjecture*

3. *implore*

■ English Learner Support

Use Cognates Tell Spanish-speaking students that they should look for cognates in the Critical Vocabulary words, such as *implore/implorar* and *splendid/espléndido*.
ALL LEVELS

LANGUAGE CONVENTIONS

Tell students that some writers make frequent use of parentheses, whereas others do not; using parentheses is a matter of taste or style.

Explain that parentheses are most often used to enclose side details within a sentence. Call students' attention to the sample sentence about the bike. Explain that the most important information in the sentence is that the flat tire means the writer needed to walk to school; the fact that this is the second flat tire in a month is less important information and can therefore be enclosed in parentheses.

✎ ANNOTATION MODEL

Point out that the student making these annotations used underlining and wrote margin notes to focus his or her attention on certain details. Remind students that they may have annotation methods that work better for them, but point out that many students find underlining and margin notes to be effective.

 GET READY

CRITICAL VOCABULARY

implore   **splendid**   **conjecture**

To see how many Critical Vocabulary words you already know, use them to complete the sentences.

1. The event was _____ , thanks to everyone's hard work and preparation.

2. Once the results became clear, we learned that his _____ was correct.

3. I _____ you to stay longer because I will struggle without your help.

LANGUAGE CONVENTIONS

Parentheses In this lesson, you will learn how to use parentheses to enclose less important details or comments without interrupting the flow of a sentence, as in the example below.

My bike had a flat tire (second time this month), so I walked to school.

As you read *The Diary of a Young Girl*, note Anne Frank's use of parentheses.

ANNOTATION MODEL   **NOTICE & NOTE**

As you read, notice primary source elements that help you learn about Anne Frank. In the model, you can see one reader's notes about *The Diary of a Young Girl.*

MONDAY EVENING, NOVEMBER 8, 1943

Dearest Kitty,

1   If you were to read all my letters in one sitting, you'd be struck by the fact that they were written in a variety of moods. It annoys me to be so dependent on the moods here in the Annex, but I'm not the only one: we're all subject to them.

> Anne addresses her diary as "Kitty" and uses the pronoun "you" to suggest how Kitty would respond.

> Anne understands that everyone is struggling to cope with life in the Annex.

BACKGROUND

Anne Frank (1929–1945) was 13 years old when she and her family went into hiding to avoid being sent to concentration camps by the Nazis. During the two years she spent living in an attic, she kept a diary. After the war, Anne's father, the only family member to survive the concentration camps to which the family was eventually sent, chose to publish the diary. The selection you are about to read consists of entries taken from throughout the work.

from
The Diary of a Young Girl

Diary by Anne Frank

SETTING A PURPOSE

As you read, think about which of Anne's thoughts and feelings are similar to those of any teenager and which are unique to her family's particularly dire, or urgent, situation.

Notice & Note

Use the side margins to notice and note signposts in the text.

MONDAY EVENING, NOVEMBER 8, 1943

Dearest Kitty,

1   If you were to read all my letters in one sitting, you'd be struck by the fact that they were written in a variety of moods. It annoys me to be so dependent on the moods here in the Annex, but I'm not the only one: we're all subject to them. If I'm engrossed in a book, I have to rearrange my thoughts before I can mingle with other people, because otherwise they might think I was strange. As you can see, I'm currently in the middle of a depression. I couldn't really tell you what set it off, but I think it stems from my cowardice, which confronts me at every turn. This evening, when Bep was still here, the doorbell rang long and loud. I instantly turned white, my stomach churned, and my heart beat wildly—and all because I was afraid.

The Diary of a Young Girl   503

BACKGROUND

Read aloud the background note. Remind students that World War II and the Holocaust took place long before they were born and that Anne Frank's diary serves as a valuable primary source for learning what it was like to be Jewish in Hitler's Europe.

SETTING A PURPOSE

Point out that Anne Frank's living situation in the early 1940s was much different from the living situations of typical American teenagers today. Explain that in some ways, however, this diary reads much like that of a modern adolescent. Have students read carefully to determine where the ideas and mood of the diary seem specific to Anne Frank's circumstances and where they seem typical for any teenager.

NOTICE AND NOTE

Remind students that they should always annotate when they read a new text and that they should be sure to include their reactions to the signposts they notice in the text.

For **listening support** for students at varying proficiency levels, see the **Text X-Ray** on page 500C.

ENGLISH LEARNER SUPPORT

Use Learning Strategies   Have students make a simple flow chart to show the order of events as described by Anne. Discuss using order words such as *first, next,* and *last.*

- Help students fill in the flow chart with events described in paragraph 1. Ask them to say an appropriate order word to describe each event. **SUBSTANTIAL**

- Have student pairs fill in the flow chart with events described in paragraph 1. Have partners take turns describing the events using order words. **MODERATE**

- Have students complete the flow chart and write a paragraph describing the sequence of events using order words to transition between sentences. **LIGHT**

ENGLISH LEARNER SUPPORT

Comprehend Language Structures Explain that an article in English is an adjective that indicates whether a noun is specific or general. Discuss the diffences of *a/an* and *the*. Some languages, such as Vietnamese and Urdu, lack articles. Work with students from these language backgrounds to explain the meanings of phrases such as *the streets*, *the Annex*, and *a castle*.
SUBSTANTIAL

MAKE INFERENCES

Remind students that texts often contain information that is not stated directly, but that readers can often use other means to determine what the author is saying. Explain that the expression *castle in the air* is an example of figurative language, and tell students that they can use the context of the sentence to understand why Anne used this particular image. (**Answer:** *Her family is trapped in the Annex, and the news they receive from the outside world regarding the course of the war is discouraging. Anne is saying that on some level she does not really believe that "after the war" is ever going to happen.*)

LANGUAGE CONVENTIONS

Have students identify the text in parentheses and explain how the information relates to the remainder of the sentence. Ask students why they think this information was set in parentheses. (**Answer:** *The first phrase gives information about the pen and the second about Anne's grandmother, but the details are not part of the sentence grammatically but provide additional information about the fountain pen and its origin.*)

CRITICAL VOCABULARY

implore: To implore implies asking for something, but with a feeling of desperation. People implore one another when what they want seems extremely important.

ASK STUDENTS why *implore* works well in this sentence, but *ask* would not be so successful. (*The writer very badly wants what she asks for. Ask is not a strong enough word to get across the intensity of her feelings.*)

 NOTICE & NOTE

2   At night in bed I see myself alone in a dungeon, without Father and Mother. Or I'm roaming the streets, or the Annex is on fire, or they come in the middle of the night to take us away and I crawl under my bed in desperation. I see everything as if it were actually taking place. And to think it might all happen soon!

3   Miep often says she envies us because we have such peace and quiet here. That may be true, but she's obviously not thinking about our fear.

4   I simply can't imagine the world will ever be normal again for us. I do talk about "after the war," but it's as if I were talking about a castle in the air, something that can never come true.

5   I see the eight of us in the Annex as if we were a patch of blue sky surrounded by menacing black clouds. The perfectly round spot on which we're standing is still safe, but the clouds are moving in on us, and the ring between us and the approaching danger is being pulled tighter and tighter. We're surrounded by darkness and danger, and in our desperate search for a way out we keep bumping into each other. We look at the fighting down below and the peace and beauty up above. In the meantime, we've been cut off by the dark mass of clouds, so that we can go neither up nor down. It looms before us like an impenetrable wall, trying to crush us, but not yet able to. I can only cry out and **implore**, "Oh, ring, ring, open wide and let us out!"

Yours, Anne

THURSDAY, NOVEMBER 11, 1943

Dearest Kitty,

6   I have a good title for this chapter:
     Ode to My Fountain Pen
     In Memoriam

7   My fountain pen was always one of my most prized possessions; I valued it highly, especially because it had a thick nib, and I can only write neatly with thick nibs. It has led a long and interesting fountain-pen life, which I will summarize below.

8   When I was nine, my fountain pen (packed in cotton) arrived as a "sample of no commercial value" all the way from Aachen,[1] where my grandmother (the kindly donor) used to live. I lay in bed with the flu, while the February winds howled

---
[1] **Aachen** (ä´kən): a city in Germany.

MAKE INFERENCES
Annotate: In paragraph 4, mark what Anne compares to "a castle in the air."

Infer: What reasons might Anne have for making this comparison?

implore
(ĭm-plôr´) *v.* To *implore* is to beg for something urgently.

LANGUAGE CONVENTIONS
Annotate: Parentheses can be used to enclose information that is helpful but not essential to the meaning of a sentence. In paragraph 8, mark the text in parentheses.

Analyze: Explain how the details in parentheses relate to the rest of the sentence.

around the apartment house. This **splendid** fountain pen came in a red leather case, and I showed it to my girlfriends the first chance I got. Me, Anne Frank, the proud owner of a fountain pen.

9   When I was ten, I was allowed to take the pen to school, and to my surprise, the teacher even let me write with it. When I was eleven, however, my treasure had to be tucked away again, because my sixth-grade teacher allowed us to use only school pens and inkpots. When I was twelve, I started at the Jewish Lyceum and my fountain pen was given a new case in honor of the occasion. Not only did it have room for a pencil, it also had a zipper, which was much more impressive. When I was thirteen, the fountain pen went with me to the Annex, and together we've raced through countless diaries and compositions. I'd turned fourteen and my fountain pen was enjoying the last year of its life with me when . . .

10   It was just after five on Friday afternoon. I came out of my room and was about to sit down at the table to write when I was roughly pushed to one side to make room for Margot and Father, who wanted to practice their Latin. The fountain pen remained unused on the table, while its owner, sighing, was forced to make do with a very tiny corner of the table, where she began rubbing beans. That's how we remove mold from the beans and restore them to their original state. At a quarter to six I swept the floor, dumped the dirt into a newspaper, along with the rotten beans, and tossed it into the stove. A giant flame shot up, and I thought it was wonderful that the stove, which had been gasping its last breath, had made such a miraculous recovery.

splendid
(splĕn´dĭd) *adj.* If something is *splendid*, it is magnificent or very good.

MAKE INFERENCES
Annotate: Mark details in paragraph 10 that describe Anne's actions.

Infer: What can you infer about Anne's relationship with her family based on these details?

APPLYING ACADEMIC VOCABULARY

☑ **communicate** ☐ **draft** ☐ **liberation** ☑ **philosophy** ☐ **publish**

Write and Discuss Have students turn to a partner to discuss the following questions. Guide students to include the Academic Vocabulary words *communicate* and *philosophy* in their responses. Ask students to share their responses with the class.

- What is the best way to **communicate** your ideas to a wide audience?
- How can a diary help you express your **philosophy**?

 MAKE INFERENCES

Have students read the prompt and then look closely at paragraph 10 to identify Anne's actions. Remind students that readers often need to make inferences when the writer does not state things directly, and that this paragraph is an example of that. Have students share the inferences they make with a partner or the class. (***Answer:*** *Inferences may include that Anne feels left out and believes that the other family members treat her as being less important than they are.*)

■ English Learner Support

Use Reading Strategies To improve oral reading skills, have students read paragraph 10 aloud as a group. Have them use choral reading, in which they all read in unison, or shared reading, in which they are led in reading together by a teacher. Help students pay attention to intonations in English sentences. **MODERATE**

For **reading support** for students at varying proficiency levels, see the **Text X-Ray** on page 500D.

CRITICAL VOCABULARY

splendid: This is a strongly positive word which suggests that someone or something is marvelous or outstanding.

ASK STUDENTS what they have done lately that others might call a *splendid* achievement.

Entertainment/Getty Images

ANALYZE A PRIMARY SOURCE

Have students annotate in accordance with the prompt on page 507. Then have them use what Anne writes about these people to make inferences about their characters. Point out that Anne's diary is a primary source about the van Daans and others mentioned in the text, because Anne actually knew these people. (**Answer:** *Mr. Kugler seems kind and generous. Mr. Dussel appears inconsiderate of others. The van Daans and the Franks seem to be upset with each other; Mother is losing patience with the van Daans. Peter shares Anne's dismay about the others' negative behavior.*)

CRITICAL VOCABULARY

conjecture: To *conjecture* is to guess, usually based on some evidence. In some disciplines, such as mathematics, the noun *conjecture* is used in much the same way as *hypothesis* or *theory*.

ASK STUDENTS why Anne uses the word *conjectured* here instead of a word such as *said* or *stated*. (*To indicate that Father is not certain what happened; he is only making an educated guess.*)

NOTICE & NOTE

11   All was quiet again. The Latin students had left, and I sat down at the table to pick up where I'd left off. But no matter where I looked, my fountain pen was nowhere in sight. I took another look. Margot looked, Mother looked, Father looked, Dussel looked. But it had vanished .

12   "Maybe it fell into the stove, along with the beans!" Margot suggested.

13   "No, it couldn't have!" I replied.

14   But that evening, when my fountain pen still hadn't turned up, we all assumed it had been burned, especially because celluloid is highly inflammable. Our darkest fears were confirmed the next day when Father went to empty the stove and discovered the clip, used to fasten it to a pocket, among the ashes. Not a trace of the gold nib was left. "It must have melted into stone," Father **conjectured**.

15   I'm left with one consolation, small though it may be: my fountain pen was cremated,[2] just as I would like to be someday!

conjecture
(kən-jěk´chər) *v.* If you *conjecture*, you guess or suppose.

SATURDAY, JANUARY 15, 1944

My dearest Kitty,

16   There's no reason for me to go on describing all our quarrels and arguments down to the last detail. It's enough to tell you that we've divided many things like meat and fats and oils and are frying our own potatoes. Recently we've been eating a little extra rye bread because by four o'clock we're so hungry for dinner we can barely control our rumbling stomachs.

17   Mother's birthday is rapidly approaching. She received some extra sugar from Mr. Kugler, which sparked off jealousy on the part of the van Daans, because Mrs. van D. didn't receive any on her birthday. But what's the point of boring you with harsh words, spiteful conversations and tears when you know they bore us even more?

18   Mother has expressed a wish, which isn't likely to come true any time soon: not to have to see Mr. van Daan's face for two whole weeks. I wonder if everyone who shares a house sooner or later ends up at odds with their fellow residents. Or have we just had a stroke of bad luck? At mealtime, when Dussel helps himself to a quarter of the half-filled gravy boat and leaves the rest of us to do without, I lose my appetite and feel like jumping to my feet, knocking him off his chair and throwing him out the door.

ANALYZE A PRIMARY SOURCE
Annotate: Mark names and third-person pronouns in paragraphs 17–19.

Draw Conclusions: Although diaries are written from the first-person point of view, clues in the text may provide insight into the character traits and feelings of others. What conclusions can you draw about the people Anne mentions based on the details she includes?

---

[2] **cremated** (krē´māt´əd): burned to ashes.

WHEN STUDENTS STRUGGLE . . .

Learning Strategy   Have students create a simple graphic organizer to help them understand what they can infer from the text. On the left, guide students to list facts from the text, such as *Mr. Dussel took most of the gravy.* On the right, have them list what the fact implies, such as *Mr. Dussel is selfish.* Have students work with partners or guide the entire class to create a group chart.

For additional support, go to the **Reading Studio** and assign the following **LEVEL** **Level Up tutorial: Making Inferences About Characters.**

19   Are most people so stingy and selfish? I've gained some insight into human nature since I came here, which is good, but I've had enough for the present. Peter says the same.

20   The war is going to go on despite our quarrels and our longing for freedom and fresh air, so we should try to make the best of our stay here.

21   I'm preaching, but I also believe that if I live here much longer, I'll turn into a dried-up old beanstalk. And all I really want is to be an honest-to-goodness teenager!

Yours, Anne

NOTICE & NOTE

ANALYZE A PRIMARY SOURCE

Annotate: Mark words and phrases that suggest Anne's feelings and outlook on life in paragraphs 20–21.

Analyze: In what ways does Anne's outlook relate to her current situation? Which emotions are shared by many teenagers?

CHECK YOUR UNDERSTANDING

Answer these questions before moving on to the **Analyze the Text** section on the following page.

1 Which word from paragraph 1 helps the reader understand the meaning of <u>cowardice</u>?

   A *depression*

   B *confront*

   C *churned*

   D *afraid*

2 The story of Anne's fountain pen allows her to recall —

   F events that led her to stop writing

   G pleasant memories from her past

   H her fondness for her sister

   J her fear of the future

3 In paragraphs 16–17, Anne explains that she will not describe many details about the arguments among her family members and the van Daans because —

   A she wants to avoid dwelling on the conflicts

   B she disagrees with the way her parents interpret events

   C the information was included in earlier entries

   D writing about the quarrels will make her hungry

The Diary of a Young Girl   507

TEACH

ANALYZE A PRIMARY SOURCE

Remind students that when they analyze a primary source they often need to do two things: They need to find and mark important evidence in the text, and they need to interpret that evidence, which often includes drawing inferences and conclusions about what the writer says. Have students read paragraphs 20–21, follow the prompt, and decide which of Anne's feelings are typical of adolescents in general and which are specific to her difficult situation. (**Answer:** *Anne's expression of optimistic hopeful feelings along with pessimistic feelings of despair are certainly shared by many teenagers, but the intensity of her feelings—especially her pessimism—likely does stem from the difficulty of her current situation.*)

CHECK YOUR UNDERSTANDING

Have students answer the questions independently.

Answers:

1. D

2. G

3. A

If they answer any questions incorrectly, have them reread the text to confirm their understanding. Then they may proceed to ANALYZE THE TEXT on p. 508.

ENGLISH LEARNER SUPPORT

Oral Assessment Use the following questions to assess students' comprehension and speaking skills:

1. Look at paragraph 1. Find the word *cowardice*. Which word tells what *cowardice* means? *(afraid)*

2. Anne tells the story of her pen. What does she remember in the story? *(pleasant memories from her past)*

3. Look at paragraphs 16–17. Why does she not want to tell about arguments? *(She does not want to think about the conflicts all the time.)*
    SUBSTANTIAL/MODERATE

ANALYZE THE TEXT

Possible answers:

1. **DOK 2:** *Anne feels depressed and isolated but recognizes that the other residents of the annex feel the same. In paragraph 5, she imagines everyone as "surrounded by menacing black clouds" and "bumping into each other" as they search for "a way out."*

2. **DOK 2:** *Anne says they are surrounded by danger looming "like an impenetrable wall," threatening to crush them. The simile describes her fear of what will happen if they are found.*

3. **DOK 3:** *Anne starts her entry with a "chapter title" as though she is writing a novel. She changes the form to tell a story rather than focus on her feelings. The form may suggest a desire to be a writer.*

4. **DOK 3:** *In paragraphs 1–2, Anne describes herself as depressed and losing patience. In paragraphs 17–18, we see her doing the same—she has "had enough"—and also shows anger. Anne's feelings of depression, anger, impatience, and anxiety support her assertion that she experiences "a variety of moods."*

5. **DOK 3:** *The entries span over two months, during which the residents have been quarreling more often. The Franks and Van Daans are now dividing food. Based on Anne's description, the residents' supply of food may have also become more limited.*

RESEARCH

SOL 8.9

Remind students that sources such as Wikipedia should not be considered "online encyclopedias" as there is no consistent editorial process and thus no way to ensure that information is accurate. Have students use reliable sources to answer the questions.

Connect Have students consider what might have been different had the diary been published in a different format.

 RESPOND

ANALYZE THE TEXT

Support your responses with evidence from the text.   NOTEBOOK

1. **Infer** What is Anne Frank's view of the tension among all eight people living in the Annex? Cite evidence to support your response.

2. **Interpret** A **simile** makes a comparison between two unlike things using the word *like* or *as*. Reread paragraph 5. What does Anne reveal about her perspective with her use of the simile "I see the eight of us in the Annex as if we were a patch of blue sky surrounded by menacing black clouds"?

3. **Draw Conclusions** Review the introduction to the entry for Thursday, November 11, 1943. Notice that the elements of this entry differ from the others. Why might Anne have used a slightly different form here?

4. **Compare** How does Anne's emotional state in paragraphs 1–2 compare with her feelings in paragraphs 18–21? Does your comparison support Anne's statement that her reader would be "struck by the fact" that her entries are "written in a variety of moods"? Explain.

5. **Draw Conclusions** Over what span of time are the entries in this excerpt from the diary written? What does Anne reveal has been happening during this period?

RESEARCH

> **RESEARCH TIP**
> Online encyclopedias provide reliable information about prominent historical figures and works of literature. When researching a particular work, official websites of authors, publishers, museums, or historical organizations may provide helpful information.

Using at least two sources, research how Anne Frank's diary was found and became published. Record what you learn in the chart.

QUESTION	ANSWER
How did Otto Frank receive his daughter's diary?	*Miep Gies saved Anne's writings after the residents of the Annex were arrested. Otto Frank returned following the war, and Miep gave him the writings after he received news of Anne's death.*
How was the published format of the diary decided?	*Anne's writings included her original diaries along with rewritten entries on loose sheets of paper. Otto Frank decided to print a third version that combined entries from both of Anne's versions.*
What was the response to the published book?	*The book became a best-seller and was translated into more than 65 languages.*

Connect Consider what you have learned about how the published format of *The Diary of a Young Girl* was chosen. In a small group, discuss ways in which different decisions in creating the published form of the diary may have affected responses to the book.

 LEARNING MINDSET

Write a Paragraph Have students consider the hypothetical situation in which Anne Frank is brought to a concentration camp but survives the war and returns to the Netherlands to collect her diary from Miep Gies. Ask students what they think would have happened afterward. Tell them to discuss whether the diary would have been published as it was or in some other format, whether Anne would have wanted it published, and what sort of adult Anne would have become. Then have students write a paragraph explaining their ideas and reasons for their thinking.

CREATE AND DISCUSS

Create a Comic Create an illustrated comic retelling of the fountain pen story that Anne shares in *The Diary of a Young Girl*.

- ❏ Review Anne's November 11, 1943, entry for details of the fountain pen story. Decide which elements you will include in your comic.
- ❏ Plan what words and images each panel will show, and create a layout of the number and size of your panels.
- ❏ Sketch your comic. Then create a final version by adding elements such as ink, color, captions, and word balloons.

Discuss with a Partner How do Anne's ideas and reactions compare with yours and those of your friends? Discuss this question with a partner.

- ❏ Review The *Diary of a Young Girl* to identify ideas and reactions with which you agree or disagree. Connect each idea or reaction with a particular value or trait to which you can relate.
- ❏ Discuss your ideas with a partner. Share any questions you generated in your discussion with the rest of the class.

RESPOND TO THE ESSENTIAL QUESTION

 What can we learn from Anne Frank?

Gather Information Review your annotations and notes on *The Diary of a Young Girl*. Then, add relevant details to your Response Log. As you determine which details to include, think about:

- what you learn about Anne and what life was like in the Annex
- reasons Anne includes certain details and descriptions
- ways in which Anne is similar to other teenagers

At the end of the unit, you can use your notes to help you write a personal narrative.

Go to the **Speaking and Listening Studio: Participating in Collaborative Discussions** for help with having a discussion.

ACADEMIC VOCABULARY

As you write and discuss what you learned from the diary, be sure to use the Academic Vocabulary words. Check off each of the words that you use.

- ❏ **communicate**
- ❏ **draft**
- ❏ **liberation**
- ❏ **philosophy**
- ❏ **publish**

CREATE AND DISCUSS

Create a Comic Remind students that they will need to use organizational strategies to ensure that they include all the appropriate elements of the story in the comic without making it too long. Model how to create a storyboard that will serve as an outline for the finished product.

For **writing support** for students at varying proficiency levels, see the **Text X-Ray** on page 500D.

Discuss with a Partner Tell students that there are no right or wrong answers to these questions; on the contrary, different students may respond to the same question in very different ways. Point out that students are trying to determine, here as they did earlier, how much of Anne's way of looking at the world is a function of her difficult living situation and how much is the result of her being a fairly typical teenager.

RESPOND TO THE ESSENTIAL QUESTION

Allow time for students to add details from "The Diary of a Young Girl" to their Unit 6 Response Logs.

ENGLISH LEARNER SUPPORT

Create a Comic Suggest to students that one of the best ways of ensuring that dialogue is effective is to read it aloud. Have students work in small groups to read aloud the dialogue they have written for their comics. Work with students on expressive reading, proper intonation, and pronunciation. For example, the phrase *fountain pen* is typically spoken with the stress on the first syllable of *fountain*. Help students make revisions to their dialogue as needed.

MODERATE/LIGHT

CRITICAL VOCABULARY

Answers:

1. *guessing an answer; to conjecture is to make an educated guess without knowing for sure*

2. *begging for help; when you implore someone you are desperate for assistance*

3. *a lovely view; something that is splendid is magnificent or wonderful, and a lovely view would be a good example of that*

VOCABULARY STRATEGY:
Connotation and Denotation

Answers:

1. *Prison* is any place where people are jailed, but *dungeon* implies an especially miserable atmosphere, especially one that is dark and gloomy.

2. *Splendid* suggests something really outstanding or even marvelous, while *fine* suggests that something is okay but not great.

3. *Conflicts* suggests disagreements, but *battles* suggests more arguments that border on violent.

RESPOND

WORD BANK
implore
splendid
conjecture

Go to the **Vocabulary Studio** for more on connotation and denotation.

CRITICAL VOCABULARY

Practice and Apply To demonstrate that you understand the Critical Vocabulary words, choose an appropriate response to each question below and explain why you chose it.

1. Which of the following would you describe as conjecturing? Why?
   explaining a problem   guessing an answer

2. Which of the following would you describe as imploring? Why?
   correcting a mistake   begging for help

3. Which of the following would you describe as splendid? Why?
   a lovely view   a draft of a story

VOCABULARY STRATEGY:
Connotation and Denotation

Many words have both a denotation and a connotation. A word's **denotation** is its dictionary definition. A word's **connotations** are the ideas and feelings associated with the word. You can use your knowledge of a word's connotation as a context clue to help you determine the meaning of other words. Study this example from *The Diary of a Young Girl.*

> **Are most people so stingy and selfish?**

While the denotation of *stingy* is "giving or spending reluctantly," the negative connotation of *selfish* can help you realize that stingy also has a negative connotation. *Stingy* suggests unkindness, in contrast to its synonyms *sparing* or *frugal*, which have more positive connotations and suggest carefulness and a desire to avoid waste.

Practice and Apply Tell how the meaning of each sentence would change if the underlined word were replaced by the word in parentheses.

1. Anne dreams of being in a prison without her parents. (dungeon)

2. The view from a certain window in the Annex was splendid. (fine)

3. Anne was bothered by the conflicts between the families. (battles)

LANGUAGE CONVENTIONS:
Parentheses

Parentheses are punctuation marks that are used to set off useful but less-important information that does not fit neatly into the sentence. The chart shows some reasons writers use parentheses.

REASON	EXAMPLE
to enclose information that is related but not of primary importance	The play (we all loved it) runs about ninety minutes.
to add directions or other information that explains or clarifies something	Lizzi's (the bakery) is giving out free samples today.
to repeat numbers or figures to ensure accuracy	The fee for the service is thirty dollars ($30).

Use parentheses so that information that you want to include but that is not of great importance doesn't interrupt the flow of a sentence.

Practice and Apply For each sentence, put parentheses around the word or words that should be enclosed by them.

1. Antonio introduced us to Deshawn (I think his last name is Jackson) at the party last weekend.

2. Paris (often called the City of Lights) is one of the world's most popular tourist destinations.

3. The banquet will be held at Nicholson Hall (on Harris Street) on Tuesday evening.

4. Our team won by 6 points (48–42.)

LANGUAGE CONVENTIONS:
Parentheses

Remind students that parentheses are frequently used to set off information that is interesting, but not essential to the meaning of a text. Review that parentheses have a beginning and an end and that the information is contained inside the two parts.

Review the examples with students, calling students' attention to the first example in particular. Point out that the main idea in the sentence has to do with the length of the play. The writer wants the reader to know how much audience members liked the play, but this is not the central message; thus, enclosing this information in parentheses makes sense. Tell students that there are other ways to write sentences like these, including setting off phrases with commas, but that many writers like to use parentheses. For example, the first sentence could begin *The play, which we all loved . . .*

Have students complete the Practice and Apply task on their own.

EL ENGLISH LEARNER SUPPORT

Language Conventions Use the following supports for students at varying proficiency levels:

- Give students a simple sentence, such as *Jose is good at soccer.* Show them how to add a parenthetical statement to make a more complex sentence, such as *Jose (my brother) is good at soccer.* Model how to read the sentence with a parenthetical. Have students echo read each sentence. **SUBSTANTIAL**

- Have students write a simple sentence about a friend, using the sentence frame *My friend likes to _____.* Then have them add a parenthetical statement that gives the friend's name and read their new sentence aloud. **MODERATE**

- Have students write a simple sentence about a friend or family member. Have them add a parenthetical statement about the person and read their sentence aloud. **LIGHT**

AFTER AUSCHWITZ
Speech by Elie Wiesel

GENRE ELEMENTS
SPEECH

Remind students that the purpose of **speeches** is to share information orally with a group of people. They can be impromptu or planned, formal or informal, long or short, and humorous or serious. Point out that speeches may inform, persuade, entertain, or a combination of these purposes. The purpose typically ties directly to the audience. Speeches are often delivered on special occasions.

LEARNING OBJECTIVES

- Cite evidence to support analysis of persuasive appeals.
- Research Elie Wiesel's work as a humanitarian and activist.
- Discuss efforts to fight religious fanaticism and racial hate.
- Analyze rhetorical devices.
- Create a poster depicting a quotation.
- **Language** Pronounce words with the inflected ending -*ed*.

TEXT COMPLEXITY

Quantitative Measures	After Auschwitz
	Ideas Presented More than one purpose; implied but easy to infer.
Quantitative Measures	**Structures Used** Organization of main ideas and details is complex but mostly explicit.
	Language Used Some unfamiliar, academic, or domain-specific words.
	Knowledge Required Specialized knowledge required.

RESOURCES

- Unit 6 Response Log
- Selection Audio
- Reading Studio: Notice & Note
- Speaking and Listening Studio: Giving a Presentation; Participating in Collaborative Discussions
- "After Auschwitz" Selection Test

SUMMARIES

English

This selection is a transcript of a speech by Elie Wiesel, a survivor of the Auschwitz concentration camp, delivered in 1995 to mark the 50th anniversary of the liberation of Auschwitz. He reflects on the horrible crimes committed by the Nazis and calls on the members of his audience and the rest of the world to reject and strongly oppose religious fanaticism and racial hatred so that such horrible crimes do not happen in the future.

English

Esta selección es una transcripción de un discurso de Elie Wiesel, un superviviente del campo de concentración de Auschwitz, dado en 1995 para conmemorar el quincuagésimo aniversario de la liberación de Auschwitz. Él reflexiona acerca de los horribles crímenes cometidos por los nazis y exhorta a los miembros del público y al resto del mundo a rechazar y a oponerse fuertemente en contra del fanatismo religioso y el odio racial para que estos crímenes no ocurran en el futuro.

 ## SMALL-GROUP OPTIONS

Have students work in small groups to read and discuss the selection.

Reciprocal Teaching

Have students read the speech manuscript. Then, have them use these question stems to each write three to five questions about the speech:

- *Why does Elie Wiesel . . . ?*
- *What does Wiesel mean by . . . ?*
- *What is his purpose in talking about . . . ?*
- *What did listeners . . . ?*

Make sure students understand that they can ask questions without knowing the answer.

Have students discuss question answers in small groups, decide by consensus on the best answer, and find text evidence to support it.

Think-Pair-Share

Present this background and question to students:

Where was this speech given and how do you know?

- Have students individually think about the question and make notes.
- Then, pair students and have them listen, discuss, and formulate a common response.
- Finally, have students share responses with the class.

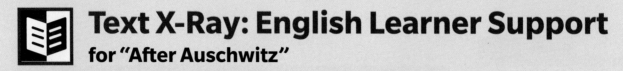

Text X-Ray: English Learner Support
for "After Auschwitz"

Use the Text X-Ray and the supports and scaffolds in the Teacher's Edition to help guide students at different proficiency levels through the selection.

INTRODUCE THE SELECTION
DISCUSS LEARNING FROM PAST MISTAKES

In this lesson, students will need to be able to discuss some horrible past mistakes in the world and think about what people can learn from the past. In addition, because of the nature of the content, which presents atrocities committed against adults, children, and whole families as well as whole groups of people, students might have to deal with strong emotions while reading. Students may need to stop and discuss at times simply to deal with the emotions. Assign one of the four phrases listed below to partners or small groups. Have students discuss the phrases to help understand the selection:

- *human condition* (paragraph 1)
- *inflict suffering and humiliation* (paragraph 4)
- *demented mind* (paragraph 10)
- *religious fanaticism and racial hate* (paragraph 17)

CULTURAL REFERENCES

The following words and phrases may be unfamiliar to students:

- *stateless, faceless and nameless victims* (paragraph 5): victims who were taken from their homes and treated as if they were not human beings
- *nocturnal processions* (paragraph 5): people walking in lines during the night
- *exiles drawn by death* (paragraph 7): people kicked out of their homes and brought to the camps
- *question of all questions* (paragraph 10): the most important question of all

LISTENING

Understand Word Choices

Draw students' attention to the beginning of each sentence at the start of paragraphs 3–6. Discuss that speeches have some "in the moment" wording that is not found in text intended to be understood in only a written form.

Have students listen as you read aloud. Use the following supports with students at varying proficiency levels:

- Ask students questions about what you just read aloud. Slowly reread the sentence in paragraph 3. Have them underline the words that would only be part of a speech. (*I speak*) **SUBSTANTIAL**
- Slowly reread paragraphs 3 and 4 to students. Have them underline the words that would only be part of a speech. (*I speak; I speak*) **MODERATE**
- Slowly reread paragraphs 3–5 to students. Have them underline the words that would only be part of a speech. (*I speak; I speak; In this place of darkness . . . here*) **LIGHT**

SPEAKING

Pronounce English Words Correctly

Have student explore the different pronunciations of -ed. Circulate around the room to make sure students are using the key term correctly.

Use the following supports with students at varying proficiency levels:

- Write these words from the text on the board: *killed, died, happened*. Model their pronunciations and have students repeat them. Ask: *What sound does ed make in these words?* (d) **SUBSTANTIAL**
- Write these words from the text on the board: *worked, killed, died, happened, condemned*. Model their pronunciations and have students repeat them. Ask: *What sound does ed make?* (t and d) **MODERATE**
- Pair students. Have students sort the past-tense verbs in paragraph 11 in a table. Have them practice using correct pronunciations. Remind students that many English past tense verbs end in *ed* that sounds like */-t/, /-d/,* or */id/*. **LIGHT**

READING

Identify Rhetorical Devices

Draw students' attention to some of the phrases in the speech that enhance arguments and communications in appeals. Discuss that the author uses these to reinforce his meaning.

Use the following supports with students at varying proficiency levels:

- Copy these sentences from paragraph 11 on the board. "In the towns nearby, what happened?" and "In the lands nearby, what happened?" Have students read these sentences and ask whether they understand the meanings. **SUBSTANTIAL**
- Have students read these sentences in paragraph 11: "In the towns nearby, what happened?" and "In the lands nearby, what happened?" Point out that these questions are examples of rhetorical devices. Ask students to discuss the meanings. (*Why did no one do anything?*) **MODERATE**
- Have students read this sentence from paragraph 10: "What kind of demented mind could have invented this system?" Pair students and ask them to discuss the meaning of the sentence in the context of the paragraph. (*What horrible person could have come up with such atrocities?*) **LIGHT**

WRITING

Create a Poster

Work with students to read the writing assignment on p. 521.

Use the following supports with students after they choose a meaningful quotation from the passage:

- Have students copy their chosen quotations into their notebooks. Use this sentence frame to help them discuss the meaning. *The quotation _____ is meaningful because _____.* **SUBSTANTIAL**
- Have students discuss what type of information they could place on their poster and what research they need to do to gather facts, dates, and other details supporting the message. **MODERATE**
- Pair students and have them discuss whether the information they gathered is relevant or needs adjustments. Have them check that all spelling should be accurate. **LIGHT**

AFTER AUSCHWITZ

Speech by **Elie Wiesel**

? Connect to the
ESSENTIAL QUESTION

"After Auschwitz" provides an overview of concentration camps as well as a plea for people worldwide to learn from the horrific situation that we will neither perpetuate nor tolerate either religious fanaticism or racial hatred.

? ESSENTIAL QUESTION:

What can we learn from Anne Frank?

 LEARNING MINDSET

Plan Remind students that planning is essential to completing work efficiently and exceptionally. Encourage students to make a plan for completing the reading assignment and the activities that follow. Point out that, for parts of the activities, such as creating the poster, it makes sense to map out steps that can help them finish as required and on time. Make sure students understand that planning will help them learn discipline, which will benefit them throughout their lives.

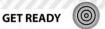

QUICK START

The speech you are about to read was given at a ceremony to mark the 50th anniversary of the liberation of Auschwitz, a Nazi concentration camp. With the class, discuss why people take the time to hold such ceremonies. Why might it be important to remember horrible crimes committed in the past?

ANALYZE APPEALS

In "After Auschwitz," Elie Wiesel's goal is to persuade, or convince, his audience to adopt a particular viewpoint and support his claim. To do so, he appeals to his audience's feelings and values. Appeals are one kind of rhetorical device used to make an argument more persuasive.

- An **emotional appeal** is a message that creates strong feelings in order to make an impact. These appeals can tap into people's feelings such as fear, pity, or vanity. In the passage from his speech provided on the chart, Elie Wiesel appeals to feelings of sympathy and compassion for others.

- In an **ethical appeal**, a speaker or writer links a claim to a widely accepted value in order to gain moral support for the claim and to establish a bond with the audience as someone who shares their values. In his speech, Wiesel appeals to the established belief that human beings should neither murder one another nor be indifferent to suffering.

View the chart below for examples of each kind of appeal. As you read the speech, notice other places Wiesel appeals to his audience's emotions and their ethics.

GENRE ELEMENTS: SPEECH

- is a talk or public address presented to an audience
- may have one or more purposes, such as to entertain, to explain, or to persuade
- is often delivered on a special occasion
- may be recorded or transcribed for later reading and analysis

TYPE OF APPEAL	EXAMPLES FROM THE SPEECH
Emotional appeal	Close your eyes and listen. Listen to the silent screams of terrified mothers, the prayers of anguished old men and women. Listen to the tears of children, Jewish children . . .
Ethical appeal	And it worked. The killers killed, the victims died and the world was the world and everything else was going on, life as usual.

After Auschwitz **513**

QUICK START

Have students read the Quick Start question and invite them to share their reactions to holding memorial ceremonies and why it might be important to remember horrible crimes from the past.

ANALYZE APPEALS

Help students understand and recognize persuasive appeals. Make sure students realize that appeals are one type of rhetorical device that people use when trying to persuade others. Point out that, although Elie Wiesel used appeals quite a bit in his speech, other people working with other topics might not use appeals at all. Discuss both types of appeals that are discussed on p. 513 (emotional and ethical) and how each is used. Then point out that the author uses both types of appeals throughout his speech, such as shown in the Type of Appeal chart.

 ENGLISH LEARNER SUPPORT

Use Articles Write these nouns on the board: emotional appeal, ethical appeal, audience, impact. Ask students to read the Analyze Appeals information on p. 513 and then to write four sentences—one using each word. Remind them that English almost always requires the use of articles before singular common nouns. Make sure they remember that the words *a*, *an*, and *the* are articles. Tell them, in this case, to be especially careful to use the article "an," which is required when using nouns that begin with vowels. **MODERATE**

ANALYZE RHETORICAL DEVICES

Point out to students that two other types of rhetorical devices that the author uses include repetition and parallelism. Make sure students realize that there are many other types of rhetorical devices that the author did not use. Have students identify the repetition in the sample sentences. *(After Auschwitz)* Have students identify the parallelism in the sample sentence and explain why it is considered parallelism. *(The words* stateless, faceless, *and* nameless *together are an example of parallelism because the three words have a similar "noun + less" structure; they emphasize that the people were robbed of their identify, and the three words used together produce a rhythm.)*

■ English Learner Support

Identify Suffixes Point out to students that the suffix *less* means "without." Ask students to write the words *stateless, faceless,* and *nameless* in a list and draw lines between the base words and the suffix. Then, have them add an equal sign after each word and write "without state," "without face," and "without name" after the words.

SUBSTANTIAL/MODERATE

ANNOTATION MODEL

Point out that annotating the text has many benefits, including these four:

- It is a good way to respond to questions.

- It allows readers to easily re-find key information.

- It serves as a form of notetaking.

- It lets readers actually use the text rather than only talk about the text.

 GET READY

ANALYZE RHETORICAL DEVICES

Appeals to emotion and ethics are just two of many **rhetorical devices,** or techniques writers use to enhance their arguments and communications. Here are two other rhetorical devices that writers often use to enhance the effectiveness of speeches in particular.

- **Repetition** is a rhetorical device in which a sound, word, phrase, clause, or line is repeated for emphasis or to give a text or speech a sense of unity. Repetition also helps reinforce meaning and can create an appealing rhythm, as in this example.

  After Auschwitz, the human condition is no longer the same. After Auschwitz, nothing will ever be the same.

- **Parallelism** is the use of words, phrases, clauses, or lines that have a similar structure or grammatical form. Like repetition, parallelism can emphasize meaning and also produce an engaging rhythm.

  In this place of darkness and malediction we can but stand in awe and remember its stateless, faceless and nameless victims.

As you read and analyze the speech, pay attention to the rhetorical devices Elie Wiesel uses.

ANNOTATION MODEL   **NOTICE & NOTE**

As you read, note examples of the speaker's appeals to both emotions and ethics, and examine other rhetorical devices. This model shows one reader's notes about the beginning of "After Auschwitz."

1 *"After Auschwitz, the <u>human condition</u> is not the same, nothing will be the same."*
2   Here heaven and earth are on fire.
3   I speak to you as a man, who 50 years and nine days ago had <u>no name, no hope, no future</u> and was known only by his number, A7713.

> "human condition" suggests ethical concerns

> parallel phrases with "no" create a rhythm that produces a tone of hopelessness

Elie Wiesel (1928–2016) was born in Romania. After the Germans invaded his town, he and his family were sent to Auschwitz, a concentration camp. Only Wiesel and two of his sisters survived. Wiesel wrote about his experiences in the book Night, which has sold millions of copies in many different languages. After its publication, Wiesel devoted himself to ensuring that the deaths of millions of Jews would never be forgotten, and that other human beings would never be subjected to such crimes. In 1986, Wiesel was awarded the Nobel Peace Prize for his life's work.

AFTER AUSCHWITZ

Speech by Elie Wiesel

BACKGROUND

The Auschwitz concentration camp complex opened in 1940 in southern Poland. Concentration camps were used to incarcerate Jews and other supposed enemies of the state. Auschwitz played a major role in the Nazi plan to exterminate all the Jews in Europe. Inside, Nazis forced prisoners into hard labor. Anyone unable to work was executed upon arrival. Between 1940 and 1945, more than one million Jews and others including Poles, Roma, and Soviet prisioners of war were sent to Auschwitz. Few survived. Auschwitz was finally abandoned by German soldiers as the Soviet army advanced upon it in 1945.

SETTING A PURPOSE

The horrible crimes committed in Nazi concentration camps occurred long ago. As you read, think about why the author continues to reflect on these events. Why does he believe people need to be reminded of them? Write down any questions you have.

> **Notice & Note**
>
> Use the side margins to notice and note signposts in the text.

After Auschwitz **515**

BACKGROUND

Have students read the background and information about the author, Elie Wiesel. Supplement the information by telling students about the place where the speech was made. The combined sites of Auschwitz and its mass-extermination center at Birkenau are considered the biggest cemetery in the world.

The Auschwitz-Birkenau State Museum is an exhibition of Nazi prisons and death chambers. The museum, originally devised by Holocaust survivors during the 1950s, is the most visited tourist site in Poland.

Prepare students to recognize the line of prayer repeated throughout the speech. Explain that the text set off in boldface is an English transliteration of Aramaic, the language spoken by Jews in ancient times. The words are the beginning of a solemn prayer that is also known as the mourner's prayer.

SETTING A PURPOSE

Direct students to use the Setting a Purpose question to focus their reading.

IMPROVE READING FLUENCY

Targeted Passage Tell students that a speech is more effective when the speaker uses appropriate expression in his or her voice. Project lines 1–9 on the board. Define unfamiliar words, and then read the lines aloud with appropriate expression. Call on volunteers to highlight the words and phrases that they hear most clearly. Read the paragraphs again, and have students chorally repeat them in a solemn and strong tone, emphasizing the highlighted words and phrases.

📖 Go to the **Reading Studio** for additional support in developing fluency.

EXTREME OR ABSOLUTE LANGUAGE

Point out that extreme or absolute language is often a feature of both persuasive speeches and emotional speeches, and that, in this case, the speech is both persuasive and emotional. **(Answer:** *These absolute statements emphasize Wiesel's claim that Auschwitz and the Holocaust in general changed humanity forever because they showed the depths of cruelty and dehumanization to which people could sink.)*

ENGLISH LEARNER SUPPORT

Learn Argument Terms Provide these Spanish cognates to students: *emotion = emoción* and *ethical = ético*. Tell them to use the cognates to help them understand that a persuasive speaker uses **emotional** and **ethical appeals** to influence listeners' opinions. Display paragraph 5 and read it aloud. Guide students to see the emotional appeal. **LIGHT**

 ANALYZE APPEALS

Explain that asking the audience to do something is a main feature of persuasive speeches. Point out that using rhetorical devices, such as appeals, can persuade audiences to do as asked. **(Answer:** *These words appeal to the audience's emotions. He is asking them to imagine seeing and hearing horrible events that create emotional responses in listeners.)*

 For **listening support** for students at varying proficiency levels, see the **Text X-Ray** on page 512C.

 NOTICE & NOTE

EXTREME OR ABSOLUTE LANGUAGE

Notice & Note: In paragraphs 1–3, mark words and phrases that suggest certainty or completeness.

Infer: What can you infer from these statements about Wiesel's perspective on Auschwitz?

ANALYZE APPEALS

Annotate: Mark the words in paragraph 6 in which Wiesel asks the audience to do something.

Analyze: Does this paragraph appeal to the audience's emotions or ethics? Explain the effect it would most likely have on an audience.

1 "After Auschwitz, the human condition is not the same, nothing will be the same."

2 Here heaven and earth are on fire.

3 I speak to you as a man, who 50 years and nine days ago had no name, no hope, no future and was known only by his number, A7713.[1]

4 I speak as a Jew who has seen what humanity has done to itself by trying to exterminate an entire people and inflict suffering and humiliation and death on so many others.

5 In this place of darkness and malediction[2] we can but stand in awe and remember its stateless, faceless and nameless victims. Close your eyes and look: endless nocturnal processions are converging here, and here it is always night. Here heaven and earth are on fire.

6 Close your eyes and listen. Listen to the silent screams of terrified mothers, the prayers of anguished old men and women. Listen to the tears of children, Jewish children, a beautiful little girl among them, with golden hair, whose vulnerable tenderness has never left me. Look and listen as they quietly walk towards dark flames so gigantic that the planet itself seemed in danger.

---

[1] **A7713:** the identification number tattooed on Wiesel at Auschwitz.
[2] **malediction** (mălˈ ĭ-dĭkˈshən): curse.

WHEN STUDENTS STRUGGLE . . .

Use Learning Strategy The imagery of Wiesel's speech might be challenging for some readers. Suggest that they use a chart to record the sights and sounds the author describes.

Sights	Sounds
"heaven and earth are on fire"	*"silent screams of terrified mothers"*
"here it is always night"	*"the tears of children"*

 For additional support, go to the **Reading Studio** and assign the following **Level Up tutorial: Prose Forms.**

7   All these men and women and children came from everywhere, a gathering of exiles drawn by death.

8   **Yitgadal veyitkadash, Shmay Rabba.**[3]

9   In this kingdom of darkness there were many people. People who came from all the occupied lands of Europe. And then there were the Gypsies and the Poles and the Czechs … It is true that not all the victims were Jews. But all the Jews were victims.

10   Now, as then, we ask the question of all questions: what was the meaning of what was so routinely going on in this kingdom of eternal night. What kind of demented mind could have invented this system?

11   And it worked. The killers killed, the victims died and the world was the world and everything else was going on, life as usual. In the towns nearby, what happened? In the lands nearby, what happened? Life was going on where God's creation was condemned to blasphemy[4] by their killers and their accomplices.

12   **Yitgadal veyitkadash, Shmay Rabba.**

---

[3] **Yitgadal veyitkadash, Shmay Rabba:** the words that begin a Jewish prayer for the dead.
[4] **blasphemy** (blăs´fə-mē): a disrespect for religion.

APPLYING ACADEMIC VOCABULARY

☑ **communicate** ☐ draft ☑ **liberation** ☐ philosophy ☐ publish

Write and Discuss Have students turn to a partner to discuss the following questions. Guide students to include the Academic Vocabulary words *communicate* and *liberation* in their responses. Ask volunteers to share their responses with the class.

- What message is Elie Wiesel trying to **communicate**?
- When did the **liberation** of Auschwitz take place?

 ENGLISH LEARNER SUPPORT

Analyze Word Choice Explain to students that a writer's use of certain words may reveal a certain emotion, attitude, or tone that the writer may feel.

Write the idiom "the question of all questions" from paragraph 10 on the board and read it. Explain that when looking at the words alone, they may seem very simple. Discuss that when this happens, students may look back at the previous text, even the previous paragraph, to understand what the writer's message may be. Have them discuss whether the effect of using the idiom instead of saying "the most important question of all," gets the writer's message across. **MODERATE/LIGHT**

For **reading support** for students at varying proficiency levels, see the **Text X-Ray** on page 512D.

 ENGLISH LEARNER SUPPORT

Summarize Main Ideas Support students in understanding the main points of the prayer. Have students scan the prayer, looking for key words they understand. Explain that readers often summarize main ideas of a text using key words. Model scanning the paragraph, calling out the easily understandable language (i.e., people came from all of Europe, not all victims were Jews, all the Jews were victims). Say: *The main idea of paragraph 9 is that Jews and other people in Europe were victims.* Allow students time to scan paragraphs 10 and 11 and summarize the main idea in one sentence. (**Possible answers:** *Paragraph 10: Why did someone make this system?, Paragraph 11: While people were being hurt, other people were living normal lives.*) Encourage students to compare their summaries with a partner. **MODERATE**

TEACH

ANALYZE RHETORICAL DEVICES

Discuss that **repetition** is a commonly used rhetorical device that can produce a wide range of effects. *(Answer: He is expressing the same thought in different words; both are statements of extreme anguish. Students may note that "After Auschwitz" is the title of the speech, and these sentences are his thesis statement.)*

ANALYZE APPEALS

Remind students that a persuasive speaker uses emotional and **ethical appeals** to influence listeners' opinions by addressing their emotions and ethics. *(Answer: The rhetorical question makes an ethical appeal and suggests that the answer is so obvious there can be no disagreement—Auschwitz reminds us that if we are not guided by moral principles, terrible actions become possible. The statement in paragraph 18 makes a powerful emotional appeal about protecting children. The effect of the two together is to tell the listener this: If you are not motivated by your principles, then do good for your children.)*

ENGLISH LEARNER SUPPORT

Spelling Suffixes -*ful*, -*ness* Remind students that suffixes add meaning to base words. Then explain the following spelling rule: if a base word ends in consonant *-y*, change the *y* to *i* before adding the suffix. Write the following words on the board: *ready, beauty, plenty, happy.* Have students work in pairs to add the suffixes *–ful* or *–ness* to each word correctly. Have student check their work in a dictionary and share their responses with the class. **ALL LEVELS**

NOTICE & NOTE

ANALYZE RHETORICAL DEVICES

Annotate: Mark the phrase that is repeated in paragraph 13.

Connect: What effect does the repetition of this phrase help to create and what is the resulting impact of that effect?

ANALYZE APPEALS

Annotate: Mark words and phrases in paragraphs 17–18 that Wiesel uses to appeal to the audience's emotions and ethics.

Compare: Paragraph 17 uses a **rhetorical question**—that is, a question that Wiesel does not expect the audience to answer—to be persuasive. Compare this question to the statement in the next paragraph. What impact does each have on the audience?

13   Turning point or watershed,[5] Birkenau[6] produced a mutation[7] on a cosmic scale, affecting man's dreams and endeavours. After Auschwitz, the human condition is no longer the same. After Auschwitz, nothing will ever be the same.

14   **Yitgadal veyitkadash, Shmay Rabba.**

15   As we remember the solitude and the pain of its victims, let us declare this day marks our commitment to commemorate their death, not to celebrate our own victory over death.

16   As we reflect upon the past, we must address ourselves to the present and the future. In the name of all that is sacred in memory, let us stop the bloodshed in Bosnia, Rwanda and Chechnia; the vicious and ruthless terror attacks against Jews in the Holy Land.[8] Let us reject and oppose more effectively religious fanaticism and racial hate.

17   Where else can we say to the world *"Remember the morality of the human condition,"* if not here?

18   For the sake of our children, we must remember Birkenau, so that it does not become their future.

[5] **watershed:** a place that marks a change of course or direction.
[6] **Birkenau:** the sub-camp at Auschwitz where prisoners were killed.
[7] **mutation** (myo͞o-tāˊshən): change.
[8] **Holy Land:** the ancient kingdom of Israel.

TO CHALLENGE STUDENTS . . .

Analyze the Speaker Have students reread the speech with a focus on Elie Wiesel as a person. Prompt them to identify what they learn about Wiesel's life and experiences and to infer what his speech suggests about his personality.

Ask students to work in small groups to use their findings to develop a brief description that might have been used to introduce Wiesel prior to his speech. Point out that while such introductions often focus on a person's accomplishments, they should emphasize Wiesel's personal qualities.

19   **Yitgadal veyitkadash, Shmay Rabba:** Weep for Thy children whose death was not mourned then: weep for them, our Father in heaven, for they were deprived of their right to be buried, for heaven itself became their cemetery.

CHECK YOUR UNDERSTANDING

Answer these questions before moving on to the **Analyze the Text** section on the following page.

1 Why does Wiesel use the present tense in paragraph 2, "Here heaven and earth are on fire"?

  A He is telling a story about the concentration camp.

  B He wants Auschwitz to be burned down and forgotten.

  C He believes Auschwitz still affects us today.

  D He is still angry about what happened to him.

2 What is the main idea of paragraph 16?

  F Nothing in today's world is as bad as the Holocaust.

  G We must forget what happened at Auschwitz and move on.

  H People who are being persecuted should fight back against their oppressors.

  J The example of the Holocaust should make us oppose similar persecutions today.

3 The speech's title means that after Auschwitz —

  A Wiesel not only survived but became a successful man

  B the world is a dark place haunted by the ghosts of the dead

  C former enemies can be friends if they acknowledge the evil that was done

  D people can no longer be indifferent to the suffering of others

✎ **CHECK YOUR UNDERSTANDING**

Have students answer the questions independently.

Answers:

  1. *C*

  2. *J*

  3. *D*

If they answer any questions incorrectly, have them reread the text to confirm their understanding. Then they may proceed to ANALYZE THE TEXT on p. 520.

 ENGLISH LEARNER SUPPORT

Oral Assessment Use the following questions to assess students' comprehension and speaking skills:

1. Read this sentence from paragraph 2: "Here heaven and earth are on fire"? Why does the author use the present tense? (*He believes Auschwitz still affects us today.*)

2. Look at paragraph 16. What is the main idea? (*The example of the Holocaust should make us oppose similar persecutions today.*)

3. What does the title of the speech mean? What happened after Auschwitz? (*People can no longer be indifferent to the suffering of others.*)

SUBSTANTIAL/MODERATE

ANALYZE THE TEXT

Possible answers:

1. **DOK 4:** *The words are repeated in a slightly different form in paragraph 13. By repeating his thesis that nothing is the same after Auschwitz, Wiesel unifies the speech.*

2. **DOK 4:** *The parallel sentences that begin the paragraphs—"I speak to you as a man/I speak as a Jew"—emphasize the universality of Wiesel's experience. The phrases "no name, no hope, no future" evoke his desperation as his identity was taken from him.*

3. **DOK 2:** *Wiesel uses the image of fire to evoke the horror of the Holocaust—the deaths of innocents and the burning of their bodies in crematoria.*

4. **DOK 3:** *Wiesel uses this opening line of a prayer that is said in the Jewish rite of mourning as an effective rhetorical device. It is a hymn of praise to God that affirms the mourners' faith even in the face of loss. Its effect is to remind the listener of the tragedy that befell the victims of the Holocaust and to show that the faith of the Jewish people is not shaken by what happened.*

5. **DOK 4:** *Wiesel is calling on his audience to learn from the past and not turn a blind eye to genocide and other forms of discrimination that are occurring in the present. When he says that "we must address ourselves to the present and the future" and "we must remember Birkenau," his ethical appeal is strengthened by his certainty and forcefulness.*

RESEARCH

Remind students to be careful to spell their search words correctly. Explain that sometimes a misspelled word or name will still lead to the search you want but that, other times, it might lead to something entirely different.

Extend Make sure students remember to share/discuss.

 RESPOND

ANALYZE THE TEXT

Support your responses with evidence from the text. 📓 NOTEBOOK

1. **Analyze** Wiesel's speech begins: "After Auschwitz, the human condition is not the same, nothing will be the same." Identify where similar language is repeated later in his speech. What is the effect of this repetition?

2. **Analyze** Reread paragraphs 3–4 and identify the examples of parallelism. What impact does the parallelism create? How does it contribute to the writer's **tone,** or the attitude he expresses?

3. **Interpret** Imagery consists of descriptive words and phrases that create sensory experiences for the reader. Wiesel writes: "Here heaven and earth are on fire." What image is he communicating? What effect might it have on his audience?

4. **Evaluate** The sentence *Yitgadal veyitkadash, Shmay Rabba* is repeated three times in the speech. Is Wiesel's use of this prayer as a rhetorical device effective? Why or why not?

5. **Notice & Note** Review Wiesel's ethical appeal in paragraphs 16–18. What values is he asking his audience to consider? What impact does his use of absolute language have on this appeal?

RESEARCH TIP
You just read the transcription of a speech. You can use the Internet to find video or audio recordings of many speeches. Hearing and seeing the speaker can enhance the impact of a speech that you have read.

RESEARCH

The Nobel Peace Prize is one of the highest honors in the world. With a partner, research more about Elie Wiesel's work as a humanitarian and activist. Use what you learn to answer these questions, as well as one additional question you have about him after reading the speech.

QUESTION	ANSWER
What genre is Wiesel's most famous book, *Night*?	*Memoir*
Aside from writing and activism, what was Wiesel's primary vocation?	*He was a teacher/professor.*
Finish this quote: "The opposite of love is not hate, but _____."	*Chairman of the President's Commission on the Holocaust* "The opposite of love is not hate, but indifference." The full quote: "The opposite of love is not hate, it's indifference. The opposite of art is not ugliness, it's indifference. The opposite of faith is not heresy, it's indifference. And the opposite of life is not death, it's indifference."
Question:	

Extend Share your questions and answers with the class and discuss any similarities and differences you find among them.

 LEARNING MINDSET

Problem Solving Remind students that there are many different ways to solve problems, such as being patient, changing strategies, and asking for help. Explain that everyone runs into problems when learning new things and everyone solves problems in their own way. Point out that every problem you solve makes you smarter.

CREATE AND PRESENT

Make a Poster Choose a quotation from "After Auschwitz" that moved you. You might find it by reading the notes you took on the selection or by rereading the speech. Then create a poster that amplifies the message of this quotation.

- ❏ Write the quotation prominently on your poster.
- ❏ Research the Holocaust and/or current events to find facts, dates, and other details that support the message expressed by the quotation you chose.
- ❏ Add to your poster the most powerful pieces of relevant information and visual details you found during your research.
- ❏ Explain your completed work to the class in an oral presentation.

Discuss with a Group In a small group, discuss how you might follow Wiesel's direction to "reject and oppose more effectively religious fanaticism and racial hate." What successful efforts do you know of? What problems exist today, and how might you help solve them?

- ❏ Choose a persecuted group that you know of from reading the news or doing research.
- ❏ Discuss these questions: Why is the group being persecuted? What global or national groups are helping the persecuted?
- ❏ Using your knowledge of how conflicts between groups of people have been resolved before, discuss how you think the current conflict can come to a just resolution.

 RESPOND

 Go to the **Speaking and Listening Studio** for help with giving a presentation and participating in a discussion.

RESPOND TO THE ESSENTIAL QUESTION

? What can we learn from Anne Frank?

Gather Information Review your annotations and notes on "After Auschwitz." Then, add relevant details to your Response Log. As you determine which information to include, think about:

- why it is important to know what happened in World War II concentration camps
- the best way to respond to that knowledge

At the end of the unit, you can use your notes to help you write a personal narrative.

ACADEMIC VOCABULARY

As you write and discuss what you learned from the speech, be sure to use the Academic Vocabulary words. Check off each of the words that you use.

- ❏ **communicate**
- ❏ **draft**
- ❏ **liberation**
- ❏ **philosophy**
- ❏ **publish**

After Auschwitz **521**

CREATE AND PRESENT

Make a Poster Point out to students that they can create their poster by hand or they can create pieces in a computer, print them out, and put them on their poster. Explain that a poster should not be overly wordy, but rather it should contain only the most important broad pieces of information.

For **writing support** for students at varying proficiency levels, see the **Text X-Ray** on page 512D.

Discuss with a Group Remind students that they do not have to take on large projects to help solve today's problems. Point out that small efforts, such as talking about the problems to raise awareness and refusing to go along with problem supporters, also helps.

RESPOND TO THE ESSENTIAL QUESTION

Allow time for students to add details from "After Auschwitz" to their Unit 6 Response Logs.

ENGLISH LEARNER SUPPORT

Understand Special Phrases Make sure students fully understand the meaning of "persecuted group." Write the word on the board in the middle of a word web. As a group, come up with words and phrases that might describe a persecuted group and fill these in around the web.

SUBSTANTIAL/MODERATE

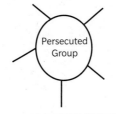

Persecuted Group

THERE BUT FOR THE GRACE

Poem by Wislawa Szymborska

DAYS

Poem by Billy Collins

GENRE ELEMENTS
POETRY

Remind students that a **poem** uses imagery and figurative language, such as similes and metaphors, to convey its meaning and mood, in addition to using sound devices to unify the poem. Poems have a speaker, or narrator, that speaks to the reader. Just as in a novel, poems contain a theme or message about life.

LEARNING OBJECTIVES

- Analyze sound devices and figurative language.
- Research Holocaust memorials and sites devoted to tolerance.
- Create a drawing or other artwork to represent figurative language.
- Recite a poem.
- Compare and contrast poems.
- **Language** Discuss figurative language using the word *metaphor*.

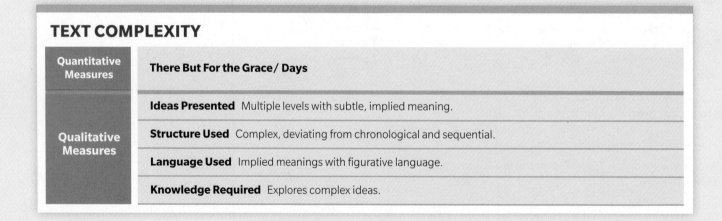

TEXT COMPLEXITY

Quantitative Measures	There But For the Grace / Days
Qualitative Measures	**Ideas Presented** Multiple levels with subtle, implied meaning.
	Structure Used Complex, deviating from chronological and sequential.
	Language Used Implied meanings with figurative language.
	Knowledge Required Explores complex ideas.

Online ⓔd

RESOURCES

- Unit 6 Response Log
- 🔊 Selection Audio
- 📖 Reading Studio: Notice & Note
- ✒ "There But for the Grace" and "Days" Selection Test

SUMMARIES

English

"There But for the Grace" recounts the randomness of cheating death on a daily basis. It recounts factors, such as proximity and location, that result in one person's death instead of another's.

"Days" shares how each day is a gift and we truly do not know whether we will have another because of how quickly things can change.

Spanish

En "Le podría pasar a cualquiera" se recuenta la aleatoriedad de engañar a la muerte diariamente. Recuenta factores, tales como la proximidad y la ubicación, que resultan en la muerte de una persona en vez de otra.

"Días" comparte cómo cada día es un regalo y que nosotros no sabemos realmente si tendremos otro debido a lo rápido que cambian las cosas.

SMALL-GROUP OPTIONS

Have students work in small groups to read and discuss the selection.

Reciprocal Teaching

- After students have read the poems, present the class with a list of generic question stems.
- Have students work individually to use the question stems to write three to five questions about the poems.
- Group students into learning groups of up to three students.
- Each student offers two questions for discussion without duplicating other students' questions.
- The group reaches consensus on the answer to each question and finds text evidence to support it.

Think-Pair-Share

- After students have read and analyzed the poems, pose this question: *What do the poems say about the fragility of life?*
- Have students think about the question individually and take notes.
- Then, have pairs discuss their ideas about the question.
- Finally, ask pairs to share their responses with the class.

Text X-Ray: English Learner Support
for "There But for the Grace" and "Days"

Use the Text X-Ray and the supports and scaffolds in the Teacher's Edition to help guide students at different proficiency levels through the selection.

INTRODUCE THE SELECTION
CHARACTERISTICS OF POETRY

To prepare students' discussion of the characteristics of poetry, review vowel and consonant sounds as well as the meanings of alliteration, repetition, assonance, and consonance.

- *Review short and long vowel sounds with students. Tell students that assonance is the repetition of vowel sounds. Help students find words with repeating vowel sounds, such as grace and later.*

- *Tell students that consonance is the repetition of consonant sounds. Remind students that consonants are all letters that are not vowels. Help students find words with repeating consonant sounds, such as had and happen.*

- *Tell students that alliteration is the repetition of a sound. Help students find examples of alliteration, such as what would.*

- *Point out that repeat is the root word of repetition. Help students find examples of repetition, such as you survived and because.*

CULTURAL REFERENCES

The following words and phrases may be unfamiliar to students:

- *forehead* ("Days" stanza 1): the area of the head between the eyes and hairline
- *turrets* ("Days" stanza 2): small towers
- *precariously* ("Days" stanza 3): unstable
- *clink* ("Days" stanza 6): a high-pitched sound made when two objects hit each other

LISTENING

Understand Mood

Tell students that poetry must often be listened to several times to be understood. Explain that a poem's mood is the feeling and emotions the reader feels from the poem.

Have students listen as you read aloud "Days." Use the following supports with students at varying proficiency levels:

- Read the first two stanzas aloud several times. Ask: *Is the mood of these stanzas positive, negative, or neutral?* Model that they should give a thumbs up if the answer is positive, a thumbs down if it is negative, and a shrug for neutral. **SUBSTANTIAL**

- Read the first three stanzas aloud several times. Have students identify the mood of the stanzas. Ask: *How would you summarize the scene the poet describes?* **MODERATE**

- After listening to the poem read aloud, ask students to work in pairs to list details that describe the mood of the poem. **LIGHT**

SPEAKING

Recite a Poem

In a small group, students will recite "There But for the Grace" or "Days" for the class. Circulate around the room to help students who may need help pronouncing some of the words in the poems.

Use the following supports with students at varying proficiency levels:

- Read each line of the first two stanzas of "There But for the Grace" or "Days." As you read, have students repeat after you focusing on their pronunciation. **SUBSTANTIAL**
- Read aloud of the first two stanzas of "There But for the Grace" or "Days." Have students circle the words you emphasize and mark an *x* where you pause. Then have students choral read with you, paying attention to the emphasized words and pauses. **MODERATE**
- Pair students with a native English speaker. Have students select one of the poems to recite. Have students practice reciting the poem aloud together. **LIGHT**

READING

Understand Figurative Language

Tell students that authors use figurative language to help readers see things in new ways. Explain that two types of figurative language, simile and metaphor, make a comparison between two unlike things.

Work with students to read "There But for the Grace." Use the following supports with students at varying proficiency levels:

- Review the definitions of *simile* and *metaphor* with students. Encourage them to think of examples of similes and metaphors. Discuss how similes and metaphors make everyday language colorful and interesting. Ask: *How do similes and metaphors help readers "see" what they are reading?* **SUBSTANTIAL**
- Have students complete the following sentence frames: *That statue is as tall as a_____. This bedroom is a _____.* Ask: *Which sentence is a simile? Which is a metaphor?* **MODERATE**
- Write examples of similes and metaphors on the board. Have student pairs work together to identify what objects are being compared. Ask: *How are these objects alike?* **LIGHT**

WRITING

Write Figurative Language

Work with students to write examples of figurative language.

Use the following supports with students at varying proficiency levels:

- Work with students to create a Venn diagram comparing and contrasting two things. Write the words that the two have in common in the center. Then use the details to write the similes and metaphors on the board. Have students copy the sentences in their notebooks. **SUBSTANTIAL**
- Provide sentence frames, such as the following, that students can use to write similes and metaphors: *The rain storm turned our yard into a _____. He was as nervous as a _____. That tall yellow building is _____ in the night sky. My brother looks like a _____ when he goes out with his girlfriend.* **MODERATE**
- Have students write two to three sentences describing a short scene with metaphors. Then have students exchange papers and, at the bottom, write a brief summary description of their partner's scene. **LIGHT**

TEACH

Connect to the
ESSENTIAL QUESTION

The poems "There But for the Grace" and "Days" expand upon the idea of the fragility of life introduced in the Anne Frank text. Throughout the poems, the authors emphasize how fleeting and quickly changing life can be.

COMPARE POEMS

After students read the Compare Poems note, ask them to think about how poets can use techniques such as sound devices and figurative language to convey a theme. Remind students that they will collaborate on a project after reading the poems.

POEM
THERE BUT FOR THE GRACE

by **Wisława Szymborska**
pages 525–527

COMPARE POEMS

The poems you are about to read have similar messages and moods. As you read, compare the ways in which each poet uses techniques such as sound devices or figurative language to convey the theme. After reading, you will collaborate with a small group on a final project.

ESSENTIAL QUESTION:

What can we learn from Anne Frank?

POEM
DAYS

by **Billy Collins**
pages 528–529

522   Unit 6

LEARNING MINDSET

Persistence Encourage students to not give up when something is challenging. Remind students that challenges are part of learning and effort is the key to growth. Model positive self-talk such as, "I know I can do this if I keep at it."

QUICK START

Think of a "close call" you had. It could be a time when you narrowly avoided an accident or almost made a mistake. Write down how you felt during and after the close call.

WHAT HAPPENED	HOW I FELT

ANALYZE SOUND DEVICES

Like songs, poems are meant to be heard. When poets choose certain words for their connection to the sense of hearing, they're using **sound devices.** The use of sound devices not only affects how a poem sounds. It can also create **mood** (the feeling or atmosphere that a writer creates for the reader), reveal **tone** (the writer's attitude toward the subject), and contribute to a poet's **voice** (the unique use of language that suggests a personality behind the words).

As you read each poem, look for these sound devices. Consider why the poet chose that device. How does it affect you as a reader?

GENRE ELEMENTS: POETRY

- uses imagery and figurative language to convey meaning and mood
- uses sound devices such as alliteration and assonance to unify the poem
- expresses a theme, or a message about life
- includes a speaker who "talks" to the reader, like a narrator in fiction; the speaker is not necessarily the poet

SOUND DEVICE	DEFINITION	EXAMPLE FROM THE POEMS
alliteration	repetition of consonant sounds at the beginnings of words	What would have happened had not a hand . . .
assonance	repetition of vowel sounds within non-rhyming words	or set upon your forehead moments before you open your eyes.
consonance	repetition of consonant sounds within and at the ends of words	It happened sooner. Later. Nearer. Farther.
onomatopoeia	the use of words whose sounds echo their meanings	you whisper, then holding your breath, place this cup on yesterday's saucer without the slightest clink.
repetition	a technique in which a sound, word, phrase, or line is repeated for emphasis or unity	It could have happened. It had to happen. It happened sooner. Later.

© Houghton Mifflin Harcourt Publishing Company

There But for the Grace / Days   523

QUICK START

Have students read the Quick Start comments, and invite them to share a story about a time they had a close call. Ask students how they felt during and after the close call.

ANALYZE SOUND DEVICES

Help students understand the terms and concepts related to the sound devices used in poetry. Remind students of the differences between mood, tone, and voice. Discuss the sound devices of alliteration, assonance, consonance, and repetition. Point out that sound devices add unity to a poem, in addition to helping create a poem's mood, tone, and voice.

EL ENGLISH LEARNER SUPPORT

Understand Directionality Reinforce the directionality of English by reviewing how to read the Analyze Sound Devices chart. Explain that each column heading applies to the text in all the rows beneath it. To read the chart, students should begin at the top left. The top row, left column introduces the first sound device—alliteration. After reading this term, students should track to the middle column to see the definition. They should move on to the right column to see the example of the term. Then they should move on to the second row, left column. Ask a volunteer to trace the order that a reader would read the information in the chart.

SUBSTANTIAL

ANALYZE FIGURATIVE LANGUAGE

Tell students that figurative language is a way of using words to express something other than their literal meaning. Remind students that understanding figurative language often requires the reader to draw inferences. Review the definitions of simile and metaphor with students and point out the example metaphor. As students read, ask them to look for similes and metaphors in the poems.

■ English Learner Support

Use Cognates Tell students that several of the figurative language words have Spanish cognates: *figurative/ figurativo/a, simile/símil, metaphor/ metáfora.*

ALL LEVELS

 ## ANNOTATION MODEL

Students can review the Reading Model introduction if they have questions about any of the signposts. Suggest that they underline important phrases or circle key words that help them identify signposts. They may want to color-code their annotations by using a different color highlighter for each signpost. Point out that they may follow this suggestion or use their own system for marking up the selections in their write-in texts.

 GET READY

ANALYZE FIGURATIVE LANGUAGE

Writers—especially poets—use **figurative language** to help readers see things in new ways. Figurative language is language used imaginatively in ways that go beyond literal definitions.

A **simile** is one type of figurative language that compares two unlike things using the words *like* or *as*. For instance, you might say, "My little sister's face is *like* a storm cloud." A **metaphor** is also a comparison between things that are basically unlike. However, unlike a simile, a metaphor does not contain the words *like* or *as*. In the example below from "Days," the poet compares a window to a "calm eye."

EXAMPLE FROM "DAYS"	EFFECT
Through the calm eye of the window	emphasizes the peacefulness of the scene

While reading "There But for the Grace" and "Days," consider the impact of the poets' use of figurative language. In what ways does the figurative language add interest and support meaning?

ANNOTATION MODEL

NOTICE & NOTE

As you read, mark striking examples of sound devices and figurative language, and jot down notes about their impact and meaning. In the model below, you can see one reader's notes about the first two stanzas of "Days."

> Each one is a gift, no doubt,
> mysteriously placed in your waking hand
> or set upon your forehead
> moments before you open your eyes.
>
> 5 Today begins cold and bright,
> the ground heavy with snow
> and the thick masonry of ice,
> the sun glinting off the turrets of clouds.

The title "Days," and the word "Today" at the beginning of the second stanza help me infer that "each one" refers to "each day." The metaphor comparing each day to a gift highlights the idea that we never know what each day will bring.

BACKGROUND

On September 1, 1939, Germany invaded Poland, triggering the start of World War II. Many Polish soldiers and citizens were slaughtered by the German army. Surviving Polish political leaders, Jews, and others were later gathered and sent to concentration camps. By the end of the war, more than five million Poles had died. Poet **Wisława Szymborska** *(1923–2012) was born in a small town in western Poland. She was in high school when Germany invaded her country, and she was fortunate to avoid imprisonment and death. She published more than a dozen poetry collections and won the Nobel Prize for Literature in 1996.*

There But for the Grace

Poem by Wisława Szymborska

PREPARE TO COMPARE

As you read the poem, note how the author uses sound devices and figurative language to emphasize ideas and convey mood.

It could have happened.
It had to happen.
It happened sooner. Later.
Nearer. Farther.
5 It happened not to you.

~~You survived because you were the first.~~
~~You survived because you were the last.~~
~~Because you were alone. Because of people.~~
~~Because you turned left. Because you turned right.~~
10 ~~Because rain fell. Because a shadow fell.~~
~~Because sunny weather prevailed.¹~~

---

¹ **prevailed:** was common or frequent.

Notice & Note

Use the side margins to notice and note signposts in the text.

ANALYZE SOUND DEVICES
Annotate: Mark the repetition in lines 6–11.

Analyze: How does the repetition in these lines impact the mood and meaning of the poem?

BACKGROUND

After students read the Background note, point out that more than five million Polish people died or were murdered in Nazi concentration camps during World War II. Remind students that these people were killed for no other reason than for their religious background.

PREPARE TO COMPARE

Direct students to use the Prepare to Compare prompt to focus their reading.

ANALYZE SOUND DEVICES

Remind students that **repetition** is a technique in which a sound, word, phrase, or line is repeated or emphasized. Have students mark the repetition in lines 6–11. Then, have students answer the question to determine how the repetition impacts the mood and meaning of the poem. (**Answer:** *Students may say that the repetition emphasizes how many reasons there may have been for people surviving. Some of the reasons are opposites of each other. This repetition and randomness helps the poet emphasize that people had little or no control over whether they lived or died.*)

EL ENGLISH LEARNER SUPPORT

Repetition Explain to students that the root word of *repetition* is *repeat*, which means to do something over and over again. Read aloud the first two lines of the second stanza. Ask volunteers to point out the words that are repeated in both lines. Ask them for a definition of the word *survive*, "to continue to live." Give them synonyms, such as "get through" and "hold on," and say these words with emphasis to indicate striving. Have students read the lines with you again and include emphasis on repeating *survived*. Then read lines 8–11 and model for students that they should tap their chests softly once for each repeated word they hear.

SUBSTANTIAL

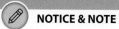

Luckily there was a wood.
Luckily there were no trees.
Luckily there was a rail, a hook, a beam, a brake,
15 a frame, a bend, a millimeter, a second.
Luckily a straw was floating on the surface.

Thanks to, because, and yet, in spite of.
What would have happened had not a hand, a foot,
by a step, a hairsbreadth[2]
20 by sheer coincidence.

_____
[2] **hairsbreadth:** a tiny space.

WHEN STUDENTS STRUGGLE . . .

Graphic Support Help students understand what is occurring in the poem by encouraging them to look at the image. Ask students what the image shows. Have students describe how it relates to the poem.

For additional support, go to the **Reading Studio** and assign the following **Level Up tutorial: Elements of Poetry.**

So you're here? Straight from a moment still ajar?
The net had one eyehole, and you got through it?
There's no end to my wonder, my silence.
Listen
25 how fast your heart beats in me.

NOTICE & NOTE

ANALYZE FIGURATIVE LANGUAGE

Annotate: Mark the metaphor that relates to survival in lines 21–25.

Analyze: What does this metaphor mean? What ideas does this use of figurative language emphasize?

CHECK YOUR UNDERSTANDING

Answer these questions about "There But for the Grace" before moving on to the next selection.

1 In lines 10–11, the words <u>rain</u>, <u>shadow</u>, and <u>sunny weather</u> most likely —

   A relate to good times and hard times

   B describe the hopes of the speaker

   C convey an upbeat, jaunty tone

   D add to the positive, optimistic mood

2 In lines 12–16, the speaker most likely repeats the word <u>luckily</u> to —

   F express gratitude that the world is such a lucky place

   G emphasize that survival often depends on luck

   H encourage people to focus on the positive

   J explain steps people can take to survive a tragedy

3 What is an important idea in "There But for the Grace"?

   A Being prepared can help people avoid tragedy.

   B Nature and hope are comforts in times of trouble.

   C Nothing is impossible with a positive attitude.

   D Good or bad fortune can suddenly change a life.

ANALYZE FIGURATIVE LANGUAGE

Remind students that a **metaphor** is a type of figurative language that compares two unlike things but does not use the words *like* or *as*. In lines 21–25, have students mark the metaphor. Then have students answer the question to determine what the metaphor means and what the use of figurative language emphasizes. (*Answer: The metaphor compares survival to escaping through a net with a single small opening. This emphasizes the randomness of survival under conditions of wartime. People survived not because of worth, strength, or skill, but because of chance.*)

CHECK YOUR UNDERSTANDING

Have students answer the questions independently.

Answers

1. *A*

2. *G*

3. *D*

If they answer any questions incorrectly, have them reread the text to confirm their understanding. Then they may proceed to "Days" on p. 528.

ENGLISH LEARNER SUPPORT

Oral Assessment Use the following questions to assess students' comprehension and speaking skills:

1. Read lines 10–11. What do the words *rain* and *shadow* and *sunny weather* do? (*The words have to do with good times and bad times.*)

2. Read lines 12–16. Why is the word *luckily* repeated? (*The word is emphasized to show that survival often depends on luck.*)

3. What is an important idea in the poem? (*Good or bad luck can suddenly change a life.*) **SUBSTANTIAL/MODERATE**

BACKGROUND

After students read the Background note, point out that Billy Collins is interested in how poetry can become part of everyday life. Ask students how the topic of days lends itself to that goal.

PREPARE TO COMPARE

Direct students to use the Prepare to Compare prompt to focus their reading.

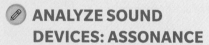

ANALYZE SOUND DEVICES: ASSONANCE

Remind students that **assonance** is the repetition of vowel sounds within non-rhyming words. In lines 5–8, have students mark the examples of assonance. Then have students answer the question to determine how assonance affects the mood of the poem. (**Answer:** *Students may say that the assonance makes the scene the poet is describing sound crisp and brisk.*)

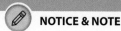
NOTICE & NOTE

BACKGROUND

Billy Collins (b. 1941) is perhaps the most popular poet in North America. When he served as the U.S. Poet Laureate from 2001 to 2003, he created the 180 Project, which provided high schools across the country with poems to be read along with daily announcements. His goal was to make poetry part of everyday life for young people.

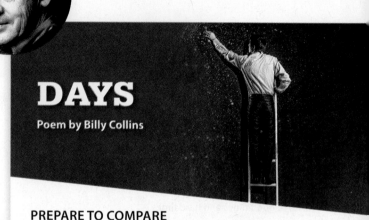

DAYS

Poem by Billy Collins

Notice & Note

Use the side margins to notice and note signposts in the text.

PREPARE TO COMPARE

As you read, think about how the poet uses figurative language to create vivid images and help convey a message, or theme. As you read the poem, note how the author uses sound devices and figurative language to emphasize ideas and convey mood.

Each one is a gift, no doubt,
mysteriously placed in your waking hand
or set upon your forehead
moments before you open your eyes.

ANALYZE SOUND DEVICES: ASSONANCE

Annotate: Mark examples of assonance in lines 5–8.

Analyze: How does the assonance affect the mood of the poem?

5   Today begins cold and bright,
the ground heavy with snow
and the thick masonry of ice,
the sun glinting off the turrets of clouds.

Through the calm eye of the window
10 everything is in its place
but so precariously
this day might be resting somehow

528   Unit 6

ENGLISH LEARNER SUPPORT

Vowel Sounds   Remind students of the five vowels and their sounds. Provide students with some examples of words with each type of vowel sound, such as *gray, key, find, go,* and *cute.* Explain that these words all have the long vowel sound, meaning they are all pronounced the same as the name of the letter. For example, the /o/ is pronounced like "oh," not like "aw," which would be the sound of a short vowel. **SUBSTANTIAL**

on the one before it,
all the days of the past stacked high
15 like the impossible tower of dishes
entertainers used to build on stage.

No wonder you find yourself
perched on the top of a tall ladder
hoping to add one more.
20 Just another Wednesday

you whisper,
then holding your breath,
place this cup on yesterday's saucer
without the slightest clink.

NOTICE & NOTE

ANALYZE FIGURATIVE LANGUAGE

Annotate: Mark the simile in lines 12–16.

Analyze: What two unlike things does the speaker compare? How does this comparison impact the meaning of the poem?

ANALYZE SOUND DEVICES: ONOMATOPOEIA

Annotate: Mark the words in line 21–24 that sound like their meaning.

Analyze: Describe how these words help you hear Billy Collins's voice.

CHECK YOUR UNDERSTANDING

Answer these questions about "Days" before moving on to the **Analyze the Text** section on the following page.

1 The figurative language in the poem suggests that the days in a life are —

   A beautiful and limitless

   B cold yet calm

   C precious but fragile

   D boring and repetitive

2 Which of the following lines in the poem contains alliteration?

   F *Today begins cold and bright*

   G *perched on the top of a tall ladder*

   H *Just another Wednesday*

   J *then holding your breath*

3 Line 14 emphasizes that —

   A a person's life can come crashing down without warning

   B there is beauty even in bitterly cold winter weather

   C it's important to keep track of events and tasks before they pile up

   D entertaining others is the key to a happy life

ENGLISH LEARNER SUPPORT

Oral Assessment Use the following questions to assess students' comprehension and speaking skills:

1. How are days described in the poem? (*precious but fragile*)

2. Which line has alliteration? (*line 18; perched on the **t**op of a **t**all ladder*)

3. What does line 14 suggest? (*that a person's life can come crashing down without warning*)

   SUBSTANTIAL/MODERATE

ANALYZE FIGURATIVE LANGUAGE

Remind students that a **simile** is a type of figurative language that compares two unlike things using the words *like* or *as*. In lines 12–16, have students mark the simile. Then have students answer the question to determine how this comparison impacts the meaning of the poem. (**Answer:** *The poet compares the past days of a person's life to an incredibly tall stack of dishes. Students may say that the metaphor makes the poem more serious—even somber—since a precarious pile of dishes is almost certain to fall, and a person's life is certain to end.*)

ANALYZE SOUND DEVICES: ONOMATOPOEIA

Explain to students that onomatopoeia is a word that imitates the natural sound of the object or action it refers to. For example, *hiss, swish, plop, huff, bark,* and *meow* are all examples of onomatopoeia. Have students think of other common words that imitate the sound they describe. (**Answer:** *The poet's voice is heard in onomatopoeia by the fact that these words that imitate sound have a singular auditory meaning, which is a sound that is made by a human voice.*)

CHECK YOUR UNDERSTANDING

Have students answer the questions independently.

Answers:

1. *C*

2. *G*

3. *A*

If they answer any questions incorrectly, have them reread the text to confirm their understanding. Then they may proceed to ANALYZE THE TEXT on p. 530.

ANALYZE THE TEXT

Possible answers:

1. **DOK 2:** *The repetition in lines 12–15 includes the word luckily. The speaker describes factors in the person's environment that may have saved the life of the person the speaker addresses as "you." Many of the things cited are opposites, and the last line of the stanza is "Luckily a straw was floating on the surface"—something incredibly small and unimportant. This repetition helps communicate the message of the poem: Sometimes people survive for minor reasons, for contradictory reasons, or for no reason at all.*

2. **DOK 2:** *I think the metaphor about the heart means that the speaker of the poem feels close to the person he or she addresses as "you." For most of the poem, the speaker tells "you" about all the minor and possibly meaningless reasons that "you" survived. When the speaker says, "Listen/how fast your heart beats in me," the speaker is saying that he or she is very much like the "you" in the poem.*

3. **DOK 4:** *The sound device used is assonance. Students should note that the short a sound unifies most of the words (a, straw, was, surface) in the line and together produce a sense of finality in the stanza.*

4. **DOK 3:** *Lines 1–4 of "Days" give the poem an upbeat and optimistic mood. The speaker's message is that each of the days in the title "is a gift, no doubt/mysteriously placed in your waking hand." However, the mood shifts later in the poem. By lines 21–24, the words "whisper" and "hold your breath" make the mood anxious. The message of the last stanza is that life is fragile and can come crashing down with even a slight mistake.*

5. **DOK 4:** *Lines 11–13 and lines 15–24 relate to the simile. The extended comparison helps connect the present to the past and emphasizes how "precariously" the days rest on each other.*

RESEARCH

Remind students to include full citations for all sources and images they use in their research.

 RESPOND

ANALYZE THE TEXT

Support your responses with evidence from the texts. 📓 NOTEBOOK

1. **Identify Patterns** Choose an example of repetition in "There But for the Grace," and explain how the repetition helps emphasize the message of the poem.

2. **Infer** Reread lines 21–25 of "There But for the Grace." In your opinion, what does the metaphor about the heart mean? How does this metaphor impact the meaning of the poem?

3. **Analyze** Examine line 16. Identify the sound device used, and explain how it affects the ending of the stanza.

4. **Compare** How does the mood of lines 1–4 of "Days" compare with the mood of lines 21–24?

5. **Evaluate** What other words and phrases in "Days" relate to the simile in lines 14–16? What impact does this extended comparison have on the poem's overall meaning? Cite text evidence in your response.

RESEARCH TIP
Because you will be presenting your research results to the class, you may want to display photographs of statues, memorials, museums, or other sites. Keep track of where you find each image, and include a credit line that lists source information. For print sources, include the title, author, publisher, publication date, and page number. For online sources, include the website, URL, article title, author, and access date.

RESEARCH

Both the poems you read in this lesson have to do with the fragility and temporary nature of life. Wisława Szymborska survived the Holocaust, but millions of people did not. In what ways do people remember victims of the Holocaust? With a partner, research Holocaust memorials or other sites dedicated to promoting remembrance and tolerance. What do these memorials have in common? What effect do they have on visitors?

MEMORIAL	DESCRIPTION

Extend With your group, share your research findings with the class. Identify a museum or memorial focused on tolerance that is near you, or present a suggestion for a new memorial. Come up with one or two questions that you would like to continue to explore.

⚙️ **LEARNING MINDSET**

Problem Solving If students get stuck when trying to respond to the Analyze the Text questions, help them by asking them to apply problem-solving strategies as they work through the questions. Encourage students to look at the question from a different angle or to try a different learning strategy.

CREATE AND RECITE

Illustrate Figurative Language Make a drawing or other artwork to represent one of the examples of figurative language in "There But for the Grace" or "Days."

❏ Review the poems to select an example of figurative language. Think about which example appeals most to you.

❏ Decide how you will represent the figurative language visually.

❏ Create your artwork. Your illustration could be a drawing, collage, or painting.

❏ Present your artwork to the class. Explain what the illustration shows and how it represents the example of figurative language.

Recite a Poem With a small group, present a recitation of "There But for the Grace" or "Days" for the class.

❏ Work with your group to select which poem you will present.

❏ Plan how you will present the poem. Will you take turns reciting different stanzas, or recite stanzas in unison?

❏ Memorize your lines and rehearse with your group.

❏ Present the poem with appropriate rate, volume, and expression.

RESPOND TO THE ESSENTIAL QUESTION

 What can we learn from Anne Frank?

Gather Information Review your annotations and notes on both poems. Then, add relevant details to your Response Log. As you determine which information to include, think about:

• literary devices each poet uses to convey meaning
• ways in which the messages in both poems relate to other selections in the unit
• connections you make between the poems, your own life, and society

At the end of the unit, you will use your notes to help you write a personal narrative.

ACADEMIC VOCABULARY
As you write and discuss what you learned from the poems, be sure to use the Academic Vocabulary words. Check off each of the words that you use.

❏ **communicate**
❏ **draft**
❏ **liberation**
❏ **philosophy**
❏ **publish**

CREATE AND RECITE

Illustrate Figurative Language Remind students that their artwork should relate to a metaphor in one of the poems. Students should be able to explain what the artwork depicts and in what ways it is relevant to the chosen metaphor.

 For **writing support** for students at varying proficiency levels, see the **Text X-Ray** on page 522D.

Recite a Poem Groups should recite one stanza from "There But for the Grace" or "Days." Choral recitations should include some variation rather than having all group members recite every word. Student recitations should be polished, expressive, and at appropriate volume.

 For **speaking support** for students at varying proficiency levels, see the **Text X-Ray** on page 522D.

RESPOND TO THE ESSENTIAL QUESTION

Allow time for students to add details from "There But for the Grace" and "Days" to their Unit 6 Response Logs.

ENGLISH LEARNER SUPPORT

Syllabication Read the selection "Days" slowly and in a modulated and expressive tone. Then read it again, telling students to listen carefully and to focus on each syllable in each word. Next, ask students to pronounce selected words from the first two stanzas and then determine the number of syllables in each one. Repeat with selected words from each stanza. Remind students that concentrating on syllables can help them read and pronounce words correctly. **SUBSTANTIAL**

COMPARE POEMS

Before groups work on the chart, emphasize that they are discussing not just the poems' themes but also the text evidence that supports the themes. In determining the themes, encourage students to consider the implicit and explicit meanings of the texts, as well as the writer's tone.

ANALYZE THE TEXTS

Possible answers:

1. **DOK 2:** *Both of these poems have implicit messages that life is wondrous yet fragile. "There But for the Grace" focuses on the idea of survival by chance, while "Days" emphasizes the idea that life can change unexpectedly.*

2. **DOK 3:** *I believe that "Days" has a more compelling theme. "Days" uses examples about life in general, not about escaping a specific time in history. The idea that each day is a gift "mysteriously placed in your waking hand" but that the days pile up "like an impossible tower of dishes" is a theme that I think most people can relate to and understand.*

3. **DOK 3:** *Both poems have significant shifts in tone. The tone of "There But for the Grace" stays stern until the last two lines. The person the speaker is addressing survived danger "by a step, a hairsbreadth/by sheer coincidence" (lines 19–20). But the last two lines of the poem are "Listen/ how fast your heart beats in me" (lines 24–25). The speaker suddenly expresses sympathy with the person he or she is speaking to because they are both fortunate survivors. The tone of "Days" starts off grateful "Each one is a gift" (line 1). However, about halfway through the poem the tone changes to one of anxiety or even fear. Lines 10–11 say "everything is in its place/but so precariously." Then the speaker compares the days of our lives to an impossibly tall stack of dishes, ready to crash down.*

4. **DOK 2:** *In line 22 of "There But for the Grace," the speaker asks, "The net had one eyehole, and you got through it?" Based on the content of the rest of the poem, the net with one eyehole is a metaphor for a dangerous situation. The speaker is saying that the person he or she is addressing had a lucky escape against great odds. The "impossible tower of dishes/entertainers used to build on stage" in lines 15–16 of "Days" is also a metaphor for life. The "Days" speaker is saying that life is like a precarious pile of dishes that may fall at any moment.*

RESPOND

Collaborate & Compare

THERE BUT FOR THE GRACE
Poem by Wisława Szymborska

DAYS
Poem by Billy Collins

COMPARE POEMS

Both "There But for the Grace" and "Days" have similar themes—in other words, similar messages about life. To analyze a poem's theme, ask yourself these questions:

- ❏ What is your first reaction after reading the poem? What message do you believe the poet wants to share?
- ❏ What evidence do you have to support your reaction? How does the poet use word choice and figurative language to get his or her message across?
- ❏ What is the on-the-surface (explicit) meaning of the poem, and what is the beneath-the-surface (implicit) meaning?
- ❏ What is the writer's tone, or attitude toward the subject?

Now that you have had time to read and think about both poems, compare and contrast their themes. In a small group, use this chart to record your thoughts. Summarize each poem's theme, and list words or phrases from the poem that support your interpretation of the theme.

POEM	THEME	EVIDENCE FROM POEM
"There But for the Grace"		
"Days"		

ANALYZE THE TEXTS

Discuss these questions in your group.

1. **Compare** With your group, review the details in your chart. In what ways are the themes of both poems similar? In what ways are they different? Explain.

2. **Critique** Which poem do you believe has a stronger or a more compelling theme? Cite evidence to support your ideas.

3. **Compare** Does the tone of each poem remain the same, or change? Explain.

4. **Interpret** How does the figurative language in each poem emphasize its theme? Include evidence from the poems to support your answer.

ENGLISH LEARNER SUPPORT

Discuss Theme Remind students that a theme is the overlying message that runs throughout a text. Tell them that the theme usually discusses human nature or the human experience. Arrange students in pairs. Then say: "Tell a story about a time you were afraid. Explain what you were afraid of and how you got over your fears." Encourage students to ask questions to monitor their understanding of their partner's story. Have students take turns telling their stories to each other. Then ask each student what important idea, or message, was relayed in the story. **MODERATE**

ANALYZE AND SHARE

Continue exploring the ideas in these poems by analyzing their connections to the other selections in this unit. Follow these steps:

1. **Identify Connections** Think about similarities between these poems and the other Unit 6 selections. Ask yourself:
   - ❏ How are the themes (messages about life) related?
   - ❏ What ideas do they share?
   - ❏ How are their explicit and implicit meanings similar?
   - ❏ Which poem connects more closely to the other selections in the unit? Why?

Use this chart to record your thoughts.

RESPOND

Go to the **Speaking and Listening Studio** for a lesson on having a collaborative discussion.

OTHER UNIT SELECTIONS	CONNECTIONS TO "THERE BUT FOR THE GRACE"	CONNECTIONS TO "DAYS"
The Diary of Anne Frank	The poem is about people who escaped; the play is about people who did it.	In the Poem and the play, each day could bring about a huge change.
The Diary of a Young Girl	Both are reactions to terrible events.	The diary and poem each include reflections about life.
"After Auschwitz"	Both are by people who experienced the Holocaust.	Both emphasize the fragility and preciousness of life.

2. **Discuss Ideas** Join a group and compare the connections you have made. Discuss your interpretations of the themes. Listen carefully, and make sure to speak respectfully even if you disagree with others' interpretations. Be willing to adjust your responses to the poems based on what others say.

3. **Select Information** Working independently, use the information you generated on your own and in the group to decide which poem is a better fit for the unit.

4. **Draft and Share** Write an analysis that explains which poem best captures the spirit of the unit and why. Cite text evidence to support your ideas. Share your analysis with a partner, and use your partner's feedback to revise your analysis.

5. **Publish Your Analysis** Include your analysis in a collection you can share with the whole class.

Collaborate & Compare   533

APPLYING ACADEMIC VOCABULARY

❏ **communicate** ☑ **draft** ❏ **liberation** ❏ **philosophy** ☑ **publish**

Write and Discuss Have students write their answers then turn to a partner to discuss the following questions. Guide students to include the Academic Vocabulary words *draft* and *publish* in their answers.

- What are the most important ideas in your **draft**?
- How did you prepare to **publish** your analysis?

APPLY

ANALYZE AND SHARE

Explain that even though texts may have similar themes, they may approach the themes in different ways.

1. **Identify Connections**

   The Diary of Anne Frank: The poem is about people who escaped; the play is about people who did not. In both, each day could bring about a huge change.

   The Diary of a Young Girl: Both are reactions to terrible events. The diary and poem each include reflections about life.

   "After Auschwitz": Both are by people who experienced the Holocaust. Both emphasize the fragility and preciousness of life.

2. **Discuss Ideas** Discuss the ideas about the themes of the texts, such as the frailty of life, the importance of chance in survival, and taking each day as a gift. Make sure all students understand how to connect the theme to the writing.

3. **Select Information** Remind students to organize the information they have collected so they can make an informed decision about which poem the information best supports.

4. **Draft and Share** Remind students how to cite textual evidence in their writing. Make sure all students understand what an analysis should include.

5. **Publish Your Analysis** Remind students to copyedit their analysis before adding it to their published collection.

There But for the Grace/ Days   **533**

INDEPENDENT READING

READER'S CHOICE

Setting a Purpose Have students review their Unit 6 Response Log and think about what they've already learned about the legacy of Anne Frank. As they select their Independent Reading selections, encourage them to consider what more they want to know.

NOTICE NOTE

Explain that some selections may contain multiple signposts; others may contain only one. The same type of signpost can occur many times in the same text.

 LEARNING MINDSET

Grit Explain to students that independent reading requires perseverance. You have to continue reading even if the work is long and sometimes confusing. Having a learning mindset means that you "stick to it" and have stamina for the reading task. You keep reading confidently until you complete the work.

 INDEPENDENT READING

? **ESSENTIAL QUESTION:**

What can we learn from Anne Frank?

Reader's Choice

Setting a Purpose Select one or more of these options from your eBook to continue your exploration of the Essential Question.

- Read the descriptions to see which text grabs your interest.
- Think about which genres you enjoy reading.

Notice & Note

In this unit, you practiced noticing and noting three signposts: **Words of the Wiser, Memory Moment,** and **Contrasts and Contradictions.** As you read independently, these signposts and others will aid your understanding. Below are the anchor questions to ask when you read literature and nonfiction.

Reading Literature: Stories, Poems, and Plays		
Signpost	**Anchor Question**	**Lesson**
Contrasts and Contradictions	Why did the character act that way?	p. 3
Aha Moment	How might this change things?	p. 3
Tough Questions	What does this make me wonder about?	p. 152
Words of the Wiser	What's the lesson for the character?	p. 406
Again and Again	Why might the author keep bringing this up?	p. 2
Memory Moment	Why is this memory important?	p. 153

Reading Nonfiction: Essays, Articles, and Arguments		
Signpost	**Anchor Question(s)**	**Lesson**
Big Questions	What surprised me? What did the author think I already knew? What challenged, changed, or confirmed what I already knew?	p. 77
Contrasts and Contradictions	What is the difference, and why does it matter?	p. 241
Extreme or Absolute Language	Why did the author use this language?	p. 76
Numbers and Stats	Why did the author use these numbers or amounts?	p. 325
Quoted Words	Why was this person quoted or cited, and what did this add?	p. 77
Word Gaps	Do I know this word from someplace else? Does it seem like technical talk for this topic? Do clues in the sentence help me understand the word?	p. 240

 ENGLISH LEARNER SUPPORT

Support Independent Reading Have students read silently with increasing ease and comprehension for longer periods. To gauge their independent reading level, encourage students to evaluate their progress. Ask them why they chose the work and how they reacted to it. Did they enjoy it and if so, why? What did they learn? How did they address words they didn't know?

- Listen carefully to their responses and give feedback where appropriate.
- Make additional recommendations to encourage further reading.

- Work with the school librarian for other books to read independently.
- Encourage students to think about their reading habits and interests as they select new titles.
ALL LEVELS

Go to the **Reading Studio** for additional support in developing fluency.

You can preview these texts in Unit 6 of your eBook.

Then, check off the text or texts that you select to read on your own.

ESSAY
Peace Can Happen
Christine Kingery

Forgiveness and compassion can heal all wounds—one person at a time.

POEMS
The Butterfly
Pavel Friedmann
On a Sunny Evening
Anonymous

Young prisoners in a concentration camp hunger for the natural world.

SHORT STORY
The Singing Women
Rebecca Makkai

An attempt to preserve a fragile culture puts it in harm's way.

ARTICLE
from **A Tragedy Revealed: A Heroine's Last Days**
Ernst Schnabel

This historical account details the fate of Anne and the other residents of the Secret Annex.

SPEECH
Nobel Prize Acceptance Speech
Elie Wiesel

A survivor of the Holocaust argues for our common humanity and against injustice.

Collaborate and Share   With a partner, discuss what you learned from at least one of your independent readings.

- Give a brief synopsis or summary of the text.
- Describe any signposts that you noticed in the text and explain what they revealed to you.
- Describe what you most enjoyed or found most challenging about the text. Give specific examples.
- Decide if you would recommend the text to others. Why or why not?

 Go to the **Reading Studio** for more resources on **Notice & Note.**

MATCHING STUDENTS TO TEXTS

Use the following information to guide students in choosing their texts.

Peace Can Happen   Lexile: 720L
   Genre: diary
   Overall Rating: Accessible

The Butterfly/On a Sunny Evening
   Genre: poems
   Overall Rating: Accessible

The Singing Women   Lexile: 970L
   Genre: short story
   Overall Rating: Challenging

**A Tragedy Revealed:
A Heroine's Last Days**   Lexile: 990L
   Genre: article
   Overall Rating: Accessible

Nobel Prize Acceptance Speech   Lexile: 790L
   Genre: speech
   Overall Rating: Accessible

Collaborate and Share   To assess how well students read the selections, walk around the room and listen to their conversations. Encourage students to be focused and specific in their comments.

 Online **Ed** **for Assessment**

- Independent Reading Selection Tests

 Encourage students to visit the **Reading Studio** to download a handy handbook of **NOTICE & NOTE** signposts.

WHEN STUDENTS STRUGGLE . . .

Keep a Reading Log As students read their selected texts, have them keep a reading log for each selection to note signposts and their thoughts about them. Use their logs to assess how well they are noticing and reflecting on elements of the texts.

Reading Log for (title)		
Page and Paragraph	**Signpost I Noticed**	**My Notes About It**

UNIT (6) Tasks

• WRITE A PERSONAL NARRATIVE

MENTOR TEXT

THE DIARY OF A YOUNG GIRL

Diary by ANNE FRANK

LEARNING OBJECTIVES

Writing Task

- Write a personal narrative.
- Use strategies to plan and organize your personal narrative.
- Use the Mentor Text as a model for writing an engaging introduction and using dialogue.
- Use an organizational chart as a guide to writing a well-structured sequence of events with vivid, specific details.
- Write a conclusion that reveals why the experience was meaningful to you.
- Revise your draft, incorporating feedback from peers.
- Edit your draft, checking it for the proper use of standard English conventions and correcting any misspellings.
- Post your personal narrative on a classroom or school website.
- Use a scoring guide to evaluate your personal narrative.
- **Language** As part of the editing process, check your personal narrative for correct capitalization.

Assign the writing Task in *Ed.*

Online

RESOURCES

- Unit 6 Response Log
- Reading Studio: Notice & Note
- Writing Studio: Writing Narratives; Writing as a Process
- Grammar Studio : Module 13: Capital Letters

Language X-Ray: English Language Support

Use the instruction below and the supports and scaffolds in the Teacher's Edition to help you guide students of different proficiency levels.

INTRODUCE THE WRITING TASK

Make sure students understand that a personal narrative is a story about real people and events that usually reflects the writer's experiences, feelings, and personality. Remind students that a successful personal narrative establishes a situation and introduces a narrator and characters. It organizes a well-structured sequence of events and uses narrative techniques, such as dialogue, pacing, relevant descriptive details, and reflection to develop experiences. It also provides a conclusion that reflects on the narrated experiences and events.

WRITING

Use Correct Capitalization

Tell students that they can prepare their personal narratives for publication by capitalizing proper nouns and words derived from them. Students should not capitalize common nouns.

Use the following supports with students at varying proficiency levels:

- Display the following sentence, say it aloud with students, and then have several volunteers read it aloud: Last week, I learned about Abraham Lincoln. Ask students which words in the sentence begin with capital letters. (*Last, I, Abraham, Lincoln*) **SUBSTANTIAL**

- Ask volunteers to explain the reason why the four words in the sentence displayed must be capitalized. (Last *is capitalized because it is the first word in a sentence;* I *is capitalized because it is the personal pronoun I;* Abraham Lincoln *is capitalized because it is the name of a person.*) **MODERATE**

- Display the following sentences, and call on volunteers to read them aloud: abraham lincoln, who was born in kentucky, died on april 15, 1865. John wilkes booth assassinated him on the night of april 14, 1865 at ford's theatre in washington, d.c. Then have volunteers edit the sentences to provide correct capitalization. (*Abraham Lincoln, Kentucky, April, Wilkes Booth, April, Ford's Theatre, Washington, D.C.*) **LIGHT**

WRITING

WRITE A PERSONAL NARRATIVE

Introduce students to the Writing Task by reading the introductory paragraph with them. Remind students to refer to the notes they recorded in the Unit 6 Response Log as they plan and draft their personal narratives. The Response Log should contain ideas about the legacy of Anne Frank. Drawing on these different perspectives will make their own writing more interesting and well informed. Tell students that a good personal narrative is a story about real people and events that usually reflect the writer's experiences, feelings, and personality.

 For **writing support** for students at varying proficiency levels, see the **Language X-Ray** on page 536B.

USE THE MENTOR TEXT

Point out that their personal narratives will be similar to Anne Frank's memoir *The Diary of a Young Girl* in that they will present events in chronological order and include dialogue. However, their personal narratives will be much shorter than Anne Frank's memoir and will focus on a specific object that they value.

WRITING PROMPT

Review the prompt with students. Encourage them to ask questions about any part of the assignment that is unclear. Make sure they understand that the purpose of their personal narrative is to relate an experience involving an object that they value.

 **WRITING TASK**

Write a Personal Narrative

 Go to the **Writing Studio** for help writing a personal narrative.

This unit focuses on Anne Frank, a Jewish girl in the Netherlands whose family hid from the Nazis during World War II. In her diary, she wrote about a pen she valued. For this writing task, create a short personal narrative about an emotional experience involving an object you value. For a narrative you can use as a mentor text, review the entry for November 11, 1943, in *The Diary of a Young Girl*.

As you write your personal narrative, you can use the notes from your Response Log, which you filled out after reading the texts in this unit.

Writing Prompt

Read the information in the box below.

> This is the context or inspiration for your personal narrative.

> One of Anne Frank's most treasured possessions was a fountain pen, which was inadvertently destroyed while she was in hiding in the Secret Annex with her family.

Think carefully about the following question.

> This is the Essential Question for this unit. How would you answer this question, based on the texts in the unit?

> What can we learn from Anne Frank?

> Now mark the words that identify exactly what you are being asked to produce.

Write a personal narrative about an experience involving an object that you value.

Be sure to —

> Review these points as you write and again when you finish. Make any needed changes or edits.

- ❏ provide an attention-getting opening
- ❏ focus on a single incident
- ❏ include vivid, specific, and sensory details
- ❏ describe events in an order that makes sense
- ❏ use transitions to make the sequence of events clear and to connect ideas within and across paragraphs
- ❏ include your thoughts and feelings
- ❏ conclude by explaining why the experience was meaningful to you

536 Unit 6

 LEARNING MINDSET

Asking for Help As students plan and develop their personal narratives, encourage them to ask for help from you, their classmates, their friends, or their parents as needed. Help them understand that asking for help is a sign of strength, not weakness.

Asking for help is an important way to cultivate a growth mindset. The people around you can help you acquire or develop strategies.

1 Plan

Before you start writing your first draft, you need to plan your personal narrative. Think about the prompt. What object has been meaningful to you? What event demonstrates its importance? To help you gather ideas, jot down a list of some of your most treasured objects, going all the way back to early childhood. Discuss ideas with a classmate, and also review Anne Frank's diary or other personal narratives.

Next, consider your purpose and audience. Who might most enjoy hearing about your experience? Keep in mind that your word choice and tone for a group of classmates or friends may differ from what it would be for a group of adults.

Use the table below for help in planning your draft.

Personal Narrative Planning Table	
Genre	Personal narrative
Topic	An experience with a valued object
Some of my most valued objects	
Ideas from discussion with classmates	
Ideas from reading other narratives	
Purpose	
Audience	

Background Reading Review the notes you took in your Response Log after reading *The Diary of a Young Girl*. Your responses to Anne's diary might give you ideas for your own personal narrative.

Go to **Writing as a Process: Task, Purpose, and Audience** for help planning your personal narrative.

Notice & Note

From Reading to Writing

As you plan your personal narrative, apply what you've learned about signposts to your own writing. Remember that writers use common features, called signposts, to help convey their message to readers. Think about how you can incorporate a **Memory Moment** into your narrative.

 Go to the **Reading Studio** for more resources on Notice & Note.

Use the notes from your Response Log as you plan your personal narrative.

---

1 PLAN

Tell students that they should think back over their lives while brainstorming ideas for their personal narratives. Have them list objects that they valued and think about which of these objects would be interesting to others. Then have students choose the single object that they want to write about.

▶ NOTICE & NOTE

From Reading to Writing Remind students that they can use **Quoted Words** to include the opinions or conclusions of someone who is an expert on the topic. Students can also use Quoted Words to provide support for a point they are trying to make. Remind students to format direct quotations correctly and to give credit to the source.

Background Reading As they plan their personal narratives, remind students to refer to the notes they took in the Response Log. They may also review the selections to find additional facts and examples to support ideas.

TO CHALLENGE STUDENTS . . .

Structure Your Narrative Challenge students to reorder the events in their narratives so they are not presented chronologically. Ask students to discuss what might be gained by the use of flashbacks or foreshadowing, for example. Have them read both the original and the new version to a small group. Then, have students discuss which structure is more effective in telling the story.

WRITING

Organize Your Ideas Tell students that a personal narrative, like a short story, has a narrative structure that includes a beginning, a middle, and an end. Tell students that creating a timeline might be a helpful planning tool. Students should list all parts of the event in time order. For each part, they should jot down who was involved, where it happened, and the significant details. When the list is finished, students can decide which parts to include in their personal narratives and which parts to condense or skip in order to maintain focus and reader's interest.

② DEVELOP A DRAFT

Remind students that most personal narratives allow readers to see inside the mind of the writer. Before students begin to write their first drafts, remind them to let readers know what their feelings and thoughts were about the object that they value. Tell students that the purpose of drafting is to generate ideas, not to achieve perfect expression.

■ English Learner Support

Link Events Provide students with a list of transitional words and phrases. Have them copy the phrases into their notebooks and check off the ones they use.

At first	Finally
From the start of . . .	In the end
After a while	After all
Next	
Then	

SUBSTANTIAL/MODERATE

Go to **Writing as a Process: Planning and Drafting** for help organizing your ideas.

Organize Your Ideas After you have planned your narrative, you need to organize your ideas in a way that will help you write your first draft. You can use the chart below to record each part of the experience in chronological order.

Main Topic: Experience with a Valued Possession		
How the valued object entered your life	**Experience that caused you to appreciate its importance to you**	**Reflection on the event and the significance of the object**
Key Details	Key Details	Key Details

② Develop a Draft

You may prefer to draft your personal narrative online.

When you're ready to begin drafting, refer to the chart above, as well as any notes you took as you studied *The Diary of a Young Girl*. These will provide a kind of map for you to follow as you write.

Your personal narrative should include the following elements:

- a well-structured, effectively paced sequence of events
- vivid, specific details about the incident
- your thoughts and feelings about the experience
- reflection on why the experience was meaningful to you

WHEN STUDENTS STRUGGLE . . .

Organize Details Have students meet with partners to help them organize their writing. Tell them to describe a significant event. As students talk, their partners should take notes about which descriptive details belong at the beginning, middle, and end of the event. Then, students can transfer the notes to the chart on this page.

For additional support, go to the **Reading Studio** and assign the following **Level Up tutorial: Revising for Unity, Coherence, and Organization.**

WRITING TASK

Use the Mentor Text

Author's Craft
Your introduction is the first place to get your reader's attention as you present your topic in an engaging way. Note how Anne Frank opens the following passage from *The Diary of a Young Girl*.

> *Dearest Kitty,*
>
> **I have a good title for this chapter:**
> *Ode to My Fountain Pen*
> *In Memoriam*

The author (Anne) begins with a humorous title. Odes are poems that express strong feelings of love or respect. Here, the author suggests that she has such feelings about a simple object—a pen—that is unimportant to most people.

Apply What You've Learned To capture your reader's attention, you might open your narrative with a surprising, unexpected comparison or an unusual expression.

Genre Characteristics
To develop an important idea and draw readers into a narrative, writers sometimes include dialogue. Notice how Anne Frank uses dialogue to convey her feelings about the lost fountain pen.

> . . . Margot looked, Mother looked, Father looked, Dussel looked. But it had vanished.
>
> "Maybe it fell into the stove, along with the beans!" Margot suggested.
>
> "No, it couldn't have!" I replied.

The author's frantic denial of her sister's suggestion indicates that she greatly valued the pen.

Apply What You've Learned To help your readers better understand the events in your narrative, consider adding dialogue. Think about other people who were part of the experience that you have chosen. What did you say to them—or what did they say to you—that might help show why you valued the object or why the experience was an emotional one?

Write a Personal Narrative **539**

WHY THIS MENTOR TEXT?

The Diary of a Young Girl serves as a mentor text for a personal narrative because it provides a unique glimpse into the writer's thoughts and feelings at a particular time. Using a chronological structure, Anne Frank tells about the loss of an object she cherished—a fountain pen—and uses dialogue to strengthen the narrative.

USE THE MENTOR TEXT

Author's Craft Tell students that a useful strategy for writing an engaging introduction is to open the paragraph with something that surprises the reader or with a startling use of figurative language. Something unexpected or unusual will hook readers, pulling them into the narrative and whetting the appetite for more.

Genre Characteristics Tell students that conversations between real people in a memoir or personal narrative often resemble the dialogue between characters in a short story. A writer's skillful use of dialogue reveals character and helps advance the plot. Remind students to consider context as they write dialogue and to enclose a speaker's exact words within quotation marks.

EL ENGLISH LEARNER SUPPORT

Recognize Formal and Informal Language Remind students of the differences between formal and informal language. Then, explain that the language they use in dialogue should be informal to reflect the way people speak in real life. Write several examples of both:

"Hey. Hurry up, would you?" someone yelled from behind me. (*Informal*)

"Excuse me. Would you please walk faster?" someone asked from behind me. (*formal*)
    MODERATE

WRITING

3 REVISE

As students revise their drafts, tell them their descriptive details must fit the situation or feeling of their narrative. Students should consider not only a word's denotation but its connotation. For example, *murmur* and *mutter* both refer to a low flow of words or sounds. But *mutter* usually suggests anger. An unhappy customer would probably *mutter* about slow service, but a happy mother would *murmur* (not mutter) a lullaby to her baby.

With a Partner As students evaluate their narratives, ask peer reviewers to provide specific feedback about how to add realistic dialogue that reveals character or advances the action. Remind students that their narratives should naturally lead to their reflections about what they learned.

WRITING TASK

3 Revise

Go to **Writing as a Process: Revising and Editing** for help revising your personal narrative.

On Your Own Once you have written your draft, you'll want to go back and look for ways to improve it. As you reread and revise, think about whether you have achieved your purpose. The Revision Guide will help you focus on specific elements to make your writing stronger.

Revision Guide

Ask Yourself	Tips	Revision Techniques
1. Does my opening grab readers' attention?	**Underline** interesting or surprising statements.	**Add** an attention-getting statement.
2. Are events in an order that makes sense? Do transitions connect paragraphs and make the sequence of events clear?	**Number** the events in the narrative. **Check** that they are in the correct order. **Underline** transitional words and phrases.	**Rearrange** events in the order in which they occurred, if necessary. **Add** transitions to link events and make connections between paragraphs.
3. Is dialogue relevant to the purpose?	**Note** any dialogue that seems unnecessary.	**Add** dialogue that reveals character and advances the action.
4. Do vivid sensory details make the experience seem real?	**Highlight** vivid, specific, and sensory details.	**Add** more sensory details. **Delete** irrelevant details.
5. Have I included my thoughts and feelings?	**Put a check mark** next to statements of feelings or thoughts.	**Add** specific details about feelings and thoughts, if necessary.
6. Does my conclusion reveal why the experience was meaningful to me?	**Underline** the statement about why the experience was meaningful.	**Add** a statement that explains why the experience was important.

ACADEMIC VOCABULARY
As you conduct your **peer review,** be sure to use these words.

- ❏ communicate
- ❏ draft
- ❏ liberation
- ❏ philosophy
- ❏ publish

With a Partner Once you and your partner have worked through the Revision Guide on your own, exchange papers and evaluate each other's draft in a **peer review.** Focus on providing revision suggestions for at least three of the items mentioned in the chart. Explain why you think your partner's draft should be revised and what your specific suggestions are.

When receiving feedback from your partner, listen attentively and ask questions to make sure you fully understand the revision suggestions.

ENGLISH LEARNER SUPPORT

Use Modal Expressions Point out that precise word choice helps readers understand the narrator's experience. Have pairs do the following:

- Discuss the different meanings for each word choice in the following sentences: *I can/may look for another job. It is possible/likely that she learned from that experience.* Make sure students understand how these words can express shades of meaning.

- Have students look at their own narratives and identify words that may be substituted with more precise word choices. Then have them discuss these with their partners to see whether the new words better express the intended meanings. **LIGHT**

4 Edit

Improve your personal narrative. Edit it for the proper use of standard English conventions and correct any misspellings or grammatical errors.

Language Conventions

Correct Capitalization When editing your draft, check for correct capitalization. Keep these categories in mind:

> Go to the **Grammar Studio** to learn more about using correct capitalization.

CATEGORY	EXAMPLES
Capitalize the first word in a sentence.	"Burn them. All of them."
Capitalize the pronoun *I*.	I'm seething with rage, yet I can't show it.
Capitalize proper nouns.	
Names of people and animals	Anne Frank, Father, Mrs. Van Daan, Mouschi, Tom Cat
Nationalities, races, peoples	Jewish, German, Dutch, Europeans, Maccabees
Languages	Dutch, Latin, German, English
Organizations, government bodies	Jewish Lyceum, Nazis, Green Police, Allies
Historical periods and events	World War II, the Holocaust
Days, months, and holidays	Friday, February, Hanukkah, St. Nicholas's Day
Titles of literary works	*The Diary of a Young Girl*, "Ode to My Fountain Pen"
Capitalize geographical names.	
Cities, states, countries, continents	Chicago, Texas, Switzerland, Europe
Regions, bodies of water, mountains	the West, Atlantic Ocean, Alps
Buildings, bridges, monuments	Westertoren, London Bridge, the Annex

Example of correct capitalization from *The Diary of a Young Girl*

It was just after five on **Friday** afternoon. **I** came out of my room and was about to sit down at the table to write when **I** was roughly pushed to one side to make room for **Margot** and **Father**, who wanted to practice their **Latin**.

5 Publish

Choose one of these options for sharing your personal narrative:
- Post your personal narrative on a classroom or school website.
- Submit your personal narrative to a literary magazine.

4 EDIT

Tell students to proofread their work several times. For example, the first reading could be to check that their narrative is complete and makes sense. The second reading could identify errors in grammar and usage. The third reading could pinpoint errors in spelling, punctuation, and mechanics.

LANGUAGE CONVENTIONS

Use Correct Capitalization Remind students of the difference between common nouns and proper nouns. For example, the word *month* is a common noun. The word *December*, however, is a proper noun because it is the name of a specific month. Proper nouns are capitalized; common nouns are not.

5 PUBLISH

Students might consider posting their personal narratives as a blog on a school website. Encourage readers to post comments and questions after reading the personal narrative. The author can also respond to those comments and questions.

WHEN STUDENTS STRUGGLE...

Visualize Details Have students work in pairs to visualize events from their narratives that need more detail. Have one student sit with eyes closed while the other asks questions, such as "What do you see?"; and "What do you hear?" Tell the listening student to take notes as the visualizing partner answers the questions.

 For additional support, go to the **Reading Studio** and assign the following Level Up tutorial: **Revising to Add Supporting Details.**

WRITING

USE THE SCORING GUIDE

Have students exchange the final draft of their personal narratives with a partner. Ask students to score each other's personal narrative and to write a brief paragraph using the language of the scoring guide to explain the reasons for their scores.

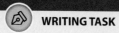
WRITING TASK

Use the scoring guide to evaluate your personal narrative.

	Writing Task Scoring Guide: Personal Narrative		
	Organization/Progression	**Development of Ideas**	**Use of Language and Conventions**
4	• The narrative has a coherent sequence that builds to a logical conclusion. • Well-chosen events result in effective pacing. • Transitions clearly show the sequence of events.	• The opening catches the reader's attention and sets the scene. • The focus is on a single incident. • The conclusion of the narrative makes clear the significance of the experience to the writer.	• Precise words and vivid, sensory language are used throughout to bring people, places, and events to life. • Spelling is correct. • Grammar, usage, and mechanics are correct.
3	• Some events are presented in a sensible order, but others are not. • Pacing is, for the most part, effective. • A few more transitions are needed to clarify the sequence of events and other details.	• The opening could be more engaging. The scene is set adequately. • The narrative focuses primarily on a single incident but includes some extraneous events. • The conclusion of the narrative suggests but doesn't make clear the significance of the event to the writer.	• Precise words and vivid, sensory details are often used to describe people, places, and events. • There are only a few spelling errors. • Grammar, usage, and mechanics are mostly correct with only a few errors.
2	• The sequence of events is confusing. • Pacing is uneven. • More transitions are needed to show the sequence of events.	• The opening is not very engaging. • The narrative may relate more than one incident but still focuses on the most important one. • The conclusion of the narrative offers conflicting interpretations of the significance of the event to the writer.	• Precise words and vivid details are used only occasionally; descriptions are often vague and general. • Spelling is often incorrect but does not make reading difficult. • Some grammatical and usage errors exist but do not obscure the writer's meaning.
1	• Events are presented in random order, with no logical connections. • Pacing is dull. • No transitions are used, making the narrative difficult to follow.	• The opening is uninteresting or is missing altogether. • The narrative wanders from incident to incident, with little or no focus. • The conclusion of the narrative fails to convey the significance of the event to the writer.	• Language is vague and confusing. • Many spelling errors are present. • Many grammatical and usage errors confuse the writer's ideas.

Reflect on the Unit

By completing your personal narrative, you have created a writing product that takes inspiration from Anne Frank's writing and explores how everyday objects and moments can be meaningful. Now reflect on what you have learned throughout this unit.

Reflect on the Essential Question

- What can we learn from Anne Frank? How did your answer to this question change as you read the selections in this unit?

- What are some examples from the texts you've read that show the kinds of lessons people can learn from Anne Frank's experiences?

Reflect on Your Reading

- Which selections were the most interesting or surprising to you?

- Did you prefer reading Anne Frank's diary or the play based on her diary? Why?

- From which selection did you learn the most about the lessons we can learn from Anne Frank?

Reflect on the Writing Task

- What was the most exciting or vivid detail in your narrative? Why do you think so?

- How did writing a personal narrative help you better understand how you felt about your experience or what its significance might be?

- What improvements did you make to your personal narrative as you were revising?

UNIT 6 SELECTIONS
- *The Diary of Anne Frank*
- *The Diary of a Young Girl*
- "After Auschwitz"
- "There But for the Grace"
- "Days"

Reflect on the Unit   543

REFLECT ON THE UNIT

Have students reflect on the questions independently and write some notes in response to each one. Then have students meet with partners or in small groups to discuss their reflections. Circulate during these discussions to identify the questions that are generating the liveliest conversations. Wrap up with a whole-class discussion focused on these questions.

 LEARNING MINDSET

Self-Reflection As they complete and publish their personal narratives, encourage students to set aside some time to reflect on what they have accomplished through their work on this unit. Ask them to think about the questions they explored and the ones they might explore later. How did writing a personal narrative help them better understand how they feel about experiences or what the significance of an incident might be? What strategies helped them become more effective learners?

HMH |  (into) **Literature**

Student Resources

 Online **HMH** *Into Literature* **Studios**

For more instruction and practice, visit the HMH *Into Literature* Studios.

 Reading Studio

 Writing Studio

 Speaking & Listening Studio

 Grammar Studio

 Vocabulary Studio

UNIT 1
RESPONSE LOG

Use this Response Log to record your ideas about how each of the texts in Unit 1 relates to or comments on the **Essential Question.**

(?) **Essential Question:**
Does technology improve or control our lives?

The Brave Little Toaster	
Are Bionic Superhumans on the Horizon?	
Interflora	
The Automation Paradox	
Heads Up, Humans	

UNIT 2
RESPONSE LOG

? **Essential Question:**
Why do we sometimes like to feel frightened?

What Is the Horror Genre?	
The Tell-Tale Heart	
The Hollow	
The Monkey's Paw (short story)	
from The Monkey's Paw (film clip)	

UNIT 3 RESPONSE LOG

Use this Response Log to record your ideas about how each of the texts in Unit 3 relates to or comments on the **Essential Question.**

? **Essential Question:**
What are the places that shape who you are?

My Favorite Chaperone	
from The Book of Unknown Americans	
The Powwow at the End of the World	
New Immigrants Share Their Stories	
A Common Bond: Teens Forge Friendships Despite Differences	

UNIT 4
RESPONSE LOG

Use this Response Log to record your ideas about how each of the texts in Unit 4 relates to or comments on the **Essential Question.**

? **Essential Question:**
What will people risk to be free?

from Narrative of the Life of Frederick Douglass, an American Slave	
from Harriet Tubman: Conductor on the Underground Railroad	
The Drummer Boy of Shiloh	
O Captain! My Captain!	
Not My Bones	
from Fortune's Bones	

UNIT 5
RESPONSE LOG

Use this Response Log to record your ideas about how each of the texts in Unit 5 relates to or comments on the **Essential Question.**

? **Essential Question:**
How do your teenage years prepare you for adulthood?

The Debt We Owe to the Adolescent Brain	
from Bronx Masquerade	
Hanging Fire	
Summer of His Fourteenth Year	
from It's Complicated: The Social Lives of Networked Teens	
Outsmart Your Smartphone	

UNIT 6
RESPONSE LOG

Use this Response Log to record your ideas about how each of the texts in Unit 6 relates to or comments on the **Essential Question.**

? **Essential Question:**
What can we learn from Anne Frank?

The Diary of Anne Frank	
from The Diary of a Young Girl	
After Auschwitz	
There But for the Grace	
Days	

© Houghton Mifflin Harcourt Publishing Company

Using a Glossary

A glossary is an alphabetical list of vocabulary words. Use a glossary just as you would a dictionary—to determine the meanings, parts of speech, pronunciation, and syllabification of words. (Some technical, foreign, and more obscure words in this book are defined for you in the footnotes that accompany many of the selections.)

Many words in the English language have more than one meaning. This glossary gives the meanings that apply to the words as they are used in the selections in this book.

The following abbreviations are used to identify parts of speech of words:

adj. adjective   *adv.* adverb   *n.* noun   *v.* verb

Each word's pronunciation is given in parentheses. A guide to the pronunciation symbols appears in the Pronunciation Key below. The stress marks in the Pronunciation Key are used to indicate the force given to each syllable in a word. They can also help you determine where words are divided into syllables.

For more information about the words in this glossary or for information about words not listed here, consult a dictionary.

Pronunciation Key

Symbol	Examples	Symbol	Examples	Symbol	Examples
ă	pat	m	mum	ûr	urge, term, firm, word, heard
ā	pay	n	no, sudden* (sud´n)	v	valve
ä	father	ng	thing	w	with
âr	care	ŏ	pot	y	yes
b	bib	ō	toe	z	zebra, xylem
ch	church	ô	caught, paw	zh	vision, pleasure, garage
d	deed, milled	oi	noise	ə	about, item, edible, gallop, circus
ĕ	pet	ŏŏ	took		
ē	bee	ōō	boot	ər	butter
f	fife, phase, rough	ŏŏr	lure		
g	gag	ôr	core	**Sounds in Foreign Words**	
h	hat	ou	out	KH	*German* ich, ach; *Scottish* loch
hw	which	p	pop		
ĭ	pit	r	roar	N	*French*, bon (bôN)
ī	pie, by	s	sauce	œ	*French* feu, œuf; *German* schön
îr	pier	sh	ship, dish		
j	judge	t	tight, stopped	ü	*French* tu; *German* über
k	kick, cat, pique	th	thin		
l	lid, needle* (nēd´l)	*th*	this		
		ŭ	cut		

*In English the consonants *l* and *n* often constitute complete syllables by themselves.

Stress Marks

The relative emphasis with which the syllables of a word or phrase are spoken, called stress, is indicated in three different ways. The strongest, or primary, stress is marked with a bold mark (´). An intermediate, or secondary, level of stress is marked with a similar but lighter mark (´). The weakest stress is unmarked. Words of one syllable show no stress mark.

GLOSSARY OF ACADEMIC VOCABULARY

access (ăk´sĕs) *n.* a way of approaching or making use of

civil (sĭv´əl) *adj.* of, or related to, citizens and their relations with each other and the state

commentary (kŏm´ən-tĕr´ē) *n.* explanation or interpretation in the form of comments or observations

communicate (kə-myōō´nĭ-kāt´) *v.* to convey information or exchange ideas

contribute (kən-trĭb´yōōt) *v.* to give or supply for a common purpose

convention (kən-vĕn´shən) *n.* a practice or procedure widely used by a group; a custom

debate (dĭ-bāt´) *v.* to engage in arguments by discussing opposing points

deduce (dĭ-dōōs´) *v.* to reach a conclusion or decision through reasoning

demonstrate (dĕm´ən-strāt´) *v.* to show clearly and deliberately

document (dŏc´yə-mənt) *n.* written or printed paper that provides evidence or information

draft (drăft) *n.; v.* an early version or stage of a written document or plan; to write such a version

immigrate (ĭm´ĭ-grāt´) *v.* to enter and settle in a new country

liberation (lĭb´ə-rā´shən) *n.* the act of freeing or the state of being free

license (lī´səns) *n.* a document that is issued as proof of legal permission to do something

occupation (ŏk´yə-pā´shən) *n.* an activity that serves as one's source of income

option (ŏp´shən) *n.* something chosen or available as a choice

philosophy (fĭ-lŏs´ə-fē) *n.* an underlying theory or set of ideas relating to life as a whole

predict (prĭ-dĭkt´) *v.* to tell about in advance, especially on the basis of special knowledge

psychology (sī-kŏl´ə-jē) *n.* the study of mental processes and behaviors

publish (pŭb´lĭsh) *v.* to prepare and issue a book or other material to the public

reaction (rē-ăk´shən) *n.* a response to something

relocate (rē-lō´kāt) *v.* to move to a new place

shifting (shĭft´ĭng) *adj.* changing attitudes, judgments, or emphases

speculate (spĕk´yə-lāt´) *v.* to reason or form a theory about something based on available evidence

sufficient (sə-fĭsh´ənt) *adj.* being enough, or as much as needed

summary (sŭm´ə-rē) *n.* a condensed, or shorter, report that includes the main points of a text or event

symbolize (sĭm´bə-līz´) *v.* to serve as a symbol of, or represent, something else

technique (tĕk-nēk´) *n.* the systematic or orderly procedure by which a task is accomplished

technology (tĕk-nŏl´ə-jē) *n.* the application of science to make products; electronic or digital products and systems

trend (trĕnd) *n.* the general direction of something; a current style

GLOSSARY OF CRITICAL VOCABULARY

abode (ə-bōd´) *n.* An *abode* is a home.

adaptable (ə-dăp´tə-bəl) *adj.* *Adaptable* means able to survive under certain conditions.

ample (ăm´pəl) *adj.* To be *ample* is to be plentiful or enough.

anonymous (ə-nŏn´ə-məs) *adj.* To be *anonymous* means to be unknown or unidentified by name.

appalled (ə-pôld´) *adj.* To be *appalled* is to feel horror and shock about something.

appease (ə-pēz´) *v.* To *appease* means to pacify or lessen the anger of, usually by making concessions.

apprehension (ăp´rĭ-hĕn´shən) *n.* *Apprehension* is the fear or dread of the future.

askew (ə-skyōō´) *adj.* When something is *askew,* it is off center.

assimilate (ə-sĭm´ə-lāt´) *v.* To *assimilate* means to blend into or become similar to the prevailing culture.

assure (ə-shoŏr´) *v.* To *assure* is to state something positively, so as to remove doubt about it.

audacity (ô-dăs´ĭ-tē) *n.* *Audacity* is shameless daring or boldness.

cajole (kə-jōl´) *v.* When you *cajole,* you coax or urge gently.

capitalize (kăp´ĭ-tl-īz´) *v.* To *capitalize* on something means to use it to one's advantage.

chafe (chāf) *v.* To *chafe* is to annoy or bother someone.

collaborate (kə-lăb´ə-rāt´) *v.* To *collaborate* means to work together.

commence (kə-mĕns´) *v.* When things *commence,* they begin or start.

compensation (kŏm´pən-sā´shən) *n.* *Compensation* is something, such as money, that is received as payment.

conceive (kən-sēv´) *v.* When you *conceive* an idea, you think of it.

condole (kən-dōl´) *v.* If you *condole* with someone, you express sympathy or sorrow.

confer (kən-fûr´) *v.* To *confer* is to share ideas or make a decision with one or more other people.

confide (kən-fīd´) *v.* To *confide* means to share private or secret information.

conjecture (kən-jĕk´chər) *v.* If you *conjecture,* you guess or suppose.

conspicuous (kən-spĭk´yōō-əs) *adj.* Something *conspicuous* is obvious or very easy to see.

consternation (kŏn´stər-nā´shən) *n.* *Consternation* is a feeling of alarm or fear.

convene (kən-vēn´) *v.* To *convene* is to come together for a purpose.

credulity (krĭ-dōō´lĭ-tē) *n.* *Credulity* is a tendency to believe too readily.

crevice (krĕv´ĭs) *n.* A *crevice* is a narrow crack.

deliberate (dĭ-lĭb´ər-ĭt) *adj.* *Deliberate* decision-making activity is the process of making a choice only after carefully considering its likely effects.

denunciation (dĭ-nŭn´sē-ā´shən) *n.* A *denunciation* is the public condemnation of something as wrong or evil.

dependent (dĭ-pĕn´dənt) *adj.* *Dependent* means relying on or requiring the aid or support of another.

deplete (dĭ-plēt´) *v.* To *deplete* means to use up or to reduce to a very small amount.

derision (dĭ-rĭzh´ən) *n.* *Derision* is jeering laughter or ridicule.

diagnostics (dī´əg-nŏs´tĭks) *n.* *Diagnostics* are tools a computer uses to identify problems.

disheveled (dĭ-shĕv´əld) *adj.* When something is *disheveled,* it is messy or untidy.

dispatcher (dĭs-păch´ər) *n.* A *dispatcher* is a person who sends out vehicles according to a schedule.

GLOSSARY OF CRITICAL VOCABULARY

dispel (dĭ-spĕl´) v. When you *dispel* something, you drive it away.

dynamic (dī-năm´ĭk) n. A *dynamic* is a system in which conflicting or competing forces are at work.

eligible (ĕl´ĭ-jə-bəl) adj. *Eligible* means qualified to be selected.

eloquence (ĕl´ə-kwəns) n. *Eloquence* is the ability to speak powerfully and persuasively.

embrace (ĕm-brās´) v. To *embrace* an idea means to accept and support it.

enhancement (ĕn-hăns´mənt) n. An *enhancement* improves or adds to the quality or function of something.

evoke (ĭ-vōk´) v. When you *evoke* something, you bring it to mind.

exotic (ĕg-zŏt´ĭk) adj. Something that is *exotic* is unusual or different.

expansive (ĕk-spăns´ĭv) adj. *Expansive* means broad in size, range, or degree of openness.

fate (fāt) n. *Fate* is a power that is thought to determine the course of events.

froth (frôth) n. A *froth* is a fit of frustration or excitement.

grimace (grĭm´ĭs) n. A *grimace* is a facial expression of pain or disgust.

hunker (hŭng´kər) v. To *hunker* down means to stay in a place and focus on a task for a period of time.

hypocritical (hĭp´ə-krĭt´ĭ-kəl) adj. If someone is *hypocritical,* the person is false or deceptive.

implant (ĭm-plănt´) v. To *implant* a device means to place it inside the body through surgery.

implore (ĭm-plôr´) v. To *implore* is to beg for something urgently.

impulsive (ĭm-pŭl´sĭv) adj. To be *impulsive* means to act quickly, before thinking about the consequences.

inarticulate (ĭn´är-tĭk´yə-lĭt) adj. Someone who is *inarticulate* is unable to speak in a clear way.

indignantly (ĭn-dĭg´nənt-lē) adv. Someone who does something *indignantly* acts in a way that shows anger or shock over something that is unjust or unfair.

inert (ĭn-ûrt´) adj. *Inert* means unable to move or act.

inhibited (ĭn-hĭb´ĭt-əd) adj. If you feel *inhibited* you feel restrained, held back, or self-conscious.

instill (ĭn-stĭl´) v. When you *instill* something, you establish or implant it gradually.

insulate (ĭn´sə-lāt´) v. To *insulate* means to surround or cover to prevent the passage of heat, electricity, or sound.

integrity (ĭn-tĕg´rĭ-tē) n. *Integrity* is following a strict code of ethical conduct.

intensify (ĭn-tĕn´sə-fī´) v. If you *intensify* something, you make it grow in strength.

intimacy (ĭn´tə-mə-sē) n. *Intimacy* refers to a state of personal closeness that is usually experienced in privacy.

justify (jŭs´tə-fī´) v. If you *justify* something, you prove it is right or valid.

legitimately (lə-jĭt´ə-mĭt-lē) adv. When you do something *legitimately,* you do it lawfully.

lethal (lē´thəl) adj. *Lethal* means causing or capable of causing death.

linger (lĭng´gər) v. To *linger* is to remain or stay longer.

loathe (lōth) v. To *loathe* something is to dislike it very much.

melodrama (mĕl´ə-drä´mə) n. *Melodrama* is behavior characterized by exaggerated emotions.

muted (myōō´tĭd) adj. When something is *muted,* it is softened or muffled.

ostentatiously (ŏs´tĕn-tā´shəs-lē) adv. Someone who does something *ostentatiously* acts in an exaggerated way in order to attract attention.

paradox (păr´ə-dŏks´) n. A *paradox* is a person, thing, or situation that is contradictory.

parallel (păr´ə-lĕl´) adj. If things are *parallel,* they have comparable or similar parts.

GLOSSARY OF CRITICAL VOCABULARY

peril (pĕr´əl) *n.* A *peril* is something that is dangerous.

perspective (pər-spĕk´tĭv) *n.* A *perspective* is a viewpoint on or understanding of something.

predominantly (prĭ-dŏm´ə-nənt-lē) *adv.* *Predominantly* refers to the most important, obvious, or typical aspect(s) of something.

prosaic (prō-zā´ĭk) *adj.* If something is *prosaic,* it is dull or ordinary.

prudence (prōōd´ns) *n.* *Prudence* is the wise handling of practical matters.

quest (kwĕst) *n.* A *quest* is a search.

ravage (răv´ĭj) *v.* To *ravage* is to cause serious damage or destruction.

redistribute (rē´dĭ-strĭb´yōōt) *v.* To *redistribute* means to distribute again but differently.

reintegrate (rē-ĭn´tĭ-grāt´) *v.* To *reintegrate* is to come together, as when similar materials are collected for recycling.

relevant (rĕl´ə-vənt) *adj.* Something is *relevant* to a topic when it is related or important to that topic.

relish (rĕl´ĭsh) *v.* To *relish* is to take great joy or pleasure in something.

reminisce (rĕm´ə-nĭs´) *v.* When you *reminisce,* you think or talk about past experiences.

renowned (rĭ-nound´) *adj.* Someone or something that is *renowned* is famous.

resignation (rĕz´ĭg-nā´shən) *n.* *Resignation* is the acceptance of something that is inescapable.

resolute (rĕz´ə-lōōt´) *adj.* If you are *resolute,* you are firm or determined.

retract (rĭ-trăkt´) *v.* To *retract* is to pull in.

robustly (rō-bŭst´lē) *adv.* *Robustly* means in a strong, healthy way.

scrutinize (skrōōt´n-īz´) *v.* To *scrutinize* is to examine or inspect with great care.

scuffle (skŭf´əl) *n.* A *scuffle* is a disorderly fight.

sector (sĕk´tər) *n.* A *sector* is a part or division, as of a city or a national economy.

snicker (snĭk´ər) *n.* A *snicker* is a superior, partially suppressed laugh.

solemn (sŏl´əm) *adj.* If an event is *solemn,* it is deeply serious.

splendid (splĕn´dĭd) *adj.* If something is *splendid,* it is magnificent or very good.

sponsor (spŏn´sər) *v.* If you *sponsor* someone, you support his or her admission into a group.

stifle (stī´fəl) *v.* If you *stifle* something, you smother it.

stimulant (stĭm´yə-lənt) *n.* A *stimulant* is an agent that excites or temporarily speeds up mental and/or physical functions.

strew (strōō) *v.* If you *strew* something, you spread it here and there, or scatter it.

stun (stŭn) *v.* To *stun* someone is to make him or her feel shocked or dazed.

sullen (sŭl´ən) *adj.* *Sullen* people show silent resentment.

tirade (tī´rād) *n.* A *tirade* is a long, angry speech.

unabated (ŭn´ə-bā´tĭd) *adj.* If something is *unabated,* it keeps its full force without decreasing.

unrest (ŭn-rĕst´) *n.* *Unrest* refers to an unstable or turbulent condition that is often marked by protests or riots.

vehemently (vē´ə-mənt-lē) *adv.* If you do something *vehemently,* you do it with intense emotion.

vex (vĕks) *v.* If you *vex* someone, you annoy that person.

vindication (vĭn´dĭ-kā´shən) *n.* *Vindication* is the evidence or proof that someone's claim is correct.

vindictive (vĭn-dĭk´tĭv) *adj.* Something is *vindictive* if it is intended to hurt or punish someone.

whimper (hwĭm´pər) *v.* To *whimper* is to sob or let out a soft cry.

Index of Skills

Key

Teacher's Edition subject entries and page references are printed in **boldface** type. Subject entries and page references that apply to both the Student Edition and the Teacher's Edition appear in lightface type.

context clues, 14, 182, 350, 374

denotation, 510

dictionary use, 46, 102, 198

figures of speech, 286

multiple-meaning words, 224

prefixes, 498

suffixes, 88

synonyms and antonyms, 26

use resources, 336

word families, 388

word roots, 58, 130, 252, 272

voice, 50, 59, 255, 523

voice modulation and pitch, 72, 402

voice-over, 209, 222

volume of speech, 72, 402

W

When Students Struggle, 3, 9, 20, 24, 32, 34, 44, 54, 63, 66, 69, 72, 77, 83, 96, 110, 119, 124, 138, 141, 144, 145, 148, 152, 161, 174, 175, 193, 194, 196, 206, 214, 218, 227, 229, 232, 235, 241, 248, 264, 280, 292, 303, 306, 308, 311, 314, 317, 320, 325, 332, 344, 360, 370, 382, 386, 387, 388, 389, 390, 391, 393, 396, 407, 414, 442, 468, 480, 484, 506, 516, 526, 527, 528, 529, 535, 538, 541

Word Gaps (Notice & Note), 20, 65, 240, 244, 248, 310

Word Networks, 75, 239, 323, 405

word origin, 46, 102, 198

words. *See also* Critical Vocabulary; Vocabulary Strategy

commonly confused, 18, 23, 27

connotation, 510

context clues for, 14, 182, 224, 286, 350, 374

denotation, 510

prefixes, 498

roots, 58, 75, 130, 239, 252, 272, 323, 405

suffixes, 88

word families, 388

Words of the Wiser (Notice & Note), 119, 281, 359, 406, 410, 424, 435, 476, 485, 493, 534

writing activities

argumentative text, 394–400

comic, 509

informational text, 25, 64–70

letters, 87, 223, 335, 387

literary analysis, 142–148, 251

opinion piece, 373

paragraph, 197

personal narrative, 536–542

personal response, 129

persuasive essay, 45

poetry, 111, 207, 295, 349

reports, 285

research report, 312–318

response to literature, 361

scene writing and dramatization, 101

short story, 230–236

sonnet, 35

speeches, 271

storyboard, 137

summaries, 13, 181

writing process. *See* develop a draft; edit; plan for writing; publish; revise

writing prompts

argument, 394

informational essay, 64

literary analysis, 142

personal narrative, 536

research report, 312

short story, 230

INDEX OF TITLES AND AUTHORS

ACKNOWLEDGMENTS

"After Auschwitz" by Elie Wiesel. Text copyright © 1995 by Elie Wiesel. Reprinted by permission of Georges Borchardt, Inc.

Excerpts from *The American Heritage Dictionary of The English Language, Fifth Edition.* Text copyright © 2016 by Houghton Mifflin Harcourt Publishing Company. Reprinted by permission of Houghton Mifflin Harcourt Publishing Company.

"Are Bionic Superhumans on the Horizon" by Ramez Naam from CNN.com April 25, 2013. Text copyright © 2013 by Turner Broadcast Systems. Reprinted by permission of PARS International on behalf of Turner Broadcast Systems. All rights reserved. Protected by the Copyright Laws of the United States. The printing, copying, redistribution, or retransmission of this Content without express written permission is prohibited. http://www.cnn.com

"The Automation Paradox" by James Bessen, from *The Atlantic Monthly*, January 19, 2016. Text copyright © 2016 by The Atlantic Monthly. Reprinted by permission of Tribune Content Agency.

Excerpt from *The Book of Unknown Americans* by Cristina Henríquez. Text copyright © 2014 by Cristina Henríquez. Reprinted by permission of Alfred A. Knopf, an imprint of the Knopf Doubleday Publishing Group, a division of Penguin Random House LLC and Canongate Books. All rights reserved. Any third party use of this material, outside this publication, is prohibited. Interested parties must apply directly to Penguin Random House LLC for permission.

"The Brave Little Toaster" from *TRSF* by Cory Doctorow. Text copyright © 2014 by Cory Doctorow. Reprinted by permission of Cory Doctorow.

"Days" from *The Art of Drowning* by Billy Collins. Text copyright © 1995 by Billy Collins. Reprinted by permission of University of Pittsburgh Press.

"The Debt We Owe to the Adolescent Brain" by Jeanne Miller from *Odyssey* March 2015. Text copyright © 2015 by Carus Publishing Company. Reprinted by permission of Carus Publishing Company. All Cricket Media material is copyrighted by Carus Publishing Company d/b/a Cricket Media, and/or various authors and illustrators. Any commercial use or distribution of material without permission is strictly prohibited. Please visit http://cricketmedia.com/licensing for licensing and http://www.cricketmedia.com for subscriptions.

"Devon Hope" by Nikki Grimes; "Open Mike: Bronx Masquerade" by Devon Hope; "Open Mike: If" by Diondra Jordan; "Diondra Jordan," and "Tyrone" from *Bronx Masquerade* by Nikki Grimes. Text copyright © 2002 by Nikki Grimes. Reprinted by permission of Dial Books for Young Readers, an imprint of Penguin Young Readers Group, a division of Penguin Random House LLC, Curtis Brown Limited and Recorded Books. All rights reserved. Any third party use of this material, outside this publication, is prohibited. Interested parties must apply directly to Penguin Random House LLC for permission.

Excerpt from *The Diary of a Young Girl: The Definitive Editions* by Anne Frank, edited by Otto H. Frank and Mirjam Pressler, translated by Susan Massotty. Translation copyright © 1995 by Penguin Random House LLC. Reprinted by permission of Doubleday, an imprint of the Knopf Doubleday Publishing Group, a division of Penguin Random House LLC and Penguin Books UK. All rights reserved. Any third-party use of this material, outside of this publication, is prohibited. Interested parties must apply directly to Penguin Random House LLC for permission.

The Diary of Anne Frank by Frances Goodrich and Albert Hackett. Text copyright © 1956 by Albert Hackett, Frances Goodrich Hackett and Otto Frank. Copyright renewed 1984 by Albert Hackett. Reprinted by permission of Random House, an imprint and division of Penguin Random House LLC and Flora Roberts, Inc. All rights reserved. Any third-party use of this material, outside of this publication, is prohibited. Interested parties must apply directly to Penguin Random House LLC for permission.

"The Drummer Boy of Shiloh" from *The Saturday Evening Post,* April 30, 1960 by Ray Bradbury. Text copyright © 1960 by the Curtis Publishing Company, renewed 1988 by Ray Bradbury. Reprinted by permission of Don Congdon Associates, Inc.

"Fortune's Bones" from *Fortune's Bones: The Manumission Requiem* by Marilyn Nelson. Text copyright © 2004 by Pamela Espeland. Reprinted by permission of Highlights for Children, Inc.

"Hanging Fire" from *The Collected Poems of Audre Lorde* by Audre Lorde. Text copyright © 1978 by The Audre Lorde Estate. Reprinted by permission of W.W. Norton and Company and Charlotte Sheedy Literary Agency.

Harriet Tubman: Conductor on the Underground Railroad by Ann Petry. Text copyright © 1955, © 1983 by Ann Petry. Reprinted by permission of Hannigan Salky Getzler Agency as agents for the author.

"The Hollow" by Kelly Deschler. Text copyright by Kelly Deschler. Reprinted by permission of Kelly Deschler.

"Interflora" by Susan Hamlyn. Text copyright and permission by Susan Hamyln.

Excerpt from *It's Complicated: The Social Lives of Networked Teens* by Danah Boyd. Text copyrighted © 2014 by Danah Boyd. Reprinted by permission of Yale University Press.

"My Favorite Chaperone" by Jean Davies Okimoto. Text copyright © 2004 by Jean Davies Okimoto. Reprinted with permission of Jean Davies Okimoto.

"Not My Bones" from *Fortune's Bones: The Manumission Requiem* by Marilyn Nelson. Text copyright © 2004 by Marilyn Nelson. Reprinted by permission of Highlights for Children, Inc.

"The Powwow at the End of the World" from *The Summer of Black Widows* by Sherman Alexie. Text copyright © 1996 by Sherman Alexie. Reprinted by permission of Hanging Loose Press.

ACKNOWLEDGMENTS

Quote by Henning Mankell from "All along the watchtower" by Nick Hasted from *The Guardian*, January 11, 2002. Text copyright © 2002 by Guardian News & Media Limited. Reprinted courtesy of Guardian News & Media Limited.

"Summer of His Fourteenth Year" from *Wind Chimes* by Gloria Amescua. Text copyright © 2004 by Altura Press. Reprinted by permission of Gloria Amescua.

"There But for the Grace" from *Sounds, Feelings, Thoughts: Seventy Poems by Wislawa Szymborska* by Wislawa Szymborska translated by Magnus J. Krynski and Robert A. Maguire. Text copyright © 1981 by Princeton University Press. Reprinted by permission Copyright Clearance Center on behalf of Princeton University Press.

Excerpt from "What is the Horror Genre?" by Stephen King from *Stephen King: a Critical Companion* by Sharon A. Russell. Text copyright © 1996 by Sharon A. Russell. Reprinted by permission of Copyright Clearance Center.